Literature and Ourselves

A Thematic Introduction for Readers and Writers

SIXTH EDITION

Gloria Mason Henderson
Gordon College

Anna Higgins
Gordon College

Bill Day
Gordon College
Professor Emeritus

Sandra Stevenson Waller
Georgia Perimeter College
Associate Professor Emerita of Humanities

PEARSON
Longman

New York San Francisco Boston
London Toronto Sydney Tokyo Singapore Madrid
Mexico City Munich Paris Cape Town Hong Kong Montreal

Senior Acquisitions Editor: Vivian Garcia
Development Editor: Marijane Wright
Executive Marketing Manager: Joyce Nilsen
Senior Supplements Editor: Donna Campion
Production Manager: Eric Jorgensen
Project Coordination, Text Design, and Electronic Page Makeup: Electronic
Publishing Services Inc., NYC
Cover Design Manager: Wendy Ann Fredericks
Cover Art: Jeff Ripple/Fine Art Landscape Photographer–Natural History Author
Photo Researcher: Anita Dickhuth
Senior Manufacturing Buyer: Dennis J. Para
Printer and Binder: Courier Corp., Westford
Cover Printer: Phoenix Color Corporation

For permission to use copyrighted material, grateful acknowledgment is made to the
copyright holders on pp. 1171–1181, which are hereby made part of this copyright
page.

Library of Congress Cataloging-in-Publication Data
Literature and ourselves : a thematic introduction for readers and writers / Gloria
Mason Henderson, Anna Higgins, Bill Day, Sandra Stevenson Waller. -- 6th ed.
     p. cm.
    Includes bibliographical references and index.
    ISBN 978-0-205-60638-2
    1. Literature--Collections. I. Henderson, Gloria Mason, II. Higgins, Anna,
III. Day, William, IV. Waller, Sandra Stevenson.
PN6014.L5562 2006
808.8--dc22

                                                              2008020333

Visit us at www.pearsonhighered.com

ISBN-13: 978-0-205-60638-2
ISBN-10:   0-205-60638-5

1 2 3 4 5 6 7 8 9 10—CRW—11 10 09 08

Contents

THEMATIC ANTHOLOGY

FAMILY   40

MEN AND WOMEN   228

Writing about Men and Women   230

Essays

Fiction

Poetry

Drama

Casebook on Robert Frost

Drama

FREEDOM AND RESPONSIBILITY   692

Writing about Freedom and Responsibility   694

Essays

Fiction

Poetry

CREATIVITY   838

QUEST   966

Poetry

Drama

Casebook on Flannery O'Connor

Alternate Contents by Genre

Fiction

Poetry

Drama

Preface

What's New in the 6th Edition?

Revised Introduction

The new Introduction is designed to foster student confidence and precision and to enhance accessibility. Some changes are cosmetic; the breaking up of spaces and the incorporation of a limited number of box features achieve a more reader-friendly text that is easily navigated. We have also adopted a more encouraging narrative voice woven into a process-oriented approach to reading and interpreting literature that demonstrates how natural it is to move from engagement with literature to response and then to interpretation and persuasive writing. Located in Part One, a guided reading illustrates the everyday nature of initial reactions to a piece of literature, assuring students that they can trust their instincts. An explanatory passage combined with a sample Reader's Journal offers a strategy for prewriting. The questions at the end of each discussion of the elements of genre have been reconfigured and now appear in box features that highlight their importance in equipping students with the tools they need to analyze literature. Located early in Part Two, the recast discussion of classical argument aims to produce careful writers, aware of their own prejudices in attempting to persuade an audience to see their views. Given the increasingly interconnected nature of our world, an understanding of opposing views is beneficial. A four-step writing instruction aids in producing confidence by walking students through the processes, one step at a time.

New Selections–both Classic and Contemporary–in all Genres

New selections in every genre from varied ethnicities have been added to enhance student engagement, which ultimately benefits the quality of the students' analytical writing as well. These new additions are located in every thematic unit, encouraging students to recognize the universality of human experience that is the basis of literature, to become familiar with customs and points of view from other cultures, and to take part in the world community.

New Casebooks

Continuing our tradition of mixing classic and contemporary literature from differing ethnicities, we have added *Casebooks* on Robert Frost and Alice Walker, located in Men and Women and Creativity respectively. As with the other *Casebooks*, these sections contain primary texts, secondary sources, and a sample student essay that incorporates evidence from both the primary works and the secondary sources. These self-contained units are keyed to discussions in the Introduction and effectively demonstrate the processes that move students from engagement and response to analysis to interpretation and a well-crafted argument paper.

Recasting of Thematic Units

Thematic units have been reconfigured in ways that enhance accessibility, classroom discussion, and relevance. Two units now have titles that reflect their new focus. For example, *Vulnerability*, formerly *Human Vulnerability*, has new selections and now adds flexibility for teachers who focus on ecological and political as well as human vulnerability. Imagination and *Reality* has been recast as *Creativity* in order to foster conversations on the act of creating. Additionally, several works popular with teachers have been moved from one unit to another. For instance, Joyce Carol Oates' "Where Are You Going, Where Have You Been?" is given new life by joining the *Family* unit, encouraging discussion about such relevant topics as the dysfunctional family. To enhance student learning, the introduction to each unit is keyed to the reading and writing instruction and to the discussion of Argument in the newly revised Introduction.

New and Revised End-of-the-Selection Questions and Suggestions for Crafting Arguments

End-of-the-selection questions and suggestions have been revised to follow the process-oriented structure of the Introduction. To produce more provocative, carefully constructed essays, the writing suggestions have been reconfigured: to aid the teacher, personal narrative writing prompts have been moved to the Instructor's Manual as have some Reader's Journal assignments; other prompts have been recast to draw on the students' understanding of argument. Students are also now encouraged to return to the box features included in the discussion of elements in order to deepen their reading experience.

Revised Appendix on Film

Because so many of our teachers have appreciated the flexibility of an appendix that focuses on film, we have completely rewritten this text as well. To reflect the process orientation of our newly revised Introduction, this section now moves students through the same processes of engagement, response, and analysis to effective argument. The appendix provides a concise survey of the terms and concepts of film to enrich classroom discussion via a shared language and to produce stronger papers; wherever possible, we connect the film terminology with the literary terminology to enhance the book's overall coherence for the student. The appendix also includes passages that foster persuasive writing in papers on film adaptation, keyed to the Introduction's discussion of classical argument. Students learn to examine their own claims more critically so that those whose views differ from theirs will listen to what they have to say about a given adaptation. The sample student paper demonstrates what is covered in the text.

Preface for Instructors

For teachers attempting to motivate students to read and then craft arguments about literature, the challenges are different. Some of these challenges are the result of under-prepared students or students who have been shaped by the immediate gratification mentality of our age. The goal for a textbook addressing such challenges is to be as accessible and engaging as possible. The sixth edition of *Literature and Ourselves: A Thematic Introduction for Readers and Writers* offers to guide students to critical reading, insightful analysis, and careful argumentation through step-by-step processes. The title's reflexive pronoun suggests our philosophy: Literature makes visible the invisible and at times unfathomable reality that we are all connected, that the many voices of literature tell "our" story, the one human story. We believe that literature can be accessible; that students can read perceptively and come to a debatable claim about what they read; and that a textbook can offer instruction in encouraging prose that fosters critical skills without hindering the students' enjoyment of the literature or the teacher's teaching.

The Organization of *Literature and Ourselves*

Literature and Ourselves opens with a two-part introduction based on the premise that stronger readers make stronger thinkers who make stronger writers, a stance we illustrate by providing process-oriented reading and writing instruction. To foster critical reading and thinking skills, Part One: Reading Literature discusses the techniques of annotation, journaling, and close textual analysis. A guided reading, a sample student Reader's Journal, questions for critical reading, and specific examples from the anthology provide support for explanations. To produce stronger student writers, Part Two: Writing about Literature provides instruction on classical argument and a step-by-step method for preparing persuasive literary arguments. Box features and a model student paper promote student learning by concrete illustration.

The literature in the anthology is divided into six engaging themes—Family, Men and Women, Vulnerability, Freedom and Responsibility, Creativity, and Quest—that move from the self, the familiar, and the concrete to the larger community, the more abstract. Each thematic unit begins with an introduction and concludes with a Casebook and unit writing prompts. The selections within each unit are introduced with author background and arranged by genre; within genre, selections are ordered chronologically.

For greater flexibility, *Literature and Ourselves* includes three appendices. *Appendix A: Critical Approaches to Literature* briefly discusses some of the major literary approaches. *Appendix B: Writing about Film* introduces students to the techniques and terminology needed to enjoy, interpret, and write effective, perceptive essays about film and the relationship of film to literary sources. *Appendix C: Documenting a Research Paper: MLA Format* enhances classroom discussion of such crucial matters as summary, paraphrase, and quotation; internal documentation; plagiarism; and the construction of a bibliography/works cited page. The glossary recaps key terms associated with reading and writing about literature.

Enduring Features

The sixth edition of *Literature and Ourselves* builds on the following distinct features of previous editions.

Culturally Diverse Literary Selections

Included works are historically, culturally, and stylistically diverse and range from classic to contemporary, written from the perspective of both genders and many ethnicities and dealing with both traditional themes and those that are particular to our times.

Casebooks

Located at the end of each thematic unit, *Casebooks* contain primary text(s) related to the theme, scholarship that speaks to the literary text(s), and a sample student essay that includes support from both the primary text(s) and the secondary sources. Teachers tell us that the *Casebooks* demonstrate to students exactly how the strategies of close reading can transform a strong reader into a strong writer. In particular, the *Casebooks* illustrate the movement from engagement to response to analysis and interpretation, and they function as powerful pedagogical tools for instructors' discussions concerning crucial matters such as

- reading and analyzing literature
- creating debatable claims
- establishing warrants and gathering supporting evidence
- structuring papers
- writing strong introductions and conclusions
- revising for voice and clarity
- making connections between personal interpretation, primary sources, and secondary sources
- comprehending the difference between summary, paraphrase, and quotation
- understanding strategies for avoiding plagiarism
- integrating secondary sources
- integrating quotations smoothly and grammatically
- documenting in proper MLA format

The Casebooks can also function as a springboard for in-depth research projects.

Emphasis on Argument

Located in Part Two of the Introduction and woven throughout the entire text and the appendix on Film, a concise discussion of classical argument fosters deeper critical thinking and more careful, persuasive papers that exhibit keen audience awareness. Students versed in argument are better equipped to comprehend the difference between essays with debatable claims and pertinent supporting evidence and essays with factual thesis statements propped up with mere plot summary.

End-of-Selection Questions

Questions and writing prompts after each selection stimulate class discussions and guide student reading and writing via the same processes covered in the Introduction.

Focus on Film

Because a growing number of teachers use film to engage their visually-oriented students, we include coverage of film adaptations of literary works. Questions about film adaptations follow many of the works in our anthology. Located at the end of each unit, Writing about Film asks students to apply the strategies gained from studying literature to studying film. The revised Appendix B includes a sample student paper about the film *Under the Tuscan Sun*.

Resources for Students and Instructors

- **Instructor's Manual (ISBN 0-205-61637-2).** An instructor's manual with detailed comments and suggestions for teaching each selection is available. This important resource, entirely written by the authors of the text, also contains references to critical articles and books that we have found to be most useful.

- **MyLiteratureLab.com** is a Web-based, state-of-the-art, interactive learning system designed to enhance introductory literature courses. It adds a whole new dimension to the study of literature with Longman Lectures—evocative, richly illustrated audio readings along with advice on how to read, interpret, and write about literary works from our own roster of Longman authors. This powerful program also features Diagnostic Tests, Interactive Readings with clickable prompts, student sample papers, Literature Timelines, Avoiding Plagiarism and research aids, Grade Tracker, and "Exchange," an electronic instructor/peer feedback tool.

- **MyLiteratureLab Faculty Teaching Guide (0-321-33213-X).** This helpful resource gives instructors step-by-step advice for integrating the features of MyLiteratureLab into their classroom, including detailed instructions in how to use Exchange, an electronic instructor/peer feedback tool.

- **Penguin Discount Novel Program.** In cooperation with Penguin Group (USA) Inc., a leading U.S. trade book publisher, Longman is proud to offer a variety of Penguin paperbacks at a significant discount—most 60% off the retail price—when packaged with any Longman title. To review the list of titles available for other disciplines, visit the Longman/Penguin Putnam website at www.pearsonhighered.com/penguin.

- **Sourcebooks Shakespeare.** Longman Publishers, in conjunction with Sourcebooks, Inc., proudly offers The Sourcebooks Shakespeare. This revolutionary new book + CD format offers the complete text of the play with rich illustrations and extensive explanatory and production notes. An accompanying audio CD, narrated by acclaimed actor Sir Derek Jacobi, features recordings of key scenes from memorable productions to allow students to compare different interpretations of the play and its characters. Contact your local representative.

- **What Every Student Should Know about Citing Sources with MLA Documentation, Michael Greer (0-321-44737-9).** This brief guide provides specific instructions on writing and documenting in the Modern Language Association (MLA) style. It offers a comprehensive listing of in-text and works cited models for a wide variety of print, electronic, and online sources. Also included are frequently asked questions about MLA style and guidelines for formatting research papers.

- **What Every Student Should Know about Avoiding Plagiarism (0-321-44689-5).** This brief guide teaches students to take plagiarism seriously and understand its consequences. Here, source usage methods—summary, paraphrase and quotation—are explained, with examples. The most common types of plagiarism are discussed, from simple mistakes such as forgetting to use quotation marks when using someone else's exact words, to wholesale fraudulence, such as purchasing student papers from online sites and claiming them as one's own work. A brief essential guide to citing sources using both MLA and APA documentation styles is also included.

- **What Every Student Should Know About Researching Online, David Munger and Shireen Campbell (0-321-44531-7).** This brief guide teaches students how to conduct research in the first place they will look: the Web. It covers how to use search engines and databases, how to evaluate sources, how to document borrowed materials, and how to avoid online plagiarism. Annotated screen shots of Web pages show students where to locate the information they need to create a proper citation; numerous examples of properly cited online and electronic sources are also provided.

- **Responding to Literature: A Writer's Journal, Daniel Kline (0-321-09542-1).** This spiral-bound journal provides students with their own space for recording their reactions to the literature they read. Guided writing prompts, suggested writing assignments, and overviews of literary terms provide students with the tools and ideas they need for responding to fiction, poetry, and drama.

- **The Longman Literature Timeline, Heidi L.M. Jacobs (0-321-14315-9).** This laminated four-page timeline provides students with a chronological overview of the major literary works. In addition, the timeline also lists major sociocultural and political events to provide students with historical and contextual insights into the impact historical events have had on writers and their works . . . and vice versa.

- **Video Program.** For qualified adopters, an impressive selection of videotapes is available to enrich students' experience of literature. Contact your local representative.

Acknowledgments

We are deeply indebted to many people for their assistance in the sixth edition of *Literature and Ourselves*. Our acquisitions editors, Matthew Wright and Vivian Garcia, have encouraged and guided us through the changes in this new edition. Erika Berg, our first development editor, gave us invaluable advice, inspired us by sharing her enthusiasm for the book, and encouraged us to make the contents even better. Our second development editor, Marijane Wright, has been our lifeline, sharing her innovative ideas, keeping us informed at each stage of our work, and offering constant encouragement. Our families have been supportive, patient, and helpful. In particular, we would like to thank Peter Higgins and Mary Dunlap.

We are also deeply indebted to many colleagues at Gordon College. We want to thank Dr. Richard Baskin, Chair of the Division of Humanities at Gordon College; Dr. Robert Vaughan, Vice President of Academics at Gordon; and Dr. Lawrence V. Weill, President of Gordon College, for their encouragement and support. We are also deeply appreciative of our colleagues on the English faculty at Gordon College, who suggested works and/or revisions that added both diversity and excellence to the new edition. In particular, we want to thank Rhonda Wilcox, David Janssen, and the 2007–2008 Accel class. The librarians at Gordon College, under the leadership of head librarian Nancy Anderson, were extremely helpful in ordering and locating materials for the text. Beth Pye, reference librarian at Gordon, has helped both with valuable suggestions and with locating information when we had become frustrated in our searches. Brett Cox, English professor at Norwich University, shared his love of science fiction and suggestions about selections. We also wish again to thank Dr. Michael Montgomery of Life College in Atlanta for his valuable suggestions about selections. Finally, we would like to thank the instructors who reviewed our manuscript at various phases of the writing process and who provided invaluable feedback to us. We are certainly grateful for their assistance: Mary Anne Bernal, San Antonio College; Roberta Eisel, Citrus College; Thomas J. Ernster, Kirkwood Community College; Katherine Fischer, Clarke College; Tina Hultgren, Kishwaukee College; Elizabeth Joseph, Eastfield College; Catherine L. Keohane, Montclair State University; Jane M. Kinney, Valdosta State University; Tiina Lombard, Miami Dade College; Amanda Loos, Harold Washington College; Michael N. Morris, Eastfield College; Caesar Perkowski, Gordon College; Pennie Pflueger, Southeast Missouri State University; Teresa M. Purvis, Lansing Community College;David B. Raymond, Northern Maine Community College; Michael Trovato, Ohio State University–Newark.

GLORIA MASON HENDERSON
ANNA DUNLAP HIGGINS

Introduction

Part One: Reading Literature

Why do people read literature? Why in a culture of drive-through-speed electronic entertainment do we find people huddled over a cup of coffee or waiting at a bus stop with a book in their hands? The reflexive pronoun in the title *Literature and Ourselves* suggests one answer: literature makes visible the invisible and at times unfathomable reality that we are all connected, that the many voices of literature tell "our" story. If the literature is crafted by a writer in our own heritage, it tells us who we are by reminding us of who we have been. When the literature is the art of someone outside our own particular heritage, it invites us into that culture, an especially salient benefit given the increasingly interconnected nature of our global community. A short story created by a woman allows a man to see life from the female perspective; a poem by one familiar with poverty invites those who know only wealth to understand deprivation. Some of us find joy in reading literature because it tells the one human story, at times beautiful and peaceful, at times ugly and angry.

Perhaps that rationale for literature's allure touches a chord in you. Look up the term "literature" in a literary handbook, and you will see a definition something like this one: literature is the body of written works of a certain period or culture, including works originally existing in an oral tradition. Often such definitions are followed by a quotation from a famous author. Henry David Thoreau penned one of the most famous lines about the power of literature: "Books are the carriers of civilization. Without books, history is silent, literature dumb, science crippled, thought and speculation at a standstill." Consider especially the last few words, "thought and speculation at a standstill." Literature invites us to experience what is felt, seen, and heard by the writer; it also triggers a response in us. The nineteenth-century poet Emily Dickinson once said that she recognized poetry by her own reaction: if she read something and felt that the top of her head had been "taken off," then she knew it was poetry. Have you ever read something that caused such a powerful response in you: perhaps a newspaper article applauding the sacrificial act of a firefighter, or a self-help book that hit home, or a novel that left you breathless? As Thoreau suggested, literature creates a response in us, stimulating our minds and leading us to speculation, celebration, meditation, or even rebuttal. We read literature for the love of the words on the page and for the love of what those words trigger in us.

1

Critical Reading: Engagement, Response, and Analysis

What about those who find literature irrelevant? The question for those readers goes beyond asking why people read literature to asking why teachers find ways to get students to read, then talk about, and then write about literature? Why must we analyze it? When you think about it, the whole world is a text that we analyze. Every day, we perform the act of moving from initial impression to engagement, response, and analysis to personal opinion because every day, we participate in the kind of thinking that reading literature stimulates. You read and interpret all kinds of texts, from road signs to e-mail and IM messages. Consciously or not, you read and are influenced by what the media and advertising companies put before your eyes. You also "read" people: facial expressions, actions, and tone of voice. All of these "texts" elicit in you what literature does because to live is to think.

What is reading but thinking that begins with the written word? In academia, this act is refered to as "critical thinking." With regard to literature, critical thinking or critical reading simply means engaging with a text, responding to it, breaking down its components for study, examining the way in which those components function as a part of the whole, and then forming an overall interpretation. Part One of this Introduction offers strategies that will enhance your critical thinking/close reading skills. Then, in Part Two you will examine argument, an excellent vehicle for expressing your thoughts about literature in such a way that others may be persuaded to find what you say worthwhile and convincing.

Engaging with a Text: Annotation

Texts speak to us. Speaking back is a very human urge. When a friend's e-mail carries shocking news, you probably begin drafting a response immediately. Similarly, when an author makes a comment that astounds you, you probably have an urge to talk back to the writer. Perhaps you have even scribbled your reaction in the margin of a book. If so, you are engaging in critical reading. Writing down reactions in the margins is actually an excellent critical thinking strategy because speaking back keeps you engaged with the text. Your comments are called "marginalia," and the name of the reading strategy is "annotation."

The first step in enhancing the kind of critical reading that elicits annotation is just what you might imagine: careful reading. Find a comfortable, private space. If you read while being distracted, you drown your own responses. Listen to your inner monologue as you read. Enjoy whatever reaction the literature is causing in you. Talk back to the text, circling or underlining and jotting down your thoughts. Write down the definitions of words that are unfamiliar. Reading this way moves you from engagement and response to analysis and interpretation—and, later, to writing in ways you perhaps never thought you could. Below is a short story called "Bread," written by Sandra Cisneros. As you read this story, you will notice the marginalia, circling, and underlining of Andie Howard, a nursing major who is showcased throughout this Introduction. Note that Andie simply wrote what she felt while she was reading. She circled and underlined word choices that puzzled her (for example, "filled"), and she called the man in the story names. You will also note some marginalia that open with "Class Notes," which Andie jotted down later during class discussion as her professor pointed out literary elements.

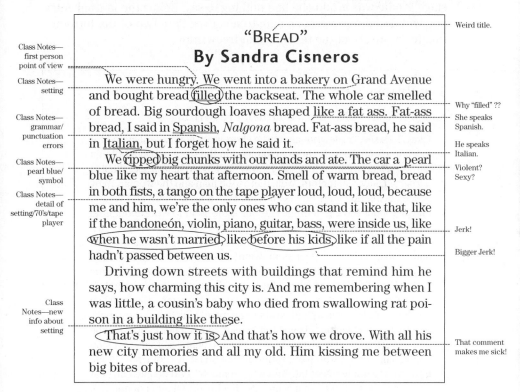

"BREAD"

By Sandra Cisneros

We were hungry. We went into a bakery on Grand Avenue and bought bread. filled the backseat. The whole car smelled of bread. Big sourdough loaves shaped like a fat ass. Fat-ass bread, I said in Spanish, *Nalgona* bread. Fat-ass bread, he said in Italian, but I forget how he said it.

We ripped big chunks with our hands and ate. The car a pearl blue like my heart that afternoon. Smell of warm bread, bread in both fists, a tango on the tape player loud, loud, loud, because me and him, we're the only ones who can stand it like that, like if the bandoneón, violin, piano, guitar, bass, were inside us, like when he wasn't married, like before his kids, like if all the pain hadn't passed between us.

Driving down streets with buildings that remind him he says, how charming this city is. And me remembering when I was little, a cousin's baby who died from swallowing rat poison in a building like these.

That's just how it is. And that's how we drove. With all his new city memories and all my old. Him kissing me between big bites of bread.

Marginalia:
- Weird title.
- Class Notes—first person point of view
- Class Notes—setting
- Why "filled" ??
- She speaks Spanish.
- Class Notes—grammar/punctuation errors
- He speaks Italian.
- Class Notes—pearl blue/symbol
- Violent? Sexy?
- Class Notes—detail of setting/70's/tape player
- Jerk!
- Bigger Jerk!
- Class Notes—new info about setting
- That comment makes me sick!

Responding to a Text: The Reader's Journal

Annotating is immediate and active response. You can feel the immediacy of Andie's comment "jerk." What happens when a piece of literature elicits more response than the margins allow? Imagine meeting someone who tells you an amazing story. Perhaps the story is about a man so enraged with jealousy that he kills his wife. Now imagine hearing such an account and being told you could think only a few words about the story and no more. That would be an impossible feat. Literature records the stories of human experience, and few of its stories elicit only a couple of words. Whether we have walked in a character's shoes or this is our first exposure to such an experience, we have a human urge to respond to story. A Reader's Journal, also called a Reader's Log, is a tool that benefits your critical reading and also moves you in the direction of paper topics. The journal works best if you record your impressions immediately, jotting down any questions, ideas, or thoughts that were too wordy for the margins. You may later discover hidden gems in these initial impressions that will become the core idea for a paper. Below is a page of free writing from Andie Howard's Reader's Journal. She had been given an assignment to select one of the short stories that the class had read and craft an essay of 750–1,000 words that would analyze either character development or an author's use of a certain symbol. At this stage, Andie was afraid she had nothing to say. Below the journal entry, you will find the professor's note to her. (See Part Two of the Introduction for more about the technique of freewriting.)

THE READER'S BOX

Sample Student Reader's Journal: Freewriting

Okay, let's see. "Freewrite about the short story you have selected for our literary analysis. Is there a character in the story or a symbol that garners your attention in a special way?" Okay, well, let's see. What is garners? Okay. Characters. Well, there's the man and the woman. Why is she seeing this guy? She is an idiot. He's a jerk. That's all I've got. Maybe I should change stories. This one is too short to write about. And what is up with the title?! Ha. I just remembered the day that we discussed this story the guy in the back was amazed when I said the man and woman were having an affair. Weird. I mean, isn't it obvious? Anyway, back to my freewrite. Character or symbol. Okay. Characters. Why is she doing this? I don't even think the guy makes her happy. And he's a jerk. I don't know if I can go anywhere with character—that's all I've got. Symbol? In class, we talked about her pearl blue heart—hey, that's my point. She's seeing this guy but he isn't making her happy. Maybe that's why they bought all that bread—she's so depressed she can't stop eating. They better watch out eating all that bread. It's not whole grain, guys, you're going to get fat. And why so much? Two people can't eat a whole back seat full. What is up with that bread? Okay. I got nothing. Okay. Maybe I should change stories. Okay. Back to the bread, I mean the man and woman. That's funny. Bread. The title is bread. Why? SC could have called it An Affair to Forget. I guess the woman can't get over him? Or she thinks he'll make her happy? How can I figure anything out about these people? The story is so short. There's nothing here to work with. Well, I guess I think they're having an affair. I mean the story doesn't say that but isn't it clear? So why? Dumb question. But really, why? I mean I can understand stuffing your face with bread but why an affair? Okay, Dr. H is looking at her watch. Time's up!

Professor's note: Andie, although you said in conference that you could not find a topic. I believe that this journal entry points to something very interesting. Read what you have written here. You are clearly puzzled by this woman. Can you analyze her? What is her motivation? You also seem very interested in the bread. As you say, "What is up with the bread?" Since the story is so short, perhaps some elements of plot function also as symbols that say something about characterization. What do you think? Good start!

Analyzing a Text

Once you have engaged with and responded to the piece of literature, you are ready to go even deeper, into the **analysis** of a text. Simply phrased, to analyze means to break down into components in order to study the whole more deeply. To some students, this act seems quite artificial. Yet analysis is an everyday act, the mind's natural movement from impression to interpretation. For example, when you meet someone new, you begin forming an impression from the first moment. That impression changes, moving toward interpretation of character as you view the person's actions and listen to the person's words. You eventually come to an opinion because—perhaps without always being conscious of it—you naturally analyze other people's words and actions. The next step is to translate these terms to literary analysis. Just as you need a bit of insight into human nature in order to understand the new person you met, you will benefit from a familiarity with the various genres and their elements.

Before you begin analyzing your selected text, note that not everyone goes about this method of study in the same way. Many interpretations stem from three basic approaches to analysis: author-oriented approaches, reader-oriented approaches, and text-oriented approaches.

Approaches: Author-, Reader-, and Text-Oriented Approaches   In adopting an author-oriented approach, a reader studies an author's life and culture to better understand the literature. This approach requires research. For example, in preparing to analyze the poetry of Emily Dickinson, the author-oriented reader would research Dickinson's life, education, and poetic career. Such an approach would also probably include research into the condition of women's lives in nineteenth-century America—Amherst, Massachusetts, in particular. In addition to biographical and historical study, the author-oriented reader would perhaps research other contemporary authors, the history of women's literature, and other literary works that influenced the poet. Other texts by the author being studied, including letters, draft poetry, statements of artistic purpose, and reviews, can also enhance an author-oriented reader's understanding of a literary work. Some of the questions and suggestions in the Casebooks reflect an author-oriented approach.

A reader-oriented approach is based upon the concept that each reader brings a unique set of experiences and expectations to literature. In its extreme form, the reader-oriented approach argues that a work of literature is recreated each time it is read, that it is produced by the mind of the reader. In a moderate form, a reader-oriented approach values a range of interpretation, conditioned by the reader's particular expectations. For instance, such an approach would expect men and women to react differently to the poetry of Emily Dickinson because each gender would bring a different understanding to the works. Some of the suggestions for work in a Reader's Journal are reader-response in nature.

When adopting a text-oriented approach, a reader analyzes a work of literature as complete in itself without relating it to the outside world. In its extreme form, this approach insists that the author's life and time as well as readers' responses to a literary work are not only unnecessary but irrelevant. In a more moderate form, text-oriented reading refers to a kind of analysis that includes close attention to words and to the parts that make up the whole. For example, a text-oriented reader would focus closely on Emily Dickinson's poems, on such elements as word choices, images, metaphors, and meter. Both the questions and writing prompts at the end of selections and the upcoming breakdown of literary elements encourage close textual analysis.

In analyzing literature, you may decide that the most satisfying method for you is one that incorporates all three approaches. You may also want to see Appendix A: Critical Approaches to Literature to learn more about the various ways to analyze literature. For now, consider the literary elements of genre. The term **genre**, derived from the Latin word *genus*, meaning kind, functions in literary study as a means of classifying literature in terms of common patterns and/or characteristics, often called elements. Below is a breakdown of four literary genres: essays, fiction, poetry, and drama. Following each genre section is a box feature containing Questions for Engagement, Response, and Analysis. To enhance your critical reading, you may want to turn back to these boxes each time you read a piece of literature.

The Elements of the Essay   In this anthology, essay refers to a short, unified work of nonfiction prose, often presenting the personal views of the author. Essays are often defined as having one of three purposes: to inform, to entertain, or to persuade. Included in this anthology are many kinds of essays, such as expository essays, critical essays, sermons, epistolary essays, biographical essays, critical essays, personal essays, and even essays excerpted from books. Students often find the essay the most accessible genre to read. This is, after all, the genre most students themselves write. The elements of the essay can be broken down into style, tone, and theme.

Style   Three powerful tools of the essayist's style are diction, syntax, and figurative language. All of us are familiar with this power: words and the way we say them mean a great deal in our everyday lives. If we choose the wrong words or phrase them poorly, we may find ourselves in a dispute with a close friend, family member, or associate. A good essayist is attentive, choosing words very carefully and phrasing sentences in a way that best expresses the intended point. Because a word's meaning may change over time or take on a different connotation, essayists pay particular attention to **diction**. In particular, an essayist looks closely at both the **connotative** meanings of words, their suggested or implied meanings, and the **denotative**, or explicit, meanings. An essayist is also careful with the level of diction, choosing between slang or formal and uncommon or common words. Such choices affect a reader's interpretation of tone and theme. You may sense, for example, that the elevated diction of the Declaration of Independence reinforces the document's seriousness.

An author's **syntax**, the patterns and structures of a writer's sentences, often further enhances the essay's overall effect. The sentences may be predominantly short and simple, even abrupt; they may be predominantly long, ornate, and complex; or they may be a mixture of both. The Declaration of Independence has long been studied as a masterpiece of syntax: the relationships between ideas—articulated frequently in periodic sentence structures—logically build up to the text's overall point. With its introductory element of over forty words, the oft-quoted opening sentence is an example of striking syntax. In fact, this first line suggests what a rich resource an essay can be for writing an argument about style.

Another stylistic tool available to the essayist is the one that students sometimes feel is the least accessible. As with the other elements, though, the use of **figurative language** is an everyday act. Children jumping off furniture declare that they are "Superman," and angry drivers yell out their windows that other, slower drivers are "grandmas." These statements are not literal but figurative. Figurative language refers to the use of such stylistic tools as metaphors, imagery, and hyperbole. Such tools are used by an author to create a mental picture for the reader. For example, in his "Letter from Birmingham City Jail," Dr. Martin Luther King Jr. paints a picture of "the stinging darts of segregation," but it seems doubtful that he is speaking of the game of darts. You will find many examples of figurative language in this anthology that lend themselves well to paper topics.

Tone   Like figurative language, **tone** is an everyday term. You have definitely recognized tone of voice when someone was angry with you. You may have also recognized tone by word choice. For example, the word choices of a person who claims to be unbiased sometimes conflict with that assertion. In essays, as in life, tone speaks to attitude, in particular to an author's attitude toward his or her subject. Tone is established by such devices as word choice, imagery, syntax, and level of diction and by the incorporation of comments with an ironic, humorous, or sad twist. Essays in this anthology range in tone from bitter to joyful, from sad to humorous. Some essays are known for their tone, for example Dr. King's calm tone in his "Letter," Jonathan Swift's satiric tone in his "A Modest Proposal," and Abraham Lincoln's elegiac tone in "The Gettysburg Address." Frances Mayes's "*Bramare*: (Archaic) To Yearn For," an essay richly enthusiastic in its many descriptions of the eighteenth-century Tuscan villa that will soon be the author's new home, feels very warm and personal. When you read an essay, especially if you are going to write a paper about it, take care to consider tone, noting the details with which it is conveyed and its effect on the overall essay.

Theme   You will probably recognize the term **theme** from your everyday life, also. A manager may call a meeting, the theme of which is that some employees are forgetting the store's motto that the customer is always right. The theme of an essay is the main idea it articulates, the point that all evidence, examples, and/or reasons support. In some essays, you might be able to underscore a line that seems to sum up the entire essay. Some students underline the phrase "all men are created equal" as summing up Jefferson's theme in the Declaration of Independence. Some readers feel that the repetition of the words "Blessed are" in Matthew's "Beatitudes" drives home the theme that suffering leads to spiritual blessing. Sometimes the theme of an essay seems much more subtle, more obliquely stated. In such essays, you may find no thesis, no single passage or group of words that fairly summarizes the author's theme. Because no two people will articulate the theme of a given piece of literature in exactly the same way, especially when it is implicit instead of explicit, theme lends itself well to papers.

THE READER'S BOX

Questions for Engagement, Response, and Analysis: Essay

Style

1. How does the writer's diction contribute to the theme and tone of the essay?
2. Is the writer's syntax complex, elaborate, simple, precise? What is the effect?
3. What kinds of figurative language does the essay contain? What is the effect?

Tone

1. How would you describe the essay's tone?
2. How is tone established?
3. What does the tone lend to the essay's overall effect?

Theme

1. What is the author's theme? What are the supporting details?
2. How do the style and tone help develop the theme?
3. How do the author's subpoints and examples develop his or her theme?

The Elements of Fiction   Fiction is often thought of as the opposite of fact, but it may be based on facts and certainly can include factual material. As a narrative, fiction tells a sequence of events, though not always in a way we immediately recognize. Short fiction has long been a source of enjoyment and instruction in such forms as parables, fables, anecdotes, and jokes. A relatively new form, short stories differ from other forms of short fiction in purpose. **Parables** and **fables** teach a lesson or a moral; anecdotes generally illustrate a point; and jokes entertain through humor. Most short stories are both brief and unified, all their parts working together to create a coherent whole. Writers make every word count. Ernest Hemingway once described the nature of the short story by comparing it to an iceberg: to paraphrase Hemingway, what is visible in a short story is only the tip of the story; in order to fathom the rest, readers need to dive deep. To read a short story carefully, consider point of view, setting, style, character, plot, and theme.

Point of View   Because it determines what readers know and do not know, **point of view**, the focus from which the story is told, is a crucial element. Some fiction is written from the **objective point of view**, which simply describes observable events. Some fiction has an **omniscient**, all-knowing, point of view that allows the author, writing in third person, to tell readers what any or all of the characters think, feel, and do. You can recognize this point of view by the author's use of third-person pronouns.

First-person point of view allows readers to see the action through the eyes of one character and to know only that character's thoughts, whether that character is the main character or a minor character. You can recognize this point of view by the author's use of "I." Tim O'Brien's narrator in "The Man I Killed" never speaks out loud to the other characters in the story, but we recognize the use of first-person point of view when he thinks "the man I killed would have listened to stories." When an author uses first-person point of view, you need to decide whether the narrator is reliable or unreliable. An unreliable narrator may alter details or provide partial details or may simply be unable to perceive the truth. The narrator in Charlotte Perkins Gilman's "The Yellow Wallpaper" obviously is an unreliable narrator because she is losing her mind.

You can recognize **third-person-limited** point of view by the author's use of third-person pronouns. Unlike omniscient, which also uses third-person pronouns, third-person-limited point of view allows readers to know the thoughts of only one character and to follow only that one character throughout the action. Carson McCullers uses this point of view in "A Domestic Dilemma," sharing only Martin's feelings and theories about the causes of Emily's behavior rather than letting readers into her mind. In providing the history of the changes in Emily, McCullers writes from

Martin's perspective: "He encountered a latent coarseness in Emily, inconsistent with her natural simplicity." Readers do not get to hear Emily's side of the story. If you write an essay about point of view, ask yourself what would be lost if the story were written in another point of view. This exercise often reveals what a particular point of view adds to the text.

Setting   A story's **setting**—the time, place, and culture in which the action occurs—may be extremely significant. For instance, many readers argue that setting is an integral element in James Baldwin's "Sonny's Blues," for neither the music nor the racial relationships would be the same in another setting. Ursula LeGuin's "The Ones Who Walk Away from Omelas," on the other hand, gains universality for some readers through its unknown mythic time and place. Setting can even be symbolic. For example, some readers interpret the highways and backroads of Flannery O'Connor's "A Good Man Is Hard to Find" as representing the condition of the soul—its journeys and its habit of getting lost on dark paths. If you choose to prepare an argument about setting, you can offer a claim concerning the setting's significance in revealing theme or character or its symbolic function.

Style   Style refers to the author's choices concerning word selection (**diction**), sentence structure (**syntax**), and **figurative language** (for example, **imagery**, **symbolism**, and **metaphor**). Some writers use fairly simple, straightforward sentences, especially if they are using a first-person narrator who is unsophisticated. In "A Christmas Memory," for instance, Truman Capote's narrator recalls his childhood using both simple diction and syntax and imagery that captures childlike wonder, as when he says of his dog, "Queenie tries to eat an angel." Some writers, William Faulkner for example, are known for styles that are extremely complex, even poetic. Such authors employ poetic tools such as rhythm and symbolic language. Another example of figurative language, a **symbol** stands for both the thing it names and something else. Some symbols are almost universal: for instance, light is often used to symbolize a growth in knowledge, a realization, or enlightenment. Other elements become symbolic within the context of a particular story and may be interpreted differently by different readers. Examples of symbols that make sense within the context of the story in which they appear are the tiny hand on Georgiana's cheek in Nathaniel Hawthorne's "The Birthmark" and Emily's bedroom in William Faulkner's "A Rose for Emily."

Authors' stylistic choices may seem casual, but they seldom are. For example, Flannery O'Connor's **simile** in "A Good Man Is Hard to Find" describing the forest as being "like a dark open mouth" is often seen as foreshadowing the imminent future of the family. Elements of style also help the author create the tone of the story. The unusual alliterative sounds with which the narrator describes her perceptions in Charlotte Perkins Gilman's "The Yellow Wallpaper" are often seen as establishing an ominous and foreboding atmosphere: "The color is repellent, almost revolting: a smouldering unclean yellow, strangely faded by the slow-turning sunlight. It is a dull yet lurid orange in some places, a sickly sulphur tint in others." An argument may certainly be made that this description seems almost to be hissing at the reader. If you would like to write an argument concerning the effect of style on character, theme, or tone, you will find rich choices in this anthology.

Character   **Character** refers to the people authors create to inhabit their stories. The main character is the **protagonist**. An opposing force or character that combats with or clashes with the protagonist is the **antagonist**. For example, in Joyce Carol Oates's "Where Are You Going, Where Have You Been?" Connie is the protagonist, and Arnold Friend is the antagonist. Usually, authors try to create believable, consistent characters. Consistency requires that any action or change in character be sufficiently motivated by what happens in the story. Authors may reveal characters in a variety of ways: by telling about them directly, by letting their actions and speech reveal their personalities, or by having other characters describe them.

The major characters in a piece of fiction are usually **round, dynamic characters**. Their personalities are well developed and believable, and they often change or grow as the story progresses. Sometimes this change is brought about by an **epiphany**, a sudden revelation or understanding, as in James Joyce's "Araby" when the boy comes face-to-face with reality. Characters who neither change nor grow are **flat, static characters**. Students tend to enjoy writing character analyses because studying someone's personality is familiar. For instance, you may wonder whether or not there is an aspect of Georgiana's personality in Hawthorne's "The Birthmark" that motivates her to go along with her husband's wishes.

Plot   **Plot** refers to the pattern of the action. Some short stories function just as they do in life: when you tell a story, you probably try to "start at the beginning." The "beginning" of the story in a piece of fiction may or may not be the beginning of the action. The fictional story may begin at some high point in the action and use **flashback** or some other technique to fill in the information necessary for an understanding of the situation. Usually plot includes **exposition**—information about the setting and the characters—and a **complication** or **conflict** that occurs within the main character, between that character and some force in nature, or between that character and another. This conflict builds until the story reaches a **climax**, a peak of action or suspense. The story's end presents the **resolution**, an unraveling of the conflict, also called the **denouement**. If plot details are out of the usual, everyday order, as in William Faulkner's "A Rose for Emily," creating a time line may help you understand the story more thoroughly. Plots such as this one just seem to beg us to write essays about their significance.

Theme   **Theme** is the major idea of a short story, the deeper meaning to which all the elements seem to be pointing. Because so much is hidden in a short story—remember Hemingway's iceberg image—theme is often difficult to articulate. For instance, do you feel the theme of Carson McCullers's "A Domestic Dilemma" is that the complexities of love serve as a trap; that modern mobility causes insecurity; or that the conflict between love for a spouse and love for one's children may pose ethical dilemmas? While we may disagree about themes, a story without a theme often seems trivial. We expect the author to use point of view, setting, style, character, and plot to offer us insight into human behavior, to leave us feeling as if we have learned something about our world and about ourselves. This new insight may be repugnant or inspirational, sad or delightful; it may make us aware of human bestiality or nobility, of the wonders of relationships, or of the complexities of love. Whatever it says to you and however you respond, the theme is the heart of the short story, its reason for being—and, thus, it is a rich element to investigate in a paper.

THE READER'S BOX

Questions for Engagement, Response, and Analysis: Short Stories

Point of View
1. What is the point of view in the story? What does that point of view add to the story?
2. If it is first-person or third-person limited, through which character do readers see the story? Is the character a reliable narrator or observer? How does his or her personality affect your perception of the action or of other characters?

Setting
1. Where and when does the story take place? Does the setting seem symbolic in any way?
2. What would be changed if the story were set somewhere else? What does the particular setting of a story add to its overall effect?

Style
1. How would you describe the diction and syntax? Are they child-like, simple, complex? What does the style add to the story?
2. Examine the author's figurative language. Do any of these devices give "clues" about character or foreshadow later actions or events?
3. Look for any symbols that really intrigue you. What do they represent in the story, and how do they enrich its meaning?
4. What is the tone of the story? How is it achieved?

Character
1. How would you describe the personalities of the characters in the story?
2. Do any of the characters develop or change in the story? Is this change one of the major points of the story?
3. Does a character take—or fail to take—an action that puzzles you? What is the motivation for that action or inaction?

Plot
1. What is the conflict in the story? When does the reader first realize there is a conflict?
2. List the steps in the development of the plot. Does it begin with "the beginning" of the story?
3. Where does the conflict reach a climax, and what is the resolution?
4. What effect does the particular plot have on this story?

Theme
1. What is the theme of the story?
2. How do all of the elements of the story work together to convey the theme?
3. Does the theme provide an insight into the human condition?
4. Does a character experience an epiphany that seems to articulate the story's reason for being?

The Elements of Poetry   Some readers find poetry to be an intimidating genre. After all, the primary units of poetry are not the familiar sentences and paragraphs but lines and stanzas; expansive human emotions are expressed in an extremely condensed format; and the wording is often metaphoric. Do you recall the comment from Emily Dickinson that she recognized poetry because it made her feel as if the top of her head had been taken off? Poetry is a powerful potion. As with the other genres, though, by reading critically—reading attentively and carefully—you will begin to unlock the secrets of poetry. You may want to consider situation and speaker, structure and sound, style, and theme.

Situation and Speaker   Many poems seem to arise out of a clearly defined **situation**, the details of who is talking to whom and why. Some poems are quite absurd, and ascertaining the situation is a bit like trying to locate all the body parts in a Picasso painting; in other poems, this task is simpler. One strategy for finding the situation of a poem is to employ the journalistic writing prompts *who, what, where, when, why,* and *how.* The *who* is the voice that is speaking in the poem, referred to logically as the **speaker**. Poems are crafted to be told from a certain perspective and to have a certain voice that is unique to that poem. The speaker is the voice that establishes a poem's distinct viewpoint. Avoid assuming that the speaker and the poet are one and the same. Some poems are autobiographical; some are not. To analyze a poem, you can also consider the *what, where, when, why,* and *how* of a poem's situation. Ask what is happening; where the situation is taking place and when; why events have happened and how? For instance, the situation in Robert Browning's "My Last Duchess" is often identified in this way: the Duke is taking the Count's agent on a tour of his upstairs art gallery. Some readers suspect that the *what*, a deed most foul, happened before the *when* of the poem. The journalist's *why* and *how* become very rich ground for interpretation as more and more of the Duke's personality is revealed.

Structure and Sound   The most immediately visible and audible elements of a poem derive from the poet's approach to structure and sound: you look at a page or hear something read and declare that the text looks and sounds—or does not look and sound—like a poem. In general, a poem's structure can be closed or open. In writing a closed form poem, the poet fits words to form, making ideas and words fit the prescribed structure. The most common closed form stanza patterns in English include the couplet, the quatrain, and the sonnet. A **couplet** is simply a pair of metrically regular, rhymed lines. Couplets are tightly controlled and challenging to write because of the difficulty of finding rhymes in English. **Quatrains**, stanzas of four lines using various rhyme schemes and metrical patterns, are the most often used stanza in English poetry, perhaps because they are the most flexible of the three stanza forms. The **sonnet** is a tightly controlled poem of fourteen lines written in iambic pentameter. The **Italian sonnet** consists of two parts, an eight-line octave rhyming *abbaabba* and a six-line sestet usually rhyming *cdecde* or *cdcdcd.* The **English** or **Shakespearean sonnet** consists of three quatrains followed by a couplet, rhyming *abab cdcd efef gg.* In writing an open form poem, sometimes referred to as free verse or organic structure, the poet allows the words to create form. Poets who chose to employ open forms prefer to let ideas and the natural music of language create structure. Open form poems may or may not have rhymes, and many have unique structure. Poets like e. e. cummings have shown how language can create its own form in both playful and serious style.

Meter, or rhythm, refers to the regular pattern of accented (stressed) and unaccented (unstressed) syllables in a poetic line. There are five basic metrical patterns in English: iambic, trochaic, anapestic, dactylic, and spondaic. An **iambic foot**, or metrical unit, consists of an unaccented syllable followed by an accented one. The line "Ĭ sháll bŭt lóve thĕe béttĕr áftĕr deáth" from Elizabeth Barrett Browning's "Sonnet 43" is in iambic meter. A **trochaic foot** consists of an accented foot followed by an unaccented foot, for example in the word "*childhood.*" An **anapestic foot**, consisting of three syllables, accents the third syllable, "*with a love,*" for instance; and a **dactylic foot**, also containing three syllables, accents the first, as in "*poetry.*" A **spondaic foot** consists of two consecutive accented syllables, as in Browning's "*Smiles, tears.*" The terms *monometer, dimeter, trimeter, tetrameter, pentameter, hexameter, septameter,* and *octameter* refer to the number of feet in a line. When we join metrical unit with number of feet, we know more particularly the sound of a poem, or its rhythmic pattern. The line "Nŏr wóuld Ĭ lóve ăt lówĕr ráte" from Andrew Marvell's "To His Coy Mistress," for example, is iambic and has four accented feet, so we call it iambic tetrameter. Because iambic is by far the most natural and common metrical pattern in English, other feet often direct readers' attention to some aspect of theme or tone. For instance, "To His Coy Mistress" is a very regular poem, using the tightly controlled couplet. Note that Marvell breaks the regularity by opening line four with a strong trochaic foot: "Désĕrts ŏf vást ĕtérnĭty." You may certainly argue that this inverted accent emphasizing the word *deserts* enhances the poem's sense of urgency.

Other than the poem's meter or rhythm, rhyme is an element of a poem's sound that readers immediately notice. A **rhyme** occurs when the final accented syllables of words sound alike, as in height and sight. Rhymes usually occur at the end of poetic lines and are designated by letters so that the first sound is designated *a* and each new sound gets the next letter in the alphabet. In the following lines from Elizabeth Barrett Browning's "Sonnet 43," the rhyme scheme is *abba*:

I love thee to the level of everyday's	a
Most quiet need, by sun and candlelight.	b
I love thee freely, as men strive for Right;	b
I love thee purely, as they turn from Praise.	a

The process of determining patterns of rhythm and rhyme is called **scansion**. Together, meter and rhyme define the stanza patterns of poems.

Clearly, meter and rhyme create sound; poets also have at their disposal a veritable arsenal of devices with which to lend the poem sound effects, so to speak. A poet may, for instance, create a euphonious or melodic sound in a poem, with the liquid consonants "r" and "l," the nasal consonants "m" and "n," and the gentle consonants "f," "v," "th," and "sh" creating a soothing effect. At the other end of the sound spectrum, the poet could create a cacophonous sound, with the explosive consonants "p," "b," "d," "k," "t," and hard "g" booming through. **Alliteration** is the repetition of consonants in stressed syllables, and **assonance** is the repetition of vowel sounds. Compare the line "I love thee freely" of Barrett's sonnet with the line "I woke to black flak" of Randall Jarrell's "The Death of the Ball Turret Gunner" to see how sound can underscore theme. By examining the tools of structure and sound, you will find rich ground for arguable paper topics.

Style   Because of the condensed, economical nature of poems, every stylistic choice a poet makes about words and phrasing is vital. If, as Hemingway argued, what readers see on the page of a short story is but the tip of an iceberg, then what we see of a poem is but an atom sitting atop the tip. First is the figurative language, a stylistic tool that a poet uses to create images that convey deep truths in language we must study in order to interpret. Emily Dickinson speaks of "dwell[ing] in Posssibility." To understand a poem, we have to unpack such metaphors by studying the poem carefully. We need also to look at the speaker's tone (conveyed especially by imagery, the level of diction, and syntax), which can range from the very metaphoric and complex to vulgar and profane. For example, in Robert Browning's "My Last Duchess," the Duke's language is very formal and aristocratic; in Emily Dickinson's "I cannot dance upon my Toes," the tone is fun and joyful. These examples alone tell us that style is a strong subject for analysis.

Theme   Studying theme calls for synthesis, for considering all the elements together and forming a statement about life or the human experience that the poet seems to be making. Of course, not all poems have a theme that can be paraphrased. What words would we use to sum up a theme in Browning's "My Last Duchess"? Still, many poems do lend themselves well to such inquiry. For example, Marvell's "To His Coy Mistress" is famous for its carpe diem theme, the young man pleading with the young woman to stop playing hard to get and get on with living while she is still alive. In thinking about theme, ideas for papers really begin to sizzle.

THE READER'S BOX

Questions for Engagement, Response, and Analysis: Poetry

Situation and Speaker

1. Can you solve the who, what, where, when, why, and how of the poem's situation?

2. Who is the speaker? What do you learn about the speaker during the poem?
3. Is there reason to equate the speaker with the poet?

Structure and Sound

1. What effects are created by the sounds and location of particular words?
2. Does the poem move quickly or slowly? Does it flow smoothly, or does it contain abrupt shifts, stops, and starts? Does its pacing change at some point?
3. How regular is the meter of the poem? If the poet uses a regular metrical pattern, what is that pattern? If the regular meter is changed, what effect is created?
4. Does the poem use rhyme or alliteration? If so, what effects are created?

Style

1. What is the level of the poem's diction? What kind of sentence structures are employed? What is the overall effect of these matters of style?
2. What is the tone of the poem?
3. Turn to the Glossary and read the definition of paradox and irony. Does the poet use either of these devices?
4. What other figurative language or symbols does the poet use? What effects are created by the use of figurative language?

Theme

1. Does the poem have a paraphrasable theme? What is it?
2. In what ways is the theme revealed or developed?
3. How do all the elements come together to express the poem's theme?

The Elements of Drama   Drama holds a unique place in literature because it is the only genre created to be performed. Like all literature, drama ultimately tells part of the human story. Playwrights can tell that story realistically, abstractly, surrealistically, or absurdly. The playwright can also combine human drama with critical or even solemn discussions of issues pertinent to that author's agenda. In reading a play deeply, look especially at several elements: dialogue and stage directions, setting, style, character, plot, and theme.

Dialogue and Stage Directions   In some ways, reading a play demands more from us than reading a novel does because most of the text of a play is composed of **dialogue**, the characters' speaking lines.

The playwright does not have the option, as does the fiction writer, of using narrative points of view to reveal necessary background information or a character's innermost thoughts. Rather, the playwright must rely almost exclusively on dialogue to develop character, to move the plot along, and to handle exposition (the background information necessary to the audience's understanding). The playwright also relies on instructions called **stage directions** to assist directors and actors in bringing the written word to life. Students sometimes "skip" the stage directions, but this text is just as important as is the dialogue. Together, they allow us to imagine the world created by the dramatist, to envision what the play would be like performed live. Included in the stage directions are descriptions having to do with such matters as set, staging, exits, entrances, costumes, volume, and props. In some plays, stage directions are vague or unspecified, leaving the set, movement, and gestures almost entirely to the interpretation of directors and actors; other plays contain extensive stage directions. Directions concerning **blocking** (the gestures, body language, interactions, and movements of characters) are quite important to read because they often reveal character and theme. For instance, an argument can certainly be made connecting theme in Susan Glaspell's *Trifles* with the women's movements.

Setting   Setting includes time, place, and cultural environment. In Henrik Ibsen's *A Doll's House*, set in 1870s Norway, for example, the nineteenth-century attitude toward women is crucial in understanding the play. Similarly, the New England farmhouse kitchen in Glaspell's *Trifles*—the site of hurried, unfinished domestic duties—is crucial in understanding Minnie Wright's situation. Readers know these women better, know the story the playwrights tell about them, by understanding where their stories take place. Likewise, the cultural environment of an African-American family struggling with racial prejudice in the 1950s clarifies family relationships and deepens the understanding of August Wilson's *Fences*. If you choose to write about setting, you can argue what part it plays in creating the overall effect of a particular work.

Style   The playwright's **style** refers to manner of expression, including the way characters present information to the audience, and to the diction, syntax, and figurative language of the dialogue. Sometimes a dramatist uses **soliloquy**, a stylistic technique in which one character alone on stage voices thoughts aloud to the audience. Soliloquies can reveal much. In William Shakespeare's *Othello*, for example, Iago reveals to the audience through soliloquies the motives that he wants to conceal from the other characters. Iago's soliloquies also reveal his personality. He presents himself as a blunt military man, unable to embellish a compliment to women; yet his soliloquies are riddled with complex sexual and animal imagery. Another stylistic device available to the dramatist is the **aside**, a passage or remark the characters speak to the audience or to themselves. The aside gives the illusion that, while the audience hears the character, other characters on stage do not. Close readings of style, especially soliloquies and asides, almost always lead to strong argument topics.

Character   The term character refers to the people created by the playwright and brought to life by the actors. The main character in a play is the protagonist; his or her opponent or opposing force is the antagonist. Othello is the protagonist of Shakespeare's *Othello*; Iago is his antagonist. Minor characters can also play a role in establishing meaning in a play. Christine Linde, for example, seldom appears on stage in Ibsen's *A Doll's House*, yet she is often seen as a **dramatic foil** for Nora, the protagonist. Dramatic characters may be classified as dynamic or static. A character who changes or grows during the course of the play is characterized as dynamic. A character who is flat and/or fails to change or grow is referred to as static.

Motivation is the driving force or incentive for a character's action or inaction. For instance, the women in Glaspell's *Trifles* choose to conceal evidence. You may write an essay that argues the motivation behind their decision. Similarily, you may want to argue why Troy Maxson in August Wilson's *Fences* is driven to act the way he does. Sometimes the motivation is determined by a character flaw or defect, called **hamartia** by the ancient Greek philosopher Aristotle. In classical Greek tragedy, this hamartia leads to the downfall of the protagonist. In Sophocles's *Oedipus Rex*, for example, the audience or reader is acutely aware of the ways in which Oedipus' quick temper and his rush to judgment—qualities of which he is unaware—contribute to his devastating reversal of fortune, or **peripeteia**.

In drama, a character's epiphany is often refered to as **anagnorisis**, another of Aristotle's terms. Anagnorsis describes a character's recognition or discovery of an important truth, which, in turn, leads to the protagonist's self-awareness, a very important part of character development. One of drama's most famous examples of anagnorisis occurs in *Oedipus Rex*, but you can find such self-discovery in many plays. Studying characters—their antagonistic relationships, their motivation, their flaws, their moments of perception and change—offers a wealth of topic choices for writing arguments.

Plot   In his *Poetics*, Aristotle claims that the most important element of a play is its plot. Most dramatists rely on plot as a framework, using a pattern of exposition, conflict, complication, climax, and resolution. A playwright may also use flashback techniques to convey missing information, breaking into the chronology of the play to return to a previous time. As a plot approaches its climax (the high point of the action), **dramatic tension** (the audience's desire to see the conflict resolved) increases. In Sophocles's *Oedipus Rex*, for instance, readers and spectators learn immediately that Oedipus and Creon are at odds. This tension builds when the chorus, Creon, and the blind Teiresias all tell Oedipus that his arrogance may cause suffering. As Oedipus ignores everyone, the dramatic tension builds. **Dramatic irony**, which often increases the dramatic tension of the plot, occurs when an important character, lacking information the audience knows, behaves in a way that is diametrically opposed to his or her own best interest or unknowingly says something that has a double meaning. You may choose to write a paper that offers your interpretation of this famous plot twist or of others in the anthology.

Modern experimental playwrights sometimes eliminate one or more of the traditional parts, sometimes deliberately avoiding a chronological sequence or obscuring altogether any sense that one event necessarily follows or causes another. As you read the plays in this anthology, decide whether you think the playwright is experimental or more traditional in approaching plot. In writing an essay about plot, you may choose to focus on making a claim about the effect of a play's particular plot strategy on character or theme.

Theme   Theme refers to the major ideas or moral precepts that the play embodies. Sometimes it is impossible for any two people to agree upon the exact words that summarize the theme(s) of a piece of literature because moral positions and abstract principles are, naturally, more difficult to express than concrete facts. In many cases, themes can also be related to complex social problems. For instance, Troy's dilemma in *Fences* is a product of the culture in which he lives as well as of his own personality. Though drama may elucidate problems, it seldom advocates solutions to them. Glaspell's *Trifles*, for example, raises questions about responsibility that it does not answer. The elusive nature of theme is one reason you may select an argument about theme: the plays themselves invite such inquiry.

THE READER'S BOX

Questions for Engagement, Response, and Analysis: Drama

Dialogue and Stage Directions

1. What purpose of the playwright do dialogue and stage directions reveal?
2. Is blocking significant? In what way?
3. How does the set as it is described in the stage directions help develop character, plot, theme, and setting?

Setting

1. How does the playwright use the setting to convey character traits, theme, conflict, or irony?

2. Of what importance is the cultural and/or physical environment of the play?

Style

1. Are characters distinguished from each other by their speaking style—their use of figurative language, diction, and syntax?
2. How does the playwright use language to convey information about characters?

Character

1. How does the playwright develop character? What does the dialogue reveal about characters? Does the playwright also use stage movements, gestures, or facial expressions to develop characters?
2. How does the playwright impart to the audience the thoughts, feelings, and ideas a character wants to conceal from other characters?
3. What motivates the protagonist, antagonist, and/or minor characters? What changes, if any, do they experience?
4. Does the protagonist have a tragic flaw (hamartia)? If so, how does this defect in character or mistake in deduction lead to his or her downfall?

Plot

1. Is the plot the traditional Aristotelian plot of beginning, middle, and end? If it is not traditional, what structure does the play-wright use? How do the acts and/or scenes contribute to the overall understanding of the play?
2. What is the basic conflict in the play? Is it between two characters, within a character, or between a character and some larger force such as fate, the environment, or an institution?
3. Is dramatic irony used to reinforce dramatic tension? If so, how does the playwright overcome the problem of revealing to the audience what he or she does not want a character to know?

Theme

1. What questions does the play raise or illuminate? Does it attempt to answer the questions or to solve a problem?
2. What is the play's theme?
3. How do the plot, character, setting, style, and conflict develop the play's theme or central issue?

Part Two: Writing About Literature

Why write about literature? Simply phrased, we write about literature because there is no deeper means of engagement with a text than attempting to articulate an interpretation of it in writing. We write to discover, to uncover our own ideas. This kind of discovery happens in everyday life. Indeed, it is the ground of talk therapy, the idea that the solution to a problem always lies within the person who owns the problem. When a client finally reaches deep down and confesses, "I am afraid to say no because I was never allowed to in my childhood," there is that eureka moment of discovering something that always lay at hand but was somehow buried. When you read what you have to say about literature, you will most likely be amazed at yourself because the act of writing unearths ideas.

Perhaps it is even natural to write about literature. When we read something, our minds cannot literally ignore what was read, as if time could be rewound and played back with those words missing. Engagement with a text, whether oral or written, is an everyday, immediate, active experience. If we read actively, literature involves us in a world outside of ourselves; it confronts us, sometimes even gets in our faces. At times, we respond so vehemently that we protest certain books. Literature demands our participation; our urge to speak back is a natural response. We write about literature because writing is a means of powerful inquiry and discovery and because doing so is to take part in the ongoing human story.

Critical Writing: Argument

Why write arguments about literature? The simplest answer is that employing the rhetorical strategy of argument greatly benefits a paper's quality. It does so by encouraging critical thinking and careful articulation of ideas. Although our culture tends to imagine scenes from talk shows or bar room brawls when someone says "argue," that is not what the term means in an English class; neither is classical argumentation a way to say "I am right, and you are wrong." To write about literature using the strategy of argument is to engage even more deeply with the processes of analytical inquiry. Your responses to all the elements of essay, fiction, poetry, and drama reviewed in Part One of the Introduction are incomplete until clarified by the critical thinking that argument triggers.

Consider the terms of rhetorical **argument**. In rhetoric, the term argue means to give voice to an idea in such a way that others may be persuaded to find what you say worthwhile and convincing. Argument is born out of a rhetorical situation when a debatable subject is introduced and our critical minds—"critical" meaning characterized by careful, exact evaluation and judgment—begin to ponder the topic. Sooner or later, we come to our own positions on the issue at hand and express our views, now referred to as our **claims**. If we are with people whose opinions differ, we may begin to anticipate opposing ideas, or **counterclaims**. To show respect to this opposing view, we speak of common ground, that area of the topic on which we can all agree; or we may choose to qualify our claim by introducing qualifying terms such as *probably, likely, often,*

Say what
you do/don't like Introduction   23
why you don't like
and give evidence

most, and *perhaps.* Then we begin to list the **warrants**, the reasons underlying our belief system that led to our claim in the first place. **Evidence**—facts, examples, and details—supports our warrants. We attempt to persuade our audience via the approach that best fits the rhetorical situation. An appeal to the sense of ethics, pointing out that the claim is ethical, is a strategy of *ethos*. An appeal to the emotions, offering details that affect the emotions, is a strategy of *pathos*. An appeal to reason, stressing the logical nature of a claim, is a strategy of *logos*.

In applying the argumentative process to writing about literature, you may benefit from employing more familiar terms. The debatable subject is an element about the literary text that is open to interpretation, the claim is the **thesis**, and warrants are the **topic sentences**. Evidence is the combination of our own analysis and textual details. Ethos, pathos, and logos are the various ways you craft a paper that is persuasive but not bullying: your warrants and evidence appeal to a reader's ethics, emotions, or logic. That, briefly stated, is the process of inquiry called argument. Of course, any definition is only as good as our ability to use what we can define. Exactly how do we write an argument about literature? In the following section are four steps you may want to follow in preparing an argument about a piece of literature.

Steps for Writing Arguments about Literature

According to family stories, Kate Chopin, an author included in this anthology, would get an idea for a story, sit down, and write it. Period. No pacing back and forth. No days of dreading the task. Do your essays come about like Chopin's? If not, relax. Few of us function that way. Actually, writing in stages benefits your papers in two ways. First, you will have more time for careful, clear articulation of ideas. Second, breaking the writing process up into more manageable steps reduces anxiety and fits more easily into a busy lifestyle. Your teacher may in fact assign certain steps. If not, you may want to consider the advantages of the following steps: Establishing Purpose and Audience; Generating a Working Thesis; Gathering Evidence; and Drafting, Revising, and Editing.

Step One: Establishing Purpose and Audience

Speaking generally, the purpose of your paper is the reason you are writing it, the claim you want to prove; the audience is the individual or group whom you are addressing. Purpose and audience may be provided to you by the teacher as part of the assignment, or they may arise naturally in the classroom. In the latter case, you may read a particular piece of literature and then discuss it in class. As other students share their ideas, you may realize that your interpretation of the text differs from that of the person sitting right beside you. Your audience is that student. Your purpose is not to prove that person wrong; your goal is to articulate your interpretation clearly in a way that shows that it is also a valid way to read the text.

Modes   In assigning arguments about literature, some teachers employ **modes**, models or prescribed formats that assist writers in articulating ideas. Some assignments call for complete adherence to a specific model; others ask students to use modes as needed to accomplish certain effects or purposes. A few popular modes that appear on literary argument assignment sheets are Explication, Analysis, and Comparison/Contrast.

Explication derives from a Latin word meaning to unfold, to explain, to make clear the meaning of something. Explication involves deep examination and extensive explanation of a literary piece. Think of having tunnel vision that allows you to focus on only the words on the page: a paper that explicates a work of literature zooms in closely, explaining thoroughly the text's meaning, line by line or passage by passage. Because such close study helps students to comprehend poems, explication is a very popular mode for poetry assignments.

Analysis comes from the term *analyze*, which means to break down into component parts in order to gain understanding of the whole. Analysis examines one aspect of a literary piece as it contributes to an understanding of the whole text. For example, you may examine how a particular character in a story influences the story's outcome, how a play turns on a critical scene, how an image in a poem contributes to the poem's overall theme, or how irony affects our understanding of a character.

Comparison/Contrast is a particular kind of analysis that looks simultaneously at two different aspects of one text or at two separate works. Comparison/contrast essays tend to fall into two methods of organization, block and alternating. The block method devotes a separate block of writing to each of the two subjects; the alternating method focuses on one common characteristic at a time, referring alternately to one subject, then to the other. If you craft a block Comparison/Contrast analyzing Alice Walker's "Everyday Use," for example, you might create one section focusing on Dee and another on Maggie; if you select to write in the alternating format, you might talk about both sisters in each paragraph, focusing on particular topics, such as self-image, attitudes toward heritage, or education.

Debatable Topics   In writing about literature, students are often tempted to paraphrase the piece of literature, merely retelling what has already been told. To avoid this common pitfall, ask yourself questions about your thesis and your audience. A strong claim does more than state a fact from the story; it offers a particular interpretation. For example, a thesis stating that the two characters in Ernest Hemingway's short story "Hills Like White Elephants" are sitting at a train station is neither debatable nor very intriguing. Who would want to read a paper that argued something that everyone can readily see? Your purpose in writing an academic essay is to make a specific claim about your selected literary work, an explanation that argues specifically how you feel the work communicates its idea. Especially if your teacher does not assign a purpose and audience but asks you to allow those elements to evolve organically as you read and participate in classroom activities, you need to focus on debatable topics. Remember that debatable means that one reader's way of interpreting is not the only way, that there is no one answer—worded in only one way—to a given question about a topic. A common method for examining a text for debabtable topics is to focus on "hot spots," areas that are difficult to navigate because meaning is not clear or because certain details are withheld. For example, solid, debatable arguments can be based on puzzling actions taken by a character. Symbols and imagery are certainly "hot spots" open to interpretation. Offering your interpretation of either the couple's discussion or the symbolic function of the landscape in Hemingway's "Hills Like White Elephants" would lend itself nicely to a strong, debatable thesis.

Audience   As in everyday life, it is imperative to know your audience, the reader(s) of your paper, especially an audience holding an opposing view. Anticipating what your audience already thinks and now needs to know will help you compose a convincing, effective paper that avoids the common pitfall of stating the obvious for a thesis and then giving plot summary as evidence. If you focus on audience, you can instead provide only the particular details and analysis required to help your reader see your point of view about a debatable topic. Here are a few questions to ask yourself:

- Who is my audience?
- How much does my audience already know about this topic? What more does the audience need to know?
- How does my audience feel about this topic? What is the counterclaim? Do my audience and I share any common ground of interpretation?
- What questions might my audience have about my interpretation?
- What is the best order for presenting my reasons and supporting evidence?
- What persuasive approach might work best with my particular audience and topic? What qualifiers (such as *perhaps* and *possibly*) could I use to ensure a respectful tone?

Step Two: Generating a Working Thesis
The title of this section was carefully selected: the "thesis," or claim, at this point in the writing process is a "working thesis." Even though it is a work-in-progress, considering your claim at this juncture is a solid second step. Several strategies are available to assist you at this point.

Re-Reading   First, return to the text. Re-reading a piece of literature once it includes your own marginalia and annotation is a very effective technique. If a piece of marginalia is really insightful or zeroes in on a portion of the text that is confusing, highlight that comment. As other ideas begin to percolate, write them down as well. You can also re-read the assignment sheet—an especially beneficial step when you begin to move deeper into understanding the point at which the assignment and your idea are coming together. Now re-read the literary piece with all your new notes. You may discover a great idea sitting right before your eyes: this is your "working thesis." Now you are ready to develop your idea.

Prewriting Strategies   **Brainstorming** is a very effective method for generating ideas because it encourages the free flow of ideas by removing editing (a later step in writing) from the early prewriting stage. **Freewriting** is one popular brainstorming technique that has only one rule: do not stop writing/typing. Set a timer for a comfortable session, perhaps ten minutes—you can always keep going if you are on a roll. If you have a tentative thesis prepared, you may want to use it as a focus point, perhaps jotted on the top of your paper or on a Post-It-Note on the side of the computer screen. Andie Howard, the student showcased in this Introduction, performed a freewriting which appears in Part One of the Introduction. If you turn back to that sample, you will notice that Andie kept writing until her teacher called time, even when all she could think to do was to write the word "okay" and then tell herself to go back to freewriting.

Two other pre-writing strategies are particularly beneficial if you are more visually oriented. As the name implies, **listing** entails writing a list of ideas, for example your thesis, topic sentences, and supporting evidence. The list can be composed of fragments or sentences, whichever you prefer. Another strategy, **clustering**, is very visual. Write down your working thesis (or even just a focus word) on a piece of paper. Draw a circle around it. Surround the thesis with as many possible warrants as you can think of, drawing a circle around each. To envision this technique, imagine a mobile of the solar system with the planets floating around the sun: the sun is your main idea or working thesis; the planets are the topic sentences or warrants. You can also draw lines connecting the supporting points to the working thesis, like strings hooking planets to the sun on a mobile. Repeat this process as evidence, or supporting details, and analysis come to mind.

The purpose of prewriting is to produce ideas, not to criticize and stifle the free flow of your thoughts. The Writer's Box below reproduces two other samples of Andie Howard's prewriting. In the clustering session, Andie was trying to choose between two possible paper topics. The prewriting sample is a list that she constructed as she tried to narrow her thesis and build support.

The Writer's Box

Sample Student Brainstorming: Clustering and Listing

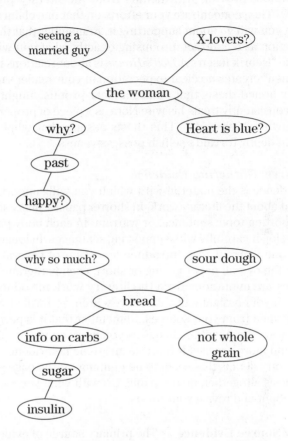

Working Thesis: the affair is like the bread, tastes good but won't satisfy

Support #1: tastes good	Support #2: empty
"Filled"	info on whole grain
affair	info on white bread
past lovers	insulin reaction
clueless man	she's in denial
Sex!	"just the way it is"!

Honing the Thesis   Perhaps the most important piece of advice you need to hear—which is why it is repeated here—is that at this point you are still dealing with a work-in-progress. You still have time to backtrack to another idea if you need to do so. If your essay involves outside research, you may in fact wish to locate your sources before committing to the final topic. (See below for tips on researching.) One key to focusing your thesis is to ask yourself this question: "What one claim am I most excited about proving with details from the literary piece(s) that I selected?" Then concentrate your efforts on that one claim and the ways in which you will go about supporting it. Remember that the final thesis will function as a contract, promising exactly what you will provide. A claim like "Henrik Ibsen's *A Doll's House* is about relations between men and women" creates no clear expectation in your reader's mind. A more precisely honed thesis that makes a clear promise might be "Torvald Helmer consistently treats his wife Nora as a piece of property to be used for his own selfish ends." This thesis asserts that what follows will discuss in depth Torvald's selfish possessiveness.

Step Three: Gathering Evidence

Your evidence is the material with which you will support your overall argument about the literary work. In shorter papers, many students place one supporting topic sentence, or warrant, in each body paragraph and then develop it carefully with supporting sentences. In longer researched papers, one warrant may introduce a section of several paragraphs. Whether the overall paper is long or short, each paragraph's supporting sentences are quotations from the literary work introduced into your analysis. If your assignment calls for research, you will also include evidence gleaned from your sources. Remember that it is perfectly normal for the thesis statement to change as you work on your topic, becoming clearer and more precise. If there seems to be no evidence to gather, or if the literary details that seem to be jumping off the page support a different thesis altogether, do not panic. Go with what you seem most passionate about and revise your thesis.

Primary Source Evidence   The primary source of evidence for your paper is the work of literature itself. Anticipate your audience—their counterclaims, their questions, and the amount of evidence they will need in order to understand your points. Ask yourself exactly which images, actions, words, or scenes are vital to clarifying your interpretation. Often at least three or four passages or examples will develop a topic well. You may want to highlight these details in the text, perhaps using a different color highlighter for each warrant or body paragraph. You may benefit from looking at the sample student paper at the end of the Introduction, in particular at the topic sentences and the evidence used to support them. Do you feel the details "add up" to clarify Andie's overall claim? You may also want to look at the sample scholarly and student essays in the Casebooks.

Secondary Source Evidence   Some literary assignments call for research, critical interpretations or historical materials relevant to your literary piece. In the library, online catalogs make available every book in your school's library—and frequently those in other libraries as well. Periodical indexes lead to articles in literary journals. Reference works that focus on authors and literature are also beneficial. Two espeically popular indexes for literary study are the *MLA International Bibliography* and the *Essay and General Literature Index*. Ask your librarian to point to scholarly research sites that can lead you to a global collection of material. Because availability varies from institution to institution, try to attend a library research orientation at your college or university.

Outside sources call for caution: you need to make certain that secondary sources are reliable. Always consider the credentials of the writer and the reputation of the publication and/or site. Ask yourself if the source's author demonstrates by credentials (profession, degrees, firsthand experience, scholarly publications) a wide range of knowledge about the subject. Also, consider the domain of electronic sources. The four most common are recognizable by their endings: sites produced by educational institutions end with .edu; sites maintained by nonprofit organizations such as churches end with .org; sites produced by commerical organizations end in .com; and sites maintained by governmental agencies end in .gov. In general, an Internet source is reliable if it is an online version of a reliable print source, if it is written by a scholar in the field, or if it has been produced by a reliable agency.

Once you have found a source that you think will be helpful, record the bibliographic information immediately, especially if the source is located on the Internet. Some students prefer the traditional way of recording this information on $3'' \times 5''$ cards; others simply type bibliographic information into an electronic file and later paste the information onto the Works Cited/Bibliography page. Carefully documenting sources not only gives credit to the source but also helps readers locate information for further study. To document means to acknowledge material in your paper that is not your own. Failure to document sources is **plagiarism**, presenting someone else's work as your own, an act that is both unethical and illegal. While it is not necessary to document common knowledge, such as dates, facts, or ideas that are generally known, you may want to document any information that is new to you. In your literature papers, document primary and secondary sources when

- Quoting the source's exact words
- Paraphrasing the secondary sources' words
- Referencing a counterclaim or opposing interpretation

Step Four: Drafting, Revising, and Editing
You have re-read the literary piece, reconsidered your own position, and perhaps even reviewed some secondary sources. Now comes the drafting stage. Some students prepare a structured and detailed outline up front, complete with Roman numerals and indented subpoints; other

students prefer simply to begin writing or typing; and still others prefer a method referred to as blocking, which is the arrangement and rearrangement of ideas in groups or "blocks." Blocking produces not a finished order but a series of starting points from which to work, a method that allows you to rearrange the blocks until you arrive at a pattern that seems promising. However you begin the task of writing, remembering that the paper is a draft is vital: at this stage, neither neatness nor correctness is important, except when you are quoting and documenting. Your primary goal in drafting should be to get your ideas down. If you find that you cannot continue with one paragraph, begin another and return later to the difficult one. You may want to leave gaps or write marginal notes in your manuscript to indicate omissions or changes you want to make later.

Writing the Introduction   Though it may or may not be the first paragraph you write, the introduction is the first paragraph your audience reads. An effective introduction invites a reader to enter the world created by the essay. Some students like to open their introduction with the thesis and then preview their supporting warrants. Other students open with a "grabber" or "hook," then narrow the focus and place the thesis as the last sentence. Popular hooks include quotations, questions, anecdotes, interesting facts, definitions, and surprising statements. Pick the strategy that best fits both the assignment and your personal style. Sample student papers, scholarly essays in the Casebooks, and the professional essays in the anthology offer a wealth of introductions for your review.

Crafting Body Paragraphs and Making Transitions   A body paragraph is a group of sentences with a central idea governing order, focus, and development. Within the paragraph, there are usually three types of sentences: the topic sentence, supporting sentences, and transitional sentences. The characteristics of a paragraph are unity, coherence, and development. In a unified paragraph, the central idea serves as the core point of the paragraph with all other sentences supporting it. The core point, referred to as the topic sentence or warrant, often appears as the first or one of the first sentences in the paragraph. To be an effective topic sentence, the warrant should support the paper's overall thesis or claim, introduce the topic of the body paragraph, and connect smoothly and logically to other topic sentences. **Supporting sentences** develop the claim of the topic sentence and include the writer's own ideas and analysis, examples and details from the piece of literature, and information gathered from outside sources, if appropriate. Think of the support sentences as "proving" the topic sentence.

Transition sentences offer coherence, linking sentences within paragraphs and linking one paragraph with the other paragraphs. The internal coherence of a body paragraph can be achieved by connecting two points through phrasing or by the use of transitional expressions such as *in addition, yet, moreover, therefore, however, furthermore, meanwhile, likewise, also, since, before, hence, on the other hand, as well,* and *thus.* Another natural and effective way to create transition is to repeat key words and phrases. Transitional sentences also act like verbal glue, connecting the body paragraphs into a cohesive unit and promoting the essay's readability.

Some students are puzzled when assignments call for paragraphs that are well-developed. After all, paragraphs have no required length in order to be called paragraphs. So, what makes a well-developed paragraph? Short, choppy paragraphs often sacrifice clarity and leave the reader with unanswered questions; on the other hand, an essay composed of very long, detailed paragraphs might prove tiresome and confusing to the reader. Aim for a comfortable length that answers all the questions you raise, remembering that a paragraph presents a single unified idea. Begin a new paragraph when your subject changes. You may find the list of prompts below beneficial for constructing organized, coherent, well-developed body paragraphs.

- Organize material logically into the various body paragraphs.
- Early on, perhaps as the first sentence, include a topic sentence that expresses the core point of the paragraph.
- Fully support and explain the core point; eliminate off-focus sentences.
- Use transitional sentences and phrases to make sure paragraphs flow well and link smoothly with each other.

Concluding Well   The job of the conclusion is to pull together all the points made in the paper. Beware of a common pitfall: the temptation simply to repeat verbatim what you have already said elsewhere in the paper. You may want to review the list of possibilities for openers to find a powerful way to end—quotations, questions, and anecdotes especially lend themselves well to conclusions. Be careful, though, that you do not throw in evidence or a question that opens a brand new paper. You want the reader to feel satisfied, to feel that all issues and questions raised have been supported and answered. You may enjoy examining sample conclusions in this textbook by professional writers, scholars, and students.

Integrating Source Evidence   Whether placed in the introduction, body, or conclusion, source evidence (primary and secondary) helps you develop your points. Several guidelines can assist you in avoiding the common pitfall of "dumping" quotations into your literary argument. First, incorporate sources in such a way that your reader knows which passages of text are yours and which are from the source. For example, a signal phrase such as "Shakespeare writes" or "Othello says" effectively identifies the author/speaker. A second guideline to consider when integrating sources concerns the nature of the borrowed material: text that is paraphrased is not placed in quotation marks but does require a parenthetical citation; text that is quoted must be quoted exactly, placed within quotation marks, and followed by a citation. Any material added to a quotation must be placed in brackets, and an omission must be indicated with ellipses.

A third guideline for integrating textual evidence is to blend quoted material so that it flows with your own prose. You do not want the reader to feel that you simply stuck evidence in anywhere. Achieve a smooth integration by considering grammatical and contextual flow. Blend a quoted fragment by fitting it into your own sentence structure. You may use your own independent clause followed by a colon in order to introduce a quotation that is a rather lengthy fragment or a complete sentence. Another grammatically correct way to integrate a quotation is to place a signal/anchoring phrase (such as "says," "according to," etc.) in front of, in the middle of, or after the quoted material. Achieve contextual flow by placing the quotations in your paper in such a way that they make sense. The material should function as support for a point you have made. You will also want to comment on any quotation you include because not everyone reads literature in the same way. An excellent strategy for checking for a nice flow between quoted words and your own is to read the paper out loud. For further guidance on handling source materials, see Appendix C: Documenting a Research Paper: MLA Format.

THE WRITER'S BOX
Avoiding Common Pitfalls at the Drafting Stage

- Is your introduction inviting?
- Is your thesis a debatable claim?
- Does your paper maintain a respectful tone throughout?
- Do you consider an opposing interpretation?
- Do you have strong topic sentences that act as warrants supporting the thesis?
- Do your body paragraphs avoid mere plot summary by combining your analysis with textual evidence?
- Have you blended quotations into the flow of your paper?
- Are all quotations identified and anchored? Do all quotation have quotation marks around them?
- Do you have parenthetical citations for all quotations and paraphrases?
- Does your conclusion end convincingly?

Revising and Editing   Revision means exactly what it says, gaining new vision on what you have said. The best way to achieve new vision is with distance. Put your draft aside for as long as time permits in order to gain objectivity; then reread it, asking yourself the questions in the Writer's Box above. Rearranging or adding paragraphs or sections may create a clearer, more convincing essay. If you move or add sections, be aware that you may need to revise the thesis and/or transitional sentences to reflect the new order. Look also for ideas that seem out of place or sound awkward, passages that lack adequate support and detail, and evidence that does not really support your claim. Do not be afraid to make substantive changes because that is what revision is all about, making sure the paper says what you want it to say. The strange truth about writing is this: often we simply do not know what we want to say until we have said it.

Editing your paper is not the same as revising it. Editing focuses on grammar, sentence errors, punctuation, word choices, and stylistic decisions. Read your paper carefully. Mark errors and passages that fail to articulate your idea clearly. Take advantage of any tutoring centers at your institution, and certainly make use of your computer's spelling and grammar checks—do not rely solely on them though because they miss errors such as the accidental use of "there" for "their." One strategy for the common tendency toward sentence errors like comma splices, run ons, and fragments is to follow this two-part technique: first, go through the paper with a colored marker, pen, or pencil and place triangles around all commas and squares around all periods; then read the paper backward, sentence by sentence, to check for complete sentences and proper comma usage. Another strategy, this one to check for style and appropriate voice, is to read the paper aloud to a friend or family member. Reading to a live audience does wonders for catching errors and for strengthening your style because what listeners demand of us—that we are clear, that we are organized and coherent, that our words are appropriate for the situation, that we refrain from rambling on and on when our point is made—is what readers demand of us as well. You may want to take advantage of the following Writer's Box as you edit.

The Writer's Box
Avoiding Common Pitfalls in the Editing Stage

- Maintain the literary present tense. For example, Iago *speaks* (not spoke) to Othello.
- Maintain active voice. Although grammatically correct—and even preferable at times—passive voice can slow down the flow of a paper or distance the reader from your material. In active voice, you make your agent "actively" perform an action: the sentence "Othello is talked to by Iago" is passive, but the sentence "Iago talks to Othello" is active and, thus, preferable.
- Ask for your teacher's preference for person. Some teachers prefer that arguments maintain third person.
- The first time you use an author's name, use the full name as it is published, for instance, T. S. Eliot. After that use the last name

> only. Do not refer to authors by their first name only unless that is all we know, for example, in the case of Luke.
> - Maintain positive persuasion. Avoid logical fallacies, for example, the exaggerated claim that "all readers know."
> - Print out copies of drafts for proofreading. Do not rely solely on spelling and grammar checks.
> - Always double-check for the most common errors in college-level papers: misspelling, fragments, run ons, comma splices, omitted commas, unnecessary commas, subject/verb agreement errors, misplaced apostrophes, pronoun reference errors, missing or incorrect transitional terms, omitted words, and exclusive language.
> - Double-check all MLA format issues—from top matter, through the paper, to the end of the Works Cited page.

Mark Twain once said, "Let us guess that whenever we read a sentence and like it, we unconsciously store it away in our model-chamber; and it goes, with the myriad of its fellows, to the building, brick by brick, of the eventual edifice which we call our style." Rest assured: you have what it takes to craft essays about literature. The literature itself helps you by encouraging you to "store away" writing styles while you search for your own. When you get ready to consider writing about the literature, get away to a quiet spot and simply enjoy what you are reading. Engage with it. Speak back to the author by jotting down your reactions in the margin or a journal. Be a careful reader, looking up words you do not know. Go through the questions at the end of the selection, and turn back to the appropriate Reader's Box for the genre you are reading. Ask yourself some of these questions in order to enrich your understanding. The quality of a paper is often determined by the quality of the questions you ask yourself about what you have read. Once you move from analysis to crafting the essay, be a careful writer. Understand your assignment. Carve out time for drafting, revising, and editing. Proof, proof, and proof again. Last, congratulate yourself on a job well done.

Sample Student Paper

The assignment particulars and the history of this student's sample paper are discussed throughout the Introduction.

MLA format. The paper is double spaced with one-inch margins. Here and on each page, Andie has placed her header (name and the page number) so that it is flush with the right margin. Flush with the left margin and double spaced is Andie's identifying information in proper format. There is no extra double spacing between this top matter and the title or between the title and the body of the paper. Andie's title is centered with quotation marks around both a quotation from the story used as title and the title of the short story itself.

Howard 1

Andie Howard

Professor Higgins

English 1102

28 February 2008

"We were hungry": the Image of Bread in Sandra

Cisneros' Short Story "Bread"

What can a reader say about Sandra Cisneros' short story "Bread"? The story is extremely short, under twenty sentences, and many of those are fragments. The plot can be summarized as a man and a woman ride through a city eating bread. The point of view is first person, the woman's perspective. Despite the story's brevity, it is powerful, and it is made even more meaningful because of the bread. For some readers, the bread is a narrative detail that adds to the setting. Such a reading is certainly valid: the bread imagery is so vivid that readers can almost smell and taste it. Perhaps there is even more significance to the bread. Cisneros <u>did</u> choose the word to be her title. In this very short, short story, the bread represents the nature of the extramarital relationship between the man and woman, one which seems to fill a hunger but is ultimately unsatisfying.

First of all, the bread represents the hunger in the couple's relationship. Beginning with the very first line, readers are witness to the hunger in this relationship. The opening words are "We were hungry" (3). Perhaps a more precise term would be ravenous. The couple did not just pick up a light snack at the bakery; they "[f]illed the backseat" with sourdough bread (3). They feel hungry enough to eat a backseat full of bread. From this very first detail, readers begin to sense also that the hunger is not just physical but sexual as well. The first paragraph is breathless with fragments. Sentences rush by, describing one sensual

Andie chose a question to open her paper with a hook. After her opening hook, Andie then provides a very brief summary of the story.

Note that Andie anticipates an opposing interpretation, acknowledging that others may see the bread differently than she does.

Andie uses the qualifying word "Perhaps" in order to acknowledge those who may disagree with her interpretation.

Andie's thesis is a debatable claim that the bread is not simply an element of the setting but a powerful symbol. In the paper, she will attempt to show a connection between the lack of nutritional value of this kind of bread and the unsatisfactory nature of this affair.

MLA format: there is no extra spacing between paragraphs.

MLA format: the bracketed [f] here indicates that Andie changed the letter, from capital "F" to lowercase.

Note Andie's handling of evidence here and throughout the paper. This particular quotation fits within the context of Andie's comments. It is also anchored, placed in quotation marks, and followed by a parenthetical citation. She is also careful to follow the quotation with commentary about it. The author's name is not used in the citation because there is only one source.

Howard 3

image after another. The car is filled with the aroma of
the warm bread. The couple eats not daintily but with
urgency: the narrator says, "We ripped big chunks with our
hands and ate. . . . bread in both fists" (3). They also
do not just listen to music but play a tango that is "loud,
loud, loud" (3). Is there any sexier music than a tango?
Also, we once again see a theme of overabundance: the
couple can get neither enough bread nor enough volume.
Perhaps they cannot get enough of each other either. From
her story, we begin to see that this hungry couple has a
history: she knows that they are the only people in each
other's lives who can stand music so loud; she knew him
before he got married and had children; pain has passed
between them; and they are both incredibly nonchalant about
the fact that he is driving while kissing her. They are
back together again, and they cannot wait to get out of the
car to initiate intimacy but do so as they drive along.

Second, the bread represents the ultimately
unsatisfactory nature of the couple's relationship.
Cisneros' second sentence makes clear that the couple
had purchased the bread in order to satisfy the hunger
described in the first sentence. But will it? Why is there
so much? Look closely at the bread. It is sourdough, which
is not a whole grain bread. Granted, it is acidic and
therefore absorbed more slowly than some "kiddie"
bread. Still, because it is made with processed flour,
the nutrients which are bound up with the fiber in
whole grain breads are already broken down. Processed flour
goes into the body like sugar, pumping up our blood
chemistry and giving us a quick high, but then those very
carbohydrates abandon us. White bread is almost all empty

Andie's topic sentences
support the thesis, introduce the topic of their
paragraph, and function
as transitions.

"Kiddie" is in quotation
marks without a citation
because it is an instance
of quotation mark usage
for special sense.

Howard 4

calories and cannot actually quench hunger. Isn't that the
nature of an extramarital affair? People who have
affairs sometimes claim that they need to feel
wanted, desired, appreciated. But does an affair
fill that need? The narrator in the story has an
overabundance of bread—and music and kisses;
still, her heart is "a pearl blue" (3). Rather than hanging
on her lover's words, she "forget[s]" how he says things
(3). She knows that he is married and has kids. She sees
the city they are in realistically, recalling "a cousin's
baby who died from swallowing rat poison" in the buildings;
the man finds the city "charming" (3). The woman even
admits that a great deal of pain has "passed between" them,
perhaps when he chose his current wife over her (3). Yet
she dismisses all these signals that this relationship will
not quench her needs with the offhand comment, "That's just
how it is" (3).

> Here with the word "sometimes" and two sentences above with the word "almost," Andie includes qualifying terms in order to avoid logical fallacy.

Remember the chip company's famous claim that "no one
can eat just one"? This slogan may be simply an
advertising gimmick, but it makes a valid
argument. Our bodies have to work really hard to
retrieve the nutrients of a food that is fiber rich. This
is slow metabolic work that is ultimately good for us.
Similarly, a marriage is incredibly hard work. Compromise,
unconditional love, and selfless care are found only by
reaching deeply within. For some married people, the
craving for the sexual high is so strong that they turn to
an affair, believing falsely that the high will last.
Eating foods with low fiber count will initially seem to
meet a need; it may even change blood chemistry enough to
produce a momentary high. If, like the couple in "Bread,"

> Andie chose to close with another hook, this time a question that includes a famous quotation from American culture.

one eats only foods that are basically pure carbohydrate,
the body will lose the ability to process sugars and
starches at all; it will then go into starvation mode and
hoard every gram of fat it can get its arteries on. Insulin
resistance could be the end result, or heart attack. The
man and woman in Cisneros' story are gorging on
sourdough bread, a vivid image and also a powerful
symbol. Like the bread, the affair is hot. The couple
eats and kisses with urgency—while in a moving
vehicle. But both the bread and the extramarital affair are
merely sugar rushes waiting to crash.

With the words "a vivid image," Andie once again acknowledges the validity of an opposing viewpoint.

LA format: Andie's
s Cited starts on its
ge and is formatted
s a reprint from this
ogy. All our sample
papers are format-
n this way. You may
structed to set your
ks Cited page up in
way, or you may be
sked to format your
iographic entry as a
selection from an
anthology.

Works Cited

Cisneros, Sandra. "Bread." *Woman Hollering Creek and Other*

    Stories. New York: Vintage Books, 1991. 1. Rpt. in

    Henderson, Higgins, Day, and Waller 3.

Henderson, Gloria Mason, Anna Dunlap Higgins, Bill Day, and

    Sandra Stevenson Waller, eds. *Literature and Ourselves: A*

    Thematic Introduction for Readers and Writers. 6th ed. New

    York: ABLongman. 2009.

Family

A scene from *It's a Wonderful Life*. RKO/The Kobal Collection.

The earliest and usually the strongest influence on each of us is the family. Throughout history, people from every walk of life have accused or thanked, bemoaned or celebrated members of their own families. As a result, family relationships have provided the subject matter for a wide variety of literature. Some families may seem destructive; others are loving and supportive. As readers, we can sympathize with, perhaps even identify with, authors or narrators as they share their own family experiences and as they cope with problems involving parents, siblings, and other family members.

Through the characters in literature, we can vicariously experience family life in a variety of times, on different economic levels, and through diverse cultures. We can understand the joys and sorrows of a mother-daughter relationship as we read Joan Didion and Joyce Carol Oates or gain insight into the dynamics of a father-son relationship by reading Luis Omar Salinas, Li-Young Lee, and Edward Whitelock. We can empathize with parents who want only the best for their children while reading William Butler Yeats' "A Prayer for my Daughter." Writers like Sherman Alexie, Nikki Giovanni, Jhumpa Lahiri, and Janice Mirikitani, coming from diverse backgrounds, share with us what family relationships are like in their communities.

Literature also allows us to experience vicariously the agony of dealing with problems we hope never to face in real life. We can empathize with the dilemmas of families whose lives are complicated by problems with drugs or alcohol in James Baldwin's "Sonny's Blues" and Carson McCullers' "A Domestic Dilemma." By allowing us to participate in the hardships and confusion of modern dysfunctional families such as those portrayed by McCullers, Oates, and August Wilson, literature helps us to understand that the "immense complexity of love" sometimes causes problems that have no easy solutions.

In addition, literature teaches us the value of laughter and tenderness in dealing with family situations. We can laugh at the experience shared by the narrator and his cousin when they visit Mr. Haha in Truman Capote's "A Christmas Memory" and enjoy Bill Cosby's humorous solutions to raising a family in *Fatherhood*. McCullers, in "A Domestic Dilemma," vividly describes Martin's tender love for his children, and Li-Young Lee portrays two generations who will benefit from the father's "gift."

Authors also share with us the realization that even the most disparate family members can work through problems to reach solutions and an even greater depth of love. James Baldwin lets us share in the stories of two brothers and participate in their reconciliation. Capote, drawing from his real-life experiences, tells of the beautiful friendship between a little boy and his much older cousin. Most important, through the enjoyment of this literature—the tears, the curses, the prayers, and the laughter—we can deepen our own understanding of others and of ourselves.

Writing about Family

The essays you write about the works in the Family unit will be diverse. First, consider which genre you want to write about and which work or works you prefer. As you plan your essays, you may want to reread the Questions for Engagement, Response, and Analysis in Part One of the Introduction for the genre you have selected. Next, consult the Suggestions for Crafting Arguments after individual works and at the end of the thematic unit.

If you choose to write on an essay, you might prefer to write on style, selecting an essay that is rich in metaphorical devices and focusing your essay on the ways that the metaphors expand, clarify, or enrich the work. For example, you could examine the way that Frances Mayes, in "*Bramare*," uses both metaphors and a variety of sound devices to create the feelings and sounds of a peaceful time that lives in the narrator's memory. If you prefer a humorous essay, you might claim that Bill Cosby in *Fatherhood* skillfully uses style to create humor.

If you prefer to write about fiction, you might write about point of view in Baldwin's "Sonny's Blues" or argue that Baldwin's use of the story-within-a-story effectively reinforces the theme. You might choose to examine the symbolism in Capote's "A Christmas Memory" or argue that the attitudes of Connie's family in "Where Are You Going, Where Have You Been?" contribute to her decisions.

If you choose to write about a poem, you might write an essay explaining how W. B. Yeats uses the images of the horn of plenty and the laurel tree to convey the kind of life he wishes for his daughter. You might claim that the many allusions in Sylvia Plath's "Daddy" create the startling tone or that the metaphors in Li-Young Lee's "The Gift" vividly convey the son's pain and his love for his father. If you choose to write on theme, you might consider what Whitelock's "Future Connected By" says about the rights of parents to steer their children away from certain careers, especially their own, or what it suggests about the generation gap.

Fences, the play by August Wilson, suggests a wide variety of topics, using both primary and secondary sources. For example, you might argue that Troy's behavior toward Rose or toward Cory is or is not justified or claim that Troy does his best to be a good husband or father. You might analyze the effect of setting—time, place, and culture—on the actions and opinions of the characters or on the theme. If you prefer analyzing characters, you might examine Rose's motivation or Gabriel's role in revealing the motivations of other characters.

When he was assigned an essay using the Casebook, Jim Fowler, a history major, first carefully read the play. Then, in order to get an overall picture of the assignment, he read the articles about the author and about the play. Because of his personal interest in baseball and because baseball is so important to the main character, he chose for his subject the effect of baseball on Troy. Before deciding on a more specific claim, Jim listed the many references to baseball and his interpretations of them in random order. He also listed any supporting passages in the critical articles. After examining the lists for ideas, Jim arranged them into three categories: language, lifestyle, and character. His preliminary thesis statement was "The reader can easily conclude that Troy's baseball experience has a very significant effect upon his language, his lifestyle, and even his moral character." Jim was now ready to write his first draft, using the ideas he had listed by category as the building blocks and tying them together coherently. At this point, Jim took his draft to his professor to see if he was on the right track. The professor made a few suggestions and corrections, such as changing the few instances in which Jim used the past tense instead of the literary present tense in writing about events in the play. After making a few changes and adding his documentation, Jim double-checked his quotations and paraphrases to ensure that he had not plagiarized any material. Believing that the conclusion could also be improved, he rewrote it and selected a title for his essay, "Baseball Metaphors in *Fences*," which is included at the end of the Casebook in this unit.

ESSAYS

Joan Didion (b. 1934)

Didion, an American novelist and journalist who grew up in California, writes both fiction and nonfiction. Her novel The Last Thing He Wanted *(1996) is a tightly plotted story about an American journalist who investigated the sale of arms in Central America. She also collaborated with her husband, John Gregory Dunn, on screenplays. In elegant essays such as those collected in* Slouching Toward Bethlehem *(1967), from which "On Going Home" comes, she examines contemporary Americans' loss of communal values and direction. Later essay collections include* The White Album *(1978) and* Political Fictions *(2001). The Year of* Magical Thinking *(2005), a poignant account of Didion's grief after the death of her beloved husband and her simultaneous coping with her daughter's fatal illness, was made into a Broadway play starring Vanessa Redgrave.*

ON GOING HOME   (1967)

1   I am home for my daughter's first birthday. By "home" I do not mean the house in Los Angeles where my husband and I and the baby live, but the place where my family is, in the Central Valley of California. It is a vital although troublesome distinction. My husband likes my family but is uneasy in their house, because once there I fall into their ways, which are difficult, oblique, deliberately inarticulate, not my husband's ways. We live in dusty houses ("D-U-S-T," he once wrote with his finger on surfaces all over the house, but no one noticed it) filled with mementos quite without value to him (what could the Canton dessert plates mean to him? how could he have known about the assay scales, why should he care if he did know?), and we appear to talk exclusively about people we know who have been committed to mental hospitals, about people we know who have been booked on drunk-driving charges, and about property, particularly about property, land, price per acre and C-2 zoning and assessments and freeway access. My brother does not understand my husband's inability to perceive the advantage in the rather common real-estate transaction known as "sale-leaseback," and my husband in turn does not understand why so many of the people he hears about in my father's house have recently been committed to mental hospitals or booked on drunk-driving charges. Nor does he understand that when we talk about sale-leasebacks and right-of-way condemnations we are talking in code about things we like best, the yellow fields and the cottonwoods and the rivers rising and falling and the mountain roads closing when the heavy snow comes in. We miss each other's points, have another drink and regard the fire. My brother refers to my husband, in his presence, as "Joan's husband." Marriage is the classic betrayal.

2   Or perhaps it is not any more. Sometimes, I think that those of us who are now in our thirties were born into the last generation to carry the burden of "home," to find in family life the source of all tension and drama. I had by all objective accounts a "normal" and a "happy" family situation, and yet I was almost thirty years old before I could talk to my family on the telephone without crying after I had hung up. We did not fight. Nothing was wrong. And yet some nameless anxiety colored the emotional charges between me and the place that I came from. The question of whether or not you could go home again was a very real part of the sentimental and largely literary baggage with which we left home in the fifties; I suspect that it is irrelevant to the children born of the fragmentation after World War II. A few weeks ago in a San Francisco bar I saw a pretty young girl on crystal take off her clothes and dance for the cash prize in an "amateur-topless" contest. There was no particular sense of moment about this, none of the effect of romantic degradation, of "dark journey," for which my generation strived so assiduously. What sense could that girl possibly make of, say, *Long Day's Journey into Night*? Who is beside the point?

3   That I am trapped in this particular irrelevancy is never more apparent to me than when I am home. Paralyzed by the neurotic lassitude engendered by meeting one's past at every turn, around every corner, inside every cupboard, I go aimlessly from room to room. I decide to meet it head-on and clear out a drawer, and I spread the contents on the bed. A bathing suit I wore the summer I was seventeen. A letter of rejection from *The Nation*, an aerial photograph of the site for a shopping center my father did not build in 1954. Three teacups hand-painted with cabbage roses and signed "E.M.," my grandmother's initials. There is no final solution for letters of rejection from *The Nation* and teacups handpainted in 1900. Nor is there any answer to snapshots of one's grandfather as a young man on skis, surveying around Donner Pass in the year 1910. I smooth out the snapshot and look into his face, and do and do not see my own. I close the drawer, and have another cup of coffee with my mother. We get along very well, veterans of a guerilla war we never understood.

4   Days pass. I see no one. I come to dread my husband's evening call, not only because he is full of news of what by now seems to me our remote life in Los Angeles, people he has seen, letters which require attention, but because he asks what I have been doing, suggests uneasily that I get out, drive to San Francisco or Berkeley. Instead I drive across the river to a family graveyard. It has been vandalized since my last visit and the monuments are broken, overturned in the dry grass. Because I once saw a rattlesnake in the grass I stay in the car and listen to a country-and-Western station. Later I drive with my father to a ranch he has in the foothills. The man who runs his cattle on it asks us to the round-up, a week from Sunday, and although I know that I will be in Los Angeles I say, in the oblique way my family talks, that I will come. Once home I mention the broken monuments in the graveyard. My mother shrugs.

5   I go to visit my great-aunts. A few of them think now that I am my cousin, or their daughter who died young. We recall an anecdote about a relative last seen in 1948, and they ask if I still like living in New York City. I have lived in Los Angeles for three years, but I say that I do. The baby is offered a horehound drop, and I am slipped a dollar bill "to buy a treat." Questions trail off, answers are abandoned, the baby plays with the dust motes in a shaft of the afternoon sun.

6   It is time for the baby's birthday party: a white cake, strawberry-marshmallow ice cream, a bottle of champagne saved from another party. In the evening, after she has gone to sleep, I kneel beside the crib and touch her face, where it is pressed against the slats, with mine. She is an open and trusting child, unprepared for and unaccustomed to the ambushes of family life, and perhaps it is just as well that I can offer her little of that life. I would like to give her more. I would like to promise her that she will grow up with a sense of her cousins and of rivers and her great-grandmother's teacups, would like to pledge her a picnic on a river with fried chicken and her hair uncombed, would like to give her *home* for her birthday, but we live differently now and I can promise her nothing like that. I give her a xylophone and a sundress from Madeira, and promise to tell her a funny story.

Questions for Engagement, Response, and Analysis

1. What does Didion mean when she says, "Marriage is the classic betrayal"? What is the source of tension between Didion's family and her husband? Why is the distinction between where she and her husband and daughter live and where her "family" lives "vital although troublesome"?

2. Explain Didion's statement that she and her mother are "veterans of a guerilla war we never understood."

3. Why, in an essay about going home, does Didion begin and end with her daughter's first birthday?

Crafting Arguments

1. In an essay, give your interpretation of Didion's definition of home. Are there examples of symbolism or figurative language that will help you support your claim?

Bill Cosby (b. 1937)

William Henry Cosby, actor, comedian, teacher, producer, and philanthropist, has been a role model for three generations of American families. After a stint in the navy, Cosby went to Temple University on a track and field scholarship, completing his B.A. in 1961. He later earned an M.A. and

Ed.D. from the University of Massachusetts. As costar with Robert Culp in I Spy *from 1965 to 1968, Cosby won Emmys for outstanding actor in a dramatic series. He produced and acted in several television series, the most famous and influential of which,* The Cosby Show, *ran from 1984 to 1992 and is still in reruns. His animated series, such as* Fat Albert *(1972-1985) and* Little Bill, *(1999) have entertained and educated children for decades. Cosby's book* Fatherhood, *from which the following essay is taken, has been a favorite Father's Day present since its publication in 1986.*

DR. SPOCK NEVER PROMISED US A ROSE GARDEN
FROM *FATHERHOOD*   (1986)

7   When a man has children, the first thing he has to learn is that he is not the boss of the house. I am certainly not the boss of *my* house. However, I have seen the boss's job and I don't want it, for sometimes the boss ends up sitting alone in a room and talking to herself as if the enemy were there: "What do you *mean* you don't want to do it? When I *tell* you to do something, you *do* it and you don't stand there practicing for law school!"

8   In spite of all the love, joy, and gratification that children bring, they do cause a certain amount of stress that takes its toll on parents. My wife and I have five children, and the reason we have five is that we did not want six.

9   Before we were married, my wife was a stunningly beautiful woman. Today she is a stunningly beautiful woman whose mouth droops and who has conversations with herself. She also sounds like my mother: "I'm gonna knock you into the middle of next week!" The middle of next week, by the way, is where their father wouldn't mind going: I would have four days by myself.

10   From time to time, my wife also threatens to knock the children to Kingdom Come. If she ever *does* knock them there, she's going to ask me to go get them, and I will not know where it is.

11   "You know where it is," she'll say. "You just don't want to find them."

12   You new fathers will learn that almost all mothers are like my wife and have conversations with themselves. These maternal monologists, however, have developed a lovely retaliation. They put a curse on their children: *I just hope that when you get married, you have children who act just like you.* (And, of course, the curse always works, proving that God has a sense of humor.) My own wish is not a curse but a simple prayer: I just want the children to get out of the house before we die.

13   There is no wisdom I can give you new fathers more profound than what I said at the start of this chapter: you are *not* the boss of this house that you want the children out of within thirty years and you are *not* allowed to give them permission for anything. When one of them comes to you and says, "Dad, can I go explore the Upper Nile?" your answer must be, "Go ask your mother."

14   Only once did I make the great permission mistake. One of the children came to me and said, "Dad, can I go out and play?"

15   "Sure," I replied. "I don't see why not."

16   That was the last time I couldn't see why not. My wife came in and said, "Did you let that child go out?"

17   "Yeah," I said.

18   "Well, the next time you check with *me*. He's being punished."

19   From that day on, I knew my place; and whenever a child starts to say, "Dad, can I . . ." even though it's my name, I always reply, "What did your mother say?"

20   And even if the child says that she got permission, I still say, "Very fine. Just bring me a note from your mother. It doesn't have to be notarized. A simple signature and date will do."

21   Ironically, even though the father is not the boss of the house, the mother will try to use him as a threat: "When your father comes home, he's going to shoot you in the face with a bazooka. And this time I'm not going to stop him."

MY WIFE'S CLEAN HANDS

22   You see, the wives *pretend* to turn over the child-raising job to us fathers, but they don't really mean it. One day, my wife said to me, "He's *your* child. I wash my hands of him."

23   Where is this sink where you can wash your hands of a child? I want to wash my hands too, and then the boy can go free.

24   For someone who supposedly had washed her hands of the child, my wife still sounded unwashed to me.

25   "You go and talk to him right now."

26   "I certainly will," I said.

27   "But the thing is, Bill, you always let him have his own way."

28   "Look, you've washed your hands; he's not yours, he's mine. So let me handle it."

29   "I want you to be hard on him."

30   She was singing this song now; but three years before, when I had wanted to set him on fire, she'd said, "Oh, *please* don't. He's such a little boy."

31   And I had said, "No, burn him now."

32   Yes, amid all the love, there are still dark threats in any normal family, especially if a man and woman have been reckless enough to allow the joy of making love to lead to something as dangerous as children.

33   The problem is consistency: there isn't any. New parents quickly learn that raising children is a kind of desperate improvisation. If *I* ever get angry at the children, my wife collects them under her wing and says, "Come away with me, darlings. Your father's gone mad."

34   Of course, people who spend more than six minutes trying to discipline children learn that consistency and logic are never a part of things.

Usually, however, my wife gives the orders in our house. Late one afternoon, I came home from playing tennis, gave her a warm kiss on the cheek, and said, "How ya feeling, pud?"

35   And she softly replied, "I want you to go upstairs and kill that boy."

36   "Very fine," I said, feeling pretty happy because *I* wasn't the one in trouble.

37   When I reached the boy's room, we had that nice thoughtful talk I mentioned earlier, the one in which he could not remember when he had shaved his head; and then, being a father who likes to probe to the very souls of those I love, I said, "So tell me, son, how are things?"

38   "Okay," he said.

39   "Is there any problem you'd like to discuss with Dad?"

40   "It's okay."

41   And, as every father knows, "Okay" means "*I haven't killed anyone.*"

42   Such descriptions of his own good behavior do not seem to stop his mother from making the poor boy the target of a hit, and I'm not the only one with a contract. His four sisters—two older, two younger—are also interested in wiping him out. Because some girls are both cleaner and more mature than boys, they had a meeting recently about his habit of leaving the toilet seat up. They conducted this meeting with the maturity that they all possess; and when it was over, they decided to fix him. You see, the two most important things to the American female are man's prevention of nuclear war and man's putting the toilet seat down. Their brother can't seem to learn the latter and may have to pay the ultimate price.

43   A father has a right to get tired of such constant sibling rivalry. Unfortunately, a father's job is *not* to get tired of what he has a right to get tired of: for example, small people who keep doing things that you tell them not to do, and when you ask them why they keep doing these things, they reply, "I don't know."

44   It is also possible to get tired of a small person who yells to another, "Will you stop *touching* me!"

45   "What's going on?" you say.

46   "She's *touching* me!"

47   "Look, don't touch her anymore, okay?"

48   "But she touched me *first.*"

49   And then you resolve the dispute with wisdom worthy of Solomon: "I don't want anyone in this house to touch another person as long as you live."

TALES FROM THE FUNNY FARM

50   No matter how calmly you try to referee, parenting will eventually produce bizarre behavior, and I'm not talking about the kids. *Their* behavior is always normal, a norm of acting incomprehensibly with sweetly blank looks. But *you* will find yourself strolling down the road to the funny farm—like my mother, who used to get so angry that she would forget my name:

51   "All right, come *over* here, Bar—uh, Bernie, . . . uh, uh—Biff . . . uh—
what *is* your name, boy? And don't lie to me 'cause you live here and I'll
find out who you are and take a stick and knock your brains out!"

52   All during my stormy boyhood years, I wanted to get some calves'
brains and keep them in my pocket. Then, when my mother hit me in the
head, I would throw them on the floor. Knowing her, however, she merely
would have said, "Put your brains back in your head! Don't *ever* let your
brains fall out of your head! Have you lost your *mind?*"

53   And thus, in spite of the joys that children do bring, does parenting
take its toll on both father and mother. Mothers who have experience in
the trenches of family warfare are sometimes even driven to what I call
anticipatory parenting. They ask a child a question, he tries to answer,
and they say, "You shut up! When I ask you a question, you keep your
mouth shut! You think I'm talking to hear myself talk? *Answer* me!"

54   This is a pitiable condition in a mother, but my hold on my own
sanity has also been a tenuous one because of the behavior of what was
created by a few delightful seconds of sex. Believe me, I have paid for those
delights. My three-year-old, for example, used to grab things belonging
to her close relatives and cry, "Mine! Mine! Mine!" It was a sound that ric-
ocheted through the house for a while and then went up your spinal cord:
"Mine! Mine! Mine!" If you followed the sound to its source, you would
always find an older child pulling on the end of what the three-year-old
had stolen, saying, "You took this from my *room!*"

55   "Why don't you let her have it?" I would tell the older one. "Don't you
hear how it's upsetting her?"

56   Okay, so I *haven't* been Solomon, perhaps because I've felt more like
Noah, just lost at sea. But the truth is that parents are not really interested in justice. They just want quiet.

57   No matter how much the pressure on your spinal cord builds up, *never*
let these small people know that you have gone insane. There is an excellent reason for this: they want the house; and at the first sign that something is wrong with you, they will take you right to a home.

58   When I reach sixty-five, I plan to keep a gun in my hand, for I know
that the moment I spill something on my lap, they'll come to me and say,
"We're sorry, Dad, but you can't control yourself and you've got to go."

59   Whether or not I manage to avoid eviction, I hope that these young
adversaries appreciate that my wife and I have tried not to make the mistakes that our parents made with us. For example, we have always been
against calling the children idiots. This philosophy has been basic for my
wife and me. And we proudly lived by it until the children came along.

Questions for Engagement, Response, and Analysis

1. What is the tone of this essay? How does Cosby create this tone?
2. What is the "great permissions mistake"?
3. Define "anticipatory parenting."

4. In your Reader's Journal, analyze and classify the expressions that are repeatedly used by parents in your home, even if you are the parent.

Crafting Arguments

1. Using details from the essay, compare Cosby's definitions of the father's and the mother's roles.

Frances Mayes (b. 1940)

A native of Fitzgerald, Georgia, Frances Mayes is a gourmet cook and the author of numerous articles on food and cooking as well as five books of poetry. Mayes became famous nationwide with the publication of Under the Tuscan Sun *(1996) which, along with the later volume,* Bella Tuscany *(1999), celebrates with passion and gusto not only the centuries-old villa Mayes bought near Cortona, Italy, but also the centuries-old traditions and culture of the surrounding Tuscan hill country. In 2003, a film version of* Under the Tuscan Sun *starring Diane Lane featured a fictionalized version of Mayes' book. Her first novel,* Swan, *was published in 2002. Mayes and her husband live alternately in North Carolina and in her villa near Cortona.*

BRAMARE: (ARCHAIC) TO YEARN FOR   (1996)

60   I am about to buy a house in a foreign country. A house with the beautiful name of Bramasole. It is tall, square, and apricot-colored with faded green shutters, ancient tile roof, and an iron balcony on the second level, where ladies might have sat with their fans to watch some spectacle below. But below, overgrown briars, tangles of roses, and knee-high weeds run rampant. The balcony faces southeast, looking into a deep valley, then into the Tuscan Apennines. When it rains or when the light changes, the facade of the house turns gold, sienna, ocher; a previous scarlet paint job seeps through in rosy spots like a box of crayons left to melt in the sun. In places where the stucco has fallen away, rugged stone shows what the exterior once was. The house rises above a *strada bianca*, a road white with pebbles, on a terraced slab of hillside covered with fruit and olive trees. Bramasole: from *bramare*, to yearn for, and *sole*, sun: something that yearns for the sun, and yes, I do.

61   The family wisdom runs strongly against this decision. My mother has said "Ridiculous," with her certain and forceful stress on the second syllable, "RiDICulous," and my sisters, although excited, fear I am eighteen, about to run off with a sailor in the family car. I quietly have my own doubts. The upright seats in the *notaio*'s outer office don't help. Through my thin white linen dress, spiky horsehairs pierce me every time I shift, which is often in the hundred-degree waiting room. I look over to see what Ed is writing on the back of a receipt: Parmesan, salami, coffee,

bread. How can he? Finally, the signora opens her door and her torrential Italian flows over us.

62   The *notaio* is nothing like a notary; she's the legal person who conducts real-estate transactions in Italy. Ours, Signora Mantucci, is a small, fierce Sicilian woman with thick tinted glasses that enlarge her green eyes. She talks faster than any human I have ever heard. She reads long laws aloud. I thought all Italian was mellifluous; she makes it sound like rocks crashing down a chute. Ed looks at her raptly; I know he's in thrall to the sound of her voice. The owner, Dr. Carta, suddenly thinks he has asked too little; he *must* have, since we have agreed to buy it. We think his price is exorbitant. We *know* his price is exorbitant. The Sicilian doesn't pause; she will not be interrupted by anyone except by Giuseppe from the bar downstairs, who suddenly swings open the dark doors, tray aloft, and seems surprised to see his *Americani* customers sitting there almost cross-eyed in confusion. He brings the signora her midmorning thimble of espresso, which she downs in a gulp, hardly pausing. The owner expects to claim that the house cost one amount while it really cost much more. "That is just the way it's done," he insists. "No one is fool enough to declare the real value." He proposes we bring one check to the *notaio*'s office, then pass him ten smaller checks literally under the table.

63   Anselmo Martini, our agent, shrugs.

64   Ian, the English estate agent we hired to help with translation, shrugs also.

65   Dr. Carta concludes, "You Americans! You take things so seriously. And, *per favore*, date the checks at one-week intervals so the bank isn't alerted to large sums."

66   Was that the same bank I know, whose sloe-eyed teller languidly conducts a transaction every fifteen minutes, between smokes and telephone calls? The signora comes to an abrupt halt, scrambles the papers into a folder and stands up. We are to come back when the money and papers are ready.

67   A window in our hotel room opens onto an expansive view over the ancient roofs of Cortona, down to the dark expanse of the Val di Chiana. A hot and wild wind—the *scirocco*—is driving normal people a little crazy. For me, it seems to reflect my state of mind. I can't sleep. In the United States, I've bought and sold a few houses before—loaded up the car with my mother's Spode, the cat, and the ficus for the five- or five-thousand-mile drive to the next doorway where a new key would fit. You *have* to churn somewhat when the roof covering your head is at stake, since to sell is to walk away from a cluster of memories and to buy is to choose where the future will take place. And the place, never neutral of course, will cast its influence. Beyond that, legal complications and contingencies must be worked out. But here, absolutely everything conspires to keep me staring into the dark.

68   Italy always has had a magnetic north pull on my psyche. Houses have been on my mind for four summers of renting farmhouses all over

Tuscany. In the first place Ed and I rented with friends, we started calculating on the first night, trying to figure out if our four pooled savings would buy the tumbled stone farm we could see from the terrace. Ed immediately fell for farm life and roamed over our neighbors' land looking at the work in progress. The Antolinis grew tobacco, a beautiful if hated crop. We could hear workers shout *"Vipera!"* to warn the others of a poisonous snake. At evening, a violet blue haze rose from the dark leaves. The well-ordered farm looked peaceful from the vantage point of our terrace. Our friends never came back, but for the next three vacations, the circuitous search for a summer home became a quest for us— whether we ever found a place or not, we were happening on places that made pure green olive oil, discovering sweet country Romanesque churches in villages, meandering the back roads of vineyards, and stopping to taste the softest Brunello and the blackest Vino Nobile. Looking for a house gives an intense focus. We visited weekly markets not just with the purchase of picnic peaches in mind; we looked carefully at all the produce's quality and variety, mentally forecasting birthday dinners, new holidays, and breakfasts for weekend guests. We spent hours sitting in piazzas or sipping lemonade in local bars, secretly getting a sense of the place's ambiance. I soaked many a heel blister in a hotel bidet, rubbed bottles of lotion on my feet, which had covered miles of stony streets. We hauled histories and guides and wildflower books and novels in and out of rented houses and hotels. Always we asked local people where they liked to eat and headed to restaurants our many guidebooks never mentioned. We both have an insatiable curiosity about each jagged castle ruin on the hillsides. My idea of heaven still is to drive the gravel farm roads of Umbria and Tuscany, very pleasantly lost.

69   Cortona was the first town we ever stayed in and we always came back to it during the summers we rented near Volterra, Florence, Montisi, Rignano, Vicchio, Quercegrossa, all those fascinating, quirky houses. One had a kitchen two people could not pass in, but there was a slice of a view of the Arno. Another kitchen had no hot water and no knives, but the house was built into medieval ramparts overlooking vineyards. One had several sets of china for forty, countless glasses and silverware, but the refrigerator iced over every day and by four the door swung open, revealing a new igloo. When the weather was damp, I got a tingling shock if I touched anything in the kitchen. On the property, Cimabue, legend says, discovered the young Giotto drawing a sheep in the dirt. One house had beds with back-crunching dips in the middles. Bats flew down the chimney and buzzed us, while worms in the beams sent down a steady sifting of sawdust onto the pillows. The fireplace was so big we could sit in it while grilling our veal chops and peppers.

70   We drove hundreds of dusty miles looking at houses that turned out to be in the flood plain of the Tiber or overlooking strip mines. The Siena agent blithely promised that the view would be wonderful again in twenty years; replanting stripped areas was a law. A glorious medieval village

house was wildly expensive. The saw-toothed peasant we met in a bar tried to sell us his childhood home, a windowless stone chicken house joined to another house, with snarling dogs lunging at us from their ropes. We fell hard for a farm outside Montisi; the *contessa* who owned it led us on for days, then decided she needed a sign from God before she could sell it. We had to leave before the sign arrived.

71   As I think back over those places, they suddenly seem preposterously alien and Cortona does, too. Ed doesn't think so. He's in the piazza every afternoon, gazing at the young couple trying to wheel their new baby down the street. They're halted every few steps. Everyone circles the carriage. They're leaning into the baby's face, making noises, praising the baby. "In my next life," Ed tells me, "I want to come back as an Italian baby." He steeps in the piazza life: the sultry and buffed man pushing up his sleeve so his muscles show when he languidly props his chin in his hand; the pure flute notes of Vivaldi drifting from an upstairs window; the flower seller's fan of bright flowers against the stone shop; a man with no neck at all unloading lambs from his truck. He slings them like flour sacks over his shoulder and the lambs' eyeballs bulge out. Every few minutes, Ed looks up at the big clock that has kept time for so long over this piazza. Finally, he takes a stroll, memorizing the stones in the street.

72   Across the hotel courtyard a visiting Arab chants his prayers toward dawn, just when I finally can fall asleep. He sounds as though he is gargling with salt water. For hours, he rings the voice's changes over a small register, over and over. I want to lean out and shout, "Shut up!" Now and then I have to laugh. I look out, see him nodding in the window, a sweet smile on his face. He reminds me so much of tobacco auctioneers I heard in hot warehouses in the South as a child. I am seven thousand miles from home, plunking down my life savings on a whim. Is it a whim? It feels very close to falling in love and that's never really whimsical but comes from some deep source. Or does it?

73   Each time we step out of the cool, high rooms of the hotel and into the sharp-edged sun, we walk around town and like it more and more. The outdoor tables at Bar Sport face the Piazza Signorelli. A few farmers sell produce on the steps of the nineteenth-century *teatro* every morning. As we drink espresso, we watch them holding up rusty hand scales to weigh the tomatoes. The rest of the piazza is lined with perfectly intact medieval or Renaissance *palazzi*. Easily, someone might step out any second and break into *La Traviata*. Every day we visit each keystoned medieval gate in the Etruscan walls, explore the Fiat-wide stone streets lined with Renaissance and older houses and the even narrower *vicoli*, mysterious pedestrian passageways, often steeply stepped. The bricked-up fourteenth-century "doors of the dead" are still visible. These ghosts of doors beside the main entrance were designed, some say, to take out the plague victims—bad luck for them to exit by the main entrance. I notice in the regular doors, people often leave their keys in the lock.

74   Guidebooks describe Cortona as "somber" and "austere." They misjudge. The hilltop position, the walls and upright, massive stone buildings give a distinctly vertical feel to the architecture. Walking across the piazza, I feel the abrupt, angular shadows fall with Euclidean purity. I want to stand up straight—the upright posture of the buildings seems to carry over to the inhabitants. They walk slowly, with very fine, I want to say, *carriage.* I keep saying, "Isn't she beautiful?" "Isn't he gorgeous?" "Look at *that* face—pure Raphael." By late afternoon, we're sitting again with our espressi, this time facing the other piazza. A woman of about sixty with her daughter and the teenage granddaughter pass by us, strolling, their arms linked, sun on their vibrant faces. We don's know why light has such a luminous quality. Perhaps the sunflower crops radiate gold from the surrounding fields. The three women look peaceful, proud, impressively pleased. There should be a gold coin with their faces on it.

75   Meanwhile, as we sip, the dollar is falling fast. We rouse ourselves from the piazza every morning to run around to all the banks, checking their posted exchange rates. When you're cashing traveler's checks for a last-minute spree at the leather market, the rate doesn't matter that much, but this is a house with five acres and every lira counts. A slight drop at those multiples makes the stomach drop also. Every hundred lire it falls, we calculate how much more expensive the house becomes. Irrationally, I also calculate how many pairs of shoes that could buy. Shoes, before, have been my major purchase in Italy, a secret sin. Sometimes I'd go home with nine new pairs: red snake-skin flats, sandals, navy suede boots, and several pairs of black pumps of varying heels.

76   Typically, the banks vary in how much commission they bite when they receive a large transfer from overseas. We want a break. It looks like a significant chunk of interest they'll collect, since clearing a check in Italy can take weeks.

77   Finally, we have a lesson in the way things work. Dr. Carta, anxious to close, calls his bank—the bank his father and his father-in-law use—in Arezzo, a half hour away. Then he calls us. "Go there," he says. "They won't take a commission for receiving the money at all, and they'll give you whatever the posted rate is when it arrives."

78   His savvy doesn's surprise me, though he has seemed spectacularly uninterested in money the entire time we have negotiated—just named his high price and stuck to it. He bought the property from the five old sisters of an landowning family in Perugia the year before, thinking, he said, to make it a summer place for his family. However, he and his wife inherited property on the coast and decided to use that instead. Was that the case, or had he scooped up a bargain from ladies in their nineties and now is making a bundle, possibly buying coast property with our money? Not that I begrudge him. He's smart.

79   Dr. Carta, perhaps fearing we might back out, calls and asks to meet us at the house. He roars up in his Alfa 164, Armani from stem to stern.

"There is something more," he says, as though continuing a conversation. "If you follow me, I will show you something." A few hundred feet down the road, he leads us up a stone path through fragrant yellow broom. Odd, the stone path continues up the hill, curving along a ridge. Soon we come to a two-hundred-degree view of the valley, with the cypress-lined road below us and a mellow landscape dotted with tended vineyards and olive groves. In the distance lies a blue daub, which is Lake Trasimeno; off to the right, we see the red-roofed silhouette of Cortona cleanly outlined against the sky, Dr. Carta turns to us triumphantly. The flat paving stones widen here. "The Romans—this road was built by the Romans—it goes straight into Cortona." The sun is broiling. He goes on and on about the large church at the top of the hill. He points out where the rest of the road might have run, right through Bramasole's property.

80   Back at the house he turns on an outside faucet and splashes his face. "You'll enjoy the finest water, truly your own abundant *acqua minerale*, excellent for the liver. *Eccellente!*" He manages to be at once enthusiastic and a little bored, friendly and slightly condescending. I am afraid we have spoken too bluntly about money. Or maybe he has interpreted our law-abiding American expectations about the transaction as incredibly naive. He lets the faucet run, cupping his hand under the water, somehow leaning over for a drink without dislodging the well-cut linen coat tossed over his shoulders. "Enough water for a swimming pool," he insists, "which would be perfect out on the point where you can see the lake, overlooking right where Hannibal defeated the Romans."

81   We're dazzled by the remains of a Roman road over the hill covered with wildflowers. We will follow the stone road into town for a coffee late in the afternoons. He shows us the old cistern. Water is precious in Tuscany and was collected drop by drop. By shining a flashlight into the opening, we've already noticed that the underground cistern has a stone archway, obviously some kind of passageway. Up the hill in the Medici fortress, we saw the same arch in the cistern there and the caretaker told us that a secret underground escape route goes downhill to the valley, then to Lake Trasimeno. Italians take such remains casually. That one is allowed to own such ancient things seems impossible to me.

82   When I first saw Bramasole, I immediately wanted to hang my summer clothes in an *armadio* and arrange my books under one of those windows looking out over the valley. We'd spent four days with Signor Martini, who had a dark little office on Via Sacco e Vanzetti down in the lower town. Above his desk hung a photo of him as a soldier, I assumed for Mussolini. He listened to us as though we spoke perfect Italian. When we finished describing what we thought we wanted, he rose, put on his Borsolino, and said one word, "*Andiamo*," let's go. Although he'd recently had a foot operation, he drove us over nonexistent roads and pushed through jungles of thorns to show us places only he knew about. Some were farmhouses with roofs collapsed onto the floor, miles from town and costing

the earth. One had a tower built by the Crusaders, but the *contessa* who owned it cried and doubled the price on the spot when she saw that we really were interested. Another was attached to other farmhouses where chickens were truly free range—they ran in and out of the houses. The yard was full of rusted farm equipment and hogs. Several felt airless or sat hard by the road. One would have required putting in a road—it was hidden in blackberry brambles and we could only peer in one window because a coiled black snake refused to budge from the threshold.

83   We took Signor Martini flowers, thanked him and said goodbye. He seemed genuinely sorry to see us go.

84   The next morning we ran into him in the piazza after coffee. He said, "I just saw a doctor from Arezzo. He might be interested in selling a house. *Una bella villa*," he added emphatically. The house was within walking distance of Cortona.

85   "How much?" we asked, although we knew by then he cringes at being asked that direct question.

86   "Let's just go take a look," was all he said. Out of Cortona, he took the road that climbs and winds to the other side of the hill. He turned onto the *strada bianca* and, after a couple of kilometers, pulled into a long, sloping driveway. I caught a glimpse of a shrine, then looked up at the three-story house with a curly iron fanlight above the front door and two tall, exotic palm trees on either side. On that fresh morning, the facade seemed radiant, glazed with layers of lemon, rouge, and terra-cotta. We both became silent as we got out of the car. After all the turns into unknown roads, the house seemed just to have been waiting all along.

87   "Perfect, we'll take it," I joked as we stepped through the weeds. Just as he had at other houses, Signor Martini made no sales pitch; he simply looked with us. We walked up to the house under a rusted pergola leaning under the weight of climbing roses. The double front door squawked like something alive when we pushed it open. The house's walls, thick as my arm is long, radiated coolness. The glass in the windows wavered. I scuffed through silty dust and saw below it smooth brick floors in perfect condition. In each room, Ed opened the inside window and pushed open the shutters to one glorious view after another of cypresses, rippling green hills, distant villas, a valley. There were even two bathrooms that functioned. They were not beautiful, but *bathrooms*, after all the houses we'd seen with no floors, much less plumbing. No one had lived there in thirty years and the grounds seemed like an enchanted garden, overgrown and tumbling with blackberries and vines. I could see Signor Martini regarding the grounds with a countryman's practiced eye. Ivy twisted into the trees and ran over fallen terrace walls. "*Molto lavoro*," much work, was all he said.

88   During several years of looking, sometimes casually, sometimes to the point of exhaustion, I never heard a house say *yes* so completely. However, we were leaving the next day, and when we learned the price, we sadly said no and went home.

89   During the next months, I mentioned Bramasole now and then. I stuck a photo on my mirror and often wandered the grounds or rooms in my mind. The house is a metaphor for the self, of course, but it also is totally real. And a *foreign* house exaggerates all the associations houses carry. Because I had ended a long marriage that was not supposed to end and was establishing a new relationship, this house quest felt tied to whatever new identity I would manage to forge. When the flying fur from the divorce settled, I had found myself with a grown daughter, a full-time university job (after years of part-time teaching), a modest securities portfolio, and an entire future to invent. Although divorce was harder than a death, still I felt oddly returned to myself after many years in a close family. I had the urge to examine my life in another culture and move beyond what I knew. I wanted something of a *physical* dimension that would occupy the mental volume the years of my former life had. Ed shares my passion for Italy completely and also shares the boon of three-month summer breaks from university teaching. There we would have long days for exploring and for our writing and research projects. When he is at the wheel, he'll *always* take the turn down the intriguing little road. The language, history, art, places in Italy are endless—two lifetimes wouldn't be enough. And, ah, the foreign self. The new life might shape itself to the contours of the house, which already is at home in the landscape, and to the rhythms around it.

90   In the spring, I called a California woman who was starting a real-estate development business in Tuscany. I asked her to check on Bramasole; perhaps if it had not sold, the price had come down. A week later, she called from a bar after meeting with the owner. "Yes, it's still for sale, but with that particular brand of Italian logic, the price has been raised. The dollar," she reminded me, "has fallen. And that house needs a lot of work."

91   Now we've returned. By this time, with equally peculiar logic, I've become fixed on buying Bramasole. After all, the only thing wrong is the expense. We both love the setting, the town, the house and land. If only one little thing is wrong, I tell myself, go ahead.

92   Still, this costs a *sacco di soldi*. It will be an enormous hassle to recover the house and land from neglect. Leaks, mold, tumbling stone terraces, crumbling plaster, one funky bathroom, another with an adorable metal hip bathtub and a cracked toilet.

93   Why does the prospect seem fun, when I found remodeling my kitchen in San Francisco a deep shock to my equilibrium? At home, we can't even hang a picture without knocking out a fistful of plaster. When we plunge the stopped-up sink, forgetting once again that the disposal doesn't like artichoke petals, sludge seems to rise from San Francisco Bay.

94   On the other hand, a dignified house near a Roman road, an Etruscan (Etruscan!) wall looming at the top of the hillside, a Medici fortress in sight, a view toward Monte Amiata, a passageway underground, one hundred and seventeen olive trees, twenty plums, and still uncounted apricot, almond, apple, and pear trees. Several figs seem to thrive near the

well. Beside the front steps there's a large hazelnut. Then, proximity to one of the most superb towns I've ever seen. Wouldn't we be crazy not to buy this lovely house called Bramasole?

95   What if one of us is hit by a potato chip truck and can't work? I run through a litany of diseases we could get. An aunt died of a heart attack at forty-two, my grandmother went blind, all the ugly illnesses. . . . What if an earthquake shakes down the universities where we teach? The Humanities Building is on a list of state structures most likely to fall in a moderately severe quake. What if the stock market spirals down?

96   I leap out of bed at three AM and step in the shower, letting my whole face take the cold water. Coming back to bed in the dark, feeling my way, I jam my toe on the iron bed frame. Pain jags all the way up my backbone. "Ed, wake up. I think I've broken my toe. How can you sleep?"

97   He sits up. "I was just dreaming of cutting herbs in the garden. Sage and lemon balm. Sage is *salvia* in Italian." He has never wavered from his belief that this is a brilliant idea, that this is heaven on earth. He clicks on the bedside lamp. He's smiling.

98   My half-on toenail is hanging half off, ugly purple spreading underneath. I can's bear to leave it or to pull it off. "I want to go home," I say.

99   He puts a Band-Aid around my toe. "You mean Bramasole, don't you?" he asks.

100   This sack of money in question has been wired from California but has not arrived. How can that be, I ask at the bank, money is wired, it arrives instantaneously. More shrugs. Perhaps the main bank in Florence is holding it. Days pass. I call Steve, my broker in California, from a bar. I'm shouting over the noise of a soccer match on the TV. "You'll have to check from that end;" he shouts back, "it's long gone from here and did you know the government there has changed forty-seven times since World War II? This money was well invested in tax-free bonds and the best growth funds. Those Australian bonds of yours earned seventeen percent. Oh well, *la dolce vita*."

101   The mosquitoes (*zanzare* they're called, just like they sound) invade the hotel with the desert wind. I spin in the sheets until my skin burns. I get up in the middle of the night and lean out the shuttered window, imagining all the sleeping guests, blisters on their feet from the stony streets, their guidebooks still in their hands. We could still back out. Just throw our bags in the rented Fiat and say *arrivederci*. Go hang out on the Amalfi coast for a month and head home, tanned and relaxed. Buy lots of sandals. I can hear my grandfather when I was twenty: "Be realistic. Come down out of the clouds." He was furious that I was studying poetry and Latin etymology, something utterly useless. Now, what am I thinking of? Buying an abandoned house in a place where I hardly can speak the language. He probably has worn out his shroud turning over in his grave. We don't have a mountain of reserves to bale us out in case that mysterious something goes wrong.

102   What is this thrall for houses? I come from a long line of women who open their handbags and take out swatches of upholstery material, colored squares of bathroom tile, seven shades of yellow paint samples, and strips of flowered wallpaper. We love the concept of four walls. "What is her house like?" my sister asks, and we both know she means what is *she* like. I pick up the free real-estate guide outside the grocery store when I go somewhere for the weekend, even if it's close to home. One June, two friends and I rented a house on Majorca; another summer I stayed in a little *casa* in San Miguel de Allende in which I developed a serious love for fountained courtyards and bedrooms with bougainvillea cascading down the balcony, the austere Sierra Madre. One summer in Santa Fe, I started looking at adobes there, imagining I would become a Southwesterner, cook with chilies, wear squash blossom turquoise jewelry—a different life, the chance to be extant in another version. At the end of a month I left and never have wanted to return.

103   I love the islands off the Georgia coast, where I spent summers when I was growing up. Why not a weathered gray house there, made of wood that looks as though it washed up on the beach? Cotton rugs, peach iced tea, a watermelon cooling in the creek, sleeping with waves churning and rolling outside the window. A place where my sisters, friends, and their families could visit easily. But I keep remembering that anytime I've stepped in my own footprints again, I haven't felt renewed. Though I'm susceptible to the pull to the known, I'm just slightly more susceptible to surprise. Italy seems endlessly alluring to me—why not, at this point, consider the opening of *The Divine Comedy*: What must one do in order to grow? Better to remember my father, the son of my very literal-minded, penny-pinching grandfather. "The family motto," he'd say, "is 'Packing and Unpacking.'" And also, "If you can't go first class, don't go at all."

104   Lying awake, I feel the familiar sense of The Answer arriving. Like answers on the bottom of the black fortune-telling eight ball that I loved when I was ten, often I can feel an idea or the solution to a dilemma floating up through murky liquid, then it is as if I see the suddenly clear white writing. I like the charged zone of waiting, a mental and physical sensation of the bends as something mysterious zigzags to the surface of consciousness.

105   What if you did *not* feel uncertainty, the white writing says. Are you exempt from doubt? Why not rename it excitement? I lean over the wide sill just as the first gilded mauve light of sunrise begins. The Arab is still sleeping. The undulant landscape looks serene in every direction. Honey-colored farmhouses, gently placed in hollows, rise like thick loaves of bread set out to cool. I know some Jurassic upheaval violently tossed up the hills, but they appear rounded as though by a big hand. As the sun brightens, the land spreads out a soft spectrum: the green of a dollar bill gone through the wash, old cream, blue sky like a blind person's eye. The Renaissance painters had it just right. I never thought of Perugino, Giotto,

Signorelli, et al., as realists, but their background views are still here, as most tourists discover, with dark cypress trees brushed in to emphasize each composition the eye falls on. Now I see why the red boot on a gold and blond angel in the Cortona museum has such a glow, why the Madonna's cobalt dress looks intense and deep. Against this landscape and light, everything takes on a primary outline. Even a red towel drying on a line below becomes totally saturated with its own redness.

106   Think: What if the sky doesn't fall? What if it's glorious? What if the house is transformed in three years? There will be by then hand-printed labels for the house's olive oil, thin linen curtains pulled across the shutters for siesta, jars of plum jam on the shelves, a long table for feasts under the linden trees, baskets piled by the door for picking tomatoes, arugula, wild fennel, roses, and rosemary. And who are we in that strange new life?

107   Finally the money arrives, the account is open. However, they have no checks. This enormous bank, the seat of dozens of branches in the gold center of Italy, has no checks to give us. "Maybe next week," Signora Raguzzi explains. "Right now, nothing." We sputter. Two days later, she calls. "I have ten checks for you." What is the big deal with checks? I get boxes of them at home. Signora Raguzzi parcels them out to us. Signora Raguzzi in tight skirt, tight T-shirt, has lips that are perpetually wet and pouting. Her skin glistens. She is astonishingly gorgeous. She wears a magnificent square gold necklace and bracelets on both wrists that jangle as she stamps our account number on each check.

108   "What great jewelry. I love those bracelets," I say.

109   "All we have here is gold," she replies glumly. She is bored with Arezzo's tombs and piazzas. California sounds good to her. She brightens every time she sees us. "Ah, California," she says as greeting. The bank begins to seem surreal. We're in the back room. A man wheels in a cart stacked with gold ingots—actual small bricks of gold. No one seems to be on guard. Another man loads two into dingy manila folders. He's plainly dressed, like a workman. He walks out into the street, taking the ingots somewhere. So much for Brinks delivery—but what a clever plain-clothes disguise. We turn back to the checks. There will be no insignia of boats or palm trees or pony express riders, there will be no name, address, driver's license, Social Security number. Only these pale green checks that look as though they were printed in the twenties. We're enormously pleased. That's close to citizenship—a bank account.

110   Finally we are gathered in the *notaio*'s office for the final reckoning. It's quick. Everyone talks at once and no one listens. The baroque legal terms leave us way behind. A jackhammer outside drills into my brain cells. There's something about two oxen and two days. Ian, who's translating, stops to explain this archaic spiral of language as an eighteenth-century legal description of the amount of land, measured by how long it would take two oxen to plow it. We have, it seems, two plowing days worth of property.

111   I write checks, my fingers cramping over all the times I write *milione*. I think of all the nice dependable bonds and utility stocks and blue chips from the years of my marriage magically turning into a terraced hillside and a big empty house. The glass house in California where I lived for a decade, surrounded by kumquat, lemon, mock orange, and guava, its bright pool and covered patio with wicker and flowered cushions—all seem to recede, as though seen through the long focus in binoculars. *Million* is such a big word in English it's hard to treat it casually. Ed carefully monitors the zeros, not wanting me to unwittingly write *miliardo*, billion, instead. He pays Signor Martini in cash. He never has mentioned a fee; we have found out the normal percentage from the owner. Signor Martini seems pleased, as though we've given him a gift. For me this is a confusing but delightful way to conduct business. Handshakes all around. Is that a little cat smile on the mouth of the owner's wife? We're expecting a parchment deed, lettered in ancient script, but no, the *notaio* is going on vacation and she'll try to get to the paperwork before she leaves. *"Normale,"* Signor Martini says. I've noticed all along that someone's word is still taken for that. Endless contracts and stipulations and contingencies simply have not come up. We walk out into the brutally hot afternoon with nothing but two heavy iron keys longer than my hand, one to a rusted iron gate, the other to the front door. They look nothing like the keys to anything I've ever owned. There is no hope for spare copies.

112   Giuseppe waves from the door of the bar and we tell him we have bought a house. "Where is it?" he wants to know.

113   "Bramasole," Ed begins, about to say where it is.

114   "Ah, Bramasole, *una bella villa!*" He has picked cherries there as a boy. Although it is only afternoon, he pulls us in and pours a *grappa* for us. "Mama!" he shouts. His mother and her sister come in from the back and everyone toasts us. They're all talking at once, speaking of us as the *stranieri*, foreigners. The *grappa* is blindingly strong. We drink ours as fast as Signora Mantucci nips her espresso and wander out in the sun. The car is as hot as a pizza oven. We sit there with the doors open, suddenly laughing and laughing.

115   We'd arranged for two women to clean and for a bed to be delivered while we signed the final papers. In town we picked up a bottle of cold *prosecco*, then stopped at the *rosticceria* for marinated zucchini, olives, roast chicken, and potatoes.

116   We arrive at the house dazed by the events and the *grappa*. Anna and Lucia have washed the windows and exorcised layers of dust, as well as many spiders' webs. The second-floor bedroom that opens onto a brick terrace gleams. They've made the bed with the new blue sheets and left the terrace door open to the sound of cuckoos and wild canaries in the linden trees. We pick the last of the pink roses on the front terrace and fill two old Chianti bottles with them. The shuttered room with its white-washed walls, just-waxed floors, pristine bed with new sheets, and sweet

roses on the windowsill, all lit with a dangling forty-watt bulb, seems as pure as a Franciscan cell. As soon as I walk in, I think it is the most perfect room in the world.

117   We shower and dress in fresh clothes. In the quiet twilight, we sit on the stone wall of the terrace and toast each other and the house with tumblers of the spicy *prosecco*, which seems like a liquid form of the air. We toast the cypress trees along the road and the white horse in the neighbor's field, the villa in the distance that was built for the visit of a pope. The olive pits we toss over the wall, hoping they will spring from the ground next year. Dinner is delicious. As the darkness comes, a barn owl flies over so close that we hear the whir of wings and, when it settles in the black locust, a strange cry that we take for a greeting. The Big Dipper hangs over the house, about to pour on the roof. The constellations pop out, clear as a star chart. When it finally is dark, we see that the Milky Way sweeps right over the house. I forget the stars, living in the ambient light of a city. Here they are, all along, spangling and dense, falling and pulsating. We stare up until our necks ache. The Milky Way looks like a flung bolt of lace unfurling. Ed, because he likes to whisper, leans to my ear. "Still want to go home," he asks, "or can this be home?"

Questions for Engagement, Response, and Analysis

1. Mayes says of moving, "to sell is to walk away from a cluster of memories and to buy is to choose where the future will take place." To what extent is her move affected by her divorce?

2. Freewrite in your Reader's Journal about how Mayes' comment that "anytime I've stepped in my own footprints again, I haven't felt renewed" has proven true in your own life.

3. Mayes says, "[T]he circuitous search for a summer house became a quest for us." In what ways is the search for a place to live a kind of quest? What are the goals of such a quest?

4. How does the author build to the climax of buying Bramasole? What other stylistic techniques does she use throughout the essay?

Crafting Arguments

1. Using evidence from the essay, explain Mayes' statement: "The house is a metaphor for the self."

2. In an essay explain why, in spite of the difficulties and the alien culture, Mayes and Ed buy Bramasole.

3. After watching the 2003 film *Under the Tuscan Sun*, write an essay comparing one aspect of Mayes' factual account with the fictionalized film version OR argue that the film version does or does not retain the mood and obvious love of this Italian home.

FICTION

Carson McCullers (1917–1967)

*Born in Columbus, Georgia, Carson Smith McCullers is
famous for her portrayal of lonely and insecure people. Some
of her short stories and novels are described as modern
Gothic.* Her most famous novels include The Heart Is a
Lonely Hunter (1940), The Ballad of the Sad Cafe *(1951),
and* The Member of the Wedding *(1946), which was made
into an award-winning play and into a movie starring
Julie Harris and Ethel Waters. McCullers learned about suffering firsthand: her health began to deteriorate because of
a misdiagnosis of rheumatic fever while she was still in
high school, and her marriage to Reeves McCullers was
marked by many separations.*

A DOMESTIC DILEMMA   (1951)

1   On Thursday Martin Meadows left the office early enough to make the
first express bus home. It was the hour when the evening lilac glow was
fading in the slushy streets, but by the time the bus had left the Mid-town
terminal the bright city night had come. On Thursdays the maid had a
half-day off and Martin liked to get home as soon as possible, since for
the past year his wife had not been—well. This Thursday he was very
tired and, hoping that no regular commuter would single him out for conversation, he fastened his attention to the newspaper until the bus had
crossed the George Washington Bridge. Once on 9-W Highway Martin
always felt that the trip was halfway done, he breathed deeply, even in
cold weather when only ribbons of draught cut through the smoky air of
the bus, confident that he was breathing country air. It used to be that at
this point he would relax and begin to think with pleasure of his home.
But in this last year nearness brought only a sense of tension and he did
not anticipate the journey's end. This evening Martin kept his face close
to the window and watched the barren fields and lonely lights of passing
townships. There was a moon, pale on the dark earth and areas of late,
porous snow; to Martin the countryside seemed vast and somehow
desolate that evening. He took his hat from the rack and put his folded
newspaper in the pocket of his overcoat a few minutes before time to pull
the cord.

2   The cottage was a block from the bus stop, near the river but not
directly on the shore; from the living-room window you could look across
the street and opposite yard and see the Hudson. The cottage was modern, almost too white and new on the narrow plot of yard. In summer the
grass was soft and bright and Martin carefully tended a flower border and
a rose trellis. But during the cold, fallow months the yard was bleak and
the cottage seemed naked. Lights were on that evening in all the rooms

in the little house and Martin hurried up the front walk. Before the steps he stopped to move a wagon out of the way.

3   The children were in the living room, so intent on play that the opening of the front door was at first unnoticed. Martin stood looking at his safe, lovely children. They had opened the bottom drawer of the secretary and taken out the Christmas decorations. Andy had managed to plug in the Christmas tree lights and the green and red bulbs glowed with out-of-season festivity on the rug of the living room. At the moment he was trying to trail the bright cord over Marianne's rocking horse. Marianne sat on the floor pulling off an angel's wings. The children wailed a startling welcome. Martin swung the fat little baby girl up to his shoulder and Andy threw himself against his father's legs.

4   "Daddy, Daddy, Daddy!"

5   Martin set down the little girl carefully and swung Andy a few times like a pendulum. Then he picked up the Christmas tree cord.

6   "What's all this stuff doing out? Help me put it back in the drawer. You're not to fool with the light socket. Remember I told you that before. I mean it, Andy."

7   The six-year-old child nodded and shut the secretary drawer. Martin stroked his fair soft hair and his hand lingered tenderly on the nape of the child's frail neck.

8   "Had supper yet, Bumpkin?"

9   "It hurt. The toast was hot."

10   The baby girl stumbled on the rug and, after the first surprise of the fall, began to cry; Martin picked her up and carried her in his arms back to the kitchen.

11   "See, Daddy," said Andy. "The toast—"

12   Emily had laid the children's supper on the uncovered porcelain table. There were two plates with the remains of cream-of-wheat and eggs and silver mugs that had held milk. There was also a platter of cinnamon toast, untouched except for one tooth-marked bite. Martin sniffed the bitten piece and nibbled gingerly. Then he put the toast into the garbage pail.

13   "Hoo—phui—What on earth!"

14   Emily had mistaken the tin of cayenne for the cinnamon.

15   "I like to have burnt up," Andy said. "Drank water and ran outdoors and opened my mouth. Marianne didn't eat none."

16   "Any," corrected Martin. He stood helpless, looking around the walls of the kitchen. "Well, that's that, I guess," he said finally. "Where is your mother now?"

17   "She's up in you alls' room."

18   Martin left the children in the kitchen and went up to his wife. Outside the door he waited for a moment to still his anger. He did not knock and once inside the room he closed the door behind him.

19   Emily sat in the rocking chair by the window of the pleasant room. She had been drinking something from a tumbler and as he entered she put the glass hurriedly on the floor behind the chair. In her attitude

there was confusion and guilt which she tried to hide by a show of spurious vivacity.

20   "Oh, Marty! You home already? The time slipped up on me. I was just going down—" She lurched to him and her kiss was strong with sherry. When he stood unresponsive she stepped back a pace and giggled nervously.

21   "What's the matter with you? Standing there like a barber pole. Is anything wrong with you?"

22   "Wrong with me?" Martin bent over the rocking chair and picked up the tumbler from the floor. "If you could only realize how sick I am—how bad it is for all of us."

23   Emily spoke in a false, airy voice that had become too familiar to him. Often at such times she affected a slight English accent, copying perhaps some actress she admired. "I haven't the vaguest idea what you mean. Unless you are referring to the glass I used for a spot of sherry. I had a finger of sherry—maybe two. But what is the crime in that, pray tell me? I'm quite all right. Quite all right."

24   "So anyone can see."

25   As she went into the bathroom Emily walked with careful gravity. She turned on the cold water and dashed some on her face with her cupped hands, then patted herself dry with the corner of a bath towel. Her face was delicately featured and young, unblemished.

26   "I was just going down to make dinner." She tottered and balanced herself by holding to the door frame.

27   "I'll take care of dinner. You stay up here. I'll bring it up."

28   "I'll do nothing of the sort. Why, whoever heard of such a thing?"

29   "Please," Martin said.

30   "Leave me alone. I'm quite all right. I was just on the way down—"

31   "Mind what I say."

32   "Mind your grandmother."

33   She lurched toward the door, but Martin caught her by the arm. "I don't want the children to see you in this condition. Be reasonable."

34   "Condition!" Emily jerked her arm. Her voice rose angrily. "Why, because I drink a couple of sherries in the afternoon you're trying to make me out a drunkard. Condition! Why, I don't even touch whiskey. As well you know. I don't swill liquor at bars. And that's more than you can say. I don't even have a cocktail at dinnertime. I only sometimes have a glass of sherry. What, I ask you, is the disgrace of that? Condition!"

35   Martin sought words to calm his wife. "We'll have a quiet supper by ourselves up here. That's a good girl." Emily sat on the side of the bed and he opened the door for a quick departure.

36   "I'll be back in a jiffy."

37   As he busied himself with the dinner downstairs he was lost in the familiar question as to how this problem had come upon his home. He himself had always enjoyed a good drink. When they were still in Alabama they had served long drinks or cocktails as a matter of course.

For years they had drunk one or two—possibly three drinks before dinner, and at bedtime a long nightcap. Evenings before holidays they might get a buzz on, might even become a little tight. But alcohol had never seemed a problem to him, only a bothersome expense that with the increase in the family they could scarcely afford. It was only after his company had transferred him to New York that Martin was aware that certainly his wife was drinking too much. She was tippling, he noticed, during the day.

38   The problem acknowledged, he tried to analyze the source. The change from Alabama to New York had somehow disturbed her; accustomed to the idle warmth of a small Southern town, the matrix of the family and cousinship and childhood friends, she had failed to accommodate herself to the stricter, lonelier mores of the North. The duties of motherhood and housekeeping were onerous to her. Homesick for Paris City, she had made no friends in the suburban town. She read only magazines and murder books. Her interior life was insufficient without the artifice of alcohol.

39   The revelations of incontinence insidiously undermined his previous conceptions of his wife. There were times of unexplainable malevolence, times when the alcoholic fuse caused an explosion of unseemly anger. He encountered a latent coarseness in Emily, inconsistent with her natural simplicity. She lied about drinking and deceived him with unsuspected strategems.

40   Then there was an accident. Coming home from work one evening about a year ago, he was greeted with screams from the children's room. He found Emily holding the baby, wet and naked from her bath. The baby had been dropped, her frail, frail skull striking the table edge, so that a thread of blood was soaking into the gossamer hair. Emily was sobbing and intoxicated. As Martin cradled the hurt child, so infinitely precious at that moment, he had an affrighted vision of the future.

41   The next day Marianne was all right. Emily vowed that never again would she touch liquor, and for a few weeks she was sober, cold and downcast. Then gradually she began—not whiskey or gin—but quantities of beer, or sherry, or outlandish liqueurs; once he had come across a hatbox of empty crème de menthe bottles. Martin found a dependable maid who managed the household competently. Virgie was also from Alabama and Martin had never dared tell Emily the wage scale customary in New York. Emily's drinking was entirely secret now, done before he reached the house. Usually the effects were almost imperceptible—a looseness of movement or the heavy-lidded eyes. The times of irresponsibilities, such as the cayenne-pepper toast were rare, and Martin could dismiss his worries when Virgie was at the house. But, nevertheless, anxiety was always latent, a threat of undefined disaster that underlaid his days.

42   "Marianne!" Martin called, for even the recollection of that time brought the need for reassurance. The baby girl, no longer hurt, but no

less precious to her father, came into the kitchen with her brother. Martin went on with the preparations for the meal. He opened a can of soup and put two chops in the frying pan. Then he sat down by the table and took his Marianne on his knees for a pony ride. Andy watched them, his fingers wobbling the tooth that had been loose all that week.

43   "Andy-the-candyman!" Martin said. "Is that old critter still in your mouth? Come closer, let Daddy have a look."

44   "I got a string to pull it with." The child brought from his pocket a tangled thread. "Virgie said to tie it to the tooth and tie the other end to the doorknob and shut the door real suddenly."

45   Martin took out a clean handkerchief and felt the loose tooth carefully. "That tooth is coming out of my Andy's mouth tonight. Otherwise I'm awfully afraid we'll have a tooth tree in the family."

46   "A what?"

47   "A tooth tree," Martin said. "You'll bite into something and swallow that tooth. And the tooth will take root in poor Andy's stomach and grow into a tooth tree with sharp little teeth instead of leaves."

48   "Shoo, Daddy," Andy said. But he held the tooth firmly between his grimy little thumb and forefinger. "There ain't any tree like that. I never seen one."

49   "There isn't any tree like that and I never saw one."

50   Martin tensed suddenly. Emily was coming down the stairs. He listened to her fumbling footsteps, his arm embracing the little boy with dread. When Emily came into the room he saw from her movements and her sullen face that she had again been at the sherry bottle. She began to yank open drawers and set the table.

51   "Condition!" she said in a furry voice. "You talk to me like that. Don't think I'll forget. I remember every dirty lie you say to me. Don't you think for a minute that I forget."

52   "Emily!" he begged. "The children—"

53   "The children—yes! Don't think I don't see through your dirty plots and schemes. Down here trying to turn my own children against me. Don't think I don't see and understand."

54   "Emily! I beg you—please go upstairs."

55   "So you can turn my children—my very own children—" Two large tears coursed rapidly down her cheeks. "Trying to turn my little boy, my Andy, against his own mother."

56   With drunken impulsiveness Emily knelt on the floor before the startled child. Her hands on his shoulders balanced her. "Listen, my Andy— you wouldn't listen to any lies your father tells you? You wouldn't believe what he says? Listen, Andy, what was your father telling you before I came downstairs?" Uncertain, the child sought his father's face. "Tell me. Mama wants to know."

57   "About the tooth tree."

58   "What?"

59   The child repeated the words and she echoed them with unbelieving terror. "The tooth tree!" She swayed and renewed her grasp on the child's

shoulder. "I don't know what you're talking about. But listen, Andy, Mama is all right, isn't she?" The tears were spilling down her face and Andy drew back from her, for he was afraid. Grasping the table edge, Emily stood up.

60 "See! You have turned my child against me."

61 Marianne began to cry, and Martin took her in his arms.

62 "That's all right, you can take your child. You have always shown partiality from the very first. I don't mind, but at least you can leave me my little boy."

63 Andy edged close to his father and touched his leg. "Daddy," he wailed.

64 Martin took the children to the foot of the stairs. "Andy, you take up Marianne and Daddy will follow you in a minute."

65 "But Mama?" the child asked, whispering.

66 "Mama will be all right. Don't worry."

67 Emily was sobbing at the kitchen table, her face buried in the crook of her arm. Martin poured a cup of soup and set it before her. Her rasping sobs unnerved him; the vehemence of her emotion, irrespective of the source, touched in him a strain of tenderness. Unwillingly he laid his hand on her dark hair. "Sit up and drink the soup." Her face as she looked up at him was chastened and imploring. The boy's withdrawal or the touch of Martin's hand had turned the tenor of her mood.

68 "Ma-Martin," she sobbed. "I'm so ashamed."

69 "Drink the soup."

70 Obeying him, she drank between gasping breaths. After a second cup she allowed him to lead her up to their room. She was docile now and more restrained. He laid her nightgown on the bed and was about to leave when a fresh round of grief, the alcoholic tumult, came again.

71 "He turned away. My Andy looked at me and turned away."

72 Impatience and fatigue hardened his voice, but he spoke warily. "You forget that Andy is still a little child—he can't comprehend the meaning of such scenes."

73 "Did I make a scene? Oh, Martin, did I make a scene before the children?"

74 Her horrified face touched and amused him against his will. "Forget it. Put on your nightgown and go to sleep."

75 "My child turned away from me. Andy looked at his mother and turned away. The children—"

76 She was caught in the rhythmic sorrow of alcohol. Martin withdrew from the room saying: "For God's sake go to sleep. The children will forget by tomorrow."

77 As he said this he wondered if it was true. Would the scene glide so easily from memory—or would it root in the unconscious to fester in the after-years? Martin did not know, and the last alternative sickened him. He thought of Emily, foresaw the morning-after humiliation: the shards of memory, the lucidities that glared from the obliterating darkness of shame. She would call the New York office twice—possibly three or four times. Martin anticipated his own embarrassment, wondering if the

others at the office could possibly suspect. He felt that his secretary had divined the trouble long ago and that she pitied him. He suffered a moment of rebellion against his fate; he hated his wife.

78   Once in the children's room he closed the door and felt secure for the first time that evening. Marianne fell down on the floor, picked herself up and calling: "Daddy, watch me," fell again, got up, and continued the falling-calling routine. Andy sat in the child's low chair, wobbling the tooth. Martin ran the water in the tub, washed his own hands in the lavatory, and called the boy into the bathroom.

79   "Let's have another look at that tooth." Martin sat on the toilet, holding Andy between his knees. The child's mouth gaped and Martin grasped the tooth. A wobble, a quick twist and the nacreous milk tooth was free. Andy's face was for the first moment split between terror, astonishment, and delight. He mouthed a swallow of water and spat into the lavatory.

80   "Look, Daddy! It's blood. Marianne!"

81   Martin loved to bathe his children, loved inexpressibly the tender, naked bodies as they stood in the water so exposed. It was not fair of Emily to say that he showed partiality. As Martin soaped the delicate boy-body of his son he felt that further love would be impossible. Yet he admitted the difference in the quality of his emotions for the two children. His love for his daughter was graver, touched with a strain of melancholy, a gentleness that was akin to pain. His pet names for the little boy were the absurdities of daily inspiration—he called the little girl always Marianne, and his voice as he spoke it was a caress. Martin patted dry the fat baby stomach and the sweet little genital fold. The washed child faces were radiant as flower petals, equally loved.

82   "I'm putting the tooth under my pillow. I'm supposed to get a quarter."

83   "What for?"

84   "You know, Daddy. Johnny got a quarter for his tooth."

85   "Who puts the quarter there?" asked Martin. "I used to think the fairies left it in the night. It was a dime in my day, though."

86   "That's what they say in kindergarden."

87   "Who does put it there?"

88   "Your parents," Andy said. "You!"

89   Martin was pinning the cover on Marianne's bed. His daughter was already asleep. Scarcely breathing, Martin bent over and kissed her forehead, kissed again the tiny hand that lay palm-upward, flung in slumber beside her head.

90   "Good night, Andy-man."

91   The answer was only a drowsy murmur. After a minute Martin took out his change and slid a quarter underneath the pillow. He left a night light in the room.

92   As Martin prowled about the kitchen making a late meal, it occurred to him that the children had not once mentioned their mother or the scene that must have seemed to them incomprehensible. Absorbed in the instant—the tooth, the bath, the quarter—the fluid passage of child-time

had borne these weightless episodes like leaves in the swift current of a shallow stream while the adult enigma was beached and forgotten on the shore. Martin thanked the Lord for that.

93   But his own anger, repressed and lurking, arose again. His youth was being frittered by a drunkard's waste, his very manhood subtly undermined. And the children, once the immunity of incomprehension passed—what would it be like in a year or so? With his elbows on the table he ate his food brutishly, untasting. There was no hiding the truth—soon there would be gossip in the office and in the town; his wife was a dissolute woman. Dissolute. And he and his children were bound to a future of degradation and slow ruin.

94   Martin pushed away from the table and stalked into the living room. He followed the lines of a book with his eyes but his mind conjured miserable images: he saw his children drowned in the river, his wife a disgrace on the public street. By bedtime the dull, hard anger was like a weight upon his chest and his feet dragged as he climbed the stairs.

95   The room was dark except for the shafting light from the half-opened bathroom door. Martin undressed quietly. Little by little, mysteriously, there came in him a change. His wife was asleep, her peaceful respiration sounding gently in the room. Her high-heeled shoes with the carelessly dropped stockings made to him a mute appeal. Her underclothes were flung in disorder on the chair. Martin picked up the girdle and the soft, silk brassière and stood for a moment with them in his hands. For the first time that evening he looked at his wife. His eyes rested on the sweet forehead, the arch of the fine brow. The brow had descended to Marianne, and the tilt at the end of the delicate nose. In his son he could trace the high cheekbones and pointed chin. Her body was full-bosomed, slender and undulant. As Martin watched the tranquil slumber of his wife the ghost of the old anger vanished. All thoughts of blame or blemish were distant from him now. Martin put out the bathroom light and raised the window. Careful not to awaken Emily he slid into the bed. By moonlight he watched his wife for the last time. His hand sought the adjacent flesh and sorrow paralleled desire in the immense complexity of love.

Questions for Engagement, Response, and Analysis

1. What clues early in the story **foreshadow** the problem in this family?

2. In your Reader's Journal, freewrite about what you would do if you were in Martin's position.

3. What particular scenes and actions affect your judgment of Martin as a father and as a husband?

4. How is the theme of the story summed up in the phrase "the immense complexity of love"?

Crafting Arguments

1. Argue what you think Martin should do in this situation. Justify your position with evidence from the story.
2. Craft a character analysis of either Martin or Emily.

James Baldwin (1924–1987)

James Baldwin knew firsthand the rigors of poverty in Harlem, for he grew up there along with eight half-brothers and -sisters. His mother worked as a domestic; his stepfather, a laborer and part-time preacher, seemed to resent his small, unattractive stepson. Thus Baldwin learned early the importance of family and the need for love, themes that appear in "Sonny's Blues" and in his other works. Baldwin's novels, essays, and stories reveal both his talent as a writer and his intolerance of bigotry. To escape American racial prejudice, he spent much of his life in France. His most famous novels are Go Tell It on the Mountain *(1953) and* Giovanni's Room *(1956). Baldwin's essays, collected in* Notes of a Native Son *(1955),* Nobody Knows My Name *(1961), and* The Fire Next Time *(1963), strongly influenced his contemporaries.*

SONNY'S BLUES   (1957)

96   I heard about it in the paper, in the subway, on my way to work. I read it, and I couldn't believe it, and I read it again. Then perhaps I just stared at it, at the newsprint spelling out his name, spelling out the story. I stared at it in the swinging lights of the subway car, and in the faces and bodies of the people, and in my own face, trapped in the darkness which roared outside.

97   It was not to be believed and I kept telling myself that, as I walked from the subway station to the high school. And at the same time I couldn't doubt it. I was scared, scared for Sonny. He became real to me again. A great block of ice got settled in my belly and kept melting there slowly all day long, while I taught my classes algebra. It was a special kind of ice. It kept melting, sending trickles of ice water all up and down my veins, but it never got less. Sometimes it hardened and seemed to expand until I felt my guts were going to come spilling out or that I was going to choke or scream. This would always be at a moment when I was remembering some specific thing Sonny had once said or done.

98   When he was about as old as the boys in my classes his face had been bright and open, there was a lot of copper in it; and he'd had wonderfully direct brown eyes, and great gentleness and privacy. I wondered what he looked like now. He had been picked up, the evening before, in a raid on an apartment downtown, for peddling and using heroin.

99   I couldn't believe it: but what I mean by that is that I couldn't find any room for it anywhere inside me. I had kept it outside me for a long time. I hadn't wanted to know. I had had suspicions, but I didn't name them, I kept putting them away. I told myself that Sonny was wild, but he wasn't crazy. And he'd always been a good boy, he hadn't ever turned hard or evil or disrespectful, the way kids can, so quick, so quick, especially in Harlem, I didn't want to believe that I'd ever see my brother going down, coming to nothing, all that light in his face gone out, in the condition I'd already seen so many others. Yet it had happened and here I was, talking about algebra to a lot of boys who might, every one of them for all I knew, be popping off needles every time they went to the head. Maybe it did more for them than algebra could.

100   I was sure that the first time Sonny had ever had horse, he couldn't have been much older than these boys were now. These boys, now, were living as we'd been living then, they were growing up with a rush and their heads bumped abruptly against the low ceiling of their actual possibilities. They were filled with rage. All they really knew were two darknesses, the darkness of their lives, which was now closing in on them and the darkness of the movies, which had blinded them to that other darkness, and in which they now, vindictively, dreamed, at once more together than they were at any other time, and more alone.

101   When the last bell rang, the class ended, I let out my breath. It seemed I'd been holding it for all that time. My clothes were wet—I may have looked as though I'd been sitting in a steam bath, all dressed up, all afternoon. I sat alone in the classroom a long time. I listened to the boys outside, downstairs, shouting and cursing and laughing. Their laughter struck me for perhaps the first time. It was not the joyous laughter which—God knows why—one associates with children. It was mocking and insular, its intent was to denigrate. It was disenchanted, and in this, also, lay the authority of their curses. Perhaps I was listening to them because I was thinking about my brother and in them I heard my brother. And myself.

102   One boy was whistling a tune, at once very complicated and very simple, it seemed to be pouring out of him as though he were a bird, and it sounded very cool and moving through all that harsh, bright air, only just holding its own through all those other sounds.

103   I stood up and walked over to the window and looked down into the courtyard. It was the beginning of the spring and the sap was rising in the boys. A teacher passed through them every now and again, quickly, as though he or she couldn't wait to get out of that courtyard, to get those boys out of their sight and off their minds. I started collecting my stuff. I thought I'd better get home and talk to Isabel.

104   The courtyard was almost deserted by the time I got downstairs. I saw this boy standing in the shadow of a doorway, looking just like Sonny. I almost called his name. Then I saw that it wasn't Sonny, but somebody we used to know, a boy from around our block. He'd been Sonny's friend.

He'd never been mine, having been too young for me, and anyway, I'd never liked him. And now, even though he was a grown-up man, he still hung around that block, still spent hours on the street corners, was always high and raggy. I used to run into him from time to time and he'd often work around to asking me for a quarter or fifty cents. He always had some real good excuse, too, and I always gave it to him. I don't know why.

105   But now, abruptly, I hated him. I couldn't stand the way he looked at me, partly like a dog, partly like a cunning child. I wanted to ask him what the hell he was doing in the school courtyard.

106   He sort of shuffled over to me, and he said, "I see you got the papers. So you already know about it."

107   "You mean about Sonny? Yes, I already know about it. How come they didn't get you?"

108   He grinned. It made him repulsive and it also brought to mind what he'd looked like as a kid. "I wasn't there. I stay away from them people."

109   "Good for you." I offered him a cigarette and I watched him through the smoke. "You come all the way down here just to tell me about Sonny?"

110   "That's right." He was sort of shaking his head and his eyes looked strange, as though they were about to cross. The bright sun deadened his damp dark brown skin and it made his eyes look yellow and showed up the dirt in his kinked hair. He smelled funky. I moved a little away from him and I said, "Well, thanks. But I already know about it and I got to get home."

111   "I'll walk you a little ways," he said. We started walking. There were a couple of kids still loitering in the courtyard and one of them said goodnight to me and looked strangely at the boy beside me.

112   "What're you going to do?" he asked me. "I mean, about Sonny?"

113   "Look. I haven't seen Sonny for over a year, I'm not sure I'm going to do anything. Anyway, what the hell *can* I do?"

114   "That's right," he said quickly, "ain't nothing you can do. Can't much help old Sonny no more, I guess."

115   It was what I was thinking and so it seemed to me he had no right to say it.

116   "I'm surprised at Sonny, though," he went on—he had a funny way of talking, he looked straight ahead as though he were talking to himself—"I thought Sonny was a smart boy, I thought he was too smart to get hung."

117   "I guess he thought so too," I said sharply, "and that's how he got hung. And how about you? You're pretty goddamn smart, I bet."

118   Then he looked directly at me, just for a minute. "I ain't smart," he said. "If I was smart, I'd have reached for a pistol a long time ago."

119   "Look. Don't tell *me* your sad story, if it was up to me, I'd give you one." Then I felt guilty—guilty, probably, for never having supposed that the poor bastard *had* a story of his own, much less a sad one, and I asked, quickly, "What's going to happen to him now?"

120   He didn't answer this. He was off by himself some place. "Funny thing," he said, and from his tone we might have been discussing the quickest way to get to Brooklyn, "when I saw the papers this morning, the first thing I asked myself was if I had anything to do with it. I felt sort of responsible."

121   I began to listen more carefully. The subway station was on the corner, just before us, and I stopped. He stopped, too. We were in front of a bar and he ducked slightly, peering in, but whoever he was looking for didn't seem to be there. The juke box was blasting away with something black and bouncy and I half watched the barmaid as she danced her way from the juke box to her place behind the bar. And I watched her face as she laughingly responded to something someone said to her, still keeping time to the music. When she smiled one saw the little girl, one sensed the doomed, still-struggling woman beneath the battered face of the semiwhore.

122   "I never *give* Sonny nothing," the boy said finally, "but a long time ago I come to school high and Sonny asked me how it felt." He paused, I couldn't bear to watch him, I watched the barmaid, and I listened to the music which seemed to be causing the pavement to shake. "I told him it felt great." The music stopped, the barmaid paused and watched the juke box until the music began again. "It did."

123   All this was carrying me some place I didn't want to go. I certainly didn't want to know how it felt. It filled everything, the people, the houses, the music, the dark, quicksilver barmaid, with menace; and this menace was their reality.

124   "What's going to happen to him now?" I asked again.

125   "They'll send him away some place and they'll try to cure him." He shook his head. "Maybe he'll even think he's kicked the habit. Then they'll let him loose"—he gestured, throwing his cigarette into the gutter. "That's all."

126   "What do you mean, that's *all*?"

127   But I knew what he meant.

128   "I *mean*, that's *all*." He turned his head and looked at me, pulling down the corners of his mouth. "Don't you know what I mean?" he asked, softly.

129   "How the hell *would* I know what you mean?" I almost whispered it, I don't know why.

130   "That's right," he said to the air, "how would *he* know what I mean?" He turned toward me again, patient and calm, and yet I somehow felt him shaking, shaking as though he were going to fall apart. I felt that ice in my guts again, the dread I'd felt all afternoon; and again I watched the barmaid, moving about the bar, washing glasses, and singing. "Listen. They'll let him out and then it'll just start all over again. That's what I mean."

131   "You mean—they'll let him out. And then he'll just start working his way back in again. You mean he'll never kick the habit. Is that what you mean?"

132   "That's right," he said, cheerfully. "*You* see what I mean."

133   "Tell me," I said at last, "why does he want to die? He must want to die, he's killing himself, why does he want to die?"

134   He looked at me in surprise. He licked his lips. "He don't want to die. He wants to live. Don't nobody want to die, ever."

135   Then I wanted to ask him—too many things. He could not have answered, or if he had, I could not have borne the answers. I started walking. "Well, I guess it's none of my business."

136   "It's going to be rough on old Sonny," he said. We reached the subway station. "This is your station?" he asked. I nodded. I took one step down. "Damn!" he said, suddenly. I looked up at him. He grinned again. "Damn it if I didn't leave all my money home. You ain't got a dollar on you, have you? Just for a couple of days, is all."

137   All at once something inside gave and threatened to come pouring out of me. I didn't hate him any more. I felt that in another moment I'd start crying like a child.

138   "Sure," I said, "Don't sweat." I looked in my wallet and didn't have a dollar, I only had a five. "Here," I said. "That hold you?"

139   He didn't look at it—he didn't want to look at it. A terrible, closed look come over his face, as though he were keeping the number on the bill a secret from him and me. "Thanks," he said, and now he was dying to see me go. "Don't worry about Sonny. Maybe I'll write him or something."

140   "Sure," I said. "You do that. So long."

141   "Be seeing you," he said. I went on down the steps.

142   And I didn't write Sonny or send him anything for a long time. When I finally did, it was just after my little girl died, he wrote me back a letter which made me feel like a bastard.

143   Here's what he said:

144   Dear brother,

145   You don't know how much I needed to hear from you. I wanted to write you many a time but I dug how much I must have hurt you and so I didn't write. But now I feel like a man who's been trying to climb up out of some deep, real deep and funky hole and just saw the sun up there, outside. I got to get outside.

146   I can't tell you much about how I got here. I mean I don't know how to tell you. I guess I was afraid of something or I was trying to escape from something and you know I have never been very strong in the head (smile). I'm glad Mama and Daddy are dead and can't see what's happened to their son and I swear if I'd known what I was doing I would never have hurt you so, you and a lot of other fine people who were nice to me and who believed in me.

147   I don't want you to think it had anything to do with me being a musician. It's more than that. Or maybe less than that. I can't get anything straight in my head down here and I try not to think about what's going to happen to me when I get outside again. Sometime I think I'm going to flip and *never* get outside and sometime I think I'll come straight back. I tell you one thing, though, I'd rather blow my brains out than go through this

again. But that's what they all say, so they tell me. If I tell you when I'm coming to New York and if you could meet me, I sure would appreciate it. Give my love to Isabel and the kids and I was sure sorry to hear about little Gracie. I wish I could be like Mama and say the Lord's will be done, but I don't know it seems to me that trouble is the one thing that never does get stopped and I don't know what good it does to blame it on the Lord. But maybe it does some good if you believe it.

148   Your brother,
149   Sonny

150   Then I kept in constant touch with him and I sent him whatever I could and I went to meet him when he came back to New York. When I saw him many things I thought I had forgotten came flooding back to me. This was because I had begun, finally, to wonder about Sonny, about the life that Sonny lived inside. This life, whatever it was, had made him older and thinner and it had deepened the distant stillness in which he had always moved. He looked very unlike my baby brother. Yet, when he smiled, when we shook hands, the baby brother I'd never known looked out from the depths of his private life, like an animal waiting to be coaxed into the light.

151   "How you been keeping?" he asked me.
152   "All right. And you?"
153   "Just fine." He was smiling all over his face. "It's good to see you again."
154   "It's good to see you."
155   The seven years' difference in our ages lay between us like a chasm: I wondered if these years would ever operate between us as a bridge. I was remembering, and it made it hard to catch my breath, that I had been there when he was born; and I had heard the first words he had ever spoken. When he started to walk, he walked from our mother straight to me. I caught him just before he fell when he took the first steps he ever took in this world.
156   "How's Isabel?"
157   "Just fine. She's dying to see you."
158   "And the boys?"
159   "They're fine, too. They're anxious to see their uncle."
160   "Oh, come on. You know they don't remember me."
161   "Are you kidding? Of course they remember you."
162   He grinned again. We got into a taxi. We had a lot to say to each other, far too much to know how to begin.
163   As the taxi began to move, I asked, "You still want to go to India?"
164   He laughed. "You still remember that. Hell, no. This place is Indian enough to me."
165   "It used to belong to them," I said.
166   And he laughed again. "They damn sure knew what they were doing when they got rid of it."
167   Years ago, when he was around fourteen, he'd been all hipped up on the idea of going to India. He read books about people sitting on rocks,

naked, in all kinds of weather, but mostly bad, naturally, and walking barefoot through hot coals and arriving at wisdom. I used to say that it sounded to me as though they were getting away from wisdom as fast as they could. I think he sort of looked down on me for that.

168 "Do you mind," he asked "if we have the driver drive alongside the park? On the west side—I haven't seen the city in so long."

169 "Of course not," I said. I was afraid that I might sound as though I were humoring him, but I hoped he wouldn't take it that way.

170 So we drove along, between the green of the park and the stony, lifeless elegance of hotels and apartment buildings, toward the vivid, killing streets of our childhood. These streets hadn't changed, though housing projects jutted up out of them now like rocks in the middle of a boiling sea. Most of the houses in which we had grown up had vanished, as had the stores from which we had stolen, the basements in which we had first tried sex, the rooftops from which we had hurled tin cans and bricks. But houses exactly like the houses of our past yet dominated the landscape, boys exactly like the boys we once had been found themselves smothering in these houses, came down into the streets for light and air and found themselves encircled by disaster. Some escaped the trap, most didn't. Those who got out always left something of themselves behind, as some animals amputate a leg and leave it in the trap. It might be said, perhaps, that I had escaped, after all, I was a school teacher; or that Sonny had, he hadn't lived in Harlem for years. Yet, as the cab moved uptown through streets which seemed, with a rush, to darken with dark people, and as I covertly studied Sonny's face, it came to me that what we both were seeking through our separate cab windows was that part of ourselves which had been left behind. It's always at the hour of trouble and confrontation that the missing member aches.

171 We hit 110th Street and started rolling up Lenox Avenue. And I'd known this avenue all my life, but it seemed to me again, as it had seemed on the day I'd first heard about Sonny's trouble, filled with a hidden menace which was its very breath of life.

172 "We almost there," said Sonny.

173 "Almost." We were both too nervous to say anything more.

174 We live in a housing project. It hasn't been up long. A few days after it was up it seemed uninhabitably new, now, of course, it's already rundown. It looks like a parody of the good, clean, faceless life—God knows the people who live in it do their best to make it a parody. The beat-looking grass lying around isn't enough to make their lives green, the hedges will never hold out the streets, and they know it. The big windows fool no one, they aren't big enough to make space out of no space. They don't bother with the windows, they watch the TV screen instead. The playground is most popular with the children who don't play at jacks, or skip rope, or roller skate, or swing, and they can be found in it after dark. We moved in partly because it's not too far from where I teach, and partly for the kids; but it's really just like the houses in which Sonny and I grew up. The same things

happen, they'll have the same things to remember. The moment Sonny and I started into the house I had the feeling that I was simply bringing him back into the danger he had almost died trying to escape.

175   Sonny has never been talkative. So I don't know why I was sure he'd be dying to talk to me when supper was over the first night. Everything went fine, the oldest boy remembered him, and the youngest boy liked him, and Sonny had remembered to bring something for each of them; and Isabel, who is really much nicer than I am, more open and giving, had gone to a lot of trouble about dinner and was genuinely glad to see him. And she's always been able to tease Sonny in a way that I haven't. It was nice to see her face so vivid again and to hear her laugh and watch her make Sonny laugh. She wasn't, or, anyway, she didn't seem to be, at all uneasy or embarrassed. She chatted as though there were no subject which had to be avoided and she got Sonny past his first, faint stiffness. And thank God she was there, for I was filled with that icy dread again. Everything I did seemed awkward to me, and everything I said sounded freighted with hidden meaning. I was trying to remember everything I'd heard about dope addiction and I couldn't help watching Sonny for signs. I wasn't doing it out of malice. I was trying to find out something about my brother. I was dying to hear him tell me he was safe.

176   "Safe!" my father grunted, whenever Mama suggested trying to move to a neighborhood which might be safer for children. "Safe, hell! Ain't no place safe for kids, nor nobody."

177   He always went on like this, but he wasn't, ever, really as bad as he sounded, not even on weekends, when he got drunk. As a matter of fact, he was always on the lookout for "something a little better," but he died before he found it. He died suddenly, during a drunken weekend in the middle of the war, when Sonny was fifteen. He and Sonny hadn't ever got on too well. And this was partly because Sonny was the apple of his father's eye. It was because he loved Sonny so much and was frightened for him, that he was always fighting with him. It doesn't do any good to fight with Sonny. Sonny just moves back, inside himself, where he can't be reached. But the principal reason that they never hit it off is that they were so much alike. Daddy was big and rough and loud-talking, just the opposite of Sonny, but they both had—that same privacy.

178   Mama tried to tell me something about this, just after Daddy died. I was home on leave from the army.

179   This was the last time I ever saw my mother alive. Just the same, this picture gets all mixed up in my mind with pictures I had of her when she was younger. The way I always see her is the way she used to be on Sunday afternoon, say, when the old folks were talking after the big Sunday dinner. I always see her wearing pale blue. She'd be sitting on the sofa. And my father would be sitting in the easy chair, not far from her. And the living room would be full of church folks and relatives. There they sit, on chairs all around the living room, and the night is creeping up outside, but nobody knows it yet. You can see the darkness growing

against the windowpanes and you hear the street noises every now and again, or maybe the jangling beat of a tambourine from one of the churches close by, but it's real quiet in the room. For a moment nobody's talking, but every face looks darkening, like the sky outside. And my mother rocks a little from the waist, and my father's eyes are closed. Everyone is looking at something a child can't see. For a minute they've forgotten the children. Maybe a kid is lying on the rug, half asleep. Maybe somebody's got a kid in his lap and is absent-mindedly stroking the kid's head. Maybe there's a kid, quiet and big-eyed, curled up in a big chair in the corner. The silence, the darkness coming, and the darkness in the faces frightens the child obscurely. He hopes that the hand which strokes his forehead will never stop—will never die. He hopes that there will never come a time when the old folks won't be sitting around the living room, talking about where they've come from, and what they've seen, and what's happened to them and their kinfolk.

180   But something deep and watchful in the child knows that this is bound to end, is already ending. In a moment someone will get up and turn on the light. Then the old folks will remember the children and they won't talk any more that day. And when light fills the room, the child is filled with darkness. He knows that every time this happens he's moved just a little closer to that darkness outside. The darkness outside is what the old folks have been talking about. It's what they've come from. It's what they endure. The child knows that they won't talk any more because if he knows too much about what's happened to *them*, he'll know too much too soon, about what's going to happen to *him*.

181   The last time I talked to my mother, I remember I was restless. I wanted to get out and see Isabel. We weren't married then and we had a lot to straighten out between us.

182   There Mama sat, in black, by the window. She was humming an old church song, *Lord, you brought me from a long ways off.* Sonny was out somewhere. Mama kept watching the streets.

183   "I don't know," she said, "if I'll ever see you again, after you go off from here. But I hope you'll remember the things I tried to teach you."

184   "Don't talk like that," I said, and smiled. "You'll be here a long time yet."

185   She smiled, too, but she said nothing. She was quiet for a long time. And I said, "Mama, don't you worry about nothing. I'll be writing all the time, and you be getting the checks. . . ."

186   "I want to talk to you about your brother," she said, suddenly. "If anything happens to me he ain't going to have nobody to look out for him."

187   "Mama," I said, "ain't nothing going to happen to you *or* Sonny. Sonny's all right. He's a good boy and he's got good sense."

188   "It ain't a question of his being a good boy," Mama said, "nor of his having good sense. It ain't only the bad ones, nor yet the dumb ones that gets sucked under." She stopped, looking at me. "Your Daddy once had a brother," she said, and she smiled, in a way that made me feel she was in pain. "You didn't never know that, did you?"

189   "No," I said, "I never knew that," and I watched her face.

190   "Oh, yes," she said, "your Daddy had a brother." She looked out of the window again. "I know you never saw your Daddy cry. But I did—many a time, through all these years."

191   I asked her, "What happened to his brother? How come nobody's ever talked about him?"

192   This was the first time I ever saw my mother look old.

193   "His brother got killed," she said, "when he was just a little younger than you are now. I knew him. He was a fine boy. He was maybe a little full of the devil, but he didn't mean nobody no harm."

194   Then she stopped and the room was silent, exactly as it had sometimes been on those Sunday afternoons. Mama kept looking out into the streets.

195   "He used to have a job in the mill," she said, "and, like all young folks, he just liked to perform on Saturday nights. Saturday nights, him and your father would drift around to different places, go to dances and things like that, or just sit around with people they knew, and your father's brother would sing, he had a fine voice, and play along with himself on his guitar. Well, this particular Saturday night him and your father was coming home from some place, and they were both a little drunk and there was a moon that night, it was bright like day. Your father's brother was feeling kind of good, and he was whistling to himself, and he had his guitar slung over his shoulder. They was coming down a hill and beneath them was a road that turned off from the highway. Well, your father's brother, being always kind of frisky, decided to run down this hill, and he did, with that guitar banging and clanging behind him, and he ran across the road, and he was making water behind a tree. And your father was sort of amused at him and he was still coming down the hill, kind of slow. Then he heard a car motor and that same minute his brother stepped from behind the tree, into the road, in the moonlight. And he started to cross the road. And your father started to run down the hill, he says he don't know why. This car was full of white men. They was all drunk, and when they seen your father's brother they let out a great whoop and holler and they aimed the car straight at him. They was having fun, they just wanted to scare him, the way they do sometimes, you know. But they was drunk. And I guess the boy, being drunk, too, and scared, kind of lost his head. By the time he jumped it was too late. Your father says he heard his brother scream when the car rolled over him, and he heard the wood of that guitar when it give, and he heard them strings go flying, and he heard them white men shouting and the car kept on a-going and it ain't stopped till this day. And, time your father got down the hill, his brother weren't nothing but blood and pulp."

196   Tears were gleaming on my mother's face. There wasn't anything I could say.

197   "He never mentioned it," she said, "because I never let him mention it before you children. Your Daddy was like a crazy man that night and for many a night thereafter. He says he never in his life seen anything as dark

as that road after the lights of that car had gone away. Weren't nothing, weren't nobody on that road, just your Daddy and his brother and that busted guitar. Oh, yes. Your Daddy never did really get right again. Till the day he died he weren't sure but that every white man he saw was the man that killed his brother."

198   She stopped and took out her handkerchief and dried her eyes and looked at me.

199   "I ain't telling you all this," she said, "to make you scared or bitter or to make you hate nobody. I'm telling you this because you got a brother. And the world ain't changed."

200   I guess I didn't want to believe this. I guess she saw this in my face. She turned away from me, toward the window again, searching those streets.

201   "But I praise my Redeemer," she said at last, "that He called your Daddy home before me. I ain't saying it to throw no flowers at myself, but, I declare, it keeps me from feeling too cast down to know I helped your father get safely through this world. Your father always acted like he was the roughest, strongest man on earth. And everybody took him to be like that. But if he hadn't had *me* there—to see his tears!"

202   She was crying again. Still I couldn't move. I said, "Lord, Lord, Mama, I didn't know it was like that."

203   "Oh, honey," she said, "there's a lot that you don't know. But you are going to find it out." She stood up from the window and came over to me. "You got to hold on to your brother," she said, "and don't let him fall, no matter what it looks like is happening to him and no matter how evil you gets with him. You going to be evil with him many a time. But don't you forget what I told you, you hear?"

204   "I won't forget," I said. "Don't you worry, I won't forget. I won't let nothing happen to Sonny."

205   My mother smiled as though she were amused at something she saw in my face. Then, "You may not be able to stop nothing from happening. But you got to let him know you's *there*."

206   Two days later I was married, and then I was gone. And I had a lot of things on my mind and I pretty well forgot my promise to Mama until I got shipped home on a special furlough for her funeral.

207   And, after the funeral, with just Sonny and me alone in the empty kitchen, I tried to find out something about him.

208   "What do you want to do?" I asked him.

209   "I'm going to be a musician," he said.

210   For he had graduated, in the time I had been away, from dancing to the juke box to finding out who was playing what, and what they were doing with it, and he had bought himself a set of drums.

211   "You mean, you want to be a drummer?" I somehow had the feeling that being a drummer might be all right for other people but not for my brother Sonny.

212   "I don't think," he said, looking at me very gravely, "that I'll ever be a good drummer. But I think I can play a piano."

213   I frowned. I'd never played the role of the older brother quite so
seriously before, had scarcely ever, in fact, *asked* Sonny a damn thing.
I sensed myself in the presence of something I didn't really know how to
handle, didn't understand. So I made my frown a little deeper as I asked:
"What kind of musician do you want to be?"

214   He grinned. "How many kinds do you think there are?"

215   "Be *serious*," I said.

216   He laughed, throwing his head back, and then looked at me. "I *am*
serious."

217   "Well, then, for Christ's sake, stop kidding around and answer a serious question. I mean, do you want to be a concert pianist, you want to
play classical music and all that, or—or what?" Long before I finished he
was laughing again. "For Christ's *sake*, Sonny!"

218   He sobered, but with difficulty. "I'm sorry. But you sound so—*scared!*"
and he was off again.

219   "Well, you may think it's funny now, baby, but it's not going to be so
funny when you have to make your living at it, let me tell you *that*." I was
furious because I knew he was laughing at me and I didn't know why.

220   "No," he said, very sober now, and afraid, perhaps, that he'd hurt me,
"I don't want to be a classical pianist. That isn't what interests me. I
mean"—he paused, looking hard at me, as though his eyes would help
me to understand, and then gestured helplessly, as though perhaps his
hand would help—"I mean, I'll have a lot of studying to do, and I'll have
to study *everything*, but, I mean, I want to play *with*—jazz musicians."
He stopped. "I want to play jazz," he said.

221   Well, the word had never before sounded as heavy, as real, as it
sounded that afternoon in Sonny's mouth. I just looked at him and I
was probably frowning a real frown by this time. I simply couldn't see
why on earth he'd want to spend his time hanging around nightclubs,
clowning around on bandstands, while people pushed each other
around a dance floor. It seemed—beneath him, somehow. I had never
thought about it before, had never been forced to, but I suppose I had
always put jazz musicians in a class with what Daddy called "good-
time people."

222   "Are you *serious?*"

223   "Hell, *yes*, I'm serious."

224   He looked more helpless than ever, and annoyed, and deeply hurt.

225   I suggested, helpfully: "You mean—like Louis Armstrong?"

226   His face closed as though I'd struck him. "No. I'm not talking about
none of that old-time, down home crap."

227   "Well, look, Sonny, I'm sorry, don't get mad. I just don't altogether get
it, that's all. Name somebody—you know a jazz musician you admire."

228   "Bird."

229   "Who?"

230   "Bird! Charlie Parker! Don't they teach you nothing in the
goddamn army?"

231   I lit a cigarette. I was surprised and then a little amused to discover that I was trembling. "I've been out of touch," I said. "You'll have to be patient with me. Now. Who's this Parker character?"

232   "He's just one of the greatest jazz musicians alive," said Sonny, sullenly, his hands in his pockets, his back to me. "Maybe *the* greatest," he added, bitterly, "that's probably why *you* never heard of him."

233   "All right," I said, "I'm ignorant. I'm sorry. I'll go out and buy all the cat's records right away, all right?"

234   "It don't" said Sonny, with dignity, "make any difference to me. I don't care what you listen to. Don't do me no favors."

235   I was beginning to realize that I'd never seen him so upset before. With another part of my mind I was thinking that this would probably turn out to be one of those things kids go through and that I shouldn't make it seem important by pushing it too hard. Still, I didn't think it would do any harm to ask: "Doesn't all this take a lot of time? Can you make a living at it?"

236   He turned back to me and half leaned, half sat, on the kitchen table. "Everything takes time," he said, "and—well, yes, sure, I can make a living at it. But what I don't seem to be able to make you understand is that it's the only thing I want to do."

237   "Well, Sonny," I said, gently, "you know people can't always do exactly what they *want* to do—"

238   "*No*, I don't know that," said Sonny, surprising me. "I think people *ought* to do what they want to do, what else are they alive for?"

239   "You getting to be a big boy," I said desperately, "it's time you started thinking about your future."

240   "I'm thinking about my future," said Sonny, grimly. "I think about it all the time."

241   I gave up. I decided, if he didn't change his mind, that we could always talk about it later. "In the meantime," I said, "you got to finish school." We had already decided that he'd have to move in with Isabel and her folks. I knew this wasn't the ideal arrangement because Isabel's folks are inclined to be dicty and they hadn't especially wanted Isabel to marry me. But I didn't know what else to do. "And we have to get you fixed up at Isabel's."

242   There was a long silence. He moved from the kitchen table to the window. "That's a terrible idea. You know it yourself."

243   "Do you have a *better* idea?"

244   He just walked up and down the kitchen for a minute. He was as tall as I was. He had started to shave. I suddenly had the feeling that I didn't know him at all.

245   He stopped at the kitchen table and picked up my cigarettes. Looking at me with a kind of mocking, amused defiance, he put one between his lips. "You mind?"

246   "You smoking already?"

247   He lit the cigarette and nodded, watching me through the smoke. "I just wanted to see if I'd have the courage to smoke in front of you."

He grinned and blew a great cloud of smoke to the ceiling. "It was easy." He looked at my face. "Come on, now. I bet you was smoking at my age, tell the truth."

248   I didn't say anything but the truth was on my face, and he laughed. But now there was something very strained in his laugh. "Sure. And I bet that ain't all you was doing."

249   He was frightening me a little. "Cut the crap," I said. "We already decided that you was going to go and live at Isabel's. Now what's got into you all of a sudden?"

250   "*You* decided it," he pointed out. "*I* didn't decide nothing." He stopped in front of me, leaning against the stove, arms loosely folded. "Look, brother. I don't want to stay in Harlem no more, I really don't." He was very earnest. He looked at me, then over toward the kitchen window. There was something in his eyes I'd never seen before, some thoughtfulness, some worry all his own. He rubbed the muscle of one arm. "It's time I was getting out of here."

251   "Where do you want to go, Sonny?"

252   "I want to join the army. Or the navy, I don't care. If I say I'm old enough, they'll believe me."

253   Then I got mad. It was because I was so scared. "You must be crazy. You goddamn fool, what the hell do you want to go and join the *army* for?"

254   "I just told you. To get out of Harlem."

255   "Sonny, you haven't even finished *school*. And if you really want to be a musician, how do you expect to study if you're in the *army?*"

256   He looked at me, trapped, and in anguish. "There's ways. I might be able to work out some kind of deal. Anyway, I'll have the G.I. Bill when I come out."

257   "*If* you come out." We stared at each other. "Sonny, please. Be reasonable. I know the setup is far from perfect. But we got to do the best we can."

258   "I ain't learning nothing in school," he said. "Even when I go." He turned away from me and opened the window and threw his cigarette out into the narrow alley. I watched his back. "At least, I ain't learning nothing you'd want me to learn." He slammed the window so hard I thought the glass would fly out, and turned back to me. "And I'm sick of the stink of these garbage cans!"

259   "Sonny," I said, "I know how you feel. But if you don't finish school now, you're going to be sorry later that you didn't." I grabbed him by the shoulders. "And you only got another year. It ain't so bad. And I'll come back and I swear I'll help you do *whatever* you want to do. Just try to put up with it till I come back. Will you please do that? For me?"

260   He didn't answer and he wouldn't look at me.

261   "Sonny. You hear me?"

262   He pulled away. "I hear you. But you never hear anything I say."

263   I didn't know what to say to that. He looked out of the window and then back at me. "OK," he said, and sighed. "I'll try."

264   Then I said, trying to cheer him up a little, "They got a piano at Isabel's. You can practice on it."

265   And as a matter of fact, it did cheer him up for a minute. "That's right," he said to himself. "I forgot that." His face relaxed a little. But the worry, the thoughtfulness, played on it still, the way shadows play on a face which is staring into the fire.

266   But I thought I'd never hear the end of that piano. At first, Isabel would write me, saying how nice it was that Sonny was so serious about his music and how, as soon as he came in from school, or wherever he had been when he was supposed to be at school, he went straight to that piano and stayed there until suppertime. And, after supper, he went back to that piano and stayed there until everybody went to bed. He was at the piano all day Saturday and all day Sunday. Then he bought a record player and started playing records. He'd play one record over and over again, all day long sometimes, and he'd improvise along with it on the piano. Or he'd play one section of the record, one chord, one change, one progression, then he'd do it on the piano. Then back to the record. Then back to the piano.

267   Well, I really don't know how they stood it. Isabel finally confessed that it wasn't like living with a person at all, it was like living with sound. And the sound didn't make any sense to her, didn't make any sense to any of them—naturally. They began, in a way, to be afflicted by this presence that was living in their home. It was as though Sonny were some sort of god, or monster. He moved in an atmosphere which wasn't like theirs at all. They fed him and he ate, he washed himself, he walked in and out of their door; he certainly wasn't nasty or unpleasant or rude, Sonny isn't any of those things; but it was as though he were all wrapped up in some cloud, some fire, some vision all his own; and there wasn't any way to reach him.

268   At the same time, he wasn't really a man yet, he was still a child, and they had to watch out for him in all kinds of ways. They certainly couldn't throw him out. Neither did they dare to make a great scene about that piano because even they dimly sensed, as I sensed, from so many thousands of miles away, that Sonny was at that piano playing for his life.

269   But he hadn't been going to school. One day a letter came from the school board and Isabel's mother got it—there had apparently, been other letters but Sonny had torn them up. This day, when Sonny came in, Isabel's mother showed him the letter and asked where he'd been spending his time. And she finally got it out of him that he'd been down in Greenwich Village, with musicians and other characters, in a white girl's apartment. And this scared her and she started to scream at him and what came up, once she began—though she denies it to this day—was what sacrifices they were making to give Sonny a decent home and how little he appreciated it.

270   Sonny didn't play the piano that day. By evening, Isabel's mother had calmed down but then there was the old man to deal with, and Isabel

herself. Isabel says she did her best to be calm but she broke down and started crying. She says she just watched Sonny's face. She could tell, by watching him, what was happening with him. And what was happening was that they penetrated his cloud, they had reached him. Even if their fingers had been a thousand times more gentle than human fingers ever are, he could hardly help feeling that they had stripped him naked and were spitting on that nakedness. For he also had to see that his presence, that music, which was life or death to him, had been torture for them, and that they had endured it, not at all for his sake, but only for mine. And Sonny couldn't take that. He can take it a little better today than he could then but he's still not very good at it and, frankly, I don't know anybody who is.

271   The silence of the next few days must have been louder than the sound of all the music ever played since time began. One morning, before she went to work, Isabel was in his room for something and she suddenly realized that all of his records were gone. And she knew for certain that he was gone. And he was. He went as far as the navy would carry him. He finally sent me a postcard from some place in Greece and that was the first I knew that Sonny was still alive. I didn't see him any more until we were both back in New York and the war had long been over.

272   He was a man by then, of course, but I wasn't willing to see it. He came by the house from time to time, but we fought almost every time we met. I didn't like the way he carried himself, loose and dreamlike all the time, and I didn't like his friends, and his music seemed to be merely an excuse for the life he led. It sounded just that weird and disordered.

273   Then we had a fight, a pretty awful fight, and I didn't see him for months. By and by I looked him up, where he was living, in a furnished room in the Village, and I tried to make it up. But there were lots of other people in the room and Sonny just lay on his bed, and he wouldn't come downstairs with me, and he treated these other people as though they were his family and I weren't. So I got mad and then he got mad, and then I told him that he might just as well be dead as live the way he was living. Then he stood up and he told me not to worry about him any more in life, that he *was* dead as far as I was concerned. Then he pushed me to the door and the other people looked on as though nothing were happening, and he slammed the door behind me. I stood in the hallway, staring at the door. I heard somebody laugh in the room and then the tears came to my eyes. I started down the steps, whistling to keep from crying, I kept whistling to myself, *You going to need me, baby, one of these cold, rainy days.*

274   I read about Sonny's trouble in the spring. Little Grace died in the fall. She was a beautiful little girl. But she only lived a little over two years. She died of polio and she suffered. She had a slight fever for a couple of days, but it didn't seem like anything and we just kept her in bed. And we would certainly have called the doctor, but the fever dropped, she seemed to be all right. So we thought it had just been a cold. Then, one

day, she was up, playing, Isabel was in the kitchen fixing lunch for the two boys when they'd come in from school, and she heard Grace fall down in the living room. When you have a lot of children you don't always start running when one of them falls, unless they start screaming or something. And, this time, Grace was quiet. Yet, Isabel says that when she heard that *thump* and then that silence, something happened in her to make her afraid. And she ran to the living room and there was little Grace on the floor, all twisted up, and the reason she hadn't screamed was that she couldn't get her breath. And when she did scream, it was the worst sound, Isabel says, that she'd ever heard in all her life, and she still hears it sometimes in her dreams. Isabel will sometimes wake me up with a low, moaning, strangled sound and I have to be quick to awaken her and hold her to me and where Isabel is weeping against me seems a mortal wound.

275   I think I may have written Sonny the very day that little Grace was buried. I was sitting in the living room in the dark, by myself, and I suddenly thought of Sonny. My trouble made his real.

276   One Saturday afternoon, when Sonny had been living with us, or, anyway, been in our house, for nearly two weeks, I found myself wandering aimlessly about the living room, drinking from a can of beer, and trying to work up the courage to search Sonny's room. He was out, he was usually out whenever I was home, and Isabel had taken the children to see their grandparents. Suddenly I was standing still in front of the living room window, watching Seventh Avenue. The idea of searching Sonny's room made me still. I scarcely dared to admit to myself what I'd be searching for. I didn't know what I'd do if I found it. Or if I didn't.

277   On the sidewalk across from me, near the entrance to a barbecue joint, some people were holding an old-fashioned revival meeting. The barbecue cook, wearing a dirty white apron, his conked hair reddish and metallic in the pale sun, and a cigarette between his lips, stood in the doorway, watching them. Kids and older people paused in their errands and stood there, along with some older men and a couple of very tough-looking women who watched everything that happened on the avenue, as though they owned it, or were maybe owned by it. Well, they were watching this, too. The revival was being carried on by three sisters in black, and a brother. All they had were their voices and their Bibles and a tambourine. The brother was testifying and while he testified two of the sisters stood together, seeming to say, amen, and the third sister walked around with the tambourine outstretched and a couple of people dropped coins into it. Then the brother's testimony ended and the sister who had been taking up the collection dumped the coins into her palm and transferred them to the pocket of her long black robe. Then she raised both hands, striking the tambourine against the air, and then against one hand, and she started to sing. And the two other sisters and the brother joined in.

278   It was strange, suddenly, to watch, though I had been seeing these street meetings all my life. So, of course, had everybody else down there.

Yet, they paused and watched and listened and I stood still at the window. *"Tis the old ship of Zion,"* they sang and the sister with the tambourine kept a steady, jangling beat, *"it has rescued many a thousand!"* Not a soul under the sound of their voices was hearing this song for the first time, not one of them had been rescued. Nor had they seen much in the way of rescue work being done around them. Neither did they especially believe in the holiness of the three sisters and the brother, they knew too much about them, knew where they lived, and how. The woman with the tambourine, whose voice dominated the air, whose face was bright with joy, was divided by very little from the woman who stood watching her, a cigarette between her heavy, chapped lips, her hair a cuckoo's nest, her face scarred and swollen from many beatings, and her black eyes glittering like coal. Perhaps they both knew this, which was why, when, as rarely, they addressed each other, they addressed each other as Sister. As the singing filled the air the watching, listening faces underwent a change, the eyes focusing on something within; the music seemed to soothe a poison out of them; and time seemed, nearly, to fall away from the sullen, belligerent, battered faces, as though they were fleeing back to their first condition, while dreaming of their last. The barbecue cook half shook his head and smiled, and dropped his cigarette and disappeared into his joint. A man fumbled in his pockets for change and stood holding it in his hand impatiently, as though he had just remembered a pressing appointment further up the avenue. He looked furious. Then I saw Sonny, standing on the edge of the crowd. He was carrying a wide, flat notebook with a green cover, and it made him look, from where I was standing, almost like a school-boy. The coppery sun brought out the copper in his skin, he was very faintly smiling, standing very still. Then the singing stopped, the tambourine turned into a collection plate again. The furious man dropped in his coins and vanished, so did a couple of the women, and Sonny dropped some change in the plate, looking directly at the woman with a little smile. He started across the avenue, toward the house. He has a slow, loping walk, something like the way Harlem hipsters walk, only he's imposed on this his own half-beat. I had never really noticed it before.

279   I stayed at the window, both relieved and apprehensive. As Sonny disappeared from my sight, they began singing again. And they were still singing when his key turned in the lock.

280   "Hey," he said.

281   "Hey, yourself. You want some beer?"

282   "No. Well, maybe." But he came up to the window and stood beside me, looking out. "What a warm voice," he said.

283   They were singing *If I could only hear my mother pray again!*

284   "Yes," I said, "and she can sure beat that tambourine."

285   "But what a terrible song," he said, and laughed. He dropped his notebook on the sofa and disappeared into the kitchen. "Where's Isabel and the kids?"

286   "I think they went to see their grandparents. You hungry?"

287   "No." He came back into the living room with his can of beer. "You want to come some place with me tonight?"

288   I sensed, I don't know how, that I couldn't possibly say no. "Sure. Where?"

289   He sat down on the sofa and picked up his notebook and started leafing through it. "I'm going to sit in with some fellows in a joint in the Village."

300   "You mean, you're going to play, tonight?"

301   "That's right." He took a swallow of his beer and moved back to the window. He gave me a sidelong look. "If you can stand it."

302   "I'll try," I said.

303   He smiled to himself and we both watched as the meeting across the way broke up. The three sisters and their brother, heads bowed, were singing *God be with you till we meet again.* The faces around them were very quiet. Then the song ended. The small crowd dispersed. We watched the three women and the lone man walk slowly up the avenue.

304   "When she was singing before," said Sonny, abruptly, "her voice reminded me for a minute of what heroin feels like sometimes—when it's in your veins. It makes you feel sort of warm and cool at the same time. And distant. And—and sure." He sipped his beer, very deliberately not looking at me. I watched his face. "It makes you feel—in control. Sometimes you've got to have that feeling."

305   "Do you?" I sat down slowly in the easy chair.

306   "Sometimes." He went to the sofa and picked up his notebook again. "Some people do."

307   "In order," I asked, "to play?" And my voice was very ugly, full of contempt and anger.

308   "Well"—he looked at me with great, troubled eyes, as though, in fact, he hoped his eyes would tell me things he could never otherwise say— "they *think* so. And *if* they think so—!"

309   "And what do *you* think?" I asked.

310   He sat on the sofa and put his can of beer on the floor. "I don't know," he said, and I couldn't be sure if he was answering my question or pursuing his thoughts. His face didn't tell me. "It's not so much to *play*. It's to *stand* it, to be able to make it at all. On any level." He frowned and smiled: "In order to keep from shaking to pieces."

311   "But these friends of yours," I said, "they seem to shake themselves to pieces pretty goddamn fast."

312   "Maybe." He played with the notebook. And something told me that I should curb my tongue, that Sonny was doing his best to talk, that I should listen. "But of course you only know the ones that've gone to pieces. Some don't—or at least they haven't *yet* and that's just about all any of us can say." He paused. "And then there are some who just live, really, in hell, and they know it and they see what's happening and they go right on. I don't know." He sighed, dropped the notebook, folded his

arms. "Some guys, you can tell from the way they play, they on something *all* the time. And you can see that, well, it makes something real for them. But of course," he picked up his beer from the floor and sipped it and put the can down again, "they *want* to, too, you've got to see that. Even some of them that say they don't—*some*, not all."

313   "And what about you?" I asked—I couldn't help it. "What about you? Do *you* want to?"

314   He stood up and walked to the window and remained silent for a long time. Then he sighed. "Me," he said. Then: "While I was downstairs before, on my way here, listening to that woman sing, it struck me all of a sudden how much suffering she must have had to go through—to sing like that. It's *repulsive* to think you have to suffer that much."

315   I said: "But there's no way not to suffer—is there, Sonny?"

316   "I believe not," he said and smiled, "but that's never stopped anyone from trying." He looked at me. "Has it?" I realized, with this mocking look, that there stood between us, forever, beyond the power of time or forgiveness, the fact that I had held silence—so long!—when he needed human speech to help him. He turned back to the window. "No, there's no way not to suffer. But you try all kinds of ways to keep from drowning in it, to keep on top of it, and to make it seem—well, like *you*. Like you did something, all right, and now you're suffering for it. You know?" I said nothing. "Well you know," he said, impatiently, "why *do* people suffer? Maybe it's better to do something to give it a reason, *any* reason."

317   "But we just agreed," I said, "that there's no way not to suffer. Isn't it better, then, just to—take it?"

318   "But nobody just takes it," Sonny cried, "that's what I'm telling you! *Everybody* tries not to. You're just hung up on the *way* some people try— it's not *your* way!"

319   The hair on my face began to itch, my face felt wet. "That's not true," I said, "that's not true. I don't give a damn what other people do, I don't even care how they suffer. I just care how *you* suffer." And he looked at me. "Please believe me," I said, "I don't want to see you—die—trying not to suffer."

320   "I won't," he said, flatly, "die trying not to suffer. At least, not any faster than anybody else."

321   "But there's no need," I said, trying to laugh, "is there? in killing yourself."

322   I wanted to say more, but I couldn't. I wanted to talk about will power and how life could be—well, beautiful. I wanted to say that it was all within; but was it? or, rather, wasn't that exactly the trouble? And I wanted to promise that I would never fail him again. But it would all have sounded—empty words and lies.

323   So I made the promise to myself and prayed that I would keep it.

324   "It's terrible sometimes, inside," he said, "that's what's the trouble. You walk these streets, black and funky and cold, and there's not really a living ass to talk to, and there's nothing shaking, and there's no way of

getting it out—that storm inside. You can't talk it and you can't make love with it, and when you finally try to get with it and play it, you realize *nobody's* listening. So *you've* got to listen. You got to find a way to listen."

325   And then he walked away from the window and sat on the sofa again, as though all the wind had suddenly been knocked out of him. "Sometimes you'll do *anything* to play, even cut your mother's throat." He laughed and looked at me. "Or your brother's." Then he sobered. "Or your own." Then: "Don't worry. I'm all right now and I think I'll *be* all right. But I can't forget—where I've been. I don't mean just the physical place I've been, I mean where I've *been*. And *what* I've been."

326   "What have you been, Sonny?" I asked.

327   He smiled—but sat sideways on the sofa, his elbow resting on the back, his fingers playing with his mouth and chin, not looking at me. "I've been something I didn't recognize, didn't know I could be. Didn't know anybody could be." He stopped, looking inward, looking helplessly young, looking old. "I'm not talking about it now because I feel *guilty* or anything like that—maybe it would be better if I did, I don't know. Anyway, I can't really talk about it. Not to you, not to anybody," and now he turned and faced me. "Sometimes, you know, and it was actually when I was most *out* of the world, I felt that I was in it, that I was *with* it, really, and I could play or I didn't really have to *play*, it just came out of me, it was there. And I don't know how I played, thinking about it now, but I know I did awful things, those times, sometimes, to people. Or it wasn't that I *did* anything to them—it was that they weren't real." He picked up the beer can; it was empty; he rolled it between his palms: "And other times—well, I needed a fix, I needed to find a place to lean, I needed to clear a space to *listen*—and I couldn't find it, and I—went crazy, I did terrible things to *me*, I was terrible *for* me." He began pressing the beer can between his hands, I watched the metal begin to give. It glittered, as he played with it, like a knife, and I was afraid he would cut himself, but I said nothing. "Oh well. I can never tell you. I was all by myself at the bottom of something, stinking and sweating and crying and shaking, and I smelled it, you know? *my* stink, and I thought I'd die if I couldn't get away from it and yet, all the same, I knew that everything I was doing was just locking me in with it. And I didn't know," he paused, still flattening the beer can, "I didn't know, I still *don't* know, something kept telling me that maybe it was good to smell your own stink, but I didn't think that *that* was what I'd been trying to do—and—who can stand it?" and he abruptly dropped the ruined beer can, looking at me with a small, still smile, and then rose, walking to the window as though it were the lodestone rock. I watched his face, he watched the avenue. "I couldn't tell you when Mama died—but the reason I wanted to leave Harlem so bad was to get away from drugs. And then, when I ran away, that's what I was running from—really. When I came back, nothing had changed, *I* hadn't changed, I was just—older." And he stopped, drumming with his fingers on the windowpane. The sun had vanished, soon darkness would fall. I watched his

face. "It can come again," he said, almost as though speaking to himself. Then he turned to me. "It can come again," he repeated. "I just want you to know that."

328 "All right," I said, at last. "So it can come again. All right."

329 He smiled, but the smile was sorrowful. "I had to try to tell you," he said.

330 "Yes," I said. "I understand that."

331 "You're my brother," he said, looking straight at me, and not smiling at all.

332 "Yes," I repeated, "yes. I understand that."

333 He turned back to the window, looking out. "All that hatred down there," he said, "all that hatred and misery and love. It's a wonder it doesn't blow the avenue apart."

334 We went to the only nightclub on a short, dark street, downtown. We squeezed through the narrow, chattering, jam-packed bar to the entrance of the big room, where the bandstand was. And we stood there for a moment, for the lights were very dim in this room and we couldn't see. Then, "Hello, boy," said a voice and an enormous black man, much older than Sonny or myself, erupted out of all that atmospheric lighting and put an arm around Sonny's shoulder. "I been sitting right here," he said, "waiting for you."

335 He had a big voice, too, and heads in the darkness turned toward us.

336 Sonny grinned and pulled a little away, and said, "Creole, this is my brother. I told you about him."

337 Creole shook my hand. "I'm glad to meet you, son," he said, and it was clear that he was glad to meet me *there*, for Sonny's sake. And he smiled, "You got a real musician in *your* family," and he took his arm from Sonny's shoulder and slapped him, lightly, affectionately, with the back of his hand.

338 "Well. Now I've heard it all," said a voice behind us. This was another musician, a friend of Sonny's, a coal-black, cheerful-looking man, built close to the ground. He immediately began confiding to me, at the top of his lungs, the most terrible things about Sonny, his teeth gleaming like a lighthouse and his laugh coming up out of him like the beginning of an earthquake. And it turned out that everyone at the bar knew Sonny, or almost everyone; some were musicians, working there, or nearby, or not working, some were simply hangers-on, and some were there to hear Sonny play. I was introduced to all of them and they were all very polite to me. Yet, it was clear that, for them, I was only Sonny's brother. Here, I was in Sonny's world. Or, rather: his kingdom. Here, it was not even a question that his veins bore royal blood.

339 They were going to play soon and Creole installed me, by myself, at a table in a dark corner. Then I watched them, Creole, and the little black man, and Sonny, and the others, while they horsed around, standing just below the bandstand. The light from the bandstand spilled just a little short of them and, watching them laughing and gesturing and moving about, I had the feeling that they, nevertheless, were being most careful not to step into that circle of light too suddenly: that if they moved into

the light too suddenly, without thinking, they would perish in flame. Then, while I watched, one of them, the small, black man, moved into the light and crossed the bandstand and started fooling around with his drums. Then—being funny and being, also, extremely ceremonious—Creole took Sonny by the arm and led him to the piano. A woman's voice called Sonny's name and a few hands started clapping. And Sonny, also being funny and being ceremonious, and so touched, I think, that he could have cried, but neither hiding it nor showing it, riding it like a man, grinned, and put both hands to his heart and bowed from the waist.

340   Creole then went to the bass fiddle and a lean, very bright-skinned brown man jumped up on the bandstand and picked up his horn. So there they were, and the atmosphere on the bandstand and in the room began to change and tighten. Someone stepped up to the microphone and announced them. Then there were all kinds of murmurs. Some people at the bar shushed others. The waitress ran around, frantically getting in the last orders, guys and chicks got closer to each other, and the lights on the bandstand, on the quartet, turned to a kind of indigo. Then they all looked different there. Creole looked about him for the last time, as though he were making certain that all his chickens were in the coop, and then he— jumped and struck the fiddle. And there they were.

341   All I know about music is that not many people ever really hear it. And even then, on the rare occasions when something opens within, and the music enters, what we mainly hear, or hear corroborated, are personal, private, vanishing evocations. But the man who creates the music is hearing something else, is dealing with the roar rising from the void and imposing order on it as it hits the air. What is evoked in him, then, is of another order, more terrible because it has no words, and triumphant, too, for that same reason. And his triumph, when he triumphs, is ours. I just watched Sonny's face. His face was troubled, he was working hard, but he wasn't with it. And I had the feeling that, in a way, everyone on the bandstand was waiting for him, both waiting for him and pushing him along. But as I began to watch Creole, I realized that it was Creole who held them all back. He had them on a short rein. Up there, keeping the beat with his whole body, wailing on the fiddle, with his eyes half closed, he was listening to everything, but he was listening to Sonny. He was having a dialogue with Sonny. He wanted Sonny to leave the shoreline and strike out for the deep water. He was Sonny's witness that deep water and drowning were not the same thing—he had been there, and he knew. And he wanted Sonny to know. He was waiting for Sonny to do the thing on the keys which would let Creole know that Sonny was in the water.

342   And, while Creole listened, Sonny moved, deep within, exactly like someone in torment. I had never before thought of how awful the relationship must be between the musician and his instrument. He has to fill it, this instrument, with the breath of life, his own. He has to make it do what he wants it to do. And a piano is just a piano. It's made out of so

much wood and wires and little hammers and big ones, and ivory. While there's only so much you can do with it, the only way to find this out is to try; to try and make it do everything.

343   And Sonny hadn't been near a piano for over a year. And he wasn't on much better terms with his life, not the life that stretched before him now. He and the piano stammered, started one way, got scared, stopped; started another way, panicked, marked time, started again; then seemed to have found a direction, panicked again, got stuck. And the face I saw on Sonny I'd never seen before. Everything had been burned out of it, and, at the same time, things usually hidden were being burned in, by the fire and fury of the battle which was occurring in him up there.

344   Yet, watching Creole's face as they neared the end of the first set, I had the feeling that something had happened, something I hadn't heard. Then they finished, there was scattered applause, and then, without an instant's warning, Creole started into something else, it was almost sardonic, it was *Am I Blue*. And, as though he commanded, Sonny began to play. Something began to happen. And Creole let out the reins. The dry, low, black man said something awful on the drums, Creole answered, and the drums talked back. Then the horn insisted, sweet and high, slightly detached perhaps, and Creole listened, commenting now and then, dry, and driving, beautiful and calm and old. Then they all came together again, and Sonny was part of the family again. I could tell this from his face. He seemed to have found, right there beneath his fingers, a damn brand-new piano. It seemed that he couldn't get over it. Then, for awhile, just being happy with Sonny, they seemed to be agreeing with him that brand-new pianos certainly were a gas.

345   Then Creole stepped forward to remind them that what they were playing was the blues. He hit something in all of them, he hit something in me, myself, and the music tightened and deepened, apprehension began to beat the air. Creole began to tell us what the blues were all about. They were not about anything very new. He and his boys up there were keeping it new, at the risk of ruin, destruction, madness, and death, in order to find new ways to make us listen. For, while the tale of how we suffer, and how we are delighted, and how we may triumph is never new, it always must be heard. There isn't any other tale to tell, it's the only light we've got in all this darkness.

346   And this tale, according to that face, that body, those strong hands on those strings, has another aspect in every country, and a new depth in every generation. Listen, Creole seemed to be saying listen. Now these are Sonny's blues. He made the little black man on the drums know it, and the bright, brown man on the horn. Creole wasn't trying any longer to get Sonny in the water. He was wishing him Godspeed. Then he stepped back, very slowly, filling the air with the immense suggestion that Sonny speak for himself.

347   Then they all gathered around Sonny and Sonny played. Every now and again one of them seemed to say, amen. Sonny's fingers filled the air

with life, his life. But that life contained so many others. And Sonny went all the way back, he really began with the spare, flat statement of the opening phrase of the song. Then he began to make it his. It was very beautiful because it wasn't hurried and it was no longer a lament. I seemed to hear with what burning he had made it his, with what burning we had yet to make it ours, how we could cease lamenting. Freedom lurked around us and I understood, at last, that he could help us to be free if we would listen, that he would never be free until we did. Yet, there was no battle in his face now. I heard what he had gone through, and would continue to go through until he came to rest in earth. He had made it his: that long line, of which we knew only Mama and Daddy. And he was giving it back, as everything must be given back, so that, passing through death, it can live forever. I saw my mother's face again, and felt, for the first time, how the stones of the road she had walked on must have bruised her feet. I saw the moonlit road where my father's brother died. And it brought something else back to me, and carried me past it, I saw my little girl again and felt Isabel's tears again, and I felt my own tears begin to rise. And I was yet aware that this was only a moment, that the world waited outside, as hungry as a tiger, and that trouble stretched above us, longer than the sky.

348   Then it was over. Creole and Sonny let out their breath, both soaking wet, and grinning. There was a lot of applause and some of it was real. In the dark, the girl came by and I asked her to take drinks to the bandstand. There was a long pause, while they talked up there in the indigo light and after awhile I saw the girl put a Scotch and milk on top of the piano for Sonny. He didn't seem to notice it, but just before they started playing again, he sipped from it and looked toward me, and nodded. Then he put it back on top of the piano. For me, then, as they began to play again, it glowed and shook above my brother's head like the very cup of trembling.

Questions for Engagement, Response, and Analysis

1. What does the narrator mean when he says of his students, "All they really knew were two darknesses, the darkness of their lives . . . and the darkness of the movies"? What is suggested by these and other references to darkness?

2. What is the **point of view** in this short story? How does it affect our perception of other characters?

3. Explain the narrator's attitude toward Sonny.

4. Explain the significance of the story within a story, the mother's tale of the narrator's father and his brother.

5. In the last scene, the narrator enters Sonny's world for the first time. Explain the symbolism of the location, the jazz, and the drink.

Crafting Arguments

1. In an essay, explain what you think Sonny is willing to sacrifice for music and why.

2. Write an essay illustrating the ways in which the narrator changes in the story and the causes for these changes.

3. Baldwin's symbolism enriches "Sonny's Blues." Write an essay exploring the use of one or more of the symbols.

4. One of the major themes in literature is that we learn wisdom through suffering. Write an essay arguing that this is or is not a major theme in this story.

Truman Capote (1924–1984)

Truman Capote, born Truman Streckfus Persons in New Orleans, spent much of his childhood in Alabama, the background for "A Christmas Memory." He took the surname of his stepfather and during his adolescence lived in Greenwich, Connecticut, and New York City. Capote began to write as a copy boy for The New Yorker. *His first short story,* "Miriam," *was published in 1946;* Other Voices, Other Rooms, *a novel, was published in 1948. From that point he became what he called a media presence; moving to Hollywood, he wrote the script for* Breakfast at Tiffany's. *The publication of* In Cold Blood: A True Account of a Multiple Murder and Its Consequences *in 1965 marked the beginning of a new genre called the nonfiction novel. A collection of short essays,* Music for Chameleon, *was published in 1980. His unfinished novel,* Answered Prayers, *was published after his death.*

A CHRISTMAS MEMORY   (1956)

349   Imagine a morning in late November. A coming of winter morning more than twenty years ago. Consider the kitchen of a spreading old house in a country town. A great black stove is its main feature; but there is also a big round table and a fireplace with two rocking chairs placed in front of it. Just today the fireplace commenced its seasonal roar.

350   A woman with shorn white hair is standing at the kitchen window. She is wearing tennis shoes and a shapeless gray sweater over a summery calico dress. She is small and sprightly, like a bantam hen; but, due to a long youthful illness, her shoulders are pitifully hunched. Her face is remarkable—not unlike Lincoln's, craggy like that, and tinted by sun and wind; but it is delicate too, finely boned, and her eyes are sherry-colored and timid. "Oh my," she exclaims, her breath smoking the windowpane, "it's fruitcake weather!"

351   The person to whom she is speaking is myself. I am seven; she is sixty-something. We are cousins, very distant ones, and we have lived together—well, as long as I can remember. Other people inhabit the house, relatives; and though they have power over us, and frequently make us cry, we are not, on the whole, too much aware of them. We are each other's best friend. She calls me Buddy, in memory of a boy who was formerly her best friend. The other Buddy died in the 1880's, when she was still a child. She is still a child.

352   "I knew it before I got out of bed," she says, turning away from the window with a purposeful excitement in her eyes. "The courthouse bell sounded so cold and clear. And there were no birds singing; they've gone to warmer country, yes indeed. Oh, Buddy, stop stuffing biscuit and fetch our buggy. Help me find my hat. We've thirty cakes to bake."

353   It's always the same: a morning arrives in November, and my friend, as though officially inaugurating the Christmas time of year that exhilarates her imagination and fuels the blaze of her heart, announces: "It's fruitcake weather! Fetch our buggy. Help me find my hat."

354   The hat is found, a straw cartwheel corsaged with velvet roses out-of-doors has faded: it once belonged to a more fashionable relative. Together, we guide our buggy, a dilapidated baby carriage, out to the garden and into a grove of pecan trees. The buggy is mine; that is, it was bought for me when I was born. It is made of wicker, rather unraveled, and the wheels wobble like a drunkard's legs. But it is a faithful object; spring-times, we take it to the woods and fill it with flowers, herbs, wild fern for our porch pots; in the summer we pile it with picnic paraphernalia and sugar-cane fishing poles and roll it down to the edge of a creek; it has its winter uses, too: as a truck for hauling firewood from the yard to the kitchen, as a warm bed for Queenie, our tough little orange and white rat terrier who has survived distemper and two rattlesnake bites. Queenie is trotting beside it now.

355   Three hours later we are back in the kitchen hulling a heaping buggy-load of windfall pecans. Our backs hurt from gathering them: how hard they were to find (the main crop having been shaken off the trees and sold by the orchard's owners, who are not us) among the concealing leaves, the frosted, deceiving grass. Caarackle! A cheery crunch, scraps of miniature thunder sound as the shells collapse and the golden mound of sweet oily ivory meat mounts in the milk-glass bowl. Queenie begs to taste, and now and again my friend sneaks her a mite, though insisting we deprive ourselves. "We mustn't, Buddy. If we start, we won't stop. And there's scarcely enough as there is. For thirty cakes." The kitchen is growing dark. Dusk turns the window into a mirror: our reflections mingle with the rising moon as we work by the fireside in the firelight. At last, when the moon is quite high, we toss the final hull into the fire and, with joined sighs, watch it catch flame. The buggy is empty, the bowl is brimful.

356   We eat our supper (cold biscuits, bacon, blackberry jam) and discuss tomorrow. Tomorrow the kind of work I like best begins: buying. Cherries and citron, ginger and vanilla and canned Hawaiian pineapple, rinds and raisins and walnuts and whiskey and oh, so much flour, butter, so many eggs, spices, flavorings: why, we'll need a pony to pull the buggy home.

357   But before these purchases can be made, there is the question of money. Neither of us has any. Except for skinflint sums persons in the house occasionally provide (a dime is considered very big money); or what we earn ourselves from various activities: holding rummage sales, selling buckets of hand-picked blackberries, jars of homemade jam and apple jelly and peach preserves, rounding up flowers for funerals and weddings. Once we won seventy-ninth prize, five dollars, in a national football contest. Not that we know a fool thing about football. It's just that we enter any contest we hear about: at the moment our hopes are centered on the fifty-thousand-dollar Grand Prize being offered to name a new brand of coffee (we suggested "AM"; and, after some hesitation, for my friend thought it perhaps sacrilegious, the slogan "AM! Amen!"). To tell the truth, our only really profitable enterprise was the Fun and Freak Museum we conducted in a back-yard woodshed two summers ago. The Fun was a stereopticon with slide views of Washington and New York lent us by a relative who had been to those places (she was furious when she discovered why we'd borrowed it); the Freak was a three-legged biddy chicken hatched by one of our own hens. Everybody hereabouts wanted to see that biddy: we charged grownups a nickel, kids two cents. And took in a good twenty dollars before the museum shut down due to the decease of the main attraction.

358   But one way and another we do each year accumulate Christmas savings, a Fruitcake Fund. These moneys we keep hidden in an ancient bead purse under a loose board under the floor under a chamber pot under my friend's bed. The purse is seldom removed from this safe location except to make a deposit, or, as happens every Saturday, a withdrawal; for on Saturdays I am allowed ten cents to go to the picture show. My friend has never been to a picture show, nor does she intend to: "I'd rather hear you tell the story, Buddy. That way I can imagine it more. Besides, a person my age shouldn't squander their eyes. When the Lord comes, let me see Him clear." In addition to never having seen a movie, she has never: eaten in a restaurant, traveled more than five miles from home, received or sent a telegram, read anything except funny papers and the Bible, worn cosmetics, cursed, wished someone harm, told a lie on purpose, let a hungry dog go hungry. Here are the few things she has done, does do: killed with a hoe the biggest rattlesnake ever seen in this county (sixteen rattles), dip snuff (secretly), tame hummingbirds (just try it) till they balance on her finger, tell ghost stories (we both believe in ghosts) so tingling they chill you in July, talk to herself, take walks in the rain, grow the prettiest japonicas in town, know the recipe for every sort of old-time Indian cure, including a magical wart-remover.

359   Now, with supper finished, we retire to the room in a faraway part of the house where my friend sleeps in a scrap-quilt-covered iron bed painted rose pink, her favorite color. Silently, wallowing in the pleasures of conspiracy, we take the bead purse from its secret place and spill its contents on the scrap quilt. Dollar bills, tightly rolled and green as May buds. Somber fifty-cent pieces, heavy enough to weight a dead man's eyes. Lovely dimes, the liveliest coin, the one that really jingles. Nickels and quarters, worn smooth as creek pebbles. But mostly a hateful heap of bitter-odored pennies. Last summer others in the house contracted to pay us a penny for every twenty-five flies we killed. Oh, the carnage of August: the flies that flew to heaven! Yet it was not work in which we took pride. And, as we sit counting pennies, it is as though we were back tabulating dead flies. Neither of us has a head for figures; we count slowly, lose track, start again. According to her calculations, we have $12.73. According to mine, exactly $13. "I do hope you're wrong, Buddy. We can't mess around with thirteen. The cakes will fall. Or put somebody in the cemetery. Why, I wouldn't dream of getting out of bed on the thirteenth." This is true: she always spends thirteenths in bed. So, to be on the safe side, we subtract a penny and toss it out the window.

360   Of the ingredients that go into our fruitcakes, whiskey is the most expensive, as well as the hardest to obtain: State laws forbid its sale. But everybody knows you can buy a bottle from Mr. Haha Jones. And the next day, having completed our more prosaic shopping, we set out for Mr. Haha's business address, a "sinful" (to quote public opinion) fish-fry and dancing café down by the river. We've been there before, and on the same errand; but in previous years our dealings have been with Haha's wife, an iodine-dark Indian woman with brassy peroxided hair and a dead-tired disposition. Actually, we've never laid eyes on her husband, though we've heard that he's an Indian too. A giant with razor scars across his cheeks. They call him Haha because he's so gloomy, a man who never laughs. As we approach his café (a large log cabin festooned inside and out with chains of garish-gay naked light bulbs and standing by the river's muddy edge under the shade of river trees where moss drifts through the branches like gray mist) our steps slow down. Even Queenie stops prancing and sticks close by. People have been murdered in Haha's café. Cut to pieces. Hit on the head. There's a case coming up in court next month. Naturally these goings-on happen at night when the colored lights cast crazy patterns and the victrola wails. In the daytime Haha's is shabby and deserted. I knock at the door, Queenie barks, my friend calls: "Mrs. Haha, ma'am? Anyone to home?"

361   Footsteps. The door opens. Our hearts overturn. It's Mr. Haha Jones himself! And he is a giant; he does have scars; he doesn't smile. No, he glowers at us through Satan-tilted eyes and demands to know: "What you want with Haha?"

362   For a moment we are too paralyzed to tell. Presently my friend half-finds her voice, a whispery voice at best: "If you please, Mr. Haha, we'd like a quart of your finest whiskey."

363   His eyes tilt more. Would you believe it? Haha is smiling! Laughing, too. "Which one of you is a drinkin' man?"

364   "It's for making fruitcakes, Mr. Haha. Cooking."

365   This sobers him. He frowns. "That's no way to waste good whiskey." Nevertheless, he retreats into the shadowed café and seconds later appears carrying a bottle of daisy-yellow unlabeled liquor. He demonstrates its sparkle in the sunlight and says: "Two dollars."

366   We pay him with nickels and dimes and pennies. Suddenly, as he jangles the coins in his hand like a fistful of dice, his face softens. "Tell you what," he proposed, pouring the money back into our bead purse, "just send me one of them fruitcakes instead."

367   "Well," my friend remarks on our way home, "there's a lovely man. We'll put an extra cup of raisins in his cake."

368   The black stove, stoked with coal and firewood, glows like a lighted pumpkin. Eggbeaters whirl, spoons spin round in bowls of butter and sugar, vanilla sweetens the air, ginger spices it; melting, nose-tingling odors saturate the kitchen, suffuse the house, drift out to the world on puffs of chimney smoke. In four days our work is done. Thirty-one cakes, dampened with whiskey, bask on window sills and shelves.

369   Who are they for?

370   Friends. Not necessarily neighbor friends: indeed, the larger share is intended for persons we've met maybe once, perhaps not at all. People who've struck our fancy. Like President Roosevelt. Like the Reverend and Mrs. J. C. Lucey, Baptist missionaries to Borneo who lectured here last winter. Or the little knife grinder who comes through town twice a year. Or Abner Packer, the driver of the six o'clock bus from Mobile, who exchanges waves with us every day as he passes in a dust-cloud whoosh. Or the young Wistons, a California couple whose car one afternoon broke down outside the house and who spent a pleasant hour chatting with us on the porch (young Mr. Wiston snapped our picture, the only one we've ever had taken). Is it because my friend is shy with everyone except strangers that these strangers, and merest acquaintances, seem to us our truest friends? I think yes. Also the scrapbooks we keep of thank-you's on White House stationery, time-to-time communications from California and Borneo, the knife grinder's penny post cards, make us feel connected to eventful worlds beyond the kitchen with its view of a sky that stops.

371   Now a nude December fig branch grates against the window. The kitchen is empty, the cakes are gone; yesterday we carted the last of them to the post office, where the cost of stamps turned our purse inside out. We're broke. That rather depresses me, but my friend insists on celebrating—with two inches of whiskey left in Haha's bottle. Queenie has a spoonful in a bowl of coffee (she likes her coffee chicory-flavored and strong). The rest we divide between a pair of jelly glasses. We're both quite awed at the prospect of drinking straight whiskey; the taste of it brings screwed-up expressions and sour shudders. But by and by we

begin to sing, the two of us singing different songs simultaneously. I don't know the words to mine, just: Come on along, come on along, to the dark-town strutters' ball. But I can dance: that's what I mean to be, a tap-dancer in the movies. My dancing shadow rollicks on the walls; our voices rock the chinaware; we giggle: as if unseen hands were tickling us. Queenie rolls on her back, her paws plow the air, something like a grin stretches her black lips. Inside myself, I feel warm and sparky as those crumbling logs, carefree as the wind in the chimney. My friend waltzes round the stove, the hem of her poor calico skirt pinched between her fingers as though it were a party dress: Show me the way to go home, she sings, her tennis shoes squeaking on the floor. Show me the way to go home.

372   Enter: two relatives. Very angry. Potent with eyes that scold, tongues that scald. Listen to what they have to say, the words tumbling together into a wrathful tune: "A child of seven! whiskey on his breath! are you out of your mind? feeding a child of seven! must be loony! road to ruina-tion! remember Cousin Kate? Uncle Charlie? Uncle Charlie's brother-in-law? shame! scandal! humiliation! kneel, pray, beg the Lord!"

373   Queenie sneaks under the stove. My friend gazes at her shoes, her chin quivers, she lifts her skirt and blows her nose and runs to her room. Long after the town has gone to sleep and the house is silent except for the chimings of clocks and the sputter of fading fires, she is weeping into a pillow already as wet as a widow's handkerchief.

374   "Don't cry," I say, sitting at the bottom of her bed and shivering despite my flannel nightgown that smells of last winter's cough syrup, "don't cry," I beg, teasing her toes, tickling her feet, "you're too old for that."

375   "It's because," she hiccups, "I am too old. Old and funny."

376   "Not funny. Fun. More fun than anybody. Listen. If you don't stop crying you'll be so tired tomorrow we can't go cut a tree."

377   She straightens up. Queenie jumps on the bed (where Queenie is not allowed) to lick her cheeks. "I know where we'll find real pretty trees, Buddy. And holly, too. With berries big as your eyes. It's way off in the woods. Farther than we've ever been. Papa used to bring us Christmas trees from there: carry them on his shoulder. That's fifty years ago. Well, now: I can't wait for morning."

378   Morning. Frozen rime lusters the grass; the sun, round as an orange and orange as hot-weather moons, balances on the horizon, burnishes the silvered winter woods. A wild turkey calls. A renegade hog grunts in the undergrowth. Soon, by the edge of knee-deep, rapid-running water we have to abandon the buggy. Queenie wades the stream first, paddles across barking complaints at the swiftness of the current, the pneumonia-making coldness of it. We follow, holding our shoes and equipment (a hatchet, a burlap sack) above our heads. A mile more: of chastising thorns, burs and briers that catch at our clothes; of rusty pine needles brilliant with gaudy fungus and molted feathers. Here, there, a flash, a flutter, an ecstasy of shrillings remind us that not all the birds have flown

south. Always, the path unwinds through lemony sun pools and pitch-black vine tunnels. Another creek to cross: a disturbed armada of speckled trout froths the water round us, and frogs the size of plates practice belly flops; beaver workmen are building a dam. On the farther shore, Queenie shakes herself and trembles. My friend shivers, too: not with cold but enthusiasm. One of her hat's ragged roses sheds a petal as she lifts her head and inhales the pine-heavy air. "We're almost there; can you smell it, Buddy?" she says, as though we were approaching an ocean.

379   And, indeed, it is a kind of ocean. Scented acres of holiday trees, prickly-leafed holly. Red berries shiny as Chinese bells: black crows swoop upon them screaming. Having stuffed our burlap sacks with enough greenery and crimson to garland a dozen windows, we set about choosing a tree. "It should be," muses my friend, "twice as tall as a boy. So a boy can't steal the star." The one we pick is twice as tall as me. A brave handsome brute that survives thirty hatchet strokes before it keels with a creaking rending cry. Lugging it like a kill, we commence the long trek out. Every few yards we abandon the struggle, sit down and pant. But we have the strength of triumphant huntsmen; that and the tree's virile, icy perfume revive us, goad us on. Many compliments accompany our sunset return along the red clay road to town; but my friend is sly and noncommittal when passersby praise the treasure perched in our buggy: what a fine tree and where did it come from? "Yonderways," she murmurs vaguely. Once a car stops and the rich mill owner's lazy wife leans out and whines: "Giveya two-bits cash for that ol tree." Ordinarily my friend is afraid of saying no; but on this occasion she promptly shakes her head: "We wouldn't take a dollar." The mill owner's wife persists. "A dollar, my foot! Fifty cents. That's my last offer. Goodness, woman, you can get another one." In answer, my friend gently reflects: "I doubt it. There's never two of anything."

380   Home: Queenie slumps by the fire and sleeps till tomorrow, snoring loud as a human.

381   A trunk in the attic contains: a shoebox of ermine tails (off the opera cape of a curious lady who once rented a room in the house), coils of frazzled tinsel gone gold with age, one silver star, a brief rope of dilapidated, undoubtedly dangerous candy-like light bulbs. Excellent decorations, as far as they go, which isn't far enough: my friend wants our tree to blaze "like a Baptist window," droop with weighty snows of ornament. But we can't afford the made-in-Japan splendors at the five-and-dime. So we do what we've always done: sit for days at the kitchen table with scissors and crayons and stacks of colored paper. I make sketches and my friend cuts them out: lots of cats, fish too (because they're easy to draw), some apples, some watermelons, a few winged angels devised from saved-up sheets of Hershey-bar tin foil. We use safety pins to attach these creations to the tree; as a final touch, we sprinkle the branches with shredded cotton (picked in August for this purpose). My friend, surveying the effect, clasps her hands together. "Now honest, Buddy. Doesn't it look good enough to eat?" Queenie tries to eat an angel.

382   After weaving and ribboning holly wreaths for all the front windows, our next project is the fashioning of family gifts. Tie-dye scarves for the ladies, for the men a home-brewed lemon and licorice and aspirin syrup to be taken "at the first Symptoms of a Cold and after Hunting." But when it comes time for making each other's gift, my friend and I separate to work secretly. I would like to buy her a pearl-handled knife, a radio, a whole pound of chocolate-covered cherries (we tasted some once, and she always swears: "I could live on them, Buddy, Lord yes I could—and that's not taking His name in vain"). Instead, I am building her a kite. She would like to give me a bicycle (she's said so on several million occasions: "If only I could, Buddy. It's bad enough in life to do without something you want; but confound it, what gets my goat is not being able to give somebody something you want them to have. Only one of these days I will, Buddy. Locate you a bike. Don't ask how. Steal it, maybe"). Instead, I'm fairly certain that she is building me a kite—the same as last year, and the year before: the year before that we exchanged slingshots. All of which is fine by me. For we are champion kite-fliers who study the wind like sailors; my friend, more accomplished than I, can get a kite aloft when there isn't enough breeze to carry clouds.

383   Christmas Eve afternoon we scrape together a nickel and go to the butcher's to buy Queenie's traditional gift, a good gnawable beef bone. The bone, wrapped in funny paper, is placed high in the tree near the silver star. Queenie knows it's there. She squats at the foot of the tree staring up in a trance of greed: when bedtime arrives she refuses to budge. Her excitement is equaled by my own. I kick the covers and turn my pillow as though it were a scorching summer's night. Somewhere a rooster crows: falsely, for the sun is still on the other side of the world.

384   "Buddy, are you awake?" It is my friend, calling from her room, which is next to mine; and an instant later she is sitting on my bed holding a candle. "Well, I can't sleep a hoot," she declares. "My mind's jumping like a jack rabbit. Buddy, do you think Mrs. Roosevelt will serve our cake at dinner?" We huddle in the bed, and she squeezes my hand I-love-you. "Seems like your hand used to be so much smaller, I guess I hate to see you grow up. When you're grown up, will we still be friends?" I say always. "But I feel so bad, Buddy. I wanted so bad to give you a bike. I tried to sell my cameo Papa gave me. Buddy"—she hesitates, as though embarrassed—"I made you another kite." Then I confess that I made her one, too; and we laugh. The candle burns too short to hold. Out it goes, exposing the starlight, the stars spinning at the window like a visible caroling that slowly, slowly daybreak silences. Possibly we doze; but the beginnings of dawn splash us like cold water: we're up, wide-eyed and wandering while we wait for others to waken. Quite deliberately my friend drops a kettle on the kitchen floor. I tap-dance in front of closed doors. One by one the household emerges, looking as though they'd like to kill us both; but it's Christmas so they can't. First, a gorgeous breakfast: just everything you can imagine—from flapjacks and fried squirrel

to hominy grits and honey-in-the-comb. Which puts everyone in a good humor except my friend and me. Frankly, we're so impatient to get at the presents we can't eat a mouthful.

385   Well, I'm disappointed. Who wouldn't be? With socks, a Sunday school shirt, some handkerchiefs, a hand-me-down sweater and a year's subscription to a religious magazine for children. The Little Shepherd. It makes me boil. It really does.

386   My friend has a better haul. A sack of Satsumas, that's her best present. She is proudest, however, of a white wool shawl knitted by her married sister. But she says her favorite gift is the kite I built her. And it is very beautiful; though not as beautiful as the one she made me, which is blue and scattered with gold and green Good Conduct stars; moreover, my name is painted on it, "Buddy."

387   "Buddy, the wind is blowing."

388   The wind is blowing, and nothing will do till we've run to a pasture below the house where Queenie has scooted to bury her bone (and where, a winter hence, Queenie will be buried, too). There, plunging through the healthy waist-high grass we unreel our kites, feel them twitching at the string like sky fish as they swim into the wind. Satisfied, sun-warmed, we sprawl in the grass and peel Satsumas and watch our kites cavort. Soon I forget the socks and hand-me-down sweater. I'm as happy as if we'd already won the fifty-thousand-dollar Grand Prize in the coffee-naming contest.

389   "My, how foolish I am!" my friend cries, suddenly alert, like a woman remembering too late she has biscuits in the oven. "You know what I've always thought?" she asks in a tone of discovery, and not smiling at me but a point beyond. "I've always thought a body would have to be sick and dying before they saw the Lord. And I imagined that when He came it would be like looking at the Baptist window: pretty as colored glass with the sun pouring through, such a shine you don't know it's getting dark. And itbeen a comfort: to think of that shine taking away all the spooky feeling. But I'll wager it never happens. I'll wager at the very end a body realizes the Lord has already shown Himself. That things as they are"—her hand circles in a gesture that gathers clouds and kites and grass and Queenie pawing earth over her bone—"just what they've always seen, was seeing Him. As for me, I could leave the world with today in my eyes."

390   This is our last Christmas together.

391   Life separates us. Those who Know Best decide that I belong in a military school. And so follows a miserable succession of bugle-blowing prisons, grim reveille-ridden summer camps. I have a new home too. But it doesn't count. Home is where my friend is, and there I never go.

392   And there she remains, puttering around the kitchen. Alone with Queeie. Then alone. ("Buddy dear," she writes in her wild hard-to-read script, "yesterday Jim Macy's horse kicked Queenie bad. Be thankful she didn't feel much. I wrapped her in a Fine Linen sheet and rode her in the

buggy down to Simpson's pasture where she can be with all her Bones . . . "). For a few Novembers she continues to bake her fruitcakes single-handed; not as many, but some: and, of course, she always sends me "the best of the batch." Also, in every letter she encloses a dime wadded in toilet paper: "See a picture show and write me the story." But gradually in her letters she tends to confuse me with her other friend, the Buddy who died in the 1880's; more and more thirteenths are not the only days she stays in bed: a morning arrives in November, a leafless birdless coming of winter morning, when she cannot rouse herself to exclaim: "Oh my, it's fruitcake weather!"

393   And when that happens, I know it. A message saying so merely confirms a piece of news some secret vein had already received, severing from me an irreplaceable part of myself, letting loose like a kite on a broken string. That is why, walking across a school campus on this particular December morning, I keep searching the sky. As if I expected to see, rather like hearts, a lost pair of kites hurrying toward heaven.

Questions for Engagement, Response, and Analysis

1. What is the **point of view** in this story? Why is this point of view essential to the story? Why is it written in present tense? How would this story differ in style and diction if the narrator were still a child?

2. Why do the two friends go to the great trouble and expense of making and mailing fruitcakes every Christmas?

3. Explain the narrator's friend's statement "'As for me, I could leave the world with today in my eyes.'"

4. Explain the symbolism of the kites.

Crafting Arguments

1. In an essay, analyze the relationships Buddy and his friend have with other people, both nearby and far away.

2. One of the strengths of the story is the vivid sensory detail given in the descriptions. In an essay, examine Capote's use of such details, supporting each of your claims with quotations from the descriptions.

3. The narrator writes that "Home is where my friend is, and there I never go." In an essay, argue that home is a place as in Mayes' "Bramare" or that home is people.

Joyce Carol Oates (b. 1938)

Joyce Carol Oates, a highly skilled and extraordinarily productive American writer of poems, criticism, and fiction, is best known for her more than twenty darkly violent novels. From Them *(1969), which won a National Book Award,*

to The Gravedigger's Daughter *(2007), Oates' novels represent an unusually large body of distinguished achievement.
Oates published her first book on short stories,* By the North
Gate, *in 1963, and her most recent,* The Museum of
Dr. Moses: Tales of Mystery and Suspense, *in 2007. Born a
Roman Catholic, Oates depicts a world devoid of saving
grace. A realistic writer whose characters speak a colloquial
dialogue full of allusions to popular culture, Oates explores
the surrealistic, nightmarish encounters that haunt the
empty, lost souls she creates.*

WHERE ARE YOU GOING,
WHERE HAVE YOU BEEN?   (1970)

FOR BOB DYLAN

394   Her name was Connie. She was fifteen and she had a quick nervous
giggling habit of craning her neck to glance into mirrors, or checking
other people's faces to make sure her own was all right. Her mother, who
noticed everything and knew everything and who hadn't much reason
any longer to look at her own face, always scolded Connie about it. "Stop
gawking at yourself, who are you? You think you're so pretty?" she would
say. Connie would raise her eyebrows at these familiar complaints and
look right through her mother, into a shadowy vision of herself as she
was right at that moment: she knew she was pretty and that was everything. Her mother had been pretty once too, if you could believe those
old snapshots in the album, but now her looks were gone and that was
why she was always after Connie.

395   "Why don't you keep your room clean like your sister? How've you got
your hair fixed—what the hell stinks? Hair spray? You don't see your
sister using that junk."

396   Her sister June was twenty-four and still lived at home. She was a
secretary in the high school Connie attended, and if that wasn't bad
enough—with her in the same building—she was so plain and chunky
and steady that Connie had to hear her praised all the time by her mother
and her mother's sisters. June did this, June did that, she saved money and
helped clean the house and cooked and Connie couldn't do a thing,
her mind was all filled with trashy daydreams. Their father was away at
work most of the time and when he came home he wanted supper and
he read the newspaper at supper and after supper he went to bed. He
didn't bother talking much to them, but around his bent head Connie's
mother kept picking at her until Connie wished her mother was dead and
she herself was dead and it was all over. "She makes me want to throw
up sometimes," she complained to her friends. She had a high, breathless, amused voice which made everything she said sound a little forced,
whether it was sincere or not.

397   There was one good thing: June went places with girl friends of hers,
girls who were just as plain and steady as she, and so when Connie

wanted to do that her mother had no objections. The father of Connie's
best girl friend drove the girls the three miles to town and left them off
at a shopping plaza, so that they could walk through the stores or go to
a movie, and when he came to pick them up again at eleven he never
bothered to ask what they had done.

398   They must have been familiar sights, walking around that shopping
plaza in their shorts and flat ballerina slippers that always scuffed the
sidewalk, with charm bracelets jingling on their thin wrists; they would
lean together to whisper and laugh secretly if someone passed by who
amused or interested them. Connie had long dark blond hair that drew
anyone's eye to it, and she wore part of it pulled up on her head and
puffed out and the rest of it she let fall down her back. She wore a pull-
over jersey blouse that looked one way when she was at home and
another way when she was away from home. Everything about her had
two sides to it, one for home and one for anywhere that was not home:
her walk that could be childlike and bobbing, or languid enough to make
anyone think she was hearing music in her head, her mouth which was
pale and smirking most of the time, but bright and pink on these evenings
out, her laugh which was cynical and drawling at home—"Ha, ha, very
funny"—but high-pitched and nervous anywhere else, like the jingling of
the charms on her bracelet.

399   Sometimes they did go shopping or to a movie, but sometimes they
went across the highway, ducking fast across the busy road, to a drive-in
restaurant where older kids hung out. The restaurant was shaped like a
big bottle, though squatter than a real bottle, and on its cap was a revolving figure of a grinning boy who held a hamburger aloft. One night in mid-
summer they ran across, breathless with daring, and right away someone
leaned out a car window and invited them over, but it was just a boy from
high school they didn't like. It made them feel good to be able to ignore
him. They went up through the maze of parked and cruising cars to the
bright-lit, fly-infested restaurant, their faces pleased and expectant as if
they were entering a sacred building that loomed out of the night to give
them what haven and what blessing they yearned for. They sat at the
counter and crossed their legs at the ankles, their thin shoulders rigid
with excitement, and listened to the music that made everything so good:
the music was always in the background like music at a church service,
it was something to depend upon.

400   A boy named Eddie came in to talk with them. He sat backwards on
his stool, turning himself jerkily around in semi-circles and then stopping
and turning again, and after a while he asked Connie if she would like
something to eat. She said she did and so she tapped her friend's arm on
her way out—her friend pulled her face up into a brave droll look—and
Connie said she would meet her at eleven, across the way. "I just hate to
leave her like that," Connie said earnestly, but the boy said that she
wouldn't be alone for long. So they went out to his car and on the way
Connie couldn't help but let her eyes wander over the windshields and

faces all around her, her face gleaming with a joy that had nothing to do with Eddie or even this place; it might have been the music. She drew her shoulders up and sucked in her breath with the pure pleasure of being alive, and just at that moment she happened to glance at a face just a few feet from hers. It was a boy with shaggy black hair, in a convertible jalopy painted gold. He stared at her and then his lips widened into a grin. Connie slit her eyes at him and turned away, but she couldn't help glancing back and there he was still watching her. He wagged a finger and laughed and said, "Gonna get you, baby," and Connie turned away again without Eddie noticing anything.

401   She spent three hours with him, at the restaurant where they ate hamburgers and drank Cokes in wax cups that were always sweating, and then down an alley a mile or so away, and when he left her off at five to eleven only the movie house was still open at the plaza. Her girl friend was there, talking with a boy. When Connie came up the two girls smiled at each other and Connie said, "How was the movie?" and the girl said, "*You* should know." They rode off with the girl's father, sleepy and pleased, and Connie couldn't help but look at the darkened shopping plaza with its big empty parking lot and its signs that were faded and ghostly now, and over at the drive-in restaurant where cars were still circling tirelessly. She couldn't hear the music at this distance.

402   Next morning June asked her how the movie was and Connie said, "So-so."

403   She and that girl and occasionally another girl went out several times a week that way, and the rest of the time Connie spent around the house—it was summer vacation—getting in her mother's way and thinking, dreaming, about the boys she met. But all the boys fell back and dissolved into a single face that was not even a face, but an idea, a feeling, mixed up with the urgent insistent pounding of the music and the humid night air of July. Connie's mother kept dragging her back to the daylight by finding things for her to do or saying, suddenly, "What's this about the Pettinger girl?"

404   And Connie would say nervously, "Oh, her. That dope." She always drew thick clear lines between herself and such girls, and her mother was simple and kindly enough to believe her. Her mother was so simple, Connie thought, that it was maybe cruel to fool her so much. Her mother went scuffling around the house in old bedroom slippers and complained over the telephone to one sister about the other, then the other called up and the two of them complained about the third one. If June's name was mentioned her mother's tone was approving, and if Connie's name was mentioned it was disapproving. This did not really mean she disliked Connie and actually Connie thought that her mother preferred her to June because she was prettier, but the two of them kept up a pretense of exasperation, a sense that they were tugging and struggling over something of little value to either of them. Sometimes, over coffee, they were almost friends, but something would come up—some vexation that was

like a fly buzzing suddenly around their heads—and their faces went hard with contempt.

405   One Sunday Connie got up at eleven—none of them bothered with church—and washed her hair so that it could dry all day long, in the sun. Her parents and sister were going to a barbecue at an aunt's house and Connie said no, she wasn't interested, rolling her eyes to let her mother know just what she thought of it. "Stay home alone then," her mother said sharply. Connie sat out back in a lawn chair and watched them drive away, her father quiet and bald, hunched around so that he could back the car out, her mother with a look that was still angry and not at all softened through the windshield, and in the back seat poor old June all dressed up as if she didn't know what a barbecue was, with all the running yelling kids and the flies. Connie sat with her eyes closed in the sun, dreaming and dazed with the warmth about her as if this were a kind of love, the caresses of love, and her mind slipped over onto thoughts of the boy she had been with the night before and how nice he had been, how sweet it always was, not the way someone like June would suppose but sweet, gentle, the way it was in movies and promised in songs; and when she opened her eyes she hardly knew where she was, the back yard ran off into weeds and a fence-line of trees and behind it the sky was perfectly blue and still. The asbestos "ranch house" that was now three years old startled her—it looked small. She shook her head as if to get awake.

406   It was too hot. She went inside the house and turned on the radio to drown out the quiet. She sat on the edge of her bed, barefoot, and listened for an hour and a half to a program called XYZ Sunday Jamboree, record after record of hard, fast, shrieking songs she sang along with, interspersed by exclamations from "Bobby King": "An' look here you girls at Napoleon's—Son and Charley want you to pay real close attention to this song coming up!"

407   And Connie paid close attention herself, bathed in a glow of slow pulsed joy that seemed to rise mysteriously out of the music itself and lay languidly about the airless little room, breathed in and breathed out with each gentle rise and fall of her chest.

408   After a while she heard a car coming up the drive. She sat up at once, startled, because it couldn't be her father so soon. The gravel kept crunching all the way in from the road—the driveway was long—and Connie ran to the window. It was a car she didn't know. It was an open jalopy, painted a bright gold that caught the sunlight opaquely. Her heart began to pound and her fingers snatched at her hair, checking it, and she whispered "Christ. Christ," wondering how bad she looked. The car came to a stop at the side door and the horn sounded four short taps as if this were a signal Connie knew.

409   She went into the kitchen and approached the door slowly, then hung out the screen door, her bare toes curling down off the step. There were two boys in the car and now she recognized the driver: he had shaggy, shabby black hair that looked crazy as a wig and he was grinning at her.

410   "I ain't late, am I?" he said.

411   "Who the hell do you think you are?" Connie said.

412   "Toldja I'd be out, didn't I?"

413   "I don't even know who you are."

414   She spoke sullenly, careful to show no interest or pleasure, and he spoke in a fast bright monotone. Connie looked past him to the other boy, taking her time. He had fair brown hair, with a lock that fell onto his forehead. His sideburns gave him a fierce, embarrassed look, but so far he hadn't even bothered to glance at her. Both boys wore sunglasses. The driver's glasses were metallic and mirrored everything in miniature.

415   "You wanta come for a ride?" he said.

416   Connie smirked and let her hair fall loose over one shoulder.

417   "Don'tcha like my car? New paint job," he said. "Hey."

418   "What?"

419   "You're cute."

420   She pretended to fidget, chasing flies away from the door.

421   "Don'tcha believe me, or what?" he said.

422   "Look, I don't even know who you are," Connie said in disgust.

423   "Hey, Ellie's got a radio, see. Mine's broke down." He lifted his friend's arm and showed her the little transistor the boy was holding, and now Connie began to hear the music. It was the same program that was playing inside the house.

424   "Bobby King?" she said.

425   "I listen to him all the time. I think he's great."

426   "He's kind of great," Connie said reluctantly.

427   "Listen, that guy's *great*. He knows where the action is."

428   Connie blushed a little, because the glasses made it impossible for her to see just what this boy was looking at. She couldn't decide if she liked him or if he was just a jerk, and so she dawdled in the doorway and wouldn't come down or go back inside. She said "What's all that stuff painted on your car?"

429   "Can'tcha read it?" He opened the door very carefully, as if he was afraid it might fall off. He slid out just as carefully, planting his feet firmly on the ground, the tiny metallic world in his glasses slowing down like gelatine hardening and in the midst of it Connie's bright green blouse. "This here is my name, to begin with," he said. ARNOLD FRIEND was written in tarlike black letters on the side, with a drawing of a round grinning face that reminded Connie of a pumpkin, except it wore sunglasses. "I wanta introduce myself, I'm Arnold Friend and that's my real name and I'm gonna be your friend, honey, and inside the car's Ellie Oscar, he's kinda shy." Ellie brought his transistor radio up to his shoulder and balanced it there. "Now these numbers are a secret code, honey," Arnold Friend explained. He read off the numbers 33, 19, 17 and raised his eyebrows at her to see what she thought of that, but she didn't think much of it. The left rear fender had been smashed and around it was written, on the gleaming gold background: DONE BY CRAZY WOMAN DRIVER.

Connie had to laugh at that. Arnold Friend was pleased at her laughter and looked up at her. "Around the other side's a lot more—you wanta come and see them?"

430   "No."

431   "Why not?"

432   "Why should I?"

433   "Don'tcha wanta see what's on the car? Don'tcha wanta go for a ride?"

434   "I don't know."

435   "Why not?"

436   "I got things to do."

437   "Like what?"

438   "Things."

439   He laughed as if she had said something funny. He slapped his thighs. He was standing in a strange way, leaning back against the car as if he were balancing himself. He wasn't tall, only an inch or so taller than she would be if she came down to him. Connie liked the way he was dressed, which was the way all of them dressed: tight faded jeans stuffed into black, scuffed boots, a belt that pulled his waist in and showed how lean he was, and a white pull-over shirt that was a little soiled and showed the hard small muscles of his arms and shoulders. He looked as if he probably did hard work, lifting and carrying things. Even his neck looked muscular. And his face was a familiar face, somehow: the jaw and chin and cheeks slightly darkened, because he hadn't shaved for a day or two, and the nose long and hawk-like, sniffing as if she were a treat he was going to gobble up and it was all a joke.

440   "Connie, you ain't telling the truth. This is your day set aside for a ride with me and you know it," he said, still laughing. The way he straightened and recovered from his fit of laughing showed that it had been all fake.

441   "How do you know what my name is?" she said suspiciously.

442   "It's Connie."

443   "Maybe and maybe not."

444   "I know my Connie," he said, wagging his finger. Now she remembered him even better, back at the restaurant, and her cheeks warmed at the thought of how she sucked in her breath just at the moment she passed him—how she must have looked to him. And he had remembered her. "Ellie and I come out here especially for you," he said. "Ellie can sit in back. How about it?"

445   "Where?"

446   "Where what?"

447   "Where're we going?"

448   He looked at her. He took off the sunglasses and she saw how pale the skin around his eyes was, like holes that were not in shadow but instead in light. His eyes were chips of broken glass that catch the light in an amiable way. He smiled. It was as if the idea of going for a ride somewhere, to some place, was a new idea to him.

449   "Just for a ride, Connie sweetheart."

450   "I never said my name was Connie," she said.

451   "But I know what it is. I know your name and all about you, lots of things," Arnold Friend said. He had not moved yet but stood still leaning back against the side of his jalopy. "I took a special interest in you, such a pretty girl, and found out all about you like I know your parents and sister are gone somewheres and I know where and how long they're going to be gone, and I know who you were with last night, and your best girl friend's name is Betty. Right?"

452   He spoke in a simple lilting voice, exactly as if he were reciting the words to a song. His smile assured her that everything was fine. In the car, Ellie turned up the volume on his radio and did not bother to look around at them.

453   "Ellie can sit in the back seat," Arnold Friend said. He indicated his friend with a casual jerk of his chin, as if Ellie did not count and she should not bother with him.

454   "How'd you find out all that stuff?" Connie said.

455   "Listen: Betty Schultz and Tony Fitch and Jimmy Pettinger and Nancy Pettinger," he said, in a chant. "Raymond Stanley and Bob Hutter—"

456   "Do you know all those kids?"

457   "I know everybody."

458   "Look, you're kidding. You're not from around here."

459   "Sure."

460   "But—how come we never saw you before?"

461   "Sure you saw me before," he said. He looked down at his boots, as if he were a little offended. "You just don't remember."

462   "I guess I'd remember you," Connie said.

463   "Yeah?" He looked up at this, beaming. He was pleased. He began to mark time with the music from Ellie's radio, tapping his fists lightly together. Connie looked away from his smile to the car, which was painted so bright it almost hurt her eyes to look at it. She looked at that name, ARNOLD FRIEND. And up at the front fender was an expression that was familiar—MAN THE FLYING SAUCERS. It was an expression kids had used the year before, but didn't use this year. She looked at it for a while as if the words meant something to her that she did not yet know.

464   "What're you thinking about? Huh?" Arnold Friend demanded. "Not worried about your hair blowing around in the car, are you?"

465   "No."

466   "Think I maybe can't drive good?"

467   "How do I know?"

468   "You're a hard girl to handle. How come?" he said. "Don't you know I'm your friend? Didn't you see me put my sign in the air when you walked by?"

469   "What sign?"

470   "My sign." And he drew an X in the air, leaning out toward her. They were maybe ten feet apart. After his hand fell back to his side the X was

still in the air, almost visible. Connie let the screen door close and stood perfectly still inside it, listening to the music from her radio and the boy's blend together. She stared at Arnold Friend. He stood there so stiffly relaxed, pretending to be relaxed, with one hand idly on the door handle as if he were keeping himself up that way and had no intention of ever moving again. She recognized most things about him, the tight jeans that showed his thighs and buttocks and the greasy leather boots and the tight shirt, and even that slippery friendly smile of his, that sleepy dreamy smile that all the boys used to get across ideas they didn't want to put into words. She recognized all this and also the singsong way he talked, slightly mocking, kidding, but serious and a little melancholy, and she recognized the way he tapped one fist against the other in homage to the perpetual music behind him. But all these things did not come together.

471   She said suddenly, "Hey, how old are you?"

472   His smile faded. She could see then that he wasn't a kid, he was much older—thirty, maybe more. At this knowledge her heart began to pound faster.

473   "That's a crazy thing to ask. Can'tcha see I'm your own age?"

474   "Like hell you are."

475   "Or maybe a couple years older, I'm eighteen."

476   "Eighteen?" she said doubtfully.

477   He grinned to reassure her and lines appeared at the corners of his mouth. His teeth were big and white. He grinned so broadly his eyes became slits and she saw how thick the lashes were, thick and black as if painted with a black tarlike material. Then he seemed to become embarrassed, abruptly, and looked over his shoulder at Ellie. "*Him*, he's crazy," he said. "Ain't he a riot, he's a nut, a real character." Ellie was still listening to the music. His sunglasses told nothing about what he was thinking. He wore a bright orange shirt unbuttoned halfway to show his chest, which was a pale, bluish chest and not muscular like Arnold Friend's. His shirt collar was turned up all around and the very tips of the collar pointed out past his chin as if they were protecting him. He was pressing the transistor radio up against his ear and sat there in a kind of daze, right in the sun.

478   "He's kinda strange," Connie said.

479   "Hey, she says you're kinda strange! Kinda strange!" Arnold Friend cried. He pounded on the car to get Ellie's attention. Ellie turned for the first time and Connie saw with shock that he wasn't a kid either—he had a fair, hairless face, cheeks reddened slightly as if the veins grew too close to the surface of his skin, the face of a forty-year-old baby. Connie felt a wave of dizziness rise in her at this sight and she stared at him as if waiting for something to change the shock of the moment, make it all right again. Ellie's lips kept shaping words, mumbling along, with the words blasting in his ear.

480   "Maybe you two better go away," Connie said faintly.

481   "What? How come?" Arnold Friend cried. "We come out here to take you for a ride. It's Sunday." He had the voice of the man on the radio now. It was the same voice, Connie thought. "Don'tcha know it's Sunday all day and honey, no matter who you were with last night today you're with Arnold Friend and don't you forget it!—Maybe you better step out here," he said, and this last was in a different voice. It was a little flatter, as if the heat was finally getting to him.

482   "No. I got things to do."

483   "Hey."

484   "You two better leave."

485   "We ain't leaving until you come with us."

486   "Like hell I am—"

487   "Connie, don't fool around with me. I mean, I mean, don't fool *around*," he said, shaking his head. He laughed incredulously. He placed his sunglasses on top of his head, carefully, as if he were indeed wearing a wig, and brought the stems down behind his ears. Connie stared at him, another wave of dizziness and fear rising in her so that for a moment he wasn't even in focus but was just a blur, standing there against his gold car, and she had the idea that he had driven up the driveway all right but had come from nowhere before that and belonged nowhere and that everything about him and even about the music that was so familiar to her was only half real.

488   "If my father comes and sees you—"

489   "He ain't coming. He's at the barbecue."

490   "How do you know that?"

491   "Aunt Tillie's. Right now they're—uh—they're drinking. Sitting around," he said vaguely, squinting as if he were staring all the way to town and over to Aunt Tillie's backyard. Then the vision seemed to get clear and he nodded energetically. "Yeah. Sitting around. There's your sister in a blue dress, huh? And high heels, the poor sad bitch—nothing like you, sweetheart! And your mother's helping some fat woman with the corn, they're cleaning the corn—husking the corn—"

492   "What fat woman?" Connie cried.

493   "How do I know what fat woman. I don't know every goddam fat woman in the world!" Arnold Friend laughed.

494   "Oh, that's Mrs. Hornby. . . . Who invited her?" Connie said. She felt a little light-headed. Her breath was coming quickly.

495   "She's too fat. I don't like them fat. I like them the way you are, honey," he said, smiling sleepily at her. They stared at each other for awhile, through the screen door. He said softly, "Now what you're going to do is this: you're going to come out that door. You're going to sit up front with me and Ellie's going to sit in the back, the hell with Ellie, right? This isn't Ellie's date. You're my date. I'm your lover, honey."

496   "What? You're crazy—"

497   "Yes, I'm your lover. You don't know what that is but you will," he said. "I know that too. I know all about you. But look: it's real nice and you

couldn't ask for nobody better than me, or more polite. I always keep my word. I'll tell you how it is, I'm always nice at first, the first time. I'll hold you so tight you won't think you have to try to get away or pretend anything because you'll know you can't. And I'll come inside you where it's all secret and you'll give in to me and you'll love me—"

498   "Shut up! You're crazy!" Connie said. She backed away from the door. She put her hands against her ears as if she'd heard something terrible, something not meant for her. "People don't talk like that, you're crazy," she muttered. Her heart was almost too big now for her chest and its pumping made sweat break out all over her. She looked out to see Arnold Friend pause and then take a step toward the porch lurching. He almost fell. But, like a clever drunken man, he managed to catch his balance. He wobbled in his high boots and grabbed hold of one of the porch posts.

499   "Honey?" he said. "You still listening?"

500   "Get the hell out of here!"

501   "Be nice, honey. Listen."

502   "I'm going to call the police—"

503   He wobbled again and out of the side of his mouth came a fast spat curse, an aside not meant for her to hear. But even this "Christ!" sounded forced. Then he began to smile again. She watched this smile come, awkward as if he were smiling from inside a mask. His whole face was a mask, she thought wildly, tanned down onto his throat but then running out as if he had plastered make-up on his face but had forgotten about his throat.

504   "Honey—? Listen, here's how it is. I always tell the truth and I promise you this: I ain't coming in that house after you."

505   "You better not! I'm going to call the police if you—if you don't—"

506   "Honey," he said, talking right through her voice, "honey, I'm not coming in there but you are coming out here. You know why?"

507   She was panting. The kitchen looked like a place she had never seen before, some room she had run inside but which wasn't good enough, wasn't going to help her. The kitchen window had never had a curtain, after three years, and there were dishes in the sink for her to do—probably—and if you ran your hand across the table you'd probably feel something sticky there.

508   "You listening, honey? Hey?"

509   "—going to call the police—"

510   "Soon as you touch the phone I don't need to keep my promise and can come inside. You won't want that."

511   She rushed forward and tried to lock the door. Her fingers were shaking. "But why lock it," Arnold Friend said gently, talking right into her face. "It's just a screen door. It's just nothing." One of his boots was at a strange angle, as if his foot wasn't in it. It pointed out to the left, bent at the ankle. "I mean, anybody can break through a screen door and glass and wood and iron or anything else if he needs to, anybody at all and specially Arnold Friend. If the place got lit up with a fire honey you'd

come running out into my arms, right into my arms and safe at home—
like you knew I was your lover and'd stopped fooling around. I don't mind
a nice shy girl but I don't like no fooling around." Part of those words
were spoken with a slight rhythmic lilt, and Connie somehow recognized
them—the echo of a song from last year, about a girl rushing into her boy
friend's arms and coming home again—

512   Connie stood barefoot on the linoleum floor, staring at him. "What do
you want?" she whispered.

513   "I want you," he said.

514   "What?"

515   "Seen you that night and thought, that's the one, yes sir. I never needed
to look any more."

516   "But my father's coming back. He's coming to get me. I had to wash
my hair first—" She spoke in a dry, rapid voice, hardly raising it for him
to hear.

517   "No, your daddy is not coming and yes, you had to wash your hair and
you washed it for me. It's nice and shining and all for me, I thank you,
sweetheart," he said, with a mock bow, but again he almost lost his balance. He had to bend and adjust his boots. Evidently his feet did not go
all the way down; the boots must have been stuffed with something so
that he would seem taller. Connie stared out at him and behind him Ellie
in the car, who seemed to be looking off toward Connie's right, into nothing.
This Ellie said, pulling the words out of the air one after another as if he
were just discovering them, "You want me to pull out the phone?"

518   "Shut your mouth and keep it shut," Arnold Friend said, his face red
from bending over or maybe from embarrassment because Connie had
seen his boots. "This ain't none of your business."

519   "What—what are you doing? What do you want?" Connie said. "If I call
the police they'll get you, they'll arrest you—"

520   "Promise was not to come in unless you touch that phone, and I'll keep
that promise," he said. He resumed his erect position and tried to force
his shoulders back. He sounded like a hero in a movie, declaring something important. He spoke too loudly and it was as if he were speaking
to someone behind Connie. "I ain't made plans for coming in that house
where I don't belong but just for you to come out to me, the way you
should. Don't you know who I am?"

521   "You're crazy," she whispered. She backed away from the door but did
not want to go into another part of the house, as if this would give
him permission to come through the door. "What do you . . . You're crazy,
you . . ."

522   "Huh? What're you saying, honey?"

523   Her eyes darted everywhere in the kitchen. She could not remember
what it was, this room.

524   "This is how it is, honey: you come out and we'll drive away, have a
nice ride. But if you don't come out we're gonna wait till your people
come home and then they're all going to get it."

525   "You want that telephone pulled out?" Ellie said. He held the radio away from his ear and grimaced, as if without the radio the air was too much for him.

526   "I toldja shut up, Ellie," Arnold Friend said, "you're deaf, get a hearing aid, right? Fix yourself up. This little girl's no trouble and's gonna be nice to me, so Ellie keep to yourself, this ain't your date—right? Don't hem in on me. Don't hog. Don't crush. Don't bird dog. Don't trail me," he said in a rapid meaningless voice, as if he were running through all the expressions he'd learned but was no longer sure which one of them was in style, then rushing on to new ones, making them up with his eyes closed, "Don't crawl under my fence, don't squeeze in my chipmunk hole, don't sniff my glue, suck my popsicle, keep your own greasy fingers on yourself!" He shaded his eyes and peered in at Connie, who was backed against the kitchen table. "Don't mind him honey he's just a creep. He's a dope. Right? I'm the boy for you and like I said you come out here nice like a lady and give me your hand, and nobody else gets hurt. I mean, your nice old bald-headed daddy and your mummy and your sister in her high heels. Because listen: why bring them in this?"

527   "Leave me alone," Connie whispered.

528   "Hey, you know that old woman down the road, the one with the chickens and stuff—you know her?"

529   "She's dead!"

530   "Dead? What? You know her?" Arnold Friend said.

531   "She's dead—"

532   "Don't you like her?"

533   "She's dead—she's—she isn't here any more—"

534   "But don't you like her, I mean, you got something against her? Some grudge or something?" Then his voice dipped as if he were conscious of a rudeness. He touched the sunglasses perched on top of his head as if to make sure they were still there. "Now you be a good girl."

535   "What are you going to do?"

536   "Just two things, or maybe three," Arnold Friend said. "But I promise it won't last long and you'll like me that way you get to like people you're close to. You will. It's all over for you here, so come on out. You don't want your people in any trouble, do you?"

537   She turned and bumped against a chair or something, hurting her leg, but she ran into the back room and picked up the telephone. Something roared in her ear, a tiny roaring, and she was so sick with fear that she could do nothing but listen to it—the telephone was clammy and very heavy and her fingers groped down to the dial but were too weak to touch it. She began to scream into the phone, into the roaring. She cried out, she cried for her mother, she felt her breath start jerking back and forth in her lungs as if it were something Arnold Friend were stabbing her with again and again with no tenderness. A noisy sorrowful wailing rose all about her and she was locked inside it the way she was locked inside the house.

538   After a while she could hear again. She was sitting on the floor with her wet back against the wall.

539   Arnold Friend was saying from the door, "That's a good girl. Put the phone back."

540   She kicked the phone away from her.

541   "No, honey. Pick it up. Put it back right."

542   She picked it up and put it back. The dial tone stopped.

543   "That's a good girl. Now come outside."

544   She was hollow with what had been fear, but what was now just an emptiness. All that screaming had blasted it out of her. She sat, one leg cramped under her, and deep inside her brain was something like a pinpoint of light that kept going and would not let her relax. She thought, I'm not going to see my mother again. She thought, I'm not going to sleep in my bed again. Her bright green blouse was all wet.

545   Arnold Friend said, in a gentle—loud voice that was like a stage voice, "The place where you came from ain't there any more, and where you had in mind to go is cancelled out. This place you are now—inside your daddy's house—is nothing but a cardboard box I can knock down any time. You know that and always did know it. You hear me?"

546   She thought, I have got to think. I have to know what to do.

547   "We'll go out to a nice field, out in the country here where it smells so nice and it's sunny," Arnold Friend said. "I'll have my arms around you so you won't need to try to get away and I'll show you what love is like, what it does. The hell with this house! It looks solid all right," he said. He ran a fingernail down the screen and the noise did not make Connie shiver, as it would have the day before. "Now put your hand on your heart, honey. Feel that? That feels solid too but we know better, be nice to me, be sweet like you can because what else is there for a girl like you but to be sweet and pretty and give in?—and get away before her people come back?"

548   She felt her pounding heart. Her hand seemed to enclose it. She thought for the first time in her life that it was nothing that was hers, that belonged to her, but just a pounding, living thing inside this body that wasn't really hers either.

549   "You don't want them to get hurt," Arnold Friend went on. "Now get up, honey. Get up all by yourself."

550   She stood up.

551   "Now turn this way. That's right. Come over here to me—Ellie, put that away, didn't I tell you? You dope. You miserable creepy dope," Arnold said. His words were not angry but only part of an incantation. The incantation was kindly. "Now come out through the kitchen to me honey and let's see a smile, try it, you're a brave sweet little girl and now they're eating corn and hotdogs cooked to bursting over an outdoor fire, and they don't know one thing about you and never did and honey you're better than them because not a one of them would have done this for you."

552   Connie felt the linoleum under her feet; it was cool. She brushed her hair back out of her eyes. Arnold Friend let go of the post tentatively and opened his arms for her, his elbows pointing in toward each other and his wrists limp, to show that this was an embarrassed embrace and a little mocking, he didn't want to make her self-conscious.

553   She put out her hand against the screen. She watched herself push the door slowly open as if she were safe back somewhere in the other doorway, watching this body and this head of long hair moving out into the sunlight where Arnold Friend waited.

554   "My sweet little blue-eyed girl," he said, in a half-sung sigh that had nothing to do with her brown eyes but was taken up just the same by the vast sunlit reaches of the land behind him and on all sides of him, so much land that Connie had never seen before and did not recognize except to know that she was going to it.

Questions for Engagement, Response, and Analysis

1. What does the interaction between Connie and her mother reveal about each of them?

2. Analyze the role of music in the story.

3. How does Arnold know so much about Connie? Why does Arnold Friend fake laughter and pretend to be a teenager even though he must know Connie will see through his charade? What attracts Connie to Arnold and Ellie? What frightens her?

4. How does Arnold convince Connie that she is powerless before him?

5. What does the evidence in the story suggest will happen to Connie?

Crafting Arguments

1. In an essay, discuss the particulars of Connie's family life and/or culture that affect her fate.

2. This story might be seen as suggesting the difficulty of distinguishing good from evil. After carefully analyzing the characters of Arnold Friend and of Connie, write an essay supporting or disagreeing with this claim.

3. Write an essay arguing that Arnold Friend is or is not the incarnation of evil.

Sherman Alexie (b. 1966)

Sherman Alexie was born on the Spokane Indian Reservation in Wellpinit, Washington. His mother is a Spokane Indian and his father a Coeur d'Alene Indian. Alexie attended Gonzaga University and Washington State University. His first two books of poetry—The Business of Fancydancing (1991) and I Would Steal Horses (1993)—

*were published while he was still in his early twenties, and
his remarkable first collection of short stories,* The
Lone Ranger and Tonto Fistfight in Heaven *(1993), from
which the following story is taken, received a PEN/
Hemingway Award for Best First Book of Fiction and a
Lila Wallace-Reader's Digest Writers' Award. One story
from this collection—"This Is What It Means to Say
Phoenix, Arizona"—was the basis for the award-winning
film* Smoke Signals *(1998). A prolific writer, Alexie has
continued to publish poetry, short stories, and novels.
In 2007, Alexie published both a novel,* Flight, *and his
first young adult novel,* The Absolutely True Diary of a
Part-Time Indian. *His unique style and his sense of humor
have made him popular with both scholars and general
readers.*

BECAUSE MY FATHER ALWAYS SAID HE WAS THE
ONLY INDIAN WHO SAW JIMI HENDRIX PLAY
"THE STAR-SPANGLED BANNER" AT WOODSTOCK (1993)

555   During the sixties, my father was the perfect hippie, since all the
hippies were trying to be Indians. Because of that, how could anyone
recognize that my father was trying to make a social statement?

556   But there is evidence, a photograph of my father demonstrating in
Spokane, Washington, during the Vietnam war. The photograph made it
onto the wire service and was reprinted in newspapers throughout the
country. In fact, it was on the cover of *Time.*

557   In the photograph, my father is dressed in bell-bottoms and flowered
shirt, his hair in braids, with red peace symbols splashed across his face
like war paint. In his hands my father holds a rifle above his head,
captured in that moment just before he proceeded to beat the shit out of
the National Guard private lying prone on the ground. A fellow demonstrator holds a sign that is just barely visible over my father's left shoulder. It reads MAKE LOVE NOT WAR.

558   The photographer won a Pulitzer Prize, and editors across the country had a lot of fun creating captions and headlines. I've read many of
them collected in my father's scrapbook, and my favorite was run in the
Seattle Times. The caption under the photograph read DEMONSTRATOR
GOES TO WAR FOR PEACE. The editors capitalized on my father's Native
American identity with other headlines like ONE WARRIOR AGAINST WAR
and PEACEFUL GATHERING TURNS INTO NATIVE UPRISING.

559   Anyway, my father was arrested, charged with attempted murder,
which was reduced to assault with a deadly weapon. It was a high-
profile case so my father was used as an example. Convicted and sen-
tenced quickly, he spent two years in Walla Walla State Penitentiary.
Although his prison sentence effectively kept him out of the war, my
father went through a different kind of war behind bars.

560   "There was Indian gangs and white gangs and black gangs and Mexican gangs," he told me once. "And there was somebody new killed every day. We'd hear about somebody getting it in the shower or wherever and the word would go down the line. Just one word. Just the color of his skin. Red, white, black, or brown. Then we'd chalk it up on the mental scoreboard and wait for the next broadcast."

561   My father made it through all that, never got into any serious trouble, somehow avoided rape, and got out of prison just in time to hitchhike to Woodstock to watch Jimi Hendrix play "The Star-Spangled Banner."

562   "After all the shit I'd been through," my father said, "I figured Jimi must have known I was there in the crowd to play something like that. It was exactly how I felt."

563   Twenty years later, my father played his Jimi Hendrix tape until it wore down. Over and over, the house filled with the rockets' red glare and the bombs bursting in air. He'd sit by the stereo with a cooler of beer beside him and cry, laugh, call me over and hold me tight in his arms, his bad breath and body odor covering me like a blanket.

564   Jimi Hendrix and my father became drinking buddies. Jimi Hendrix waited for my father to come home after a long night of drinking. Here's how the ceremony worked:

1. I would lie awake all night and listen for the sounds of my father's pickup.
2. When I heard my father's pickup, I would run upstairs and throw Jimi's tape into the stereo.
3. Jimi would bend his guitar into the first note of "The Star-Spangled Banner" just as my father walked inside.
4. My father would weep, attempt to hum along with Jimi, and then pass out with his head on the kitchen table.
5. I would fall asleep under the table with my head near my father's feet.
6. We'd dream together until the sun came up.

565   The days after, my father would feel so guilty that he would tell me stories as a means of apology.

566   "I met your mother at a party in Spokane," my father told me once. "We were the only two Indians at the party. Maybe the only two Indians in the whole town. I thought she was so beautiful. I figured she was the kind of woman who could make buffalo walk on up to her and give up their lives. She wouldn't have needed to hunt. Every time we went walking, birds would follow us around. Hell, tumbleweeds would follow us around."

567   Somehow my father's memories of my mother grew more beautiful as their relationship became more hostile. By the time the divorce was final, my mother was quite possibly the most beautiful woman who ever lived.

568   "Your father was always half crazy," my mother told me more than once. "And the other half was on medication."

569   But she loved him, too, with a ferocity that eventually forced her to leave him. They fought each other with the kind of graceful anger that

only love can create. Still, their love was passionate, unpredictable, and selfish. My mother and father would get drunk and leave parties abruptly to go home and make love.

570   "Don't tell your father I told you this," my mother said. "But there must have been a hundred times he passed out on top of me. We'd be right in the middle of it, he'd say *I love you*, his eyes would roll backwards, and then out went his lights. It sounds strange, I know, but those were good times."

571   I was conceived during one of those drunken nights, half of me formed by my father's whiskey sperm, the other half formed by my mother's vodka egg. I was born a goofy reservation mixed drink, and my father needed me just as much as he needed every other kind of drink.

572   One night my father and I were driving home in a near-blizzard after a basketball game, listening to the radio. We didn't talk much. One, because my father didn't talk much when he was sober, and two, because Indians don't need to talk to communicate.

573   "Hello out there, folks, this is Big Bill Baggins, with the late-night classics show on KROC, 97.2 on your FM dial. We have a request from Betty in Tekoa. She wants to hear Jimi Hendrix's version of 'The Star-Spangled Banner' recorded live at Woodstock."

574   My father smiled, turned the volume up, and we rode down the highway while Jimi led the way like a snowplow. Until that night, I'd always been neutral about Jimi Hendrix. But, in that near-blizzard with my father at the wheel, with the nervous silence caused by the dangerous roads and Jimi's guitar, there seemed to be more to all that music. The reverberation came to mean something, took form and function.

575   That song made me want to learn to play guitar, not because I wanted to be Jimi Hendrix and not because I thought I'd ever play for anyone. I just wanted to touch the strings, to hold the guitar tight against my body, invent a chord, and come closer to what Jimi knew, to what my father knew.

576   "You know," I said to my father after the song was over, "my generation of Indian boys ain't ever had no real war to fight. The first Indians had Custer to fight. My great-grandfather had World War I, my grandfather had World War II, you had Vietnam. All I have is video games."

577   My father laughed for a long time, nearly drove off the road into the snowy fields.

578   "Shit," he said. "I don't know why you're feeling sorry for yourself because you ain't had to fight a war. You're lucky. Shit, all you had was that damn Desert Storm. Should have called it Dessert Storm because it just made the fat cats get fatter. It was all sugar and whipped cream with a cherry on top. And besides that, you didn't even have to fight it. All you lost during that war was sleep because you stayed up all night watching CNN."

579   We kept driving through the snow, talked about war and peace.

580   "That's all there is," my father said. "War and peace with nothing in between. It's always one or the other."

581   "You sound like a book," I said.

582   "Yeah, well, that's how it is. Just because it's in a book doesn't make it not true. And besides, why the hell would you want to fight a war for this country? It's been trying to kill Indians since the very beginning. Indians are pretty much born soldiers anyway. Don't need a uniform to prove it."

583   Those were the kinds of conversations that Jimi Hendrix forced us to have. I guess every song has a special meaning for someone somewhere. Elvis Presley is still showing up in 7–11 stores across the country, even though he's been dead for years, so I figure music just might be the most important thing there is. Music turned my father into a reservation philosopher. Music had powerful medicine.

584   "I remember the first time your mother and I danced," my father told me once. "We were in this cowboy bar. We were the only real cowboys there despite the fact that we're Indians. We danced to a Hank Williams song. Danced to that real sad one, you know. 'I'm So Lonesome I Could Cry.' Except your mother and I weren't lonesome or crying. We just shuffled along and fell right goddamn down into love."

585   "Hank Williams and Jimi Hendrix don't have much in common," I said.

586   "Hell, yes, they do. They knew all about broken hearts," my father said.

587   "You sound like a bad movie."

588   "Yeah, well, that's how it is. You kids today don't know shit about romance. Don't know shit about music either. Especially you Indian kids. You all have been spoiled by those drums. Been hearing them beat so long, you think that's all you need. Hell, son, even an Indian needs a piano or guitar or saxophone now and again."

589   My father played in a band in high school. He was the drummer. I guess he'd burned out on those. Now, he was like the universal defender of the guitar.

590   "I remember when your father would haul that old guitar out and play me songs," my mother said. "He couldn't play all that well but he tried. You could see him thinking about what chord he was going to play next. His eyes got all squeezed up and his face turned all red. He kind of looked that way when he kissed me, too. But don't tell him I said that."

591   Some nights I lay awake and listened to my parents' lovemaking. I know white people keep it quiet, pretend they don't ever make love. My white friends tell me they can't even imagine their own parents getting it on. I know exactly what it sounds like when my parents are touching each other. It makes up for knowing exactly what they sound like when they're fighting. Plus and minus. Add and subtract. It comes out just about even.

592   Some nights I would fall asleep to the sounds of my parents' lovemaking. I would dream Jimi Hendrix. I could see my father standing in the front row in the dark at Woodstock as Jimi Hendrix played "The Star-Spangled Banner." My mother was at home with me, both of us waiting for my father to find his way back home to the reservation. It's amazing to realize I was alive, breathing and wetting my bed, when Jimi was alive and breaking guitars.

593   I dreamed my father dancing with all these skinny hippie women, smoking a few joints, dropping acid, laughing when the rain fell. And it did rain there. I've seen actual news footage. I've seen the documentaries. It rained. People had to share food. People got sick. People got married. People cried all kinds of tears.

594   But as much as I dream about it, I don't have any clue about what it meant for my father to be the only Indian who saw Jimi Hendrix play at Woodstock. And maybe he wasn't the only Indian there. Most likely there were hundreds but my father thought he was the only one. He told me that a million times when he was drunk and a couple hundred times when he was sober.

595   "I was there," he said. "You got to remember this was near the end and there weren't as many people as before. Not nearly as many. But I waited it out. I waited for Jimi."

596   A few years back, my father packed up the family and the three of us drove to Seattle to visit Jimi Hendrix's grave. We had our photograph taken lying down next to the grave. There isn't a gravestone there. Just one of those flat markers.

597   Jimi was twenty-eight when he died. That's younger than Jesus Christ when he died. Younger than my father as we stood over the grave.

598   "Only the good die young," my father said.

599   "No," my mother said. "Only the crazy people choke to death on their own vomit."

590   "Why you talking about my hero that way?" my father asked.

591   "Shit," my mother said. "Old Jesse WildShoe choked to death on his own vomit and he ain't anybody's hero."

592   I stood back and watched my parents argue. I was used to these battles. When an Indian marriage starts to fall apart, it's even more destructive and painful than usual. A hundred years ago, an Indian marriage was broken easily. The woman or man just packed up all their possessions and left the tipi. There were no arguments, no discussions. Now, Indians fight their way to the end, holding onto the last good thing, because our whole lives have to do with survival.

593   After a while, after too much fighting and too many angry words had been exchanged, my father went out and bought a motorcycle. A big bike. He left the house often to ride that thing for hours, sometimes for days. He even strapped an old cassette player to the gas tank so he could listen to music. With that bike, he learned something new about running away. He stopped talking as much, stopped drinking as much. He didn't do much of anything except ride that bike and listen to music.

594   Then one night my father wrecked his bike on Devil's Gap Road and ended up in the hospital for two months. He broke both his legs, cracked his ribs, and punctured a lung. He also lacerated his kidney. The doctors said he could have died easily. In fact, they were surprised he made it through surgery, let alone survived those first few hours when he lay on the road, bleeding. But I wasn't surprised. That's how my father was.

595   And even though my mother didn't want to be married to him anymore and his wreck didn't change her mind about that, she still came to see him every day. She sang Indian tunes under her breath, in time with the hum of the machines hooked into my father. Although my father could barely move, he tapped his finger in rhythm.

596   When he had the strength to finally sit up and talk, hold conversations, and tell stories, he called for me.

597   "Victor," he said. "Stick with four wheels."

598   After he began to recover, my mother stopped visiting as often. She helped him through the worst, though. When he didn't need her anymore, she went back to the life she had created. She traveled to powwows, started to dance again. She was a champion traditional dancer when she was younger.

599   "I remember your mother when she was the best traditional dancer in the world," my father said. "Everyone wanted to call her sweetheart. But she only danced for me. That's how it was. She told me that every other step was just for me."

600   "But that's only half of the dance," I said.

601   "Yeah," my father said. "She was keeping the rest for herself. Nobody can give everything away. It ain't healthy."

602   "You know," I said, "sometimes you sound like you ain't even real."

603   "What's real? I ain't interested in what's real. I'm interested in how things should be."

604   My father's mind always worked that way. If you don't like the things you remember, then all you have to do is change the memories. Instead of remembering the bad things, remember what happened immediately before. That's what I learned from my father. For me, I remember how good the first drink of that Diet Pepsi tasted instead of how my mouth felt when I swallowed a wasp with the second drink.

605   Because of all that, my father always remembered the second before my mother left him for good and took me with her. No. I remembered the second before my father left my mother and me. No. My mother remembered the second before my father left her to finish raising me all by herself.

606   But however memory actually worked, it was my father who climbed on his motorcycle, waved to me as I stood in the window, and rode away. He lived in Seattle, San Francisco, Los Angeles, before he finally ended up in Phoenix. For a while, I got postcards nearly every week. Then it was once a month. Then it was on Christmas and my birthday.

607   On a reservation, Indian men who abandon their children are treated worse than white fathers who do the same thing. It's because white men have been doing that forever and Indian men have just learned how. That's how assimilation can work.

608   My mother did her best to explain it all to me, although I understood most of what happened.

609   "Was it because of Jimi Hendrix?" I asked her.

610   "Part of it, yeah," she said. "This might be the only marriage broken up by a dead guitar player."

611   "There's a first time for everything, enit?"

612   "I guess. Your father just likes being alone more than he likes being with other people. Even me and you."

613   Sometimes I caught my mother digging through old photo albums or staring at the wall or out the window. She'd get that look on her face that I knew meant she missed my father. Not enough to want him back. She missed him just enough for it to hurt.

614   On those nights I missed him most I listened to music. Not always Jimi Hendrix. Usually I listened to the blues. Robert Johnson mostly. The first time I heard Robert Johnson sing I knew he understood what it meant to be Indian on the edge of the twenty-first century, even if he was black at the beginning of the twentieth. That must have been how my father felt when he heard Jimi Hendrix. When he stood there in the rain at Woodstock.

615   Then on the night I missed my father most, when I lay in bed and cried, with that photograph of him beating that National Guard private in my hands, I imagined his motorcycle pulling up outside. I knew I was dreaming it all but I let it be real for a moment.

616   "Victor," my father yelled. "Let's go for a ride."

617   "I'll be right down. I need to get my coat on."

618   I rushed around the house, pulled my shoes and socks on, struggled into my coat, and ran outside to find an empty driveway. It was so quiet, a reservation kind of quiet, where you can hear somebody drinking whiskey on the rocks three miles away. I stood on the porch and waited until my mother came outside.

619   "Come on back inside," she said. "It's cold."

620   "No," I said. "I know he's coming back tonight."

621   My mother didn't say anything. She just wrapped me in her favorite quilt and went back to sleep. I stood on the porch all night long and imagined I heard motorcycles and guitars, until the sun rose so bright that I knew it was time to go back inside to my mother. She made breakfast for both of us and we ate until we were full.

Questions for Engagement, Response, and Analysis

1. Explain the statement that "Music turned my father into a reservation philosopher." How does the narrator feel about his father? Why does Jimi Hendrix's version of "The Star-Spangled Banner" appeal to the narrator and his father?

2. What does the father mean when he says, "War and peace with nothing in between. It's always one or the other"?

3. Explain the narrator's claim that he is "a goofy reservation mixed drink."

4. In your Reader's Journal, write your definition of what it means to be a hippie.

Crafting Arguments

1. In an essay, analyze the narrator's claim that "music just might be the most important thing there is. . . . Music had powerful medicine."

P O E T R Y

William Butler Yeats (1865–1939)

*An Irish poet and playwright, William Butler Yeats is
regarded by many as one of the greatest twentieth-century
poets. Yeats' first poems were published in 1885. Active in
the Irish National Theatre, he became a leader in the Irish
literary revival. His* Collected Poems *(1933), spanning fifty
years, shows his extraordinary range and his growth as a
poet. Much of Yeats's poetry is powerfully and elaborately
symbolic, referring to his vision of a spiritual world and his
cyclical theory of history.*

A PRAYER FOR MY DAUGHTER   (1919)

Once more the storm is howling, and half hid
Under this cradle-hood and coverlid
My child sleeps on. There is no obstacle
But Gregory's Wood and one bare hill
5   Whereby the haystack and roof-levelling wind,
Bred on the Atlantic, can be stayed;
And for an hour I have walked and prayed
Because of the great gloom that is in my mind.

I have walked and prayed for this young child an hour,
10   And heard the sea-wind scream upon the tower,
And under the arches of the bridge, and scream
In the elms above the flooded stream;
Imagining in excited reverie
That the future years had come
15   Dancing to a frenzied drum
Out of the murderous innocence of the sea.

May she be granted beauty, and yet not
Beauty to make a stranger's eye distraught,
Or hers before a looking-glass; for such,
20   Being made beautiful overmuch,
Consider beauty a sufficient end,
Lose natural kindness, and maybe
The heart-revealing intimacy
That chooses right, and never find a friend.

25   Helen, being chosen, found life flat and dull,
And later had much trouble from a fool;
While that great Queen that rose out of the spray,
Being fatherless, could have her way,

Yet chose a bandy-leggèd smith for man.
30   It's certain that fine women eat
A crazy salad with their meat
Whereby the Horn of Plenty is undone.

In courtesy I'd have her chiefly learned;
Hearts are not had as a gift, but hearts are earned
35   By those that are not entirely beautiful.
Yet many, that have played the fool
For beauty's very self, has charm made wise;
And many a poor man that has roved,
Loved and thought himself beloved,
40   From a glad kindness cannot take his eyes.

May she become a flourishing hidden tree,
That all her thoughts may like the linnet be,
And have no business but dispensing round
Their magnanimities of sound;
45   Nor but in merriment begin a chase,
Nor but in merriment a quarrel.
Oh, may she live like some green laurel
Rooted in one dear perpetual place.

My mind, because the minds that I have loved,
50   The sort of beauty that I have approved,
Prosper but little, has dried up of late,
Yet knows that to be choked with hate
May well be of all evil chances chief.
If there's no hatred in a mind
55   Assault and battery of the wind
Can never tear the linnet from the leaf.

An intellectual hatred is the worst,
So let her think opinions are accursed.
Have I not seen the loveliest woman born
60   Out of the mouth of Plenty's horn,
Because of her opinionated mind
Barter that horn and every good
By quiet natures understood
For an old bellows full of angry wind?

65   Considering that, all hatred driven hence,
The soul recovers radical innocence
And learns at last that it is self-delighting,
Self-appeasing, self-affrighting,
And that its own sweet will is heaven's will,
70   She can, though every face should scowl

And every windy quarter howl
Or every bellows burst, be happy still.

And may her bridegroom bring her to a house
Where all's accustomed, ceremonious;
75   For arrogance and hatred are the wares
Peddled in the thoroughfares.
How but in custom and in ceremony
Are innocence and beauty born?
Ceremony's a name for the rich horn,
80   And custom for the spreading laurel tree.

Questions for Engagement, Response, and Analysis

1. What is the **situation** in the poem?
2. Why does the speaker pray that his daughter not be "beautiful overmuch"?
3. Why does Yeats declare "opinions accursed"?
4. What do the last two lines mean?

Crafting Arguments

1. Write an essay that offers your interpretation of Yeats' "A Prayer for My Daughter."
2. Throughout the poem Yeats uses the images of the Horn of Plenty and "a flourishing hidden" laurel tree, and he returns to these in the last two lines of the poem. In an essay, explain what these images suggest that the narrator wants for his daughter as a result of his own experiences.

Theodore Roethke (1908–1963)

Theodore Roethke was both an acclaimed poet and an exuberant and popular professor of poetry. Partly because he threw himself wholeheartedly into both professions, he often suffered from exhaustion and mental breakdowns. Roethke's relationship with his own father, a German-American who combined authoritarianism with sensitivity, seems to have been ambivalent. His father died when Roethke was fourteen. Roethke received many awards during his long literary career, including two Guggenheim Fellowships, two Ford Foundation Grants, and a Pulitzer Prize in poetry in 1954 for The Waking: Poems 1933–53.

MY PAPA'S WALTZ   (1942)

The whiskey on your breath
Could make a small boy dizzy;
But I hung on like death:
Such waltzing was not easy.

5   We romped until the pans
Slid from the kitchen shelf;
My mother's countenance
Could not unfrown itself.

The hand that held my wrist
10 Was battered on one knuckle;
At every step you missed
My right ear scraped a buckle.

You beat time on my head
With a palm caked hard by dirt,
15 Then waltzed me off to bed
Still clinging to your shirt.

Questions for Engagement, Response, and Analysis

1. What details does Roethke use to describe the father? What do these details suggest?

2. To what does the word *waltz* in the title refer? As he is "waltzed" to bed, the boy is "still clinging" to his father. What does this reaction indicate about the boy's feelings for his father?

3. Roethke uses the three-beat line, which reflects the three beats of the waltz. Does the total effect of the poem reflect the smooth gliding motion of the dance? Why or why not?

Crafting Arguments

1. Use specific details from this poem to argue that this family is functional or dysfunctional.

2. Write an essay, using this poem and Giovanni's "Nikki-Rosa," to analyze why memories that may seem negative to some adults are not so to children.

Gwendolyn Brooks (1917–2001)

Born in Topeka, Kansas, Gwendolyn Brooks began writing while still a teenager. In high school, she met Langston Hughes, who encouraged her to write and follow her literary ambitions. Brooks is the author of more than twenty books of poetry, including A Street in Bronzeville *(1945);* The

Bean Eaters *(1960); and* Children Coming Home *(1991).*
She also wrote other works such as the novel Maud Martha
(1953) and a book of essays, Young Poet's Primer *(1981). In*
1950, Brooks became the first African American to win the
Pulitzer Prize in literature, for Annie Allen. *In 1968, she*
became the poet laureate for the state of Illinois, and from
1985 to 1986 she was Consultant in Poetry for the Library
of Congress.

THE MOTHER   (1945)

Abortions will not let you forget.
You remember the children you got that you did not get,
The damp small pulps with a little or with no hair,
The singers and workers that never handled the air.
5   You will never neglect or beat
Them, or silence or buy with a sweet.
You will never wind up the sucking-thumb
Or scuttle off ghosts that come.
You will never leave them, controlling your luscious sigh,
10   Return for a snack of them, with gobbling mother-eye.

I have heard in the voices of the wind the voices of my dim killed
children.
I have contracted. I have eased
My dim dears at the breasts they could never suck.
15   I have said, Sweets, if I sinned, if I seized
Your luck
And your lives from your unfinished reach,
If I stole your births and your names,
Your straight baby tears and your games,
20   Your stilted or lovely loves, your tumults, your marriages, aches,
and your deaths,
If I poisoned the beginnings of your breaths,
Believe that even in my deliberateness I was not deliberate.
Though why should I whine,
25   Whine that the crime was other than mine?—
Since anyhow you are dead.
Or rather, or instead,
You were never made.
But that too, I am afraid,
30   Is faulty: oh, what shall I say, how is the truth to be said?
You were born, you had body, you died.
It is just that you never giggled or planned or cried.

Believe me, I loved you all.
Believe me, I knew you, though faintly, and I loved, I loved you
35   All.

Questions for Engagement, Response, and Analysis

1. Who is the narrator in this poem?
2. Why does the narrator call the aborted fetuses "killed children"? What is the impact of negative words such as "stole," "poisoned," "crime," and "dead"?
3. In your Reader's Journal, freewrite about your reaction to this poem. You may want to research the psychological effects of abortions on some women.

Crafting Arguments

1. If the narrator loved the children, why did she abort them? Explain your claim using evidence from the poem.

Sylvia Plath (1932–1963)

Born in 1932 in Boston, Massachusetts, Sylvia Plath showed an aptitude for writing and a tremendous drive to excel even in childhood. In 1956 she married English poet Ted Hughes. Plath's poetry demonstrates a passionate engagement with language and a rare gift for image and metaphor; it also displays an impressive array of subjects, voices, and tones. Although her poems about death are her most frequently anthologized works, she also wrote books for children and splendid poems about motherhood. Though much of her poetry is written in free verse, she also handles rhyme and verse forms adeptly. A number of her poems, such as "Daddy," address her relationship with her father, Otto Plath, who died when she was eight years old. In her poetry, she often draws on history and myth to explore her obsessive love for her father and her unresolved feelings about his early death. Whatever her subject, her poems are invariably well-crafted, marked by a playful, wide-ranging imagination and a tireless love of language. In The Colossus *(1962) and* Crossing the Water *(eventually published in 1971), she was still developing her own distinctive poetic style; but in* Ariel, *published posthumously in 1966, she found her own voice. Sadly, most of the recognition she received for her writing came after her death. Her autobiographical novel,* The Bell Jar, *was published shortly before her death, but* Ariel *did not appear until well after Plath had killed herself in 1963. Approximately twenty years after her death, her* Collected Poems *(1981), compiled and edited by Ted Hughes, was awarded the Pulitzer Prize.*

DADDY   (1963)

You do not do, you do not do
Any more, black shoe
In which I have lived like a foot
For thirty years, poor and white,
5   Barely daring to breathe or Achoo.

Daddy, I have had to kill you.
You died before I had time—
Marble-heavy, a bag full of God,
Ghastly statue with one grey toe
10   Big as a Frisco seal

And a head in the freakish Atlantic
Where it pours bean green over blue
In the waters off beautiful Nauset.
I used to pray to recover you.
15   Ach, du.

In the German tongue, in the Polish town
Scraped flat by the roller
Of wars, wars, wars.
But the name of the town is common.
20   My Polack friend

Says there are a dozen or two.
So I never could tell where you
Put your foot, your root,
I never could talk to you.
25   The tongue stuck in my jaw.

It stuck in a barb wire snare.
Ich, ich, ich, ich,
I could hardly speak.
I thought every German was you.
30   And the language obscene

An engine, an engine
Chuffing me off like a Jew.
A Jew to Dachau, Auschwitz, Belsen.
I began to talk like a Jew.
35   I think I may well be a Jew.

The snows of the Tyrol, the clear beer of Vienna
Are not very pure or true.
With my gypsy ancestress and my weird luck
And my Taroc pack and my Taroc pack
40   I may be a bit of a Jew.

I have always been scared of *you*,
With your Luftwaffe, your gobbledygoo.
And your neat moustache
And your Aryan eye, bright blue
45   Panzer-man, panzer-man, O You—

Not God but a swastika
So black no sky could squeak through.
Every woman adores a Fascist,
The boot in the face, the brute
50   Brute heart of a brute like you.

You stand at the blackboard, daddy,
In the picture I have of you,
A cleft in your chin instead of your foot
But no less a devil for that, no not
55   Any less the black man who

Bit my pretty red heart in two.
I was ten when they buried you.
At twenty I tried to die
And get back, back, back to you.
60   I thought even the bones would do.

But they pulled me out of the sack.
And they stuck me together with glue.
And then I knew what to do.
I made a model of you,
65   A man in black with a Meinkampf look

And a love of the rack and the screw.
And I said I do, I do.
So daddy, I'm finally through.
The black telephone's off at the root,
70   The voices just can't worm through.

If I've killed one man, I've killed two—
The vampire who said he was you
And drank my blood for a year,
Seven years, if you want to know.
75   Daddy, you can lie back now.

There's a stake in your fat black heart
And the villagers never liked you.
They are dancing and stamping on you.
They always *knew* it was you.
80   Daddy, daddy, you bastard, I'm through.

Questions for Engagement, Response, and Analysis

1. What role do rhyme and assonance play in the overall meaning of the poem?
2. What is the significance of the heart imagery in the poem?
3. In "Daddy," the speaker describes her own suffering in terms of the Jews' suffering during the Holocaust. Other poets, some of them Plath's contemporaries, have objected to this comparison, for a variety of reasons. What valid objections might they have?
4. Examine Plath's use of surprising or shocking allusions and their effect on tone and meaning in "Daddy."

Crafting Arguments

1. Research the allusions to either mythology or history in this poem, and write an essay showing how these allusions add to the depth of meaning and universality of the poem.
2. Contrast Plath's response to loss in "Daddy" with that revealed in Lahiri's "A Temporary Matter" or Mukherjee's "The Management of Grief."
3. In an essay, discuss the nature of the speaker's relationship to her father.

Luis Omar Salinas (b. 1938)

Salinas, an influential leader of Chicano poets, was born in Robstown, Texas, but moved with his family to Monterrey, Mexico. After his mother's death, the family moved back to Robstown. Salinas later lived in several towns in California, where his exposure to the majority white culture and the lack of overt racism such as he had experienced in Texas influenced his feelings of loneliness and alienation, themes often examined in his poems. Salinas has written several volumes of poetry, including his first, Crazy Gipsy *(1970), and the most recent,* Elegy for Desire *(2005). Salinas' problems with mental illness probably influenced his perceptivity and his sensitivity in his portrayal of character.*

MY FATHER IS A SIMPLE MAN   (1987)

I walk to town with my father
to buy a newspaper. He walks slower
than I do so I must slow up.
The street is filled with children.
5 We argue about the price
of pomegranates, I convince
him it is the fruit of scholars.

He has taken me on this journey
and it's been lifelong.
10   He's sure I'll be healthy
so long as I eat more oranges,
and tells me the orange
has seeds and so is perpetual;
and we too will come back
15   like the orange trees.
I ask him what he thinks
about death and he says
he will gladly face it when
it comes but won't jump
20   out in front of a car.
I'd gladly give my life
for this man with a sixth
grade education, whose kindness
and patience are true . . .
25   The truth of it is, he's the scholar,
and when the bitter-hard reality
comes at me like a punishing
evil stranger, I can always
remember that here was a man
30   who was a worker and provider,
who learned the simple facts
in life and lived by them,

who held no pretense.
And when he leaves without
35   benefit of fanfare or applause
I shall have learned what little
there is about greatness.

Questions for Engagement, Response, and Analysis

1. What does the argument over pomegranates versus oranges tell about the character of the father and son?
2. What is the lifelong journey on which the father has taken the narrator? What is its destination?
3. List the father's character traits as shown in this short poem.

Crafting Arguments

1. Using evidence from the poem to support your claims, write an essay describing the relationship between the narrator and his father.
2. Write an essay comparing Salinas' father with Whitelock's father or with Li-Young Lee's father.

Nikki Giovanni (b. 1943)

Yolande Cornelia Giovanni Jr. was born in Knoxville, Tennessee. She received her B.A. from Fisk University in 1967 and attended both the University of Pennsylvania and Columbia University. Giovanni has published many books of poetry, beginning with Black Feeling Black Talk *(1968) and* Spin a Soft Black Song: Poems for Children *(1971).* Grand Mothers: A Multicultural Anthology of Poems, Reminiscences, and Short Stories about the Keepers of Our Traditions *was published in 1994, and in 2003 Giovanni published* The Collected Poetry of Nikki Giovanni. *Known as a militant African American poet, Giovanni also writes very personal poetry. Since 1987 Giovanni has been a University Distinguished Professor of English at Virginia Tech.*

NIKKI-ROSA (1968)

childhood remembrances are always a drag
if you're Black
you always remember things like living in Woodlawn
with no inside toilet
5   and if you become famous or something
they never talk about how happy you were to have your mother
all to yourself and
how good the water felt when you got your bath from one of those
big tubs that folk in chicago barbecue in
10   and somehow when you talk about home
it never gets across how much you
understood their feelings
as the whole family attended meetings about Hollydale
and even though you remember
15   your biographers never understand
your father's pain as he sells his stock
and another dream goes
and though you're poor it isn't poverty that
concerns you
20   and though they fought a lot
it isn't your father's drinking that makes any difference
but only that everybody is together and you
and your sister have happy birthdays and very good christmasses
and I really hope no white person ever has cause to write about me
25   because they never understand Black love is Black wealth and they'll
probably talk about my hard childhood and never understand that
all the while I was quite happy

Questions for Engagement, Response, and Analysis

1. Who is the narrator in this poem?
2. Analyze the structure and sound of this poem. Note also its approach to punctuation. What are the effects of the poet's choices on the meaning of the poem?
3. What stereotype does Giovanni attack in this poem? Why does Giovanni not want a white biographer?

Crafting Arguments

1. What attitude does the poem take toward poverty? What matters most to Giovanni about her childhood?
2. Using evidence from the poem, identify the theme and show how the speaker's attitude is reflected in the poem.

Li-Young Lee (b. 1957)

Li-Young Lee was born of Chinese parents in Jakarta, Indonesia. The family moved to the United States in 1964. Lee has written three highly regarded books of poems, including Rose *(1986), which contains "The Gift";* City in Which I Love You, *which won the Lamont Poetry Award of the Academy of American Poets for 1990; and* Book of My Nights *(2001). In 1995, Lee published a memoir,* The Winged Seed: A Remembrance. Breaking the Alabaster Jar: Conversations with Li-Young Lee *(2006) is a collection of interviews. Lee has been strongly influenced by his father, a physician, philosopher, writer, and minister who spent a year as a political prisoner in an Indonesian prison.*

THE GIFT   (1986)

To pull the metal splinter from my palm
my father recited a story in a low voice.
I watched his lovely face and not the blade.
Before the story ended he'd removed
5   the iron sliver I thought I'd die from.
I can't remember the tale
but hear his voice still, a well
of dark water, a prayer.
And I recall his hands,
10   two measures of tenderness
he laid against my face,
the flames of discipline
he raised above my head.
Had you entered that afternoon

15   you would have thought you saw a man
     planting something in a boy's palm,
     a silver tear, a tiny flame.
     Had you followed that boy
     you would have arrived here,
20   where I bend over my wife's right hand.
     Look how I shave her thumbnail down
     so carefully she feels no pain.
     Watch as I lift the splinter out.
     I was seven when my father
25   took my hand like this,
     and I did not hold that shard
     between my fingers and think,
     Metal that will bury me,
     christen it Little Assassin,
30   Ore Going Deep for My Heart.
     And I did not lift up my wound and cry,
     Death visited here!
     I did what a child does
     when he's given something to keep.
35   I kissed my father.

Questions for Engagement, Response, and Analysis

1. What is the **situation** in this poem?
2. What techniques does Lee employ to tell this story?
3. Who is the narrator in this poem? Explain the gift that the narrator receives and gives to his family.
4. What is meant by *"Metal that will bury me,"* "Little Assassin," and *"Death visited here!"*? Why does the speaker use these words in this gentle poem?

Crafting Arguments

1. Using specific examples from the poem to support your claims, write an essay describing the relationship between the narrator and his father.
2. Write an essay interpreting the metaphors in this poem.

Edward J. Whitelock (b. 1966)

A poet, an essayist, and a professor, Edward J. Whitelock received his B.A. and M.A. degrees from Millersville University of Pennsylvania and his Ph.D. from Indiana University of Pennsylvania. He has taught at Gordon College since 1998. He is the co-author with David A. Janssen of

Apocalypse Jukebox: The End of the World in American
Popular Music, *a critical analysis of rock-and-roll music.
Whitelock's poems, mainly about the working class, have
been published in* Exquisite Corpse, Paper Street, *and*
Lifeboat: A Journal of Memoir. *In this autobiographical
poem, "Future Connected By," Whitelock contrasts the son's
pride in his father's work with the father's desire for a
different profession for his son.*

FUTURE CONNECTED BY (2002)

"A good handshake makes a good impression."
All of a Sunday afternoon.
My dad and a work buddy,
supposed to be fixing the basement toilet.
5   Drinking beer. Smoking cigarettes.
    "Make sure it's strong, certain."
Benny or Red or Smitty. Whoever he was.
He squeezed my hand til my knuckles rattled.
    "You don't want anyone to get the wrong impression."
10   These were *men.*
Every day balanced on girders a hundred feet up.
Eating lunch, feet dangling over the Delaware River.
    "You lose your grip, last thing you'll lose."
    "Yup, your butt becomes a suction cup."
15   Eleven hour days. Dinner. A couple beers with tv.
    But weekends were for hanging around.

    Another time.
A snow day home from school day.
My father came home early.
20   No blood in his face.
Late morning, opened a beer in his chair.
    "They sent me home.
    I slipped off a girder, but I caught myself."
    Feet dangling over the Delaware River.
25   "It's okay."
We watched cartoons all day. Ate dinner.
He went to bed early.
And back the next day.

I was an every weekend tagalong,
30   under foot and into everything.
Once, when one of his buddies asked,
    "So, what're you gonna be when you grow up?"
I had been waiting for the question,
and looked longingly up to my father.
35   "I'm going to be a welder, just like my dad."

I waited for the proud pat on the head,
but got instead that first, finalizing denial.
 "No yer not. Yer too smart for that.
 Yer gonna go'ta college and getta good job.
40 Gonna make it with your head, not your back."
The words spilled like stone from a gravel truck,
the raw materials of a wall I knew would be too high to see over.
Dad's buddy nodded his approval, so I just said "Okay."
I'd be the good son. I'd leave him behind.

Questions for Engagement, Response, and Analysis

1. Analyze Whitelock's structure and style. How do poetic techniques allow him to tell this story so vividly?

2. In what ways do the "*men*" affect the speaker's definition of masculinity?

3. How do the structure of the poem and the diction help to contrast the father's and the son's lives?

4. What does the title ask or imply?

Crafting Arguments

1. Write an essay analyzing the relationship between the father and son in this poem and explaining why although the son wants to be "'just like [his] dad,'" the dad doesn't want the son to be like him. What does the last line mean?

2. Using the poem as the basis for an argumentative essay, persuade your audience that the son is right to admire his father and want to enter his profession or that his father is right to want more for his son.

Casebook
on August Wilson

This casebook on August Wilson's play *Fences* provides a glimpse into the joys and sorrows of a complex family at a time in United States history when opportunities for black people were limited. After you have carefully read the play and formed your own ideas about elements such as the themes, characters, and symbols, you can use the essays about *Fences* to expand your knowledge of the writer and the play. The essays included here also allow you to write a brief documented essay using the play as your primary source and the essays as secondary sources.

August Wilson (1945–2005)

August Wilson grew up in a Pittsburgh, Pennsylvania, ghetto probably much like the one in which Fences *is set. Able to read by age four, Wilson dropped out of high school at age fifteen, bought a typewriter, and began writing poetry. Still searching for his distinctive voice as poet and dramatist, Wilson in 1967 founded the Black Horizons Theater Company. Wilson chose to write a ten-play cycle about the experiences of Black Americans in the twentieth century. Besides his Pulitzer Prize–winning* Fences, *first produced by the Yale Repertory Theater in 1985, Wilson's plays include* Ma Rainey's Black Bottom *(1984);* Joe Turner's Come and Gone *(1986), which was voted Broadway play of the 1987–1988 season by the New York Drama Critics' Circle;* The Piano Lesson *(1986), which in 1990 won Wilson a second Pulitzer Prize;* Two Trains Running *(1990);* Seven Guitars *(1995); and* King Hedley II *(2001). Wilson completed the last play in the cycle,* Radio Golf, *in 2005.*

FENCES   (1985)

List of Characters

TROY MAXSON
JIM BONO:	Troy's friend
ROSE:	Troy's wife
LYONS:	Troy's oldest son by previous marriage
GABRIEL:	Troy's brother
CORY:	Troy and Rose's son
RAYNELL:	Troy's daughter

SETTING

The setting is the yard which fronts the only entrance to the Max-
son household, an ancient two-story brick house set back off a
small alley in a big-city neighborhood. The entrance to the house is
gained by two or three steps leading to a wooden porch badly in
need of paint.

A relatively recent addition to the house and running its full
width, the porch lacks congruence. It is a sturdy porch with a flat
roof. One or two chairs of dubious value sit at one end where the
kitchen window opens onto the porch. An old-fashioned icebox
stands silent guard at the opposite end.

The yard is a small dirt yard, partially fenced, except for the
last scene, with a wooden sawhorse, a pile of lumber, and other
fencebuilding equipment set off to the side. Opposite is a tree from
which hangs a ball made of rags.

A baseball bat leans against the tree. Two oil drums serve as
garbage receptacles and sit near the house at right to complete the
setting.

THE PLAY

Near the turn of the century, the destitute of Europe sprang on the
city with tenacious claws and an honest and solid dream. The city
devoured them. They swelled its belly until it burst into a thousand
furnaces and sewing machines, a thousand butcher shops and bak-
ers' ovens, a thousand churches and hospitals and funeral parlors
and moneylenders. The city grew. It nourished itself and offered
each man a partnership limited only by his talent, his guile, and
his willingness and capacity for hard work. For the immigrants of
Europe, a dream dared and won true.

The descendants of African slaves were offered no such welcome
or participation. They came from places called the Carolinas and
the Virginias, Georgia, Alabama, Mississippi, and Tennessee.
They came strong, eager, searching. The city rejected them and
they fled and settled along the riverbanks and under bridges in

*shallow, ramshackle houses made of sticks and tarpaper. They
collected rags and wood. They sold the use of their muscles and their
bodies. They cleaned houses and washed clothes, they shined shoes,
and in quiet desperation and vengeful pride, they stole, and lived
in pursuit of their own dream so that they could breathe free,
finally, and stand to meet life with the force of dignity and whatever eloquence the heart could call upon.*

*By 1957, the hard-won victories of the European immigrants
had solidified the industrial might of America. War had been
confronted and won with new energies that used loyalty and patriotism as its fuel. Life was rich, full, and flourishing. The Milwaukee Braves won the World Series, and the hot winds of change that
would make the sixties a turbulent, racing, dangerous, and
provocative decade had not yet begun to blow full.*

ACT 1
SCENE 1

*It is 1957. Troy and Bono enter the yard, engaged in conversation.
Troy is fifty-three years old, a large man with thick, heavy hands; it
is this largeness that he strives to fill out and make an accommodation with. Together with his blackness, his largeness informs his
sensibilities and the choices he has made in his life.*

*Of the two men, Bono is obviously the follower. His commitment
to their friendship of thirty-odd years is rooted in his admiration
of Troy's honesty, capacity for hard work, and his strength, which
Bono seeks to emulate.*

*It is Friday night, payday, and the one night of the week the two
men engage in a ritual of talk and drink. Troy is usually the most
talkative and at times he can be crude and almost vulgar, though he
is capable of rising to profound heights of expression. The men carry
lunch buckets and wear or carry burlap aprons and are dressed in
clothes suitable to their jobs as garbage collectors.*

BONO: Troy, you ought to stop that lying!

TROY: I ain't lying! The nigger had a watermelon this big. *(He indicates
with his hands.)* Talking about . . . "What watermelon, Mr. Rand?"
I liked to fell out! "What watermelon, Mr. Rand?" . . . And it sitting
there big as life.

BONO: What did Mr. Rand say?

TROY: Ain't said nothing. Figure if the nigger too dumb to know he
carrying a watermelon, he wasn't gonna get much sense out of him.
Trying to hide that great big old watermelon under his coat. Afraid
to let the white man see him carry it home.

BONO: I'm like you . . . I ain't got no time for them kind of people.

TROY: Now what he look like getting mad cause he see the man from
the union talking to Mr. Rand?

BONO: He come to me talking about . . . "Maxson gonna get us fired."
I told him to get away from me with that. He walked away from me
calling you a trouble maker. What Mr. Rand say?

TROY: Ain't said nothing. He told me to go down the Commissioner's
office next Friday. They called me down there to see them.

BONO: Well, as long as you got your complaint filed, they can't fire you.
20   That's what one of them white fellows tell me.

TROY: I ain't worried about them firing me. They gonna fire me cause I
asked a question? That's all I did. I went to Mr. Rand and asked him,
"Why? Why you got the white mens driving and the colored lifting?"
Told him, "what's the matter, don't I count? You think only white
fellows got sense enough to drive a truck. That ain't no paper job!
Hell, anybody can drive a truck. How come you got all white driving
and the colored lifting?" He told me "take it to the union." Well, hell
that's what I done! Now they wanna come up with this pack of lies.

BONO: I told Brownie if the man come and ask him any questions . . .
30   just tell the truth! It ain't nothing but something they done trumped
up on you cause you filed a complaint on them.

TROY: Brownie don't understand nothing. All I want them to do is
change the job description. Give everybody a chance to drive the
truck. Brownie can't see that. He ain't got that much sense.

BONO: How you figure he be making out with that gal be up at Taylors'
all the time . . . that Alberta gal?

TROY: Same as you and me. Getting just as much as we is. Which is to
say nothing.

BONO: It is, huh? I figure you doing a little better than me . . . and I ain't
40   saying what I'm doing.

TROY: Aw, nigger, look here . . . I know you. If you had got anywhere
near that gal, twenty minutes later you be looking to tell somebody.
And the first one you gonna tell . . . that you gonna want to brag
to . . . is gonna be me.

BONO: I ain't saying that. I see where you be eyeing her.

TROY: I eye all the women. I don't miss nothing. Don't never let nobody
tell you Troy Maxson don't eye the women.

BONO: You been doing more than eyeing her. You done bought her a
drink or two.

50   TROY: Hell yeah, I bought her a drink! What that mean? I bought you
one, too. What that mean cause I buy her a drink? I'm just being
polite.

BONO: It's all right to buy her one drink. That's what you call being
polite. But when you wanna be buying two or three . . . that's what
you call eyeing her.

TROY: Look here, as long as you known me . . . you ever known me to
chase after women?

BONO: Hell yeah! Long as I done known you. You forgetting I knew you
when.

60 TROY: Naw, I'm talking about since I been married to Rose?

BONO: Oh, not since you been married to Rose. Now, that's the truth, there. I can say that.

TROY: All right then! Case closed.

BONO: I see you be walking up around Alberta's house. You supposed to be at Taylors' and you be walking up around there.

TROY: What you watching where I'm walking for? I ain't watching after you.

BONO: I seen you walking around there more than once.

TROY: Hell, you liable to see me walking anywhere! That don't mean
70   nothing cause you see me walking around there.

BONO: Where she come from anyway? She just kinda showed up one day.

TROY: Tallahassee. You can look at her and tell she one of them Florida gals. They got some big healthy women down there. Grow them right up out the ground. Got a little bit of Indian in her. Most of them niggers down in Florida got some Indian in them.

BONO: I don't know about that Indian part. But she damn sure big and healthy. Woman wear some big stockings. Got them great big old legs and hips as wide as the Mississippi River.

80 TROY: Legs don't mean nothing. You don't do nothing but push them out of the way. But them hips cushion the ride!

BONO: Troy, you ain't got no sense.

TROY: It's the truth! Like you riding on Goodyears!

(Rose enters from the house. She is ten years younger than Troy, her devotion to him stems from her recognition of the possibilities of her life without him: a succession of abusive men and their babies, a life of partying and running the streets, the Church, or aloneness with its attendant pain and frustration. She recognizes Troy's spirit as a fine and illuminating one and she either ignores or forgives his faults, only some of which she recognizes. Though she doesn't drink, her presence is an integral part of the Friday night rituals. She alternates between the porch and the kitchen, where supper preparations are under way.)

ROSE: What you all out here getting into?

TROY: What you worried about what we getting into for? This is men talk, woman.

ROSE: What I care what you all talking about? Bono, you gonna stay for supper?

BONO: No, I thank you, Rose. But Lucille say she cooking up a pot
90   of pigfeet.

TROY: Pigfeet! Hell, I'm going home with you! Might even stay the night if you got some pigfeet. You got something in there to top them pigfeet, Rose?

ROSE: I'm cooking up some chicken. I got some chicken and collardgreens.

TROY: Well, go on back in the house and let me and Bono finish what we was talking about. This is men talk. I got some talk for you later. You know what kind of talk I mean. You go on and powder it up.

ROSE: Troy Maxson, don't you start that now!

TROY *(puts his arm around her)*: Aw, woman . . . come here. Look
100　　here, Bono . . . when I met this woman . . . I got out that place, say, "Hitch up my pony, saddle up my mare . . . there's a woman out there for me somewhere. I looked here. Looked there. Saw Rose and latched on to her." I latched on to her and told her—I'm gonna tell you the truth—I told her, "Baby, I don't wanna marry, I just wanna be your man." Rose told me . . . tell him what you told me, Rose.

ROSE: I told him if he wasn't the marrying kind, then move out the way so the marrying kind could find me.

TROY: That's what she told me. "Nigger, you in my way. You blocking the view! Move out the way so I can find me a husband." I thought it
110　　over two or three days. Come back—

ROSE: Ain't no two or three days nothing. You was back the same night.

TROY: Come back, told her . . . "Okay, baby . . . but I'm gonna buy me a banty rooster and put him out there in the backyard . . . and when he sees a stranger come, he'll flap his wings and crow . . ." Look here, Bono, I could watch the front door by myself . . . it was that back door I was worried about.

ROSE: Troy, you ought not talk like that. Troy ain't doing nothing but telling a lie.

TROY: Only thing is . . . when we first got married . . . forget the rooster
120　　. . . we ain't had no yard!

BONO: I hear you tell it. Me and Lucille was staying down there on Logan Street. Had two rooms with the outhouse in the back. I ain't mind the outhouse none. But when the goddamn wind blow through there in the winter . . . that's what I'm talking about! To this day I wonder why in the hell I ever stayed down there for six long years. But see, I didn't know I could do no better. I thought only white folks had inside toilets and things.

ROSE: There's a lot of people don't know they can do no better than
130　　they doing now. That's just something you got to learn. A lot of folks still shop at Bella's.

TROY: Ain't nothing wrong with shopping at Bella's. She got fresh food.

ROSE: I ain't said nothing about if she got fresh food. I'm talking about what she charge. She charge ten cents more than the A&P.

TROY: The A&P ain't never done nothing for me. I spends my money where I'm treated right. I go down to Bella, say, "I need a loaf of bread, I'll pay you Friday." She give it to me. What sense that make when I got money to go and spend it somewhere else and ignore the person who done right by me? That ain't in the Bible.

140　　ROSE: We ain't talking about what's in the Bible. What sense it make to shop there when she overcharge?

TROY: You shop where you want to. I'll do my shopping where the people been good to me.

ROSE: Well, I don't think it's right for her to overcharge. That's all I was saying.

BONO: Look here . . . I got to get on. Lucille going be raising all kind of hell.

TROY: Where you going, nigger? We ain't finished this pint. Come here, finish this pint.

BONO: Well, hell, I am . . . if you ever turn the bottle loose.

TROY (*hands him the bottle*): The only thing I say about the A&P is I'm glad Cory got that job down there. Help him take care of his school clothes and things. Gabe done moved out and things getting tight around here. He got that job. . . . He can start to look out for himself.

ROSE: Cory done went and got recruited by a college football team.

TROY: I told that boy about that football stuff. The white man ain't gonna let him get nowhere with that football. I told him when he first come to me with it. Now you come telling me he done went and got more tied up in it. He ought to go and get recruited in how to fix cars or something where he can make a living.

ROSE: He ain't talking about making no living playing football. It's just something the boys in school do. They gonna send a recruiter by to talk to you. He'll tell you he ain't talking about making no living playing football. It's a honor to be recruited.

TROY: It ain't gonna get him nowhere. Bono'll tell you that.

BONO: If he be like you in the sports . . . he's gonna be all right. Ain't but two men ever played baseball as good as you. That's Babe Ruth and Josh Gibson. Them's the only two men ever hit more home runs than you.

TROY: What it ever get me? Ain't got a pot to piss in or a window to throw it out of.

ROSE: Times have changed since you was playing baseball, Troy. That was before the war. Times have changed a lot since then.

TROY: How in hell they done changed?

ROSE: They got lots of colored boys playing ball now. Baseball and football.

BONO: You right about that, Rose. Times have changed, Troy. You just come along too early.

TROY: There ought not never have been no time called too early! Now you take that fellow . . . what's that fellow they had playing right field for the Yankees back then? You know who I'm talking about Bono. Used to play right field for the Yankees.

ROSE: Selkirk?

TROY: Selkirk! That's it! Man batting .269, understand? .269. What kind of sense that make? I was hitting .432 with thirty-seven home runs! Man batting .269 and playing right field for the Yankees! I saw Josh Gibson's daughter yesterday. She walking around with raggedy shoes on her feet. Now I bet you Selkirk's

daughter ain't walking around with raggedy shoes on her feet!
I bet you that!

ROSE: They got a lot of colored baseball players now. Jackie Robinson
was the first. Folks had to wait for Jackie Robinson.

TROY: I done seen a hundred niggers play baseball better than Jackie
Robinson. Hell, I know some teams Jackie Robinson couldn't even
190   make! What you talking about Jackie Robinson. Jackie Robinson
wasn't nobody. I'm talking about if you could play ball then they
ought to have let you play. Don't care what color you were. Come
telling me I come along too early. If you could play . . . then they
ought to have let you play.

(Troy takes a long drink from the bottle.)

ROSE: You gonna drink yourself to death. You don't need to be drinking
like that.

TROY: Death ain't nothing. I done seen him. Done wrassled with him.
You can't tell me nothing about death. Death ain't nothing but a
fastball on the outside corner. And you know what I'll do to that!
200   Lookee here, Bono . . . am I lying? You get one of them fastballs,
about waist high, over the outside corner of the plate where you can
get the meat of the bat on it . . . and good god! You can kiss it goodbye. Now, am I lying?

BONO: Naw, you telling the truth there. I seen you do it.

TROY: If I'm lying . . . that 450 feet worth of lying! *(Pause.)* That's all
death is to me. A fastball on the outside corner.

ROSE: I don't know why you want to get on talking about death.

TROY: Ain't nothing wrong with talking about death. That's part of life.
210   Everybody gonna die. You gonna die, I'm gonna die. Bono's gonna
die. Hell, we all gonna die.

ROSE: But you ain't got to talk about it. I don't like to talk about it.

TROY: You the one brought it up. Me and Bono was talking about baseball . . . you tell me I'm gonna drink myself to death. Ain't that right,
Bono? You know I don't drink this but one night out of the week.
That's Friday night. I'm gonna drink just enough to where I can handle it. Then I cuts it loose. I leave it alone. So don't you worry about
me drinking myself to death. 'Cause I ain't worried about Death. I
done seen him. I done wrestled with him.
220   Look here, Bono . . . I looked up one day and Death was marching
straight at me. Like Soldiers on Parade! The Army of Death was
marching straight at me. The middle of July, 1941. It got real cold
just like it be winter. It seem like Death himself reached out and
touched me on the shoulder. He touch me just like I touch you. I got
cold as ice and Death standing there grinning at me.

ROSE: Troy, why don't you hush that talk.

TROY: I say . . . What you want, Mr. Death? You be wanting me? You done
brought your army to be getting me? I looked him dead in the eye.

I wasn't fearing nothing. I was ready to tangle. Just like I'm ready to
230   tangle now. The Bible say be ever vigilant. That's why I don't get but
so drunk. I got to keep watch.

ROSE: Troy was right down there in Mercy Hospital. You remember he had
pneumonia? Laying there with a fever talking plumb out of his head.

TROY: Death standing there staring at me . . . carrying that sickle in his
hand. Finally he say, "You want bound over for another year?" See,
just like that . . . "You want bound over for another year?" I told
him, "Bound over hell! Let's settle this now!"

    It seem like he kinda fell back when I said that, and all the cold went
out of me. I reached down and grabbed that sickle and threw it just
240   as far as I could throw it . . . and me and him commenced to
wrestling.

    We wrestled for three days and three nights. I can't say where
I found the strength from. Every time it seemed like he was gonna
get the best of me, I'd reach way down deep inside myself and find
the strength to do him one better.

ROSE: Every time Troy tell the story he find different ways to tell it. Different things to make up about it.

TROY: I ain't making up nothing. I'm telling you the facts of what happened. I wrestled with Death for three days and three nights and I'm
250   standing here to tell you about it. *(Pause.)* All right. At the end of
the third night we done weakened each other to where we can't
hardly move. Death stood up, throwed on his robe . . . had him a
white robe with a hood on it. He throwed on that robe and went off
to look for his sickle. Say, "I'll be back." Just like that. "I'll be back." I
told him, say, "Yeah, but . . . you gonna have to find me!" I wasn't no
fool. I wasn't going looking for him. Death ain't nothing to play with.
And I know he's gonna get me. I know I got to join his army . . . his
camp followers. But as long as I keep my strength and see him
coming . . . as long as I keep up my vigilance . . . he's gonna have to
260   fight to get me. I ain't going easy.

BONO: Well, look here, since you got to keep up your vigilance . . . let
me have the bottle.

TROY: Aw hell, I shouldn't have told you that part. I should have left out
that part.

ROSE: Troy be talking that stuff and half the time don't even know what
he be talking about.

TROY: Bono know me better than that.

BONO: That's right, I know you. I know you got some Uncle Remus in
your blood. You got more stories than the devil got sinners.

270   TROY: Aw hell, I done seen him too! Done talked with the devil.

ROSE: Troy, don't nobody wanna be hearing all that stuff.

*(Lyons enters the yard from the street. Thirty-four years old, Troy's
son by a previous marriage, he sports a neatly trimmed goatee, sport*

coat, white shirt, tieless and buttoned at the collar. Though he fancies himself a musician, he is more caught up in the rituals and "idea" of being a musician than in the actual practice of the music. He has come to borrow money from Troy, and while he knows he will be successful, he is uncertain as to what extent his lifestyle will be held up to scrutiny and ridicule.)

LYONS: Hey, Pop.

TROY: What you come "Hey, Popping" me for?

LYONS: How you doing, Rose? *(He kisses her.)* Mr. Bono. How you doing?

BONO: Hey, Lyons . . . how you been?

TROY: He must have been doing all right. I ain't seen him around here last week.

ROSE: Troy, leave your boy alone. He come by to see you and you wanna start all that nonsense.

TROY: I ain't bothering Lyons. *(Offers him the bottle.)* Here . . . get you a drink. We got an understanding. I know why he come by to see me and he know I know.

LYONS: Come on, Pop . . . I just stopped by to say hi . . . see how you was doing.

TROY: You ain't stopped by yesterday.

ROSE: You gonna stay for supper, Lyons? I got some chicken cooking in the oven.

LYONS: No, Rose . . . thanks. I was just in the neighborhood and thought I'd stop by for a minute.

TROY: You was in the neighborhood alright, nigger. You telling the truth there. You was in the neighborhood cause it's my payday.

LYONS: Well, hell, since you mentioned it . . . let me have ten dollars.

TROY: I'll be damned! I'll die and go to hell and play blackjack with the devil before I give you ten dollars.

BONO: That's what I wanna know about . . . that devil you done seen.

LYONS: What . . . Pop done seen the devil? You too much, Pops.

TROY: Yeah, I done seen him. Talked to him too!

ROSE: You ain't seen no devil. I done told you that man ain't had nothing to do with the devil. Anything you can't understand, you want to call it the devil.

TROY: Look here, Bono . . . I went down to see Hertzberger about some furniture. Got three rooms for two-ninety-eight. That what it say on the radio. "Three rooms . . . two-ninety-eight." Even made up a little song about it. Go down there . . . man tell me I can't get no credit. I'm working every day and can't get no credit. What to do? I got an empty house with some raggedy furniture in it. Cory ain't got no bed. He's sleeping on a pile of rags on the floor. Working every day and can't get no credit. Come back here—Rose'll tell you—madder than hell. Sit down . . . try to figure what I'm gonna do. Come a knock on

the door. Ain't been living here but three days. Who know I'm here?
Open the door . . . devil standing there bigger than life. White fellow . . .
got on good clothes and everything. Standing there with a clipboard
in his hand. I ain't had to say nothing. First words come out of his
mouth was . . . "I understand you need some furniture and can't get
no credit." I liked to fell over. He say, "I'll give you all the credit you
want, but you got to pay the interest on it." I told him, "Give me
three rooms worth and charge whatever you want." Next day a truck
320   pulled up here and two men unloaded them three rooms. Man what
drove the truck give me a book. Say send ten dollars, first of every
month to the address in the book and everything will be alright. Say
if I miss a payment the devil was coming back and it'll be hell to pay.
That was fifteen years ago. To this day . . . the first of the month I
send my ten dollars, Rose'll tell you.

ROSE: Troy lying.

TROY: I ain't never seen that man since. Now you tell me who else that
could have been but the devil? I ain't sold my soul or nothing like
that, you understand. Naw, I wouldn't have truck with the devil
about nothing like that. I got my furniture and pays my ten dollars
330   the first of the month just like clockwork.

BONO: How long you say you been paying this ten dollars a month?

TROY: Fifteen years!

BONO: Hell, ain't you finished paying for it yet? How much the man
done charged you.

TROY: Aw hell, I done paid for it. I done paid for it ten times over! The
fact is I'm scared to stop paying it.

ROSE: Troy lying. He got that furniture from Mr. Glickman. He ain't
paying no ten dollars a month to nobody.

TROY: Aw hell, woman. Bono know I ain't that big a fool.

340   LYONS: I was just getting ready to say . . . I know where there's a bridge
for sale.

TROY: Look here, I'll tell you this . . . it don't matter to me if he was the
devil. It don't matter if the devil give credit. Somebody had got to give it.

ROSE: It ought to matter. You going around talking about having truck
with the devil . . . God's the one you gonna have to answer to. He's
the one gonna be at the Judgment.

LYONS: Yeah, well, look here, Pop . . . let me have that ten dollars. I'll
give it back to you. Bonnie got a job working at the hospital.

TROY: What I tell you, Bono? The only time I see this nigger is when he
350   wants something. That's the only time I see him.

LYONS: Come on, Pop, Mr. Bono don't want to hear all that. Let me have
the ten dollars. I told you Bonnie working.

TROY: What that mean to me? "Bonnie working." I don't care if she
working. Go ask her for the ten dollars if she working. Talking about
"Bonnie working." Why ain't you working?

LYONS: Aw, Pop, you know I can't find no decent job. Where am I gonna get a job at? You know I can't get no job.

TROY: I told you I know some people down there. I can get you on the rubbish if you want to work. I told you that the last time you came by here asking me for something.

360 LYONS: Naw, Pop . . . thanks. That ain't for me. I don't wanna be carrying nobody's rubbish. I don't wanna be punching nobody's time clock.

TROY: What's the matter, you too good to carry people's rubbish? Where you think that ten dollars you talking about come from? I'm just supposed to haul people's rubbish and give my money to you cause you too lazy to work. You too lazy to work and wanna know why you ain't got what I got.

ROSE: What hospital Bonnie working at? Mercy?

LYONS: She's down at Passavant working in the laundry.

TROY: I ain't got nothing as it is. I give you that ten dollars and I got to eat

370 beans the rest of the week. Naw . . . you ain't getting no ten dollars here.

LYONS: You ain't got to be eating no beans. I don't know why you wanna say that.

TROY: I ain't got no extra money. Gabe done moved over to Miss Pearl's paying her the rent and things done got tight around here. I can't afford to be giving you every payday.

LYONS: I ain't asked you to give me nothing. I asked you to loan me ten dollars. I know you got ten dollars.

TROY: Yeah. I got it. You know why I got it? Cause I don't throw my money away out there in the streets. You living the fast life . . . wanna

380 be a musician . . . running around in them clubs and things . . . then, you learn to take care of yourself. You ain't gonna find me going and asking nobody for nothing. I done spent too many years without.

LYONS: You and me is two different people, Pop.

TROY: I done learned my mistake and learned to do what's right by it. You still trying to get something for nothing. Life don't owe you nothing. You owe it to yourself. Ask Bono. He'll tell you I'm right.

LYONS: You got your way of dealing with the world . . . I got mine. The only thing that matters to me is the music.

TROY: Yeah, I can see that! It don't matter how you gonna eat . . . where

390 your next dollar is coming from. You telling the truth there.

LYONS: I know I got to eat. But I got to live too. I need something that gonna help me to get out of the bed in the morning. Make me feel like I belong in the world. I don't bother nobody. Just stay with my music cause that's the only way I can find to live in the world. Otherwise there ain't no telling what I might do. Now I don't come criticizing you and how you live. I just come by to ask you for ten dollars. I don't wanna hear all that about how I live.

TROY: Boy, your mama did a hell of a job raising you.

400 LYONS: You can't change me, Pop. I'm thirty-four years old. If you wanted to change me, you should have been there when I was growing up. I come by to see you . . . ask for ten dollars and you

want to talk about how I was raised. You don't know nothing about how I was raised.

ROSE: Let the boy have ten dollars, Troy.

TROY *(to Lyons)*: What the hell you looking at me for? I ain't got no ten dollars. You know what I do with my money. *(To Rose)* Give him ten dollars if you want him to have it.

ROSE: I will. Just as soon as you turn it loose.

TROY *(handing Rose the money)*: There it is. Seventy-six dollars and forty-two cents. You see this, Bono? Now, I ain't gonna get but six of
410   that back.

ROSE: You ought to stop telling that lie. Here, Lyons. *(She hands him the money.)*

LYONS: Thanks, Rose. Look . . . I got to run . . . I'll see you later.

TROY: Wait a minute. You gonna say, "thanks, Rose" and ain't gonna look to see where she got that ten dollars from? See how they do me, Bono?

LYONS: I know she got it from you, Pop. Thanks. I'll give it back to you.

TROY: There he go telling another lie. Time I see that ten dollars . . . he'll be owing me thirty more.

420   LYONS: See you, Mr. Bono.

BONO: Take care, Lyons!

LYONS: Thanks, Pop. I'll see you again.

(Lyons exits the yard.)

TROY: I don't know why he don't go and get him a decent job and take care of that woman he got.

BONO: He'll be alright, Troy. The boy is still young.

TROY: The *boy* is thirty-four years old.

ROSE: Let's not get off into all that.

BONO: Look here . . . I got to be going. I got to be getting on. Lucille gonna be waiting.

430   TROY *(puts his arm round Rose)*: See this woman, Bono? I love this woman. I love this woman so much it hurts. I love her so much . . . I done run out of ways of loving her. So I got to go back to basics. Don't you come by my house Monday morning talking about time to go to work . . . 'cause I'm still gonna be stroking!

ROSE: Troy! Stop it now!

BONO: I ain't paying him no mind. Rose. That ain't nothing but gin-talk. Go on, Troy. I'll see you Monday.

TROY: Don't you come by my house, nigger! I done told you what I'm gonna be doing.

(The lights go down to black.)

SCENE 2

The lights come up on Rose hanging up clothes. She hums and sings softly to herself. It is the following morning.

440   ROSE *(sings)*: Jesus, be a fence all around me every day.
       Jesus, I want you to protect me as I travel on my way
       Jesus, be a fence all around me every day.

       (Troy enters from the house.)

       ROSE *(continues)*:
       Jesus, I want you to protect me
       As I travel on my way.
       (To Troy) 'Morning. You ready for breakfast? I can fix it soon as I
       finish hanging up these clothes.

       TROY: I got the coffee on. That'll be all right. I'll just drink some of that
450   this morning.

       ROSE: That *651* hit yesterday. That's the second time this month. Miss
       Pearl hit for a dollar . . . seem like those that need the least always
       get lucky. Poor folks can't get nothing.

       TROY: Them numbers don't know nobody. I don't know why you fool
       with them. You and Lyons both.

       ROSE: It's something to do.

       TROY: You ain't doing nothing but throwing your money away.

       ROSE: Troy, you know I don't play foolishly. I just play a nickel here and
       a nickel there.

460   TROY: That's two nickels you done thrown away.

       ROSE: Now I hit sometimes . . . that makes up for it. It always comes in
       handy when I do hit. I don't hear you complaining then.

       TROY: I ain't complaining now. I just say it's foolish. Trying to guess out
       of six hundred ways which way the number gonna come. If I had all
       the money niggers, these Negroes, throw away on numbers for one
       week—just one week—I'd be a rich man.

       ROSE: Well, you wishing and calling it foolish ain't gonna stop folks
       from playing numbers. That's one thing for sure. Besides . . . some
       good things come from playing numbers. Look where Pope done
470   bought him that restaurant off of numbers.

       TROY: I can't stand niggers like that. Man ain't had two dimes to rub
       together. He walking around with his shoes all run over bumming
       money for cigarettes. All right. Got lucky there and hit the numbers . . .

       ROSE: Troy, I know all about it.

       TROY: Had good sense, I'll say that for him. He ain't throwed his money
       away. I seen niggers hit the numbers and go through two thousand
       dollars in four days. Man bought him that restaurant down there . . .
       fixed it up real nice . . . and then didn't want nobody to come in it! A
       Negro go in there and can't get no kind of service. I seen a white fell-
480   ow come in there and order a bowl of stew. Pope picked all the
       meat out the pot for him. Man ain't had nothing but a bowl of meat!
       Negro come behind him and ain't got nothing but the potatoes and
       carrots. Talking about what numbers do for people, you picked a
       wrong example. Ain't done nothing but make a worser fool out of
       him than he was before.

ROSE: Troy, you ought to stop worrying about what happened at work yesterday.

TROY: I ain't worried. Just told me to be down there at the Commissioner's office on Friday. Everybody think they gonna fire me. I ain't worried about them firing me. You ain't got to worry about that.

490 *(Pause.)* Where's Cory? Cory in the house? *(Calls)* Cory?

ROSE: He gone out.

TROY: Out, huh? He gone out cause he know I want him to help me with this fence. I know how he is. That boy scared of work.

(Gabriel enters. He comes halfway down the alley and, hearing Troy's voice, stops.)

TROY *(continues)*: He ain't done a lick of work in his life.

ROSE: He had to go to football practice. Coach wanted them to get in a little extra practice before the season start.

500 TROY: I got his practice . . . running out of here before he get his chores done.

ROSE: Troy, what is wrong with you this morning? Don't nothing set right with you. Go on back in there and go to bed . . . get up on the other side.

TROY: Why something got to be wrong with me? I ain't said nothing wrong with me.

ROSE: You got something to say about everything. First it's the numbers . . . then it's the way the man runs his restaurant . . . then you done got on Cory. What's it gonna be next? Take a look up there and

510 see if the weather suits you . . . or is it gonna be how you gonna put up the fence with the clothes hanging in the yard.

TROY: You hit the nail on the head then.

ROSE: I know you like I know the back of my hand. Go on in there and get you some coffee . . . see if that straighten you up. 'Cause you ain't right this morning.

(Troy starts into the house and sees Gabriel. Gabriel starts singing. Troy's brother, he is seven years younger than Troy. Injured in World War II, he has a metal plate in his head. He carries an old trumpet tied around his waist and believes with every fiber of his being that he is the Archangel Gabriel. He carries a chipped basket with an assortment of discarded fruits and vegetables he has picked up in the strip district and which he attempts to sell.)

GABRIEL*(singing)*:
Yes, ma'am, I got plums.
You ask me how I sell them
Oh ten cents apiece
Three for a quarter
520 Come and buy now

'Cause I'm here today
And tomorrow I'll be gone

(Gabriel enters.)

Hey, Rose!

ROSE: How you doing, Gabe?

GABRIEL: There's Troy . . . Hey, Troy!

TROY: Hey, Gabe. *(Exits into kitchen.)*

ROSE *(to Gabriel)*: What you got there?

GABRIEL: You know what I got, Rose. I got fruits and vegetables.

530 ROSE *(looking in basket)*: Where's all these plums you talking about?

GABRIEL: I ain't got no plums today, Rose. I was just singing that. Have
some tomorrow. Put me in a big order for plums. Have enough
plums tomorrow for St. Peter and everybody.

(Troy re-enters from kitchen, crosses to steps.)

(To Rose) Troy's mad at me.

TROY: I ain't mad at you. What I got to be mad at you about? You ain't
done nothing to me.

GABRIEL: I just moved over to Miss Pearl's to keep out from in your way.
540   I ain't mean no harm by it.

TROY: Who said anything about that? I ain't said anything about that.

GABRIEL: You ain't mad at me, is you?

TROY: Naw . . . I ain't mad at you, Gabe. If I was mad at you I'd tell you
about it.

GABRIEL: Got me two rooms. In the basement. Got my own door, too.
Wanna see my key? *(He holds up a key.)* That's my own key! Ain't
nobody else got a key like that. That's my key! My two rooms!

TROY: Well, that's good, Gabe. You got your own key . . . that's good.

ROSE: You hungry, Gabe? I was just fixing to cook Troy his breakfast.

550 GABRIEL: I'll take some biscuits. You got some biscuits? Did you know
when I was in heaven . . . every morning me and St. Peter would sit
down by the gate and eat some big fat biscuits? Oh, yeah! We had us
a good time. We'd sit there and eat us them biscuits and then St.
Peter would go off to sleep and tell me to wake him up when it's
time to open the gates for the judgment.

ROSE: Well, come on . . . I'll make up a batch of biscuits.

(Rose exits into the house.)

GABRIEL: Troy . . . St. Peter got your name in the book. I seen it. It say . . .
Troy Maxson. I say . . . I know him! He got the same name like what I
got. That's my brother!

560 TROY: How many times you gonna tell me that, Gabe?

GABRIEL: Ain't got my name in the book. Don't have to have my name.
I done died and went to heaven. He got your name though. One
morning St. Peter was looking at his book . . . marking it up for

the judgment . . . and he let me see your name. Got it in there under M. Got Rose's name . . . I ain't seen it like I seen yours . . . but I know it's in there. He got a great big book. Got everybody's name what was ever been born. That's what he told me. But I seen your name. Seen it with my own eyes.

TROY: Go on in the house there. Rose going to fix you something to eat.

570 GABRIEL: Oh, I ain't hungry. I done had breakfast with Aunt Jemimah. She come by and cooked me up a whole mess of flapjacks. Remember how we used to eat them flapjacks?

TROY: Go on in the house and get you something to eat now.

GABRIEL: I got to sell my plums. I done sold some tomatoes. Got me two quarters. Wanna see? *(He shows Troy his quarters.)* I'm gonna save them and buy me a new horn so St. Peter can hear me when it's time to open the gates. *(Gabriel stops suddenly. Listens.)* Hear that? That's the hellhounds. I got to chase them out of here . . . Go on get out of here! Get out! *(Gabriel exits singing.)*

580 Better get ready for the judgment
Better get ready for the judgment
My Lord is coming down

(Rose enters from the house.)

TROY: He gone off somewhere.

GABRIEL *(offstage)*: Better get ready for the judgment
Better get ready for the judgment morning
Better get ready for the judgment
My God is coming down

ROSE: He ain't eating right. Miss Pearl say she can't get him to eat noth-
590 ing.

TROY: What you want me to do about it, Rose? I done did everything I can for the man. I can't make him get well. Man got half his head blown away . . . what you expect?

ROSE: Seem like something ought to be done to help him.

TROY: Man don't bother nobody. He just mixed up from that metal plate he got in his head. Ain't no sense for him to go back into the hospital.

ROSE: Least he be eating right. They can help him take care of himself.

TROY: Don't nobody wanna be locked up, Rose. What you wanna lock him up for? Man go over there and fight the war . . . messin' around with them Japs . . . get half his head blown off . . . and they give him
600 a lousy three thousand dollars. And I had to swoop down on that.

ROSE: Is you fixing to go into that again?

TROY: That's the only way I got a roof over my head . . . cause of that metal plate.

ROSE: Ain't no sense you blaming yourself for nothing. Gabe wasn't in no condition to manage that money. You done what was right by him. Can't nobody say you ain't done what was right by him. Look how long you took care of him . . . till he wanted to have his own place and moved over there with Miss Pearl.

610 TROY: That ain't what I'm saying, woman! I'm just stating the facts. If my brother didn't have that metal plate in his head . . . I wouldn't have a pot to piss in or a window to throw it out of. And I'm fifty-three years old. Now see if you can understand that!

(Troy gets up from the porch and starts to exit the yard.)

ROSE: Where you going off to? You been running out of here every Saturday for weeks. I thought you was gonna work on this fence?

TROY: I'm gonna walk down to Taylors'. Listen to the ball game. I'll be back in a bit. I'll work on it when I get back.

(He exits the yard. The lights go to black.)

SCENE 3

The lights come up on the yard. It is four hours later. Rose is taking down the clothes from the line. Cory enters carrying his football equipment.

ROSE: Your daddy like to had a fit with you running out of here without doing your chores.

620 CORY: I told you I had to go to practice.

ROSE: He say you were supposed to help him with this fence.

CORY: He been saying that the last four or five Saturdays, and then he don't never do nothing, but go down to Taylors'. Did you tell him about the recruiter?

ROSE: Yeah, I told him.

CORY: What he say?

ROSE: He ain't said nothing too much. You get in there and get started on your chores before he gets back. Go on and scrub down them steps before he gets back here hollering and carrying on.

630 CORY: I'm hungry. What you got to eat, Mama?

ROSE: Go on and get started on your chores. I got some meat loaf in there. Go on and make you a sandwich . . . and don't leave no mess in there. *(Cory exits into the house. Rose continues to take down the clothes. Troy enters the yard and sneaks up and grabs her from behind.)* Troy! Go on, now. You liked to scared me to death. What was the score of the game? Lucille had me on the phone and I couldn't keep up with it.

TROY: What I care about the game? Come here, woman. *(He tries to kiss her.)*

640 ROSE: I thought you went down Taylors' to listen to the game. Go on, Troy! You supposed to be putting up this fence.

TROY *(attempting to kiss her again)*: I'll put it up when I finish with what is at hand.

ROSE: Go on, Troy. I ain't studying you.

TROY (*chasing after her*): I'm studying you . . . fixing to do my homework!

ROSE: Troy, you better leave me alone.

TROY: Where's Cory? That boy brought his butt home yet?

ROSE: He's in the house doing his chores.

TROY (*calling*): Cory! Get your butt out here, boy!

650

*(Rose exits into the house with the laundry. Troy goes over to the pile
of wood, picks up a board, and starts sawing. Cory enters from the
house.)*

TROY: You just now coming in here from leaving this morning?

CORY: Yeah, I had to go to football practice.

TROY: Yeah, what?

CORY: Yessir.

TROY: I ain't but two seconds off you noway. The garbage sitting in
there overflowing . . . you ain't done none of your chores . . . and you
come in here talking about "Yeah."

CORY: I was just getting ready to do my chores now, Pop . . .

TROY: Your first chore is to help me with this fence on Saturday. Everything else come after that. Now get that saw and cut them boards.

660

*(Cory takes the saw and begins cutting the boards. Troy continues
working. There is a long pause.)*

CORY: Hey, Pop . . . why don't you buy a TV?

TROY: What I want with a TV? What I want one of them for?

CORY: Everybody got one. Earl, Ba Bra . . . Jesse!

TROY: I ain't asked you who had one. I say what I want with one?

CORY: So you can watch it. They got lots of things on TV. Baseball
games and everything. We could watch the World Series.

TROY: Yeah . . . and how much this TV cost?

CORY: I don't know. They got them on sale for around two hundred dollars.

TROY: Two hundred dollars, huh?

670 CORY: That ain't that much, Pop.

TROY: Naw, it's just two hundred dollars. See that roof you got over
your head at night? Let me tell you something about that roof. It's
been over ten years since that roof was last tarred. See now . . . the
snow come this winter and sit up there on that roof like it is . . . and
it's gonna seep inside. It's just gonna be a little bit . . . ain't gonna
hardly notice it. Then the next thing you know, it's gonna be leaking
all over the house. Then the wood rot from all that water and you
gonna need a whole new roof. Now, how much you think it cost to
get that roof tarred?

680 CORY: I don't know.

TROY: Two hundred and sixty-four dollars . . . cash money. While you
thinking about a TV, I got to be thinking about the roof . . . and

whatever else go wrong around here. Now if you had two hundred dollars, what would you do . . . fix the roof or buy a TV?

CORY: I'd buy a TV. Then when the roof started to leak . . . when it needed fixing . . . I'd fix it.

TROY: Where you gonna get the money from? You done spent it for a TV. You gonna sit up and watch the water run all over your brand new TV.

CORY: Aw, Pop. You got money. I know you do.

690 TROY: Where I got it at, huh?

CORY: You got it in the bank.

TROY: You wanna see my bankbook? You wanna see that seventy-three dollars and twenty-two cents I got sitting up in there?

CORY: You ain't got to pay for it all at one time. You can put a down payment on it and carry it on home with you.

TROY: Not me. I ain't gonna owe nobody nothing if I can help it. Miss a payment and they come and snatch it right out of your house. Then what you got? Now, soon as I get two hundred dollars clear, then I'll buy a TV. Right now, as soon as I get two hundred and sixty-four dol-

700 lars, I'm gonna have this roof tarred.

CORY: Aw . . . Pop!

TROY: You go on and get your two hundred dollars and buy one if ya want it. I got better things to do with my money.

CORY: I can't get no two hundred dollars. I ain't never seen two hundred dollars.

TROY: I'll tell you what . . . you get a hundred dollars and I'll put the other hundred with it.

CORY: All right, I'm gonna show you.

TROY: You gonna show me how you can cut them boards right now.

(Cory begins to cut the boards. There is a long pause.)

710 CORY: The Pirates won today. That make five in a row.

TROY: I ain't thinking about the Pirates. Got an all-white team. Got that boy . . . that Puerto Rican boy . . . Clemente. Don't even half-play him. That boy could be something if they give him a chance. Play him one day and sit him on the bench the next.

CORY: He gets a lot of chances to play.

TROY: I'm talking about playing regular. Playing every day so you can get your timing. That's what I'm talking about.

CORY: They got some white guys on the team that don't play everyday. You can't play everybody at the same time.

720 TROY: If they got a white fellow sitting on the bench . . . you can bet your last dollar he can't play! The colored guy got to be twice as good before he get on the team. That's why I don't want you to get all tied up in them sports. Man on the team and what it get him? They got colored on the team and don't use them. Same as not having them. All them teams the same.

CORY: The Braves got Hank Aaron and Wes Covington. Hank Aaron hit two home runs today. That makes forty-three.

TROY: Hank Aaron ain't nobody. That's what you supposed to do. That's
how you supposed to play the game. Ain't nothing to it. It's just a
730   matter of timing . . . getting the right follow-through. Hell, I can hit
forty-three home runs right now!

CORY: Not off no major-league pitching, you couldn't.

TROY: We had better pitching in the Negro leagues. I hit seven home
runs off of Satchel Paige. You can't get no better than that!

CORY: Sandy Koufax. He's leading the league in strike-outs.

TROY: I ain't thinking of no Sandy Koufax.

CORY: You got Warren Spahn and Lew Burdette. I bet you couldn't hit
no home runs off of Warren Spahn.

TROY: I'm through with it now. You go on and cut them boards. *(Pause.)*
740   Your mama tell me you done got recruited by a college football
team? Is that right?

CORY: Yeah. Coach Zellman say the recruiter gonna be coming by to
talk to you. Get you to sign the permission papers.

TROY: I thought you supposed to be working down there at the A&P.
Ain't you suppose to be working down there after school?

CORY: Mr. Stawicki say he gonna hold my job for me until after the football season. Say starting next week I can work weekends.

TROY: I thought we had an understanding about this football stuff? You
suppose to keep up with your chores and hold that job down at the
750   A&P. Ain't been around here all day on a Saturday. Ain't none of your
chores done . . . and now you telling me you done quit your job.

CORY: I'm gonna be working weekends.

TROY: You damn right you are! And ain't no need for nobody coming
around here to talk to me about signing nothing.

CORY: Hey, Pop . . . you can't do that. He's coming all the way from
North Carolina.

TROY: I don't care where he coming from. The white man ain't gonna let
you get nowhere with that football noway. You go on and get your
book-learning so you can work yourself up in that A&P or learn how
760   to fix cars or build houses or something, get you a trade. That way
you have something can't nobody take away from you. You go on
and learn how to put your hands to some good use. Besides hauling
people's garbage.

CORY: I get good grades, Pop. That's why the recruiter wants to talk
with you. You got to keep up your grades to get recruited. This way
I'll be going to college. I'll get a chance . . .

TROY: First you gonna get your butt down there to the A&P and get
your job back.

CORY: Mr. Stawicki done already hired somebody else cause I told him I
770   was playing football.

TROY: You a bigger fool than I thought . . . to let somebody take away
your job so you can play some football. Where you gonna get your
money to take out your girlfriend and whatnot? What kind of
foolishness is that to let somebody take away your job?

CORY: I'm still gonna be working weekends.

TROY: Naw . . . naw. You getting your butt out of here and finding you another job.

CORY: Come on, Pop! I got to practice. I can't work after school and play football, too. The team needs me. That's what Coach Zellman say . . .

780   TROY: I don't care what nobody else say. I'm the boss . . . you understand? I'm the boss around here. I do the only saying what counts.

CORY: Come on, Pop!

TROY: I asked you . . . did you understand?

CORY: Yeah . . .

TROY: What?!

CORY: Yessir.

TROY: You go on down there to that A&P and see if you can get your job back. If you can't do both . . . then you quit the football team. You've got to take the crookeds with the straights.

CORY: Yessir. *(Pause.)* Can I ask you a question?

790   TROY: What the hell you wanna ask me? Mr. Stawicki the one you got the questions for.

CORY: How come you ain't never liked me?

TROY: Liked you? Who the hell say I got to like you? What law is there say I got to like you? Wanna stand up in my face and ask a damn foolass question like that. Talking about liking somebody. Come here, boy, when I talk to you.

(Cory comes over to where Troy is working. He stands slouched over and Troy shoves him on his shoulder.)

Straighten up, goddammit! I asked you a question . . . what law is there say I got to like you?

CORY: None.

800   TROY: Well, all right then! Don't you eat every day? *(Pause.)* Answer me when I talk to you! Don't you eat every day?

CORY: Yeah.

TROY: Nigger, as long as you in my house, you put that sir on the end of it when you talk to me!

CORY: Yes . . . sir.

TROY: You eat every day.

CORY: Yessir!

TROY: Got a roof over your head.

CORY: Yessir!

810   TROY: Got clothes on your back.

CORY: Yessir.

TROY: Why you think that is?

CORY: Cause of you.

TROY: Aw, hell I know it's cause of me . . . but why do you think that is?

CORY *(hesitant)*: Cause you like me.

TROY: Like you? I go out of here every morning . . . bust my butt . . . putting up with them crackers every day . . . cause I like you? You about the biggest fool I ever saw. *(Pause.)* It's my job. It's my
820   responsibility! You understand that? A man got to take care of his family. You live in my house . . . sleep you behind on my bedclothes . . . fill you belly up with my food . . . cause you my son. You my flesh and blood. Not cause I like you! Cause it's my duty to take care of you. I owe a responsibility to you!

    Let's get this straight right here . . . before it go along any further . . . I ain't got to like you. Mr. Rand don't give me money come payday cause he likes me. He gives me cause he owe me. I done give you everything I had to give you. I gave you your life! Me and your mama worked that out between us. And liking your black ass wasn't part of
830   the bargain. Don't you try and go through life worrying about if somebody like you or not. You best be making sure they doing right by you. You understand what I'm saying, boy?

CORY: Yessir.

TROY: Then get the hell out of my face, and get on down to that A&P.

(Rose has been standing behind the screen door for much of the scene. She enters as Cory exits.)

ROSE: Why don't you let the boy go ahead and play football, Troy? Ain't no harm in that. He's just trying to be like you with the sports.

TROY: I don't want him to be like me! I want him to move as far away from my life as he can get. You the only decent thing that ever happened to me. I wish him that. But I don't wish him a thing else from
840   my life. I decided seventeen years ago that boy wasn't getting involved in no sports. Not after what they did to me in the sports.

ROSE: Troy, why don't you admit you was too old to play in the major leagues? For once . . . why don't you admit that?

TROY: What do you mean too old? Don't come telling me I was too old. I just wasn't the right color. Hell, I'm fifty-three years old and can do better then Selkirk's .269 right now!

ROSE: How's was you gonna play ball when you were over forty? Sometimes I can't get no sense out of you.

TROY: I got good sense, woman. I got sense enough not to let my boy
850   get hurt over playing no sports. You been mothering that boy too much. Worried about if people like him.

ROSE: Everything that boy do . . . he do for you. He wants you to say "Good job, son." That's all.

TROY: Rose, I ain't got time for that. He's alive. He's healthy. He's got to make his own way. I made mine. Ain't nobody gonna hold his hand when he get out there in that world.

ROSE: Times have changed from when you was young, Troy. People change. The world's changing around you and you can't even see it.

860   TROY (*slow, methodical*): Woman . . . I do the best I can do. I come in here every Friday. I carry a sack of potatoes and a bucket of lard. You all line up at the door with your hand out. I give you the lint from my pockets. I give you my sweat and my blood. I ain't got no tears. I done spent them. We go upstairs in that room at night . . . and I fall down on you and try to blast a hole into forever. I get up Monday morning . . . find my lunch on the table. I go out. Make my way. Find my strength to carry me through to the next Friday. (*Pause.*) That's all I got, Rose. That's all I got to give. I can't give nothing else.

(*Troy exits into the house. The lights go down to black.*)

SCENE 4

It is Friday. Two weeks later. Cory starts out of the house with his football equipment. The phone rings.

CORY (*calling*): I got it!

(*He answers the phone and stands in the screen door talking.*)

870   Hello? Hey, Jesse. Naw . . . I was just getting ready to leave now.
ROSE (*calling*): Cory!
CORY: I told you, man, them spikes is all tore up. You can use them if you want, but they ain't no good. Earl got some spikes.
ROSE (*calling*): Cory!
CORY (*calling to Rose*): Mam? I'm talking to Jesse. (*Into phone*) When she say that? (*Pause.*) Aw, you lying, man. I'm gonna tell her you said that.
ROSE (*calling*): Cory, don't you go nowhere!
CORY: I got to go to the game, Ma! (*Into the phone*) Yeah, hey, look, I'll
880   talk to you later. Yeah, I'll meet you over Earl's house. Later. Bye, Ma.

(*Cory exits the house and starts out the yard.*)

ROSE: Cory, where you going off to? You got that stuff all pulled out and thrown all over your room.
CORY (*in the yard*): I was looking for my spikes. Jesse wanted to borrow my spikes.
ROSE: Get up there and get that cleaned up before your daddy get back in here.
CORY: I got to go to the game! I'll clean it up when I get back.

(*Cory exits.*)

ROSE: That's all he need to do is see that room all messed up.

(*Rose exits into the house. Troy and Bono enter the yard. Troy is dressed in clothes other than his work clothes.*)

890   BONO: He told him the same thing he told you. Take it to the union.

TROY: Brownie ain't got that much sense. Man wasn't thinking about nothing. He wait until I confront them on it . . . then he wanna come crying seniority. *(Calls)* Hey Rose!

BONO: I wish I could have seen Mr. Rand's face when he told you.

TROY: He couldn't get it out of his mouth! Liked to bit his tongue! When they called me down there to the Commissioner's office . . . he thought they was gonna fire me. Like everybody else.

BONO: I didn't think they was gonna fire you. I thought they was gonna put you on the warning paper.

900 TROY: Hey, Rose! *(To Bono)* Yeah, Mr. Rand like to bit his tongue.

(Troy breaks the seal on the bottle, takes a drink, and hands it to Bono.)

BONO: I see you run right down to Taylors' and told that Alberta gal.

TROY *(calling)*: Hey Rose! *(To Bono)* I told everybody. Hey, Rose! I went down there to cash my check.

ROSE *(entering from the house)*: Hush all that hollering, man! I know you out here. What they say down there at the Commissioner's office?

TROY: You supposed to come when I call you, woman. Bono'll tell you that. *(To Bono)* Don't Lucille come when you call her?

910 ROSE: Man, hush your mouth. I ain't no dog . . . talk about "come when you call me."

TROY *(puts his arm around Rose)*: You hear this Bono? I had me an old dog used to get uppity like that. You say, "C'mere, Blue!" . . . and he just lay there and look at you. End up getting a stick and chasing him away trying to make him come.

ROSE: I ain't studying you and your dog. I remember you used to sing that old song.

TROY *(he sings)*:
  Hear it ring! Hear it ring!
920   I had a dog and his name was Blue.

ROSE: Don't nobody wanna hear you sing that old song.

TROY *(sings)*: You know Blue was mighty true.

ROSE: Used to have Cory running around here singing that song.

BONO: Hell, I remember that song myself.

TROY *(sings)*:
  You know Blue was a good old dog
  Blue treed a possum in a hollow log.
  That was my daddy's song. My daddy made up that song.

ROSE: I don't care who made it up. Don't nobody wanna hear you sing it.

930 TROY *(makes a sound like calling a dog)*: Come here, woman.

ROSE: You come in here carrying on, I reckon they ain't fired you. What they say down there at the Commissioner's office?

TROY: Look here, Rose . . . Mr. Rand called me into his office today when I got back from talking to them people down there . . . it come from up top . . . he called me in and told me they was making me a driver.

ROSE: Troy, you kidding!

TROY: No I ain't. Ask Bono.

ROSE: Well, that's great, Troy. Now you don't have to hassle them people no more.

(Lyons enters from the street.)

940   TROY: Aw hell, I wasn't looking to see you today. I thought you was in jail. Got it all over the front page of the *Courier* about them raiding Sefus' place . . . where you be hanging out with all them thugs.

LYONS: Hey, Pop . . . that ain't got nothing to do with me. I don't go down there gambling. I go down there to sit in with the band. I ain't got nothing to do with the gambling part. They got some good music down there.

LROY: They got some rogues . . . is what they got.

LYONS: How you been, Mr. Bono? Hi, Rose.

950   BONO: I see where you playing down at the Crawford Grill tonight.

ROSE: How come you ain't brought Bonnie like I told you. You should have brought Bonnie with you, she ain't been over in a month of Sundays.

LYONS: I was just in the neighborhood . . . thought I'd stop by.

TROY: Here he come . . .

BONO: Your daddy got a promotion on the rubbish. He's gonna be the first colored driver. Ain't got to do nothing but sit up there and read the paper like them white fellows.

LYONS: Hey, Pop . . . if you knew how to read you'd be all right.

BONO: Naw . . . naw . . . you mean if the nigger knew how to drive he'd

960   be all right. Been fighting with them people about driving and ain't even got a license. Mr. Rand know you ain't got no driver's license?

TROY: Driving ain't nothing. All you do is point the truck where you want it to go. Driving ain't nothing.

BONO: Do Mr. Rand know you ain't got no driver's license? That's what I'm talking about. I ain't asked if driving was easy. I asked if Mr. Rand know you ain't got no driver's license.

TROY: He ain't got to know. The man ain't got to know my business. Time he find out, I have two or three driver's licenses.

LYONS *(going into his pocket)*: Say look here, Pop . . .

970   TROY: I knew it was coming. Didn't I tell you, Bono? I know what kind of "Look here, Pop" that was. The nigger fixing to ask me for some money. It's Friday night. It's my payday. All them rogues down there on the avenue . . . the ones that ain't in jail . . . and Lyons is hopping in his shoes to get down there with them.

LYONS: See, Pop . . . if you give somebody else a chance to talk sometime, you'd see that I was fixing to pay you back your ten dollars like I told you. Here . . . I told you I'd pay you when Bonnie got paid.

TROY: Naw . . . you go ahead and keep that ten dollars. Put it in the bank. The next time you feel like you wanna come by here and ask

980   me for something . . . you go on down there and get that.

LYONS: Here's your ten dollars, Pop. I told you I don't want you to give me nothing. I just wanted to borrow ten dollars.

TROY: Naw . . . you go on and keep that for the next time you want to ask me.

LYONS: Come on, Pop . . . here go your ten dollars.

ROSE: Why don't you go on and let the boy pay you back, Troy?

LYONS: Here you go, Rose. If you don't take it I'm gonna have to hear about it for the next six months. *(He hands her the money.)*

ROSE: You can hand yours over here too, Troy.

TROY: You see this, Bono. You see how they do me.

BONO: Yeah, Lucille do me the same way.

990

(Gabriel is heard singing offstage. He enters.)

GABRIEL: Better get ready for the Judgment! Better get ready for . . . Hey! . . . Hey! . . . There's Troy's boy!

LYONS: How you doing, Uncle Gabe?

GABRIEL: Lyons . . . The King of the Jungle! Rose . . . hey, Rose. Got a flower for you. *(He takes a rose from his pocket.)* Picked it myself. That's the same rose like you is!

ROSE: That's right nice of you, Gabe.

LYONS: What you been doing, Uncle Gabe?

1000　GABRIEL: Oh, I been chasing hellhounds and waiting on the time to tell St. Peter to open the gates.

LYONS: You been chasing hellhounds, huh? Well . . . you doing the right thing, Uncle Gabe. Somebody got to chase them.

GABRIEL: Oh, yeah . . . I know it. The devil's strong. The devil ain't no pushover. Hellhounds snipping at everybody's heels. But I got my trumpet waiting on the judgment time.

LYONS: Waiting on the Battle of Armageddon, huh?

GABRIEL: Ain't gonna be too much of a battle when God get to waving that Judgment sword. But the people's gonna have a hell of a time
1010　trying to get into heaven if them gates ain't open.

LYONS *(putting his arm around Gabriel)*: You hear this, Pop. Uncle Gabe, you all right!

GABRIEL *(laughing with Lyons)*: Lyons! King of the Jungle.

ROSE: You gonna stay for supper, Gabe. Want me to fix you a plate?

GABRIEL: I'll take a sandwich, Rose. Don't want no plate. Just wanna eat with my hands. I'll take a sandwich.

ROSE: How about you, Lyons? You staying? Got some short ribs cooking.

1020　LYONS: Naw, I won't eat nothing till after we finished playing. *(Pause.)* You ought to come down and listen to me play, Pop.

TROY: I don't like that Chinese music. All that noise.

ROSE: Go on in the house and wash up, Gabe . . . I'll fix you a sandwich.

GABRIEL *(to Lyons, as he exits)*: Troy's mad at me.

LYONS: What you mad at Uncle Gabe for, Pop?

ROSE: He thinks Troy's mad at him cause he moved over to Miss Pearl's.

TROY: I ain't mad at the man. He can live where he want to live at.

LYONS: What he move over there for? Miss Pearl don't like nobody.

ROSE: She don't mind him none. She treats him real nice. She just don't
1030   allow all that singing.

TROY: She don't mind that rent he be paying . . . that's what she don't mind.

ROSE: Troy, I ain't going through that with you no more. He's over there
cause he want to have his own place. He can come and go as he please.

TROY: Hell, he could come and go as he please here. I wasn't stopping
him. I ain't put no rules on him.

ROSE: It ain't the same thing, Troy. And you know it. *(Gabriel comes to
the door.)* Now that's the last I wanna hear about that. I don't wanna
hear nothing else about Gabe and Miss Pearl. And next week . . .

1040   GABRIEL: I'm ready for my sandwich, Rose.

ROSE: And next week when that recruiter come from that school . . .
I want you to sign that paper and go on and let Cory play football.
Then that'll be the last I have to hear about that.

TROY *(to Rose as she exits into the house)*: I ain't thinking about Cory
nothing.

LYONS: What . . . Cory got recruited? What school he going to?

TROY: That boy walking around here smelling his piss . . . thinking he's
grown. Thinking he's gonna do what he want, irrespective of what I
say. Look here, Bono . . . I left the Commissioner's office and went
1050   down to the A&P . . . that boy ain't working down there. He lying to
me. Telling me he got his job back . . . telling me he working weekends . . . telling me he working after school . . . Mr. Stawicki tell me
he ain't working down there at all!

LYONS: Cory just growing up. He's just busting at the seams trying to fill
out your shoes.

TROY: I don't care what he's doing. When he get to the point where he
wanna disobey me . . . then it's time for him to move on. Bono'll tell
you that. I bet he ain't never disobeyed his daddy without paying the
consequences.

1060   BONO: I ain't never had a chance. My daddy came on through . . . but I
ain't never knew him to see him . . . or what he had on his mind or
where he went. Just moving on through. Searching out the New
Land. That's what the old folks used to call it. See a fellow moving
around from place to place . . . woman to woman . . . called it searching out the New Land. I can't say if he ever found it. I come along,
didn't want no kids. Didn't know if I was gonna be in one place long
enough to fix on them right as their daddy. I figured I was going
searching, too. As it turned out I been hooked up with Lucille near
about as long as your daddy been with Rose. Going on sixteen years.

1070   TROY: Sometimes I wish I hadn't known my daddy. He ain't cared nothing about no kids. A kid to him wasn't nothing. All he wanted was
for you to learn how to walk so he could start you to working. When
it come time for eating . . . he ate first. If there was anything left over,

that's what you got. Man would sit down and eat two chickens and give you the wing.

LYONS: You ought to stop that, Pop. Everybody feed their kids. No matter how hard times is . . . everybody care about their kids. Make sure they have something to eat.

TROY: The only thing my daddy cared about was getting them bales of cotton in to Mr. Lubin. That's the only thing that mattered to him. Sometimes I used to wonder why he was living. Wonder why the devil hadn't come and got him "Get them bales of cotton in to Mr. Lubin" and find out he owe him money . . .

LYONS: He should have just went on and left when he saw he couldn't get nowhere. That's what I would have done.

TROY: How he gonna leave with eleven kids? And where he gonna go? He ain't knew how to do nothing but farm. No, he was trapped and I think he knew it. But I'll say this for him . . . he felt a responsibility toward us. Maybe he ain't treated us the way I felt he should have . . . but without that responsibility he could have walked off and left us . . . made his own way.

BONO: A lot of them did. Back in those days what you talking about . . . they walk out their front door and just take on down one road or another and keep on walking.

LYONS: There you go! That's what I'm talking about.

BONO: Just keep on walking till you come to something else. Ain't you never heard of nobody having the walking blues? Well, that's what you call it when you just take off like that.

TROY: My daddy ain't had them walking blues! What you talking about? He stayed right there with his family. But he was just as evil as he could be. My mama couldn't stand him. Couldn't stand that evilness. She run off when I was about eight. She sneaked off one night after he had gone to sleep. Told me she was coming back for me. I ain't never seen her no more. All his women run off and left him. He wasn't good for nobody.

When my turn come to head out, I was fourteen and got to sniffing around Joe Canewell's daughter. Had us an old mule we called Greyboy. My daddy sent me out to do some plowing and I tied Greyboy and went to fooling around with Joe Canewell's daughter. We done found us a nice little spot, got real cozy with each other. She about thirteen and we done figured we was grown anyway . . . so we down there enjoying ourselves . . . ain't thinking about nothing. We didn't know Greyboy had got loose and wandered back to the house and my daddy was looking for me. We down there by the creek enjoying ourselves when my daddy come up on us. Surprised us. He had them leather straps off the mule and commenced to whupping me like there was no tomorrow. I jumped up, mad and embarrassed. I was scared of my daddy. When he commenced to whupping on me . . . quite naturally I run to get out of the way. *(Pause.)*

Now I thought he was mad cause I ain't done my work. But I see
1120   where he was chasing me off so he could have the gal for himself.
When I see what the matter of it was, I lost all fear of my daddy. Right
there is where I become a man . . . at fourteen years of age. *(Pause.)*
Now it was my turn to run him off. I picked up them same reins
that he had used on me. I picked up them reins and commenced to
whupping on him. The gal jumped up and run off . . . and when my
daddy turned to face me, I could see why the devil had never come
to get him . . . cause he was the devil himself. I don't know what happened. When I woke up, I was laying right there by the creek, and
Blue . . . this old dog we had . . . was licking my face. I thought I was
1130   blind. I couldn't see nothing. Both my eyes were swollen shut. I
layed there and cried. I didn't know what I was gonna do. The only
thing I knew was the time had come for me to leave my daddy's
house. And right there the world suddenly got big. And it was a long
time before I could cut it down to where I could handle it.

Part of that cutting down was when I got to the place where I
could feel him kicking in my blood and knew that the only thing that
separated us was the matter of a few years.

(Gabriel enters from the house with a sandwich.)

1140   LYONS: What you got there, Uncle Gabe?

GABRIEL: Got me a ham sandwich. Rose gave me a ham sandwich.

TROY: I don't know what happened to him. I done lost touch with everybody except Gabriel. But I hope he's dead. I hope he found some
peace.

LYONS: That's a heavy story, Pop. I didn't know you left home when you
was fourteen.

TROY: And didn't know nothing. The only part of the world I knew was
the forty-two acres of Mr. Lubin's land. That's all I knew about life.

LYONS: Fourteen's kinda young to be out on your own. *(Phone rings.)* I
1150   don't even think I was ready to be out on my own at fourteen. I don't
know what I would have done.

TROY: I got up from the creek and walked on down to Mobile. I was
through with farming. Figured I could do better in the city. So I
walked the two hundred miles to Mobile.

LYONS: Wait a minute . . . you ain't walked no two hundred miles, Pop.
Ain't nobody gonna walk no two hundred miles. You talking about
some walking there.

BONO: That's the only way you got anywhere back in them days.

LYONS: Shhh. Damn if I wouldn't have hitched a ride with somebody!

1160   TROY: Who you gonna hitch it with? They ain't had no cars and things
like they got now. We talking about 1918.

ROSE *(entering)*: What you all out here getting into?

TROY *(to Rose)*: I'm telling Lyons how good he got it. He don't know
nothing about this I'm talking.

ROSE: Lyons, that was Bonnie on the phone. She say you supposed to
pick her up.

LYONS: Yeah, okay, Rose.

TROY: I walked on down to Mobile and hitched up with some of them fellows that was heading this way. Got up here and found out . . . not only couldn't you get a job . . . you couldn't find no place to live. I thought I was in freedom. Shhh. Colored folks living down there on the riverbanks in whatever kind of shelter they could find for themselves. Right down there under the Brady Street Bridge. Living in shacks made of sticks and tarpaper. Messed around there and went from bad to worse. Started stealing. First it was food. Then I figure, hell, if I steal money I can buy me some food. Buy me some shoes, too! One thing led to another. Met your mama and had you. What I do that for? Now I got to worry about feeding you and her. Got to steal three times as much. Went out one day looking for somebody to rob . . . that's what I was, a robber. I'll tell you the truth. I'm ashamed of it today. But it's the truth. Went to rob this fellow . . . pulled out my knife . . . and he pulled out a gun. Shot me in the chest. It felt just like somebody had taken a hot branding iron and laid it on me. When he shot me I jumped at him with my knife. They told me I killed him and they put me in the penitentiary and locked me up for fifteen years. That's where I met Bono. That's where I learned how to play baseball. Got out that place and your mama had taken you and went on to make life without me. Fifteen years was a long time for her to wait. But that fifteen years cured me of that robbing stuff. Rose'll tell you. She asked me when I met her if I had gotten all that foolishness out of my system. And I told her "Baby, it's you and baseball all what count with me." You hear me, Bono? I meant it, too. She say, "Which one comes first?" I told her, "Baby, ain't no doubt it's baseball . . . but you stick and get old with me and we'll both outlive this baseball." Am I right, Rose? And it's true.

ROSE: Man, hush your mouth. You ain't said no such thing. Talking about "Baby, you know you'll always be number one with me." That's what you was talking.

TROY: You hear that, Bono. That's why I love her.

BONO: Rose'll keep you straight. You get off the track, she'll straighten you up.

ROSE: Lyons, you better get on up and get Bonnie. She waiting on you.

LYONS (gets up to go): Hey, Pop, why don't you come on down to the Grill and hear me play?

TROY: I ain't going down there. I'm too old to be sitting around in them clubs.

BONO: You got to be good to play down at the Grill.

LYONS: Come on, Pop . . .

TROY: I got to get up in the morning.

LYONS: You ain't got to stay long.

TROY: Naw, I'm gonna get my supper and go on to bed.

LYONS: Well, I got to go. I'll see you again.

TROY: Don't you come around my house on my payday.

ROSE: Pick up the phone and let somebody know you coming. And bring Bonnie with you. You know I'm always glad to see her.

LYONS: Yeah, I'll do that, Rose. You take care now. See you, Pop. See you, Mr. Bono. See you, Uncle Gabe.

GABRIEL: Lyons! King of the Jungle!

(Lyons exits.)

TROY: Is supper ready, woman? Me and you got some business to take care of. I'm gonna tear it up, too.

ROSE: Troy, I done told you now!

1220 TROY *(puts his arm around Bono)*: Aw hell, woman . . . this is Bono. Bono like family. I done known this nigger since . . . how long I done know you?

BONO: It's been a long time.

TROY: I done known this nigger since Skippy was a pup. Me and him done been through some times.

BONO: You sure right about that.

TROY: Hell, I done know him longer than I known you. And we still standing shoulder to shoulder. Hey, look here, Bono . . . a man can't ask for no more than that. *(Drinks to him.)* I love you, nigger.

1230 BONO: Hell, I love you too . . . but I got to get home see my woman. You got yours in hand. I got to go get mine.

(Bono starts to exit as Cory enters the yard, dressed in his football uniform. He gives Troy a hard, uncompromising look.)

CORY: What you do that for, Pop? *(He throws his helmet down in the direction of Troy.)*

ROSE: What's the matter? Cory . . . what's the matter?

CORY: Pa done went up to the school and told Coach Zellman I can't play football no more. Wouldn't even let me play the game. Told him to tell the recruiter not to come.

ROSE: Troy . . .

TROY: What you Troying me for. Yeah, I did it. And the boy know why
1240   I did it.

CORY: Why you wanna do that to me? That was the one chance I had.

ROSE: Ain't nothing wrong with Cory playing football, Troy.

TROY: The boy lied to me. I told the nigger if he wanna play football . . . to keep up his chores and hold down that job at the A&P. That was the conditions. Stopped down there to see Mr. Stawicki . . .

CORY: I can't work after school during the football season, Pop! I tried to tell you that Mr. Stawicki's holding my job for me. You don't never want to listen to nobody. And then you wanna go and do this to me!

TROY: I ain't done nothing to you. You done it to yourself.

1250 CORY: Just cause you didn't have a chance! You just scared I'm gonna be better than you, that's all.

TROY: Come here.

ROSE: Troy . . .

(Cory reluctantly crosses over to Troy.)

TROY: All right! See. You done made a mistake.

CORY: I didn't even do nothing!

TROY: I'm gonna tell you what your mistake was. See . . . you swung at the ball and didn't hit it. That's strike one. See, you in the batter's box now. You swung and you missed. That's strike one. Don't you strike out!

(Lights fade to black.)

ACT 2

SCENE 1

The following morning. Cory is at the tree hitting the ball with the bat. He tries to mimic Troy, but his swing is awkward, less sure. Rose enters from the house.

1260   ROSE: Cory, I want you to help me with this cupboard.

CORY: I ain't quitting the team. I don't care what Poppa say.

ROSE: I'll talk to him when he gets back. He had to go see about your Uncle Gabe. The police done arrested him. Say he was disturbing the peace. He'll be back directly. Come on in here and help me clean out the top of this cupboard.

(Cory exits into the house. Rose sees Troy and Bono coming down the alley.)

Troy . . . what they say down there?

TROY: Ain't said nothing. I give them fifty dollars and they let him go. I'll talk to you about it. Where's Cory?

ROSE: He's in there helping me clean out these cupboards.

1270   TROY: Tell him to get his butt out here.

(Troy and Bono go over to the pile of wood. Bono picks up the saw and begins sawing.)

TROY *(to Bono)*: All they want is the money. That makes six or seven times I done went down there and got him. See me coming they stick out their *hands.*

BONO: Yeah. I know what you mean. That's all they care about . . . that money. They don't care about what's right. *(Pause.)* Nigger, why you got to go and get some hard wood? You ain't doing nothing but building a little old fence. Get you some soft pine wood. That's all you need.

TROY: I know what I'm doing. This is outside wood. You put pine wood inside the house. Pine wood is inside wood. This here is outside

1280   wood. Now you tell me where the fence is gonna be?

BONO: You don't need this wood. You can put it up with pine wood and it'll stand as long as you gonna be here looking at it.

TROY: How you know how long I'm gonna be here, nigger? Hell, I might just live forever. Live longer than old man Horsely.

BONO: That's what Magee used to say.

TROY: Magee's a damn fool. Now you tell me who you ever heard of gonna pull their own teeth with a pair of rusty pliers.

BONO: The old folks . . . my granddaddy used to pull his teeth with pliers. They ain't had no dentists for the colored folks back then.

1290   TROY: Get clean pliers! You understand? Clean, pliers! Sterilize them! Besides we ain't living back then. All Magee had to do was walk over to Doc Goldblum's.

BONO: I see where you and that Tallahassee gal . . . that Alberta . . . I see where you all done got tight.

TROY: What do you mean "got tight?"

BONO: I see where you be laughing and joking with her all the time.

TROY: I laughs and jokes with all of them, Bono. You know me.

BONO: That ain't the kind of laughing and joking I'm talking about.

(Cory enters from the house.)

CORY: How you doing, Mr. Bono?

1300   TROY: Cory? Get that saw from Bono and cut some wood. He talking about the wood's too hard to cut. Stand back there, Jim, and let that young boy show you how it's done.

BONO: He's sure welcome to it.

(Cory takes the saw and begins to cut the wood.)

Whew-e-e! Look at that. Big old strong boy. Look like Joe Louis. Hell, must be getting old the way I'm watching that boy whip through that wood.

CORY: I don't see why Mama want a fence around the yard noways.

TROY: Damn if I know either. What the hell she keeping out with it? She ain't got nothing nobody want.

1310   BONO: Some people build fences to keep people out . . . and other people build fences to keep people in. Rose wants to hold on to you all. She loves you.

TROY: Hell, nigger, I don't need nobody to tell me my wife loves me.

Cory . . . go on in the house and see if you can find that other saw.

CORY: Where's it at?

TROY: I said find it! Look for it till you find it!

(Cory exits into the house.)

What's that supposed to mean? Wanna keep us in?

BONO: Troy . . . I done known you seem like damn near my whole life. You and Rose both. I done know both of you all for a long time. I

1320   remember when you met Rose. When you was hitting them baseball

out the park. A lot of them old gals was after you then. You had the pick of the litter. When you picked Rose, I was happy for you. That was the first time I knew you had any sense. I said . . . My man Troy knows what he's doing . . . I'm gonna follow this nigger . . . he might take me somewhere. I been following you, too. I done learned a whole heap of things about life watching you. I done learned how to tell where the shit lies. How to tell it from the alfalfa. You done learned me a lot of things. You showed me how to not make the same mistakes . . . to take life as it comes along and keep putting one
1330   foot in front of the other. *(Pause.)* Rose a good woman, Troy.

TROY: Hell, nigger, I know she a good woman. I been married to her for eighteen years. What you got on your mind, Bono?

BONO: I just say she a good woman. Just like I say anything. I ain't got to have nothing on my mind.

TROY: You just gonna say she a good woman and leave it hanging out there like that? Why you telling me she a good woman?

BONO: She loves you, Troy. Rose loves you.

TROY: You saying I don't measure up. That's what you trying to say. I don't measure up cause I'm seeing this other gal. I know what you
1340   trying to say.

BONO: I know what Rose means to you, Troy. I'm just trying to say I don't want to see you mess up.

TROY: Yeah, I appreciate that, Bono. If you was messing around on Lucille I'd be telling you the same thing.

BONO: Well that's all I got to say. I just say that because I love you both.

TROY: Hell, you know me . . . I wasn't out there looking for nothing. You can't find a better woman than Rose. I know that. But seems like this woman just stuck onto me where I can't shake her loose. I done wrestled with it, tried to throw her off me . . . but she just stuck on tighter. Now she's stuck on for good.

1350 BONO: You's in control . . . that's what you tell me all the time. You responsible for what you do.

TROY: I ain't ducking the responsibility of it. As long as it sets right in my heart . . . then I'm okay. Cause that's all I listen to. It'll tell me right from wrong every time. And I ain't talking about doing Rose no bad turn. I love Rose. She done carried me a long ways and I love and respect her for that.

BONO: I know you do. That's why I don't want to see you hurt her. But what you gonna do when she find out? What you got then? If you try to juggle both of them . . . sooner or later you gonna drop one of
1360   them. That's common sense.

TROY: Yeah, I hear what you saying, Bono. I been trying to figure a way to work it out.

BONO: Work it out right, Troy. I don't want to be getting all up between you and Rose's business . . . but work it so it come out right.

TROY: Aw hell, I get all up between you and Lucille's business. When you gonna get that woman that refrigerator she been wanting? Don't tell me you ain't got no money now. I know who your banker is. Mellon don't need that money bad as Lucille want that refrigerator. I'll tell you that.

1370

BONO: Tell you what I'll do . . . when you finish building this fence for Rose . . . I'll buy Lucille that refrigerator.

TROY: You done stuck your foot in your mouth now! *(Troy grabs up a board and begins to saw. Bono starts to walk out the yard.)* Hey, nigger . . . where you going?

BONO: I'm going home. I know you don't expect me to help you now. I'm protecting my money. I wanna see you put that fence up by yourself. That's what I want to see. You'll be here another six months without me.

1380

TROY: Nigger, you ain't right.

BONO: When it comes to my money . . . I'm right as fireworks on the Fourth of July.

TROY: All right, we gonna see now. You better get out your bankbook.

(Bono exits, and Troy continues to work. Rose enters from the house.)

ROSE: What they say down there? What's happening with Gabe?

TROY: I went down there and got him out. Cost me fifty dollars. Say he was disturbing the peace. Judge set up a hearing for him in three weeks. Say to show cause why he shouldn't be recommitted.

ROSE: What was he doing that cause them to arrest him?

TROY: Some kids was teasing him and he run them off home. Say he was howling and carrying on. Some folks seen him and called the police. That's all it was.

1390

ROSE: Well, what's you say? What'd you tell the Judge?

TROY: Told him I'd look after him. It didn't make no sense to recommit the man. He stuck out his big greasy palm and told me to give him fifty dollars and take him on home.

ROSE: Where's he at now? Where'd he go off to?

TROY: He's gone on about his business. He don't need nobody to hold his hand.

ROSE: Well, I don't know. Seem like that would be the best place for him if they did put him into the hospital. I know what you're gonna say. But that's what I think would be best.

1400

TROY: The man done had his life ruined fighting for what? And they wanna take and lock him up. Let him be free. He don't bother nobody.

ROSE: Well, everybody got their own way of looking at it I guess. Come on and get your lunch. I got a bowl of lima beans and some cornbread in the oven. Come on get something to eat. Ain't no sense you fretting over Gabe.

(Rose turns to go into the house.)

TROY: Rose . . . got something to tell you.

ROSE: Well, come on . . . wait till I get this food on the table.

TROY: Rose! *(She stops and turns around.)* I don't know how to say this. *(Pause.)* I can't explain it none. It just sort of grows on you till it gets out of hand. It starts out like a little bush . . . and the next thing you know it's a whole forest.

ROSE: Troy . . . what is you talking about?

TROY: I'm talking, woman, let me talk. I'm trying to find a way to tell you . . . I'm gonna be a daddy. I'm gonna be somebody's daddy.

ROSE: Troy . . . you're not telling me this? You're gonna be . . . what?

TROY: Rose . . . now . . . see . . .

ROSE: You telling me you gonna be somebody's daddy? You telling your *wife* this?

(Gabriel enters from the street. He carries a rose in his hand.)

GABRIEL: Hey, Troy! Hey, Rose!

ROSE: I have to wait eighteen years to hear something like this.

GABRIEL: Hey, Rose . . . I got a flower for you. *(He hands it to her.)* That's a rose. Same rose like you is.

ROSE: Thanks, Gabe.

GABRIEL: Troy, you ain't mad at me is you? Them bad mens come and put me away. You ain't mad at me is you?

TROY: Naw, Gabe, I ain't mad at you.

ROSE: Eighteen years and you wanna come with this.

GABRIEL *(takes a quarter out of his pocket)*: See what I got? Got a brand new quarter.

TROY: Rose . . . it's just . . .

ROSE: Ain't nothing you can say, Troy. Ain't no way of explaining that.

GABRIEL: Fellow that give me this quarter had a whole mess of them. I'm gonna keep this quarter till it stop shining.

ROSE: Gabe, go on in the house there. I got some watermelon in the frigidaire. Go on and get you a piece.

GABRIEL: Say, Rose . . . you know I was chasing hellhounds and them bad mens come and get me and take me away. Troy helped me. He come down there and told them they better let me go before he beat them up. Yeah, he did!

ROSE: You go on and get you a piece of watermelon, Gabe. Them bad mens is gone now.

GABRIEL: Okay, Rose . . . gonna get me some watermelon. The kind with the stripes on it.

(Gabriel exits into the house.)

ROSE: Why, Troy? Why? After all these years to come dragging this in to me now. It don't make no sense at your age. I could have expected this ten or fifteen years ago, but not now.

TROY: Age ain't got nothing to do with it, Rose.

ROSE: I done tried to be everything a wife should be. Everything a wife could be. Been married eighteen years and I got to live to see the

1450   day you tell me you been seeing another woman and done fathered a
        child by her. And you know I ain't never wanted no half nothing in
        my family. My whole family is half. Everybody got different fathers
        and mothers . . . my two sisters and my brother. Can't hardly tell
        who's who. Can't never sit down and talk about Papa and Mama. It's
        your papa and your mama and my papa and my mama . . .

TROY: Rose . . . stop it now.

ROSE: I ain't never wanted that for none of my children. And now you
        wanna drag your behind in here and tell me something like this.

TROY: You ought to know. It's time for you to know.

1460   ROSE: Well, I don't want to know, goddamn it!

TROY: I can't just make it go away. It's done now. I can't wish the cir-
        cumstance of the thing away.

ROSE: And you don't want to either. Maybe you want to wish me and
        my boy away. Maybe that's what you want? Well, you can't wish us
        away. I've got eighteen years of my life invested in you. You ought to
        have stayed upstairs in my bed where you belong.

TROY: Rose . . . now listen to me . . . we can get a handle on this thing. We
        can talk this out . . . come to an understanding.

ROSE: All of a sudden it's "we." Where was "we" at when you was down
1470   there rolling around with some god-forsaken woman? "We" should
        have come to an understanding before you started making a damn
        fool of yourself. You're a day late and a dollar short when it comes
        to an understanding with me.

TROY: It's just . . . She gives me a different idea . . . a different under-
        standing about myself. I can step out of this house and get away
        from the pressures and problems . . . be a different man. I ain't got to
        wonder how I'm gonna pay the bills or get the roof fixed. I can just
        be a part of myself that ain't never been.

ROSE: What I want to know . . . is do you plan to continue seeing her.
1480   That's all you can say to me.

TROY: I can sit up in her house and laugh. Do you understand what I'm
        saying. I can laugh out loud . . . and it feels good. It reaches all the way
        down to the bottom of my shoes. *(Pause.)* Rose, I can't give that up.

ROSE: Maybe you ought to go on and stay down there with her . . . if
        she a better woman than me.

TROY: It ain't about nobody being a better woman or nothing. Rose, you
        ain't the blame. A man couldn't ask for no woman to be a better wife
        than you've been. I'm responsible for it. I done locked myself into a
1490   pattern trying to take care of you all that I forget about myself.

ROSE: What the hell was I there for? That was my job, not somebody
        else's.

TROY: Rose, I done tried all my life to live decent . . . to live a clean . . .
        hard . . . useful life. I tried to be a good husband to you. In every way I
        knew how. Maybe I come into the world backwards, I don't know.
        But . . . you born with two strikes on you before you come to the

plate. You got to guard it closely . . . always looking for the curve-ball on the inside corner. You can't afford to let none get past you. You can't afford a call strike. If you going down . . . you going down swinging. Everything lined up against you. What you gonna do. I fooled them, Rose. I bunted. When I found you and Cory and a halfway decent job . . . I was safe. Couldn't nothing touch me. I wasn't gonna strike out no more. I wasn't going back to the penitentiary. I wasn't gonna lay in the streets with a bottle of wine. I was safe. I had me a family. A job. I wasn't gonna get that last strike. I was on first looking for one of them boys to knock me in. To get me home.

ROSE: You should have stayed in my bed, Troy.

TROY: Then when I saw that gal . . . she firmed up my backbone. And I got to thinking that if I tried . . . I just might be able to steal second. Do you understand after eighteen years I wanted to steal second.

ROSE: You should have held me tight. You should have grabbed me and held on.

TROY: I stood on first base for eighteen years and I thought . . . well, goddamn it . . . go on for it!

ROSE: We're not talking about baseball! We're talking about you going off to lay in bed with another woman . . . and then bring it home to me. That's what we're talking about. We ain't talking about no baseball.

TROY: Rose, you're not listening to me. I'm trying the best I can to explain it to you. It's not easy for me to admit that I been standing in the same place for eighteen years.

ROSE: I been standing with you! I been right here with you, Troy. I got a life too. I gave eighteen years of my life to stand in the same spot with you. Don't you think I ever wanted other things? Don't you think I had dreams and hopes? What about my life? What about me? Don't you think it ever crossed my mind to want to know other men? That I wanted to lay up somewhere and forget about my responsibilities? That I wanted someone to make me laugh so I could feel good? You not the only one who's got wants and needs. But I held on to you, Troy. I took all my feelings, my wants and needs, my dreams . . . and I buried them inside you. I planted a seed and watched and prayed over it. I planted myself inside you and waited to bloom. And it didn't take me no eighteen years to find out the soil was hard and rocky and it wasn't never gonna bloom.

But I held on to you, Troy. I held on tighter. You was my husband. I owed you everything I had. Every part of me I could find to give you. And upstairs in that room . . . with the darkness falling in on me . . . I gave everything I had to try and erase the doubt that you wasn't the finest man in the world. And wherever you was going . . . I wanted to be there with you. Cause you was my husband. Cause that's the only way I was gonna survive as your wife. You always talking about what you give . . . and what you don't have to give. But you take, too. You take . . . and don't even know nobody's giving!

(Rose turns to exit into the house; Troy grabs her arm.)

TROY: You say I take and don't give!
ROSE: Troy! You're hurting me!
TROY: You say I take and don't give.
ROSE: Troy . . . you're hurting my arm! Let go!
TROY: I done give you everything I got. Don't you tell that lie on me.
ROSE: Troy!
1550   TROY: Don't you tell that lie on me!

(Cory enters from the house.)

CORY: Mama!
ROSE: Troy. You're hurting me.
TROY: Don't you tell me about no taking and giving.

(Cory comes up behind Troy and grabs him. Troy, surprised, is thrown off balance just as Cory throws a glancing blow that catches him on the chest and knocks him down. Troy is stunned, as is Cory.)

ROSE: Troy. Troy. No!

(Troy gets to his feet and starts at Cory.)

Troy . . . no. Please! Troy!

(Rose pulls on Troy to hold him back. Troy stops himself.)

TROY *(to Cory)*: All right. That's strike two. You stay away from around me, boy. Don't you strike out. You living with a full count. Don't you strike out.

(Troy exits out the yard as the lights go down.)

SCENE 2

It is six months later, early afternoon. Troy enters from the house and starts to exit the yard. Rose enters from the house.

ROSE: Troy, I want to talk to you.
1560   TROY: All of a sudden, after all this time, you want to talk to me, huh? You ain't wanted to talk to me for months. You ain't wanted to talk to me last night. You ain't wanted no part of me then. What you wanna talk to me about now?
ROSE: Tomorrow's Friday.
TROY: I know what day tomorrow is. You think I don't know tomorrow's Friday? My whole life I ain't done nothing but look to see Friday coming and you got to tell me it's Friday.
ROSE: I want to know if you're coming home.
TROY: I always come home, Rose. You know that. There ain't never been
1570   a night I ain't come home.

ROSE: That ain't what I mean . . . and you know it. I want to know if you're coming straight home after work.

TROY: I figure I'd cash my check . . . hang out at Taylors' with the boys . . . maybe play a game of checkers . . .

ROSE: Troy, I can't live like this. I won't live like this. You livin' on borrowed time with me. It's been going on six months now you ain't been coming home.

TROY: I be here every night. Every night of the year. That's 365 days.

ROSE: I want you to come home tomorrow after work.

1580   TROY: Rose . . . I don't mess up my pay. You know that now. I take my pay and I give it to you. I don't have no money but what you give me back. I just want to have a little time to myself . . . a little time to enjoy life.

ROSE: What about me? When's my time to enjoy life?

TROY: I don't know what to tell you, Rose. I'm doing the best I can.

ROSE: You ain't been home from work but time enough to change your clothes and run out . . . and you wanna call that the best you can do?

TROY: I'm going over to the hospital to see Alberta. She went into the hospital this afternoon. Look like she might have the baby early. I
1590   won't be gone long.

ROSE: Well, you ought to know. They went over to Miss Pearl's and got Gabe today. She said you told them to go ahead and lock him up.

TROY: I ain't said no such thing. Whoever told you that is telling a lie. Pearl ain't doing nothing but telling a big fat lie.

ROSE: She ain't had to tell me. I read it on the papers.

TROY: I ain't told them nothing of the kind.

ROSE: I saw it right there on the papers.

TROY: What it say, huh?

ROSE: It said you told them to take him.

1600   TROY: Then they screwed that up, just the way they screw up everything. I ain't worried about what they got on the paper.

ROSE: Say the government send part of his check to the hospital and the other part to you.

TROY: I ain't got nothing to do with that if that's the way it works. I ain't made up the rules about how it work.

ROSE: You did Gabe just like you did Cory. You wouldn't sign the paper for Cory . . . but you signed for Gabe. You signed that paper.

(The telephone is heard ringing inside the house.)

TROY: I told you I ain't signed nothing, woman! The only thing I signed was the release form. Hell, I can't read, I don't know what they had
1610   on that paper! I ain't signed nothing about sending Gabe away.

ROSE: I said send him to the hospital . . . you said let him be free . . . now you done went down there and signed him to the hospital for half his money. You went back on yourself, Troy. You gonna have to answer for that.

TROY: See now . . . you been over there talking to Miss Pearl. She done got mad cause she ain't getting Gabe's rent money. That's all it is. She's liable to say anything.

ROSE: Troy, I seen where you signed the paper.

1620   TROY: You ain't seen nothing I signed. What she doing got papers on my brother anyway? Miss Pearl telling a big fat lie. And I'm gonna tell her about it too! You ain't seen nothing I signed. Say . . . you ain't seen nothing I signed.

(Rose exits into the house to answer the telephone. Presently she returns.)

ROSE: Troy . . . that was the hospital. Alberta had the baby.

TROY: What she have? What is it?

ROSE: It's a girl.

TROY: I better get on down to the hospital to see her.

ROSE: Troy.

TROY: Rose . . . I got to see her now. That's only right . . . what's the matter . . . the baby's all right, ain't it?

1630   ROSE: Alberta died having the baby.

TROY: Died . . . you say she's dead? Alberta's dead?

ROSE: They said they done all they could. They couldn't do nothing for her.

TROY: The baby? How's the baby?

ROSE: They say it's healthy. I wonder who's gonna bury her.

TROY: She had family, Rose. She wasn't living in the world by herself.

ROSE: I know she wasn't living in the world by herself.

TROY: Next thing you gonna want to know if she had any insurance.

ROSE: Troy, you ain't got to talk like that.

1640   TROY: That's the first thing that jumped out your mouth. "Who's gonna bury her?" Like I'm fixing to take on that task for myself.

ROSE: I am your wife. Don't push me away.

TROY: I ain't pushing nobody away. Just give me some space. That's all. Just give me some room to breathe.

(Rose exits into the house. Troy walks about the yard.)

TROY *(with a quiet rage that threatens to consume him)*: All right . . . Mr. Death. See now . . . I'm gonna tell you what I'm gonna do. I'm gonna take and build me a fence around this yard. See? I'm gonna build me a fence around what belongs to me. And then I want you to stay on the other side. See? You stay over there until you're ready for me. Then you come
1650   on. Bring your army. Bring your sickle. Bring your wrestling clothes. I ain't gonna fall down on my vigilance this time. You ain't gonna sneak up on me no more. When you ready for me . . . when the top of your list say Troy Maxson . . . that's when you come around here. You come up and knock on the front door. Ain't nobody else got nothing to do with this. This is between you and me. Man to man. You stay on the other

side of that fence until you ready for me. Then you come up and knock on the front door. Anytime you want. I'll be ready for you.

(The lights go down to black.)

SCENE 3

The lights come up on the porch. It is late evening three days later. Rose sits listening to the ball game waiting for Troy. The final out of the game is made and Rose switches off the radio. Troy enters the yard carrying an infant wrapped in blankets. He stands back from the house and calls.

Rose enters and stands on the porch. There is a long, awkward silence, the weight of which grows heavier with each passing second.

TROY: Rose . . . I'm standing here with my daughter in my arms. She ain't but a wee bittie little old thing. She don't know nothing about 1660 grownups' business. She innocent . . . and she ain't got no mama.

ROSE: What you telling me for, Troy?

(She turns and exits into the house.)

TROY: Well . . . I guess we'll just sit out here on the porch.

(He sits down on the porch. There is an awkward indelicateness about the way he handles the baby. His largeness engulfs and seems to swallow it. He speaks loud enough for Rose to hear.)

A man's got to do what's right for him. I ain't sorry for nothing I done. It felt right in my heart. *(To the baby)* What you smiling at? Your daddy's a big man. Got these great big old hands. But sometimes he's scared. And right now your daddy's scared cause we sitting out here and ain't got no home. Oh, I been homeless before. I ain't had no little baby with me. But I been homeless. You just be out on the road by your lonesome and you see one of them trains 1670 coming and you just kinda go like this . . . *(He sings as a lullaby)*:
Please, Mr. Engineer let a man ride the line
Please, Mr. Engineer let a man ride the line
I ain't got no ticket please let me ride the blinds

(Rose enters from the house. Troy, hearing her steps behind him, stands and faces her.)

She's my daughter, Rose. My own flesh and blood. I can't deny her no more than I can deny them boys. *(Pause.)* You and them boys is my family. You and them and this child is all I got in the world. So I guess what I'm saying is . . . I'd appreciate it if you'd help me take care of her.

ROSE: Okay, Troy . . . you're right. I'll take care of your baby for you . . . 1680 cause . . . like you say . . . she's innocent . . . and you can't visit the sins of the father upon the child. A motherless child has got a hard time.

(She takes the baby from him.) From right now . . . this child got a mother. But you a womanless man.

(Rose turns and exits into the house with the baby. Lights go down to black.)

SCENE 4

It is two months later. Lyons enters from the street. He knocks on the door and calls.

LYONS: Hey, Rose! *(Pause.)* Rose!

ROSE *(from inside the house)*: Stop that yelling. You gonna wake up Raynell. I just got her to sleep.

LYONS: I just stopped by to pay Papa this twenty dollars I owe him. Where's Papa at?

ROSE: He should be here in a minute. I'm getting ready to go down to the church. Sit down and wait on him.

LYONS: I got to go pick up Bonnie over her mother's house.

ROSE: Well, sit it down there on the table. He'll get it.

LYONS *(enters the house and sets the money on the table)*: Tell Papa I said thanks. I'll see you again.

ROSE: All right, Lyons. We'll see you.

(Lyons starts to exit as Cory enters.)

CORY: Hey, Lyons.

LYONS: What's happening, Cory. Say man, I'm sorry I missed your graduation. You know I had a gig and couldn't get away. Otherwise, I would have been there, man. So what you doing?

CORY: I'm trying to find a job.

LYONS: Yeah I know how that go, man. It's rough out here. Jobs are scarce.

CORY: Yeah, I know.

LYONS: Look here, I got to run. Talk to Papa . . . he know some people. He'll be able to help get you a job. Talk to him . . . see what he say.

CORY: Yeah . . . all right, Lyons.

LYONS: You take care. I'll talk to you soon. We'll find some time to talk.

(Lyons exits the yard. Cory wanders over to the tree, picks up the bat and assumes a batting stance. He studies an imaginary pitcher and swings. Dissatisfied with the result, he tries again. Troy enters. They eye each other for a beat. Cory puts the bat down and exits the yard. Troy starts into the house as Rose exits with Raynell. She is carrying a cake.)

TROY: I'm coming in and everybody's going out.

ROSE: I'm taking this cake down to the church for the bake sale. Lyons was by to see you. He stopped by to pay you your twenty dollars. It's laying in there on the table.

TROY *(going into his pocket)*: Well . . . here go this money.

ROSE: Put it in there on the table, Troy. I'll get it.

TROY: What time you coming back?

ROSE: Ain't no use you studying me. It don't matter what time I come back.

TROY: I just asked you a question, woman. What's the matter . . . can't I ask you a question?

ROSE: Troy, I don't want to go into it. Your dinner's in there on the stove. All you got to do is heat it up. And don't you be eating the rest of them cakes in there. I'm coming back for them. We having a bake 1720   sale at the church tomorrow.

(Rose exits the yard. Troy sits down on the steps, takes a pint bottle from his pocket, opens it and drinks. He begins to sing.)

TROY:
Hear it ring! Hear it ring!
Had an old dog his name was Blue
You know Blue was mighty true
You know Blue was a good old dog
Blue treed a possum in a hollow log
You know from that he was a good old dog

(Bono enters the yard.)

BONO: Hey, Troy.

TROY: Hey, what's happening, Bono?

1730   BONO: I just thought I'd stop by to see you.

TROY: What you stop by and see me for? You ain't stopped by in a month of Sundays. Hell, I must owe you money or something.

BONO: Since you got your promotion I can't keep up with you. Used to see you every day. Now I don't even know what route you working.

TROY: They keep switching me around. Got me out in Greentree now . . . hauling white folks' garbage.

BONO: Greentree, huh? You lucky, at least you ain't got to be lifting them barrels. Damn if they ain't getting heavier. I'm gonna put in my two years and call it quits.

1740   TROY: I'm thinking about retiring myself.

BONO: You got it easy. You can *drive* for another five years.

TROY: It ain't the same, Bono. It ain't like working the back of the truck. Ain't got nobody to talk to . . . feel like you working by yourself. Naw, I'm thinking about retiring. How's Lucille?

BONO: She all right. Her arthritis get to acting up on her sometime. Saw Rose on my way in. She going down to the church, huh?

TROY: Yeah, she took up going down there. All them preachers looking for somebody to fatten their pockets. *(Pause.)* Got some gin here.

BONO: Naw, thanks. I just stopped by to say hello.

1750   TROY: Hell, nigger . . . you can take a drink. I ain't never known you to say no to a drink. You ain't got to work tomorrow.

BONO: I just stopped by. I'm fixing to go over to Skinner's. We got us a domino game going over his house every Friday.

TROY: Nigger, you can't play no dominoes. I used to whup you four
games out of five.

BONO: Well, that learned me. I'm getting better.

TROY: Yeah? Well, that's all right.

BONO: Look here . . . I got to be getting on. Stop by sometime, huh?

TROY: Yeah, I'll do that, Bono. Lucille told Rose you bought her a new
1760   refrigerator.

BONO: Yeah, Rose told Lucille you had finally built your fence . . . so I
figured we'd call it even.

TROY: I knew you would.

BONO: Yeah . . . okay. I'll be talking to you.

TROY: Yeah, take care, Bono. Good to see you. I'm gonna stop over.

BONO: Yeah. Okay, Troy.

(Bono exits. Troy drinks from the bottle.)

TROY:

Old Blue died and I dig his grave
Let him down with a golden chain
1770   Every night when I hear old Blue bark
I know Blue treed a possum in Noah's Ark.
Hear it ring! Hear it ring!

*(Cory enters the yard. They eye each other for a beat. Troy is sitting
in the middle of the steps. Cory walks over.)*

CORY: I got to get by.

TROY: Say what? What's you say?

CORY: You in my way. I got to get by.

TROY: You got to get by where? This is my house. Bought and paid for.
Took me fifteen years. And if you wanna go in my house and I'm sitting on the steps . . . you say excuse me. Like your mama taught you.

1780   CORY: Come on, Pop . . . I got to get by.

*(Cory starts to maneuver his way past Troy. Troy grabs his leg and
shoves him back.)*

TROY: You just gonna walk over top of me?

CORY: I live here, too!

TROY *(advancing toward him)*: You just gonna walk over top of me in
my own house?

CORY: I ain't scared of you.

TROY: I ain't asked if you was scared of me. I asked you if you was fixing to walk over top of me in my own house? That's the question.
You ain't gonna say excuse me? You just gonna walk over top of me?

1790   CORY: If you wanna put it like that.

TROY: How else am I gonna put it?

CORY: I was walking by you to go into the house cause you sitting on the
steps drunk, singing to yourself. You can put it like that.

TROY: Without saying excuse me???

(Cory doesn't respond.)

I asked you a question. Without saying excuse me???

CORY: I ain't got to say excuse me to you. You don't count around here no more.

TROY: Oh, I see . . . I don't count around here no more. You ain't got to say excuse me to your daddy. All of a sudden you done got so grown that your daddy don't count around here no more . . . Around here in his own house and yard that he done paid for with the sweat of his brow. You done got so grown to where you gonna take over. You gonna take over my house. Is that right? You gonna wear my pants. You gonna go in there and stretch out on my bed. You ain't got to say excuse me cause I don't count around here no more. Is that right?

CORY: That's right. You always talking this dumb stuff. Now, why don't you just get out my way.

TROY: I guess you got someplace to sleep and something to put in your belly. You got that, huh? You got that? That's what you need. You got that, huh?

CORY: You don't know what I got. You ain't got to worry about what I got.

TROY: You right! You one hundred percent right! I done spent the last seventeen years worrying about what you got. Now it's your turn, see? I'll tell you what to do. You grown . . . we done established that. You a man. Now, let's see you act like one. Turn your behind around and walk out this yard. And when you get out there in the alley . . . you can forget about this house. See? Cause this is my house. You go on and be a man and get your own house. You can forget about this. Cause this is mine. You go on and get yours cause I'm through with doing for you.

CORY: You talking about what you did for me . . . what'd you ever give me?

TROY: Them feet and bones! That pumping heart, nigger! I give you more than anybody else is ever gonna give you.

CORY: You ain't never gave me nothing! You ain't never done nothing but hold me back. Afraid I was gonna be better than you. All you ever did was try and make me scared of you. I used to tremble every time you called my name. Every time I heard your footsteps in the house. Wondering all the time . . . what's Papa gonna say if I do this? . . . What's he gonna say if I do that? . . . What's Papa gonna say if I turn on the radio? And Mama, too . . . she tries . . . but she's scared of you.

TROY: You leave your mama out of this. She ain't got nothing to do with this.

CORY: I don't know how she stands you . . . after what you did to her.

TROY: I told you to leave your mama out of this!

(He advances toward Cory.)

CORY: What you gonna do . . . give me a whupping? You can't whup me no more. You're too old. You just an old man.

TROY *(shoves him on his shoulder)*: Nigger! That's what you are. You just another nigger on the street to me!

CORY: You crazy! You know that?

TROY: Go on now! You got the devil in you. Get on away from me!

CORY: You just a crazy old man . . . talking about I got the devil in me.

TROY: Yeah, I'm crazy! If you don't get on the other side of that yard . . . I'm
1840   gonna show you how crazy I am! Go on . . . get the hell out of my yard.

CORY: It ain't your yard. You took Uncle Gabe's money he got from the
army to buy this house and then you put him out.

TROY (*advances on Cory*): Get your black ass out of my yard!

(*Troy's advance backs Cory up against the tree. Cory grabs up the bat.*)

CORY: I ain't going nowhere! Come on . . . put me out! I ain't scared of
you.

TROY: That's my bat!

CORY: Come on!

TROY: Put my bat down!

CORY: Come on, put me out.

(*Cory swings at Troy, who backs across the yard.*)

What's the matter? You so bad . . . put me out!

(*Troy advances toward Cory.*)

1850   CORY (*backing up*): Come on! Come on!

TROY: You're gonna have to use it! You wanna draw that bat back on
me . . . you're gonna have to use it.

CORY: Come on! . . . Come on!

(*Cory swings the bat at Troy a second time. He misses. Troy continues to advance toward him.*)

TROY: You're gonna have to kill me! You wanna draw that bat back on
me. You're gonna have to kill me.

(*Cory, backed up against the tree, can go no farther. Troy taunts
him. He sticks out his head and offers him a target.*)

Come on! Come on!

1860   (*Cory is unable to swing the bat. Troy grabs it.*)

TROY: Then I'll show you.

(*Cory and Troy struggle over the bat. The struggle is fierce and fully
engaged. Troy ultimately is the stronger, and takes the bat from Cory
and stands over him ready to swing. He stops himself.*)

Go on and get away from around my house.

(*Cory, stung by his defeat, picks himself up, walks slowly out of the
yard and up the alley.*)

CORY: Tell Mama I'll be back for my things.

1870   TROY: They'll be on the other side of that fence.

(*Cory exits.*)

TROY: I can't taste nothing. Helluljah! I can't taste nothing no more.

(Troy assumes a batting posture and begins to taunt Death, the fast-ball in the outside corner.) Come on! It's between you and me now! Come on! Anytime you want! Come on! I be ready for you . . . but I ain't gonna be easy.

(The lights go down on the scene.)

SCENE 5

The time is 1965. The lights come up in the yard. It is the morning of Troy's funeral. A funeral plaque with a light hangs beside the door. There is a small garden plot off to the side. There is noise and activity in the house as Rose, Lyons, and Bono have gathered. The door opens and Raynell, seven years old, enters dressed in a flannel night-gown. She crosses to the garden and pokes around with a stick. Rose calls from the house.

ROSE: Raynell!
RAYNELL: Mam?
ROSE: What you doing out there?
RAYNELL: Nothing.

(Rose comes to the door.)

ROSE: Girl, get in here and get dressed. What you doing?
RAYNELL: Seeing if my garden growed.
ROSE: I told you it ain't gonna grow overnight. You got to wait.
RAYNELL: It don't look like it never gonna grow. Dag!
1880   ROSE: I told you a watched pot never boils. Get in here and get dressed.
RAYNELL: This ain't even no pot, Mama.
ROSE: You just have to give it a chance. It'll grow. Now you come on and do what I told you. We got to be getting ready. This ain't no morning to be playing around. You hear me?
RAYNELL: Yes, Mam.

(Rose exits into the house. Raynell continues to poke at her garden with a stick. Cory enters. He is dressed in a Marine corporal's uniform, and carries a duffel bag. His posture is that of a military man, and his speech has a clipped sternness.)

CORY *(to Raynell)*: Hi. *(Pause.)* I bet your name is Raynell.
RAYNELL: Uh huh.
CORY: Is your mama home?

(Raynell runs up on the porch and calls through the screen door.)

RAYNELL: Mama . . . there's some man out here. Mama?

(Rose comes to the door.)

1890   ROSE: Cory? Lord have mercy! Look here, you all!

(Rose and Cory embrace in a tearful reunion as Bono and Lyons enter from the house dressed in funeral clothes.)

BONO: Aw, looka here . . .

ROSE: Done got all grown up!

CORY: Don't cry, Mama. What you crying about?

ROSE: I'm just so glad you made it.

CORY: Hey, Lyons. How you doing, Mr. Bono.

(Lyons goes to embrace Cory.)

LYONS: Look at you, man. Look at you. Don't he look good, Rose? Got them Corporal stripes.

ROSE: What took you so long?

CORY: You know how the Marines are, Mama. They got to get all their
1900   paperwork straight before they let you do anything.

ROSE: Well, I'm sure glad you made it. They let Lyons come. Your Uncle Gabe's still in the hospital. They don't know if they gonna let him out or not. I just talked to them a little while ago.

LYONS: A Corporal in the United States Marines.

BONO: Your daddy knew you had it in you. He used to tell me all the time.

LYONS: Don't he look good, Mr. Bono?

BONO: Yeah, he remind me of Troy when I first met him. *(Pause.)* Say, Rose, Lucille's down at the church with the choir. I'm gonna
1910   go down and get the pallbearers lined up. I'll be back to get you all.

ROSE: Thanks, Jim.

CORY: See you, Mr. Bono.

LYONS *(with his arm around Raynell)*: Cory . . . look at Raynell. Ain't she precious? She gonna break a whole lot of hearts.

ROSE: Raynell, come and say hello to your brother. This is your brother, Cory. You remember Cory.

RAYNELL: No, Mam.

CORY: She don't remember me, Mama.

1920   ROSE: Well, we talk about you. She heard us talk about you.
(To Raynell) This is your brother, Cory. Come on and say hello.

RAYNELL: Hi.

CORY: Hi. So you're Raynell. Mama told me a lot about you.

ROSE: You all come on into the house and let me fix you some break-fast. Keep up your strength.

CORY: I ain't hungry, Mama.

LYONS: You can fix me something, Rose. I'll be in there in a minute.

ROSE: Cory, you sure you don't want nothing? I know they ain't feeding
1930   you right.

CORY: No, Mama . . . thanks. I don't feel like eating. I'll get something later.

ROSE: Raynell . . . get on upstairs and get that dress on like I told you.

(Rose and Raynell exit into the house.)

LYONS: So . . . I hear you thinking about getting married.

CORY: Yeah, I done found the right one, Lyons. It's about time.

LYONS: Me and Bonnie been split up about four years now. About the time Papa retired. I guess she just got tired of all them changes I was putting her through. *(Pause.)* I always knew you was gonna make something out yourself. Your head was always in the right direction.
So . . . you gonna stay in . . . make it a career . . . put in your twenty years?

CORY: I don't know. I got six already. I think that's enough.

LYONS: Stick with Uncle Sam and retire early. Ain't nothing out here. I guess Rose told you what happened with me. They got me down the workhouse. I thought I was being slick cashing other people's checks.

CORY: How much time you doing?

LYONS: They give me three years. I got that beat now. I ain't got but nine more months. It ain't so bad. You learn to deal with it like anything else. You got to take the crookeds with the straights. That's what Papa used to say. He used to say that when he struck out. I seen him strike out three times in a row . . . and the next time up he hit the ball over the grandstand. Right out there in Homestead Field. He wasn't satisfied hitting in the seats . . . he want to hit it over everything! After the game he had two hundred people standing around waiting to shake his hand. You got to take the crookeds with the straights. Yeah, Papa was something else.

CORY: You still playing?

LYONS: Cory . . . you know I'm gonna do that. There's some fellows down there we got us a band . . . we gonna try and stay together when we get out . . . but yeah, I'm still playing. It still helps me to get out of bed in the morning. As long as it do that I'm gonna be right there playing and trying to make some sense out of it.

ROSE *(calling)*: Lyons, I got these eggs in the pan.

LYONS: Let me go on and get these eggs, man. Get ready to go bury Papa. *(Pause.)* How you doing? You doing all right?

(Cory nods. Lyons touches him on the shoulder and they share a moment of silent grief. Lyons exits into the house. Cory wanders about the yard. Raynell enters.)

RAYNELL: Hi.

CORY: Hi.

RAYNELL: Did you used to sleep in my room?

CORY: Yeah . . . that used to be my room.

RAYNELL: That's what Papa call it. "Cory's room." It got your football in the closet.

(Rose comes to the door.)

ROSE: Raynell, get in there and get them good shoes on.

RAYNELL: Mama, can't I wear these? Them other ones hurt my feet.

ROSE: Well, they just gonna have to hurt your feet for a while. You ain't said they hurt your feet when you went down to the store and got them.

RAYNELL: They didn't hurt then. My feet done got bigger.

1980   ROSE: Don't you give me no backtalk now. You get in there and get them shoes on. *(Raynell exits into the house.)* Ain't too much changed. He still got that piece of rag tied to that tree. He was out here swinging that bat. I was just ready to go back in the house. He swung that bat and then he just fell over. Seem like he swung it and stood there with this grin on his face . . . and then he just fell over. They carried him on down to the hospital, but I knew there wasn't no need . . . why don't you come on in the house?

CORY: Mama . . . I got something to tell you. I don't know how to tell you this . . . but I've got to tell you . . . I'm not going to Papa's funeral.

1990   ROSE: Boy, hush your mouth. That's your daddy you talking about. I don't want hear that kind of talk this morning. I done raised you to come to this? You standing there all healthy and grown talking about you ain't going to your daddy's funeral?

CORY: Mama . . . listen . . .

ROSE: I don't want to hear it, Cory. You just get that thought out of your head.

CORY: I can't drag Papa with me everywhere I go. I've got to say no to him. One time in my life I've got to say no.

ROSE: Don't nobody have to listen to nothing like that. I know you and
2000   your daddy ain't seen eye to eye, but I ain't got to listen to that kind of talk this morning. Whatever was between you and your daddy . . . the time has come to put it aside. Just take it and set it over there on the shelf and forget about it. Disrespecting your daddy ain't gonna make you a man, Cory. You got to find a way to come to that on your own. Not going to your daddy's funeral ain't gonna make you a man.

CORY: The whole time I was growing up . . . living in his house . . . Papa was like a shadow that followed you everywhere. It weighed on you and sunk into your flesh. It would wrap around you and lay there
2010   until you couldn't tell which one was you anymore. That shadow digging in your flesh. Trying to crawl in. Trying to live through you. Everywhere I looked, Troy Maxson was staring back at me . . . hiding under the bed . . . in the closet. I'm just saying I've got to find a way to get rid of that shadow, Mama.

ROSE: You just like him. You got him in you good.

CORY: Don't tell me that, Mama.

ROSE: You Troy Maxson all over again.

CORY: I don't want to be Troy Maxson. I want to be me.

ROSE: You can't be nobody but who you are, Cory. That shadow wasn't nothing but you growing into yourself. You either got to grow into it or cut it down to fit you. But that's all you got to make life with. That's all you got to measure yourself against that world out there. Your daddy wanted you to be everything he wasn't . . . and at the same time he tried to make you into everything he was. I don't know if he was right or wrong . . . but I do know he meant to do more good than he meant to do harm. He wasn't always right. Sometimes when he touched he bruised. And sometimes when he took me in his arms he cut.

When I first met your daddy I thought . . . Here is a man I can lay down with and make a baby. That's the first thing I thought when I seen him. I was thirty years old and had done seen my share of men. But when he walked up to me and said, "I can dance a waltz that'll make you dizzy," I thought, Rose Lee, here is a man that you can open yourself up to and be filled to bursting. Here is a man that can fill all them empty spaces you been tipping around the edges of. One of them empty spaces was being somebody's mother.

I married your daddy and settled down to cooking his supper and keeping clean sheets on the bed. When your daddy walked through the house he was so big he filled it up. That was my first mistake. Not to make him leave some room for me. For my part in the matter. But at that time I wanted that. I wanted a house that I could sing in. And that's what your daddy gave me. I didn't know to keep up his strength I had to give up little pieces of mine. I did that. I took on his life as mine and mixed up the pieces so that you couldn't hardly tell which was which anymore. It was my choice. It was my life and I didn't have to live it like that. But that's what life offered me in the way of being a woman and I took it. I grabbed hold of it with both hands.

By the time Raynell came into the house, me and your daddy had done lost touch with one another. I didn't want to make my blessing off of nobody's misfortune . . . but I took on to Raynell like she was all them babies I had wanted and never had. *(The phone rings.)* Like I'd been blessed to relive a part of my life. And if the Lord see fit to keep up my strength . . . I'm gonna do her just like your daddy did you . . . I'm gonna give her the best of what's in me.

RAYNELL *(entering, still with her old shoes)*: Mama . . . Reverend Tollivier on the phone.

(Rose exits into the house.)

RAYNELL: Hi.

CORY: Hi.

RAYNELL: You in the Army or the Marines?

CORY: Marines.

2060 RAYNELL: Papa said it was the Army. Did you know Blue?

CORY: Blue? Who's Blue?

RAYNELL: Papa's dog what he sing about all the time.

CORY *(singing)*:

> Hear it ring! Hear it ring!
> I had a dog his name was Blue
> You know Blue was mighty true
> You know Blue was a good old dog
> Blue treed a possum in a hollow log
> You know from that he was a good old dog.
2070 Hear it ring! Hear it ring!

(Raynell joins in singing.)

CORY AND RAYNELL:

> Blue treed a possum out on a limb
> Blue looked at me and I looked at him
> Grabbed that possum and put him in a sack
> Blue stayed there till I came back
> Old Blue's feets was big and round
> Never allowed a possum to touch the ground.
> Old Blue died and I dug his grave
> I dug his grave with a silver spade
2080 Let him down with a golden chain
> And every night I call his name
> Go on Blue, you good dog you
> Go on Blue, you good dog you.

RAYNELL:

> Blue laid down and died like a man
> Blue laid down and died . . .

BOTH: Blue laid down and died like a man

> Now he's treeing possums in the Promised Land
> I'm gonna tell you this to let you know
2090 Blue's gone where the good dogs go
> When I hear old Blue bark
> When I hear old Blue bark
> Blue treed a possum in Noah's Ark
> Blue treed a possum in Noah's Ark.

(Rose comes to the screen door.)

ROSE: Cory, we gonna be ready to go in a minute.

CORY *(to Raynell)*: You go on in the house and change them shoes like Mama told you so we can go to Papa's funeral.

RAYNELL: Okay, I'll be back.

(Raynell exits into the house. Cory gets up and crosses over to the tree. Rose stands in the screen door watching him. Gabriel enters from the alley.)

GABRIEL *(calling)*: Hey, Rose!

2100   ROSE: Gabe?

GABRIEL: I'm here, Rose. Hey Rose, I'm here!

(Rose enters from the house.)

ROSE: Lord . . . Look here, Lyons!

LYONS: See, I told you, Rose . . . I told you they'd let him come.

CORY: How you doing, Uncle Gabe?

LYONS: How you doing, Uncle Gabe?

GABRIEL: Hey, Rose. It's time. It's time to tell St. Peter to open the gates.
Troy, you ready? You ready, Troy. I'm gonna tell St. Peter to open the
gates. You get ready now.

*(Gabriel, with great fanfare, braces himself to blow. The trumpet is
without a mouthpiece. He puts the end of it into his mouth and
blows with great force, like a man who has been waiting some
twenty-odd years for this single moment. No sound comes out of the
trumpet. He braces himself and blows again with the same result. A
third time he blows. There is a weight of impossible description that
falls away and leaves him bare and exposed to a frightful realization. It is a trauma that a sane and normal mind would be unable
to withstand. He begins to dance. A slow, strange dance, eerie and
life-giving. A dance of atavistic signature and ritual. Lyons
attempts to embrace him. Gabriel pushes Lyons away. He begins to
howl in what is an attempt at song, or perhaps a song turning back
into itself in an attempt at speech. He finishes his dance and the
gates of heaven stand open as wide as God's closet.)*

That's the way that go!

Blackout

Questions for Engagement, Response, and Analysis

Act I

Scene 1

1. In the introduction, Wilson describes Troy as "a large man with thick,
   heavy hands" and says it is "this largeness that he strives to fill out and
   make an accommodation with. Together with his blackness, his largeness informs his sensibilities and the choices he has made in his life."
   After you have read the play, interpret this description.

2. Troy says, "Death ain't nothing but a fastball on the outside corner."
   Explain what he means by this baseball imagery.

3. What does Troy's story about wrestling with death reveal about his
   attitude toward life?

4. Why does Troy call the man who gave him credit to buy furniture the
   devil? Explain similar financial practices that exist today.

5. Lyons says that he cannot find a job. What would be a more accurate statement about his situation? Why does Troy hassle him before giving him money?

6. Explain the relationship between Troy and Lyons.

Scene 2

1. Compare Rose's and Troy's attitudes toward gambling.

2. Explain Troy's treatment of Gabriel.

Scene 3

1. What does Cory view as his two primary jobs? What does Troy believe Cory's responsibilities should be?

2. Troy asks Cory, "What law is there I got to like you?" What does this question reveal about Troy's concept of fatherhood?

3. Explain Troy's statement to Rose at the end of scene 3.

Scene 4

1. Why does Troy, who cannot read and has no driver's license, want to drive the garbage truck?

2. Gabriel's severance money, which he received as a result of his injury while fighting for his country, pays for the house Troy lives in. Why, then, does Gabriel want to live at Miss Pearl's, where he has to pay rent?

3. Both Rose and Lyons tell Troy that Cory is trying to live up to Troy's example. Why does this assertion not please Troy?

4. Describe Troy's father's behavior. In what ways has his experience with his father influenced Troy's behavior toward Lyons and Cory?

5. What does Lyons' comment that Troy's father "should have just went on and left when he saw he couldn't get nowhere" reveal about Lyons's attitude toward responsibility?

6. Why does Troy sabotage Cory's chances to play football?

Act II

Scene 1

1. How and why do Troy's and Rose's opinions about Gabriel's being institutionalized differ?

2. Troy says that the situation with Alberta "starts out like a little bush . . . and the next thing you know it's a whole forest" and that at Alberta's "I can . . . get away from the pressures and problems . . . and be a different man . . . . I can just be a part of myself that ain't never been." Analyze what these two statements reveal about Troy's character.

3. Interpret the baseball analogy with which Troy tries to explain the situation with Alberta.

4. Explain Rose's analogy about the seed.

Scene 2

1. Explain Rose's statement to Troy that "You did Gabe just like you did Cory. You wouldn't sign the paper for Cory . . . but you signed for Gabe." Why did Troy sign Gabriel's commitment papers?

2. Why, after Alberta's death, does Troy tell death that he is going to finish the fence?

Scene 3

1. Explain Rose's statement at the end of this scene: "From right now . . . this child got a mother. But you a womanless man."

Scene 4

1. Interpret the symbolism of Cory's threatening Troy with a baseball bat. Why does Troy drive his own son away from home?

Scene 5

1. Discuss the contrasting attitudes of Lyons and Cory about responsibility and their consequent adult roles.

2. Support or argue against Cory's statement that his father was "trying to live through" him when Cory was growing up and Rose's answer that "Your daddy wanted you to be everything he wasn't . . . and at the same time he tried to make you into everything he was."

3. Analyze Rose's explanation of her marriage to Troy.

4. Troy sings a favorite song, "Old Blue," when he is drinking, and Raynell and Cory sing "Old Blue" at the end of the play. Analyze the significance of this song.

THE DRAMATIC VISION OF AUGUST WILSON

SANDRA SHANNON

1   According to Wilson, he began *Fences* "with the image of a man standing in his yard with a baby in his arms" (DeVries 25). From the play's inception, he was aware of the amount of dramatic leverage provided by this visually powerful image, born of his desire to prove that, contrary to myth, black men are responsible: "We have been told so many times how irresponsible we are as black males that I try and present positive images of responsibility" (25). But Troy appears not to pose much of a challenge to this myth. Although he heroically acknowledges the infant as his own—"She's my daughter, Rose. My own flesh and blood" (*F* 79)—his idea of responsibility is seen in his decision to hand over the child to someone who apparently is more responsible than he. Indeed, Wilson's perspective on responsibility might appear dubious to those unfamiliar with his decidedly male ethos, which he links to the history of black male-female relations in America. In an interview with Mark Rocha, Wilson states:

You've got to understand the sociology of it. The transition from slavery to freedom was a cultural shock for blacks. All of a sudden black men had to ask themselves things like, "What is money?" "What is marriage?" Black women, for all their own struggles, were relatively stable. Economically, they had control of the house. But what were black men supposed to do to make a living? (Rocha 38).

2   Still, for Wilson or any member of an audience to view Troy's actions as "responsible" depends on focusing not on the responsibility of the distraught middle-aged garbageman for the entire situation but on his responsibility in honoring his daughter and ultimately facing the evils of his own making. That he does not simply flee apparently saves him from the total damnation heaped upon so many black men caught in similar dilemmas.

3   Troy's entertaining anecdotes and searing monologues only seem incongruous with his station in life: in fact, language has become his most effective defense against victimization. That his own father was essentially a failure and a victim of the ruthless tenant farming system rests heavily upon Troy, for, as a young boy, he witnessed firsthand his father's destruction: "Sometimes I use to wonder why he was living. . . . He ain't knew how to do nothing but farm. No, he was trapped and I think he knew it"(*F* 51). Unfortunately, Troy's predicament is not very far removed from the bleak conditions that doomed his father—a dead-end job and no chance for a better life. Still, Troy's words portray him as the ultimate warrior, even though circumstances suggest otherwise. Expansive rhetoric justifies his wrongdoing, appeases his family, and apparently soothes his conscience.

4   Troy's fondness for talk is grounded in the African American oral tradition not yet affected by the cultural shock that followed the invention of the television and the spread of modern audiovisual devices. In fact, the Maxsons do not own a television set, and, as Troy explains to Cory, patching their leaky roof will most certainly take precedence over purchasing an electronic gadget. In the absence of such diversions, verbal communication becomes an art form for Troy. Rarely does he spare words when he has an opportunity to dominate center stage. When Rose cautions him against consuming too much liquor, he launches into a speech on death based upon a series of metaphors that provide a window to his character. By invoking the rules of baseball, he familiarizes death's power: "Death ain't nothing but a fastball on an outside corner" (10). By borrowing images from the military, he acknowledges and, to some extent, admires death's persistence: "I looked up one day and Death was marching straight at me. The middle of July, 1941" (11). And by alluding to wrestling, he suggests that he, as if heeding the speaker of Dylan Thomas's poem, will not "go gentle into that good night": "We wrestled for three days and three nights. I can't say where I found the strength

from. Every time it seemed like he was gonna get the best of me, I'd reach way down deep inside myself and find the strength to do him one better" (12).

5   In addition to being a master at metaphors, Troy is skilled at using language to deflect attention from his faults. One of the most dramatically poignant moments in *Fences* occurs when Troy scrambles to find suitable words to explain to his wife of eighteen years that he has fathered a child with another woman: "I'm trying to find a way to tell you . . . I'm gonna be a daddy. I'm gonna be somebody's daddy" (66). He is moving as he justifies his relationship with Alberta, the "other woman": "I can sit up in her house and laugh. Do you understand what I'm saying. I can laugh . . . and it feels good. It reaches all the way down to the bottom of my shoes" (69). He even succeeds at presenting a convincing plea to Rose to take in and raise his orphaned daughter as her own. Apparently language creates a larger-than-life reality for Troy. In each of these situations, Troy's words redirect any feelings of guilt away from himself. He seems free from remorse and actually appears heroic against all charges while a less eloquent man might appear villainous.

6   Like all of Wilson's plays to date, *Fences* is very much a black man's story. Black women do have appreciable roles in his dramas; however, they seldom are as developed as the men, who freely commune with other black men, whether in a dingy bandroom, on a back porch stoop, at a kitchen table, or in a one- room cafe. Wilson's sharply drawn male characters are, no doubt, also the result of his early devotion to listening to their conversations in the barrooms and tobacco houses of Pittsburgh. As a young, inexperienced poet who admitted that his verse suffered because he knew nothing of the world, he unconsciously absorbed the larger-than-life narratives of these storytellers. Also, deep within the psyche of young Wilson was (and still is) an urge to search for and create the image of a father he never had, one who would fill his son's head with his wisdom and guide him toward a responsible adulthood. As evidenced by Troy, Wilson assembles from the variety of black men that he has encountered a paternal image—by no means angelic, but an image of a father nonetheless.

❥

7   Regardless of the process behind Wilson's depictions of his characters, the women's realities are decidedly different from those of the men around them and are limited to those possibilities sustained and promoted by Western culture. Critic and novelist Marilyn French sees a general dualism in the portrayal of women: "This split in principle of nature, the feminine principle, still exists in our perception of actual women; there is the mother madonna, and the whore; the nourisher and the castrator. This split in the feminine principle I call inlaw and outlaw aspects of it" (23). According to French, the outlaw is described in terms of "darkness, chaos, flesh, the sinister, magic and above all, sexuality,"

while the inlaw suggests completely different values: "nutritiveness, compassion, mercy, and the ability to create felicity" (24).

8   These two categories can be usefully applied to the women in *Fences*. Consider Troy's mistress Alberta as an "outlaw": she disrupts the Maxson family circle, sundering relationships between husband and wife and father and son as well as the deeply fraternal bond between Troy and Bono. She represents everything that sticks its tongue out at the responsibility that Troy faces as a family man and as head of the household. She demands nothing of him—not his loyalty, not his money, not even his time. She provides a haven from the chronic concerns of survival weighing down upon the frustrated garbage collector and would-be Major Leaguer, a place where he can simply laugh out loud. Nevertheless, Alberta is not blamed as the "whore," though she is the key to the disintegration of the Maxson family and ultimately to Troy's tragic demise. When Rose Ïfinally does learn about Troy's affair, her fury is directed solely at her husband as a willing party, not at Alberta as his temptress. Never physically appearing in the play, known only through conversations about her, Alberta becomes merely a manifestation of Troy's own flawed character.

9   While the outlaw Alberta appeals to Troy's hedonistic nature, the "inlaw" Rose reminds him of responsibility. She manages the home, wrestles with daily worries over money, and single-handedly tries to keep the Maxson family together. She does all of this while willfully neglecting to establish time and space for her own growth. As her name suggests, Rose thrives amid adversity and stands out from the moral squalor around her. While few might be expected to withstand the amount of humiliation she endures, Rose seems to thrive upon it; she is able to transform a motherless infant into a stable young girl and pull the loose threads of her family together at the play's end.

10   Rose Maxson lingers half in the shadows during the entire first act of *Fences*, speaking largely in reaction to her husband's exaggerated stories about himself. However, when she finally discovers her voice, she is convincing even as her character transforms. Though before she was the predictable image of temperance, she suddenly becomes a woman who stands eye-to-eye with her egoistic husband: "I been standing with you! I been right here with you, Troy. I got a life too. I gave eighteen years of my life to stand in the same spot with you. Don't you think I ever wanted other things? Don't you think I had dreams and hopes?" (70–71). In one impassioned scene, Rose's entire history rushes forward out of nearly two decades of dormancy. Yet this moment of revelation does not lessen Rose Maxson's extreme altruism. She is so thoroughly and persistently moral that her character becomes more obviously symbolic than realistic. She is her husband's conscience, quite literally his better half. Like Alberta, she is basically an extension of Troy's ego, not one whose own story requires a full hearing. Her eighteen-year suppression of self and allegiance to

family perfectly match the mold of the inlaw, for as French describes it, the inlaw prototype "requires volitional subordination[;] . . . it values above all the good of the whole . . . and finds pleasure in that good rather than in assertion of self" (24).

❥

11   Wilson's symbolic depictions of black women such as Rose have their basis in his capabilities as a poet. Also a by-product of his grounding in poetry is a conscious tendency to incorporate powerful metaphors to communicate his plays' larger thematic concerns. He believes this to be an important part of his strength as a dramatist: "The idea of metaphor . . . is a very large idea in my plays and something that I find lacking in most other contemporary plays. . . . I think I write the kinds of plays that I do because I have twenty-six years of writing poetry underneath all that" (interview).

12   The title image of *Fences*, the third play in Wilson's black history chronicle, very appropriately conveys a number of realities for the black family of late '50s America. It raises issues ranging from economic and professional deprivation to emotional and moral isolation. The fence, which may either inhibit or protect, is both a positive and negative image to various members of the Maxson family. To Rose, who nags Troy about completing this wooden border, the fence promises to keep in those whom she loves, preventing them from leaving the fortress she so lovingly sustains for them. To Cory, however, the fence becomes a tangible symbol of all that stands in the way of his independence. His work on it is merely an exercise in obedience and a reminder that he is not yet a man—at least not to Troy. To Troy, the fence represents added restrictions placed upon him. Thus he half-heartedly erects one section of the fence at a time and completes the job only after accepting a challenge from Bono, who agrees to buy his wife, Lucille, a refrigerator as soon as Troy completes the fence. It takes Bono to explain to him the importance of the fence:

> CORY: I don't know why Mama want a fence around the yard noways.
> TROY: Damn if I know either. What the hell she keeping out with it? She ain't got nothing nobody want.
> BONO: Some people build fences to keep people out . . . and other people build fences to keep people in. Rose wants to hold on to you all. She loves you. (*F* 61)

13   On a deeper level, Troy sees the fence's completion as a reminder of his own mortality; he senses that he is erecting his own monument. His anxiety about death's inevitability emerges when his longtime friend questions Troy's choice of wood:

> BONO: You don't need this wood [hard wood]. You can put it up with pine wood and it'll stand as long as you gonna be here looking at it.

TROY: How you know how long I'm gonna be here, nigger? Hell,
I might just live forever. Live longer than old man Horsely. (60)

14   Troy's reluctance to complete the fence seems ominous, for shortly after finishing it for Rose, he dies. The fence, then, becomes a gauge for his life, during which he experiences both literal and figurative incarceration. He is fenced off from society during a lengthy prison term; he is fenced out of the Major Leagues because of racial segregation; and after he initiates the breakup of his family, he is fenced out of his home as well as out of the hearts of Rose and Cory.

15   Other metaphors that the poet-turned-playwright effectively weaves throughout *Fences* adopt their imagery from the game of baseball. Images of the game loom large in the consciousness of the onetime Negro Leaguer, Troy, who often borrows the behavioral codes of this game to suit various situations in his life. Part of the tragedy of *Fences* is Troy's belief that he would have surpassed current black players and the white Major League players of his youth had he been allowed to play among them. His ego and professional potential have been devastated because he has been cheated out of at least a chance to play Major League ball. As an outward manifestation of the blues he surely feels because of this loss, Troy adopts the language of the game in order to explain the "deprivation of possibility" (Reed 93) that has hurt him so deeply.

16   For Troy, life is a baseball game riddled with fast balls, curve balls, sacrifice flies, and an occasional strikeout, but too few homeruns. Although the conflict of the ball game lasts for only nine innings, Troy sees himself as being constantly at bat. From keeping death at bay to announcing a "full count" against his defiant son Cory, Troy flavors his conversation with baseball metaphors at every chance he gets. The various rules of the game become his basis for interpreting his actions and another avenue for expressing his blues. His preoccupation with images associated with the traditionally masculine, extremely competitive sport robs him of the candor necessary to handle the delicate relationships in his life. In one of the most intense moments of the play, Troy struggles to explain to his wife that he has not only been unfaithful to her but has also fathered a child outside of their marriage bed: "I fooled them, Rose. I bunted. When I found you and Cory and a halfway decent job . . . I was safe. Couldn't nothing touch me. I wasn't gonna strike out no more. . . . I stood on first base for eighteen years and I thought . . . well, goddamn it . . . go on for it!" (*F* 70). In using this second language, Troy comes to live it. He completely alienates both his son and his wife by forcing upon them his very selfish view of life. Consequently, he cannot see past immediate self-gratification; he cannot compromise, nor can he ask for forgiveness.

17   Wilson's use of metaphor in *Fences* extends to include Gabriel, Troy's disabled brother. Gabriel's war injury, a severe head wound, required that

a metal plate be surgically implanted in his head. The brain-damaged Gabriel fantasizes that he is Archangel Gabriel, whose tasks are to open Heaven's pearly gates and to chase away hellhounds. When Troy is certain of Gabriel's irreversible condition, he claims the $3,000 compensation awarded his brother and uses it to purchase the home where he, Rose, Cory, and Gabriel live.

18   Gabriel is what Wilson refers to as a "spectacle character" (interview) whose role, as its label suggests, is to command attention and to force both acknowledgment and understanding of issues that are sooner ignored. Here, he serves as a glaring reminder of the crippling injustices black men endure at the hands of their own country. Wilson notes, "This black man had suffered this wound fighting for a country in which his brother could not play baseball." America cannot hide the shame of thousands of black veterans like Gabriel, who sacrificed dearly in the service of their country yet possibly faced homelessness, prison, or the insane asylum upon their return. Gabriel's payment of $3,000 is ludicrously low for an injury that has maimed him for life.

19   Although Gabriel is not crucial to the central conflict of *Fences*, his presence gives Troy another dimension. In addition to being an embarrassing emblem of America's darker side, Gabriel is also a manifestation of the worst in Troy. He exposes a man who has become immune to the emotions of self-pity and remorse; a man who, after capitalizing on his brother's misfortune, has him committed to a mental institution. Troy has become so devastated by his own deferred dreams that nothing, save pleasing himself, matters to him. He can sign papers to prevent his son from receiving free tuition as a football recruit; he can sign papers to put his brother away indefinitely. To Wilson, Gabriel has a significant function in *Fences*, and he is bothered by critics who dismiss this wounded man as a halfwit:

> They [critics] make me mad when I read the reviews and they would refer to Gabriel as an idiot. . . . Gabriel is one of those self-sufficient characters. He gets up and goes to work every day. He goes out and collects those discarded fruit and vegetables, but he's taking care of himself. He doesn't want Troy to take care of him. He moves out of Troy's house and lives down there and pays his rent to the extent that he is able. (interview)

20   Wilson plays upon the dramatic tension inherent in the spectacle of Gabriel's character, but he also relies upon this highly sensitive man to introduce an identifiable element of African American culture: belief in a spiritual world. Although Gabriel's perceptions of Christianity and images associated with the afterlife are apparently the results of his dementia, he articulates several myths that have their origins in traditional religious beliefs among African Americans. For example, he

revives the myth of Saint Peter, so-called keeper of the pearly gates, and keeps alive the fear of Judgment Day: "Ain't gonna be too much of a battle when God get to waving that Judgment sword. But the people's gonna have a hell of a time trying to get into heaven if them gates ain't open" (*F* 47–48).

21   Gabriel also confirms the existence of a great Judgment Book in which Saint Peter records "everybody's name what was ever been born" (26). Gabriel, who believes he has already died and gone to Heaven, is a privileged soul, for, according to him, Saint Peter has allowed him to see both Troy and Rose's names recorded in the ledger. And, again, according to Gabriel, he sometimes relieves Saint Peter from the eternal task of guarding the pearly gates: "Did you know when I was in heaven . . . every morning me and St. Peter would sit down by the gate and eat some big fat biscuits? Oh, yeah! We had us a good time. We'd sit there and eat us them biscuits and then St. Peter would go off to sleep and tell me to wake him up when it's time to open the gates for the judgment" (26).

22   Each encounter with Gabriel convinces one to look beyond his surface disability and concentrate instead upon the spiritual and mythical worlds he creates and the realms of possibility that these worlds offer. Gabriel's ability to look beyond the literal is his own means of negotiating an indifferent world, yet it also exemplifies a long-standing Christian belief among African Americans to look toward things-not-seen for salvation. He has adopted both a frame of mind and a vision that get him through the daily drudgery of his condition. This special vision is most evident in the final scene of *Fences*, when the Maxson family prepares to bury Troy. At this time Gabriel experiences "a trauma that a sane and normal mind would be unable to withstand. He begins to dance. A slow, strange dance, eerie and life-giving. A dance of atavistic signature and ritual. . . . He finishes his dance and the gates of heaven stand open as wide as God's closet" (101). As a spectacle character, Gabriel's significance is in providing a flawed icon of African Americans' cultural past. He is a cultural paradox—not taken seriously by those around him yet conveying in his distorted sensibilities the cultural bedrock of generations past and to come.

Works Cited

De Vries, Hillary. "A Song in Search of Itself." *American Theater* January 1987, 22–25.

Reed, Ishmael. "In Search of August Wilson." *Connoisseur* 217 (March 1987): 92–97.

Rocha, Mark. "A Conversation with August Wilson." *Diversity: A Journal of Multicultural Issues* 1 (Spring 1993): 24–42.

Wilson, August. *Fences*. New York: New American Library, 1987.

BOUNDARIES, LOGISTICS, AND IDENTITY: THE PROPERTY OF METAPHOR IN *FENCES* AND *JOE TURNER'S COME AND GONE*

ALAN NADEL

1   In Fences, August Wilson . . . describes Troy Maxson's struggle to build a fence around his property. . . . . A fifty-three-year-old garbageman who owns a small house in a run-down section of Pittsburgh, in 1957, Troy during the course of the play works at building a small fence around his meager back yard. At the same time, he works constantly to delineate his rights and responsibilities, as husband, brother, worker, friend, and father. His name, Maxson, suggests a shortened "Mason-Dixon,"[1] a personalized version of the national division over the properties of blackness. His character similarly embodies the personal divisions that come from living in a world where the Mason-Dixon line exists as the ubiquitous circumscription of black American claims to human rights.

2   Troy lives in a house with Rose, his wife of eighteen years, and their seventeen-year-old son, Cory. The down payment for the house came from the $3,000 his brother Gabriel received in compensation for a World War II head wound that left him a virtual half-wit, harboring the belief "with every fiber of his being that he is the Archangel Gabriel" (23). Troy takes pride at having housed and cared for Gabriel since the injury, and at the same time expresses shame at having had to rely on Gabriel's misfortune to provide the down payment he could never have acquired through years of honest labor. Having run away from a cruel and abusive father when he was a teenager, he found his way to the city, where he married and supported his family through theft until he was convicted of assault and armed robbery and sent to jail for fifteen years. There he learned to play baseball and give up robbery. By the time he was released, his wife having left him, he met Rose, remarried, and after playing baseball in the Negro Leagues, became a garbageman.

3   The central conflicts in the play arise from his refusal to let his son play football or accept a football scholarship to college, and from his having fathered a daughter through an extramarital affair. But these are framed by conflicts with the father he fled, the major leagues that wouldn't let him play baseball, and Death himself, with whom Troy had once wrestled. Whatever else he loses, he vigilantly maintains his property and his property rights, demanding his authority within its confines, eventually building a fence around his yard and guarding the entrance with all of his human power against the force of Death, whose representation in human form is generally perceived to be metaphoric.

4   It is on these grounds—and on his home ground—that Troy chooses to be sized up. For in all other locales he is a large man who has been underestimated. As a baseball player and even as a garbageman, the

---

[1]In *Ma Rainey's Black Bottom*, in fact, Levee refers to it as the "Maxon-Dixon line" (82).

world has not taken his measure. To "take the measure of a man" is to make a metaphor derived from a set of primary physical traits. "To measure up" means to fulfill a role in the same way one fills out a suit of clothes; "to take measure of oneself" means to assess one's ability to fill a specific role in the same way that one selects that suit of clothes. Implicit in all these metaphors is a set of objective physical standards— what Locke called primary characteristics—against which such intangibles as character, courage, loyalty, skill, or talent can be determined.

5   In the logistics of *Fences*, however, these standards form the variables measured against the standard of Troy Maxson's largeness. From the outset of the play, his size is a given: "Troy is fifty-three years old, a large man with thick heavy hands; it is this largeness that he strives to fill out and make an accommodation with. Together with his blackness, his largeness informs his sensibilities and the choices he has made in life" (1). And after his death, as Rose explains to Cory, "When I first met your daddy, . . . I thought here is a man you can open yourself up to and be filled to bursting. Here is a man that can fill all them empty spaces you been tipping around the edges of. . . . When your daddy walked through the house, he filled it up" (93). Cory perceived Troy as "a shadow that followed you everywhere. It weighed on you and sunk in your flesh. It would wrap around you and lay there until you couldn't tell which one was you any more" (93), but Rose argues that Cory is just like his father:

> That shadow wasn't nothing but you growing into yourself. You either got to grow into it or cut it down to fit you. But that's all you got to make life with. That's all you got to measure yourself against that world out there. Your daddy wanted you to be everything he wasn't . . . and at the same time he tried to make you into everything he was. (93)

6   In addition to establishing Troy's size as the standard, both negative and positive, Rose is setting that standard against the standards asserted by the dominant white culture. Cory, in other words, is being urged not to measure himself against Troy but to use Troy's size as a defense against the other, implicitly figurative, norms of "that world out there."

7   In so doing, Rose is asking him, in fact, to continue his father's quest. For the problem of the play can be seen as Troy's attempt to take measure of himself in a world that has denied him the external referents. His struggle is to act in the literal world in such a way as to become not just the literal but the figurative father, brother, husband, man he desires to be. The role of father is the most complex because he is the father of three children from three different women. The children, precisely seventeen years apart, represent Troy's paternal responsibilities to three successive generations of black children. As each of these children makes demands on him, he must measure up to his responsibilities, and for each generation he measures up differently.

8   When his older son, Lyons, a would-be musician, for example, regularly borrows money from him, Troy puts Lyons through a ritual of humiliation constructed out of the process of differentiating Lyons from

himself: "I done learned my mistake and learned to do what's right by it. You still trying to get something for nothing. Life don't owe you nothing. You owe it to yourself." At issue here is not only Troy's sense of himself as role model but also his sense of himself as negative example. He is both the father to emulate and the father not to emulate: Lyons should be like Troy by not making Troy's mistake. This lesson has a double edge, though, because the earlier, error-ridden life that Troy has learned to reject included not only his criminal acts but also his marriage to Lyons's mother and his fathering of Lyons. At that point in his life, we later learn, he felt he was not ready to be a father or to accept the responsibilities of fatherhood. For Lyons to recognize Troy's mistakes, then, is for him to acknowledge the inappropriateness of his own existence.

9   Troy deals with his younger son, Cory, in the same way. Like Troy, Cory is a talented athlete. A superstar in the Negro baseball leagues, Troy was never given an opportunity to play in the white leagues. Believing that white America would never allow a black to be successful in professional sports, he refuses to allow his son to go to college on a football scholarship. Once again, he becomes what he sees as a positive example for his son by virtue of his ability to reject himself. In a completely self-contained economy, he becomes both the model of error and the model of correction.

10   In regard to sports, particularly, he does this by constructing a division between personal history and American history. An extraordinary baseball player whose talents are compared with those of Babe Ruth and Josh Gibson, Troy was unfortunately over forty years old when professional baseball was first integrated. Within the time frame of American history, as his friend Bono says, "Troy just come along too early" (9). Troy rejects Bono's opinion with a triple negative: "There ought not never have been no time called too early" (9). "I'm talking about," he explains, "if you could play ball then they ought to have let you play. Don't care what color you were. Come telling me I come along too early. If you could play, then they ought to have let you play"(9).

11   After the death in childbirth of his girlfriend . . . Troy issues his challenge to Death in terms of the wall he is constructing between himself and it:

> I'm gonna build me a fence around what belongs to me. And I want you to stay on the other side. See? You stay over there until you're ready for me. Then you come on. Bring your army. Bring your sickle. Bring your wrestling clothes. I ain't gonna fall down on my vigilance this time. You ain't gonna sneak up on me no more. When you ready for me . . . that's when you come around here . . . .Then we gonna find out what manner of man you are. . . . You stay on the other side of that fence until you ready for me.

12   This is the metaphoric fence constructed to complement the literal fence Rose had been requesting from the outset. When Death accepts

Troy's challenge, he confirms Troy's mastery over the literal, his power to turn his property into the visible recognition of his human properties, such that his responsibilities to his family, his athletic prowess, and his physical presence confirm his ability to confront Death—and hence to construct his life—on his own terms. In his terms, as he stated earlier in the play, "Death ain't nothing but a fastball on the outside corner" (10). Rose's description of Troy's death confirms that terminology: "He was out there swinging that bat and then he just fell over. Seem like he swung it and stood there with this grin on his face . . . and then he just fell over" (91). The inference is not only that he had protected his family by striking a final blow at Death but, more significantly, that he was able to do so because Troy made Death come to him on Troy's terms. Although Troy's challenge may be seen as figurative, Death's accepting it makes it literal, and thus the man-to-man battle between Troy and Death becomes a literal fight and simultaneously affirms Troy's power to create a site—however small—in which the figurative becomes literal. The conversion not only reduces Death to a man but also affirms Troy's status as one.

13   Within the context of the play, moreover, Wilson affirms the literal status of that conversion by having Gabriel perform a similar feat. Released from the mental hospital in order to attend Troy's funeral, Gabriel arrives carrying his trumpet. Although it has no mouthpiece, he uses it to "tell St. Peter to open the gates" (99). After three attempts, with no sound coming from the trumpet, "he begins to dance. A slow, strange dance, eerie and life-giving. A dance of atavistic signature and ritual. He begins to howl in what is an attempt at song, or perhaps a song turning back into itself in an attempt at speech. He finishes his song and the gates of heaven stand open as wide as God's closet" (100).

14   Gabriel's ability to invert the literal and the figurative thus confirms our understanding of Troy's death, at the same time that it revises our understanding of Gabriel's marginality or "madness." For we can read his wound as a function of attributing literal power to such figurative institutions as nation and warfare. As a soldier in World War II, he invested his primary literal claim to human rights—his human life—in support of a figurative structure—the United States—that on the very site of his investment, the segregated armed forces, denied the status of that life as human. One can only assume that the part of his brain blown away in the war contained the beliefs and conceptions that allowed him to accept the figurative status of his own humanity. Lacking that part of his brain, he is not functional within the dominant white culture, as is evidenced by his numerous arrests as well as his institutionalizations.

15   The Mason-Dixon line, marking off the site where he may consider himself literally human, has become for Gabriel the walls of the mental institution. By the end of the play—providing a virtual survey of the institutionalized power critiqued by Michel Foucault—all the Maxsons are disciplined within figurative Mason-Dixon lines. With Gabriel in the

mental hospital, Cory in the armed services, Lyons in prison (we could conceivably even add Rose's recent involvement with the church), they find only this moment of relief within the boundary of the fence that Troy built. In the play's final pronouncement, with Gabriel speaking now as prophet and miracle worker rather than as marginalized madman, he asserts and demonstrates that the order of things—the relationship of figurative to literal—should be reversed: "And that's the way that go!" (100).

16   This is a tactical victory, a method of subverting and resisting the strategic power of the dominant culture. For that culture has urged the black American man to flight with the implication that his humanity was the function of logistics; confined by sites that denied literal confirmation of that humanity, the culture has offered the promise of an elsewhere, a site where the literal and figurative reconfigure. To pursue that promise, to seek that site, often meant sacrificing familial responsibilities. Instead of pursuing that site at the expense of his family, Troy created it in order to protect them. As Rose, referring to the fence, noted to Cory: "Oh, that's been up there ever since Raynell wasn't but a wee little bitty old thing. Your daddy finally got around to putting that up to keep her in the yard" (91).

17   In this way, Troy fought not only Death, but also history. For the normative discourse of white. American history, in 1957, was one of progress and assimilation. Textbooks promoted the idea of the melting pot and of upward mobility; historical films and dramas reinscribed the myth of the nuclear family; and despite the continued presence of Jim Crow laws, segregated schools and facilities, rampant denial of voter rights, and extensive discrimination in housing and employment, American history and, more important, its popularizations represented the United States as a land of equal opportunity, with liberty and justice for all. Those whose personal narratives failed to confirm this hegemonic discourse became invisible; as Ralph Ellison so dramatically illustrated in *Invisible Man*, they fell outside of history. Despairing of the possibility of altering dominant historical discourse, Troy devotes himself to reconfiguring the paternal patterns that compose his personal history.

18   In thus making himself both the positive and the negative model for his sons, he also makes his father a positive and a negative model. For unlike many men of his generation—Bono's father, for example—Troy's father refused to leave the family, however much he detested it. As Troy points out, "He felt a responsibility toward us. May be he ain't treated us the way I felt he should have, but without that responsibility he could have walked off and left us, made his own way" (49). In contrast, as Bono points out, "Back in those days what you talking about, niggers used to travel all over. They get up one day and see where the day ain't sitting right with them and they walk out their front door and just take on down one road or another and keep on walking. . . . Just walk on till you come

to something else. Ain't you never heard of nobody having the walking blues?" (50–51).

Works Cited

Wilson, August. *Fences*. New York: New American Library, Plume, 1986.
————. *Ma Rainey's Black Bottom*. New York: New American Library, Plume, 1985.

FILLING THE TIME:
READING HISTORY IN THE DRAMA
OF AUGUST WILSON

JOHN TIMPANE

1   In the prefatorial piece "The Play," Wilson locates *Fences* in a "big-city neighborhood" of an eastern industrial town—probably Pittsburgh—in 1957. In 1957, "the Milwaukee Braves won the World Series, and the hot winds of change that would make the sixties a turbulent, racing, dangerous, and provocative decade had not yet begun to blow full."[1] The year 1957, as Wilson does not mean us to forget, was the year of Little Rock, when Eisenhower reluctantly ordered regular army paratroops to prevent interference with court-ordered racial integration at Little Rock Central High School. That was the year of H.R. 6127, the Civil Rights Act of 1957, passed after virulent debate and filibuster in the Senate. Texas, Tennessee, Delaware, Maryland, and other states were in the throes of court-ordered desegregation; Little Rock stood out because of the prospect that state and federal troops might face each other. The winds of change blew both hot and cold. The possibility of new positivities coexisted with the fact of ancient recalcitrance. Only three weeks before Little Rock, Ku Klux Klan members had castrated a black man outside of Zion, Alabama. And Louis "Satchmo" Armstrong, in a public gesture that attracted both widespread praise and widespread blame, canceled a much-publicized tour of the USSR, saying that "the way they are treating my people in the South, the government can go to hell. . . . It's getting almost so bad, a colored man hasn't got any country."

2   In *Fences*, baseball operates metonymically, as a metaphoric stand-in for the troubled changes of 1957. Much of the action takes place just before the Milwaukee Braves' victory over the New York Yankees in the 1957 World Series. That victory signified a year of many changes in baseball, changes that reflected the social upheavals of 1957. One change, very much in progress, was the emergence of the black ballplayer. Black players had played prominent roles in previous World Series—Willie Mays in the 1954 series and Jackie Robinson in the Brooklyn Dodgers' victory over the Yankees in 1955. Milwaukee was the first non–New York

[1]Richards, Introduction, pp. vii, xviii.

team led by a black star to win a World Series. Hank Aaron, the most powerful hitter in baseball history, played alongside Eddie Mathews, white and a great slugger, and alongside three excellent white pitchers: Warren Spahn, Bob Buhl, and Lew Burdette. Because of the quick rise to prominence of Mays, Aaron, Roberto Clemente, and Frank Robinson, the question was no longer whether blacks would play but whether they could become leaders. As the success of the Braves portended, the answer was yes: Aaron led the league in power statistics, hit a home run on the last day of the season to give the Braves the pennant, rampaged through Yankee pitching to give his team the World Series, and won the National League Most Valuable Player Award for 1957.

3   Yet the Braves were far from being a truly integrated team, and integration was far from complete in baseball. Though blacks had been playing in the major leagues since 1947, it would take until 1959 for each major league team to have at least one black player. Behind the grudging, piecemeal process of integration in sports lies a Foucaultian "disjunction"—World War II—and a resultant "redistribution": the postwar move west. Hard times in postwar Boston meant dwindling patronage for the Boston Braves, so the team moved west to Milwaukee in 1953. In 1957, the Dodgers left Brooklyn for Los Angeles, and the New York Giants left for San Francisco. In so doing, these teams mirrored an accelerating westward shift in the center of population. Further, the war probably created new social potential (to this day not completely realized) for women and blacks. For baseball, all this meant new teams, new audiences, and new pressures to tap at last the large pool of talented black players. The National League led in this regard. Indeed, it was not until Frank Robinson was traded from the Cincinnati Reds to the Baltimore Orioles and won the Triple Crown in 1966 that a black player dominated American League pitching the way Mays, Clemente, and Aaron had done in the National League.

4   Changes in baseball and changes in American life complicate the ability of anyone who, like Troy, bases his assumptions about reality on the facts of a prewar world. In the first scene of *Fences*, Troy pits his reading of things against those of Bono, Rose, and Lyons. Troy intersperses lies with truths, claiming he has seen and contended with Death and the devil. Rose challenges the way Troy presents these tales: "Anything you can't understand, you want to call it the devil" (14). Rose and Bono are a chorus parenthesizing Troy's insistence on his reading:

ROSE: Times have changed since you was playing baseball, Troy. That was before the war. Times have changed a lot since then.
TROY: How in hell they done changed?
ROSE: They got lots of colored boys playing ball now. Baseball and football.
BONO: You right about that, Rose. Times have changed, Troy. You done come along too early.
TROY: There ought not never have been no time called too early! (9)

5   James calls the present "a saddle-back . . . from which we look in two directions into time."2 Throughout Fences, Troy Maxson straddles this saddleback, constantly constructing a present selectively out of memory (the past) and desire (the future).

6   Desire figures most clearly in his conflict with his son, Cory. Troy is affronted by Cory's desire to try out before a college football recruiter from North Carolina. Troy's own sport, and the source of his personal language of metaphors, is baseball; Cory's choice of football galls him. American popular culture has forgotten that integration had come to major league football long before Jackie Robinson signed a baseball contract. Fritz Pollard had played with the Akron Indians beginning in 1919, and black players played professional football until 1933, when the disruption of the Depression made football a whites-only sport for thirteen years.

7   As with baseball, this redistribution was tied to the postwar westward push. The National Football League (NFL) had originally centered in the Midwest, gradually adding franchises in eastern industrial centers. Longstanding interest in starting a franchise on the West Coast was realized when the Cleveland Rams moved to Los Angeles after the war. A rival league, the All-American Football Conference (AAFC), started up in 1946. Though the two leagues would soon merge, the AAFC forced some innovative moves, including the initiation of western franchises (the Los Angeles Dons and the San Francisco 49ers) and the signing of black players. That same year, the Los Angeles Rams signed Kenny Washington and Woody Strode, and the Cleveland Browns signed Bill Willis and Marion Motley. Motley became a record-breaking rusher, beginning a strong tradition of black running backs that included Joe Perry, who, while playing for the San Francisco 49ers and Baltimore Colts, broke all rushing records through the 1950s. (His heir-apparent was Jim Brown.) By 1953, a black collegiate running back, J. C. Caroline of the University of Illinois, had broken the hallowed records of "Red" Grange, a white runner of the 1920s and 1930s. By the late 1950s, black athletes had established a prominence in football that at least equaled the standing of Mays, Aaron, and the Robinsons in baseball.[3]

8   With the stronger tradition of integration, football was on the verge of becoming a truly national sport in 1957. Cory believes, as Troy does not, that a talented black athlete can get a chance. This disagreement emerges when they discuss Roberto Clemente, now in his third year with the local baseball club, the Pittsburgh Pirates.

> TROY: I ain't thinking about the Pirates. Got an all-white team. Got that boy . . . that Puerto Rican boy . . . Clemente. Don't even half-play him. That boy could be something if they give him a chance. Play him one day and sit him on the bench the next.

[2]James, *Principles of Psychology*, p. 574.
[3]For a more detailed discussion about the vexed issue of integration in professional football, see Ocania Chalk, *Pioneers of Black Sport* (New York: Dodd, Mead, 1975).

CORY: He gets a lot of chances to play.

TROY: I'm talking about playing regular. Playing every day so you can get your timing. That's what I'm talking about.

CORY: They got some white guys on the team that don't play every day. You can't play everybody at the same time.

TROY: If they got a white fellow sitting on the bench . . . you can bet your last dollar he can't play! The colored guy got to be twice as good before he get on the team. That's why I don't want you to get all tied up in them sports. Man on the team and what it get him? They got colored on the team and don't use them. Same as not having them. All them teams the same.

CORY: The Braves got Hank Aaron and Wes Covington. Hank Aaron hit two home runs today. That makes forty-three.

TROY: Hank Aaron ain't nobody. (33–34)

9   Far beyond baseball, the ulterior difference here is over whether a change has occurred in American society. Generational differences indicate a difference in reading. All Cory knows are the achievements of Aaron (who would hit forty-four home runs in 1957), Covington, and Clemente; these seem incontrovertible evidence that his dreams have a foundation.

10   What Troy knows is his own frustration as a great player in the Negro Leagues. His success was also his self-sacrifice: The Negro Leagues began to die as soon as black players began to be accepted in numbers into professional baseball. What killed Troy's career was, ironically, the *advent* of integrated baseball. Although he is clearly aware of these facts, and clearly damaged by them, Troy insists that history is continuous, that what was once true is still true. Cory assumes that what is true is new— that there is now a new form of positivity, a sudden redistribution—and this assumption on Cory's part outrages his father. For one the gap signifies the death he constantly pits himself against, and for the other it signifies a life in the future, liberated from his father's limitations. Granted, Troy's knowing dictum that "the colored guy got to be twice as good before he get on the team" was quite true in 1957 and is still a widely shared perception today. But Cory is not arguing that his chance is likely; he is arguing that it is possible.

11   Troy gives many names to his resistance. Compassion is one. As he says to Rose, "I got sense enough not to let my boy get hurt over playing no sports" (39). Jealousy is another. Cory is getting a chance while he is still young, whereas even in 1947 Troy was "too old to play in the major leagues" (39). Both these "reasons" are versions of his resistance to reading the change that is making Clemente and Aaron into national heroes. Both Troy's compassion for his son and his jealousy of him are ways to deny his own death.

12   Here, we may remember one of Foucault's more disturbing claims: that the traditional view of history as a seamless continuity really disguised the quest to construct the self as authoritative, continuous,

integrated, and eternal. In *Archaeology of Knowledge* he pictures the outraged author crying, "Must I suppose that in my discourse I can have no survival? And that in speaking I am not banishing my death, but actually establishing it?"[4] For Troy, to acknowledge the possibility of Cory's success is to acknowledge that his own time has passed. Thus his repression of a fact that would have been available to any avid baseball fan in Pittsburgh—that Roberto Clemente really is getting a chance to play. Clemente had 543 at-bats in 1956 and 451 in 1957.[5] Thus his claim that Aaron is "nobody." Note the extreme care with which Wilson has placed the action of the third act: quite late in September 1957, seemingly to show that reality takes no heed of Troy's judgments. Aaron would win the home-run and runs-batted-in titles, earning him the Most Valuable Player Award. Clemente would go on to 3,000 hits and the Hall of Fame.

Works Cited

Foucault, Michel. *Archaeology of Knowledge*. Trans. by A. M. Sheridan Smith. New York: Pantheon, 1972.

James, William. *Principles of Psychology*. Ed. by Frederick H. Burkhardt. Vol. 1. Cambridge: Harvard University Press, 1981.

Neft, David S., and Richard M. Cohen. *The Sports Encyclopedia: Baseball*. New York: St. Martin's Press, 1989.

Richards, Lloyd. Introduction to *Fences*, by August Wilson, vii–viii. New York: New American Library, Plume, 1986.

Wilson, August. *Fences*. New York: New American Library, Plume, 1986.

[4]Foucault, *Archaeology of Knowledge*, p. 210.,
[5]Neft and Cohen, *Sports Encyclopedia*, pp. 309, 312.

AUGUST WILSON'S WOMEN

HARRY ELAM JR.

1   The idea of a woman "needing a man" is . . . implicit in the action of *Fences*. It underlines Rose Maxson's reasons for marrying her husband, Troy, and remaining married to him despite his infidelity. Rose Maxson in Fences reflects strong traditional values associated with black women and yet asserts a strong feminist voice. Unlike the other women discussed, she is both wife and mother. In these roles she sacrifices self, supports her family, and holds it together. Barbara Christian notes that in African American communities, "the idea that mothers should lead lives of sacrifice has become the norm."[1] Rose embodies this norm. Christian observes that the literature of black males has often perpetuated this image.[2] Yet with Rose, Wilson expands on the stereotype while exploring this question of need as well as consistent truths of black female experience as wife and mother.

[1]Christian, *Black Feminist Criticism*, p. 234.
[2]Ibid., p. 236.

2   Rose exudes both love and strength. Each Friday her husband, Troy, hands over his paycheck to Rose. He relinquishes this element of economic authority, and she controls the household budget. From a position of "outsider-within" she observes the weekly payday rituals of the men. When necessary and from a distance, she participates, playfully teasing Troy, always bolstering his authority and publicly demonstrating her support for her man. As mother she nurtures her son, Cory. Aggressively, she defends Cory against the stubborn will of his father.

3   Rose understands that she has consigned herself to the limits imposed upon her by marriage and social expectations. Unlike Risa or Berniece, Rose articulates her perspective and the motivation for her actions. When Troy rationalizes his infidelity to her, she reaffirms her commitment to the relationship and castigates him for not doing the same.

> But I held onto you, Troy. I took all my feelings, my wants and needs, my dreams and I buried them inside you. I planted a seed and watched and prayed over it. I planted myself inside you and waited to bloom. And it didn't take me no eighteen years to find out the soil was hard and rocky and it wasn't never gonna bloom. But I held onto you, Troy. I held tighter. You was my husband. I owed you everything I had. Every part of me I could find to give you. And upstairs in that room, with the darkness falling in on me, I gave everything I had to try and erase the doubt that you wasn't the finest man in the world. And wherever you was going I wanted to be there with you. 'Cause you was my husband, 'cause that's the only way I was gonna survive as your wife. (165)

4   Rose's verbal assault on Troy earns the audience's sympathy. Faced with the realities and imperfections of marriage, she is determined to make their marriage work. Still, Rose clearly accepts her own material oppression. "I *owed* you everything I had," she says. Troy's adultery provides that catalyst that propels her to reassess her position, to gain a greater self-awareness and to change.

5   Quite powerfully, Rose, hurt and betrayed, asserts her independence. When Troy presents her with his illegitimate, motherless daughter, Rose informs him, "Okay Troy. You're right. I'll take care of your baby for you 'cause, like you say, she's innocent and you can't visit the sins of the father upon the child. A motherless child has got a hard time. From right now . . . this child has a mother. But you a womanless man" (173). In the Broadway production, when Mary Alice as Rose accented this line by taking the baby and then slamming the back door in Troy's face, the audience, particularly black female spectators, erupted with cheers and applause. For at that moment Rose stands as a champion of black women, of any woman who has suffered under the constraints of a restrictive and inequitable marriage.

6   The avenues into which Rose channels her new freedom, nevertheless, affirm rather than assault traditional gender limitations and hegemonic legitimacy. She finds solace in the church and the mothering of her adopted daughter, Raynell. While Rose spiritually distances herself from

Troy, she does not leave the marriage. The church becomes a surrogate. Collins argues that institutions such as the church can be "contradictory locations," where black women not only learn independence but also "learn to subordinate our interests as women to the allegedly greater good of the larger African American community."[3] Thus Rose, despite her spiritual independence, continues to conform to the traditional expectations and limitations placed on women. Black feminist scholar bell hooks criticizes the play and Rose for their conformity:

> *Fences* poignantly portrays complex and negative contradictions within black masculinity in a white supremacist context. However, patriarchy is not critiqued, and even though tragic expressions of conventional masculinity are evoked, sexist values are re-inscribed via the black woman's redemption message as the play ends.[4]

7   Rose's words at the end of the play, however, both critique and confirm the patriarchy. She tells Cory, who has returned for his father's funeral:

> That was my first mistake. Not to make him leave some room for me, for my part in the matter. But at that time I wanted that. I wanted a house that I could sing in. And that's what your daddy gave me. I didn't know to keep his strength I had to give up little pieces of mine. I did that. I took his life as mine and mixed up the pieces so that I couldn't hardly tell which was which anymore. It was my choice. It was my life and I didn't have to live it like that. But that's what life offered me in the way of being a woman, and I took it. (189–90)

8   As a black woman in 1957, Rose had extremely restricted options. Marriage required compromise and, quite often for women, a loss of self. The traditional nature of their marriage allowed Troy to dominate, while Rose suppressed her will and desires. Rose reflects on this reality, on a historic truth experienced by many black women. Thus her words call attention to the limitations of gender roles and critique the patriarchal system that created these limitations. Yet Rose also professes her own complicity. Rose's acceptance of the blame, her internalization of external conditions of oppression, prevent her from challenging the status quo. She chooses to accept her subservient position in her marriage; this she believes is what "life offers her as a woman."

Works Cited

Christian, Barbara. *Black Feminist Criticism*. New York: Pergamon Press, 1985.

Collins, Patricia Hill. *Black Feminist Thought*. Boston: Unwin Hyman, 1990.

hooks, bell. *Yearning: Race, Gender, and Cultural Politics*. Boston: South End Press, 1990.

[3]Collins, *Black Feminist Thought*, p. 86.
[4]hooks, *Yearning*, p. 18.

Wilson, August. *Three Plays: "Ma Rainey's Black Bottom," "Fences,"
"Joe Turner's Come and Gone."* Pittsburgh: University of Pittsburgh
Press, 1991.

AN INTERVIEW WITH AUGUST WILSON

BONNIE LYONS

1   This interview took place in February 1997 in Merchants Cafe in Pioneer Square in downtown Seattle, near August Wilson's office. Dressed
in a white dress shirt and tie coupled with a casual jacket and a cap, Wilson was soft-spoken and somewhat restrained at first. He became more
and more animated as he spoke about his passion for black life in America and for his plays. Wilson is well aware that he created his characters,
but he spoke of them with such knowledge and affection that I was
reminded of the famous story of Balzac calling for his characters on his
deathbed.

Q. Elsewhere you've talked about writing as a way of effecting social
change and said that all your plays are political, but that you try not
to make them didactic or polemical. Can you talk a little about how
plays can effect social change without being polemical or didactic?

A. I don't write primarily to effect social change. I believe writing can do
that, but that's not why I write. I work as an artist. However, all art is
political in the sense that it serves the politics of someone. Here in
America whites have a particular view of blacks, and I think my plays
offer them a different and new way to look at black Americans. For
instance, in *Fences* they see a garbageman, a person they really don't
look at, although they may see a garbageman every day. By looking at
Troy's life, white people find out that the content of this black
garbageman's life is very similar to their own, that he is affected by
the same things—love, honor, beauty, betrayal, duty. Recognizing that
these things are as much a part of his life as of theirs can be revolutionary and can affect how they think about and deal with black people in their lives.

Q. How would that same play, *Fences*, affect a black audience?

A. Blacks see the content of their lives being elevated into art. They don't
always know that is possible, and it's important to know that.

Q. You've talked about how important black music was for your development. Was there any black literature that showed you that black
lives can be the subject of great art?

A. *Invisible Man.* When I was fourteen I discovered the Negro section
of the library. I read *Invisible Man*, Langston Hughes, and all the
thirty or forty books in the section, including the sociology. I remember reading a book that talked about the "Negro's power of hard
work" and how much that phrase affected me.... Forty years ago we
had few black writers compared to today. There have been forty years

of education and many more college graduates. And it's important to remember that blacks don't have a long history of writing. We come from an oral tradition. At one point in America it was a crime to teach blacks to read and write. So it's only in the past 150 years that we've been writing in this country.

&

Q. You're self-educated. How do you feel about schools and self-education?
A. The schools are horrible and don't teach anybody anything. From about the fifth grade on, I was always butting heads with my teachers. I would ask them questions and they would say, "Shut up. Sit down," because they didn't know the answers. So I'd go to the library to find out. When I quit school at fourteen, I didn't want my mother to know, so I'd get up and go to the library and stay there until three o'clock. My mother taught me to read when I was four years old, and in the library for the first time in my life I felt free. I could read whole books on subjects that interested me. I'd read about the Civil War or theology. By the time I left the library, I thought, "Okay, I'm ready. I know a lot of stuff." It always amazed me that libraries were free.

&

Q. When you look at your work as a whole, what patterns do you see?
A. *Fences* is the odd man out because it's about one individual and everything focuses around him. The others are ensemble plays. I think I need to write another one like *Fences* to balance it out.

&

Q. How were things better in the forties?
A. We used to have our own black baseball league, for example. Everything was black-owned. On a Sunday black families would go over to the field, and some would sell peanuts or chicken sandwiches and so on. We were more self-sufficient. When blacks were finally allowed to play in the white leagues, the loss for the black community was great. Similarly in the forties black women were not allowed to go downtown and try on dresses in the department stores. So we had our own dress stores in the neighborhood and the doctors and dentists and teachers and business owners all lived in the same neighborhood and we had a thriving community. Then the doctors and dentists started moving out, and the whole community began to fall down. So now we're in a situation in which the basketball league is 99 percent black, but it's owned by whites. If all the money made from black sports and black music were in black hands, if it were spent in our neighborhoods, things would be very different.
Q. Elsewhere you've said you want your audience to see your characters as Africans, not just black folks in America. Can you talk about that?

A. I'm talking about black Americans having uniquely African ways of participating in the world, of doing things, different ways of socializing. I have no fascination with Africa itself. I've never been to Africa and have no desire to go.

Q. You've said that you try not to create characters who are victims. Yet aren't all these scars a sign that they have been victimized? Is the issue how they deal with their victimization, how they respond to it?

A. We're all victims of white America's paranoia. My characters don't respond as victims. No matter what society does to them, they are engaged with life, wrestling with it, trying to make sense out of it. Nobody is sitting around saying, "Woe is me."

Jim Fowler

Professor Henderson

English 1102

14 April 2006

Baseball Metaphors in *Fences*

Jim Fowler

1   Many factors related to life experience work together to influence an individual's thought and character. In August Wilson's play *Fences*, the character Troy Maxson is an excellent portrayal of how numerous factors influence the complex personality of a black man in the 1950's. One very influential factor which is highlighted throughout the play involves Troy's experience as a former Negro league baseball player. Troy's baseball experience has a significant effect upon his language, his lifestyle, and even his character.

2   Troy Maxson uses the language of baseball to express many of his thoughts and emotions. As Sandra Shannon states, "Troy flavors his conversation with baseball metaphors at every chance he gets" (204). Troy deals with many issues in his personal life by using baseball terms and experiences to reflect how he feels. One illustration of how baseball affects his emotional expression occurs when he and his son Cory are fighting. Troy angrily informs Cory that he already has two strikes, and he cautions his son, "Don't you strike out" (175). On another occasion, Troy uses baseball lingo to reveal the thrill and excitement he experiences when he engages in an extramarital affair. Troy attempts to explain his infidelity by stating to his wife, "Do you understand after eighteen years I wanted to steal second" (181). When he refers to his more serious emotions

involving the duties and responsibility of wife and family, he uses the analogy of bunting his way on base and states, "I was safe. I had me a family. A job. I wasn't gonna get that last strike" (181).

3   Troy's lifestyle is certainly affected in significant ways by his prior baseball experience. Playing the sport of baseball has probably contributed to Troy's self-centered and egotistical behavior. His friend tells Troy, "When you was hitting them baseballs out the park. A lot of them old gals was after you then" (176-77). Troy seems to miss the excitement and fun of baseball, and at times he resents the demanding responsibilities of work and his family. Baseball also influenced Troy's lifestyle by affecting his parenting. Because of the injustice Troy experienced when he played in the Negro league before the integration of baseball, he robs his son Cory of a chance to enjoy playing collage football and possibly to make something of himself in sports. In response to his own personal experience, Troy states, "I got sense enough not to let my boy get hurt over playing no sports" (165). Troy's decision not to allow his son to make his own choices and decisions causes anger and resentment in their relationship.

4   His experiences with baseball also affect Troy's character in significant ways. Troy describes his perception of the black person's experience when he states, "you born with two strikes on you before you come to the plate" (180-81). Facing the obstacles of life as a black man in a hostile society makes Troy very strong-willed and independent. Because of his experiences in baseball, Troy believes that black athletes will always be treated unfairly. Unlike his son, Troy cannot believe that "a

change has occurred in American society" (Timpane 215). He
somewhat pessimistically accepts the unfairness of his life and
tries to deal with his difficulties in his own manner. The way
in which Troy views his life also strongly impacts his attitude
toward death. Troy refers to death as a "fastball on the outside
corner" (150). This analogy indicates that Troy believes that
although he cannot hold power over death, he can try his best to
fight it off. When he receives a fastball on the outside corner,
he may not hit a home run, but he has a very good chance of
defending the plate. Troy is able "to confront Death—and hence
to construct his life—on his own terms" (Nadel 210).

5   In the play *Fences*, August Wilson reveals how environmental
factors contribute to the character formation of Troy Maxson.
Troy Maxson's life is strongly affected by his experience of
playing baseball in the Negro league prior to World War II. At
this time in the history of the sport, Troy realized that having
the athletic ability to play baseball did not guarantee African
American players equal opportunities with white players. Troy's
bitter disappointment over this experience of injustice has a
great impact on shaping his perception of the world and his
lifestyle choices. The baseball metaphors and images in the play
provide excellent insight into the character of Troy Maxson.

Works Cited

Henderson, Gloria Mason, Anna Dunlap Higgins, William Day, and

Sandra Stevenson Waller, eds. *Literature and Ourselves: A*

Thematic Introduction for Readers and Writers. 6th ed. New

York: ABLongman, 2009.

Nadel, Alan. "Boundaries, Logistics, and Identity: The Property

of Metaphor in *Fences and Joe Turner's Come and Gone." May*

All Your Fences Have Gates: Essays on the Drama of August

Wilson. Ed. Alan Nadel. Iowa City: U of Iowa P, 1994.

Henderson, Higgins, Day, and Waller, eds. 207-12.

Shannon, Sandra G. *The Dramatic Vision of August Wilson.*

Washington, DC: Howard UP, 1995. 103-17. Henderson,

Higgins, Day, and Waller 199-206.

Timpane, John. "Filling the Time: Reading History in the Drama of

August Wilson." *May All Your Fences Have Gates: Essays on*

the Drama of August Wilson. Ed. Alan Nadel. Iowa City: U of

Iowa P, 1994. Henderson, Higgins, Day, and Waller 212-16.

Wilson, August. *Fences.* N.p.: New American Library, 1986.

Henderson, Higgins, Day, and Waller 144-97.

Crafting Arguments

1. What is Troy's conception of a husband's responsibilities? Write an essay arguing that Troy is or is not a good husband.

2. Explain the symbolism of fences in the play. Why is Troy building a fence? Why does it take him so long to finish it?

3. Using the primary and secondary sources in this casebook, discuss in detail how baseball has affected Troy's lifestyle, his language, and his character.

4. Analyze the means by which Troy uses language to justify himself.

5. Write an essay comparing Troy's sons.

6. Troy tells Rose that in Alberta's house he can "laugh out loud." Beginning with this idea, contrast Troy's relationship with Rose to his relationship with Alberta.

7. Write an essay using the primary and secondary sources to support one of the following statements:

Troy uses his own past to justify his unfair treatment of Cory and Rose.

Troy sincerely tries to make the best decisions for his family.

Family: Crafting Arguments

1. Use at least two of the works in this unit to point out how the themes emphasize what is or is not necessary for a family to be happy.

2. Select two of the stories in this unit and analyze the ways that the authors' portrayal of problems faced by families and their ways of solving or failing to solve them is central to the themes of the stories.

3. Analyze the effectiveness of the authors' selection of point of view in at least two of the stories in this unit.

4. Several of the poems in the Family unit portray complex fathers. Select two poems and compare the character of the fathers or analyze the tone created by the child's portrayal of the father.

5. In some families, the parents are such high achievers that the children find it difficult to live up to their parents' standards. In other families, as in Whitelock's "Future Connected By," the child is encouraged not to emulate the parent. Select one or more works from Family or Men and Women and craft an essay to show the importance of family role models for sons or daughters or to discuss the need for sons or daughters to be distinct individuals.

6. Examine the tone of two of the three essays in Family and write an essay analyzing how the authors create the tone and illustrating how tone differs in the two essays.

Family: Writing about Film

See Appendix B: Writing about Film for help with these essays.

1. Dysfunctional families are at the heart of many works of literature and, therefore, many film adaptations, from the many versions of *Hamlet* to *Oliver Twist*, *The Adventures of Huckleberry Finn*, *Tobacco Road*, *The Little Foxes*, *The Color Purple*, *Beloved*, and *Hotel New Hampshire*. Select your favorite dysfunctional literary family and view the film version. Craft a paper that analyzes the ways the director handles this popular theme. Is the overall atmosphere of the film dark or light, and how is that tone achieved?

2. One classic film adaptation about family is not about the kind of family we often think of when we hear that word: Francis Ford Coppola's *The Godfather* (1972) and its sequels focus on the nuclear family and also on larger "families." Write a Classification paper examining the

types of family in these classic films. What message does the film offer about "family"?

3. E. B. White's novels *Stuart Little* and *Charlotte's Web* have been adapted more than once. Although appropriate for children, these movies have also been described as "inspiring" for the adult viewer. Write a paper that examines what these films have to say about acceptance, endurance, and family. What film techniques are important in conveying the film's message?

4. The Appendix on film includes a sample student paper analyzing a film adaptation of Frances Mayes' *Under the Tuscan Sun*, a text that offers an important message about struggle and survival after divorce. View the movie and prepare your own analysis of the film. You might prefer another film adaptation that focuses on the healing within a family, such as the classic *It's a Wonderful Life* (1947) or one of the versions of *A Christmas Carol*.

Men and Women

A scene from *Atonement*. Focus Features/Everett Collection.

G ender issues have long fascinated us. Reportedly, women are from Venus, and men are from Mars. According to the old nursery rhyme, girls are made of sugar and spice and everything nice; boys are made of snails and puppy dog tails. Some Americans denounce the culture's continued gender stereotyping. They point, for example, to toy manufacturers' production of scantily clad dolls based on pop icons as evidence that our culture sexualizes girls. Other Americans point to the success of ad campaigns featuring fathers tenderly caressing babies as evidence that the country has moved away from historic gender constructions. When it comes to gender, we all seem to have something to say.

The selections in this unit are sure to stir discussions about gender. The authors' perspectives offer insight into gendered issues covering a wide range of time and place and heritage: William Shakespeare's Elizabethan era England, Henrik Ibsen's nineteenth-century Norway, Kate Chopin's end of the nineteenth-century southern America, Jhumpa Lahiri's late–twentieth-century America. Included in this section are some of the most important voices in women's literature and African American women's literature: Virginia Woolf, Kate Chopin, Charlotte Perkins Gilman, Zora Neale Hurston, Maya Angelou, Marge Piercy, and Rita Dove. Male authors long considered classic—Shakespeare, Robert Browning, Nathaniel Hawthorne, Ibsen, Ernest Hemingway, and Robert Frost—join with newer voices—Max Shulman and David Osborne—to provide a male perspective.

Some of the works in this unit speak to the struggle of power between the genders, to what has been called the sexual politics of the male/female relationship. Addressing an audience of women, Virginia Woolf argues that in order for women to carve out a professional niche in a patriarchal society, they must "kill" the Angel in the House, the imprisoning gender stereotype affecting women's behavior and thoughts. In his hilarious essay "Love Is a Fallacy," Max Shulman deconstructs the male power base when the supposedly less intelligent girl outsmarts the smart guy. Both Zora Neal Hurston's "The Gilded Six-Bits" and Jhumpa

Lahiri's "A Temporary Matter" showcase couples struggling with issues involving power, trust, communication, and forgiveness. David Osborne's "Beyond the Cult of Fatherhood" shares the male perspective when a couple defies traditional gender roles and attempts to negotiate parental authority. Because they refuse to offer easy answers to the complexities of gendered relations, the stories and essays in this unit invite discussion.

The literary works included in this section also delve into issues that affect us all, regardless of gender. Both men and women struggle with self-image and purpose. Georgiana in Nathaniel Hawthorne's "The Birthmark" and the girl in Marge Piercy's "Barbie Doll" are affected by what others say about them. Both even allow others to convince them that their worth can be measured by physical attractiveness; the consequences are tragic when they themselves accept that they fail to measure up to the standard. The speaker in Maya Angelou's "Phenomenal Woman" exudes confidence. Charismatic, comfortable in the company of men and of women, the speaker addresses us directly, suggesting that her confidence should inspire our own. In Zora Neale Hurston's "The Gilded Six-Bits," the usually peaceful Joe must decide how to act when an interloper attempts to destroy his family; once he is betrayed, he must then chose how he will respond.

Many of the works in this unit portray beautiful and at times complex love relationships, such as those found in the Frost Casebook. The lines created by Elizabeth Barrett Browning expressing her unconditional love are so beautifully crafted that to this day they are often sung in wedding ceremonies. In literature as in life, men and women sometimes find themselves attempting to navigate the ebb and flow of love, a "course" that William Shakespeare once claimed never runs smoothly. Despite their best efforts, neither the narrator in Lahiri's short story nor the speaker in Andrew Marvell's poem wins his love. The narrator in Shulman's essay outsmarts himself in his attempt to get the girl. The love offered by the husband in Kate Chopin's "Desiree's Baby" is literally only skin deep.

Writing about Men and Women

The works in this unit provide a rich source for essays about men and women. Once you have selected the work or works of literature you intend to use in your essay, you should re-read the Questions for Engagement, Response, and Analysis about that particular genre in the Introduction. For help in selecting a suitable topic, you can also re-read the suggestions for Crafting Arguments after the selections and those at the end of this unit.

If you decide to write about an essay, you might compare the approaches to parenting of the author and his wife in David Osborne's "Beyond the Cult of Fatherhood" or argue that the motivation of the narrator in Max Shulman's "Love Is a Fallacy" is less than noble. If you prefer to examine style, you might compare Polly's speech patterns at the beginning of "Love Is a Fallacy" with her answers after her introduction to logical fallacies.

If you choose to write on a work of fiction, you might, for example, write an analysis of a complex character like Joe in "The Gilded Six-Bits" or Shoba in "A Temporary Matter," or you might argue that Charlotte Perkins Gilman's use of the wallpaper as a symbol in "The Yellow Wallpaper" effectively conveys the narrator's mental deterioration. If you prefer Comparison/Contrast essays, you might discuss how different characters interpret the birthmark in Hawthorne's story, or you might compare the types of control exercised by Armand in Chopin's "Desiree's Baby" with those of the man in Hemingway's "Hills Like White Elephants." If you prefer to argue about a character's motivation, you might analyze the reasons for Shoba's choice at the end of "A Temporary Matter" or for Joe's decision at the end of "The Gilded Six-Bits."

If you choose to write on poetry, you might claim that Andrew Marvell uses traditional rules of argument in an attempt to persuade his mistress to give in to him. If you prefer to write about style, you could examine one or more of the six sonnets in this unit and argue that the sonnet form is especially appropriate for poems about love, or you could examine the metaphorical devices Elizabeth Barrett Browning uses in "Sonnet 43" and explain their appropriateness as expressions of her love. The varying tones in the poems are also a rich source of essay topics. If you enjoy Robert Frost's poetry, you can choose from many interesting topics suggested at the end of the Casebook.

The play in this unit also offers you a variety of essay types and topics. If you choose to write on *A Doll's House*, you may want to examine the writing suggestions at the end of the play. For example, you might write an essay contrasting Nora's behavior at the beginning of the play with her actions at the end, or you might analyze the causes of her behavior. You might wish to argue that Nora is jointly responsible for her dilemma, that Helmer bears most of the responsibility, or that Nora does or does not make the right choice at the end of the play.

No matter what topic you choose for your essay, you will probably want first to study the work of literature carefully and select convincing examples to prove your claims. For example, when Daniel Wilkinson was asked to write an essay on Frost using the materials in the Casebook, he first read all of the poems closely in order to form his own opinions about them before reading the opinions of critics. He decided on a working thesis. Then he read the critical essays to see what additional support he might find for his claims. Since Daniel is an English major, his background in literature made writing the essay easier for him, and once he had selected a thesis, he wrote an excellent first draft. He set it aside for a day or two to "forget" what he had written—long enough to clean up a few argumentative gaps and the grammar mistakes he had passed over in the writing process. He also realized that he needed to consult his handbook in order to polish the MLA form that his professor required. Then he e-mailed a copy of the essay to his professor, who suggested only a few changes. Finally, Daniel revised and edited his essay and submitted the final copy, which is included at the end of the Frost Casebook.

ESSAYS

Virginia Woolf (1882–1941)

*Though plagued throughout her lifetime by nervous break-
downs, Virginia Stephen Woolf became a major influence on
English literature. Today she is considered one of the most
significant writers in the field of women's literature. Woolf
was a member of the famous Bloomsbury circle, a group that
stressed culture and opposed many restrictive Victorian
standards. She excelled as a novelist with such works as*
Mrs. Dalloway *(1925) and* To the Lighthouse *(1927); as a
critic; and as an essayist with* A Room of One's Own *(1929)
and* Three Guineas *(1938). This speech was presented to the
Women's Service League, a group of career women, in 1936.*

PROFESSIONS FOR WOMEN (1936)

1   When your secretary invited me to come here, she told me that your
Society is concerned with the employment of women and she suggested
that I might tell you something about my own professional experiences.
It is true I am a woman; it is true I am employed; but what professional
experiences have I had? It is difficult to say. My profession is literature;
and in that profession there are fewer experiences for women than in any
other, with the exception of the stage—fewer, I mean, that are peculiar
to women. For the road was cut many years ago—by Fanny Burney, by
Aphra Behn, by Harriet Martineau, by Jane Austen, by George Eliot—
many famous women, and many more unknown and forgotten, have been
before me, making the path smooth, and regulating my steps. Thus, when
I came to write, there were very few material obstacles in my way. Writing was a reputable and harmless occupation. The family peace was not
broken by the scratching of a pen. No demand was made upon the family purse. For ten and sixpence one can buy paper enough to write all the
plays of Shakespeare—if one has a mind that way. Pianos and models,
Paris, Vienna and Berlin, masters and mistresses, are not needed by a
writer. The cheapness of writing paper is, of course, the reason why
women have succeeded as writers before they have succeeded in the
other professions.

2   But to tell you my story—it is a simple one. You have only got to figure to yourselves a girl in a bedroom with a pen in her hand. She had only
to move that pen from left to right—from ten o'clock to one. Then it
occurred to her to do what is simple and cheap enough after all—to slip
a few of those pages into an envelope, fix a penny stamp in the corner,
and drop the envelope in the red box at the corner. It was thus that I
became a journalist; and my effort was rewarded on the first day of the
following month—a very glorious day it was for me—by a letter from an
editor containing a cheque for one pound ten shillings and sixpence. But

to show you how little I deserve to be called a professional woman, how little I know of the struggles and difficulties of such lives, I have to admit that instead of spending that sum upon bread and butter, rent, shoes and stockings, or butcher's bills, I went out and bought a cat—a beautiful cat, a Persian cat, which very soon involved me in bitter disputes with my neighbours.

3   What could be easier than to write articles and to buy Persian cats with the profits? But wait a moment. Articles have to be about something. Mine, I seem to remember, was about a novel by a famous man. And while I was writing this review, I discovered that if I were going to review books I should need to do battle with a certain phantom. And the phantom was a woman, and when I came to know her better I called her after the heroine of a famous poem, The Angel in the House. It was she who used to come between me and my paper when I was writing reviews. It was she who bothered me and wasted my time and so tormented me that at last I killed her. You who come of a younger and happier generation may not have heard of her—you may not know what I mean by the Angel in the House. I will describe her as shortly as I can. She was intensely sympathetic. She was immensely charming. She was utterly unselfish. She excelled in the difficult arts of family life. She sacrificed herself daily. If there was chicken, she took the leg; if there was a draught she sat in it—in short she was so constituted that she never had a mind or a wish of her own, but preferred to sympathize always with the minds and wishes of others. Above all—I need not say it—she was pure. Her purity was supposed to be her chief beauty—her blushes, her great grace. In those days—the last of Queen Victoria—every house had its Angel. And when I came to write I encountered her with the very first words. The shadow of her wings fell on my page; I heard the rustling of her skirts in the room. Directly, that is to say, I took my pen in hand to review that novel by a famous man, she slipped behind me and whispered: "My dear, you are a young woman. You are writing about a book that has been written by a man. Be sympathetic; be tender; flatter; deceive; use all the arts and wiles of our sex. Never let anybody guess that you have a mind of your own. Above all, be pure." And she made as if to guide my pen. I now record the one act for which I take some credit to myself, though the credit rightly belongs to some excellent ancestors of mine who left me a certain sum of money—shall we say five hundred pounds a year?—so that it was not necessary for me to depend solely on charm for my living. I turned upon her and caught her by the throat. I did my best to kill her. My excuse, if I were to be had up in a court of law, would be that I acted in self-defence. Had I not killed her she would have killed me. She would have plucked the heart out of my writing. For, as I found, directly I put pen to paper, you cannot review even a novel without having a mind of your own, without expressing what you think to be the truth about human relations, morality, sex. And all these questions, according to the Angel in the House, cannot be dealt with freely and openly by women;

they must charm, they must conciliate, they must—to put it bluntly—tell lies if they are to succeed. Thus, whenever I felt the shadow of her wing or the radiance of her halo upon my page, I took up the inkpot and flung it at her. She died hard. Her fictitious nature was of great assistance to her. It is far harder to kill a phantom than a reality. She was always creeping back when I thought I had despatched her. Though I flatter myself that I killed her in the end, the struggle was severe; it took much time that had better have been spent upon learning Greek grammar; or in roaming the world in search of adventures. But it was a real experience; it was an experience that was bound to befall all women writers at that time. Killing the Angel in the House was part of the occupation of a woman writer.

4   But to continue my story. The Angel was dead; what then remained? You may say that what remained was a simple and common object—a young woman in a bedroom with an inkpot. In other words, now that she had rid herself of falsehood, that young woman had only to be herself. Ah, but what is "herself"? I mean, what is a woman? I assure you, I do not know. I do not believe that you know. I do not believe that anybody can know until she has expressed herself in all the arts and professions open to human skill. That indeed is one of the reasons why I have come here—out of respect for you, who are in process of showing us by your experiments what a woman is, who are in process of providing us, by your failures and successes, with that extremely important piece of information.

5   But to continue the story of my professional experiences. I made one pound ten and six by my first review; and I bought a Persian cat with the proceeds. Then I grew ambitious. A Persian cat is all very well, I said; but a Persian cat is not enough. I must have a motor car. And it was thus that I became a novelist—for it is a very strange thing that people will give you a motor car if you will tell them a story. It is a still stranger thing that there is nothing so delightful in the world as telling stories. It is far pleasanter than writing reviews of famous novels. And yet, if I am to obey your secretary and tell you my professional experiences as a novelist, I must tell you about a very strange experience that befell me as a novelist. And to understand it you must try first to imagine a novelist's state of mind. I hope I am not giving away professional secrets if I say that a novelist's chief desire is to be as unconscious as possible. He has to induce in himself a state of perpetual lethargy. He wants life to proceed with the utmost quiet and regularity. He wants to see the same faces, to read the same books, to do the same things day after day, month after month, while he is writing, so that nothing may break the illusion in which he is living—so that nothing may disturb or disquiet the mysterious nosings about, feelings round, darts, dashes and sudden discoveries of that very shy and illusive spirit, the imagination. I suspect that this state is the same both for men and women. Be that as it may, I want you to imagine me writing a novel in a state of trance. I want you to figure to yourselves a girl sitting with a pen in her hand, which for

minutes, and indeed for hours, she never dips into the inkpot. The image that comes to my mind when I think of this girl is the image of a fisherman lying sunk in dreams on the verge of a deep lake with a rod held out over the water. She was letting her imagination sweep unchecked round every rock and cranny of the world that lies submerged in the depths of our unconscious being. Now came the experience, the experience that I believe to be far commoner with women writers than with men. The line raced through the girl's fingers. Her imagination had rushed away. It had sought the pools, the depths, the dark places where the largest fish slumber. And then there was a smash. There was an explosion. There was foam and confusion. The imagination had dashed itself against something hard. The girl was roused from her dream. She was indeed in a state of the most acute and difficult distress. To speak without figure she had thought of something, something about the body, about the passions which it was unfitting for her as a woman to say. Men, her reason told her, would be shocked. The consciousness of what men will say of a woman who speaks the truth about her passions had roused her from her artist's state of unconsciousness. She could write no more. The trance was over. Her imagination could work no longer. This I believe to be a very common experience with women writers—they are impeded by the extreme conventionality of the other sex. For though men sensibly allow themselves great freedom in these respects, I doubt that they realize or can control the extreme severity with which they condemn such freedom in women.

6   These then were two very genuine experiences of my own. These were two of the adventures of my professional life. The first—killing the Angel in the House—I think I solved. She died. But the second, telling the truth about my own experiences as a body, I do not think I solved. I doubt that any woman has solved it yet. The obstacles against her are still immensely powerful—and yet they are very difficult to define. Outwardly, what is simpler than to write books? Outwardly, what obstacles are there for a woman rather than for a man? Inwardly, I think, the case is very different; she has still many ghosts to fight, many prejudices to overcome. Indeed it will be a long time still, I think, before a woman can sit down to write a book without finding a phantom to be slain, a rock to be dashed against. And if this is so in literature, the freest of all professions for women, how is it in the new professions which you are now for the first time entering?

7   Those are the questions that I should like, had I time, to ask you. And indeed, if I have laid stress upon these professional experiences of mine, it is because I believe that they are, though in different forms, yours also. Even when the path is nominally open—when there is nothing to prevent a woman from being a doctor, a lawyer, a civil servant—there are many phantoms and obstacles, as I believe, looming in her way. To discuss and define them is I think of great value and importance; for thus only can the labour be shared, the difficulties be solved. But besides this,

it is necessary also to discuss the ends and the aims for which we are fighting, for which we are doing battle with these formidable obstacles. Those aims cannot be taken for granted; they must be perpetually questioned and examined. The whole position, as I see it—here in this hall surrounded by women practicing for the first time in history I know not how many different professions—is one of extraordinary interest and importance. You have won rooms of your own in the house hitherto exclusively owned by men. You are able, though not without great labour and effort, to pay the rent. You are earning your five hundred pounds a year. But this freedom is only a beginning; the room is your own, but it is still bare. It has to be furnished; it has to be decorated; it has to be shared. How are you going to furnish it, how are you going to decorate it? With whom are you going to share it, and upon what terms? These, I think are questions of the utmost importance and interest. For the first time in history you are able to ask them; for the first time you are able to decide for yourselves what the answers should be. Willingly would I stay and discuss those questions and answers—but not tonight. My time is up; and I must cease.

Questions for Engagement, Response, and Analysis

1. Describe Woolf's style and tone. In what ways are they designed to appeal to her original audience?

2. In your Reader's Journal, discuss the degree to which the "Angel in the House" haunts you or women you know. Discuss other angels that a person might have to kill off, such as the Angel at Work, the Angel at School, the Angel in the Family, or the Angel of Friendship.

3. What obstacle other than the "Angel in the House" does Woolf face? Why has she not overcome that obstacle?

4. What, according to Woolf, can a man talk about or write about that a woman cannot? What limits on free expression do women today face?

Crafting Arguments

1. Analyze Woolf's analogy between women pioneering in professions and an unfurnished room.

2. Define Woolf's "Angel in the House." Who is she? Why did the author have to kill the "Angel"?

Max Shulman (1919–1988)

*American humorist Max Shulman wrote short stories, nov-
els, plays, and screenplays. He adapted many of his works
for film or television, often serving as composer and lyri-
cist as well. His collection titled* The Many Loves of Dobie
Gillis, *from which the following essay is taken, was made
into the 1953 movie called* The Affairs of Dobie Gillis,
*starring Debbie Reynolds, and into a 1959 television series
starring Dwayne Hickman as Dobie and Bob Denver as his
friend Maynard G. Krebs. His 1955 play* The Tender Trap
*was rewritten as a movie for Debbie Reynolds and Frank
Sinatra, and the movie made from the 1958 novel* Rally
Round the Flag, Boys! *starred Paul Newman and Joanne
Woodward.*

LOVE IS A FALLACY   (1951)

1   Cool was I and logical. Keen, calculating, perspicacious, acute and
astute—I was all of these. My brain was as powerful as a dynamo, as precise as a chemist's scales, as penetrating as a scalpel. And—think of it!—
I was only eighteen.

2   It is not often that one so young has such a giant intellect. Take, for
example, Petey Burch, my roommate at the University of Minnesota.
Same age, same background, but dumb as an ox. A nice enough fellow,
you understand, but nothing upstairs. Emotional type. Unstable. Impressionable. Worst of all, a faddist. Fads, I submit, are the very negation of
reason. To be swept up in every new craze that comes along, to surrender yourself to idiocy just because everybody else is doing it—this, to me,
is the acme of mindlessness. Not, however, to Petey.

3   One afternoon I found Petey lying on his bed with an expression of
such distress on his face that I immediately diagnosed appendicitis.
"Don't move," I said. "Don't take a laxative. I'll get a doctor."

4   "Raccoon," he mumbled thickly.

5   "Raccoon?" I said, pausing in my flight.

6   "I want a raccoon coat," he wailed.

7   I perceived that his trouble was not physical, but mental. "Why do you
want a raccoon coat?"

8   "I should have known it," he cried, pounding his temples. "I should have
known they'd come back when the Charleston came back. Like a fool I
spent all my money for textbooks, and now I can't get a raccoon coat."

9   "Can you mean," I said incredulously, "that people are actually wearing raccoon coats again?"

10   "All the Big Men on Campus are wearing them. Where've you been?"

11   "In the library," I said, naming a place not frequented by Big Men
on Campus.

12   He leaped from the bed and paced the room. "I've got to have a raccoon coat," he said passionately. "I've got to!"

13   "Petey, why? Look at it rationally. Raccoon coats are unsanitary. They shed. They smell bad. They weigh too much. They're unsightly."

14   You don't understand," he interrupted impatiently. "It's the thing to do. Don't you want to be in the swim?"

15   "No," I said truthfully.

16   "Well, I do," he declared. "I'd give anything for a raccoon coat. Anything!"

17   My brain, that precision instrument, slipped into high gear. "Anything?" I asked, looking at him narrowly.

18   "Anything," he affirmed in ringing tones.

19   I stroked my chin thoughtfully. It so happened that I knew where to get my hands on a raccoon coat. My father had had one in his under-graduate days; it lay now in a trunk in the attic back home. It also hap-pened that Petey had something I wanted. He didn't *have* it exactly, but at least he had first rights on it. I refer to his girl, Polly Espy.

20   I had long coveted Polly Espy. Let me emphasize that my desire for this young woman was not emotional in nature. She was, to be sure, a girl who excited the emotions, but I was not one to let my heart rule my head. I wanted Polly for a shrewdly calculated, entirely cerebral reason.

21   I was a freshman in law school. In a few years I would be out in prac-tice. I was well aware of the importance of the right kind of wife in fur-thering a lawyer's career. The successful lawyers I had observed were, almost without exception, married to beautiful, gracious, intelligent women. With one omission, Polly fitted these specifications perfectly.

22   Beautiful she was. She was not yet of pin-up proportions, but I felt sure that time would supply the lack. She already had the makings.

23   Gracious she was. By gracious I mean full of graces. She had an erect-ness of carriage, an ease of bearing, a poise that clearly indicated the best of breeding. At table her manners were exquisite. I had seen her at the Kozy Kampus Korner eating the specialty of the house—a sandwich that contained scraps of pot roast, gravy, chopped nuts, and a dipper of sauer-kraut—without even getting her fingers moist.

24   Intelligent she was not. In fact, she veered in the opposite direction. But I believed that under my guidance she would smarten up. At any rate, it was worth a try. It is, after all, easier to make a beautiful dumb girl smart than to make an ugly smart girl beautiful.

25   "Petey," I said, "are you in love with Polly Espy?"

26   "I think she's a keen kid," he replied, "but I don't know if you'd call it love. Why?"

27   "Do you," I asked, "have any kind of formal arrangement with her? I mean are you going steady or anything like that?"

28   "No. We see each other quite a bit, but we both have other dates."

29   "Is there," I asked, "any other man for whom she has a particular fondness?"

30   "Not that I know of. Why?"

31   I nodded with satisfaction. "In other words, if you were out of the pic-ture, the field would be open. Is that right?"

32   "I guess so. What are you getting at?"

33   "Nothing, nothing," I said innocently, and took my suitcase out of the closet.

34   "Where are you going?" asked Petey.

35   "Home for the weekend." I threw a few things into the bag.

36   "Listen," he said, clutching my arm eagerly, "while you're home, you couldn't get some money from your old man, could you, and lend it to me so I can buy a raccoon coat?"

37   "I may do better than that," I said with a mysterious wink and closed my bag and left.

38   "Look," I said to Petey when I got back Monday morning. I threw open the suitcase and revealed the huge, hairy, gamy object that my father had worn in his Stutz Bearcat in 1925.

39   "Holy Toledo!" said Petey reverently. He plunged his hands into the raccoon coat and then his face. "Holy Toledo!" he repeated fifteen or twenty times.

40   "Would you like it?" I asked.

41   "Oh yes!" he cried, clutching the greasy pelt to him. Then a canny look came into his eyes. "What do you want for it?"

42   "Your girl," I said, mincing no words.

43   "Polly?" he said in a horrified whisper. "You want Polly?"

44   "That's right."

45   He flung the coat from him. "Never," he said stoutly.

46   I shrugged. "Okay. If you don't want to be in the swim, I guess it's your business."

47   I sat down in a chair and pretended to read a book, but out of the corner of my eye I kept watching Petey. He was a torn man. First he looked at the coat with the expression of a waif at a bakery window. Then he turned away and set his jaw resolutely. Then he looked back at the coat, with even more longing in his face. Then he turned away, but with not so much resolution this time. Back and forth his head swiveled, desire waxing, resolution waning. Finally he didn't turn away at all; he just stood and stared with mad lust at the coat.

48   "It isn't as though I was in love with Polly," he said thickly. "Or going steady or anything like that."

49   "That's right," I murmured.

50   "What's Polly to me, or me to Polly?"

51   "Not a thing," said I.

52   "It's just been a casual kick—just a few laughs, that's all."

53   "Try on the coat," said I.

54   He complied. The coat bunched high over his ears and dropped all the way down to his shoe tops. He looked like a mound of dead raccoons. "Fits fine," he said happily.

55   I rose from my chair. "Is it a deal?" I asked, extending my hand.

56   He swallowed. "It's a deal," he said and shook my hand.

57   I had my first date with Polly the following evening. This was in the nature of a survey; I wanted to find out just how much work I had to do to get her mind up to the standard I required. I took her first to dinner. "Gee, that was a delish dinner," she said as we left the restaurant. Then I took her to a movie. "Gee, that was a marvy movie," she said as we left the theater. And then I took her home. "Gee, I had a sensaysh time," she said as she bade me good night.

58   I went back to my room with a heavy heart. I had gravely underestimated the size of my task. This girl's lack of information was terrifying. Nor would it be enough merely to supply her with information. First she had to be taught to *think*. This loomed as a project of no small dimensions, and at first I was tempted to give her back to Petey. But then I got to thinking about her abundant physical charms and about the way she entered a room and the way she handled a knife and fork, and I decided to make an effort.

59   I went about it, as in all things, systematically. I gave her a course in logic. It happened that I, as a law student, was taking a course in logic myself, so I had all the facts at my finger tips. "Polly," I said to her when I picked her up on our next date, "tonight we are going over to the Knoll and talk."

60   "Oo, terrif," she replied. One thing I will say for this girl: you would go far to find another so agreeable.

61   We went to the Knoll, the campus trysting place, and we sat down under an old oak, and she looked at me expectantly. "What are we going to talk about?" she asked.

62   "Logic."

63   She thought this over for a minute and decided she liked it. "Magnif," she said.

64   "Logic," I said, clearing my throat, "is the science of thinking. Before we can think correctly, we must first learn to recognize the common fallacies of logic. These we will take up tonight."

65   "Wow-dow!" she cried, clapping her hands delightedly.

66   I winced, but went bravely on. "First let us examine the fallacy called Dicto Simpliciter."

67   "By all means," she urged, batting her lashes eagerly.

68   "Dicto Simpliciter means an argument based on an unqualified generalization. For example: Exercise is good. Therefore everybody should exercise."

69   "I agree," said Polly earnestly. "I mean exercise is wonderful. I mean it builds the body and everything."

70   "Polly," I said gently, "the argument is a fallacy. *Exercise is good* is an unqualified generalization. For instance, if you have heart disease, exercise is bad, not good. Many people are ordered by their doctors *not* to exercise. You must *qualify* the generalization. You must say exercise is *usually* good, or exercise is good *for most people*. Otherwise you have committed a Dicto Simpliciter. Do you see?"

71   "No," she confessed. "But this is marvy. Do more! Do more!"

72   "It will be better if you stop tugging at my sleeve," I told her, and when she desisted, I continued. "Next we take up a fallacy called Hasty Generalization. Listen carefully: You can't speak French. I can't speak French. Petey Burch can't speak French. I must therefore conclude that nobody at the University of Minnesota can speak French."

73   "Really?" said Polly, amazed. "*Nobody?*"

74   I hid my exasperation. "Polly, it's a fallacy. The generalization is reached too hastily. There are too few instances to support such a conclusion."

75   "Know any more fallacies?" she asked breathlessly. "This is more fun than dancing even."

76   I fought off a wave of despair. I was getting nowhere with this girl, absolutely nowhere. Still, I am nothing if not persistent. I continued. "Next comes Post Hoc. Listen to this: Let's not take Bill on our picnic. Every time we take him out with us, it rains."

77   "I know somebody just like that," she exclaimed. "A girl back home— Eula Becker, her name is. It never fails. Every single time we take her on a picnic—"

78   "Polly," I said sharply, "it's a fallacy. Eula Becker doesn't *cause* the rain. She has no connection with the rain. You are guilty of Post Hoc if you blame Eula Becker."

79   "I'll never do it again," she promised contritely. "Are you mad at me?"

80   I sighed deeply. "No, Polly, I'm not mad."

81   "Then tell me some more fallacies."

82   "All right. Let's try Contradictory Premises."

83   "Yes, let's," she chirped, blinking her eyes happily.

84   I frowned, but plunged ahead. "Here's an example of Contradictory Premises: If God can do anything, can He make a stone so heavy that He won't be able to lift it?"

85   "Of course," she replied promptly.

86   "But if He can do anything, He can lift the stone," I pointed out.

87   "Yeah," she said thoughtfully. "Well, then I guess He can't make the stone."

88   "But He can do anything," I reminded her.

89   She scratched her pretty, empty head. "I'm all confused," she admitted.

90   "Of course you are. Because when the premises of an argument contradict each other, there can be no argument. If there is an irresistible force, there can be no immovable object. If there is an immovable object, there can be no irresistible force. Get it?"

91   "Tell me some more of this keen stuff," she said eagerly.

92   I consulted my watch. "I think we'd better call it a night. I'll take you home now, and you go over all the things you've learned. We'll have another session tomorrow night."

93   I deposited her at the girls' dormitory, where she assured me that she had had a perfectly terrif evening, and I went glumly home to my room. Petey lay snoring in his bed, the raccoon coat huddled like a great hairy beast at his feet. For a moment I considered waking him and telling him that he could have his girl back. It seemed clear

that my project was doomed to failure. The girl simply had a logic-proof head.

94   But then I reconsidered. I had wasted one evening; I might as well waste another. Who knew? Maybe somewhere in the extinct crater of her mind, a few embers still smoldered. Maybe somehow I could fan them into flame. Admittedly it was not a prospect fraught with hope, but I decided to give it one more try.

95   Seated under the oak the next evening I said, "Our first fallacy tonight is called Ad Misericordiam."

96   She quivered with delight.

97   "Listen closely," I said. "A man applies for a job. When the boss asks him what his qualifications are, he replies that he has a wife and six children at home, the wife is a helpless cripple, the children have nothing to eat, no clothes to wear, no shoes on their feet, there are no beds in the house, no coal in the cellar, and winter is coming."

98   A tear rolled down each of Polly's pink cheeks. "Oh, this is awful, awful," she sobbed.

99   "Yes, it's awful," I agreed, "but it's no argument. The man never answered the boss's question about his qualifications. Instead he appealed to the boss's sympathy. He committed the fallacy of Ad Misericordiam. Do you understand?"

100   "Have you got a handkerchief?" she blubbered.

101   I handed her a handkerchief and tried to keep from screaming while she wiped her eyes. "Next," I said in a carefully controlled tone, "we will discuss False Analogy. Here is an example: Students should be allowed to look at their textbooks during examinations. After all, surgeons have X-rays to guide them during an operation, lawyers have briefs to guide them during a trial, carpenters have blueprints to guide them when they are building a house. Why, then, shouldn't students be allowed to look at their textbooks during an examination?"

102   "There now," she said enthusiastically, "is the most marvy idea I've heard in years."

103   "Polly," I said testily, "the argument is all wrong. Doctors, lawyers, and carpenters aren't taking a test to see how much they have learned, but students are. The situations are altogether different, and you can't make an analogy between them."

104   "I still think it's a good idea," said Polly.

105   "Nuts," I muttered. Doggedly I pressed on. "Next we'll try Hypothesis Contrary to Fact."

106   "Sounds yummy," was Polly's reaction.

107   "Listen: If Madame Curie had not happened to leave a photographic plate in a drawer with a chunk of pitchblende, the world today would not know about radium."

108   "True, true," said Polly, nodding her head. "Did you see the movie? Oh, it just knocked me out. That Walter Pidgeon is so dreamy. I mean he fractures me."

109   "If you can forget Mr. Pidgeon for a moment," I said coldly, "I would like to point out that the statement is a fallacy. Maybe Madame Curie would have discovered radium at some later date. Maybe somebody else would have discovered it. Maybe any number of things would have happened. You can't start with a hypothesis that is not true and then draw any supportable conclusions from it."

110   "They ought to put Walter Pidgeon in more pictures," said Polly. "I hardly ever see him any more."

111   One more chance, I decided. But just one more. There is a limit to what flesh and blood can bear. "The next fallacy is called Poisoning the Well."

112   "How cute!" she gurgled.

113   "Two men are having a debate. The first one gets up and says, 'My opponent is a notorious liar. You can't believe a word that he is going to say.' . . . Now, Polly, think. Think hard. What's wrong?"

114   I watched her closely as she knit her creamy brow in concentration. Suddenly a glimmer of intelligence—the first I had seen—came into her eyes. "It's not fair," she said with indignation. "It's not a bit fair. What chance has the second man got if the first man calls him a liar before he even begins talking?"

115   "Right!" I cried exultantly. "One hundred percent right. It's not fair. The first man has *poisoned the well* before anybody could drink from it. He has hamstrung his opponent before he could even start. . . . . Polly, I'm proud of you."

116   "Pshaw," she murmured, blushing with pleasure.

117   "You see, my dear, these things aren't so hard. All you have to do is concentrate. Think—examine—evaluate. Come now, let's review everything we have learned."

118   "Fire away," she said with an airy wave of her hand.

119   Heartened by the knowledge that Polly was not altogether a cretin, I began a long, patient review of all I had told her. Over and over and over again I cited instances, pointed out flaws, kept hammering away without let-up. It was like digging a tunnel. At first everything was work, sweat, and darkness. I had no idea when I would reach the light, or even *if* I would. But I persisted. I pounded and clawed and scraped, and finally I was rewarded. I saw a chink of light. And then the chink got bigger and the sun came pouring in and all was bright.

120   Five grueling nights this took, but it was worth it. I had made a logician out of Polly; I had taught her to think. My job was done. She was worthy of me at last. She was a fit wife for me, a proper hostess for my many mansions, a suitable mother for my well-heeled children.

121   It must not be thought that I was without love for this girl. Quite the contrary. Just as Pygmalion loved the perfect woman he had fashioned, so I loved mine. I determined to acquaint her with my feelings at our very next meeting. The time had come to change our relationship from academic to romantic.

122   "Polly," I said when next we sat beneath our oak, "tonight we will not discuss fallacies."

123   "Aw, gee," she said, disappointed.

124   "My dear," I said, favoring her with a smile, "we have now spent five evenings together. We have gotten along splendidly. It is clear that we are well matched."

125   "Hasty Generalization," said Polly brightly.

126   "I beg your pardon," said I.

127   "Hasty Generalization," she repeated. "How can you say that we are well matched on the basis of only five dates?"

128   I chuckled with amusement. The dear child had learned her lessons well. "My dear," I said, patting her hand in a tolerant manner, "five dates is plenty. After all, you don't have to eat a whole cake to know that it's good."

129   "False Analogy," said Polly promptly. "I'm not a cake. I'm a girl."

130   I chuckled with somewhat less amusement. The dear child had learned her lessons perhaps too well. I decided to change tactics. Obviously the best approach was a simple, strong, direct declaration of love. I paused for a moment while my massive brain chose the proper words. Then I began:

131   "Polly, I love you. You are the whole world to me, and the moon and the stars and the constellations of outer space. Please, my darling, say that you will go steady with me, for if you will not, life will be meaningless. I will languish. I will refuse my meals. I will wander the face of the earth, a shambling, hollow-eyed hulk."

132   There, I thought, folding my arms, that ought to do it.

133   "Ad Misericordiam," said Polly.

134   I ground my teeth. I was not Pygmalion; I was Frankenstein, and my monster had me by the throat. Frantically I fought back the tide of panic surging through me. At all costs I had to keep cool.

135   "Well, Polly," I said, forcing a smile, "you certainly have learned your fallacies."

136   "You're darn right," she said with a vigorous nod.

137   "And who taught them to you, Polly?"

138   "You did."

139   "That's right. So you do owe me something, don't you, my dear? If I hadn't come along you never would have learned about fallacies."

140   "Hypothesis Contrary to Fact," she said instantly.

141   I dashed perspiration from my brow. "Polly," I croaked, "you mustn't take all these things so literally. I mean this is just classroom stuff. You know that the things you learn in school don't have anything to do with life."

142   "Dicto Simpliciter," she said, wagging her finger at me playfully.

143   That did it. I leaped to my feet, bellowing like a bull. "Will you or will you not go steady with me?"

144   "I will not," she replied.

145   "Why not?" I demanded.

146   "Because this afternoon I promised Petey Burch that I would go steady with him."

147   I reeled back, overcome with the infamy of it. After he promised, after he made a deal, after he shook my hand! "The rat!" I shrieked, kicking up great chunks of turf. "You can't go with him, Polly. He's a liar. He's a cheat. He's a rat."

148   "Poisoning the Well," said Polly, "and stop shouting. I think shouting must be a fallacy too."

149   With an immense effort of will, I modulated my voice. "All right," I said. "You're a logician. Let's look at this thing logically. How could you choose Petey Burch over me? Look at me—a brilliant student, a tremendous intellectual, a man with an assured future. Look at Petey—a knothead, a jitterbug, a guy who'll never know where his next meal is coming from. Can you give me one logical reason why you should go steady with Petey Burch?"

150   "I certainly can," declared Polly. "He's got a raccoon coat."

Questions for Engagement, Response, and Analysis

1. What is the point of view? How is this point of view necessary to create the humor in the essay? How would it differ if it were written from Polly's point of view?

2. Analyze the style and tone of the essay.

3. Describe the narrator's opinion of Polly. Of Petey. Of himself.

4. Explain the literary allusions to Pygmalion and Frankenstein. How does their inclusion add to the humor?

5. How does the narrator's final date illustrate the limits of logic?

Crafting Arguments

1. Write a character sketch of the narrator, presumably Dobie Gillis. Support each of your claims with examples and quotations from the essay.

2. Trace the ways in which Polly's speech patterns differ before and after she learns about fallacies.

David Osborne (b. 1951)

David Osborne, a political journalist and a consultant to the Clinton presidential campaign in 1992 and later to Al Gore, has published articles in many prestigious magazines. His book Reinventing Government *(1992), coauthored with Ted Gaebler, presents guidelines and suggestions for changes in government;* Banishing Bureaucracy *(1997) suggests strategies for implementing these changes. In 2004 Osborne published* The Price of Government: Getting the Results We Need in an Age of Permanent Fiscal Crisis. *Osborne and his wife,*

Rose, an obstetrician and gynecologist, and their four children live in Essex, Massachusetts.

BEYOND THE CULT OF FATHERHOOD   (1985)

1   If I ever finish this article, it will be a miracle. Nicholas woke up this morning with an earache and a temperature, and I spent half the day at the doctor's office and pharmacy. Another ear infection.

2   Nicholas is my son. Twenty months old, a stout little bundle of energy and affection.

3   I will never forget the moment when I realized how completely Nick would change my life. My wife is a resident in obstetrics and gynecology, which means, among other things, that she works 100 hours a week, leaves the house every day by six and works all night several times a week, and often all weekend too. I'm not a househusband; I take Nick to day care five days a week. But I come about as close to house-husbandry as I care to. I am what you might call a "nontraditional" father.

4   Nick was three weeks old when I learned what that actually meant. Rose had just gone back to work, and Nick and I were learning about bottles. I don't remember if it was Rose's first night back or her second, but she wasn't home.

5   I stayed up too late; I had not yet learned that, with a baby in the house, you grab sleep whenever you can—even if it means going to bed at nine. Just as I drifted off, about 11:30, Nick woke up. I fed him and rocked him and put him back to sleep. About 2 AM he woke again, crying, and I rocked him for 45 minutes before he quieted down.

6   When he started screaming at four, I was in the kitchen by the time I woke up. As every parent knows, the sound of an infant—your infant—screaming sends lightning bolts up the spine. Bells ring in the head; nerves jangle. Racing against my son's hunger, I boiled water, poured it into the little plastic sack, slipped the sack into the plastic bottle, put on the top, and plunged the bottle into a bowl of cold water to cool it. I had not yet learned that in Connecticut, where I live, the water need not be sterilized. (Fathers are the last to know.)

7   It takes a long time to boil water and cool it back to body temperature, and I was dead on my feet even before the screams rearranged my vertebrae. By the time the water had cooled, I was half-crazed, my motions rapid and jerky. I mixed in the powdered formula and slipped the nipple back on. I ran toward Nick's room, shaking the bottle as hard as I could to make sure it was thoroughly mixed. As I reached his crib, the top flew off—and the contents sprayed all over the room.

8   At that point, I lost it. I swore at the top of my lungs, I stomped around the room, I slammed the changing table, and I swore some more. That was when I realized what I had gotten myself into—and how much I had to learn.

9   With baby boomers well ensconced in the nation's newsrooms, father-hood is sweeping American journalism. You can pick up the *New York Times Magazine*, or *Esquire*, or Bob Greene's best-seller, *Good Morning, Merry Sunshine: A Father's Journal of His Child's First Year* (Penguin), and read all about the wonders of being a father.

10   By all accounts, today's fathers are more involved and more sensitive than their own fathers were. But as warm and tender as their writing may be, it rings false. Rosalie Ziomek, a mother in Evanston, Illinois, said it perfectly in a letter to the *New Republic*, after it printed a scathing review of Bob Greene's book. "I was enraged by Greene's book," Ziomek wrote. "Anyone taking care of a newborn infant doesn't have time to write about it. Greene was cashing in on the experiences that most women have quietly and painfully lived without the glorification of fame and money. Meanwhile, because of the structure of his work/social life, which he is unwilling to alter, he avoids the thing that is the hardest part of new motherhood: the moment-to-moment dependency of a tiny, help-less, and demanding human being. I have more to say on the subject, but I have three children to take care of and writing is a luxury I can't afford right now."

11   Ziomek is right. I've been trying to keep a journal as Greene did, and it's impossible. There's no time. And how do you capture the essence of an exhausting, never-ending 24-hour day in a few paragraphs? Snapshots work if you spend an hour or two with a child, but if you spend days, everything dissolves in a blur.

12   My experience is different from that of the fathers I read about. Cer-tainly I am not fulfilling the role of a traditional mother, and certainly no child could ask for a more loving mother than Nick has. But I do fix most of the meals and do most of the laundry and change a lot of the diapers and get Nick up and dressed in the morning and shuttle him back and forth to day care and cart him to the grocery store and sing him to sleep and clean up his toys and wipe his nose and deal with his tantrums and cuddle with him and tickle him and all the other wonderful and exhaust-ing things mothers do. If you ask me what it all means, I can't say. After 20 months, I'm still dizzy, still desperate for a free hour or two, and still hopelessly in love with my little boy. All I have to offer are fragments; profound thoughts are for people who have more time. But if you want to go beyond the cult of fatherhood, I think I've been there.

13   My day starts about 6:30 or 7 AM, when Nick stands up in his crib and calls out for me. I stumble into his room, pick him up, give him a kiss and a "Good morning, Pumpkin," and carry him back to bed. I lay him down on his mother's empty pillow, lie down beside him, and sometimes I drowse again before it's really time to get up. But most mornings Nick is ready to start his day, and he gradually drags me up toward conscious-ness. He smiles at me, climbs up on me, and rests his head against my cheek—even kisses me if I'm really lucky, or sits on my bladder and

bounces, if I'm not. I tickle him, and he laughs and squirms and shrieks for more.

14   Sometimes he lies there for a few minutes, thinking his little boy thoughts, before sliding himself backward off the bed and going in search of something to do. Often he arrives back with a toy or two and asks to be picked "Up! Up!" Then he plays for a few minutes, making sure to keep an eye on my progress toward wakefulness. When he has waited long enough, he hands me my glasses, takes my hand, and pulls me out of bed.

15   While I shower, Nick plays in the bathroom, sitting on the floor with his toys. By the time I'm dressed, the kettle is whistling, and he's ready for breakfast. We always eat together, he has hot cereal, I have cold cereal, and often we share a bagel. I wish you could hear him say "cream cheese."

16   The rough times come on weekends. After 24 hours, I'm ready to be hung out on the line to dry. After 48 hours, I'm ready to pin medals on women who stay home every day with their kids. For single mothers, I'm ready to build monuments.

17   Don't let anyone tell you otherwise: traditional mothers work harder than anyone else can even imagine. They are on duty 24 hours a day, 365 days a year. I remember wondering, as a youth, why my own mother always rushed around with such urgency when she was cooking or cleaning. To me, she was like a woman possessed. Now I do the same thing. When you have a young child (or two, or three), you have very little time to get the dishes done, or cook dinner, or vacuum, or do the laundry so when you get a moment, you proceed with all possible haste. If your children are asleep, they might wake up. If they're playing, they might get bored and demand your attention.

18   Friends who visit me nowadays probably think I'm crazy, the way I rush compulsively to get dinner ready or mow the lawn or finish the laundry. I do feel somewhat self-conscious about it. But the fact is, if I'm cooking, Nick is going to start demanding his meal soon, and if it's not ready, he's going to get very cranky. And with all the chores that pile up on a weekend—the lawn, the laundry, the groceries, and so on—I have to seize every possible instant. If he naps, that may give me an hour and a half. If he wakes up before I'm done, whatever I'm doing will never get finished.

19   In any case, it is on weekends alone with Nick that I feel the full brunt of child-rearing. Consider a typical weekend: Nick wakes at 7:00, and we lie in bed and play for half an hour before getting up. But this morning he feels feverish, so I take his temperature. It is 101.6—not high for a young child, but a fever nonetheless.

20   The first thing I do is call Maureen, who takes care of him during the week. Both of her kids have a bug, and I want to find out what the symptoms are, to see if Nick has the same thing. From what we can tell, he does. On that basis, I decide to give him Tylenol for the fever, rather than taking him in to the pediatrician to see if he's got an ear infection.

Besides, he wants to lie down for a nap at 10:00, before I have decided, and doesn't wake until 1:00. By then the office is closed.

21   After lunch he feels much better—cool, happy, and bubbling. We play with his lock-blocks for a while, then watch a basketball game. He's very cuddly, because he's not feeling well. After the game it's off to the bank and grocery store. He falls asleep on the way home, at 5:45. It's an awkward time for a nap, but he only sleeps until 6:30. He wakes up crying, with a high fever, feeling miserable.

22   To get him to swallow more Tylenol, which he hates, I promise him ice cream. I give him half an ice-cream sandwich while I rush around the kitchen cooking dinner, and when he finishes it, he cries for the other half. I tell him he can have it after he eats his dinner. But when dinner is ready, he won't eat; he just sits there pointing at the freezer, where the ice cream is, and wailing. This is a major tantrum—hot tears, red face. I can't help but sympathize, though, because it's born of feeling absolutely wretched. How should I respond? I don't want to give in and teach him he can get his way by screaming. I try to comfort him by holding him in my lap, but he just sobs. Finally I take him into his room and rock him, holding him close. Gradually the sobs subside, and after 10 minutes I take him back into the kitchen, hold him on my lap, and feed him myself. He doesn't eat much, but enough to deserve his ice cream.

23   Though Nick gets over the incident in no time, I am traumatized. The fever is frightening—it has hit 102 by dinnertime, and it only drops to 101.4 by 8 p.m. Should I have taken him to the doctor? Will he spike a really high fever tonight? Am I being too relaxed? And what will Rose say? I cannot stop worrying; I feel heartsick as I read him his bedtime stories, though he cools down as he drifts to sleep in my arms. Would a mother feel so uncertain, I wonder? Do mothers feel adequate at moments like this? Or am I in a father's territory here?

24   Sunday morning Nick wakes at 6:30 and devours his breakfast, but pretty soon his temperature begins to rise. I call our pediatrician, who reassures me that it doesn't sound like an ear infection, and that I'm doing the right thing. Still, Nick isn't feeling well, and it makes him more demanding. He wants to be held; he wants me with him constantly; he insists that I do what he wants me to do and cries if I balk. It is a wearing day. He naps late, and when I wake him at seven, he is again miserable—temperature at 102.4, crying, refusing to let me change his diaper. But after more Tylenol and a good dinner he feels better.

25   I haven't heard from Rose all weekend, so I decide to call her at the hospital. She is furious that I haven't taken Nick to the doctor. A child who gets ear infections as often as he does has to be checked, she yells at me. He could blow out an eardrum! And why haven't I called her— she's his mother, for God's sake! I'm exhausted, I've been busting my hump all weekend, alone, doing the best I can, and now I'm being abused. I don't like it. My first impulse is to hang up on her, but instead I hand the

phone to Nicholas, who has a long talk with her. He says "Mommy!" she says "Nicholas!" and he laughs and laughs.

26   Rose may be right, I know, but that doesn't help my anger. We part tersely, and I promise to take him to the pediatrician the next morning before I leave for California on an article assignment. After that's out of the way, Nick and I have a good evening. We read books, and several times he leads me into his room to get another handful. A short bath, more books, then off to bed. He wants to take two of his trucks to bed with him—a new wrinkle—but I finally convince him to say "night-night" to his trucks and turn out the lights.

27   I have several hours of work to do before I leave, so I don't get to bed until after midnight. I'm absolutely shot. When the alarm rings at 6:00, I haul myself out of bed, shower, get dressed, and get Nick up and fed and dressed. We speed down to the library to return several books, then to the doctor's office. No ear infection; it's just a bug, says the doc, and he should be over it by nightfall. I drop Nick off at Maureen's by 9:30, race home, and spend the next hour packing, vacuuming, cleaning up the dishes and defrosting something for Rose and Nick's dinner. When I get to the airport, I realize I've misread my ticket and I'm half an hour early. I'm exhausted, and the trip has yet to begin.

28   Two nights later I call Rose. When I ask how she is, she bursts into tears. Nicholas has fallen at Maureen's and cut his forehead on a metal toy. Rose was caught in an ice storm between the hospital and home, so Maureen had to take her own kids to a neighbor's and rush Nick to the pediatrician's office for stitches. They gave him a local anesthetic, but he screamed the whole time.

29   "I feel so awful," Rose sobs, over and over. "I should have been there. I just feel awful." Guilt floods in, but it is nothing to match Rose's guilt. This is one of the differences I have discovered between mothers and fathers.

30   Rose has felt guilty since the day she went back to work—the hardest single thing I've ever watched her do. Deep inside her psyche lies a powerful message that she belongs at home, that if she is not with her child she is terribly irresponsible.

31   I feel guilty only occasionally. When I dropped Nick off at day care the first day after returning from California, and he sobbed because he thought I was leaving him again, the guilt just about killed me. I turned into a classic mother: as soon as I got home, I called to see if he was still crying. (He was.) Two guilt-ridden hours later I called again, desperate to hear that everything was fine. (It was.)

32   Deep within my psyche, however, the most powerful message is that I belong at work, that if I am not out making my mark on the world I am worth nothing.

33   The contradiction between family and career is nothing new; it is perhaps the central unresolved conflict in the lives of American women

today. What I did not expect was the force with which that conflict would erupt in my life.

34   Like an addict, I now find myself squeezing in every last minute of work that I can. I wait until the last possible instant before rushing out the door to pick Nick up in the afternoon. I dart out to my study while he naps on weekends, using a portable intercom to listen for his cries. At night I compulsively page through old newspapers that pile up because I can no longer read them over breakfast, afraid I've missed something important. As I hit deadline time, I pray that Nicholas doesn't get sick. I have even tried writing on a Saturday afternoon, with Nick playing in my studio. That experiment lasted half an hour, at which point he hit the reset button on the back of my computer and my prose was lost to the ages.

35   This frantic effort to keep up is clearly not good for me, but I cannot seem to abandon it. I constantly feel as if I live in a pressure cooker. I long for a free day, even a free hour. But my career has taken off just as my responsibilities as a father have hit their peak, and I cannot seem to scale down my commitment to either.

36   When Nick was four months old, I took him to a Christmas party, one Saturday when Rose was working. After an hour or so he got cranky, so I took him upstairs with a bottle. A little girl followed, and soon her brother and sister—equally bored by the goings-on downstairs—had joined us. It wasn't long before Dad came looking for them.

37   We introduced ourselves and talked for a bit. His wife, it turned out, was also a doctor. The curious part came when I asked what he did. First he told me all the things he had done in the past: carpentry, business, you name it. Then he said he'd done enough—he was about 40—and felt no need to prove himself any more. Finally he told me he stayed at home with the kids. And frankly, he pulled it off with far more dignity and less stammering than I would have, had our places been reversed.

38   I don't think I could do what he does. If I were to stay home full-time with Nick, I would quickly lose my self- esteem, and within months I would be deep into an identity crisis. Part of the reason I love my role as a father is that I am secure in my role as a writer. Without that, I would not feel good enough about myself to be the kind of father I am.

39   This is not simply a problem inside male heads. How many women would be content with men who stayed home with the kids? Not many, I'll wager. And not my wife, I know. From my experience, modern women want a man who will share the responsibilities at home but still be John Wayne in the outside world. They don't want any wimps wearing aprons. And men know it.

40   We are in a Burger King, in Fall River, Massachusetts. We are not having a good day. We drove two hours to shop in the factory outlets here, and all but a handful are closed because it's Sunday.

41   Nick likes Burger King, but he's not having a great day either. He has recently learned about tantrums, and as we get ready to leave, he

decides to throw one. He doesn't want to leave; he doesn't want to put on his coat; he just doesn't want to be hauled around any more. So he stands up and wails.

42   Rose is mortified; she takes any misbehavior in public as an advertisement of her failings as a mother. It triggers all her guilt about working. This time, the timing couldn't be worse, because she is already on edge.

43   Our tantrum strategy is generally to let him yell, to ignore him, and thus to teach him that it does no good. But in a public restaurant, I don't have the stamina to ignore him, so I cross the room to pick him up.

44   Rose orders me away from him, in no uncertain terms. There are no negotiations, no consultations. We are going to do this her way or no way.

45   That lights my fuse, of course, and after simmering for 10 minutes, I bring it up. "Let it go," she tells me, almost in tears over Nicholas. "It's not important."

46   It's not important.

47   Ah, the double bind. You're in charge one day, playing mother and father all wrapped into one, depended upon to feed him and clothe him and change him and bathe him and rock him and meet his every need. And the next day you're a third wheel, because Mom is around. You are expected to put in the long hours, but to pretend in public that you don't, for fear of undercutting your wife's sense of self-worth as a mother. How could she be doing her job, her psyche seems to whisper, if she's letting someone else make half the decisions and give half the care? There are many double binds in modern relationships, and this is the one I like the least.

48   I didn't let it drop that day, of course. At home, when Rose asserts the traditional mother's prerogative to make decisions and handle problems alone, on her terms, I often let it go. But when it happens in public, or in front of family, it is too much. It is as if my entire contribution to raising Nicholas is being denied, as if the world is being told that I am nothing more than a spectator. Luckily, as Nick grows older, and it becomes clear to Rose that she will always be number one in his heart, she has begun to relax her public vigilance, and this problem seems to have abated.

49   This is the first time I've ever been part of a woman's world. I'm not really a part of it, of course; the chasm between the sexes is too wide to step across so lightly. But when it comes to children, I have instant rapport with most mothers. We talk about the same things, think about the same things, joke about the same things. With men, it is almost never that way, even when the men are fathers and the subject is kids. We can share enthusiasms, but the sense of being there, on the inside—the unspoken understanding that comes out of shared experience—that is missing.

50   In fact, most men don't have the slightest idea what my life with Nick is like. When I tell colleagues—even those with children—that I have no time to read, or to watch television, I get blank stares. (I never tell mothers that; they already know. Who has time to read?) One friend, also a

writer, stopped in the middle of a recent conversation and said, "You have Nick at home while you're working, don't you? What do you do with him?" No such thought could pass a mother's lips.

51   None of this would have been possible had I not been forced into taking care of Nick on my own much of the time. In fact, my entire relationship with Nick would have been different had I not been forced off the sidelines. I am convinced that in our society, when Mom is home with the kids, it is almost impossible for Dad to be an equal partner in their upbringing, even if he wants to be.

52   I believe this because for three weeks, while Rose was home after Nick's birth, it felt impossible to me. Rose had carried Nick for nine months; Rose had been through labor; and Rose was nursing him. For nine months he had listened to her heartbeat, felt her pulse, been a part of her being. Now he hunted her scent and drank from her body, and the bond between them was awesome. I was like some voyeur, peeking through the window at an ancient and sacred rite.

53   Then Rose went back to work, and I had no choice but to get off the sidelines. I *had* to get Nick dressed in the morning. I *had* to feed him. I *had* to burp him and rock him and change him and get up with him in the night. He may have wanted his mother, but she wasn't there.

54   Gradually, it all began to come naturally. I learned to carry him on my (nonexistent) hip and do anything—or any combination of things—with one hand. I learned to whip up a bottle in no time, to change a diaper and treat diaper rash and calm his tears.

55   Even on vacation, it is remarkably easy to slip back into a traditional role—for both Rose and me. But the day Rose goes back to work, I am always yanked back to reality. I complain a lot, but in truth, this is my great good fortune.

56   Last night Nick asked to go to the beach—"Go? Beach? Go? Beach?" I walked him the two blocks down, one of his hands firmly in mine, the other proudly holding the leash for Sam, our dog. We played on the swings for a long time, then strolled along the beach while Sam went swimming. It was that very still hour before dark, when the world slows to a hush, and little boys and girls slowly wind down. It was almost dark when we returned. Nick asked his daddy to give him his bath, then his mommy to put him to bed.

57   This morning when I woke he was lying beside me, on his mother's empty pillow. I looked over and he gave me a big smile, his eyes shining with that special, undiluted joy one sees only in children. Then he propped himself up on his elbows, leaned over and kissed me. If there are any better moments in life, I've never found them.

Questions for Engagement, Response, and Analysis

1. Describe Osborne's tone.
2. To what does the title of Osborne's essay refer?
3. What are the purposes of the anecdotes in this essay?
4. Osborne's staying home with his son defies traditional family roles. As he says, however, it also differs from that of traditional mothers. Describe the difficulties and the joys of his role.
5. Osborne quotes a letter by Rosalie Ziomek to the *New Republic* as describing "'the hardest part of new motherhood: the moment-to-moment dependency of a tiny, helpless, and demanding human being.'" Precisely what does that dependency entail? How does Osborne's essay develop the consequences of that dependency?

Crafting Arguments

1. Craft a Comparison/Contrast essay that offers your interpretation of Osborne's and his wife's roles in and reactions to raising Nicholas.
2. Osborne declares that he could not stay at home full time: "Part of the reason I love my role as a father is that I am secure in my role as a writer. Without that, I would not feel good enough about myself to be the kind of father I am." Why must he prove himself in ways other than fatherhood? Does Osborne share the "unresolved conflict" he attributes to women?

FICTION

Nathaniel Hawthorne (1804–1864)

One of America's greatest fiction writers, Nathaniel Hawthorne was born in Salem, Massachusetts, and was strongly influenced by his Puritan heritage. The Scarlet Letter *(1850) is considered an American classic.* The House of Seven Gables *(1851) and* The Blithedale Romance *(1852) continued his stories about New England, but in his last novel,* The Marble Faun *(1860), Hawthorne chose Italy as his setting. In his short story collections—*Twice-Told Tales *(1837),* Mosses from an Old Manse *(1846), and* The Snow-Image, and Other Twice-Told Tales *(1851)—Hawthorne gave American literature some of its most memorable short fiction Many of these stories, like "The Birth-Mark," portray men who overestimate their own intelligence and power over science and consequently lose touch with the heart of humanity. Though Hawthorne seldom portrayed successful marriages in his fiction, his own marriage was a loving and lasting one.*

THE BIRTH-MARK   (1843)

1   In the latter part of the last century, there lived a man of science—an eminent proficient in every branch of natural philosophy—who, not long before our story opens, had made experience of a spiritual affinity, more attractive than any chemical one. He had left his laboratory to the care of an assistant, cleared his fine countenance from the furnace-smoke, washed the stain of acids from his fingers, and persuaded a beautiful woman to become his wife. In those days, when the comparatively recent discovery of electricity, and other kindred mysteries of nature, seemed to open paths into the region of miracle, it was not unusual for the love of science to rival the love of woman, in its depth and absorbing energy. The higher intellect, the imagination, the spirit, and even the heart, might all find their congenial aliment in pursuits which, as some of their ardent votaries believed, would ascend from one step of powerful intelligence to another, until the philosopher should lay his hand on the secret of creative force, and perhaps make new worlds for himself. We know not whether Aylmer possessed this degree of faith in man's ultimate control over nature. He had devoted himself, however, too unreservedly to scientific studies, ever to be weaned from them by any second passion. His love for his young wife might prove the stronger of the two; but it could only be by intertwining itself with his love of science, and uniting the strength of the latter to its own.

2   Such a union accordingly took place, and was attended with truly remarkable consequences, and a deeply impressive moral. One day, very

soon after their marriage, Aylmer sat gazing at his wife, with a trouble in his countenance that grew stronger, until he spoke.

3   "Georgiana," said he, "has it never occurred to you that the mark upon your cheek might be removed?"

4   "No, indeed," said she, smiling; but perceiving the seriousness of his manner, she blushed deeply. "To tell you the truth, it has been so often called a charm, that I was simple enough to imagine it might be so."

5   "Ah, upon another face, perhaps it might," replied her husband. "But never on yours! No, dearest Georgiana, you came so nearly perfect from the hand of Nature, that this slightest possible defect—which we hesitate whether to term a defect or a beauty—shocks me, as being the visible mark of earthly imperfection."

6   "Shocks you, my husband!" cried Georgiana, deeply hurt; at first reddening with momentary anger, but then bursting into tears. "Then why did you take me from my mother's side? You cannot love what shocks you!"

7   To explain this conversation, it must be mentioned, that, in the centre of Georgiana's left cheek, there was a singular mark, deeply interwoven, as it were, with the texture and substance of her face. In the usual state of her complexion,—a healthy, though delicate bloom,—the mark wore a tint of deeper crimson, which imperfectly defined its shape amid the surrounding rosiness. When she blushed, it gradually became more indistinct, and finally vanished amid the triumphant rush of blood, that bathed the whole check with its brilliant glow. But, if any shifting emotion caused her to turn pale, there was the mark again, a crimson stain upon the snow, in what Aylmer sometimes deemed an almost fearful distinctness. Its shape bore not a little similarity to the human hand, though of the smallest pigmy size. Georgiana's lovers were wont to say, that some fairy, at her birth-hour, had laid her tiny hand upon the infant's cheek, and left this impress there, in token of the magic endowments that were to give her such sway over all hearts. Many a desperate swain would have risked life for the privilege of pressing his lips to the mysterious hand. It must not be concealed, however, that the impression wrought by this fairy sign-manual varied exceedingly, according to the difference of temperament in the beholders. Some fastidious persons—but they were exclusively of her own sex—affirmed that the Bloody Hand, as they chose to call it, quite destroyed the effect of Georgiana's beauty, and rendered her countenance even hideous. But it would be as reasonable to say that one of those small blue stains, which sometimes occur in the purest statuary marble, would convert the Eve of Powers to a monster. Masculine observers, if the birth-mark did not heighten their admiration, contented themselves with wishing it away, that the world might possess one living specimen of ideal loveliness, without the semblance of a flaw. After his marriage—for he thought little or nothing of the matter before—Aylmer discovered that this was the case with himself.

8   Had she been less beautiful—if Envy's self could have found aught else to sneer at—he might have felt his affection heightened by the prettiness of this mimic hand, now vaguely portrayed, now lost, now stealing forth again and glimmering to-and-fro with every pulse of emotion that throbbed within her heart. But, seeing her otherwise so perfect, he found this one defect grow more and more intolerable, with every moment of their united lives. It was the fatal flaw of humanity, which Nature, in one shape or another, stamps ineffaceably on all her productions, either to imply that they are temporary and finite, or that their perfection must be wrought by toil and pain. The Crimson Hand expressed the ineludible gripe, in which mortality clutches the highest and purest of earthly mould, degrading them into kindred with the lowest, and even with the very brutes, like whom their visible frames return to dust. In this manner, selecting it as the symbol of his wife's liability to sin, sorrow, decay, and death, Alymer's sombre imagination was not long in rendering the birth-mark a frightful object, causing him more trouble and horror than ever Georgiana's beauty, whether of soul or sense, had given him delight.

9   At all the seasons which should have been their happiest, he invariable and without intending it—nay, in spite of a purpose to the contrary—reverted to this one disastrous topic. Trifling as it at first appeared, it so connected itself with innumerable trains of thought, and modes of feeling, that it became the central point of all. With the morning twilight, Aylmer opened his eyes upon his wife's face, and recognized the symbol of imperfection; and when they sat together at the evening hearth, his eyes wandered stealthily to her cheek, and beheld, flickering with the blaze of the wood fire, the spectral Hand that wrote mortality, where he would fain have worshipped. Georgiana soon learned to shudder at his gaze. It needed but a glance, with the peculiar expression that his face often wore, to change the roses of her cheek into a deathlike paleness, amid which the Crimson Hand was brought strongly out, like a bas-relief of ruby on the whitest marble.

10   Late, one night, when the lights were growing dim, so as hardly to betray the stain on the poor wife's cheek, she herself, for the first time, voluntarily took up the subject.

11   "Do you remember, my dear Aylmer," said she, with a feeble attempt at a smile—"have you any recollection of a dream, last night, about this odious Hand?"

12   "None!—none whatever!" replied Aylmer, starting; but then he added in a dry, cold tone, affected for the sake of concealing the real depth of his emotion:—"I might well dream of it; for before I fell asleep, it had taken a pretty firm hold of my fancy."

13   "And you did dream of it," continued Georgiana, hastily; for she dreaded lest a gush of tears should interrupt what she had to say—"A terrible dream! I wonder that you can forget it. Is it possible to forget this one expression?—'It is in her heart now—we must have

it out'—Reflect, my husband; for by all means I would have you recall that dream."

14   The mind is in a sad note, when Sleep, the all-involving, cannot confine her spectres within the dim region of her sway, but suffers them to break forth, affrighting this actual life with secrets that perchance belong to a deeper one. Aylmer now remembered his dream. He had fancied himself, with his servant Aminadab, attempting an operation for the removal of the birth-mark. But the deeper went the knife, the deeper sank the Hand, until at length its tiny grasp appeared to have caught hold of Georgiana's heart; whence, however, her husband was inexorably resolved to cut or wrench it away.

15   When the dream had shaped itself perfectly in his memory, Aylmer sat in his wife's presence with a guilty feeling. Truth often finds its way to the mind close-muffled in robes of sleep, and then speaks with uncompromising directness of matters in regard to which we practise an unconscious self-deception, during our waking moments. Until now, he had not been aware of the tyrannizing influence acquired by one idea over his mind, and of the lengths which he might find in his heart to go, for the sake of giving himself peace.

16   "Aylmer," resumed Georgiana, solemnly, "I know not what may be the cost to both of us, to rid me of this fatal birth-mark. Perhaps its removal may cause cureless deformity. Or, it may be, the stain goes as deep as life itself. Again, do we know that there is a possibility, on any terms, of unclasping the firm gripe of this little Hand, which was laid upon me before I came into the world?"

17   "Dearest Georgiana, I have spent much thought upon the subject," hastily interrupted Aylmer—"I am convinced of the perfect practicability of its removal."

18   "If there be the remotest possibility of it," continued Georgiana, "let the attempt be made, at whatever risk. Danger is nothing to me; for life—while this hateful mark makes me the object of your horror and disgust—life is a burthen which I would fling down with joy. Either remove this dreadful Hand, or take my wretched life! You have deep science! All the world bears witness of it. You have achieved great wonders! Cannot you remove this little little mark, which I cover with the tips of two small fingers? Is this beyond your power, for the sake of your own peace, and to save your poor wife from madness?"

19   "Noblest—dearest—tenderest wife!" cried Aylmer, rapturously. "Doubt not my power. I have already given this matter the deepest thought—thought which might almost have enlightened me to create a being less perfect than yourself. Georgiana, you have led me deeper than ever into the heart of science. I feel myself fully competent to render this dear cheek as faultless as its fellow; and then, most beloved, what will be my triumph, when I shall have corrected what Nature left imperfect, in her fairest work! Even Pygmalion, when his sculptured woman assumed life, felt not greater ecstasy than mine will be."

20   "It is resolved, then," said Georgiana, faintly smiling,—"And, Aylmer, spare me not, though you should find the birth-mark take refuge in my heart at last."

21   Her husband tenderly kissed her cheek—her right cheek—not that which bore the impress of the Crimson Hand.

22   The next day, Aylmer apprized his wife of a plan that he had formed, whereby he might have opportunity for the intense thought and constant watchfulness, which the proposed operation would require; while Georgiana, likewise, would enjoy the perfect repose essential to its success. They were to seclude themselves in the extensive apartments occupied by Aylmer as a laboratory, and where, during his toilsome youth, he had made discoveries in the elemental powers of nature, that had roused the admiration of all the learned societies in Europe. Seated calmly in this laboratory, the pale philosopher had investigated the secrets of the highest cloud-region, and of the profoundest mines; he had satisfied himself of the causes that kindled and kept alive the fires of the volcano; and had explained the mystery of fountains, and how it is that they gush forth, some so bright and pure, and others with such rich medicinal virtues, from the dark bosom of the earth. Here, too, at an earlier period, he had studied the wonders of the human frame, and attempted to fathom the very process by which Nature assimilates all her precious influences from earth and air, and from the spiritual world to create and foster Man, her masterpiece. The latter pursuit, however Aylmer had long laid aside, in unwilling recognition of the truth, against which all seekers sooner or later stumble, that our great creative Mother while she amuses us with apparently working in the broadest sunshine, is yet severely careful to keep her own secrets, and, in spite of her pretended openness, shows us nothing but results. She permits us indeed, to mar, but seldom to mend, and, like a jealous patentee, on no account to make. Now, however, Aylmer resumed these half-forgotten investigations; not, of course, with such hopes or wishes as first suggested them; but because they involved much physiological truth, and lay in the path of his proposed scheme for the treatment of Georgiana.

23   As he led her over the threshold of the laboratory, Georgiana was cold and tremulous. Aylmer looked cheerfully into her face, with intent to reassure her, but was so startled with the intense glow of the birth-mark upon the whiteness of her cheek, that he could not restrain a strong convulsive shudder. His wife fainted.

24   "Aminadab! Aminadab!" shouted Aylmer, stamping violently on the floor.

25   Forthwith, there issued from an inner apartment a man of low stature, but bulky frame, with shaggy hair hanging about his visage, which was grimed with the vapors of the furnace. This personage had been Aylmer's underworker during his whole scientific career, and was admirably fitted for that office by his great mechanical readiness, and the skill with which, while incapable of comprehending a single principle, he executed

all the practical details of his master's experiments. With his vast strength, his shaggy hair, his smoky aspect, and the indescribable earthiness that incrusted him, he seemed to represent man's physical nature; while Aylmer's slender figure, and pale, intellectual face, were no less apt a type of the spiritual element.

26   "Throw open the door of the boudoir, Aminadab," said Aylmer, "and burn a pastille."

27   "Yes, master," answered Aminadab, looking intently at the lifeless form of Georgiana; and then he muttered to himself:-"If she were my wife, I'd never part with that birth-mark."

28   When Georgiana recovered consciousness, she found herself breathing an atmosphere of penetrating fragrance, the gentle potency of which had recalled her from her deathlike faintness. The scene around her looked like enchantment. Aylmer had converted those smoky, dingy, sombre rooms, where he had spent his brightest years in recondite pursuits, into a series of beautiful apartments, not unfit to be the secluded abode of a lovely woman. The walls were hung with gorgeous curtains, which imparted the combination of grandeur and grace, that no other species of adornment can achieve; and as they fell from the ceiling to the floor, their rich and ponderous folds, concealing all angles and straight lines, appeared to shut in the scene from infinite space. For aught Georgiana knew, it might be a pavilion among the clouds. And Aylmer, excluding the sunshine, which would have interfered with his chemical processes, had supplied its place with perfumed lamps, emitting flames of various hue, but all uniting in a soft, empurpled radiance. He now knelt by his wife's side, watching her earnestly, but without alarm; for he was confident in his science, and felt that he could draw a magic circle round her, within which no evil might intrude.

29   "Where am I?—Ah, I remember!" said Georgiana, faintly; and she placed her hand over her cheek, to hide the terrible mark from her husband's eyes.

30   "Fear not, dearest!" exclaimed he. "Do not shrink from me! Believe me, Georgiana, I even rejoice in this single imperfection, since it will be such rapture to remove it."

31   "Oh, spare me!" sadly replied his wife—"Pray do not look at it again. I never can forget that convulsive shudder."

32   In order to soothe Georgiana, and, as it were, to release her mind from the burthen of actual things, Aylmer now put in practice some of the light and playful secrets, which science had taught him among its profounder lore. Airy figures, absolutely bodiless ideas, and forms of unsubstantial beauty came and danced before her, imprinting their momentary footsteps on beams of light. Though she had some indistinct idea of the method of these optical phenomena, still the illusion was almost perfect enough to warrant the belief that her husband possessed sway over the spiritual world. Then again, when she felt a wish to look forth from her seclusion, immediately, as if her thoughts were answered, the procession

of external existence flitted across a screen. The scenery and the figures of actual life were perfectly represented, but with that bewitching, yet indescribable difference, which always makes a picture, an image, or a shadow, so much more attractive than the original. When wearied of this, Aylmer bade her cast her eyes upon a vessel, containing a quantity of earth. She did so, with little interest at first, but was soon startled, to perceive the germ of a plant, shooting upward from the soil. Then came the slender stalk—the leaves gradually unfolded themselves—and amid them was a perfect and lovely flower.

33   "It is magical!" cried Georgiana, "I dare not touch it."

34   "Nay, pluck it," answered Aylmer, "pluck it, and inhale its brief perfume while you may. The flower will wither in a few moments, and leave nothing save its brown seed-vessels—but thence may be perpetuated a race as ephemeral as itself."

35   But Georgiana had no sooner touched the flower than the whole plant suffered a blight, its leaves turning coal-black, as if by the agency of fire.

36   "There was too powerful a stimulus," said Aylmer thoughtfully.

37   To make up for this abortive experiment, he proposed to take her portrait by a scientific process of his own invention. It was to be effected by rays of light striking upon a polished plate of metal. Georgiana assented—but, on looking at the result, was affrighted to find the features of the portrait blurred and indefinable; while the minute figure of a hand appeared where the cheek should have been. Aylmer snatched the metallic plate and threw it into a jar of corrosive acid.

38   Soon, however, he forgot these mortifying failures. In the intervals of study and chemical experiment, he came to her, flushed and exhausted, but seemed invigorated by her presence, and spoke in glowing language of the resources of his art. He gave a history of the long dynasty of the Alchemists, who spent so many ages in quest of the universal solvent, by which the Golden Principle might be elicited from all things vile and base. Aylmer appeared to believe that, by the plainest scientific logic, it was altogether within the limits of possibility to discover this long-sought medium; but, he added, a philosopher who should go deep enough to acquire the power would attain too lofty a wisdom to stoop to the exercise of it. Not less singular were his opinions in regard to the Elixir Vitae. He more than intimated that it was his option to concoct a liquid that should prolong life for years—perhaps interminably—but that it would produce a discord in nature, which all the world, and chiefly the quaffer of the immortal nostrum, would find cause to curse.

39   "Aylmer, are you in earnest?" asked Georgiana, looking at him with amazement and fear; "it is terrible to possess such power, or even to dream of possessing it!"

40   "Oh, do not tremble, my love!" said her husband, "I would not wrong either you or myself by working such inharmonious effects upon our lives. But I would have you consider how trifling, in comparison, is the skill requisite to remove this little Hand."

41   At the mention of the birth-mark, Georgiana, as usual, shrank, as if a red-hot iron had touched her cheek.

42   Again, Aylmer applied himself to his labors. She could hear his voice in the distant furnace-room, giving directions to Aminadab, whose harsh, uncouth, misshapen tones were audible in response, more like the grunt or growl of a brute than human speech. After hours of absence, Aylmer reappeared, and proposed that she should now examine his cabinet of chemical products and natural treasures of the earth. Among the former he showed her a small vial, in which, he remarked, was contained a gentle yet most powerful fragrance, capable of impregnating all the breezes that blow across a kingdom. They were of inestimable value, the contents of that little vial; and, as he said so, he threw some of the perfume into the air, and filled the room with piercing and invigorating delight.

43   "And what is this?" asked Georgiana, pointing to a small crystal globe, containing a gold-colored liquid. "It is so beautiful to the eye, that I could imagine it the Elixir of Life."

44   "In one sense it is," replied Aylmer, "or rather the Elixir of Immortality. It is the most precious poison that ever was concocted in this world. By its aid, I could apportion the lifetime of any mortal at whom you might point your finger. The strength of the dose would determine whether he were to linger out years, or drop dead in the midst of a breath. No king, on his guarded throne, could keep his life, if I, in my private station, should deem that the welfare of millions justified me in depriving him of it."

45   "Why do you keep such a terrific drug?" inquired Georgiana in horror.

46   "Do not mistrust me, dearest!" said her husband, smiling; "its virtuous potency is yet greater than its harmful one. But, see! here is a powerful cosmetic. With a few drops of this, in a vase of water, freckles may be washed away as easily as the hands are cleansed. A stronger infusion would take the blood out of the cheek, and leave the rosiest beauty a pale ghost."

47   "Is it with this lotion that you intend to bathe my cheek?" asked Georgiana anxiously.

48   "Oh, no!" hastily replied her husband—"this is merely superficial. Your case demands a remedy that shall go deeper."

49   In his interviews with Georgiana, Aylmer generally made minute inquiries as to her sensations, and whether the confinement of the rooms, and the temperature of the atmosphere, agreed with her. These questions had such a particular drift that Georgiana began to conjecture that she was already subjected to certain physical influences, either breathed in with the fragrant air, or taken with her food. She fancied likewise—but it might be altogether fancy—that there was a stirring up of her system,— a strange indefinite sensation creeping through her veins, and tingling, half painfully, half pleasurably, at her heart. Still, whenever she dared to look into the mirror, there she beheld herself, pale as a white rose, and with the crimson birth-mark stamped upon her cheek. Not even Aylmer now hated it so much as she.

50   To dispel the tedium of the hours which her husband found it necessary to devote to the processes of combination and analysis, Georgiana
turned over the volumes of his scientific library. In many dark old tomes,
she met with chapters full of romance and poetry. They were the works
of the philosophers of the middle ages, such as Albertus Magnus, Cor-
nelius Agrippa, Paracelsus, and the famous friar who created the
prophetic Brazen Head. All these antique naturalists stood in advance of
their centuries, yet were imbued with some of their credulity, and therefore were believed, and perhaps imagined themselves, to have acquired
from the investigation of nature a power above nature, and from physics
a sway over the spiritual world. Hardly less curious and imaginative were
the early volumes of the Transactions of the Royal Society, in which the
members, knowing little of the limits of natural possibility, were continually recording wonders, or proposing methods whereby wonders might
be wrought.

51   But, to Georgiana, the most engrossing volume was a large folio from
her husband's own hand, in which he had recorded every experiment of
his scientific career, with its original aim, the methods adopted for its
development, and its final success or failure, with the circumstances to
which either event was attributable. The book, in truth, was both the history and emblem of his ardent, ambitious, imaginative, yet practical and
laborious life. He handled physical details, as if there were nothing
beyond them; yet spiritualized them all, and redeemed himself from materialism, by his strong and eager aspiration towards the infinite. In his
grasp, the veriest clod of earth assumed a soul. Georgiana, as she read,
reverenced Aylmer, and loved him more profoundly than ever, but with
a less entire dependence on his judgment than heretofore. Much as he
had accomplished, she could not but observe that his most splendid successes were almost invariably failures, if compared with the ideal at
which he aimed. His brightest diamonds were the merest pebbles, and
felt to be so by himself, in comparison with the inestimable gems which
lay hidden beyond his reach. The volume, rich with achievements that
had won renown for its author, was yet as melancholy a record as ever
mortal hand had penned. It was the sad confession, and continual exem-
plification, of the short-comings of the composite man—the spirit bur-
thened with clay and working in matter—and of the despair that assails
the higher nature at finding itself so miserably thwarted by the earthly
part. Perhaps every man of genius, in whatever sphere, might recognize
the image of his own experience in Aylmer's journal.

52   So deeply did these reflections affect Georgiana that she laid her face
upon the open volume and burst into tears. In this situation she was
found by her husband.

53   "It is dangerous to read in a sorcerer's books," said he, with a smile,
though his countenance was uneasy and displeased. "Georgiana, there
are pages in that volume, which I can scarcely glance over and keep my
senses. Take heed lest it prove as detrimental to you!"

54   "It has made me worship you more than ever," said she.

55   "Ah! wait for this one success," rejoined he, "then worship me if you will. I shall deem myself hardly unworthy of it. But, come! I have sought you for the luxury of your voice. Sing to me, dearest!"

56   So she poured out the liquid music of her voice to quench the thirst of his spirit. He then took his leave, with a boyish exuberance of gaiety, assuring her that her seclusion would endure but a little longer, and that the result was already certain. Scarcely had he departed, when Georgiana felt irresistibly impelled to follow him. She had forgotten to inform Aylmer of a symptom, which, for two or three hours past, had begun to excite her attention. It was a sensation in the fatal birth-mark, not painful, but which induced a restlessness throughout her system. Hastening after her husband, she intruded, for the first time, into the laboratory.

57   The first thing that struck her eye was the furnace, that hot and feverish worker, with the intense glow of its fire, which, by the quantities of soot clustered above it, seemed to have been burning for ages. There was a distilling apparatus in full operation. Around the room were retorts, tubes, cylinders, crucibles, and other apparatus of chemical research. An electrical machine stood ready for immediate use. The atmosphere felt oppressively close, and was tainted with gaseous odors, which had been tormented forth by the processes of science. The severe and homely simplicity of the apartment, with its naked walls and brick pavement, looked strange, accustomed as Georgiana had become to the fantastic elegance of her boudoir. But what chiefly, indeed almost solely, drew her attention, was the aspect of Aylmer himself.

58   He was pale as death, anxious, and absorbed, and hung over the furnace as if it depended upon his utmost watchfulness whether the liquid, which it was distilling, should be the draught of immortal happiness or misery. How different from the sanguine and joyous mien that he had assumed for Georgiana's encouragement!

59   "Carefully now, Aminadab! Carefully, thou human machine! Carefully, thou man of clay!" muttered Aylmer, more to himself than his assistant. "Now, if there be a thought too much or too little, it is all over!"

60   "Ho! ho!" mumbled Aminadab—"look, master, look!"

61   Aylmer raised his eyes hastily, and at first reddened, then grew paler than ever, on beholding Georgiana. He rushed towards her, and seized her arm with a gripe that left the print of his fingers upon it.

62   "Why do you come hither? Have you no trust in your husband?" cried he impetuously. "Would you throw the blight of that fatal birth-mark over my labors? It is not well done. Go, prying woman, go!"

63   "Nay, Aylmer," said Georgiana, with the firmness of which she possessed no stinted endowment, "it is not you that have a right to complain. You mistrust your wife! You have concealed the anxiety with which you watch the development of this experiment. Think not so unworthily of me, my husband! Tell me all the risk we run; and fear not that I shall shrink, for my share in it is far less than your own!"

64   "No, no, Georgiana!" said Aylmer impatiently, "it must not be."

65   "I submit," replied she calmly. "And, Aylmer, I shall quaff whatever draught you bring me; but it will be on the same principle that would induce me to take a dose of poison, if offered by your hand."

66   "My noble wife," said Aylmer, deeply moved, "I knew not the height and depth of your nature, until now. Nothing shall be concealed. Know, then, that this Crimson Hand, superficial as it seems, has clutched its grasp into your being, with a strength of which I had no previous conception. I have already administered agents powerful enough to do aught except to change your entire physical system. Only one thing remains to be tried. If that fail us, we are ruined!"

67   "Why did you hesitate to tell me this?" asked she.

68   "Because, Georgiana," said Aylmer, in a low voice, "there is danger!"

69   "Danger? There is but one danger—that this horrible stigma shall be left upon my cheek!" cried Georgiana. "Remove it! remove it!—whatever be the cost—or we shall both go mad!"

70   "Heaven knows, your words are too true," said Aylmer, sadly. "And now, dearest, return to your boudoir. In a little while, all will be tested."

71   He conducted her back, and took leave of her with a solemn tenderness, which spoke far more than his words how much was now at stake. After his departure, Georgiana became wrapt in musings. She considered the character of Aylmer, and did it completer justice than at any previous moment. Her heart exulted, while it trembled, at his honorable love, so pure and lofty that it would accept nothing less than perfection, nor miserably make itself contented with an earthlier nature than he had dreamed of. She felt how much more precious was such a sentiment, than that meaner kind which would have borne with the imperfection for her sake, and have been guilty of treason to holy love, by degrading its perfect idea to the level of the actual. And, with her whole spirit, she prayed, that, for a single moment, she might satisfy his highest and deepest conception. Longer than one moment, she well knew, it could not be; for his spirit was ever on the march—ever ascending—and each instant required something that was beyond the scope of the instant before.

72   The sound of her husband's footsteps aroused her. He bore a crystal goblet, containing a liquor colorless as water, but bright enough to be the draught of immortality. Aylmer was pale; but it seemed rather the consequence of a highly wrought state of mind, and tension of spirit, than of fear or doubt.

73   "The concoction of the draught has been perfect," said he, in answer to Georgiana's look. "Unless all my science have deceived me, it cannot fail."

74   "Save on your account, my dearest Aylmer," observed his wife, "I might wish to put off this birth-mark of mortality by relinquishing mortality itself, in preference to any other mode. Life is but a sad possession to

those who have attained precisely the degree of moral advancement at which I stand. Were I weaker and blinder, it might be happiness. Were I stronger, it might be endured hopefully. But, being what I find myself, methinks I am of all mortals the most fit to die."

75   "You are fit for heaven without tasting death!" replied her husband. "But why do we speak of dying? The draught cannot fail. Behold its effect upon this plant!"

76   On the window-seat there stood a geranium, diseased with yellow blotches which had overspread all its leaves. Aylmer poured a small quantity of the liquid upon the soil in which it grew. In a little time, when the roots of the plant had taken up the moisture, the unsightly blotches began to be extinguished in a living verdure.

77   "There needed no proof," said Georgiana, quietly. "Give me the goblet. I joyfully stake all upon your word."

78   "Drink, then, thou lofty creature!" exclaimed Aylmer, with fervid admiration. "There is no taint of imperfection on thy spirit. Thy sensible frame, too, shall be all perfect!"

79   She quaffed the liquid, and returned the goblet to his hand.

80   "It is grateful," said she, with a placid smile. "Methinks it is like water from a heavenly fountain; for it contains I know not what of unobtrusive fragrance and deliciousness. It allays a feverish thirst that had parched me for many days. Now, dearest, let me sleep. My earthly senses are closing over my spirit like the leaves round the heart of a rose at sunset."

81   She spoke the last words with a gentle reluctance, as if it required almost more energy than she could command to pronounce the faint and lingering syllables. Scarcely had they loitered through her lips, ere she was lost in slumber. Aylmer sat by her side, watching her aspect with the emotions proper to a man, the whole value of whose existence was involved in the process now to be tested. Mingled with this mood, however, was the philosophic investigation, characteristic of the man of science. Not the minutest symptom escaped him. A heightened flush of the cheek—a slight irregularity of breath—a quiver of the eyelid—a hardly perceptible tremor through the frame—such were the details which, as the moments passed, he wrote down in his folio volume. Intense thought had set its stamp upon every previous page of that volume; but the thoughts of years were all concentrated upon the last.

82   While thus employed, he failed not to gaze often at the fatal Hand, and not without a shudder. Yet once, by a strange and unaccountable impulse, he pressed it with his lips. His spirit recoiled, however, in the very act, and Georgiana, out of the midst of her deep sleep, moved uneasily and murmured as if in remonstrance. Again, Aylmer resumed his watch. Nor was it without avail. The Crimson Hand, which at first had been strongly visible upon the marble paleness of Georgiana's cheek now grew more faintly outlined. She remained not less pale than ever; but the birth-mark,

with every breath that came and went, lost somewhat of its former distinctness. Its presence had been awful; its departure was more awful still. Watch the stain of the rainbow fading out of the sky; and you will know how that mysterious symbol passed away.

83   "By Heaven, it is well nigh gone!" said Aylmer to himself, in almost irrepressible ecstasy. "I can scarcely trace it now. Success! Success! And now it is like the faintest rose-color. The slightest flush of blood across her cheek would overcome it. But she is so pale!"

84   He drew aside the window-curtain and suffered the light of natural day to fall into the room and rest upon her cheek. At the same time, he heard a gross, hoarse chuckle, which he had long known as his servant Aminadab's expression of delight.

85   "Ah, clod! Ah, earthly mass!" cried Aylmer, laughing in a sort of frenzy. "You have served me well! Matter and Spirit—Earth and Heaven—have both done their part in this! Laugh, thing of senses! You have earned the right to laugh."

86   These exclamations broke Georgiana's sleep. She slowly unclosed her eyes and gazed into the mirror, which her husband had arranged for that purpose. A faint smile flitted over her lips, when she recognized how barely perceptible was now that Crimson Hand, which had once blazed forth with such disastrous brilliancy as to scare away all their happiness. But then her eyes sought Aylmer's face, with a trouble and anxiety that he could by no means account for.

87   "My poor Aylmer!" murmured she.

88   "Poor? Nay, richest! Happiest! Most favored!" exclaimed he. "My peerless bride, it is successful! You are perfect!"

89   "My poor Aylmer!" she repeated, with a more than human tenderness. "You have aimed loftily!—you have done nobly! Do not repent, that, with so high and pure a feeling, you have rejected the best that earth could offer. Aylmer—dearest Aylmer—I am dying!"

90   Alas, it was too true! The fatal Hand had grappled with the mystery of life, and was the bond by which an angelic spirit kept itself in union with a mortal frame. As the last crimson tint of the birth-mark—that sole token of human imperfection—faded from her cheek, the parting breath of the now perfect woman passed into the atmosphere, and her soul, lingering a moment near her husband, took its heavenward flight. Then a hoarse, chuckling laugh was heard again! Thus ever does the gross Fatality of Earth exult in its invariable triumph over the immortal essence, which, in this dim sphere of half-development, demands the completeness of a higher state. Yet, had Aylmer reached a profounder wisdom, he need not thus have flung away the happiness, which would have woven his mortal life of the self-same texture with the celestial. The momentary circumstance was strong for him; he failed to look beyond the shadowy scope of Time, and living once for all in Eternity, to find the perfect Future in the present.

Questions for Engagement, Response, and Analysis

1. Describe the view of science that, according to Hawthorne, existed for some people at the end of the eighteenth century. Explain why or how "the love of science" might "rival the love of woman." Why would the two be opposing forces? How does Aylmer try to blend the two?

2. How does the birthmark affect those who see it? How does Georgiana herself view it?

3. How do Aylmer's dream and the pattern of the results in Aylmer's experiments foreshadow the end of the story?

4. What do Aylmer and Aminadab represent?

5. Does the last sentence give Hawthorne's theme? Defend your opinion.

Crafting Arguments

1. The story is full of symbols, from the birthmark itself to nature. In an essay, analyze and interpret the symbols, using quotations and examples to support your claims.

2. In an essay, offer your interpretation of the theme of Hawthorne's story, supporting your claim with specific examples from the story.

3. Contrast Georgiana's situation with that of the girl child in "Barbie Doll."

Kate Chopin (1850–1904)

Katherine O'Flaherty was born in St. Louis, Missouri, but moved to Louisiana when she married Oscar Chopin in 1870. New Orleans and the Grande Isle are the setting for most of her stories and for her novel The Awakening *(1899), which shocked readers because of her treatment of adultery and suicide. Chopin's stories deal with marriages that are failing, women in the process of achieving independence, or subjects such as miscegenation and integration. "Désirée's Baby" deals honestly with women's emotions.*

DÉSIRÉE'S BABY (1894)

1   As the day was pleasant, Madame Valmondé drove over to L'Abri to see Désirée and the baby.

2   It made her laugh to think of Désirée with a baby. Why, it seemed but yesterday that Désirée was little more than a baby herself; when Monsieur in riding through the gateway of Valmondé had found her lying asleep in the shadow of the big stone pillar.

3   The little one awoke in his arms and began to cry for "Dada." That was as much as she could do or say. Some people thought she might have strayed there of her own accord, for she was of the toddling age.

The prevailing belief was that she had been purposely left by a party of Texans, whose canvas-covered wagon, late in the day, had crossed the ferry that Coton Maïs kept, just below the plantation. In time Madame Valmondé abandoned every speculation but the one that Désirée had been sent to her by a beneficent Providence to be the child of her affection, seeing that she was without child of the flesh. For the girl grew to be beautiful and gentle, affectionate and sincere—the idol of Valmondé.

4   It was no wonder, when she stood one day against the stone pillar in whose shadow she had lain asleep, eighteen years before, that Armand Aubigny riding by and seeing her there, had fallen in love with her. That was the way all the Aubignys fell in love, as if struck by a pistol shot. The wonder was that he had not loved her before; for he had known her since his father brought him home from Paris, a boy of eight, after his mother died there. The passion that awoke in him that day, when he saw her at the gate, swept along like an avalanche, or like a prairie fire, or like anything that drives headlong over all obstacles.

5   Monsieur Valmondé grew practical and wanted things well considered: that is, the girl's obscure origin. Armand looked into her eyes and did not care. He was reminded that she was nameless. What did it matter about a name when he could give her one of the oldest and proudest in Louisiana? He ordered the *corbeille* from Paris, and contained himself with what patience he could until it arrived; then they were married.

6   Madame Valmondé had not seen Désirée and the baby for four weeks. When she reached L'Abri she shuddered at the first sight of it, as she always did. It was a sad looking place, which for many years had not known the gentle presence of a mistress, old Monsieur Aubigny having married and buried his wife in France, and she having loved her own land too well ever to leave it. The roof came down steep and black like a cowl, reaching out beyond the wide galleries that encircled the yellow stuccoed house. Big, solemn oaks grew close to it, and their thick-leaved, far-reaching branches shadowed it like a pall. Young Aubigny's rule was a strict one, too, and under it his negroes had forgotten how to be gay, as they had been during the old master's easy-going and indulgent lifetime.

7   The young mother was recovering slowly, and lay full length, in her soft white muslins and laces, upon a couch. The baby was beside her, upon her arm, where he had fallen asleep, at her breast. The yellow nurse woman sat beside a window fanning herself.

8   Madame Valmondé bent her portly figure over Désirée and kissed her, holding her an instant tenderly in her arms. Then she turned to the child.

9   "This is not the baby!" she exclaimed, in startled tones. French was the language spoken at Valmondé in those days.

10   "I knew you would be astonished," laughed Désirée, "at the way he has grown. The little *cochon de lait!* Look at his legs, mamma, and his hands and fingernails,—real finger-nails. Zandrine had to cut them this morning. Isn't it true, Zandrine?"

11   The woman bowed her turbaned head majestically, "Mais si, Madame."

12   "And the way he cries," went on Désirée, "is deafening. Armand heard him the other day as far away as La Blanche's cabin."

13   Madame Valmondé had never removed her eyes from the child. She lifted it and walked with it over to the window that was lightest. She scanned the baby narrowly, then looked as searchingly at Zandrine, whose face was turned to gaze across the fields.

14   "Yes, the child has grown, has changed," said Madame Valmondé, slowly, as she replaced it beside its mother. "What does Armand say?"

15   Désirée's face became suffused with a glow that was happiness itself.

16   "Oh, Armand is the proudest father in the parish, I believe, chiefly because it is a boy, to bear his name; though he says not,—that he would have loved a girl as well. But I know it isn't true. I know he says that to please me. And mamma," she added, drawing Madame Valmondé's head down to her, and speaking in a whisper, "he hasn't punished one of them—not one of them—since baby is born. Even Négrillon, who pretended to have burnt his leg that he might rest from work—he only laughed, and said Négrillon was a great scamp. Oh, mamma, I'm so happy; it frightens me."

17   What Désirée said was true. Marriage, and later the birth of his son, had softened Armand Aubigny's imperious and exacting nature greatly. This was what made the gentle Désirée so happy, for she loved him desperately. When he frowned she trembled, but loved him. When he smiled, she asked no greater blessing of God. But Armand's dark, handsome face had not often been disfigured by frowns since the day he fell in love with her.

18   When the baby was about three months old, Désirée awoke one day to the conviction that there was something in the air menacing her peace. It was at first too subtle to grasp. It had only been a disquieting suggestion; an air of mystery among the blacks; unexpected visits from far-off neighbors who could hardly account for their coming. Then a strange, an awful change in her husband's manner, which she dared not ask him to explain. When he spoke to her, it was with averted eyes, from which the old love-light seemed to have gone out. He absented himself from home; and when there, avoided her presence and that of her child, without excuse. And the very spirit of Satan seemed suddenly to take hold of him in his dealings with the slaves. Désirée was miserable enough to die.

19   She sat in her room, one hot afternoon, in her *peignoir*, listlessly drawing through her fingers the strands of her long, silky brown hair that hung about her shoulders. The baby, half naked, lay asleep upon her own great mahogany bed, that was like a sumptuous throne, with its satin lined half-canopy. One of La Blanche's little quadroon boys—half naked too—stood fanning the child slowly with a fan of peacock feathers. Désirée's eyes had been fixed absently and sadly upon the baby, while she was striving to penetrate the threatening mist that she felt closing about her. She looked from her child to the boy who stood beside him, and back again; over and over. "Ah!" It was a cry that she could not help, which she was

not conscious of having uttered. The blood turned like ice in her veins, and a clammy moisture gathered upon her face.

20   She tried to speak to the little quadroon boy; but no sound would come, at first. When he heard his name uttered, he looked up, and his mistress was pointing to the door. He laid aside the great, soft fan, and obediently stole away, over the polished floor, on his bare tiptoes.

21   She stayed motionless, with gaze riveted upon her child, and her face the picture of fright.

22   Presently her husband entered the room, and without noticing her, went to a table and began to search among some papers which covered it.

23   "Armand," she called to him, in a voice which must have stabbed him, if he was human. But he did not notice. "Armand," she said again. Then she rose and tottered toward him. "Armand," she panted once more, clutching his arm, "look at our child. What does it mean? Tell me."

24   He coldly but gently loosened her fingers from about his arm and thrust the hand away from him. "Tell me what it means!" she cried despairingly.

25   "It means," he answered lightly, "that the child is not white; it means that you are not white."

26   A quick conception of all that this accusation meant for her nerved her with unwonted courage to deny it. "It is a lie; it is not true, I am white! Look at my hair, it is brown; and my eyes are gray, Armand, you know they are gray. And my skin is fair," seizing his wrist. "Look at my hand; whiter than yours, Armand," she laughed hysterically.

27   "As white as La Blanche's," he returned cruelly; and went away leaving her alone with their child.

28   When she could hold a pen in her hand, she sent a despairing letter to Madame Valmondé.

29   "My mother, they tell me I am not white. Armand has told me I am not white. For God's sake tell them it is not true. You must know it is not true. I shall die. I must die. I cannot be so unhappy, and live."

30   The answer that came was as brief:

31   "My own Désirée: Come home to Valmondé; back to your mother who loves you. Come with your child."

32   When the letter reached Désirée she went with it to her husband's study, and laid it open upon the desk before which he sat. She was like a stone image: silent, white, motionless after she placed it there.

33   In silence he ran his cold eyes over the written words. He said nothing. "Shall I go, Armand?" she asked in tones sharp with agonized suspense.

34   "Yes, go."

35   "Do you want me to go?"

36   "Yes, I want you to go."

37   He thought Almighty God had dealt cruelly and unjustly with him; and felt, somehow, that he was paying Him back in kind when he stabbed thus into his wife's soul. Moreover he no longer loved her,

because of the unconscious injury she had brought upon his home and his name.

38   She turned away like one stunned by a blow, and walked slowly towards the door, hoping he would call her back.

39   "Good-by, Armand," she moaned.

40   He did not answer her. That was his last blow at fate.

41   Désirée went in search of her child. Zandrine was pacing the sombre gallery with it. She took the little one from the nurse's arms with no word of explanation, and descending the steps, walked away, under the live-oak branches.

42   It was an October afternoon; the sun was just sinking. Out in the still fields the negroes were picking cotton.

43   Désirée had not changed the thin white garment nor the slippers which she wore. Her hair was uncovered and the sun's rays brought a golden gleam from its brown meshes. She did not take the broad, beaten road which led to the far-off plantation of Valmondé. She walked across a deserted field, where the stubble bruised her tender feet, so delicately shod, and tore her thin gown to shreds.

44   She disappeared among the reeds and willows that grew thick along the banks of the deep, sluggish bayou; and she did not come back again.

45   Some weeks later there was a curious scene enacted at L'Abri. In the centre of the smoothly swept back yard was a great bonfire. Armand Aubigny sat in the wide hallway that commanded a view of the specta-cle; and it was he who dealt out to a half dozen negroes the material which kept this fire ablaze.

46   A graceful cradle of willow, with all its dainty furbishings, was laid upon the pyre, which had already been fed with the richness of a price-less *layette*. Then there were silk gowns, and velvet and satin ones added to these; laces, too, and embroideries; bonnets and gloves; for the *corbeille* had been of rare quality.

47   The last thing to go was a tiny bundle of letters; innocent little scrib-blings that Désirée had sent to him during the days of their espousal. There was the remnant of one back in the drawer from which he took them. But it was not Désirée's; it was part of an old letter from his mother to his father. He read it. She was thanking God for the blessing of her hus-band's love:-

48   "But, above all," she wrote, "night and day, I thank the good God for having so arranged our lives that our dear Armand will never know that his mother, who adores him, belongs to the race that is cursed with the brand of slavery."

Questions for Engagement, Response, and Analysis

1. What is the point of view in this story? What does Chopin achieve with this point of view?

2. Explain the importance of the setting to this story.

3. Why does Armand suddenly find love with Désirée after having known her since they were children?

4. What does Chopin gradually reveal about Armand's character as the story builds? What details reveal this? How consistent is Désirée as a character?

Crafting Arguments

1. For a surprise ending to be artistically effective, the author should give readers clues that such an eventuality is possible. Argue that the readers are or are not sufficiently prepared for the end of the story.

2. Write a character analysis of Armand or of Désirée.

3. Désirée's value as a person in the eyes of her society and in her own eyes is redefined and reduced due to one element of background over which she has no control. Examine the ramifications of her loss of or redefinition of identity, using specific examples to justify your claims.

Charlotte Perkins Gilman (1860–1935)

Charlotte Perkins Gilman was best known during her life-time as a lecturer and author of books on the rights of women and on socialism. Yet today she is most famous for what is generally acknowledged as her best short story, "The Yellow Wallpaper." According to Gilman, the story was writ-ten after she had suffered a nervous breakdown. A special-ist in nervous diseases, consulted as a result of Gilman's depression, advised her first husband to allow her to par-ticipate only in domestic life and to terminate her painting and writing. After three months of this treatment, she was near a mental breakdown. Unlike the narrator of "The Yel-low Wallpaper," Gilman went on to a successful second mar-riage and a career. She continued to suffer from depression at times and committed suicide in 1935 as a result of severe pain caused by cancer.

THE YELLOW WALLPAPER   (1899)

1   It is very seldom that mere ordinary people like John and myself secure ancestral halls for the summer.

2   A colonial mansion, a hereditary estate, I would say a haunted house and reach the height of romantic felicity—but that would be asking too much of fate!

3   Still I will proudly declare that there is something queer about it.

4   Else, why should it be let so cheaply? And why have stood so long untenanted?

5   John laughs at me, of course, but one expects that.

6   John is practical in the extreme. He has no patience with faith, an intense horror of superstition, and he scoffs openly at any talk of things not to be felt and seen and put down in figures.

7   John is a physician, and *perhaps*—(I would not say it to a living soul, of course, but this is dead paper and a great relief to my mind)—*perhaps* that is one reason I do not get well faster.

8   You see, he does not believe I am sick! And what can one do?

9   If a physician of high standing, and one's own husband, assures friends and relatives that there is really nothing the matter with one but temporary nervous depression—a slight hysterical tendency—what is one to do?

10   My brother is also a physician, and also of high standing, and he says the same thing.

11   So I take phosphates or phosphites—whichever it is—and tonics, and air and exercise, and journeys, and am absolutely forbidden to "work" until I am well again.

12   Personally, I disagree with their ideas.

13   Personally, I believe that congenial work, with excitement and change, would do me good.

14   But what is one to do?

15   I did write for a while in spite of them; but it *does* exhaust me a good deal—having to be so sly about it, or else meet with heavy opposition.

16   I sometimes fancy that in my condition, if I had less opposition and more society and stimulus—but John says the very worst thing I can do is to think about my condition, and I confess it always makes me feel bad.

17   So I will let it alone and talk about the house.

18   The most beautiful place! It is quite alone, standing well back from the road, quite three miles from the village. It makes me think of English places that you read about, for there are hedges and walls and gates that lock, and lots of separate little houses for the gardeners and people.

19   There is a *delicious* garden! I never saw such a garden—large and shady, full of box-bordered paths, and lined with long grape-covered arbors with seats under them.

20   There were greenhouses, but they are all broken now.

21   There was some legal trouble, I believe, something about the heirs and co-heirs; anyhow, the place has been empty for years.

22   That spoils my ghostliness, I am afraid, but I don't care—there is something strange about the house—I can feel it.

23   I even said so to John one moonlight evening, but he said what I felt was a draught, and shut the window.

24   I get unreasonably angry with John sometimes. I'm sure I never used to be so sensitive. I think it is due to this nervous condition.

25   But John says if I feel so I shall neglect proper self-control; so I take pains to control myself—before him, at least, and that makes me very tired.

26   I don't like our room a bit. I wanted one downstairs that opened onto the piazza and had roses all over the window, and such pretty old-fashioned chintz hangings! But John would not hear of it.

27   He said there was only one window and not room for two beds, and no near room for him if he took another.

28   He is very careful and loving, and hardly lets me stir without special direction.

29   I have a schedule prescription for each hour in the day; he takes all care from me, and so I feel basely ungrateful not to value it more.

30   He said he came here solely on my account, that I was to have perfect rest and all the air I could get. "Your exercise depends on your strength, my dear," said he, "and your food somewhat on your appetite; but air you can absorb all the time." So we took the nursery at the top of the house.

31   It is a big, airy room, the whole floor nearly, with windows that look all ways, and air and sunshine galore. It was nursery first, and then play-room and gymnasium, I should judge, for the windows are barred for lit-tle children, and there are rings and things in the walls.

32   The paint and paper look as if a boys' school had used it. It is stripped off—the paper—in great patches all around the head of my bed, about as far as I can reach, and in a great place on the other side of the room low down. I never saw a worse paper in my life. One of those sprawling, flam-boyant patterns committing every artistic sin.

33   It is dull enough to confuse the eye in following, pronounced enough constantly to irritate and provoke study, and when you follow the lame uncertain curves for a little distance they suddenly commit suicide—plunge off at outrageous angles, destroy themselves in unheard-of contradictions.

34   The color is repellent, almost revolting: a smouldering unclean yellow, strangely faded by the slow-turning sunlight. It is a dull yet lurid orange in some places, a sickly sulphur tint in others.

35   No wonder the children hated it! I should hate it myself if I had to live in this room long.

36   There comes John, and I must put this away—he hates to have me write a word.

37   We have been here two weeks, and I haven't felt like writing before, since that first day.

38   I am sitting by the window now, up in this atrocious nursery, and there is nothing to hinder my writing as much as I please, save lack of strength.

39   John is away all day, and even some nights when his cases are serious.

40   I am glad my case is not serious!

41   But these nervous troubles are dreadfully depressing.

42   John does not know how much I really suffer. He knows there is no reason to suffer, and that satisfies him.

43   Of course it is only nervousness. It does weigh on me so not to do my duty in any way!

44   I meant to be such a help to John, such a real rest and comfort, and here I am a comparative burden already!

45   Nobody would believe what an effort it is to do what little I am able—to dress and entertain, and order things.

46   It is fortunate Mary is so good with the baby. Such a dear baby!

47   And yet I *cannot* be with him, it makes me so nervous.

48   I suppose John never was nervous in his life. He laughs at me so about this wallpaper!

49   At first he meant to repaper the room, but afterward he said that I was letting it get the better of me, and that nothing was worse for a nervous patient than to give way to such fancies.

50   He said that after the wallpaper was changed it would be the heavy bedstead, and then the barred windows, and then the gate at the head of the stairs, and so on.

51   "You know the place is doing you good," he said, "and really, dear, I don't care to renovate the house just for a three months' rental."

52   "Then do let us go downstairs," I said. "There are such pretty rooms there."

53   Then he took me in his arms and called me a blessed little goose, and said he would go down cellar, if I wished, and have it whitewashed into the bargain.

54   But he is right enough about the beds and windows and things.

55   It is as airy and comfortable a room as anyone need wish, and, of course, I would not be so silly as to make him uncomfortable just for a whim.

56   I'm really getting quite fond of the big room, all but that horrid paper.

57   Out of one window I can see the garden—those mysterious deep-shaded arbors, the riotous old-fashioned flowers, and bushes and gnarly trees.

58   Out of another I get a lovely view of the bay and a little private wharf belonging to the estate. There is a beautiful shaded lane that runs down there from the house. I always fancy I see people walking in these numerous paths and arbors, but John has cautioned me not to give way to fancy in the least. He says that with my imaginative power and habit of story-making, a nervous weakness like mine is sure to lead to all manner of excited fancies, and that I ought to use my will and good sense to check the tendency. So I try.

59   I think sometimes that if I were only well enough to write a little it would relieve the press of ideas and rest me.

60   But I find I get pretty tired when I try.

61   It is so discouraging not to have any advice and companionship about my work. When I get really well, John says we will ask Cousin Henry and Julia down for a long visit; but he says he would as soon put fireworks in my pillow-case as to let me have those stimulating people about now.

62   I wish I could get well faster.

63   But I must not think about that. This paper looks to me as if it *knew* what a vicious influence it had!

64   There is a recurrent spot where the pattern lolls like a broken neck and two bulbous eyes stare at you upside down.

65   I get positively angry with the impertinence of it and the everlasting-ness. Up and down and sideways they crawl, and those absurd unblinking

eyes are everywhere. There is one place where two breadths didn't match, and the eyes go all up and down the line, one a little higher than the other.

66   I never saw so much expression in an inanimate thing before, and we all know how much expression they have! I used to lie awake as a child and get more entertainment and terror out of blank walls and plain furniture than most children could find in a toy-store.

67   I remember what a kindly wink the knobs of our big old bureau used to have, and there was one chair that always seemed like a strong friend.

68   I used to feel that if any of the other things looked too fierce I could always hop into that chair and be safe.

69   The furniture in this room is no worse than inharmonious, however, for we had to bring it all from downstairs. I suppose when this was used as a playroom they had to take the nursery things out, and no wonder! I never saw such ravages as the children have made here.

70   The wallpaper, as I said before, is torn off in spots, and it sticketh closer than a brother—they must have had perseverance as well as hatred.

71   Then the floor is scratched and gouged and splintered, the plaster itself is dug out here and there, and this great heavy bed, which is all we found in the room, looks as if it had been through the wars.

72   But I don't mind it a bit—only the paper.

73   There comes John's sister. Such a dear girl as she is, and so careful of me! I must not let her find me writing.

74   She is a perfect and enthusiastic housekeeper, and hopes for no better profession. I verily believe she thinks it is the writing which made me sick!

75   But I can write when she is out, and see her a long way off from these windows.

76   There is one that commands the road, a lovely shaded winding road, and one that just looks off over the country. A lovely country, too, full of great elms and velvet meadows.

77   This wallpaper has a kind of sub-pattern in a different shade, a particularly irritating one, for you can only see it in certain lights, and not clearly then.

78   But in the places where it isn't faded and where the sun is just so—I can see a strange, provoking, formless sort of figure that seems to skulk about behind that silly and conspicuous front design.

79   There's sister on the stairs!

80   Well, the Fourth of July is over! The people are all gone, and I am tired out. John thought it might do me good to see a little company, so we just had Mother and Nellie and the children down for a week.

81   Of course I didn't do a thing. Jennie sees to everything now.

82   But it tired me all the same.

83   John says if I don't pick up faster he shall send me to Weir Mitchell in the fall.

84   But I don't want to go there at all. I had a friend who was in his hands once, and she says he is just like John and my brother, only more so!

85   Besides, it is such an undertaking to go so far.

86   I don't feel as if it was worthwhile to turn my hand over for anything, and I'm getting dreadfully fretful and querulous.

87   I cry at nothing, and cry most of the time.

88   Of course I don't when John is here, or anybody else, but when I am alone.

89   And I am alone a good deal just now. John is kept in town very often by serious cases, and Jennie is good and lets me alone when I want her to.

90   So I walk a little in the garden or down that lovely lane, sit on the porch under the roses, and lie down up here a good deal.

91   I'm getting really fond of the room in spite of the wallpaper. Perhaps *because* of the wallpaper.

92   It dwells in my mind so!

93   I lie here on this great immovable bed—it is nailed down, I believe—and follow that pattern about by the hour. It is as good as gymnastics, I assure you. I start, we'll say, at the bottom, down in the corner over there where it has not been touched, and I determine for the thousandth time that I *will* follow that pointless pattern to some sort of a conclusion.

94   I know a little of the principle of design, and I know this thing was not arranged on any laws of radiation, or alternation, or repetition, or symmetry, or anything else that I ever heard of.

95   It is repeated, of course, by the breadths, but not otherwise.

96   Looked at in one way, each breadth stands alone; the bloated curves and flourishes—a kind of "debased Romanesque" with delirium tremens—go waddling up and down in isolated columns of fatuity.

97   But, on the other hand, they connect diagonally, and the sprawling outlines run off in great slanting waves of optic horror, like a lot of wallowing sea-weeds in full chase.

98   The whole thing goes horizontally, too, at least it seems so, and I exhaust myself trying to distinguish the order of its going in that direction.

99   They have used a horizontal breadth for a frieze, and that adds wonderfully to the confusion.

100   There is one end of the room where it is almost intact, and there, when the crosslights fade and the low sun shines directly upon it, I can almost fancy radiation after all—the interminable grotesque seems to form around a common center and rush off in headlong plunges of equal distraction.

101   It makes me tired to follow it. I will take a nap, I guess.

102   I don't know why I should write this.

103   I don't want to.

104   I don't feel able.

105   And I know John would think it absurd. But I *must* say what I feel and think in some way—it is such a relief!

106   But the effort is getting to be greater than the relief.

107   Half the time now I am awfully lazy, and lie down ever so much. John says I mustn't lose my strength, and has me take cod liver oil and lots of tonics and things, to say nothing of ale and wine and rare meat.

108   Dear John! He loves me very dearly, and hates to have me sick. I tried to have a real earnest reasonable talk with him the other day, and tell him how I wish he would let me go and make a visit to Cousin Henry and Julia.

109   But he said I wasn't able to go, nor able to stand it after I got there; and I did not make out a very good case for myself, for I was crying before I had finished.

110   It is getting to be a great effort for me to think straight. Just this nervous weakness, I suppose.

111   And dear John gathered me up in his arms, and just carried me upstairs and laid me on the bed, and sat by me and read to me till it tired my head.

112   He said I was his darling and his comfort and all he had, and that I must take care of myself for his sake, and keep well.

113   He says no one but myself can help me out of it, that I must use my will and self-control and not let any silly fancies run away with me.

114   There's one comfort—the baby is well and happy, and does not have to occupy this nursery with the horrid wallpaper.

115   If we had not used it, that blessed child would have! What a fortunate escape! Why, I wouldn't have a child of mine, an impressionable little thing, live in such a room for worlds.

116   I never thought of it before, but it is lucky that John kept me here after all; I can stand it so much easier than a baby, you see.

117   Of course I never mention it to them any more—I am too wise—but I keep watch for it all the same.

118   There are things in that wallpaper that nobody knows about but me, or ever will.

119   Behind that outside pattern the dim shapes get clearer every day.

120   It is always the same shape, only very numerous.

121   And it is like a woman stooping down and creeping about behind that pattern. I don't like it a bit. I wonder—I begin to think—I wish John would take me away from here!

122   It is so hard to talk with John about my case, because he is so wise, and because he loves me so.

123   But I tried it last night.

124   It was moonlight. The moon shines in all around just as the sun does.

125   I hate to see it sometimes, it creeps so slowly, and always comes in by one window or another.

126   John was asleep and I hated to waken him, so I kept still and watched the moonlight on that undulating wallpaper till I felt creepy.

127   The faint figure behind seemed to shake the pattern, just as if she wanted to get out.

128   I got up softly and went to feel and see if the paper *did* move, and when I came back John was awake.

129   "What is it, little girl?" he said. "Don't go walking about like that—you'll get cold."

130   I thought it was a good time to talk, so I told him that I really was not gaining here, and that I wished he would take me away.

131   "Why, darling!" said he. "Our lease will be up in three weeks, and I can't see how to leave before."

132   "The repairs aren't done at home, and I cannot possibly leave town just now. Of course, if you were in any danger, I could and would, but you really are better, dear, whether you can see it or not. I am a doctor, dear, and I know. You are gaining flesh and color, your appetite is better, I feel really much easier about you."

133   "I don't weigh a bit more," said I, "not as much; and my appetite may be better in the evening when you are here but it is worse in the morning when you are away!"

134   "Bless her little heart!" said he with a big hug. "She shall be as sick as she pleases! But now let's improve the shining hours by going to sleep, and talk about it in the morning!"

135   "And you won't go away?" I asked gloomily.

136   "Why, how can I, dear? It is only three weeks more and then we will take a nice little trip of a few days while Jennie is getting the house ready. Really, dear, you are better!"

137   "Better in body perhaps—" I began, and stopped short, for he sat up straight and looked at me with such a stern, reproachful look that I could not say another word.

138   "My darling," said he, "I beg of you, for my sake and for our child's sake, as well as for your own, that you will never for one instant let that idea enter your mind! There is nothing so dangerous, so fascinating, to a temperament like yours. It is a false and foolish fancy. Can you not trust me as a physician when I tell you so?"

139   So of course I said no more on that score, and we went to sleep before long. He thought I was asleep first, but I wasn't, and lay there for hours trying to decide whether that front pattern and the back pattern really did move together or separately.

140   On a pattern like this, by daylight, there is a lack of sequence, a defiance of law, that is a constant irritant to a normal mind.

141   The color is hideous enough, and unreliable enough, and infuriating enough, but the pattern is torturing.

142   You think you have mastered it, but just as you get well under way in following, it turns a back-somersault and there you are. It slaps you in the face, knocks you down, and tramples upon you. It is like a bad dream.

143   The outside pattern is a florid arabesque, reminding one of a fungus. If you can imagine a toadstool in joints, an interminable string of toadstools, budding and sprouting in endless convolutions—why, that is something like it.

144   That is, sometimes!

145   There is one marked peculiarity about this paper, a thing nobody seems to notice but myself, and that is that it changes as the light changes.

146   When the sun shoots in through the east window—I always watch for that first long, straight ray—it changes so quickly that I never can quite believe it.

147   That is why I watch it always.

148   By moonlight—the moon shines in all night when there is a moon—I wouldn't know it was the same paper.

149   At night in any kind of light, in twilight, candlelight, lamplight, and worst of all by moonlight, it becomes bars! The outside pattern, I mean, and the woman behind it is as plain as can be.

150   I didn't realize for a long time what the thing was that showed behind, that dim sub-pattern, but now I am quite sure it is a woman.

151   By daylight she is subdued, quiet. I fancy it is the pattern that keeps her so still. It is so puzzling. It keeps me quiet by the hour.

152   I lie down ever so much now. John says it is good for me, and to sleep all I can.

153   Indeed he started the habit by making me lie down for an hour after each meal.

154   It is a very bad habit, I am convinced, for you see, I don't sleep.

155   And that cultivates deceit, for I don't tell them I'm awake—oh, no!

156   The fact is I am getting a little afraid of John.

157   He seems very queer sometimes, and even Jennie has an inexplicable look.

158   It strikes me occasionally, just as a scientific hypothesis, that perhaps it is the paper!

159   I have watched John when he did not know I was looking, and come into the room suddenly on the most innocent excuses, and I've caught him several times *looking at the paper!* And Jennie too. I caught Jennie with her hand on it once.

160   She didn't know I was in the room, and when I asked her in a quiet, a very quiet voice, with the most restrained manner possible, what she was doing with the paper, she turned around as if she had been caught stealing, and looked quite angry—asked me why I should frighten her so!

161   Then she said that the paper stained everything it touched, that she had found yellow smooches on all my clothes and John's and she wished we would be more careful!

162   Did not that sound innocent? But I know she was studying that pattern, and I am determined that nobody shall find it out but myself!

163   Life is very much more exciting now than it used to be. You see, I have something more to expect, to look forward to, to watch. I really do eat better, and am more quiet than I was.

164   John is so pleased to see me improve! He laughed a little the other day, and said I seemed to be flourishing in spite of my wallpaper.

165   I turned it off with a laugh. I had no intention of telling him it was *because* of the wallpaper—he would make fun of me. He might even want to take me away.

166   I don't want to leave now until I have found it out. There is a week more, and I think that will be enough.

167   I'm feeling so much better!

168   I don't sleep much at night, for it is so interesting to watch developments; but I sleep a good deal during the daytime.

169   In the daytime it is tiresome and perplexing.

170   There are always new shoots on the fungus, and new shades of yellow all over it. I cannot keep count of them, though I have tried conscientiously.

171   It is the strangest yellow, the wallpaper! It makes me think of all the yellow things I ever saw—not beautiful ones like buttercups, but old, foul, bad yellow things.

172   But there is something else about that paper—the smell! I noticed it the moment we came into the room, but with so much air and sun it was not bad. Now we have had a week of fog and rain, and whether the windows are open or not, the smell is here.

173   It creeps all over the house.

174   I find it hovering in the dining-room, skulking in the parlor, hiding in the hall, lying in wait for me on the stairs.

175   It gets into my hair.

176   Even when I go to ride, if I turn my head suddenly and surprise it— there is that smell!

177   Such a peculiar odor, too! I have spent hours in trying to analyze it, to find what it smelled like.

178   It is not bad—at first—and very gentle, but quite the subtlest, most enduring odor I ever met.

179   In this damp weather it is awful. I wake up in the night and find it hanging over me.

180   It used to disturb me at first. I thought seriously of burning the house—to reach the smell.

181   But now I am used to it. The only thing I can think of that it is like is the *color* of the paper! A yellow smell.

182   There is a very funny mark on this wall, low down, near the mopboard. A streak that runs round the room. It goes behind every piece of furniture, except the bed, a long, straight, even *smooch*, as if it had been rubbed over and over.

183   I wonder how it was done and who did it, and what they did it for. Round and round and round—round and round and round—it makes me dizzy!

184   I really have discovered something at last.

185   Through watching so much at night, when it changes so, I have finally found out.

186   The front pattern *does* move—and no wonder! The woman behind shakes it!

187   Sometimes I think there are a great many women behind, and sometimes only one, and she crawls around fast, and her crawling shakes it all over.

188   Then in the very bright spots she keeps still, and in the very shady spots she just takes hold of the bars and shakes them hard.

189   And she is all the time trying to climb through. But nobody could climb through that pattern—it strangles so; I think that is why it has so many heads.

190   They get through and then the pattern strangles them off and turns them upside down, and makes their eyes white!

191   If those heads were covered or taken off it would not be half so bad.

192   I think that woman gets out in the daytime!

193   And I'll tell you why—privately—I've seen her!

194   I can see her out of every one of my windows!

195   It is the same woman, I know, for she is always creeping, and most women do not creep by daylight.

196   I see her in that long shaded lane, creeping up and down. I see her in those dark grape arbors, creeping all around the garden.

197   I see her on that long road under the trees, creeping along, and when a carriage comes she hides under the blackberry vines.

198   I don't blame her a bit. It must be very humiliating to be caught creeping by daylight!

199   I always lock the door when I creep by daylight. I can't do it at night, for I know John would suspect something at once.

200   And John is so queer now that I don't want to irritate him. I wish he would take another room! Besides, I don't want anybody to get that woman out at night but myself.

201   I often wonder if I could see her out of all the windows at once.

202   But, turn as fast as I can, I can only see out of one at one time.

203   And though I always see her, she *may* be able to creep faster than I can turn! I have watched her sometimes away off in the open country, creeping as fast as a cloud shadow in a wind.

204   If only that top pattern could be gotten off from the under one! I mean to try it, little by little.

205   I have found out another funny thing, but I shan't tell it this time! It does not do to trust people too much.

206   There are only two more days to get this paper off, and I believe John is beginning to notice. I don't like the look in his eyes.

207   And I heard him ask Jennie a lot of professional questions about me. She had a very good report to give.

208   She said I slept a good deal in the daytime.

209   John knows I don't sleep very well at night, for all I'm so quiet!

210   He asked me all sorts of questions, too, and pretended to be very loving and kind.

211   As if I couldn't see through him!

212   Still, I don't wonder he acts so, sleeping under this paper for three months.

213 It only interests me, but I feel sure John and Jennie are affected by it.

214 Hurrah! This is the last day, but it is enough. John is to stay in town over night, and won't be out until this evening.

215 Jennie wanted to sleep with me—the sly thing; but I told her I should undoubtedly rest better for a night all alone.

216 That was clever, for really I wasn't alone a bit! As soon as it was moonlight and that poor thing began to crawl and shake the pattern, I got up and ran to help her.

217 I pulled and she shook. I shook and she pulled, and before morning we had peeled off yards of that paper.

218 A strip about as high as my head and half around the room.

219 And then when the sun came and that awful pattern began to laugh at me, I declared I would finish it today!

220 We go away tomorrow, and they are moving all my furniture down again to leave things as they were before.

221 Jennie looked at the wall in amazement, but I told her merrily that I did it out of pure spite at the vicious thing.

222 She laughed and said she wouldn't mind doing it herself, but I must not get tired.

223 How she betrayed herself that time!

224 But I am here, and no person touches this paper but Me—not *alive!*

225 She tried to get me out of the room—it was too patent! But I said it was so quiet and empty and clean now that I believed I would lie down again and sleep all I could, and not to wake me even for dinner—I would call when I woke.

226 So now she is gone, and the servants are gone, and the things are gone, and there is nothing left but that great bedstead nailed down, with the canvas mattress we found on it.

227 We shall sleep downstairs tonight, and take the boat home tomorrow.

228 I quite enjoy the room, now it is bare again.

229 How those children did tear about here!

230 This bedstead is fairly gnawed!

231 But I must get to work.

232 I have locked the door and thrown the key down into the front path.

233 I don't want to go out, and I don't want to have anybody come in, till John comes.

234 I want to astonish him.

235 I've got a rope up here that even Jennie did not find. If that woman does get out, and tries to get away, I can tie her!

236 But I forgot I could not reach far without anything to stand on!

237 This bed will *not* move!

238 I tried to lift and push it until I was lame, and then I got so angry I bit off a little piece at one corner—but it hurt my teeth.

239 Then I peeled off all the paper I could reach standing on the floor. It sticks horribly and the pattern just enjoys it! All those strangled heads and bulbous eyes and waddling fungus growths just shriek with derision!

240   I am getting angry enough to do something desperate. To jump out of the window would be admirable exercise, but the bars are too strong even to try.

241   Besides I wouldn't do it. Of course not. I know well enough that a step like that is improper and might be misconstrued.

242   I don't like to *look* out of the windows even—there are so many of those creeping women and they creep so fast.

243   I wonder if they all come out of that wallpaper as I did?

244   But I am securely fastened now by my well-hidden rope—you don't get *me* out in the road there!

245   I suppose I shall have to get back behind the pattern when it comes night, and that is hard!

246   It is so pleasant to be out in this great room and creep around as I please!

247   I don't want to go outside. I won't, even if Jennie asks me to.

248   For outside you have to creep on the ground, and everything is green instead of yellow.

249   But here I can creep smoothly on the floor, and my shoulder just fits in that long smooch around the wall, so I cannot lose my way.

250   Why, there's John at the door!

251   It is no use, young man, you can't open it!

252   How he does call and pound!

253   Now he's crying to Jennie for an axe.

254   It would be a shame to break down that beautiful door!

255   "John, dear!" said I in the gentlest voice. "The key is down by the front steps, under a plantain leaf!"

256   That silenced him for a few moments.

257   Then he said, very quietly indeed, "Open the door, my darling!"

258   "I can't," said I. "The key is down by the front door under a plantain leaf!" And then I said it again, several times, very gently and slowly, and said it so often that he had to go and see, and he got it of course, and came in. He stopped short by the door.

259   "What is the matter?" he cried. "For God's sake, what are you doing!"

260   I kept on creeping just the same, but I looked at him over my shoulder.

261   "I've got out at last," said I, "in spite of you and Jane. And I've pulled off most of the paper, so you can't put me back!"

262   Now why should that man have fainted? But he did, and right across my path by the wall, so that I had to creep over him every time!

Questions for Engagement, Response, and Analysis

1. What is the point of view of this story? Why is it crucial to the effectiveness of the story? How does the point of view create an ironic tone?

2. Describe in detail the setting of this story.

3. How does John's profession affect his relationship with his wife? What is the significance of the narrator's repeatedly saying "but John says" after having given her opinion?

4. What is the significance of the narrator's not being allowed to see her baby? What role do Mary and Jennie play in the story?

Crafting Arguments

1. Trace the changes in the narrator's attitude toward the wallpaper and explain how they depict her state of mind.

2. Write an essay examining the symbolism and supporting each of your claims with specific examples from the story.

Zora Neale Hurston (1891–1960)

Born in Alabama, Hurston moved with her family to Eatonville, Florida, the first "Negro" community to be incorporated; from there she moved to Jacksonville, Baltimore, and then New York. In New York she received good reviews for "Spunk" in 1925 and became part of the Harlem Renaissance. Hurston published four novels, two volumes of poetry, and an autobiography. One of her novels, Their Eyes Were Watching God *(1937), has been praised by modern critics. Hurston spent five years traveling the rural South, collecting folklore and music, information she assimilated into her stories. Much of her writing uses as a setting the general store porch because she felt that that part of the community was the most interesting place in town, even though women were excluded from it.*

THE GILDED SIX-BITS   (1933)

1   It was a Negro yard around a Negro house in a Negro settlement that looked to the payroll of the G. and G. Fertilizer works for its support.

2   But there was something happy about the place. The front yard was parted in the middle by a sidewalk from gate to doorstep, a sidewalk edged on either side by quart bottles driven neck down into the ground on a slant. A mess of homey flowers planted without a plan but blooming cheerily from their helter-skelter places. The fence and house were white-washed. The porch and steps scrubbed white.

3   The front door stood open to the sunshine so that the floor of the front room could finish drying after its weekly scouring. It was Saturday. Everything clean from the front gate to the privy house. Yard raked so that the strokes of the rake would make a pattern. Fresh newspaper cut in fancy edge on the kitchen shelves.

4   Missie May was bathing herself in the galvanized washtub in the bedroom. Her dark-brown skin glistened under the soapsuds that skittered

down from her washrag. Her stiff young breasts thrust forward aggressively, like broad-based cones with the tips lacquered in black.

5   She heard men's voices in the distance and glanced at the dollar clock on the dresser.

6   "Humph! Ah'm way behind time t'day! Joe gointer be heah 'fore Ah git mah clothes on if Ah don't make haste."

7   She grabbed the clean mealsack at hand and dried herself hurriedly and began to dress. But before she could tie her slippers, there came the ring of singing metal on wood. Nine times.

8   Missie May grinned with delight. She had not seen the big tall man come stealing in the gate and creep up the walk grinning happily at the joyful mischief he was about to commit. But she knew that it was her husband throwing silver dollars in the door for her to pick up and pile beside her plate at dinner. It was this way every Saturday afternoon. The nine dollars hurled into the open door, he scurried to a hiding place behind the Cape jasmine bush and waited.

9   Missie May promptly appeared at the door in mock alarm.

10   "Who dat chunkin' money in mah do'way?" she demanded. No answer from the yard. She leaped off the porch and began to search the shrubbery. She peeped under the porch and hung over the gate to look up and down the road. While she did this, the man behind the jasmine darted to the chinaberry tree. She spied him and gave chase.

11   "Nobody ain't gointer be chunkin' money at me and Ah not do 'em nothin'," she shouted in mock anger. He ran around the house with Missie May at his heels. She overtook him at the kitchen door. He ran inside but could not close it after him before she crowded in and locked with him in a rough-and-tumble. For several minutes the two were a furious mass of male and female energy. Shouting, laughing, twisting, turning, tussling, tickling each other in the ribs; Missie May clutching onto Joe and Joe trying, but not too hard, to get away.

12   "Missie May, take yo' hand out mah pocket!" Joe shouted out between laughs.

13   "Ah ain't, Joe, not lessen you gwine gimme whateve' it is good you got in yo' pocket. Turn it go, Joe, do. Ah'll tear yo' clothes."

14   "Go on tear 'em. You de one dat pushes de needles round heah. Move yo' hand, Missie May."

15   "Lemme git dat paper sak out yo' pocket. Ah bet it's candy kisses."

16   "Tain't. Move yo' hand. Woman ain't got no business in a man's clothes nohow. Go way."

17   Missie May gouged way down and gave an upward jerk and triumphed.

18   "Unhhunh! Ah got it! It 'tis so candy kisses. Ah knowed you had somethin' for me in yo' clothes. Now Ah got to see whut's in every pocket you got."

19   Joe smiled indulgently and let his wife go through all of his pockets and take out the things that he had hidden there for her to find. She bore off the chewing gum, the cake of sweet soap, the pocket handkerchief as

if she had wrested them from him, as if they had not been bought for the sake of this friendly battle.

20   "Whew! dat play-fight done got me all warmed up!" Joe exclaimed. "Got me some water in de kittle?"

21   "Yo' water is on de fire and yo' clean things is cross de bed. Hurry up and wash yo'self and get changed so we kin eat. Ah'm hongry." As Missie said this, she bore the steaming kettle into the bedroom.

22   "You ain't hongry, sugar," Joe contradicted her. "Youse jus' a little empty. Ah'm de one what's hongry. Ah could eat up camp meetin', back off 'ssociation, and drink Jurdan dry. Have it on de table when Ah get out de tub."

23   "Don't you mess wid mah business, man. You get in yo' clothes. Ah'm a real wife, not no dress and breath. Ah might not look lak one, but if you burn me, you won't git a thing but wife ashes."

24   Joe splashed in the bedroom and Missie May fanned around in the kitchen. A fresh red-and-white checked cloth on the table. Big pitcher of buttermilk beaded with pale drops of butter from the churn. Hot fried mullet, crackling bread, ham hock atop a mound of string beans and new potatoes, and perched on the windowsill a pone of spicy potato pudding.

25   Very little talk during the meal but that little consisted of banter that pretended to deny affection but in reality flaunted it. Like when Missie May reached for a second helping of the tater pone. Joe snatched it out of her reach.

26   After Missie May had made two or three unsuccessful grabs at the pan, she begged, "Aw, Joe, gimme some mo' dat tater pone."

27   "Nope, sweetenin' is for us menfolks. Y'all pritty li'l frail eels don't need nothin' lak dis. You too sweet already."

28   "Please, Joe."

29   "Naw, naw. Ah don't want you to git no sweeter than whut you is already. We goin' down de road a lil piece t'night so you go put on yo' Sunday-go-to-meetin' things."

30   Missie May looked at her husband to see if he was playing some prank. "Sho nuff, Joe?"

31   "Yeah. We goin' to de ice cream parlor."

32   "Where de ice cream parlor at, Joe?"

33   "A new man done come heah from Chicago and he done got a place and took and opened it up for a ice cream parlor, and bein' as it's real swell, Ah wants you to be one de first ladies to walk in dere and have some set down."

34   "Do Jesus, Ah ain't knowed nothin' bout it. Who de man done it?"

35   "Mister Otis D. Slemmons, of spots and places—Memphis, Chicago, Jacksonville, Philadelphia and so on."

36   "Dat heavyset man wid his mouth full of gold teeths?"

37   "Yeah. Where did you see 'im at?"

38   "Ah went down to de sto' tuh git a box of lye and Ah seen 'im standin' on de corner talkin' to some of de mens, and Ah come on back and went

to scrubbin' de floor, and he passed and tipped his hat whilst Ah was scourin' de steps. Ah thought 'Ah never seen *him* befo'.'"

39   Joe smiled pleasantly. "Yeah, he's up-to-date. He got de finest clothes Ah ever seen on a colored man's back."

40   "Aw, he don't look no better in his clothes than you do in yourn. He got a puzzlegut on 'im and he so chuckleheaded he got a pone behind his neck."

41   Joe looked down at his own abdomen and said wistfully: "Wisht Ah had a build on me lak he got. He ain't puzzlegutted, honey. He jes' got a corperation. Dat make 'm look lak a rich white man. All rich mens is got some belly on 'em."

42   "Ah seen de pitchers of Henry Ford and he's a spare-built man and Rockefeller look lak he ain't got but one gut. But Ford and Rockefeller and dis Slemmons and all de rest kin be as many-gutted as dey please, Ah'm satisfied wid you jes' lak you is, baby. God took pattern after a pine tree and built you noble. Youse a pretty still man, and if Ah knowed any way to make you mo' pritty Ah'd take and do it."

43   Joe reached over gently and toyed with Missie May's ear. "You jes' say dat cause you love me, but Ah know Ah can't hold no light to Otis D. Slemmons. Ah ain't never been nowhere and Ah ain't got nothin' but you."

44   Missie May got on his lap and kissed him and he kissed back in kind. Then he went on. "All de womens is crazy 'bout 'im everywhere he go."

45   "How you know dat, Joe?"

46   "He tole us so hisself."

47   "Dat don't make it so. His mouf is cut crossways, ain't it? Well, he kin lie jes' lak anybody else."

48   "Good Lawd, Missie! You womens sho is hard to sense into things. He's got a five-dollar gold piece for a stickpin and he got a ten-dollar gold piece on his watch chain and his mouf is jes' crammed full of gold teeths. Sho wisht it wuz mine. And what make it so cool, he got money 'cumulated. And womens give it all to 'im."

49   "Ah don't see whut de womens see on 'im. Ah wouldn't give 'im a wink if de sheriff wuz after 'im."

50   "Well, he tole us how de white womens in Chicago give 'im all dat gold money. So he don't 'low nobody to touch it at all. Not even put dey finger on it. Dey told 'im not to. You kin make 'miration at it, but don't tetch it."

51   "Whyn't he stay up dere where dey so crazy 'bout 'im?"

52   "Ah reckon dey done made 'im vast-rich and he wants to travel some. He says dey wouldn't leave 'im hit a lick of work. He got mo' lady people crazy 'bout him than he kin shake a stick at."

53   "Joe, Ah hates to see you so dumb. Dat stray nigger jes' tell y'all anything and y'all b'lieve it."

54   "Go 'head on now, honey, and put on yo' clothes. He talkin' 'bout his pritty womens—Ah wan 'im to see *mine*."

55   Missie May went off to dress and Joe spent the time trying to make his stomach punch out like Slemmons's middle. He tried the rolling swagger of the stranger, but found that his tall bone-and-muscle stride fitted ill

with it. He just had time to drop back into his seat before Missie May came in dressed to go.

56   On the way home that night Joe was exultant. "Didn't Ah say ole Otis was swell? Can't he talk Chicago talk? Wuzn't dat funny whut he said when great big fat ole Ida Armstrong come in? He asted me, 'Who is dat broad wid de forty shake?' Dat's a new word. Us always thought forty was a set of figgers but he showed us where it means a whole heap of things. Sometimes he don't say forty, he jes' say thirty-eight and two and dat mean de same thing. Know whut he told me when Ah wuz payin' for our ice cream? He say, "Ah have to hand it to you, Joe. Dat wife of yours is jes' thirty-eight and two. Yessuh, she's forty!' Ain't he killin'?"

57   "He'll do in case of a rush. But he sho is got uh heap uh gold on 'im. Dat's de first time Ah ever seed gold money. It lookted good on him sho nuff, but it'd look a whole heap better on you."

58   "Who, me? Missie May, youse crazy! Where would a po' man lak me git gold money from?"

59   Missie May was silent for a minute, then she said, "Us might find some goin' long de road some time. Us could."

60   "Who would be losin' gold money round heah? We ain't even seen none dese white folks wearin' no gold money on dey watch chain. You must be figgerin' Mister Packard or Mister Cadillac goin' pass through heah."

61   "You don't know whut been lost 'round heah. Maybe somebody way back in memorial times lost they gold money and went on off and it ain't never been found. And then if we wuz to find it, you could wear some 'thout havin' no gang of womens lak dat Slemmons say he got."

62   Joe laughed and hugged her. "Don't be so wishful 'bout me. Ah'm satisfied de way Ah is. So long as Ah be yo' husband. Ah don't keer 'bout nothin' else. Ah'd ruther all de other womens in de world to be dead than for you to have de toothache. Less we go to bed and get our night rest."

63   It was Saturday night once more before Joe could parade his wife in Slemmons's ice cream parlor again. He worked the night shift and Saturday was his only night off. Every other evening around six o'clock he left home, and dying dawn saw him hustling home around the lake, where the challenging sun flung a flaming sword from east to west across the trembling water.

64   That was the best part of life—going home to Missie May. Their whitewashed house, the mock battle on Saturday, the dinner and ice cream parlor afterwards, church on Sunday nights when Missie outdressed any woman in town—all, everything, was right.

65   One night around eleven the acid ran out at the G. and G. The foreman knocked off the crew and let the steam die down. As Joe rounded the lake on his way home, a lean moon rode the lake in a silver boat. If anybody had asked Joe about the moon on the lake, he would have said he hadn't paid it any attention. But he saw it with his feelings. It made him yearn painfully for Missie. Creation obsessed him. He thought about children. They had been married more than a year now. They had money put

away. They ought to be making little feet for shoes. A little boy child would be about right.

66   He saw a dim light in the bedroom and decided to come in through the kitchen door. He could wash the fertilizer dust off himself before presenting himself to Missie May. It would be nice for her not to know that he was there until he slipped into his place in bed and hugged her back. She always liked that.

67   He eased the kitchen door open slowly and silently, but when he went to set his dinner bucket on the table he bumped it into a pile of dishes, and something crashed to the floor. He heard his wife gasp in fright and hurried to reassure her.

68   "Iss me, honey. Don't git skeered."

69   There was a quick, large movement in the bedroom. A rustle, a thud, and a stealthy silence. The light went out.

70   What? Robbers? Murderers? Some varmint attacking his helpless wife, perhaps. He struck a match, threw himself on guard and stepped over the doorsill into the bedroom.

71   The great belt on the wheel of Time slipped and eternity stood still. By the match light he could see the man's legs fighting with his breeches in his frantic desire to get them on. He had both chance and time to kill the intruder in his helpless condition—half in and half out of his pants—but he was too weak to take action. The shapeless enemies of humanity that live in the hours of Time had waylaid Joe. He was assaulted in his weakness. Like Samson awakening after his haircut. So he just opened his mouth and laughed.

72   The match went out and he struck another and lit the lamp. A howling wind raced across his heart, but underneath its fury he heard his wife sobbing and Slemmons pleading for his life. Offering to buy it with all that he had. "Please, suh, don't kill me. Sixty-two dollars at de sto'. Gold money."

73   Joe just stood. Slemmons looked at the window, but it was screened. Joe stood out like a rough-backed mountain between him and the door. Barring him from escape, from sunrise, from life.

74   He considered a surprise attack upon the big clown that stood there laughing like a chessy cat. But before his fist could travel an inch, Joe's own rushed out to crush him like a battering ram. Then Joe stood over him.

75   "Git into yo' damn rags, Slemmons, and dat quick."

76   Slemmons scrambled to his feet and into his vest and coat. As he grabbed his hat, Joe's fury overrode his intentions and he grabbed at Slemmons with his left hand and struck at him with his right. The right landed. The left grazed the front of his vest. Slemmons was knocked a somersault into the kitchen and fled through the open door. Joe found himself alone with Missie May, with the golden watch charm clutched in his left fist. A short bit of broken chain dangled between his fingers.

77   Missie May was sobbing. Wails of weeping without words. Joe stood, and after a while he found out that he had something in his hand. And then he stood and felt without thinking and without seeing with his

natural eyes. Missie May kept on crying and Joe kept on feeling so much, and not knowing what to do with all his feelings, he put Slemmons's watch charm in his pants pocket and took a good laugh and went to bed.

78   "Missie May, whut you cryin' for?"

79   "Cause Ah love you so hard and Ah know you don't love *me* no mo'."

80   Joe sank his face into the pillow for a spell, then he said huskily, "You don't know de feelings of dat yet, Missie May."

81   "Oh Joe, honey, he said he wuz gointer give me dat gold money and he jes' kept on after me—"

82   Joe was very still and silent for a long time. Then he said, "Well, don't cry no mo', Missie May. Ah got yo' gold piece for you."

83   The hours went past on their rusty ankles. Joe still and quiet on one bed rail and Missie May wrung dry of sobs on the other. Finally the sun's tide crept upon the shore of night and drowned all its hours. Missie May with her face stiff and streaked towards the window saw the dawn come into her yard. It was day. Nothing more. Joe wouldn't be coming home as usual. No need to fling open the front door and sweep off the porch, making it nice for Joe. Never no more breakfast to cook; no more washing and starching of Joe's jumper-jackets and pants. No more nothing. So why get up?

84   With this strange man in her bed, she felt embarrassed to get up and dress. She decided to wait till he had dressed and gone. Then she would get up, dress quickly and be gone forever beyond reach of Joe's looks and laughs. But he never moved. Red light turned to yellow, then white.

85   From beyond the no-man's land between them came a voice. A strange voice that yesterday had been Joe's.

86   "Missie May, ain't you gonna fix me no breakfus'?"

87   She sprang out of bed. "Yeah, Joe. Ah didn't reckon you wuz hongry."

88   No need to die today. Joe needed her for a few more minutes anyhow.

89   Soon there was a roaring fire in the cookstove. Water bucket full and two chickens killed. Joe loved fried chicken and rice. She didn't deserve a thing and good Joe was letting her cook him some breakfast. She rushed hot biscuits to the table as Joe took his seat.

90   He ate with his eyes in his plate. No laughter, no banter.

91   "Missie May, you ain't eatin' yo' breakfus'."

92   "Ah don't choose none, Ah thank yuh."

93   His coffee cup was empty. She sprang to refill it. When she turned from the stove and bent to set the cup beside Joe's plate, she saw the yellow coin on the table between them.

94   She slumped into her seat and wept into her arms.

95   Presently Joe said calmly, "Missie May, you cry too much. Don't look back lak Lot's wife and turn to salt."

96   The sun, the hero of every day, the impersonal old man that beams as brightly on death as on birth, came up every morning and raced across the blue dome and dipped into the sea of fire every morning. Water ran downhill and birds nested.

97   Missie knew why she didn't leave Joe. She couldn't. She loved him too much, but she could not understand why Joe didn't leave her. He was polite, even kind at times, but aloof.

98   There were no more Saturday romps. No ringing silver dollars to stack beside her plate. No pockets to rifle. In fact, the yellow coin in his trousers was like a monster hiding in the cave of his pockets to destroy her.

99   She often wondered if he still had it, but nothing could have induced her to ask nor yet to explore his pockets to see for herself. Its shadow was in the house whether or no.

100   One night Joe came home around midnight and complained of pains in the back. He asked Missie to rub him down with liniment. It had been three months since Missie had touched his body and it all seemed strange. But she rubbed him. Grateful for the chance. Before morning youth triumphed and Missie exulted. But the next day, as she joyfully made up their bed, beneath her pillow she found the piece of money with the bit of chain attached.

101   Alone to herself, she looked at the thing with loathing, but look she must. She took it into her hands with trembling and saw first thing that it was no gold piece. It was a gilded half dollar. Then she knew why Slemmons had forbidden anyone to touch his gold. He trusted village eyes at a distance not to recognize his stickpin as a gilded quarter, and his watch charm as a four-bit piece.

102   They were man and wife again. Then another thought came clawing at her. He had come home to buy from her as if she were any woman in the longhouse. Fifty cents for her love. As if to say that he could pay as well as Slemmons. She slid the coin into his Sunday pants pocket and dressed herself and left his house.

103   Halfway between her house and the quarters she met her husband's mother, and after a short talk she turned and went back home. Never would she admit defeat to that woman who prayed for it nightly. If she had not the substance of marriage she had the outside show. Joe must leave *her*. She let him see she didn't want his old gold four-bits, too.

104   She saw no more of the coin for some time though she knew that Joe could not help finding it in his pocket. But his health kept poor, and he came home at least every ten days to be rubbed.

105   The sun swept around the horizon, trailing its robes of weeks and days. One morning as Joe came in from work, he found Missie May chopping wood. Without a word he took the ax and chopped a huge pile before he stopped.

106   "You ain't got no business choppin' wood, and you know it."

107   "How come? Ah been choppin' it for the last longest."

108   "Ah ain't blind. You makin' feet for shoes."

109   "Won't you be glad to have a lil baby chile, Joe?"

110   "You know dat 'thout astin' me."

111   "Iss gointer be a boy chile and de very spit of you."

112   "You reckon, Missie May?"

113   "Who else could it look lak?"

114   Joe said nothing, but he thrust his hand deep into his pocket and fingered something there.

115   It was almost six months later Missie May took to bed and Joe went and got his mother to come wait on the house.

116   Missie May was delivered of a fine boy. Her travail was over when Joe came in from work one morning. His mother and the old woman were drinking great bowls of coffee around the fire in the kitchen.

117   The minute Joe came into the room his mother called him aside.

118   "How did Missie May make out?" he asked quickly.

119   "Who, dat gal? She strong as a ox. She gointer have plenty mo'. We done fixed her wid de sugar and lard to sweeten her for de nex' one."

120   Joe stood silent awhile.

121   "You ain't ask 'bout de baby, Joe. You oughter be mighty proud cause he sho is de spittin' image of yuh, son. Dat's yourn all right, if you never git another one, dat un is yourn. And you know Ah'm mighty proud too, son, cause Ah never thought well of you marryin' Missie May cause her ma used tuh fan her foot round right smart and Ah been mighty skeered dat Missie May wuz gointer git misput on her road."

122   Joe said nothing. He fooled around the house till late in the day, then, just before he went to work, he went and stood at the foot of the bed and asked his wife how she felt. He did this every day during the week.

123   On Saturday he went to Orlando to make his market. It had been a long time since he had done that.

124   Meat and lard, meal and flour, soap and starch. Cans of corn and tomatoes. All the staples. He fooled around town for a while and bought bananas and apples. Way after while he went around to the candy store.

125   "Hellow, Joe," the clerk greeted him. "Ain't seen you in a long time."

126   "Nope, Ah ain't been heah. Been round in spots and places."

127   "Want some of them molasses kisses you always buy?"

128   "Yessuh." He threw the gilded half dollar on the counter. "Will dat spend?"

129   "What is it, Joe? Well, I'll be doggone! A gold-plated four-bit piece. Where'd you git it, Joe?"

130   "Offen a stray nigger dat come through Eatonville. He had it on his watch chain for a charm—goin' round making out iss gold money. Ha ha! He had a quarter on his tiepin and it wuz all golded up too. Tryin' to fool people. Makin' out he so rich and everything. Ha! Ha! Tryin' to tote off folkses wives from home."

131   "How did you git it, Joe? Did he fool you, too?"

132   "Who, me? Naw suh! He ain't fooled me none. Know what Ah done? He come round me wid his smart talk. Ah hauled off and knocked 'im down and took his old four-bits away from 'im. Gointer buy my wife some good ole lasses kisses wid it. Gimme fifty cents worth of dem candy kisses."

133   "Fifty cents buys a mighty lot of candy kisses, Joe. Why don't you split it up and take some chocolate bars, too? They eat good, too."

134   "Yessuh, dey do, but Ah wants all dat is kisses. Ah got a lil boy chile home now. Tain't a week old yet, but he kin suck a sugar tit and maybe eat one them kisses hisself."

135   Joe got his candy and left the store. The clerk turned to the next customer. "Wisht I could be like these darkies. Laughin' all the time. Nothin' worries 'em."

136   Back in Eatonville, Joe reached his own front door. There was the ring of singing metal on wood. Fifteen times. Missie May couldn't run to the door, but she crept there as quickly as she could.

137   "Joe Banks, Ah hear you chunkin' money in mah do'way. You wait till Ah got mah strength back and Ah'm gointer fix you for dat."

Questions for Engagement, Response, and Analysis

1. What is the point of view? How does it affect the reader's reaction to the plot?
2. How does the first sentence set the stage for the story?
3. What does Joe's opinion of Otis D. Slemmons reveal about him?
4. What is the significance of the "gold piece" under the pillow? Explain the title of the story.
5. Is Joe's decision at the end of the story responsible? Why or why not?
6. How would you describe this story's theme?

Crafting Arguments

1. Prepare a character sketch of either Missie May or Joe.
2. In an essay, show how Hurston reveals the complexity of characters who appear to the outside world to be simple and happy.
3. This story may be interpreted to describe a conflict in which one character's pursuit of freedom, even if the character has unselfish intentions, infringes on the dignity of a more responsible character. Discuss how the story explores and defines the limits of freedom.
4. Write an essay arguing that Joe is or is not a better husband than Troy in *Fences* or than John in "The Yellow Wallpaper."

Ernest Hemingway (1899–1961)

Hemingway began his literary career as a cub reporter for the Kansas City Star. *There he learned a style of writing that many critics believe had a lasting influence on his fiction: his frequent use of short, simple or compound sentences. Hemingway continued his newspaper writing as a foreign correspondent throughout much of his life. As his works became famous, Hemingway also became a celebrity, often living the kind of adventures he wrote about: he fought in World War I, supported the Spanish Civil War, hunted in Africa, and married four times. His most famous novels include* The Sun Also Rises *(1926),* A Farewell to Arms *(1929),* For Whom the Bell Tolls *(1940), and* The Old Man and the Sea *(1952). In 1954, Hemingway was awarded the Nobel Prize for Literature.*

HILLS LIKE WHITE ELEPHANTS (1927)

1   The hills across the valley of the Ebro were long and white. On this side there was no shade and no trees and the station was between two lines of rails in the sun. Close against the side of the station there was the warm shadow of the building and a curtain, made of strings of bamboo beads, hung across the open door into the bar, to keep out flies. The American and the girl with him sat at a table in the shade, outside the building. It was very hot and the express from Barcelona would come in forty minutes. It stopped at this junction for two minutes and went on to Madrid.

2   "What should we drink?" the girl asked. She had taken off her hat and put it on the table.

3   "It's pretty hot," the man said.

4   "Let's drink beer."

5   "Dos cervezas," the man said into the curtain.

6   "Big ones?" a woman asked from the doorway.

7   "Yes. Two big ones."

8   The woman brought two glasses of beer and two felt pads. She put the felt pads and the beer glasses on the table and looked at the man and the girl. The girl was looking off at the line of hills. They were white in the sun and the country was brown and dry.

9   "They look like white elephants," she said.

10   "I've never seen one," the man drank his beer.

11   "No, you wouldn't have."

12   "I might have," the man said. "Just because you say I wouldn't have doesn't prove anything."

13   The girl looked at the bead curtain. "They've painted something on it," she said. "What does it say?"

14   "Anis del Toro. It's a drink."

15   "Could we try it?"

16 The man called "Listen" through the curtain. The woman came out from the bar.

17 "Four reales."

18 "We want two Anis del Toro."

19 "With water?"

20 "Do you want it with water?"

21 "I don't know," the girl said. "Is it good with water?"

22 "It's all right."

23 "You want them with water?" asked the woman.

24 "Yes, with water."

25 "It tastes like licorice," the girl said and put the glass down.

26 "That's the way with everything."

27 "Yes," said the girl. "Everything tastes of licorice. Especially all the things you've waited so long for, like absinthe."

28 "Oh, cut it out."

29 "You started it," the girl said. "I was being amused. I was having a fine time."

30 "Well, let's try and have a fine time."

31 "All right. I was trying. I said the mountains looked like white elephants. Wasn't that bright?"

32 "That was bright."

33 "I wanted to try this new drink. That's all we do, isn't it—look at things and try new drinks?"

34 "I guess so."

35 The girl looked across at the hills.

36 "They're lovely hills," she said. "They don't really look like white elephants. I just meant the coloring of their skin through the trees."

37 "Should we have another drink?"

38 "All right."

39 The warm wind blew the bead curtain against the table.

40 "The beer's nice and cool," the man said.

41 "It's lovely," the girl said.

42 "It's really an awfully simple operation, Jig," the man said. "It's not really an operation at all."

43 The girl looked at the ground the table legs rested on.

44 "I know you wouldn't mind it, Jig. It's really not anything. It's just to let the air in."

45 The girl did not say anything.

46 "I'll go with you and I'll stay with you all the time. They just let the air in and then it's all perfectly natural."

47 "Then what will we do afterward?"

48 "We'll be fine afterward. Just like we were before."

49 "What makes you think so?"

50 "That's the only thing that bothers us. It's the only thing that's made us unhappy."

51   The girl looked at the bead curtain, put her hand out and took hold of two of the strings of beads.

52   "And you think then we'll be all right and be happy."

53   "I know we will. You don't have to be afraid. I've known lots of people that have done it."

54   "So have I," said the girl. "And afterward they were all so happy."

55   "Well," the man said, "if you don't want to you don't have to. I wouldn't have you do it if you didn't want to. But I know it's perfectly simple."

56   "And you really want to?"

57   "I think it's the best thing to do. But I don't want you to do it if you don't really want to."

58   "And if I do it you'll be happy and things will be like they were and you'll love me?"

59   "I love you now. You know I love you."

60   "I know. But if I do it, then it will be nice again if I say things are like white elephants, and you'll like it?"

61   "I'll love it. I love it now but I just can't think about it. You know how I get when I worry."

62   "If I do it you won't ever worry?"

63   "I won't worry about that because it's perfectly simple."

64   "Then I'll do it. Because I don't care about me."

65   "What do you mean?"

66   "I don't care about me."

67   "Well, I care about you."

68   "Oh, yes. But I don't care about me. And I'll do it and then everything will be fine."

69   "I don't want you to do it if you feel that way."

70   The girl stood up and walked to the end of the station. Across, on the other side, were fields of grain and trees along the banks of the Ebro. Far away, beyond the river, were mountains. The shadow of a cloud moved across the field of grain and she saw the river through the trees.

71   "And we could have all this," she said. "And we could have everything and every day we make it more impossible."

72   "What did you say?"

73   "I said we could have everything."

74   "We can have everything."

75   "No, we can't."

76   "We can have the whole world."

77   "No, we can't."

78   "We can go everywhere."

79   "No, we can't. It isn't ours any more."

80   "It's ours."

81   "No, it isn't. And once they take it away, you never get it back."

82   "But they haven't taken it away."

83   "We'll wait and see."

84   "Come on back in the shade," he said. "You mustn't feel that way."

85   "I don't feel any way," the girl said. "I just know things."

86   "I don't want you to do anything that you don't want to do—"

87   "Nor that isn't good for me," she said. "I know. Could we have another beer?"

88   "All right. But you've got to realize—"

89   "I realize," the girl said. "Can't we maybe stop talking?"

90   They sat down at the table and the girl looked across at the hills on the dry side of the valley and the man looked at her and at the table.

91   "You've got to realize," he said, "that I don't want you to do it if you don't want to. I'm perfectly willing to go through with it if it means anything to you."

92   "Doesn't it mean anything to you? We could get along."

93   "Of course it does. But I don't want anybody but you. I don't want any one else. And I know it's perfectly simple."

94   "Yes, you know it's perfectly simple."

95   "It's all right for you to say that, but I do know it."

96   "Would you do something for me now?"

97   "I'd do anything for you."

98   "Would you please please please please please please please stop talking?"

99   He did not say anything but looked at the bags against the wall of the station. There were labels on them from all the hotels where they had spent nights.

100   "But I don't want you to," he said, "I don't care anything about it."

101   "I'll scream," the girl said.

102   The woman came out through the curtains with two glasses of beer and put them down on the damp felt pads. "The train comes in five minutes," she said.

103   "What did she say?" asked the girl.

104   "That the train is coming in five minutes."

105   The girl smiled brightly at the woman, to thank her.

106   "I'd better take the bags over to the other side of the station," the man said. She smiled at him.

107   "All right. Then come back and we'll finish the beer."

108   He picked up the two heavy bags and carried them around the station to the other tracks. He looked up the tracks but could not see the train. Coming back, he walked through the barroom, where people waiting for the train were drinking. He drank an Anis at the bar and looked at the people. They were all waiting reasonably for the train. He went out through the bead curtain. She was sitting at the table and smiled at him.

109   "Do you feel better?" he asked.

110   "I feel fine," she said. "There's nothing wrong with me. I feel fine."

Questions for Engagement, Response, and Analysis

1. What is the point of view in this story? What effect does it have on the reading experience?

2. In your Reader's Journal, sketch the setting, using details concerning the station and the landscapes on either side. What role does setting appear to have in the overall story?

3. As best you can with the details you are given, describe the couple's relationship at the beginning of the story.

4. How would you describe the woman's tone during the couple's conversation? How would you describe the man's tone? How do you interpret the woman's final words?

Crafting Arguments

1. Analyze the way each character views the situation.

2. In an essay, discuss how the relationship between the man and woman changes through the course of this very short story.

3. Write an essay in which you argue that the man is using persuasive techniques in an attempt to convince the woman to do something she does not want to do.

Jhumpa Lahiri (b. 1967)

Born in London to parents who were born and reared in India, Jhumpa Lahiri grew up in Rhode Island. She was educated at Barnard College, earning a B.A. in English, and at Boston College, receiving M.A.'s in English, Creative Writing, and Comparative Literature and the Arts, and a Ph.D. in Renaissance Studies. The New Yorker *published three of her stories in 1998, and her 1999 short story collection* Interpreter of Maladies, *from which this story is taken, received the 2000 Pulitzer Prize for Fiction. Lahiri's 2003 novel,* The Namesake, *like her stories, has been praised for its quiet language and realistic and compassionate portrayal of South Asians in the United States and their search for identity. A film version of* The Namesake *appeared in 2007. Lahiri's 2008 short story collection,* Unaccustomed Earth, *explores Hawthorne's suggestion in the "The Custom House" that people may benefit from putting down roots in "unaccustomed earth."*

A TEMPORARY MATTER   (1999)

1   The notice informed them that it was a temporary matter: for five days their electricity would be cut off for one hour, beginning at eight PM. A line had gone down in the last snowstorm, and the repairmen were going to take advantage of the milder evenings to set it right. The work would affect only the houses on the quiet tree-lined street, within walking distance of a row of brick-faced stores and a trolley stop, where Shoba and Shukumar had lived for three years.

2   "It's good of them to warn us," Shoba conceded after reading the notice aloud, more for her own benefit than Shukumar's. She let the strap of her leather satchel, plump with files, slip from her shoulders, and left it in the

hallway as she walked into the kitchen. She wore a navy blue poplin rain-coat over gray sweatpants and white sneakers, looking, at thirty-three, like the type of woman she'd once claimed she would never resemble.

3   She'd come from the gym. Her cranberry lipstick was visible only on the outer reaches of her mouth, and her eyeliner had left charcoal patches beneath her lower lashes. She used to look this way sometimes, Shukumar thought, on mornings after a party or a night at a bar, when she'd been too lazy to wash her face, too eager to collapse into his arms. She dropped a sheaf of mail on the table without a glance. Her eyes were still fixed on the notice in her other hand. "But they should do this sort of thing during the day."

4   "When I'm here, you mean," Shukumar said. He put a glass lid on a pot of lamb, adjusting it so only the slightest bit of steam could escape. Since January he'd been working at home, trying to complete the final chapters of his dissertation on agrarian revolts in India. "When do the repairs start?"

5   "It says March nineteenth. Is today the nineteenth?" Shoba walked over to the framed corkboard that hung on the wall by the fridge, bare except for a calendar of William Morris wallpaper patterns. She looked at it as if for the first time, studying the wallpaper pattern carefully on the top half before allowing her eyes to fall to the numbered grid on the bottom. A friend had sent the calendar in the mail as a Christmas gift, even though Shoba and Shukumar hadn't celebrated Christmas that year.

6   "Today then," Shoba announced. "You have a dentist appointment next Friday, by the way."

7   He ran his tongue over the tops of his teeth; he'd forgotten to brush them that morning. It wasn't the first time. He hadn't left the house at all that day, or the day before. The more Shoba stayed out, the more she began putting in extra hours at work and taking on additional projects, the more he wanted to stay in, not even leaving to get the mail, or to buy fruit or wine at the stores by the trolley stop.

8   Six months ago, in September, Shukumar was at an academic confer-ence in Baltimore when Shoba went into labor, three weeks before her due date. He hadn't wanted to go to the conference, but she had insisted; it was important to make contacts, and he would be entering the job mar-ket next year. She told him that she had his number at the hotel, and a copy of his schedule and flight numbers, and she had arranged with her friend Gillian for a ride to the hospital in the event of an emergency. When the cab pulled away that morning for the airport, Shoba stood waving good-bye in her robe, with one arm resting on the mound of her belly as if it were a perfectly natural part of her body.

9   Each time he thought of that moment, the last moment he saw Shoba pregnant, it was the cab he remembered most, a station wagon, painted red with blue lettering. It was cavernous compared to their own car. Although Shukumar was six feet tall, with hands too big ever to rest com-fortably in the pockets of his jeans, he felt dwarfed in the back seat. As the cab sped down Beacon Street, he imagined a day when he and Shoba

might need to buy a station wagon of their own, to cart their children back and forth from music lessons and dentist appointments. He imagined himself gripping the wheel, as Shoba turned around to hand the children juice boxes. Once, these images of parenthood had troubled Shukumar, adding to his anxiety that he was still a student at thirty-five. But that early autumn morning, the trees still heavy with bronze leaves, he welcomed the image for the first time.

10   A member of the staff had found him somehow among the identical convention rooms and handed him a stiff square of stationery. It was only a telephone number, but Shukumar knew it was the hospital. When he returned to Boston it was over. The baby had been born dead. Shoba was lying on a bed, asleep, in a private room so small there was barely enough space to stand beside her, in a wing of the hospital they hadn't been to on the tour for expectant parents. Her placenta had weakened and she'd had a cesarean, though not quickly enough. The doctor explained that these things happen. He smiled in the kindest way it was possible to smile at people known only professionally. Shoba would be back on her feet in a few weeks. There was nothing to indicate that she would not be able to have children in the future.

11   These days Shoba was always gone by the time Shukumar woke up. He would open his eyes and see the long black hairs she shed on her pillow and think of her, dressed, sipping her third cup of coffee already, in her office downtown, where she searched for typographical errors in textbooks and marked them, in a code she had once explained to him, with an assortment of colored pencils. She would do the same for his dissertation, she promised, when it was ready. He envied her the specificity of her task, so unlike the elusive nature of his. He was a mediocre student who had a facility for absorbing details without curiosity. Until September he had been diligent if not dedicated, summarizing chapters, outlining arguments on pads of yellow lined paper. But now he would lie in their bed until he grew bored, gazing at his side of the closet which Shoba always left partly open, at the row of the tweed jackets and corduroy trousers he would not have to choose from to teach his classes that semester. After the baby died it was too late to withdraw from his teaching duties. But his adviser had arranged things so that he had the spring semester to himself. Shukumar was in his sixth year of graduate school. "That and the summer should give you a good push," his adviser had said. "You should be able to wrap things up by next September."

12   But nothing was pushing Shukumar. Instead he thought of how he and Shoba had become experts at avoiding each other in their three-bedroom house, spending as much time on separate floors as possible. He thought of how he no longer looked forward to weekends, when she sat for hours on the sofa with her colored pencils and her files, so that he feared that putting on a record in his own house might be rude. He thought of how long it had been since she looked into his eyes and smiled, or whispered

his name on those rare occasions they still reached for each other's bodies before sleeping.

13   In the beginning he had believed that it would pass, that he and Shoba would get through it all somehow. She was only thirty-three. She was strong, on her feet again. But it wasn't a consolation. It was often nearly lunchtime when Shukumar would finally pull himself out of bed and head downstairs to the coffeepot, pouring out the extra bit Shoba left for him, along with an empty mug, on the countertop.

14   Shukumar gathered onion skins in his hands and let them drop into the garbage pail, on top of the ribbons of fat he'd trimmed from the lamb. He ran the water in the sink, soaking the knife and the cutting board, and rubbed a lemon half along his fingertips to get rid of the garlic smell, a trick he'd learned from Shoba. It was seven-thirty. Through the window he saw the sky, like soft black pitch. Uneven banks of snow still lined the sidewalks, though it was warm enough for people to walk about without hats or gloves. Nearly three feet had fallen in the last storm, so that for a week people had to walk single file, in narrow trenches. For a week that was Shukumar's excuse for not leaving the house. But now the trenches were widening, and water drained steadily into grates in the pavement.

15   "The lamb won't be done by eight," Shukumar said. "We may have to eat in the dark."

16   "We can light candles," Shoba suggested. She unclipped her hair, coiled neatly at her nape during the days, and pried the sneakers from her feet without untying them. "I'm going to shower before the lights go," she said, heading for the staircase. "I'll be down."

17   Shukumar moved her satchel and her sneakers to the side of the fridge. She wasn't this way before. She used to put her coat on a hanger, her sneakers in the closet, and she paid bills as soon as they came. But now she treated the house as if it were a hotel. The fact that the yellow chintz armchair in the living room clashed with the blue-and-maroon Turkish carpet no longer bothered her. On the enclosed porch at the back of the house, a crisp white bag still sat on the wicker chaise, filled with lace she had once planned to turn into curtains.

18   While Shoba showered, Shukumar went into the downstairs bathroom and found a new toothbrush in its box beneath the sink. The cheap, stiff bristles hurt his gums, and he spit some blood into the basin. The spare brush was one of many stored in a metal basket. Shoba had bought them once when they were on sale, in the event that a visitor decided, at the last minute, to spend the night.

19   It was typical of her. She was the type to prepare for surprises, good and bad. If she found a skirt or a purse she liked she bought two. She kept the bonuses from her job in a separate bank account in her name. It hadn't bothered him. His own mother had fallen to pieces when his father died, abandoning the house he grew up in and moving back to Calcutta, leaving Shukumar to settle it all. He liked that Shoba was different. It

astonished him, her capacity to think ahead. When she used to do the shopping, the pantry was always stocked with extra bottles of olive and corn oil, depending on whether they were cooking Italian or Indian. There were endless boxes of pasta in all shapes and colors, zippered sacks of basmati rice, whole sides of lambs and goats from the Muslim butchers at Haymarket, chopped up and frozen in endless plastic bags. Every other Saturday they wound through the maze of stalls Shukumar eventually knew by heart. He watched in disbelief as she bought more food, trailing behind her with canvas bags as she pushed through the crowd, arguing under the morning sun with boys too young to shave but already missing teeth, who twisted up brown paper bags of artichokes, plums, gingerroot, and yams, and dropped them on their scales, and tossed them to Shoba one by one. She didn't mind being jostled, even when she was pregnant. She was tall, and broad-shouldered, with hips that her obstetrician assured her were made for childbearing. During the drive back home, as the car curved along the Charles, they invariably marveled at how much food they'd bought.

20   It never went to waste. When friends dropped by, Shoba would throw together meals that appeared to have taken half a day to prepare, from things she had frozen and bottled, not cheap things in tins but peppers she had marinated herself with rosemary, and chutneys that she cooked on Sundays, stirring boiling pots of tomatoes and prunes. Her labeled mason jars lined the shelves of the kitchen, in endless sealed pyramids, enough, they'd agreed, to last for their grandchildren to taste. They'd eaten it all by now. Shukumar had been going through their supplies steadily, preparing meals for the two of them, measuring out cupfuls of rice, defrosting bags of meat day after day. He combed through her cookbooks every afternoon, following her penciled instructions to use two teaspoons of ground coriander seeds instead of one, or red lentils instead of yellow. Each of the recipes was dated, telling the first time they had eaten the dish together. April 2, cauliflower with fennel. January 14, chicken with almonds and sultanas. He had no memory of eating those meals, and yet there they were, recorded in her neat proofreader's hand. Shukumar enjoyed cooking now. It was the one thing that made him feel productive. If it weren't for him, he knew, Shoba would eat a bowl of cereal for her dinner.

21   Tonight, with no lights, they would have to eat together. For months now they'd served themselves from the stove, and he'd taken his plate into his study, letting the meal grow cold on his desk before shoving it into his mouth without pause, while Shoba took her plate to the living room and watched game shows, or proofread files with her arsenal of colored pencils at hand.

22   At some point in the evening she visited him. When he heard her approach he would put away his novel and begin typing sentences. She would rest her hands on his shoulders and stare with him into the blue glow of the computer screen. "Don't work too hard," she would say after

a minute or two, and head off to bed. It was the one time in the day she sought him out, and yet he'd come to dread it. He knew it was something she forced herself to do. She would look around the walls of the room, which they had decorated together last summer with a border or marching ducks and rabbits playing trumpets and drums. By the end of August there was a cherry crib under the window, a white changing table with mint-green knobs, and a rocking chair with checkered cushions. Shukumar had disassembled it all before bringing Shoba back from the hospital, scraping off the rabbits and ducks with a spatula. For some reason the room did not haunt him the way it haunted Shoba. In January, when he stopped working at his carrel in the library, he set up his desk there deliberately, partly because the room soothed him, and partly because it was a place Shoba avoided.

23   Shukumar returned to the kitchen and began to open drawers. He tried to locate a candle among the scissors, the eggbeaters and whisks, the mortar and pestle she'd bought in a bazaar in Calcutta, and used to pound garlic cloves and cardamom pods, back when she used to cook. He found a flashlight, but no batteries, and a half-empty box of birthday candles. Shoba had thrown him a surprise birthday party last May. One hundred and twenty people had crammed into the house—all the friends and the friends of friends they now systematically avoided. Bottles of vinho verde had nested in a bed of ice in the bathtub. Shoba was in her fifth month, drinking ginger ale from a martini glass. She had made a vanilla cream cake with custard and spun sugar. All night she kept Shukumar's long fingers linked with hers as they walked among the guests at the party.

24   Since September their only guest had been Shoba's mother. She came from Arizona and stayed with them for two months after Shoba returned from the hospital. She cooked dinner every night, drove herself to the supermarket, washed their clothes, put them away. She was a religious woman. She set up a small shrine, a framed picture of a lavender-faced goddess and a plate of marigold petals, on the bedside table in the guest room, and prayed twice a day for healthy grandchildren in the future. She was polite to Shukumar without being friendly. She folded his sweaters with an expertise she had learned from her job in a department store. She replaced a missing button on his winter coat and knit him a beige and brown scarf, presenting it to him without the least bit of ceremony, as if he had only dropped it and hadn't noticed. She never talked to him about Shoba; once, when he mentioned the baby's death, she looked up from her knitting, and said, "But you weren't even there."

25   It struck him as odd that there were no real candles in the house. That Shoba hadn't prepared for such an ordinary emergency. He looked now for something to put the birthday candles in and settled on the soil of a potted ivy that normally sat on the windowsill over the sink. Even though the plant was inches from the tap, the soil was so dry that he had to water

it first before the candles would stand straight. He pushed aside the things on the kitchen table, the piles of mail, the unread library books. He remembered their first meals there, when they were so thrilled to be married, to be living together in the same house at last, that they would just reach for each other foolishly, more eager to make love than to eat. He put down two embroidered place mats, a wedding gift from an uncle in Lucknow, and set out the plates and wineglasses they usually saved for guests. He put the ivy in the middle, the white-edged, star- shaped leaves girded by ten little candles. He switched on the digital clock radio and tuned it to a jazz station.

26 "What's all this?" Shoba said when she came downstairs. Her hair was wrapped in a thick white towel. She undid the towel and draped it over a chair, allowing her hair, damp and dark, to fall across her back. As she walked absently toward the stove she took out a few tangles with her fingers. She wore a clean pair of sweatpants, a T-shirt, an old flannel robe. Her stomach was flat again, her waist narrow before the flare of her hips, the belt of the robe tied in a floppy knot.

27 It was nearly eight. Shukumar put the rice on the table and the lentils from the night before into the microwave oven, punching the numbers on the timer.

28 "You made *rogan josh*," Shoba observed, looking through the glass lid at the bright paprika stew.

29 Shukumar took out a piece of lamb, pinching it quickly between his fingers so as not to scald himself. He prodded a larger piece with a serving spoon to make sure the meat slipped easily from the bone. "It's ready," he announced.

30 The microwave had just beeped when the lights went out, and the music disappeared.

31 "Perfect timing," Shoba said.

32 "All I could find were birthday candles." He lit up the ivy, keeping the rest of the candles and a book of matches by his plate.

33 "It doesn't matter," she said, running a finger along the stem of her wineglass. "It looks lovely."

34 In the dimness, he knew how she sat, a bit forward in her chair, ankles crossed against the lowest rung, left elbow on the table. During his search for the candles, Shukumar had found a bottle of wine in a crate he had thought was empty. He clamped the bottle between his knees while he turned in the corkscrew. He worried about spilling, and so he picked up the glasses and held them close to his lap while he filled them. They served themselves, stirring the rice with their forks, squinting as they extracted bay leaves and cloves from the stew. Every few minutes Shukumar lit a few more birthday candles and drove them into the soil of the pot.

35 "It's like India," Shoba said, watching him tend his makeshift candelabra. "Sometimes the current disappears for hours at a stretch. I once had to attend an entire rice ceremony in the dark. The baby just cried and cried. It must have been so hot."

36   Their baby had never cried, Shukumar considered. Their baby would never have a rice ceremony, even though Shoba had already made the guest list, and decided on which of her three brothers she was going to ask to feed the child its first taste of solid food, at six months if it was a boy, seven if it was a girl.

37   "Are you hot?" he asked her. He pushed the blazing ivy pot to the other end of the table, closer to the piles of books and mail, making it even more difficult for them to see each other. He was suddenly irritated that he couldn't go upstairs and sit in front of the computer.

38   "No. It's delicious," she said, tapping her plate with her fork. "It really is."

39   He refilled the wine in her glass. She thanked him.

40   They weren't like this before. Now he had to struggle to say something that interested her, something that made her look up from her plate, or from her proofreading files. Eventually he gave up trying to amuse her. He learned not to mind the silences.

41   "I remember during power failures at my grandmother's house, we all had to say something," Shoba continued. He could barely see her face, but from her tone he knew her eyes were narrowed, as if trying to focus on a distant object. It was a habit of hers.

42   "Like what?"

43   "I don't know. A little poem. A joke. A fact about the world. For some reason my relatives always wanted me to tell them the names of my friends in America. I don't know why the information was so interesting to them. The last time I saw my aunt she asked after four girls I went to elementary school with in Tucson. I barely remember them now."

44   Shukumar hadn't spent as much time in India as Shoba had. His parents, who settled in New Hampshire, used to go back without him. The first time he'd gone as an infant he'd nearly died of amoebic dysentery. His father, a nervous type, was afraid to take him again, in case something were to happen, and left him with his aunt and uncle in Concord. As a teenager he preferred sailing camp or scooping ice cream during the summers to going to Calcutta. It wasn't until after his father died, in his last year of college, that the country began to interest him, and he studied its history from course books as if it were any other subject. He wished now that he had his own childhood story of India.

45   "Let's do that," she said suddenly.

46   "Do what?"

47   "Say something to each other in the dark."

48   "Like what? I don't know any jokes."

49   "No, no jokes." She thought for a minute. "How about telling each other something we've never told before."

50   "I used to play this game in high school," Shukumar recalled. "When I got drunk."

51   "You're thinking of truth or dare. This is different. Okay, I'll start." She took a sip of wine. "The first time I was alone in your apartment, I looked in your address book to see if you'd written me in. I think we'd known each other two weeks."

52   "Where was I?"

53   "You went to answer the telephone in the other room. It was your mother, and I figured it would be a long call. I wanted to know if you'd promoted me from the margins of your newspaper."

54   "Had I?"

55   "No. But I didn't give up on you. Now it's your turn."

56   He couldn't think of anything, but Shoba was waiting for him to speak. She hadn't appeared so determined in months. What was there left to say to her? He thought back to their first meeting, four years earlier at a lecture hall in Cambridge, where a group of Bengali poets were giving a recital. They'd ended up side by side, on folding wooden chairs. Shukumar was soon bored; he was unable to decipher the literary diction, and couldn't join the rest of the audience as they sighed and nodded solemnly after certain phrases. Peering at the newspaper folded in his lap, he studied the temperatures of cities around the world. Ninety-one degrees in Singapore yesterday, fifty-one in Stockholm. When he turned his head to the left, he saw a woman next to him making a grocery list on the back of a folder, and was startled to find that she was beautiful.

57   "Okay," he said, remembering. "The first time we went out to dinner, to the Portuguese place, I forgot to tip the waiter. I went back the next morning, found out his name, left money with the manager."

58   "You went all the way back to Somerville just to tip a waiter?"

59   "I took a cab."

60   "Why did you forget to tip the waiter?"

61   The birthday candles had burned out, but he pictured her face clearly in the dark, the wide tilting eyes, the full grape-toned lips, the fall at age two from her high chair still visible as a comma on her chin. Each day, Shukumar noticed, her beauty, which had once overwhelmed him, seemed to fade. The cosmetics that had seemed superfluous were necessary now, not to improve her but to define her somehow.

62   "By the end of the meal I had a funny feeling that I might marry you," he said, admitting it to himself as well as to her for the first time. "It must have distracted me."

63   The next night Shoba came home earlier than usual. There was lamb left over from the evening before, and Shukumar heated it up so that they were able to eat by seven. He'd gone out that day, through the melting snow, and bought a packet of taper candles from the corner store, and batteries to fit the flashlight. He had the candles ready on the countertop, standing in brass holders shaped like lotuses, but they ate under the glow of the copper-shaded ceiling lamp that hung over the table.

64   When they had finished eating, Shukumar was surprised to see that Shoba was stacking her plate on top of his, and then carrying them over to the sink. He had assumed she would retreat to the living room, behind her barricade of files.

65   "Don't worry about the dishes," he said, taking them from her hands.

66   "It seems silly not to," she replied, pouring a drop of detergent onto a sponge. "It's nearly eight o'clock."

67   His heart quickened. All day Shukumar had looked forward to the lights going out. He thought about what Shoba had said the night before, about looking in his address book. It felt good to remember her as she was then, how bold yet nervous she'd been when they first met, how hopeful. They stood side by side at the sink, their reflections fitting together in the frame of the window. It made him shy, the way he felt the first time they stood together in a mirror. He couldn't recall the last time they'd been photographed. They had stopped attending parties, went nowhere together. The film in his camera still contained pictures of Shoba, in the yard, when she was pregnant.

68   After finishing the dishes, they leaned against the counter, drying their hands on either end of a towel. At eight o'clock the house went black. Shukumar lit the wicks of the candles, impressed by their long, steady flames.

69   "Let's sit outside," Shoba said. "I think it's warm still."

70   They each took a candle and sat down on the steps. It seemed strange to be sitting outside with patches of snow still on the ground. But everyone was out of their houses tonight, the air fresh enough to make people restless. Screen doors opened and closed. A small parade of neighbors passed by with flashlights.

71   "We're going to the bookstore to browse," a silver-haired man called out. He was walking with his wife, a thin woman in a windbreaker, and holding a dog on a leash. They were the Bradfords, and they had tucked a sympathy card into Shoba and Shukumar's mailbox back in September. "I hear they've got their power."

72   "They'd better," Shukumar said. "Or you'll be browsing in the dark."

73   The woman laughed, slipping her arm through the crook of her husband's elbow. "Want to join us?"

74   "No thanks," Shoba and Shukumar called out together. It surprised Shukumar that his words matched hers.

75   He wondered what Shoba would tell him in the dark. The worst possibilities had already run through his head. That she'd had an affair. That she didn't respect him for being thirty-five and still a student. That she blamed him for being in Baltimore the way her mother did. But he knew those things weren't true. She'd been faithful, as had he. She believed in him. It was she who had insisted he go to Baltimore. What didn't they know about each other? He knew she curled her fingers tightly when she slept, that her body twitched during bad dreams. He knew it was honeydew she favored over cantaloupe. He knew that when they returned from the hospital the first thing she did when she walked into the house was pick out objects of theirs and toss them into a pile in the hallway: books from the shelves, plants from the windowsills, paintings from walls, photos from tables, pots and pans that hung from the hooks over the stove. Shukumar had stepped out of her way, watching as she moved methodically from room to room. When she was satisfied, she stood there staring at the pile she'd made, her lips drawn back in such distaste that Shukumar had thought she would spit. Then she'd started to cry.

76   He began to feel cold as he sat there on the steps. He felt that he needed her to talk first, in order to reciprocate.

77   "That time when your mother came to visit us," she said finally. "When I said one night that I had to stay late at work, I went out with Gillian and had a martini."

78   He looked at her profile, the slender nose, the slightly masculine set of her jaw. He remembered that night well; eating with his mother, tired from teaching two classes back to back, wishing Shoba were there to say more of the right things because he came up with only the wrong ones. It had been twelve years since his father had died, and his mother had come to spend two weeks with him and Shoba, so they could honor his father's memory together. Each night his mother cooked something his father had liked, but she was too upset to eat the dishes herself, and her eyes would well up as Shoba stroked her hand. "It's so touching," Shoba had said to him at the time. Now he pictured Shoba with Gillian, in a bar with striped velvet sofas, the one they used to go to after the movies, making sure she got her extra olive, asking Gillian for a cigarette. He imagined her complaining, and Gillian sympathizing about visits from in-laws. It was Gillian who had driven Shoba to the hospital.

79   "Your turn," she said, stopping his thoughts.

80   At the end of their street Shukumar heard sounds of a drill and the electricians shouting over it. He looked at the darkened facades of the houses lining the street. Candles glowed in the windows of one. In spite of the warmth, smoke rose from the chimney.

81   "I cheated on my Oriental Civilization exam in college," he said. "It was my last semester, my last set of exams. My father had died a few months before. I could see the blue book of the guy next to me. He was an American guy, a maniac. He knew Urdu and Sanskrit. I couldn't remember if the verse we had to identify was an example of a *ghazal* or not. I looked at his answer and copied it down."

82   It had happened over fifteen years ago. He felt relief now, having told her.

83   She turned to him, looking not at his face, but at his shoes—old moccasins he wore as if they were slippers, the leather at the back permanently flattened. He wondered if it bothered her, what he'd said. She took his hand and pressed it. "You didn't have to tell me why you did it," she said, moving closer to him.

84   They sat together until nine o'clock, when the lights came on. They heard some people across the street clapping from their porch, and televisions being turned on. The Bradfords walked back down the street, eating ice-cream cones and waving. Shoba and Shukumar waved back. Then they stood up, his hand still in hers, and went inside.

85   Somehow, without saying anything, it had turned into this. Into an exchange of confessions—the little ways they'd hurt or disappointed each other, and themselves. The following day Shukumar thought for hours about what to say to her. He was torn between admitting that he

once ripped out a photo of a woman in one of the fashion magazines she used to subscribe to and carried it in his books for a week, or saying that he really hadn't lost the sweater-vest she bought him for their third wedding anniversary but had exchanged it for cash at Filene's, and that he had gotten drunk alone in the middle of the day at a hotel bar. For their first anniversary, Shoba had cooked a ten-course dinner just for him. The vest depressed him. "My wife gave me a sweater-vest for our anniversary," he complained to the bartender, his head heavy with cognac. "What do you expect?" the bartender had replied. "You're married."

86   As for the picture of the woman, he didn't know why he'd ripped it out. She wasn't as pretty as Shoba. She wore a white sequined dress, and had a sullen face and lean, mannish legs. Her bare arms were raised, her fists around her head, as if she were about to punch herself in the ears. It was an advertisement for stockings. Shoba had been pregnant at the time, her stomach suddenly immense, to the point where Shukumar no longer wanted to touch her. The first time he saw the picture he was lying in bed next to her, watching her as she read. When he noticed the magazine in the recycling pile he found the woman and tore out the page as carefully as he could. For about a week he allowed himself a glimpse each day. He felt an intense desire for the woman, but it was a desire that turned to disgust after a minute or two. It was the closest he'd come to infidelity.

87   He told Shoba about the sweater on the third night, the picture on the fourth. She said nothing as he spoke, expressed no protest or reproach. She simply listened, and then she took his hand, pressing it as she had before. On the third night, she told him that once after a lecture they'd attended, she let him speak to the chairman of his department without telling him that he had a dab of pâté on his chin. She'd been irritated with him for some reason, and so she'd let him go on and on, about securing his fellowship for the following semester, without putting a finger to her own chin as a signal. The fourth night, she said that she never liked the one poem he'd ever published in his life, in a literary magazine in Utah. He'd written the poem after meeting Shoba. She added that she found the poem sentimental.

88   Something happened when the house was dark. They were able to talk to each other again. The third night after supper they'd sat together on the sofa, and once it was dark he began kissing her awkwardly on her forehead and her face, and though it was dark he closed his eyes, and knew that she did, too. The fourth night they walked carefully upstairs, to bed, feeling together for the final step with their feet before the landing, and making love with a desperation they had forgotten. She wept without sound, and whispered his name, and traced his eyebrows with her finger in the dark. As he made love to her he wondered what he would say to her the next night, and what she would say, the thought of it exciting him. "Hold me," he said, "hold me in your arms." By the time the lights came back on downstairs, they'd fallen asleep.

89   The morning of the fifth night Shukumar found another notice from the electric company in the mailbox. The line had been repaired ahead of schedule, it said. He was disappointed. He had planned on making shrimp *malai* for Shoba, but when he arrived at the store he didn't feel like cooking anymore. It wasn't the same, he thought, knowing that the lights wouldn't go out. In the store the shrimp looked gray and thin. The coconut milk tin was dusty and overpriced. Still, he bought them, along with a beeswax candle and two bottles of wine.

90   She came home at seven-thirty. "I suppose this is the end of our game," he said when he saw her reading the notice.

91   She looked at him. "You can still light candles if you want." She hadn't been to the gym tonight. She wore a suit beneath the raincoat. Her makeup had been retouched recently.

92   When she went upstairs to change, Shukumar poured himself some wine and put on a record, a Thelonius Monk album he knew she liked.

93   When she came downstairs they ate together. She didn't thank him or compliment him. They simply ate in a darkened room, in the glow of a beeswax candle. They had survived a difficult time. They finished off the shrimp. They finished off the first bottle of wine and moved on to the second. They sat together until the candle had nearly burned away. She shifted in her chair, and Shukumar thought that she was about to say something. But instead she blew out the candle, stood up, turned on the light switch, and sat down again.

94   "Shouldn't we keep the lights off?" Shukumar asked.

95   She set her plate aside and clasped her hands on the table. "I want you to see my face when I tell you this," she said gently.

96   His heart began to pound. The day she told him she was pregnant, she had used the very same words, saying them in the same gentle way, turning off the basketball game he'd been watching on television. He hadn't been prepared then. Now he was.

97   Only he didn't want her to be pregnant again. He didn't want to have to pretend to be happy.

98   "I've been looking for an apartment and I've found one," she said, narrowing her eyes on something, it seemed, behind his left shoulder. It was nobody's fault, she continued. They'd been through enough. She needed some time alone. She had money saved up for a security deposit. The apartment was on Beacon Hill, so she could walk to work. She had signed the lease that night before coming home.

99   She wouldn't look at him, but he stared at her. It was obvious that she'd rehearsed the lines. All this time she'd been looking for an apartment, testing the water pressure, asking a Realtor if heat and hot water were included in the rent. It sickened Shukumar, knowing that she had spent these past evenings preparing for a life without him. He was relieved and yet he was sickened. This was what she'd been trying to tell him for the past four evenings. This was the point of her game.

100   Now it was his turn to speak. There was something he'd sworn he would never tell her, and for six months he had done his best to block it from his

mind. Before the ultrasound she had asked the doctor not to tell her the sex of their child, and Shukumar had agreed. She had wanted it to be a surprise.

101   Later, those few times they talked about what had happened, she said at least they'd been spared that knowledge. In a way she almost took pride in her decision, for it enabled her to seek refuge in a mystery. He knew that she assumed it was a mystery for him, too. He'd arrived too late from Baltimore—when it was all over and she was lying on the hospital bed. But he hadn't. He'd arrived early enough to see their baby, and to hold him before they cremated him. At first he had recoiled at the suggestion, but the doctor said holding the baby might help him with the process of grieving. Shoba was asleep. The baby had been cleaned off, his bulbous lids shut tight to the world.

102   "Our baby was a boy," he said. "His skin was more red than brown. He had black hair on his head. He weighed almost five pounds. His fingers were curled shut, just like yours in the night."

103   Shoba looked at him now, her face contorted with sorrow. He had cheated on a college exam, ripped a picture of a woman out of a magazine. He had returned a sweater and got drunk in the middle of the day instead. These were the things he had told her. He had held his son, who had known life only within her, against his chest in a darkened room in an unknown wing of the hospital. He had held him until a nurse knocked and took him away, and he promised himself that day that he would never tell Shoba, because he still loved her then, and it was the one thing in her life that she had wanted to be a surprise.

104   Shukumar stood up and stacked his plate on top of hers. He carried the plates to the sink, but instead of running the tap he looked out the window. Outside the evening was still warm, and the Bradfords were walking arm in arm. As he watched the couple the room went dark, and he spun around. Shoba had turned the lights off. She came back to the table and sat down, and after a moment Shukumar joined her. They wept together, for the things they now knew.

Questions for Engagement, Response, and Analysis

1. What event precipitated the alienation between Shoba and Shukumar? How and why has it affected each of them?

2. When Shoba decides that they each should tell the other something they've not told before, Shukumar wonders, "What was there left to say to her?" Why would he have nothing new to say? What does that reveal about his relationship to Shoba?

3. Why does Shukumar look forward to the lights' going out? Why are the revelations they make during the blackouts so meaningful and important to him? What, according to Shukumar, is "the point of this game"?

4. What is the point of view? How would the story differ if told from the point of view of the other spouse?

5. Why, when Shoba tells Shukumar that she has found an apartment, does he feel both sickened and relieved?

6. What does the last line, "They wept together for the things they now knew" mean for their relationship?

7. Explain the meaning of the title of this story.

Crafting Arguments

1. Write an essay in which you explain how the varied elements of Lahiri's style enable her to portray vivid emotional reactions.

2. In an essay, compare this couple's reaction to the death of their son to the reaction of Amy and her husband in Frost's "Home Burial."

POETRY

William Shakespeare (1564–1616)

The biography of William Shakespeare precedes Othello *in the Vulnerability Unit.*

SONNET 138 (1609)

When my love swears that she is made of truth,
I do believe her, though I know she lies,
That she might think me some untutor'd youth,
Unlearned in the world's false subtleties.
5   Thus vainly thinking that she thinks me young,
Although she knows my days are past the best,
Simply I credit her false-speaking tongue:
On both sides thus is simple truth supprest.
But wherefore says she not she is unjust?
10   And wherefore say not I that I am old?
O, love's best habit is in seeming trust,
And age in love loves not to have years told:
    Therefore I lie with her, and she with me,
    And in our faults by lies we flatter'd be.

Questions for Engagement, Response, and Analysis

1. Analyze Shakespeare's use of the three quatrains to describe the causes for the actions of the two lovers and of the couplet to present the effect.

Crafting Arguments

1. Using as a basis for your claims the puns on the word *lie*, write an essay analyzing the relationship between the narrator and his companion.

Andrew Marvell (1621–1678)

Andrew Marvell was a Puritan, a vocal advocate of personal freedom, and a member of the British Parliament. He, like John Donne, was one of the poets whom Samuel Johnson later called metaphysical. Marvell is known today for the exquisite craftsmanship of such poems as "The Garden," "To His Coy Mistress," and "An Horatian Ode upon Cromwell's Return from Ireland."

TO HIS COY MISTRESS   (1681)

Had we but world enough, and time,
This coyness, Lady, were no crime.
We would sit down, and think which way
To walk, and pass our long love's day.
5   Thou by the Indian Ganges' side
Shouldst rubies find: I by the tide
Of Humber would complain. I would
Love you ten years before the flood:
And you should, if you please, refuse
10 Till the conversion of the Jews.
My vegetable love should grow
Vaster than empires, and more slow.
An hundred years should go to praise
Thine eyes, and on thy forehead gaze.
15 Two hundred to adore each breast:
But thirty thousand to the rest.
An age at least to every part,
And the last age should show your heart:
For, Lady, you deserve this state;
20 Nor would I love at lower rate.
  But at my back I always hear
Time's wingèd chariot hurrying near:
And yonder all before us lie
Deserts of vast eternity.
25 Thy beauty shall no more be found;
Nor, in thy marble vault, shall sound
My echoing song: then worms shall try
That long-preserved virginity:
And your quaint honour turn to dust;
30 And into ashes all my lust.
The grave's a fine and private place,
But none, I think, do there embrace.
  Now, therefore, while the youthful hew
Sits on thy skin like morning dew,
35 And while thy willing soul transpires
At every pore with instant fires,
Now let us sport us while we may;
And now, like amorous birds of prey,
Rather at once our time devour,
40 Than languish in his slow-chapped power.
Let us roll all our strength, and all
Our sweetness, up into one ball:
And tear our pleasures with rough strife,

Thorough the iron gates of life.
45   Thus, though we cannot make our sun
Stand still, yet we will make him run.

Questions for Engagement, Response, and Analysis

1. How does the tone of the poem change from the first stanza to the second to the last?
2. Who is the speaker in the poem? Do you think he genuinely loves his listener, or is he just feeding her a line? Defend your answer.

Crafting Arguments

1. Define *carpe diem*, and explain how Marvell's narrator uses this concept to further his seduction.
2. Analyze and illustrate the persuasive techniques that the speaker uses.

Elizabeth Barrett Browning (1806–1861)

Elizabeth Barrett was famous as a well-educated and precocious poet. By the time Robert Browning fell in love with her, she had become a semi-invalid forbidden by her tyrannical father to marry. After Elizabeth and Robert eloped to Italy, her health improved. The depth of her love for her husband is beautifully illustrated by the Sonnets from the Portuguese *(1850), forty-four verses tracing the progress of her love for Robert, who called her his little Portuguese. "How Do I Love Thee?" is the most famous of these sonnets.*

SONNET 43   (1850)

How do I love thee? Let me count the ways.
I love thee to the depth and breadth and height
My soul can reach, when feeling out of sight
For the ends of Being and ideal Grace.
5   I love thee to the level of everyday's
Most quiet need, by sun and candlelight.
I love thee freely, as men strive for Right;
I love thee purely, as they turn from Praise.
I love thee with the passion put to use
10   In my old griefs, and with my childhood's faith.
I love thee with a love I seemed to lose
With my lost saints—I love thee with the breath,
Smiles, tears, of all my life!—and, if God choose,
I shall but love thee better after death.

Questions for Engagement, Response, and Analysis

1. How and why does Browning use this tightly controlled form to express boundless love?

2. According to this sonnet, what are the different types of love necessary for a marriage to last?

Crafting Arguments

1. Browning uses a series of metaphorical devices—**personification, metonymy**, and **synecdoche**—to describe her love. These are combined with poetic sound devices such as **anaphora, alliteration, assonance**, and **caesura**. Write an essay explaining how these devices, as well as the sonnet form, enable Browning to express great depths of feeling in the confined space of a sonnet.

2. Compare the depth of love described in this sonnet with the love portrayed in one of Robert Frost's poems.

Robert Browning (1812–1889)

The English poet Robert Browning is famous for his perfection of the dramatic monologue, for the depth and breadth of knowledge displayed in his poetry, for his ideas, and for his role in one of the most famous love stories of the nineteenth century. His wife, Elizabeth Barrett Browning, immortalized their love in her Sonnets from the Portuguese. *Robert Browning's most admired books,* Men and Women *(1855) and* Dramatis Personae *(1864), contain many of his frequently read poems. His book-length poem* The Ring and the Book *(1868), an account of a murder trial in seventeenth-century Rome, experiments with multiple points of view and is a precursor of the nonfiction novel.*

MY LAST DUCHESS (1842)

FERRARA

That's my last Duchess painted on the wall,
Looking as if she were alive. I call
That piece a wonder, now: Frà Pandolf's hands
Worked busily a day, and there she stands.
5   Will't please you sit and look at her? I said
"Frà Pandolf" by design, for never read
Strangers like you that pictured countenance,
The depth and passion of its earnest glance,
But to myself they turned (since none puts by
10   The curtain I have drawn for you, but I)

And seemed as they would ask me, if they durst,
How such a glance came there; so, not the first
Are you to turn and ask thus. Sir, 'twas not
Her husband's presence only, called that spot
15 Of joy into the Duchess' cheek: perhaps
Frà Pandolf chanced to say "Her mantle laps
Over my lady's wrist too much," or "Paint
Must never hope to reproduce the faint
Half-flush that dies along her throat": such stuff
20 Was courtesy, she thought, and cause enough
For calling up that spot of joy. She had
A heart—how shall I say?—too soon made glad,
Too easily impressed; she liked whate'er
She looked on, and her looks went everywhere.
25 Sir, 'twas all one! My favor at her breast,
The dropping of the daylight in the West,
The bough of cherries some officious fool
Broke in the orchard for her, the white mule
She rode with round the terrace—all and each
30 Would draw from her alike the approving speech,
Or blush, at least. She thanked men—good! but thanked
Somehow—I know not how—as if she ranked
My gift of a nine-hundred-years-old name
With anybody's gift. Who'd stoop to blame
35 This sort of trifling? Even had you skill
In speech—(which I have not)—to make your will
Quite clear to such an one, and say, "Just this
Or that in you disgusts me; here you miss,
Or there exceed the mark"—and if she let
40 Herself be lessoned so, nor plainly set
Her wits to yours, forsooth, and made excuse
—E'en then would be some stooping; and I choose
Never to stoop. Oh sir, she smiled, no doubt,
Whene'er I passed her; but who passed without
45 Much the same smile? This grew; I gave commands;
Then all smiles stopped together. There she stands
As if alive. Will't please you rise? We'll meet
The company below, then. I repeat,
The Count your master's known munificence
50 Is ample warrant that no just pretense
Of mine for dowry will be disallowed;
Though his fair daughter's self, as I avowed
At starting, is my object. Nay, we'll go
Together down, sir. Notice Neptune, though,
55 Taming a sea horse, thought a rarity,
Which Claus of Innsbruck cast in bronze for me!

Questions for Engagement, Response, and Analysis

1. What qualities of the deceased Duchess annoyed the Duke?
2. Why does the Duke want to make plain to this particular listener what he disliked about his deceased wife?
3. What do Ferrara's diction and sentence structure suggest about his character?

Crafting Arguments

1. This dramatic monologue in which the Duke describes his deceased wife reveals more about him than about her. Using his statements about her and about himself, write a character sketch of the Duke.

Maya Angelou (b. 1928)

Marguerita Johnson, who later changed her name to Maya Angelou, was born in St. Louis but spent her childhood in Stamps, Arkansas, and in California. Before she became famous as a writer, she tried a wide variety of occupations, from streetcar conductor to cook to dancer and singer. Angelou has written five autobiographical books, the first, I Know Why the Caged Bird Sings *(1969), being the most popular. In addition, she excels in many areas: writing essays, novels, and short fiction; acting and directing; and participating in civil-rights activities. Maya Angelou is a colorful and popular speaker. At Bill Clinton's presidential inauguration in January 1993, Angelou read her poem "On the Pulse of Morning," written for the occasion. Two of her recent books of essays are* A Song Flung Up from Heaven *(2002) and* Halleluyah! The Welcome Table *(2004), a book of reminiscences and recipes.*

PHENOMENAL WOMAN   (1978)

Pretty women wonder where my secret lies.
I'm not cute or built to suit a fashion model's size
But when I start to tell them,
They think I'm telling lies.
5   I say,
It's in the reach of my arms,
The span of my hips,
The stride of my step,
The curl of my lips.
10 I'm a woman
Phenomenally.
Phenomenal woman,

That's me.

I walk into a room
15   Just as cool as you please,
And to a man,
The fellows stand or
Fall down on their knees.
Then they swarm around me,
20   A hive of honey bees.
I say,
It's the fire in my eyes,
And the flash of my teeth,
The swing in my waist,
25   And the joy in my feet.
I'm a woman
Phenomenally.
Phenomenal woman,
That's me.

30   Men themselves have wondered
What they see in me.
They try so much
But they can't touch
My inner mystery.
35   When I try to show them,
They say they still can't see.
I say,
It's in the arch of my back,
The sun of my smile,
40   The ride of my breasts,
The grace of my style.
I'm a woman
Phenomenally,
Phenomenal woman,
45   That's me.

Now you understand
Just why my head's not bowed.
I don't shout or jump about
Or have to talk real loud.
50   When you see me passing,
It ought to make you proud.
I say,
It's in the click of my heels,
The bend of my hair,
55   the palm of my hand,

The need for my care.
'Cause I'm a woman
Phenomenally.
Phenomenal woman,
60   That's me.

Questions for Engagement, Response, and Analysis

1. Describe the narrator's personality.
2. What do others say is her attraction?
3. What does the narrator believe to be her secret?

Crafting Arguments

1. Examine Angelou's use of diction and syntax to create the tone and emphasize the theme of the poem.
2. Get a copy of the words to Helen Reddy's song "I Am Woman" or Christina Aguilera's "Beautiful" and compare these lyrics with Angelou's poem.

Marge Piercy (b. 1936)

Piercy was born in Detroit to an imaginative, active Jewish mother and a Presbyterian father. Leaving home at seventeen, she struggled through such jobs as secretary, switchboard operator, artist's model, and salesclerk while trying unsuccessfully to get her novels published. She and her second husband were active in the civil-rights movement and protested against the Vietnam War. She has recently become involved in the Jewish renewal movement. Seriously involved in political causes all of her life, Piercy considers herself a political writer. She has published more than thirty books, including novels, poetry, essays, and a play. Her most recent works are a poetry collection, Colors Passing Through Us *(2003), and the novel* Sex Wars *(2005).*

BARBIE DOLL   (1970)

This girlchild was born as usual
and presented dolls that did pee-pee
and miniature GE stoves and irons
and wee lipsticks the color of cherry candy.
5   Then in the magic of puberty, a classmate said:
You have a great big nose and fat legs.

She was healthy, tested intelligent,
possessed strong arms and back,
abundant sexual drive and manual dexterity.

10   She went to and fro apologizing.
      Everyone saw a fat nose on thick legs.

      She was advised to play coy,
      exhorted to come on hearty,
      exercise, diet, smile and wheedle.
15   Her good nature wore out
      like a fan belt.
      So she cut off her nose and her legs
      and offered them up.

      In the casket displayed on satin she lay
20   with the undertaker's cosmetics painted on,
      a turned-up putty nose,
      dressed in a pink and white nightie.
      Doesn't she look pretty? everyone said.
      Consummation at last.
25   To every woman a happy ending.

Questions for Engagement, Response, and Analysis

1. What is significant about the gifts "this girlchild" received?

2. Why is she not named but rather referred to generically as "this girl-child"?

3. Explain the irony of the last verse. At what stereotypes is Piercy's satire directed?

Crafting Arguments

1. In an essay, contrast the girlchild in "Barbie Doll" with the speaker in "Phenomenal Woman."

Janice Mirikitani (b. 1942)

Poet, teacher, and activist Janice Mirikitani is a third-generation Japanese American who was interned during World War II. After a painful childhood and an earlier marriage, Mirikitani married her minister from Glide Memorial United Methodist Church. Both her life and her poetry reflect her empathy with and support for those in need. She is president of the Glide Foundation, where she directs fifty programs that serve the poor and homeless of San Francisco. As a founding member of Third World Communications, Mirikitani has edited many works of struggling Japanese American writers. Her own works, which express her outrage against racism, sexism, and oppression of any kind, include several volumes of poetry: Awake in the River *(1978),* Shedding Silence *(1987), and* We the

Dangerous (1995). Much of her work shows a dichotomy between traditional Japanese customs and beliefs and a newer Japanese American or American identity.

BREAKING TRADITION (1987)

for my Daughter

My daughter denies she is like me,
Her secretive eyes avoid mine.
She reveals the hatreds of womanhood
already veiled behind music and smoke and telephones.
5   I want to tell her about the empty room
of myself.
This room we lock ourselves in
where whispers live like fungus,
giggles about small breasts and cellulite,
10   where we confine ourselves to jealousies,
bedridden by menstruation.
This waiting room where we feel our hands
are useless, dead speechless clamps
that need hospitals and forceps and kitchens
15   and plugs and ironing boards to make them useful.
I deny I am like my mother. I remember why:
She kept her room neat with silence,
defiance smothered in requirements to be otonashii,
passion and loudness wrapped in an obi,
20   her steps confined to ceremony,
the weight of her sacrifice she carried like
a foetus. Guilt passed on in our bones.
I want to break tradition—unlock this room
where women dress in the dark.
25   Discover the lies my mother told me.
The lies that we are small and powerless.
that our possibilities must be compressed
to the size of pearls, displayed only as
passive chokers, charms around our neck.
30   Break Tradition.
I want to tell my daughter of this room
of myself
filled with tears of violins,
the light in my hands,
35   poems about madness,
the music of yellow guitars—
sounds shaken from barbed wire and
goodbyes and miracles of survival.
This room of open window where daring ones escape.

40   My daughter denies she is like me
       her secretive eyes are walls of smoke
       and music and telephones,
       her pouting ruby lips, her skirts
       swaying to salsa, teena marie and the stones,
45   her thighs displayed in carnivals of color.
       I do not know the contents of her room.
     She mirrors my aging.
     She is breaking tradition.

Questions for Engagement, Response, and Analysis

1. To what is the speaker referring by "this room we lock ourselves in,"
   and "she kept her room neat with silence"? Why does she want to
   "unlock this room / where women dress in the dark"?
2. What are "the hatreds of womanhood" that the daughter expresses?
   What is the poem about other than the generation gap?
3. What is the speaker's tone? How is it achieved?
4. Mirikitani addresses the poem "for my daughter." How does she also
   use addresses to her daughter to structure the poem?

Crafting Arguments

1. Three generations are portrayed in the poem. Analyze the reasons
   each daughter denies being like her mother and the ways in which
   each claims to differ.

Julia Alvarez (b. 1950)

*Born in New York but raised in the Dominican Republic
until the age of ten, Julia Alvarez is a poet, an essayist, and
a novelist. She graduated from Abbot Academy in 1967 and
from Middlebury College in 1971 and received a Masters in
Creative Writing from Syracuse University in 1975. After
teaching English and Creative Writing at a variety of
schools and universities, she returned to Middlebury as a
professor and writer-in-residence. Alvarez's most famous
prose work,* How the Garcia Girls Lost Their Accents *(1991),
is a collection of fifteen connected stories about four girls
from the Dominican Republic who have moved to New York
and are seeking to find their identity between two very different cultures. Her novel* In the Time of Butterflies *(1994)
is based on the lives of the Mirabal sisters, who lost their
lives in the struggle to free the Dominican Republic from an
oppressive dictatorship. Alvarez published her first book of
poetry,* Homecoming, *in 1984. "Abbot Academy" is from her
2004 collection,* The Woman I Kept to Myself.*

ABBOT ACADEMY   (1984)

Mami sent me to Abbot where they tamed
wild girls—or so she'd heard—into ladies,
who knew to hold their skirts down in a breeze
and say "Excuse me" if compelled to speak;
5   ladies who married well, had lovely kids,
then inexplicably went mad and had
gin and tonics or the gardener for breakfast—
that part my mother hadn't heard; ladies
who learned to act like blondes even if they
10   were dark-haired, olive-skinned, spic-chicks like me.

And so that fall, with everything checked off
the master list—3 tea dresses, 2 pairs
of brown oxfords, white gloves, 4 cardigans—
I was deposited at Draper Hall
15   to have my edges rounded off, my roots
repotted in American soil.
I bit my nails, cracked my knuckles hard,
habits the handbook termed unladylike—
(*sins*, the nuns called them back at Catholic school).
20   I said my first prayer in months that night.
"Ay Dios," I begged, "help me survive this place."
And for the first time in America,
He listened: the next day for English class
I was assigned to Miss Ruth Stevenson
25   who closed the classroom door and said, "Ladies,
let's have ourselves a hell of a good time!"
And we did, reading Austen, Dickinson,
Eliot, Woolf, until we understood
we'd come to train—not tame—the wild girls
30   into the women who would run the world.

Questions for Engagement, Response, and Analysis

1. Who is the narrator in this poem? What are her mother's expectations
   of Abbot Academy? What are the narrator's? How are these expectations fulfilled?
2. What do the four writers whom Miss Stevenson's class studied have
   in common?

Crafting Arguments

1. Examine the lives and works of at least two of the four writers Alvarez
   mentions (Dickinson and Woolf are included in this textbook), and
   write an essay arguing that the lessons the narrator would learn from

them would indeed help to make her into one of "the women who
would run the world."

2. Compare the differing views of different generations in this poem with
those in Mirikitani's "Breaking Tradition."

Judith Ortiz Cofer (b. 1952)

Born in Puerto Rico, Judith Cofer spent part of her child-
hood in Paterson, New Jersey, where the library became an
oasis to her literary yearnings. In 1987, she published two
books of poetry, Terms of Survival *and* Reaching for the Main-
land, *and in 1990 she published personal essays and poems*
in Silent Dancing: A Partial Remembrance of a Puerto Rican
Childhood *and a novel,* The Line of the Sun. *Her 1993 book,*
The Latin Deli, *vividly reveals the dichotomy of a woman*
who is pulled between two cultures. An Island Like You: Stories of the Barrio *(1995) was a Best Book of the Year selec-*
tion of the American Library Association. Her recent works
include The Meaning of Consuelo *(2003),* A Love Story
Beginning in Spanish, *and* Call Me Maria *(2004), a novel for*
children. Cofer is presently a professor of English and
Creative Writing at the University of Georgia.

ANNIVERSARY   (1993)

Lying in bed late, you will sometimes read to me
about a past war that obsesses you;
about young men, like our brothers once,
who each year become more like our sons
5   because they died the year we met,
or the year we got married
or the year our child was born.
                              You read to me
about how they dragged their feet through a green maze
10 where they fell, again and again, victims
to an enemy wily enough to be the critter hero
of some nightmare folktale, with his booby traps
in the shape of human children, and his cities
under the earth; and how, even when they survived,
15 these boys left something behind
in the thick brush or muddy swamp where no one
can get it back—caught like a baseball cap
on a low-hanging tree branch.
                              And I think about you and me,
20 nineteen, angry, and in love, in that same year
when America broke out in violence
like a late-blooming adolescent, deep in a turmoil
it could neither understand nor control;

how we marched in the rough parade
25   decorated with the insignias of our rebellion:
peace symbols and scenes of Eden
embroidered on our torn and faded jeans,
necks heavy with beads we did not count on
for patience, singing *Revolution*—
30   a song we misconstrued for years.
                                 Death was a slogan
to shout about with raised fists or hang on banners.
But here we are,
listening more closely than ever to the old songs,
35   sung for new reasons by new voices. We are survivors
of an undeclared war someone might decide to remake
like a popular tune. Sometimes, in the dark, alarmed
by too deep a silence, I will lay my hand on your chest,
for the familiar, steady beat to which I have attuned
40   my breathing for so many years.

Questions for Engagement, Response, and Analysis

1. What war does the narrator describe? What clues identify the time and the war? In what ways are the details of the description universal?

2. Explain the statement "We are survivors / of an undeclared war someone might decide to remake / like a popular tune."

3. What kind of marriage do this husband and wife celebrate? What clues in the poem reveal the relationship they have? How does the description of the relationship help to create the tone?

Crafting Arguments

1. In an essay, show how Cofer uses the tone and the details of the anniversaries and of the relationship between the husband and wife to craft her powerful theme.

Rita Dove (b. 1952)

Rita Dove has the distinction of being both the first African American and the youngest poet laureate of the United States. Born in Akron, Ohio, Dove graduated summa cum laude with a B.A. from Miami University in 1973. In 1977 she received an M.F.A. from the University of Iowa. Her works include books of poetry, The Yellow House on the Corner *(1980),* Museum *(1983), and* Grace Notes *(1989); a collection of short stories,* Fifth Sunday *(1985); and a novel,* Through the Ivory Gate *(1992). Dove won the Pulitzer Prize in poetry in 1987 for her biographical poems about her maternal grandparents,* Thomas and Beulah *(1986). Her most recent book of poetry is* American Smooth *(2004).*

Currently she is Commonwealth Professor of English at the University of Virginia.

COURTSHIP   (1986)

FROM *THOMAS AND BEULAH*

1.

Fine evening may I have
the pleasure . . .
up and down the block
waiting—for what? A
5   magnolia breeze, someone
to trot out the stars?

But she won't set a foot
in his turtledove Nash,
it wasn't proper.
10   Her pleated skirt fans
softly, a circlet of arrows.

King of the Crawfish
in his yellow scarf,
mandolin belly pressed tight

15   to his hounds-tooth vest—
his wrist flicks for the pleats
all in a row, sighing . . .

2.

. . . so he wraps the yellow silk
still warm from his throat
20   around her shoulders. (He made
good money; he could buy another.)
A gnat flies
in his eye and she thinks
he's crying.

25   Then the parlor festooned
like a ship and Thomas
twirling his hat in his hands
wondering how did I get here.
China pugs guarding a fringed settee
30   where a father, half-Cherokee,
smokes and frowns.
I'll give her a good life—

what was he doing,
selling all for a song?
35   His heart fluttering shut
then slowly opening.

Questions for Engagement, Response, and Analysis

1. Describe the events on this night or several nights of courtship from Thomas' viewpoint.
2. The fifth verse changes the tone and location. What has taken place between the fourth and the fifth verse? Why does Thomas wonder how he got there?
3. Explain the meaning of the last two lines.

COURTSHIP, DILIGENCE   (1986)

A yellow scarf runs through his fingers
as if it were melting.
Thomas dabbing his brow.

And now his mandolin in a hurry
5   though the night, as they say,
is young,
though she is *getting on.*

Hush, the strings tinkle. *Pretty gal.*

Cigar-box music!
10   She'd much prefer a pianola
and scent in a sky-colored flask

Not that scarf, bright as butter.
Not his hands, cool as dimes.

Questions for Engagement, Response, and Analysis

1. Describe the events of this courtship from Beulah's point of view and then from Thomas'. How do they differ? What are some of the courting conventions employed by both Thomas and Beulah?
2. According to the poems, how much control do each of the two people in this courtship have over the interaction and over the result?
3. How does Dove create the tone in the poem? How does the tone reflect the feelings of the couple?
4. Explain the meaning of the last two lines of "Courtship, Diligence."

Crafting Arguments

1. In an essay, use evidence from both poems to describe the progress of this relationship and to support your interpretation of the theme.

DRAMA

Henrik Ibsen (1828–1906)

*Norwegian playwright Henrik Ibsen is often called the
father of modern drama. His early Romantic plays were
written in verse. In his plays, Ibsen established the tradition of realism in drama, of plays that attempt to imitate
life faithfully. His most famous realistic plays, A Doll's
House (1879), Ghosts (1881), and Hedda Gabler (1890), are
also described as theater of ideas or problem plays, those
that deal with social issues or depict social problems.*

*A Doll's House caused immediate controversy when it
was first produced, for it was performed before audiences
accustomed to viewing a wife as virtually the property of
her husband. When A Doll's House was followed by Ghosts,
a play about inherited venereal disease, Ibsen was forced to
leave Norway. Later, when praised by leaders of the Women's
Rights League for defending women's rights, Ibsen pointed
out that he was describing all humanity in his plays. One
reason for the continued popularity of A Doll's House is that
it raises questions about the rights of women and about the
gendered roles played by men and women.*

A DOLL'S HOUSE   (1879)

Characters

NORA HELMER

TORVALD HELMER,
a lawyer and Nora's husband

DR. RANK

MRS. LINDE

NILS KROGSTAD, a bank clerk

THE HELMERS' THREE SMALL CHILDREN

ANNA MARIE, the children's nurse

HELENE, a maid

A DELIVERY BOY

ACT 1

*A comfortable, tastefully but not expensively furnished room. There
is a door in the back right wall that leads to the front hallway of the
apartment. A doorway on the left leads to Torvald's study. Between
the doors is a piano. Halfway down the stage left wall is another
door and a window. Near the window is a round table, an armchair,
and a sofa. Halfway down the stage right wall is a door and near it
a porcelain stove, two armchairs, and a rocking chair. Between the*

stove and the door is a small table. There are engravings on the walls. There is an etagere with small china figures and objets d'art; a small bookcase with richly bound leather books. There is a carpet on the floor, a fire burning in the stove. It is a winter day.

A bell rings in the hallway. Shortly after, we hear the front door being opened. Nora enters. She is humming happily to herself. She is wearing street clothes and is carrying an armful of wrapped packages, which she puts down on the table. She leaves the hall door open. Through it we can see the delivery boy. He is holding a Christmas tree and a basket, which he hands to the maid who had let them in.

NORA: Hide the tree carefully, Helene. The children mustn't catch a glimpse of it until this evening. Not until we've decorated it. *(to the delivery boy)* How much do I owe you? *(taking out her purse)*

DELIVERY BOY: Fifty pence, ma'am.

NORA: There's a hundred. No, keep the change.

(The boy thanks her and leaves. Nora shuts the door and begins to take off her street clothes. She is laughing softly to herself. She takes a bag of macaroons from her pocket, eats a couple, then crosses quietly to Torvald's door and listens carefully.) Mmm! He's home. *(hums as she crosses to the table)*

TORVALD: *(from the study)* Is that my little lark twittering away out there?

10   NORA: *(opening packages)* Yes it is!

TORVALD: Is that my little squirrel fussing about in there?

NORA: Yes.

TORVALD: And when did she come home?

NORA: *(putting the bag of macaroons back in her pocket and wiping her mouth)* A minute ago. Do come in, Torvald. Come and see what I've bought.

TORVALD: I'm busy. *(soon after, he opens the door and looks in, pen in hand)* Did you say *bought*? All that? Has Madam Extravagant been throwing money away again?

NORA: But Torvald. . . .This year we should . . . oh, let ourselves go a little. It's the first Christmas we haven't had to count the pennies.

20   TORVALD: But we can't just go wasting money.

NORA: I know, Torvald. But we can waste just a little bit, can't we? Just a teeny bit? You've got a big salary now . . . you're going to make piles and piles of money.

TORVALD: Yes. After New Year's. And even then it's a full three months before the whole raise comes through.

NORA: Pah! We can borrow money until then.

TORVALD: Nora! *(taking her playfully by the ear)* There you go again! Scatterbrain! Look, what if I borrowed a thousand crowns today and

30   you spent the lot over Christmas, and then on New Year's eve a tile fell off the roof, hit me on the head, and I lay there . . .

NORA: *(hand on her mouth)* Oh! Don't say such things!

TORVALD: Yes, but what if it actually happened—then what?

NORA: If something so terrible happened, I wouldn't care if I had debts or not.

TORVALD: But what about the people I'd borrowed from?

NORA: Them? Who cares about them? I don't know them.

TORVALD: Nora, Nora! Just like a woman! I am serious. Nora, you know how I feel about all that. NO DEBTS. Never borrow! When a home
40   has its foundations built upon borrowing, upon debt, then some part of its freedom, some part of its beauty is lost. Until now we have fought a brave battle, the two of us. And we will keep on fighting for the little while that we still have to.

NORA: Whatever you say, Torvald. *(at the stove)*

TORVALD: *(following her)* My little songbird's wings must not droop. Come now. Don't be a sulky little squirrel. *(takes out his wallet)* Nora! Guess what I have here!

NORA: *(turning quickly)* Money!

TORVALD: There, *(handing her some money)* you see? I know how
50   expensive it is to run a house at Christmas.

NORA: Ten, twenty, thirty, forty. Oh thank you, Torvald. I can really take care of everything with this.

TORVALD: Well, you'll have to.

NORA: I promise. I promise. But come and see all that I bought. It was so cheap! Look, some new clothes for Ivar—and a little sword. A horsie and a trumpet for Robert. And a doll with its own little bed for Emmy. They're not very good, but she'll break them to bits in no time anyway. And I bought some dress material and some handkerchiefs for the maids. Old Anna Marie really deserves something better.

60   TORVALD: And what's in that package there?

NORA: No. Torvald, no! Not until tonight!

TORVALD: I see. But tell me, Little Miss Extravagant, what did you think of for yourself?

NORA: For me? Oh I don't want anything.

TORVALD: Of course you do. Now tell me, what would you really— within reason of course . . . like to have?

NORA: I honestly don't know. Although, Torvald . . .

TORVALD: Yes?

NORA: *(playing with the buttons on his jacket—but not looking at him)* If you really want to give me something—then maybe—maybe
70   you could . . .

TORVALD: Out with it, come on.

NORA: *(speaking fast)* You could give me money, Torvald. No more than you think you can spare. . . .Then . . . one of these days I'll buy something with it.

TORVALD: But Nora—

NORA: Oh please, Torvald my darling, please. Do that for me. And I could wrap the money in pretty gold paper and hang it on the tree. Wouldn't that be fun?

TORVALD: What do we call those little birds that fly through their money?

80 NORA: I know. Spendthrifts! Yes, yes, I know. But do what I ask, Torvald, and then I'll have time to make up my mind about what I need most. Now that's sensible of me, isn't it?

TORVALD: *(smiling)* Yes, very . . . if you could actually hang onto the money I gave you and then spend it on something for yourself. But it would go for the house—or something frivolous. And then I'd only have to give you some more.

NORA: Oh but Torvald—

TORVALD: Don't contradict me, Nora. Sweet Nora. . . . Spendthrifts *are* sweet, but they spend an awful lot of money. You have no idea what

90 it costs a man to feed these little birds.

NORA: How can you say that! I save everything I can!

TORVALD: *(laughing)* I know, I know. Everything you can. But that adds up to nothing at all!

NORA: *(humming again and with a smile of satisfaction)* Mmmm. . . . If only you knew . . . if only you knew . . . songbirds and squirrels have a lot of expenses.

TORVALD: You're so strange, so like your father. You can find money anywhere and everywhere. But the moment you have it, it runs right through your fingers. You have no idea what you've done with it. Ah

100 well, one takes you as you are. It runs in the blood. It's ingrained— these things are hereditary, Nora.

NORA: I wish I'd inherited many of Papa's qualities.

TORVALD: And I wish you to be only as you are, my songbird, my sweet little lark. Wait a minute . . . I have the feeling . . . no . . . how should I put it . . . ? You look very guilty about . . . something . . .

NORA: I do?

TORVALD: Yes, you do. Look me straight in the eye.

NORA: *(looking at him)* Well?

TORVALD: *(shaking his finger)* Little Miss Sweet Tooth! Have you been

110 running wild in town again today?

NORA: No. What gives you that idea?

TORVALD: Little Miss Sweet Tooth didn't make a little detour down to the patisserie?

NORA: No. Honestly, Torvald.

TORVALD: Not even a little nibble?

NORA: No. Not a bite.

TORVALD: Not even a macaroon or two . . . ?

NORA: No, Torvald. Honestly, I prom—

TORVALD: It's all right, it's all right . . . I'm only joking.

120 NORA: I could never deceive you.

TORVALD: I know, I know and you *have* given me your word. *(crossing to her)* Well, keep your little Christmas secrets to yourself. Nora, my darling, I'm sure they'll all be revealed this evening when we light the tree.

NORA: Did you remember to ask Dr. Rank?

TORVALD: No. But there is no need. It is assumed he will dine with us. All the same, I'll invite him when he stops by this morning. I've ordered some superb wine. Nora, you have no idea how much I'm looking forward to this evening.

130   NORA: Me too! And the children will be so happy, Torvald.

TORVALD: It's such a gratifying feeling . . . to have a safe, secure job . . . a comfortable salary. It . . . it gives one such . . . satisfaction.

NORA: Oh it's wonderful.

TORVALD: Remember last Christmas? For three whole weeks you locked yourself up in your room. Every night. Making flowers for the Christmas tree. Till well past midnight. And other decorations to surprise us. That was one of the most boring periods of my entire life.

NORA: I wasn't bored.

TORVALD: But the results, Nora, were . . . well . . . pretty pathetic.

140   NORA: Don't bring all that up again. I couldn't help it that the cat tore everything to shreds.

TORVALD: No, it wasn't your fault. You tried so hard to please us all. And that's what counts. But . . . I'm so glad the hard times are over.

NORA: Yes. It's really wonderful.

TORVALD: This year I don't have to sit in my study alone, boring myself to death. And you don't have to tire your precious eyes and your beautiful, delicate hands.

NORA: *(clapping her hands)* No. It's true . . . it's true, Torvald . . . . I don't have to, do I? I love to hear you say that. *(taking his*

150   *arm)* Now. Let me tell you what I think we should do. Right after Christmas—*(doorbell)* The doorbell! *(tidying the room)* Someone *would* have to come just now. What a bore!

TORVALD: I'm not at home to visitors, don't forget.

MAID: *(from the hallway)* Ma'am, a lady to see you—

NORA: All right, show her in.

MAID: *(to Torvald)* And the doctor's just come too.

TORVALD: Did he go to my study?

MAID: Yes sir, he did.

(Torvald goes back to his room. The maid ushers in Mrs. Linde, who is dressed in traveling clothes, then shuts the door.)

MRS. LINDE: *(hesitant and somewhat dejected)* Hello, Nora.

160   NORA: *(uncertainly)* Hello . . .

MRS. LINDE: You don't recognize me.

NORA: No. . . . I'm not sure. . . . Wait a minute. . . . It can't . . . Kristine! Is that you?

MRS. LINDE: Yes, it's me.

NORA: Kristine! To think I didn't recongnized you! But then . . . how could . . . ? *(in a quieter voice)* You've changed so much, Kristine.

MRS. LINDE: Yes. No doubt I have. It's been nine—ten long years.

NORA: Has it been that long since we last met? Yes. Yes, it has. For me these last eight years have been so truly happy. And so you've

170   come into town too now. Made the long trip in winter. That was
       brave of you.
MRS. LINDE: The ship got in this morning.
NORA: So you came to enjoy yourself here over Christmas. Of course.
       That's wonderful! And we will enjoy ourselves. But take your coat
       off. *(helps her)* There now, let's sit here and be warm and cozy by
       the stove. No, sit in the easy chair. I'll take the rocker. . . . *(takes her
       hands)* Yes, now you look like your old self again. It was just that
       first moment. But you look paler, Kristine . . . paler and maybe a lit-
       tle bit thinner.
180 MRS. LINDE: And much much older, Nora.
NORA: Yes . . . perhaps a bit older . . . a teeny weeny bit older. But not
       much. *(suddenly serious)* But how thoughtless of me to sit here
       chattering away. Sweet Kristine, I'm so sorry, so sorry.
MRS. LINDE: What do you mean?
NORA: You lost your husband.
MRS. LINDE: Yes, there years ago.
NORA: I knew about it, of course. I read it in the newspapers. Kristine, I
       meant to write. I really did . . . but I kept putting it off . . . there was
       always something . . .
190 MRS. LINDE: Nora, I understand completely.
NORA: No! . . . it was awful of me, Kristine. How much you must have
       suffered. And he left you nothing?
MRS. LINDE: Nothing.
NORA: And there were no children?
MRS. LINDE: No.
NORA: You have nothing then?
MRS. LINDE: Not even a sense of loss. Nothing to . . . touch me.
NORA: *(looking incredulously at her)* But Kristine, how could that be?
MRS. LINDE: *(smiling, tired, and smoothing her hair)* Oh, it happens
200   sometimes.
NORA: So completely alone. That must be impossibly hard for you. I
       have three beautiful children. You can't see them at the
       moment—they're out with the maid. But you must talk to me, tell
       me everything—
MRS. LINDE: No! No no, tell me about you.
NORA: No, you first. Today I don't want to be selfish. Today it's all about
       you. But there *is* something I must tell you about. Did you hear
       about the extra ordinary good luck we just had?
MRS. LINDE: No, tell me about it.
210 NORA: Torvald has been made manager of the bank. Isn't that
       extraordinary?
MRS. LINDE: Your husband? That's wonderful.
NORA: Isn't it? You can't always depend on an income if you're a lawyer
       . . . especially if you won't go near cases that aren't aboveboard and
       . . . and honorable. And of course Torvald would never do that . . .
       and I'm completely behind him on that. . . . Oh we are both

absolutely thrilled! He'll start work at the bank right after New
Year's, and he'll get a huge salary and lots of commissions. From
now on we can live quite differently . . . we can live as we want. Oh
220   Kristine, I feel so happy, so free. Won't it be wonderful to have piles
of money and not a care in the world?
MRS. LINDE: Well, it would be wonderful to have enough to meet one's
daily needs.
NORA: No! Not just daily needs. But piles and piles of money!
MRS. LINDE: *(smiling)* Nora! Nora! You still haven't come to your
senses! Even at school you just loved to spend money.
NORA: *(with a quiet laugh)* Yes, that's what Torvald still says about me.
(wagging her finger) But this "Nora! Nora!" isn't quite as silly as
you all think. We were in no position for me to waste any money. We
230   had to work. . . . Both of us.
MRS. LINDE: You too?
NORA: Yes. I did a few odd jobs—needlework, embroidery, crochet-
ing—that sort of thing *(casually)* . . . and some other things too.
You know that Torvald left his department when we got married? He
had no chance of being promoted in his firm. And of course he
needed to earn more money. That first year he drove himself so
hard. He took on all kinds of extra work. He didn't stop from morn-
ing to night. It took its toll. He became deathly ill. His doctors said it
was essential for him to go south and travel.
240   MRS. LINDE: Didn't you spend a whole year in Italy?
NORA: Yes. But it wasn't easy to get away. I'd just had the baby . . .
Ivar. But we *had* to go. Oh, it was a wonderful trip—and it saved
Torvald's life. But it was terrifyingly expensive, Kristine.
MRS. LINDE: I'm sure it was.
NORA: Four thousand eight hundred crowns. That is *so* much money!
MRS. LINDE: It's lucky you had it when you needed it.
NORA: Well, the fact is we got it from Papa.
MRS. LINDE: Oh, I see. That was about the time your father died.
NORA: Yes. Just about then. But I couldn't even go and see him. I
250   couldn't look after him. I had to stay here. I was expecting Ivar,
and I had to take care of my poor sick Torvald. Oh my dear Papa! I
never saw him again, Kristine. That was the worst time in all my
married life.
MRS. LINDE: I know how much you loved him. And then you went to
Italy?
NORA: Yes. We could afford it now, and the doctors insisted. We left a
month later.
MRS. LINDE: And your husband came home completely cured.
NORA: Fit as a fiddle.
260   MRS. LINDE: But . . . the doctor?
NORA: Who?

MRS. LINDE: The man who came in with me. . . . I thought the maid called him "doctor."

NORA: Oh! Yes, that's Dr. Rank. But he's not making a house call. He's our best friend. He stops by at least once a day. No, Torvald has been completely healthy since we got back, and the children are strong and fit. And so am I. *(she jumps up and claps her hands)* Oh dear God, Kristine, it's so wonderful to be alive and happy! But how awful of me—here I am talking only about myself. *(sitting on a stool next to Kristine and placing her arms across her knees)* Don't be angry with me. Tell me, is it true that you weren't in love with your husband? Why did you marry him then?

MRS. LINDE: Well, my mother was still alive, but she was an invalid confined to her bed—and I had my two younger brothers to look after. In all good conscience, I didn't think I could refuse his offer.

NORA: No, of course not. Was he a rich man?

MRS. LINDE: I think he was very well off . . . .But the business was precarious, Nora, and when he died everything fell apart and there was nothing left.

NORA: And then—?

MRS. LINDE: Well, I had to scratch out a living somehow. I had a little shop. I did a little teaching and whatever else I could find. The last three years have been work work work without a moment's rest. But it's over now, Nora. My poor mother doesn't need me any more. She's passed on. And my brothers—they've got jobs and are taking care of themselves.

NORA: You must feel so free. . . .

MRS. LINDE: Oh no . . . just unspeakably empty. I have nothing to live for. *(she gets up and is visibly anxious)* That's why I couldn't stand it any more in that godforsaken place. Perhaps it will be easier here to find something to do . . . to occupy my mind. If only I were lucky enough to find a steady job, maybe some office work.

NORA: But Kristine, that would be exhausting. You already look so tired. You'd be far better off going to a health spa.

MRS. LINDE: *(moving to the window)* I have no father to give me money to go traveling, Nora.

NORA: *(getting up)* Oh, don't be angry with me.

MRS. LINDE: *(going to her)* Oh Nora, don't *you* be angry with me! The worst part of this whole situation is all the bitterness stored up inside me. You've got no one to work *for* . . . and yet you've got to grab every opportunity. You have to live . . . and you become selfish. You know when you told me about all your good luck I was happier for myself than for you.

NORA: What do you mean? Oh I see. You thought perhaps Torvald could do something for you.

MRS. LINDE: Yes. Exactly.

NORA: And he will, Kristine. Just leave it to me. I'll bring it up so . . .
310 delicately. I'll find something nice to humor him with. Oh, I can't
wait to help you.

MRS. LINDE: You are so kind, Nora, to be thinking of me—more than
kind when you know so little about the hardships of this life.

NORA: I—? I know so little?

MRS. LINDE: *(smiling)* Well, good heavens, a little bit of needlework
and things like that. . . . Nora, you are still a child.

NORA: *(with a toss of her head, she begins to pace)* Well, you don't
have to act so superior.

MRS. LINDE: Oh?

320 NORA: You're like everybody else. You all think I'm incapable of doing
anything serious . . .

MRS. LINDE: Oh come . . .

NORA: . . . or of ever having to face the brutality of life . . .

MRS. LINDE: Nora, my dear. You've just been telling me what you've
been through.

NORA: Oh, that was nothing. I haven't told you about the really important thing.

MRS. LINDE: The important thing? What was that?

NORA: I'm not surprised that you look down on me, Kristine. But you
330 have no right to. You're proud of yourself because you worked so
hard all those years looking after your mother.

MRS. LINDE: I'm not looking down on anyone. But I *am* proud . . . of
course, and happy that I know I was able to make my mother's last
days a little more comfortable.

NORA: And you're proud of what you did for your brothers.

MRS. LINDE: I think I have every right to be.

NORA: I think so too. But let me tell you something, Kristine. I have
something to be proud of too.

MRS. LINDE: I'm sure you do. Tell me about it.

340 NORA: Keep your voice down. . . . Just think if Torvald were to hear us!
He mustn't find out. Not for the world. *No one* must find out. . . . No
one but you, Kristine.

MRS. LINDE: Find out what?

NORA: *(pulling her over to the sofa)* Come over here. Oh yes, I've got
something to be proud of. It was I who saved Torvald's life.

MRS. LINDE: Saved his life? How?

NORA: I told you about our trip to Italy. Well, Torvald would never have
recovered if we hadn't gone there.

MRS. LINDE: Yes. But your father gave you all the money. . . .

350 NORA: *(smiling)* That's what Torvald thinks, and so does everyone else,
but . . .

MRS. LINDE: What?

NORA: Papa never gave us a penny. I raised all the money myself.

MRS. LINDE: You? All that money?

NORA: Four thousand eight hundred crowns. What do you think of that?

MRS. LINDE: Nora! How could you do that? Did you win the lottery?

NORA: *(with a touch of contempt)* The lottery! Pah! How could I be proud of that?

360 MRS. LINDE: Where did you get it then?

NORA: *(smiling and then humming a little tune)* Aha! Tum tee tum.

MRS. LINDE: Well, you couldn't have borrowed it.

NORA: Oh, why not?

MRS. LINDE: Because it's not possible for a wife to borrow money without her husband's consent.

NORA: *(tossing her head)* Oh, that's not true. . . . Not when a wife has a little talent for business. . . . A wife who knows how to get things done.

MRS. LINDE: But Nora, I don't see how . . .

370 NORA: No, there's no reason you should. Anyway, I never said anything about *borrowing* the money. There are all kinds of ways I could have got my hands on it. *(stretching back on the sofa)* I could have gotten it from some admirer—after all, I am rather attractive. . . .

MRS. LINDE: Please be serious.

NORA: You really are dying to find out, aren't you, Kristine?

MRS. LINDE: Nora, my dear, listen. You haven't done anything . . . that you might regret?

NORA: How could I regret saving my husband's life?

MRS. LINDE: You might regret that you did something behind his back.

380 NORA: But I couldn't possibly tell him. Good heavens! Can't you see? It would have been terrible if he had found out how sick he really was. The doctors came to *me* and told *me* that his life was in danger . . . he would only survive if I took him to the South. Well, of course I tried coaxing him to go at first. I told him it would be so nice for me to take a holiday abroad—like other young wives. I tried everything. I cried. I begged. I told him that he had a duty to think of my . . . condition. . . . That he had to be a sweetheart and do what I asked. I dropped hints . . . oh . . . that he could easily borrow the money. Kristine, he nearly exploded in anger. He accused me of being frivo-
390 lous. He said it was his duty as a husband not to give in to what I think he called my "little whims and daydreams." So I thought to myself, "All right, but your life is going to be saved somehow." Then I thought of a way to do it.

MRS. LINDE: But . . . but your father must have told him that you didn't get the money from *him*.

NORA: No—it was just about then that Papa died. I had always intended to tell him and ask him to keep it a secret. But he was so sick . . . and in the end, well, unfortunately I didn't need to tell him.

MRS. LINDE: And you—you've never told your husband?

400   NORA: Good heavens, no! How could I? He has such strict rules about
these sorts of things. And, well, like most men, Torvald has his pride.
He'd feel humiliated—hurt, even—if he thought he was indebted to
me in any way. It would spoil everything. This lovely, happy home
would never be the same.

MRS. LINDE: Aren't you ever going to tell him?

NORA: *(smiling and thoughtful)* Well, maybe someday. But not for a
long time. When I'm no longer pretty. No, don't laugh, what I mean is
. . . when Torvald doesn't love me as much as he does now. When he
no longer enjoys watching me dancing and dressing up and reciting
410   little poems. It might be a good idea to have that up my sleeve. . . .
(breaking off) But that's all nonsense. That time will never come.
So? Kristine, what do you think of my great secret? I'm not so useless
after all? And it hasn't been easy, I can tell you. It's a huge worry to
have to meet your obligations on time. In the business world there
are things called quarterly payments and installments. They're always
so terribly hard to pay on time. So whenever I could, I've scraped
together a little bit here, a little bit there. There wasn't much I could
save out of the housekeeping money. Torvald has to live a comfortable life, and the children have to look nice. I didn't think I should
420   touch the money I'd set aside for my little sweethearts.

MRS. LINDE: So it all had to come out of your allowance? Oh poor Nora!

NORA: Of course it did. After all, this was my choice. So if Torvald gave
me money for a new dress or something, I never spent more than
half. I bought the simplest, cheapest things. Thank heavens I look
good in almost anything. So . . . Torvald never even noticed. But,
Kristine, it hasn't been easy. Isn't it nice to be beautifully dressed?

MRS. LINDE: Yes, it is.

NORA: And I found other ways of making money. Last winter I was very
lucky. I got a lot of copying to do, and I locked myself away and sat
430   there writing—often till after midnight. Oh, sometimes I got so tired.
But, you know, it was so much fun sitting there, working, earning
money. It almost felt like being a man.

MRS. LINDE: How much have you been able to pay off?

NORA: Well, I don't exactly know. It's difficult with something like that
to know how much you owe. I know this much . . . every penny I've
made, scraped together, I've paid. Oh God, sometimes I've been at
my wit's end. *(she smiles)* I used to sit here and think of some rich
old man who'd fallen in love with me . . . and . . .

MRS. LINDE: Who? Who was that?

440   NORA: Wait . . . and that he died and that in his will in huge letters it
said, "All my money is to go to the beautiful Nora Helmer, cash in
hand."

MRS. LINDE: But Nora . . . who is this man?

NORA: Oh good heavens, don't you understand? There's no "old man." I
just sat here and imagined him . . . oh so many times. I had nowhere

to go, nowhere to look for money. But that's all done with now. That stupid old man can stay where he is. I don't care. He's gone and the will is gone. My troubles are over. *(she jumps up)* Oh Kristine, just think . . . nothing to worry about anymore, no more! I can laugh and
450   play with the children. I can buy all the new modern things for the house—which Torvald loves. And soon it will be spring. Blue skies will come back, maybe we'll go away for a little while, maybe we'll see the sea again. Oh, isn't it wonderful to be happy and full of life? *(doorbell rings in the hallway)*

MRS. LINDE: *(getting up)* That's the door—perhaps I should go. . . .

NORA: No, stay. It's for Torvald. They won't come in here.

MAID: *(at door)* Excuse me, there's someone to see the lawyer.

NORA: The bank manager.

MAID: Yes, the bank manager. But I didn't know . . . since the doctor's with him.

460 NORA: Who is it?

KROGSTAD: *(in doorway)* It's me, Mrs. Helmer.

(Mrs. Linde is startled, collects herself, turns to window)

NORA: *(very tense and in a low voice)* What is it? Why do you want to see my husband?

KROGSTAD: Bank business. In a way. I have a small job in savings at the bank, and I've heard that your husband is to be the new manager, so . . .

NORA: So it's only . . .

KROGSTAD: Only business, Mrs. Helmer, boring business. Nothing else whatsoever.

470 NORA: Well, he is in his study. *(She gives a brief bow and shuts the door. Then she tends to the stove.)*

MRS. LINDE: Nora, who was that?

NORA: His name is Krogstad. He's a lawyer.

MRS. LINDE: So, it *was* him. . . .

NORA: You know him?

MRS. LINDE: I used to . . . years ago. He worked in a lawyer's office in my hometown.

NORA: Yes, he did.

MRS. LINDE: He's changed.

NORA: He had a very unhappy marriage.

480 MRS. LINDE: Then he's a widower now?

NORA: Yes, with lots of children. *(she closes the door of the stove and shifts her rocking chair)* There, that should burn well now.

MRS. LINDE: I hear he's involved in all kinds of business deals.

NORA: Really? Well you may have heard right. I don't know anything about . . . But let's stop talking about business . . . it's so boring.

(Dr. Rank comes out of Torvald's study)

DR. RANK: *(in doorway)* No no, my dear man. I don't want to be in your way. And anyway, I'd like to see your wife for a while. *(he shuts the door and notices Mrs. Linde)* Oh, I beg your pardon. I seem to be in the way here too.

490 NORA: Of course you're not! Dr. Rank—Mrs. Linde.

DR. RANK: I keep on hearing that name in this house! Didn't I pass you on the stairs on the way up?

MRS. LINDE: Yes. I don't like stairs. I have to go very slowly.

DR. RANK: You're not feeling well?

MRS. LINDE: Just tired, I think. I've been working too hard.

DR. RANK: That's all? So you've come to town for a rest? Lots of parties, eh?

MRS. LINDE: I've come to look for work.

DR. RANK: Not a very clever cure for exhaustion.

500 MRS. LINDE: One has to live, Doctor.

DR. RANK: Yes, current opinion seems to be in favor of it.

NORA: Now, Dr. Rank, you want to live as much as anybody.

DR. RANK: Indeed I do. However terrible I may actually feel, I want to prolong the agony. For as long as possible. My patients all seem to have the same idea. And it even applies to those whose sickness is moral. At this moment there is a man in there with Helmer who's a moral cripple.

MRS. LINDE: *(softly)* Ahhh.

NORA: Who do you mean?

510 DR. RANK: Oh, you wouldn't know him . . . he's a lawyer by the name of Krogstad. He's a thoroughly rotten human being. But the first words out of his mouth—as if it were important—"Oh, but I have to live."

NORA: Oh, what did he want to see Torvald about?

DR. RANK: I've no idea. I think he said something about the bank.

NORA: I didn't know that Krog . . . the lawyer had anything to do with the bank.

DR. RANK: Yes, he has some sort of job there. *(to Mrs. Linde)* I don't know if the same thing happens in your town, but here there are people who go around sniffing out moral corruption, and when

520 they've found it they *reward* the owner with a well-paid job—just so they can keep an eye on him. An honest man will find himself left out in the cold.

MRS. LINDE: Well, perhaps the sick do need looking after.

DR. RANK: *(with a shrug of his shoulders)* There you are, you see. That's the sort of opinion that's turning society into a home for the diseased.

NORA: *(She has been deep in her own thoughts. She suddenly gives a quiet chuckle and claps her hands.)*

DR. RANK: Why do you laugh at what I said? Do you really understand what society means?

NORA: Oh, what do I care about your boring old society? I was
530   laughing about something else, something very funny. Tell me,
Dr. Rank, do all the people who work at the bank have to report
to Torvald now?

DR. RANK: Do you find that so "very funny"?

NORA: *(smiling and humming)* Ah . . . that's my business. *(walking
around the room)* Well, yes, it really is very funny to think that we—
that Torvald has so much power over so many people. *(taking the
paper bag from her pocket)* Dr. Rank, would you like a macaroon?

DR. RANK: Macaroons? Well! I thought they were forbidden in this
house.

540   NORA: They are. But Kristine gave these to me.

MRS. LINDE: *(somewhat frightened)* What? I . . . I . . .

NORA: Nothing to be frightened of. You didn't know that Torvald had
forbidden them. The fact is, he's afraid they will ruin my teeth. But
. . . pah . . . once in a while . . . that's all right, isn't it, Dr. Rank?
(putting one in his mouth) Here! Have one. And one for you, Kristine. And I'll have one too . . . just a teeny one. No more than two!
(walking about again) Oh I'm *so* happy! There's just one thing
more that I would *love* to do.

DR. RANK: And what is that?

550   NORA: Something I've been *longing* to say in front of Torvald.

DR. RANK: Why can't you say it?

NORA: Oh, I couldn't . . . it's very bad.

MRS. LINDE: Bad?

DR. RANK: Then you'd better not . . . though perhaps in front of *us*?
What is it that you'd *love* to say in front of Torvald?

NORA: I'd love to say—Well, I'll be damned!

DR. RANK: You must be mad!

MRS. LINDE: Nora! My dear . . .

DR. RANK: Well, go ahead! . . . he's coming out.

560   NORA: *(hiding the macaroons)* Sh! Sh! Sh!

*(Torvald comes out with his coat over his arm and his hat in his
hand)*

NORA: *(crossing to him)* So. Torvald, my dear, you got rid of him?

TORVALD: Yes. He's just left.

NORA: Let me introduce you—this is Kristine. She just came into town.

TORVALD: Kristine . . . ? I beg your pardon . . . I don't remember . . .

NORA: Mrs. Linde, dear. Kristine Linde.

TORVALD: Oh yes. You and my wife were at school together, weren't
you?

MRS. LINDE: Yes. That's when we met.

NORA: Just think, she came all this way to see you!

570   TORVALD: To see me?

NORA: Kristine is extremely good at office work. And she really wants to work for a man who knows what he's doing so she can perfect her skills.

TORVALD: That's a wise choice, Mrs. Linde.

NORA: So when she heard you'd been made manager of the bank— there was a telegram or something—she came here as quickly as she could. You'll be able to do something for Kristine, won't you, Torvald, for my sake?

TORVALD: Well, it's not impossible. . . . I presume you are a widow, Mrs.
580   Linde?

MRS. LINDE: Yes.

TORVALD: And you've had some experience in accountancy?

MRS. LINDE: Yes. A fair amount.

TORVALD: Then it's more than likely I can find a position for you.

NORA: *(clapping her hands)* There you are. Didn't I tell you?

TORVALD: You came at the right moment, Mrs. Linde.

MRS. LINDE: How can I ever thank you?

TORVALD: There's no need . . . *(putting on his overcoat)* But now you must excuse me . . .

590   DR. RANK: Wait a moment. I'll come with you. *(getting his fur coat from the hall and warming it by the stove)*

NORA: Come back soon, Torvald my dear.

TORVALD: I won't be more than an hour.

NORA: Are you going too, Kristine?

MRS. LINDE: *(putting on her coat)* Yes. I must go. I have to find a room.

TORVALD: Then perhaps we can all walk down the street together.

NORA: *(helping her)* It's such a shame that we don't have more room . . . but we couldn't possibly—

MRS. LINDE: Don't even think of it! Goodbye, my dear Nora. And thank you.

600   NORA: Goodbye for now—you'll come back this evening, won't you? And you too, Dr. Rank. What? "If you feel up to it"? Of course you will. Wrap yourself up warmly.

(They all go out into the hallway still talking. Then the children's voices are heard on the stairs.)

NORA: Here they are. Here they are!! *(She runs to open the door. Anna Marie, the Nurse, comes in with the children.)* Come on in! Come in! *(she bends down and kisses them)* Oh, my little sweethearts! Look at them, Kristine, aren't they darling?

DR. RANK: Let's not stand here in the draft.

TORVALD: Come along, Mrs. Linde. Only a mother could stand to be here now!

(They go down the stairs. The children, the Nurse, and Nora come back into the room.)

610   NORA: Oh, you look so nice and healthy. Pink cheeks—like apples! . . .
       no, like roses! *(the children chatter through the following)* Did you
       have a good time? Oh that's good! You gave Emmy and Bob a ride on
       your sled? Both of them? At the same time? Oh my goodness! You're
       such a big boy, Ivar. Let me take her for a moment, Anna, my little
       baby doll! *(taking the baby from the Nurse and dancing with her)*
       Yes. Mummy will dance with Bobby too! What? You played snow-
       balls? Oh, I wish I'd been there. Leave them, Nanny. I'll take their
       things off . . . let me do it . . . it's such fun. You go off now, Anna
       Marie, you look half frozen. There's some hot coffee on the stove in
620   there. *(The Nurse goes into the room on the left. Nora takes off the
       children's outdoor clothes, throwing them on the floor. They keep
       talking to her all at once.)* What? A big doggie ran after you? But he
       didn't bite you. No, big doggies don't bite little doll babies . . . Ivar!
       No! Don't open the parcels. What's inside? Wouldn't you like to
       know! Oh no, it's nothing nice at all! You want to play a game? What
       do you want to play? Hide-and-seek? Yes. Let's play hide-and-seek.
       Bob, you hide first. Me? All right, I'll go first.

       *(The children and Nora play the game both in the living room and
       in the room next to it. They are screaming with laughter. Nora hides
       under the table. The children run about looking but can't find her.
       Then the sound of her muffled laughter makes them run to the table
       and lift the cloth and they see her. Lots of shouting. She comes out
       on all fours trying to mock-frighten them. More shouts. There has
       been a knocking at the front door. No one has noticed. The door half
       opens. Krogstad is standing there waiting as the game continues.)*

       KROGSTAD: Excuse me, Mrs. Helmer . . .
       NORA: *(stifles a cry and starts to get up)* Oh! What do you want?
       KROGSTAD: I'm sorry . . . but the front door was open. Perhaps some-
630   one forgot to shut it.
       NORA: *(rising)* My husband is out, Mr. Krogstad.
       KROGSTAD: I know.
       NORA: What do you want then?
       KROGSTAD: A word with you.
       NORA: Me! *(to the children, gently)* Go in and see Nanny. What? No.
       The strange man won't hurt mummy . . . as soon as he's gone we'll
       finish our game. *(She takes the children into the other room and
       shuts the door. She is tense and wary.)* You want to see me?
       KROGSTAD: Yes, I do.
640   NORA: Today? But it's not the first of the month yet. . . .
       KROGSTAD: No. It's Christmas Eve. And it's up to you whether you have
       a merry Christmas or not.
       NORA: What do you want? I can't spare anything today. . . .
       KROGSTAD: We'll talk about that later. This is about something else.
       Perhaps you can spare me a moment?

NORA: Well . . . yes . . . I can . . . but . . .

KROGSTAD: Good. I was sitting in Olsen's restaurant and saw your husband going down the street . . .

NORA: Well?

650 KROGSTAD: With a lady.

NORA: So . . . ?

KROGSTAD: May I be so bold as to ask if it was a Mrs. Linde?

NORA: It was.

KROGSTAD: She just arrived in town?

NORA: Yes. Today.

KROGSTAD: She's a good friend of yours?

NORA: Yes, she is. But I don't see . . .

KROGSTAD: I knew her too. Once upon a time.

NORA: Yes. I know.

660 KROGSTAD: Oh? You know about it? I thought so. In that case I can ask
you straight out: Is Mrs. Linde going to get a job at the bank?

NORA: How dare you question me, Mr. Krogstad. . . . You, one of my
husband's subordinates. But since you ask I will tell you. Yes, Mrs.
Linde is going to work at the bank. And it was I who recommended
her, Mr. Krogstad. Now you know.

KROGSTAD: Well, that's what I suspected.

NORA: *(pacing)* So. . . . It seems that I have a little influence. Just
because one is a woman doesn't necessarily mean—and a subordinate, Mr. Krogstad, should be careful not to cross anyone who has . . .

670 well . . .

KROGSTAD: Influence?

NORA: Exactly.

KROGSTAD: *(changing his tone of voice)* Mrs. Helmer, I expect you will
be good enough to use your influence on my behalf.

NORA: What do you mean?

KROGSTAD: That you will be kind enough to see to it that I don't lose my
subordinate position at the bank.

NORA: What do you mean? Who is proposing to take it away from you?

KROGSTAD: Oh, you don't have to pretend you don't know. I completely

680 understand. . . . Your friend is not particularly keen to come into
contact with me again. And I quite understand whom I'd have to
thank for being fired.

NORA: But I assure you . . .

KROGSTAD: I'm sure you do. But to come to the point. I think it's time
for you to use your influence to make sure that doesn't happen.

NORA: But, Mr. Krogstad! I have no influence!

KROGSTAD: You don't? I thought you just said . . .

NORA: Well, naturally I didn't intend you to think *that's* what I meant.
Me? Why would you think that I have any influence of that kind on

690 my husband?

KROGSTAD: Oh, I've known your husband since we were students. I
don't think he's less . . . susceptible . . . than other husbands.

NORA: If you continue to speak disrespectfully of my husband, I will
turn you out of the house.

KROGSTAD: That's very brave, Mrs. Helmer.

NORA: I'm not afraid of you any more. After the New Year, I will be
finished with the whole thing.

KROGSTAD: *(controlling himself)* Now you listen to me, Mrs. Helmer. If
necessary I am ready to fight for my little job at the bank as if I were
700   fighting for my life.

NORA: I can see that.

KROGSTAD: It's not just for the money. In fact that's the least important
thing. It's something else—I might as well tell you. It's this. I'm sure
you know, like everybody else, that some years ago I made an
unfortunate mistake.

NORA: I've heard something about it.

KROGSTAD: It never went to trial. But after that, all doors were closed to
me. So I turned to the business that brought us together. I had to
make a living. And to tell the truth, I haven't been as bad as some
710   others. But it's time for me to be done with all that. My sons are
growing up. And for their sake I must regain my reputation in this
town. The job at the bank was the first step up for me—and now
your husband is going to kick me back down into the mud.

NORA: You must believe me, Mr. Krogstad. I have no power to help you.

KROGSTAD: But if you set your mind to it. . . . You should be aware that I
have the means to force you . . .

NORA: Are you threatening to tell my husband that I owe you money?

KROGSTAD: Well, what if I did tell him?

NORA: That would be a totally contemptible thing to do. *(sobbing)* I
720   have kept this from him with pride and with happiness. I could not
bear to have him find out like that—from *you*—in such an ugly,
clumsy way. It would be terribly unpleasant for me.

KROGSTAD: Just unpleasant? . . .

NORA: *(impetuously)* All right, then—tell him. But it'll be all the worse
for you. My husband will see for himself what a monster you are.
And there is no way that you will keep your job.

KROGSTAD: I meant—do you think that it would be "unpleasant" for you
only at home?

NORA: If my husband does find out, he will of course immediately pay
730   you what is still owed. And then we will have nothing more to do
with you.

KROGSTAD: *(moving toward her)* Listen, Mrs. Helmer. Either I have a
bad memory or you don't know much about business. I think I have
to remind you of a few details.

NORA: What do you mean?

KROGSTAD: When your husband was ill, you came to me to borrow four thousand eight hundred crowns.

NORA: I didn't know where else to go.

KROGSTAD: I promised to get you the money . . .

740 NORA: Yes. And you did.

KROGSTAD: . . . I promised to get you the money on certain conditions. You were so worried about your husband's health, so anxious to get the money for your trip, that I don't think you paid much attention to the details. So. I think it's appropriate that I remind you. I promised to get the money if you would sign a security bond, which I then drew up.

NORA: And I signed it.

KROGSTAD: Exactly. Underneath your signature was a clause naming your father as security. He was supposed to sign this clause.

750 NORA: Supposed to? He did.

KROGSTAD: I'd left the date blank. In other words, your father was to enter the date on the day he signed it. Do you remember that?

NORA: Yes, I think so.

KROGSTAD: Then I gave you the document for you to mail to your father? Is that correct?

NORA: Yes.

KROGSTAD: And obviously you mailed it immediately because—oh, just five or six days later—you brought it to me, duly signed by your father. And I gave you the money.

760 NORA: So? Haven't I been paying it off regularly?

KROGSTAD: Yes. Pretty regularly. But—to get back to my point—you were having a very hard time then, weren't you, Mrs. Helmer?

NORA: I certainly was.

KROGSTAD: Your father was very sick, I believe.

NORA: He was near the end.

KROGSTAD: And he died soon afterward?

NORA: Yes.

KROGSTAD: Tell me, Mrs. Helmer, do you by any chance remember the day he died? The date, I mean.

770 NORA: Papa died on the 29th of September.

KROGSTAD: That is correct. I've made sure of that for myself. And that's what's so strange. (producing the paper) I can't explain it.

NORA: What is strange?

KROGSTAD: What is strange, Mrs. Helmer, is that your father signed this contract three days after his death.

NORA: What? I don't understand.

KROGSTAD: Your father died on the 29th of September. But if you look here, you'll see that he dated his signature "October 2nd." Isn't that strange, Mrs. Helmer? (Nora is silent) Can you explain it? (Nora

780 is still silent) It's also strange that "October 2nd" and the year aren't in your father's handwriting, though I do think I recognize the hand. Now, of course, that could be explained—your father

might have forgotten to date his signature, and someone else might
just have guessed the date *before* they knew of his death. Nothing
wrong with that. It's the signature that's important. That *is* genuine, isn't it, Mrs. Helmer? Your father really did sign his own
name, didn't he?

NORA: *(pauses, then looks him straight in the eye and with a toss of
her head)* No, he did not. I signed Papa's name.

KROGSTAD: Mrs. Helmer! You realize that is a very dangerous
790   confession?

NORA: Why? You'll get your money back soon enough.

KROGSTAD: Let me ask you something. Why didn't you mail the contract
to your father?

NORA: I couldn't. He was much too sick. If I'd asked him for his signature, I'd have had to tell him what the money was for. And in his
condition, I couldn't tell him my husband was deathly ill. I couldn't
possibly.

KROGSTAD: It would have been better for you if you'd canceled the trip.

NORA: That was impossible! That trip was to save my husband's life. I
800   couldn't cancel it.

KROGSTAD: But did it never occur to you that you were deceiving me?

NORA: Why should I worry about that? I wasn't thinking about you at
all. I hated the way you handled everything—so coldhearted, making
everything so difficult—even though you knew how desperately ill
my husband was.

KROGSTAD: Mrs. Helmer. It's obvious that you don't understand what it
is that you are guilty of. Just let me tell you about what *I* did—the
thing that ruined my reputation. It was nothing more and nothing
worse than what you did.

810   NORA: You? Are you trying to tell me that *you* would have had the
courage to try to save your wife's life?

KROGSTAD: The law doesn't care about motives.

NORA: Then the law is stupid.

KROGSTAD: Stupid or not, it is the law that will judge you if I produce
this paper in court.

NORA: I don't believe it. Is a daughter not allowed to protect her dying
father from worry and care? Is a wife not allowed to save her husband's
life? I don't know much about the law. But I'm sure that there must *be*
laws that allow things like that. You are a lawyer. You must know about
820   laws like that. You must be a very poor lawyer, Mr. Krogstad.

KROGSTAD: Perhaps. But when it comes to business—the kind of business you and I have engaged in—don't you think I know about that?
All right. Do as you like. But I tell you this. If I lose my job again, I'll
bring you down with me. *(he bows and exits)*

NORA: *(she seems buried in thought for a short time, then tosses her
head)* That's nonsense! He's just trying to frighten me! I'm not so

stupid as he thinks. *(she starts clearing up the children's things)* And yet—? No, it can't be true. I did it because I love my husband.

THE CHILDREN: *(in the doorway, sharing the conversation)* Mother, the strange man has gone out through the front gate.

830 NORA: Yes, sweethearts, I know. But don't tell anyone about the strange man. Do you hear me? Not even Papa.

CHILDREN: No, Mother. Let's go play!

NORA: No, not now.

CHILDREN: But, Mama, you promised!

NORA: Yes, but I can't now. Run on in. . . . I've got such a lot to do. Off you go, my sweethearts! *(She shuttles them into the room one by one, then shuts the door. She sits on the sofa and starts doing some needle work, but soon stops.)* No! *(she throws down the needle-work, gets up, goes to the hall door, and calls out)* Helene? Bring the tree in! *(goes to the table on the left, opens a drawer, and then*

840 *stops)* No! No! It can't be true!

MAID: *(coming in with tree)* Where shall I put it, Madam?

NORA: Here. In the middle of the room.

MAID: Can I get you anything else?

NORA: No, thank you, I've got everything.

(Maid exits)

NORA: *(starting to dress the tree)* I'll put a candle here—flowers there—oh, that awful man! Everything's fine. The tree will look beautiful. I'll do everything I can to please you, Torvald—I'll sing for you, dance for you. *(Torvald comes in with some papers under his arm)* Oh, are you back already?

850 TORVALD: Yes. Was anyone here?

NORA: Here? No.

TORVALD: That's strange. I saw Krogstad leaving by the front gate.

NORA: Oh, did you? Oh yes, I forgot. Krogstad was here for a short while.

TORVALD: Nora . . . I can see from your face that he's been here, begging you to put in a good word for him.

NORA: Yes.

TORVALD: And you were supposed to make it seem like it was your idea. You were to hide the fact that he'd been here. Isn't that what he

860 asked you?

NORA: Yes, Torvald. But . . .

TORVALD: Nora, Nora. And you would agree to something like that? Even to have a conversation with a man like that, to promise him anything? And on top of everything, to lie to me?

NORA: Lie?

TORVALD: Didn't you just say that no one had been here? *(shaking his finger at her)* My little songbird must never do that again. A songbird must sing with a pure voice—no false notes. *(putting his arm*

around her waist) Isn't that right? Yes, I know it is. *(letting her go)*
870   We'll say no more about it. *(sitting down by the stove)* How warm
and cozy it is in here. *(going through his papers)*
NORA: *(after a short pause, during which she dresses the tree)*
Torvald?
TORVALD: Yes?
NORA: I am *so* looking forward to the fancy dress ball at the Stenborgs
the day after tomorrow.
TORVALD: And I am "*so*" curious to see how you're going to surprise me.
NORA: Oh, I've been so very silly.
TORVALD: What do you mean?
NORA: I can't think of anything to wear! Everything seems so silly and
880   unimportant.
TORVALD: Ah. Does my little Nora finally realize that?
NORA: *(standing behind his chair with her hands on the back of it)*
Are you very busy, Torvald?
TORVALD: Well—
NORA: What are all those papers?
TORVALD: Bank business.
NORA: Already?
TORVALD: I asked the retiring manager to give me the authority to make
the necessary changes in staff and to reorganize the workload.
I have to spend Christmas week doing that. Everything has to be
890   ready for the new year.
NORA: Was that why this poor man, Krogstad—
TORVALD: Hmm.
NORA: *(leaning against the back of the chair and stroking his hair)*
If you weren't so busy, I'd ask you a really big favor, Torvald.
TORVALD: What? Tell me.
NORA: You have the best taste of anyone I know. And I do want to look
nice at the fancy dress ball. Torvald, couldn't you help me decide
what I should go as, what sort of dress I should wear?
TORVALD: Aha! So the stubborn little lady needs someone to come to
her rescue?
900   NORA: Yes, Torvald. I can't do a thing without you.
TORVALD: All right, I'll think it over. I'm sure we'll come up with
something.
NORA: That's so sweet of you. *(Going to the Christmas tree. Short
pause.)* The red flowers look really pretty. Tell me, did Krogstad do
something very bad?
TORVALD: He forged someone's name. Have you any idea what that means?
NORA: Isn't it possible that he had no choice?
TORVALD: Yes. But in many cases like this, it was probably—indiscretion. I'm not without compassion. I won't condemn a man altogether
910   just because of one mistake.
NORA: I know you wouldn't, Torvald.

TORVALD: There have been many men who have been rehabilitated if
they confess their faults and take their punishment.

NORA: Punishment?

TORVALD: But Krogstad did nothing of the kind. He got himself out of it
by trickery. And that is why he is now completely ruined.

NORA: Do you think it would—

TORVALD: *(interrupting)* Just think how a guilty man like that has to lie
and be a hypocrite with everyone, how he has to put on a false mask
920   even in front of those he loves, even in front of his own wife and
children. And the children—that's the worst thing of all, Nora.

NORA: How?

TORVALD: Because an atmosphere of lies infects and poisons the entire
household. Every breath the children take is filled with the germs
of evil.

NORA: *(coming near to him)* How can you be sure of that?

TORVALD: My dear, I've seen it many times in my career as a lawyer.
Most of the people who get into trouble early in life have had a
mother who lies and cheats.

930   NORA: Why do you only say the mother?

TORVALD: It usually seems to come from the mother's influence,
although of course a lying father would have the same effect.
All lawyers are familiar with the scenario. This man Krogstad has
been consistently poisoning his own children with his lies and
deception. That is why I say that he is a moral degenerate. *(holding
out his hands to her)* And that is why my sweet little Nora must
promise not to speak on his behalf. Give me your hand on it. Come
on, what's this? Give me your hand! There now, that's settled. I can
assure you it would be quite impossible for me to work with him. I
940   literally feel physically sick in the presence of such people.

NORA: *(taking her hand out of his and going to the other side of the
Christmas tree)* It's so hot in here. And I have so much to do.

TORVALD: *(getting up and putting his papers in order)* Yes. I must try
to get through some of these before dinner. And I must think about
your fancy dress too! Oh, and maybe I have a little something
wrapped in gold paper to hang on the tree. . . . *(patting her on the
head)* My sweet little songbird. *(he goes to his room and shuts the
door)*

NORA: *(after a pause, whispering)* No. It can't be true. It can't be. It
can't be.

(Nurse opens the door on the left)

NURSE: The children are pestering me to let them come in and see their
950   Mama.

NORA: No. No. Don't let them come in to me. Stay with them, Anna.

NURSE: Very well, Madam. *(she shuts the door)*

NORA: *(her face pale with fright)* Corrupt my little children? Poison my home? *(short pause, then, with a toss of her head)* It's not true. It can't possibly be true.

ACT 2

The same setting as Act 1. But the Christmas tree is now in the corner by the piano, stripped of its ornaments and with burned-down candles on its somewhat tattered branches. Nora's cloak and hat are lying on the sofa. She is pacing the room, visibly uncomfortable. She stops by the sofa and picks up her cloak.

NORA: *(dropping the cloak)* Is that someone coming? *(goes to the door and listens)* No—there's no one there. Nobody will come on Christmas day—or tomorrow either. But perhaps— *(opens the door and looks out)* There's nothing in the mailbox. It's empty. *(reentering the room)* Nonsense! Of course he can't be serious. It just couldn't happen. . . . No! I have three small children.

(the Nurse enters from the room on the left with a big cardboard box)

NURSE: I finally found the box with the fancy dress.
NORA: Thanks, put it on the table.
NURSE: It's badly in need of repair.
NORA: I'd love to tear it into thousands of little pieces.
NURSE: Good heavens! It can easily be put right with a little bit of patience.
NORA: Yes. Well, I'll go and get Mrs. Linde to give me a hand with it.
NURSE: Going out again? In this weather? You'll catch your death of cold, Madam.
NORA: Worse things could happen. How are the children?
NURSE: The poor little dears are playing with their Christmas presents, but—
NORA: Are they asking for me all the time?
NURSE: Well, they're so used to having their Mama with them. . . .
NORA: Well, Anna, I won't be able to be with them as much any more.
NURSE: Oh well, little children get used to everything.
NORA: Do you think so? Do you think they'd forget their mother if she went away for good?
NURSE: Good heavens. . . . Went away for good?
NORA: I want you to tell me something I've often wondered about— how did you have the heart to give your child away to people you didn't know?
NURSE: I had no choice—if I was to be my little Nora's nanny.
NORA: Yes, but how could you be *willing* to do it?
NURSE: Well, I was going to get a good position, wasn't I? A poor girl who's got into trouble should count herself lucky. Besides, that terrible man wasn't going to do a thing to help.
NORA: I expect your daughter has forgotten all about you.

NURSE: No. Indeed she hasn't. She wrote to me when she got confirmed
990   and when she got married.

NORA: *(putting her arms around her neck)* Dear old Anna Marie, you
were such a good mother to me when I was a little girl.

NURSE: Well, my poor little Nora had no other mother but me.

NORA: And if my little ones had no other mother, I'm sure you'd—oh
what nonsense I'm talking. *(opening the box)* Go in and see them—.
Now I have to—you'll see tomorrow how beautiful I will look.

NURSE: I know there'll be no one more beautiful than you at the ball.
(goes into the room on the left)

NORA: *(starts to unpack the box, then pushes it away)* I wish
I were brave enough to go out. Oh, I hope nobody comes. I hope
1000   everything will be all right here at home. Oh what nonsense!
Nobody'll come. I just mustn't think about it. Let me brush the
muff. Oh what beautiful, beautiful gloves. Stop thinking about it.
Stop! One, two, three, four, five, six . . . *(she gives a little scream)*
There's someone coming! *(starts for the door, then stands
uncertainly)*

*(Mrs. Linde enters from the hall, where she has taken off her cloak
and hat)*

NORA: Oh it's you, Kristine! There's no one else outside, is there? How
nice of you to come.

MRS. LINDE: They told me you were asking for me.

NORA: Yes, I was just passing by. As a matter of fact, there is something
you could help me with. Sit down by me on the sofa. Look at this.
1010   Tomorrow night there's a fancy dress ball upstairs at the Stenborgs.
Torvald wants me to go as a Neapolitan fishergirl. He wants me to
dance the tarantella that I learned in Capri.

MRS. LINDE: I see. So you're going in character.

NORA: That's what Torvald wants. Here's the dress. Look. Torvald had it
made for me there. But it's torn, and I have no idea—

MRS. LINDE: Well, we can easily fix that. Some of the trimming has come
loose here and there, that's all. Needle and thread? Now then, that's
all we need. *(starting to sew)* So. You're going to be all dressed up
tomorrow, Nora. I'll tell you what—I'll pop in for a moment to see
1020   you in all your finery. Oh, I forgot to thank you for a wonderful
evening yesterday.

NORA: *(gets up and crosses the room)* Well, I don't think yesterday was
all that wonderful. You should have come to town a little bit sooner,
Kristine. But Torvald really knows how to make a house look
beautiful.

MRS. LINDE: And so do you. You're not your father's daughter for nothing. But tell me, is Dr. Rank always as depressed as he was last
night?

NORA: No, last night it was very noticeable. I have to tell you—he's got
1030   a life-threatening disease. It's a form of consumption—and it affects
his spine. Oh the poor man. His father was a terrible creature who
lived a life of excess—and his son was sickly from childhood—do
you understand what I mean?

MRS. LINDE: *(putting down her sewing)* My dear Nora, how do you
know about such things?

NORA: *(walking about)* Ah, when you've had three children as I have,
well, people drop by, married women—and they know quite a bit
about medical problems—and they talk—about one thing and another.

MRS. LINDE: *(Resumes her sewing. A short silence.)* Does Dr. Rank
1040   come here every day?

NORA: Every day. He's Torvald's best friend, and a good friend of mine
too. He's just like one of the family.

MRS. LINDE: But tell me—can he be trusted? I mean, isn't he the sort of
man who is always eager to please?

NORA: Not in the least. What makes you think that?

MRS. LINDE: Well. When you introduced me to him yesterday, he said
that he had often heard my name mentioned in this house. But afterward I noticed that your husband hadn't the slightest idea who I
was. So how could Dr. Rank . . . ?

1050 NORA: You're quite right, Kristine. Torvald loves me so much that
he wants me all to himself. That's what he says. Early on, he
seemed, well, jealous if I even mentioned the people I was so
fond of at home. So naturally I stopped doing that. But I often
talk about things like that with Dr. Rank because he likes to
listen to me.

MRS. LINDE: Now you listen to *me*, Nora. You're still almost a child in
many ways. I'm a little bit more mature, a little bit more experienced.
I must tell you this—you ought to put a stop to this with Dr. Rank.

NORA: Put a stop to what?

1060 MRS. LINDE: Two things, I think. Yesterday there was some silly talk
about a rich admirer who would leave you money—

NORA: An admirer who doesn't exist. Unfortunately. What else?

MRS. LINDE: Dr. Rank is a wealthy man?

NORA: Yes, he is.

MRS. LINDE: And he has no dependents?

NORA: No. No one, but . . .

MRS. LINDE: And he comes here every day?

NORA: That's what I said.

MRS. LINDE: How could a gentleman be so tactless?

1070 NORA: I don't understand what you mean.

MRS. LINDE: Don't pretend, Nora. Do you think I can't guess who lent
you the four thousand eight hundred crowns?

NORA: Are you out of your mind? How could you think that? A friend of both of us who comes here every day? Can't you see how terribly awkward that would be?

MRS. LINDE: It's really not him?

NORA: No. Absolutely not. It would never have entered my head for a moment. Besides, he had no money to lend at the time. He inherited it afterward.

1080   MRS. LINDE: Well, Nora, that was lucky for you, I think.

NORA: No, it would never have entered my head to ask Dr. Rank. Although I'm quite sure that if I had asked him—

MRS. LINDE: But you wouldn't—?

NORA: Of course not. There's no need as far as I can see. . . . But I'm quite sure that if I told Dr. Rank—

MRS. LINDE: Behind your husband's back?

NORA: Well, I have to put a stop to things with the other person—and *that* will be behind his back. I *must* put a stop to it with him.

MRS. LINDE: Yes. That's what I told you yesterday, but—

1090   NORA: *(pacing)* It's so much easier for a *man* to put things like that right—

MRS. LINDE: One's husband, yes.

NORA: Nonsense. *(stops pacing)* When you pay off a debt you get your contract back, don't you?

MRS. LINDE: Yes. That's the normal procedure.

NORA: And you can tear it up into thousands of pieces, and throw it on the fire—nasty filthy piece of paper.

MRS. LINDE: *(puts down her sewing and, looking Nora straight in the eye, gets up slowly)* Nora, you're hiding something from me, aren't you?

NORA: Do I look as if I were?

MRS. LINDE: Something has happened since yesterday morning. Nora,
1100   what is it?

NORA: *(crossing to her)* Kristine— *(stops and listens)* Sh! Torvald just came back. Do you mind going into the children for a moment? Torvald hates to see sewing things in this room. Let Anna Marie give you a hand.

MRS. LINDE: *(gathering up some of the things)* Of course. But I'm not leaving here until we've had this out with each other. *(she goes into the room on the left just as Torvald comes in)*

NORA: *(crossing to him)* I've missed you so much, Torvald.

TORVALD: Was that the dressmaker?

NORA: No, it was Kristine. She's helping me mend my dress. You'll see,
1110   I'll look really pretty.

TORVALD: Wasn't that a good idea I had?

NORA: Wonderful. But don't you think it's nice of me to do what you want?

TORVALD: Nice? To do as your husband wishes? You little scamp! But I'm sure you didn't mean it like that. But . . . I mustn't disturb you. You'll want to be trying on your dress, I'm sure.

NORA: You're going to be working?

TORVALD: *(showing her a bundle of papers)* Yes, look at this. I've just been to the bank. *(going into his room)*

NORA: Torvald!

1120 TORVALD: Yes?

NORA: If your little squirrel asked you for something, and she was very, very nice . . .

TORVALD: What?

NORA: Would you do it?

TORVALD: I'd want to hear what it was first.

NORA: Your little squirrel would run all over the place and do her little tricks. You must have to be nice and do what she wants.

TORVALD: Tell me what you mean.

NORA: Your skylark would sing, warble in every room, singing loud,
1130 singing soft . . .

TORVALD: Well, she does that anyway.

NORA: I'd be a fairy and dance for you in the moonlight, Torvald.

TORVALD: Nora, you're not talking about—the thing you asked of me this morning. . . .

NORA: *(going toward him)* Yes, Torvald. I beg you, I beg you.

TORVALD: How dare you bring up that business again?

NORA: You *must* do as I ask. You *must* let Krogstad keep his job at the bank.

TORVALD: My dear Nora, I have arranged to give his position to
1140 Mrs. Linde.

NORA: Yes, I know you've been really kind about that. But you could just as easily fire someone other than Krogstad.

TORVALD: You are being *incredibly* stubborn. Just because you chose to give him so thoughtless a promise—that you would speak on his behalf—I'm supposed to—

NORA: That's not the reason, Torvald. I'm doing this for you. This man writes for the most dreadful, slanderous newspapers. You told me so yourself. He can do you a terrible amount of harm. I'm scared to death of him—

1150 TORVALD: Oh, I understand. You're thinking about the past and you're afraid.

NORA: What do you mean?

TORVALD: Well, of course you're thinking about your father.

NORA: Yes. Yes, that's it. Just remember what those malicious people wrote in the papers about Papa, how they slandered him. I'm sure they would have had him dismissed if the Department had not sent you over to look into the matter, and if you hadn't been so kind and helpful to him.

TORVALD: My dear Nora. There's a very important difference between
1160 your father and me. Your father's reputation as a public official was not above suspicion. Mine *is*—and I hope it will remain so, as long as I hold my position.

NORA: But you can never tell what these people might do to you! We ought to have enough money to be comfortable, we ought to be cozy and happy in our quiet little home. We should have no cares. You and I and the children. That is why I'm begging you.

TORVALD: And it's just because you *are* pleading on his behalf that you make it impossible for me to keep him on. Everyone at the bank
1170   already knows that I intend to dismiss Krogstad. Are people going to say now that the new manager has changed his mind just because his wife asked him?

NORA: And what if they did?

TORVALD: Oh yes. Just so this stubborn little woman can get her own way. Do you think I'm going to make myself look like a fool in front of my whole staff? Do you think I'm going to let people think I'm a man who will change his mind because of outside pressures? I can assure you I'd feel the consequences of that pretty quickly. And in any case, there's one thing that makes it impossible for me to keep
1180   Krogstad at the bank as long as I am the manager.

NORA: What's that?

TORVALD: I might perhaps have overlooked his moral failings if I had to—

NORA: Yes, you could, couldn't you?

TORVALD: —and I hear that he's a hard worker. *But* I knew him when we were boys. It was one of those impulsive friendships that often haunt one in later life. I might as well tell you quite plainly that we were once on very intimate terms with one another. But this man has no tact when other people are around. On the contrary, he
1190   thinks our past friendship gives him the right to be on familiar terms with me. All the time it's "Hi there, Torvald, old pal!" That sort of thing. It is *extremely* difficult for me. He would make my position in the bank totally intolerable.

NORA: Torvald, I can't believe you mean that.

TORVALD: Can't you? Why not?

NORA: Because it's such a narrow-minded way of looking at things.

TORVALD: Narrow-minded? What do you mean? Do you think I'm narrow-minded?

NORA: No, just the opposite, my love. And that is why . . .

1200   TORVALD: No. You said that I had a narrow-minded way of looking at things. Well then, *I* myself must be narrow-minded. All right. I'm going to put an end to this. *(he goes to the hall door and calls out)* Helene!

NORA: What are you going to do?

TORVALD: *(rummaging through his papers)* Settle it once and for all. *(Maid enters)* Here. Take this letter, go downstairs, and find a messenger. Immediately. Tell him to deliver it right away. The address is on it. Here's the money.

MAID: Yes, sir. *(exits with the letter)*

1210   TORVALD: *(putting his papers together)* Now then, Madam Stubborn.

NORA: *(almost out of breath)* Torvald, what was that letter?

TORVALD: Krogstad's dismissal.

NORA: Call her back, Torvald. There's still time. Torvald, call her back! Do it for me, do it for you, do it for the children. Do you hear me, Torvald, call her back! You don't know what this letter can do to us.

TORVALD: It's too late.

NORA: Yes, it's too late.

TORVALD: My dear Nora. I can forgive you for being so upset. But it really is an insult to me. Isn't it an insult to think that I should be
1220   afraid of a starving pen pusher? But I forgive you because, in its own way, it speaks so eloquently of your love for me. *(he takes her in his arms)* And that is how it should be, my darling Nora. You can be sure that whatever happens, I will be brave and strong. You'll see that I am man enough to take everything upon myself.

NORA: *(her voice is horror-stricken)* What do you mean by that?

TORVALD: Everything . . .

NORA: *(recovering)* You'll never have to do that.

TORVALD: Well, well, we'll share the burden, Nora, as man and wife should. That's how it's going to be. *(putting his arms around her)*
1230   Are you happy now? There, there. No more frightened little dove's eyes. It's all in your imagination. So. You must go and rehearse the tarantella and practice on the tambourine. I'll go into the office and shut the door, and I will hear nothing. You can make as much noise as you like. *(turns back at the door)* And when Dr. Rank comes, tell him where he can find me. *(nods to her, takes his papers, goes into his room, and shuts the door)*

NORA: *(Nora is rooted to the spot, very bewildered, and whispers to herself)* He actually could do it. He *will* do it. He'll do it in spite of everything. No, no, no. Never, never. Anything rather than that. I need help . . . anything. *(the doorbell rings in a familiar pattern)* Dr. Rank! Anything! Anything other than that . . . *(She puts her hands over her face, pulls herself together, opens the door. Rank is standing in the hall, hanging up his coat. During the following conversation, it begins to grow dark.)*
1240   NORA: Good day, Dr. Rank. I recognized your ring. But you mustn't go in to Torvald now. I think he's busy.

DR. RANK: And you?

NORA: *(ushers him in and shuts the door)* Oh, you know that I always have time for you.

DR. RANK: Thank you. I shall take advantage of that for as long as I can.

NORA: What do you mean by that? For as long as you can?

DR. RANK: Does that alarm you?

NORA: It was such a strange way of putting it. Is something going to happen?

1250 DR. RANK: Nothing that I haven't been preparing for. But I didn't expect
it to happen so soon.

NORA: *(holding him tightly by the arm)* What did they tell you?
Dr. Rank, you must talk to me.

DR. RANK: *(sitting down by the stove)* It's all over. Nothing can be done.

NORA: *(with a sigh of relief)* Are you talking about yourself?

DR. RANK: Who else? You can't lie to yourself. I'm the worst of all my
patients, Mrs. Helmer. Recently I've been assessing my internal net
worth. And I'm bankrupt. Perhaps within a month I'll lie rotting in
the graveyard.

1260 NORA: What a disgusting thing to say!

DR. RANK: Well, it *is* disgusting. And the fact is that I will have to endure
so much more before the graveyard. I will make only one more
examination of myself. When I've done that I will know—with some
certainty—when the disintegration will begin. There's something I
want to tell you. Torvald . . . is a very refined man. That makes him
absolutely incapable of facing anything that is unpleasant. I won't
have him visit me in my sick room.

NORA: Oh but Dr. Rank . . .

DR. RANK: I won't have him in there. Not under any circumstances. My
1270 door is locked to him. As soon as I am absolutely sure that the end is
coming, I will send you my card with a black cross on it. And then
you will know that the pain and suffering is coming to an end.

NORA: You are talking nonsense. I wanted you to be so happy today.

DR. RANK: With death watching my every move? To have to suffer this
because of another man's sin. There's no justice. In every single family, in one way or another, there is some inexorable curse which
brings retribution.

NORA: *(putting her hands over her ears)* Nonsense. Talk about something happy!

1280 DR. RANK: Oh, we can laugh about the whole thing! My innocent spine has
to suffer because my father, well, enjoyed himself when he was young.

NORA: *(sitting at the table on the left)* You mean that he loved asparagus and pâté de foie gras and that sort of thing, don't you?

DR. RANK: Yes, and truffles.

NORA: Yes, truffles. And oysters too, I'm sure.

DR. RANK: Oysters, yes of course.

NORA: And gallons of port and champagne. It's so sad that all these
wonderful things should attack our bodies.

DR. RANK: Especially sad that they should take revenge on the bodies of
1290 those who didn't have the chance to enjoy them.

NORA: Yes. That's the worst part.

DR. RANK: *(looking at her carefully)* Hmm.

NORA: *(after a short pause)* Why did you smile?

DR. RANK: No, it was you.

NORA: No, it was you, Dr. Rank.

DR. RANK: *(getting up)* You're a much greater tease than I thought.

NORA: Well, I'm in a silly mood today.

DR. RANK: So it seems.

NORA: *(putting her hands on his shoulders)* Dear, dear, Dr. Rank.
1300   Death cannot ever take you away from Torvald and me.

DR. RANK: Oh, you'd easily recover from the loss. The departed are
soon forgotten.

NORA: *(looking at him anxiously)* Do you believe that?

DR. RANK: People form new friendships.

NORA: Who will form new friendships?

DR. RANK: You and Torvald, when I'm gone. You're already well on the
way, I think. What did Mrs. Linde want here last night?

NORA: Aha! You don't mean to say that you're jealous
of Kristine?

1310   DR. RANK: Yes, I am. She will take over from me in this house. When I'm
gone this woman will—

NORA: Shh! Keep your voice down. She's in the other room.

DR. RANK: Today again. You see?

NORA: She's only come to sew my dress for me. Good heavens,
you're totally unreasonable. *(sitting down on the sofa)* Now be
nice, Dr. Rank. And tomorrow you'll see how beautifully I shall
dance. And you can think that I'm dancing all for you—and for
Torvald too, of course. *(taking various things out of the box)*
Dr. Rank, come and sit down over here. I want to show
1320   you something.

DR. RANK: *(sitting down)* What is it?

NORA: Just look at these.

DR. RANK: Silk stockings.

NORA: Flesh-colored. Aren't they beautiful? It's so dark in here now, but
tomorrow—no, no, no! You must only look at the feet! Oh well. You
can have a little look at the legs too.

DR. RANK: Hmm.

NORA: Why do you look so doubtful? Don't you think they'll fit me?

DR. RANK: I have no way of forming an opinion on that.

1330   NORA: *(looking at him for a moment)* Shame on you! *(hitting him
lightly on the ear with the stockings)* That's to punish you. *(folding
them up again)*

DR. RANK: And what other nice little things am I going to be allowed to see?

NORA: Not a thing more. Nothing. You were so naughty. *(she looks
among the things humming to herself)*

DR. RANK: *(after a short silence)* When I'm sitting here, talking to you,
so intimately, I can't imagine—even for a second—what would have
happened to me if I'd never come into this house.

NORA: *(smiling)* I think you really do feel at home with us.

DR. RANK: *(in a low voice, looking straight ahead)* And to have to
leave it all.

1340   NORA: Nonsense. You're not going to leave it all.

DR. RANK: *(recovering)* And not to be able to leave behind even the slightest token of one's thanks, not even a fleeting regret—nothing but an empty place which the first person who comes will fill as well as anyone else.

NORA: And if I asked you now for a—no . . .

DR. RANK: For what?

NORA: For something that really proves the depth of your friendship.

DR. RANK: Yes, yes.

NORA: I mean a really big favor.

1350   DR. RANK: Would you honestly make me so happy, just for once?

NORA: But you don't know what it is yet.

DR. RANK: No, but tell me.

NORA: I really can't, Dr. Rank. It's something that makes no sense. I need advice, I need help, I need a favor.

DR. RANK: The bigger it is, the better. I've no idea what you mean. Tell me. Can't you trust me?

NORA: More than anyone else. I know you are my best, my truest friend. So I will tell you what it is. Dr. Rank, it is something you must help me stop from happening. You know how much Torvald

1360   loves me, how devoted he is, how inexpressibly deep his love for me is. He'd never, even for a second, hesitate to give his life for me.

DR. RANK: *(leaning toward her)* Nora—do you think he's the only one? . . .

NORA: *(with a slight start)* The only one?

DR. RANK: The only one who would give his life for you. . . .

NORA: *(sadly)* Ah. Is that it?

DR. RANK: I was determined that you should know that before I . . . went away. There will never be a better opportunity than now. So

1370   now you know, Nora. And now you know too that you can trust me in a way that you couldn't trust anyone else.

NORA: *(rising deliberately and quietly)* Let me get by you.

DR. RANK: *(making room for her to pass by but sitting still)* Nora.

NORA: *(at the hall door)* Helene! Bring in the lamp! *(going over to the stove)* Dear Dr. Rank, that was really awful of you.

DR. RANK: To have loved you as much as everybody else? Was that awful?

NORA: No. But to *tell* me! There was really no need.

DR. RANK: What do you mean? Did you know? *(Maid enters with lamp,*

1380   *sets it down on the table, and exits)* Nora—Mrs. Helmer—tell me, did you have any idea of this?

NORA: Oh, how would I know whether I had any idea or not? I really can't tell you. But for you to be so clumsy, Dr. Rank! We were getting on so well.

DR. RANK: In any case, now you know that you can have your way with me, body and soul. So, won't you tell me what's on your mind?

NORA: *(looking at him)* After what just happened?

DR. RANK: I beg you. Tell me what it is.

NORA: I can't tell you anything now.

1390 DR. RANK: No, no, you mustn't punish me like that. Let me do for you whatever a man can do.

NORA: You can do nothing for me now. Anyway, I really don't need any help. You'll find that the whole thing is just . . . my imagination. It really is! Of course it is! *(sitting down in the rocking chair and smiling)* You're really a terrible man, aren't you, Dr. Rank? Aren't you ashamed of yourself now that the light is on?

DR. RANK: Not at all. But perhaps I had better go—go for good.

NORA: No you will not. You must come here every day, just as before.

1400 You know very well that Torvald needs you.

DR. RANK: Yes. And you?

NORA: Oh, I'm always wonderfully happy when you come.

DR. RANK: That's exactly what confused me. You are an enigma to me. I have often thought that you would just as soon share my company as Torvald's.

NORA: Yes, you see there are those whom one loves and those whom one would choose to spend one's time with.

DR. RANK: There's something in that.

NORA: When I was at home I loved Papa most of all. But I always had

1410 great fun sneaking off to the maids' quarters. They never passed judgment, and they always talked to each other about such amusing things.

DR. RANK: Oh, I see—I've taken *their* place.

NORA: *(jumping up and going to him)* Oh dear, sweet Dr. Rank. That's not what I meant at all. But I'm sure you understand that being with Torvald is a little bit like being with Papa. . . .

(Maid enters from the hallway)

MAID: Excuse me, ma'am. *(whispers and hands her a card)*

NORA: *(glancing at card)* Oh! *(puts card in her pocket)*

DR. RANK: Is anything the matter?

1420 NORA: No, no, nothing at all. It's just . . . just . . . it's my new dress. . . .

DR. RANK: But your dress is over there.

NORA: Oh yes, that one. This is a new one. I ordered it. Torvald mustn't find out about it—

DR. RANK: So that was your great secret!

NORA: Of course, of course. Just go in to him. He's sitting in the inner room. Keep him there as long as you—

DR. RANK: You can rest assured I won't let him get away. *(goes into Torvald's study)*

NORA: *(to Maid)* He's waiting in the kitchen?

MAID: Yes, he came up the back stairs.

1430 NORA: Didn't you tell him no one was home?

MAID: Yes. But that didn't do any good.

NORA: He won't go away?

MAID: No. He says he won't go till he sees you, ma'am.

NORA: Well, let him come in. But quietly! Helene, you mustn't say a
word about this to anybody. It's a surprise—for my husband.

MAID: Yes, ma'am. I understand. *(exit)*

NORA: It's going to happen! This terrible, terrible thing. I can't do anything to stop it. No, no, no, it can't happen. It will not happen.
*(She bolts the door of the study. The Maid opens the hall door for
Krogstad and then closes it. He is wearing a fur coat and hat and
high boots.)*

NORA: *(going toward him)* Keep your voice down—my husband is at
1440 home.

KROGSTAD: It doesn't matter about that.

NORA: What do you want from me?

KROGSTAD: I want you to explain something.

NORA: Hurry up, then. What is it?

KROGSTAD: I'm sure you know that I have been dismissed.

NORA: There was nothing I could do, Mr. Krogstad. I tried to interfere,
I really, really did, but it was no use.

KROGSTAD: Does your husband have so little love for you? He knows
what damage I can do to you, and yet he persists—

1450 NORA: How could you think that he knows anything about this?

KROGSTAD: No. I suppose not. It would not be at all like our respected
Torvald Helmer to have the courage—

NORA: Please, Mr. Krogstad, show my husband some respect.

KROGSTAD: All the respect he deserves. So. You've kept all this business
to yourself. Then I guess you've got a clearer picture than you had
yesterday of what it is that you have done.

NORA: More than you could ever show me.

KROGSTAD: Yes, I'm such a "poor lawyer."

NORA: What do you want from me?

1460 KROGSTAD: I only wanted to see how you were, Mrs. Helmer. I've been
thinking about you all day. I'm just a clerk, a pen-pusher, a—well,
even a man like me has some feelings, you know.

NORA: Then why don't you show them? Think of my little children.

KROGSTAD: Did you or your husband ever think of mine? Never mind
about that. I came to tell you that you mustn't worry too much. First
of all, I am not going to bring any formal charges.

NORA: No, of course, I was sure you wouldn't.

KROGSTAD: The whole thing can be settled quite amicably. There's no
reason why anyone should know anything about it. We'll keep it a
1470 secret between the three of us.

NORA: My husband must never find out anything about it.

KROGSTAD: And how will you stop that? Are you saying that you can pay off the balance?

NORA: No, not just at the moment.

KROGSTAD: Perhaps you have a plan for raising the money fairly soon?

NORA: No plan that I would put into practice.

KROGSTAD: Well, in any case it wouldn't have been any use. If you stood there with your hands full of money, I still wouldn't give you back

1480 the contract.

NORA: And what do you intend doing with it?

KROGSTAD: Nothing. I shall just hold on to it—keep it in my possession. No one who's not involved need know anything about it. So if you've been thinking of doing something desperate—

NORA: I have.

KROGSTAD: If you've been thinking of running away from home—

NORA: I have.

KROGSTAD: —or even worse—

NORA: How did you know?

1490 KROGSTAD: —then give up the idea.

NORA: How did you know I had thought of *that*?

KROGSTAD: Most of us think of that at first. I did too. But I didn't have the courage.

NORA: *(faintly)* Neither did I.

KROGSTAD: *(sounding relieved)* No. That's it, isn't it? You didn't have the courage.

NORA: No. I haven't, I haven't.

KROGSTAD: Besides, it would have been a very foolish thing to do. Once the first domestic storm has passed—. Well, I have a letter for your

1500 husband in my pocket.

NORA: Telling him everything?

KROGSTAD: As gently as possible.

NORA: *(quickly)* He mustn't get that letter. Tear it up. I'll get some money somehow.

KROGSTAD: But Mrs. Helmer, I think I told you just now—

NORA: I'm not talking about the money I owe you. Just tell me how much you're asking my husband for, and I'll get it for you.

KROGSTAD: I'm not asking your husband for a penny.

NORA: What do you want then?

1510 KROGSTAD: Listen. I want to get my reputation back, Mrs. Helmer. And your husband is going to have to help me. For the past year and a half my life has been exemplary—even though it was a struggle and I had very little money. I was happy to make my way up step by step. But now I've been thrown back down again. And it's not going to be enough for me just to be taken back in again. I tell you—I want to

get ahead. I want to get back into the bank but in a better job. Your
husband must find a place for me—

NORA: He will never do that.

KROGSTAD: Oh yes he will. I know him. He won't utter a peep. And as

1520   soon as I'm back in there again, with him, you'll see! Within a year
I'll be the manager's right-hand man. It'll be Nils Krogstad, not
Torvald Helmer, who's running the bank.

NORA: You'll never see the day. . . .

KROGSTAD: Do you mean that you will—?

NORA: Now I have the courage.

KROGSTAD: You don't frighten me. A fine, pampered lady like you—

NORA: You'll see, you'll see.

KROGSTAD: Under the ice, perhaps? Down, down into the black, icy
water. And then in the spring you'll float up to the surface all bloated

1530   and unrecognizable, your hair fallen out.

NORA: You don't frighten me.

KROGSTAD: Nor you me. Mrs. Helmer, people don't do such things. In any
case, what would be the use? He would still be completely in my power.

NORA: Even then? When I am no longer—

KROGSTAD: Don't forget that I am in complete control of your reputation.
(Nora is speechless and just stares at him) So. Now I have warned
you. Don't do anything foolish. When Torvald has gotten my letter, I
expect a reply from him. And don't you forget that it is your husband
who has forced me to do this sort of thing again. I can never forgive

1540   him for that. Goodbye, Mrs. Helmer. *(exits through the hall)*

NORA: *(goes to the hall door, opens it slightly, and listens)* He's going.
He's not putting the letter in the box. No. No. It couldn't happen!
(opens the door slowly) What? He's standing outside and not going
down stairs. Did he change his mind? Is he . . . ? *(The letter is
dropped in the box, and Krogstad's footsteps can be heard going
down the stairs. Nora stifles a cry, then runs across the room to
the table by the sofa. A short pause.)* It's in the mailbox. *(crosses
back to the door)* There it is. Oh Torvald, Torvald, there's no hope for
us now!

(Mrs. Linde comes in from the room on the left with the dress)

MRS. LINDE: There. I think it's all done. Would you like to try it on—?

NORA: *(in a hoarse whisper)* Kristine, come here.

1550   MRS. LINDE: *(throwing the dress down on the sofa)* What's the matter?
You look so upset!

NORA: Come here. Do you see that letter? There, look—you can see it
through the glass in the mailbox.

MRS. LINDE: Yes, I can see it.

NORA: That letter is from Krogstad.

MRS. LINDE: Nora—Krogstad lent you the money!

NORA: Yes. And now Torvald will find out all about it.

MRS. LINDE: Believe me, Nora, that's the best thing that could happen—
for both of you.

1560 NORA: But there's something you don't know—I forged a signature.

MRS. LINDE: Good heavens—!

NORA: I'm telling this only to you, Kristine. I want you to be my witness.

MRS. LINDE: Your witness? What do you mean? What do you want me
to—?

NORA: If I should lose my mind—no, it could easily happen—

MRS. LINDE: Nora!

NORA: Or if anything else should happen to me—anything . . . and I
weren't to be here . . .

MRS. LINDE: Nora! Nora, you're out of your mind.

1570 NORA: And if it turned out that someone wanted to take all the responsibility, all the blame . . . you understand? . . .

MRS. LINDE: Yes. Yes. But how could you think . . . ?

NORA: You must be my witness that *it is not true*. Kristine, I am not out
of my mind. In fact I have come to my senses. And I repeat: no one
else knows anything about this. I and I alone did it. Remember that.

MRS. LINDE: I promise you I will. But I don't understand all of this.

NORA: How could you? A miracle is about to happen. . . .

MRS. LINDE: A miracle?

NORA: Yes. A miracle. But it's so devastating, Kristine. It mustn't

1580 happen—not for all the world.

MRS. LINDE: I will go and see Krogstad right away.

NORA: No. You mustn't. He might do you some harm.

MRS. LINDE: There was a time when he would have done anything for
me.

NORA: Krogstad?

MRS. LINDE: Where does he live?

NORA: How would I know? Oh yes— *(feeling in her pocket)* here's his
card. But the letter, the letter—!

TORVALD: *(calling from his room, knocking on the door)* Nora!

1590 NORA: *(anxiously)* What is it? What do you want?

TORVALD: Don't be alarmed. We're not coming in. You've locked the
door. Are you trying on your dress?

NORA: Yes, I am. I look so nice, Torvald.

MRS. LINDE: *(she has read the card)* He lives just round the corner.

NORA: But it's no use. It's hopeless. The letter is lying there in the box.

MRS. LINDE: And your husband has the key?

NORA: Yes. He always has it.

MRS. LINDE: Krogstad must ask for his letter back before your husband
reads it. He must make up some excuse.

1600 NORA: But Torvald always at this time of day—

MRS. LINDE: Find some way of stopping him. Go in and see him while
I'm gone. I'll be back as soon as I can. *(she goes out quickly)*

NORA: *(goes to Torvald's door, opens it, and peeps in)* Torvald!

TORVALD: *(from inside)* Well? Am I finally allowed into my own room? Come along, Rank, now you're going to see— *(stopping in the doorway)* What's this?

NORA: What's what, dear?

TORVALD: Rank had led me to believe there would be a wonderful transformation.

1610 DR. RANK: *(in doorway)* That's what I thought. But evidently I was wrong.

NORA: Well, no one can admire me in my dress until tomorrow night.

TORVALD: My dear Nora, you look exhausted. Have you been doing too much rehearsing?

NORA: No. I've not rehearsed at all.

TORVALD: But you'll have to . . .

NORA: Yes, Torvald, I know I do. But I can't make any progress at all without you. I've totally forgotten the whole thing.

TORVALD: Oh, we'll soon get it right again.

1620 NORA: Yes, help me Torvald. Promise me. I'm so nervous about it. All those people. . . . You must give me all your time this evening. No more business—you mustn't even pick up a pen. Promise me, Torvald dear.

TORVALD: I promise. This evening I will be totally at your service, you helpless little creature. Oh, but while I think of it, I'll just go and— *(goes toward the hall door)*

NORA: Where are you going?

TORVALD: To see if there's any mail.

NORA: No. No, don't do that, Torvald.

TORVALD: Why not?

1630 NORA: Torvald, please don't. There's nothing there.

TORVALD: Well, let me look. *(Turns to go to the mailbox. Nora goes to the piano and plays the first bars of the tarantella. Torvald stops in the doorway.)* Aha!

NORA: I can't dance tomorrow if I don't rehearse.

TORVALD: *(going to her)* Are you really so nervous about it?

NORA: Yes, I really am. Let me rehearse right now. There's time before we go to dinner. Sit down and play for me, Torvald. You can make criticisms and correct me if I do the wrong steps.

TORVALD: Well, if you want me to—with pleasure! *(sits at piano)*

NORA: *(Takes a tambourine out of the box along with a long, brightly colored shawl, which she drapes around her shoulders. She leaps to the front of the room and calls out.)* Now play for me. I'm going to

1640 dance. *(Torvald plays and Nora dances. Dr. Rank stands behind Torvald at the piano and watches.)*

TORVALD: *(playing)* Slower! Slower!

NORA: This is the only way I know how!

TORVALD: Not so violently, Nora!

NORA: No, this is right!

TORVALD: *(stopping playing)* No. No. That's all wrong.

NORA: Didn't I tell you?

DR. RANK: Let me play for her.

TORVALD: *(getting up)* Yes, do. It'll be easier for me to correct her.

(Dr. Rank sits down and plays. Nora dances more and more wildly. Torvald is standing by the stove and gives her frequent instructions. She seems oblivious. Her hair falls down over her shoulders. She pays no attention to it and goes on dancing. Enter Mrs. Linde.)

MRS. LINDE: *(standing in awe at the door)* Oh!!

1650   NORA: *(dancing)* It's such fun, Kristine.

TORVALD: Nora, my darling, you're dancing as if your life depended on it.

NORA: It does, it does.

TORVALD: Stop, Rank, stop! This is sheer madness. Stop, I tell you.

(Dr. Rank stops playing. Nora suddenly stands still. Torvald goes up to her.) I would never have believed it. You've forgotten everything I taught you.

NORA: *(tossing aside the tambourine)* There you are, you see?

TORVALD: You need a lot of coaching.

NORA: Yes, I really do. You must teach me right up to the last minute.

1660   Promise me, Torvald!

TORVALD: You can depend on me.

NORA: You must think only of me—nothing else. Not today or tomorrow. You mustn't open a single letter, not even go near the mailbox—

TORVALD: So, you're still afraid of that man—

NORA: Yes, I am.

TORVALD: Nora, I can tell by your face that there's a letter from him out there.

NORA: I don't know. Perhaps there is. But you mustn't read anything

1670   like that right now. We mustn't let anything dreadful come between us until this is all over.

DR. RANK: *(whispers to Torvald)* You mustn't contradict her.

TORVALD: *(taking her in his arms)* My little one shall have her own way. But tomorrow night, after you've danced—

NORA: You will be free—

(the Maid appears in the doorway on the right)

MAID: Dinner is served, ma'am.

NORA: We will have champagne, Helene.

MAID: Very good, ma'am.

TORVALD: Well, well, well—we're having a banquet!

1680   NORA: Yes. A champagne banquet till the wee small hours. *(calling out)* And—Helene—some macaroons! Lots. Just for once!

TORVALD: Calm down! Don't be so nervous! Be my own little lark, as always.

NORA: Yes, dear, I will. But go in now. You too, Dr. Rank. Kristine, would you help me put my hair up?

DR. RANK: *(whispering to Torvald as they go out)* There isn't anything, um . . . She's not expecting . . . ?

TORVALD: Oh no, nothing like that. . . . It's just another instance of this childlike nervousness I was telling you about. *(they exit to the right)*

1690 NORA: Well?

MRS. LINDE: Gone out of town.

NORA: I could tell from your face.

MRS. LINDE: He's coming back tomorrow evening. I left him a note.

NORA: You shouldn't have done anything. You must let everything take its course. In a way, it's wonderful to be waiting for a miracle.

MRS. LINDE: And what are you waiting for?

NORA: Oh, you wouldn't understand. Go in and join them. I'll be in in a moment. *(Mrs. Linde goes into the dining room. Nora stands still for a while, as if regaining her composure. Then she looks at her watch.)* Five o'clock. Seven hours till midnight. Then twenty-four

1700 hours till the next midnight. Then the tarantella will be finished. Twenty-four plus seven? Thirty-one hours to live.

TORVALD: *(from the doorway)* Where's my little lark?

NORA: *(going to him with her arms outstretched)* Here she is!

ACT 3

The same setting. The table has been placed in the center of the room, with chairs around it. A lamp is on the table. The hallway door is open. Music is heard from upstairs. Mrs. Linde is sitting at the table, slowly turning the pages of a book. She tries to concentrate but cannot. Every now and then she listens for a sound from the hallway.

MRS. LINDE: He's not here yet . . . *(looking at her watch)* . . . and the time is nearly up. If he doesn't— *(Goes to the outer hall and opens the downstairs door carefully. Quiet footsteps are heard on the stairs. She whispers.)* Come in. There's no one here.

KROGSTAD: *(in the doorway)* I got the note from you at home. What is this all about?

MRS. LINDE: *I have* to talk to you.

1710 KROGSTAD: Really? And do *I have* to be *here*?

MRS. LINDE: Look, I couldn't possibly meet with you where I live. There's no private entrance to my rooms. Come in. We are quite alone. The maid is asleep, and the Helmers are at the party upstairs.

KROGSTAD: Are the Helmers really going to a party tonight?

MRS. LINDE: Yes. Why not?

KROGSTAD: Of course, why not?

MRS. LINDE: Now, Nils, we must have a talk.

KROGSTAD: What can we two possibly have to talk about?

1720 MRS. LINDE: A great deal, I think.

KROGSTAD: I wouldn't have thought so.

MRS. LINDE: No. I don't think you ever really understood me.

KROGSTAD: What was there to understand? The whole world saw exactly what was happening—a woman without any feelings was leaving her man when a more lucrative prospect showed up.

MRS. LINDE: Do you really believe that I have no feelings? And do you think it was so easy for me to do it?

KROGSTAD: Wasn't it?

MRS. LINDE: Nils, did you really think so?

1730 KROGSTAD: If your version of events is right, then why did you write me that letter?

MRS. LINDE: What else could I do? I *had* to break up with you. And so it was my duty to kill any feelings you had for me.

KROGSTAD: *(flexing his hands)* So that was it. All that—all for money.

MRS. LINDE: Remember that I had an invalid mother and two little brothers to take care of. We couldn't wait for you, Nils. You didn't have any prospects at the time.

KROGSTAD: That may be true. But you had no right to leave me for another man.

1740 MRS. LINDE: I don't know, I don't know. I've asked myself many times if I had that right.

KROGSTAD: *(in a gentler tone)* When I lost you, I felt as if the ground beneath my feet had given way. Look at me now—I'm like a shipwrecked man clinging to a piece of wreckage.

MRS. LINDE: But help may be near.

KROGSTAD: It *was* near. But then you came and got in my way.

MRS. LINDE: I didn't intend to, Nils. I only found out today that I was going to take your place at the bank.

KROGSTAD: If you say so, I believe you. But now that you know, aren't

1750 you going to let me keep it?

MRS. LINDE: No, because there would be no benefit for you at all.

KROGSTAD: "Benefit, benefit!"—that's what *I* would do.

MRS. LINDE: I have learned to think carefully before I act. Life and bitter necessity have taught me that.

KROGSTAD: And life has taught me not to trust fine speeches.

MRS. LINDE: Then life has taught you something very useful. But surely you must believe in actions?

KROGSTAD: What do you mean?

MRS. LINDE: You said you were like a shipwrecked man clinging to a

1760 piece of wreckage.

KROGSTAD: I had every reason to say that.

MRS. LINDE: Well, I'm like a shipwrecked woman clinging to a piece of wreckage—no one to mourn for, to care for.

KROGSTAD: You made that choice.

MRS. LINDE: At that time there was no other choice.

KROGSTAD: Well, what about now?

MRS. LINDE: Nils, what would you think of us two shipwrecked people joining together?

KROGSTAD: What do you mean?

1770 MRS. LINDE: Two people on the same piece of wreckage would stand a better chance than on their own.

KROGSTAD: Kristine!

MRS. LINDE: Why do you think I came to town?

KROGSTAD: You mean that you were thinking of me?

MRS. LINDE: I couldn't bear to live without working. All my life, for as long as I can remember, I have worked. It has been my greatest, my only pleasure. But now I'm all alone in the world. My life is empty, and I feel lost. There is no pleasure at all in working for oneself. Nils, give me something, give me someone

1780 to work for.

KROGSTAD: How can I trust that? It's just a woman's overly exaggerated sense of decency that makes you suggest that.

MRS. LINDE: Have you ever noticed such a thing in me before?

KROGSTAD: Could you really do this? You know all about my past?

MRS. LINDE: Yes.

KROGSTAD: And you know my reputation in this town?

MRS. LINDE: Just now you seemed to imply that if you'd been with me, you might have been a different man.

KROGSTAD: I'm sure of it.

1790 MRS. LINDE: Is it too late?

KROGSTAD: Have you thought about this carefully, Kristine? Yes, I'm sure you have. I can see it in your face. Do you really have the courage—?

MRS. LINDE: I want to be a mother to someone. Your children need a mother. And we two need each other. Nils, I have faith in the real you—I can face anything with you.

KROGSTAD: (taking her hands) Thank you, thank you, Kristine. Now I must find a way to regain my reputation in the world. Oh, but I forgot—

1800 MRS. LINDE: (listening) Sh! The tarantella! Go, go now.

KROGSTAD: Why? What is it?

MRS. LINDE: Can't you hear them upstairs? When the dance is over, they'll be downstairs immediately.

KROGSTAD: Yes, I'll go. But none of this is any use. I'm sure you don't know what steps I've taken as regards the Helmers.

MRS. LINDE: Yes, I know all about that.

KROGSTAD: And you still can—?

MRS. LINDE: I can understand to what lengths a man like you might go when you have no hope.

1810 KROGSTAD: If only I could undo what I have done.

MRS. LINDE: You can't. Your letter is out there in the mailbox.

KROGSTAD: Are you sure?

MRS. LINDE: Quite sure, but—

KROGSTAD: *(looking at her carefully)* Is that what all this is about? You want to save your friend no matter the cost? Tell me . . . tell me honestly, is that it?

MRS. LINDE: Nils, a woman who has sold out once before to help someone else doesn't do it a second time.

KROGSTAD: I'll ask for my letter back.

MRS. LINDE: No.

1820 KROGSTAD: Yes, of course I will. I'll wait here until Torvald comes down. I'll tell him he must give me my letter back—that it's only about my dismissal—that he mustn't read it.

MRS. LINDE: No, Nils, you mustn't ask for your letter back.

KROGSTAD: Tell me the truth. Isn't that why you asked me to meet you here?

MRS. LINDE: At first, yes. I was frightened. But twenty-four hours have passed since then, and in that time I have observed some incredible things happening in this house. Torvald must find out all about it. This painful secret must be revealed. They must come to a complete

1830 understanding between themselves. That is impossible with all this deception, this hiding of the truth.

KROGSTAD: All right. As long as you take full responsibility. But there is one thing I can do. And I will do it at once.

MRS. LINDE: *(listening)* You must go quickly. The dance is over, it's not safe for us here any longer.

KROGSTAD: I will wait for you down below.

MRS. LINDE: Yes, wait for me. You'll walk me home.

KROGSTAD: I've never had such an amazing piece of luck in my life. *(he goes out through the outer door, but the door between the living room and the hall remains open)*

MRS. LINDE: *(tidying up the room and getting her hat and cloak ready)* What a difference, what a difference! Someone to work for,

1840 someone to live for—a home to take care of. And I will do that. I wish they'd hurry up and come—*(listens)* There they are now. I'd better put on my things. *(takes up her hat and cloak)*

(Torvald and Nora can be heard talking outside. A key is turned. Torvald brings Nora almost forcibly into the hall. She is wearing her Italian costume and a large black shawl. Torvald is in evening dress with a black cloak open over his shoulders.)

NORA: *(struggling with Torvald in the doorway)* No, no, don't make me go in. I want to go back upstairs. I don't want to leave so early.

1930 TORVALD: But my dearest Nora . . .

NORA: Please, Torvald dear, *Please*—just for an hour longer.

TORVALD: Not for a minute, my sweet Nora, You know that's what we agreed. Gome in here. You'll catch a cold out there. *(he brings her gently into the room even though she resists)*

1850   MRS. LINDE: Good evening.

NORA: Kristine!

TORVALD: You're so late, Mrs. Linde?

MRS. LINDE: Yes. Please excuse me. I really wanted to see Nora in her
dress.

NORA: And you've been sitting here waiting for me?

MRS. LINDE: Yes. Unfortunately, I came too late, you'd already gone upstairs.
And I thought to myself that I couldn't leave without seeing you.

TORVALD: *(taking off Nora's shawl)* Well? Have a good look at her.
I think she's worth a look. Isn't she beautiful. Mrs. Linde?

1860   MRS. LINDE: Yes, she really is.

TORVALD: Doesn't she look remarkably lovely? Everyone thought so at
the ball. But this sweet little thing is terribly stubborn. What are we
going to do with her? It's hard to believe, but I almost had to drag
her away.

NORA: Torvald, you will be very sorry for not letting me stay, even for
just half an hour.

TORVALD: Listen to her, Mrs. Linde! She danced the tarantella. She
was an enormous success, and she deserved it. Although perhaps
the performance was somewhat too realistic—a little more . . . I

1870   mean . . . than artistic conventions demanded. But never mind.
The important thing is, she was a success. She was an enormous
success. Do you think I'd let her stay after that, and spoil the
effect? No indeed. I put my arm around the lovely little girl from
Capri—my *Capri*cious little girl from Capri, I should say. We made
one round of the room, we bowed to either side, and, as they say
in romantic novels, the beautiful vision disappeared. An exit
always ought to be perfectly timed, Mrs. Linde. But I can't make
Nora understand that! Phew! This room is hot. *(throws his cloak
on a chair and opens the door of his study)* Oh! It's all dark in

1880   here. Oh, of course—excuse me—*(he goes in and lights some
candles)*

NORA: *(quickly and in a whisper)* Well?

MRS. LINDE: *(in a low voice)* I've talked with him.

NORA: Yes, and?

MRS. LINDE: Nora, you've got to tell your husband all about it.

NORA: *(without any expression)* I knew it.

MRS. LINDE: You have nothing to be afraid of from Krogstad. But you
must tell your husband.

NORA: I won't tell him.

MRS. LINDE: Then the letter will.

1890   NORA: Thank you, Kristine. Now I know what I have to do. Sh!

TORVALD: *(coming in)* Well, Mrs. Linde, have you admired her?

MRS. LINDE: Yes, and now I must say good night.

TORVALD: Already? Is this knitting yours?

MRS. LINDE: *(picking it up)* Yes, thank you. I'd almost forgotten it.

TORVALD: So you knit?

MRS. LINDE: Of course.

TORVALD: You know, you ought to take up embroidery.

MRS. LINDE: Really? Why?

TORVALD: It's much more . . . becoming. Watch me. You hold the
1900   embroidery like this in your left hand, with the needle in your
right—like this—making a long, graceful curve. Do you see?

MRS. LINDE: Yes. Perhaps—

TORVALD: Yes, but knitting! That will always be *un*becoming.
Watch—your arms are close together, the needles go up and
down—it looks sort of Chinese. They had really excellent
champagne.

MRS. LINDE: Well, good night, Nora. Don't be stubborn anymore.

TORVALD: That's right, Mrs. Linde.

MRS. LINDE: Good night, Mr. Helmer.
1910   TORVALD: *(walking her to the door)* Good night, good night. I hope
you'll get home all right. I'd be very happy to—but you don't have far
to go. Good night, good night. *(she goes out, he shuts the door after
her, and comes back in)* Ah! At last! At last we've gotten rid of her.
She's such an old bore, that woman.

NORA: Aren't you tired. Torvald?

TORVALD: Not in the least.

NORA: You're not sleepy?

TORVALD: Not at all. On the contrary, I feel full of life. And you? You
look tired and quite sleepy.
1920   NORA: Yes, I am very tired. I want to go to sleep right away.

TORVALD: There! I was right not to let you stay any longer.

NORA: Everything you do is right, Torvald.

TORVALD: *(kissing her on the forehead)* Finally my little lark is speaking
the truth. Did you notice that Dr. Rank was in really good spirits
tonight?

NORA: Really? Was he? I didn't talk to him at all.

TORVALD: I didn't say much to him. But I haven't seen him having such a
good time for ages. *(looking at her for a while and then going
nearer to her)* It's delicious to be home again, all by ourselves, to be
1930   alone with you—you fascinating, lovely little creature.

NORA: Don't look at me like that, Torvald.

TORVALD: Why shouldn't I look at the thing I love most? All that
beauty—and it's mine, all mine.

NORA: *(going to the other side of the table)* No, Torvald, you mustn't
say things like that to me tonight.

TORVALD: *(following her)* I can see you've still got the tarantella in your
blood. It makes you more captivating than ever. Listen, the guests
are beginning to leave. *(in a lower voice)* Nora, soon the whole
house will be quiet.
1940   NORA: Yes. I hope so.

TORVALD: Yes, my own darling Nora. Do you know, when I'm out
at a party with you, like tonight, do you know why I don't talk
to you very much, stay away from you, and only occasionally
cast a furtive glance in your direction? Do you know why? It's
because I pretend to myself that we are secretly in love and you are
my secret fiancée. And that no one knows there is anything at all
between us.

NORA: Yes, yes. I know that you're thinking about me all the time.

TORVALD: And then, when we're leaving and I'm putting the shawl over
1950   your lovely young shoulders, on your beautiful neck, then I pretend
to myself that you are my young bride. And that we've just come
from our wedding, and that I'm bringing you home for the first
time—and that I'm going to be alone with you for the first time—all
alone with my shy little darling. This whole evening I've been longing only for you. When I watched the sensual movements of the
tarantella, my blood was on fire. I couldn't stand it any longer, and
that's why I brought you down so early.

NORA: Go now, Torvald. You must let me go. I don't want—

TORVALD: What? You must be joking! My little Nora, you don't want? I'm
1960   your husband, aren't I?

(a knock at the outer door)

NORA: *(with a start)* Did you hear that?

TORVALD: *(going into the hall)* Who is it?

DR. RANK: *(outside)* It's me. May I come in for a moment?

TORVALD: *(in an annoyed whisper)* Oh, what does he want now?
(aloud) Can you wait a moment? *(unlocking the door)* Come in! It's
kind of you not to just pass by.

DR. RANK: I thought I heard your voice. I felt that I'd like to drop in.
(quickly looking around the room) Ah yes—these dear rooms that I
know so well. You're very happy and cozy in here, you two.

1970   TORVALD: I think you made yourself quite happy upstairs too.

DR. RANK: Very much so. And why shouldn't I? Why shouldn't I enjoy all
the world has to offer—at least as much as I can for as long as I can.
The wine was superb.

TORVALD: Especially the champagne.

DR. RANK: You noticed that too? I can hardly believe how much I managed to put away.

NORA: Torvald drank a large amount of champagne tonight too.

DR. RANK: Did he?

NORA: Yes. And he's always in such good spirits afterward.

1980   DR. RANK: Well, why shouldn't you enjoy a happy evening after a hard
day's work?

TORVALD: Hard day's work? I'm afraid I can't lay claim to that.

DR. RANK: *(clapping him on the back)* But *I* can.

NORA: Dr. Rank, have you been working on some scientific experiments?

DR. RANK: Exactly.

TORVALD: Listen to that. Little Nora talking about scientific experiments.

NORA: May I congratulate you on the result?

1990   DR. RANK: Indeed you may.

NORA: It was favorable, then?

DR. RANK: Best possible result for both doctor and patient. Certainty.

NORA: *(quickly and inquiringly)* Certainty?

DR. RANK: Absolute certainty. So didn't I have the right to enjoy myself tonight?

NORA: Yes, you certainly did, Dr. Rank.

TORVALD: I agree. As long as you don't have to pay for it in the morning.

DR. RANK: Ah well, in this life nothing comes without a price.

NORA: Dr. Rank, do you enjoy these fancy dress balls?

2000   DR. RANK: Yes, if there are lots of pretty costumes.

NORA: Tell me, what shall we two wear next year?

TORVALD: You little featherbrain! You're thinking about next year already?

DR. RANK: We two? Well, I can tell you. You will go as a guardian angel.

TORVALD: What do you think would be an appropriate costume for that?

DR. RANK: Your wife should go dressed as she is in everyday life.

TORVALD: That was a nice turn of phrase. But tell us what you would go as?

DR. RANK: Well, my dear friend, I've already made up my mind about

2010   that.

TORVALD: Well?

DR. RANK: At the next fancy dress ball I will be invisible.

TORVALD: That's very funny!

DR. RANK: I'll have a big black hat—did you ever hear of hats that make you invisible? If you put one on, nobody can see you.

TORVALD: *(suppressing a smile)* Yes, yes, quite right.

DR. RANK: But I'm totally forgetting what I came for. Torvald, give me a cigar. One of the black Havanas.

TORVALD: With the greatest of pleasure. *(offering him his case)*

2020   DR. RANK: *(taking a cigar and cutting off the end)* Thank you.

NORA: *(striking a match)* Let me give you a light.

DR. RANK: Thank you. *(she holds the match for him to light the cigar)* And now, goodbye.

TORVALD: Goodbye, goodbye, you dear old man.

NORA: Sleep well, Dr. Rank.

DR. RANK: Thank you for the wish.

NORA: Wish me the same.

DR. RANK: You? Well, if that's what you want—sleep well. And thank you for the light. *(he nods to both of them and goes out)*

2030   TORVALD: *(in a quiet voice)* He's drunk more than he should.

NORA: *(absently)* Perhaps. *(Torvald takes a bunch of keys out of his
pocket and goes into the hall)* Torvald, what are you doing out
there?

TORVALD: Emptying the letterbox. It's full. There'll be no room for the
newspaper in the morning.

NORA: Are you going to work tonight?

TORVALD: You know very well that I'm not. What's this? Someone's been
picking at the lock!

NORA: The lock?

2040   TORVALD: Yes, someone's been . . . what's . . . ? I'm sure the maid
wouldn't— Here's a broken hairpin. Nora, it's one of yours.

NORA: *(quickly)* It must have been the children, then.

TORVALD: You must teach them not to do things like that. There, I've got
it open. *(taking out the letters and calling out to the kitchen)*
Helene! Helene! Put the front door light out. *(Comes back in the
room, shuts the hall door. His hands are full of letters.)* Look at
this. Look at this pile of letters. *(sorting through them)* What on
earth is this?

NORA: *(at the window)* The letter. No, Torvald, no!

2050   TORVALD: Two of Dr. Rank's cards.

NORA: Dr. Rank's?

TORVALD: *(looking at them)* Yes, they were on top. He must have put
them in on his way out.

NORA: Did he write anything on them?

TORVALD: There's a black cross over his name. Look at that. That's so
disturbing. It looks as if he were announcing his own death.

NORA: That's exactly what he's doing.

TORVALD: What? Do you know anything about this? Has he spoken
to you?

2060   NORA: Yes. He told me that when the cards arrived it would be his way
of saying goodbye. He's going to lock himself if away and die.

TORVALD: My poor old friend! Of course I knew we wouldn't have him
with us for very long. But so soon! And he's hiding himself away like
a wounded animal.

NORA: If it has to happen, it's best that it should be done without a
word. Don't you think so, Torvald?

TORVALD: *(walking up and down)* He'd become part of our lives. I can't
think of him as having left us. He suffered and he was lonely. He was
like a cloud, a dark background to our sunlit happiness. Well, per-

2070   haps it's for the best. For him anyway. *(standing still)* And perhaps
it is for us too, Nora. We have only ourselves now. *(putting his
arms around her)* My wife, my darling, I don't feel I can hold you
tight enough. You know, Nora, I've often wished that you might be in
some great danger, so that I could risk my life, everything, just
for you.

NORA: *(disengaging herself and speaking in a firm, clear voice)* You must read your letters now, Torvald.

TORVALD: No, not tonight. I want to be with you. I want to be with my darling wife.

2080 NORA: When your best friend is dying?

TORVALD: Yes, you're right. It's touched us both. Something ugly has come between us. The thought of mortality in all its horror. We must try to empty our minds of that. Until we do—we'll each go to our own room.

NORA: *(hanging on to his neck)* Good night, Torvald, good night.

TORVALD: *(kissing her on the forehead)* Good night, my little songbird. Sleep well, Nora. I'm going to read my letters. *(he takes the mail and goes into his study, shutting the door)*

NORA: *(groping around the room, picks up Torvald's cloak, throws it around her, speaking in quick, broken whispers)* Never to see him again. Never, never. *(putting her shawl over her head)* Never to see

2090 my children again—never again. Never, never—the black icy water—deep, deep down. If only it were all over. He's got it now and he's reading it. Goodbye, Torvald. Goodbye, my children. *(she's about to rush out through the hall when Torvald opens his door quickly and stands with the letter in his hand)*

TORVALD: Nora!

NORA: Ah.

TORVALD: What's this? Do you know what's in this letter?

NORA: Yes, I know. Let me go. Let me get out of here.

TORVALD: *(holding her back)* Where are you going?

NORA: *(trying to get free)* You can't save me, Torvald.

TORVALD: *(staggering)* Is this true? Is this true? It's . . . horrible. No,

2100 no! It *can't* be true.

NORA: It is true. I have loved you more than anything else in the world.

TORVALD: Oh, don't give me any silly excuses.

NORA: *(stepping toward him)* Torvald.

TORVALD: You . . . miserable thing. What have you done?

NORA: Let me go. You're not going to suffer for my sake. You're not going to take this upon yourself.

TORVALD: Let's have no melodrama here. *(locking the hall door)* You're going to stay here and give me an explanation. Do you understand what you've done? Answer me! Do you understand what you've done?

2110 NORA: *(looking steadily at him, with her face hardening)* Yes. I'm beginning to understand everything.

TORVALD: *(pacing around the room)* What a rude awakening. These eight years, she who was my pride and joy was a hypocrite. A liar. No, worse, worse—a criminal. It's so unspeakably awful. For shame, for shame! *(Nora is silent and looks steadily at him. He stands in front of her.)* I should have suspected that something like this would happen. I should've known. Your father's total lack of principle—

don't interrupt—his total lack of principle has finally come out in
you. No religion, no ethics, no sense of duty. I'm being punished now
2120   for turning a blind eye to all that he did. And I did that just for you.
And this is how you repay me.

NORA: Yes. This is how.

TORVALD: You've destroyed all my happiness. You've ruined my future.
I can't bear to think of it. I'm in the hands of a man with no scruples.
He can do what he likes with me. He can ask anything he wants,
order me to do anything—and I dare not say no. And I have to sink
to such depths of agony, all because of a thoughtless woman.

NORA: When I am gone, you will be free.

TORVALD: Don't play with words, please. Your father was always very
2130   good at that. What good would it do me if you were "gone," as you
say? None at all. He can tell the world about all this, and if he does,
I may be suspected, falsely, of having been a partner in your crime.
In fact, most people would probably think that I was behind it—that
it was I who suggested it. And I have you to thank for all of this. You,
the one I have loved throughout our married life. Do you understand
what it is you have done to me?

NORA: *(coldly and quietly)* Yes.

TORVALD: It's so hard to believe—I can't take it all in! But—you and I
must come to some understanding. Take off that shawl. Take it off, I
2140   tell you! I must find a way of appeasing him. We've got to make sure
that this business is hushed up, no matter the cost. As for you and
me, we've got to make it look like everything between us is just as it
was before. Naturally, that's only for the eyes of the world. You will
still remain here in my house. That is taken for granted. But you will
not be allowed to raise the children. I could not trust you with them.
To think that I have to say that to someone I have loved so deeply—
someone I still—no, that is all over. From this moment on, it's not a
question of happiness. All there is now is saving what's left of our
shattered lives, keeping up appearances. *(front doorbell rings,*
2150   *Torvald jumps)* What's that? At this time? It can't get any worse, he
can't . . . Keep out of sight, Nora. Say you're ill. *(Nora does not
move. Torvald goes and unlocks the hall door. The Maid, half
dressed, comes to the door.)*

MAID: A letter for the mistress.

TORVALD: Give it to me. *(he takes the letter and shuts the door)* It's
from him. You can't have it—I'll read it myself.

NORA: Yes, read it.

TORVALD: *(standing by the lamp)* I can hardly bring myself to do it. This
could be the ruin of us both. No, I have to know. *(he tears open the
letter, reads a few lines, looks at a piece of paper enclosed, and gives
a shout)* Nora! *(she looks at him with questions in her eyes)* Nora!
No, I've got to read it again. It's true! Yes, I'm saved. Nora, I'm saved!

2160   NORA: And I?

TORVALD: You too, of course. We're both saved. The two of us. Look! He's sent you the contract back. He says that he's sorry. He apologizes . . . there's a happy change of events in his life. Oh, never mind what he says . . . we're saved, Nora! No one can do anything to you. Oh, Nora, Nora—no, first I must destroy these terrible things. Let me see . . . *(looking at the contract)* No, no, I don't want to look at it. The whole thing will be nothing but a bad dream. *(tears up the contract and the letters, throws them into the stove, and watches them burn)* There. Now they're gone forever. He said that since Christmas Eve . . . you . . . these past three days must have been agonizing for you, Nora.

NORA: I've been fighting a hard battle.

TORVALD: And you must have suffered. There was no way out except— but no, we mustn't think about all the horror you went through. All we must do is shout with joy and keep telling each other it's over, it's over! Listen to me, Nora, you don't seem to understand that it's all over. What's the matter?—such a cold, hard face. Oh my poor Nora, I quite understand. You can hardly believe that I have forgiven you. But it's true, Nora, I swear to you. I've forgiven you. Totally. I know that what you did you did because you love me.

NORA: That is true.

TORVALD: You loved me as a wife should love her husband. You were just too naive to understand the implications of what you were doing. But do you think I love you the less because you didn't understand how to do things on your own? No, no. You must rely on me. I will advise you and give you directions. I wouldn't be a man if this female helplessness didn't make you twice as attractive to me. You must forget the harsh things I said when I was so upset at first. I thought my whole world was collapsing about me. I have forgiven you, Nora. I swear to you, I have forgiven you.

NORA: Thank you for forgiving me. *(she goes out through the door on the right)*

TORVALD: No, don't go—*(looking in)* What are you doing in there?

NORA: *(inside)* Taking off my costume.

TORVALD *(standing by the open door)* Yes. Do that. Try to calm yourself down. Put your mind at ease, my frightened little songbird. You're safe now, and my big broad wings will protect you. *(walking to and fro by the door)* Nora, our home is so warm and cozy. Here you will always be safe. I will protect you—like a hunted dove that I've saved from the talons of a hawk. I will calm your poor beating heart. Little by little it will happen. Trust me, Nora. Tomorrow morning you'll think about it quite differently. Soon everything will be as it was before. In no time you won't need me to assure you that I have forgiven you. You will be absolutely sure that I have. Surely you can't imagine that I would reject you or even reproach you? You can't imagine what a real man's heart is like, Nora. It is so indescribably

sweet and satisfying for a man to know that he has forgiven his
wife—completely forgiven her and with all his heart. It's as if that
simple act has made her doubly his own. It's as if he had given her a
new life. And so, in a way she is now both wife and child to him. That
is what you will be for me from now on, little frightened helpless dar-
2210   ling. You mustn't worry about anything, Nora. All you have to do is be
open, frank, and honest with me, and I will be the conscience and the
will for you and . . . What's this? Not in bed? You've changed.

NORA: *(in her everyday clothes)* Yes, Torvald. I've changed.

TORVALD: But why?—It's so late.

NORA: I won't go to sleep tonight.

TORVALD: But my dear Nora—

NORA: *(looking at her watch)* It's not that late. Sit down, Torvald. You
and I have a lot to say to each other. *(she sits down at one side of
the table)*

TORVALD: Nora—what's this?—your eyes are so cold!

2220   NORA: Sit down. This will take some time; we have a lot to talk
about.

TORVALD: *(sits down at the opposite side of the table)* You're frightening me, Nora!—I don't understand you.

NORA: No, that's just it. You don't understand me, and I've never understood you either—until tonight. No, you mustn't interrupt me. I want
you to just listen to what I have to say. Torvald, it's time we settled
our accounts.

TORVALD: What do you mean by that?

NORA: *(after a short silence)* Doesn't anything strike you as strange in
2230   our sitting here like this?

TORVALD: What would that be?

NORA: We've been married now for eight years. Do you realize that this
is the first time that we two, you and I, man and wife, have had a
serious conversation?

TORVALD: What do you mean serious?

NORA: In all these eight years—no, longer than that—from the moment
we first met, we have never exchanged a *word* on any serious
subject.

TORVALD: Well, why would I keep on talking to you about my worries?
2240   There was nothing you could do to help.

NORA: I'm not talking about business. What I'm saying is that we have
never really sat down together to try and get to the bottom of
anything.

TORVALD: But, my dear Nora, what good would that have done you?

NORA: That's just it. You have never understood me. I have been greatly
wronged, Torvald—first by Papa and then by you.

TORVALD: What! By your father and me?—the two men who loved you
more than anyone else in the world?

NORA: *(shaking her head)* You have never loved me. You just thought it
was pleasant to be *in* love with me.

TORVALD: Nora, what are you saying?

NORA: It's perfectly true, Torvald. When I was at home with Papa, he
gave me his opinions on everything. So I had the same opinions as
he did. If I disagreed with him I concealed the fact, because he
wouldn't have liked it. He called me his doll-child, and he played
with me just as I used to play with my dolls. And when I came to live
in your house—

TORVALD: What a way to talk about our marriage!

NORA: *(undisturbed)* I mean that I was simply handed over from Papa
to you. You arranged everything to suit your own tastes, and so I had
the same tastes as you—or else I pretended to. I'm really not sure
which—I think sometimes the one and sometimes the other. When I
look back on it, it seems to me that I was living here like a pauper—
from hand to mouth. The whole reason for my existence was to perform tricks for you, Torvald. But that's what you wanted. You and
Papa have committed a great sin against me. It is your fault that I
have made nothing of my life.

TORVALD: How unreasonable and how ungrateful, Nora! Haven't you
been happy here?

NORA: No, I have never been happy. I thought I was, but I haven't been.

TORVALD: Not—happy!

NORA: No. Just cheerful. You have always been so kind to me. But our
home has been nothing but a playroom. I have been your doll-wife,
just as at home I was Papa's doll-child; and in this house the children
have been my dolls. I thought it was great fun when you played with
me, and they thought it was great fun when I played with them. That
is what our marriage has been, Torvald.

TORVALD: There's some truth in what you say—though you've exaggerated and made too much of it. But in the future things will be different. Playtime is over, and it's time for lessons.

NORA: Whose lessons? Mine or the children's?

TORVALD: Yours *and* the children's, Nora, my darling.

NORA: I'm sorry, Torvald, but you are not the man to teach me how to
be a proper wife to you.

TORVALD: How can you say that!

NORA: And how am I fit to bring up the children?

TORVALD: Nora!

NORA: Didn't you say yourself a little while ago—that you dare not trust
me to bring them up?

TORVALD: That was in a moment of anger! Why do you pay any attention
to that?

NORA: No, you were perfectly right. I am not fit to bring them up. There
is something else I must do first. I must try to educate myself—and

you are not the man to help me do that. I must do that by myself.
That is why I am leaving you.

TORVALD: *(springing up)* What did you say?

NORA: I must be by myself if I'm going to understand myself and the
world around me. That is why I can't stay with you any longer.

TORVALD: Nora, Nora!

2300   NORA: I am leaving, right away. I'm sure Kristine will take me in for the
night—

TORVALD: You're out of your mind! I won't allow it! I forbid you!

NORA: There's no point in forbidding me anything any longer. I'll take with
me only what belongs to me. I'll take nothing from you—now or later.

TORVALD: What kind of mad behavior is this?

NORA: Tomorrow I will go home—to my old home, I mean. It will be
easier for me to find something to do there.

TORVALD: You foolish woman! You can't see what you're doing!

NORA: I must try and make some sense of all this, Torvald.

2310   TORVALD: You're deserting your home, your husband, and your children!
Think what people will say!

NORA: I can't think about that at all. All I know is that I have no other
option.

TORVALD: I am deeply shocked. Is this how you neglect your most
sacred duties?

NORA: What do you think are my most sacred duties?

TORVALD: Do I need to tell you? Your duty to your husband and your
children!

NORA: I have another duty just as sacred.

2320   TORVALD: No, you don't. What duty could that be?

NORA: My duty to myself.

TORVALD: Before everything else, you are a wife and a mother.

NORA: I don't believe that any more. I believe that before everything I
am a thinking human being, just as you are—or, at any rate, that I
must try to become one. I know very well, Torvald, that most people
would think you are right, and that your views would be supported
in books. But I can no longer be satisfied with what most people say

2330   or what's written in books. I must think things over for myself and
try to understand them.

TORVALD: Why not try to understand your place in your own home?
Haven't you got a dependable guide in things like—your religion?

NORA: I'm afraid, Torvald, I don't really know what religion is.

TORVALD: What are you saying?

NORA: All I know is what my pastor told me when I was confirmed. He
told us that religion was this, that, and the other. When I have left all
this behind, when I am alone, I will look into that too. I will find out
if what the pastor said is true, or at least if it is true for me.

TORVALD: This is unheard of in a girl like you! But if religion can't put
you on the right path, then let me try to prick your conscience. You

2340 have *some* moral sense, don't you? Or—now answer me—am I supposed to think that you don't?

NORA: Well, Torvald, that is not an easy question to answer. I really don't know. I am totally perplexed. All I know is that you and I look at it very differently. And I am finding out too that the law is very different from what I thought. I find it impossible to convince myself that the law is right. According to the law, a woman has no right to protect her old and dying father, or to save her husband's life. I can't believe that.

TORVALD: You're talking like a child. You don't understand the world we 2350 live in.

NORA: No, I don't. But I intend to try. I'm going to find out which is right, the world or I.

TORVALD: You are not well, Nora, you must have a fever. I almost think you may be out of your mind.

NORA: My mind has never been so clear and determined as tonight.

TORVALD: And with this clear mind of yours you are determined to abandon your husband and your children?

NORA: Yes.

TORVALD: Then there is only one possible explanation.

2360 NORA: What?

TORVALD: You do not love me anymore.

NORA: No, that is just it.

TORVALD: Nora!—how can you say that?

NORA: It's very painful, Torvald. You have always been so kind to me, but I can't help it. I don't love you anymore.

TORVALD: *(regaining his composure)* Are you clear and determined about that too?

NORA: Yes, absolutely clear and determined. That is why I won't stay here any longer.

2370 TORVALD: And can you tell me what I have done to lose your love?

NORA: Yes, I can. It was tonight, when the miracle didn't happen. It was then that I saw you were not the man I thought you were.

TORVALD: Please explain yourself—I don't understand.

NORA: I had waited so patiently for eight years. Goodness knows, I didn't think that miracles happen every day. Then this . . . this . . . disaster fell upon me, and I felt quite sure that the miracle was finally going to happen. When Krogstad's letter was in the mailbox, never for a moment did I think you would accept his conditions. I was absolutely sure that you would say to him: Go ahead! Publish it. Let the whole 2380 world know! And after that—

TORVALD: Yes, what then?—after I had exposed my wife to shame and disgrace?

NORA: After that—I was absolutely sure that you would step forward and assume all the blame and say, "I am the guilty one."

TORVALD: Nora—!

NORA: What you are thinking is that I would never have accepted a
     sacrifice like that from you. No, of course I wouldn't. But what
     would my word have been against yours? That was the miracle I was
     hoping for. The miracle I was afraid of. It was to make sure that did
2390   not happen that I was ready to kill myself.
TORVALD: I would slave night and day for you, Nora—I would endure
     sorrow and poverty for your sake. But no man would sacrifice his
     honor even for the one he loves.
NORA: Thousands of women have done that.
TORVALD: You're thinking and talking like a stupid child.
NORA: Perhaps. But you don't think or talk like the man I could spend
     the rest of my life with. As soon as you stopped being frightened—
     and you weren't afraid of what was happening to me, you were
     afraid of what was happening to you—when it was over, as far as
2400   you were concerned it was just as if nothing had happened. Exactly
     as before. I was your little lark. I was your doll. Of course you would
     handle it twice as gently. It was so delicate and fragile. *(getting up)*
     Torvald—it was then it dawned on me that for eight years I've been
     living with a stranger and I had borne him three children—. Oh, I
     can't bear to think of it! I could tear myself to pieces!
TORVALD: *(sadly)* Yes. I see. I see. A gulf has opened up between us—
     I see that now. But Nora, couldn't we bridge that gulf?
NORA: The woman I am now is no wife for you.
TORVALD: I could change who I am—
2410 NORA: Perhaps—if your doll is taken away from you.
TORVALD: But to lose you!—to lose you forever! No, no, Nora, I can't
     accept that.
NORA: *(going out to the right)* That is why it must happen. *(she comes
     back with her cloak and hat and a small bag which she puts on a
     chair by the table)*
TORVALD: Nora. Nora, not now! Wait until tomorrow.
NORA: *(putting on her cloak)* I can't spend the night in the house of a
     stranger.
TORVALD: But we could live here like brother and sister—?
NORA: *(putting on her hat)* You know that that wouldn't last. *(puts the
     cloak round her)* Goodbye, Torvald. I won't see my children. I know
2420   they're in better hands than mine. The woman I am now would be
     no use to them.
TORVALD: But someday, Nora—someday?
NORA: How can I answer that? I've no idea of what's going to become
     of me.
TORVALD: But you are my wife, whatever happens to you.
NORA: Listen, Torvald. I have heard that when a wife leaves her hus-
     band's house, as I am doing now, he is legally freed from all obliga-
     tions toward her. In any case, *I* am setting you free. You're not to feel
     like a prisoner in any way. I will not feel that way at all. There must be
2430   perfect freedom on both sides. Here is your ring back. Give me mine.

TORVALD: That too?

NORA: That too.

TORVALD: Here it is.

NORA: There. Now it's all over. I've put the keys here. The maids know all about running the house—much better than I do. Tomorrow, after I've left, Kristine will come and pack the things I brought with me from home. I'll have them sent on to me.

TORVALD: It's all over! All over!—Nora, will you never think of me again?

2440   NORA: I know that I will often think of you . . . and the children . . . and this house.

TORVALD: May I write to you, Nora?

NORA: No—never. You must never do that.

TORVALD: But at least let me send you—

NORA: Nothing—nothing—

TORVALD: Just let me help you if you ever need it.

NORA: No. I can never accept anything from a stranger.

TORVALD: Nora—can I never be anything more than a stranger to you?

NORA: *(taking her bag)* Oh, Torvald, the greatest miracle of all would

2450   have to happen.

TORVALD: What would that be?

NORA: You and I would have to change so much that—. Oh, Torvald, I don't believe in miracles anymore.

TORVALD: But I will. Tell me!—changed so much that—?

NORA: That our life together would be a real marriage. Goodbye. *(she goes out through the hall)*

TORVALD: *(sinks down on a chair at the door and buries his face in his hands)* Nora! Nora! *(looks round and rises)* Empty. She's gone. *(a glimmer of hope flashes across his face)* The greatest miracle of all—?

(the sound of a door shutting is heard from below)

Questions for Engagement, Response, and Analysis

Act 1

1. What is the setting of this play? How does Ibsen reveal early in the play the importance of and shortage of money in this family?

2. What are the qualities Torvald admires in Nora?

3. What does Nora believe to be of primary importance to Torvald?

Act 2

1. What do Torvald's statements about himself reveal about his self-concept? What would these statements lead Nora to expect?

2. What does Rank's refusal to let Torvald visit him in the hospital suggest about Rank's opinion of Torvald?

3. Explain Nora's statement to Dr. Rank that "there are some people whom one loves and those whom one would choose to spend one's time with."

4. List the pet names that Torvald calls Nora and explain the implications of each.

Act 3

1. Explain the significance of the play's title.

2. From the opening scene of the play until the beginning of the last scene, Nora lies to Torvald. Why?

3. Explain Nora's statement to Torvald, "You don't understand me. And I've never understood you either—until tonight."

4. Why would Nora's statement that she has a duty toward herself be so astonishing to a nineteenth-century audience? What would be the probable reaction of an audience today?

5. How is Nora's situation at the end of the play different from what it would be for a woman today?

6. In what ways does Nora misjudge all of the males in her life? Explain.

7. What does Nora think Torvald will do when he learns the truth? How does her expectation make the reality even worse?

8. What is the theme of this play?

Crafting Arguments

1. Several events in Act 1, such as Torvald's attitude toward his clients and his statements about Krogstad, foreshadow Torvald's reactions in Act 3. In an essay, analyze Torvald's behavior in Act 1 and his statements in Act 2, and argue that (1) they prepare the reader or viewer for his behavior in Act 3 or (2) they make his behavior in Act 3 even more ironic.

2. Contrast Nora's behavior at the beginning of the play with her behavior at the end of Act 3 and explain the reasons for the change.

3. In an essay, explain the ironic contrast between Torvald's statements to Nora about protecting her and his actual behavior toward her.

4. Look up the definition of a dramatic foil in the glossary. Then, write an essay arguing that Kristine Linde is a dramatic foil for Nora.

5. Write an argumentative essay on one of the following:

   Nora's decision at the end of the play is unrealistic and misguided.

   Nora's decision at the end of the play is necessary for her self-preservation.

   Torvald is just as trapped by society's expectations of a husband as Nora is as a wife.

Casebook
on Robert Frost

Though Frost is often described as a nature poet, he claimed that all but two of his poems include people. In this Casebook, nine poems, ranging from beautiful love sonnets to longer narrative poems in blank verse and even to descriptions of terrifying encounters, depict the complex relationships between men and women. The critical articles and the interview by Robert Penn Warren and Cleanth Brooks allow you to craft an argument that uses the poems as your primary sources and the critical works as your secondary.

Robert Frost (1874–1963)

Robert Frost's life, like many of his poems, was filled with ironies. Known as a New England poet, Frost was born in San Francisco and named after Robert E. Lee. When his poetry was not recognized in the United States, he moved to England and there published his first books of poetry, A Boy's Will *(1913) and* North of Boston *(1914). When he returned to the United States, his fame as a poet was already established.*

Frost had more than his share of family tragedies, however, and was always aware of the darker side of life. Even his famous definition of poetry as a "momentary stay against confusion" in "The Figure a Poem Makes" emphasizes the complexities of life and the necessity of finding ways to manage life's ambiguities. For Frost, precise form in poetry is one of those ways; as a master craftsman, he uses traditional poetic form so skillfully that he seems to recreate the natural speech patterns of the New England characters in his dialogues and monologues, and he adds to the meaning of his poems by using such tight forms as the sonnet and terza rima.

THE PASTURE   (1914)

I'm going out to clean the pasture spring;
I'll only stop to rake the leaves away
(And wait to watch the water clear, I may):
I shan't be gone long.—You come too.

5   I'm going out to fetch the little calf
That's standing by the mother. It's so young
It totters when she licks it with her tongue.
I shan't be gone long.—You come too.

Questions for Engagement, Response, and Analysis

1. This poem is placed first in the collected works of Frost and is an obvious invitation. What are the possible interpretations of this invitation and to whom might they be addressed?

2. Examine the form and language of this poem and explain how they do or do not suggest qualities of Frost's poetry, both in this poem and in the others included in this text.

THE SILKEN TENT   (1939)

She is as in a field a silken tent
At midday when a sunny summer breeze
Has dried the dew and all its ropes relent,
So that in guys it gently sways at ease,
5   And its supporting central cedar pole,
That is its pinnacle to heavenward
And signifies the sureness of the soul,
Seems to owe naught to any single cord,
But strictly held by none, is loosely bound
10   By countless silken ties of love and thought
To everything on earth the compass round,
And only by one's going slightly taut
In the capriciousness of summer air
Is of the slightest bondage made aware.

Questions for Engagement, Response, and Analysis

1. This poem uses one predominating metaphor. Examine and interpret each of the images that are part of this metaphor in the poem: the silken tent, the guys, and the central pole.
2. The sonnet is a strict and somewhat rigidly stylized form. Why might Frost have chosen this form for this subject?
3. What is the tone of this poem? Support your answer by using specific examples from the poem.

NEVER AGAIN WOULD BIRDS' SONG BE THE SAME (1946)

He would declare and could himself believe
That the birds there in all the garden round
From having heard the daylong voice of Eve
Had added to their own an oversound,
5   Her tone of meaning but without the words.
Admittedly an eloquence so soft
Could only have had an influence on birds
When call or laughter carried it aloft.
Be that as may be, she was in their song.
10   Moreover her voice upon their voices crossed
Had now persisted in the woods so long
That probably it never would be lost.
Never again would birds' song be the same.
And to do that to birds was why she came.

Questions for Engagement, Response, and Analysis

1. Frost described this poem as "an old fashioned praise poem." What traditional form is it written in?
2. Whom is the narrator praising in the poem? Is the praise for one woman only? What are the qualities for which he praises her?
3. Compare the tone of this poem with that of "The Silken Tent."

MEETING AND PASSING   (1930)

As I went down the hill along the wall
There was a gate I had leaned at for the view
And had just turned from when I first saw you
As you came up the hill. We met. But all
5   We did that day was mingle great and small
Footprints in summer dust as if we drew
The figure of our being less than two
But more than one as yet. Your parasol

Pointed the decimal off with one deep thrust.
10   And all the time we talked you seemed to see
Something down there to smile at in the dust.
(Oh, it was without prejudice to me!)
Afterward I went past what you had passed
Before we met, and you what I had passed.

Questions for Engagement, Response, and Analysis

1. This poem describes a chance encounter. Who is the narrator?
2. What clues suggest the future of the two people in this encounter?
3. Why is the dot made by the parasol a decimal point rather than a period?

PUTTING IN THE SEED   (1914)

You come to fetch me from my work tonight
When supper's on the table, and we'll see
If I can leave off burying the white
Soft petals fallen from the apple tree
5   (Soft petals, yes, but not so barren quite,
Mingled with these, smooth bean and wrinkled pea),
And go along with you ere you lose sight
Of what you came for and become like me,
Slave to a springtime passion for the earth.
10   How Love burns through the Putting in the Seed
On through the watching for that early birth
When, just as the soil tarnishes with weed,
The sturdy seedling with arched body comes
Shouldering its way and shedding the earth crumbs.

Questions for Engagement, Response, and Analysis

1. Who is the speaker in this poem?
2. Like "The Silken Tent," this sonnet has one predominating metaphor. Using the details of the poem, suggest at least two interpretations of this metaphor.
3. What is the tone of this poem?

THE SUBVERTED FLOWER   (1949)

She drew back; he was calm;
"It is this that had the power."
And he lashed his open palm
With the tender-headed flower.

5   He smiled for her to smile,
       But she was either blind
       Or willfully unkind.
       He eyed her for a while
       For a woman and a puzzle.
10   He flicked and flung the flower,
       And another sort of smile
       Caught up like fingertips
       The corners of his lips
       And cracked his ragged muzzle.
15   She was standing to the waist
       In goldenrod and brake,
       Her shining hair displaced.
       He stretched her either arm
       As if she made it ache
20   To clasp her—not to harm;
       As if he could not spare
       To touch her neck and hair.
       "If this has come to us
       And not to me alone————"
25   So she thought she heard him say;
       Though with every word he spoke
       His lips were sucked and blown
       And the effort made him choke
       Like a tiger at a bone.
30   She had to lean away.
       She dared not stir a foot,
       Lest movement should provoke
       The demon of pursuit
       That slumbers in a brute.
35   It was then her mother's call
       From inside the garden wall
       Made her steal a look of fear
       To see if he could hear
       And would pounce to end it all
40   Before her mother came.
       She looked and saw the shame:
       A hand hung like a paw,
       An arm worked like a saw
       As if to be persuasive,
45   An ingratiating laugh
       That cut the snout in half,
       An eye become evasive.
       A girl could only see
       That a flower had marred a man,
50   But what she could not see

Was that the flower might be
Other than base and fetid:
That the flower had done but part,
And what the flower began
55   Her own too meager heart
Had terribly completed.
She looked and saw the worst.
And the dog or what it was,
Obeying bestial laws,
60   A coward save at night,
Turned from the place and ran.
She heard him stumble first
And use his hands in flight.
She heard him bark outright.
65   And oh, for one so young
The bitter words she spit
Like some tenacious bit
That will not leave the tongue.
She plucked her lips for it,
70   And still the horror clung.
Her mother wiped the foam
From her chin, picked up her comb,
And drew her backward home.

Questions for Engagement, Response, and Analysis

1. Through whose eyes is this encounter seen?
2. What changes take place in the boy as this encounter progresses? To what extent do the girl's actions and reactions influence his behavior?
3. Examine and interpret the animal imagery in the poem.
4. One meaning of the word *subvert* is to "corrupt by an undermining of morals." How does this meaning relate to the flower in the poem, which the title says is "subverted"?
5. What is the tone of this poem?

HOME BURIAL   (1914)

He saw her from the bottom of the stairs
Before she saw him. She was starting down,
Looking back over her shoulder at some fear.
She took a doubtful step and then undid it
5   To raise herself and look again. He spoke
Advancing toward her: "What is it you see
From up there always?—for I want to know."
She turned and sank upon her skirts at that,

And her face changed from terrified to dull.
10 He said to gain time: "What is it you see?"
Mounting until she cowered under him.
"I will find out now—you must tell me, dear."
She, in her place, refused him any help,
With the least stiffening of her neck and silence.
15 She let him look, sure that he wouldn't see,
Blind creature; and awhile he didn't see.
But at last he murmured, "Oh," and again, "Oh."

"What is it—what?" she said.

        "Just that I see."

"You don't," she challenged. "Tell me what it is."

20 "The wonder is I didn't see at once.
I never noticed it from here before.
I must be wonted to it—that's the reason.
The little graveyard where my people are!
So small the window frames the whole of it.
25 Not so much larger than a bedroom, is it?
There are three stones of slate and one of marble,
Broad-shouldered little slabs there in the sunlight
On the sidehill. We haven't to mind *those*.
But I understand: it is not the stones,
30 But the child's mound—"

        "Don't, don't, don't,

    don't," she cried.

She withdrew, shrinking from beneath his arm
That rested on the banister, and slid downstairs;
And turned on him with such a daunting look,
He said twice over before he knew himself:
35 "Can't a man speak of his own child he's lost?"

"Not you!—Oh, where's my hat? Oh, I don't need it!
I must get out of here. I must get air.—
I don't know rightly whether any man can."

"Amy! Don't go to someone else this time.
40 Listen to me. I won't come down the stairs."
He sat and fixed his chin between his fists.
"There's something I should like to ask you, dear."

"You don't know how to ask it."

        "Help me, then."

Her fingers moved the latch for all reply.

45 "My words are nearly always an offense.
I don't know how to speak of anything
So as to please you. But I might be taught,
I should suppose. I can't say I see how.
A man must partly give up being a man
50 With womenfolk. We could have some arrangement
By which I'd bind myself to keep hands off
Anything special you're a-mind to name.
Though I don't like such things 'twixt those that love.
Two that don't love can't live together without them.
55 But two that do can't live together with them."
She moved the latch a little. "Don't—don't go.
Don't carry it to someone else this time.
Tell me about it if it's something human.
Let me into your grief. I'm not so much
60 Unlike other folks as your standing there
Apart would make me out. Give me my chance.
I do think, though, you overdo it a little.
What was it brought you up to think it the thing
To take your mother-loss of a first child
65 So inconsolably—in the face of love.
You'd think his memory might be satisfied—"

"There you go sneering now!"

               "I'm not, I'm not!

You make me angry. I'll come down to you.
God, what a woman! And it's come to this,
70 A man can't speak of his own child that's dead."

"You can't because you don't know how to speak.
If you had any feelings, you that dug
With your own hand—how could you?—his little grave;
I saw you from that very window there,
75 Making the gravel leap and leap in air,
Leap up, like that, like that, and land so lightly
And roll back down the mound beside the hole.
I thought, Who is that man? I didn't know you.
And I crept down the stairs and up the stairs
80 To look again, and still your spade kept lifting.
Then you came in. I heard your rumbling voice
Out in the kitchen and I don't know why,
But I went near to see with my own eyes,
You could sit there with the stains on your shoes
85 Of the fresh earth from your own baby's grave
And talk about your everyday concerns.
You had stood the spade up against the wall

Outside there in the entry, for I saw it."
"I shall laugh the worst laugh I ever laughed.
90   I'm cursed. God, if I don't believe I'm cursed."

"I can repeat the very words you were saying:
'Three foggy mornings and one rainy day
Will rot the best birch fence a man can build.'
Think of it, talk like that at such a time!
95   What had how long it takes a birch to rot
To do with what was in the darkened parlor?
You *couldn't* care! The nearest friends can go
With anyone to death, comes so far short
They might as well not try to go at all.
100   No, from the time when one is sick to death,
One is alone, and he dies more alone.
Friends make pretense of following to the grave,
But before one is in it, their minds are turned
And making the best of their way back to life
105   And living people, and things they understand.
But the world's evil. I won't have grief so
If I can change it. Oh, I won't, I won't!"

"There, you have said it all and you feel better.
You won't go now. You're crying. Close the door.
110   The heart's gone out of it: why keep it up?
Amy! There's someone coming down the road!"

"*You*—oh, you think the talk is all. I must go—
Somewhere out of this house. How can I make you—"

"If—you—do!" She was opening the door wider.

115   "Where do you mean to go? First tell me that.
I'll follow and bring you back by force. I *will!*—"

Questions for Engagement, Response, and Analysis

1. The husband says, "'A man must partly give up being a man / With womenfolk.'" Explain these lines and agree or disagree with the husband's claim.

2. Explain the significance of Amy's statement about the rotting birch. Why does the husband's statement about the birch offend Amy? With whom do you agree? Why?

3. In what ways does the physical movement of Amy and her husband reflect their differences of opinion and their emotional reaction to one another?

4. Does the title have more than one possible meaning?

The Death of the Hired Man   (1914)

Mary sat musing on the lamp-flame at the table,
Waiting for Warren. When she heard his step,
She ran on tiptoe down the darkened passage
To meet him in the doorway with the news
5   And put him on his guard. "Silas is back."
She pushed him outward with her through the door
And shut it after her. "Be kind," she said.
She took the market things from Warren's arms
And set them on the porch, then drew him down
10   To sit beside her on the wooden steps.

"When was I ever anything but kind to him?
But I'll not have the fellow back," he said.
"I told him so last haying, didn't I?
If he left then, I said, that ended it.
15   What good is he? Who else will harbor him
At his age for the little he can do?
What help he is there's no depending on.
Off he goes always when I need him most.
He thinks he ought to earn a little pay,
20   Enough at least to buy tobacco with,
So he won't have to beg and be beholden.
'All right,' I say, 'I can't afford to pay
Any fixed wages, though I wish I could.'
'Someone else can.' 'Then someone else will have to.'
25   I shouldn't mind his bettering himself
If that was what it was. You can be certain,
When he begins like that, there's someone at him
Trying to coax him off with pocket money—
In haying time, when any help is scarce.
30   In winter he comes back to us. I'm done."

"Sh! not so loud: he'll hear you," Mary said.

"I want him to: he'll have to soon or late."
"He's worn out. He's asleep beside the stove.
When I came up from Rowe's I found him here,
35   Huddled against the barn door fast asleep,
A miserable sight, and frightening, too—
You needn't smile—I didn't recognize him—
I wasn't looking for him—and he's changed.
Wait till you see."

          "Where did you say he'd been?"
40   "He didn't say. I dragged him to the house,
And gave him tea and tried to make him smoke.
I tried to make him talk about his travels.

Nothing would do: he just kept nodding off."

"What did he say? Did he say anything?"

45   "But little."

        "Anything? Mary confess
He said he'd come to ditch the meadow for me."

"Warren!"

        "But did he? I just want to know."

"Of course he did. What would you have him say?
Surely you wouldn't grudge the poor old man
50   Some humble way to save his self-respect.
He added, if you really care to know,
He meant to clear the upper pasture, too.
That sounds like something you have heard before?
Warren, I wish you could have heard the way
55   He jumbled everything. I stopped to look
Two or three times—he made me feel so queer—
To see if he was talking in his sleep.
He ran on Harold Wilson—you remember—
The boy you had in haying four years since.
60   He's finished school, and teaching in his college.
Silas declares you'll have to get him back.
He says they two will make a team for work:
Between them they will lay this farm as smooth!
The way he mixed that in with other things.
65   He thinks young Wilson a likely lad, though daft
On education—you know how they fought
All through July under the blazing sun,
Silas up on the cart to build the load,
Harold along beside to pitch it on."

70   "Yes, I took care to keep well out of earshot."

"Well, those days trouble Silas like a dream.
You wouldn't think they would. How some things linger!
Harold's young college-boy's assurance piqued him.
After so many years he still keeps finding
75   Good arguments he sees he might have used.
I sympathize. I know just how it feels
To think of the right thing to say too late.
Harold's associated in his mind with Latin.
He asked me what I thought of Harold's saying
80   He studied Latin, like the violin,
Because he liked it—that an argument!
He said he couldn't make the boy believe

He could find water with a hazel prong—
Which showed how much good school had ever done him.
85 He wanted to go over that. But most of all
He thinks if he could have another chance
To teach him how to build a load of hay—"

"I know, that's Silas' one accomplishment.
He bundles every forkful in its place,
90 And tags and numbers it for future reference,
So he can find and easily dislodge it
In the unloading. Silas does that well.
He takes it out in bunches like big birds' nests.
You never see him standing on the hay
95 He's trying to lift, straining to lift himself."

"He thinks if he could teach him that, he'd be
Some good perhaps to someone in the world.
He hates to see a boy the fool of books.
Poor Silas, so concerned for other folk,
100 And nothing to look backward to with pride,
And nothing to look forward to with hope,
So now and never any different."

Part of a moon was falling down the west,
Dragging the whole sky with it to the hills.
105 Its light poured softly in her lap. She saw it
And spread her apron to it. She put out her hand
Among the harplike morning-glory strings,
Taut with the dew from garden bed to eaves,
As if she played unheard some tenderness
110 That wrought on him beside her in the night.
"Warren," she said, "he has come home to die:
You needn't be afraid he'll leave you this time."
"Home," he mocked gently.

"Yes, what else but home?
It all depends on what you mean by home.
115 Of course he's nothing to us, any more
Than was the hound that came a stranger to us
Out of the woods, worn out upon the trail."

"Home is the place where, when you have to go there,
They have to take you in."

"I should have called it
120 Something you somehow haven't to deserve."

Warren leaned out and took a step or two,
Picked up a little stick, and brought it back

And broke it in his hand and tossed it by.
"Silas has better claim on us you think
125   Than on his brother? Thirteen little miles
As the road winds would bring him to his door.
Silas has walked that far no doubt today.
Why doesn't he go there? His brother's rich,
a somebody—director in the bank."

130   He never told us that."

      "We know it, though."

"I think his brother ought to help, of course.
I'll see to that if there is need. He ought of right
To take him in, and might be willing to—
He may be better than appearances.
135   But have some pity on Silas. Do you think
If he had any pride in claiming kin
Or anything he looked for from his brother,
He'd keep so still about him all this time?"

"I wonder what's between them."

      "I can tell you.
140   Silas is what he is—we wouldn't mind him—
But just the kind that kinsfolk can't abide.
He never did a thing so very bad.
He don't know why he isn't quite as good
As anybody. Worthless though he is,
145   He won't be made ashamed to please his brother."

"*I* can't think Si ever hurt anyone."

No, but he hurt my heart the way he lay
And rolled his old head on that sharp-edged chair-back.
He wouldn't let me put him on the lounge.
150   You must go in and see what you can do.
I made the bed up for him there tonight.
You'll be surprised at him—how much he's broken.
His working days are done; I'm sure of it."

"I'd not be in a hurry to say that."

155   "I haven't been. Go, look, see for yourself.
But, Warren, please remember how it is:
He's come to help you ditch the meadow.
He has a plan. You mustn't laugh at him.
He may not speak of it, and then he may.
160   I'll sit and see if that small sailing cloud
Will hit or miss the moon."

It hit the moon.
Then there were three there, making a dim row,
The moon, the little silver cloud, and she.
Warren returned—too soon, it seemed to her—
165   Slipped to her side, caught up her hand and waited.

"Warren?" she questioned.

"Dead," was all he answered.

Questions for Engagement, Response, and Analysis

1. Examine the passages describing the cloud, the moon, and the stick, and explain their significance or symbolism.

2. Why it is so important to Silas that Warren and Mary understand that he has returned to work for them? Why does he not go to his brother's home?

3. Support or challenge Mary's statement that Silas had "'nothing to look backward to with pride, / And nothing to look forward to with hope.'"

4. Silas thinks that Harold's studying "'Latin, like the violin, / Because he liked it'" is ridiculous. Support or oppose Harold's point of view.

5. Warren and Mary handle the same situation differently. How do their similarities and their differences define their personalities?

BEREFT   (1929)

Where had I heard this wind before
Change like this to a deeper roar?
What would it take my standing there for,
Holding open a restive door,
5   Looking downhill to a frothy shore?
Summer was past and day was past.
Somber clouds in the west were massed.
Out in the porch's sagging floor
Leaves got up in a coil and hissed,
10   Blindly struck at my knee and missed.
Something sinister in the tone
Told me my secret must be known:
Word I was in the house alone
Somehow must have gotten abroad,
15   Word I was in my life alone,
Word I had no one left but God.

Questions for Engagement, Response, and Analysis

1. The title of this poem implies that the speaker has suffered a devastating loss. Explain the effective metaphorical devices that illustrate this devastation.

2. This poem is one of many that together frame Frost's concept of the relationship of humans to nature. What does this poem suggest about that relationship?

3. What is the tone of this poem? Does the last line alter that tone?

FROST'S POETRY OF METAPHOR
JUDITH OSTER

1   "Metaphor is the whole of poetry." "Poetry is simply made of metaphor ... Every poem is a new metaphor inside or it is nothing." (*CPPP*, 786)[1] Such are the burdens Robert Frost placed upon metaphor, and on himself as a poet. He went even farther in his claiming that metaphor is the whole of thinking, and that, therefore, to be educated by poetry—note: by poetry—is to be taught to think (*CPPP*, 786). In "Education by Poetry," an essay that originated in a talk at Amherst, he says:

> [T]he teacher must teach the pupil to think. . . . We still ask boys in college to think, . . . but we seldom tell them it is just putting this and that together, it is saying one thing in terms of another. To tell them is to set their feet on the first rung of a ladder the top of which reaches to the sky . . . The metaphor whose manage we are best taught in poetry—that is all there is of thinking. It may not seem far for the mind to go, but it is the mind's furthest. The richest accumulation of the ages is the noble metaphors we have rolled up.

(*CPPP*, 723;725)

2   But he also cautions that all metaphors break down somewhere, as of course they must because a metaphor, no matter how rich or how apt, is not an identity, never an exact correspondence. On one hand, this means that one must be wary when thinking by means of metaphor, and one must be wary when reading or hearing the metaphors of others. As examples he gives scientific theories such as evolution (a plant metaphor), a mechanistic universe (a machine—all right—but where's the lever, or button, or pedal?), and concludes; "Unless you have had your proper poetical education in the metaphor, you are not safe anywhere. Because you are not at ease in figurative values: you don't know the metaphor in its strength and its weakness . . . You are not safe in science; you are not safe in history" (721). We must understand that a metaphor will take us only so far before it "breaks down." My love may be a rose in her softness, her sweetness, her beauty, or even her tendency to hurt me. But she

[1]Robert Frost, *Collected Poems, Prose, and Plays*, New York: Library of America, 1995.

does not grow outside in the garden on a stem. The human lover is infinitely more complicated than the rose.

3   On the other hand, the fact that metaphors are not merely correspondences or strict analogies is their glory. In their richness, great metaphors enlarge our thinking and our imaginations as we "play" with their possibilities, but also test their limits. How far can we take one up that ladder before we fall? How good are we at creating our own metaphors, and what do we risk when we do so? This is very serious "play"—to Frost, "play for mortal stakes," as he writes in "Two Tramps in Mud Time." The "game" in "Mending Wall" ("Oh, just another kind of outdoor game, / One on a side. It comes to little more"), as well as the playfulness of its tone, never successfully masks the seriousness of that poem or its mysteries. What is the "something" that does not love a wall? What can be meant by "know[ing] what I was walling in or walling out"? What is it that requires "walling in"?

4   Possibly related to reading and writing metaphors is one of Frost's metaphors of poetry: "I wouldn't have a poem that hadn't doors. I wouldn't leave them open, though."[2] The basic conceptual metaphor, is that of a structure (which a poem, after all, is). If a poem has doors that open and close, it may be represented as a house, where leaving doors open could leave the resident vulnerable to intrusion, even theft or harm. We may ask once again whether closing the door means walling in or walling out, or both. On the other hand, a house with doors can also be inviting; the one standing outside may be invited in. A door, after all, is meant to be opened as well as shut. A word like "something," for example, used as Frost uses it, opens it at least a crack: "Something there is that doesn't love a wall" ("Mending Wall," *CPPP*, 39); or: "What was that whiteness? / Truth? A pebble of quartz? For once, then, something" ("For Once, Then, Something," *CPPP*, 208). A poem, then, can be an invitation, but not an unlimited one, not always, and not to everyone. We may get invited in and challenged to play the game, but we are not assured of a perfect score.

5   A person who does not realize that this is an open-ended game with no one "correct" answer may be too timid to accept the challenge. This is true of many who "fear" poetry, and this can include serious students of literature. . . .

6   To understand poetry—come close to it, as Frost would say—is to know it at its strongest and largest, but to know it at its weakest as well; to know how far one may take it, where it breaks down, and where it breaks out and soars beyond itself. To read poetry like much of Frost's is to keep open the widest range of possibilities, but, as Frost says elsewhere, to "stay unassuming," not daring to close down or be conclusive where the poem stays open. This is especially true in poems where we can only suspect that we are reading metaphor, or, where we are not given a second term or situation with shared attributes, but are somehow

[2]Frost's English notebook, quoted in Lawrance Thompson's *Robert Frost: The Early Years, 1874–1915* (New York: Holt, Rinehart, and Winston, 1966), p. 397.

convinced that this image or small drama has meaning beyond itself, that it is indeed metaphor, and because its referent is left open, can be "about" many things, none of them mutually exclusive. . . . A poem like "Birches," for example, practically forces us to ask: what is this poem *about*? Not "what does it mean" or "what do birches stand for?" or "what is the poet telling us?" but what is the poet asking us to explore or connect with; think about, and feel? While those birches may present us with a beautiful New England image, the real picture we are given is not a static tableau of trees, but a powerful, dynamic drama of *climbing* birches, of a boy testing the limits of his daring, keeping his balance in a precarious position of his own choosing. Too far from town to play baseball, too alone to be challenged by others, he challenges himself. It is true that the trees and the boy's actions are described metaphorically:

> You may see their trunks arching in the woods
> . . .
> Like girls on hands and knees that throw their hair
> Before them over their heads to dry in the sun.

> > he always kept his poise
> To the top branches, climbing carefully
> With the same pains you use to fill a cup
> Up to the brim, and even above the brim.

7   We must also keep in mind that even the literal description of the boy and his actions are being imagined wistfully by the speaker—the trees have, in reality, been bent down to stay by ice storms; and these are also described metaphorically in terms of crazed enamel, broken glass, and the inner dome of heaven. Ironically, that magnificent picture is called "matter-of-fact" because it is Truth—ice storms, not boys—even though it is expressed in language that is not matter-of-fact at all. There is no lack, then, of metaphor, even metaphor within metaphor and metaphoric playing *in* the poem, but what of the significance of that whole scene and its drama—the whole poem as metaphor, or, in another word, the story-as-metaphor we term "parable"? What are those arching girls doing there? Why, suddenly, does the speaker declare: "Earth's the right place for love," when he has just been talking about pain and weariness, memories of being himself a swinger of birches, of a pathless wood, and a weeping eye?

8   By the time he says "It's when I'm weary of considerations, / And life is too much like a pathless wood" it is clear that we are not just talking about trees and boys climbing them; the question is, at what point before this did the poem begin to push toward parable? That the poem encompasses more we would probably all agree, but we would have trouble agreeing on, or even identifying the exact line where we began to feel those larger meanings—life and death, the risks and costs and joys of love, or art, or climbing in every sense—the absolute need for both daring and balance when we do so. In fact, even in our own subsequent readings we would most likely point to different places. But that is the

strength of the poem. Its supreme art lies precisely in the way it blurs the distinctions between concrete fact and imagination, between catching us up in the experience of the poem and forcing us to contemplate it in a more detached manner—the same tension, of course, between experience and contemplation that is everywhere *in* the poem.

9   In some poems we need to ask a question more fundamental even than where metaphor begins or what it signifies: are we in the presence of metaphor at all? Perhaps the most debated work in the Frost canon is that best-known and best-loved poem "Stopping by Woods on a Snowy Evening" (*CPPP*, 207). It has been read as "simply" a beautiful lyric, as a suicide poem, as recording a single autobiographical incident, and everything in between. Ours is not to adjudicate, nor to "fix" a meaning, but to allow the poem its openness, its fullest possible range; at the same time, to ask how such a delicate lyric, so satisfying in its perfect blend of description, sound, feeling, and form, has still prompted its readers to find, or seek, something more. Why hasn't it just been taken literally? What triggers those readings? To choose just one of any possible starting points, the word "promises." In this context of beautiful scene the word "pulls down" the experience from the merely aesthetic and sensual, but does so without diminishing that beauty or that feeling, without weighing down the poem. What results is a conflict between two undiminished forces: "promises" that would lead the speaker onward, and his desire to give in to his intoxication with the beauty and peacefulness of the woods. The pull between those alternatives can be seen as that between obligation and temptation, or most literally, between stopping and going on.

10   If we decide to look at the situation literally, we would think about what staying might mean. Most obvious is simply that it's too cold to stay there safely. The restfulness—the "ease" of "easy wind" and the "down" of "downy flake" begin to suggest an implicit metaphor, especially when combined with the "sleep" which must be postponed until promises are kept ("and miles to go before I sleep")—that of a bed. Sleeping before stopping, then, adds to the notion of not-yet-doing the danger of no-longer-being. Whether a beautiful momentary diversion from "promises," a fleeting wish that one *could* postpone promises, or a more dangerous temptation, the scene offers escape, aided by the hypnotic effect created by the beauty of the scene. The reader, too, is lulled by the scene, and by the rhythmic perfection of the poem.

11   What *does* the poem mean? Frost would probably say "Read it. It means what it says." What *can* the poem mean? That is another issue: whatever those words in those combinations will allow without distorting their meanings, without introducing elements that cannot fit in the context of the poem as a whole. What will it mean to a particular reader at a particular moment of reading? That must be flexible: one could follow Frost's advice to a graduate student to take his poetry "all the way." Or one could feel chastised by Frost's ridicule of those who say this is a "suicide poem." Or one could ignore Frost altogether.

12   It is just such questions, fueled by our desire to make meaning, or to explore the possibilities and limitations of words, that make Frost such a challenge to his readers despite the accessibility of his language and his "dramas." What does "The woods are lovely, dark and deep" mean? Can a line be more literal than this? But then we might be influenced by other associations we have built up with a word like "dark." Our everyday discourse uses "dark" metaphorically with no reference to poems, for example: we are kept in the dark (ignorance of the situation); we have deep, dark secrets (those we are ashamed to divulge, perhaps); someone gave me a dark look (menacing or unfriendly); theologians write of a dark night of the soul. On the most literal level, children are often afraid of the dark, most probably because they cannot see what is there, and nothing is more frightening than the unknown, than imagining what might be there that we cannot see. Even the least imaginative adults are afraid when they cannot see their way, for they might trip over some object, or bang into it, or get lost. . . .

13   One poem that contains no contextual clues within it, no language loaded with emotional weight, is "The Pasture" (*CPPP*, 3), that invitation to join the speaker as he goes "out to clean the pasture spring," to "rake the leaves away / And wait to watch the water clear." Both stanzas end with "You come too." The speaker issues an invitation and repeats it. We need make nothing more of it. But once we notice that this poem stands at the front of every one of Frost's collections, we assume it has a greater significance to him. We see this poem in a context, even though the context is outside the poem itself. We may assume (as others have) that it is either a love poem, or an invitation into his poetry. And once we assume that, the words, so innocent of metaphorical weight up to that point, are open to re-examination—where else does he write of pastures, and water (clear or in need of clearing); where else of leaves, and mothers, of being gone long? The answer: in many places. One has only to peruse his body of work to find a broad range of experiences, emotions, speculations, and conflicts expressed through and among leaves, or water, or clearing, or wandering. Still, the poem, like "Stopping by Woods," remains a lovely lyric.

14   What if there are no contextual clues to guide us, or to force us into metaphor? Usually, we can take an image or leave it, seeing a poem more, or less, richly, fearing under- or over-reading, with nothing very much at stake. In "Home Burial," however, there is a moment when everything could depend on whether or not the words were metaphor, and if they were, on what an "interpretive reading" might have been able to achieve. The grief-stricken wife, it will be remembered, cannot reconcile herself to the death of her baby, and cannot forgive her husband for his failure to grieve. The poem does indeed dramatize the burial of that home and that marriage, bringing the reader into a frustratingly anguished scene of confrontation and failed (or non-existent) communication. After much

urging, the wife has finally given voice to what has been upsetting her so much—her husband's digging of the infant's grave:

> "If you had any feelings, you that dug
> With your own hand—how could you?—his little grave;
> . . .
> I thought, Who is that man? I didn't know you.
> . . .
> Then you came in. I heard your rumbling voice
> Out in the kitchen, . . .
> . . .
> You could sit there with the stains on your shoes
> Of the fresh earth from your own baby's grave
> And talk about your everyday concerns.
> . . .
> I can repeat the very words you were saying:
> 'Three foggy mornings and one rainy day
> Will rot the best birch fence a man can build.'
> Think of it, talk like that at such a time!
> What had how long it takes a birch to rot
> To do with what was in the darkened parlor?" (*CPPP*, 58)

15   The answer, if he had been speaking metaphorically, could have been "Everything!" Wetness rotting a birch fence, talked of "at such a time," could have been his way of commenting on death, projecting onto a fence what would happen to the best coffin one could build, and to whatever it contained. But she did not see that possibility; he did not explain it, and even though we readers understand what such a metaphor could have meant, we can also understand how callous he either seemed to one who could not think metaphorically, or how callous he really was, if the words were, literally, about his everyday concerns.

16   We cannot resolve in any definitive way which of the alternatives is "right." The husband's obtuseness elsewhere in the dialogue would not lead us to suspect him of much poetry; still, he reacts to her accusations by saying, "I'm cursed!" Again, does that mean for his wrongs, or in his having a wife who cannot understand *him* any better than he understands her. He has, after all, made some effort. But the issue of not "getting" a metaphor, as if some sort of test has been failed, can be looked at quite apart from the drama of "Home Burial." How much should have to be explained, and how much should be expected of the reader or listener? Frost's statement: "Success in taking figures of speech is as intoxicating as making figures of speech" (*CPPP*, 814) implies that the reader (or listener) must also be somewhat of a poet, must read creatively, or at least sensitively and imaginatively enough not to miss metaphors and their possibilities. For a poet to place a good reading on a par with a poet's "making" is not only a supreme compliment to readers, but to the whole process of reading. Readers have traditionally looked up to the poets they read, and here is a poet valuing what we do, implying that he may need us as much as we need him.

Looked at in another way, though, such a statement places tremendous responsibility and expectation on a reader. The other side of the coin of "success" is failure—Frost would fail those who did not "take" the metaphor, those who failed his "test.". . .

17   In other poems the lesson is more subtle, more of a demonstration, and we may be helped by what he has written and said about poetry in conversations and on platforms. Not surprisingly, much of his poetry talk centered on the importance of metaphor. As might also be expected, the best of his comments on poetry or definitions of metaphor were themselves metaphors, for example: Frost spoke of a poem as a napkin going into a napkin ring, with the ring as the poem and the napkin spreading out again for other people.[3] Another time he used the image of a current carrying the eel grass with it, combing it like hair; it thus combs it in different directions without uprooting it from its initial clarity, its fixed meaning. What to the poet is his "fixed meaning" would most probably be, to us, the words on the page, "holding down" our readings even as they are pushed and pulled by the "currents" of possible meaning. A similar "swaying" metaphor Frost used was that of a boat at anchor: "The poetry that sways on its anchor has both deftness and definiteness."[4]

18   What all these metaphors of poetry/metaphor have in common is an underlying image of radiating (a term Frost also used). Words, metaphors, poems should radiate meaning(s) outward from the words on the page, becoming more than their literal selves, but never at the expense of losing their moorings, coming loose from the actual words and images that "anchor" them, or hold them "rooted" to the poet's text. One could also relate the image of radiating to Frost's metaphor of a poet's getting his ideas to "flash out new" like quicksilver rolling in a dish: just lying there it is dull, but a roll of the dish makes the quicksilver flash bright. The poet's freshness is his own knack for "breaking through" the dulling oxidation.[5]

19   But "radiation" is not the only conceptual metaphor of metaphor recurring in Frost. The creative and procreative possibilities of making and taking metaphor were not lost on him and he was fond of expressing this in sexual terms. Frost noted that some metaphors seemed sexual—a bringing together of a male and female element to create propagation of thought. He welcomed Thompson's term "engendering," and went on to call the process "pollenating." Certainly some of Frost's greatest love poetry can be seen as poems about poetry: the new creation that arises in "Putting in the Seed" (*CPPP*, 120) for example, resulting out of love "burn[ing] through" in a "springtime passion for the earth," is, literally, a seedling; but the language of its sprouting: "the sturdy seedling with arched body comes / Shouldering its way and shedding the earth crumbs" presents us with an image that powerfully suggests both sexual union and the birth of a baby. At the same time, if, to use Frost's famous comparison, "the figure

[3]Lecture, University of Maryland, 1941.
[4]The eel grass metaphor is quoted by Thompson in his "Notes on Frost" 415kkk.
[5]Thompson's "Notes on Frost," 2/18/40.

[for poetry] is the same as for love," we may view these passions and creations—love and planting—as potentially applicable to the passion for poetry and the creation that results from it. "Never Again Would Birds' Song Be the Same" (*CPPP*, 308) evokes Eve in the garden, and (a) man whose life would never be the same since "she came," but what that man "believes," hears, and "declares" seems to arise equally out of love and imagination. In so many of the poems, the loved one addressed is assumed to be sharing imagination as well as love with the speaker. . . .

20   Metaphor, then, creates out of difference: items from disparate categories are associated, shown their likeness, and seen newly. To use Frost's term, they "pollenate," engender, "propagate" thought. But another way of showing "one thing in terms of another" is to show one thing becoming another—transformation rather than generation (born out in the Greek and Latin roots of the word). Frost shows both operating in his saying: "A poem is not a string but a web. It is like a sapling. Set it and watch it proliferate."[6] Frost showed this phenomenon often in poems, but did not talk about it much in lectures or prose. One famous exception, though, is his metaphor of poetic making: "Like a piece of ice on a hot stove the poem must ride on its own melting" (*CPPP*, 778). Now *there's* a becoming, a transformation: ice becomes water, a cold solid becomes a warm liquid, a static object is put into motion, and all by means of heat, which is also a metaphor, though one we have begun to use unthinkingly—the heat of passion, the heat of creative energy, the heat of a gripping idea. What we are really talking about is the transformative power of passion, whether it be for love, creation, or commitment to anything we care about deeply. . . .

21   A very different sort of passion transforms the metaphors in "The Subverted Flower" (*CPPP*, 308) even as it transforms the boy and the girl in the drama. This poem has been variously analyzed, but I see it as a youthful sexual confrontation whose sudden and newly experienced passion frightens them both with its power. What begins as a flower ("'it is this that had the power.' / And he lashed his open palm / With the tender-headed flower") becomes subverted, and the imagery describing the boy becomes animalistic, bestial: "ragged muzzle," "a tiger at the bone," a snout. The images are plainly there for us to see, but we, the readers, are also constantly being made aware that we are seeing them through others' eyes:

> She looked and saw the shame:
> A hand hung like a paw,
> . . .
> A girl could only see
> That a flower had marred a man,
> But what she could not see

---

[6]*Prose Jottings of Robert Frost*, ed. Edward Connery Lathem and Hyde Cox (Lunenburg, VT: Northeast Kingdom Publishers, 1982), 15–16.

Was that the flower might be
Other than base and fetid:
That the flower had done but part,
And what the flower began
Her own too meager heart
Had terribly completed
She looked and saw the worst.

22 And we are hearing the judgment of the girl through another's voice, one
that has already described her "in goldenrod and brake, / Her shining hair
displaced"; described the boy's either arm stretched "as if she made it
ache / to clasp her—not to harm." In this highly charged dramatization of
an encounter, we also see operating the principle of interactive metaphor,
combined with the principle of metaphor as transformation; for we see
not only his transformation into a beast, but hers as well: "The bitter
words she spit / Like some tenacious bit . . . Her mother wiped the foam /
from her chin . . ." The flower has become "a brute," but how? in whose
eyes? And we must ask, . . . to what extent her vision, her images of him
effected that transformation; to what extent her own transformation was
a metaphor applied to what she (and also probably he) was not yet able
to understand or explain.

23 Of course expressing the inexpressible is one of the chief values
metaphor holds for us. Putting this and that together, or saying this is like
that, may be the only way we can understand or explain a "this" we cannot define, a feeling or experience or concept so abstract, or so new or
so powerful that we have no adequate word for it. What the couple saw,
though, was not just a flower and an animal, but a flower turning into an
animal. In such cases, the analogical process of metaphor, the interac-
tivity we have discussed between subjects, might more often be one
between the reader and the drama of the transformation in the poem. . . .

24 When the relationship between "this" and "that" is dynamic, "this"
becomes "that" because some force or power, be it will or nature, an outside agent or a creative urge, has activated the process. The whole
process, then, opens us up to its metaphoric possibilities; it is we who
will make connections with life and death, the story of Circe, or ice cubes
melted by a hot stove.

25 If "metaphor is the whole of poetry," where does that leave form,
which Frost spoke of just as often—sound, meter, sentence-sounds;
forming as a way of saving our sanity?[7] He had noted early on, in his English notebook, that "metaphor is not only in thought it is in sentence
sounds as well." As one might suspect, he depended on metaphor (one

---

[7]"There is at least so much good in the world that it admits of form and the making of
form. And not only admits of it, but calls for it. . .The artist, the poet might be expected
to be the most aware of such assurance. But it is really everybody's sanity to feel and live
by it . . . The background is hugeness and confusion shading away . . . into utter chaos;
and against the background any small man-made figure of order and concentration"
(*CPPP*, 740).

of loving coupling and creation at that) to show how integral form is to the poem: "Form in language is such a disjected lot of old broken pieces it almost seems as nonexistent as the spirit till the two embrace in the sky. They are not to be thought of as encountering in rivalry but in creation" (*CPPP*, 790). One can take this the further step I suspect he wanted us to take: when they form a perfect union, the poem reaches the sky. In both a tribute to poetry and to a woman, he invokes a "heavenward" direction. "The Silken Tent" (*CPPP*, 302) he has written "in praise of [a woman's] poise" has at its center a pole that is its pinnacle to heaven. This poem of woman in relation seems to me unsurpassed in the way it marries form and its central metaphor, and the way both work together as metaphor(s) of "She." Frost was very proud of his feat in creating a sonner in a single sentence — a sentence that *as* a sentence merits very close attention along with the image. . . . This poem is a tribute to the kind of woman who, because of her loving and thoughtful ties to others, becomes proud, erect, and beautiful even as she exists as a shelter, creating a home, or providing a haven of privacy and emotional protection.

26   The silken tent swaying gently at ease presents an image not only of beauty but of dignity and free movement—the tent swaying "in guys" sways also in the "guise" of freedom of movement. But one guy going taut, a summer breeze, or increased moisture remind her occasionally of "the slightest bondage." Because these are ties of love and thought, however, because they are "silken ties," the slightest bondage is not undesirable. What is necessary and positive about such bondage only becomes fully apparent when we realize that in giving she receives; that those "ties" to others are what keep her erect; that were those ties to snap, the tent would collapse; that heavenward pinnacle signifying the sureness of the soul would fall, for nothing emanates simply from the pole. The pole stands only in relation to the guys.[8] It is important too that the ties are many, for that very diversity is what keeps the pole balanced at the center. In the relationship between heavenward pole and guys, it is almost as if the ties of love and thought are in fact her claim to heaven.

27   This poem of loving bondage and of an existence based upon it is a perfect example of form and words, form and idea "embracing" What seems so remarkable about this sonnet/sentence is the way in which the structure of this sentence is analogous to the metaphor itself and to the relationship the metaphor expresses. The single sentence construction provides, even more firmly than the sonnet form, a unified tightness which corresponds to the tightness of the single image and the tightness of the ropes controlling the very existence of the silken structure. At the same time, the sentence, like the tent "swaying" in the breeze, comes perilously close to going out of control with its multiplication of subordinate clauses (a guise of freedom). Sentence structure has become metaphor.

---

[8]"Guys" is derived from the French "guier," which means to guide, another aspect of such relationship.

28   When one identifies the subordinate clauses, their subjects, verbs, and antecedents, one discovers that the sentence raises some real syntactical questions: for one, what is the main clause? For another, if "as" is used as a conjunction of comparison, it must introduce a clause—a subject and a predicate. If we assume that "tent" is the subject, what verb completes the clause—what verb that is not inside another clause and governed by its own subject? We find that "tent" actually governs no verb in the poem. It is "pole" not "tent" that is the subject of the verbs in the "and" clause; reduced to its simplest terms the sentence would read: "and its pole seems to owe naught to any single cord, but loosely held by countless ties to earth, and only by one's going taut is of the slightest bondage made aware." Grammatically, it would be the pole that is "made aware." We are made aware of "its" [the pole's] centrality to the erectness of the tent, and thus its connection to it; our intuition, though, tells us that only "she," the human subject, can be made aware. The logic of our intuition has supplied a human subject, grammar has supplied "pole" as subject, with "tent" as inseparable from it, with the result that we have a metaphoric fusion of woman, her soul, tent, and pole.

29   This may work as a complex metaphor, but it does not solve the issue of the subject "tent" left with no verb. Only by supplying an implied but unstated "is" can it be solved: "She is as is . . . a silken tent in a field at midday." The parallelism then is one based on existence—analogous existence, and we must see this in relation to Frost's choice of "as" over "like." There would have been no grammatical problem had Frost written: "She is like a silken tent . . . ," which would make perfect sense. The way he did write the poem—with "as"—he has rejected the easier comparison between woman and tent, and forced the comparison, not of nouns, but of relationships. She is not like a tent; she exists in the same manner as a tent does, by means of the same conflicting, balancing pulls. The main clause, then, is simply: "She is." The rest of the poem shows how such existence is maintained and kept upright. In addition to the image of tent and pole being bound by ties of love and thought we are reminded that these are ties "to everything on earth the compass round." "Earth's the right place for love," after all; without the tie to earth that pole could not rise heavenward.

30   As with the metaphor of transformation and process, of climbing birches, what is being compared is not the more usual noun to noun, but verb to verb—in this case the verb of existence, comparing the way she *is* to the way that silken tent *is*. We do not see that second "is," though, any more than we see the pole/soul that does the supporting. The process we undergo to "see" what is implicit but not obvious or explicit is also analogous to the way we must read a poet who expresses himself through indirection.

Poetry provides the one permissible way of saying one thing and meaning another. People say, "Why don't you say what you mean?" We never

do that, do we, being all of us too much poets. We like to talk in parables
and hints and indirections—whether from diffidence or some other
instinct.

(CPPP, 719–20)

31   Why "permissible," and what might "some other instinct" be? Perhaps
permissible because, as noted at the outset, metaphors do open doors,
but not always, and not to everyone. They do not lie, they hint and veil.
And veils allow us to see through them, their partial concealing, partial
revealing no small part of their attraction. Perhaps "other instincts" might
be both to protect the self, yet at the same time to be attractive and inviting. Frost used to mark his students according to how close they came
to poetry, and it may well be that we too are being tested, or perhaps
invited. But there is more to share than the feelings or insights or understanding or experience available in a poem: we are also being invited to
share his considerable intellect. To use Frost's metaphor that combines
these qualities: "I for my part would not be afraid to go in for enthusiasm
. . . [b]ut the enthusiasm I mean is taken through the prism of the intellect . . . such enthusiasm is one object of all teaching in poetry . . . I
would be willing to throw away everything but that: enthusiasm tamed
by metaphor" (<i>CPPP</i>, 719). Metaphor then is the ground on which we
meet a poet's "enthusiasms" and his intellect. But how shall we be
marked? How shall we know if we are at least passing the test of taking
metaphors, if not making them?

32   One test may very well be whether we are enjoying the experience—
the game, the play, the seriousness, sharing both enthusiasm and intellect with the poet. This may be one way that, as Stevens says, "Poetry
helps us live our lives," providing not only connection with the feeling
and mind of another, but play; not only new ways of expressing our feelings and experiences, but new ways of seeing them. A good metaphor
can be a lens through which we see newly; to use Frost's metaphor, a
"prism of the intellect," which, as we know, not only allows us to see
through it, but allows us to see a spectrum, a range of color. Our "new"
vision is, in more ways than one, an enlarged vision. A fragmentary note
in one of Frost's memorandum books (English notebook) speaks of walls
of books with here and there a window in them. "The books are part of
what we perceive with in looking out the window." This is an arresting
metaphor of how literature can work, how Frost hoped it would work:
the reader seeing <i>through</i> not just <i>into</i> a text, using that text to look <i>out</i>,
and not simply <i>in</i> (whether into the text, the self, or the author). Poetry,
which to Frost <i>is</i> metaphor or nothing, would surely be the clearest of
such windows, the sharpest of such lenses, the most color-producing of
prisms.

33   But there is yet another "lesson," perhaps the most important of all:
the glorious possibilities of language. We are encouraged to risk in it, to
test and enlarge its possibilities while ever being mindful of its

constraints. "Feeling free in harness" (*I*, 135) Frost used to say; swaying in the guise of freedom, at anchor—language controls and keeps us anchored, "on earth," even as it opens itself—and us—to almost infinite possibilities of perceiving and creating. Coming to realize the power of language, the beauty of it, even as we chafe at its limitations may very well be the real education by poetry. The fun begins when we accept its invitations to join in the game.

"The Place Is the Asylum": Women and Nature in Robert Frost's Poetry[1]

Katherine Kearns

1 . . . Frost's poetry subtly but persistently reiterates a vision of sexual anarchy. Men and women possess the power to make each other mad. . . . Women are powerful, active, magnetic in their madness, which is manifested in escape from the asylum of households into nature. Men are rendered impotent: they can only pursue unsuccessfully or withdraw into themselves. They have nowhere else to go, because Frost's world is controlled by a powerful femininity. As brides or as keepers, women dominate households. Their houses embody them so that symbolically every threshold is sexually charged; "cellar holes" become pits that represent female sexuality, birth, death, and the grave, and attics are minds filled with the bones of old lovers. Frost's men can no more fulfill their women than they can fill the houses with life and children, and so the women run away and the men follow. Yet the pursuit is dangerous, for it leads into nature that is equally female and thus potentially deadly. While Frost fills his outside world with walls, and with ceilings of dark leaves, and with the bars of birch and hickory trees, nature resists containment and defies control as surely as a woman does. . . .

2 Men in Frost's poetry are thus potentially circumscribed in their movements . . . .

3 "Home Burial" may be used to clarify Frost's intimate relationships between sex, death, and madness. The physical iconography is familiar—a stairwell, a window, a doorway, and a grave—elements which Frost reiterates throughout his poetry. The marriage in "Home Burial" has been destroyed by the death of a first and only son. The wife is in the process of leaving the house, crossing the threshold from marital asylum into freedom. The house is suffocating her. Her window view of the graveyard is not enough and is, in fact, a maddening reminder that she could not enter the earth with her son. With its transparent barrier, the window is a mockery of a widened vision throughout Frost's poetry and seems to incite escape rather than quelling it; in "Home Burial" the woman can

---

[1]All quotations from Frost's poetry are from *The Poetry of Robert Frost*, ed. Edward Connery Lathem, 2nd ed. (New York: Holt, 1979).

"see" through the window and into the grave in a way her husband cannot, and the fear is driving her down the steps toward the door—"She was starting down—/ Looking back over her shoulder at some fear"—even before she sees her husband. He threatens to follow his wife and bring her back by force, as if he is the cause of her leaving, but his gesture will be futile because it is based on the mistaken assumption that she is escaping him. Pathetically, he is merely an obstacle toward which she reacts at first dully and then with angry impatience. He is an animate part of the embattled household, but her real impetus for movement comes from the grave.

4   The house itself, reduced symbolically and literally to a womb-like passageway between the bedroom and the threshold, is a correlative for the sexual tension generated by the man's insistence on his marital rights. He offers to "give up being a man" by binding himself "to keep hands off," but their marriage is already sexually damaged and empty. The man and woman move in an intricate dance, she coming downward and then retracing a step, he "Mounting until she cower[s] under him," she "shrinking from beneath his arm" to slide downstairs. Randall Jarrell examines the image of the woman sinking into "a modest, compact, feminine bundle" upon her skirts;[2] it might be further observed that this childlike posture is also very much a gesture of sexual denial, body bent, knees drawn up protectively against the breasts, all encompassed by voluminous skirts. The two are in profound imbalance, and Frost makes the wife's speech and movements the poetic equivalent of stumbling and resistance; her lines are frequently eleven syllables, and often are punctuated by spondees whose forceful but awkward slowness embodies the woman's vacillations "from terrified to dull," and from frozen and silent immobility to anger. Her egress from the house will be symbolic verification of her husband's impotence, and if she leaves it and does not come back, the house will rot as the best birch fence will rot. Unfilled, without a woman with child, it will fall into itself, an image that recurs throughout Frost's poetry. Thus the child's grave predicts the dissolution of household . . . almost a literal "home burial."

5   The husband . . . will learn the lesson *because* of the grave of his son, the once and future rival for his wife's attention. Yet that the grave exists at all is proof of their fruitful sexual union, and it sets them apart from Frost's other couples. In relatively few Frost poems is a marriage specifically delineated as productive of children. . . . There are no children to batten down the doors, or to embody passion in a form that lasts, and so women simply walk away. The son in "Home Burial" lies now in the dirt, to which the mother wishes desperately to commit herself, and while earth is associated again and again in Frost with love, nothing will come of this planting except the dissolution of marriage.

---

[2]"Robert Frost's 'Home Burial,'" in *The Moment of Poetry*, ed. Don Cameron Allen (Baltimore: Johns Hopkins Univ. Press, 1962), p. 104.

6   The family graveyard in "Home Burial" is, in the husband's words, "not much larger than a bedroom," an observation that ties not just his own sexuality to the earth and to death but that of all previous generations as well. Jarrell explicates the gravedigging scene in "Home Burial" as perceived by the grieving mother: as if in a dream, she climbs the stairs and looks out to see her husband plunging his spade again and again into the earth. Then she walks down to see her husband's shoes stained with fresh earth, his spade standing against the wall in the entryway. Jarrell says, "Such things have a sexual force, a sexual meaning, as much in our waking hours as in our dreams. . . . When the plowman digs his plow into the earth, Mother Earth, to make her bear, this does not have a sexual appropriateness only in the dreams of neurotic patients—it is something we all understand, whether or not we admit we understand."[3] "Home Burial," in its committing to earth the proof of a couple's sexual love, predicts a pattern of imagery, rich and ambivalent, that throughout Frost's poetry relates earth at once both to sexuality and to death. The grave, with its natural and domestic correlatives, becomes a remarkably potent conflation of the point at which desire and death merge into inextricable ecstasy and despair. . . .

7   When there are accessible doors and windows, entry can be forced or escape can be accomplished. Each has ominous possibilities. Often women in Frost's poems stand and look out windows, and what they see, as in "Home Burial," is both troubling and seductive. . . .

8   "The Subverted Flower" adds a final dimension to the incomplete metamorphoses in these poems, for, because the woman will not become the flower, the man becomes, quite literally, a beast. According to Thompson, the ambiguous accusation made against the flower—"It is this that had the power,"—suggests that the speaker blames the flower for his unchecked desire and his importuning of the woman. He is both man and beast early in the poem, his smile of apology replaced by a smile of desire that "crack[s] his ragged muzzle" when he sees her "standing to the waist / In goldenrod and brake, / Her shining hair displaced." This is indeed a provocative image, and he stretches out his arms instinctively "As if he could not spare / To touch her neck and hair." Beast-like he is deprived of language, words choking him "Like a tiger at a bone." Unprotected because she has gone outside the garden walls, she is afraid to move lest she wake "the demon of pursuit / That slumbers in a brute." She is terrified that he will "pounce to end it all." She sees him as some sort of powerful animal, a tiger, a lion, a wolf, perhaps, until he drops his hands from their outstretched position so that they hang like paws, and laughs ingratiatingly. He drops his eyes in subjection. At this point he no longer has a muzzle, but a "snout," and is an ugly creature which becomes frightened and runs away.

9   The poem seems straightforward in its allegory of the man turned to beast through sexual desire. But it takes a subtle turn that pulls it back

[3]Jarrell, p. 123.

towards many of the poems examined thus far. The woman has the power to madden the man and to make him bestial with her rejection of the sexuality implicit in standing waist deep in flowers with her hair disarranged. She can only see that the flower on which he blames his desire is "base and fetid," words that speak connotatively of sexual corruption and decay. Yet she is herself a beast because she rejects her role as flower. In the battle against the man she has forced him downward from a tiger to a pig with a snout, or a dog, or some worse creature, and she has shamed him into lowering his eyes, a mark of servility in animals. She watches him run and stumble, and she hears him bark, but then she "spits" bitter words like a snake spits venom or a cat spits in fury. She "plucks her lips" ineffectually, much as the man has earlier pawed the air, and she foams at the mouth like a rabid dog. She must, finally, be "drawn backward home" by her mother. She is not a beast in the beginning because she is too much like a flower among flowers, but the metamorphosis of both lovers suggests the inescapable power of denied and subverted sexuality. She is, like the women in "The Housekeeper," "A Servant to Servants," "The Hill Wife," and "Maple," abetted by her mother, who replaces her comb and takes her back into a walled garden. Only a dryad stepping out of her mother tree is free to walk into the woods and set up housekeeping. If the lover wants to come to this subverted flower it will be on the mother's terms, inside walls and into the asylum of marriage, where the cycle of madness and despair will be perpetuated.

10   Frost's woods can be as lovely, dark, and deep as a woman, but the attraction has all the complexity inherent in our fallen natures. Eve is contaminated by knowledge, and Adam in his pursuit of her becomes a beast. Desire, domesticated by marriage and contained in household, is eviscerated into childlessness and impotent dread, but when doors are thrown open, thresholds crossed, and escapes effected, it becomes, embodied in the women who run away, irresistibly powerful. All the women who have ever escaped into the world from the asylum of marriage seem, in Frost's poetry, to have died into the earth, like leaves trodden into the mire, to be reborn into nature. Their femininity is both alluring and deadly, provocative of madness and of delight. The only "safe" place is in the cage of hickory bars in the upper floor of the isolated cabin. There the naked and love-crossed madman can "talk" about love, much as the poet writes about it: without endangering himself or anyone else.

THE CRAFT OF POETRY

ROBERT PENN WARREN

AND CLEANTH BROOKS

In 1959, immediately after his eighty-fifth-birthday celebration, RF recorded with poets Cleanth Brooks and Robert Penn Warren a discussion centering upon technical aspects of verse, made for inclusion in a tape entitled "Conversations on the Craft of Poetry," which was issued by Holt, Rinehart and Winston, Inc. to accompany their third edition of Brooks and Warren's book Understanding Poetry. *Also participating in the session was Holt editor Kenney Withers.*

The following extracts are drawn from a printed transcript that was published in booklet form as a companion piece to the recording.

WITHERS: Mr. Frost, I once heard you say that for a poem to stick it must have a dramatic accent.

FROST: If it doesn't, it will not stay in anybody's head. It won't be *catchy.* [. . .]

Catchiness has a lot to do with it, all of it, all the way up from the ballads you hear on the street to the lines in Shakespeare that stay with you without your trying to remember them. I just say catchy. They stick on you like burrs thrown on you in holiday foolery. You don't have to try to remember them. It's from the way they're said,
10 you know, an archness or something.

WARREN: Well, I'm sure you're right about the dramatic quality being the basic quality of good poetry. That would bring up the relation of meter and rhythm to the dramatic moment—moment by moment— in a poem, wouldn't it?

FROST: That's right.

WARREN: I'd like to hear you say it in your way, how meter enters into this picture—the dramatic quality.

FROST: The meter seems to be the basis of—the waves and the beat of the heart seems to be basic in all making of poetry in all languages—
20 some sort of meter.

WARREN: The strain of the rhythm against the meter. Is that itself just a dramatic fact that permeates a poem?

FROST: From those two things rises what we call this tune that's different from the tune of the other kind of music. It's a music of itself. And when people say that this will easily turn into—be set to music, I think it's bad writing. It ought to fight being set to music if it's got expression in it.

BROOKS: Yes, there's something resistant and unique in it; you can't just turn it into something else. This is to overstate the matter, but I do
30 want to get it clear, if I can for myself: Would you say that even though the meter is based on the human pulse or some kind of basic rhythm in our natures, still for the poet it's something to be played over against—it's something to be fought with, to be tussled with? It's not directly expressive—ta-DA, ta-DA, ta-DA, ta-DA, ta-DA.

FROST: No, it's doggerel when you do that. You see, and how you save it from doggerel is having enough dramatic meaning in it for the other thing to break the doggerel. And it mustn't break *with* it.

I said years ago that it reminds me of a donkey and a donkey cart;
for some of the time the cart is on the tugs and some of the time on
40   the hold-backs. You see it's that way all the time. The one's doing
that and the other—the one's holding the thing back and the other's
pushing it forward—and so on, back and forward. . . . I puzzled over
it many years and tried to make people see what I meant. They use
the word "rhythm" about a lot of free verse; and gee, what's the good
of the rhythm unless it is on something that trips it—that it ruffles?
You know, it's got to ruffle the meter.

BROOKS: Isn't this the fault of—to name the name of a man who did
write some very fine poems, I think: Vachel Lindsay depends too
much on just the doggerel—the stamp of the. . . .

50   FROST: Singsong, yes. And you know when he had something else, he
thought he ought to put a note about it in the margin. Did you notice
that?

BROOKS: Yes, to tell you how to read it.

FROST: "Say this in a golden tone," he says. You ought not to have to say
that in the margin.

BROOKS: No, no. It's built in.

FROST: That ought to be in the meaning. This is why you have to have a
meaning, 'cause you don't know what to do with anything if you
don't have a meaning. It makes you act up; you've got to act up.

60   "What sayest thou, old barrelful of lies?" Chaucer says. What
d'you say, "old barrelful of lies"? And you can hear it talk just the
same today—and all of it. That's why it exists. It's beautiful, anywhere you look into Chaucer:

> Since I from love escaped am so fat,
> I never think to have been in his prison lean;
> Since I am free, I count him not a bean.

This is Chaucer talking too. It's just the same now. I hear the
country people talking, England and here, with these same ways of
acting up. Put it that way—call it "acting up."

70   You act up when you talk. Some do more than others. Some little
children do: some just seem to be rather straight line, but some
switch their whole body when they talk—switch their skirts.
Expressiveness comes over them. Words aren't enough.

And of course all before words came the expressiveness—groans
and murmurs and things like that emerging into words. And some
few of these linger, like "um-hnm" and "unh-unh" and "mmm" and all
our groans. By myself sometimes I groan at something already done
that I'd like to avert.

WARREN: From a groan to a sonnet's a straight line.

80   FROST: Yes, that's right.

WARREN: You are distinguishing, then, the meaning in the most limited
sense from the over-all, felt meaning of the whole thing. Is that it?

FROST: That's your whole guide, the over-all meaning.

WARREN: That's your guide and your end product.

FROST: Yes, your end product. And also, you know, one of the funny things is that this *mood* you're writing in foretells the end product. See, it begins sort of that way and a way of talking that foretells the end product. There's a logic of that sort of thing.

90   Somebody said to be a master writer you don't have to wait for your moods. That'd be like Browning as he got older. You get to be a virtuoso, and you aren't a poet any more. He'd lost his moods somewhere. He'd got to be a master. We don't want to be masters.

WARREN: In other words you don't want even to be master—is that right?—of the particular poem. Before you start you're moving from mood to the exploration of the mood, is that it?

BROOKS: Poem is a discovery. . . .

FROST: Yes, that's right. You're on a little voyage of discovery. And there's a logic in it. You're going to come out somewhere with great certainty. And you can tell whether you've lost it on the way. And

100   you throw the poem away—if you lose it.

WARREN: Yes.

FROST: Down the years, looking back over it all. And you see, a good many who think they're writing free verse are really writing old-fashioned iambic. A good deal of Whitman's like that, and a lot of Masters is like that: he just never got away from blank verse—the sound of blank verse.

And so there are places where this thing takes place that I'm talking about—there's both the meter and the expressiveness on it—and so we get a poem.

110   Ezra Pound used to say that you've got to get all the meter out of it—extirpate the meter. If you do, maybe you've got true free verse, and I don't want any of it!

WARREN: Well, you can go at it another way: I guess it's Winters who said that behind all good free verse—I may be misinterpreting him, but I think that's what he says—behind all good free verse there's a shadow of formal verse.

FROST: That's right. And if we hadn't had the years of formal verse, this stuff wouldn't be any good, you know. The shadow is there; that's what gives it any charm it has. You see, I'm hard on free verse a

120   little—too hard, I know.

BROOKS: Would you be hard, Mr. Frost, also, on the business of the beatniks and chanting poetry to jazz? Is that letting too much of music—of the wrong side of music come in?

FROST: Yes, absolutely. Death! Hang 'em all!

This fellow that's going to talk with me (A. P. Herbert from London) tomorrow, they've told me what his prejudices are, you know, to see if they couldn't rouse me to say something to him. He's in favor of hanging delinquent children. That's the funniest prejudice.

And he'd be in favor of exterminating the free-verse writers, I'm pretty sure. I'm not as bad as that.

130   Let's put it this way, that prose and verse are alike in having high poetic possibilities of ideas, and free verse is anywhere you want to be between those two things, prose and verse. I like to say, guardedly, that I could define poetry this way: It is that which is lost out of both prose and verse in translation. That means something in the way the words are curved and all that—the way the words are taken, the way you take the words.

WARREN: The best-order notion: the old Coleridgean best-order notion.

FROST: Yes, I'm pretty extreme about it.

You know, I've given offense by saying that I'd as soon write free
140   verse as play tennis with the net down. I want something there—the other thing—something to hold and something for me to put a strain on; and I'd be lost in the air with just cutting loose—unless I'm in my other mood of making it prose right out, you know, and I don't write much of that. But that's another thing. [. . .]

BROOKS: Speaking of tune, Yeats said that he started a poem with a little tune in his head.

FROST: Yeats said a good many things, and I've talked with him about that. He said that nothing he hated more than having his poems set to music. It stole the show. It wasn't the tune he heard in his ear.
150   And what this other thing is. . . . If he meant a tune, it doesn't seem to go with that, does it?

Burns without any doubt had old music—old songs—in his head that he wrote from. But I don't think that of Yeats; I don't know what he meant by that. But if he meant a tune. . . . I have a tune, but it's a tune of the blend of these two things. Something rises—it's neither one of these things. It's neither the meter nor the rhythm; it's a tune arising from the stress on those—same as your fingers on the strings, you know. The twang!

WARREN: The twang.
160   FROST: The twang of one on the other. And I don't know what he meant. I think he must have meant what we mean: from a result of something beginning to rise from it right away when you're playing one on the other; that's what he carried. There must be a oneness as you're doing it. You aren't putting two things together—laying them together. It isn't synthetic like that; no.

BROOKS: No, it's growing a plant, not building a wall.

WARREN: Growing in terms of this dominating mood—is that right?— that you referred to as a germ of the poem?

FROST: Yes.
170   WARREN: The tune is the mood groping for its logic, is that it? Something like that?

FROST: That's right; that's right, yes. I'm glad that we feel that way together. Yes, you know that, when I begin a poem I don't know—

I don't want a poem that I can tell was written toward a good ending—one sentence, you know. That's trickery. You've got to be the happy discoverer of your ends.

BROOKS: That's a very fine way of phrasing it, "the happy discoverer of your end." Because otherwise it is contrived. You can see it coming a mile off.

FROST: A mile away.

I've often said that another definition of poetry is dawn—that it's something dawning on you while you're writing it. It comes off if it really dawns when the light comes at the end. And the feeling of dawn—the freshness of dawn—that you didn't think this all out and write it in prose first and then translate it into verse. That's abhorrent! [. . .]

One of the things that I notice with myself is that I can't make certain word sounds go together, sometimes; they won't say. This has got something to do with the way one vowel runs into another, the way one syllable runs into another. And then I never know—I don't like to reason about that too much. I don't understand it, but I've changed lines because there was something about them that my ear refused. And I suppose it has something to do with this vowels and consonants.

You know what I've thought sometimes: that the mouth and throat are like this, that it's certain sounds are here, and you can't go right from this one to that one; you've got to go like this. The mouth's got to be doing that inside. I don't know.

But gee, you know, I don't want any science of it. It's got to be—not trial and error. You don't correct it if you're going well—if you're felicitous—if you're having a happy day.

Well, we've come a good way. And it's fun. I don't often sit with somebody to talk about it this way. Sometimes from the platform I say some of these things, you know. And I used to do it more than I do it now. I had a notion I had to tell the public how to read lines. Then I decided no; that's in them anyway. They all had Mother Goose and everything. Don't you see that you throw them back on their Mother Goose? And then all with the play of ideas in it; how deep the Mother Goose is, you see:

Pussy cat, pussy cat, where have you been?
I've been to London to see the Coronation!

To pervert a little:

Pussy cat, pussy cat, what did you see there?
I saw nothing but what I might have seen just
    as well by staying right here in Nashville!
I saw a mouse run under a chair.

And that's very deep. But it's so pretty the way it's set off, you know, and nobody need see it at all unless they're any discerning.

"I saw a mouse run under a chair." That's meant a lot to me, that has,
220 all my life.

WARREN: That's a good one.

FROST: That's what makes regionalists, you see. You could stay right at
home and see it all.

You know another thing I think belongs to poetry is fresh observation, don't you? All the time, little insights. They say "nothing
new," but there is all the time. For instance, I was saying about
women the other day—they were plaguing me to leave some boys I
wanted to talk to; they thought I was getting tired or something.
Finally I turned on them, and I said, "A woman would rather take
230 care of you than listen to you think."

WARREN: That's a mark of a good woman.

FROST: And then I softened that to them by saying, "That's why we like
you, my dears. You see, because we know that what we think doesn't
amount to much anyway, we men." You see, that was a fresh
observation.

WARREN: Well, the mere observation of just the facts of the world is a
constant refresher for poetry. It's a waking up of yourself when you
get the least little turn of an observation of the way a leaf or a light
is, or something.

240 FROST: Little insights into a character and a little observation of something growing. You know how it does, something with life.[. . .]

Wilkinson 1

Daniel Wilkinson

Professor Henderson

English 1102

2 May 2007

The Necessity of Escape

1 Few poets of the twentieth century have had the widespread

appeal of Robert Frost. Frost's poems do not require the level

of patience or the symbol-hunting talents that the poetry of

contemporaries such as T. S. Eliot, Wallace Stevens, and Ezra

Pound demands. Much of Frost's poetry, beyond its pastoral

surroundings that echo the Romanticists of old, seems almost

wholly preoccupied with the question of how the genders relate

to one another. Indeed, from the pervasive Freudian images of

"Putting in the Seed" to the rather nervous meeting of man and woman recounted in "Meeting and Passing," Frost's poetry, while simpler in form and language than the Modernist works from the same period, gives provocative insights into how the genders interact. These shorter works are, of course, narrower in scope when compared to the longer narrative poems that provide a more in-depth look at the relationships between the genders. "Home Burial" and "The Death of the Hired Man" are, essentially, conversations between husband and wife that concern themselves not only with one another in matters of love outright but also with the influence of love on more sober circumstances. In both narrative poems, man-made structures both tangible and intangible become means of imprisonment from which characters must flee to gain a measure of peace.

2   From the very beginning, "The Death of the Hired Man" strikes a somber tone, for readers see Mary alone at a lamp-lit table, waiting to recount Silas's return to her husband Warren (Frost 1-2). Even the names of the characters add to the rather dark nature of the poem: all the names—Mary, Warren, and Silas—are in trochaic meter, whose second unaccented syllable rather "dies off" at the end of each foot. Mary's unsettling news concerning Silas's return must not be delivered inside the house. In turn, Mary feels the need to meet Warren at the door to deliver her news, before he can get inside. Practically, such a move to the porch might serve to allow Silas to sleep through the resulting conversation; such behavior would certainly be befitting of a good host to her houseguest. However, she nevertheless "ran on tiptoe down the darkened passage" at the first sign of Warren's return (Frost 3), as if the house must not be allowed to hold her nor her news any longer than necessary. Warren at first seems rather angry; his statements

often begin with spondees that sound reminiscent of frustration.
Line eleven begins with three staccato syllables in "When was
I," line thirteen begins with two spondees in "I told him so,"
and line seventeen has another two spondees in "What help he
is." At hearing the news, Warren is indeed in a man-made
structure, but it is not a physical one. Rather, Warren's
memories of Silas consist of blanket generalizations that the
reader cannot verify and that are likely products of the
moment's shock. Indeed, his memories are largely in the present
tense—not the past tense of concrete remembrance—and look to be
rather hastily constructed in the heat of the moment. However,
once Mary assures Warren that Silas has said that he has
returned to help at the farm, Warren's rhetoric softens and
loses its spondees and frustrated tone (Frost 48). Mary produces
within Warren a calming effect that counteracts Warren's
seemingly impatient nature very well. Mary further pleads
Silas's case when she gives Warren a concrete memory to hang
onto: Silas's times with Harold Wilson and the old man's talent
at building haystacks (Frost 88-95). Mary, in effect, keeps
Warren out of the physical confines of the house and the mental
confines of Warren's own supposed bad times with Silas.

Like Mary, Silas seems to have a deeply ingrained
proclivity toward spurning both societal and physical shelter.
In his younger days, Silas proved himself to be quite the
competent field hand who held steadfast to old homespun wisdom
so that he would not become trapped within words like Harold
Wilson—a "fool of books" (Frost 98). Silas refuses even to trust
familial institutions, as he refuses to contact his brother, a
rather wealthy banker, when his health begins to decline. The
reader learns from Mary that the relationship between Silas and

his brother had likely been a bad one and that by going to his
brother, Silas would have been "ashamed" (Frost 145). Forsaking
man-made structures of familial bonds, he returns "home": the
farm. Mary recounts that she found him "[h]uddled against the
barn door fast asleep" (Frost 35). Though Silas might have been
forced to stay outdoors due to the absence of people at the
farmhouse, Mary admits that she had to "[drag] him to the house"
(Frost 40). Once inside, Silas refuses to go any farther into
the house than necessary and chooses to sleep next to the stove,
likely on the floor, for readers learn later that he refused to
use the lounge set out for him (Frost 149). Even at death's
door, Silas clings to a uniquely pastoral, Thoreauvian
independence in his reluctance to take part in the comforts the
house offers and thus accept what he might believe to be
obligatory kindnesses from Mary.

4   In "Home Burial," the foreboding intangible structures are
far more destructive than Silas's refusal to rely on his
brother. Katherine Kearns has already documented the
imprisonment experienced by Amy in the poem, yet she absolves
Amy's husband from the responsibility and effectually puts Amy
into her own tortured world. Clearly, in Amy's mind, the husband
deserves at least part of the blame for her leaving, if not all
of it, for she must escape the confines of what her husband has
made. Amy's movement is not out of a "womb-like passage" from
"marital asylum into freedom" (Kearns 418). Rather, the
transformation is much simpler: in leaving the house, Amy moves
from death to life, from marital enshrinement to the physical
world. The house is just as much of a grave as is the one the
husband dug for the child. The opening scene is a fairly
familiar one: a beautiful woman is at the top of the stairs, and

her husband stares up at her as if she stands on a pedestal.
Unfortunately for him, Amy is bent on climbing down the stairs,
leaving the house, and thus completely dismantling that
pedestal. The grave will haunt her for as long as she lives in
that house, and thus she must exit it for her own well-being.
The whole property in this poem is the masculine realm, unlike
in the previous poem, where the men forged their own world in
the fields; the house is quite literally the pedestal on which
the husband places his wife, if his vow to "bring [her] back by
force" is any indication (Frost 116). Amy's husband has
unwittingly forged for his wife a home where her grief is
expected to be silenced, just as she perceives that her husband
silences his; he is not "merely an obstacle" (Kearns 418). Just
as he may believe that he is demonstrating love for the child by
digging the grave, the man likely demonstrates his love for Amy
by putting the house around her. At seeing her husband digging
from inside the house, Amy forever links him to that grave and
the child therein. The house for Amy is solely the dwelling of a
cold and heartless man who can understand neither her nor her
problems. By leaving the house, she can leave behind the
troubles her husband has created and thus escape the physical
structure of the house and the social imprisonment of their
failing marriage.

5   Amy's problem might manifest itself in her disconsolation
over her deceased son, but its root is her husband's perceived
lack of remorse at the child's death. Amy recounts with stark
detail the nonchalance with which her husband dug the boy's
grave and his concern that "Three foggy mornings and one rainy
day / Will rot the best birch fence a man can build" (Frost
92-93). Her husband has found a means to channel his grief in
digging his son's grave, a physical task that makes an inverse

sort of physical structure, but a structure nevertheless.

Indeed, the man compares the burial ground to the house when he

describes it as "not much larger than a bedroom" (Frost 25).

Such a description might have the sexual connotation noted by

Kearns (419), yet its simpler comparison to the house must be

the one that resonates within Amy. Her husband has become the

very embodiment of mindless physical labor, for only someone

with his mind completely free of sorrow could dig that "little

grave" with "[his] own hand" (Frost 73). Amy is unwilling and

perhaps incapable of understanding this means of channeling

grief, and therefore his action is interpreted as a lack of

grief, instead of as an expression of it. That grave is just

another man-made structure from which she must flee, and that

birch fence is yet another. Her husband's remark might have been

an attempt at diffusing some of the situation's tension or

taking his own mind off of his son's death; only the most hard-

hearted of individuals would truly be concerned about fences at

such a time. Amy, from her point of view, might as well join her

son, for living in the house of a man concerned with commonplace

and pedestrian fences in a time of crisis is no way to spend a

life, and thus she must go "Somewhere out of this house" (Frost

113). Her husband's culpability does not particularly matter to

her in this case. Katherine Kearns's idea of an "enticing

nature" is obviated by the fact that nearly anywhere would be

enticing to a woman in Amy's state. If anything, nature rather

looms in the background and becomes another foe to Amy's husband

as he vows to bring her back from wherever she may go (Frost

116).

6   Narrative poems like "The Death of the Hired Man" and "Home

Burial" often present a special problem to readers, for while

their language remains solidly in the realm of the poetically ambiguous, the events and people therein leap off the page and into the realm of the lifelike. Indeed, these poems are the stuff of novels, for they turn the events of secluded New England areas into transcendent literature with a viable message for a wide audience. In a conversation with critic Cleanth Brooks and fellow poet Robert Penn Warren, Frost said that one could "stay right home and see it all" (426). Frost, however briefly, constructs a world in the narrative poems where people can struggle mightily with the little necessities of family and society. Those like Warren and Mary, with one another to fall back on, can survive the structures of life while still managing to be true to one another and to the lives they have built together. Amy, after deeming her husband unfit to lean upon during times of trouble, decides to leave the physical and familial home for a chance at a life somewhere far away from what haunts her. The ideal resolutions to the problems presented in Frost's narrative poems might not lie in granting humanity a rugged, lonely, Thoreau-style independence from physical and societal constructs. Rather, Frost's ideal independence seems to be in spite of those constructs: true, lasting independence seems to stem from an indomitable will to use those constructs to form a more peaceful self.

Works Cited

Brooks, Cleanth and Robert Penn Warren. "The Craft of Poetry."

   Understanding Poetry. 3rd ed. New York: Holt, 1959.

   199-206. Rpt. in Henderson, Higgins, Day, and Waller

   420-26.

Frost, Robert. "The Death of the Hired Man." *The Poetry of*

   Robert Frost. Ed. Edward C. Latham. New York: Holt, 1979.

   34-40. Rpt. in Henderson, Higgins, Day, and Waller 400-04.

———. "Home Burial." *The Poetry of Robert Frost*. Ed. Edward C.

   Latham. New York: Holt, 1979. 51-55. Rpt. in Henderson,

   Higgins, Day, and Waller 396-99.

Henderson, Gloria Mason, Anna Dunlap Higgins, Bill Day, and

   Sandra Stevenson Waller, eds. *Literature and Ourselves:*

   A Thematic Introduction for Readers and Writers. 6th ed.

   New York: Longman, 2009.

Kearns, Katherine. "'The Place Is the Asylum'": Women and Nature

   in Frost's Poetry." *American Literature* 59.2 (1987):

   190-210. Rpt. in Henderson, Higgins, Day, and Waller

   417-20.

Crafting Arguments

1. The tone of the nine poems included in this casebook varies dramatically, from playful to somber and from loving to terrifying. Select two of the poems, and write a Comparison/Contrast essay that suggests the ways in which Frost creates the tone(s).

2. Four of the poems in this Casebook are sonnets but not all use the same form. Look at the discussion of the sonnet in Part One of the Introduction. Then pick two of the sonnets and write an essay that supports your claims about why Frost selected that particular form for those subjects or themes.

3. Using the poem "Home Burial," contrast Amy's view about death with the husband's.

4. Write an essay comparing the marriage in "The Death of the Hired Man" with that in "Home Burial."

5. The two dialogue poems by Frost, "Home Burial" and "The Death of the Hired Man," depicting the conversations between a husband and wife, are written in blank verse. Write an essay on one or both of these poems illustrating Frost's skill in writing poetry that successfully imitates conversation.

6. Warren in "The Death of the Hired Man" and Amy's husband in "Home Burial" have definite ideas about what a man should and should not be. Use specific examples from the poems to write an essay about what these two men believe about manhood.

7. Select two love poems or two poems that include sexual imagery and write an essay about Frost's varied portrayals of relationships between men and women.

8. Frost is famous for the layers of meaning and for the consequent variety of possibilities for interpreting his poems. Select at least one poem and argue that more than one interpretation is possible.

Men and Women: Crafting Arguments

1. Choose two of the sonnets in this unit and write an essay comparing the authors' use of the sonnet form and of metaphorical or sound devices to create tone and theme.

2. Several of the poems in this section deal with courtship. Use two or more of these poems to write an essay about the rituals of courtship.

3. Analyze the problems faced by men or by women in their relationships with one another and their methods of dealing with the problems in one or more of the following: *A Doll's House*, "Beyond the Cult of Fatherhood," "The Gilded Six-Bits," "Désirée's Baby," "The Yellow Wallpaper," "Hills like White Elephants," or "A Temporary Matter."

4. Select two or three of the love poems in this unit and write an essay explaining what attributes of the lovers have caused the love to last and deepen.

5. In an essay, compare the expectations of women for women in "Phenomenal Woman," "Barbie Doll," and "Abbot Academy."

Men and Women: Writing about Film

See Appendix B: Writing about Film for help with these essays.

1. The classic films *Vertigo* (1958) and *My Fair Lady* (1964), adapted from literary works by the French authors Pierre Boileau and Thomas Narcejac and by George Bernard Shaw, deal with the same kinds of gender issues that we see in several works in this unit. View these two movies and prepare a Comparison/Contrast paper in which you examine the treatment of gender issues in each. Which film techniques help convey theme?

2. Hollywood adaptations of fairy tales are very popular. Some support the myth of the original tale, some question the myth, and some poke fun at the myth. Read a classic fairy tale and then select an adaptation of it. For example, you could select "Cinderella" and then view a film such as *Pretty Woman, Ever After*, or *Happily N'Ever After*; or you could choose "Beauty and the Beast" or "Sleeping Beauty" and then view one of Disney's adaptations of these tales or a movie like *Shrek*. In your essay, craft an argument about the director's interpretation of the fairy tale or compare some aspect of the movie with the original tale.

3. Many classic pieces of literature famous for a male/female relationship at their center have been adapted to film; some have been adapted numerous times. A few titles include *Othello, Romeo and Juliet, West Side Story, Madame Bovary, Clueless, Emma, Pride and Prejudice, The Scarlet Letter, Little Women, A Doll's House, Gone with the Wind, Cat on a Hot Tin Roof, Streetcar Named Desire, The Great Gatsby, Sophie's Choice, The Lover, Ethan Frome, Terms of Endearment,* and *My Fair Lady*. Select one of these adaptations or another adaptation approved by your instructor and compare its portrayal of the male/female theme with that of the piece of literature. Does the filmmaker change the source's message? What techniques of filmmaking does the director employ to highlight the movie's particular approach to this theme?

4. Some viewers feel that Forest Whitaker's adaptation *Waiting to Exhale* (1995) offers examples of strong, independent, responsible black women; other viewers have attacked the lead characters as co-dependent and irresponsible. View this adaptation and add your voice to the dialogue.

Vulnerability

A scene from *The Joy Luck Club*. Buena Vista/Photofest.

When thousands of people died as the twin towers of the World Trade Center collapsed after a terrorist attack on September 11, 2001, our entire nation stood still, watching in outraged grief. However much we may have known in our hearts that we are always and everywhere vulnerable, the terrorist attacks on September 11 came as a shock. Mere quivering, soft, easily crushed masses that we are, how are we to live with the knowledge of such frightening vulnerability? Such questions have haunted writers since time immemorial, puzzling the ever-patient Job, the great tragedians of ancient Athens, and the religous thinkers of quite diverse cultures and times.

No matter how we try to protect ourselves with security systems, storm warnings, airbags, and quake-resistant structures, violence constantly threatens us. We are all vulnerable, fearing and suffering pain and heartbreak, the loss of loved ones, the loss of memory or physical ability, the constant threat of accidental death or violent assault. The threat may come from outside in the form of terrorism as described in the essays of Stephen Sloan and Leonard Weinberg or as the ghastly devastation of war depicted in such poems as Wilfred Owen's "*Dulce et Decorum Est*" or Randall Jarrell's "The Death of the Ball Turret Gunner." Perhaps more frighteningly, it may also threaten us from within ourselves. Othello, in William Shakespeare's tragedy, twisted and manipulated by the evil Iago, struggles with jealousy so violent that it leads him to kill his wife, Desdemona. Like Othello, we may live in an illusion of security until the seductive face of evil draws us into its violent maw.

Even if we manage to avoid such violence, we all must face the reality that every day our world changes. Sometimes those changes occur through our careless misuse of our environment as described by Bill McKibben in "Happiness Is" or through our cruel or thoughtless treatment of others. As Barbara Kingsolver points out in "A Pure, High Note of Anguish," "The mortal citizens of a planet are praying right now that we will bear in mind . . . that no kind of bomb ever built will extinguish hatred."

How we face our common vulnerability defines us as people. As the narrator in Bharati Mukherjee's eloquent story "The Management of

Grief" says, "we must all grieve in our own way"; similarly, we must all handle fear in our own ways, whether with the extraordinary courage in the face of doom of a Todd Beamer (leader in forcing Al Qaeda terrorists to crash United Airlines flight 93 in Pennsylvania on September 11, 2001) or with the crazed rage of Othello. Confronted by the terrible brutality of Auschwitz, Pinhas, a rabbi in Elie Wiesel's essay "Yom Kippur: The Day without Forgiveness," doubts whether God knows what He is doing. Others, like the speaker in "Do Not Go Gentle into That Good Night" by Dylan Thomas, may fight death with every ounce of will and courage they can muster. Still others, like Shakespeare's Othello, may choose self-inflicted death over a life of humiliation or poverty or guilt. However it may confront them, great literature does not ignore the horrors of evil in the world. Great literature reflects the extraordinary variety of our responses to them.

Writing about Vulnerability

As you prepare your essay on one or more of the works in this section, consider that just as each genre allows you to take different approaches to the works, so too does each kind of essay. After selecting the work or works of literature you intend to use in your essay, you should reread the Questions for Engagement, Response, and Analysis about that particular genre in Part One of the Introduction. You can also reread the suggestions for Crafting Arguments after the selections and those at the end of this unit for ideas about suitable subjects.

If you decide to write about an essay, you might, for example, examine the different kinds of discrimination portrayed in the works in this unit, such as religious discrimination in Wiesel's "Yom Kippur," or, using the same essay, you might analyze the effectiveness of personal acts of defiance on those who are left behind. Perhaps you might argue after reading Stephen Sloan's essay "The Meaning of Terrorism: The Problem of Definition Revisited" that one or more of his claims is or is not sufficiently supported. You might prefer to examine a claim that is more difficult to prove, such as Bill McKibben's assertion that happiness is not increased by an accumulation of more and more possessions, and then argue the effectiveness of his evidence.

If you prefer to write on a work of fiction, you might choose one of the stories from the Casebook on Amy Tan. For example, you might write an essay analyzing Olivia's motivation for returning to China in "Young Girl's Wish" or the reasons for Precious Auntie's behavior toward the narrator in "Heart." Using Anton Chekhov's "The Lottery Ticket," you might compare the attitudes of the couple at the beginning and at the conclusion of the story or analyze their reasons for not checking the winning lottery number earlier. If you prefer, you might attempt to prove that the town in William Faulkner's "A Rose for Emily" is complicit in Miss Emily's behavior.

Both the form and the content of the poems in this unit offer good possibilities for essays. For example, you might choose to analyze how Percy Bysshe Shelley's use of the sonnet form and of synecdoche creates a living portrait of a dead ruler. You might examine e. e. cummings' playful use of form to write about the serious subject of death in "Buffalo Bill's Defunct" or analyze the way that Billy Collins uses humorous details to develop a poem about "Forgetfulness." If you prefer to write a Comparison/ Contrast essay, you could examine the different attitudes toward death described in Dylan Thomas's villanelle "Do Not Go Gentle into That Good Night."

Because so much excellent scholarship on *Othello* is available, you might write a researched essay on the seemingly gratuitous evil of Iago or analyze the changes in Othello's language and personality. If you prefer to analyze characters, you could write on Emilia's motivation in first helping and then exposing her husband. You might also choose to argue that though Iago manipulates Othello, ultimately Othello falls because of a flaw within himself.

When Gael Fowler, a communications major, was asked to write an essay using the Casebook on Amy Tan, she began by reading both stories and all of the critical essays. At first she considered writing on both of the stories, but after trying several thesis statements, she could not decide on one that included both. She finally chose to write on the types of death in "Heart."

Gael actually started several essays but in the end went back to her original idea. She sent her completed draft to her professor by e-mail to see if she was following the directions of the assignment. The professor suggested a few additions and said that Gael needed to make it clear that the stories told by Precious Auntie were a retelling of things that happened in the past. At this point, Gael added to the introduction a part about what had happened to the main character of the story. The new version, because it focused more on the main character, made a better essay. Gael felt that this change caused the paper as a whole to flow more smoothly. This revision also solved a problem she had faced about the verb tenses because the whole paper now was written in present tense, except for the quotations. Next, she polished the essay and rearranged and reworded her original conclusion. Gael chose her title after she wrote the first draft. Her final essay is included at the end of the Casebook.

E S SA Y S

Black Elk (c. 1863–1950)

A member of the Sioux tribe and a relative of Crazy Horse, Black Elk witnessed the Battle of Little Big Horn in 1876. After a brief, unpleasant experience as part of Buffalo Bill's Wild West Show in 1886, he returned to the reservation in 1889. Black Elk was injured in the massacre at Wounded Knee in 1890. Early in the twentieth century, he converted to Roman Catholicism, though without giving up his Sioux beliefs. Late in life, he told the story of his life to John G. Neihardt, who edited and published the account as Black Elk Speaks *(1932). He described Sioux beliefs and sacred Sioux rituals to Joseph Epes Brown, who published them under the title* In the Sacred Pipe *in 1953.*

From BLACK ELK SPEAKS

The Butchering at Wounded Knee   (1932)

1   That evening before it happened, I went in to Pine Ridge and heard these things, and while I was there, soldiers started for where the Big Foots were. These made about five hundred soldiers that were there next morning. When I saw them starting I felt that something terrible was going to happen. That night I could hardly sleep at all. I walked around most of the night.

2   In the morning I went out after my horses, and while I was out I heard shooting off toward the east, and I knew from the sound that it must be wagon-guns (cannon) going off. The sounds went right through my body, and I felt that something terrible would happen.

3   When I reached camp with the horses, a man rode up to me and said: "Hey-hey-hey! The people that are coming are fired on! I know it!"

4   I saddled up my buckskin and put on my sacred shirt. It was one I had made to be worn by no one but myself. It had a spotted eagle outstretched on the back of it, and the daybreak star was on the left shoulder, because when facing south that shoulder is toward the east. Across the breast, from the left shoulder to the right hip, was the flaming rainbow, and there was another rainbow around the neck, like a necklace, with a star at the bottom. At each shoulder, elbow, and wrist was an eagle feather; and over the whole shirt were red streaks of lightning. You will see that this was from my great vision, and you will know how it protected me that day.

5   I painted my face all red, and in my hair I put one eagle feather for the One Above.

6   It did not take me long to get ready, for I could still hear the shooting over there.

7   I started out alone on the old road that ran across the hills to Wounded Knee. I had no gun. I carried only the sacred bow of the west that I had

seen in my great vision. I had gone only a little way when a band of young men came galloping after me. The first two who came up were Loves War and Iron Wasichu. I asked what they were going to do, and they said they were just going to see where the shooting was. Then others were coming up, and some older men.

8   We rode fast, and there were about twenty of us now. The shooting was getting louder. A horseback from over there came galloping very fast toward us, and he said: "Hey-hey-hey! They have murdered them!" Then he whipped his horse and rode away faster toward Pine Ridge.

9   In a little while we had come to the top of the ridge where, looking to the east, you can see for the first time the monument and the burying ground on the little hill where the church is. That is where the terrible thing started. Just south of the burying ground on the little hill a deep dry gulch runs about east and west, very crooked, and it rises westward to nearly the top of the ridge where we were. It had no name, but the Wasichus sometimes call it Battle Creek now. We stopped on the ridge not far from the head of the dry gulch. Wagon guns were still going off over there on the little hill, and they were going off again where they hit along the gulch. There was much shooting down yonder, and there were many cries, and we could see cavalrymen scattered over the hills ahead of us. Cavalrymen were riding along the gulch and shooting into it, where the women and children were running away and trying to hide in the gullies and the stunted pines.

10   A little way ahead of us, just below the head of the dry gulch, there were some women and children who were huddled under a clay bank, and some cavalrymen were there pointing guns at them.

11   We stopped back behind the ridge, and I said to the others: "Take courage. These are our relatives. We will try to get them back." Then we all sang a song which went like this:

"A thunder being nation I am, I have said.
A thunder being nation I am, I have said.
You shall live.
You shall live.
You shall live.
You shall live."

12   Then I rode over the ridge and the others after me, and we were crying: "Take courage! It is time to fight!" The soldiers who were guarding our relatives shot at us and then ran away fast, and some more cavalrymen on the other side of the gulch did too. We got our relatives and sent them across the ridge to the northwest where they would be safe.

13   I had no gun, and when we were charging, I just held the sacred bow out in front of me with my right hand. The bullets did not hit us at all.

14   We found a little baby lying all alone near the head of the gulch. I could not pick her up just then, but I got her later and some of my people

adopted her. I just wrapped her up tighter in a shawl that was around her and left her there. It was a safe place, and I had other work to do.

15   The soldiers had run eastward over the hills where there were some more soldiers, and they were off their horses and lying down. I told the others to stay back, and I charged upon them holding the sacred bow out toward them with my right hand. They all shot at me, and I could hear bullets all around me, but I ran my horse right close to them, and then swung around. Some soldiers across the gulch began shooting at me too, but I got back to the others and was not hurt at all.

16   By now many other Lakotas, who had heard the shooting, were coming up from Pine Ridge, and we all charged on the soldiers. They ran eastward toward where the trouble began. We followed down along the dry gulch, and what we saw was terrible. Dead and wounded women and children and little babies were scattered all along there where they had been trying to run away. The soldiers had followed along the gulch, as they ran, and murdered them in there. Sometimes they were in heaps because they had huddled together, and some were scattered all along. Sometimes bunches of them had been killed and torn to pieces where the wagon guns hit them. I saw a little baby trying to suck its mother, but she was bloody and dead.

17   There were two little boys at one place in this gulch. They had guns and they had been killing soldiers all by themselves. We could see the soldiers they had killed. The boys were all alone there, and they were not hurt. These were very brave little boys.

18   When we drove the soldiers back, they dug themselves in, and we were not enough people to drive them out from there. In the evening they marched off up Wounded Knee Creek, and then we saw all that they had done there.

19   Men and women and children were heaped and scattered all over the flat at the bottom of the little hill where the soldiers had their wagon-guns, and westward up the dry gulch all the way to the high ridge, the dead women and children and babies were scattered.

20   When I saw this I wished that I had died too, but I was not sorry for the women and children. It was better for them to be happy in the other world, and I wanted to be there too. But before I went there I wanted to have revenge. I thought there might be a day, and we should have revenge.

21   After the soldiers marched away, I heard from my friend, Dog Chief, how the trouble started, and he was right there by Yellow Bird when it happened. This is the way it was:

22   In the morning the soldiers began to take all the guns away from the Big Foots, who were camped in the flat below the little hill where the monument and burying ground are now. The people had stacked most of their guns, and even their knives, by the tepee where Big Foot was lying sick. Soldiers were on the little hill and all around, and there were soldiers across the dry gulch to the south and over east along Wounded Knee

Creek too. The people were nearly surrounded, and the wagon-guns were pointing at them.

23   Some had not yet given up their guns, and so the soldiers were searching all the tepees, throwing things around and poking into everything. There was a man called Yellow Bird, and he and another man were standing in front of the tepee where Big Foot was lying sick. They had white sheets around and over them, with eyeholes to look through, and they had guns under these. An officer came to search them. He took the other man's gun, and then started to take Yellow Bird's. But Yellow Bird would not let go. He wrestled with the officer, and while they were wrestling, the gun went off and killed the officer. Wasichus and some others have said he meant to do this, but Dog Chief was standing right there, and he told me it was not so. As soon as the gun went off, Dog Chief told me, an officer shot and killed Big Foot who was lying sick inside the tepee.

24   Then suddenly nobody knew what was happening, except that the soldiers were all shooting and the wagon-guns began going off right in among the people.

25   Many were shot down right there. The women and children ran into the gulch and up west, dropping all the time, for the soldiers shot them as they ran. There were only about a hundred warriors and there were nearly five hundred soldiers. The warriors rushed to where they had piled their guns and knives. They fought soldiers with only their hands until they got their guns.

26   Dog Chief saw Yellow Bird run into a tepee with his gun, and from there he killed soldiers until the tepee caught fire. Then he died full of bullets.

27   It was a good winter day when all this happened. The sun was shining. But after the soldiers marched away from their dirty work, a heavy snow began to fall. The wind came up in the night. There was a big blizzard, and it grew very cold. The snow drifted deep in the crooked gulch, and it was one long grave of butchered women and children and babies, who had never done any harm and were only trying to run away.

The End of the Dream

28   After the soldiers marched away, Red Crow and I started back toward Pine Ridge together, and I took the little baby that I told you about. Red Crow had one too.

29   We were going back to Pine Ridge, because we thought there was peace back home; but it was not so. While we were gone, there was a fight around the Agency, and our people had all gone away. They had gone away so fast that they left all the tepees standing.

30   It was nearly dark when we passed north of Pine Ridge where the hospital is now, and some soldiers shot at us, but did not hit us. We rode into the camp, and it was all empty. We were very hungry because we had not eaten anything since early morning, so we peeped into the tepees until we saw where there was a pot with papa (dried meat) cooked in it. We

sat down in there and began to eat. While we were doing this, the soldiers shot at the tepee, and a bullet struck right between Red Crow and me. It threw dust in the soup, but we kept right on eating until we had our fill. Then we took the babies and got on our horses and rode away. If that bullet had only killed me, then I could have died with papa in my mouth.

31   The people had fled down Clay Creek, and we followed their trail. It was dark now, and late in the night we came to where they were camped without any tepees. They were just sitting by little fires, and the snow was beginning to blow. We rode in among them and I heard my mother's voice. She was singing a death song for me, because she felt sure I had died over there. She was so glad to see me that she cried and cried.

32   Women who had milk fed the little babies that Red Crow and I brought with us.

33   I think nobody but the little children slept any that night. The snow blew and we had no tepees.

34   When it was getting light, a war party went out and I went along; but this time I took a gun with me. When I started out the day before to Wounded Knee, I took only my sacred bow, which was not made to shoot with; because I was a little in doubt about the Wanekia religion at that time, and I did not really want to kill anybody because of it.

35   But I did not feel like that any more. After what I had seen over there, I wanted revenge; I wanted to kill.

36   We crossed White Clay Creek and followed it up, keeping on the west side. Soon we could hear many guns going off. So we struck west, following a ridge to where the fight was. It was close to the Mission, and there are many bullets in the Mission yet.

37   From this ridge we could see that the Lakotas were on both sides of the creek and were shooting at soldiers who were coming down the creek. As we looked down, we saw a little ravine, and across this was a big hill. We crossed and rode up the hillside.

38   They were fighting right there, and a Lakota cried to me: "Black Elk, this is the kind of a day in which to do something great!" I answered: "How!"[1]

39   Then I got off my horse and rubbed earth on myself, to show the Powers that I was nothing without their help. Then I took my rifle, got on my horse and galloped up to the top of the hill. Right below me the soldiers were shooting, and my people called out to me not to go down there; that there were some good shots among the soldiers and I should get killed for nothing.

40   But I remembered my great vision, the part where the geese of the north appeared. I depended upon their power. Stretching out my arms with my gun in the right hand, like a goose soaring when it flies low to turn in a change of weather, I made the sound the geese make—br-r-r-p, br-r-r-p, br-r-r-p; and, doing this, I charged. The soldiers saw, and began

[1]Signifying assent.

shooting fast at me. I kept right on with my buckskin running, shot in their faces when I was near, then swung wide and rode back up the hill.

41   All this time the bullets were buzzing around me and I was not touched. I was not even afraid. It was like being in a dream about shooting. But just as I had reached the very top of the hill, suddenly it was like waking up, and I was afraid. I dropped my arms and quit making the goose cry. Just as I did this, I felt something strike my belt as though some one had hit me there with the back of an ax. I nearly fell out of my saddle, but I managed to hold on, and rode over the hill.

42   An old man by the name of Protector was there, and he ran up and held me, for now I was falling off my horse. I will show you where the bullet struck me sidewise across the belly here (showing a long deep scar on the abdomen). My insides were coming out. Protector tore up a blanket in strips and bound it around me so that my insides would stay in. By now I was crazy to kill, and I said to Protector: "Help me on my horse! Let me go over there. It is a good day to die, so I will go over there!" But Protector said: "No, young nephew! You must not die to-day. That would be foolish. Your people need you. There may be a better day to die." He lifted me into my saddle and led my horse away down hill. Then I began to feel very sick.

43   By now it looked as though the soldiers would be wiped out, and the Lakotas were fighting harder; but I heard that, after I left, the black Wasichu soldiers came, and the Lakotas had to retreat.

44   There were many of our children in the Mission, and the sisters and priests were taking care of them. I heard there were sisters and priests right in the battle helping wounded people and praying.

45   There was a man by the name of Little Soldier who took charge of me and brought me to where our people were camped. While we were over at the Mission Fight, they had fled to the O-ona-gazhee [2] and were camped on top of it where the women and children would be safe from soldiers. Old Hollow Horn was there. He was a very powerful bear medicine man, and he came over to heal my wound. In three days I could walk, but I kept a piece of blanket tied around my belly.

46   It was now nearly the middle of the Moon of Frost in the Tepee (January). We heard that soldiers were on Smoky Earth River and were coming to attack us in the O-ona-gazhee. They were near Black Feather's place. So a party of about sixty of us started on the war-path to find them. My mother tried to keep me at home, because, although I could walk and ride a horse, my wound was not all healed yet. But I would not stay; for, after what I had seen at Wounded Knee, I wanted a chance to kill soldiers.

47   We rode down Grass Creek to Smoky Earth, and crossed, riding down stream. Soon from the top of a little hill we saw wagons and cavalry guarding them. The soldiers were making a corral of their wagons and getting ready to fight. We got off our horses and went behind some hills

[2]Sheltering place, an elevated plateau in the Badlands, with precipitous sides, and inaccessible save by one narrow neck of land easily defended.

to a little knoll, where we crept up to look at the camp. Some soldiers were bringing harnessed horses down to a little creek to water, and I said to the others: "If you will stay here and shoot at the soldiers, I will charge over there and get some good horses." They knew of my power, so they did this, and I charged on my buckskin while the others kept shooting. I got seven of the horses; but when I started back with these, all the soldiers saw me and began shooting. They killed two of my horses, but I brought five back safe and was not hit. When I was out of range, I caught up a fine bald-faced bay and turned my buckskin loose. Then I drove the others back to our party.

48   By now more cavalry were coming up the river, a big bunch of them, and there was some hard fighting for a while, because there were not enough of us. We were fighting and retreating, and all at once I saw Red Willow on foot running. He called to me: "Cousin, my horse is killed!" So I caught up a soldier's horse that was dragging a rope and brought it to Red Willow while the soldiers were shooting fast at me. Just then, for a little while, I was a wanekia [3] myself. In this fight Long Bear and another man, whose name I have forgotten, were badly wounded; but we saved them and carried them along with us. The soldiers did not follow us far into the Badlands, and when it was night we rode back with our wounded to the O-ona-gazhee.

49   We wanted a much bigger war-party so that we could meet the soldiers and get revenge. But this was hard, because the people were not all of the same mind, and they were hungry and cold. We had a meeting there, and were all ready to go out with more warriors, when Afraid-of-His-Horses came over from Pine Ridge to make peace with Red Cloud, who was with us there.

50   Our party wanted to go out and fight anyway, but Red Cloud made a speech to us something like this: "Brothers, this is a very hard winter. The women and children are starving and freezing. If this were summer, I would say to keep on fighting to the end. But we cannot do this. We must think of the women and children and that it is very bad for them. So we must make peace, and I will see that nobody is hurt by the soldiers."

51   The people agreed to this, for it was true. So we broke camp next day and went down from the O-ona-gazhee to Pine Ridge, and many, many Lakotas were already there. Also, there were many, many soldiers. They stood in two lines with their guns held in front of them as we went through to where we camped.

52   And so it was all over.

53   I did not know then how much was ended. When I look back now from this high hill of my old age, I can still see the butchered women and children lying heaped and scattered all along the crooked gulch as plain as when I saw them with eyes still young. And I can see that something else died there in the bloody mud, and was buried in the blizzard. A people's dream died there. It was a beautiful dream.

[3] A "make-live," savior.

54   And I, to whom so great a vision was given in my youth,—you see me now a pitiful old man who has done nothing, for the nation's hoop is broken and scattered. There is no center any longer, and the sacred tree is dead.

Questions for Engagement, Response, and Analysis

1. What is the tone of most of this essay? How does it change in the conclusion?
2. What is the theme of the essay?
3. What details reveal Black Elk's religious views? What do they suggest about this religion?
4. In your Reader's Journal, freewrite a description of this event from the point of view of a soldier in the United States Army.
5. Reread the last two paragraphs and explain what, according to Black Elk, died at Wounded Knee.

Crafting Arguments

1. If you are not already familiar with the history of the battle of Wounded Knee, read an account in a history book. Then, write an essay explaining how point of view in this essay affects readers' perception of the event.

Elie Wiesel (b. 1928)

Elie Wiesel was born in the village of Sighet in a part of Romania often claimed by Hungary. In 1944, the Nazis sent Wiesel and his family, along with all the other Jews of their village and region, to Auschwitz, where Wiesel's mother and younger sister were killed. Moved to Buchenwald, Wiesel and his father worked as slaves under horrendous conditions, which ultimately killed his father. Wiesel survived to become the foremost chronicler of the horrors of the Holocaust. Naturalized as a U.S. citizen in 1963, Wiesel has served as a faculty member in humanities at Boston University since 1976 and in 1978 was named chair of the U.S. Holocaust Museum. In 1985, he was awarded the National Medal of Freedom and, in 1986, the Nobel Peace Prize. Among his many books are And the World Has Remained Silent *(1956), a powerful novel of life in Auschwitz from the point of view of a young boy, later translated and abridged as* Night: The Town Beyond the Wall *(1962);* Legends of Our Time, *from which the following selection is taken;* The Forgotten *(1989);* All Rivers Run to the Sea: A Memoir *(1995); and* The Time of the Uprooted *(2005).*

Yom Kippur: The Day Without Forgiveness   (1968)

1   With a lifeless look, a painful smile on his face, while digging a hole in the ground, Pinhas moved his lips in silence. He appeared to be arguing with someone within himself and, judging from his expression, seemed close to admitting defeat.

2   I had never seen him so downhearted. I knew that his body would not hold out much longer. His strength was already abandoning him, his movements were becoming more heavy, more chaotic. No doubt he knew it too. But death figured only rarely in our conversations. We preferred to deny its presence, to reduce it, as in the past, to a simple allusion, something abstract, inoffensive, a word like any other.

3   "What are you thinking about? What's wrong?"

4   Pinhas lowered his head, as if to conceal his embarrassment, or his sadness, or both, and let a long time go by before he answered, in a voice scarcely audible: "Tomorrow is Yom Kippur."

5   Then I too felt depressed. My first Yom Kippur in the camp. Perhaps my last. The day of judgment, of atonement. Tomorrow the heavenly tribunal would sit and pass sentence: "And like unto a flock, the creatures of this world shall pass before thee." Once upon a time—last year—the approach of this day of tears, of penitence and fear, had made me tremble. Tomorrow, we would present ourselves before God, who sees everything and who knows everything, and we would say: "Father, have pity on your children." Would I be capable of praying with fervor again? Pinhas shook himself abruptly. His glance plunged into mine.

6   "Tomorrow is the Day of Atonement and I have just made a decision: I am not going to fast. Do you hear? I am not going to fast."

7   I asked for no explanation. I knew he was going to die and suddenly I was afraid that by way of justification he might declare: "It is simple, I have decided not to comply with the law anymore and not to fast because in the eyes of man and of God I am already dead, and the dead can disobey the commandments of the Torah." I lowered my head and made believe I was not thinking about anything but the earth I was digging up under a sky more dark than the earth itself.

8   We belonged to the same Kommando. We always managed to work side by side. Our age difference did not stop him from treating me like a friend. He must have been past forty. I was fifteen. Before the war, he had been *Rosh-Yeshiva*, director of a rabbinical school somewhere in Galicia. Often, to outwit our hunger or to forget our reasons for despair, we would study a page of the Talmud from memory. I relived my childhood by forcing myself not to think about those who were gone. If one of my arguments pleased Pinhas, if I quoted a commentary without distorting its meaning, he would smile at me and say: "I should have liked to have you among my disciples."

9   And I would answer: "But I am your disciple, where we are matters little."

10   That was false, the place was of capital importance. According to the law of the camp I was his equal; I used the familiar form when I addressed him. Any other form of address was inconceivable.

11   "Do you hear?" Pinhas shouted defiantly. "I will not fast."

12   "I understand. You are right. One must not fast. Not at Auschwitz. Here we live outside time, outside sin. Yom Kippur does not apply to Auschwitz."

13   Ever since Rosh Hashana, the New Year, the question had been bitterly debated all over camp. Fasting meant a quicker death. Here everybody fasted all year round. Every day was Yom Kippur. And the book of life and death was no longer in God's hands, but in the hands of the executioner. The words *mi yichye umi yamut*, "who shall live and who shall die," had a terrible real meaning here, an immediate bearing. And all the prayers in the world could not alter the *Gzar-din*, the inexorable movement of fate. Here, in order to live, one had to eat, not pray.

14   "You are right, Pinhas," I said, forcing myself to withstand his gaze. "You *must* eat tomorrow. You've been here longer than I have, longer than many of us. You need your strength. You have to save your strength, watch over it, protect it. You should not go beyond your limits. Or tempt misfortune. That would be a sin."

15   Me, his disciple? I gave him lessons, I gave him advice, as if I were his elder, his guide.

16   "That is not it," said Pinhas, getting irritated. "I could hold out for one day without food. It would not be the first time."

17   "Then what is it?"

18   "A decision. Until now, I've accepted everything. Without bitterness, without reservation. I have told myself: 'God knows what he is doing.' I have submitted to his will. Now I have had enough, I have reached my limit. If he knows what he is doing, then it is serious; and it is not any less serious if he does not. Therefore, I have decided to tell him: 'It is enough.'"

19   I said nothing. How could I argue with him? I was going through the same crisis. Every day I was moving a little further away from the God of my childhood. He had become a stranger to me; sometimes, I even thought he was my enemy.

20   The appearance of Edek put an end to our conversation. He was our master, our king. The Kapo. This young Pole with rosy cheeks, with the movements of a wild animal, enjoyed catching his slaves by surprise and making them shout with fear. Still an adolescent, he enjoyed possessing such power over so many adults. We dreaded his changeable moods, his sudden fits of anger: without unclenching his teeth, his eyes half-closed, he would beat his victims long after they had lost consciousness and had ceased to moan.

21   "Well?" he said, planting himself in front of us, his arms folded. "Taking a little nap? Talking over old times? You think you are at a resort? Or in the synagogue?"

22   A cruel flame lit his blue eyes, but it went out just as quickly. An aborted rage. We began to shovel furiously, not thinking about anything

but the ground which opened up menacingly before us. Edek insulted us a few more times and then walked off.

23   Pinhas did not feel like talking anymore, neither did I. For him the die had been cast. The break with God appeared complete.

24   Meanwhile, the pit under our legs was becoming wider and deeper. Soon our heads would hardly be visible above the ground. I had the weird sensation that I was digging a grave. For whom? For Pinhas? For myself? Perhaps for our memories.

25   On my return to camp, I found it plunged in feverish anticipation: they were preparing to welcome the holiest and longest day of the year. My barracks neighbors, a father and son, were talking in low voices. One was saying: "Let us hope the roll-call does not last too long." The other added: "Let us hope that the soup is distributed before the sun sets, otherwise we will not have the right to touch it."

26   Their prayers were answered. The roll-call unfolded without incident, without delay, without public hanging. The section-chief hurriedly distributed the soup; I hurriedly gulped it down. I ran to wash, to purify myself. By the time the day was drawing to a close, I was ready.

27   Some days before, on the eve of Rosh Hashana, all the Jews in camp— Kapos included—had congregated at the square where roll was taken, and we had implored the God of Abraham, Isaac, and Jacob to end our humiliation, to change sides, to break his pact with the enemy. In unison we had said *Kaddish* for the dead and for the living as well. Officers and soldiers, machine guns in hand, had stood by, amused spectators, on the other side of the barbed wire.

28   Now, we did not go back there for *Kol Nidre*. We were afraid of a selection: in preceding years, the Day of Atonement had been turned into a day of mourning. Yom Kippur had become *Tisha b'Av*, the day the Temple was destroyed.

29   Thus, each barracks housed its own synagogue. It was more prudent. I was sorry, because Pinhas was in another block.

30   A Hungarian rabbi officiated as our cantor. His voice stirred my memories and evoked that legend according to which, on the night of Yom Kippur, the dead rise from their graves and come to pray with the living. I thought: "Then it is true; that is what really happens. The legend is confirmed at Auschwitz."

31   For weeks, several learned Jews had gathered every night in our block to transcribe from memory—by hand, on toilet paper—the prayers for the High Holy Days. Each cantor received a copy. Ours read in a loud voice and we repeated each verse after him. The *Kol Nidre*, which releases us from all vows made under constraint, now seemed to me anachronistic, absurd, even though it had been composed in similar circumstances, in Spain, right near the Inquisition stakes. Once a year the converts would assemble and cry out to God: "Know this, all that we have said is unsaid, all that we have done is undone." *Kol Nidre?* A sad joke.

Here and now we no longer had any secret vows to make or to deny: everything was clear, irrevocable.

32   Then came the *Vidui*, the great confession. There again, everything rang false, none of it concerned us anymore. *Ashamnu*, we have sinned. *Bagadnu*, we have betrayed. *Gazalnu*, we have stolen. What? Us? *We* have sinned? Against whom? By doing what? *We* have betrayed? Whom? Undoubtedly this was the first time since God judged his creation that victims beat their breasts accusing themselves of the crimes of their executioners.

33   Why did we take responsibility for sins and offenses which not one of us could ever have had the desire or the possibility of committing? Perhaps we felt guilty despite everything. Things were simpler that way. It was better to believe our punishments had meaning, that we had deserved them; to believe in a cruel but just God was better than not to believe at all. It was in order not to provoke an open war between God and his people that we had chosen to spare him, and we cried out: "You are our God, blessed be your name. You smite us without pity, you shed our blood, we give thanks to you for it, O Eternal One, for you are determined to show us that you are just and that your name is justice!"

34   I admit having joined my voice to the others and implored the heavens to grant me mercy and forgiveness. At variance with everything my lips were saying, I indicted myself only to turn everything into derision, into farce. At any moment I expected the Master of the universe to strike me dumb and to say: "That is enough—you have gone too far." And I like to think I would have replied: "You, also, blessed be your name, you also."

35   Our services were dispersed by the camp bell. The section-chiefs began to yell: "Okay, go to sleep! If God hasn't heard you, it's because he is incapable of hearing."

36   The next day, at work, Pinhas joined another group. I thought: "He wants to eat without being embarrassed by my presence." A day later, he returned. His face even more pale, even more gaunt than before. Death was gnawing at him. I caught myself thinking: "He will die because he did not observe Yom Kippur."

37   We dug for several hours without looking at each other. From far off, the shouting of the Kapo reached us. He walked around hitting people relentlessly.

38   Toward the end of the afternoon, Pinhas spoke to me: "I have a confession to make."

39   I shuddered, but went on digging. A strange, almost child-like smile appeared on his lips when he spoke again: "You know, I fasted."

40   I remained motionless. My stupor amused him.

41   "Yes, I fasted. Like the others. But not for the same reasons. Not out of obedience, but out of defiance. Before the war, you see, some Jews rebelled against the divine will by going to restaurants on the Day of Atonement; here, it is by observing the fast that we can make our

indignation heard. Yes, my disciple and teacher, know that I fasted. Not for love of God, but against God."

42   He left me a few weeks later, victim of the first selection.

43   He shook my hand: "I would have liked to die some other way and elsewhere. I had always hoped to make of my death, as of my life, an act of faith. It is a pity. God prevents me from realizing my dream. He no longer likes dreams."

44   Nonetheless, he asked me to say *Kaddish* for him after his death, which, according to his calculations, would take place three days after his departure from camp.

45   "But why?" I asked, "since you are no longer a believer?"

46   He took the tone he always used when he explained a passage in the Talmud to me: "You do not see the heart of the matter. Here and now, the only way to accuse him is by praising him."

47   And he went, laughing, to his death.

Questions for Engagement, Response, and Analysis

1. What is the speaker's relationship to Pinhas in the essay? What is his age?

2. Yom Kippur is the one opportunity for divine forgiveness Pinhas will have during the year. He is unlikely to live until the next Day of Atonement. Why, then, does he tell the narrator that he will not fast and will thereby willfully disobey God?

3. The narrator says, "Once upon a time—last year—the approach of this day of tears, of penitence and fear, had made me tremble." Why does he refer to a time as recently as "last year" as "once upon a time"? How and why has his attitude toward Yom Kippur changed?

4. Why would the inhabitants of Auschwitz want to reduce death to "a simple allusion, something abstract, inoffensive, a word like any other"?

5. Discuss Pinhas's statement "The only way to accuse him is by praising him."

6. Why does Pinhas die laughing?

Crafting Arguments

1. Write a character analysis of Edek, the "master of the camp."

2. Craft an essay in which you explain why both Pinhas and the narrator have such a hard time accepting God. Why might Pinhas doubt that God knows what he is doing? What are the implications of God's not knowing "what he is doing"? What are the implications of his knowing but nevertheless allowing a horror like the Holocaust to continue?

Bill McKibben (b. 1960)

Bill McKibben, an American writer whose subjects include the environment and the economy, stresses the ways to improve quality of life. At Harvard University, McKibben wrote for the Harvard Crimson *newspaper, and he continued his writing as a staff writer for* The New Yorker. The End of Nature *(1989), McKibben's first book, which helped to increase awareness of climate change, was updated in 2006. His latest book,* Deep Economy: The Wealth of Communities and the Durable Future *(2007), discusses his continued concern for the environment and the economy and his efforts to share ways to increase real happiness. In addition to his books, McKibben publishes in magazines such as* Harpers *and the* Atlantic. *As an active member of the Methodist church, McKibben often stresses spiritual happiness rather than happiness through increased ownership. At Middlebury College in Vermont, McKibben 'is a scholar in residence.*

HAPPINESS IS . . . (2007)

1   Climate change isn't just a threat. It's an opportunity for us to live happier, more fulfilling lives. The fossil fuel age changed every detail of western human life—where we lived, how we travelled (and how much), what we ate, how our economies worked. But there were two changes in particular that it wrought—huge changes. Changes so huge they redefine the meaning of huge.

2   One is physical—the sudden onset of a rapid warming that will change the Very geography of the planet in almost unbelievable fashion over the next century. We live on a different earth already, and it is going to get worse fast. Way worse. The other is psychological—cheap fossil fuel tipped the balance in the modern mind between self as individual and self as member of community. It made us different people.

3   Worse people. And so here's the good news—fighting either problem means fighting them both. We've been backed into a corner and the only way out is the right way . . .

4   Let's look at the physical problem first. In the last three years or so, the environmental movement has been busy morphing into the global warming movement. And with good reason. For a long time, environmentalists have been declaring that unless we change our course, Something Bad will happen. Now we know what. The earth is warming—indeed, it's warming more rapidly, and with far more devastating effect, than we would have guessed just a few years ago.

5   I wrote the first book for a general audience about climate change back in 1989; at the time, we thought the phenomenon would be epochal (I called my account *The End of Nature*), but we also thought it would be relatively linear, a gradually heating planet with gradually rising seas.

Most scientists guessed that both negative and positive feedback effects would appear—for instance, we'd see more clouds, which would help cool the earth and keep the temperature rise at least a little under control. But those ameliorating effects haven't shown up; instead, we've seen—as documented in each issue of *Nature*—yet more evidence of just how badly we've unhinged the basic physical systems of our home planet. To wit:

- Soils, as they've warmed, have become more microbially active, leading to higher rates of decay, and hence giving off more carbon dioxide. The classic study was done in the UK, and it showed that the flux out of the soils is roughly equal to everything Britain has done since 1990 to reduce carbon emissions.
- Everything frozen on earth is now melting, and melting very quickly. Arctic sea ice has failed to fully re-freeze for the past two winters— the first time anything like that has been observed. If you look at the earth from a satellite, it looks remarkably different than it did a decade or two ago—those Apollo shots of our lonely blue/white orb in the darkness of space are now more blue and less white.
- Hot ocean water is leading—much faster than anyone would have predicated a decade ago—to more massive storms. In 2005, Hurricane Wilma set the Atlantic record for the lowest barometric pressure ever recorded in the hemisphere.

6   All of which leads scientists to a new kind of despair. In the winter of 2006, James Lovelock famously announced that we had already passed the point of no return—billions would perish, while a remnant of civilization might survive if wise leaders led them north towards the pole. Less feverishly, but at least as ominously, the planet's foremost climate scientist, America's James Hansen, defied a White House gag order in the winter of 2005 to declare that unless we started putting less carbon into the atmosphere in the next ten years, we'd soon inhabit a "totally different planet." He seemed most spooked by new data from Greenland showing ice sheets breaking up at a faster-than-expected rate, and thus threatening to raise sea levels by many metres. Ten years. And that was a year ago.

7   So the Something Bad is here. And it's big—as big or bigger than the effects of a thermonuclear exchange. What we need to note is where it came from.

8   Environmentalists have spent most of their time working on the periphery of our economic life: we stuck filters on smokestacks and filters on effluent pipes and filters on car exhausts. The theory was that our basic scheme of life—getting more money then buying more stuff— worked pretty well, it just needed some filtering.

9   It turns out that idea was wrong. The basic scheme of things was the problem. There's no filter you can stick on a car that will keep it from emitting carbon dioxide. What you need is, for instance, a train. Or a

bicycle. Which is to say, a different basic scheme. We can change all our light bulbs for low-energy light bulbs (and we should), but if we don't change the set of attitudes that produces tomatoes in January, or a Ryanair flight across the globe whenever we're chilly, and two people to a house well, that nifty light bulb will be shining on a "totally different planet." The best guess? Stabilizing climate at current levels of disruption would require an immediate, worldwide, 70 percent reduction in carbon emission. That's a lot of light bulbs.

10   There's a reason, of course, why environmentalists have concentrated on light bulbs and filters. It's easy, at least relatively. It doesn't require engaging in discussion about the bigger questions about how we live, and we haven't wanted to engage with those because we assumed we'd lose any argument. Assumed that people liked the way they lived so much they couldn't imagine changing it. Indeed, that's been the biggest operating assumption of our time, the thought that underlay the career of Tony Blair or Bill ("It's the economy, stupid") Clinton. All change needed to come around the edges—we were so deeply enmeshed in the rhythms of consumer culture that challenging it in any real way seemed anathema. You could really see this attitude at work in the negotiations around the World Trade Organization. Relentless expansion of the international economy was the central business at hand—labour and environmental concerns could be discussed, but as "side agreements." We were, literally, in the margins; the economic worldview loomed so large that all else was in its shadow.

11   But that's begun to change or soon will. Or could, anyway, if environmentalism begins to transform itself from a fixation on filters and light bulbs to a new fixation—on human satisfaction.

12   For a very long time, "happiness" has been considered a soft topic, something that hippies and sandal-wearers bothered themselves with and the actual world ignored as it went about the important business of More. In the past decade, however, economists, aided by psychologists and sociologists, have begun to question some of their assumptions. In the old view, you measured happiness by what people bought—under the principle of utility maximization, your credit card statement held the answer to what satisfied you. Ipso facto.

13   But some academics began wondering: why not ask people if they were happy? The first problem was, would their answers be meaningful? An immense amount of research went into trying to answer this question—people undergoing colonoscopies were prodded about the precise level of pain they were feeling, researchers looked at "biases in recall of menstrual symptoms" or "fearlessness and courage in novice paratroopers undergoing training." Some of the early papers had a distinctly academic ring: "The Importance of Taking Part in Daily Life," for instance. (Or the discovery by another analyst that "there is no context in which cutting oneself shaving will be a pleasant experience.")

14   Eventually, however, the various researchers (led in some ways by Princeton's Daniel Kahneman, who won the 2002 Nobel Prize in

Economics—despite not being an economist—for his work on this and other problems) converged on the idea that people really could decide whether they were happy or not. British economist Richard Layard, who has written a great deal about this work, says: "We now know that what people say about how they feel corresponds closely to the actual levels of activity in different parts of the brain, which can be measured in standard scientific ways." People who call themselves happy also seem happier to their friends, live healthier lives, and so forth.

15   Which allows you to start doing something interesting. It allows you to start reversing two centuries of reductionism. Instead of asking: "What did you buy?" you can ask someone: "Is your life good?" And once you've asked that, you're in position to ask the most subversive question there could be: "Is 'more' better?"

16   Because if more really is better, then environmentalism is a lost cause. There aren't enough PowerPoint slides of calving icebergs to turn things around.

17   But if more isn't necessarily better, then there are possibilities.

18   And so here's the bottom line. We've become significantly richer, but not significantly happier. In a sense, you could say that the years since the second World War have been a loosely controlled experiment designed to answer this precise question.

19   The environmentalist Alan Durning found that compared to 1950, the average American family now owns twice as many cars, uses 21 times as much plastic, and travels 25 times farther by air. Gross domestic product per capita has tripled since 1950 in the U.S. We obviously eat more calories. And yet—the satisfaction meter seems not to have budged. More Americans say their marriages are unhappy, their jobs are hideous, and that they don't like the place where they live. The number who, all things considered, say they are "very happy" with their lives has slid steadily over that period. During the rapid economic boom of the Clinton years, the decline in satisfaction seemed, if anything, to accelerate—for instance, a report from the National Opinion Research Center showed increasing numbers of relationships breaking up. As one journalist summarized the findings, "there's more misery in people's lives today."

20   As always, the United States leads the way, but the rest of the world doesn't trail terribly far behind. In the United Kingdom, per capita gross domestic product grew 66 percent between 1973 and 2001 and yet people's satisfaction with their lives changed not a whit. Nor did it budge in Japan, despite a fivefold increase in income in the postwar years.

21   Depression has risen steadily across the advanced world. As the British researcher Richard Douthwaite noted, the doubling of UK income corresponded with rises in everything from crime to divorce. Which doesn't necessarily mean that getting richer caused these problems, but it surely didn't alleviate them. Taken as a whole, we got both more stuff and less happiness.

22   Why did this happen? Though the study of satisfaction is in fact an infant science, the data suggests powerfully that what modern westerners lack is community — we've lost the connections to other people that as evolved primates we need in order to thrive. In the U.S., for instance, studies show that if you find one of the tens of millions of Americans who doesn't belong to anything and convince them to join a church choir or a baseball fan club or any other league of fellow humans, their mortality risk—the chance that they will die in the next year—drops by half. That's not a very subtle effect. People have many fewer friends on average then they did a generation ago, and they visit with those friends—and with family and neighbours — considerably less often. We have, in effect, privatized our lives; an emergent species, the hyper-individual, is on the ascendant.

23   And here's what's interesting. It's fossil fuel that let that happen, just as surely as it's fossil fuel that's melting the ice caps. In America, for instance, cheap gas meant building suburbs—in 1920, Americans lived, on average, about ten persons to an acre. By the year 2000, new subdivisions averaged two people per acre. And once you've moved out to the edge, cheap electricity and heating oil lead people to build with ever-greater grandiosity. The average new home in America has doubled in size since 1970—there are entire suburbs that look like they were built for entry-level monarchs, every home with turrets.

24   But it's not just big cars and big houses. As Felicity Lawrence and Joanna Blythman have shown in their reporting on the transformation of European agriculture, it's also our most basic habits. Forget about relying on your neighbours—the farmer, the butcher, the baker—for your food. Why not, since it's always summer somewhere, simply order take-out from across the globe every single night? Supermarkets, says Blythman, peddle the dream that it is "feasible, and indeed reasonable, for the UK shopper to expect virtually every horticultural product on the planet every day." But you can only get Californian lettuce to London if you're willing to spend 100 calories of fossil energy for every calorie of food. And, so far, we are willing—refrigerated air transport is the fastest growing sector of the food economy.

25   Think I'm overstating the case? Consider the greatest television phenomenon of our time, the show *Survivor*, which touched off the wave of "reality" television. It operates from the premise that, even in an emergency, the obvious goal is to end up alone on the island, to manipulate and scheme until everyone else disappears and leaves you by yourself with your money. The Soviets and the Chinese failed in their 20th-century efforts to build the New Man. But we've evolved one in the West, a hardy hyper-individualist. Margaret Thatcher at the zenith of her power once said, "there is no such thing as 'society.' There are individual men and women and there are families." The only problem is, the individuals aren't all that happy and they're starting to get kind of hot.

26   In a new world like this, we need a new environmentalism. It begins with, say a carrot. Slightly gnarled, perhaps—not a "baby carrot" lathed

to millimetric precision and entombed in a plastic sack, but a real one. Or a potato. Or even a parsnip. The winter before last, I decided on an experiment. Could I make it through the winter in our northern valley eating only the food that came from the fields around me? I wasn't sure— winter's long here (though not as long as it once was, sigh) and an awful lot of our agricultural infrastructure has disappeared. (America now has more prisoners than farmers.) But it turned out that in fact there were enough old farmers hanging on, and enough new ones starting up, to make it a delicious eight months. Root vegetables, but also every kind of cheese and yogurt. Apples from the county's lovely orchards, stored properly for the winter and pressed weekly for cider (even though, in the local supermarket, all the apples were arriving from China and South Africa). Even good beer from our local brewery, made with wheat from a neighbour's field.

27   And it wasn't just the food that was so satisfying. It was the network of new friends—the orchardist, the guy who grew 40 kinds of potatoes on three acres, the fellow raising fallow deer on an old cow pasture. Yes, all this took more time—but the time was the benefit. I felt more connected instead of less.

28   It turns out that I'm not alone. A pair of sociologists recently followed shoppers as they made their rounds, first at the supermarket and then at the local farmers' market. Everyone knows the supermarket experience—light trance, quick tour of the same stations of the culinary cross, back out to the parking lot. At the farmers' market, people had 10 times as many conversations as they had at the supermarket—an order of magnitude more community. Something like an order of magnitude less energy used, too. That's an environmentalism that might start adding up to the scale of change that the planet requires, and that we require. And you don't need to stop with food—you can do the same analysis with energy, with wood, even with entertainment. Why does music, like milk, need to be downloaded from some distant location? Why can't your neighbours make it with you? That's why it's good news when British officials report a resurgence of live music in pubs and clubs, and touring jam bands—descendants of the wandering bards—are making more money in America than the MTV stars.

29   In a weird way, the marketers had figured out all of this years ago, long before the academics and the politicians. Hence advertisements gradually went from being straightforward (this car has more cylinders) to being straightforwardly devious (buy this car and have sex with this girl) to being incredibly bent: buy this car or beer or cosmetic and you will have the community that you crave. If only it were true—if only buying a Heineken could make you part of a world that worked for you—then we'd be fine. But since it's not true, then it's up to the rest of us to make good on the promise.

30   Environmentalists, in other words, need to build a world where that kind of satisfaction really is possible. A world where we rely on each

other for something real again. The kind of world, not incidentally, that needs less coal and gas and oil to make it run.

31   In autumn 2005, the New Economics Foundation released a truly mind-blowing study, which attempted to rank the nations of the world by how much human satisfaction they'd achieved, with how little environmental devastation. Most of the headlines about the study focused on the abysmal rankings of the richest nations (the U.S. was 150th and 178th). But just as interesting was the group that did best: regardless of income, the citizens of island nations were counted as both happier and less spendthrift. Which makes sense. No man is an island, and on an island he's more likely to figure that out. It's a finding every bit as important as the news about Greenland's melting glaciers.

32   We know, after the long experience of the 20th century, all the things that don't work for human satisfaction (centrally planned economies, endlessly repeated ideologies, ever more accumulation). We know, from what the scientists now tell us weekly, what doesn't work for the planet (burning hydrocarbons). Environmentalism is now the art of putting those two sets of facts together.

33   Nothing more, but nothing less.

Questions for Engagement, Response, and Analysis

1. What is the thesis of this essay? How does it differ from the theses of most articles about the environment? Explain.

2. Define the "consumer culture."

3. What kind of research does McKibben ridicule? In your opinion, why does he ridicule it?

4. List the examples of McKibben's use of humor. Why do you believe he uses humor in this discussion of a serious subject?

5. Freewrite in your Reader's Journal about what, if anything, you can do about this problem.

Crafting Arguments

1. Starting with your answer to question number one above, examine McKibben's support for his claims. Then in an essay in which you support each of your claims, argue that his thesis is or is not accurate.

Barbara Kingsolver (b. 1955)

Born in Annapolis, Maryland, Barbara Kingsolver grew up in Kentucky. Though she went to DePauw University on a piano scholarship, she graduated with a degree in biology and took graduate courses in evolutionary biology at the University of Arizona. Kingsolver's first novel, The Bean Trees *(1988), has been translated into several other languages and is still in print. A prolific writer, she has published more novels, including* Pigs in Heaven *(1993),* The Poisonwood Bible *(1998), and* Prodigal Summer *(2000); short stories; and essays. Her 2007 book,* Animal, Vegetable, Miracle, *describes her family's experiment with eating only what they could grow or what they could purchase at local farms. Kingsolver and her family presently live in Virginia. Her essay included here was published twelve days after the September 11, 2001, attacks.*

A PURE, HIGH NOTE OF ANGUISH (2001)

1   Tucson—I want to do something to help right now. But I can't give blood (my hematocrit always runs too low), and I'm too far way to give anybody shelter or a drink of water. I can only give words. My verbal hemoglobin never seems to wane, so words are what I'll offer up in this time that asks of us the best citizenship we've ever mustered. I don't mean to say I have a cure. Answers to the main questions of the day— Where was that fourth plane headed? How did they get knives through security?—I don't know any of that. I have some answers, but only to the questions nobody is asking right now but my 5-year-old. Why did all those people die when they didn't do anything wrong? Will it happen to me? Is this the worst thing that's ever happened? Who were those children cheering that they showed for just a minute, and why were they glad? Please, will this ever, ever happen to me?

2   There are so many answers, and none: It is desperately painful to see people die without having done anything to deserve it, and yet this is how lives end nearly always. We get old or we don't, we get cancer, we starve, we are battered, we get on a plane thinking we're going home but never make it. There are blessings and wonders and horrific bad luck and no guarantees. We like to pretend life is different from that, more like a game we can actually win with the right strategy, but it isn't. And, yes, it's the worst thing that's happened, but only this week. Two years ago, an earthquake in Turkey killed 17,000 people in a day, babies and mothers and businessmen, and not one of them did a thing to cause it. The November before that, a hurricane hit Honduras and Nicaragua and killed even more, buried whole villages and erased family lines and even now, people wake up there empty-handed. Which end of the world shall we talk about? Sixty years ago, Japanese airplanes bombed Navy boys who were sleeping on ships in gentle Pacific waters. Three and a half years later, American planes bombed a plaza in Japan where men and women were going to work, where schoolchildren were playing, and more humans died at once than anyone thought possible. Seventy thousand in a minute. Imagine. Then twice that many more, slowly, from the inside.

3   There are no worst days, it seems. Ten years ago, early on a January morning, bombs rained down from the sky and caused great buildings in the city of Baghdad to fall down—hotels, hospitals, palaces, buildings

with mothers and soldiers inside—and here in the place I want to love best, I had to watch people cheering about it. In Baghdad, survivors shook their fists at the sky and said the word "evil." When many lives are lost all at once, people gather together and say words like "heinous" and "honor" and "revenge," presuming to make this awful moment stand apart somehow from the ways people die a little each day from sickness or hunger. They raise up their compatriots' lives to a sacred place—we do this, all of us who are human—thinking our own citizens to be more worthy of grief and less willingly risked than lives on other soil. But broken hearts are not mended in this ceremony, because, really, every life that ends is utterly its own event—and also in some way it's the same as all others, a light going out that ached to burn longer. Even if you never had the chance to love the light that's gone, you miss it. You should. You bear this world and everything that's wrong with it by holding life still precious, each time, and starting over.

4   And those children dancing in the street? That is the hardest question. We would rather discuss trails of evidence and whom to stamp out, even the size and shape of the cage we might put ourselves in to stay safe, than to mention the fact that our nation is not universally beloved; we are also despised. And not just by "The Terrorist," that lone, deranged non-man in a bad photograph whose opinion we can clearly dismiss, but by ordinary people in many lands. Even by little boys—whole towns full of them it looked like—jumping for joy in school shoes and pilled woolen sweaters.

5   There are a hundred ways to be a good citizen, and one of them is to look finally at the things we don't want to see. In a week of terrifying events, here is one awful, true thing that hasn't much been mentioned: Some people believe our country needed to learn how to hurt in this new way. This is such a large lesson, so hatefully, wrongfully taught, but many people before us have learned honest truths from wrongful deaths. It still may be within our capacity of mercy to say this much is true: We didn't really understand how it felt when citizens were buried alive in Turkey or Nicaragua or Hiroshima. Or that night in Baghdad. And we haven't cared enough for the particular brothers and mothers taken down a limb or a life at a time, for such a span of years that those little, briefly jubilant boys have grown up with twisted hearts. How could we keep raining down bombs and selling weapons, if we had? How can our president still use that word "attack" so casually, like a move in a checker game, now that we have awakened to see that word in our own newspapers, used like this: Attack on America.

6   Surely, the whole world grieves for us right now. And surely it also hopes we might have learned, from the taste of our own blood, that every war is both won and lost, and that loss is a pure, high note of anguish like a mother singing to any empty bed. The mortal citizens of a planet are praying right now that we will bear in mind, better than ever before, that no kind of bomb ever built will extinguish hatred.

7   "Will this happen to me?" is the wrong question, I'm sad to say. It always was.

Questions for Engagement, Response, and Analysis

1. What is the tone of this essay? How is it created?
2. What is Kingsolver's theme or thesis?
3. Interpret Kingsolver's claim that life is not "like a game we can actually win with the right strategy. . . ."
4. Kingsolver says that we can discuss "the size and shape of the cage we might put ourselves in to stay safe." What could the cage be? Why would it be a cage? Explain whether it would be worth it.

Crafting Arguments

1. List the examples of imagery in this essay. Then in an essay interpret the images and explain what they add to the tone and meaning of the essay.
2. If "'Will this happen to me?'" is the wrong question, what would be the right question or questions? Defend your answer in an essay.

Stephen Sloan (b. 1936)

Stephen Sloan has been publishing books on terrorism since 1980. He received his M.A. and Ph.D. from New York University in 1962 and 1967 respectively. Most recently he coauthored a Historical Dictionary of Terrorism *(1995) and wrote* Terrorism: The Present Threat in Context *(2006), from which "The Meaning of Terrorism" is taken. Sloan is a professor in the Department of Political Science at the University of Oklahoma.*

THE MEANING OF TERRORISM

CUTTING THROUGH THE SEMANTIC JUNGLE   (2006)

1   In the academic, political and operational world of terrorism, there is little agreement on the definition of terrorism. Existing definitions range from "you know it when you see it" to the most complex formulations that appear to have been jerry-built—and indeed, a number of them have been by committee. In fact, according to one leading authority, there are more than two hundred recognized definitions and even each one of them can be subject to interpretation.

2   It is not that the definitional issue is not important. At the outset, the definition can help to establish what the scope of the inquiry is. That is, how does one differentiate acts of terrorism from other forms of violence? Moreover, the question of definition has both policy and operational implications. For example, if terrorism is primarily considered to be a criminal act, the focus is on law enforcement—a primarily preventative and reactive approach with a minimum use of force and strong

emphasis on the collection of evidence. If, on the other hand, terrorism is viewed to be a form of warfare, the focus would be a military approach with an emphasis on collection of intelligence for planning operations—an offensive approach and, as required, a maximum use of force.

3   Perhaps the most vexing of all of this is that the word "terrorism" is itself an emotionally laden one. As the saying goes: one man's terrorist is another man's freedom fighter. In sum, terrorism is largely defined on the basis of one's ideological and political vantage point. This is to be expected, since the use of terrorism in both rhetoric and action has taken on a pejorative meaning. Therefore, while it may be intellectually stimulating to debate its meaning, debates on definition often lead to frustration and semantic deadlock.

4   It may be more useful to parse the definition of terrorism by identifying its major characteristics. By effectively dissecting the anatomy of terrorism, one can have a basis for understanding its major characteristics without falling into the emotional and political motivation that often accompanies the definition issue. What are the major characteristics of terrorism? . . .

Terrorism Is Not Mindless Violence: It's an Instrumental Act

5   The image of a suicide bomber in Sri Lanka, Israel or Iraq; the killing of children in Russia; the poisoning of passengers in a subway in Tokyo and other acts of carnage reinforce the view that terrorists are deranged individuals whose motivation for action is either unfathomable, primal or both. While on occasion an individual may be mentally ill, most are quite rational in their actions. It is because the public can neither understand nor justify what they have witnessed that the perpetrators are characterized as being sociopaths or, in a more colloquial sense, crazies. That public perception is largely predicated on the view that what the terrorists do is not rational. Somehow, ascribing rationality to an action is viewed as justifying it. The tragic fact is that one moves toward the dehumanization process used to describe adversaries in war. We are therefore forced to recognize the "ordinariness" of most terrorists. They represent what Hannah Arendt referred to in regard to Adolf Eichman, the organizer of mass killings and genocide, who was a manifestation of "the banality of evil."

6   When individuals resort to acts of violence as individuals or members of a particular group—no matter how repugnant—they are involved in a form of collective behavior as part of a larger ideology. In the fullest sense, terrorism is purposeful violence.

7   To achieve some goal—short- or long-term, realistic or fantastical—it should be recognized that terrorism, in most cases, is instrumental—a means to an end and a way to achieve various goals. An understanding of the purposeful act provides the necessary basis to understand terrorism. The understanding brings necessary analytic order and a degree of

objectivity that would be impossible to achieve if one simply said that terrorism was just mindless violence. This understanding does not suggest that there are not those who for whatever reason engage in violence for violence's sake, but most individuals and groups involved in terrorism are goal-directed—not only in regard to objectives achieved in this life but, as in the case of suicide bombers, also the next.

Terrorism as Strategy and Tactics

8   Since those who engage in terrorism are not involved in mindless violence, what brings a sense of direction, planning and cohesion to the individual acts and campaigns of terrorism? Similar to the case of its definition, the line between strategies and tactics may be blurred.

9   *Strategy* refers to the big picture—the broader and ultimate goals of an organization, be it military or civilian. In contrast, *tactics* refer to those measures that are utilized to achieve strategic objectives. In understanding the characteristics of terrorism, the arbitrary division between the two is often obscured.

10   To many terrorist groups, particularly those motivated by fundamentalist religious beliefs, the strategy is both preordained and transcendental. The ultimate objective will become a reality based on one's religious belief or a commitment to a particular ideology. It is set in stone by either religious interpretation or a worldview based on a particular vision of human nature and history. In some ways strategy is faith in a certain outcome, rather than an objective that will be ultimately realized, by the "true believer." This interpretation of strategy is akin to dogma—it is the revealed truth that, while subject to some interpretation, is immutable.

11   Consequently, the strategy often addresses very broad goals which can be defined in terms of religious transformations or the secular assertion of a political ideology. Even here the line is blurred because to the religious fundamentalist the line between Church and State, the divine and the secular, does not exist. Thus, the individuals and groups who adhere to fundamental beliefs need not be concerned with addressing tactics because all will be accomplished as articles of faith—that is, the terrorist knows that his or her success is ordained and, therefore, cannot fail. Whether an anarchist group that seeks to destroy the old order or a religious group that seeks to replace another, there is no need to define the tactics in a world where the present and future have already been ordained. The vision may be faulty and cannot objectively be achieved, but that makes no difference. Despite the hardships and barriers in the communities of both the religious and the secular, the strategy will be realized as an article of faith.

12   This does not mean that religious and secular tactics don't have a part to play in the pursuit of the ultimate goal, but such tactics are short-term, part of a temporal world, fleeting and may or may not be connected to the strategic vision. It is this blurring of the line between tactics and

strategy that is both a great strength and a great weakness to those who engage in terrorism.

13   The strength of having a strategic vision rests in the fact that, whatever the odds or setbacks, those who believe in the vision can engage in a protracted conflict against great adversaries with the firm realization not only that their cause is just, but that, given time, its goals will be achieved. In contrast, governments opposing terrorism—particularly democracies—must address the continuing shift of public opinion, contentious and fractious political forces, competition for tangible resources and diverse policy alternatives. And all of this must be done to address effectively any immediate and short-term crises. Despite the desire to have a strategic vision, governments have little time to address long-term strategic goals. Forced to address what may be considered tactical considerations, the political leadership does not have the luxury to think, much less act, strategically against adversaries with a long-term commitment.

14   The pressure to do something in the face of the latest terrorist act places intense pressure on governments. Even the attempt to focus on the tactical dimensions of combating terrorism is fraught with difficulties. Since most terrorist groups do not differentiate between civilians, the military and law-enforcement personnel, they all exist as a global target of opportunity. The public demands effective security measures as if total protection could be provided. This is an impossibility because the results would be an undemocratic transformation of the political order, replaced with a repressive "surveillance society." How does one establish the appropriate cost for security in monetary, liberty and political currencies? This does not suggest that there are not tactical measures that can effectively counter threats and acts of terrorism, but they are beyond the scope of this book.

15   What is most important, strategically and tactically, is what the reader and his or her family, friends and community can do to meet the threat. The basic requirement of doing so is to understand terrorism and to respond neither blindly nor emotionally to the images which bombard us on a daily basis. In order to develop the necessary understanding, one must address the following question: What are the various forms of terrorism and how do they impact the immediate victims and the audience?

Terrorism as a Form of Individual and Collective Psychological Operations

16   Since terrorism is violence with a purpose, what is its prime goal? On this there appears to be a consensus by most authorities despite problems associated with seeking a universal definition. Terrorism is first and foremost a form of psychological warfare. As noted earlier, the attacks are primarily instigated to affect the audience. This does suggest that the death, pain and anguish of the immediate victims is not very real and important, but it is the second-order effect—the impact on a broader

audience—that makes terrorism such an invidious and profound weapon. If you recognize the psychological objectives of the terrorist toward individuals and groups, there is a better chance that you can better adjust to the realities of terrorism. This lessens the magnification of the threat that causes one to engage in what can rightfully be called autoterrorism—that is, the terrorizing of oneself.

17   The impact of terrorism on the individual is intimately related to the nature of terror. . . . Terror is a mental state, primarily a fear of what might happen to us. All of us have varying degrees of stated and unstated concerns about situations that create a sense of fear or dread within. In most instances they lie below the mental surface and do not have an impact on our behavior, but when a fear is so strong that it rises to our consciousness and has a profound impact on our mental well being and physical behavior, it can become a phobia. Phobias can paralyze both individuals and societies, which is why it is vital that we do not react primally when we hear of a terrorist attack.

18   We all have various agendas of fear, things that can intimidate us, things that go bump in the night. In most instances we grow out of them. But, terrorists have created an agenda of fear that can influence our behavior. For example, while the public may have some generalized concerns about flying, most individuals will fly since it is the fastest and most convenient form of long-distance travel. While passenger traffic increased because of availability and price, since the introduction of skyjacking in the 1960s most people will look around their gate at the airport and profile other passengers, asking themselves how they would react if their concerns become a reality. They have become secondary victims of terrorism. When their behavior changes and they won't fly because of terrorist acts, they become first-hand victims of terrorism. While they are not the immediate victims held hostage in a cabin, they have fallen victim because it has changed both their mental and physical behaviors.

19   Governments which practice terrorism from above—regime repression—have also created agendas of fear to change attitudes and behaviors and enforce compliance among their citizens. The classic technique of arresting individuals at night, the shock of being taken away from the warmth and security of a bed by the police, has tempered individuals who would normally speak out against a government and its policies. Even more invidious is the fact that a government, through psychological manipulation, will seek to probe the weaknesses and fears of someone and use the threat of turning those fears into a reality as a means of seeking confession or enforcing compliance. One need only remember how the protagonist in George Orwell's *1984* was broken by the government who recognized his fear of being eaten by rats.

20   When people identify with a victim of terrorism whom they have seen on television or read about, when they can not only relate to the experience but also think "there but for the grace of God go I," then they have been subject to terrorism. If the terrorist's actions have altered the way

someone both thinks and behaves, then the audience member has been subject to a degree of terrorism that can be measured from mild to profound. The impact on the individual who witnesses, but is not directly involved in, an incident of terrorism cannot be overstated. The ability to reach out electronically and touch someone in so many ways has given terrorists the ability to export fear consciously beyond the immediate victim. . . .

21   The magnitudes of acts of terrorism have been greatly enhanced by the fact that not only are individuals subject to fear and terrorism, but also that society at large is subject to the impact of terrorist acts and campaigns. If terrorism is ultimately aimed at creating a psychological effect on the individual, then it is also a form of psychological warfare geared at mass audiences and the governments that represent them. The success of terrorism is not only in the magnification of its acts through threat and its physical coercion of the immediate victim, but also in the psychosocial coercion against a much larger group.

22   Terrorism is very successful as a fear multiplier. This multiplication is primarily the result of acts of terrorism breaking through our individual and collective desire for predictability and the accompanying sense of security. Beyond the earthly considerations is also the more transcendental impact. In the final analysis, the violence the public witnesses reminds them not only of their own vulnerability, but also of their own mortality.

23   This sense of vulnerability and mortality is readily seen among members of communities that have been subject to terrorists' attacks both directly and indirectly. Directly, as in the case of the Oklahoma City bombing or the World Trade Center attacks, where numerous people could literally say that if they had not been late to work or chosen to take the day off, they could have been in the ruins of the destroyed buildings. One can only imagine the long-term psychological impact on those individuals, but even more disturbing is the indirect psychological impact on the part of those who could have been victims. Those who witnessed the carnage from five or five thousand miles away share a common emotion in an interconnected world. Their sense of security has been threatened and, ironically, those closer to the act may be better able to cope than those further away.

24   Consider the following: Students who are in Spain during a bombing in Madrid may have the luxury of telling their parents not to worry since they were miles away on the coast. But, to the parents, distance may be irrelevant because in their eyes their children were in Spain when the attack happened. Perhaps the most coherent illustration that distance may not determine the magnitude of the psychological impact is the unfortunate trend in the seizure of schoolchildren. Attacks may be politically motivated as what happened in South Malacca, in the Netherlands and in Beslan, Russia or non-political such as the murders of high school students by fellow students in Columbine, Colorado. Such tragedies create intense psychological pain. The children were deliberately

selected as targets because their captivity, injury or death strikes at the very heart of the family structure. By their actions, the perpetrators send a chilling message to the world. Now, after 9/11, the United States understands that terrorism is not what happens to someone else in some other country.

Terrorism as a Political Weapon

25   If a psychological impact is central to the tactics and strategies of those who practice terrorism, then it is equally true that in terms of goals the primary focus of terrorism is to achieve political objectives, as Bruce Horrman states in his text *Inside Terrorism*, "terrorism is ineluctably political." Terrorists have mixed agendas, ranging from organized crime to religious crusades, but there is a common agreement that what differentiates terrorism from other forms of violence is its political dimension. Thus, while someone may be taken hostage during a bank robbery and subjected to terror, they are not victims of terrorism. To the victim, the motivation behind the action might not be significant, but to the authorities it can make quite a bit of difference. Different measures are taken when combating terrorism as opposed to apolitical criminal acts.

26   Terrorism is first and foremost a weapon used to promote a political agenda. It should be emphasized that terrorists come from all sides of the political spectrum. They range from those who wish to destroy the system to those who want to revolutionize the system and those who wish to return to an idealized system of the past. Those who have had the greatest capability in performing acts of mass terrorism hold yet another position on the political spectrum, those engaging in terrorism from above—the authoritarian and totalitarian states. Many examples of this type of terrorism exist in modern times, from the brutal crackdown on students in Burma in 1988 to the recent intimidation of the people of Zimbabwe by their President, Robert Mugabe.

27   It is also important to recognize that the position of politics in terrorism is not always clear. For example, some fundamentalist beliefs do not differentiate between religious and secular and thus no line differentiating Church and State exists. The lack of this differentiation has created one of the most potent forms of terrorism, Holy Terror, where an article of faith supersedes political ideology.

28   The scope of political change desired may also vary from issue-oriented terrorism, such as the debate over the right to have abortions and specific environmental demands. In the broader range, the political objectives may be based on calls for self-determination based on ethnic, language and territorial considerations. Beyond that, as in the case of various fundamentalist groups, objectives go beyond the nation-state and seek regional or global changes through terrorism.

29   Given the diversity of belief systems by terrorists and their organizations, it is just as dangerous to engage in generalized terrorist stereotyping as it is to engage in simplistic physical, racial and ethnic stereotyping.

Both types may bring superficial analytical order that provides simplistic and erroneous descriptions of who the terrorists are at the cost of being ineffective or even worse, promoting racism and other forms of prejudice and discrimination.

Terrorism as a Form of Warfare

30   It is common for the political leadership and the media to discuss policies in the context of the war on terrorism, but by no means is it clear whether it *is* a war and if so, what *kind* of war it is. As in the case of a general definition of terrorism, a discussion of terrorism as warfare is not simply semantic. There are policy and operational implications that result from this discussion.

31   At the outset, one must raise the issue of where terrorism fits into what is commonly referred to as the spectrum of conflict, which ranges from low intensity to mid-intensity to conventional to ultimately nuclear conflict. Traditionally, terrorism has been associated with unconventional or low-intensity conflict, which also fall under the heading of insurgency. In this context, terrorism is primarily viewed as an unconventional tactic in a territorial conflict waged by a weak organization against a strong adversary—most commonly the government in power. The insurgents (the weak side) engage in asymmetric warfare in which they attempt to overcome the strength of their enemy by playing on its vulnerabilities— a large number of targets, a cumbersome bureaucracy and often a low level of public acceptance of the conflict (i.e. legitimacy).

32   Those who engage in this type of terrorism seek to wear down their adversary psychologically through a protracted campaign of conflict. This is often a tactic used as part of a revolutionary strategy. In this type of conflict, the small numbers and clandestine nature of the insurgents makes them difficult to identify, attack and apprehend. These types of terrorist campaigns are sometimes referred to as "the war of the flea," so aptly named in honor of the exceedingly small insect that is very difficult to eradicate. . . .

33   With the advancing technologies in transportation and communication systems starting in the 1960s, we have witnessed the development of what I call "non-territorial terrorism"—a form of terrorism not confined to a clearly delineated geographic area. As a result of the introduction of jet aircraft, terrorists could literally strike at targets of opportunity thousands of miles from the territorial-based conflict. Moreover, as the events of 9/11 showed us, nonterritorial terrorists can use aircraft as what can be called a low-intensity human-guided intercontinental missile system. The balance of nuclear terror during the Cold War has now been upended by terrorists who have engaged in mass terror using planes as nonnuclear, but very potent, weapons of mass destruction.

34   Given the emergence of non-territorial terrorism, the counter terrorism strategies and tactics that have applied to terrorism as part of an insurgency may no longer be appropriate. Since the terrorists have often

selected targets far away from their base of operations, whose hearts and minds can a government win over? The victims of the attacks live nowhere near the terrorists' base. In conjunction with this, a third-party government may not only provide safe haven to the terrorists and their base of operations, but may also engage in supporting the terrorists who carry out operations beyond their borders, as was the case with Al Qaeda. When these attacks occur thousands of miles from where the terrorists make their home, a major challenge for the targeted government is the jurisdiction and territorial boundaries of its police, military and security forces.

35   Terrorism as a form of warfare has yet to be clearly defined by those who are schooled in the arts and sciences of warfare. This is not a traditional conflict between nation-states; nor is it a war with uniformed, recognizable soldiers. There are also no clearly defined laws of warfare or rules of engagement, since to all intents and purposes terrorism is a war that does not recognize the difference between combatant and noncombatant. If we do define it as war, it is a war without rules, a war without structure. In a sense, it is a new form of total war, though usually on a smaller scale.

36   By saying that terrorists do not recognize the difference between combatant and noncombatant I do not mean to suggest that civilians have not been killed or wounded as a result of war—often called collateral damage. The difference here is that terrorists intentionally target civilians as a prime objective in waging their psychological warfare.

37   Another manifestation caused by contemporary terrorism has resulted in a response by multinational corporations. Just as terrorists have created their own non-state armies, multinational corporations have developed their own counterterrorist forces. Governments have enlisted the aid of nongovernmental civilians on the battlefield to provide services for counterterrorist military operations. The new mercenary, the corporate warrior, has arisen.

38   Finally, we are entering a new phase in the transformation of warfare with the emergence of netwar. Terrorists who reject secular Western culture, but are more than willing and capable to use the latest trends in technology against industrial and postindustrial societies, have been using it effectively. . . .

Terrorism as an Evolutionary Process

39   In a sense, terrorists are like sharks that must keep swimming if they are to receive the oxygen they need to survive. . . . [T]here is continuity in the strategy and nature of terrorism. The process can be appreciated by understanding the development of doctrine, which can be applied to understanding the evolution of terrorism.

40   There is fundamental doctrine that transcends time and there is environmental doctrine affected by gradual and profound changes in the political, social, economic, religious and especially the technological

environments. Changes in any of these can cause new opportunities and dangers for terrorists. Finally, there is operational doctrine, the art and science of engaging in the carnage of terrorism. While doctrine does not offer a cognitive road map of future developments, it does provide a guide to identifying and evaluating future threats. It bears repetition that terrorism is not mindless violence. It is not a happening; it is not the product of individuals and groups running amok. Therefore, in assessing the past, present and future of terrorism, the following axioms can help us to understand terrorism as an ongoing process.

41   At the outset, terrorists must adapt to what their available resources are. They traditionally are in a weaker position than their adversary—unless they are engaged in terrorism from above or regime repression. They must not only do more with less, they must also have the imagination to outmaneuver a stronger foe. As we have noted, they have an advantage over the cumbersome, large, inflexible militaries they face. In far too many cases, bureaucratic imagination is lacking and creativity is contradictory in terms. Terrorists must also adhere to the organizational and operational mantra that "small is beautiful." The small size of terrorist organizations circumvents their liability against a much larger adversary and turns it into an asset.

42   Neither terrorists nor their targets can afford to fail. The authorities of the targeted government are faced with the near-impossible task of preventing all terrorist incidents. One major incident can be traumatic, whereas success against terrorists is ironically marked when nothing happens. In the same manner, terrorist organizations in their early organizational phase cannot afford mistakes. Given their weak position and minimal resources, one error can be fatal. As with all other people, terrorists must learn from their mistakes if they are to survive. But, while terrorists often portray themselves as being revolutionary or on the cutting edge of political and societal change, they can also be caught in their own dogma and their own prisms of belief.

Conclusion

43   While one realizes the power of images in the media and the sense of fear they can create, the fact of the matter is that few people will directly experience the anguish of terrorism. I do not mean to minimize the profound physical and emotional cost to the victims and to their families and friends, but it remains that the ability of the terrorists to instill fear in a larger audience makes their actions so effective. And, as noted earlier, if people move beyond the routine precautions and profoundly alter their lives as a result of a loss of security, they have fallen into the trap of fear as intended by the terrorists. It is also important not to understate the threat and enter a stage of denial. A balance must be established.

44   This balance can be established by increasing one's understanding of terrorism. Terrorism is not mindless violence. Whether it is a tactic or strategy, a form of psychological warfare, a political weapon, a new form

of warfare or a criminal act, it is not a monster that lurks in the dark, nor a monster that we can do nothing about. Understanding terrorism can help negate the fear that accompanies the sense of dread that comes from what we don't know. An understanding of terrorism can help us—and those responsible for providing our security—to avoid the ultimate threat: terrorizing ourselves.

Questions for Engagement, Response, and Analysis

1. Explain Sloan's claim that terrorism is "an instrumental act." Who is subject to it?

2. How may religious and political terrorism overlap?

3. According to Sloan, is terrorism a form of warfare? Why or why not? Why is it important to understand what terrorism is and is not?

Crafting Arguments

1. Using evidence from Sloan's text, craft an essay that differentiates between mindless violence, criminal violence, terrorism, and warfare.

Leonard Weinberg (b. 1939)

Author of numerous books and articles on terrorism, Leonard Weinberg has also received many awards and appointments. He was a Fulbright senior research fellow for Italy and has served as a consultant to the United Nations Office for the Prevention of Terrorism. In 1999 Weinberg received the Thornton Peace Prize for his efforts in promoting Christian-Jewish reconciliation. His recent books include Political Parties and Terrorist Groups *(2003),* Right-Wing Extremism in the Twenty-First Century *(2003),* Religious Fundamentalism and Political Extremism *(2003), and* Global Terrorism: A Beginner's Guide *(2005), from which "Why Do People Become Terrorists?" is taken. Weinberg is Foundation Professor of Political Science at the University of Nevada.*

WHY DO PEOPLE BECOME TERRORISTS?   (2005)

1   . . . Why do people join [terrorist groups]? What motivates individuals to become involved in violent attacks on bus, train, or plane passengers, passers-by in shopping malls—perfect strangers, in other words?

2   One widely discussed response is mental illness. Terrorists, or those who join terrorist organizations (the two are not necessarily the same), have personalities that dispose them to kill the helpless or unsuspecting. . . . The fundamental problem in using mental illness as a response to the "why?" question is that it is not supported by the facts. Few studies or clinical interviews with terrorists or ex-terrorists have detected serious signs

of mental disturbance. Apparently there is no such thing as a terrorist personality. Profoundly disturbed individuals who hear voices speaking to them from inanimate objects or live in a delusional world are unlikely to be admitted into terrorist organizations because, among other things, their peculiarities would make them so unreliable they would endanger the lives of other members. . . .

3   Why people join terrorist groups may have more to do with the attractions they offer than the internal mental states of those who join. With few exceptions (e.g. the Lord's Liberation Army in Uganda), terrorist organizations are voluntary. Rarely are people compelled to join. So the question becomes: What incentives or inducements do such groups possess that attract recruits?

4   The obvious answer is their strong commitment to a cause of one kind or another. Belief in the cause serves as the principal incentive for joining. Still, we would be jumping to conclusions if we accepted the group's goal as the only incentive for joining. One qualification is that there are typically far more people who believe in a goal than actually join the terrorist group committed to achieving it. Why do some join and others not? Another reservation is that in some cases individuals have joined a terrorist group without a clear understanding of what its objectives are. There are still other cases when a group's goals change depending on the circumstances in which it finds itself. For instance, the late Abu Nidal's Fatah Revolutionary Council began as an organization in 1974 because its leader rejected any means other than violence of bringing about Israel's destruction. Over time Nidal's organization became willing to carry out a terrorist attack on behalf of any cause willing to pay for its commission.

5   Other incentives: Often people join terrorist groups because doing so offers them or seems to offer them an opportunity for action. Not uncommonly, those drawn to terrorist bands are individuals who have grown weary of empty rhetoric about the need to do something about a cause. Bars, coffee houses, bookstores, school cafeterias, and other gathering sites frequently abound with individuals engaged in seemingly endless discussions about their social and political grievances. Terrorist organizations provide a way for those who wish, finally, to translate the words into reality. Individuals who wish to take up arms against a sea of troubles may be attracted to organizations that promise something beyond rhetorical condemnations of various enemies.

6   The fact that terrorist groups often attract individuals based on the opportunity for action comes with a cost. The group may need to engage in exceptionally risky and potentially self-destructive attacks because they risk losing the support of members whose strongest incentive for joining the group is the excitement stimulated by violent action.

7   Status often serves as another incentive. Superficially membership in a terrorist group seems unlikely to enhance someone's status or social standing. Joining a violent organization does not seem the equivalent of

joining an elite social club or illustrious university faculty. However, membership in a terrorist group may well confer heightened social status. For young men especially, walking down a street carrying a gun or grenade launcher, appearing tough and menacing to others, may indeed raise their status in the eyes of their peers.

8   Suicide bombers or "martyrs" in the Middle East provide examples of the benefits to be gained. The self-sacrificers (*shahids*) are rewarded for their deeds by immediate entry into paradise, a substantial improvement over their terrestrial circumstances. They achieve earthly fame because their pictures appear on posters throughout the area. Before departing on their adventure they are often filmed explaining why they are going to do what they are about to do. Film clips are then shown on television following the suicide bombings. Surviving family members are frequently regarded with enhanced status by the community at large because of their son's or daughter's willingness to die on behalf of the cause.

9   Material benefits may accrue to those who become involved in terrorism. As with social standing, it is hard to imagine money and other material incentives being significant in decisions to join terrorist organizations. But such may indeed be the case. Some terrorist organizations are quite wealthy. They may be the beneficiaries of major contributions from wealthy donors. In recent years wealthy businessmen from Saudi Arabia and the oil-rich Persian Gulf sheikdoms have contributed vast amounts of money to Islamic charities. The latter, in turn, funnel much of this money to Islamist groups in Pakistan and elsewhere, ostensibly for educational purposes. In reality the money finds its way to jihadi organizations engaged in terrorist activities directed *inter alia* against Indian-controlled Kashmir. Otherwise unemployed young men receive monetary compensation, hazardous duty pay, for carrying out terrorist attacks on Hindu Kashmiri and representatives of Indian authority in the region. The leaders of these groups, although they may be at pains to disguise it, often live lives of some luxury.

10   This situation is by no means unique to South Asia. During the 1970s the Israelis assassinated a PLO leader in front of his villa on the French Riviera. Yassir Arafat is the personal beneficiary of funds intended to benefit the Palestinians; he siphons off enough to maintain substantial banking accounts, some reportedly in Israeli banks.

11   On reflection the significance of money as an incentive should hardly be a surprise. Terrorists often support themselves by staging bank robberies, holding hostages for ransom, and participating in various money-making schemes. In Northern Ireland both the IRA and the Protestant paramilitaries are heavily involved in petty racketeering. And in Latin America, Shining Path and FARC have become major beneficiaries of the cocaine business.

12   The longer a terrorist group endures, the more likely its existing membership as well as new inductees are to find material incentives of growing importance. In some instances, such as the Muslim separatist

Abu Sayaf Group (ASG) in the Philippines (which specializes in kidnapping Westerners and holding them for ransom), it becomes hard to tell where political terrorism stops and organized criminal activity begins.

The opportunity to gain revenge for previous sufferings and humiliations may also serve as a powerful incentive for joining groups engaged in terrorism. If you or a person in your family or circle of friends has suffered at the hands of a perceived enemy the ability to retaliate may become a very powerful attraction. Women suicide bombers in the Chechen "Black Widows" and Sri Lankan "Birds of Paradise," for instance, are widely believed to have been the victims of rape at the hands of their Russian and Sinhalese antagonists.

Questions for Engagement, Response, and Analysis

1. According to Weinberg, what are the five major reasons individuals join terrorist groups?
2. What theory about terrorists is usually incorrect?

Crafting Arguments

1. Using both Sloan's and Weinberg's essays, write an essay on one of the following:

    An understanding of what terrorism is and is not is essential to devising a strategy for dealing with it.

    The best ways to discourage people from joining terrorist groups are . . . [list and support your theories].

    Because terrorism is so random and is committed by people who often appear to be perfectly ordinary, there is no way to prevent it.

FICTION

Anton Pavlovich Chekhov (1860–1904)

Anton Chekhov was born in the Ukraine but eventually followed his family to Moscow. While attending Moscow University Medical School, Chekhov began to support his family by writing short stories. He practiced medicine until 1892 but continued his writing, publishing two novels. He also began writing drama, first one-act plays and later full-length plays. His success in drama began with the production of The Seagull *in 1897. Chekhov's most famous plays are* Uncle Vanya *(1899),* The Three Sisters *(1901), and* The Cherry Orchard *(1904), widely regarded as a masterpiece.*

*Today Chekhov is considered the greatest Russian drama-
tist and one of the masters of the modern short story.*

THE LOTTERY TICKET   (1887)

1   Ivan Dmitritch, a middle-class man who lived with his family on an
income of twelve hundred a year and was very well satisfied with his lot,
sat down on the sofa after supper and began reading the newspaper.

2   "I forgot to look at the newspaper today," his wife said to him as she
cleared the table. "Look and see whether the list of drawings is there."

3   "Yes, it is," said Ivan Dmitritch, "but hasn't your ticket lapsed?"

4   "No, I took the interest on Tuesday."

5   "What is the number?"

6   "Series 9,499, number 26."

7   "All right . . . we will look . . . 9,499 and 26."

8   Ivan Dmitritch had no faith in lottery luck and would not, as a rule,
have consented to look at the lists of winning numbers, but now, as he
had nothing else to do and as the newspaper was before his eyes, he
passed his finger downward along the column of numbers. And immediately, as though in mockery of his skepticism, no further than the second
line from the top, his eye was caught by the figure 9,499! Unable to
believe his eyes, he hurriedly dropped the paper on his knees without
looking to see the number of the ticket, and, just as though someone had
given him a douche of cold water, he felt an agreeable chill in the pit of
the stomach, tingling and terrible and sweet!

9   "Masha, 9,499 is there!" he said in a hollow voice.

10   His wife looked at his astonished and panic-stricken face and realized
that he was not joking.

11   "9,499?" she asked, turning pale and dropping the folded tablecloth on
the table.

12   "Yes, yes . . . it really is there!"

13   "And the number of the ticket?"

14   "Oh yes! There's the number of the ticket too. But stay . . . wait! No, I say!
Anyway, the number of our series is there! Anyway, you understand. . . ."

15   Looking at his wife, Ivan Dmitritch gave a broad, senseless smile, like
a baby when a bright object is shown it. His wife smiled too; it was as
pleasant to her as to him that he only mentioned the series and did not
try to find out the number of the winning ticket. To torment and tantalize
oneself with hopes of possible fortune is so sweet, so thrilling!

16   "It is our series," said Ivan Dmitritch, after a long silence. "So there is
a probability that we have won. It's only a probability, but there it is!"

17   "Well, now look!"

18   "Wait a little. We have plenty of time to be disappointed. It's on the second line from the top, so the prize is seventy-five thousand. That's not
money but power, capital! And in a minute I shall look at the list, and
there—26! Eh? I say, what if we really have won?"

19   The husband and wife began laughing and staring at one another in silence. The possibility of winning bewildered them; they could not have said, could not have dreamed, what they both needed that seventy-five thousand for, what they would buy, where they would go. They thought only of the figures 9,499 and 75,000 and pictured them in their imagination, while somehow they could not think of the happiness itself which was so possible.

20   Ivan Dmitritch, holding the paper in his hand, walked several times from corner to corner and only when he had recovered from the first impression began dreaming a little.

21   "And if we have won," he said, "why, it will be a new life, it will be a transformation! The ticket is yours, but if it were mine I should, first of all, of course, spend twenty-five thousand on real property in the shape of an estate; ten thousand on immediate expenses, new furnishing . . . traveling . . . paying debts, and so on. . . . The other forty thousand I would put in the bank and get interest on it."

22   "Yes, an estate, that would be nice," said his wife, sitting down and dropping her hands in her lap.

23   "Somewhere in the Tula or Oryol provinces. . . . In the first place we shouldn't need a summer villa, and besides, it would always bring in an income."

24   And pictures came crowding on his imagination, each more gracious and poetical than the last. And in all these pictures he saw himself well-fed, serene, healthy, felt warm, even hot! Here, after eating a summer soup, cold as ice, he lay on his back on the burning sand close to a stream or in the garden under a lime tree. . . . It is hot . . . . His little boy and girl are crawling about near him, digging in the sand or catching ladybirds in the grass. He dozes sweetly, thinking of nothing, and feeling all over that he need not go to the office today, tomorrow, or the day after. Or, tired of lying still, he goes to the hayfield, or to the forest for mushrooms, or watches the peasants catching fish with a net. When the sun sets he takes a towel and soap and saunters to the bathing shed, where he undresses at his leisure, slowly rubs his bare chest with his hands and goes into the water. And in the water, near the opaque soapy circles, little fish flit to and fro and green water weeds nod their heads. After bathing there is tea with cream and milk rolls. . . . In the evening a walk or *vint* with the neighbors.

25   "Yes, it would be nice to buy an estate," said his wife, also dreaming, and from her face it was evident that she was enchanted by her thoughts.

26   Ivan Dmitritch pictured to himself autumn with its rains, its cold evenings, and its St. Martin's summer. At that season he would have to take longer walks about the garden and beside the river, so as to get thoroughly chilled, and then drink a big glass of vodka and eat a salted mushroom or a soused cucumber, and then—drink another. . . . The children would come running from the kitchen garden, bringing a carrot and a radish smelling of fresh earth. . . . And then, he would lie stretched full

length on the sofa, and in leisurely fashion turn over the pages of some illustrated magazine, or, covering his face with it and unbuttoning his waistcoat, give himself up to slumber.

27   The St. Martin's summer is followed by cloudy, gloomy weather. It rains day and night; the bare trees weep; the wind is damp and cold. The dogs, the horses, the fowls—all are wet, depressed, downcast. There is nowhere to walk: one can't go out for days together; one has to pace up and down the room, looking despondently at the gray window. It is dreary!

28   Ivan Dmitritch stopped and looked at his wife.

29   "I should go abroad, you know, Masha," he said.

30   And he began thinking how nice it would be in late autumn to go abroad somewhere to the South of France . . . to Italy . . . to India!

31   "I should certainly go abroad too," his wife said. "But look at the number of the ticket!"

32   "Wait, wait! . . ."

33   He walked about the room and went on thinking. It occurred to him: what if his wife really did go abroad? It is pleasant to travel alone, or in the society of light, careless women who live in the present, and not such as think and talk all the journey about nothing but their children, sigh, and tremble with dismay over every farthing. Ivan Dmitritch imagined his wife in the train with a multitude of parcels, baskets, and bags; she would be sighing over something, complaining that the train made her head ache, that she had spent so much money. . . . At the stations he would continually be having to run for boiling water, bread and butter. . . . She wouldn't have dinner because of its being too dear. . . .

34   "She would begrudge me every farthing," he thought, with a glance at his wife. "The lottery ticket is hers, not mine! Besides, what is the use of her going abroad? What does she want there? She would shut herself up in the hotel and not let me out of her sight. . . . I know!"

35   And for the first time in his life his mind dwelt on the fact that his wife had grown elderly and plain, and that she was saturated through and through with the smell of cooking, while he was still young, fresh, and healthy, and might well have got married again.

36   "Of course, all that is silly nonsense," he thought, "but . . . why should she go abroad? What would she make of it? And yet she would go, of course. . . . I can fancy . . . In reality it is all one to her, whether it is Naples or Klin. She would only be in my way. I should be dependent upon her. I can fancy how, like a regular woman, she will lock the money up as soon as she gets it. . . . She will hide it from me. . . . She will look after her relations and grudge me every farthing."

37   Ivan Dmitritch thought of her relations. All those wretched brothers and sisters and aunts and uncles would come crawling about as soon as they heard of the winning ticket, would begin whining like beggars, and fawning upon them with oily, hypocritical smiles. Wretched, detestable people! If they were given anything, they would ask for more, while if

they were refused, they would swear at them, slander them, and wish them every kind of misfortune.

38   Ivan Dmitritch remembered his own relations, and their faces, at which he looked impartially in the past, struck him now as repulsive and hateful.

39   "They are such reptiles!" he thought.

40   And his wife's face, too, struck him as repulsive and hateful. Anger surged up in his heart against her, and he thought malignantly:

41   "She knows nothing about money, and so she is stingy. If she won it she would give me a hundred roubles and put the rest away under lock and key."

42   And he looked at his wife, not with a smile now, but with hatred. She glanced at him, too, and also with hatred and anger. She had her own day-dreams, her own plans, her own reflections; she understood perfectly well what her husband's dreams were. She knew who would be the first to try and grab her winnings.

43   "It's very nice making daydreams at other people's expense!" is what her eyes expressed. "No, don't you dare!"

44   Her husband understood her look; hatred began stirring again in his breast, and in order to annoy his wife he glanced quickly, to spite her, at the fourth page on the newspaper and read out triumphantly:

45   "Series 9,499, number 46! Not 26!"

46   Hatred and hope both disappeared at once, and it began immediately to seem to Ivan Dmitritch and his wife that their rooms were dark and small and low-pitched, that the supper they had been eating was not doing them good, but lying heavy on their stomachs, that the evenings were long and wearisome. . . .

47   "What the devil's the meaning of it?" said Ivan Dmitritch, beginning to be ill-humored. "Wherever one steps there are bits of paper under one's feet, crumbs, husks. The rooms are never swept! One is simply forced to go out. Damnation take my soul entirely! I shall go and hang myself on the first aspen tree!"

Questions for Engagement, Response, and Analysis

1. What is the theme of this story?
2. In your opinion, why does Ivan Dmitritch delay looking at the second number?
3. Compare the dreams of Ivan Dmitritch with those of his wife.
4. Explain the irony of the ending.

Crafting Arguments

1. Write a character analysis of Ivan Dmitritch or of his wife. Support each of your claims with examples from the story.

2. Contrast the attitudes of Ivan Dmitritch at the beginning of the story with his attitudes at the end. What do the changes reveal about his character and values?

William Faulkner (1897–1962)

Born near Oxford, Mississippi, Faulkner used his home state as the setting for many of his short stories and novels. He invented an imaginary county—Yoknapatawpha—and peopled it with a variety of characters worthy of Shakespeare, from the noble members of the Sartoris family and the intellectual Quenton Compson to the Snopes family, most of whom are sneaky and self-serving. His most famous novels include The Sound and the Fury *(1929);* Light in August *(1932);* Absalom, Absalom! *(1936); and the Snopes trilogy:* The Hamlet *(1940),* The Town *(1957), and* The Mansion *(1958). In 1950, Faulkner was awarded the Nobel Prize for Literature.*

A ROSE FOR EMILY   (1930)

I

1   When Miss Emily Grierson died, our whole town went to her funeral: the men through a sort of respectful affection for a fallen monument, the women mostly out of curiosity to see the inside of her house, which no one save an old manservant—a combined gardener and cook—had seen in at least ten years.

2   It was a big, squarish frame house that had once been white, decorated with cupolas and spires and scrolled balconies in the heavily lightsome style of the seventies, set on what had once been our most select street. But garages and cotton gins had encroached and obliterated even the august names of that neighborhood; only Miss Emily's house was left, lifting its stubborn and coquettish decay above the cotton wagons and the gasoline pumps—an eyesore among eyesores. And now Miss Emily had gone to join the representatives of those august names where they lay in the cedar-bemused cemetery among the ranked and anonymous graves of Union and Confederate soldiers who fell at the battle of Jefferson.

3   Alive, Miss Emily had been a tradition, a duty, and a care; a sort of hereditary obligation upon the town, dating from that day in 1894 when Colonel Sartoris, the mayor—he who fathered the edict that no Negro woman should appear on the streets without an apron—remitted her taxes, the dispensation dating from the death of her father on into perpetuity. Not that Miss Emily would have accepted charity. Colonel Sartoris invented an involved tale to the effect that Miss Emily's father had loaned money to the town, which the town, as a matter of busi-

ness, preferred this way of repaying. Only a man of Colonel Sartoris' generation and thought could have invented it and only a woman could have believed it.

4   When the next generation, with its more modern ideas, became mayors and aldermen, this arrangement created some little dissatisfaction. On the first of the year they mailed her a tax notice. February came, and there was no reply. They wrote her a formal letter, asking her to call at the sheriff's office at her convenience. A week later the mayor wrote her himself, offering to call or to send his car for her, and received in reply a note on paper of an archaic shape, in a thin, flowing calligraphy in faded ink, to the effect that she no longer went out at all. The tax notice was also enclosed, without comment.

5   They called a special meeting of the Board of Aldermen. A deputation waited upon her, knocked at the door through which no visitor had passed since she ceased giving china painting lessons eight or ten years earlier. They were admitted by the old Negro into a dim hall from which a stairway mounted into still more shadow. It smelled of dust and disuse—a close, dank smell. The Negro led them into the parlor. It was furnished in heavy, leather-covered furniture. When the Negro opened the blinds of one window, they could see that the leather was cracked; and when they sat down, a faint dust rose sluggishly about their thighs, spinning with slow motes in the single sun-ray. On a tarnished gilt easel before the fireplace stood a crayon portrait of Miss Emily's father.

6   They rose when she entered—a small, fat woman in black, with a thin gold chain descending to her waist and vanishing into her belt, leaning on an ebony cane with a tarnished gold head. Her skeleton was small and spare; perhaps that was why what would have been merely plumpness in another was obesity in her. She looked bloated, like a body long submerged in motionless water, and of that pallid hue. Her eyes, lost in the fatty ridges of her face, looked like two small pieces of coal pressed into a lump of dough as they moved from one face to another while the visitors stated their errand.

7   She did not ask them to sit. She just stood in the door and listened quietly until the spokesman came to a stumbling halt. Then they could hear the invisible watch ticking at the end of the gold chain.

8   Her voice was dry and cold. "I have no taxes in Jefferson. Colonel Sartoris explained it to me. Perhaps one of you can gain access to the city records and satisfy yourselves."

9   "But we have. We are the city authorities, Miss Emily. Didn't you get a notice from the sheriff, signed by him?"

10   "I received a paper, yes," Miss Emily said. "Perhaps he considers himself the sheriff . . . I have no taxes in Jefferson."

11   "But there is nothing on the books to show that, you see. We must go by the—"

12   "See Colonel Sartoris. I have no taxes in Jefferson."

13   "But, Miss Emily—"

14   "See Colonel Sartoris." (Colonel Sartoris had been dead almost ten years.) "I have no taxes in Jefferson. Tobe!" The Negro appeared. "Show these gentlemen out."

II

15   So she vanquished them, horse and foot, just as she had vanquished their fathers thirty years before about the smell. That was two years after her father's death and a short time after her sweetheart—the one we believed would marry her—had deserted her. After her father's death she went out very little; after her sweetheart went away, people hardly saw her at all. A few of the ladies had the temerity to call, but were not received, and the only sign of life about the place was the Negro man— a young man then—going in and out with a market basket.

16   "Just as if a man—any man—could keep a kitchen properly," the ladies said; so they were not surprised when the smell developed. It was another link between the gross, teeming world and the high and mighty Griersons.

17   A neighbor, a woman, complained to the mayor, Judge Stevens, eighty years old.

18   "But what will you have me do about it, madam?" he said.

19   "Why, send her word to stop it," the woman said. "Isn't there a law?"

20   "I'm sure that won't be necessary," Judge Stevens said. "It's probably just a snake or a rat that nigger of hers killed in the yard. I'll speak to him about it."

21   The next day he received two more complaints, one from a man who came in diffident deprecation. "We really must do something about it, Judge. I'd be the last one in the world to bother Miss Emily, but we've got to do something." That night the Board of Aldermen met—three gray-beards and one younger man, a member of the rising generation.

22   "It's simple enough," he said. "Send her word to have her place cleaned up. Give her a certain time to do it in, and if she don't . . ."

23   "Dammit, sir," Judge Stevens said, "will you accuse a lady to her face of smelling bad?"

24   So the next night, after midnight, four men crossed Miss Emily's lawn and slunk about the house like burglars, sniffing along the base of the brickwork and at the cellar openings while one of them performed a reg-ular sowing motion with his hand out of a sack slung from his shoulder. They broke open the cellar door and sprinkled lime there, and in all the outbuildings. As they recrossed the lawn, a window that had been dark was lighted and Miss Emily sat in it, the light behind her, and her upright torso motionless as that of an idol. They crept quietly across the lawn and into the shadow of the locusts that lined the street. After a week or two the smell went away.

25   That was when people had begun to feel really sorry for her. People in our town, remembering how old lady Wyatt, her great-aunt, had gone com-

pletely crazy at last, believed that the Griersons held themselves a little too high for what they really were. None of the young men were quite good enough for Miss Emily and such. We had long thought of them as a tableau, Miss Emily a slender figure in white in the background, her father a spraddled silhouette in the foreground, his back to her and clutching a horsewhip, the two of them framed by the back-flung front door. So when she got to be thirty and was still single, we were not pleased exactly, but vindicated; even with insanity in the family she wouldn't have turned down all of her chances if they had really materialized.

26   When her father died, it got about that the house was all that was left to her; and in a way, people were glad. At last they could pity Miss Emily. Being left alone, and a pauper, she had become humanized. Now she too would know the old thrill and the old despair of a penny more or less.

27   The day after his death all the ladies prepared to call at the house and offer condolence and aid, as is our custom. Miss Emily met them at the door, dressed as usual and with no trace of grief on her face. She told them that her father was not dead. She did that for three days, with the ministers calling on her, and the doctors, trying to persuade her to let them dispose of the body. Just as they were about to resort to law and force, she broke down, and they buried her father quickly.

28   We did not say she was crazy then. We believed she had to do that. We remembered all the young men her father had driven away, and we knew that with nothing left, she would have to cling to that which had robbed her, as people will.

III

29   She was sick for a long time. When we saw her again, her hair was cut short, making her look like a girl, with a vague resemblance to those angels in colored church windows—sort of tragic and serene.

30   The town had just let the contracts for paving the sidewalks, and in the summer after her father's death they began the work. The construction company came with niggers and mules and machinery, and a foreman named Homer Barron, a Yankee—a big, dark, ready man, with a big voice and eyes lighter than his face. The little boys would follow in groups to hear him cuss the niggers, and the niggers singing in time to the rise and fall of picks. Pretty soon he knew everybody in town. Whenever you heard a lot of laughing anywhere about the square, Homer Barron would be in the center of the group. Presently we began to see him and Miss Emily on Sunday afternoons driving in the yellow-wheeled buggy and the matched team bays from the livery stable.

31   At first we were glad that Miss Emily would have an interest, because the ladies all said, "Of course a Grierson would not think seriously of a Northerner, a day laborer." But there were still others, older people, who said that even grief could not cause a real lady to forget *noblesse oblige*—without calling it *noblesse oblige*. They just said, "Poor Emily. Her kinsfolk should come to her." She had some kin in Alabama; but years ago

her father had fallen out with them over the estate of old lady Wyatt, the crazy woman, and there was no communication between the two families. They had not even been represented at the funeral.

32   And as soon as the old people said, "Poor Emily," the whispering began. "Do you suppose it's really so?" they said to one another. "Of course it is. What else could . . ." This behind their hands; rustling of craned silk and satin behind jalousies closed upon the sun of Sunday afternoon as the thin, swift clop-clop-clop of the matched team passed: "Poor Emily."

33   She carried her head high enough—even when we believed that she was fallen. It was as if she demanded more than ever the recognition of her dignity as the last Grierson; as if it had wanted that touch of earthiness to reaffirm her imperviousness. Like when she bought the rat poison, the arsenic. That was over a year after they had begun to say "Poor Emily," and while the two female cousins were visiting her.

34   "I want some poison," she said to the druggist. She was over thirty then, still a slight woman, though thinner than usual, with cold, haughty black eyes in a face the flesh of which was strained across the temples and about the eyesockets as you imagine a lighthouse-keeper's face ought to look. "I want some poison," she said.

35   "Yes, Miss Emily. What kind? For rats and such? I'd recom—"

36   "I want the best you have. I don't care what kind."

37   The druggist named several. "They'll kill anything up to an elephant. But what you want is—"

38   "Arsenic," Miss Emily said, "Is that a good one?"

39   "Is . . . arsenic? Yes, ma'am. But what you want—"

40   "I want arsenic."

41   The druggist looked down at her. She looked back at him, erect, her face like a strained flag. "Why, of course," the druggist said. "If that's what you want. But the law requires you to tell what you are going to use it for."

42   Miss Emily just stared at him, her head tilted back in order to look him eye for eye, until he looked away and went and got the arsenic and wrapped it up. The Negro delivery boy brought her the package; the druggist didn't come back. When she opened the package at home there was written on the box, under the skull and bones: "For rats."

IV

43   So the next day we all said, "She will kill herself"; and we said it would be the best thing. When she had first begun to be seen with Homer Barron, we had said, "She will marry him." Then we said, "She will persuade him yet," because Homer himself had remarked—he liked men, and it was known that he drank with the younger men in the Elks' Club—that he was not a marrying man. Later we said, "Poor Emily" behind the jalousies as they passed on Sunday afternoon in the glittering buggy, Miss Emily with her head high and Homer Barron with his hat cocked and a cigar in his teeth, reins and whip in a yellow glove.

44   Then some of the ladies began to say that it was a disgrace to the town and a bad example to the young people. The men did not want to interfere, but at last the ladies forced the Baptist minister—Miss Emily's people were Episcopal—to call upon her. He would never divulge what happened during that interview, but he refused to go back again. The next Sunday they again drove about the streets, and the following day the minister's wife wrote to Miss Emily's relations in Alabama.

45   So she had blood-kin under her roof again and we sat back to watch the developments. At first nothing happened. Then we were sure that they were to be married. We learned that Miss Emily had been to the jeweler's and ordered a man's toilet set in silver, with the letters H. B. on each piece. Two days later we learned that she had bought a complete outfit of men's clothing, including a nightshirt, and we said, "They are married." We were really glad. We were glad because the two female cousins were even more Grierson than Miss Emily had ever been.

46   So we were not surprised when Homer Barron—the streets had been finished some time since—was gone. We were a little disappointed that there was not a public blowing-off, but we believed that he had gone on to prepare for Miss Emily's coming, or to give her a chance to get rid of the cousins. (By that time it was a cabal, and we were all Miss Emily's allies to help circumvent the cousins.) Sure enough, after another week they departed. And, as we had expected all along, within three days Homer Barron was back in town. A neighbor saw the Negro man admit him at the kitchen door at dusk one evening.

47   And that was the last we saw of Homer Barron. And of Miss Emily for some time. The Negro man went in and out with the market basket, but the front door remained closed. Now and then we would see her at a window for a moment, as the men did that night when they sprinkled the lime, but for almost six months she did not appear on the streets. Then we knew that this was to be expected too; as if that quality of her father which had thwarted her woman's life so many times had been too virulent and too furious to die.

48   When we next saw Miss Emily, she had grown fat and her hair was turning gray. During the next few years it grew grayer and grayer until it attained an even pepper-and-salt iron-gray, when it ceased turning. Up to the day of her death at seventy-four it was still that vigorous iron-gray, like the hair of an active man.

49   From that time on her front door remained closed, save for a period of six or seven years, when she was about forty, during which she gave lessons in china-painting. She fitted up a studio in one of the downstairs rooms, where the daughters and granddaughters of Colonel Sartoris' contemporaries were sent to her with the same regularity and in the same spirit that they were sent to church on Sundays with a twenty-five-cent piece for the collection plate. Meanwhile her taxes had been remitted.

50   Then the newer generation became the backbone and the spirit of the town, and the painting pupils grew up and fell away and did not

send their children to her with boxes of color and tedious brushes and pictures cut from the ladies' magazines. The front door closed upon the last one and remained closed for good. When the town got free postal delivery, Miss Emily alone refused to let them fasten the metal numbers above her door and attach a mailbox to it. She would not listen to them.

51   Daily, monthly, yearly we watched the Negro grow grayer and more stooped, going in and out with the market basket. Each December we sent her a tax notice, which would be returned by the post office a week later, unclaimed. Now and then we would see her in one of the downstairs windows—she had evidently shut up the top floor of the house—like the carven torso of an idol in a niche, looking or not looking at us, we could never tell which. Thus she passed from generation to generation—dear, inescapable, impervious, tranquil, and perverse.

52   And so she died. Fell ill in the house filled with dust and shadows, with only a doddering Negro man to wait on her. We did not even know she was sick; we had long since given up trying to get any information from the Negro. He talked to no one, probably not even to her, for his voice had grown harsh and rusty, as if from disuse.

53   She died in one of the downstairs rooms, in a heavy walnut bed with a curtain, her gray head propped on a pillow yellow and moldy with age and lack of sunlight.

V

54   The Negro met the first of the ladies at the front door and let them in, with their hushed, sibilant voices and their quick curious glances, and then he disappeared. He walked right through the house and out the back and was not seen again.

55   The two female cousins came at once. They held the funeral on the second day, with the town coming to look at Miss Emily beneath a mass of bought flowers, with the crayon face of her father musing profoundly above the bier and the ladies sibilant and macabre; and the very old men—some in their brushed confederate uniforms—on the porch and the lawn, talking of Miss Emily as if she had been a contemporary of theirs, believing that they had danced with her and courted her perhaps, confusing time with its mathematical progression, as the old do, to whom all the past is not a diminishing road but, instead, a huge meadow which no winter ever quite touches, divided from them now by the narrow bottleneck of the most recent decade of years.

56   Already we knew that there was one room in that region above stairs which no one had seen in forty years, and which would have to be forced. They waited until Miss Emily was decently in the ground before they opened it.

57   The violence of breaking down the door seemed to fill this room with pervading dust. A thin, acrid pall as of the tomb seemed to lie everywhere

upon this room decked and furnished as for a bridal: upon the valance curtains of faded rose color, upon the rose-shaded lights, upon the dressing table, upon the delicate array of crystal and the man's toilet things backed with tarnished silver, silver so tarnished that the monogram was obscured. Among them lay a collar and tie, as if they had just been removed, which, lifted, left upon the surface a pale crescent in the dust. Upon a chair hung the suit, carefully folded; beneath it the two mute shoes and the discarded socks.

58   The man himself lay in the bed.

59   For a long while we just stood there, looking down at the profound and fleshless grin. The body had apparently once lain in the attitude of an embrace, but now the long sleep that outlasts love, that conquers even the grimace of love, had cuckolded him. What was left of him, rotted beneath what was left of the nightshirt, had become inextricable from the bed in which he lay; and upon him and upon the pillow beside him lay that even coating of the patient and biding dust.

60   Then we noticed that in the second pillow was the indentation of a head. One of us lifted something from it, and leaning forward, that faint and invisible dust dry and acrid in the nostrils, we saw a long strand of iron-gray hair.

Questions for Engagement, Response, and Analysis

1. From whose point of view is the story told? How would you describe the narrators' attitudes toward Miss Emily?

2. What is the relationship between the town and Miss Emily? In what sense(s) is she a "tradition, a duty, and a care"? Why does Colonel Sartoris feel obligated to her?

3. What does Miss Emily's ability to vanquish the authorities of Jefferson reveal about her attitudes and personality?

4. In what ways is the setting crucial to this story? What does the description of the parlor reveal about the house and about Miss Emily?

5. What does the last sentence of the story reveal? What hints of the ending make it believable, if shocking?

6. In your Reader's Journal write an entry in which you (1) convince a jury that Miss Emily is or is not guilty of murder or (2) support or refute the idea that Miss Emily was insane.

Crafting Arguments

1. Write an essay in which you analyze Faulkner's use of the theme of the fluidity of time.

2. In terms of the time and the environment in which she lives, explain Miss Emily's treatment by, and response to, the two men in her life.

Chinua Achebe (b. 1930)

Chinua Achebe, a Nigerian novelist and man of letters who writes in English, is among the most highly respected and influential contemporary African authors. Achebe's early novels, Things Fall Apart *(1959),* No Longer at Ease *(1962), and* Arrow of Gold *(1964), explore the conflict between traditional tribal customs and the European values introduced by colonists. His later novels,* A Man of the People *(1964) and* Anthills of the Savannah *(1988), expose the corruption and conflicts in postcolonial Nigerian politics. Achebe's* Collected Poems *was published in 2004. In 2007 Achebe received the Man Booker International Prize for fiction.*

DEAD MEN'S PATH   (1953)

1   Michael Obi's hopes were fulfilled much earlier than he had expected. He was appointed headmaster of Ndume Central School in January 1949. It had always been an unprogressive school, so the Mission authorities decided to send a young and energetic man to run it. Obi accepted this responsibility with enthusiasm. He had many wonderful ideas and this was an opportunity to put them into practice. He had had sound secondary school education which designated him a "pivotal teacher" in the official records and set him apart from the other headmasters in the mission field. He was outspoken in his condemnation of the narrow views of these older and often less-educated ones.

2   "We shall make a good job of it, shan't we?" he asked his young wife when they first heard the joyful news of his promotion.

3   "We shall do our best," she replied. "We shall have such beautiful gardens and everything will be just *modern* and delightful. . . ." In their two years of married life she had become completely infected by his passion for "modern methods" and his denigration of "these old and superannuated people in the teaching field who would be better employed as traders in the Onitsha market." She began to see herself already as the admired wife of the young headmaster, the queen of the school.

4   The wives of the other teachers would envy her position. She would set the fashion in everything. . . . Then, suddenly, it occurred to her that there might not be other wives. Wavering between hope and fear, she asked her husband, looking anxiously at him.

5   "All our colleagues are young and unmarried," he said with enthusiasm which for once she did not share. "Which is a good thing," he continued.

6   "Why?"

7   "Why? They will give all their time and energy to the school."

8   Nancy was downcast. For a few minutes she became skeptical about the new school; but it was only for a few minutes. Her little personal misfortune could not blind her to her husband's happy prospects. She looked at him as he sat folded up in a chair. He was stoop-shouldered and looked frail. But he sometimes surprised people with sudden bursts of physical

energy. In his present posture, however, all his bodily strength seemed to have retired behind his deep-set eyes, giving them an extraordinary power of penetration. He was only twenty-six, but looked thirty or more. On the whole, he was not unhandsome.

9   "A penny for your thoughts, Mike," said Nancy after a while, imitating the woman's magazine she read.

10   "I was thinking what a grand opportunity we've got at last to show these people how a school should be run."

11   Ndume School was backward in every sense of the word. Mr. Obi put his whole life into the work, and his wife hers too. He had two aims. A high standard of teaching was insisted upon, and the school compound was to be turned into a place of beauty. Nancy's dream-gardens came to life with the coming of the rains, and blossomed. Beautiful hibiscus and allamanda hedges in brilliant red and yellow marked out the carefully tended school compound from the rank neighborhood bushes.

12   One evening as Obi was admiring his work he was scandalized to see an old woman from the village hobble right across the compound, through a marigold flower-bed and the hedges. On going up there he found faint signs of an almost disused path from the village across the school compound to the bush on the other side.

13   "It amazes me," said Obi to one of his teachers who had been three years in the school, "that you people allowed the villagers to make use of this footpath. It is simply incredible." He shook his head.

14   "The path," said the teacher apologetically, "appears to be very important to them. Although it is hardly used, it connects the village shrine with their place of burial."

15   "And what has that got to do with the school?" asked the headmaster.

16   "Well, I don't know," replied the other with a shrug of the shoulders. "But I remember there was a big row some time ago when we attempted to close it."

17   "That was some time ago. But it will not be used now," said Obi as he walked away. "What will the Government Education Officer think of this when he comes to inspect the school next week? The villagers might, for all I know, decide to use the schoolroom for a pagan ritual during the inspection."

18   Heavy sticks were planted closely across the path at the two places where it entered and left the school premises. These were further strengthened with barbed wire.

19   Three days later the village priest of *Ani* called on the headmaster. He was an old man and walked with a slight stoop. He carried a stout walking-stick which he usually tapped on the floor, by way of emphasis, each time he made a new point in his argument.

20   "I have heard," he said after the usual exchange of cordialities, "that our ancestral footpath has recently been closed. . . ."

21   "Yes," replied Mr. Obi. "We cannot allow people to make a highway of our school compound."

22   "Look here, my son," said the priest bringing down his walking-stick, "this path was here before you were born and before your father was born. The whole life of this village depends on it. Our dead relatives depart by it and our ancestors visit us by it. But most important, it is the path of children coming in to be born. . . ."

23   Mr. Obi listened with a satisfied smile on his face.

24   "The whole purpose of our school," he said finally, "is to eradicate just such beliefs as that. Dead men do not require footpaths. The whole idea is just fantastic. Our duty is to teach your children to laugh at such ideas."

25   "What you say may be true," replied the priest, "but we follow the practices of our fathers. If you reopen the path we shall have nothing to quarrel about. What I always say is: let the hawk perch and let the eagle perch." He rose to go.

26   "I am sorry," said the young headmaster. "But the school compound cannot be a thoroughfare. It is against our regulations. I would suggest your constructing another path, skirting our premises. We can even get our boys to help in building it. I don't suppose the ancestors will find the little detour too burdensome."

27   "I have no more words to say," said the old priest, already outside.

28   Two days later a young woman in the village died in childbed. A diviner was immediately consulted and he prescribed heavy sacrifices to propitiate ancestors insulted by the fence.

29   Obi woke up next morning among the ruins of his work. The beautiful hedges were torn up not just near the path but right round the school, the flowers trampled to death and one of the school buildings pulled down . . . That day, the white Supervisor came to inspect the school and wrote a nasty report on the state of the premises but more seriously about the "tribal-war situation developing between the school and the village, arising in part from the misguided zeal of the new headmaster."

Questions for Engagement, Response, and Analysis

1. Why is Obi infatuated with "modern" ways and disdainful of the "narrow views" of "less-educated" people? What is his wife's response? What are Obi's two goals? Explain how and why each goal is or is not fulfilled.

2. What is the essence of the argument about the path? What is the village priest's position? Explain what the priest means when he says, "let the hawk perch and let the eagle perch."

3. What is the reaction of the local people? What is their justification?

4. What is the tone of the story? Explain the irony of the last paragraph.

Crafting Arguments

1. Write a character analysis of Michael Obi and/or of Nancy.

2. Michael says, "'Dead men do not require footpaths.'" The priest disagrees. Using specific examples from the story, write an essay supporting one of these points of view.

Bharati Mukherjee (b. 1940)

Born in Calcutta to wealthy parents, Mukherjee moved to Britain when she was eight. She received a B.A. from the University of Calcutta, an M.A. in English and Ancient Indian Culture from the University of Baroda, an M.F.A. in creative writing and a Ph.D. from the University of Iowa. After her marriage to Clark Blaize, she and her husband wrote two books: Days and Nights in Calcutta *(1977) and* The Sorrow and the Terror: The Haunting Legacy of the Air India Tragedy *(1987). Writing about the immigrant experience in America, about Indian women and their mistreatment, and about the search for identity in a multicultural world, Mukherjee has published seven novels, including* The Tiger's Daughter *(1971),* Wife *(1975),* The Holder of the World *(1993),* Desirable Daughters *(2002), and* The Tree Bride *(2004). Mukherjee is a professor at the University of California, Berkeley.*

THE MANAGEMENT OF GRIEF (1988)

1   A woman I don't know is boiling tea the Indian way in my kitchen. There are a lot of women I don't know in my kitchen, whispering and moving tactfully. They open doors, rummage through the pantry, and try not to ask me where things are kept. They remind me of when my sons were small, on Mother's Day or when Vikram and I were tired, and they would make big, sloppy omelets. I would lie in bed pretending I didn't hear them.

2   Dr. Sharma, the treasurer of the Indo-Canada Society, pulls me into the hallway. He wants to know if I am worried about money. His wife, who has just come up from the basement with a tray of empty cups and glasses, scolds him. "Don't bother Mrs. Bhave with mundane details." She looks so monstrously pregnant her baby must be days overdue. I tell her she shouldn't be carrying heavy things. "Shaila," she says, smiling, "this is the fifth." Then she grabs a teenager by his shirttails. He slips his Walkman off his head. He has to be one of her four children; they have the same domed and dented foreheads. "What's the official word now?" she demands. The boy slips the headphones back on. "They're acting evasive, Ma. They're saying it could be an accident or a terrorist bomb."

3   All morning, the boys have been muttering, Sikh bomb, Sikh bomb. The men, not using the word, bow their heads in agreement. Mrs. Sharma touches her forehead at such a word. At least they've stopped talking about space debris and Russian lasers.

4   Two radios are going in the dining room. They are tuned to different stations. Someone must have brought the radios down from my boys' bedrooms. I haven't gone into their rooms since Kusum came running across the front lawn in her bathrobe. She looked so funny, I was laughing when I opened the door.

5   The big TV in the den is being whizzed through American networks and cable channels.

6   "Damn!" some man swears bitterly. "How can these preachers carry on like nothing's happened?" I want to tell him we're not that important. You look at the audience, and at the preacher in his blue robe with his beautiful white hair, the potted palm trees under a blue sky, and you know they care about nothing.

7   The phone rings and rings. Dr. Sharma's taken charge. "We're with her," he keeps saying. "Yes, yes, the doctor has given calming pills. Yes, yes, pills are having necessary effect." I wonder if pills alone explain this calm. Not peace, just a deadening quiet. I was always controlled, but never repressed. Sound can reach me, but my body is tensed, ready to scream. I hear their voices all around me. I hear my boys and Vikram cry. "Mommy, Shaila!" and their screams insulate me, like headphones.

8   The woman boiling water tells her story again and again. "I got the news first. My cousin called from Halifax before six AM, can you imagine. He'd gotten up for prayers and his son was studying for medical exam and heard on a rock channel that something had happened to a plane. They said first it had disappeared from the radar, like a giant eraser just reached out. His father called me, so I said to him, what do you mean 'something bad'? You mean a hijacking? And he said, *Behn*, there is no confirmation of anything yet, but check with your neighbors because a lot of them must be on that plane. So I called poor Kusum straight-away. I knew Kusum's husband and daughter were booked to go yesterday."

9   Kusum lives across the street from me. She and Satish had moved less than a month ago. They said they needed a bigger place. All the people, the Sharmas and friends from the Indo-Canada Society, had been there for the housewarming. Satish and Kusum made tandoori on their big gas grill and even the white neighbors piled their plates high with that luridly red, charred, juicy chicken. Their younger daughter had danced, and even our boys had broken away from the Stanley Cup telecast to put in a reluctant appearance. Everyone took pictures for their albums and for the community newspapers—another of our families had made it big in Toronto—and now I wonder how many of those happy faces are gone. "Why does God give us so much if all along He intends to take it away?" Kusum asks me.

10   I nod. We sit on carpeted stairs, holding hands like children. "I never once told him that I loved him," I say. I was too much the well-brought-up woman. I was so well brought up I never felt comfortable calling my husband by his first name.

11   "It's all right," Kusum says. "He knew. My husband knew. They felt it. Modern young girls have to say it because what they feel is fake."

12   Kusum's daughter Pam runs in with an overnight case. Pam's in her McDonald's uniform. "Mummy! You have to get dressed!" Panic makes her cranky. "A reporter's on his way here."

13   "Why?"

14   "You want to talk to him in your bathrobe?" She starts to brush her mother's long hair. She's the daughter who's always in trouble. She dates Canadian boys and hangs out in the mall, shopping for tight sweaters. The younger one, the goody-goody one according to Pam, the one with voice so sweet that when she sang *bhajans* for Ethiopian relief even a frugal man like my husband wrote out a hundred-dollar check, *she* was on that plane. *She* was going to spend July and August with grandparents because Pam wouldn't go. Pam said she'd rather waitress at McDonald's. "If it's a choice between Bombay and Wonderland, I'm picking Wonderland," she'd said.

15   "Leave me alone," Kusum yells. "You know what I want to do? If I didn't have to look after you now, I'd hang myself."

16   Pam's young face goes blotchy with pain. "Thanks," she says, "don't let me stop you."

17   "Hush," pregnant Mrs. Sharma scolds Pam. "Leave your mother alone. Mr. Sharma will tackle the reporters and fill out the forms. He'll know what has to be said."

18   Pam stands her ground. "You think I don't know what Mummy's thinking? *Why her*? That's what. That's sick! Mummy wishes my little sister were alive and I were dead."

19   Kusum's hand in mine is trembly hot. We continue to sit on the stairs.

20   She calls before she arrives, wondering if there's anything I need. Her name is Judith Templeton and she's an appointee of the provincial government. "Multiculturalism?" I ask, and she says "partially," but that her mandate is bigger. "I've been told you knew many of the people on that flight," she says. "Perhaps if you'd agree to help us reach the others . . .?"

21   She gives me time at least to put on tea water and pick up the mess in the front room. I have a few *samosas* from Kusum's housewarming that I could fry up, but then I think, why prolong this visit?

22   Judith Templeton is much younger than she sounded. She wears a blue suit with a white blouse and a polka-dot tie. Her blond hair is cut short, her only jewelry is pearl-drop earrings. Her briefcase is new and expensive looking, a gleaming cordovan leather. She sits with it across her lap. When she looks out the front windows onto the street, her contact lenses seem to float in front of her light blue eyes.

23   "What sort of help do you want from me?" I ask. She has refused the tea, out of politeness, but I insist, along with some slightly stale biscuits.

24   "I have no experience," she admits. "That is, I have an M.S.W. and I've worked in liaison with accident victims, but I mean I have no experience with a tragedy of this scale—"

25   "Who could?" I ask.

26   "—and with the complications of culture, language, and custom. Someone mentioned that Mrs. Bhave is a pillar—because you've taken it more calmly."

27   At this, perhaps, I frown, for she reaches forward, almost to take my hand. "I hope you understand my meaning, Mrs. Bhave. There are hundreds of people in Metro directly affected, like you, and some of them speak no English. There are some widows who've never handled money or gone on a bus, and there are old parents who still haven't eaten or gone outside their bedrooms. Some houses and apartments have been looted. Some wives are still hysterical. Some husbands are in shock and profound depression. We want to help, but our hands are tied in so many ways. We have to distribute money to some people, and there are legal documents—these things can be done. We have interpreters, but we don't always have the human touch, or maybe the right human touch. We don't want to make mistakes, Mrs. Bhave, and that's why we'd like to ask you to help us."

28   "More mistakes, you mean," I say.

29   "Police matters are not in my hands," she answers.

30   "Nothing I can do will make any difference," I say. "We must all grieve in our own way."

31   "But you are coping very well. All the people said, Mrs. Bhave is the strongest person of all. Perhaps if the others could see you, talk with you, it would help them."

32   "By the standards of the people you call hysterical, I am behaving very oddly and very badly, Miss Templeton." I want to say to her, *I wish I could scream, starve, walk into Lake Ontario, jump from a bridge.* "They would not see me as a model. I do not see myself as a model."

33   I am a freak. No one who has ever known me would think of me reacting this way. This terrible calm will not go away.

34   She asks me if she may call again, after I get back from a long trip that we all must make. "Of course," I say. "Feel free to call, anytime."

35   Four days later, I find Kusum squatting on a rock overlooking a bay in Ireland. It isn't a big rock, but it juts sharply out over water. This is as close as we'll ever get to them. June breezes balloon out her sari and unpin her knee-length hair. She has the bewildered look of a sea creature whom the tides have stranded.

36   It's been one hundred hours since Kusum came stumbling and screaming across my lawn. Waiting around the hospital, we've heard many stories. The police, the diplomats, they tell us things thinking that we're strong, that knowledge is helpful to the grieving, and maybe it is. Some, I know, prefer ignorance, or their own versions. The plane broke into two, they say. Unconsciousness was instantaneous. No one suffered. My boys must have just finished their breakfasts. They loved eating on planes, they loved the smallness of plates, knives, and forks. Last year they saved the airline salt and pepper shakers. Half an hour more and they would have made it to Heathrow.

37   Kusum says that we can't escape our fate. She says that all those people—our husbands, my boys, her girl with the nightingale voice, all

those Hindus, Christians, Sikhs, Muslims, Parsis, and atheists on that plane—were fated to die together off this beautiful bay. She learned this from a swami in Toronto.

38   I have my Valium.

39   Six of us "relatives"—two widows and four widowers—chose to spend the day today by the waters instead of sitting in a hospital room and scanning photographs of the dead. That's what they call us now: relatives. I've looked through twenty-seven photos in two days. They're very kind to us, the Irish are very understanding. Sometimes understanding means freeing a tourist bus for this trip to the bay, so we can pretend to spy our loved ones through the glassiness of waves or in sun-speckled cloud shapes.

40   I could die here, too, and be content.

41   "What is that, out there?" She's standing and flapping her hands, and for a moment I see a head shape bobbing in the waves. She's standing in the water, I on the boulder. The tide is low, and a round, black headsized rock has just risen from the waves. She returns, her sari end dripping and ruined, and her face is a twisted remnant of hope, the way mine was a hundred hours ago, still laughing but inwardly knowing that nothing but the ultimate tragedy could bring two women together at six o'clock on a Sunday morning. I watch her face sag into blankness.

42   "That water felt warm, Shaila," she says at length.

43   "You can't," I say. "We have to wait for our turn to come."

44   I haven't eaten in four days, haven't brushed my teeth.

45   "I know," she says. "I tell myself I have no right to grieve. They are in a better place than we are. My swami says depression is a sign of our selfishness."

46   Maybe I'm selfish. Selfishly I break away from Kusum and run, sandals slapping against stones, to the water's edge. What if my boys aren't lying pinned under the debris? What if they aren't stuck a mile below that innocent blue chop? What if, given the strong currents . . .

47   Now I've ruined my sari, one of my best. Kusum has joined me, knee deep in water that feels to me like a swimming pool. I could settle in the water, and my husband would take my hand and the boys would slap water in my face just to see me scream.

48   "Do you remember what good swimmers my boys were, Kusum?"

49   "I saw the medals," she says.

50   One of the widowers, Dr. Ranganathan from Montreal, walks out to us, carrying his shoes in one hand. He's an electrical engineer. Someone at the hotel mentioned his work is famous around the world, something about the place where physics and electricity come together. He has lost a huge family, something indescribable. "With some good luck," Dr. Ranganathan suggests to me, "a good swimmer could make it safely to some island. It is quite possible that there may be many, many microscopic islets scattered around."

51   "You're not just saying that?" I tell Dr. Ranganathan about Vinod, my elder son. Last year he took diving as well.

52   "It's a parent's duty to hope," he says. "It is foolish to rule out possibilities that have not been tested. I myself have not surrendered hope."

53   Kusum is sobbing once again. "Dear lady," he says, laying his free hand on her arm, and she calms down.

54   "Vinod is how old?" he asks me. He's very careful, as we all are. *Is*, not was.

55   "Fourteen. Yesterday he was fourteen. His father and uncle were going to take him down to the Taj and give him a big birthday party. I couldn't go with them because I couldn't get two weeks off from my stupid job in June." I process bills for a travel agent. June is a big travel month.

56   Dr. Ranganathan whips the pockets of his suit jacket inside out. Squashed roses, in darkening shades of pink, float on the water. He tore the roses off creepers in somebody's garden. He didn't ask anyone if he could pluck the roses, but now there's been an article about it in the local papers. When you see an Indian person, it says, please give them flowers.

57   "A strong youth of fourteen," he says, "can very likely pull to safety a younger one."

58   My sons, though four years apart, were very close. Vinod wouldn't let Mithun drown. *Electrical engineering*, I think, foolishly perhaps: this man knows important secrets of the universe, things closed to me. Relief spins me lightheaded. No wonder my boys' photographs haven't turned up in the gallery of photos of the recovered dead. "Such pretty roses," I say.

59   "My wife loved pink roses. Every Friday I had to bring a bunch home. I used to say, Why? After twenty-odd years of marriage you're still needing proof positive of my love?" He has identified his wife and three of his children. Then others from Montreal, the lucky ones, intact families with no survivors. He chuckles as he wades back to shore. Then he swings around to ask me a question. "Mrs. Bhave, you are wanting to throw in some roses for your loved ones? I have two big ones left."

60   But I have other things to float: Vinod's pocket calculator; a half-painted model B-52 for my Mithun. They'd want them on their island. And for my husband? For him I let fall into the calm, glassy waters a poem I wrote in the hospital yesterday. Finally he'll know my feelings for him. "Don't tumble, the rocks are slippery," Dr. Ranganathan cautions. He holds out a hand for me to grab.

61   Then it's time to get back on the bus, time to rush back to our waiting posts on hospital benches. Kusum is one of the lucky ones. The lucky ones flew here, identified in multiplicate their loved ones, then will fly to India with the bodies for proper ceremonies. Satish is one of the few males who surfaced. The photos of faces we saw on the walls in an office at Heathrow and here in the hospital are mostly of women. Women have more body fat, a nun said to me matter-of-factly. They float better.

62   Today I was stopped by a young sailor on the street. He had loaded bodies, he'd gone into the water when—he checks my face for signs of strength—when the sharks were first spotted. I don't blush, and he

breaks down. "It's all right," I say. "Thank you." I heard about the sharks from Dr. Ranganathan. In his orderly mind, science brings understanding, it holds no terror. It is the shark's duty. For every deer there is a hunter, for every fish a fisherman.

63   The Irish are not shy; they rush to me and give me hugs and some are crying. I cannot imagine reactions like that on the streets of Toronto. Just strangers, and I am touched. Some carry flowers with them and give them to any Indian they see.

64   After lunch, a policeman I have gotten to know quite well catches hold of me. He says he thinks he has a match for Vinod. I explain what a good swimmer Vinod is.

65   "You want me with you when you look at the photos?" Dr. Ranganathan walks ahead of me into the picture gallery. In these matters he is a scientist and I am grateful. It is a new perspective. "They have performed miracles," he says. "We are indebted to them."

66   The first day or two the policemen showed us relatives only one picture at a time; now they're in a hurry, they're eager to lay out the possibles, and even the probables.

67   The face on the photo is of a boy much like Vinod; the same intelligent eyes, the same thick brows dipping into a V. But this boy's features, even his cheeks, are puffier, wider, mushier.

68   "No." My gaze is pulled by other pictures. There are five other boys who look like Vinod.

69   The nun assigned to console me rubs the first picture with a fingertip. "When they've been in the water for a while, love, they look a little heavier." The bones under the skin are broken, they said on the first day—try to adjust your memories. It's important.

70   "It's not him. I'm his mother. I'd know."

71   "I know this one!" Dr. Ranganathan cries out, and suddenly from the back of the gallery. "And this one!" I think he senses that I don't want to find my boys. "They are the Kutty brothers. They were also from Montreal." I don't mean to be crying. On the contrary, I am ecstatic. My suitcase in the hotel is packed heavy with dry clothes for my boys.

72   The policeman starts to cry. "I am so sorry. I am so sorry, ma'am. I really thought we had a match."

73   With the nun ahead of us and the policeman behind, we, the unlucky ones without our children's bodies, file out of the makeshift gallery.

74   From Ireland most of us go on to India. Kusum and I take the same direct flight to Bombay, so I can help her clear customs quickly. But we have to argue with a man in uniform. He has large boils on his face. The boils swell and glow with sweat as we argue with him. He wants Kusum to wait in line and he refuses to take authority because his boss is on a tea break. But Kusum won't let her coffins out of sight, and I shan't desert her though I know that my parents, elderly and diabetic, must be waiting in a stuffy car in a scorching lot.

75   "You bastard!" I scream at the man with the popping boils. Other passengers press closer. "You think we're smuggling contraband in those coffins!"

76   Once upon a time we were well-brought-up women; we were dutiful wives who kept our heads veiled, our voices shy and sweet.

77   In India, I become, once again, an only child of rich, ailing parents. Old friends of the family come to pay their respects. Some are Sikh, and inwardly, involuntarily, I cringe. My parents are progressive people; they do not blame communities for a few individuals.

78   In Canada it is a different story now.

79   "Stay longer," my mother pleads. "Canada is a cold place. Why would you want to be by yourself?" I stay.

80   Three months pass. Then another.

81   "Vikram wouldn't have wanted you to give up things!" they protest. They called my husband by the name he was born with. In Toronto he'd changed to Vik so the men he worked with at his office would find his name as easy as Rod or Chris. "You know, the dead aren't cut off from us!"

82   My grandmother, the spoiled daughter of a rich zamindar, shaved her head with rusty razor blades when she was widowed at sixteen. My grandfather died of childhood diabetes when he was nineteen, and she saw herself as the harbinger of bad luck. My mother grew up without parents, raised indifferently by an uncle, while her true mother slept in a hut behind the main estate house and took her food with the servants. She grew up a rationalist. My parents abhor mindless mortification.

83   The zamindar's daughter kept stubborn faith in Vedic rituals; my parents rebelled. I am trapped between two modes of knowledge. At thirty-six, I am too old to start over and too young to give up. Like my husband's spirit, I flutter between worlds.

84   Courting aphasia, we travel. We travel with our phalanx of servants and poor relatives. To hill stations and to beach resorts. We play contract bridge in dusty gymkhana clubs. We ride stubby ponies up crumbly mountain trails. At tea dances, we let ourselves be twirled twice round the ballroom. We hit the holy spots we hadn't made time for before. In Varanasi, Kalighat, Rishikesh, Hardwar, astrologers and palmists seek me out and for a fee offer me cosmic consolations.

85   Already the widowers among us are being shown new bride candidates. They cannot resist the call of custom, the authority of their parents and older brothers. They must marry; it is the duty of a man to look after a wife. The new wives will be young widows with children, destitute but of good family. They will make loving wives, but the men will shun them. I've had calls from the men over crackling Indian telephone lines. "Save me," they say, these substantial, educated, successful men of forty. "My parents are arranging a marriage for me." In a month they will have buried one family and returned to Canada with a new bride and partial family.

86   I am comparatively lucky. No one here thinks of arranging a husband for an unlucky widow.

87   Then, on the third day of the sixth month into this odyssey, in an abandoned temple in a tiny Himalayan village, as I make my offering of flowers and sweetmeats to the god of a tribe of animists, my husband descends to me. He is squatting next to a scrawny sadhu in moth-eaten robes. Vikram wears the vanilla suit he wore the last time I hugged him. The sadhu tosses petals on a butter-fed flame, reciting Sanskrit mantras and sweeps his face of flies. My husband takes my hands in his.

88   *You're beautiful*, he starts. Then, *What are you doing here?*

89   *Shall I stay?* I ask. He only smiles, but already the image is fading. *You must finish alone what we started together.* No seaweed wreathes his mouth. He speaks too fast, just as he used to when we were an envied family in our pink split-level. He is gone.

90   In the windowless altar room, smoky with joss sticks and clarified butter lamps, a sweaty hand gropes for my blouse. I do not shriek. The sadhu arranges his robe. The lamps hiss and sputter out.

91   When we come out of the temple, my mother says, "Did you feel something weird in there?".

92   My mother has no patience with ghosts, prophetic dreams, holy men, and cults.

93   "No," I lie. "Nothing."

94   But she knows that she's lost me. She knows that in days I shall be leaving.

95   Kusum's put up her house for sale. She wants to live in an ashram in Hardwar. Moving to Hardwar was her swami's idea. Her swami runs two ashrams, the one in Hardwar and another here in Toronto.

96   "Don't run away," I tell her.

97   "I'm not running away," she says. "I'm pursuing inner peace. You think you or that Ranganathan fellow are better off?"

98   Pam's left for California. She wants to do some modeling, she says. She says when she comes into her share of the insurance money she'll open a yoga-cum-aerobics studio in Hollywood. She sends me postcards so naughty I daren't leave them on the coffee table. Her mother has withdrawn from her and the world.

99   The rest of us don't lose touch, that's the point. Talk is all we have, says Dr. Ranganathan, who has also resisted his relatives and returned to Montreal and to his job, alone. He says, Whom better to talk with than other relatives? We've been melted down and recast as a new tribe.

100   He calls me twice a week from Montreal. Every Wednesday night and every Saturday afternoon. He is changing jobs, going to Ottawa. But Ottawa is over a hundred miles away, and he is forced to drive two hundred and twenty miles a day from his home in Montreal. He can't bring himself to sell his house. The house is a temple, he says; the king-sized bed in the master bedroom is a shrine. He sleeps on a folding cot. A devotee.

101   There are still some hysterical relatives. Judith Templeton's list of those needing help and those who've "accepted" is in nearly perfect balance. Acceptance means you speak of your family in the past tense and you make active plans for moving ahead with your life. There are courses at Seneca and Ryerson we could be taking. Her gleaming leather briefcase is full of college catalogues and lists of cultural societies that need our help. She has done impressive work, I tell her.

102   "In the textbooks on grief management," she replies—I am her confidante. I realize, one of the few whose grief has not sprung bizarre obsessions—"there are stages to pass through: rejection, depression, acceptance, reconstruction." She has compiled a chart and finds that six months after the tragedy, none of us still rejects reality, but only a handful are reconstructing. "Depressed acceptance" is the plateau we've reached. Remarriage is a major step in reconstruction (though she's a little surprised, even shocked, over *how* quickly some of the men have taken on new families). Selling one's house and changing jobs and cities is healthy.

103   How to tell Judith Templeton that my family surrounds me, and that like creatures in epics, they've changed shapes? She sees me as calm and accepting but worries that I have no job, no career. My closest friends are worse off than I. I cannot tell her my days, even my nights, are thrilling.

104   She asks me to help with families she can't reach at all. An elderly couple in Agincourt whose sons were killed just weeks after they had brought their parents over from a village in Punjab. From their names, I know they are Sikh. Judith Templeton and a translator have visited them twice with offers of money for airfare to Ireland, with bank forms, power-of-attorney forms, but they have refused to sign, or to leave their tiny apartment. Their sons' money is frozen in the bank. Their sons' investment apartments have been trashed by tenants, the furnishings sold off. The parents fear that anything they sign or any money they receive will end the company's or the country's obligations to them. They fear they are selling their sons for two airline tickets to a place they've never seen.

105   The high-rise apartment is a tower of Indians and West Indians, with a sprinkling of Orientals. The nearest bus-stop kiosk is lined with women in saris. Boys practice cricket in the parking lot. Inside the building, even I wince a bit from the ferocity of onion fumes, the distinctive and immediate Indianness of frying ghee, but Judith Templeton maintains a steady flow of information. These poor old people are in imminent danger of losing their place and all their services.

106   I say to her, "They are Sikh. They will not open up to a Hindu woman." And what I want to add is, as much as I try not to, I stiffen now at the sight of beards and turbans. I remember a time when we all trusted each other in this new country, it was only the new country we worried about.

107   The two rooms are dark and stuffy. The lights are off, and an oil lamp sputters on the coffee table. The bent old lady has let us in, and her

husband is wrapping a white turban over his oiled, hip-length hair. She immediately goes into the kitchen, and I hear the most familiar sound of an Indian home, tap water hitting and filling a teapot.

108   They have not paid their utility bills, out of fear and inability to write a check. The telephone is gone, electricity and gas and water are soon to follow. They have told Judith their sons will provide. They are good boys and they have always earned and looked after their parents.

109   We converse a bit in Hindi. They do not ask about the crash and I wonder if I should bring it up. If they think I am here merely as a translator, then they may feel insulted. There are thousands of Punjabi speakers, Sikhs, in Toronto to do a better job. And so I say to the old lady, "I too have lost my sons, and my husband, in the crash."

110   Her eyes immediately fill with tears. The man mutters a few words which sound like a blessing. "God provides and God takes away," he says.

111   I want to say, But only men destroy and give back nothing. "My boys and my husband are not coming back," I say. "We have to understand that."

112   Now the old woman responds. "But who is to say? Man alone does not decide these things." To this her husband adds his agreement.

113   Judith asks about the bank papers, the release forms. With a stroke of the pen, they will have a provincial trustee to pay their bills, invest their money, send them a monthly pension.

114   "Do you know this woman?" I ask them.

115   The man raises his hand from the table, turns it over, and seems to regard each finger separately before he answers. "This young lady is always coming here, we make tea for her, and she leaves papers for us to sign." His eyes scan a pile of papers in the corner of the room. "Soon we will be out of tea, then will she go away?"

116   The old lady adds, "I have asked my neighbors and no one else gets *angrezi* visitors. What have we done?"

117   "It's her job," I try to explain. "The government is worried. Soon you will have no place to stay, no lights, no gas, no water."

118   "Government will get its money. Tell her not to worry, we are honorable people."

119   I try to explain the government wishes to give money, not take. He raises his hand. "Let them take," he says. "We are accustomed to that. That is no problem."

120   "We are strong people," says the wife. "Tell her that."

121   "Who needs all this machinery?" demands the husband. "It is unhealthy, the bright lights, the cold air on a hot day, the cold food, the four gas rings. God will provide, not government."

122   "When our boys return," the mother says.

123   Her husband sucks his teeth. "Enough talk," he says.

124   Judith breaks in. "Have you convinced them?" The snaps on her cordovan briefcase go off like firecrackers in that quiet apartment. She lays the sheaf of legal papers on the coffee table. "If they can't write their names, an X will do—I've told them that."

125   Now the old lady has shuffled to the kitchen and soon emerges with a pot of tea and two cups. "I think my bladder will go first on a job like this," Judith says to me, smiling. "If only there was some way of reaching them. Please thank her for the tea. Tell her she's very kind."

126   I nod in Judith's direction and tell them in Hindi, "She thanks you for the tea. She thinks you are being very hospitable but she doesn't have the slightest idea what it means."

127   I want to say, Humor her. I want to say, My boys and my husband are with me too, more than ever. I look in the old man's eyes and I can read his stubborn, peasant's message: *I have protected this woman as best I can. She is the only person I have left. Give to me or take from what you will, but I will not sign for it. I will not pretend that I accept.*

128   In the car, Judith, says, "You see what I'm up against? I'm sure they're lovely people, but their stubbornness and ignorance are driving me crazy. They think signing a paper is signing their sons' death warrants, don't they?"

129   I am looking out the window. I want to say, *In our culture, it is a parent's duty to hope.*

130   "Now Shaila, this next woman is a real mess. She cries day and night, and she refuses all medical help. We may have to—"

131   "Let me out at the subway," I say.

132   "I beg your pardon?" I can feel those blue eyes staring at me.

133   It would not be like her to disobey. She merely disapproves, and slows at a corner to let me out. Her voice is plaintive. "Is there anything I said? Anything I did?"

134   I could answer her suddenly in a dozen ways, but I choose not to. "Shaila? Let's talk about it," I hear, then slam the door.

135   A wife and mother begins her life in a new country, and that life is cut short. Yet her husband tells her: Complete what we have started. We, who stayed out of politics and came half way around the world to avoid religious and political feuding, have been the first in the New World to die from it. I no longer know what we started, nor how to complete it. I write letters to the editors of local papers and to members of Parliament. Now at least they admit it was a bomb. One MP answers back, with sympathy, but with a challenge. You want to make a difference? Work on a campaign. Work on mine. Politicize the Indian voter.

136   My husband's old lawyer helps me set up a trust. Vikram was a saver and a careful investor. He had saved the boys' boarding school and college fees. I sell the pink house at four times what we paid for it and take a small apartment downtown. I am looking for a charity to support.

137   We are deep in the Toronto winter, gray skies, icy pavements. I stay indoors, watching television. I have tried to assess my situation, how best to live my life, to complete what we began so many years ago. Kusum has written me from Hardwar that her life is now serene. She has seen Satish and has heard her daughter sing again. Kusum was on a pilgrimage,

passing through a village, when she heard a young girl's voice, singing one of her daughter's favorite *bhajans*. She followed the music through the squalor of a Himalayan village, to a hut where a young girl, an exact replica of her daughter, was fanning coals under the kitchen fire. When she appeared, the girl cried out, "Ma!" and ran away. What did I think of that?

138   I think I can only envy her.

139   Pam didn't make it to California, but writes me from Vancouver. She works in a department store, giving makeup hints to Indian and Oriental girls. Dr. Ranganathan has given up his commute, given up his house and job, and accepted an academic position in Texas, where no one knows his story and he has vowed not to tell it. He calls me now once a week.

140   I wait, I listen and I pray, but Vikram has not returned to me. The voices and the shapes and the nights filled with visions ended abruptly several weeks ago.

141   I take it as a sign.

142   One rare, beautiful, sunny day last week, returning from a small errand on Yonge Street, I was walking through the park from the subway to my apartment. I live equidistant from the Ontario Houses of Parliament and the University of Toronto. The day was not cold, but something in the bare trees caught my attention. I looked up from the gravel, into the branches and the clear blue sky beyond. I thought I heard the rustling of larger forms, and I waited a moment for voices. Nothing.

143   "What?" I asked.

144   Then as I stood in the path looking north to Queen's Park and west to the university, I heard the voices of my family one last time. *Your time has come*, they said. *Go, be brave.*

145   I do not know where this voyage I have begun will end. I do not know which direction I will take. I dropped the package on a park bench and started walking.

Questions for Engagement, Response, and Analysis

1. What does the author's selection of the two settings suggest about the theme? What is the theme of this story?

2. Judith Templeton, the social worker, asks the narrator for help because she has heard that Mrs. Bhave has "taken it more calmly." What are Mrs. Bhave's feelings about this observation?

3. The narrator says, "'Nothing I can do will make any difference. . . . We must all grieve in our own way.'" Compare her feelings of helplessness with those of Kingsolver or of Pinhas in Wiesel's essay.

4. What details about her behavior toward her husband does the narrator, Mrs. Bhave, focus on? Analyze Mrs. Bhave's reaction to the customs agent in India. What do these reactions suggest about Mrs. Bhave?

5. Explain the last paragraph of the story.

Crafting Arguments

1. Discuss in detail the misunderstanding between the government and those who are grieving in Mukherjee's story. Then analyze the attitudes of the recipients to the government's attempt to help.

2. Compare Mukherjee's question, "Why does God give us so much if all along He intends to take it away?" with a similar expression in Weisel's "Yom Kippur."

Todd James Pierce (b. 1965)

Writer and teacher Todd James Pierce is also a tireless advocate for beginning writers. Pierce received an M.F.A. from the University of California at Irvine, an M.A. from Oregon State University, and a Ph.D. from Florida State University. His works have been published in many collections and in prestigious journals. In 2003, Pierce published The Australia Stories, *a novel later republished as* A Woman of Stone *(2006). "Newsworld II" is the last story in the collection* Newsworld *(2006). In addition to teaching fiction writing, Pierce has published a textbook on writing entitled* Behind the Short Story *(2007).*

NEWSWORLD II   (2006)

1   We watched it in Social Studies, then in World History. That Friday, September 14, we saw it again in a class called Life Studies. When the jet slammed into the north tower, Mr. Stolz, our teacher, squeezed the bridge of his nose pensively just like he did when he lectured about the dangers of credit-card debt. He shifted his eyes to us, his class of eleventh-grade boys, and asked how we felt about the attack.

2   We weren't good at talking about our feelings, though Mr. Stolz had made us read a book called *The Emotional Life of Men.* Our emotions were mysterious to us, the fine divisions between melancholy and depression, yearning and desire. We suspected that someday soon we'd be able to tell the difference between such things, the same way our parents could tell the difference between a good wine and a *very* good wine. We didn't tell Mr. Stolz much about our lives. For example, we didn't tell him that Jay Moore had videotaped the attack, then watched it after doing three lines of Ritalin. Nor did we tell him that Jeff Loeb's little brother, Seth, had laughed when he saw the first jet exploding into the tower. He'd thought it was a movie, like *Independence Day.* After his teacher explained that the planes were real, he cried for ten minutes before going to recess and kicking a red activity ball over the playground fence.

3   We sat quietly, waiting for Mr. Stolz to talk to us. From previous classes we'd learned there were special scripts for talking about your feelings. For example, there were specific things you should say to a friend with

a serious drug problem. But we didn't know the script for this situation. Alan Whidden, a boy who'd been busted for steroids, said, "It makes me angry." Mr. Stolz stood there in his starched black T-shirt and ironed jeans, regarding us with stern eyes. Harry Kessel, a JV lineman, said, "We should get whoever did this."

4   We were scared, but didn't know how to say we were scared. The men in our textbook weren't the kind of men you saw in the suburbs of Atlanta. They weren't the kind who told their sons, "Kick some ass in the game this weekend" or, "If you're going to do it, for god's sake wear a rubber." Our fathers went fishing ten times a year and rode tractor mowers around our weedy suburban lawns. They hung punching bags in our garages, the nylon casings filled with the exact amount of sand to make the bags feel like dead bodies.

5   Initially we believed the terrorist attacks were something that happened up north, a good ways above the Mason-Dixon Line. But then our airport closed. The freeway closed, the mall closed, so did the movie theater. Lastly Newsworld draped a thick black chain across the entrance to its parking lot, right in front of the attendant booths where Jeff Sanders and Jarvis White had collected the five-dollar parking fee from tourists all summer long. A professionally printed sign announced, "National Security Closure."

6   Most of us worked at Newsworld, an amusement park three miles from our school. We said we hated it, but in truth we didn't mind it so much. We sold Icees and scraped gum off the sidewalk. We stole stuffed animals from the gift shops and gave them to our girlfriends. We thought the job was educational and believed it would help us get into a good college.

7   After my evening shift I liked to walk through the park. I particularly liked The Vietnam Experience, three acres so lush you forgot you were in central Georgia, a silver mist rising from vents hidden in rocks, water dripping from irrigation hoses molded to resemble jungle vines. It was kind of creepy, the way it was laid out, the huts made of sticks, military radios and grenade launchers left beside the Main Guest Trail. Sometimes I would meet my girlfriend, Devon MacCray, in the Lost Vietnamese Village. We would make out in one of the thatched huts while a cool breeze circled around us and the soft voices of the Vietcong whispered from miniature speakers hidden in banyan trees.

8   We'd grown up with Newsworld, the way other kids had grown up with Disney or Six Flags. Our parents had taken us there when we were seven or eight so we could walk through an authentic reproduction of a 1950s diner and sit behind the wheel of a 1955 Chevy Bel Air. We were made to watch a clumsy mannequin of Martin Luther King Jr. deliver highlights from his "I Have a Dream" speech while an equally clumsy mannequin of his wife quivered beside him.

9   We were ushered into the First Interactive Museum, a newsreel of our parents' lives spun out as entertainment. As children, we loved to ride the Kentucky Derby Carousel, control the U-Fly-Em Fighter Jets, watch

Neil Armstrong step onto the moon, the gray lunar dust rising up around his opaque boot while we sat in a cozy reproduction of Mission Control, listening to the brassy fanfare of "The Star-Spangled Banner."

10　　When we were teenagers we first experienced the strangeness of boarding a ride based on a news story we'd seen on TV. As little kids, we'd watched in irritation as OJ's Bronco crawled up the freeway followed by patrol cars and TV news helicopters, the live footage interrupting *Animaniacs* and *Duck Tales*. Five years later we climbed into similar Broncos—vehicles outfitted with lap bars and individual sound systems embedded into the headrests—and were whisked into the dim sound stage of Los Angeles. Dave Fowler, my best friend in junior high, told me, "This ride totally sucks." Yet we went on it three more times, until Doug could mimic the announcer's voice, a lazy California accent that made words such as "pursuit" sound more important than they did in the South.

11　　We learned about the park's closure on September 11 while watching a team of reporters explore the wreckage of New York. A bulletin scrolled across the TV informing us that the park had been closed along with other public areas. My mother, a diet counselor for Jenny Craig, watched all day, clicking from one channel to the next. Each one showed the smoldering remains of the towers, surrounded by other buildings that experts believed would collapse as well. She ate saltines right out of the box, not from premeasured "snack baggies" she kept in the cupboard. "I shouldn't be eating these," she said, then put another one into her mouth.

12　　Over the next two days, we drove by Newsworld many times, noting how odd it was to see the parking lot empty, how naked the sky appeared over the Titanic without artificial smoke rising from the cracked hull of the ship. Though signs warned against trespassing, we walked along the twelve-foot security fence that separated Newsworld from the rest of Georgia. Ron Watson, a boy who'd been arrested twice for shoplifting, was the first to throw stones. We listened as they landed inside the park, their sharp *pock-pock-pock* across the painted cement, then the enthusiastic hush of breaking glass.

13　　We planned to break into the park on Saturday night, all of us wearing black shirts and jeans. We'd never been inside the park when it was closed. We'd never walked along Twentieth-Century Boulevard without hearing the cheerful calliope music that came from the snack wagon, nor had we seen the Boogie Nights Disco without pinwheels of colored lights spinning across the darkened front windows. Specifically we wanted to walk through an attraction called The San Francisco Earthquake, to stand among the crumpled buildings, the piles of bricks and metal covered by a fine, simulated dust. Though no one said as much, we felt we might better understand what had happened in New York if we could be inside the park for a while, on this street where buildings had been destroyed by a different tragedy.

14　　We met at the delivery entrance, most of us half-drunk on schnapps. We were anxious yet sad. Sometimes we felt so many things we thought our bodies would burst. But other times we felt as though our hearts had been scraped out with a spoon. We were worried about the draft. Would there be a draft? We'd never been in love. We'd never done anything important, though our lives *felt* as important as a big summer movie.

15   We moved quietly into the park, sliding under a dusty gap in the fence. Lonnie Mason carried a flashlight he'd taken from his father's car, though no one allowed him to turn it on. Jimmy Kendral claimed to have the keys to the security shack, but when we tried them they didn't work. We walked down a street called Legends of the '50s, past diners just like those our grandparents had known—diners with overstuffed red booths and jukebox menus at each table. We walked past the Daily Scoop, a gift shop where some of us had worked the previous summer. Dan Wheeler pressed his hands to the tinted glass so he could see inside; shadows fell across displays of news-related action figures, cash registers with their empty drawers left open, per the new employee guidelines.

16   Though we never said as much, we all felt the ragged ends of nostalgia brush against our hearts. Had we felt nostalgic before? Ron Watson missed his father who now lived across town. Jeff Loeb missed a girl who'd moved to Canada. But this was different. We ached to be fifteen again, to be washed in the silver colander of our sophomore year, a world of drivers' permits and diet-related acne. We longed to squeeze back into the snakeskin of our youth, to feel its safe snugness around our growing, muscular bodies.

17   We almost didn't recognize the park without the background music in each of its six themed lands. The Vietnam Experience looked like any other swamp. Where was the manufactured mist, the menacing chatter of the Vietcong? The large building that housed the OJ Simpson ride could have been any warehouse, without its signature neon sign and the image of OJ projected on a screen above the entrance.

18   We were disappointed because we saw how easily our childhood could be turned off, everything shut down and emptied. Behind an attraction called Hooverville, Jeff Loeb carved his initials into the soft pine exterior of a gift shop. Stephen Moore picked up a Visitors' Guide that listed the parade and show schedule for Monday, September 10. Karl Asher saw a quarter under a park bench and left it there.

19   We'd come here not knowing what to expect, though we all expected to learn something as we walked around the carefully organized debris of The San Francisco Earthquake, the piles of bricks, the broken pieces of plastic designed to look like glass. We wanted to feel something other than the vague ache we'd felt all week. We wanted emotion to fill our bodies like a golden light. Our teachers had told us the world would be different now—harder, difficult in ways we couldn't imagine.

20   Most of us had never been to New York. Our families had taken us on short vacations to New Orleans and Orlando, where we'd visited other theme parks, sometimes a zoo or a museum. Chuck Milligan, the only boy to fail his driving test, told us the Twin Towers were five times taller than

any building in Atlanta. Though Chuck was prone to exaggeration, we tried to imagine the tallest building in Atlanta stacked on top of itself five times. We'd only seen the towers on TV, only noticed their impressive gray bulk as they fell to the ground in a burning, dusty heap. We were good at understanding TV. We knew some reality shows were more real than others, yet we didn't know how to feel about what we'd seen on September 11.

21   We were surprised that we didn't find security guards on Twentieth-Century Boulevard, yet relieved as well. We had a good sense about ourselves as we neared the far end of the park, a sense that we were not just marching through the unexamined life of the average boy at our school. We felt a stirring in our chests, a fizz like carbonation, like the stirring we felt when a girl let us undo the secret plastic clasp of her bra.

22   By now we'd adjusted to the strangeness of the empty park. Park trees looked like regular trees without the choreographed spectacle of white lights flashing along their branches. As we passed by The Big '80s Shop, we were reminded of one of our private fears. We feared our lives might be slightly less real than the lives of other boys, though we all wore the same clothes, all watched the same TV shows. Brian Furgeson, the math teacher's son, stopped to look into the shop window at stacks of colorful Italian sweaters just like the ones Bill Cosby used to wear on TV.

23   We were at the edge of San Francisco, yet we were at the edge of New York as well. We felt the anticipation of children as we walked by Fisherman's Wharf, a restaurant that served chowder in sourdough bowls. Mentally we were taking down all the emotional walls our parents complained about so we could absorb this experience directly. Lonnie Mason, a religious boy, removed a votive candle from his jacket pocket and rolled it along the length of his palm.

24   We didn't see it until we were in the preshow area. There, at the entrance, we found a tall plywood barrier. We'd seen similar barriers placed around other attractions—ones under renovation—yet we knew the San Francisco Earthquake was not under renovation. Park guests had visited it all summer. Jeff Loeb was the first to speak. "Mother fucker," he said, then walked to the barrier and punched it.

25   We did our best to peer inside, pressing our eyes to the dark seams between boards, but we could see very little. We saw a few bricks littering a cracked sidewalk. We saw a broken hydrant that, during park hours, gushed water. We saw the distant outline of a wooden pushcart tipped up on its side. A few of us saw a light in the telegraph office, a hanging bulb designed to swing as though the ground had just stopped shaking.

26   Harry Kessel suggested we push through the barrier. Brian Jenks, the track star, said we should climb over it. We were at the end of an alcove, a short hallway that, like a cattle chute, funneled guests into the broken world of San Francisco. We'd already pushed against the plywood, testing its strength. Yet we tested it again, first with our hands, then our shoulders.

27   We were there, at the end of the preshow area, when two security guards found us. They held their flashlights at odd angles, like the cross-eyed gaze of an idiot. We were worried, yet we were defiant as well. We felt we should look brave, if only for each other. We felt a childish lick of shame whenever a beam from their flashlights touched our bodies. We knew they would escort us outside the park, but we stayed there, our weight against the plywood barrier, longing to know what was on the other side.

28   It was different for all of us, the disappointment. For me it was like falling in love with a pretty girl who, in the end, turns you down for a date. For Harry Kessell it was like being first alternate for the all-state team and never getting to play. We knew our lives were changing, but didn't know how they were changing. We were juniors at a very good high school, but after watching those jets curve into the towers, we had no idea where we were going nor did we know what we should do along the way.

Questions for Engagement, Response, and Analysis

1. What is the effect of Pierce's choice of a narrator? How might the story have differed if the boys had been younger or older?
2. What is the tone of the story?
3. Why do the boys go back for a final visit to Newsworld?
4. What is the theme of the story?

Crafting Arguments

1. In an essay, explain and defend your interpretation of the changes the boys experience on the days after 9/11.

POETRY

Percy Bysshe Shelley (1792–1822)

Shelley, born in Field Place, Sussex, England, was adored by his six brothers and sisters; consequently, he demanded adoration in later years. He was expelled from Oxford along with his friend Thomas Jefferson Hogg because of his revolutionary philosophy. From that point on, Shelley led a fascinating life, marrying twice and enjoying a friendship with Romantic hero George Gordon, Lord Byron. He is known for his propaganda writing, lovely lyrics, and intellectual convictions.

OZYMANDIAS   (1818)

I met a traveller from an antique land
Who said: Two vast and trunkless legs of stone
Stand in the desert . . . Near them, on the sand,
Half sunk, a shattered visage lies, whose frown,
5   And wrinkled lip, and sneer of cold command,
Tell that its sculptor well those passions read
Which yet survive, stamped on these lifeless things,
The hand that mocked them, and the heart that fed:
And on the pedestal these words appear:
10 "My name is Ozymandias, king of kings:
Look on my works, ye Mighty, and despair!"
Nothing beside remains. Round the decay
Of that colossal wreck, boundless and bare
The lone and level sands stretch far away

Questions for Engagement, Response, and Analysis

1. What is the tone of this poem? How do the last six lines affect this tone?
2. What is the theme of "Ozymandias"?
3. Examine the structure and the metaphorical devices in the poem. How do they contribute to the depiction of Ozymandias and to the theme of the poem?

Crafting Arguments

1. In an essay, show how Shelley uses the tight form and the vivid metaphorical devices to create his powerful theme.

Edwin Arlington Robinson (1869–1935)

Edwin Arlington Robinson's life provided him with a wealth of material for his poetic portraits of lonely and tragic misfits. After a series of financial and physical tragedies decimated his family, Robinson moved to Greenwich Village in New York City, where for a time he was practically destitute. Although he received Pulitzer prizes for his later work, primarily book-length blank verse poems on the Arthurian legends, Robinson is best remembered for his Tilbury Town poems, portraits of imaginary misfits who inhabit a town based on his hometown of Gardiner, Maine.

RICHARD CORY   (1897)

Whenever Richard Cory went down town,
We people on the pavement looked at him:

He was a gentleman from sole to crown,
Clean favored, and imperially slim.

5   And he was always quietly arrayed,
And he was always human when he talked;
But still he fluttered pulses when he said,
"Good-morning," and he glittered when he walked.

And he was rich—yes, richer than a king—
10   And admirably schooled in every grace:
In fine, we thought that he was everything
To make us wish that we were in his place.

So on we worked, and waited for the light,
And went without the meat, and cursed the bread;
15   And Richard Cory, one calm summer night,
Went home and put a bullet through his head.

Questions for Engagement, Response, and Analysis

1. From what point of view is the poem written? Explain how Robinson's use of this point of view allows him to control what the speakers and, therefore, the readers know about Richard Cory.

2. How does a similar point of view achieve a similar result in Faulkner's "A Rose for Emily"?

3. What is the tone of the poem?

Crafting Arguments

1. Write an essay on the symbols, images, and sound devices used in this poem—the overall symbolism of kingship; the metonymy and metaphor; the alliteration, assonance, consonance, rhyme, and rhythm. Explain how these devices help to emphasize the observers' perception of Richard Cory.

Paul Laurence Dunbar (1872–1906)

Paul Dunbar was born in Dayton, Ohio, to former slaves; however, his father, Joshua, escaped to Canada and fought in the Union army. Dunbar later wrote for The Tattler, *printed by his classmate, Orville Wright. Wanting more than Dayton could offer, Dunbar toured Europe giving readings of his poetry. He wrote poems, among them the collection* Oak and Ivy *(1892); novels, such as* The Sport of Gods *(1902); and musicals, including* Dream Lovers: An Operatic Romance *(1898). Dunbar gained recognition for his diverse accomplishments and for the use of dialect in his poems. His themes include the overt oppression of African-Americans in all aspects of life and the ramifications of brutality imposed on the human soul.*

WE WEAR THE MASK   (1913)

We wear the mask that grins and lies,
It hides our cheeks and shades our eyes,—
This debt we pay to human guile;
With torn and bleeding hearts we smile,
5   And mouth with myriad subtleties.
Why should the world be overwise,
In counting all our tears and sighs?
Nay, let them only see us, while
  We wear the mask.

10   We smile, but, O great Christ, our cries
To Thee from tortured souls arise.
We sing, but oh, the clay is vile
Beneath our feet, and long the mile;
But let the world dream otherwise,
15   We wear the mask.

Questions for Engagement, Response, and Analysis

1. Who are the speakers in this poem?
2. What is the tone? How does Dunbar reveal it?
3. What does Dunbar mean by "let the world dream otherwise, / We wear the mask"? Why does he use the word *dream?*

Crafting Arguments

1. Explain why the people in this poem believe that they have to hide behind masks. What in society causes people to conceal their true identities? In an essay, argue that the speakers in the poem are or are not like other individuals in feeling that they must conceal parts of themselves from others.

John McCrae (1872–1918)

Canadian John McCrae had resigned from the military in 1904 and pursued a successful career as a physician, but in 1914, when Canada declared war on Germany, McCrae, then forty-one years old, immediately joined the war effort. After fighting on the Western Front, he was assigned to the medical corps in France. He was still on active duty when he died of pneumonia in 1918. His only book of poetry, In Flanders Fields and Other Poems, *was published in 1919, but "In Flanders Fields," a poem written immediately after the battlefield death of a close friend, had been published in* Punch, *the English magazine, in 1915 and was already the most popular poem about World War I.*

IN FLANDERS FIELDS   (1915)

In Flanders fields the poppies blow
Between the crosses, row on row,
That mark our place; and in the sky
The larks, still bravely singing, fly
5   Scarce heard amid the guns below.

We are the Dead. Short days ago,
We lived, felt dawn, saw sunset glow,
Loved, and were loved, and now we lie
In Flanders fields.

10   Take up our quarrel with the foe:
To you from failing hands we throw
The torch; be yours to hold it high.
If ye break faith with us who die
We shall not sleep, though poppies grow
In Flanders fields.

Questions for Engagement, Response, and Analysis

1. Who are the speakers in this poem?
2. What are Flanders fields? Describe the contrast between nature here and the activities of the men.
3. What is the theme of this poem? What is the challenge issued in the third verse?

Crafting Arguments

1. Write an essay identifying and interpreting the symbols in this poem.

Claude McKay (1890–1948)

Claude McKay's poetry reflects his childhood in Jamaica and his adult life in America. His work is associated with the Harlem Renaissance, but he was often in conflict with the writers of that movement because of his political views. During the course of his life, McKay wrote lyrical poems, dialect poems, and sonnets.

IF WE MUST DIE   (1922)

If we must die, let it not be like hogs
Hunted and penned in an inglorious spot,
While round us bark the mad and hungry dogs,
Making their mock at our accursed lot.
5   If we must die, O let us nobly die,

So that our precious blood may not be shed
In vain; then even the monsters we defy
Shall be constrained to honor us though dead!
O kinsmen! we must meet the common foe!
10   Though far outnumbered let us show us brave,
And for their thousand blows deal one deathblow!
What though before us lies the open grave?
Like men we'll face the murderous, cowardly pack,
Pressed to the wall, dying, but fighting back!

Questions for Engagement, Response, and Analysis

1. Whom does McKay refer to as "we" in the poem?
2. McKay has negative words for those he wants to oppose: "mad and hungry dogs," "the monsters," and "murderous, cowardly pack." What is the effect of this loaded language?
3. What is the theme of this poem?

Crafting Arguments

1. Martin Luther King Jr. preached nonviolence; however, Claude McKay, writing a generation earlier, preached violence. Using the poem as the basis for discussion, comment on McKay's justification for not backing down from retaliation or violence.
2. Write an essay examining McKay's use of loaded language and the sonnet form to create tone and emphasize the theme in this poem.

Wilfred Owen (1893–1918)

Wilfred Owen is recognized as one of the greatest English war poets. He joined the British Army in 1915, fought as an officer in World War I, and was killed in that war on November 4, 1918, just seven days before it ended. Most of Owen's poems, which powerfully evoke the terror and inhumanity of war, were not published until after his death.

DULCE ET DECORUM EST   (1920)

Bent double, like old beggars under sacks,
Knock-kneed, coughing like hags, we cursed through sludge,
Till on the haunting flares we turned our backs
And towards our distant rest began to trudge.
5   Men marched asleep. Many had lost their boots
But limped on, blood-shod. All went lame; all blind;
Drunk with fatigue; deaf even to the hoots
Of tired, outstripped Five-Nines that dropped behind.
Gas! GAS! Quick, boys!—An ecstasy of fumbling,

10   Fitting the clumsy helmets just in time;
     But someone still was yelling out and stumbling
     And flound'ring like a man in fire or lime . . .
     Dim, through the misty panes and thick green light,
     As under a green sea, I saw him drowning.

15   In all my dreams, before my helpless sight,
     He plunges at me, guttering, choking, drowning.

     If in some smothering dreams you too could pace
     Behind the wagon that we flung him in,
     And watch the white eyes writhing in his face,
20   His hanging face, like a devil's sick of sin;
     If you could hear, at every jolt, the blood
     Come gargling from the froth-corrupted lungs,
     Obscene as cancer, bitter as the cud
     Of vile, incurable sores on innocent tongues,—
25   My friend, you would not tell with such high zest
     To children ardent for some desperate glory,
     The old Lie: *Dulce et decorum est*
     Pro patria mori.

Questions for Engagement, Response, and Analysis

1. What is the tone of this poem?
2. This poem's last sentence, from Horace, *Odes*, III, ii, 13, means "It is sweet and proper to die for one's country." Compare the realistic portrayal of war with the patriotic sentiments in the last few lines of the poem.

Crafting Arguments

1. Write a thorough analysis of this poem, examining how its tone changes from stanza to stanza and how imagery, sound, diction, and syntax develop tone.

e. e. cummings (1894–1962)

[E]dward [E]stlin [C]ummings spent his early life in Cambridge, Massachusetts. During World War I, he spent several months in a French concentration camp as a political prisoner, an experience he recalls in his first book, The Enormous Room *(1922). Best known for his poetry, which is highly experimental in typography and punctuation, cummings published twelve books of poems, including* Tulips and Chimneys *(1923),* 50 Poems *(1940), and* 95 Poems *(1958). His* Poems 1923–1954 *earned a special citation from the National Book Awards.*

BUFFALO BILL'S DEFUNCT   (1923)

Buffalo Bill's
defunct
            who used to
            ride a watersmooth-silver
5   stallion
and break onetwothreefourfive pigeonsjustlikethat
                                                      Jesus
he was a handsome man
                        and what i want to know is
10   how do you like your blueeyed boy
Mister Death

Questions for Engagement, Response, and Analysis

1. What is the effect of cummings' using the word *defunct* instead of *dead?*
2. To whom is the poem addressed? In your opinion, why would cummings choose Buffalo Bill as the subject of his poem?
3. Why are the words run together in line 6?

Crafting Arguments

1. In an essay, analyze cummings' use of form and wording to create tone.

Randall Jarrell (1914–1965)

Randall Jarrell was an American poet and critic. While some of his poems like the following one present a bleak, almost tragic vision, others present an innocent, almost childlike one. Early war poems such as "The Death of the Ball Turret Gunner" arose out of Jarrell's brief service as a pilot in World War II. Jarrell failed as a pilot, partially because he was bored by having to stay in formation and fly at one unvarying speed.

THE DEATH OF THE BALL TURRET GUNNER   (1945)

From my mother's sleep I fell into the State,
And I hunched in its belly till my wet fur froze.
Six miles from earth, loosed from its dream of life,
I woke to black flak and the nightmare fighters.
5   When I died they washed me out of the turret with a hose.

Questions for Engagement, Response, and Analysis

1. Why does Jarrell use pronouns without antecedents—I, me, they—instead of real names?

2. What is the tone of this poem? How does Jarrell's choice of words and images create this tone?

3. What do the references to "sleep," "dream," and "nightmare" suggest about the speaker's consciousness?

Crafting Arguments

1. In an essay, state what you believe to be the theme and point out the methods by which Jarrell conveys such a powerful theme.

Dylan Thomas (1914–1953)

Dylan Thomas was a Welsh poet known for his extraordinary reading voice. His most famous poems, exuberant and rich in sound and imagery, are nevertheless constructed with painstaking care, as the deceptively simple villanelle "Do Not Go Gentle into That Good Night" illustrates.

DO NOT GO GENTLE INTO THAT GOOD NIGHT (1945)

Do not go gentle into that good night,
Old age should burn and rave at close of day;
Rage, rage against the dying of the light.

Though wise men at their end know dark is right,
5   Because their words had forked no lightning they
Do not go gentle into that good night.

Good men, the last wave by, crying how bright
Their frail deeds might have danced in a green bay,
Rage, rage against the dying of the light.

10   Wild men who caught and sang the sun in flight,
And learn, too late, they grieved it on its way,
Do not go gentle into that good night.

Grave men, near death, who see with blinding sight
Blind eyes could blaze like meteors and be gay,
15   Rage, rage against the dying of the light.

And you, my father, there on the sad height,
Curse, bless, me now with your fierce tears, I pray.
Do not go gentle into that good night.
Rage, rage against the dying of the light.

Questions for Engagement, Response, and Analysis

1. Each of the middle stanzas describes a different kind of man facing death. Analyze these stanzas and interpret the metaphors in each.

2. What is the theme of this poem?

3. What does the speaker mean when he asks his father to "curse, bless" him?

Crafting Arguments

1. This poem is a *villanelle*, a form that is extremely difficult and rare in English poetry because of its patterns of repetition and rigidly patterned rhyme scheme. A villanelle is a nineteen-line poem made up of five tercets and one quatrain and rhyming *aba, aba, aba, aba, aba, abaa*. The first line is repeated in lines 6, 12, and 18; the third line is repeated in lines 9, 15, and 19. In an essay, analyze the way that Thomas uses this extremely rigid form to create the tone and reinforce the theme.

Billy Collins (b. 1941)

Award-winning poet and distinguished teacher Billy Collins was born in New York. He received a Ph.D. from the University of California, Riverside in 1971. Among his books of poetry are The Apple That Astonished Paris *(1988);* Questions about Angels *(1991), which was selected for the* Edward Hirsch National Poetry Series; The Art of Drowning *(1995);* Picnic, Lightning *(1998);* Sailing Around the Room: New and Selected Poems *(2001);* Nine Horses *(2002), and* The Trouble with Poetry and Other Poems *(2005). Collins was appointed Poet Laureate of the United States for 2001–2003 and named Poet Laureate of the state of New York during 2004–2006. He presently teaches at Herbert H. Lehman College of the City University of New York.*

FORGETFULNESS   (1991)

The name of the author is the first to go
followed obediently by the title, the plot,
the heartbreaking conclusion, the entire novel
which suddenly becomes one you have never read, never
even heard of,

5   as if, one by one, the memories you used to harbor
decided to retire to the southern hemisphere of the brain,
to a little fishing village where there are no phones.

Long ago you kissed the names of the nine Muses goodbye
and watched the quadratic equation pack its bag,
10   and even now as you memorize the order of the planets,

something else is slipping away, a state flower perhaps,
the address of an uncle, the capital of Paraguay.

Whatever it is you are struggling to remember
it is not poised on the tip of your tongue,
15   not even lurking in some obscure corner of your spleen.
It has floated away down a dark mythological river
whose name begins with an *L* as far as you can recall,
well on your own way to oblivion where you will join those
who have even forgotten how to swim and how to ride a bicycle.

20   No wonder you rise in the middle of the night
to look up the date of a famous battle in a book on war.
No wonder the moon in the window seems to have drifted
out of a love poem that you used to know by heart.

Questions for Engagement, Response, and Analysis

1. To whom does "you" refer in Collins' poem?
2. What kinds of things has the speaker forgotten?
3. Compare Collins' comments about forgetfulness with Mary's comment in Frost's poem "Death of the Hired Man": "I know just how it feels to think of the right thing to say too late."

Crafting Arguments

1. Write an essay showing how Collins uses devices such as **puns**, **metaphors**, and **allusions** to create humor in the poem.

Sharon Olds (b. 1942)

Sharon Olds, a San Francisco–born poet, was educated at Stanford and Columbia universities. Among her many awards is a National Book Critics Circle Award for poetry. Her first book of poems, Satan Says, *was published in 1980. Later publications include* The Dead and the Living *(1983);* The Gold Cell *(1987), which includes the following poem;* The Father *(1992);* The Wellspring *(1995);* Blood, Tin, Straw *(1990);* The Unswept Room *(2002); and* Strike Sparks: Selected Poems *(2004). Her poetry, noted for its vivid language and truthful images, has appeared in* The New Yorker, *the* Paris Review, *and* Ploughshares. *Olds was New York state poet from 1998 to 2000. She teaches poetry workshops at New York University.*

ON THE SUBWAY   (1987)

The boy and I face each other.
His feet are huge, in black sneakers
laced with white in a complex pattern like a
set of intentional scars. We are stuck on

5 opposite sides of the car, a couple of
   molecules stuck in a rod of light
   rapidly moving through darkness. He has the
   casual cold look of a mugger,
   alert under hooded lids. He is wearing
10 red, like the inside of the body
   exposed. I am wearing dark fur, the
   whole skin of an animal taken and
   used. I look at his raw face,
   he looks at my fur coat, and I don't
15 know if I am in his power—
   he could take my coat so easily, my
   briefcase, my life—
   or if he is in my power, the way I am
   living off his life, eating the steak
20 he does not eat, as if I am taking
   the food from his mouth. And he is black
   and I am white, and without meaning or
   trying to I must profit from his darkness,
   the way he absorbs the murderous beams of the
25 nation's heart, as black cotton
   absorbs the heat of the sun and holds it. There is
   no way to know how easy this
   white skin makes my life, this
   life he could take so easily and
30 break across his knee like a stick the way his
   own back is being broken, the
   rod of his soul that at birth was dark and
   fluid and rich as the heart of a seedling
   ready to thrust up into any available light.

Questions for Engagement, Response, and Analysis

1. What is the point of view in this poem? How would the poem differ if
   it were written from the boy's point of view?
2. Examine the images of color and light and the images of hurt and pain
   in the poem. How do they contribute to the tone and theme?
3. Does the speaker experience an epiphany in this poem? If so, what is it?

Crafting Arguments

1. Write an essay explaining how the rich similes and metaphors add to
   the visual effect and the depth of meaning.
2. In an essay, explain how the images of hurt, pain, and fear emphasize
   the contrast between the speaker and the stranger while also revealing their similarities.

Ron Rash (b. 1953)

*American poet, short story writer, and novelist Ron Rash belongs to a family whose members have lived for more than two centuries in the Appalachian mountain region. Though his themes are universal, his heritage is an important part of his literature. Rash received degrees from Gardner-Webb College and Clemson University. He is presently Parris Distinguished Professor of Appalachian Studies at Western Carolina University. His works include three books of poetry—*Eureka Mill *(1998),* Among the Believers *(2000), and* Raising the Dead *(2002)—and three short story collections—*The Night the New Jesus Fell to Earth and Other Stories from Cliffside, North Carolina *(1994),* Casualties *(2000), and* Chemistry and Other Stories *(2007). Rash has also written four novels:* One Foot in Eden *(2002),* Saints at the River *(2004),* The World Made Straight *(2006), and* Serena *(2008). The following poem from* Raising the Dead *describes the flooding of Jocassee Valley in South Carolina.*

LAST SERVICE   (2002)

Though cranes and bulldozers came,
yanked free marble and creek stones
like loose teeth, and then shovels
unearthed coffins and Christ's
5 stained glass face no longer paned
windows but like the steeple,
piano, bell, and hymnals
followed that rolling graveyard
over the quick-dying streams,
10 the soon obsolete bridges—
they still congregated there,
wading then crossing in boats
those last Sunday nights, their farms
already lost in the lake,
15 nothing but that brief island
left of their world as they lit
the church with candles and sang
from memory deep as water
old hymns of resurrection
20 before leaving that high ground
where the dead had once risen.

Questions for Engagement, Response, and Analysis

1. Examine the form of the poem, for example the number of syllables in each line and the sound devices, such as alliteration and assonance. Then explain what effect they create in the poem.

2. List the symbols in the poem and give your interpretation of their meaning.

3. Explain the implications of the last line.

4. What is the theme of the poem? How is it conveyed?

Crafting Arguments

1. In an essay, offer your interpretation of the symbols and the metaphorical devices in this poem. Is there a unifying symbol, or do several metaphors convey the image and/or theme of the poem?

Adam Zagajewski (b. 1945)

Zagajewski is a prolific and award-winning writer of poetry, fiction, and essays. Born in Poland and raised in Silesia and Cracow, he graduated from the Jagiellonian University. His early poetry, published in Communique *(1972) and* Meat Shops *(1975), features political and social issues; but later poetry, in* Traveling to Lowe *(1985) and* The Canvas *(1986), deals with the searching of young intellectuals. His novels, such as* Warm and Cold *(1975),* The Thin Line *(1983), and* Absolute Pitch, *published only in German translation, present the spiritual problems of the modern artist. His often autobiographical essays are included in* The Unpresented World *(1974),* Solidarity and Solitude *(1986),* Two Cities *(1991),* In the Beauty of Others *(1998), and* Another Beauty *(2000). Zagajewski is a professor in the creative writing program at the University of Houston.*

TRY TO PRAISE THE MUTILATED WORLD   2002

TRANSLATED FROM THE POLISH BY CLARE CAVANAGH

Try to praise the mutilated world.
Remember June's long days,
and wild strawberries, drops of wine, the dew.
The nettles that methodically overgrow
5   the abandoned homesteads of exiles.
You must praise the mutilated world.
You watched the stylish yachts and ships;
one of them had a long trip ahead of it,
while salty oblivion awaited others.
10 You've seen the refugees heading nowhere,
you've heard the executioners sing joyfully.
You should praise the mutilated world.
Remember the moments when we were together
in a white room and the curtain fluttered.

15 Return in thought to the concert where music flared.
You gathered acorns in the park in autumn
and leaves eddied over the earth's scars.
Praise the mutilated world
and the gray feather a thrush lost,
20 and the gentle light that strays and vanishes
and returns.

Questions for Engagement, Response, and Analysis

1. What evidence does the speaker give that the world is "mutilated"?
2. What is the implication of the last two lines?
3. What is the tone of the poem? What words and images set this tone?

Crafting Arguments

1. Examine the descriptions that Zagajewski includes after each repetition of "praise the mutilated world." Then write an essay illustrating how these images create and reinforce the theme.
2. In an essay, explain what Zagajewski is saying about vulnerability

DRAMA

William Shakespeare (1564–1616)

William Shakespeare is generally regarded as the greatest writer ever to have written in English. Though Shakespeare also produced an often-admired sequence of 154 sonnets and several narrative poems, his extraordinary reputation rests primarily on his plays. Notable for their sheer number and diversity, the thirty-seven plays include thirteen comedies, ten tragedies, ten history plays, and four romances.

Using language that is rich and highly allusive yet conversational and informal, the plays reveal not only a sure sense of dramatic structure and tension but also a love of human diversity. As a member of an acting company that performed both in the outdoor Globe playhouse and in the indoor Blackfriars, Shakespeare was intimately familiar with the theater of his time and with its conventions. Among the most highly regarded of his plays are the comedies As You Like It, All's Well That Ends Well, *and* Twelfth Night; *the history plays* Henry IV Part I *and* Henry IV, Part II; *the tragedies* Hamlet,

Othello, King Lear, *and* Macbeth; *and* The Tempest, *a romance generally thought to have been Shakespeare's last play.* Othello *displays the richness of language, character, and dramatic tension for which Shakespeare is justly celebrated.*

ABOUT TRAGEDY

Shakespeare's Othello *is a tragedy. In its most general literary usage, the term* **tragedy** *refers to a particular kind of play in which a good person through some character flaw destroys himself or herself.*

The most famous definition of tragedy comes from the ancient Greek philosopher Aristotle (384–322 B.C.). In his Poetics, *Aristotle defines tragedy as*

a representation *(mimesis)* of an action *(praxis)* that is serious, complete, and of a certain magnitude . . . presented, not narrated [i.e., a drama, not a story] . . . with incidents arousing pity and fear in such a way as to accomplish a purgation *(katharsis)* of such emotions. (296)

The purpose of tragedy, according to Aristotle, is to make the audience feel "pity and fear" in order somehow to purge or cleanse these emotions. The most important elements of tragedy are plot and character. The plot must present an action that is complete, with a clear beginning and an ending that gives a sense of finality, and must be unified, so that every part contributes to the whole. The best plots feature reversal **(peripeteia),** *a not improbable but unexpected 180-degree change in situation, and recognition* **(anagnorisis),** *the tragic hero's sudden understanding of his or her fate and its implications.* **A tragic hero,** *Aristotle maintains, must be good but flawed, must be aristocratic, must be believable, and must behave consistently.*

Shakespeare, writing for a different audience in a different kind of theater at a different time, produced tragedies that are rich in language and character development but less dramatically unified than Aristotle prescribes. For example, Shakespeare did not hesitate to insert into his tragedies scenes containing the broadest farce, an impropriety of which Aristotle would almost certainly have disapproved. It is a testimony to Shakespeare's dramatic genius that he could include in his tragedies such richly comic scenes without disrupting their dramatic tension. Of all Shakespeare's tragedies, Othello *is the most Aristotelian in its unity. Shakespearean in its puns and plays on words and in the diversity and fullness of such characters as Othello, Iago, Emilia, and Desdemona,* Othello *moves inexorably to its tragic conclusion.*

Work Cited

Aristotle. "The Art of Poetry." From *Aristotle*. Sel. and trans. Philip
Wheelwright. New York: Odyssey, 1951.

OTHELLO, THE MOOR OF VENICE (1604)

The Names of the Actors

OTHELLO:	the Moor
BRABANTIO:	[a senator,] father to Desdemona
CASSIO:	an honorable lieutenant [to Othello]
IAGO:	[Othello's ancient,] a villain
RODERIGO:	a gulled gentleman
DUKE OF VENICE	
SENATORS [OF VENICE]	
MONTANO:	Governor of Cyprus
GENTLEMEN OF CYPRUS	
LODOVICO AND GRATIANO:	[kinsmen to Brabantio,] two noble Venetians
SAILORS	
CLOWN	
DESDEMONA:	[daughter to Brabantio and wife to Othello]
EMILIA:	wife to Iago
BIANCA:	a courtesan [and mistress to Cassio]
A MESSENGER	
A HERALD	
A MUSICIAN	
SERVANTS, ATTENDANTS, OFFICERS, SENATORS, MUSICIANS, GENTLEMEN	

SCENE

Venice; a seaport in Cyprus

1.1

(Enter Roderigo and Iago.)

RODERIGO:

1   Tush, never tell me! I take it much unkindly
　　 That thou, Iago, who has had my purse
3   As if the strings were thine, shouldst know of this.

1.1 Location: Venice. A street.   **1 never tell me** (An expression of incredulity, like "tell me another one.")   **3 this** i.e., Desdemona's elopement

⁴ IAGO: 'Sblood, but you'll not hear me.
        If ever I did dream of such a matter,
        Abhor me.
    RODERIGO:
        Thou toldst me thou didst hold him in thy hate.
    IAGO: Despise me
        If I do not. Three great ones of the city,
        In personal suit to make me his lieutenant,
¹¹   Off-capped to him; and by the faith of man,
        I know my price, I am worth no worse a place.
        But he, as loving his own pride and purposes,
¹⁴   Evades them with a bombast circumstance
¹⁵   Horribly stuffed with epithets of war,
        And, in conclusion,
        Nonsuits my mediators. For, "Certes," says he,
        "I have already chose my officer."
        And what was he?
²⁰   Forsooth, a great arithmetician,
        One Michael Cassio, a Florentine,
²²   A fellow almost damned in a fair wife,
        That never set a squadron in the field
²⁴   Nor the division of a battle knows
²⁵   More than a spinster unless the bookish theoric,
²⁶   Wherein the togaed consuls can propose
        As masterly as he. Mere prattle without practice
        Is all his soldiership. But he, sir, had th' election;
²⁹   And I, of whom his eyes had seen the proof
        At Rhodes, at Cyprus, and on other grounds
³¹   Christened and heathen, must be beleed and calmed
³²   By debitor and creditor. This countercaster,
³³   He, in good time, must his lieutenant be,
³⁴   And I—God bless the mark!—his Moorship's ancient.

---

4 'Sblood by His (Christ's) blood   **11 him** i.e., Othello   **14 bombast circumstance**
wordy evasion. (*Bombast* is cotton padding.)   **15 epithets of war** military expressions
17 Nonsuits rejects the petition of. **Certes** certainly   **20 arithmetician** i.e., a man
whose military knowledge is merely theoretical, based on books of tactics   **22 A [. . .]**
wife (Cassio does not seem to be married, but his counterpart in Shakespeare's source
does have a woman in his house. See also 4.1.131.)   **24 division of a battle** disposition
of a military unit   **25 a spinster** i.e., a housewife, one whose regular occupation is spinning. **theoric** theory   **26 togaed** wearing the toga. **consuls** counselors, senators.
propose discuss   **29 his** i.e., Othello's   **31 Christened** Christian. **beleed and calmed**
left to leeward without wind, becalmed. (A sailing metaphor.)   **32 debitor and creditor** (A name for a system of bookkeeping, here used as a contemptuous nickname for
Cassio.) **countercaster** i.e., bookkeeper, one who tallies with *counters*, or "metal disks."
(Said contemptuously.)   **33 in good time** opportunely, i.e., forsooth   **34 God bless
the mark** (Perhaps originally a formula to ward off evil; here an expression of impatience.) **ancient** standard-bearer, ensign

RODERIGO:

35   By heaven, I rather would have been his hangman.

IAGO:

Why, there's no remedy. 'Tis the curse of service;

37   Preferment goes by letter and affection,

38   And not by old gradation, where each second

Stood heir to th' first. Now, sir, be judge yourself

40   Whether I in any just term am affined

To love the Moor.

RODERIGO: I would not follow him then.

43   IAGO: O sir, content you.

I follow him to serve my turn upon him.

We cannot all be masters, nor all masters

46   Cannot be truly followed. You shall mark

Many a duteous and knee-crooking knave

That, doting on his own obsequious bondage,

Wears out his time, much like his master's ass,

50   For naught but provender, and when he's old, cashiered.

51   Whip me such honest knaves. Others there are

52   Who, trimmed in forms and visages of duty,

Keep yet their hearts attending on themselves,

And, throwing but shows of service on their lords,

55   Do well thrive by them, and when they have lined their coats,

Do themselves homage. These fellows have some soul,

And such a one do I profess myself. For, sir,

It is as sure as you are Roderigo,

59   Were I the Moor I would not be Iago.

In following him, I follow but myself—

Heaven is my judge, not I for love and duty, ·

62   But seeming so for my peculiar end.

For when my outward action doth demonstrate

64   The native act and figure of my heart

65   In compliment extern, 'tis not long after

But I will wear my heart upon my sleeve

67   For daws to peck at. I am not what I am.

---

35 his hangman the executioner of him   37 Preferment promotion. letter and affection personal influence and favoritism   38 old gradation step-by-step seniority, the traditional way   40 term respect. affined bound   43 content you don't you worry about
that   46 truly faithfully   50 cashiered dismissed from service   51 Whip me whip, as
far as I'm concerned   52 trimmed [. . .] duty dressed up in the mere form and show of
dutifulness   55 lined their coats i.e., stuffed their purses   56 Do themselves
homage i.e., attend to self-interest solely   59 Were [. . .] Iago i.e., if I were able to
assume command, I certainly would not choose to remain a subordinate, or, I would
keep a suspicious eye on a flattering subordinate   62 peculiar particular, personal
64 native innate. figure shape, intent   65 compliment extern outward show (con-
forming in this case to the inner workings and intention of the heart)   67 daws small
crowlike birds, proverbially stupid and avaricious. I am not what I am i.e., I am not one
who wears his heart on his sleeve

RODERIGO:

68   What a full fortune does the thick-lips owe
69   If he can carry 't thus!

IAGO: Call up her father.
Rouse him, make after him, poison his delight,
Proclaim him in the streets; incense her kinsmen,

72   And, though he in a fertile climate dwell,
73   Plague him with flies. Though that his joy be joy,
74   Yet throw such chances of vexation on 't
75   As it may lose some color.

RODERIGO: Here is her father's house. I'll call aloud.

IAGO:

77   Do, with like timorous accent and dire yell
78   As when, by night and negligence, the fire
Is spied in populous cities.

RODERIGO:

What ho, Brabantio! Signor Brabantio, ho!

IAGO:

Awake! What ho, Brabantio! Thieves, thieves, thieves!
Look to your house, your daughter, and your bags!

83   Thieves, thieves!

(Brabantio [enters] above [at a window].)

BRABANTIO:

What is the reason of this terrible summons?

85   What is the matter there?

RODERIGO: Signor, is all your family within?

IAGO: Are your doors locked?

BRABANTIO: Why, wherefore ask you this?

IAGO:

89   Zounds, sir, you're robbed. For shame, put on your gown!
Your heart is burst; you have lost half your soul.
Even now, now, very now, an old black ram

92   Is tupping your white ewe. Arise, arise!
93   Awake the snorting citizens with the bell,
94   Or else the devil will make a grandsire of you.
Arise, I say!

---

68 full swelling. **thick-lips** (Elizabethans often applied the term "Moor" to Negroes.)
owe own   **69 carry 't thus** carry this off   **72–73 though [. . .] flies** though he seems
prosperous and happy now, vex him with misery   **73 Though [. . .] be joy** although he
seems fortunate and happy. (Repeats the idea of line 72.)   **74 chances of vexation** vexing changes   **75 As it may** that may cause it to. **some color** some of its fresh gloss
77 timorous frightening   **78 and negligence** i.e., by negligence   **83 s.d. at a window**
(This stage direction, from the Quarto, probably calls for an appearance on the gallery
above and rearstage.)   **85 the matter** your business   **89 Zounds** by His (Christ's)
wounds   **92 tupping** covering, copulating with. (Said of sheep.)   **93 snorting** snoring
94 the devil (The devil was conventionally pictured as black.)

BRABANTIO: what, have you lost your wits?

RODERIGO: Most reverend signor, do you know my voice?

BRABANTIO: Not I. What are you?

RODERIGO: My name is Roderigo.

BRABANTIO: The worser welcome.
    I have charged thee not to haunt about my doors.
    In honest plainness thou hast heard me say
    My daughter is not for thee; and now, in madness,
104 Being full of supper and distempering drafts,
105 Upon malicious bravery dost thou come
106 To start my quiet.

RODERIGO: Sir, sir, sir—

BRABANTIO: But thou must needs be sure
109 My spirits and my place have in their power
    To make this bitter to thee.

RODERIGO: Patience, good sir.

BRABANTIO:
    What tell'st thou me of robbing? This is Venice;
113 My house is not a grange.

RODERIGO: Most grave Brabantio,
115 In simple and pure soul I come to you.

IAGO: Zounds, sir, you are one of those that will not serve God if the
    devil bid you. Because we come to do you service and you think we
118 are ruffians, you'll have your daughter covered with a Barbary
119 horse; you'll have your nephews neigh to you; you'll have coursers
120 for cousins and jennets for germans.

BRABANTIO: What profane wretch art thou?

IAGO: I am one, sir, that comes to tell you your daughter and the Moor
    are now making the beast with two backs.

BRABANTIO: Thou art a villain.

125 IAGO: You are a senator.

BRABANTIO:
126 This thou shalt answer. I know thee, Roderigo.

RODERIGO:
    Sir, I will answer anything. But I beseech you,
128 If't be your pleasure and most wise consent—
    As partly I find it is—that your fair daughter,
130 At this odd-even and dull watch o' the night,

---

104 distempering intoxicating   **105 Upon malicious bravery** with hostile intent to
defy me   **106 start** startle, disrupt   **109 My spirits and my place** my temperament
and my authority of office. **have in** have it in   **113 grange** isolated country house
115 simple sincere   **118 Barbary** from northern Africa (and hence associated with Othello)
119 nephews i.e., grandsons. **coursers** powerful horses   **120 cousins** kinsmen.
jennets small Spanish horses. **germans** near relatives   **125 a senator** (Said with mock
politeness, as though the word itself were an insult.)   **126 answer** be held accountable
for   **128 wise** well-informed   **130 odd-even** between one day and the next, i.e., about
midnight

131 Transported with no worse nor better guard
132 But with a knave of common hire, a gondolier,
To the gross clasps of a lascivious Moor—
134 If this be known to you and your allowance
135 We then have done you bold and saucy wrongs.
136 But if you know not this, my manners tell me
We have your wrong rebuke. Do not believe
138 That, from the sense of all civility,
139 I thus would play and trifle with your reverence.
Your daughter, if you have not given her leave,
I say again, hath made a gross revolt,
142 Tying her duty, beauty, wit, and fortunes
143 In an extravagant and wheeling stranger
144 Of here and everywhere. Straight satisfy yourself.
If she be in her chamber or your house,
Let loose on me the justice of the state
For thus deluding you.
148 BRABANTIO: Strike on the tinder, ho!
Give me a taper! Call up all my people!
150 This accident is not unlike my dream.
Belief of it oppresses me already.
Light, I say, light!   (*Exit* [*above*].)
IAGO: Farewell, for I must leave you.
154 It seems not meet nor wholesome to my place
155 To be producted—as, if I stay, I shall—
Against the Moor. For I do know the state,
157 However this may gall him with some check,
158 Cannot with safety cast him, for he's embarked
159 With such loud reason to the Cyprus wars,
160 Which even now stands in act, that, for their souls,
161 Another of his fathom they have none
162 To lead their business; in which regard,
Though I do hate him as I do hell pains,
164 Yet for necessity of present life
I must show out a flag and sign of love,

---

131 with by   **132 But with a knave** than by a low fellow, a servant   **134 allowance**
permission   **135 saucy** insolent   **138 from** contrary to. **civility** good manners,
decency   **139 your reverence** the respect due to you   **142 wit** intelligence
143 extravagant expatriate, wandering far from home. **wheeling** roving about, vagabond
stranger foreigner   **144 Straight** straightway   **148 tinder** charred linen ignited by a
spark from flint and steel, used to light torches or *tapers* (lines 145, 171)   **150 accident**
occurrence, event   **154 meet** fitting. **place** position (as ensign)   **155 producted** produced (as a witness)   **157 gall** rub; oppress. **check** rebuke   **158 cast** dismiss.
embarked engaged   **159 loud reason** unanimous shout of confirmation (in the Senate)
160 stands in act are going on. **for their souls** to save themselves   **161 fathom** i.e.,
ability, depth of experience   **162 in which regard** out of regard for which   **164 life**
livelihood

Which is indeed but sign. That you shall surely find him,
167   Lead to the Sagittary the raisèd search,
168   And there will I be with him. So farewell. (*Exit*)

(*Enter [below] Brabantio [in his nightgown] with servants and torches.*)

BRABANTIO:
It is too true an evil. Gone she is;
170   And what's to come of my despisèd time
Is naught but bitterness. Now, Roderigo,
Where didst thou see her?—O unhappy girl!—
With the Moor, sayst thou?—Who would be a father!—
How didst thou know 'twas she?—O, she deceives me
Past thought!—What said she to you?—Get more tapers.
Raise all my kindred.—Are they married, think you?
RODERIGO: Truly, I think they are.
BRABANTIO:
O heaven! How got she out? O treason of the blood!
Fathers, from hence trust not your daughters' minds
180   By what you see them act. Is there not charms
181   By which the property of youth and maidhood
182   May be abused? Have you not read, Roderigo,
Of some such thing?
RODERIGO: Yes, sir, I have indeed.
BRABANTIO: Call up my brother.—O, would you had had her!—
Some one way, some another.—Do you know
Where we may apprehend her and the Moor?
RODERIGO:
188   I think I can discover him, if you please
To get good guard and go along with me.
BRABANTIO:
Pray you, lead on. At every house I'll call;
191   I may command at most.—Get weapons, ho!
And raise some special officers of night.-
193   On, good Roderigo. I will deserve your pains. (*Exeunt.*)

1.2

(*Enter Othello, Iago, attendants with torches.*)

IAGO: Though in the trade of war I have slain men,

---

167 Sagittary (An inn or house where Othello and Desdemona are staying, named for its sign of Sagittarius, or Centaur.) **raisèd search** search party roused out of sleep
168 s.d. nightgown dressing gown. (This costuming is specified in the Quarto text.)
170 time i.e., remainder of life   **180 charms** spells   **181 property** special quality, nature   **182 abused** deceived   **188 discover** reveal, uncover   **191 command** demand assistance   **193 deserve** show gratitude for

2   Yet do I hold it very stuff o' the conscience
3   To do no contrived murder. I lack iniquity
      Sometimes to do me service. Nine or ten times
5   I had thought t' have yerked him here under the ribs.
OTHELLO: 'Tis better as it is.
IAGO: Nay, but he prated,
      And spoke such scurvy and provoking terms
      Against your honor
      That, with the little godliness I have,
11   I did full hard forbear him. But, I pray you, sir,
      Are you fast married? Be assured of this,
13   That the magnifico is much beloved,
14   And hath in his effect a voice potential
      As double as the Duke's. He will divorce you,
      Or put upon you what restraint or grievance
      The law, with all his might to enforce it on,
18   Will give him cable.
OTHELLO: Let him do his spite.
20   My services which I have done the seigniory
21   Shall out-tongue his complaints. 'Tis yet to know—
      Which, when I know that boasting is an honor,
      I shall promulgate—I fetch my life and being
24   From men of royal siege, and my demerits
25   May speak unbonneted to as proud a fortune
      As this that I have reached. For know, Iago,
      But that I love the gentle Desdemona,
28   I would not my unhousèd free condition
29   Put into circumscription and confine
30   For the sea's worth. But look, what lights come yond?

(Enter Cassio [and certain officers] with torches.)

IAGO: Those are the raisèd father and his friends.
      You were best go in.
OTHELLO: Not I. I must be found.
34   My parts, my title, and my perfect soul

1.2 Location: Venice. Another street, before Othello's lodgings.   2 very stuff
essence, basic material (continuing the metaphor of *trade* from line 1)   **3 contrived** pre-
meditated   **5 yerked** stabbed. **him** i.e., Roderigo   **11 I [. . .] him** *I* restrained myself with
great difficulty from assaulting him   **13 magnifico** Venetian grandee, i.e., Brabantio   **14 in
his effect** at his command. **potential** powerful   **18 cable** i.e., scope   **20 seigniory** Venetian government   **21 yet to know** not yet widely known   **24 siege** i.e., rank. (Literally, seat
used by a person of distinction.) **demerits** deserts   **25 unbonneted** without removing the
hat, i.e., on equal terms (? Or "with hat off," "in all due modesty.")   **28 unhousèd** unconfined, undomesticated   **29 circumscription and confine** restriction and confinement
30 the sea's worth all the riches at the bottom of the sea. **s.d. officers** (The Quarto text
calls for "Cassio with lights, officers with torches.")   **34 My [. . .] soul** my natural gifts, my
position or reputation, and my unflawed conscience

Shall manifest me rightly. Is it they?

36 IAGO: By Janus, I think no.

OTHELLO: The servants of the Duke? And my lieutenant?
The goodness of the night upon you, friends!
What is the news?

CASSIO: The Duke does greet you, General,
And he requires your haste-post-haste appearance
Even on the instant.

43 OTHELLO: What is the matter, think you?

CASSIO:

44 Something from Cyprus, as I may divine.

45 It is a business of some heat. The galleys

46 Have sent a dozen sequent messengers
This very night at one another's heels,

48 And many of the consuls, raised and met,
Are at the Duke's already. You have been hotly called for;
When, being not at your lodging to be found,

51 The Senate hath sent about three several quests
To search you out.

OTHELLO: 'Tis well I am found by you.
I will but spend a word here in the house
And go with you. (*Exit.*)

56 CASSIO: Ancient, what makes he here?

IAGO:

57 Faith, he tonight hath boarded a land carrack.

58 If it prove lawful prize, he's made forever.

CASSIO: I do not understand.

IAGO: He's married.

CASSIO: To who?

(Enter Othello.)

IAGO:

62 Marry, to—Come,—Captain, will you go?

63 OTHELLO: Have with you.

CASSIO:

64 Here comes another troop to seek for you.

(Enter Brabantio, Roderigo, with officers and torches.)

---

36 Janus Roman two-faced god of beginnings   **43 matter** business   **44 divine** guess
45 heat urgency   **46 sequent** successive   **48 consuls** senators   **51 about** all over the
city. **several** separate   **56 makes** does   **57 boarded** gone aboard and seized as an act
of piracy (with sexual suggestion). **carrack** large merchant ship   **58 prize** booty
62 Marry (An oath, originally "by the Virgin Mary"; here used with wordplay on *married*.)
63 Have with you i.e., let's go   **64 s.d. officers and torches** (The Quarto text calls for
"others with lights and weapons.")

IAGO:

65   It is Brabantio. General, be advised.
      He comes to bad intent.

OTHELLO: Holla! Stand there!

RODERIGO:

      Signor, it is the Moor.

BRABANTIO: Down with him, thief!

(They draw on both sides.)

IAGO:

      You, Roderigo! Come, sir, I am for you.

OTHELLO:

71   Keep up your bright swords, for the dew will rust them.
      Good signor, you shall more command with years.
      Than with your weapons.

BRABANTIO:

      O thou foul thief, where hast thou stowed my daughter?
      Damned as thou art, thou hast enchanted her!

76   For I'll refer me to all things of sense,
      If she in chains of magic were not bound
      Whether a maid so tender, fair, and happy,
      So opposite to marriage that she shunned
      The wealthy curlèd darlings of our nation,
      Would ever have, t' incur a general mock,

82   Run from her guardage to the sooty bosom
      Of such a thing as thou—to fear, not to delight.

84   Judge me the world if 'tis not gross in sense
      That thou hast practiced on her with foul charms,

86   Abused her delicate youth with drugs or minerals

87   That weakens motion. I'll have 't disputed on;
      'Tis probable and palpable to thinking.

89   I therefore apprehend and do attach thee
      For an abuser of the world, a practicer

91   Of arts inhibited and out of warrant.—
      Lay hold upon him! If he do resist,
      Subdue him at his peril.

OTHELLO: Hold your hands,

96   Both you of my inclining and the rest.
      Were it my cue to fight, I should have known it
      Without a prompter.—Whither will you that I go

---

65 be advised be on your guard   **71 Keep up** keep in the sheath   **76 refer me** submit my case. **things of sense** common sense understandings, or, creatures possessing common sense   **82 her guardage** my guardianship of her   **84 gross in sense** obvious **86 minerals** i.e., poisons   **87 weakens motion** impair the vital faculties. **disputed on** argued in court by professional counsel, debated by experts   **89 attach** arrest   **91 arts inhibited** prohibited arts, black magic   **95 inclining** following, party

To answer this your charge?
BRABANTIO: To prison, till fit time
100   Of law and course of direct session
Call thee to answer.
OTHELLO: What if I do obey?
How may the Duke be therewith satisfied,
Whose messengers are here about my side
Upon some present business of the state
To bring me to him?
OFFICER: 'Tis true, most worthy signor.
The Duke's in council, and your noble self,
I am sure, is sent for.
BRABANTIO: How? The Duke in council?
111   In this time of the night? Bring him away.
112   Mine's not an idle cause. The Duke himself,
Or any of my brothers of the state,
Cannot but feel this wrong as 'twere their own;
For if such actions may have passage free,
Bondslaves and pagans shall our statesmen be. (*Exeunt.*)

1.3

(*Enter Duke [and] Senators [and sit at a table, with lights], and Officers.*)

[*The Duke and Senators are reading dispatches.*]

DUKE:
1   There is no composition in these news
That gives them credit.
3   FIRST SENATOR: Indeed, they are disproportioned.
My letters say a hundred and seven galleys.
DUKE:
And mine, a hundred forty.
SECOND SENATOR: And mine, two hundred.
7   But though they jump not on a just account—
8   As in these cases, where the aim reports
'Tis oft with difference—yet do they all confirm
A Turkish fleet, and bearing up to Cyprus.
DUKE:
Nay, it is possible enough to judgment.

---

100 course of direct session regular or specially convened legal proceedings
111 away right along   **112 idle** trifling   **115 have passage free** are allowed to go
unchecked   **1.3 Location: Venice. A council chamber. s.d. Enter [. . .] Officers**
(The Quarto text calls for the Duke and senators to "sit at a table with lights and attendants.")   **1 composition** consistency   **3 disproportioned** inconsistent   **7 jump**
agree. **just** exact   **8 the aim** conjecture

12   I do not so secure me in the error
   But the main article I do approve
In fearful sense.
SAILOR (*within*): What ho, what ho, what ho!

 (Enter Sailor.)

OFFICER: A messenger from the galleys.
DUKE: Now, what's the business?
SAILOR:

18   The Turkish preparation makes for Rhodes.
So was I bid report here to the state
By Signor Angelo.
DUKE:

21   How say you by this change?
FIRST SENATOR: This cannot be

23   By no assay of reason. 'Tis a pageant

24   To keep us in false gaze. When we consider
Th' importancy of Cyprus to the Turk,
And let ourselves again but understand
That, as it more concerns the Turk than Rhodes,

28   So may he with more facile question bear it,

29   For that it stands not in such warlike brace,

30   But altogether lacks th' abilities

31   That Rhodes is dressed in—if we make thought of this,

32   We must not think the Turk is so unskillful

33   To leave the latest which concerns him first,
Neglecting an attempt of ease and gain

35   To wake and wage a danger profitless,
DUKE:

Nay, in all confidence, he's not for Rhodes.
OFFICER: Here is more news.

 (Enter a Messenger.)

MESSENGER: The Ottomites, reverend and gracious,
Steering with due course toward the isle of Rhodes,

40   Have there injointed them with an after fleet.
FIRST SENATOR:

Ay, so I thought. How many, as you guess?

12–13 I do not [. . .] approve *I* do not take such (false) comfort in the discrepancies
that *I* fail to perceive the main point, i.e., that the Turkish fleet is threatening **18 preparation** fleet prepared for battle **21 by** about **23 assay** test. **pageant** mere show
24 in false gaze looking the wrong way **28 So may [. . .] it** so also he (the Turk) can
more easily capture it (Cyprus) **29 For that** since. **brace** state of defense **30 abilities** means of self-defense **31 dressed in** equipped with **32 unskillful** deficient in
judgment **33 latest** last **35 wake** stir up. **wage** risk **40 injointed them** joined
themselves. **after** second, following

MESSENGER:

42   Of thirty sail; and now they do restem
43   Their backward course, bearing with frank appearance
        Their purposes toward Cyprus. Signor Montano,
45   Your trusty and most valiant servitor,
46   With his free duty recommends you thus,
        And prays you to believe him.

DUKE: 'Tis certain then for Cyprus.
        Marcus Luccicos, is not he in town?

FIRST SENATOR: He's now in Florence.

DUKE:
        Write from us to him, post-post-haste. Dispatch.

FIRST SENATOR: Here comes Brabantio and the valiant Moor.

(Enter Brabantio, Othello, Cassio, Iago, Roderigo, and officers.)

DUKE:

53   Valiant Othello, we must straight employ you
54   Against the general enemy Ottoman.
55   *(To Brabantio.)* I did not see you; welcome, gentle signor.
        We lacked your counsel and your help tonight.

BRABANTIO:
        So did I yours. Good Your Grace, pardon me;
58   Neither my place nor aught I heard of business
        Hath raised me from my bed, nor doth the general care
60   Take hold on me, for my particular grief
61   Is of so floodgate and o'erbearing nature
62   That it engluts and swallows other sorrows
63   And it is still itself.

DUKE: Why, what's the matter?

BRABANTIO: My daughter! O, my daughter!

DUKE AND SENATORS: Dead?

BRABANTIO: Ay, to me.

68   She is abused, stol'n from me, and corrupted
        By spells and medicines bought of mountebanks;
        For nature so preposterously to err,
71   Being not deficient, blind, or lame of sense,
72   Sans witchcraft could not.

42–43 restem [. . .] course retrace their original course   **43 frank appearance** undisguised intent   **45 servitor** officer under your command   **46 free duty** freely given and loyal service. **recommends** commends himself and reports to   **53 straight** straightway   **54 general enemy** universal enemy to all Christendom   **55 gentle** noble   **58 place** official position   **60 particular** personal   **61 floodgate** i.e., overwhelming (as when floodgates are opened)   **62 engluts** engulfs   **63 is still itself** remains undiminished   **68 abused** deceived   **71 deficient** defective. **lame of sense** deficient in sensory perception   **72 Sans** without

DUKE:
> Whoe'er he be that in this foul proceeding
> Hath thus beguiled your daughter of herself,
> And you of her, the bloody book of law
> You shall yourself read in the bitter letter
77   After your own sense—yea, though our proper son
78   Stood in your action.

BRABANTIO: Humbly I thank Your Grace.
> Here is the man, this Moor, whom now it seems
> Your special mandate for the state affairs
> Hath hither brought.

ALL: We are very sorry for 't.

DUKE (*to Othello*): What, in your own part, can you say to this?

BRABANTIO: Nothing, but this is so.

OTHELLO:
> Most potent, grave, and reverend signors,
87   My very noble and approved good masters:
> That I have ta'en away this old man's daughter,
> It is most true; true, I have married her.
90   The very head and front of my offending
91   Hath this extent, no more. Rude am I in my speech,
> And little blessed with the soft phrase of peace;
93   For since these arms of mine had seven years' pith,
94   Till now some nine moons wasted, they have used
95   Their dearest action in the tented field;
> And little of this great world can I speak
> More than pertains to feats of broils and battle,
> And therefore little shall I grace my cause
> In speaking for myself. Yet, by your gracious patience,
100   I will a round unvarnished tale deliver
> Of my whole course of love—what drugs, what charms,
> What conjuration, and what mighty magic,
103   For such proceeding I am charged withal,
> I won his daughter.

BRABANTIO: A maiden never bold;
106   Of spirit so still and quiet that her motion
> Blushed at herself; and she, in spite of nature,
108   Of years, of country, credit, everything,

---

77 After [. . .] sense according to your own interpretation. **our proper** my own
78 Stood [. . .] action were under your accusation   **87 approved** proved, esteemed
90 head and front height and breadth, entire extent   **91 Rude** unpolished   **93 since
[. . .] pith** i.e., since I was seven. **pith** strength, vigor   **94 Till [. . .] wasted** until some
nine months ago (since when Othello has evidently not been on active duty, but in
Venice)   **95 dearest** most valuable   **100 round** plain   **103 withal** with
106–107 her [. . .] herself i.e., she blushed easily at herself. (*Motion* can suggest the
impulse of the soul or of the emotions, or physical movement.)   **108 years** i.e., difference in age. **credit** virtuous reputation

To fall in love with what she feared to look on!
It is a judgment maimed and most imperfect
111 That will confess perfection so could err
Against all rules of nature, and must be driven
113 To find out practices of cunning hell
114 Why this should be. I therefore vouch again
115 That with some mixtures powerful o'er the blood,
116 Or with some dram conjured to this effect,
He wrought upon her.

DUKE: To vouch this is no proof,
119 Without more wider and more overt test
120 Than these thin habits and poor likelihoods
121 Of modern seeming do prefer against him.

FIRST SENATOR: But Othello, speak.
123 Did you by indirect and forcèd courses
Subdue and poison this young maid's affections?
125 Or came it by request and such fair question
As soul to soul affordeth?

OTHELLO: I do beseech you,
Send for the lady to the Sagittary
And let her speak of me before her father.
If you do find me foul in her report,
The trust, the office I do hold of you
Not only take away, but let your sentence
Even fall upon my life.

DUKE: Fetch Desdemona hither.

OTHELLO:
Ancient, conduct them. You best know the place.

(Exeunt Iago and attendants.)

And, till she come, as truly as to heaven
137 I do confess the vices of my blood,
138 So justly to your grave ears I'll present
How I did thrive in this fair lady's love,
And she in mine.

DUKE: Say it, Othello.

OTHELLO:
Her father loved me, oft invited me,
143 Still questioned me the story of my life
From year to year—the battles, sieges, fortunes

---

111 **confess** concede (that)   113 **practices** plots   114 **vouch** assert   115 **blood** passions   116 **dram [. . .] effect** dose made by magical spells to have this effect   119 **more wider** fuller. **test** testimony   120 **habits** garments, i.e., appearances. **poor likelihoods** weak inferences   121 **modern seeming** commonplace assumption. **prefer** bring forth   123 **forcèd courses** means used against her will   125 **question** conversation   137 **blood** passions, human nature   138 **justly** truthfully, accurately   143 **Still** continually

That I have passed.
I ran it through, even from my boyish days
To th' very moment that he bade me tell it,
Wherein I spoke of most disastrous chances,
149 Of moving accidents by flood and field,
150 Of hairbreadth scapes i' th' imminent deadly breach,
Of being taken by the insolent foe
And sold to slavery, of my redemption thence,
153 And portance in my travels' history,
154 Wherein of antres vast and deserts idle,
155 Rough quarries, rocks, and hills whose heads touch heaven,
156 It was my hint to speak—such was my process—
And of the Cannibals that each other eat,
158 The Anthropophagi, and men whose heads
Do grow beneath their shoulders. These things to hear
Would Desdemona seriously incline;
But still the house affairs would draw her thence,
Which ever as she could with haste dispatch
She'd come again, and with a greedy ear
Devour up my discourse. Which I, observing,
165 Took once a pliant hour, and found good means
To draw from her a prayer of earnest heart
167 That I would all my pilgrimage dilate,
168 Whereof by parcels she had something heard,
169 But not intentively. I did consent,
And often did beguile her of her tears,
When I did speak of some distressful stroke
That my youth suffered. My story being done,
She gave me for my pains a world of sighs.
174 She swore, in faith, 'twas strange, 'twas passing strange,
'Twas pitiful, 'twas wondrous pitiful.
She wished she had not heard it, yet she wished
177 That heaven had made her such a man. She thanked me,
And bade me, if I had a friend that loved her,
I should but teach him how to tell my story,
180 And that would woo her. Upon this hint I spake.
She loved me for the dangers I had passed,
And I loved her that she did pity them.

---

149 moving accidents stirring happenings   **150 imminent [. . .] breach** death-
threatening gaps made in a fortification   **153 portance** conduct   **154 antres** caverns.
idle barren, desolate   **155 Rough quarries** rugged rock formations   **156 hint** occasion, opportunity   **158 Anthropophagi** man-eaters. (A term from Pliny's *Natural History*.)   **165 pliant** well-suiting   **167 dilate** relate in detail   **168 by parcels**
piecemeal   **169 intentively** with full attention, continuously   **174 passing** exceedingly   **177 made her** created her to be   **180 hint** opportunity. (Othello does not mean
that she was dropping hints.)

This only is the witchcraft I have used.
Here comes the lady. Let her witness it.

(Enter Desdemona, Iago, [and] attendants.)

DUKE:
I think this tale would win my daughter too.
Good Brabantio,
187 Take up this mangled matter at the best.
Men do their broken weapons rather use
Than their bare hands.

BRABANTIO: I pray you, hear her speak.
If she confess that she was half the wooer,
Destruction on my head if my bad blame
Light on the man!—Come hither, gentle mistress.
Do you perceive in all this noble company
Where most you owe obedience?

DESDEMONA: My noble Father,
I do perceive here a divided duty.
198 To you I am bound for life and education;
199 My life and education both do learn me
200 How to respect you. You are the lord of duty;
I am hitherto your daughter. But here's my husband,
And so much duty as my mother showed
To you, preferring you before her father,
204 So much I challenge that I may profess
Due to the Moor my lord.

BRABANTIO: God be with you! I have done.
Please it Your Grace, on to the state affairs.
208 I had rather to adopt a child than get it.
Come hither, Moor.   *(He joins the hands of Othello and Desdemona.)*
210 I here do give thee that with all my heart
211 Which, but thou hast already, with all my heart
212 I would keep from thee.—For your sake, jewel,
I am glad at soul I have no other child,
214 For thy escape would teach me tyranny,
215 To hang clogs on them.—I have done, my lord.

DUKE:
216 Let me speak like yourself, and lay a sentence
217 Which, as a grece or step, may help these lovers

---

187 Take [. . .] best make the best of a bad bargain   **198 education** upbringing
199 learn teach   **200 of duty** to whom duty is due   **204 challenge** claim   **208 get**
beget   **210 with all my heart** wherein my whole affection has been engaged
211 with all my heart willingly, gladly   **212 For your sake** on your account
214 escape elopement   **215 clogs** (Literally, blocks of wood fastened to the legs of
criminals or convicts to inhibit escape.)   **216 like yourself** i.e., as you would, in your
proper temper. **lay a sentence** apply a maxim   **217 grece** step

Into your favor.

219 When remedies are past, the griefs are ended
220 By seeing the worst, which late on hopes depended.
221 To mourn a mischief that is past and gone
222 Is the next way to draw new mischief on.
223 What cannot be preserved when fortune takes,
224 Patience her injury a mockery makes.
     The robbed that smiles steals something from the thief;
226 He robs himself that spends a bootless grief.

BRABANTIO:

     So let the Turk of Cyprus us beguile,
     We lose it not, so long as we can smile.
229 He bears the sentence well that nothing bears
     But the free comfort which from thence he hears,
     But he bears both the sentence and the sorrow
     That, to pay grief, must of poor patience borrow.
233 These sentences, to sugar or to gall,
     Being strong on both sides, are equivocal.
     But words are words. I never yet did hear
236 That the bruisèd heart was piercèd through the ear.
     I humbly beseech you, proceed to th' affairs of state.

DUKE: The Turk with a most mighty preparation makes for Cyprus.

239 Othello, the fortitude of the place is best known to you; and though we
240 have there a substitute of most allowed sufficiency, yet opinion, a
     sovereign mistress of effects, throws a more safer voice on you. You
242 must therefore be content to slubber the gloss of your new fortunes
243 with this more stubborn and boisterous expedition.

OTHELLO:

     The tyrant custom, most grave senators,
     Hath made the flinty and steel couch of war
246 My thrice-driven bed of down. I do agnize
     A natural and prompt alacrity
248 I find in hardness, and do undertake

---

219 remedies hopes of remedy   **220 which [. . .] depended** which griefs were sustained until recently by hopeful anticipation   **221 mischief** misfortune, injury
222 next nearest   **223 What** whatever   **224 Patience [. . .] makes** patience laughs at the injury inflicted by fortune (and thus eases the pain)   **226 spends a bootless grief** indulges in unavailing grief   **229–232 He bears [...] borrow** a person well bears out your maxim who can enjoy its platitudinous comfort, free of all genuine sorrow, but anyone whose grief bankrupts his poor patience is left with your saying and his sorrow, too. (*Bears the sentence* also plays on the meaning, "receives judicial sentence.")
 233–234 These [. . .] equivocal these fine maxims are equivocal, either sweet or bitter in their application   **236 piercèd [. . .] ear** i.e., surgically lanced and cured by mere words of advice   **239 fortitude** strength   **240 substitute** deputy. **allowed** acknowledged
240–241 opinion [. . .] on you general opinion, an important determiner of affairs, chooses you as the best man   **242 slubber** soil, sully   **243 stubborn** harsh, rough
246 thrice-driven thrice sifted, winnowed. **agnize** know in myself, acknowledge
248 hardness hardship

These present wars against the Ottomites.
250   Most humbly therefore bending to your state,
I crave fit disposition for my wife,
252   Due reference of place and exhibition,
253   With such accommodation and besort
254   As levels with her breeding.
DUKE:
Why, at her father's.
BRABANTIO: I will not have it so.
OTHELLO:
                    Nor I.
DESDEMONA: Nor I. I would not there reside,
To put my father in impatient thoughts
By being in his eye. Most gracious Duke,
261   To my unfolding lend your prosperous ear,
262   And let me find a charter in your voice,
T' assist my simpleness.
DUKE: What would you, Desdemona?
DESDEMONA:
That I did love the Moor to live with him,
266   My downright violence and storm of fortunes
267   May trumpet to the world. My heart's subdued
Even to the very quality of my lord.
I saw Othello's visage in his mind,
270   And to his honors and his valiant parts
Did I my soul and fortunes consecrate.
So that, dear lords, if I be left behind
273   A moth of peace, and he go to the war,
274   The rites for why I love him are bereft me,
And I a heavy interim shall support
By his dear absence. Let me go with him.
276   OTHELLO:
Let her have your voice.
277   Vouch with me, heaven, I therefor beg it not
To please the palate of my appetite,
280   Nor to comply with heat—the young affects

---

250 bending [. . .] state bowing or kneeling to your authority   252 reference [. . .]
exhibition provision of appropriate place to live and allowance of money   253 accommodation suitable provision. besort attendance   254 levels equals, suits. breeding
social position, upbringing   261 unfolding explanation, proposal. prosperous propi-
tious   262 charter privilege, authorization   266 My [. . .] fortunes my plain and total
breach of social custom, taking my future by storm and disrupting my whole life
267–268 My heart's [. . .] lord my heart is brought wholly into accord with Othello's
virtues; I love him for his virtues   270 parts qualities   273 moth i.e., one who consumes merely   274 rites rites of love (with a suggestion, too, of "rights," sharing)
276 dear (1) heartfelt (2) costly   277 voice consent   280 heat sexual passion. young
affects passions of youth, desires

281   In me defunct—and proper satisfaction,
282   But to be free and bounteous to her mind.
283   And heaven defend your good souls that you think
       I will your serious and great business scant
       When she is with me. No, when light-winged toys
286   Of feathered Cupid seel with wanton dullness
287   My speculative and officed instruments,
288   That my disports corrupt and taint my business,
       Let huswives make a skillet of my helm,
       And all indign and base adversities
290   Make head against my estimation!
291   DUKE:
       Be it as you shall privately determine,
       Either for her stay or going. Thè affair cries haste,
       And speed must answer it.
       A SENATOR: You must away tonight.
       DESDEMONA:
       Tonight, my lord?
       DUKE: This night.
       OTHELLO: With all my heart.
       DUKE:
       At nine i' the morning here we'll meet again.
       Othello, leave some officer behind,
       And he shall our commission bring to you,
302   With such things else of quality and respect
303   As doth import you.
       OTHELLO: So please Your Grace, my ancient;
       A man he is of honesty and trust.
       To his conveyance I assign my wife,
       With what else needful Your Good Grace shall think
       To be sent after me.
       DUKE: Let it be so.
       Good night to everyone. (*To Brabantio.*) And, noble signor,
311   If virtue no delighted beauty lack,
       Your son-in-law is far more fair than black.
       FIRST SENATOR:
       Adieu, brave Moor. Use Desdemona well.
       BRABANTIO:
       Look to her, Moor, if thou hast eyes to see.
       She has deceived her father, and may thee.

---

281 proper personal   **282 free** generous   **283 defend** forbid. **think** should think
286 seel i.e., making blind (as in falconry, by sewing up the eyes of the hawk during
training)   **287 speculative [...] instruments** eyes and other faculties used in the
performance of duty   **288 That** so that. **disports** sexual pastimes. **taint** impair
290 indign unworthy, shameful   **291 Make head** raise an army. **estimation** reputation
302 of quality and respect of importance and relevance   **303 import** concern
311 delighted capable of delighting

(Exeunt [Duke, Brabantio, Cassio, Senators and officers].)

OTHELLO:
My life upon her faith! Honest Iago,
My Desdemona must I leave to thee.
I prithee, let thy wife attend on her,
And bring them after in the best advantage.
Come, Desdemona. I have but an hour
Of love, of worldly matters and direction,
To spend with thee. We must obey the time.

([Exit with Desdemona].)

RODERIGO: Iago—
IAGO: What sayst thou, noble heart?
RODERIGO: What will I do, think'st thou?
IAGO: Why, go to bed and sleep.
RODERIGO: I will incontinently drown myself.
IAGO: If thou dost, I shall never love thee after. Why,
thou silly gentleman?
RODERIGO: It is silliness to live when to live is torment;
and then have we a prescription to die when death is
our physician.
IAGO: O villainous! I have looked upon the
world for four times seven years, and, since I could distinguish
betwixt a benefit and an injury, I never found man
that knew how to love himself. Ere I would say I
would drown myself for the love of a guinea hen, I
would change my humanity with a baboon.
RODERIGO: What should I do? I confess it is my shame
to be so fond, but it is not in my virtue to amend it.
IAGO: Virtue? A fig! 'Tis in ourselves that we are thus
or thus.Our bodies are our gardens, to the which our
wills are gardeners; so that if we will plant nettles or
sow lettuce, set hyssop and weed up thyme, supply it
with one gender of herbs or distract it with many,
either to have it sterile with idleness or manured with
industry—why, the power and corrigible authority of
this lies in our wills. If the beam of our lives had not

---

319 in [. . .] advantage at the most favorable opportunity   **321 direction** instructions   **322 the time** the urgency of the present crisis   **327 incontinently** immediately, without self-restraint   **331 prescription** (1) right based on long-established custom (2) doctor's prescription   **333 villainous** i.e., what perfect nonsense   **337 guinea hen** (A slang term for a prostitute.)   **340 fond** infatuated. **virtue** strength, nature   **341 fig** (To give a fig is to thrust the thumb between the first and second fingers in a vulgar and insulting gesture)   **344 hyssop** a herb of the mint family   **345 gender** kind. **distract it with** divide it among   **346 idleness** want of cultivation   **347 corrigible authority** power to correct   **348 beam** balance

349   one scale of reason to poise another of sensuality, the
350   blood and baseness of our natures would conduct us to
       most preposterous conclusions. But we have reason
352   to cool our raging motions, our carnal stings, our unbitted
353   lusts, whereof I take this that you call love to
354   be a sect or scion.

RODERIGO: It cannot be.

IAGO: It is merely a lust of the blood and a permission
       of the will. Come, be a man. Drown thyself? Drown
       cats and blind puppies. I have professed me thy friend,
       and I confess me knit to thy deserving with cables of
360   perdurable toughness. I could never better stead thee
       than now. Put money in thy purse. Follow thou the
362   wars; defeat thy favor with an usurped beard. I say,
       put money in thy purse. It cannot be long that Des-
       demona should continue her love to the Moor—put
       money in thy purse—nor he his to her. It was a vio-
366   lent commencement in her, and thou shalt see an
       answerable sequestration—put but money in thy purse.
368   These Moors are changeable in their wills—fill thy
       purse with money. The food that to him now is as
370   luscious as locusts shall be to him shortly as bitter as
371   coloquintida. She must change for youth; when she is
       sated with his body, she will find the error of her
       choice. She must have change, she must. Therefore
       put money in thy purse. If thou wilt needs damn thy-
375   self, do it a more delicate way than drowning. Make
376   all the money thou canst. If sanctimony and a frail vow
377   betwixt an erring barbarian and a supersubtle Vene-
       tian be not too hard for my wits and all the tribe of
       hell, thou shalt enjoy her. Therefore make money.
380   A pox of drowning thyself! It is clean out of the way.
381   Seek thou rather to be hanged in compassing thy joy
       than to be drowned and go without her.

383   RODERIGO: Wilt thou be fast to my hopes if I depend on the
384   issue?

---

349 poise counterbalance   **350 blood** natural passions   **352 motions** appetites
353 unbitted unbridled, uncontrolled   **354 sect or scion** cutting or offshoot
360 perdurable very durable. **stead** assist   **362 defeat thy favor** disguise your face.
usurped (The suggestion is that Roderigo is not man enough to have a beard of his own.)
366–367 an answerable sequestration a corresponding separation or estrangement
368 wills carnal appetites   **370 locusts** fruit of the carob tree (see Matthew 3:4), or
perhaps honeysuckle   **371 coloquintida** colocynth or bitter apple, a purgative
375 Make raise, collect   **376 sanctimony** sacred ceremony   **377 erring** wandering,
vagabond, unsteady   **380 clean [. . .] way** entirely unsuitable as a course of action
381 compassing encompassing, embracing   **383 fast** true   **384 issue** (successful)
outcome

IAGO: Thou art sure of me. Go, make money. I have
told thee often, and I retell thee again and again, I hate
387   the Moor. My cause is hearted; thine hath no less reason.
388   Let us be conjunctive in our revenge against him.
If thou canst cuckold him, thou dost thyself a pleasure,
me a sport. There are many events in the womb of tim
391   which will get delivered. Traverse, go, provide thy money.
We will have more of this tomorrow. Adieu.
RODERIGO: Where shall we meet i' the morning?
IAGO: At my lodging.
395   RODERIGO: I'll be with thee betimes.   *(He starts to leave.)*
IAGO: Go to, farewell.—Do you hear, Roderigo?
RODERIGO: What say you?
IAGO: No more of drowning, do you hear?
RODERIGO: I am changed.
IAGO: Go to, farewell. Put money enough in your purse.
RODERIGO: I'll sell my land.   *(Exit.)*
IAGO:

Thus do I ever make my fool my purse;
For I mine own gained knowledge should profane
404   If I would time expend with such a snipe
But for my sport and profit. I hate the Moor;
406   And it is thought abroad that twixt my sheets
407   He's done my office. I know not if 't be true;
But I, for mere suspicion in that kind,
409   Will do as if for surety. He holds me well;
The better shall my purpose work on him.
411   Cassio's a proper man. Let me see now:
412   To get his place and to plume up my will
In double knavery—How, how?—Let's see:
414   After some time, to abuse Othello's ear
415   That he is too familiar with his wife.
416   He hath a person and a smooth dispose
To be suspected, framed to make women false.
418   The Moor is of a free and open nature,
That thinks men honest that but seem to be so,
420   And will as tenderly be led by the nose
As asses are.

---

387 hearted fixed in the heart, heartfelt   **388 conjunctive** united   **391 Traverse** (A
military marching term.)   **395 betimes** early   **404 snipe** woodcock, i.e., fool   **406 it
is thought abroad** it is rumored   **407 my office** i.e., my sexual function as husband
409 do [. . .] surety act as if on certain knowledge. **holds me well** regards me favorably   **411 proper** handsome   **412 plume up** put a feather in the cap of, i.e., glorify,
gratify   **414 abuse** deceive   **415 he** i.e., Cassio   **416 dispose** disposition   **418 free**
frank, generous. **open** unsuspicious   **420 tenderly** readily

I have 't. It is engendered. Hell and night
Must bring this monstrous birth to the world's light.

(Exit.)

2.1

(Enter Montano and two Gentlemen.)

MONTANO: What from the cape can you discern at sea?
FIRST GENTLEMAN:
2   Nothing at all. It is a high-wrought flood.
3   I cannot, twixt the heaven and the main,
    Descry a sail.
MONTANO:
    Methinks the wind hath spoke aloud at land;
    A fuller blast ne'er shook our battlements.
7   If it hath ruffianed so upon the sea,
8   What ribs of oak, when mountains melt on them,
9   Can hold the mortise? What shall we hear of this?
SECOND GENTLEMAN:
10   A segregation of the Turkish fleet.
    For do but stand upon the foaming shore,
12   The chidden billow seems to pelt the clouds;
13   The wind-shaked surge, with high and monstrous mane,
14   Seems to cast water on the burning Bear
    And quench the guards of th' ever-fixèd pole.
16   I never did like molestation view
17   On the enchafèd flood.
18 MONTANO: If that the Turkish fleet
19   Be not ensheltered and embayed, they are drowned;
20   It is impossible to bear it out.

(Enter a [Third] Gentleman.)

THIRD GENTLEMAN: News, lads! Our wars are done.
    The desperate tempest hath so banged the Turks

2.1 Location: A seaport in Cyprus. An open place near the quay. **2 high-wrought flood** very agitated sea **3 main** ocean (also at line 42) **7 ruffianed** raged **8 mountains** i.e., of water **9 hold the mortise** hold their joints together. (A mortise is the socket hollowed out in fitting timbers.) **10 segregation** dispersal **12 chidden** i.e., rebuked, repelled (by the shore), and thus shot into the air **13 monstrous mane** (The surf is like the mane of a wild beast.) **14 the burning Bear** i.e., the constellation Ursa Minor or the Little Bear, which includes the polestar (and hence regarded as the *guards of th' ever-fixèd pole* in the next line; sometimes the term *guards* is applied to the two "pointers" of the Big Bear or Dipper, which may be intended here.) **16 like molestation** comparable disturbance **17 enchafèd** angry **18 If that** if **19 embayed** sheltered by a bay **20 bear it out** survive, weather the storm

23   That their designment halts. A noble ship of Venice
24   Hath seen a grievous wreck and sufferance
      On most part of their fleet.

MONTANO: How? Is this true?

THIRD GENTLEMAN: This ship is here put in,

28   A Veronesa; Michael Cassio,
      Lieutenant to the warlike Moor Othello,
      Is come on shore; the Moor himself at sea,
      And is in full commission here for Cyprus.

MONTANO:
      I am glad on 't. 'Tis a worthy governor.

THIRD GENTLEMAN:
      But this same Cassio, though he speak of comfort
34   Touching the Turkish loss, yet he looks sadly
      And prays the Moor be safe, for they were parted
      With foul and violent tempest.

MONTANO: Pray heaven he be,
      For I have served him, and the man commands
39   Like a full soldier. Let's to the seaside, ho!
      As well to see the vessel that's come in
      As to throw out our eyes for brave Othello,
42   Even till we make the main and the' aerial blue
43   An indistinct regard.

THIRD GENTLEMAN: Come, let's do so,
45   For every minute is expectancy
46   Of more arrivance.

(Enter Cassio.)

CASSIO:
      Thanks, you the valiant of this warlike isle,
48   That so approve the Moor! O, let the heavens
      Give him defense against the elements,
      For I have lost him on a dangerous sea.

MONTANO: Is he well shipped?

CASSIO:
      His bark is stoutly timbered, and his pilot
53   Of very expert and approved allowance;
54   Therefore my hopes, not surfeited to death,

---

23 designment design, enterprise. **halts** is lame   **24 wreck** shipwreck. **sufferance** damage, disaster   **28 Veronesa** i.e., fitted out in Verona for Venetian service, or possibly *Verennessa* (the Folio spelling), i.e., *verrinessa*, a cutter (from *verrinare*, "to cut through")   **34 sadly** gravely   **39 full** perfect   **42 the main [. . .] blue** the sea and the sky   **43 An indistinct regard** indistinguishable in our view   **45 is expectancy** gives expectation   **46 arrivance** arrival   **48 approve** admire, honor   **53 approved allowance** tested reputation   **54 surfeited to death** i.e., overextended, worn thin through repeated application or delayed fulfillment

55   Stand in bold cure.
                    (A cry within:) "A sail, a sail, a sail!"
CASSIO:
      What noise?
A GENTLEMAN:
58   The town is empty. On the brow o' the sea
      Stand ranks of people, and they cry "A sail!"
CASSIO:
60   My hopes do shape him for the governor.

                              (A shot within.)

SECOND GENTLEMAN:
61   They do discharge their shot of courtesy;
      Our friends at least.
CASSIO: I pray you, sir, go forth,
      And give us truth who 'tis that is arrived.
SECOND GENTLEMAN: I shall. *(Exit.)*
MONTANO:
      But, good Lieutenant, is your general wived?
CASSIO:
      Most fortunately. He hath achieved a maid
68   That paragons description and wild fame,
69   One that excels the quirks of blazoning pens,
70   And in th' essential vesture of creation
      Does tire the enginer.

      (Enter [Second] Gentleman.)

72   How now? Who has put in?
SECOND GENTLEMAN:
      'Tis one Iago, ancient to the General.
CASSIO:
      He's had most favorable and happy speed.
      Tempests themselves, high seas, and howling winds,
76   The guttered rocks and congregated sands—
77   Traitors ensteeped to clog the guiltless keel—
78   As having sense of beauty, do omit
79   Their mortal natures, letting go safely by
      The divine Desdemona.
MONTANO: What is she?

---

55 in bold cure in strong hopes of fulfillment   **58 brow o' the sea** cliff-edge   **60 My
[. . .] for** I hope it is   **61 discharge [. . .] courtesy** fire a salute in token of respect
and courtesy   **68 paragons** surpasses. **wild fame** extravagant report   **69 quirks** witty
conceits. **blazoning** setting forth as though in heraldic language   **70–71 in [. . .]**
enginer in her real, God-given, beauty, (she) defeats any attempt to praise her. **enginer**
engineer, i.e, poet, one who devises. **s.d. Second Gentleman** (So identified in the
Quarto text here and in lines 58, 61, 68, and 96; the Folio calls him a gentleman.)   **72 put
in** i.e., to harbor   **76 guttered** jagged, trenched   **77 ensteeped** lying under water
78 As as if. **omit** forbear to exercise   **79 mortal** deadly

CASSIO:
>She that I spake of, our great captain's captain,
>Left in the conduct of the bold Iago,
>84 Whose footing here anticipates our thoughts
>85 A sennight's speed. Great Jove, Othello guard,
>And swell his sail with thine own powerful breath,
>87 That he may bless this bay with his tall ship,
>Make love's quick pants in Desdemona's arms,
>Give renewed fire to our extincted spirits,
>And bring all Cyprus comfort!

(Enter Desdemona, Iago, Roderigo, and Emilia.)

>O, behold,
>The riches of the ship is come on shore!
>You men of Cyprus, let her have your knees.

(The gentleman make curtsy to Desdemona.)

>Hail to thee, lady! And the grace of heaven
>Before, behind thee, and on every hand
>Enwheel thee round!
>DESDEMONA: I thank you, valiant Cassio.
>What tidings can you tell me of my lord?
>CASSIO:
>He is not yet arrived, nor know I aught.
>But that he's well and will be shortly here.
>DESDEMONA:
>O, but I fear—How lost you company?
>CASSIO:
>The great contention of the sea and skies
>Parted our fellowship.
>   *(Within)* "A sail, a sail!" *(A shot.)*
>   But hark. A sail!
>SECOND GENTLEMAN:
>They give their greeting to the citadel.
>This likewise is a friend.
>CASSIO: See for the news.

(Exit Second Gentleman.)

>Good Ancient, you are welcome. *(Kissing Emilia.)*
>   Welcome, mistress.
>Let it not gall your patience, good Iago,
>112 That I extend my manners; 'tis my breeding
>That gives me this bold show of courtesy.

---

84 footing landing   **85 sennight's** week's   **87 tall** splendid, gallant   **112 extend** give scope to. **breeding** training in the niceties of etiquette

IAGO:

> Sir, would she give you so much of her lips
> As of her tongue she often bestows on me,
> You would have enough.

117 DESDEMONA: Alas, she has no speech!

IAGO: In faith, too much.

119 I find it still, when I have list to sleep.

> Marry, before your ladyship, I grant,
> She puts her tongue a little in her heart

122 And chides with thinking.

EMILIA: You have little cause to say so.

IAGO:

124 Come on, come on. You are pictures out of doors,

125 Bells in your parlors, wildcats in your kitchens,

126 Saints in your injuries, devils being offended,

127 Players in your huswifery, and huswives in your beds.

DESDEMONA: O, fie upon thee, slanderer!

IAGO:

129 Nay, it is true, or else I am a Turk.

> You rise to play, and go to bed to work.

EMILIA:

> You shall not write my praise.

IAGO: No, let me not.

DESDEMONA:

> What wouldst write of me, if thou shouldst praise me?

IAGO:

> O gentle lady, do not put me to 't,

135 For I am nothing if not critical.

DESDEMONA:

136 Come on, essay.—There's one gone to the harbor?

IAGO: Ay, madam.

DESDEMONA:

> I am not merry, but I do beguile

139 The thing I am by seeming otherwise.

> Come, how wouldst thou praise me?

IAGO:

> I am about it, but indeed my invention

142 Comes from my pate as birdlime does from frieze—

---

117 she has no speech i.e., she's not a chatterbox, as you allege   **119 still** always. **list** desire   **122 with thinking** i.e., in her thoughts only   **124 pictures out of doors** i.e., silent and well-behaved in public   **125 Bells** i.e., jangling, noisy, and brazen. **in your kitchens** i.e., in domestic affairs. (Ladies would not do the cooking.)   **126 Saints** martyrs   **127 Players** idlers, triflers, or deceivers. **huswifery** housekeeping. **huswives** hussies (i.e., women are "busy" in bed, or unduly thrifty in dispensing sexual favors)   **129 A Turk** an infidel, not to be believed   **135 critical** censorious   **136 essay** try   **139 The thing I am** i.e., my anxious self   **142 birdlime** sticky substance used to catch small birds. **frieze** coarse woolen cloth

143   It plucks out brains and all. But my Muse labors,
     And thus she is delivered:
     If she be fair and wise, fairness and wit,
146   The one's for use, the other useth it.

DESDEMONA:
147   Well praised! How if she be black and witty?

IAGO:
     If she be black, and thereto have a wit,
149   She'll find a white that shall her blackness fit.

DESDEMONA:
     Worse and worse.

EMILIA: How if fair and foolish?
     She never yet was foolish that was fair,
153   For even her folly helped her to an heir.

154 DESDEMONA: These are old fond paradoxes to make fools
     laugh i' th' alehouse. What miserable praise hast thou
156   for her that's foul and foolish?

IAGO:
157   There's none so foul and foolish thereunto,
158   But does foul pranks which fair and wise ones do.

DESDEMONA: O heavy ignorance! Thou praisest the worst
     best. But what praise couldst thou bestow on a deserving
     woman indeed, one that, in the authority of her merit,
162   did justly put on the vouch of very malice itself?

IAGO:
     She that was ever fair, and never proud,
     Had tongue at will, and yet was never loud,
165   Never lacked gold and yet went never gay,
166   Fled from her wish, and yet said, "Now I may,"
     She that being angered, her revenge being nigh,
168   Bade her wrong stay and her displeasure fly,
     She that in wisdom never was so frail
170   To change the cod's head for the salmon's tail,
     She that could think and ne'er disclose her mind,
     See suitors following and not look behind,
     She was a wight, if ever such wight were—

DESDEMONA: To do what?

---

143 labors (1) exerts herself (2) prepares to deliver a child (with a following pun on *delivered* in line 144)   **146 The one's [. . .] it** i.e., her cleverness will make use of her beauty   **147 black** dark-complexioned, brunette   **149 a white** a fair person (with wordplay on "wight," a person). **fit** (with sexual suggestion of mating)   **153 folly** (with added meaning of "lechery, wantonness"). **to an heir** i.e., to bear a child   **154 fond** foolish   **156 foul** ugly   **157 thereunto** in addition   **158 foul** sluttish   **162 put [. . .] vouch** compel the approval   **165 gay** extravagantly clothed   **166 Fled [. . .] may** avoided temptation where the choice was hers   **168 Bade [. . .] stay** i.e., resolved to put up with her injury patiently   **170 To [. . .] tail** i.e., to exchange a lackluster husband for a sexy lover (?) (*Cod's head* is slang for "penis," and *tail*, for "pudendum.")

IAGO:
175   To suckle fools and chronicle small beer.
DESDEMONA: O most lame and impotent conclusion! Do
    not learn of him, Emilia, though he be thy husband.
178   How say you, Cassio? Is he not a most profane and
179   liberal counselor?
180   CASSIO: He speaks home, madam. You may relish him more in the sol-
181   dier than in the scholar.

(Cassio and Desdemona stand together, conversing intimately.)

182   IAGO *(aside)*: He takes her by the palm. Ay, well said,
    whisper. With as little a web as this will I ensnare as
    great a fly as Cassio. Ay, smile upon her, do; I will
185   gyve thee in thine own courtship. You say true; 'tis so,
    indeed. If such tricks as these strip you out of your
    lieutenantry, it had been better you had not kissed
    your three fingers so oft, which now again you are
189   most apt to play the sir in. Very good; well kissed! An
    excellent courtesy! 'Tis so, indeed. Yet again your fingers
191   to your lips? Would they were clyster pipes for your
    sake! *(Trumpet within.)* The Moor! I know his trumpet.
CASSIO: 'Tis truly so.
DESDEMONA: Let's meet him and receive him.
CASSIO: Lo, where he comes!

(Enter Othello and attendants.)

OTHELLO:
    O my fair warrior!
DESDEMONA: My dear Othello!
OTHELLO:
    It gives me wonder great as my content
    To see you here before me. O my soul's joy,
    If after every tempest come such calms,
    May the winds blow till they have wakened death,
    And let the laboring bark climb hills of seas
    Olympus-high, and duck again as low
    As hell's from heaven! If it were now to die,
    'Twere now to be most happy, for I fear
    My soul hath her content so absolute

---

175 suckle fools breastfeed babies. **chronicle small beer** i.e., keep petty household accounts, keep track of trivial matters   **178 profane** irreverent, ribald   **179 liberal** licentious, free-spoken   **180 home** right to the target. (A term from fencing.) **relish** appreciate   **181 in** in the character of   **182 well said** well done   **185 gyve** fetter, shackle. **courtship** courtesy, show of courtly manners. **You say true** i.e., that's right, go ahead   **189 the sir** i.e., the fine gentleman   **191 clyster pipes** tubes used for enemas and douches

That not another comfort like to this
208   Succeeds in unknown fate.
DESDEMONA: The heavens forbid
      But that our loves and comforts should increase
      Even as our days do grow!
OTHELLO:
      Amen to that, sweet powers!
      I cannot speak enough of this content.
      It stops me here; it is too much of joy.
      And this, and this, the greatest discords be

      (They kiss.)

215   That e'er our hearts shall make!
IAGO *(aside)*: O, you are well tuned now!
218   But I'll set down the pegs that make this music,
219   As honest as I am.
OTHELLO: Come, let us to the castle.
      News, friends! Our wars are done, the Turks are drowned.
      How does my old acquaintance of this isle?—
223   Honey, you shall be well desired in Cyprus;
      I have found great love amongst them. O my sweet,
225   I prattle out of fashion, and I dote
      In mine own comforts.—I prithee, good Iago,
227   Go to the bay and disembark my coffers.
228   Bring thou the master to the citadel;
      He is a good one, and his worthiness
230   Does challenge much respect.—Come, Desdemona.—
      Once more, well met at Cyprus!

      (Exeunt Othello and Desdemona [and all but Iago and Roderigo].)

IAGO *(to an attendant)*: Do thou meet me presently at
      the harbor. *(To Roderigo.)* Come hither. If thou be'st
234   valiant—as, they say, base men being in love have
      then a nobility in their natures more than is native to
236   them—list me. The Lieutenant tonight watches on
237   the court of guard. First, I must tell thee this:
      Desdemona is directly in love with him.
RODERIGO: With him? Why, 'tis not possible.
240   IAGO: Lay thy finger thus, and let thy soul be instructed.

---

208 Succeeds [. . .] fate i.e., can follow in the unknown future   **215 s.d. They kiss**
(The direction is from the Quarto.)   **218 set down** loosen (and hence untune the instrument)   **219 As [. . .] I am** for all my supposed honesty   **223 desired** welcomed
225 out of fashion irrelevantly, incoherently (?)   **227 coffers** chests, baggage
228 master ship's captain   **230 challenge** lay claim to, deserve   **234 base men** even
lowly born men   **236 list** listen to   **237 court of guard** guardhouse. (Cassio is in
charge of the watch.)   **240 thus** i.e., on your lips

Mark me with what violence she first loved the Moor,
242   but for bragging and telling her fantastical lies. To love
him still for prating? Let not thy discreet heart think it.
Her eye must be fed; and what delight shall she have
to look on the devil? When the blood is made dull with
246   the act of sport, there should be, again to inflame it
247   and to give satiety a fresh appetite, loveliness in favor,
248   sympathy in years, manners, and beauties all which
the Moor is defective in. Now, for want of these
250   required conveniences, her delicate tenderness will
251   find itself abused, begin to heave the gorge, disrelish
252   and abhor the Moor. Very nature will instruct her in it
and compel her to some second choice. Now, sir, this
254   granted—as it is a most pregnant and unforced
255   position—who stands so eminent in the degree of this
256   fortune as Cassio does? A knave very voluble, no
257   further conscionable than in putting on the mere form
258   of civil and humane seeming for the better compass-
259   ing of his salt and most hidden loose affection. Why,
260   none, why, none. A slipper and subtle knave, a finder
261   out of occasions, that has an eye can stamp and
262   counterfeit advantages, though true advantage never
present itself; a devilish knave. Besides, the knave is
handsome, young, and hath all those requisites in him
265   that folly and green minds look after. A pestilent
266   complete knave, and the woman hath found him already.
RODERIGO: I cannot believe that in her. She's full of
268   most blessed condition.
269   IAGO: Blessed fig's end! The wine she drinks is made of
grapes. If she had been blessed, she would never have
271   loved the Moor. Blessed pudding! Didst thou not see
her paddle with the palm of his hand? Didst not mark that?
RODERIGO: Yes, that I did; but that was but courtesy.
274   IAGO: Lechery, by this hand. An index, an obscure prologue to the history of lust and foul thoughts. They
met so near with their lips that their breaths embraced

---

242 but only   **246 the act of sport** sex   **247 favor** appearance   **248 sympathy**
correspondence, similarity   **250 required conveniences** things conducive to sexual
compatibility   **251 abused** cheated, revolted. **heave the gorge** experience nausea
252 Very nature her very instincts   **254 pregnant** evident, cogent   **255 in [. . .] of** as
next in line for   **256 voluble** facile, glib   **257 conscionable** conscientious, conscience-
bound   **258 humane** polite, courteous   **259 salt** licentious. **affection** passion
260 slipper slippery   **261 an eye can stamp** an eye that can coin, create   **262 advantages**
favorable opportunities   **265 folly** wantonness. **green** immature   **266 found him** sized
him up, perceived his intent   **268 condition** disposition   **269 fig's end** (See 1.3.341 for
the vulgar gesture of the fig.)   **271 pudding** sausage   **274 index** table of contents.
obscure (i.e., the *lust and foul thoughts*, line 275, are secret, hidden from view)

together. Villainous thoughts, Roderigo! When these
278   mutualities so marshal the way, hard at hand comes
279   the master and main exercise, th' incorporate conclusion. Pish! But, sir, be you ruled by me. I have brought
281   you from Venice. Watch you tonight; for the command,
I'll lay't upon you. Cassio knows you not. I'll not
be far from you. Do you find some occasion to
284   anger Cassio, either by speaking too loud, or tainting
his discipline, or from what other course you please,
286   which the time shall more favorably minister.

RODERIGO: Well.

288   IAGO: Sir, he's rash and very sudden in choler, and haply
may strike at you. Provoke him that he may, for even
290   out of that will I cause these of Cyprus to mutiny,
291   whose qualification shall come into no true taste again
but by the displanting of Cassio. So shall you have a
shorter journey to your desires by the means I shall
294   then have to prefer them, and the impediment most
profitably removed, without the which there were no
expectation of our prosperity.

RODERIGO: I will do this, if you can bring it to any opportunity.

298   IAGO: I warrant thee. Meet me by and by at the citadel.
I must fetch his necessaries ashore. Farewell.

RODERIGO: Adieu. (*Exit.*)

IAGO: That Cassio loves her, I do well believe 't;
302   That she loves him, 'tis apt and of great credit.
The Moor, howbeit that I endure him not,
Is of a constant, loving, noble nature,
And I dare think he'll prove to Desdemona
A most dear husband. Now, I do love her too,
Not out of absolute lust—though peradventure
308   I stand accountant for as great a sin—
309   But partly led to diet my revenge
For that I do suspect the lusty Moor
Hath leaped into my seat, the thought whereof
Doth, like a poisonous mineral, gnaw my innards;
And nothing can or shall content my soul
Till I am evened with him, wife for wife,
Or failing so, yet that I put the Moor

---

278 mutualities exchanges, intimacies. **hard at hand** closely following   **279 incorporate** carnal   **281 Watch you** stand watch   **281–282 for the command [. . .] you** I'll arrange for you to be appointed, given orders   **284 tainting** disparaging   **286 minister** provide   **288 choler** wrath. **haply** perhaps   **290 mutiny** riot   **291 qualification** appeasement. **true taste** i.e., acceptable state   **294 prefer** advance   **298 warrant** assure. **by and by** immediately   **302 apt** probable. **credit** credibility   **308 accountant** accountable   **309 diet** feed

At least into a jealousy so strong
That judgment cannot cure. Which thing to do,
318   If this poor trash of Venice, whom I trace
319   For his quick hunting, stand the putting on,
320   I'll have our Michael Cassio on the hip,
321   Abuse him to the Moor in the rank garb—
322   For I fear Cassio with my nightcap too—
Make the Moor thank me, love me, and reward me
For making him egregiously an ass
326   And practicing upon his peace and quiet
Even to madness. 'Tis here, but yet confused.
Knavery's plain face is never seen till used. *(Exit.)*

2.2

(Enter Othello's Herald with a proclamation.)

HERALD: It is Othello's pleasure, our noble and valiant
general, that, upon certain tidings now arrived, im-
3   porting the mere perdition of the Turkish fleet, every
4   man put himself into triumph: some to dance, some to
make bonfires, each man to what sport and revels his
6   addiction leads him. For, besides these beneficial
news, it is the celebration of his nuptial. So much was
8   his pleasure should be proclaimed. All offices are open,
and there is full liberty of feasting from this present
hour of five till the bell have told eleven. Heaven bless
the isle of Cyprus and our noble general Othello!
(Exit.)

2.3

(Enter Othello, Desdemona, Cassio, and attendants.)

OTHELLO:
Good Michael, look you to the guard tonight.
2   Let's teach ourselves that honorable stop
3   Not to outsport discretion.

---

318 trace i.e., train, or follow (?), or perhaps *trash*, a hunting term, meaning to put
weights on a hunting dog in order to slow him down   **319 For** to make more eager.
stand [. . .] on respond properly when I incite him to quarrel   **320 on the hip** at my
mercy, where I can throw him. (A wrestling term.)   **321 Abuse** slander. **rank garb**
coarse manner, gross fashion   **322 with my nightcap** i.e., as a rival in my bed, as one
who gives me cuckold's horns   **325 practicing upon** plotting against   **2.2 Location:**
Cyprus. A street.   **3 mere perdition** complete destruction   **4 triumph** public celebration   **6 addiction** inclination   **8 offices** rooms where food and drink are kept
2.3. Location: Cyprus. The citadel.   **2 stop** restraint   **3 outsport** celebrate beyond
the bounds of

CASSIO:
  Iago hath direction what to do,
  But notwithstanding, with my personal eye
  Will I look to 't.
OTHELLO: Iago is most honest.
8 Michael, good night. Tomorrow with your earliest
  Let me have speech with you. (*To Desdemona.*)
  Come, my dear love,
11 The purchase made, the fruits are to ensue;
  That profit's yet to come 'tween me and you.—
  Good night.

(*Exit [Othello, with Desdemona and attendants].*)

(*Enter Iago.*)

CASSIO: Welcome, Iago. We must to the watch.
15 IAGO: Not this hour, Lieutenant; 'tis not yet ten o' the
16 clock. Our general cast us thus early for the love of his
17 Desdemona; who let us not therefore blame. He hath
  not yet made wanton the night with her, and she is
  sport for Jove.
CASSIO: She's a most exquisite lady.
IAGO: And, I'll warrant her, full of game.
CASSIO: Indeed, she's a most fresh and delicate creature.
23 IAGO: What an eye she has! Me thinks it sounds a parley
  to provocation.
CASSIO: An inviting eye, and yet methinks right modest.
26 IAGO: And when she speaks, is it not an alarum to love?
CASSIO: She is indeed perfection.
IAGO: Well, happiness to their sheets! Come, Lieutenant,
29 I have a stoup of wine, and here without are a brace of
30 Cyprus gallants that would fain have a measure to the
  health of black Othello.
CASSIO: Not tonight, good Iago. I have very poor and unhappy brains for drinking. I could well wish courtesy
  would invent some other custom of entertainment.
35 IAGO: O, they are our friends. But one cup! I'll drink for you.
CASSIO: I have drunk but one cup tonight and that was
37 craftily qualified too, and behold what innovation it

---

8 with your earliest at your earliest convenience   **11–12 The purchase [. . .] you**
i.e., though married, we haven't yet consummated our love   **15 Not this hour** not for an
hour yet   **16 cast** dismissed   **17 who** i.e., Othello   **23 sounds a parley** calls for a conference, issues an invitation   **26 alarum** signal calling men to arms (continuing the military metaphor of *parley*, line 23)   **29 stoup** measure of liquor, two quarts. **without**
outside. **brace** pair   **30 fain have a measure** gladly drink a toast   **35 for you** in your
place. (Iago will do the steady drinking to keep the gallants company while Cassio has
only one cup.)   **37 qualified** diluted. **innovation** disturbance, insurrection

38   makes here. I am unfortunate in the infirmity and
      dare not task my weakness with any more.
      IAGO: What, man? 'Tis a night of revels. The gallants
      desire it.
      CASSIO: Where are they?
      IAGO: Here at the door. I pray you, call them in.
44   CASSIO: I'll do 't, but it dislikes me.   *(Exit.)*
      IAGO: If I can fasten but one cup upon him,
      With that which he hath drunk tonight already,
47   He'll be as full of quarrel and offense
      As my young mistress' dog. Now, my sick fool Roderigo,
      Whom love hath turned almost the wrong side out,
50   To Desdemona hath tonight caroused
51   Potations pottle-deep; and he's to watch.
52   Three lads of Cyprus—noble swelling spirits,
53   That hold their honors in a wary distance,
54   The very elements of this warlike isle—
      Have I tonight flustered with flowing cups,
56   And they watch too. Now, 'mongst this flock of drunkards
      Am I to put our Cassio in some action
      That may offend the isle. But here they come.

      *(Enter Cassio, Montano, and gentlemen; [servants following with
      wine].)*

59   If consequence do but approve my dream,
60   My boat sails freely both with wind and stream.
61   CASSIO: 'Fore God, they have given me a rouse already,
      MONTANO: Good faith, a little one; not past a pint, as I am a soldier.
      IAGO: Some wine, ho!
65   *(He sings.)* "And let me the cannikin clink, clink,
             And let me the cannikin clink.
             A soldier's a man,
68   O, man's life's but a span;
             Why, then, let a soldier drink."
      Some wine, boys!
      CASSIO: 'Fore God, an excellent song.
      IAGO: I learned it in England, where indeed they are
73   most potent in potting. Your Dane, your German,

---

38 here i.e., in my head   **44 it dislikes me** i.e., I'm reluctant   **47 offense** readiness to
take offense   **50 caroused** drunk off   **51 pottle-deep** to the bottom of the tankard.
watch stand watch   **52 swelling** proud   **53 hold [. . .] distance** i.e., are extremely
sensitive of their honor   **54 very elements** typical sort   **56 watch** are members of the
guard   **59 If [. . .] dream** if subsequent events will only substantiate my scheme
60 stream current   **61 rouse** full draft of liquor   **65 cannikin** small drinking vessel
68 span brief span of time. (Compare Psalm 39:5 as rendered in the Book of Common
Prayer: "Thou hast made my days as it were a span long.")   **73 potting** drinking

and your swag-bellied Hollander—drink, ho!—are
nothing to your English.

CASSIO: Is your Englishman so exquisite in his drinking?

77 IAGO: Why, he drinks you, with facility, your Dane

78 dead drunk; he sweats not to overthrow your Almain;
he gives your Hollander a vomit ere the next pottle
can be filled.

CASSIO: To the health of our general!

82 MONTANO: I am for it, Lieutenant, and I'll do you justice.

IAGO: O sweet England!   (*He sings.*)
> "King Stephen was and-a worthy peer,
> His breeches cost him but a crown;
> He held them sixpence all too dear,
87 > With that he called the tailor lown.
> He was a wight of high renown,
> And thou art but of low degree.
> 'Tis pride that pulls the country down;
91 > Then take thy auld cloak about thee."

Some wine, ho!

CASSIO: 'Fore God, this is a more exquisite song than
the other.

IAGO: Will you hear't again?

CASSIO: No, for I hold him to be unworthy of his place
that does those things. Well, God's above all; and
there be souls must be saved, and there be souls must
not be saved.

IAGO: It's true, good Lieutenant.

CASSIO: For mine own part—no offense to the General,
102 nor any man of quality—I hope to be saved.

IAGO: And so do I too, Lieutenant.

CASSIO: Ay, but, by your leave, not before me; the lieutenant is to be saved before the ancient. Let's have no
more of this; let's to our affairs.—God forgive us our
sins!—Gentlemen, let's look to our business. Do not
think, gentlemen, I am drunk. This is my ancient; this
is my right hand, and this is my left. I am not drunk
now. I can stand well enough, and speak well enough.

GENTLEMEN: Excellent well.

CASSIO: Why, very well then; you must not think then
that I am drunk.   (*Exit.*)

MONTANO:
114 To th' platform, masters. Come, let's set the watch.

     (*Exeunt Gentlemen.*)

---

77 drinks you drinks. **your Dane** your typical Dane   **78 sweats not** i.e., need not exert
himself. **Almain** German   **82 I'll [. . .] justice** i.e., I'll drink as much as you   **87 lown**
lout, rascal   **91 auld** old   **102 quality** rank   **114 set the watch** mount the guard

IAGO:
You see this fellow that is gone before.
He's a soldier fit to stand by Caesar
And give direction; and do but see his vice.
118   'Tis to his virtue a just equinox,
The one as long as the other. 'Tis pity of him.
I fear the trust Othello puts him in,
On some odd time of his infirmity,
Will shake this island.

MONTANO: But is he often thus?

IAGO:
'Tis evermore the prologue to his sleep.
125   He'll watch the horologe a double set,
If drink rock not his cradle.

MONTANO: It were well
The General were put in mind of it.
Perhaps he sees it not, or his good nature
Prizes the virtue that appears in Cassio
And looks not on his evils. Is not this true?

(Enter Roderigo.)

IAGO *(aside to him)*: How now, Roderigo?
I pray you, after the Lieutenant; go.   *(Exit Roderigo.)*

MONTANO:
And 'tis great pity that the noble Moor
135   Should hazard such a place as his own second
136   With one of an engraffed infirmity.
It were an honest action to say so
To the Moor.

IAGO: Not I, for this fair island.
I do love Cassio well and would do much
To cure him of this evil.   *(Cry within: "Help! Help!")*
But, hark! What noise?

142   *(Enter Cassio, pursuing Roderigo.)*

CASSIO: Zounds, you rogue! You rascal!

MONTANO: What's the matter, Lieutenant?

CASSIO: A knave teach me my duty? I'll beat the knave
146   into a twiggen bottle.

RODERIGO: Beat me?

---

118 just equinox exact counterpart. (*Equinox* is an equal length of days and nights.)
125 watch [. . .] set stay awake twice around the clock or *horologe*   **135–136 hazard**
[. . .] With risk giving such an important position as his second in command to
136 engraffed engrafted, inveterate   **142 s.d. pursuing** (The Quarto text reads, "driving
in.")   **146 twiggen** wicker-covered. (Cassio vows to assail Roderigo until his skin resembles wickerwork or until he has driven Roderigo through the holes in a wickerwork.)

CASSIO: Dost thou prate, rogue?   (*He strikes Roderigo.*)

MONTANO: Nay, good Lieutenant.   (*Restraining him.*)

   I pray you, sir, hold your hand.

CASSIO: Let me go, sir, or I'll knock you o'er the

152   mazard.

MONTANO: Come, come, you're drunk.

CASSIO: Drunk?   (*They fight.*)

IAGO (*aside to Roderigo*):

155   Away, I say. Go out and cry a mutiny.

(*Exit Roderigo.*)

   Nay, good Lieutenant—God's will, gentlemen—
   Help, ho!—Lieutenant—sir—Montano—sir—
158   Help, masters!—Here's a goodly watch indeed!

(*A bell rings.*)

159   Who's that which rings the bell?—Diablo, ho!
160   The town will rise. God's will, Lieutenant, hold!
   You'll be ashamed forever.

(*Enter Othello and attendants [with weapons].*)

OTHELLO:
   What is the matter here?

MONTANO: Zounds, I bleed still.
   I am hurt to th' death. He dies! (*He thrusts at Cassio.*)

OTHELLO: Hold, for your lives!

IAGO:
   Hold, ho!
   Lieutenant—sir—Montano—gentlemen—
   Have you forgot all sense of place and duty?
   Hold! The General speaks to you. Hold, for shame!

OTHELLO:
   Why, how now, ho! From whence ariseth this?
170   Are we turned Turks, and to ourselves do that
   Which heaven hath forbid the Ottomites?
   For Christian shame, put by this barbarous brawl!
173   He that stirs next to carve for his own rage
174   Holds his soul light; he dies upon his motion.
   Silence that dreadful bell. It frights the isle
176   From her propriety. What is the matter, masters?

---

152 mazard i.e., head. (Literally, a drinking vessel.)   **155 mutiny** riot   **158 masters** sirs.
s.d. A bell rings (This direction is from the Quarto, as are *Exit Roderigo* at line 133,
They fight at line 154, and *with weapons* at line 161.)   **159 Diablo** the devil   **160 rise**
grow riotous   **170–171 to ourselves [. . .] Ottomites** inflict on ourselves the harm that
heaven has prevented the Turks from doing (by destroying their fleet)   **173 carve for** i.e.,
indulge, satisfy with his sword   **174 Holds [. . .] light** i.e., places little value on his life.
upon his motion if he moves   **176 propriety** proper state or condition

Honest Iago, that looks dead with grieving,
Speak. Who began this? On thy love, I charge thee.

IAGO:
I do not know. Friends all but now, even now,
180   In quarter and in terms like bride and groom
181   Devesting them for bed; and then, but now—
As if some planet had unwitted men—
Swords out, and tilting one at others' breasts
184   In opposition bloody. I cannot speak
185   Any beginning to this peevish odds;
And would in action glorious I had lost
Those legs that brought me to a part of it!

OTHELLO:
188   How comes it, Michael, you are thus forgot?

CASSIO: I pray you, pardon me. I cannot speak.

OTHELLO:
190   Worthy Montano, you were wont be civil;
191   The gravity and stillness of your youth
The world hath noted, and your name is great
193   In mouths of wisest censure. What's the matter
194   That you unlace your reputation thus
195   And spend your rich opinion for the name
Of a night-brawler? Give me answer to it.

MONTANO:
Worthy Othello, I am hurt to danger.
Your officer, Iago, can inform you—
199   While I spare speech, which something now offends me—
Of all that I do know; nor know I aught
By me that's said or done amiss this night,
Unless self-charity be sometimes a vice,
And to defend ourselves it be a sin
When violence assails us.

OTHELLO: Now, by heaven,
206   My blood begins my safer guides to rule,
207   And passion, having my best judgment collied,
208   Essays to lead the way. Zounds, if I stir,
Or do but lift this arm, the best of you
Shall sink in my rebuke. Give me to know
211   How this foul rout began, who set it on;

---

180 In quarter in friendly conduct, within bounds. **in terms** on good terms   **181 Devesting them** undressing themselves   **184 speak** explain   **185 peevish odds** childish quarrel
188 are thus forgot have forgotten yourself thus   **190 wont** be accustomed to be
191 stillness sobriety   **193 censure** judgment   **194 unlace** undo, lay open (as one might loose the strings of a purse containing reputation)   **195 opinion** reputation   **199 something** somewhat. **offends** pains   **206 blood** passion (of anger). **guides** i.e., reason
207 collied darkened   **208 Essays** undertakes   **211 rout** riot

212   And he that is approved in this offense,
       Though he had twinned with me, both at a birth,
214   Shall lose me. What? In a town of war
       Yet wild, the people's hearts brim full of fear,
216   To manage private and domestic quarrel?
217   In night, and on the court and guard of safety?
       'Tis monstrous. Iago, who began 't?
       MONTANO (*to Iago*):
219   If partially affined, or leagued in office,
       Thou dost deliver more or less than truth,
       Thou art no soldier.
       IAGO: Touch me not so near.
       I had rather have this tongue cut from my mouth
       Than it should do offense to Michael Cassio;
       Yet, I persuade myself, to speak the truth
       Shall nothing wrong him. Thus it is, General.
       Montano and myself being in speech,
       There comes a fellow crying out for help,
       And Cassio following him with determined sword
230   To execute upon him. Sir, this gentleman
                          (*indicating Montano*)
231   Steps in to Cassio and entreats his pause.
       Myself the crying fellow did pursue,
       Lest by his clamor—as it so fell out—
       The town might fall in fright. He, swift of foot,
235   Outran my purpose, and I returned, the rather
       For that I heard the clink and fall of swords
       And Cassio high in oath, which till tonight
       I ne'er might say before. When I came back—
       For this was brief—I found them close together
       At blow and thrust, even as again they were
       When you yourself did part them.
       More of this matter cannot I report.
243   But men are men; the best sometimes forget.
       Though Cassio did some little wrong to him,
245   As men in rage strike those that wish them best,
       Yet surely Cassio, I believe, received
       From him that fled some strange indignity,
248   Which patience could not pass.

---

212 approved in found guilty of   **214 town of** town garrisoned for   **216 manage**
undertake   **217 on [. . .] safety** at the main guardhouse or headquarters and on watch
219 partially affined made partial by some personal relationship. **leagued in office** in
league as fellow officers   **230 execute** give effect to (his anger)   **231 his pause** him to
stop   **235 rather** sooner   **243 forget** forget themselves   **245 those [. . .] best** i.e.,
even those who are well disposed   **248 pass** pass over, overlook

OTHELLO: I know, Iago,
Thy honesty and love doth mince this matter,
Making it light to Cassio. Cassio, I love thee,
But nevermore be officer of mine.

(Enter Desdemona, attended.)

Look if my gentle love be not raised up.
I'll make thee an example.
DESDEMONA:
What is the matter, dear?
OTHELLO: All's well now, sweeting;
Come away to bed. *(To Montano.)* Sir, for your hurts,
258   Myself will be your surgeon.—Lead him off.

(Montano is led off.)

Iago, look with care about the town
And silence those whom this vile brawl distracted.
Come, Desdemona. 'Tis the soldiers' life
To have their balmy slumbers waked with strife.

(Exit [with all but Iago and Cassio].)

IAGO: What, are you hurt, Lieutenant?
CASSIO: Ay, past all surgery.
IAGO: Marry, God forbid!
CASSIO: Reputation, reputation, reputation! O, I have
   lost my reputation! I have lost the immortal part of
   myself, and what remains is bestial. My reputation,
   Iago, my reputation!
IAGO: As I am an honest man, I thought you had
   received some bodily wound; there is more sense in
   that than in reputation. Reputation is an idle and most
273   false imposition, oft got without merit and lost without deserving. You have lost no reputation at all,
   unless you repute yourself such a loser. What, man,
276   there are more ways to recover the General again. You
277   are but now cast in his mood—a punishment more in
278   policy than in malice, even so as one would beat his
279   offenseless dog to affright an imperious lion. Sue to
   him again and he's yours.

---

258 be your surgeon i.e., make sure you receive medical attention   **273 false imposition** thing artificially imposed and of no real value   **276 recover** regain favor with
277 cast in his mood dismissed in a moment of anger   **277–278 in policy** done for
expediency's sake and as a public gesture   **278–279 would [. . .] lion** i.e., would make
an example of a minor offender in order to deter more important and dangerous offenders
279 Sue petition

CASSIO: I will rather sue to be despised than to deceive
282   so good a commander with so slight, so drunken, and
283   so indiscreet an officer. Drunk? And speak parrot?
And squabble? Swagger? Swear? And discourse fustian with one's own shadow? O thou invisible spirit
of wine, if thou hast no name to be known by, let us
call thee devil!

IAGO: What was he that you followed with your sword?
What had he done to you?

CASSIO: I know not.

IAGO: Is 't possible?

CASSIO: I remember a mass of things, but nothing
293   distinctly; a quarrel, but nothing wherefore. O God,
that men should put an enemy in their mouths to steal
away their brains! That we should with joy, pleasance,
296   revel, and applause transform ourselves into beasts!

IAGO: Why, but you are now well enough. How came
you thus recovered?

CASSIO: It hath pleased the devil drunkenness to give
place to the devil wrath. One unperfectness shows me
another, to make me frankly despise myself.

302   IAGO: Come, you are too severe a moraler. As the time,
the place, and the condition of this country stand, I
could heartily wish this had not befallen; but since it is
as it is, mend it for your own good.

CASSIO: I will ask him for my place again; he shall tell
307   me I am a drunkard. Had I as many mouths as Hydra,
such an answer would stop them all. To be now a
sensible man, by and by a fool, and presently a beast!
O, strange! Every inordinate cup is unblessed, and the
ingredient is a devil.

IAGO: Come, come, good wine is a good familiar
creature, if it be well used. Exclaim no more against it.
And, good Lieutenant, I think you think I love you.

315   CASSIO: I have well approved it, sir. I drunk!

316   IAGO: You or any man living may be drunk at a time,
man. I'll tell you what you shall do. Our general's wife
318   is now the general—I may say so in this respect, for
that he hath devoted and given up himself to the

---

282 slight worthless   **283 speak parrot** talk nonsense, rant. (*Discourse fustian*, lines
284–285, has much the same meaning.)   **293 wherefore** why   **296 applause** desire for
applause   **302 moraler** moralizer   **307 Hydra** the Lernaean Hydra, a monster with
many heads and the ability to grow two heads when one was cut off, slain by Hercules as
the second of his twelve labors   **315 approved** proved   **316 at a time** at one time or
another   **318–319 in [. . .] that** in view of this fact, that

320 contemplation, mark, and denotement of her parts
and graces. Confess yourself freely to her; importune
her help to put you in your place again. She is of so
323 free, so kind, so apt, so blessed a disposition, she
holds it a vice in her goodness not to do more than she
is requested. This broken joint between you and her
326 husband entreat her to splinter; and, my fortunes
327 against any lay worth naming, this crack of your love
shall grow stronger than it was before.

CASSIO: You advise me well.

330 IAGO: I protest, in the sincerity of love and honest
kindness.

332 CASSIO: I think it freely; and betimes in the morning I
will beseech the virtuous Desdemona to undertake for
334 me. I am desperate of my fortunes if they check me here.

IAGO: You are in the right. Good night, Lieutenant. I
must to the watch.

CASSIO: Good night, Honest Iago.   (*Exit Cassio.*)

IAGO:
And what's he then that says I play the villain,
339 When this advice is free I give, and honest,
340 Probal to thinking, and indeed the course
To win the Moor again? For 'tis most easy
342 Th' inclining Desdemona to subdue
343 In any honest suit; she's framed as fruitful
344 As the free elements. And then for her
To win the Moor—were't to renounce his baptism,
All seals and symbols of redeemèd sin—
His soul is so enfettered to her love
That she may make, unmake, do what she list,
349 Even as her appetite shall play the god
350 With his weak function. How am I then a villain,
351 To counsel Cassio to this parallel course
352 Directly to his good? Divinity of hell!
353 When devils will the blackest sins put on,
354 They do suggest at first with heavenly shows,

---

320 mark, and denotement (Both words mean "observation.") **parts** qualities   **323 free** generous   **326 splinter** bind with splints   **327 lay** stake, wager   **330 protest** insist, declare   **332 freely** unreservedly   **334 check** repulse   **339 free** (1) free from guile (2) freely given   **340 Probal** probable, reasonable   **342 inclining** favorably disposed. **subdue** persuade   **343 framed as fruitful** created as generous   **344 free elements** i.e., earth, air, fire, and water, unrestrained and spontaneous   **349 her appetite** her desire, or, perhaps, his desire for her   **350 function** exercise of faculties (weakened by his fondness for her)   **351 parallel** corresponding to these facts and to his best interests   **352 Divinity of hell** inverted theology of hell (which seduces the soul to its damnation)   **353 put on** further, instigate   **354 suggest** tempt

As I do now. For whiles this honest fool
Plies Desdemona to repair his fortune,
And she for him pleads strongly to the Moor,
I'll pour this pestilence into his ear,
359   That she repeals him for her body's lust;
And by how much she strives to do him good,
362   She shall undo her credit with the Moor.
So will I turn her virtue into pitch,
And out of her own goodness make the net
That shall enmesh them all.

(Enter Roderigo.)

How now, Roderigo?
RODERIGO: I do follow here in the chase, not like a
367   hound that hunts, but one that fills up the cry. My
money is almost spent; I have been tonight exceedingly well cudgeled; and I think the issue will be I shall
370   have so much experience for my pains, and so,
with no money at all and a little more wit, return again
to Venice.

IAGO:
How poor are they that have not patience!
What wound did ever heal but by degrees?
Thou know'st we work by wit, and not by witchcraft,
And wit depends on dilatory time.
Does't not go well? Cassio hath beaten thee,
378   And thou, by that small hurt, hast cashiered Cassio.
379   Though other things grow fair against the sun,
Yet fruits that blossom first will first be ripe.
Content thyself awhile. By the Mass, 'tis morning!
Pleasure and action make the hours seem short.
Retire thee; go where thou art billeted.
Away, I say! Thou shalt know more hereafter.
Nay, get thee gone.   *(Exit Roderigo.)*
Two things are to be done.
387   My wife must move for Cassio to her mistress;
I'll set her on;
Myself the while to draw the Moor apart
390   And bring him jump when he may Cassio find
Soliciting his wife. Ay, that's the way.
392   Dull not device by coldness and delay.   *(Exit.)*

---

359 repeals him attempts to get him restored   **362 pitch** i.e., (1) foul blackness (2) a
snaring substance   **367 fills up the cry** merely takes part as one of the pack   **370 so**
much just so much and no more   **378 cashiered** dismissed from service   **379–380**
Though [. . .] ripe i.e., plans that are well prepared and set expeditiously in motion will
soonest ripen into success   **387 move** plead   **390 jump** precisely   **392 device** plot.
coldness lack of zeal

3.1

(Enter Cassio [and] Musicians.)

1 CASSIO: Masters, play here—I will content your pains—
Something that's brief, and bid "Good morrow, General."
(They play.)

([Enter] Clown)

CLOWN: Why, masters, have your instruments been in
4   Naples, that they speak i' the nose thus?
A MUSICIAN: How, sir, how?
CLOWN: Are these, I pray you, wind instruments?
A MUSICIAN: Ay, marry, are they, sir.
CLOWN: O, thereby hangs a tail.
A MUSICIAN: Whereby hangs a tale, sir?
10 CLOWN: Marry, sir, by many a wind instrument that I know.
But, masters, here's money for you. *(He gives money.)*
And the General so likes your music that he desires
13   you, for love's sake, to make no more noise with it.
A MUSICIAN: Well, sir, we will not.
15 CLOWN: If you have any music that may not be heard,
to 't again; but, as they say, to hear music the General
does not greatly care.
A MUSICIAN: We have none such, sir.
19 CLOWN: Then put up your pipes in your bag, for I'll away.
Go, vanish into air, away!   *(Exeunt Musicians.)*
CASSIO: Dost thou hear, mine honest friend?
CLOWN: No, I hear not your honest friend; I hear you.
23 CASSIO: Prithee, keep up thy quillets. There's a poor
piece of gold for thee. *(He gives money.)* If the gentle-
woman that attends the General's wife be stirring, tell
26   her there's one Cassio entreats her a little favor of
speech. Wilt thou do this?
28 CLOWN: She is stirring, sir. If she will stir hither, I
29   shall seem to notify unto her.
CASSIO:
Do, good my friend.   *(Exit Clown.)*

**3.1 Location: Before the chamber of Othello and Desdemona. 1 content your
pains** reward your efforts **4 speak i' the nose** (1) sound nasal (2) sound like one
whose nose has been attacked by syphilis. (Naples was popularly supposed to have a high
incidence of venereal disease.)   **10 wind instrument** (With a joke on flatulence. The
tail, line 8, that hangs nearby the *wind instrument* suggests the penis.) **13 for love's
sake** (1) out of friendship and affection (2) for the sake of lovemaking in Othello's marriage **15 may not** cannot **19 I'll away** (Possibly a misprint, or a snatch of song?)
23 keep up do not bring out, do not use. **quillets** quibbles, puns **26–27 a little [. . .]
speech** the favor of a brief talk **28 stir** bestir herself (with a play on *stirring*, "rousing
herself from rest") **29 seem** deem it good, think fit

(Enter Iago.)

31   In happy time, Iago.

IAGO: You have not been abed, then?

CASSIO: Why, no. The day had broke
Before we parted. I have made bold, Iago,
To send in to your wife. My suit to her
Is that she will to virtuous Desdemona
Procure me some access.

IAGO: I'll send her to you presently;
And I'll devise a means to draw the Moor
Out of the way, that your converse and business
May be more free.

CASSIO:
I humbly thank you for 't. *(Exit Iago).*

44   I never knew
A Florentine more kind and honest.

(Enter Emilia.)

46   EMILIA: Good morrow, good Lieutenant. I am sorry
For your displeasure; but all will sure be well.

48   The General and his wife are talking of it,
49   And she speaks for you stoutly. The Moor replies
50   That he you hurt is of great fame in Cyprus
51   And great affinity, and that in wholesome wisdom
He might not but refuse you; but he protests he loves you
53   And needs no other suitor but his likings
To take the safest occasion by the front
To bring you in again.

CASSIO: Yet I beseech you,
If you think fit, or that it may be done,
Give me advantage of some brief discourse
With Desdemona alone.

EMILIA: Pray you, come in.

61   I will bestow you where you shall have time
To speak your bosom freely.

CASSIO: I am much bound to you.   *(Exeunt.)*

3.2

(Enter Othello, Iago, and Gentlemen.)

OTHELLO (*giving letters*): These letters give, Iago, to the pilot,

---

31 In happy time i.e., well met   **44 Florentine** i.e., even a fellow Florentine. (Iago is a
Venetian; Cassio is a Florentine.)   **46 displeasure** fall from favor   **48 stoutly** spirit-
edly   **49 fame** reputation, importance   **50 affinity** kindred, family connection
51 protests insists   **53 occasion [. . .] front** opportunity by the forelock   **61 bosom**
inmost thoughts   **3.2 Location: The citadel.**

2   And by him do my duties to the Senate.
3   That done, I will be walking on the works;
4   Repair there to me.
IAGO: Well, my good lord, I'll do't.
OTHELLO:
       This fortification, gentlemen, shall we see't?
7   GENTLEMEN: We'll wait upon your lordship.   (*Exeunt.*)

3.3

       (*Enter Desdemona, Cassio, and Emilia.*)

DESDEMONA:
       Be thou assured, good Cassio, I will do
       All my abilities in thy behalf.
EMILIA:
       Good madam, do. I warrant it grieves my husband
       As if the cause were his.
DESDEMONA:
       O, that's an honest fellow. Do not doubt, Cassio,
       But I will have my lord and you again
       As friendly as you were.
CASSIO: Bounteous madam,
       Whatever shall become of Michael Cassio,
       He's never anything but your true servant.
DESDEMONA:
       I know't. I thank you. You do love my lord;
       You have known him long, and be you well assured
13   He shall in strangeness stand no farther off
14   Than in a politic distance.
CASSIO: Ay, but lady,
       That policy may either last so long,
17   Or feed upon such nice and waterish diet,
18   Or breed itself so out of circumstance,
19   That, I being absent and my place supplied,
       My general will forget my love and service.
DESDEMONA:
21   Do not doubt that. Before Emilia here
22   I give thee warrant of thy place. Assure thee,

---

2 do my duties convey my respects   **3 works** breastworks, fortifications   **4 Repair** return, come   **7 wait upon** attend   **3.3 Location: The garden of the citadel.** **13 strangeness** aloofness   **14 politic** required by wise policy   **17 Or [. . .] diet** or sustain itself at length upon such trivial and meager technicalities   **18 breed [. . .] circumstance** continually renew itself so out of chance events, or yield so few chances for my being pardoned   **19 supplied** filled by another person   **21 doubt** fear **22 warrant** guarantee

If I do vow a friendship I'll perform it
To the last article. My lord shall never rest.
25 I'll watch him tame and talk him out of patience;
26 His bed shall seem a school, his board a shrift;
I'll intermingle everything he does
With Cassio's suit. Therefore be merry, Cassio,
29 For thy solicitor shall rather die
30 Than give thy cause away.

(Enter Othello and Iago [at a distance].)

EMILIA: Madam, here comes my lord.
CASSIO: Madam, I'll take my leave.
DESDEMONA: Why, stay, and hear me speak.
CASSIO:
Madam, not now. I am very ill at ease,
Unfit for mine own purposes.
36 DESDEMONA: Well, do your discretion.   *(Exit Cassio.)*
IAGO: Ha? I like not that.
OTHELLO: What dost thou say?
IAGO:
Nothing, my lord; or if—I know not what.
OTHELLO: Was not that Cassio parted from my wife?
IAGO:
Cassio, my lord? No, sure, I cannot think it,
That he would steal away so guiltylike,
Seeing you coming.
OTHELLO: I do believe 'twas he.
DESDEMONA: How now, my lord?
I have been talking with a suitor here.
A man that languishes in your displeasure.
OTHELLO: Who is 't you mean?
DESDEMONA:
Why, your lieutenant, Cassio. Good my lord,
If I have any grace or power to move you,
51 His present reconciliation take;
For if he be not one that truly loves you,
53 That errs in ignorance and not in cunning,
I have no judgment in an honest face.
I prithee, call him back.
OTHELLO: Went he hence now?
DESDEMONA: Yes, faith, so humbled
That he hath left part of his grief with me

---

25 watch him tame tame him by keeping him from sleeping (A term from falconry.) **out of patience** past his endurance   **26 board** dining table. **shrift** confessional   **29 solicitor** advocate   **30 away** up   **36 do your discretion** act according to your own discretion   **51 His [. . .] take** let him be reconciled to you right away   **53 in cunning** wittingly

To suffer with him. Good love, call him back.

OTHELLO:

Not now, sweet Desdemon. Some other time.

DESDEMONA: But shall 't be shortly?

OTHELLO: The sooner, sweet, for you.

DESDEMONA: Shall 't be tonight at supper?

OTHELLO: No, not tonight.

65 DESDEMONA: Tomorrow dinner, then?

OTHELLO: I shall not dine at home.

I meet the captains at the citadel.

DESDEMONA:

Why, then, tomorrow night, or Tuesday morn,

Or Tuesday noon, or night, or Wednesday morn.

I prithee, name the time, but let it not

Exceed three days. I' faith, he's penitent;

72 And yet his trespass, in our common reason—

73 Save that, they say, the wars must make example

74 Out of her best—is not almost a fault

75 T'incur a private check. When shall he come?

Tell me, Othello. I wonder in my soul

What you would ask me that I should deny,

78 Or stand so mammering on. What? Michael Cassio,

That came a-wooing with you, and so many a time,

When I have spoke of you dispraisingly,

Hath ta'en your part—to have so much to do

82 To bring him in! By 'r Lady, I could do much—

OTHELLO:

Prithee, no more. Let him come when he will;

I will deny thee nothing.

DESDEMONA: Why, this is not a boon.

'Tis as I should entreat you wear your gloves,

Or feed on nourishing dishes, or keep you warm,

88 Or sue to you to do a peculiar profit

To your own person. Nay, when I have a suit

90 Wherein I mean to touch your love indeed,

91 It shall be full of poise and difficult weight,

And fearful to be granted.

OTHELLO: I will deny thee nothing.

94 Whereon, I do beseech thee, grant me this,

To leave me but a little to myself.

---

65 dinner (the noontime meal)   **72 common reason** everyday judgments   **73–74 Save**
[. . .] best were it not that, as the saying goes, military discipline requires making an
example of the very best men. (*Her* refers to *wars* as a singular concept.)   **74 not**
almost scarcely   **75 a private check** even a private reprimand   **78 mammering**
on wavering about   **82 bring him in** restore him to favor   **88 peculiar** particular, personal
90 touch test   **91 poise** weight, heaviness; or equipoise, delicate balance involving hard
choice   **94 Whereon** in return for which

DESDEMONA:

Shall I deny you? No. Farewell, my lord.

OTHELLO:

97   Farewell, my Desdemona. I'll come to thee straight.

DESDEMONA:

98   Emilia, come.—Be as your fancies teach you;

Whate'er you be, I am obedient.   (*Exit* [*with Emilia*].)

OTHELLO:

100   Excellent wretch! Perdition catch my soul

101   But I do love thee! And when I love thee not,

Chaos is come again.

IAGO: My noble lord—

OTHELLO: What doest thou say, Iago?

IAGO:

Did Michael Cassio, when you wooed my lady,

Know of your love?

OTHELLO:

He did, from first to last. Why dost thou ask?

IAGO:

But for a satisfaction of my thought;

No further harm.

OTHELLO: Why of thy thought, Iago?

IAGO:

I did not think he had been acquainted with her.

OTHELLO:

O, yes, and went between us very oft.

IAGO: Indeed?

OTHELLO:

Indeed? Ay, indeed. Discern'st thou aught in that? Is he not honest?

IAGO: Honest, my lord?

OTHELLO: Honest. Ay, honest?

IAGO: My lord, for aught I know.

OTHELLO: What dost thou think?

IAGO: Think, my lord?

OTHELLO:

"Think, my lord?" By heaven, thou echo'st me,

As if there were some monster in thy thought

Too hideous to be shown. Thou dost mean something.

I heard thee say even now, thou lik'st not that,

When Cassio left my wife. What didst not like?

125   And when I told thee he was of my counsel

---

97 straight straightway   **98 fancies** inclinations   **100 wretch** (A term of affectionate endearment.)   **101–102 And [. . .] again,** i.e., my love for you will last forever, until the end of time when chaos will return. (But with an unconscious, ironic suggestion that, if anything should induce Othello to cease loving Desdemona, the result would be chaos.)   **125 of my counsel** in my confidence

In my whole course of wooing, thou criedst "Indeed?"
127   And didst contract and purse thy brow together
As if thou then hadst shut up in thy brain
129   Some horrible conceit. If thou dost love me,
Show me thy thought.
IAGO: My lord, you know I love you.
OTHELLO: I think thou dost;
133   And for I know thou'rt full of love and honesty,
And weigh'st thy words before thou giv'st them breath,
135   Therefore these stops of thine fright me the more;
For such things in a false disloyal knave
137   Are tricks of custom, but in a man that's just
138   They're close dilations, working from the heart
139   That passion cannot rule.
140 IAGO: For Michael Cassio,
I dare be sworn I think that he is honest.
OTHELLO:
I think so too.
IAGO: Men should be what they seem;
144   Or those that be not, would they might seem none!
OTHELLO: —
Certain, men should be what they seem.
IAGO:
Why, then, I think Cassio's an honest man.
OTHELLO: Nay, yet there's more in this.
I prithee, speak to me as to thy thinkings,
As thou dost ruminate, and give thy worst of thoughts
The worst of words.
IAGO: Good my lord, pardon me.
Though I am bound to every act of duty,
153   I am not bound to that all slaves are free to.
Utter my thoughts? Why, say they are vile and false,
As where's that palace where into foul things
Sometimes intrude not? Who has that breast so pure
But some uncleanly apprehensions
158   Keep leets and law days, and in sessions sit
159   With meditations lawful?
OTHELLO:
160   Thou dost conspire against thy friend, Iago,

---

127 purse knit   **129 conceit** fancy   **133 for** because   **135 stops** pauses   **137 of custom** customary   **138 close dilations** secret or involuntary expressions or delays
139 That passion cannot rule i.e., that are too passionately strong to be restrained (referring to the workings), or, that cannot rule its own passions (referring to the heart).   **140 For** as for   **144 none** i.e., not to be men, or not seem to be honest   **153 that** that which. **free to** free with respect to   **158 Keep leets and law days** i.e., hold court, set up their authority in one's heart. (*Leets* are a kind of manor court; *law days* are the days courts sit in session, or those sessions.)   **159 With** along with. **lawful** innocent   **160 thy friend** i.e., Othello

If thou but think'st him wronged and mak'st his ear
A stranger to thy thoughts.

IAGO: I do beseech you,

164   Though I perchance am vicious in my guess—
       As I confess it is my nature's plague

166   To spy into abuses, and oft my jealousy

167   Shapes faults that are not—that your wisdom then,

168   From one that so imperfectly conceits,
       Would take no notice, nor build yourself a trouble

170   Out of his scattering and unsure observance.
       It were not for your quiet nor your good,
       Nor for my manhood, honesty, and wisdom,
       To let you know my thoughts.

OTHELLO: What dost thou mean?

IAGO:
       Good name in man and woman, dear my lord,

176   Is the immediate jewel of their souls.
       Who steals my purse steals trash; 'tis something, nothing;
       'Twas mine, 'tis his, and has been slave to thousands;
       But he that filches from me my good name
       Robs me of that which not enriches him
       And makes me poor indeed.

OTHELLO: By heaven, I'll know thy thoughts.

IAGO:

183   You cannot, if my heart were in your hand,
       Nor shall not, whilst 'tis in my custody.

OTHELLO: Ha?

IAGO: O, beware, my lord, of jealousy.

187   It is the green-eyed monster which doth mock
       The meat it feeds on. That cuckold lives in bliss

189   Who, certain of his fate, loves not his wronger;

190   But O, what damnèd minutes tells he o'er
       Who dotes, yet doubts, suspects, yet fondly loves!

OTHELLO: O misery!

193   IAGO: Poor and content is rich, and rich enough,

194   But riches fineless is as poor as winter
       To him that ever fears he shall be poor.
       Good God, the souls of all my tribe defend

---

164 vicious wrong   **166 jealousy** suspicious nature   **167 then** on that account
168 one i.e., myself, Iago. **conceits** judges, conjectures   **170 scattering** random
176 immediate essential, most precious   **183 if** even if   **187–188 doth mock [. . .]**
on mocks and torments the heart of its victim, the man who suffers jealousy   **189 his
wronger** i.e., his faithless wife. (The unsuspecting cuckold is spared the misery of loving
his wife only to discover she is cheating on him.)   **190 tells** counts   **193 Poor [. . .]
enough** to be content with what little one has is the greatest wealth of all. (Proverbial.)
194 fineless boundless

From jealousy!

OTHELLO: Why, why is this?
　　Think'st thou I'd make a life of jealousy,
200　To follow still the changes of the moon
　　With fresh suspicions? No! To be once in doubt
202　Is once to be resolved. Exchange me for a goat
　　When I shall turn the business of my soul
204　To such exsufflicate and blown surmises
205　Matching thy inference. 'Tis not to make me jealous
　　To say my wife is fair, feeds well, loves company,
　　Is free of speech, sings, plays, and dances well;
　　Where virtue is, these are more virtuous.
　　Nor from mine own weak merits will I draw
210　The smallest fear or doubt of her revolt,
　　For she had eyes, and chose me. No, Iago,
　　I'll see before I doubt; when I doubt, prove;
　　And on the proof, there is no more but this—
　　Away at once with love or jealousy.

IAGO:
　　I am glad of this, for now I shall have reason
　　To show the love and duty that I bear you
　　With franker spirit. Therefore, as I am bound,
　　Receive it from me. I speak not yet of proof.
　　Look to your wife; observe her well with Cassio.
220　Wear your eyes thus, not jealous nor secure.
　　I would not have your free and noble nature,
222　Out of self-bounty, be abused. Look to 't.
　　I know our country disposition well;
　　In Venice they do let God see the pranks
　　They dare not show their husbands; their best conscience
　　Is not to leave 't undone, but keep 't unknown.

OTHELLO: Dost thou say so?

IAGO:
　　She did deceive her father, marrying you;
　　And when she seemed to shake and fear your looks,
　　She loved them most.

OTHELLO:　　　　　　　And so she did.

232 IAGO:　　　　　　　　　　　　Why, go to, then!

200–201 To follow [. . .] suspicions to be constantly imagining new causes for suspicion, changing incessantly like the moon　**202 once** once and for all. **resolved** free of doubt, having settled the matter　**204 exsufflicate and blown** inflated and blown up, rumored about, or spat out and fly-blown, hence loathsome, disgusting　**205 inference** description or allegation　**210 doubt [. . .] revolt** fear of her unfaithfulness　**220 not** neither. **secure** free from uncertainty　**222 self-bounty** inherent or natural goodness and generosity. **abused** deceived　**232 go to** (An expression of impatience.)

233   She that, so young, could give out such a seeming,
234   To seel her father's eyes up close as oak,
        He thought 'twas witchcraft! But I am much to blame.
        I humbly do beseech you of your pardon
        For too much loving you.
238   OTHELLO: I am bound to thee forever.
        IAGO:
        I see this hath a little dashed your spirits.
        OTHELLO: Not a jot, not a jot.
        IAGO: I' faith, I fear it has.
        I hope you will consider what is spoke
        Comes from my love. But I do see you're moved.
        I am to pray you not to strain my speech
245   To grosser issues nor to larger reach
        Than to suspicion.
        OTHELLO: I will not.
        IAGO: Should you do so, my lord,
        My speech should fall into such vile success
        Which my thoughts aimed not. Cassio's my worthy friend.
        My lord, I see you're moved.
        OTHELLO: No, not much moved.
253   I do not think but Desdemona's honest.
        IAGO:
        Long live she so! And long live you to think so!
        OTHELLO:
        And yet, how nature erring from itself—
        IAGO:
        Ay, there's the point! As—to be bold with you—
257   Not to affect many proposèd matches
258   Of her own clime, complexion, and degree,
        Whereto we see in all things nature tends—
260   Foh! One may smell in such a will most rank,
261   Foul disproportion, thoughts unnatural.
262   But pardon me. I do not in position
        Distinctly speak of her, though I may fear
264   Her will, recoiling to her better judgment,
265   May fall to match you with her country forms
266   And happily repent.

---

233 seeming false appearance   **234 seel** blind. (A term from falconry.) **oak** (A close-grained wood.)   **238 bound** indebted (but perhaps with ironic sense of "tied")
245 issues significance. **reach** meaning, scope   **249 success** effect, result   **253 honest** chaste   **257 affect** prefer, desire   **258 clime** [. . .] **degree** country, color, and social position   **260 will** sensuality, appetite   **261 disproportion** abnormality   **262 position** argument, proposition   **264 recoiling** reverting. **better** i.e., more natural and reconsidered   **265 fall** [. . .] **forms** undertake to compare you with Venetian norms of handsomeness   **266 happily repent** haply repent her marriage

OTHELLO: Farewell, farewell!
If more thou dost perceive, let me know more.
Set on thy wife to observe. Leave me, Iago.
IAGO (*going*): My lord, I take my leave.
OTHELLO:
Why did I marry? This honest creature doubtless
Sees and knows more, much more, than he unfolds.
IAGO (*returning*):
My Lord, I would I might entreat your honor
274   To scan this thing no farther. Leave it to time.
Although 'tis fit that Cassio have his place—
For, sure, he fills it up with great ability—
Yet, if you please to hold him off awhile,
278   You shall by that perceive him and his means.
279   Note if your lady strain his entertainment
With any strong or vehement importunity;
Much will be seen in that. In the meantime,
282   Let me be thought too busy in my fears—
As worthy cause I have to fear I am—
284   And hold her free, O do beseech your honor.
285   OTHELLO: Fear not my government.
IAGO: I once more take my leave.   (*Exit.*)
OTHELLO:
This fellow's of exceeding honesty,
288   And knows all qualities, with a learnèd spirit,
289   Of human dealings. If I do prove her haggard,
290   Though that her jesses were my dear heartstrings,
291   I'd whistle her off and let her down the wind
292   To prey at fortune. Haply, for I am black
293   And have not those soft parts of conversation
294   That chamberers have, or for I am declined
Into the vale of years—yet that's not much—
296   She's gone. I am abused, and my relief
Must be to loathe her. O curse of marriage,
That we can call these delicate creatures ours
And not their appetites! I had rather be a toad
And live upon the vapor of a dungeon
Than keep a corner in the thing I love
For others' uses. Yet, 'tis the plague of great ones;

---

274 scan scrutinize   **278 his means** the method he uses (to regain his post)   **279 strain
his entertainment** urge his reinstatement   **282 busy** interfering   **284 hold her free**
regard her as innocent   **285 government** self-control, conduct   **288 qualities** natures,
types   **289 haggard** wild (like a wild female hawk)   **290 jesses** straps fastened around
the legs of a trained hawk   **291 I'd [. . .] wind** i.e., I'd let her go forever. (To release a
hawk downwind was to invite it not to return.)   **292 prey at fortune** fend for herself in
the wild. **Haply, for** perhaps, because   **293 soft [. . .] conversation** pleasing graces of
social behavior   **294 chamberers** gallants   **296 abused** deceived

303   Prerogatived are they less than the base.
       'Tis destiny unshunnable, like death.
305   Even then this forkèd plague is fated to us
306   When we do quicken. Look where she comes.

(Enter Desdemona and Emilia.)

If she be false, O, then heaven mocks itself!
I'll not believe 't.
DESDEMONA: How now, my dear Othello?
310   Your dinner, and the generous islanders
311   By you invited, do attend your presence.
OTHELLO:
I am to blame.
DESDEMONA: Why do you speak so faintly?
Are you not well?
OTHELLO:
I have a pain upon my forehead here.
DESDEMONA:
316   Faith, that's with watching. 'Twill away again.

(She offers her handkerchief.)

Let me but bind it hard, within this hour
It will be well.
319   OTHELLO: Your napkin is too little.
320   Let it alone. Come, I'll go in with you.

(He puts the handkerchief from him, and it drops.)

DESDEMONA:
I am very sorry that you are not well.

(Exit [with Othello].)

EMILIA *(picking up the handkerchief)*: I am glad I have found this napkin.
This was her first remembrance from the Moor.
324   My wayward husband hath a hundred times
Wooed me to steal it, but she so loves the token—
For he conjured her she should ever keep it—
That she reserves it evermore about her
328   To kiss and talk to. I'll have the work ta'en out,

---

303 Prerogatived privileged (to have honest wives). **the base** ordinary citizens.
(Socially prominent men are especially prone to the unavoidable destiny of being cuckolded and to the public shame that goes with it.)   **305 forkèd** (An allusion to the horns
of the cuckold.)   **306 quicken** receive life. (*Quicken* may also mean to swarm with maggots as the body festers, as in 4.2.76, in which case lines 305–306 suggest that *even then*, in
death, we are cuckolded by *forkèd* worms.)   **310 generous** noble   **311 attend** await
316 watching too little sleep   **319 napkin** handkerchief   **320 Let it alone** i.e., never
mind   **324 wayward** capricious   **328 work ta'en out** design of the embroidery copied

And give 't Iago. What he will do with it
Heaven knows, not I;
331   I nothing but to please his fantasy.

(Enter Iago.)

IAGO:
How now? What do you here alone?
EMILIA:
Do not you chide. I have a thing for you.
IAGO:
334   You have a thing for me? It is a common thing—
EMILIA: Ha?
IAGO: To have a foolish wife.
EMILIA:
O, is that all? What will you give me now
For that same handkerchief?
IAGO: What handkerchief?
EMILIA: What handkerchief?
Why, that the Moor first gave to Desdemona;
That which so often you did bid me steal.
IAGO: Hast stolen it from her?
EMILIA:
No, faith. She let it drop by negligence,
345   And to th' advantage, I, being here, took 't up.
Look, here 'tis.
IAGO: A good wench! Give it me.
EMILIA: What will you do with 't, that you have been so earnest
To have me filch it?
IAGO *(snatching it)*: Why, what is that to you?
EMILIA:
If it be not for some purpose of import,
Give 't me again. Poor lady, she'll run mad
353   When she shall lack it.
354 IAGO: Be not acknown on 't.
I have use for it. Go, leave me.   *(Exit Emilia.)*
356   I will in Cassio's lodging lose this napkin
And let him find it. Trifles light as air
Are to the jealous confirmations strong
As proofs of Holy Writ. This may do something.
The Moor already changes with my poison.
361   Dangerous conceits are in their natures poisons,

---

331 fantasy whim   **334 common thing** (With bawdy suggestion; *common* suggests
coarseness and availability to all comers, and *thing* is a slang term for the pudendum.)
345 to th' advantage taking the opportunity   **353 lack** miss   **354 Be [. . .] on 't** do
not confess knowledge of it   **356 lose** (The Folio spelling, *loose*, is a normal spelling for
"lose," but may also contain the idea of "let go," "release.")   **361 conceits** fancies, ideas

362 Which at the first are scarce found to distaste,
363 But with a little act upon the blood
    Burn like the mines of sulfur.

(Enter Othello.)

          I did say so.
366 Look where he comes! Not poppy nor mandragora
    Nor all the drowsy syrups of the world
    Shall ever medicine thee to that sweet sleep
369 Which thou owedst yesterday.

OTHELLO: Ha, ha, false to me?

IAGO:
Why, how now, General? No more of that.

OTHELLO:
Avaunt! Begone! Thou hast set me on the rack.
I swear 'tis better to be much abused
Than but to know 't a little.

IAGO: How now, my lord?

OTHELLO:
What sense had I of her stolen hours of lust?
I saw 't not, thought it not, it harmed not me.
378 I slept the next night well, fed well, was free and merry;
    I found not Cassio's kisses on her lips.
380 He that is robbed, not wanting what is stolen,
    Let him not know 't and he's not robbed at all.

IAGO: I am sorry to hear this.

OTHELLO:
I had been happy if the general camp,
384 Pioners and all, had tasted her sweet body,
385 So I had nothing known. O, now, forever
    Farewell the tranquil mind! Farewell content!
387 Farewell the plumèd troops and the big wars
    That makes ambition virtue! Oh, farewell!
    Farewell the neighing steed and the shrill trump,
    The spirit-stirring drum, th' ear-piercing fife,
391 The royal banner, and all quality,
392 Pride, pomp, and circumstance of glorious war!
393 And O, you mortal engines, whose rude throats
394 Th' immortal Jove's dread clamors counterfeit,
    Farewell! Othello's occupation's gone.

---

362 distaste be distasteful   **363 act** action, working   **366 mandragora** an opiate made of the mandrake root   **369 thou owedst** you did own   **378 free** carefree **380 wanting** missing   **384 Pioners** diggers of mines, the lowest grade of soldiers **385 So** provided   **387 big** stately   **391 quality** character, essential nature   **392 Pride** rich display. **circumstance** pageantry   **393 mortal engines** i.e., cannon. (*Mortal* means "deadly.")   **394 Jove's dread clamors** i.e., thunder

IAGO: Is 't possible, my lord?

OTHELLO:

    Villain, be sure thou prove my love a whore!

    Be sure of it. Give me the ocular proof,

    Or, by the worth of mine eternal soul,

    Thou hadst been better have been born a dog

    Than answer my waked wrath!

IAGO: Is 't come to this?

OTHELLO:

    Make me to see 't, or at least so prove it

404   That the probation bear no hinge nor loop

    To hang a doubt on, or woe upon thy life!

IAGO: My noble lord—

OTHELLO:

    If thou dost slander her and torture me,

408   Never pray more; abandon all remorse;

409   On horror's head horrors accumulate;

410   Do deeds to make heaven weep, all earth amazed;

    For nothing canst thou to damnation add

    Greater than that.

IAGO: O grace! O heaven forgive me!

    Are you a man? Have you a soul or sense?

415   God b' wi' you; take mine office. O wretched fool,

416   That lov'st to make thine honesty a vice!

    O monstrous world! Take note, take note, O world,

    To be direct and honest is not safe.

419   I thank you for this profit, and from hence

420   I'll love no friend, sith love breeds such offense.

421 OTHELLO: Nay, stay. Thou shouldst be honest.

IAGO:

    I should be wise, for honesty's a fool

    And loses that it works for.

OTHELLO: By the world,

    I think my wife be honest and think she is not;

426   I think that thou art just and think thou are not.

    I'll have some proof. My name, that was as fresh

428   As Dian's visage, is now begrimed and black

    As mine own face. If there be cords, or knives,

    Poison, or fire, or suffocating streams,

---

404 probation proof   **408 remorse** pity, penitent hope for salvation   **409 horrors accu-mulate** add still more horrors   **410 amazed** confounded with horror   **415 O wretched fool** (Iago addresses himself as a fool for having carried honesty too far.)   **416 vice** failing, something overdone   **419 profit** profitable instruction. **hence** henceforth   **420 sith** since. **offense** i.e., harm to the one who offers help and friendship   **421 Thou shouldst be** It appears that you are. (But Iago replies in the sense of "ought to be.")   **426 that** what **428 Dian** Diana, goddess of the moon and of chastity

I'll not endure it. Would I were satisfied!

IAGO:

  I see, sir, you are eaten up with passion.

  I do repent me that I put it to you.

  You would be satisfied?

OTHELLO: Would? Nay, and I will.

IAGO:

  And may; but how? How satisfied, my lord?

437 Would you, the supervisor, grossly gape on?

  Behold her topped?

OTHELLO: Death and damnation! O!

IAGO:

  It were a tedious difficulty, I think,

441 To bring them to that prospect. Damn them then,

442 If ever mortal eyes do see them bolster

443 More than their own. What then? How then?

  What shall I say? Where's satisfaction?

  It is impossible you should see this,

446 Were they as prime as goats, as hot as monkeys,

447 As salt as wolves in pride, and fools as gross

  As ignorance made drunk. But yet I say,

449 If imputation and strong circumstances

  Which lead directly to the door of truth

  Will give you satisfaction, you might have 't.

OTHELLO:

  Give me a living reason she's disloyal.

IAGO: I do not like the office.

454 But sith I am entered in this cause so far,

455 Pricked to 't by foolish honesty and love,

  I will go on. I lay with Cassio lately,

  And being troubled with a raging tooth

  I could not sleep. There are a kind of men

  So loose of soul that in their sleeps will mutter

  Their affairs. One of this kind is Cassio.

  In sleep I heard him say, "Sweet Desdemona,

  Let us be wary, let us hide our loves!"

  And then, sir, would he grip and wring my hand,

  Cry "O sweet creature!", then kiss me hard,

  As if he plucked up kisses by the roots

  That grew upon my lips; then laid his leg

  Over my thigh, and sighed, and kissed, and then

---

437 supervisor onlooker   **441 Damn them then** i.e., they would have to be really incorrigible   **442 bolster** go to bed together, share a bolster   **443 More** other. **own** own eyes   **446 prime** lustful   **447 salt** wanton, sensual. **pride** heat   **449 imputation [. . .] circumstances** strong circumstantial evidence   **454 sith** since   **455 Pricked** spurred

Cried, "Cursèd fate that gave thee to the Moor!"

OTHELLO:

O monstrous! Monstrous!

IAGO: Nay, this was but his dream.

OTHELLO:

471   But this denoted a foregone conclusion.

472   'tis a shrewd doubt, though it be but a dream.

IAGO:

And this may help to thicken other proofs

That do demonstrate thinly.

OTHELLO: I'll tear her all to pieces.

IAGO:

Nay, but be wise. Yet we see nothing done;

She may be honest yet. Tell me but this:

Have you not sometimes seen a handkerchief

479   Spotted with strawberries in your wife's hand?

OTHELLO:

I gave her such a one. 'Twas my first gift.

IAGO:

I know not that; but such a handkerchief—

I am sure it was your wife's—did I today

See Cassio wipe his beard with.

OTHELLO: If it be that—

IAGO:

If it be that, or any that was hers,

It speaks against her with the other proofs.

OTHELLO:

487   O, that the slave had forty thousand lives!

One is too poor, too weak for my revenge.

Now do I see 'tis true. Look here, Iago,

490   All my fond love thus do I blow to heaven.

'Tis gone.

Arise, black vengeance, from the hollow hell!

493   Yield up, O love, thy crown and hearted throne

494   To tyrannous hate! Swell, bosom, with thy freight,

495   For 'tis of aspics' tongues!

496   IAGO: Yet be content.

OTHELLO: O, blood, blood, blood!

IAGO:

Patience, I say. Your mind perhaps may change.

---

471 foregone conclusion concluded experience or action   **472 shrewd doubt** suspicious circumstance   **479 Spotted with strawberries** embroidered with a strawberry pattern   **487 the slave** i.e., Cassio   **490 fond** foolish (but also suggesting "affectionate")   **493 hearted** fixed in the heart   **494 freight** burden   **495 aspics'** venomous serpents'   **496 content** calm

OTHELLO:

499   Never, Iago. Like to the Pontic Sea,
Whose icy current and compulsive course
Ne'er feels retiring ebb, but keeps due on
502   To the Propontic and the Hellespont,
Even so my bloody thoughts with violent pace
Shall ne'er look back, ne'er ebb to humble love,
505   Till that a capable and wide revenge
506   Swallow them up. Now, by yond marble heaven,
(*Kneeling*) In the due reverence of a sacred vow
I here engage my words.

IAGO: Do not rise yet.

510   (*He kneels.*) Witness, you ever-burning lights above,
511   You elements that clip us round about,
Witness that here Iago doth give up
513   The execution of his wit, hands, heart,
To wronged Othello's service. Let him command,
515   And to obey shall be in me remorse,
516   What bloody business ever.   (*They rise.*)

OTHELLO: I greet thy love,
Not with vain thanks, but with acceptance bounteous,
519   And will upon the instant put thee to 't.
Within these three days let me hear thee say
That Cassio's not alive.

IAGO: My friend is dead;
'Tis done at your request. But let her live.

OTHELLO:

524   Damn her, lewd minx! O, damn her, damn her!
Come, go with me apart. I will withdraw
To furnish me with some swift means of death
For the fair devil. Now art thou my lieutenant.

IAGO: I am your own forever.   (*Exeunt.*)

3.4

(*Enter Desdemona, Emilia, and Clown.*)

1   DESDEMONA: Do you know, sirrah, where Lieutenant
2   Cassio lies?

---

499 Pontic Sea Black Sea   **502 Propontic** Sea of Marmora, between the Black Sea and the Aegean. **Hellespont** Dardanelles, straits where the Sea of Marmora joins with the Aegean   **505 capable** ample, comprehensive   **506 marble** i.e., gleaming like marble and unrelenting   **510 s.d. He kneels** (In the Quarto text, Iago kneels here after Othello has knelt at line 506.)   **511 clip** encompass   **513 execution** exercise, action. **wit** mind   **515 remorse** pity (for Othello's wrongs)   **516 ever** soever   **519 to 't** to the proof   **524 minx** wanton   **3.4. Location: Before the citadel.**   **1 sirrah** (A form of address to an inferior.)   **2 lies** lodges. (But the Clown makes the obvious pun.)

CLOWN: I dare not say he lies anywhere.

DESDEMONA: Why, man?

CLOWN: He's a soldier, and for me to say a soldier lies,
'tis stabbing.

DESDEMONA: Go to. Where lodges he?

CLOWN: To tell you where he lodges is to tell
you where I lie.

DESDEMONA: Can anything be made of this?

CLOWN: I know not where he lodges, and for me to devise a lodging and
11   say he lies here, or he lies there, were to lie in mine own throat.

DESDEMONA: Can you inquire him out, and be edified
by report?

CLOWN: I will catechize the world for him;
that is, make questions, and by them answer.

16   DESDEMONA: Seek him, bid him come hither. Tell him I have moved my
lord on his behalf and hope all will be well.

CLOWN: To do this is within the compass of man's wit, and therefore I
will attempt the doing it. (*Exit Clown.*)

DESDEMONA:
Where should I lose that handkerchief, Emilia?

EMILIA: I know not, madam.

DESDEMONA:
Believe me, I had rather have lost my purse
23   Full of crusadoes; and but my noble Moor
Is true of mind and made of no such baseness
As jealous creatures are, it were enough
To put him to ill thinking.

EMILIA: Is he not jealous?

DESDEMONA:
Who, he? I think the sun where he was born
29   Drew all such humors from him.

EMILIA   Look where he comes.

(*Enter Othello.*)

DESDEMONA:
I will not leave him now till Cassio
Be called to him. How is 't with you, my lord?

OTHELLO:
Well, my good lady. (*Aside.*) O, hardness to dissemble!—
How do you, Desdemona?

DESDEMONA: Well, my good lord.

OTHELLO:
Give me your hand. (*She gives her hand.*) This hand is moist, my lady.

---

11 lie [. . .] throat (1) lie egregiously and deliberately (2) use the windpipe to speak a
lie **16 moved** petitioned **23 crusadoes** Portuguese gold coins **29 humors** (Refers
to the four bodily fluids thought to determine temperament.)

DESDEMONA: It yet hath felt no age nor known no sorrow.

39 OTHELLO: This argues fruitfulness and liberal heart.
Hot, hot, and moist. This hand of yours requires
41 A sequester from liberty, fasting and prayer,
42 Much castigation, exercise devout;
For here's a young and sweating devil here
That commonly rebels. 'Tis a good hand,
A frank one.

DESDEMONA: You may indeed say so,
For 'twas that hand that gave away my heart.

OTHELLO:
48 A liberal hand. The hearts of old gave hands,
49 But our new heraldry is hands, not hearts.

DESDEMONA:
I cannot speak of this. Come now, your promise.

51 OTHELLO: What promise, chuck?

DESDEMONA:
I have sent to bid Cassio come speak with you.

OTHELLO:
53 I have a salt and sorry rheum offends me;
Lend me thy handkerchief.

DESDEMONA: Here, my lord. (*She offers a handkerchief.*)

OTHELLO:
That which I gave you.

DESDEMONA: I have it not about me.

OTHELLO: Not?

DESDEMONA: No, faith, my lord.

OTHELLO:
That's a fault. That handkerchief
Did an Egyptian to my mother give.
62 She was a charmer, and could almost read
The thoughts of people. She told her, while she kept it
'Twould make her amiable and subdue my father
Entirely to her love, but if she lost it
Or made a gift of it, my father's eye
Should hold her loathèd and his spirits should hunt
68 After new fancies. She, dying, gave it me,

---

39 argues gives evidence of. **fruitfulness** generosity, amorousness, and fecundity. **liberal** generous and sexually free   **41 sequester** separation, sequestration   **42 castigation** corrective discipline. **exercise devout** i.e., prayer, religious meditation, etc.   **45 frank** generous, open (with sexual suggestion)   **48 The hearts [. . .] hands** i.e., in former times, people would give their hearts when they gave their hands to something   **49 But [. . .] hearts** i.e., in our decadent times, the joining of hands is no longer a badge to signify the giving of hearts   **51 chuck** (A term of endearment.)   **53 salt [. . .] rheum** distressful head cold or watering of the eyes   **62 charmer** sorceress   **68 fancies** loves

And bid me, when my fate would have me wived,
70   To give it her. I did so; and take heed on 't;
Make it a darling like your precious eye.
72   To lose 't or give 't away were such perdition
As nothing else could match.

DESDEMONA: Is 't possible?

OTHELLO:
    is true. There's magic in the web of it.
    A sibyl, that had numbered in the world
77   The sun to course two hundred compasses,
78   In her prophetic fury sewed the work;
    The worms were hallowed that did breed the silk,
80   And it was dyed in mummy which the skillful
81   Conserved of maiden's hearts.

DESDEMONA: I' faith! Is 't true?

OTHELLO:
    Most veritable. Therefore look to 't well.

DESDEMONA: Then would to God that I had never seen 't!

OTHELLO: Ha? Wherefore?

DESDEMONA:
86   Why do you speak so startingly and rash?

OTHELLO:
87   Is 't lost? Is 't gone? Speak, is 't out o' the way?

DESDEMONA: Heaven bless us!

OTHELLO: Say you?

90   DESDEMONA: It is not lost; but what an if it were?

OTHELLO: How?

DESDEMONA:
    I say it is not lost.

OTHELLO: Fetch 't, let me see 't.

DESDEMONA:
    Why, so I can, sir, but I will not now.
    This is a trick to put me from my suit.
    Pray you, let Cassio be received again.

OTHELLO:
    Fetch me the handkerchief! My mind misgives.

DESDEMONA: Come, come,
99   You'll never meet a more sufficient man.

OTHELLO:
    The handkerchief!

---

70 her i.e., to my wife   **72 perdition** loss   **77 compasses** annual circlings. (The *sibyl*, or prophetess, was two hundred years old.)   **78 prophetic fury** frenzy of prophetic inspiration. **work** embroidered pattern   **80 mummy** medicinal or magical preparation drained from mummified bodies   **81 Conserved of** prepared or preserved out of **86 startingly and rash** disjointedly and impetuously, excitedly   **87 out o' the way** lost, misplaced   **90 an if** if   **99 sufficient** able, complete

101 DESDEMONA: I pray, talk me of Cassio.
     OTHELLO:
          The handkerchief!
103 DESDEMONA: A man that all his time
          Hath founded his good fortunes on your love,
          Shared dangers with you—
     OTHELLO: The handkerchief!
     DESDEMONA: I' faith, you are to blame.
     OTHELLO: Zounds!   (*Exit Othello.*)
     EMILIA: Is not this man jealous?
     DESDEMONA: I ne'er saw this before.
          Sure, there's some wonder in this handkerchief.
          I am most unhappy in the loss of it.
     EMILIA:
113   'Tis not a year or two shows us a man.
114   They are all but stomachs, and we all but food;
115   They eat us hungerly, and when they are full
          They belch us.

          (*Enter Iago and Cassio.*)

                         Look you, Cassio and my husband.
     IAGO (*to Cassio*): There is no other way; 'tis she must do 't.
119   And, lo, the happiness! Go and importune her.
     DESDEMONA:
          How now, good Cassio? What's the news with you?
     CASSIO:
          Madam, my former suit. I do beseech you
122   That by your virtuous means I may again
          Exist and be a member of his love
124   Whom I, with all the office of my heart,
          Entirely honor. I would not be delayed.
126   If my offense be of such mortal kind
127   That nor my service past, nor present sorrows,
          Nor purposed merit in futurity
          Can ransom me into his love again,
130   But to know so must be my benefit;
          So shall I clothe me in a forced content,
132   And shut myself up in some other course,
133   To fortune's alms.

---

101 **talk** talk to   103 **all his time** throughout his career   113 **'Tis [. . .] man** i.e., you
can't really know a man even in a year or two of experience (?), or, real men come along
seldom (?)   114 **but** nothing but   115 **hungerly** hungrily   119 **the happiness** in
happy time, fortunately met   122 **virtuous** efficacious   124 **office** loyal service
126 **mortal** fatal   127 **nor [. . .] nor** neither [. . .] nor   130 **But [. . .] benefit** merely
to know that my case is hopeless will have to content me (and will be better than uncertainty)   132 **shut [. . .] in** confine myself to   133 **To fortune's alms** throwing myself
on the mercy of fortune

DESDEMONA: Alas, thrice-gentle Cassio,
135   My advocation is not now in tune.
         My lord is not my lord; nor should I know him,
137   Were he in favor as in humor altered.
         So help me every spirit sanctified
         As I have spoken for you all my best
140   And stood within the blank of his displeasure
         For my free speech! You must awhile be patient.
         What I can do I will, and more I will
         Than for myself I dare. Let that suffice you.

IAGO:
         Is my lord angry?

EMILIA: He went hence but now.
         And certainly in strange unquietness.

IAGO:
         Can he be angry? I have seen the cannon
         When it hath blown his ranks into the air,
         And like the devil from his very arm
         Puffed his own brother—and is he angry?
151   Something of moment then. I will go meet him.
         There's matter in 't indeed, if he be angry.

DESDEMONA:
         I prithee, do so.   *(Exit [Iago].)*
154   Something, sure of state,
155   Either from Venice, or some unhatched practice
         Made demonstrable here in Cyprus to him,
157   Hath puddled his clear spirit; and in such cases
         Men's natures wrangle with inferior things,
         Though great ones are their object. 'Tis even so;
160   For let our finger ache, and it indues
         Our other, healthful members even to a sense
         Of pain. Nay, we must think men are not gods,
163   Nor of them look for such observancy
164   As fits the bridal. Beshrew me much, Emilia,
165   I was, unhandsome warrior as I am,
166   Arraigning his unkindness with my soul;
167   But now I find I had suborned the witness,
         And he's indicted falsely.

---

135 **advocation** advocacy   137 **favor** appearance. **humor** mood   140 **within the blank** within point-blank range. (The *blank* is the center of the target.)   151 **of moment** of immediate importance, momentous   154 **of state** concerning state affairs   155 **unhatched practice** as yet unexecuted or undiscovered plot   157 **puddled** muddied   160 **indues** brings to the same condition   163 **observancy** attentiveness   164 **bridal** wedding (when a bridegroom is newly attentive to his bride). **Beshrew me** (A mild oath.)   165 **unhandsome** insufficient, unskillful   166 **with** before the bar of   167 **suborned the witness** induced the witness to give false testimony

EMILIA: Pray heaven it be
State matters, as you think, and no conception
171   Nor no jealous toy concerning you.
DESDEMONA:
Alas the day! I never gave him cause.
EMILIA:
But jealous souls will not be answered so;
They are not ever jealous for the cause,
175   But jealous for they're jealous. It is a monster
176   Begot upon itself, born on itself.
DESDEMONA:
Heaven keep that monster from Othello's mind!
EMILIA: Lady, amen.
DESDEMONA:
I will go seek him. Cassio, walk hereabout.
If I do find him fit, I'll move your suit
And seek to effect it to my uttermost.
CASSIO:
I humbly thank your ladyship.

                    (Exit [Desdemona with Emilia].)

                    (Enter Bianca.)

BIANCA:
183   Save you, friend Cassio!
184   CASSIO: What make you from home?
How is 't with you, my most fair Bianca?
I' faith, sweet love, I was coming to your house.
BIANCA:
And I was going to your lodging, Cassio.
What, keep a week away? Seven days and nights?
189   Eightscore-eight hours? And lovers' absent hours
190   More tedious than the dial eightscore times?
O weary reckoning!
CASSIO: Pardon me, Bianca.
I have this while with leaden thoughts been pressed;
194   But I shall, in a more continuate time,
195   Strike off this score of absence. Sweet Bianca,

                    (giving her Desdemona's handkerchief)

196   Take me this work out.

---

171 toy fancy   **175 for** because   **176 Begot upon itself** generated solely from itself
183 Save God save.   **184 make** do   **189 Eightscore-eight** one hundred sixty-eight,
the number of hours in a week   **190 the dial** a complete revolution of the clock
194 continuate uninterrupted   **195 Strike [. . .] score** settle this account   **196 Take**
[. . .] out copy this embroidery for me

BIANCA: O Cassio, whence came this?
198 This is some token from a newer friend.
To the felt absence now I feel a cause.
Is't come to this? Well, well.
CASSIO: Go to, woman!
Throw your vile guesses in the devil's teeth,
From whence you have them. You are jealous now
That this is from some mistress, some remembrance.
No, by my faith, Bianca.
BIANCA: Why, whose is it?
CASSIO:
I know not, neither. I found it in my chamber.
208 I like the work well. Ere it be demanded—
209 As like enough it will—I would have it copied.
Take it and do 't, and leave me for this time.
BIANCA: Leave you? Wherefore?
CASSIO:
I do attend here on the General,
213 And think it no addition, nor my wish,
To have him see me womaned.
BIANCA: Why, I pray you?
CASSIO: Not that I love you not.
BIANCA: But that you do not love me.
218 I pray you, bring me on the way a little,
And say if I shall see you soon at night.
CASSIO:
'Tis but a little way that I can bring you,
For I attend here; but I'll see you soon.
BIANCA:
'Tis very good. I must be circumstanced.

(Exeunt omnes.)

4.1

(Enter Othello and Iago.)

IAGO: Will you think so?
OTHELLO: Think so, Iago?
IAGO: What,
To kiss in private?
OTHELLO: An unauthorized kiss!
IAGO:
Or to be naked with her friend in bed

---

198 friend mistress   **208 demanded** inquired for   **209 like** likely   **213 addition** i.e., addition to my reputation   **218 bring** accompany   **4.1 Location: Before the citadel**.

An hour or more, not meaning any harm?

OTHELLO:

Naked in bed, Iago, and not mean harm?
It is hypocrisy against the devil.
They that mean virtuously and yet do so,
The devil their virtue tempts, and they tempt heaven.

IAGO:

12   If they do nothing, 'tis a venial slip.
But if I give my wife a handkerchief—

OTHELLO: What then?

IAGO:

Why then, 'tis hers, my lord, and being hers,
She may, I think, bestow 't on any man.

OTHELLO:

She is protectress of her honor too.
May she give that?

IAGO:

Her honor is an essence that's not seen;
20   They have it very oft that have it not.
But, for the handkerchief—

OTHELLO:

By heaven, I would most gladly have forgot it.
Thou saidst—O, it comes o'er my memory
24   As doth the raven o'er the infectious house,
Boding to all—he had my handkerchief.

IAGO: Ay, what of that?

OTHELLO: That's not so good now.

IAGO: What
If I had said I had seen him do you wrong?
30   Or heard him say—as knaves by such abroad,
Who having, by their own importunate suit,
32   Or voluntary dotage of some mistress,
33   Convincèd or supplied them, cannot choose
But they must blab—

OTHELLO: Hath he said anything?

IAGO:

He hath, my lord; but, be you well assured,
No more than he'll unswear.

OTHELLO: What hath he said?

IAGO:

Faith, that he did—I know not what he did.

OTHELLO: What? What?

---

12 **venial** pardonable   20 **They have it** i.e., they enjoy a reputation for it   24 **raven [. . .] house** (Allusion to the belief that the raven hovered over a house of sickness or infection, such as one visited by the plague.)   30 **abroad** around about   32 **voluntary dotage** willing infatuation   33 **Convincèd or supplied** seduced or sexually gratified

IAGO:
 Lie—
OTHELLO: With her?
IAGO: With her, on her; what you will.
OTHELLO: Lie with her? Lie on her? We say "lie on her"
45   when they belie her. Lie with her? Zounds, that's fulsome.
      —Handkerchief—confessions—handkerchief!
47   —To confess and be hanged for his labor—first to be
48   hanged and then to confess.—I tremble at it. Nature
      would not invest herself in such shadowing passion
50   without some instruction. It is not words that shakes
      me thus. Pish! Noses, ears, and lips.—Is 't possible?
      —Confess—handkerchief!—O devil!

(Falls in a trance.)

IAGO: Work on,
   My medicine, work! Thus credulous fools are caught,
   And many worthy and chaste dames even thus,
   All guiltless, meet reproach.—What, ho! My lord!
   My lord, I say! Othello!

(Enter Cassio.)

                    How now, Cassio?
CASSIO: What's the matter?
IAGO:
   My lord is fall'n into an epilepsy.
   This is his second fit. He had one yesterday.
CASSIO:
   Rub him about the temples.
IAGO: No, forbear.
64   The lethargy must have his quiet course.
      If not, he foams at mouth, and by and by
      Breaks out to savage madness. Look, he stirs.
      Do you withdraw yourself a little while.
      He will recover straight. When he is gone,
69   I would on great occasion speak with you.

(Exit Cassio.)

   How is it, General? Have you not hurt your head?

---

45 belie slander. **fulsome** foul   **47–48 first [. . .] to confess** (Othello reverses the
proverbial *confess and be hanged*; Cassio is to be given no time to confess before he
dies.)   **48–50 Nature [. . .] instruction** i.e., without some foundation in fact, nature
would not have dressed herself in such an overwhelming passion that comes over me
now and fills my mind with images, or in such a lifelike fantasy as Cassio had in his
dream of lying with Desdemona   **50 words** mere words   **64 lethargy** coma. **his** its
69 on great occasion on a matter of great importance

OTHELLO:

71   Dost thou mock me?

IAGO: I mock you not, by heaven.
      Would you would bear your fortune like a man!

OTHELLO:
      A hornèd man's a monster and a beast.

IAGO:
      There's many a beast then in a populous city,
76   And many a civil monster.

OTHELLO: Did he confess it?

IAGO: Good sir, be a man.

79   Think every bearded fellow that's but yoked
80   May draw with you. There's millions now alive
81   That nightly lie in those unproper beds
82   Which they dare swear peculiar. Your case is better.
      O, 'tis the spite of hell, the fiend's arch-mock,
84   To lip a wanton in a secure couch
      And to suppose her chaste! No, let me know,
86   And knowing what I am, I know what she shall be.

OTHELLO: O, thou art wise. 'Tis certain.

IAGO: Stand you awhile apart;
89   Confine yourself but in a patient list.
      Whilst you were here o'erwhelmèd with your grief—
      A passion most unsuiting such a man—
92   Cassio came hither. I shifted him away,
93   And laid good 'scuse upon your ecstasy,
      Bade him anon return and here speak with me,
95   The which he promised. Do but encave yourself
96   And mark the fleers, the gibes, and notable scorns
      That dwell in every region of his face;
      For I will make him tell the tale anew,
      Where, how, how oft, how long ago, and when
100   He hath and is again to cope your wife.
      I say, but mark his gesture. Marry, patience!
102   Or I shall say you're all-in-all in spleen,
      And nothing of a man.

OTHELLO: Dost thou hear, Iago?

---

71 mock me (Othello takes Iago's question about hurting his head to be a mocking reference to the cuckold's horns)   **76 civil** i.e., dwelling in a city   **79 yoked** (1) married
(2) put into the yoke of infamy and cuckoldry   **80 draw with you** pull as you do, like
oxen who are yoked, i.e., share your fate as cuckold   **81 unproper** not exclusively their
own   **82 peculiar** private, their own. **better** i.e., because you know the truth   **84 lip**
kiss. **secure** free from suspicion   **86 what I am** i.e., a cuckold. **she shall be** will happen to her   **89 in [. . .] list** within the bounds of patience   **92 shifted him away** used
a dodge to get rid of him   **93 ecstasy** trance   **95 encave** conceal   **96 fleers** sneers.
notable obvious   **100 cope** encounter with, have sex with   **102 all-in-all in spleen**
utterly governed by passionate impulses

I will be found most cunning in my patience;
But dost thou hear?—most bloody.

IAGO: That's not amiss;

108   But yet keep time in all. Will you withdraw?

(Othello stands apart.)

Now will I question Cassio of Bianca,
110   A huswife that by selling her desires.
Buys herself bread and clothes. It is a creature
That dotes on Cassio—as 'tis the strumpet's plague
To beguile many and be beguiled by one.
114   He, when he hears of her, cannot restrain
From the excess of laughter. Here he comes.

(Enter Cassio.)

As he shall smile, Othello shall go mad;
117   And his unbookish jealousy must conster
Poor Cassio's smiles, gestures, and light behaviors
Quite in the wrong.—How do you now, Lieutenant?

CASSIO:

120   The worser that you give me the addition
121   Whose want even kills me.

IAGO:

Ply Desdemona well and you are sure on 't.
(Speaking lower.) Now, if this suit lay in Bianca's power,
How quickly should you speed!

125   CASSIO *(laughing)*: Alas, poor caitiff!

OTHELLO *(aside)*: Look how he laughs already!

IAGO:

I never knew a woman love man so.

CASSIO:

Alas, poor rogue! I think, i' faith, she loves me.

OTHELLO:

Now he denies it faintly, and laughs it out.

IAGO:

Do you hear, Cassio?

OTHELLO: Now he importunes him

132   To tell it o'er. Go to! Well said, well said.

IAGO:

She gives it out that you shall marry her.
Do you intend it?

CASSIO: Ha, ha, ha!

---

108 keep time keep yourself steady (as in music)   **110 huswife** hussy   **114 restrain**
refrain   **117 unbookish** uninstructed. **conster** construe   **120 addition** title
121 Whose want the lack of which   **125 caitiff** wretch   **132 Go to** (An expression of
remonstrance.) **Well said** well done

OTHELLO:
136 Do you triumph, Roman? Do you triumph?
137 CASSIO: I marry her? What? A customer? Prithee, bear
some charity to my wit; do not think it so unwhole-
some. Ha, ha, ha!
140 OTHELLO: So, so, so, so! They laugh that win.
141 IAGO: Faith, the cry goes that you shall marry her.
CASSIO: Prithee, say true.
143 IAGO: I am a very villain else.
144 OTHELLO: Have you scored me? Well.
CASSIO: This is the monkey's own giving out. She is
persuaded I will marry her out of her own love and
147 flattery, not out of my promise.
148 OTHELLO: Iago beckons me. Now he begins the story.
CASSIO: She was here even now; she haunts me in every
150 place. I was the other day talking on the seabank with
151 certain Venetians, and thither comes the bauble, and,
152 by this hand, she falls thus about my neck—
        [*He embraces Iago.*]
OTHELLO: Crying, "O dear Cassio!" as it were; his gesture imports it.
CASSIO: So hangs and lolls and weeps upon me, so shakes
and pulls me. Ha, ha, ha!
OTHELLO: Now he tells how she plucked him to my
158 chamber. O, I see that nose of yours, but not that dog
I shall throw it to.
CASSIO: Well, I must leave her company.
161 IAGO: Before me, look where she comes.

(Enter Bianca [with Othello's handkerchief].)

162 CASSIO: 'Tis such another fitchew! Marry, a perfumed
one. What do you mean by this haunting of me?
164 BIANCA: Let the devil and his dam haunt you! What did
you mean by that same handkerchief you gave me
even now? I was a fine fool to take it. I must take out
167 the work? A likely piece of work, that you should find

---

136 Roman (The Romans were noted for their *triumphs* or triumphal processions.)
137 customer i.e., prostitute   **137–138 bear [. . .] wit** be more charitable to my judgment   **140 They [. . .] win** i.e., they that laugh last laugh best   **141 cry** rumor   **143 I
[. . .] else** call me a complete rogue if I'm not telling the truth   **144 scored me** scored
off me, beaten me, made up my reckoning, branded me   **147 flattery** self-flattery, self-
deception   **148 beckons** signals   **150 seabank** seashore   **151 bauble** plaything
152 by this hand I make my vow   **158–159 not [...] to** (Othello imagines himself cutting off Cassio's nose and throwing it to a dog.)   **161 Before me** i.e., on my soul
162 'Tis [. . .] fitchew what a polecat she is! Just like all the others. **fitchew** (Polecats
were often compared with prostitutes because of their rank smell and presumed lechery.)
164 dam mother   **167 A likely [. . .] work** a fine story

it in your chamber and know not who left it there!
This is some minx's token, and I must take out the
170   work? There; give it your hobbyhorse. [*She gives him
the handkerchief.*] Wheresoever you had it, I'll take out
no work on't.

CASSIO: How now, my sweet Bianca? How now? How now?

174   OTHELLO: By heaven, that should be my handkerchief!

BIANCA: If you'll come to supper tonight, you may; if
176   you will not, come when you are next prepared for.

(Exit.)

IAGO: After her, after her.

CASSIO: Faith, I must. She'll rail in the streets else.

IAGO: Will you sup there?

CASSIO: Faith, I intend so.

IAGO: Well, I may chance to see you, for I would very fain speak with you.

CASSIO: Prithee, come. Will you?

183   IAGO: Go to. Say no more.   *(Exit Cassio.)*

OTHELLO (*advancing*): How shall I murder him, Iago?

IAGO: Did you perceive how he laughed at his vice?

OTHELLO: O, Iago!

IAGO: And did you see the handkerchief?

OTHELLO: Was that mine?

IAGO: Yours, by this hand. And to see how he prizes
the foolish woman your wife! She gave it him, and he
hath given it his whore.

OTHELLO: I would have him nine years a-killing. A fine
woman! A fair woman! A sweet woman!

IAGO: Nay, you must forget that.

OTHELLO: Ay, let her rot and perish, and be damned
tonight, for she shall not live. No, my heart is turned
to stone; I strike it, and it hurts my hand. O, the world
hath not a sweeter creature! She might lie by an emperor's side and command him tasks.

200   IAGO: Nay, that's not your way.

OTHELLO: Hang her! I do but say what she is. So delicate
with her needle! An admirable musician! O, she will
sing the savageness out of a bear. Of so high and plen-
204   teous wit and invention!

IAGO: She's the worse for all this.

OTHELLO: O, a thousand, a thousand times! And then,
207   of so gentle a condition!

---

170 **hobbyhorse** harlot   174 **should be** must be   176 **when [. . .] for** when I'm ready
for you (i.e., never)   183 **Go to** (An expression of remonstrance.)   200 **your way** i.e.
the way you should think of her   204 **invention** imagination   207 **gentle a condition**
wellborn and well-bred

208 IAGO: Ay, too gentle.

OTHELLO: Nay, that's certain. But yet the pity of it, Iago!
O, Iago, the pity of it, Iago!

211 IAGO: If you are so fond over her iniquity, give her patent
to offend, for if it touch not you it comes near nobody.

213 OTHELLO: I will chop her into messes.
Cuckold me?

IAGO: O, 'tis foul in her.

OTHELLO: With mine officer?

IAGO: That's fouler.

OTHELLO: Get me some poison, Iago, this night. I'll not

218 expostulate with her, lest her body and beauty unprovide my mind again. This night, Iago.

IAGO: Do it not with poison. Strangle her in her bed,
even the bed she hath contaminated.

OTHELLO: Good, good! The justice of it pleases. Very good.

223 IAGO: And for Cassio, let me be his undertaker. You shall
hear more by midnight.

OTHELLO:
Excellent good. [*A trumpet within.*] What trumpet is that same?

IAGO: I warrant, something from Venice.

(Enter Lodovico, Desdemona, and attendants.)

'Tis Lodovico. This comes from the Duke.
See, your wife's with him.

LODOVICO:
God save you, worthy General!

230 OTHELLO: With all my heart, sir.

LODOVICO (*giving him a letter*):
The duke and the senators of Venice greet you.

OTHELLO:
I kiss the instrument of their pleasures.

(He opens the letter, and reads.)

DESDEMONA:
And what's the news, good cousin Lodovico?

IAGO:
I am very glad to see you, signor. Welcome to Cyprus.

LODOVICO:
I thank you. How does Lieutenant Cassio?

IAGO: Lives, sir.

---

208 gentle generous, yielding (to other men)   **211 fond** foolish. **patent** license
213 messes portions of meat, i.e., bits   **218–219 unprovide** weaken, render unfit
223 be his undertaker undertake to dispatch him   **230 With all my heart** i.e., I thank
you most heartily

DESDEMONA:

238   Cousin, there's fall'n between him and my lord
An unkind breach; but you shall make all well.

OTHELLO: Are you sure of that?

DESDEMONA: My lord?

OTHELLO (*reads*): "This fail you not to do, as you will—"

LODOVICO:

He did not call; he's busy in the paper.
Is there division twixt my lord and Cassio?

DESDEMONA:

A most unhappy one. I would do much
245   T' atone them, for the love I bear to Cassio.

OTHELLO: Fire and brimstone!

DESDEMONA: My lord?

OTHELLO: Are you wise?

DESDEMONA:

What, is he angry?

LODOVICO: Maybe the letter moved him;
For, as I think, they do command him home,
252   Deputing Cassio in his government.

253   DESDEMONA: By my troth, I am glad on 't.

OTHELLO: Indeed?

DESDEMONA: My lord?

256   OTHELLO: I am glad to see you mad.

DESDEMONA: Why, sweet Othello—

OTHELLO (*striking her*): Devil!

DESDEMONA: I have not deserved this.

LODOVICO:

My lord, this would not be believed in Venice,
261   Though I should swear I saw 't. 'Tis very much.
Make her amends; she weeps.

OTHELLO: O devil, devil!
264   If that the earth could teem with woman's tears,
265   Each drop she falls would prove a crocodile.
Out of my sight!

DESDEMONA: I will not stay to offend you.   (*Going.*)

LODOVICO: Truly, an obedient lady.

I do beseech your lordship, call her back.

OTHELLO: Mistress!

DESDEMONA (*returning*): My lord?

---

238 unkind unnatural, contrary to their natures; hurtful   **245 atone** reconcile
252 government office   **253 on 't** of it   **256 I am [. . .] mad** i.e., I am glad to see that
you are insane enough to rejoice in Cassio's promotion (? Othello bitterly plays on
Desdemona's *I am glad.*)   **261 very much** too much, outrageous   **264 teem** breed, be
impregnated   **265 falls** lets fall. **crocodile** (Crocodiles were supposed to weep hypocritical tears for their victims.)

272 OTHELLO: What would you with her, sir?

LODOVICO: Who, I, my lord?

OTHELLO:

Ay, you did wish that I would make her turn.
Sir, she can turn, and turn, and yet go on
And turn again; and she can weep, sir, weep;
277 And she's obedient, as you say, obedient,
Very obedient.—Proceed you in your tears.—
279 Concerning this, sir—O well—painted passion!—
I am commanded home.—Get you away;
I'll send for you anon.—Sir, I obey the mandate
And will return to Venice.—Hence, avaunt!

(Exit Desdemona.)

Cassio shall have my place. And, sir, tonight
I do entreat that we may sup together.
285 You are welcome, sir, to Cyprus.—Goats and monkeys!

(Exit.)

LODOVICO:

Is this the noble Moor whom our full Senate
Call all in all sufficient? Is this the nature
Whom passion could not shake? Whose solid virtue
The shot of accident nor dart of chance
Could neither graze nor pierce?

IAGO: He is much changed.

LODOVICO:

Are his wits safe? Is he not light of brain?

IAGO:

293 He's that he is. I may not breathe my censure
What he might be. If what he might he is not,
I would to heaven he were!

LODOVICO: What, strike his wife?

IAGO:

Faith, that was not so well; yet would I knew
That stroke would prove the worst!

299 LODOVICO: Is it his use?

300 Or did the letters work upon his blood
And new-create his fault?

---

272 What [. . .] sir (Othello implies that Desdemona is pliant and will do a *turn*, lines
274–276, for any man.)   **277 obedient** (With much the same sexual connotation as *turn*
in lines 274–276.)   **279 passion** i.e., grief   **285 Goats and monkeys** (See 3.3.446.)
293–295 I may [. . .] were i.e., I dare not venture an opinion as to whether he's of
unsound mind, as you suggest, but, if he isn't, then it might be better to wish he were in
fact insane, since only that could excuse his wild behavior   **299 use** custom
300 blood passions

IAGO: Alas, alas!
It is not honesty in me to speak
What I have seen and known. You shall observe him,
305   And his own courses will denote him so
That I may save my speech. Do but go after,
And mark how he continues.
LODOVICO:
I am sorry that I am deceived in him. (*Exeunt.*)

4.2

(Enter Othello and Emilia.)

OTHELLO: You have seen nothing then?
EMILIA:
Nor ever heard, nor ever did suspect.
OTHELLO:
Yes, you have seen Cassio and she together.
EMILIA:
But then I saw no harm, and then I heard
Each syllable that breath made up between them.
OTHELLO: What, did they never whisper?
EMILIA: Never, my lord.
OTHELLO: Nor send you out o' the way?
EMILIA: Never.
OTHELLO:
To fetch her fan, her gloves, her mask, nor nothing?
EMILIA: Never, my lord.
OTHELLO: That's strange.
EMILIA:
I durst, my lord, to wager she is honest,
14   Lay down my soul at stake. If you think other,
15   Remove your thought; it doth abuse your bosom.
If any wretch have put this in your head,
17   Let heaven requite it with the serpent's curse!
For if she be not honest, chaste, and true,
There's no man happy; the purest of their wives
Is foul as slander.
OTHELLO: Bid her come hither. Go.

(Exit Emilia.)

---

305 **courses will denote** actions will reveal **4.2 Location: The citadel. 14 at stake** as the wager **15 abuse your bosom** deceive you **17 the serpent's curse** the curse pronounced by God on the serpent for deceiving Eve, just as some man has done to Othello and Desdemona. (See Genesis 3:14.)

22   She says enough; yet she's a simple bawd
23   That cannot say as much. This is a subtle whore,
24   A closet lock and key of villainous secrets.
     And yet she'll kneel and pray; I have seen her do't.

(Enter Desdemona and Emilia.)

DESDEMONA: My lord, what is your will?
OTHELLO: Pray you, chuck, come hither.
DESDEMONA:
     What is your pleasure?
OTHELLO: Let me see your eyes.
     Look in my face.
DESDEMONA: What horrible fancy's this?
32   OTHELLO *(to Emilia)*: Some of your function, mistress.
33   Leave procreants alone and shut the door;
     Cough or cry "hem" if anybody come.
35   Your mystery, your mystery! Nay, dispatch.

(Exit Emilia.)

DESDEMONA *(kneeling)*:
     Upon my knees, what doth your speech import?
     I understand a fury in your words,
     But not the words.
OTHELLO:
     Why, what art thou?
DESDEMONA: Your wife, my lord, your true
     And loyal wife.
OTHELLO:
     Come, swear it, damn thyself,
43   Lest, being like one of heaven, the devils themselves
     Should fear to seize thee. Therefore be double damned:
     Swear thou art honest.
DESDEMONA: Heaven doth truly know it.
OTHELLO:
     Heaven truly knows that thou art false as hell.
DESDEMONA:
     To whom, my lord? With whom? How am I false?
OTHELLO [*weeping*]:
     Ah, Desdemon! Away, away, away!
DESDEMONA:
     Alas the heavy day! Why do you weep?

22–23 she's [...] much i.e., any procuress or go-between who couldn't make up as plausible a story as Emilia's would have to be pretty stupid   **23 This** i.e., Desdemona   **24 closet lock and key** i.e, concealer   **32 Some [. . .] function** i.e., practice your chosen profession, that of bawd (by guarding the door)   **33 procreants** mating couples   **35 mystery** trade, occupation   **43 being [. . .] heaven** looking like an angel

51   Am I the motive of these tears, my lord?
      If haply you my father do suspect
      An instrument of this your calling back,
      Lay not your blame on me. If you have lost him,
      I have lost him too.
      OTHELLO: Had it pleased heaven
57   To try me with affliction, had they rained
      All kinds of sores and shames on my bare head,
      Steeped me in poverty to the very lips,
      Given to captivity me and my utmost hopes,
      I should have found in some place of my soul
      A drop of patience. But, alas, to make me
63   A fixèd figure for the time of scorn
64   To point his slow and moving finger at!
      Yet could I bear that too, well, very well.
66   But there where I have garnered up my heart,
      Where either I must live or bear no life,
68   The fountain from the which my current runs
      Or else dries up to be discarded thence!
70   Or keep it as a cistern for foul toads
71   knot and gender in! Turn thy complexion there,
72   Patience, thou young and rose-lipped cherubin—
      Ay, there look grim as hell!
      DESDEMONA:
74   I hope my noble lord esteems me honest.
      OTHELLO:
75   O, ay, as summer flies are in the shambles,
76   That quicken even with blowing. O thou weed,
      Who art so lovely fair and smell'st so sweet
      That the sense aches at thee, would thou hadst ne'er been born!
      DESDEMONA:
79   Alas, what ignorant sin have I committed?
      OTHELLO:
      Was this fair paper, this most goodly book,
      Made to write "whore" upon? What committed?
82   Committed? O thou public commoner!
      I should make very forges of my cheeks,

---

51 motive cause   **57 they** i.e., heavenly powers   **63 time of scorn** i.e., scornful world
64 his its. **slow and moving finger** i.e., hour hand of the clock, moving so slowly it seems
hardly to move at all. (Othello envisages himself as being eternally pointed at by the scornful world as the numbers on a clock are pointed at by the hour hand.)   **66 garnered**
stored   **68 fountain** spring   **70 cistern** cesspool   **71 knot** couple. **gender** engender.
Turn [. . .] there change your color, grow pale, at such a sight.   **72–73 Patience [. . .]**
hell (Even Patience, that rose-lipped cherub, will look grim and pale at this spectacle.)
74 honest chaste   **75 shambles** slaughterhouse   **76 quicken** come to life. **with blow-**
ing i.e., with the puffing up of something rotten in which maggots are breeding   **79 igno-**
rant sin sin in ignorance   **82 commoner** prostitute

That would to cinders burn up modesty,
Did I but speak thy deeds. What committed?

86 Heaven stops the nose at it and the moon winks;
87 The bawdy wind, that kisses all it meets,
88 Is hushed within the hollow mine of earth
And will not hear 't. What committed?
Impudent strumpet!

DESDEMONA: By heaven, you do me wrong.
OTHELLO:
Are not you a strumpet?
DESDEMONA: No, as I am a Christian.

94 If to preserve this vessel for my lord
From any other foul unlawful touch
Be not to be a strumpet, I am none.

OTHELLO: What, not a whore?
DESDEMONA: No, as I shall be saved.
OTHELLO: Is 't possible?
DESDEMONA:
O, heaven forgive us!

101 OTHELLO: I cry you mercy, then.
I took you for that cunning whore of Venice
That married with Othello. (*Calling out.*) You, mistress,
That have the office opposite to Saint Peter
And keep the gate of hell!

(Enter Emilia.)

               You, you, ay, you!
107 We have done our course. There's money for your pains.

(He gives money.)

I pray you, turn the key and keep our counsel. (*Exit.*)
EMILIA:
109 Alas, what does this gentleman conceive?
How do you, madam? How do you, my good lady?
111 DESDEMONA: Faith, half asleep.
EMILIA:
Good madam, what's the matter with my lord?
DESDEMONA: With who?
EMILIA: Why, with my lord, madam.
DESDEMONA:
Who is thy lord?
EMILIA: He that is yours, sweet lady.

---

86 winks closes her eyes. (The moon symbolizes chastity.)   **87 bawdy** kissing one and
all   **88 mine** cave (where the winds were thought to dwell)   **94 vessel** body   **101 cry**
you mercy beg your pardon   **107 course** business (with an indecent suggestion of
"trick," turn at sex)   **109 conceive** suppose, think   **111 half asleep** i.e., dazed

DESDEMONA:

I have none. Do not talk to me, Emilia.

I cannot weep, nor answers have I none

119   But what should go by water. Prithee, tonight

Lay on my bed my wedding sheets, remember;

And call thy husband hither.

EMILIA: Here's a change indeed!   (*Exit.*)

DESDEMONA:

'Tis meet I should be used so, very meet.

124   How have I been behaved, that he might stick

125   The small'st opinion on my least misuse?

(Enter Iago and Emilia.)

IAGO:

What is your pleasure, madam? How is 't with you?

DESDEMONA:

I cannot tell. Those that do teach young babes

Do it with gentle means and easy tasks.

He might have chid me so, for, in good faith,

I am a child to chiding.

IAGO: What is the matter, lady?

EMILIA:

Alas, Iago, my lord hath so bewhored her,

Thrown such despite and heavy terms upon her,

That true hearts cannot bear it.

DESDEMONA: Am I that name, Iago?

IAGO: What name, fair lady?

DESDEMONA:

Such as she said my lord did say I was.

EMILIA:

He called her whore. A begger in his drink

139   Could not have laid such terms upon his callet.

IAGO: Why did he so?

DESDEMONA (*weeping*):

I do not know. I am sure I am none such.

IAGO: Do not weep, do not weep. Alas the day!

EMILIA:

Hath she forsook so many noble matches,

Her father and her country and her friends,

To be called whore? Would it not make one weep?

DESDEMONA:

It is my wretched fortune.

147   IAGO: Beshrew him for 't!

---

119 go by water be expressed by tears   **124 stick** attach   **125 opinion** censure. **least misuse** slightest misconduct   **139 callet** whore   **147 Beshrew** curse

148 How comes this trick upon him?

DESDEMONA: Nay, heaven doth know.

EMILIA:

150 I will be hanged if some eternal villain,
151 Some busy and insinuating rogue,
152 Some cogging, cozening slave, to get some office,
     Have not devised this slander. I will be hanged else.

IAGO:

Fie, there is no such man. It is impossible.

DESDEMONA:

If any such there be, heaven pardon him!

EMILIA:

156 A halter pardon him! And hell gnaw his bones!
     Why should he call her whore? Who keeps her company?
158 What place? What time? What form? What likelihood?
     The Moor's abused by some most villainous knave,
     Some base notorious knave, some scurvy fellow.
161 O heaven, that such companions thou'dst unfold,
     And put in every honest hand a whip
     To lash the rascals naked through the world
     Even from the east to th' west!

165 IAGO: Speak within door.

EMILIA:

166 O, fie upon them! Some such squire he was
167 That turned your wit the seamy side without
     And made you to suspect me with the Moor.

IAGO:

169 You are a fool. Go to.

DESDEMONA: Alas, Iago,
     What shall I do to win my lord again?
     Good friend, go to him; for, by this light of heaven,
     I know not how I lost him. Here I kneel.   (*She kneels.*)
     If e'er my will did trespass 'gainst his love,
175 Either in discourse of thought or actual deed,
176 Or that mine eyes, mine ears, or any sense
177 Delighted them in any other form;
178 Or that I do not yet, and ever did,
     And ever will—though he do shake me off
     To beggarly divorcement love him dearly,

---

148 **trick** strange behavior, delusion   150 **eternal** inveterate   151 **insinuating** ingratiating, fawning, wheedling   152 **cogging** cheating. **cozening** defrauding   156 **halter**
hangman's noose   158 **form** appearance, circumstance   161 **that** would that.
companions fellows. **unfold** expose   165 **within door** i.e., not so loud   166 **squire**
fellow   167 **seamy side without** wrong side out   169 **Go to** i.e., that's enough
175 **discourse of thought** process of thinking   176 **that** if. (Also in line 178.)
177 **Delighted them** took delight   178 **yet** still

181   Comfort forswear me! Unkindness may do much,
182   And his unkindness may defeat my life,
        But never taint my love. I cannot say "whore."
184   It does abhor me now I speak the word;
185   To do the act that might the addition earn
186   Not the world's mass of vanity could make me.

    (She rises.)

IAGO:
187   I pray you, be content. 'Tis but his humor.
        The business of the state does him offense,
        And he does chide with you.
DESDEMONA: If 'twere no other—
IAGO: It is but so, I warrant.   *(Trumpets within.)*
        Hark, how these instruments summon you to supper!
193   The messengers of Venice stays the meat.
        Go in, and weep not. All things shall be well.

            (Exeunt Desdemona and Emilia.)

    (Enter Roderigo.)

    How now, Roderigo?
RODERIGO: I do not find that thou deal'st justly with me.
IAGO: What in the contrary?
198   RODERIGO: Every day thou dafft'st me with some device,
        Iago, and rather, as it seems to me now, keep'st
200   from me all conveniency than suppliest me with the
201   least advantage of hope. I will indeed no longer
202   endure it, nor am I yet persuaded to put up in peace
        what already I have foolishly suffered.
IAGO: Will you hear me, Roderigo?
RODERIGO: Faith, I have heard too much, for your words
        and performances are no kin together.
IAGO: You charge me most unjustly.
RODERIGO: With naught but truth. I have wasted myself
        out of my means. The jewels you have had from me to
210   deliver Desdemona would half have corrupted a votarist.
        You have told me she hath received them and returned
212   me expectations and comforts of sudden respect and
        acquaintance, but I find none.
IAGO: Well, go to, very well.

---

181 Comfort forswear may heavenly comfort forsake   **182 defeat** destroy   **184 abhor**
(1) fill me with abhorrence (2) make me whorelike   **185 addition** title   **186 vanity**
showy splendor   **187 humor** mood   **193 stays the meat** are waiting to dine   **198 thou**
dafft'st me you put me off. **device** excuse, trick   **200 conveniency** advantage, opportunity   **201 advantage** increase   **202 put up** submit to, tolerate   **210 deliver** deliver to.
votarist nun   **212 sudden respect** immediate consideration

215 RODERIGO: "Very well"! "Go to"! I cannot go to, man,
    nor 'tis not very well. By this hand, I think it is scurvy,
217   and begin to find myself fopped in it.
    IAGO: Very well.
219 RODERIGO: I tell you 'tis not very well. I will make myself
    known to Desdemona. If she will return me my jewels,
    I will give over my suit and repent my unlawful solicita-
222   tion; if not, assure yourself I will seek satisfaction of you.
223 IAGO: You have said now?
    RODERIGO: Ay, and said nothing but what I protest
225   intendment of doing.
    IAGO: Why, now I see there's mettle in thee, and even
    from this instant do build on thee a better opinion
    than ever before. Give me thy hand, Roderigo. Thou
    hast taken against me a most just exception; but yet I
    protest I have dealt most directly in thy affair.
    RODERIGO: It hath not appeared.
    IAGO: I grant indeed it hath not appeared, and your
    suspicion is not without wit and judgment. But,
    Roderigo, if thou hast that in thee indeed which I have
    greater reason to believe now than ever—I mean
    purpose, courage, and valor—this night show it. If
    thou the next night following enjoy not Desdemona,
    take me from this world with treachery and devise
239   engines for my life.
    RODERIGO: Well, what is it? Is it within reason and compass?
    IAGO: Sir, there is especial commission come from Venice
    to depute Cassio in Othello's place.
    RODERIGO: Is that true? Why, then Othello and Desdemona
    return again to Venice.
    IAGO: O, no; he goes into Mauritania and takes away
    with him the fair Desdemona, unless his abode be
    lingered here by some accident; wherein none can be
248   so determinate as the removing of Cassio.
    RODERIGO: How do you mean, removing of him?
    IAGO: Why, by making him uncapable of Othello's
    place—knocking out his brains.
    RODERIGO: And that you would have me to do?
    IAGO: Ay, if you dare do yourself a profit and a right.

---

215 I cannot go to (Roderigo changes Iago's *go to*, an expression urging patience, to *I cannot go to*, "I have no opportunity for success in wooing.") **217 fopped** fooled, duped **219 not very well** (Roderigo changes Iago's *very well*, "all right then," to *not very well*, "not at all good.") **222 satisfaction** repayment. (The term normally means settling of accounts in a duel.) **223 You [. . .] now** have you finished? **225 intendment** intention **239 engines for** plots against **248 determinate** conclusive

254   He sups tonight with a harlotry, and thither will I go to
him. He knows not yet of his honorable fortune. If
you will watch his going thence, which I will fashion
257   to fall out between twelve and one, you may take him
at your pleasure. I will be near to second your attempt,
and he shall fall between us. Come, stand not amazed
at it, but go along with me. I will show you such a
necessity in his death that you shall think yourself
262   bound to put it on him. It is now high suppertime,
263   and the night grows to waste. About it.
RODERIGO: I will hear further reason for this.
IAGO: And you shall be satisfied.   (*Exeunt.*)

4.3

(*Enter Othello, Lodovico, Desdemona, Emilia, and attendants.*)

LODOVICO:
    I do beseech you, sir, trouble yourself no further.
OTHELLO:
    O, pardon me; 'twill do me good to walk.
LODOVICO:
    Madam, good night. I humbly thank your ladyship.
DESDEMONA:
    Your honor is most welcome.
OTHELLO: Will you walk, sir?
    O, Desdemona!
DESDEMONA: My lord?
OTHELLO: Get you to bed on th' instant. I will be returned forthwith. Dismiss your attendant there. Look 't be done.
DESDEMONA: I will my lord.

(*Exit [Othello, with Lodovico and attendants].*)

EMILIA: How goes it now? He looks gentler than he did.
DESDEMONA:
12   He says he will return incontinent,
    And hath commanded me to go to bed,
    And bid me to dismiss you.
EMILIA: Dismiss me?
DESDEMONA:
    It was his bidding. Therefore, good Emilia,
    Give me my nightly wearing, and adieu.
    We must not now displease him.
EMILIA: I would you had never seen him!

---

254 harlotry slut   **257 fall out** occur   **262 high** fully   **263 grows to waste** wastes away   **4.3. Location: The citadel.**   **12 incontinent** immediately

DESDEMONA:

21 So would not I. My love doth so approve him
That even his stubbornness, his checks, his frowns—
Prithee, unpin me—have grace and favor in them.

(Emilia prepares Desdemona for bed.)

EMILIA: I have laid those sheets you bade me on the bed.
DESDEMONA:

24 All's one. Good faith, how foolish are our minds!
If I do die before thee, prithee shroud me
In one of these same sheets.

27 EMILIA: Come, come, you talk.
DESDEMONA:

My mother had a maid called Barbary.
29 She was in love, and he she loved proved mad
And did forsake her. She had a song of "Willow."
An old thing 'twas, but it expressed her fortune,
And she died singing it. That song tonight
33 Will not go from my mind; I have much to do
But to go hang my head all at one side
And sing it like poor Barbary. Prithee, dispatch.

36 EMILIA: Shall I go fetch your nightgown?
DESDEMONA: No, unpin me here.
38   This Lodovico is a proper man.
EMILIA: A very handsome man.
DESDEMONA: He speaks well.
EMILIA: I know a lady in Venice would have walked barefoot to Palestine for a touch of his nether lip.
DESDEMONA *(singing)*:
"The poor soul sat sighing by a sycamore tree,
44 Sing all a green willow;
Her hand on her bosom, her head on her knee,
Sing willow, willow, willow.
The fresh streams ran by her and murmured her moans;
Sing willow, willow, willow;
Her salt tears fell from her, and softened the stones—"
   Lay by these.
(Singing.) "Sing willow, willow, willow—"
52   Prithee, hie thee. He'll come anon.
(Singing.) "Sing all a green willow must be my garland.
Let nobody blame him; his scorn I approve—"

---

21 stubbornness roughness. **checks** rebukes   **24 All's one** all right. It doesn't really matter   **27 talk** i.e., prattle   **29 mad** wild, i.e., faithless   **33–34 I [. . .] hang** I can scarcely keep myself from hanging   **36 nightgown** dressing gown   **38 proper** handsome   **44 willow** (A conventional emblem of disappointed love.)   **52 hie thee** hurry. **anon** right away

Nay, that's not next.—Hark! Who is 't that knocks?

EMILIA: It's the wind.

DESDEMONA (*singing*):
"I called my love false love; but what said he then?
    Sing willow, willow, willow;
If I court more women, you'll couch with more men."
    So, get thee gone. Good night. Mine eyes do itch;
    Doth that bode weeping?

EMILIA: 'Tis neither here nor there.

DESDEMONA: I have heard it said so. O, these men, these men!
Dost thou in conscience think—tell me, Emilia—

65 That there be women do abuse their husbands
In such gross kind?

EMILIA: There be some such, no question.

DESDEMONA:
Wouldst thou do such a deed for all the world?

EMILIA:
Why, would not you?

DESDEMONA: No, by this heavenly light!

EMILIA:
Nor I neither by this heavenly light;
I might do 't as well i' the dark.

DESDEMONA: Wouldst thou do such a deed for all the world?

EMILIA:
The world's a huge thing. It is a great price
For a small vice.

DESDEMONA:
Good troth, I think thou wouldst not.

EMILIA: By my troth, I think I should, and undo 't when
I had done. Marry, I would not do such a thing for a

79 joint ring, nor for measures of lawn, nor for gowns,

80 petticoats, nor caps, nor any petty exhibition. But for

81 all the whole world! Uds pity, who would not make
her husband a cuckold to make him a monarch? I
should venture purgatory for 't.

DESDEMONA:
Beshrew me if I would do such a wrong
For the whole world.

EMILIA: Why, the wrong is but a wrong i' the world, and
having the world for your labor, 'tis a wrong in your
own world, and you might quickly make it right.

DESDEMONA:
I do not think there is any such woman.

---

65 abuse deceive   **79 joint ring** a ring made in separate halves. **lawn** fine linen
80 exhibition gift   **81 Uds** God's

EMILIA: Yes, a dozen, and as many

91   To th' vantage as would store the world they played for.
      But I do think it is their husbands' faults

93   If wives do fall. Say that they slack their duties

94   And pour our treasures into foreign laps,
      Or else break out in peevish jealousies,

96   Throwing restraint upon us? Or say they strike us,

97   Or scant our former having in despite?

98   Why, we have galls, had though we have some grace,
      Yet have we some revenge. Let husbands know

100   Their wives have sense like them. They see, and smell,
      And have their palates both for sweet and sour,
      As husbands have. What is it that they do

103   When they change us for others? Is it sport?

104   I think it is. And doth affection breed it?
      I think it doth. Is 't frailty that thus errs?
      It is so, too. And have not we affections,
      Desires for sport, and frailty, as men have?
      Then let them sue us well; else let them know,
      The ills we do, their ills instruct us so.

DESDEMONA:

110   Good night, good night. God me such uses send

111   Not to pick bad from bad, but by bad mend!

                                          (Exeunt.)

5.1

(Enter Iago and Roderigo.)

IAGO:

1   Here stand behind this bulk. Straight will he come.

2   Wear thy good rapier bare, and put it home.
      Quick, quick! Fear nothing. I'll be at thy elbow.
      It makes us or it mars us. Think on that,

---

91 To th' vantage in addition, to boot. **store** populate. **played** (1) gambled (2) sported sexually   **93 duties** marital duties   **94 pour [. . .] laps** i.e., are unfaithful, give what is rightfully ours (semen) to other women   **96 Throwing [. . .] us** i.e., jealously restricting our freedom to see other men   **97 scant [. . .] despite** reduce our allowance to spite us   **98 have galls** i.e., are capable of resenting injury and insult   **100 sense** physical sense   **103 sport** sexual pastime   **104 affection** passion   **110 uses** habit, practice **111 Not [. . .] mend** i.e, not to learn bad conduct from others' badness (as Emilia has suggested women learn from men), but to mend my ways by perceiving what badness is, making spiritual benefit out of evil and adversity   **5.1 Location: A street in Cyprus. 1 bulk** framework projecting from the front of a shop   **2 bare** unsheathed

And fix most firm thy resolution.

RODERIGO:
Be near at hand. I may miscarry in 't.

IAGO:
Here, at thy hand. Be bold, and take thy stand.

(Iago stands aside. Roderigo conceals himself.)

RODERIGO:
I have no great devotion to the deed;
And yet he hath given me satisfying reasons.
'Tis but a man gone. Forth, my sword! He dies.

(He draws.)

IAGO:
11   I have rubbed this young quat almost to the sense,
And he grows angry. Now, whether he kill Cassio
Or Cassio him, or each do kill the other,
14   Every way makes my gain. Live Roderigo,
He calls me to a restitution large
16   Of gold and jewels that I bobbed from him
As gifts to Desdemona.
It must not be. If Cassio do remain,
He hath a daily beauty in his life
That makes me ugly; and besides, the Moor
21   May unfold me to him; there stand I in much peril.
No, he must die. Be 't so. I hear him coming.

(Enter Cassio.)

RODERIGO *(coming forth)*:
I know his gait, 'tis he.—Villain, thou diest!

(He attacks Cassio.)

CASSIO:
That thrust had been mine enemy indeed,
25   But that my coat is better than thou know'st.
26   I will make proof of thine.
(He draws, and wounds Roderigo.)

RODERIGO: O, I am slain! *(He falls.)*
(Iago, from behind, wounds Cassio in the leg, and exit.)

CASSIO:
I am maimed forever. Help, ho! Murder! Murder!

---

11 quat pimple, pustule. **to the sense** to the quick   **14 Live Roderigo** if Roderigo lives
16 bobbed swindled   **21 unfold** expose   **25 coat** (Possibly a garment of mail under
the outer clothing, or simply a tougher coat than Roderigo expected.)   **26 proof** a test

(Enter Othello.)

OTHELLO:
The voice of Cassio! Iago keeps his word.
RODERIGO: O, villain that I am!
OTHELLO: It is even so.
CASSIO: O, help, ho! Light! A surgeon!
OTHELLO:
'Tis he. O brave Iago, honest and just,
That hast such noble sense of thy friend's wrong!

35   Thou teachest me. Minion, your dear lies dead,
36   And your unblest fate hies. Strumpet, I come.
37   Forth of my heart those charms, thine eyes, are blotted;
    Thy bed, lust-stained, shall with lust's blood be spotted.
        (Exit Othello.)

(Enter Lodovico and Gratiano.)

CASSIO:
39   What ho! No watch? No passage? Murder! Murder!
GRATIANO:
'Tis some mischance. The voice is very direful.
CASSIO: O, help!
LODOVICO: Hark!
RODERIGO: O wretched villain!
LODOVICO:
44   Two or three groan. 'Tis heavy night;
    These may be counterfeits. Let's think 't unsafe
46   To come in to the cry without more help.

      (They remain near the entrance.)

RODERIGO:
Nobody come? Then shall I bleed to death.

      (Enter Iago [in his shirtsleeves, with a light].)

LODOVICO: Hark!
GRATIANO:
Here's one comes in his shirt, with light and weapons.
IAGO:
50   Who's there? Whose noise is this that cries on murder?
LODOVICO:
We do not know.
IAGO: Did not you hear a cry?

---

35 Minion hussy (i.e., Desdemona)   **36 hies** hastens on   **37 Forth of** from out
39 passage people passing by   **44 heavy** thick, dark   **46 come in to** approach
50 cries on cries out

CASSIO:
    Here, here! for heaven's sake, help me!

IAGO: What's the matter?
          (*He moves toward Cassio.*)

GRATIANO (*to Lodovico*):
    This is Othello's ancient, as I take it.

LODOVICO (*to Gratiano*):
    The same indeed, a very valiant fellow.

IAGO (*to Cassio*):
57   What are you here that cry so grievously?

CASSIO:
58   Iago? O, I am spoiled, undone by villains!
    Give me some help.

IAGO:
    O me, Lieutenant! What villains have done this?

CASSIO:
    I think that one of them is hereabout,
62   And cannot make away.

IAGO: O treacherous villains!
    (*To Lodovico and Gratiano.*) What are you there? Come
    in, and give me some help.   (*They advance.*)

RODERIGO: O, help me there!

CASSIO:
    That's one of them.

IAGO: O murderous slave! O villain!
      (*He stabs Roderigo.*)

RODERIGO:
    O damned Iago! O inhuman dog!

IAGO:
    Kill men i' the dark?—Where be these bloody thieves?—
    How silent is this town!—Ho! Murder, murder!—
    (*To Lodovico and Gratiano.*) What may you be? Are you of good
    or evil?

74 LODOVICO: As you shall prove us, praise us.

IAGO: Signor Lodovico?

LODOVICO: He, sir.

IAGO:
77   I cry you mercy. Here's Cassio hurt by villains.

GRATIANO: Cassio?

IAGO: How is 't, brother?

CASSIO: My leg is cut in two.

IAGO: Marry, heaven forbid!

---

57 What who (also at lines 64 and 72)   **58 spoiled** ruined, done for   **62 make** get
74 praise appraise   **77 I cry you mercy** I beg your pardon

Light, gentlemen! I'll bind it with my shirt.

(He hands them the light, and tends to Cassio's wound.)

(Enter Bianca.)

BIANCA:

What is the matter, ho? Who is 't that cried?

IAGO: Who is 't that cried?

BIANCA: O my dear Cassio!

My sweet Cassio! O Cassio, Cassio, Cassio!

IAGO:

O notable strumpet! Cassio, may you suspect

Who they should be that have thus mangled you?

CASSIO: No.

GRATIANO:

I am sorry to find you thus. I have been to seek you.

IAGO:

91   Lend me a garter. *(He applies a tourniquet.)* So.—O, for a chair,

To bear him easily hence!

BIANCA:

Alas, he faints! O Cassio, Cassio, Cassio!

IAGO:

Gentlemen all, I do suspect this trash

To be a party in this injury.—

Patience awhile, good Cassio.—Come, come;

Lend me a light. *(He shines the light on Roderigo.)*

Know we this face or no?

Alas, my friend and my dear countryman

Roderigo! No.—Yes, sure.—O heaven! Roderigo!

GRATIANO: What, of Venice?

IAGO: Even he, sir. Did you know him?

GRATIANO: Know him? Ay.

IAGO:

104   Signor Gratiano? I cry your gentle pardon.

105   These bloody accidents must excuse my manners

That so neglected you.

GRATIANO: I am glad to see you.

IAGO:

How do you, Cassio? O, a chair, a chair!

GRATIANO: Roderigo!

IAGO:

110   He, he, 'tis he. *(A litter is brought in.)* O, that's well said;

the chair.

Some good man bear him carefully from hence;

---

91 chair litter   **104 gentle** noble   **105 accidents** sudden events   **110 well said**
well done

I'll fetch the General's surgeon. (*To Bianca.*) For you, mistress,
114   Save you your labor.—He that lies slain here, Cassio,
115   Was my dear friend. What malice was between you?

CASSIO:
None in the world, nor do I know the man.

IAGO (*to Bianca*):
117   What, look you pale?—O, bear him out o' th' air.

(Cassio and Roderigo are borne off.)

118   Stay you, good gentlemen.—Look you pale, mistress?—
119   Do you perceive the gastness of her eye?—
120   Nay, if you stare, we shall hear more anon.—
Behold her well; I pray you, look upon her.
Do you see, gentlemen? Nay, guiltiness
Will speak, though tongues were out of use.

(Enter Emilia.)

EMILIA:
'Las, what's the matter? What's the matter, husband?

IAGO:
Cassio hath here been set on in the dark
By Roderigo and fellows that are scaped.
He's almost slain, and Roderigo dead.

EMILIA:
Alas, good gentleman! Alas, good Cassio!

IAGO:
This is the fruits of whoring. Prithee, Emilia,
130   Go know of Cassio where he supped tonight.
(*To Bianca.*) What, do you shake at that?

BIANCA:
He supped at my house, but I therefore shake not.

IAGO:
O, did he so? I charge you go with me.

EMILIA: O, fie upon thee, strumpet!

BIANCA:
135   I am no strumpet, but of life as honest
As you that thus abuse me.

EMILIA: As I? Faugh! Fie upon thee!

IAGO:
138   Kind gentlemen, let's go see poor Cassio dressed.—
Come, mistress, you must tell's another tale.

---

114 Save [. . .] labor i.e., never you mind tending Cassio   **115 malice** enmity   **117 bear [. . .] air** (Fresh air was thought to be dangerous for a wound.)   **118 Stay you** (Lodovico and Gratiano are evidently about to leave.)   **119 gastness** terror   **120 stare** (Iago pretends to interpret Bianca's wild looks as an involuntary confession of guilt.)   **130 know** learn   **135 honest** chaste   **138 Cassio dressed** Cassio's wounds dressed

Emilia, run you to the citadel
And tell my lord and lady what hath happed.—
Will you go on afore? (*Aside.*) This is the night
143   That either makes me or fordoes me quite.   (*Exeunt.*)

5.2

(*Enter Othello [with a light], and Desdemona in her bed.*)

OTHELLO:
1   It is the cause, it is the cause, my soul.
Let me not name it to you, you chaste stars!
It is the cause. Yet I'll not shed her blood,
Nor scar that whiter skin of hers than snow,
5   And smooth as monumental alabaster.
Yet she must die, else she'll betray more men.
7   Put out the light, and then put out the light.
8   If I quench thee, thou flaming minister,
I can again thy former light restore,
10   Should I repent me; but once put out thy light,
11   Thou cunning'st pattern of excelling nature,
12   I know not where is that Promethean heat
13   That can thy light relume. When I have plucked thy rose,
I cannot give it vital growth again;
It needs must wither. I'll smell thee on the tree.
(*He kisses her.*)
O balmy breath, that dost almost persuade
Justice to break her sword! One more, one more.
Be thus when thou art dead, and I will kill thee,
And love thee after. One more, and that's the last.
(*He kisses her.*)
So sweet was ne'er so fatal. I must weep,
21   But they are cruel tears. This sorrow's heavenly;
22   It strikes where it doth love. She wakes.
DESDEMONA: Who's there? Othello?
OTHELLO: Ay, Desdemona.
DESDEMONA: Will you come to bed, my lord?

---

143 fordoes undoes, ruins   **5.2 Location: A bedchamber in the citadel. s.d. in her bed** (Either the curtains are drawn back to reveal the bed in a recessed area backstage, or the bed is "thrust out" onstage as the scene begins.)   **1 cause** i.e., cause of justice, the offense itself, which Othello must correct as an agent of justice   **5 monumental** i.e., used in making tombs and funeral monuments   **7 the light [. . .] light** the torch or lamp [. . .] Desdemona's life   **8 flaming minister** torch or lamp that serves me   **10 repent me** change my mind   **11 Thou [. . .] pattern** you skillfully wrought perfect example   **12 Promethean heat** divine fire (Alluding to the theft of fire from heaven by Prometheus.)   **13 relume** rekindle   **21 cruel** unrelenting   **22 It [. . .] love** (Compare Hebrews 12:6: "For whom the Lord loveth he chasteneth.")

OTHELLO: Have you prayed tonight, Desdemon?

DESDEMONA: Ay, my lord.

OTHELLO:

28   If you bethink yourself of any crime

Unreconciled as yet to heaven and grace,

30   Solicit for it straight.

DESDEMONA:

Alack, my lord, what may you mean by that?

OTHELLO:

Well, do it, and be brief. I will walk by.

I would not kill thy unprepared spirit.

34   No, heaven forfend! I would not kill thy soul.

DESDEMONA:

Talk you of killing?

OTHELLO: Ay, I do.

DESDEMONA: Then heaven

Have mercy on me!

OTHELLO: Amen, with all my heart!

DESDEMONA:

If you say so, I hope you will not kill me.

OTHELLO: Humh!

DESDEMONA:

And yet I fear you; for you're fatal then

When your eyes roll so. Why I should fear I know not,

Since guiltiness I know not; but yet I feel I fear.

OTHELLO:

Think on thy sins.

46   DESDEMONA: They are loves I bear to you.

OTHELLO: Ay, and for that thou diest.

DESDEMONA:

That death's unnatural that kills for loving.

Alas, why gnaw you so your nether lip?

Some bloody passion shakes your very frame.

These are portents; but yet I hope, I hope,

52   They do not point on me.

OTHELLO: Peace, and be still!

DESDEMONA: I will so. What's the matter?

OTHELLO:

That handkerchief which I so loved and gave thee

Thou gav'st to Cassio.

DESDEMONA: No, by my life and soul!

Send for the man and ask him.

---

28 crime sin   **30 Solicit** petition, pray. **straight** immediately   **34 forfend** forbid
46 They are [. . .] you i.e., if I sinned, it was in loving you more than my father or more
than God   **52 point on** point at, predict what is to happen to

OTHELLO:

Sweet soul, take heed, take heed of perjury.

Thou art on thy deathbed.

DESDEMONA:

Ay, but not yet to die.

62 OTHELLO: Yes, presently.

Therefore confess thee freely of thy sin;

For to deny each article with oath

65 Cannot remove nor choke the strong conception

66 That I do groan withal. Thou art to die.

DESDEMONA:

Then Lord have mercy on me!

OTHELLO: I say, amen.

DESDEMONA:

And have you mercy too! I never did

70 Offend you in my life; never loved Cassio

71 But with such general warranty of heaven

As I might love. I never gave him token.

OTHELLO:

By heaven, I saw my handkerchief in 's hand.

74 O perjured woman! Thou dost stone my heart,

And makes me call what I intend to do

A murder, which I thought a sacrifice.

I saw the handkerchief.

DESDEMONA: He found it, then.

I never gave it him. Send for him hither;

Let him confess a truth.

OTHELLO: He hath confessed.

DESDEMONA: What, my lord?

OTHELLO:

That he hath used thee.

DESDEMONA: How? Unlawfully?

OTHELLO: Ay.

DESDEMONA:

He will not say so.

OTHELLO: No, his mouth is stopped;

88 Honest Iago hath ta'en order for't.

DESDEMONA:

O, my fear interprets. What, is he dead?

OTHELLO:

Had all his hairs been lives, my great revenge

Had stomach for them all.

DESDEMONA:

Alas, he is betrayed and I undone!   (*She weeps.*)

---

62 presently immediately   **65 conception** (1) belief in your guilt (2) plan in my mind
66 groan withal (1) groan at in sorrow (2) as in giving birth   **70 Offend** wrong   **71 warranty** sanction   **74 stone** turn to stone, harden   **88 ta'en order** taken measures

OTHELLO:

　　Out, strumpet! Weep'st thou for him to my face?

DESDEMONA:

　　O, banish me, my lord, but kill me not!

OTHELLO: Down, strumpet!

DESDEMONA:

　　Kill me tomorrow; let me live tonight!

OTHELLO: Nay, if you strive—

DESDEMONA:

　　But half an hour!

99　OTHELLO:　　　　　　　　　Being done, there is no pause.

DESDEMONA:

　　But while I say one prayer!

OTHELLO: It is too late.

(Smothers her.)

EMILIA *(at the door)*:

　　My lord, my lord! What, ho! My lord, my lord!

OTHELLO:

　　What noise is this? Not dead? Not yet quite dead?

　　I that am cruel am yet merciful;

　　I would not have thee linger in thy pain.

(He dispatches her.)

　　So, so.

EMILIA *(within)*: What, ho! My lord, my lord!

OTHELLO:　　　　　　　　　　　　　　　Who's there?

EMILIA *(within)*:

　　O, good my lord, I would speak a word with you!

OTHELLO:

　　Yes, 'tis Emilia.—By and by—She's dead.

　　'Tis like she comes to speak of Cassio's death.—

112　The noise was here. Ha! No more moving?

　　Still as the grave. Shall she come in? Were 't good?—

　　I think she stirs again. No. What's best to do?

　　If she come in, she'll sure speak to my wife.

　　My wife! My wife! What wife? I have no wife.

　　O, insupportable! O heavy hour!

　　Methinks it should be now a huge eclipse

　　Of sun and moon, and that th' affrighted globe

120　Should yawn at alteration.

EMILIA *(within)*:　　　　　　　　I do beseech you

　　That I may speak with you, O, good my lord!

---

99 Being done i.e., since justice has begun its relentless course　**112 here** (The Folio's
high is possible, suggesting that the commotion of the attack on Cassio was loud.)
120 yawn gape in amazement, i.e., move in an earthquake. (According to Pliny, earth-
quakes often happen during eclipses.) **at alteration** at these cataclysmic events in
nature, well suited to express the horror of Desdemona's death

OTHELLO:

 I had forgot thee. O, come in, Emilia.—

124 Soft, by and by. Let me the curtains draw—

   (He closes the bed-curtains and opens the door.)

 Where art thou?

   (Enter Emilia.)

    What's the matter with thee now?

EMILIA:

 O, my good lord, yonder's foul murders done!

OTHELLO: What, now?

EMILIA: But now, my lord.

OTHELLO:

130 It is the very error of the moon;

 She comes more nearer earth than she was wont,

 And makes men mad.

EMILIA:

 Cassio, my lord, hath killed a young Venetian

 Called Roderigo.

OTHELLO: Roderigo killed?

 And Cassio killed?

EMILIA: No, Cassio is not killed.

OTHELLO:

 Not Cassio killed? Then murder's out of tune,

 And sweet revenge grows harsh.

DESDEMONA: O, falsely, falsely murdered!

EMILIA: O Lord, what cry is that?

OTHELLO: That? What?

EMILIA:

143 Out and alas, that was my lady's voice.

   (She opens the bed-curtains.)

 Help, help, ho, help! O lady, speak again!

 Sweet Desdemona! O sweet mistress, speak!

DESDEMONA: A guiltless death I die.

EMILIA: O, who hath done this deed?

DESDEMONA: Nobody; I myself. Farewell.

 Commend me to my kind lord. O, farewell! *(She dies.)*

OTHELLO:

 Why, how should she be murdered?

EMILIA: Alas, who knows?

OTHELLO:

 You heard her say herself it was not I.

---

124 Soft wait a minute **130 error** aberration, irregularity **143 Out** (A cry of dismay, intensifying *alas.*)

EMILIA:
> She said so. I must needs report the truth.

OTHELLO:
> She's like a liar gone to burning hell!
> 'Twas I that killed her.

EMILIA: O, the more angel she,
> And you the blacker devil!

OTHELLO:
158   She turned to folly, and she was a whore.

EMILIA:
159   Thou dost belie her, and thou art a devil.

OTHELLO: She was false as water.

EMILIA: Thou art rash as fire to say
> That she was false. O, she was heavenly true!

OTHELLO:
163   Cassio did top her. Ask thy husband else.
> O, I were damned beneath all depth in hell
> But that I did proceed upon just grounds
> To this extremity. Thy husband knew it all.

EMILIA: My husband?

OTHELLO: Thy husband.

EMILIA: That she was false to wedlock?

OTHELLO:
> Ay, with Cassio. Nay, had she been true,
> If heaven would make me such another world
172   Of one entire and perfect chrysolite,
> I'd not have sold her for it.

EMILIA: My husband?

OTHELLO:
> Ay, 'twas he that told me on her first.
> An honest man he is, and hates the slime
> That sticks on filthy deeds.

EMILIA: My husband?

OTHELLO:
179   What needs this iterance, woman? I say thy husband.

EMILIA:
180   O mistress, villainy hath made mocks with love!
> My husband say she was false?

OTHELLO: He, woman;
> I say thy husband. Dost understand the word?
> My friend, thy husband, honest, honest Iago.

EMILIA:
> If he say so, may his pernicious soul

---

158 folly i.e., wantonness, fleshly sin   **159 belie** slander   **163 else** i.e., if you don't
believe me   **172 chrysolite** precious topaz   **179 iterance** iteration, repetition
180 made mocks with derided, made sport of

Rot half a grain a day! He lies to th' heart.

She was too fond of her most filthy bargain.

OTHELLO: Ha? (*He draws.*)

EMILIA: Do thy worst!

This deed of thine is no more worthy heaven

Than thou wast worthy her.

192 OTHELLO: Peace, you were best.

EMILIA:

Thou hast not half that power to do me harm

194 As I have to be hurt. O gull! O dolt!

As ignorant as dirt! Thou hast done a deed—

I care not for thy sword; I'll make thee known,

Though I lost twenty lives.—Help! Help, ho, help!

The Moor hath killed my mistress! Murder, murder!

(Enter Montano, Gratiano, and Iago.)

MONTANO:

What is the matter? How now, General?

EMILIA:

O, are you come, Iago? You have done well,

That men must lay their murders on your neck.

GRATIANO: What is the matter?

EMILIA (*to Iago*):

Disprove this villain, if thou be'st a man.

He says thou toldst him that his wife was false.

I know thou didst not; thou'rt not such a villain.

Speak, for my heart is full.

IAGO:

I told him what I thought, and told no more

208 Than what he found himself was apt and true.

EMILIA:

But did you ever tell him she was false?

IAGO: I did.

EMILIA:

You told a lie, an odious, damnèd lie!

Upon my soul, a lie, a wicked lie.

She false with Cassio? Did you say with Cassio?

IAGO:

214 With Cassio, mistress. Go to, charm your tongue.

EMILIA:

I will not charm my tongue; I am bound to speak.

My mistress here lies murdered in her bed—

ALL: O heavens forfend!

---

192 you were best it would be best for you   **194 to be hurt** i.e, to endure hurt. **gull** dupe   **208 apt** plausible   **214 charm** keep silent (as though by a magic spell)

EMILIA:
And your reports have set the murder on.

OTHELLO:
Nay, stare not, masters. It is true indeed.

GRATIANO: 'Tis a strange truth.

MONTANO:
O monstrous act!

EMILIA: Villainy, villainy, villainy!
I think upon 't—I think I smell 't! O villainy!

224   I thought so then—I'll kill myself for grief—
O villainy, villainy!

IAGO:
What, are you mad? I charge you, get you home.

EMILIA:
Good gentlemen, let me have leave to speak.
'Tis proper I obey him, but not now.
Perchance, Iago, I will ne'er go home.

OTHELLO:

230   O! O! O!   (*Othello falls on the bed.*)

EMILIA: Nay, lay thee down and roar,
For thou hast killed the sweetest innocent

233   That e'er did lift up eye.

OTHELLO (*rising*):   O, she was foul!
I scarce did know you, uncle. There lies your niece,
Whose breath indeed these hands have newly stopped.

237   I know this act shows horrible and grim.

GRATIANO:
Poor Desdemon! I am glad thy father's dead.
Thy match was mortal to him, and pure grief

240   Shore his old thread in twain. Did he live now,

241   This sight would make him do a desperate turn,
Yea, curse his better angel from his side,
And fall to reprobance.

OTHELLO:
'Tis pitiful. But yet Iago knows.
That she with Cassio hath the act of shame
A thousand times committed. Cassio confessed it;

247   And she did gratify his amorous works

248   With that recognizance and pledge of love
Which I first gave her. I saw it in his hand;

---

224 then (Perhaps at 3.3.347–349 and 4.2.150–169.)   **230 s.d. Othello [. . .] bed** (This
direction is from the Quarto, as also *He kisses her* at line 19 and *She dies* at line 149.)
233 lift up eye i.e., lift her eyes to heaven   **237 shows** looks   **240 Shore [. . .]**
thread sheared the thread of his old age (as Atropos, one of the three Fates, was thought
to do)   **241 turn** deed   **243 reprobance** damnation, i.e., suicide   **247 gratify** reward
248 recognizance token

It was a handkerchief, an antique token
My father gave my mother.

EMILIA: O God! O heavenly God!

IAGO:
Zounds, hold your peace.

EMILIA: 'Twill out, 'twill out! I peace?

208   No, I will speak as liberal as the north.
Let heaven and men and devils, let them all,
All, all, cry shame against me, yet I'll speak.

IAGO:
Be wise, and get you home.

EMILIA: I will not.

(Iago threatens Emilia.)

GRATIANO: Fie,
Your sword upon a woman?

EMILIA:
O thou dull Moor! That handkerchief thou speak'st of
I found by fortune and did give my husband;
For often, with a solemn earnestness,
265   More than indeed belonged to such a trifle,
He begged of me to steal 't.

IAGO: Villainous whore!

EMILIA:
She give it Cassio? No, alas! I found it,
And I did give 't my husband.

IAGO: Filth, thou liest!

EMILIA:
By heaven, I do not, I do not, gentlemen.
272   O murderous coxcomb! What should such a fool
Do with so good a wife?

274   OTHELLO: Are there no stones in heaven
275   But what serves for the thunder?—Precious villain!

(He runs at Iago; Montano disarms Othello, Iago, from behind, stabs Emilia.)

GRATIANO:
The woman falls! Sure he hath killed his wife.

EMILIA:
Ay, ay. O, lay me by my mistress' side.

(Exit Iago.)

---

255 liberal as the north freely as the north wind (blows)   **265 belonged** was appropriate   **272 coxcomb** fool. (Addressed to Othello.)   **274 stones** bolts, such as those used for thunderbolts   **275 Precious** i.e., arrant, utter, **s.d. He [. . .] Emilia** (The Quarto text reads, "The Moor runs at Iago. Iago kills his wife." The Quarto also specifies the exit of Iago at line 277 and the death of Emilia at line 293.)

GRATIANO:

> He's gone, but his wife's killed.

MONTANO:

> 'Tis a notorious villain. Take you this weapon,
> Which I have here recovered from the Moor.
> Come, guard the door without. Let him not pass,
> But kill him rather. I'll after that same villain,
> For 'tis a damnèd slave.

(Exit [with all but Othello and Emilia, who has been laid by Desdemona's side].)

OTHELLO: I am not valiant neither,

285 But every puny whipster gets my sword.

286 But why should honor outlive honesty?

> Let it go all.

EMILIA: What did thy song bode, lady?

> Hark, canst thou hear me? I will play the swan,
> And die in music. *(She sings.)* "Willow, willow, willow."
> Moor, she was chaste. She loved thee, cruel Moor.
> So come my soul to bliss as I speak true.
> So speaking as I think, alas, I die.   *(She dies.)*

OTHELLO:

> I have another weapon in this chamber;

295 It was a sword of Spain, the ice-brook's temper—

> O, here it is. *(He finds a sword.)* Uncle, I must come forth.

GRATIANO *(within)*:

> If thou attempt it, it will cost thee dear.
> Thou hast no weapon, and perforce must suffer.

OTHELLO:

> Look in upon me then and speak with me,

300 Or, naked as I am, I will assault thee.

(Enter Gratiano.)

GRATIANO:

> What is the matter?

OTHELLO: Behold, I have a weapon;

> A better never did itself sustain
> Upon a soldier's thigh. I have seen the day
> That, with this little arm and this good sword,
> I have made my way through more impediments

307 Than twenty times your stop. But O, vain boast!

> Who can control his fate? 'Tis not so now.

---

285 whipster contemptible fellow (one who is always ready to whip out his sword)
286 honor i.e., the bravery for which one enjoys a soldier's reputation. **honesty** true integrity   **295 the ice-brook's temper** tempered in ice-cold water   **300 naked** unarmed   **307 stop** power (to stop)

Be not afraid, though you do see me weaponed;
310 Here is my journey's end, here is my butt
311 And very seamark of my utmost sail.

(Gratiano steps back.)

312 Do you go back dismayed? 'Tis a lost fear;
313 Man but a rush against Othello's breast
And he retires. Where should Othello go?

(He turns to Desdemona.)

Now, how dost thou look now? O ill-starred wench!
316 Pale as thy smock! When we shall meet at compt,
This look of thine will hurl my soul from heaven,
And fiends will snatch at it. Cold, cold, my girl?
Even like thy chastity. O cursèd, cursèd slave!
Whip me, ye devils,
From the possession of this heavenly sight!
Blow me about in winds! Roast me in sulfur!
Wash me in steep-down gulfs of liquid fire!
O Desdemon! Dead, Desdemon! Dead! O! O!

(Enter Lodovico, Cassio [carried in a litter], Montano, and Iago [prisoner], with officers.)

LODOVICO:
Where is this rash and most unfortunate man?
OTHELLO:
That's he that was Othello. Here I am.
LODOVICO:
Where is that viper? Bring the villain forth.

(Iago is led forward.)

OTHELLO:
328 I look down towards his feet; but that's a fable.
If that thou be'st a devil, I cannot kill thee.

(He wounds Iago.)

LODOVICO:
Wrench his sword from him. *(Othello is disarmed.)*
IAGO: I bleed, sir, but not killed.
OTHELLO:
I am not sorry neither. I'd have thee live,

---

310 butt goal, limit (An archery term.)   **311 seamark** beacon (marking his destination or limit)   **312 lost** wasted, unneeded   **313 Man [. . .] rush** wield no more than a reed **316 compt** account, judgment day   **319 slave** i.e., Othello himself   **324 s.d. in a litter** (The Quarto specifies that Cassio is "in a chair.")   **328 towards his feet** i.e., to see if they are cloven, as the devil's are fabled to be

333   For in my sense 'tis happiness to die.

LODOVICO:
    O thou Othello that was once so good,

335   Fall'n in the practice of a cursèd slave,
    What shall be said to thee?

OTHELLO: Why, anything.
    An honorable murderer, if you will,
    For naught I did in hate, but all in honor.

LODOVICO:
    This wretch hath part confessed his villainy.

341   Did you and he consent in Cassio's death?

OTHELLO: Ay.

CASSIO:
    Dear General, I never gave you cause.

OTHELLO:
    I do believe it, and I ask your pardon.
    Will you, I pray, demand that demi-devil
    Why he hath thus ensnared my soul and body?

IAGO:
    Demand me nothing. What you know, you know.
    From this time forth I never will speak word.

LODOVICO: What, not to pray?

350 GRATIANO: Torments will ope your lips.

OTHELLO: Well, thou dost best.

LODOVICO:
    Sir, you shall understand what hath befall'n,
    Which, as I think, you know not. Here is a letter
    Found in the pocket of the slain Roderigo;
    And here another. (*He produces letters.*) The one of them imports
    The death of Cassio, to be undertook
    By Roderigo.

OTHELLO: O villain!

359 CASSIO: Most heathenish and most gross!

LODOVICO (*showing another paper*):

360   Now here's another discontented paper
    Found in his pocket too. And this, it seems,
    Roderigo meant t' have sent this damnèd villain;

363   But that belike Iago in the interim

364   Came in and satisfied him.

OTHELLO: O thou pernicious caitiff!—
    How came you, Cassio, by that handkerchief
    That was my wife's?

---

333 in my sense to one who feels as I do   **335 in the practice** through the plotting,
into the snare. **slave** villain   **341 consent** agree   **350 Torments** torture   **359 gross**
monstrous   **360 discontented** full of discontent   **363 belike** most likely   **364 Came**
[. . .] him interposed and gave him satisfactory explanation

CASSIO: I found it in my chamber;
And he himself confessed but even now
That there he dropped it for a special purpose
371   Which wrought to his desire.

OTHELLO: O fool, fool, fool!

CASSIO:
There is besides in Roderigo's letter
How he upbraids Iago, that he made him
375   Brave me upon the watch, whereon it came
376   That I was cast; and even but now he spake,
After long seeming dead, Iago hurt him,
Iago set him on.

LODOVICO (to Othello):
You must forsake this room and go with us.
380   Your power and your command is taken off,
And Cassio rules in Cyprus. For this slave,
If there be any cunning cruelty
383   That can torment him much and hold him long,
384   It shall be his. You shall close prisoner rest
Till that the nature of your fault be known
To the Venetian state.—Come, bring away.

OTHELLO:
387   Soft you; a word or two before you go.
I have done the state some service, and they know 't.
No more of that. I pray you, in your letters,
390   When you shall these unlucky deeds relate,
Speak of me as I am; nothing extenuate,
Nor set down aught in malice. Then must you speak
Of one that loved not wisely but too well;
394   Of one not easily jealous but, being wrought,
395   Perplexed in the extreme; of one whose hand,
396   Like the base Indian, threw a pearl away
397   Richer than all his tribe; of one whose subdued eyes,
Albeit unusèd to the melting mood,
Drops tears as fast as the Arabian trees
400   Their medicinable gum. Set you down this;
And say besides that in Aleppo once,
Where a malignant and a turbaned Turk

---

371 wrought [. . .] desire worked out as he wished, fitted in with his plan   375 Brave
defy. whereon it came whereof it came about   376 cast dismissed   380 taken off
taken away   383 hold him long keep him alive a long time (during his torture)   384 rest
remain   387 Soft you one moment   390 unlucky unfortunate   394 wrought worked
upon, worked into a frenzy   395 Perplexed distraught   396 Indian (This reading from
the Quarto pictures an ignorant savage who cannot recognize the value of a precious jewel.
The Folio reading, Iudean or Judean, i.e., infidel or disbeliever, may refer to Herod, who
slew Miriamne in a fit of jealousy, or to Judas Iscariot, the betrayer of Christ.)   397 subdued i.e., overcome by grief   400 gum i.e., myrrh

Beat a Venetian and traduced the state,
I took by th' throat the circumcisèd dog
And smote him, thus.   (*He stabs himself.*)

406   LODOVICO: O bloody period!

GRATIANO: All that is spoke is marred.

OTHELLO:
I kissed thee ere I killed thee. No way but this,
Killing myself, to die upon a kiss.

(*He kisses Desdemona and dies.*)

CASSIO:
This did I fear, but thought he had no weapon;
For he was great of heart.

412   LODOVICO (*to Iago.*):   O Spartan dog,
413   More fell than anguish, hunger, or the sea!
Look on the tragic loading of this bed.
This is thy work. The object poisons sight;
Let it be hid. Gratiano, keep the house,

(*The bed curtains are drawn.*)

417   And seize upon the fortunes of the Moor,
418   For they succeed on you. (*To Cassio.*) To you, Lord Governor,
418   Remains the censure of this hellish villain,
The time, the place, the torture. O, enforce it!

---

405 s.d. He stabs himself (This direction is in the Quarto text).   **406 period** termination, conclusion   **412 Spartan dog** (Spartan dogs were noted for their savagery and silence.)   **413 fell** cruel   **416 Let it be hid** i.e., draw the bed curtains. (No stage direction specifies that the dead are to be carried offstage at the end of the play.) **keep** remain in   **417 seize upon** take legal possession of   **418 succeed on** pass as though by inheritance to   **419 censure** sentencing

Questions for Engagement, Response, and Analysis

Act I

1. What are Iago's motives for his feelings toward Othello? What does he mean by his claim "'Tis in ourselves that we are thus or thus" (1.3.341)?

2. How does Iago feel about Othello's ethnic background? Support your answer with quotations from the play.

3. When Brabantio and Roderigo draw swords to attack Othello, the latter says, "Keep up your bright swords, for the dew will rust them" (1.2.71). What does this line reveal about Othello's character?

4. What are the qualities in Othello that cause Desdemona to fall in love with him?

5. What in Iago's character makes him particularly dangerous?

6. Why does Othello trust Iago more than he trusts Desdemona?

Act II

1. Explain the reasons for the severity of Othello's punishment of Cassio? Is Othello's punishment unjust?

2. Why is Iago adept when talking to Roderigo but inept in producing flattering verses to please Desdemona? How do Iago's apparent ineptness in flattery and bluntness of speech serve his purpose?

3. What seems to be Iago's attitude toward women and sexuality? How does the imagery he uses reveal this attitude?

4. Why does Shakespeare have the ordinarily deceptive Iago reveal his true character in his soliloquies?

Act III

1. How does Iago lead Othello to begin doubting and suspecting Cassio?

2. Iago says in 3.3.360, "The Moor already changes with my poison." When Othello begins to doubt Desdemona, how else does his character change? Does his language change? If so, how does that reveal a character change? See 3.3.287–306 and 3.3.383–95.

3. Explain the significance of the handkerchief.

4. Iago has what he initially sought—the position of lieutenant. Why then does he continue his efforts to destroy Othello?

5. Explain the foreshadowing of Othello's speech:

> Perdition catch my soul
> But I do love thee! And when I love thee not,
> Chaos is come again. (3.3.100–02)

6. Explain the truth and the irony of Iago's speech:

> Who steals my purse steals trash; 'tis something, nothing;
> 'Twas mine, 'tis his, and has been slave to thousands;
> But he that filches from me my good name
> Robs me of that which not enriches him
> And makes me poor indeed. (3.3.177–81)

Act IV

1. Discuss Iago's skill in manipulating Cassio and Desdemona.

2. What do Othello's speech and actions in this act reveal about him? How does Lodovico's speech in 4.1.286–90 reflect the extent of Othello's fall?

3. Is there any evidence of Desdemona's disobedience or unfaithfulness to Othello? How does she respond to bad treatment from him?

Support your response with references to the text. See, in particular, 4.3.63–66 and 4.3.84–85.

4. In what ways is Emilia a dramatic foil for Desdemona?

Act V

1. Why does Othello say, "Put out the light, and then put out the light" (5.2.7)?

2. How does Othello feel about killing Desdemona as he prepares to do so? See his soliloquy at 5.2.1–22.

3. How does Othello's speech at 5.2.302–24 reflect the extent of his fall?

4. What is Othello's motivation to kill Desdemona? What flaw in his character leads him to fall into Iago's trap?

5. In your opinion, why, after having explained his motives in soliloquies and conversations earlier in the play, does Iago now (5.2.348) say, "From this time forth I never will speak word"?

6. In what sense is Othello's death a triumph? Has he managed to retain any of his former dignity?

Crafting Arguments

1. Write an essay in which you examine Iago's motivation and argue that there is or is not any adequate motive that can explain the intensity of his malevolence.

2. Analyze the means by which Iago poisons Othello's mind, examining both Iago's techniques and Othello's gullibility.

3. Examine in detail the change Othello undergoes. How does jealousy change not only his attitude toward Desdemona and Cassio but also his language, his sleep, and his attitudes toward his work as a soldier—his entire personality?

4. Discuss in detail how imagery defines one or more of the major characters—Iago, Desdemona, Othello, or Cassio.

5. In *Poetics*, Aristotle describes the tragic hero as a good man who holds a high position and falls because of a flaw within himself. Write an essay in which you attempt to prove that Othello fits this definition, supporting each of your claims with examples and quotations from the play.

Casebook on Amy Tan

The two excerpts from Amy Tan's novels *The Hundred Secret Senses* and *The Bonesetter's Daughter* are excellent examples of the theme of vulnerability. They are connected to each other through the characters and Tan's physical, emotional, and cultural experiences that determine the revelations about the self. The three articles will allow you to write critically about this theme using both primary and secondary sources. They will also provide insight into Chinese and Chinese American feelings of alienation.

Amy Tan (b. 1952)

Amy Tan was born in Oakland, California, several years after her mother and father emigrated from China. Tan graduated with honors from San Jose State University, where she later earned an M.A. in linguistics. In 1989 her first novel, The Joy Luck Club, *was published and became a surprise best-seller.* The Joy Luck Club *received numerous awards and was adapted into a film in 1994. Tan is also author of* The Kitchen God's Wife *(1991),* The Hundred

Secret Senses (1995), The Bonesetter's Daughter *(2002), and* Saving Fish from Drowning *(2005). She has also written a number of short stories and essays as well as two children's books:* The Moon Lady *(1992) and* The Siamese Cat *(1994). Along with fellow writers Stephen King, Dave Barry, and Scott Turow, Tan occasionally performs with the musical group called the Rock Bottom Remainders in order to raise money for literacy programs.*

YOUNG GIRL'S WISH (1996)

1   My first morning in China, I awake in a dark hotel room in Guilin and see a figure leaning over my bed, staring at me with the concentrated look of a killer. I'm about to scream, when I hear my sister Kwan saying, in Chinese, "Sleeping on your side—so *this* is the reason your posture is so bad. From now on, you must sleep on your back. Also, do exercises."

2   She snaps on the light and proceeds to demonstrate, hands on hips, twisting at the waist like a sixties P.E. teacher. I wonder how long she's been standing by my bed, waiting for me to waken so she can present her latest bit of unsolicited advice. Her bed is already made.

3   I look at my watch and say, in a grumpy voice, "Kwan, it's only five in the morning."

4   "This is China. Everyone else is up. Only you're asleep."

5   "Not anymore."

6   We've been in China less than eight hours, and already she's taking control of my life. We're on her terrain; we have to go by her rules, speak her language. She's in Chinese heaven.

7   Snatching my blankets, she laughs. "Libby-ah, hurry and get up." Kwan has never been able to correctly pronounce my name, Olivia. "I want to go see my village and surprise everyone. I want to watch Big Ma's mouth fall open and hear her words of surprise: 'Hey, I thought I chased you away. Why are you back?'"

8   Kwan pushes open the window. We're staying at the Sheraton Guilin, which faces the Li River. Outside it's still dark. I can hear the *trnnng! trnnng!* of what sounds like a noisy pachinko parlor. I go to the window and look down. Peddlers on tricycle carts are ringing their bells, greeting one another as they haul their baskets of grain, melons, and turnips to market. The boulevard is bristling with the shadows of bicycles and cars, workers and schoolchildren—the whole world chirping and honking, shouting and laughing, as though it were the middle of the day. On the handlebar of a bicycle dangle the gigantic heads of four pigs, roped through the nostrils, their white snouts curled in death grins.

9   "Look." Kwan points down the street to a set of stalls lit by low-watt bulbs. "We can buy breakfast there, cheap and good. Better than paying nine dollars each for hotel food—and for what? Doughnut, orange juice, bacon, who wants it?"

10   I recall the admonition in our guidebooks to steer clear of food sold by street venders. "Nine dollars, that's not much," I reason.

11   "Wah! You can't think this way anymore. Now you're in China. Nine dollars is lots of money here, one week's salary."

12   "Yeah, but cheap food might come with food poisoning."

13   Kwan gestures to the street. "You look. All those people there, do they have food poisoning?"

14   Kwan is right. Who am I to begrudge carrying home a few parasites? I slip some warm clothes on and go into the hallway to knock on my husband's door. Simon answers immediately, fully dressed. "I couldn't sleep," he admits.

15   In five minutes, the three of us are on the sidewalk. We pass dozens of food stalls, some with portable propane burners, others with makeshift grills. In front of the stalls, customers squat in semicircles eating noodles and dumplings. Kwan chooses a vender who is slapping what look like floury pancakes onto the sides of a blazing-hot oil drum. "Give me three," she says, in Chinese. The vender pries the pancakes off with his blackened fingers, and Simon and I yelp as we toss the hot pancakes up and down like circus jugglers.

16   "How much?" Kwan opens her change purse.

17   "Six yuan," the pancake vender tells her.

18   I calculate the cost is a little more than a dollar, dirt cheap. By Kwan's estimation, this is tantamount to extortion. "Wah!" She points to another customer. "You charged him only fifty fen a pancake."

19   "Of course! He's a local worker. You three are tourists."

20   "What are you saying! I'm also local."

21   "You?" The vender snorts and gives her a cynical once-over. "From where, then?"

22   "Changmian."

23   His eyebrows rise in suspicion. "Really, now! Who do you know in Changmian?"

24   Kwan rattles off some names.

25   The vender slaps his thigh. "Wu Ze-min? You know Wu Ze-min?"

26   "Of course. As children, we lived across the lane from each other. I haven't seen him in over thirty years."

27   "His daughter married my son."

28   "Nonsense!"

29   The man laughs. "It's true. Two years ago. My wife and my mother opposed the match—just because the girl was from Changmian. But they have old countryside ideas, they still believe Changmian is cursed. Not me, I'm not superstitious, not anymore. And now a baby's been born, last spring, a girl, but I don't mind."

30   "Hard to believe Wu Ze-min's a grandfather. How is he?"

31   "Lost his wife twenty years ago, when they were sent to the cowsheds for counter-revolutionary thinking. They smashed his hands, but not his mind. Later he married another woman, Yang Ling-fang."

32   "That's not possible! She was the little sister of an old schoolmate of mine. I still see her as a tender young girl."

33   "Not so tender anymore. She's got *jiaoban* skin, tough as leather, been through plenty of hardships, let me tell you."

34   Kwan and the vender continue to gossip while Simon and I eat our pancakes. They taste like a cross between focaccia and a green-onion omelette. By now Kwan and the vender act like old friends, and he advises her how to get a good price on a driver to take us to Changmian.

35   "All right, older brother," Kwan says, "how much do I owe you?"

36   "Six yuan."

37   "Wah! Still six yuan? Too much, too much. I'll give you two, no more than that."

38   "Make it three, then."

39   Kwan grunts, settles up, and we leave. When we're half a block away, I whisper to Simon, "That man said Changmian is cursed."

40   Kwan overhears me. "*Tst!* That's just a story, a thousand years old. Only stupid people still think Changmian is a bad-luck place to live."

41   I translate for Simon, then ask, "What kind of bad luck?"

42   "You don't want to know."

43   I am about to insist she tell me, when Simon points to an open-air market overflowing with wicker baskets of thick-skinned pomelos, dried beans, cassia tea, chilies.

44   I inhale deeply and imagine that I'm filling my lungs with the very air that inspired my ancestors, whoever they might have been. Because we arrived late the night before, we haven't yet seen the Guilin landscape, its fabled karst peaks, its magical limestone caves, and all the other sites listed in our guidebook as the reasons this is known in China as "the most beautiful place on earth."

45   Looking up toward cloud level, we see the amazing peaks, which resemble prehistoric shark's teeth, the clichéd subject of every Chinese calendar and scroll painting. But tucked in the gums of these ancient stone formations is the blight of high-rises, their stucco exteriors grimy with industrial pollution, their signboards splashed with garish red and gilt characters. Between these are lower buildings from an earlier era, all of them painted a proletarian toothpaste-green. And here and there is the rubble of prewar houses and impromptu garbage dumps. The whole scene gives Guilin the look and stench of a pretty face marred by tawdry lipstick, gapped teeth, and an advanced case of periodontal disease.

46   "Boy, oh boy," whispers Simon. "If Guilin is China's most beautiful city, I can't wait to see what the cursed village of Changmian looks like."

47   We catch up with Kwan. "Everything is entirely different, no longer the same." Kwan must be sad to see how horribly Guilin has changed over the past thirty years. But then she says, in a proud and marvelling voice, "So much progress, everything is so much better."

48   A couple of blocks farther on, we come upon a bird market. Hanging from tree limbs are hundreds of decorative cages containing singing

finches, and exotic birds with gorgeous plumage, punk crests, and fan-like tails. On the ground are cages of huge birds, perhaps eagles or hawks, magnificent, with menacing talons and beaks. There are also the ordinary fowl—chickens and ducks, destined for the stewpot.

49   I see a man hissing at me. *"Ssssss!"* He sternly motions me to come over. What is he, the secret police?

50   The man solemnly reaches underneath a table and brings out a cage. "You like," he says, in English. Facing me is a snowy-white owl with milk-chocolate highlights. It looks like a fat Siamese cat with wings. The owl blinks its golden eyes and I fall in love.

51   "Hey, Simon, Kwan, come here. Look at this."

52   "One hundred dollar, U.S.," the man says. "Very cheap."

53   Simon shakes his head and says in a weird combination of pantomime and broken English: "Take bird on plane, not possible, customs official will say stop, not allowed, must pay big fine—"

54   "How much?" the man asks brusquely. "You say. I give you morning price, best price."

55   "There's no use bargaining," Kwan tells the man in Chinese. "We're tourists. We can't bring birds back to the United States, no matter how cheap."

56   "Aaah, who's talking about bringing it back?" the man replies in rapid Chinese. "Buy it today, then take it to that restaurant, over there. For a small price, they can cook it tonight for your dinner."

57   "Oh, my God!" I turn to Simon. "He's selling this owl as food!"

58   "That's disgusting. Tell him he's a fucking goon."

59   "You tell him!"

60   "I can't speak Chinese."

61   The man must think I am urging my husband to buy me an owl for dinner. "You're very lucky I even have *one*. The cat-eagle is rare, very rare," he brags. "Took me three weeks to catch it."

62   "I don't believe this," I tell Simon. "I'm going to be sick."

63   Then I hear Kwan saying, "A cat-eagle is not that rare, just hard to catch. Besides, I hear the flavor is ordinary."

64   "To be honest," says the man, "it's not as pungent as, say, a pangolin. But you eat a cat-eagle to give you strength and ambition, not to be fussy over taste. Also, it's good for improving your eyesight. One of my customers was nearly blind. After he ate a cat-eagle, he could see his wife for the first time in twenty years. The customer came back and cursed me: 'Shit! She's ugly enough to scare a monkey. Fuck your mother for letting me eat that cat-eagle!'"

65   Kwan laughs heartily. "Yes, yes, I've heard this about cat-eagles. It's a good story." She pulls out her change purse and holds up a hundred-yuan note.

66   "Kwan, what are you doing?" I cry. "We are *not* going to eat this owl!"

67   The man waves away the hundred yuan. "Only American money," he says firmly. "One hundred *American* dollars."

68   Kwan pulls out an American ten-dollar bill.

69   "Kwan!" I shout.

70   The man shakes his head, refusing the ten. Kwan shrugs, then starts to walk away. The man shouts to her to give him fifty, then. She comes back and holds out a ten and a five, and says, "That's my last offer."

71   "This is insane!" Simon mutters.

72   The man sighs, then relinquishes the cage, complaining, "What a shame, so little money for so much work. Look at my hands, three weeks of climbing and cutting down bushes to catch this bird."

73   As we walk away, I grab Kwan's free arm: "There's no way I'm going to let you eat this owl. I don't care if we are in China."

74   "Shh! Shh! You'll scare him!" Kwan pulls the cage out of my reach. She gives me a maddening smile, then walks over to a concrete wall, overlooking the river and sets the cage on top. She meows to the owl. "Oh, little friend, you want to go to Changmian? You want to climb with me to the top of the mountain, let my little sister watch you fly away?" The owl twists his head and blinks.

75   I almost cry with joy and guilt. Why do I think such bad things about Kwan?

76   "See that?" I hear Kwan say. "Over there." She's pointing to a cone-shaped peak off in the distance. "Just outside my village stands a sharp- headed mountain, taller than that one, even. We call it Young Girl's Wish, after a slave girl who ran away to the top of it, then flew off with a phoenix who was her lover." Kwan looks at me. "It's a story, just superstition."

77   I'm amused that she thinks she has to explain.

78   Kwan continues, "Yet all the girls in our village believed in that tale, not because they were stupid but because they wanted to hope for a better life. We thought that if we climbed to the top and made a wish, it might come true. So we raised little hatchlings, and when the birds were ready to fly we climbed to the top of Young Girl's Wish and let them go. The birds would then fly to where the phoenixes lived and tell them our wishes." Kwan sniffs. "Big Ma told me the peak was named Young Girl's Wish because a crazy girl climbed to the top. But when she tried to fly, she fell all the way down and lodged herself so firmly into the earth she became a boulder. Big Ma said that's why you can see so many boulders at the bottom of that peak—they're all the stupid girls who followed her kind of crazy thinking, wishing for hopeless things."

79   I laugh. Kwan stares at me fiercely, as if I were Big Ma, the aunt who raised her. "You can't stop young girls from wishing. No! Everyone must dream. To stop dreaming—well, that's like saying you can never change your fate. Isn't that true?"

80   "I suppose."

81   "So now you guess what I wished for."

82   "I don't know. What?"

83   "Come on, you guess."

84   "A handsome husband."

85   "No."

86   "A car."

87   Kwan laughs and slaps my arm. "You guessed wrong! O.K., I'll tell you." She looks toward the mountain peaks. "Before I left for America, I raised three birds, not just one, so I could make three wishes at the top of the peak. I told myself, If these three wishes come true, my life is complete, I can die happy. My first wish: to have a sister I could love with all my heart, only that, and I would ask for nothing more from her. My second wish: to return to China with my sister. My third wish"—Kwan's voice now quavers—"for Big Ma to see this and say she was sorry she sent me away."

88   This is the first time Kwan's ever shown me how deeply she can resent someone who's treated her wrong. "I opened the cage," she continues, "and let my three birds go free." She flings out her hand in demonstration. "But one of them beat its wings uselessly, drifting in half-circles, before it fell like a stone all the way to the bottom. Now you see, two of my wishes have already happened: I have you, and together we are in China. Last night, I realized my third wish would never come true. Big Ma will never tell me she is sorry."

89   She holds up the cage with the owl. "But now I have a beautiful cat-eagle that can carry with him my new wish. When he flies away, all my old sadnesses will go with him. Then both of us will be free."

90   Actually, Kwan is my half sister, but I never mention that publicly. That would be an insult, as if she deserved only fifty per cent of my love. She was born in China. I was born in San Francisco, after our father immigrated there and married my mother.

91   Mom calls herself "American mixed grill, a bit of everything white, fatty, and fried." She was born in Moscow, Idaho, where she was a champion baton twirler and once won a county-fair prize for growing a deformed potato that had the profile of Jimmy Durante. She told me she dreamed she'd one day grow up to be different—thin, exotic, and noble, like Luise Rainer, who won an Oscar playing O-lan in "The Good Earth." When Mom moved to San Francisco and became a Kelly girl instead, she did the next-best thing. She married our father. Mom thinks that her marrying out of the Anglo race makes her a liberal. "When Jack and I met," she still tells people, "there were laws against mixed marriages. We broke the law for love." She neglects to mention that those laws didn't apply in California.

92   None of us, including my mom, even knew that Kwan existed until shortly before my father died, of renal failure. I was not quite four when he passed away. But I still remember the last day I saw him in the hospital.

93   I was sitting on a sticky vinyl chair, eating a bowl of strawberry Jell-O cubes that my father had given me from his lunch tray. He was propped up in bed, breathing hard. Mom would cry one minute, then act cheerful. The next thing I remember, my father was whispering and Mom leaned

in close to listen. Her mouth opened wider and wider. Then her head turned sharply toward me, all twisted with horror.

94   "Your daughter?" I heard my mom say. "Bring her back?"

95   What I remember after that is a jumble: the bowl of Jell-O crashing to the floor, Mom staring at a photo, then me seeing the black-and-white snapshot of a skinny baby with patchy hair.

96   It turned out that my father had been a university student in Guilin. He used to buy live frogs for his supper at the outdoor market from a young woman named Li Chen. He later married her, and in 1944 she gave birth to a daughter. In 1948, my father's first wife died, of a lung disease, perhaps t.b. He went to Hong Kong to search for work and left Kwan in the care of his wife's younger sister, Li Bin-bin, who lived in a small mountain village called Changmian. He sent money for their support—but in 1949, after the Communists took over, it was impossible for my father to return. What else could he do? With a heavy heart, he left for America to start a new life and forget about the sadness he left behind.

97   Eleven years later, while he was dying in the hospital, the ghost of his first wife appeared at the foot of his bed. "Claim back your daughter," she warned, "or suffer the consequences after death!"

98   Looking back, I can imagine how my mom must have felt when she first heard this. Another wife? A daughter in China? We were a modern American family. We spoke English. Sure, we ate Chinese food, but take-out, like everyone else. And we lived in a ranch- style house in Daly City. My father worked for the Government Accounting Office. My mother went to P.T.A. meetings. She had never heard my father talk about Chinese superstitions before; they attended church and bought life insurance instead.

99   After my father died, my mother kept telling everyone how he had treated her "just like a Chinese empress." She made all sorts of grief-stricken promises to God and my father's grave. My mother vowed never to remarry. She vowed to teach us children to do honor to the family name. She vowed to find my father's firstborn child, Kwan, and bring her to the United States. The last promise was the only one she kept.

100   I was nearly six when Kwan arrived.

101   We head to the hotel, in search of a car that will take one local, two tourists, and a cat-eagle to Changmian village. By nine, we've procured the services of a driver, an amiable young man who knows how to do the capitalist hustle. "Clean, cheap, fast,"he declares, in Chinese. And then he makes an aside for Simon's benefit.

102   "What'd he say?" Simon asks.

103   "He's letting you know he speaks English."

104   Our driver reminds me of the slick Hong Kong youths who hang out in the trendy pool halls of San Francisco, the same pomaded hair, his inch-long pinkie nail, perfectly manicured, symbolizing that his lucky life is one without backbreaking work. He flashes us a smile, revealing a set

of nicotine-stained teeth. "You call me Rocky," he says, in heavily accented English. "Like famous movie star." He opens the door with a flourish, and we climb into a black Nissan, a late-model sedan that, curiously, lacks seat belts and safety headrests. Do the Japanese think Chinese lives aren't worth saving? "China has either better drivers or no liability lawyers," Simon concludes.

105   Rocky happily assumes we like loud music and slips in a Eurythmics tape, a gift from one of his other "excellent American customers." And so, with Kwan in the front seat and Simon, the owl, and me in back, we start our journey to Changmian, blasted by the beat of "Sisters Are Doing It for Themselves."

106   Rocky's excellent American customers have also taught him select phrases, which he recites to us: "Where you go? I know it. Jump in, let's go." "Go faster? Too fast? No way, José." "How far? Not far. Too far." "Park car? Wait a sec. Back in flash." "Not lost. No problem. Chill out."

107   Rocky explains that he is teaching himself English so he can one day go to America.

108   "My idea," he says, in Chinese, "is to become a famous movie actor, specializing in martial arts. Of course, I don't expect a big success from the start. Maybe I'll have to take a job as a taxi-driver. But I'm hardworking. In America, people don't know how to be as hardworking as we Chinese. We also know how to suffer. What's unbearable to Americans would be ordinary for me. Don't you think that's true, older sister?"

109   Kwan gives an ambiguous "Hmm." I wonder whether she is thinking of her brother-in-law, a former chemist, who immigrated to the States and now works as a dishwasher because he's too scared to speak English, lest people think he is stupid. Just then Simon's eyes grow round, and I shout, "Holy shit!" as the car nearly sideswipes two schoolgirls holding hands. Rocky blithely goes on about his dream.

110   "When I live in America, I'll save most of my money, spend only a little on food, cigarettes, maybe the movies every now and then, and, of course, a car for my taxi business. My needs are simple. Even if I don't become a movie star, I can still come back to China and live like a rich man."

111   He looks at us through the rearview mirror and gives us a thumbs-up. A second later, Simon grips the front seat, and I shout, "Holy Jesus shit!" We are about to hit a young woman on a bicycle with her baby perched on the handlebar. At the last possible moment, the cyclist wobbles to the right and out of our way.

112   Rocky laughs. "Chill out," he says. And then he explains, in Chinese, why we shouldn't worry. Kwan turns around and translates for Simon: "He said in China if driver run over somebody, driver always at fault, no matter how careless other person."

113   Simon looks at me. "This is supposed to reassure us? Did something get lost in the translation?"

114   "It doesn't make any sense," I tell Kwan, as Rocky veers in and out of traffic. "A dead pedestrian is a dead pedestrian, no matter whose fault it is."

115   *"Tst!* This American thinking," Kwan replies. The owl swings his head and stares at me, as if to say, Wise up, gringa, this is China, your American ideas don't work here. "In China," Kwan goes on, "you always responsible for someone else, no matter what. You get run over, this my fault, you my little sister. Now you understand?"

116   We drive by a strip of shops selling rattan furniture and straw hats. And then we're in the outskirts of town, both sides of the road lined with mile after mile of identical one- room restaurants. Some are in the stages of being built, their walls layers of brick, mud plaster, and whitewash. They advertise the same specialties: orange soda pop and steamy-hot noodle soup. Idle waitresses squat outside, watching our car whizz by.

117   A few miles farther on, the restaurants give way to simple wooden stalls with thatched roofs, and, even farther, peddlers, without any shelter, stand by the road, yelling at the top of their lungs, waving their string bags of pomelos, their bottles of homemade hot sauce.

118   As the stretches between villages grow longer, Kwan falls asleep, her head bobbing lower and lower. She half awakens with a snort every time we hit a pothole. After a while, she emits long, rhythmical snores, blissfully unaware that Rocky is driving faster and faster down the two-lane road. Each time he accelerates, the owl opens his wings slightly, then settles down again in the cramped cage. I'm gripping my knees, then sucking air between clenched teeth whenever Rocky swings into the left lane.

119   We are now tailgating a truck filled with soldiers in green uniforms. They wave to us. Rocky honks his horn, then swerves sharply to pass. As we go by the truck, I can see an oncoming bus bearing down on us, the urgent blare of its horn growing louder and louder. "Oh, my God, oh, my God," I whimper. I close my eyes, and Simon grabs my hand. The car jerks back into the right lane. I hear a *whoosh*, then the blare of the bus horn receding.

120   "That's it," I say in a tense whisper. "I'm going to tell him to slow down."

121   "I don't know, Olivia. He might be offended."

122   I glare at Simon. "What? You'd rather die than be rude?"

123   He affects an attitude of nonchalance. "They all drive like that."

124   "So mass suicide makes it O.K.?"

125   "Well, we haven't seen any accidents."

126   Simon stares at me. At that moment, Rocky brakes abruptly. Kwan and the owl awake with a flutter of arms and wings. Rocky rolls down the window and sticks out his head. He curses under his breath, then starts punching the car horn with the heel of his hand.

127   After a few minutes, we see the source of our delay: an accident, a bad one, to judge from the spray of glass, metal, and personal belongings that litters the road. The smells of spilled gasoline and scorched rubber hang in the air. Just as I am about to say to Simon, "See?" our car inches past a black minivan, belly up, its doors splayed like the broken wings of a squashed insect. A tire lies in a nearby vegetable field. Seconds later, we go by the other half of the impact: a red-and-white bus. The large front

window is smashed, the hound-nosed hood twisted and smeared with a hideous swath of blood. About fifty gawkers, farm tools still in hand, mill around, staring and pointing at various parts of the crumpled bus as if it were a science exhibit. And then I see a dozen or so injured people, some clutching themselves and bellowing in pain, others lying quietly in shock. Or perhaps they are already dead.

128   "Shit, I can't believe this," says Simon. "There's no ambulance, no doctors."

129   "Stop the car," I order Rocky, in Chinese. "We should help them." Why did I say that? What can I possibly do? I can barely look at the victims, let alone touch them.

130   "*Ai-ya.*" Kwan stares at the field. "So many yin people." Yin people? Kwan believes she can see ghosts, those who have died and now dwell in the World of Yin. Is she now saying there are dead people out there? The owl coos mournfully, and my hands turn slippery-cold.

131   Rocky keeps his eyes on the road ahead, driving forward, leaving the tragedy behind us. "We'd be of no use," he says, in Chinese. "We have no medicine, no bandages. Besides, it's not good to interfere, especially since you're foreigners. Don't worry, the police will be along soon."

132   I'm secretly relieved he isn't heeding my instructions.

133   "You're Americans," he continues, his voice deep with Chinese authority. "You're not used to seeing tragedies. You pity us, yes, because you can later go home to a comfortable life and forget what you've seen. For us, this type of disaster is commonplace. We have so many people, no room left for pity."

134   "Would someone please tell me what's going on!" Simon exclaims. "Why aren't we stopping?"

135   "Don't ask questions," I snap. "Remember?"

136   When we get back on the open road, Kwan gives Rocky some advice. He solemnly nods, then slows down.

137   "What'd she say?" Simon asks.

138   "Chinese logic. If we're killed, no payment. And in the next life, he'll owe us big time."

139   Another three hours pass. I know we have to be getting close to Changmian. Kwan is pointing out landmarks. "There! There!" she cries huskily, bouncing up and down like a little child. "Those two peaks. The village they surround is called Wife Waiting for Husband's Return. But where is the tree? What happened to the tree? Next to that house, there was a very big tree, maybe a thousand years old."

140   She scans ahead. "That place there! We used to hold a big market. But now look, it's just an empty field. And there—that mountain up ahead! That's the one we called Young Girl's Wish."

141   Kwan laughs, but the next second she seems puzzled. "Funny, now that mountain looks so small. Why is that? Did it shrink, washed down by the rain? Or maybe the peak was worn down by too many girls

running up there to make a wish. Or maybe it's because I've become too American and now. I see things with different eyes, everything looking smaller poorer, not as good."

142   All at once, Kwan shouts to Rocky to turn down a small dirt road we have just passed. He makes an abrupt U-turn, knocking Simon and me into each other, and causing the owl to shriek. We are rumbling along a rutted lane, past fields with pillows of moist red dirt. "Turn left, turn left!" Kwan orders. She has her hands clasped in her lap. "Too many years, too many years," she says, as if chanting.

143   We approach a stand of trees, and then, as soon as Kwan announces, "Changmian," I see it: a village nestled between two jagged peaks, their hillsides a velvety moss-green with folds deepening into emerald. More comes into view: crooked rows of buildings whitewashed with lime, their pitched tile roofs laid in the traditional pattern of dragon coils. Surrounding the village are well-tended fields and mirrorlike ponds neatly divided by stone walls and irrigation trenches. We jump out of the car. Miraculously, Changmian has avoided the detritus of modernization. I see no tin roofs or electrical power lines. In contrast to other villages we've passed, the outlying lands here haven't become dumping grounds for garbage, the alleys aren't lined with crumpled cigarette packs or pink plastic bags. Clean stone pathways crisscross the village, then thread up a cleft between the two peaks and disappear through a stone archway. In the distance is another pair of tall peaks, dark jade in color, and beyond those the purple shadows of two more. Simon and I stare at each other, wide-eyed.

144   I feel as though we've stumbled on a fabled misty land, half memory, half illusion. Are we in Chinese Nirvana? Changmian looks like the carefully cropped photos found in travel brochures advertising "a charmed world of the distant past, where visitors can step back in time." There must be something wrong, I keep warning myself. Around the corner we'll stumble on reality: the fast-food market, the tire junkyard, the signs indicating this village is really a Chinese fantasyland for tourists.

145   "I feel like I've seen this place before," I whisper to Simon.

146   "Me, too. Maybe it was in a documentary." He laughs. "Or a car commercial."

147   I gaze at the mountains and realize why Changmian seems so familiar. It's the setting for Kwan's stories, the ones that filter into my dreams. There they are: the archways, the cassia trees, the hills leading to Thistle Mountain. And being here, I feel as if the membrane separating the two halves of my life has finally been shed.

148   From out of nowhere we hear squeals and cheers. Fifty tiny schoolchildren race toward the perimeter of a fenced-in yard. As we draw closer, the children shriek, turn on their heels, and run back to the school building, laughing. After a few seconds, they come screaming toward us like a flock of birds, followed by their smiling teacher. They stand at attention, and then shout all together, in English, "A-B-C! One-two-three! How are you! Hello goodbye!"

149   We continue along the path. Two young men on bicycles slow down and stop to stare at us. We keep walking and round a corner. Kwan gasps. Farther up the path, in front of an arched gateway, stand a dozen smiling people. Kwan puts her hand to her mouth, then runs toward them. When she reaches the group, she grabs each person's hand between her two palms, then hails a stout woman and slaps her on the back.

150   "Fat!" Kwan says. "You've grown unbelievably fat!"

151   "Hey, look at you—what happened to your hair? Did you ruin it on purpose?"

152   "This is the style! What, have you been in the countryside so long you don't recognize good style?"

153   "Oh, listen to her, she's still bossy, I can tell."

154   "You were always the bossy one, not—"

155   Kwan stops in midsentence, transfixed by a stone wall. You would think it's the most fascinating sight she's ever seen.

156   "Big Ma," she murmurs. "What's happened? How can this be?"

157   A man in the crowd guffaws. "Ha! She was so anxious to see you she got up early this morning, then jumped on a bus to meet you in Guilin. And now look—you're here, she's there. Won't she be mad!"

158   Everyone laughs, except Kwan. She walks closer to the wall, calling hoarsely, "Big Ma, Big Ma." Several people whisper, and everyone draws back, frightened.

159   "Uh-oh," I say.

160   "Why is Kwan crying?" Simon whispers.

161   "Big Ma, oh, Big Ma." Tears are streaming down Kwan's cheeks. "You must believe me, this is not what I wished. How unlucky that you died on the day that I've come home." A few women gasp and cover their mouths.

162   I walk over to Kwan. "What are you saying? Why do you think she's dead?"

163   "Why is everyone so freaked?" Simon glances about.

164   I hold up my hand. "I'm not sure." I turn back to her. "Kwan?" I say gently. "Kwan?" But she does not seem to hear me. She is looking tenderly at the wall, laughing and crying.

165   "Yes, I knew this," she is saying. "Of course, I knew. In my heart, I knew all the time."

166   In the afternoon, the villagers hold an uneasy homecoming party for Kwan in the community hall. The news has spread through Changmian that Kwan has seen Big Ma's ghost. Yet she has not announced this to the village, and since there is no proof that Big Ma has died, there is no reason to call off a food-laden celebration that evidently took her friends days to prepare. During the festivities, Kwan does not brag about her car, her sofa, her English. She listens quietly as her former childhood playmates recount major events of their lives: the birth of twin sons, a railway trip to a big city, and the time a group of student intellectuals was sent to Changmian for reëducation during the Cultural Revolution.

167   "They thought they were smarter than us," recounts one woman, whose hands are gnarled by arthritis. "They wanted us to raise a fast-growing rice, three crops a year instead of two. They gave us special seeds. They brought us insect poison. Then the little frogs that swam in the rice fields and ate the insects, they all died. And the ducks that ate the frogs, they all died, too. Then the rice died."

168   A man with bushy hair shouts, "So we said, 'What good is it to plant three crops of rice that fail rather than two that are successful?'"

169   The woman with arthritic hands continues: "These same intellectuals tried to breed our mules! Ha! Can you believe it? For two years, every week, one of us would ask them, 'Any luck?' And they'd say, 'Not yet, not yet.' And we'd try to keep our faces serious but encouraging. 'Try harder, comrade,' we'd say. 'Don't give up.'"

170   We are still laughing when a young boy runs into the hall, shouting that an official from Guilin has arrived in a fancy black car. Silence. The official comes into the hall, and everyone stands. He solemnly holds up the identity card of Li Bin-bin and asks if she belonged to the village. Several people glance nervously at Kwan. She walks slowly toward the official, looks at the identity card, and nods. The official makes an announcement, and a ripple of moans and then wails fills the room.

171   Simon leans toward me. "What's wrong?"

172   "Big Ma's dead. She was killed in that bus accident we saw this morning."

173   Simon and I walk over and each put a hand on one of Kwan's shoulders. She feels so small.

174   "I'm sorry," Simon stammers.

175   Kwan gives him a teary smile. As Li Bin-bin's closest relative, she has volunteered to perform the necessary bureaucratic ritual of bringing the body back to the village the next day. The three of us are returning to Guilin.

176   As soon as Rocky sees us, he stubs out his cigarette and turns off the car radio. Someone must have told him the news. "What a tragedy," he says. "I'm sorry, big sister, I should have stopped. I'm to blame—"

177   Kwan waves off his apologies. "No one's to blame. Anyway, regrets are useless, always too late."

178   When Rocky opens the car door, we see that the owl is still in his cage on the backseat. Kwan lifts the cage gently and stares at the bird. "No need to climb the mountain anymore," she says. She sets the cage on the ground, then opens its door. The owl sticks out his head, hops to the edge of the doorway and onto the ground. He twists his head and, with a great flap of wings, takes off toward the peaks. Kwan watches him until he disappears.

179   As Rocky warms the engine, I ask Kwan, "When we passed the bus accident this morning, did you see someone who looked like Big Ma? Is that how you knew she'd died?"

180   "What are you saying? I didn't know she was dead until I saw her yin self standing by the wall."

181   "Then why did you tell her that you knew?"

182   Kwan frowns, puzzled. "I knew what?"

183   "You were telling her you knew, in your heart you knew it was true. Weren't you talking about the accident?"

184   "Ah," she says, understanding at last. "No, not the accident." She sighs. "I told Big Ma that what *she* was saying was true."

185   "What did she say?"

186   Kwan turns to the window, and I can see the reflection of her stricken face. "She said she was wrong about the story of Young Girl's Wish. She said all my wishes had already come true. She was always sorry she sent me away. But she could never tell me this. Otherwise, I wouldn't have left her for a chance at a better life."

187   I search for some way to console Kwan. "At least you can still see her," I say.

188   "Ah?"

189   "I mean as a yin person. She can visit you."

190   Kwan stares out the car window. "But it's not the same. We can no longer make new memories together. We can't change the past. Not until the next lifetime." She exhales heavily, releasing all her unsaid words.

Questions for Engagement, Response, and Analysis

1. What is the point of view in the story? What is the effect of this point of view on the theme and tone?

2. Describe the street scenes in Guilin. What does Olivia mean when she says that the city of Guilin was "a pretty face marred by tawdry lipstick, gapped teeth, and an advanced case of periodontal disease"?

3. List some of the foreshadowing elements and explain what they foreshadow.

4. What is the tale of the "Young Girl's Wish"? What are Kwan's three wishes?

5. Who are "yin people"? What other Chinese legends does the story include?

6. How does Kwan know that Big Ma is dead before anyone else does?

7. Why doesn't Kwan brag about her American possessions after Big Ma's death?

8. Explain the importance of the "cat-eagle" and of the owl?

HEART   (2001)

1   These are the things I must not forget.

2   I was raised with the Liu clan in the rocky Western Hills south of Peking. The oldest recorded name of our village was Immortal Heart. Precious Auntie taught me how to write this down on my chalkboard. *Watch now, Doggie*, she ordered, and drew the character for "heart": *See this curving stroke? That's the bottom of the heart, where blood gathers and*

flows. And the dots, those are the two veins and the artery that carry the blood in and out. As I traced over the character, she asked: *Whose dead heart gave shape to this word? How did it begin, Doggie? Did it belong to a woman? Was it drawn in sadness?*

3   I once saw the heart of a fresh-killed pig. It was red and glistening. And I had already seen plenty of chicken hearts in a bowl, waiting to be cooked. They looked like tiny lips and were the same color as Precious Auntie's scars. But what did a woman heart look like? "Why do we have to know whose heart it was?" I asked as I wrote the character.

4   And Precious Auntie flapped her hands fast: *A person should consider how things begin. A particular beginning results in a particular end.*

5   I remember her often talking about this, how things begin. Since then I have wondered about the beginning and end of many things. Like Immortal Heart village. And the people who lived there, myself included. By the time I was born, Immortal Heart was no longer lucky. The village lay between hills in a valley that dropped into a deep limestone ravine. The ravine was shaped like the curved chamber of a heart, and the heart's artery and veins were the three streams that once fed and drained the ravine. But they had gone dry. So had the divine springs. Nothing was left of the waterways but cracked gullies and the stench of a fart.

6   Yet the village began as a sacred place. According to legend, a visiting emperor himself had planted a pine tree in the middle of the valley. The tree was to honor his dead mother, and his respect for his mother was so great he vowed that the tree would live forever. When Precious Auntie first saw the tree, it was already more than three thousand years old.

7   Rich and poor alike made a pilgrimage to Immortal Heart. They hoped that the tree's vital energy would rub off on them. They stroked the trunk, patted the leaves, then prayed for baby sons or big fortunes, a cure for dying, an end to curses. Before leaving, they chipped off some bark, snapped off some twigs. They took them away as souvenirs. Precious Auntie said this was what killed the tree, too much admiration. When the tree died, the souvenirs lost their strength. And because the dead tree was no longer immortal, it was no longer famous, nor was our village. That tree was not even ancient, people said afterward, maybe only two or three hundred years old. As for the story about the emperor honoring his mother? That was a fake feudal legend to make us think the corrupt were sincere. Those complaints came out the same year that the old Ching Dynasty fell down and the new Republic sprang up.

8   The nickname of our village is easy for me to remember: Forty-six Kilometers from Reed Moat Bridge. Reed Moat Bridge is the same as Marco Polo Bridge, what people now call the turnoff point to and from Peking. GaoLing's probably forgotten the old name, but I have not. During my girlhood, the directions to get to Immortal Heart went like this: "First find the Reed Moat Bridge, then walk backward forty-six kilometers."

9   That joke made it sound as if we lived in a pitiful little hamlet of twenty or thirty people. Not so. When I was growing up, nearly two thousand

people lived there. It was crowded, packed from one edge of the valley to the other. We had a brick maker, a sack weaver, and a dye mill. We had twenty-four market days, six temple fairs, and a primary school that GaoLing and I went to when we were not helping our family at home. We had all kinds of peddlers who went from house to house, selling fresh bean curd and steamed buns, twisted dough and colorful candies. And we had lots of people to buy those goods. A few coppers, that was all you needed to make your stomach as happy as a rich man's.

10   The Liu clan had lived in Immortal Heart for six centuries. For that amount of time, the sons had been inkstick makers who sold their goods to travelers. They had lived in the same courtyard house that had added rooms, and later wings, when one mother four hundred years ago gave birth to eight sons, one a year. The family home grew from a simple three-pillar house to a compound with wings stretching five pillars each. In later generations, the number of sons was less, and the extra rooms became run-down and were rented to squabbling tenants. Whether those people laughed at coarse jokes or screamed in pain, it did not matter, the sounds were the same, ugly to hear.

11   All in all, our family was successful but not so much that we caused great envy. We ate meat or bean curd at almost every meal. We had new padded jackets every winter, no holes. We had money to give for the temple, the opera, the fair. But the men of our family also had ambitions. They were always looking for more. They said that in Peking, more people wrote important documents. Those important documents required more good ink. Peking was where more of the big money was. Around 1920, Father, my uncles, and their sons went there to sell the ink. From then on, that was where they lived most of the time, in the back room of a shop in the old Pottery-Glazing District.

12   In our family, the women made the ink. We stayed home. We all worked—me, GaoLing, my aunts and girl cousins, everybody. Even the babies and Great-Granny had a job of picking out stones from the dried millet we boiled for breakfast. We gathered each day in the ink-making studio. According to Great-Granny, the studio began as a grain shed that sat along the front wall of the courtyard house. Over the years, one generation of sons added brick walls and a tile roof. Another strengthened the beams and lengthened it by two pillars. The next tiled the floors and dug pits for storing the ingredients. Then other descendants made a cellar for keeping the inksticks away from the heat and cold. "And now look," Great-Granny often bragged. "Our studio is an ink palace."

13   Because our ink was the best quality, we had to keep the tables and the floors clean year-round. With the dusty yellow winds from the Gobi, this was not easy to do. The window openings had to be covered with both glass and thick paper. In the summer, we hung netting over the doorways to keep out the insects. In the winter, it was sheep hides to keep out the snow.

14   Summer was the worst season for ink-making. Heat upon heat. The fumes burned our eyes and nostrils and lungs. From watching Precious

Auntie tie her scarf over her marred face, we got the idea of putting a wet cloth over our mouths. I can still smell the ingredients of our ink. There were several kinds of fragrant soot: pine, cassia, camphor, and the wood of the chopped-down Immortal Tree. Father hauled home several big logs of it after lightning cracked the dead tree right down the middle, exposing its heart, which was nearly hollow because of beetles eating it inside out. There was also a glue of sticky paste mixed with many oils—serpentine, camphor, turpentine, and tung wood. Then we added a sweet poisonous flower that helped resist insects and rats. That was how special our ink was, all those lasting smells.

15   We made the ink a little at a time. If a fire broke out, as it had a couple of hundred years before, all the supplies and stock would not be lost at once. And if a batch was too sticky or too wet, too soft or not black enough, it was easier to find out who was to blame. Each of us had at least one part in a long list of things to do. First there was burning and grinding, measuring and pouring. Then came stirring and molding, drying and carving. And finally, wrapping and counting, storing and stacking. One season I had to wrap, only that. My mind could wander but my fingers still moved like small machines. Another season I had to use very fine tweezers to pluck bugs that had fallen onto the sticks. Whenever GaoLing did this, she left too many dents. Precious Auntie's job was to sit at a long table and press the sooty mixture into the stone molds. As a result, the tips of her fingers were always black. When the ink was dry, she used a long, sharp tool to carve the good-luck words and drawings into the sticks. Her calligraphy was even better than Father's.

16   It was boring work, but we were proud of our secret family recipe. It yielded just the right color and hardness. An inkstick of ours could last ten years or more. It did not dry out and crumble, or grow soggy with moisture. And if the sticks were stored in the coolness of a root cellar, as ours were, they could last from one great period of history to another. Those who used our ink said the same. It didn't matter how much heat or moisture or dirt from fingers soaked into the page, their words lasted, black and strong.

17   Mother claimed the ink was why our hair remained the blackest black. It was better for the hair than drinking black-sesame-seed soup. "Work hard all day making ink, look young at night while you sleep." That was our joke, and Great-Granny often boasted: "My hair is as black as the burnt shell of a horse chestnut and my face as wrinkly white as the meat inside." Great-Granny had a clever tongue. One time she added, "Better than having white hair and a burnt face," and everyone laughed, even though Precious Auntie was in the room.

18   In later years, however, Great-Granny's tongue was not so sharp or fast. Often she said with a worried brow, "Have you seen Hu Sen?" You could say yes, you could say no, and a moment later, she chirped like a bird, "Hu Sen? Hu Sen?" always requesting her dead grandson, very sad to hear.

19   Toward the end of her life, Great-Granny had thoughts that were like crumbling walls, stones without mortar. A doctor said her inner wind was cold and her pulse was slow, a shallow stream about to freeze. He advised foods with more heat. But Great-Granny only grew worse. Precious Auntie suspected that a tiny flea had crawled into her ear and was feasting on her brain. Confusion Itch was the name of the malady, Precious Auntie said. It is the reason people often scratch their heads when they cannot remember. Her father had been a doctor, and she had seen other patients with the same problem. Yesterday, when I could not remember Precious Auntie's name, I wondered if a flea had run in my ear! But now that I am writing down so many things, I know I don't have Great-Granny's disease. I can recall the smallest details even though they were long ago and far away.

20   The compound where we lived and worked—that comes back to me as if I were now standing before the gate. It was on Pig's Head Lane. The road started at the east, near the market square where pigs heads were sold. From the square, it hooked to the north and ran past the former location of the once famous Immortal Tree. Then it tightened into the little crooked alley where one compound bumped into another. The end of Pig's Head Lane was a narrow perch of earth above the deepest part of the ravine. Precious Auntie told me that the perch was originally made by a warlord thousands of years before. He dreamed that the insides of the mountain were made of jade. So he ordered everyone to dig, dig, don't stop. Men, women, and children dredged for his dream. By the time the warlord died, the children were old, with crooked backs, and half the mountain lay on its side.

21   Behind our compound, the perch became a cliff. And way down, if you fell head over toes, was the bottom of the ravine. The Liu family had once owned twenty *mu* of land behind the compound. But over the centuries, with each heavy rainfall, the walls of the ravine had collapsed and widened, rumbled and deepened. Each decade, those twenty *mu* of land grew smaller and smaller and the cliff crept closer to the back of our house.

22   The moving cliff gave us the feeling we had to look behind us to know what lay ahead. We called it the End of the World. Sometimes the men of our family argued among themselves whether we still owned the land that had crashed down into the ravine. One uncle said, "What you own is the spit that travels from your own mouth to the bottom of that wasteland." And his wife said, "Don't talk about this anymore. You're only inviting disaster." For what lay beyond and below was too unlucky to say out loud: unwanted babies, suicide maidens, and beggar ghosts. Everyone knew this.

23   I went to the cliff many times with my brothers and GaoLing when we were younger. We liked to roll spoiled melons and rotten cabbages over the edge. We watched them fall and splat, hitting skulls and bones. At least that was what we thought they had hit. But one time we climbed down, sliding on our bottoms, grabbing onto roots, descending into the underworld. And when we heard rustling sounds in the brush, we

screamed so loud our ears hurt. The ghost turned out to be a scavenger dog. And the skulls and bones, they were just boulders and broken branches. But though we saw no bodies, all around were bright pieces of clothing: a sleeve, a collar, a shoe, and we were sure they belonged to the dead. And then we smelled it: the stink of ghosts. A person needs to smell that only once to know what it is. It rose from the earth. It wafted toward us on the wings of a thousand flies. The flies chased us like a storm cloud, and as we scrambled back up, First Brother kicked loose a stone that gouged out a piece of Second Brother's scalp. We could not hide this wound from Mother, and when she saw it, she beat us all, then told us that if we ever went down to the End of the World again, we might as well stand outside the walls of the compound forever and not bother to come in.

24   The walls of the Liu home were made of rocks exposed from the washed-down earth. The rocks were stacked and held together with a mud, mortar, and millet paste, then plastered over with lime. They were sweaty damp in summer, moldy damp in winter. And in the many rooms of that house, here and there was always another roof leak or drafty hole in the wall. And yet when I remember that house, I have a strange home-sickness for it. Only there do I have a memory of secret places, warm or cool, of darkness where I hid and pretended I could escape to somewhere else.

25   Within those walls, many families of different positions and generations lived together at the same time, from landlord to tenants, Great-Granny to smallest niece. I guess we were thirty or more people, half of which was the Liu clan. Liu Jin Sen was the eldest of four sons. He was the one I called Father. My uncles and their wives called him Eldest Brother. My cousins called him Eldest Uncle. And by position my uncles were Big Uncle and Little Uncle, and their wives were Big Aunt and Little Aunt. When I was very small, I used to think Father and Mother were called Eldest because they were much taller than my uncles and aunts. First Brother and Second Brother were also large-boned, as was Gao-Ling, and for a long time I did not know why I was so short.

26   Baby Uncle was the fourth son, the youngest, the favorite. His name was Liu Hu Sen. He was my real father, and he would have married Precious Auntie, if only he had not died on their wedding day.

27   Precious Auntie was born in a bigger town down in the foothills, a place called Zhou's Mouth of the Mountain, named in honor of Emperor Zhou of the Shang Dynasty, whom everyone now remembers as a tyrant.

28   Our family sometimes went to the Mouth of the Mountain for temple fairs and operas. If we traveled by road, it was only about ten kilometers from Immortal Heart. If we walked through the End of the World, it was half that distance but a more dangerous way to go, especially in the summertime. That was when the big rains came. The dry ravine filled, and before you could run to the cliffs, climb up, and cry out, "Goddess of Mercy," the gullies ran by like thieves, grabbing you and whatever else was not deeply rooted in the soil. Once the rain stopped, the floodwaters

drained fast and the mouths of the caves swallowed the dirt and the trees, the bodies and the bones. They went down the mountain's throat, into its stomach, intestines, and finally the bowels, where everything got stuck. *Constipated*, Precious Auntie once explained to me. *Now you see why there are so many bones and hills: Chicken Bone Hill, Old Cow Hill, Dragon Bone Hill. Of course, it's not just dragon bones in Dragon Bone Hill. Some are from ordinary creatures, bear, elephant, hippopotamus.* Precious Auntie drew a picture of each of these animals on my chalkboard, because we had never talked about them before.

29   *I have a bone, probably from a turtle*, she told me. She fished it from a tuck in her sleeve. It looked like a dried turnip with pockmarks. *My father almost ground this up for medicine. Then he saw there was writing on it.* She turned the bone over, and I saw strange characters running up and down. *Until recently, these kinds of bones weren't so valuable, because of the scratches. Bone diggers used to smooth them with a file before selling them to medicine shops. Now the scholars call these oracle bones, and they sell for twice as much. And the words on here? They're questions to the gods.*

30   "What does it say?" I asked.

31   Who knows? The words were different then. But it must be something that should have been remembered. Otherwise, why did the gods say it, why did a person write it down?

32   "Where are the answers?"

33   Those are the cracks. The diviner put a hot nail to the bone, and it cracked like a tree hit by lightning. Then he interpreted what the cracks meant.

34   She took back the divining bone. *Someday, when you know how to remember, I'll give this to you to keep. But for now you'll only forget where you put it. Later we can go looking for more dragon bones, and if you find one with writing on it, you can keep it for yourself.*

35   In the Mouth of the Mountain, every poor man collected dragon bones when he had a chance. So did the women, but if they found one, they had to say a man found it instead, because otherwise the bone was not worth as much. Later, middlemen went around the village buying the dragon bones, and then they took them to Peking and sold them to medicine shops for high prices, and the shops sold them to sick people for higher prices yet. The bones were well known for curing anything, from wasting diseases to stupidity. Plenty of doctors sold them. And so did Precious Auntie's father. He used bones to heal bones.

36   For nine hundred years, Precious Auntie's family had been bonesetters. That was the tradition. Her father's customers were mostly men and boys who were crushed in the coal mines and limestone quarries. He treated other maladies when necessary, but bonesetting was his specialty. He did not have to go to a special school to be a bone doctor. He learned from watching his father, and his father learned from his father before him. That was their inheritance. They also passed along the secret location for finding the best dragon bones, a place called the Monkey's Jaw.

An ancestor from the time of the Sung Dynasty had found the cave in the deepest ravines of the dry riverbed. Each generation dug deeper and deeper, with one soft crack in the cave leading to another farther in. And the secret of the exact location was also a family heirloom, passed from generation to generation, father to son, and in Precious Auntie's time, father to daughter to me.

37   I still remember the directions to our cave. It was between the Mouth of the Mountain and Immortal Heart, far from the other caves in the foothills, where everyone else went to dig up dragon bones. Precious Auntie took me there several times, always in the spring or the autumn, never summer or winter. To get there, we went down into the End of the World and walked along the middle of the ravine, away from the walls, where the grown-ups said there were things that were too bad to see. Sometimes we passed by a skein of weeds, shards of a bowl, a quagmire of twigs. In my childish mind, those sights became parched flesh, a baby's skullcap, a soup of maiden bones. And maybe they were, because sometimes Precious Auntie put her hands over my eyes.

38   Of the three dry streambeds, we took the one that was the artery of the heart. And then we stood in front of the cave itself, a split in the mountain only as tall as a broom. Precious Auntie pulled aside the dead bushes that hid the cave. And the two of us took big breaths and went in. In words, it is hard to say how we made our way in, like trying to describe how to get inside an ear. I had to twist my body in an unnatural way far to the left, then rest a foot on a little ledge that I could reach only by crooking my leg close to my chest. By then I was crying and Precious Auntie was grunting to me, because I could not see her black fingers to know what she was saying. I had to follow her huffs and handclaps, crawling like a dog so I would not hit my head or fall down. When we finally reached the larger part of the cave, Precious Auntie lighted the candle lamp and hung it on a long pole with footrests, which had been left by one of her clan from long ago.

39   On the floor of the cave were digging tools, iron wedges of different sizes, hammers and claws, as well as sacks for dragging out the dirt. The walls of the cave were many layers, like an eight-treasure rice pudding cut in half, with lighter, crumbly things on top, then a thicker muddy part like bean paste below, and growing heavier toward the bottom. The highest layer was easiest to chip. The lowest was like rock. But that was where the best bones were found. And after centuries of people's digging through the bottom there was now an overhang waiting to crash down. The inside of the cave looked like the molars of a monkey that could bite you in two, which was why it was called the Monkey's Jaw.

40   While we rested, Precious Auntie talked with her inky hands. *Stay away from that side of the monkey's teeth. Once they chomped down on an ancestor, and he was ground up and gobbled with stone. My father found his skull over there. We put it back right away. Bad luck to separate a man's head from his body.*

41   Hours later, we would climb back out of the Monkey's Jaw with a sack of dirt and, if we had been lucky, one or two dragon bones. Precious Auntie held them up to the sky and bowed, thanking the gods. She believed the bones from this cave were the reason her family had become famous as bonesetters.

42   *When I was a girl,* she said once as we walked home, *I remember lots of desperate people coming to see my father. He was their last chance. If a man could not walk, he could not work. And if he could not work, his family could not eat. Then he would die, and that would be the end of his family line and all that his ancestors had worked for.*

43   For those desperate customers, Precious Auntie's father had remedies of three kinds: modern, try-anything, and traditional. The modern was the Western medicine of missionaries. The try-anything was the spells and chants of rogue monks. As for the traditional, that included the dragon bones, as well as seahorses and seaweed, insect shells and rare seeds, tree bark and bat dung, all of the highest quality. Precious Auntie's father was so talented that patients from the five surrounding mountain villages traveled to the Famous Bonesetter from the Mouth of the Mountain (whose name I will write down, once I remember it).

44   Skilled and famous though he was, he could not prevent all tragedies. When Precious Auntie was four, her mother and older brothers died of an intestine-draining disease. So did most of the other relatives from both sides of the family, dead just three days after they attended a red-egg ceremony and drank from a well infected with the body of a suicide maiden. The bonesetter was so ashamed he could not save his own family members that he spent his entire fortune and went into a lifetime of debt to hold their funerals.

45   *Because of grief,* Precious Auntie said with her hands, *he spoiled me, let me do whatever a son might do. I learned to read and write, to ask questions, to play riddles, to write eight-legged poems, to walk alone and admire nature. The old biddies used to warn him that it was dangerous that I was so boldly happy, instead of shy and cowering around strangers. And why didn't he bind my feet, they asked. My father was used to seeing pain of the worst kinds. But with me, he was helpless. He couldn't bear to see me cry.*

46   So Precious Auntie freely followed her father around in his study and shop. She soaked the splints and plucked the moss. She polished the scales and tallied the accounts. A customer could point to any jar in the shop and she could read the name of its contents, even the scientific words for animal organs. As she grew older, she learned to bleed a wound with a square nail, to use her own saliva for cleansing sores, to apply a layer of maggots for eating pus, and to wrap torn flaps with woven paper. By the time she passed from childhood to maidenhood, she had heard every kind of scream and curse. She had touched so many bodies, living, dying, and dead, that few families considered her for a bride. And while she had never been possessed by romantic love, she recognized the

throes of death. *When the ears grow soft and flatten against the head,* she once told me, *then it's too late. A few seconds later, the last breath hisses out. The body turns cold.* She taught me many facts like that.

47   For the most difficult cases, she helped her father put the injured man on a light latticework pallet of rattan. Her father lifted and lowered this by pulleys and rope, and she guided the pallet into a tub filled with salt water. There the man's crushed bones floated and were fitted into place. Afterward, Precious Auntie brought her father rattan strips that had been soaked soft. He bent them into a splint so the limb could breathe but remain still. Toward the end of the visit, the bonesetter opened his jar of dragon bones and used a narrow chisel to chip off a sliver tiny as a fingernail clipping. Precious Auntie ground this into a powder with a silver ball. The powder went into a paste for rubbing or a potion for drinking. Then the lucky patient went home. Soon he was back in the quarries all day long.

48   One day, at dinnertime, Precious Auntie told me a story with her hands that only I could understand. *A rich lady came to my father and told him to unbind her feet and mold them into more modern ones. She said she wanted to wear high-heeled shoes. "But don't make the new feet too big,"* she said, *"not like a slave girl's or a foreigner's. Make them naturally small like hers." And she pointed to my feet.*

49   I forgot that Mother and my other aunts were at the dinner table, and I said aloud, "Do bound feet look like the white lilies that the romantic books describe?" Mother and my aunts, who still had bound feet, gave me a frowning look. How could I talk so openly about a woman's most private parts? So Precious Auntie pretended to scold me with her hands for asking such a question, but what she really said was this: *They're usually crimped like flower-twist bread. But if they're dirty and knotty with calluses, they look like rotten ginger roots and smell like pig snouts three days dead.*

50   In this way, Precious Auntie taught me to be naughty, just like her. She taught me to be curious, just like her. She taught me to be spoiled. And because I was all these things, she could not teach me to be a better daughter, though in the end, she tried to change my faults.

51   I remember how she tried. It was the last week we were together. She did not speak to me for days. Instead she wrote and wrote and wrote. Finally she handed me a bundle of pages laced together with cord. *This is my true story,* she told me, *and yours as well.* Out of spite, I did not read most of those pages. But when I did, this is what I learned.

52   One late-autumn day, when Precious Auntie was nineteen by her Chinese age, the bonesetter had two new patients. The first was a screaming baby from a family who lived in Immortal Heart. The second was Baby Uncle. They would both cause Precious Auntie everlasting sorrow, but in two entirely different ways.

53   The bawling baby was the youngest son of a big-chested man named Chang, a coffinmaker who had grown rich in times of plagues. The carv-

ings on the outside of his coffins were of camphor wood. But the insides were cheap pine, painted and lacquered to look and smell like the better golden wood.

54   Some of that same golden wood had fallen from a stack and knocked the baby's shoulder out of its socket. That's why the baby was howling, Chang's wife reported with a frightened face. Precious Auntie recognized this nervous woman. Two years before, she had sat in the bonesetter's shop because her eye and jaw had been broken by a stone that must have fallen out of the open sky. Now she was back with her husband, who was slapping the baby's leg, telling him to stop his racket. Precious Auntie shouted at Chang: "First the shoulder, now you want to break his leg as well." Chang scowled at her. Precious Auntie picked up the baby. She rubbed a little bit of medicine inside his cheeks. Soon the baby quieted, yawned once, and fell asleep. Then the bonesetter snapped the small shoulder into place.

55   "What's the medicine?" the coffinmaker asked Precious Auntie. She didn't answer.

56   "Traditional things," the bonesetter said. "A little opium, a little herbs, and a special kind of dragon bone we dig out from a secret place only our family knows."

57   "Special dragon bone, eh?" Chang dipped his finger in the medicine bowl, then dabbed inside his cheek. He offered some to Precious Auntie, who sniffed in disgust, and then he laughed and gave Precious Auntie a bold look, as if he already owned her and could do whatever he pleased.

58   Right after the Changs and their baby left, Baby Uncle limped in.

59   He had been injured by his nervous horse, he explained to the bonesetter. He had been traveling from Peking to Immortal Heart, and during a rest, the horse startled a rabbit, then the rabbit startled the horse, and the horse stepped on Baby Uncle's foot. Three broken toes resulted, and Baby Uncle rode his bad horse to the Mouth of the Mountain, straight to the Famous Bonesetter's shop.

60   Baby Uncle sat in the blackwood examination chair. Precious Auntie was in the back room and could see him through the parted curtain. He was a thin young man of twenty-two. His face was refined but he did not act pompous or overly formal, and while his gown was not that of a rich gentleman, he was well groomed. She heard him joke about his accident: "My mare was so crazy with fright I thought she was going to gallop straight to the underworld with me stuck astride." When Precious Auntie stepped into the room, she said, "But fate brought you here instead." Baby Uncle fell quiet. When she smiled, he forgot his pain. When she put a dragon bone poultice on his naked foot, he decided to marry her. That was Precious Auntie's version of how they fell in love.

61   I have never seen a picture of my real father, but Precious Auntie told me that he was very handsome and smart, yet also shy enough to make a girl feel tender. He looked like a poor scholar who could rise above his circumstances, and surely he would have qualified for the imperial

examinations if they had not been canceled several years before by the new Republic.

62   The next morning, Baby Uncle came back with three stemfuls of lychees for Precious Auntie as a gift of appreciation. He peeled off the shell of one, and she ate the white-fleshed fruit in front of him. The morning was warm for late autumn, they both remarked. He asked if he could recite a poem he had written that morning: "You speak," he said, "the language of shooting stars, more surprising than sunrise, more brilliant than the sun, as brief as sunset. I want to follow its trail to eternity."

63   In the afternoon, the coffinmaker Chang brought a watermelon to the bonesetter. "To show my highest appreciation," he said. "My baby son is already well, able to pick up bowls and smash them with the strength of three boys."

64   Later that week, unbeknownst one to the other, each man went to a different fortune-teller. The two men wanted to know if their combination of birthdates with Precious Auntie's was lucky. They asked if there were any bad omens for a marriage.

65   The coffinmaker went to a fortune-teller in Immortal Heart, a man who walked about the village with a divining stick. The marriage signs were excellent, the fortune-teller said. See here, Precious Auntie was born in a Rooster year, and because Chang was a Snake, that was nearly the best match possible. The old man said that Precious Auntie also had a lucky number of strokes in her name (I will write the number down here when I remember her name). And as a bonus, she had a mole in position eleven, near the fatty part of her cheek, indicating that only sweet words fell from her obedient mouth. The coffinmaker was so happy to hear this that he gave the fortune-teller a big tip.

66   Baby Uncle went to a fortune-teller in the Mouth of the Mountain, an old lady with a face more wrinkled than her palm. She saw nothing but calamity. The first sign was the mole on Precious Auntie's face. It was in position twelve, she told Baby Uncle, and it dragged down her mouth, meaning that her life would always bring her sadness. Their combination of birth years was also inharmonious, she a fire Rooster and he a wood Horse. The girl would ride his back and peck him apart piece by piece. She would consume him with her insatiable demands. And here was the worst part. The girl's father and mother had reported the date of her birth was the sixteenth day of the seventh moon. But the fortune-teller had a sister-in-law who lived near the bonesetter, and she knew better. She had heard the newborn's wails, not on the sixteenth day, but on the fifteenth, the only day when unhappy ghosts are allowed to roam the earth. The sister-in-law said the baby sounded like this: "*Wu-wu, wu-wu*," not like a human but like a haunted one. The fortune-teller confided to Baby Uncle that she knew the girl quite well. She often saw her on market days, walking by herself. That strange girl did fast calculations in her head and argued with merchants. She was arrogant and headstrong. She was also educated, taught by her father to know the mysteries of the body. The girl

was too curious, too questioning, too determined to follow her own mind. Maybe she was possessed. Better find another marriage match, the fortune-teller said. This one would lead to disaster.

67 Baby Uncle gave the fortune-teller more money, not as a tip, but to make her think harder. The fortune-teller kept shaking her head. But after Baby Uncle had given a total of a thousand coppers, the old lady finally had another thought. When the girl smiled, which was often, her mole was in a luckier position, number eleven. The fortune-teller consulted an almanac, matched it to the hour of the girl's birth. Good news. The Hour of the Rabbit was peace-loving. Her inflexibility was just a bluff. And any leftover righteousness could be beaten down with a strong stick. It was further revealed that the fortune-teller's sister-in-law was a gossip known for exaggeration. But just to make sure the marriage went well, the fortune-teller sold Baby Uncle a Hundred Different Things charm that covered bad dates, bad spirits, bad luck, and hair loss. "But even with this, don't marry in the Dragon Year. Bad year for a Horse."

68 The first marriage proposal came from Chang's matchmaker, who went to the bonesetter and related the good omens. She boasted of the coffinmaker's respect, as an artisan descended from noted artisans. She described his house, his rock gardens, his fish ponds, the furniture in his many rooms, how the wood was of the best color, purple like a fresh bruise. As to the matter of a dowry, the coffinmaker was willing to be more than generous. Since the girl was to be a second wife and not a first, couldn't her dowry be a jar of opium and a jar of dragon bones? This was not much, yet it was priceless, and therefore not insulting to the girl's worth.

69 The bonesetter considered the offer. He was growing old. Where would his daughter go when he died? And what other man would want her in his household? She was too spirited, too set in her ways. She had no mother to teach her the manners of a wife. True, the coffinmaker would not have been his first choice of son-in-law, if he had had another, but he did not want to stand in the way of his daughter's future happiness. He told Precious Auntie about the generous offer from the coffinmaker.

70 To this, Precious Auntie huffed. "The man's a brute," she said. "I'd rather eat worms than be his wife."

71 The bonesetter had to give Chang's matchmaker an awkward answer: "I'm sorry," he said, "but my daughter cried herself sick, unable to bear the thought of leaving her worthless father." The lie would have been swallowed without disgrace, if only the offer from Baby Uncle's matchmaker had not been accepted the following week.

72 A few days after the future marriage was announced, the coffinmaker went back to the Mouth of the Mountain and surprised Precious Auntie as she was returning from the well. "You think you can insult me, then walk away laughing?"

73 "Who insulted whom? You asked me to be your concubine, a servant to your wife. I'm not interested in being a slave in a feudal marriage."

74   As she tried to leave, Chang pinched her neck, saying he should break it, then shook her as if he truly might snap off her head like a winter twig. But instead he threw her to the ground, cursing her and her dead mother's private parts.

75   When Precious Auntie recovered her breath, she sneered, "Big words, big fists. You think you can scare a person into being sorry?"

76   And he said these words, which she never forgot: "You'll soon be sorry every day of your miserable life."

77   Precious Auntie did not tell her father or Hu Sen what had happened. No sense in worrying them. And why lead her future husband to wonder if Chang had a reason to feel insulted? Too many people had already said she was too strong, accustomed to having her own way. And perhaps this was true. She had no fear of punishment or disgrace. She was afraid of almost nothing.

78   A month before the wedding, Baby Uncle came to her room late at night. "I want to hear your voice in the dark," he whispered. "I want to hear the language of shooting stars." She let him into her *k'ang* and he eagerly began the nuptials. But as Baby Uncle caressed her, a wind blew over her skin and she began to tremble and shake. For the first time, she was afraid, she realized, frightened by unknown joy.

79   The wedding was supposed to take place in Immortal Heart village, right after the start of the new Dragon Year. It was a bare spring day. Slippery pockets of ice lay on the ground. In the morning, a traveling photographer came to the bonesetter's shop in the Mouth of the Mountain. He had broken his arm the month before, and his payment was a photograph of Precious Auntie on her wedding day. She wore her best winter jacket, one with a high fur-lined collar, and an embroidered cap. She had to stare a long time into the camera, and as she did so, she thought of how her life would soon change forever. Though she was happy, she was also worried. She sensed danger, but she could not name what it was. She tried to look far into the future, but she could see nothing.

80   For the journey to the wedding, she changed her clothes to her bridal costume, a red jacket and skirt, the fancy headdress with a scarf that she had to drape over her head once she left her father's home. The bonesetter had borrowed money to rent two mule carts, one to carry gifts for the groom's family, the other for the bride's trunks of blankets and clothes.

81   There was an enclosed sedan chair for the bride herself, and the bonesetter also had to hire four sedan carriers, two carters, a flute player, and two bodyguards to watch out for bandits. For his daughter, he had procured only the best: the fanciest sedan chair, the cleanest carts, the strongest guards with real pistols and gunpowder. In one of the carts was the dowry, the jar of opium and the jar of dragon bones, the last of his supply. He assured his daughter many times not to worry about the cost. After her wedding, he could go to the Monkey's Jaw and gather more bones.

82   Halfway between the villages, two bandits wearing hoods sprang out of the bushes. "I'm the famous Mongol Bandit!" the larger one bellowed. Right away, Precious Auntie recognized the voice of Chang the coffin-maker. What kind of ridiculous joke was this? But before she could say anything, the guards threw down their pistols, the carriers dropped their poles, and Precious Auntie was thrown to the floor of the sedan and knocked out.

83   When she came to, she saw Baby Uncle's face in a haze. He had lifted her out of the sedan. She looked around and saw that the wedding trunks had been ransacked and the guards and carriers had fled. And then she noticed her father lying in a ditch, his head and neck at an odd angle, the life gone from his face. Was she in a dream? "My father," she moaned. "I want to go to him." As she bent over the body, unable to make sense of what had happened, Baby Uncle picked up a pistol that one of the guards had dropped.

84   "I swear I'll find the demons who caused my bride so much grief," he shouted, and then he fired the pistol toward heaven, startling his horse.

85   Precious Auntie did not see the kick that killed Baby Uncle, but she heard it, a terrible crack, like the opening of the earth when it was born. For the rest of her life she was to hear it in the breaking of twigs, the crackling of fire, whenever a melon was cleaved in the summer.

86   That was how Precious Auntie became a widow and an orphan in the same day. "This is a curse," she murmured, as she stared down at the bodies of the men she loved. For three sleepless days after their deaths, Precious Auntie apologized to the corpses of her father and Baby Uncle. She talked to their still faces. She touched their mouths, though this was for-bidden and caused the women of the house to fear that the wronged ghosts might either possess her or decide to stay.

87   On the third day, Chang arrived with two coffins. "He killed them!" Precious Auntie cried. She picked up a fire poker and tried to strike him. She beat at the coffins. Baby Uncle's brothers had to wrestle her away. They apologized to Chang for the girl's lunacy, and Chang replied that grief of this magnitude was admirable. Because Precious Auntie continued to be wild with admirable grief, the women of the house had to bind her from elbows to knees with strips of cloth. Then they laid her on Baby Uncle's *k'ang*, where she wiggled and twisted like a butterfly stuck in its cocoon until Great-Granny forced her to drink a bowl of medicine that made her body grow limp. For two days and nights, she dreamed she was with Baby Uncle, lying on the *k'ang* as his bride.

88   When she revived, she was alone in the dark. Her arms and legs had been unbound, but they were weak. The house was quiet. She went searching for her father and Baby Uncle. When she reached the main hall, the bodies were gone, already buried in Chang's wooden handiwork. Weeping, she wandered about the house and vowed to join them in the yellow earth. In the ink-making studio, she went looking for a length of rope, a sharp knife, matches she could swallow, anything to cause pain

greater than she felt. And then she saw a pot of black resin. She lowered a dipper into the liquid and put it in the maw of the stove. The oily ink became a soup of blue flames. She tipped the ladle and swallowed.

89   Great-Granny was the first to hear the thump-bumping sounds in the studio. Soon the other women of the household were there as well. They found Precious Auntie thrashing on the floor, hissing air out of a mouth blackened with blood and ink. "Like eels are swimming in the bowl of her mouth," Mother said. "Better if she dies."

90   But Great-Granny did not let this happen. Baby Uncle's ghost had come to her in a dream and warned that if Precious Auntie died, he and his ghost bride would roam the house and seek revenge on those who had not pitied her. Everyone knew there was nothing worse than a vengeful ghost. They caused rooms to stink like corpses. They turned bean curd rancid in a moment's breath. They let wild creatures climb over the walls and gates. With a ghost in the house, you could never get a good night's sleep.

91   Day in and day out, Great-Granny dipped cloths into ointments and laid these over Precious Auntie's wounds. She bought dragon bones, crushed them, and sprinkled them into her swollen mouth. And then she noticed that another part of Precious Auntie had become swollen: her womb.

92   Over the next few months, Precious Auntie wounds changed from pus to scars, and her womb grew like a gourd. She had once been a fine-looking girl. Now all except blind beggars shuddered at the sight of her. One day, when it was clear she was going to survive, Great-Granny said to her speechless patient: "Now that I've saved your life, where will you and your baby go? What will you do?"

93   That night, the ghost of Baby Uncle came once again to Great-Granny, and the next morning, Great-Granny told Precious Auntie: "You are to stay and be nursemaid to this baby. First Sister will claim it as hers and raise it as a Liu. To those you meet, we'll say you're a distant relation from Peking, a cousin who lived in a nunnery until it burned down and nearly took you with it. With that face, no one will recognize you."

94   And that's what happened. Precious Auntie stayed. I was the reason she stayed, her only reason to live. Five months after my birth in 1916, GaoLing was born to Mother, who had been forced by Great-Granny to claim me as her own. How could Mother say she had two babies five months apart? That was impossible. So Mother decided to wait. Exactly nine months after my birth, and on a very lucky date in 1917, GaoLing was born for sure.

95   The grown-ups knew the truth of our births. The children knew only what they were supposed to pretend. And though I was smart I was stupid. I did not ever question the truth. I did not wonder why Precious Auntie had no name. To others she was Nursemaid. To me, she was Precious Auntie. And I did not know who she really was until I read what she wrote.

96   "I am your mother," the words said.

97   I read that only after she died. Yet I have a memory of her telling me with her hands, I can see her saying this with her eyes. When it is dark, she says this to me in a clear voice I have never heard. She speaks in the language of shooting stars.

Questions for Engagement, Response, and Analysis

1. Explain the duties of a bonesetter.

2. Give examples of the geographically descriptive names of the Chinese cities and areas.

3. In what ways do superstitions influence the actions of the characters?

4. What did Chang and Baby Uncle have in common, and what were their differences? What were the results of their commonalities? Why did Precious Auntie choose Baby Uncle instead of Chang, the coffinmaker?

5. How did Precious Auntie lose the ability to speak? In what ways is Lu Ling dependent on her nursemaid? What clues early in the story suggest the relationship between Precious Auntie and Lu Ling?

6. List the vivid metaphors in the story and give your interpretation of each. Be sure to consider the metaphor in the last sentence.

AMY TAN: A CRITICAL COMPANION

E. D. HUNTLEY

1   Like a growing number of contemporary writers, Amy Tan crafts novels that resist facile and definitive classification into any of the conventional fictional genres. That the books are novels is widely acknowledged, although Tan has said that she intended *The Joy Luck Club* to be a collection of short stories. Readers and critics alike do, however, agree that Tan's work incorporates or echoes other genres including nonfiction and poetry. In fact, a significant source of the charm and artistry of the three Tan novels is their shape as fictional narratives that embrace elements of biography and autobiography, history and mythology, folk tale and Asian talk story, personal reminiscence and memoir. Tan's novels reify and reinterpret traditional genres by casting them in a variety of modes—realistic, comic, tragic, tragicomic, allegorical, fantastic, naturalistic, and heroic—that metamorphose seamlessly into each other in Tan's signature narrative style. Commentary is juxtaposed with memory, fable with history, pidgin English with California-speak, American culture with Chinese tradition, past with present in a collision of stories and voices and personalities, filtered through the point of view of an Asian American author who lives between worlds, who inhabits that border country known only to those in whose minds and sensibilities cultures clash and battle for dominance. Although Amy Tan's prose style is distinctively her own, she also owes a literary debt to other writers who, like her, inhabit the border country that shapes and inspires so many minority writers—

writers who derive their voices and narrative structures from their experiences in the neighborhoods of America's diaspora cultures.

Asian American Literature: A Definition

2   In 1982, Elaine Kim's ground-breaking study, *Asian American Literature: An Introduction to the Writings and Social Context*, essentially brought an entire body of little-known literature into the American literary consciousness, and helped Asian American literature gain recognition as a significant body of writing with both a "new tradition" of literary creation and a discernible—and very fluid—canon. In her work, Kim defined Asian American literature as "published creative writings in English by Americans of Chinese, Japanese, Korean, and Filipino descent" (xi). Although that definition lost its currency as immigrants from Cambodia, Vietnam, India, Pakistan, and other Asian countries began to make their homes in the United States and to write about their experiences, one crucial element of Kim's definition still holds true. Asian American literature is the creative work of writers of Asian descent who identify themselves as Americans and who view their own experiences and the world through the dual lenses of their American identities and their ethnic roots. More specifically, Asian American literature "elucidates the social history of Asians in the United States" (xiii). Although, as Kim points out, Asian American literature "shares with most other literature thematic concerns such as love, desire for personal freedom and acceptance, and struggles against oppression and injustice" (xii–xiii), this body of literature also is the product of other distinctive cultural forces. Like African American writing, fiction, poetry, and drama by Asian Americans is shaped by racism—both overt and disguised—and its corollaries, prejudice and discrimination. Moreover, for most Asian American writers, the Old Country and its culture are neither ancient nor buried history but very much alive and integral to the present, either in their own lives or in those of their parents and grandparents. The immigrant experience looms large in the writing of Asian Americans, and with that experience comes questions about marginality and life on the border, as well as explorations of issues of biculturalism and language, and decisions about identity . . . .

3   Although these anthologies made some Asian writing more accessible to larger numbers of readers, Asian American literature had its first significant impact on the popular American consciousness in 1976 when Maxine Hong Kingston published *The Woman Warrior*, her rivetingly powerful memoir about growing up Chinese in America. Kingston's book was well-received in literary circles, winning the National Book Critics Circle Award for the best nonfiction of 1976, and paved the way for the young writers of the next decade to prove conclusively that the Asian American voice had a powerful resonance far beyond Chinatown or Little Tokyo or the neighborhood enclaves of Korean or Filipino immigrants. Unfortunately, Kingston was condemned

by some Asian American writers who accused her of trying to "cash in" on the "feminist fad," of writing only for financial gain by creating "white-pleasing autobiography passing for pop cultural anthropology" (Kim 198). However, Kingston's detractors, although articulate and vocal, are few—limited mainly to a few male writers of Asian descent who have continued to argue that the tremendous sales and widespread popularity enjoyed by Asian American women writers undermines the masculinity of their male colleagues.

4   Kingston ushered in the 1980s with *China Men* (1980), winning the American Book Award. During that decade, Asian American writers earned recognition for the excellence and importance of their work. Among poets, Cathy Song won the Yale Series of Younger Poets competition for *Picture Bride* in 1982, Garrett Hongo was awarded the Lamont Poetry prize of the Academy of American Poets in 1987, and Li-Young Lee was invited to read his poetry on National Public Radio. A new generation of playwrights graced the American stage: Genny Lim's *Island* (1985) was featured on National Public Television, and David Henry Hwang entranced Broadway audiences and won several Tony Awards for *M. Butterfly* in 1988. Into the growing market for and interest in Asian American writing came Amy Tan and *The Joy Luck Club* in 1989. The publication of that novel helped to catapult Asian American fiction into the literary mainstream when it appeared on national bestseller lists and became a featured book-club selection. By the end of the decade, many writers, including David Mura, Jessica Hagedorn, Philip Kan Gotanda, Ping Chong, Gish Jen, and Cynthia Kadohata discovered their work—along with that of Kingston and Tan—in textbook anthologies and on required reading lists for literature courses. Years later, the final pieces of evidence that Asian American writing has entrenched itself in the popular mind are the popular film versions of works by writers as diverse as Tan and Hwang, and memoir-writer Le-Ly Hayslip.

5   Partly because of the volume of their work and certainly because they write about subjects that resonate with so many mainstream readers, Chinese American women writers have been largely but inadvertently responsible for the new and sudden popularity of Asian American writing, a development that is made more startling because Chinese women were an almost invisible minority in American society until the early 1950s. Because most of them were kept out of the United States by laws specifically excluding Chinese women (including those who were married to American-born Chinese men) from immigration quotas, these women were outnumbered by Chinese men by approximately twenty to one. Given those numbers, we should not be surprised at the relatively small number of Chinese women writers in the first half of the twentieth century—in fact, we should be amazed that so many of the significant early Chinese American writers were women.

Plot Development

6   The plot of *The Hundred Secret Senses* follows two narrative threads: Olivia's search for an integrated self, and Kwan's desire to undo the damage of a century-old mistake. Although the two are closely related, the connections between them do not immediately become obvious but emerge gradually as elements of each plot come to light and reveal echoes of the other.

7   Borrowing a technique from the classical epic, Amy Tan begins the novel *in medias res*, or—colloquially translated—in the middle of the action. Over a century earlier in China, Kwan—with the very best intentions—told a lie, fabricating a story that had the unforeseen effect of disrupting the lives of two people and abruptly terminating the romance that had begun between them. The plot that has Kwan at its center is the history of her previous existence as Nunumu; the events of her life gradually reveal the incidents that lead inexorably toward the mistake that separates Miss Banner and Yiban. Now in California, Kwan is devoting her energies to the cause of rectifying her mistake and reuniting the lovers. Meanwhile, in the narrative of Olivia's efforts to discover what she wants her life to become, Olivia and Simon already are separated and have initiated the legal transactions that will lead to divorce. Both women tell their stories, but whereas Olivia's narratives suggest interior monologues with a pervasive component of self-questioning and no identifiable audience, Kwan's stories—which are embedded in Olivia's—are clearly addressed to Olivia.

8   As Olivia sorts through the emotional chaos resulting from her separation from Simon, she repeatedly is reminded of the events of their courtship, the early years of their marriage, and their more recent attempts to revive the companionship they felt when they were younger. Because Simon was and is her first and only love, Olivia is not dealing well with the break-up of her marriage, and Kwan, who is still the protective older sister although they are both adults, worries constantly about Olivia, inviting her to dinner, dropping in for brief visits, offering the opinion that the separation is a mistake and that Olivia and Simon should reconcile. In the first half of the novel, each overture by Kwan prompts Olivia to remember a story that Kwan has told her, and each story told by Kwan in turn somehow returns the narrative to Olivia's emotional dilemma. With each new story, the outlines of connections become clearer. Initially, it appears that Kwan wants to bring the couple back together because she was responsible for the evening during which Elza—a *yin* person and Simon's first love who had been dead for a while—supposedly told Simon to forget her and to find happiness with Olivia. But Kwan's stories and everyday conversation are laced with oblique references to her belief that the rightness of Olivia's and Simon's union was determined by events in the distant past, and eventually Kwan manages to persuade Simon and Olivia to join her on a trip to China where, she points out mysteriously, they will discover the true pattern of their lives.

9   During the China trip, Olivia's and Kwan's narratives abruptly change. Removed from the familiar and confronted with a new culture, Olivia curtails her litany of past rejections and begins instead to detail events as they happen; and because she is in China, Olivia no longer has to rely on her memory of Kwan's stories—China is all around her to be experienced. Kwan, for her part, increases the number and frequency of her stories about Nunumu and Miss Banner, adding stories that Olivia has never heard—for instance, the story of Yiban and the last days in the Ghost Merchant's house, or the tale of the flight to the mountains. Early in the novel, Kwan's stories emerge as Olivia's memories, but in the final chapters, Kwan tells her stories in the immediate present. Gone is the slow gentle rhythm of memory; each tale now is urgent, immediate, triggered by the sight of a mountain or the taste of a special dish or, ultimately, the very palpable presence of a music box that Kwan claims to have hidden in a cave over a century earlier. Kwan's final stories clarify connections: Olivia and Simon are Miss Banner and Yiban, and Kwan has brought them to Changmian to reunite them. The novel ends with an epilogue narrated by Olivia. She and Simon are working toward reconciliation. More important, they have a daughter who was conceived in China, and who is— Olivia firmly believes—Kwan's final gift to them.

Narrative Strategies

10   Tan employs the juxtaposition of past and present as a narrative device for her story of the indestructibility of love and loyalty. Past and present are so closely interrelated that Olivia ultimately admits to being occasionally confused about whether an event actually occurred or is merely an episode in one of Kwan's frequently recounted stories. Toward the end of the novel, as Olivia and Kwan turn over the contents of the ancient music box that the latter says she hid in a cave more than a hundred years earlier, Olivia's logical mind races from one explanation to another. Always the rational American woman of the 1990s, Olivia is inclined to doubt what her senses suggest; nevertheless, she cannot dismiss the fact of Kwan's unflinching candor. In their time together, Olivia has never known Kwan to lie; in fact, Kwan says only what she truly believes to be true. And although Olivia knows that she should believe Kwan even now, another question surfaces: "[I]f I believe what she says, does that mean I now believe she has *yin* eyes?" (320). At that moment, Olivia realizes what she has known, has in fact believed all along—since childhood— that Kwan does remember events, the memory of which defies rational explanation.

11   Events in the past clearly and significantly influence the lives of both Olivia and Kwan. They are sisters, thanks to Jack Yee's two marriages and the shameful act of thievery that provided him with the wherewithal to abandon a wife and child, to discard an identity, and to begin a new life and new family in America. Through her conversations with her *yin* friends about Olivia's marital problems, Kwan bridges the chronological

gap between her two lives, and Olivia is forced to endure advice and comments on her marriage from a certain Lao Lu, a friend of Kwan's from the Taiping days in the Ghost Merchant's house. Not even Olivia's marriage is immune to the influence of the past: after nearly two decades of marriage, Simon still appears to be obsessed with his first love who was killed in an avalanche.

12   During the visit to China, Kwan becomes more and more insistent that she and Olivia have had a previous life together, and when the sisters are together on the mountain, Olivia begins to half believe that she does indeed recognize in her present circumstances a series of strong resonances from another time. Whether these frissons of memory are remnants of Kwan's stories or genuine recollections from Olivia's past is immaterial. What is clear is that Olivia finds the more distinctive elements of the Guilin landscape disturbingly familiar.

13   Present and past finally collide on a rain-drenched mountain just beyond Changmian. Assailed from all directions by a cascade of sensory and emotional stimuli (Kwan's final story about her last hours in the nineteenth century, a hilly landscape that possesses a dreamlike familiarity combined with jarring strangeness, Simon's disappearance into the cold mist, Kwan's rediscovery of the music box that she last saw when she was Nunumu, and finally Kwan's revelation of the truth about Simon and Elza), Olivia is drawn into an admission that her history with Kwan could have begun near this mountain in an earlier century. It remains only for Olivia to unearth the jars full of duck eggs that Kwan says Nunumu buried during the Taiping troubles. As Olivia holds the ancient crumbling duck eggs in her cupped hands, the act liberates her from the doubts that have undermined all of her relationships. And although Kwan vanishes into the Changmian caves and is never found despite an intensive and protracted search, Olivia believes that the daughter who is born to her and Simon nine months later is a gift from Kwan. The child is not Kwan, exactly, but she is connected with Kwan in some mysterious way—and in that little girl, the past and the present are fused into wholeness and the future.

14   As she does in her other novels, Tan relies on formal storytelling as a narrative strategy in *The Hundred Secret Senses*. Both Kwan's nineteenth-century existence as Nunumu and her twentieth-century childhood in Changmian before her emigration to America emerge through narrative set pieces that Kwan performs as though they are legends or folktales, artifacts of an oral tradition that she feels impelled to pass on to Olivia who is her captive audience.

15   Tan uses the flashback technique to superb effect in the novel. New words, chance remarks, familiar objects and mementos, the taste of traditional Chinese dishes, and celebrations trigger Kwan's recollections, prompting her to narrate vignettes, brief tales, events, the particulars of specific episodes in her former lives. In one instance, when she overhears the neighborhood children referring to her as "a retard" and forces Olivia

to define the word, Kwan suddenly is reminded of Miss Banner's early attempts to speak Chinese, and she tells Olivia that Nunumu initially thought that Miss Banner's inability to speak or understand Chinese indicated a lack of intelligence. On occasion, Kwan says, Nunumu actually laughed at Miss Banner's feeble attempts to converse in the vernacular. The memory prompts Kwan immediately to launch into an account of Miss Banner's first garbled description of her early life. Because Miss Banner cannot speak adequate Chinese, she ends up thoroughly confusing Nunumu by telling an impossibly surrealistic story about her origins, but Nunumu's patience with her mistress eventually results in her success at teaching Miss Banner how to view the world "exactly as a Chinese person" would (49).

16   By providing multiple versions of and varying perspectives on events that are central to the novel, Tan explores the ways through which storytellers create meaning on many levels and from different points of view. In some cases, the plurality of versions is the inadvertent result of misunderstandings, incomplete information, or even partial fabrication; in other cases, variant editions of a story signal the storyteller's intent to deceive. Tan seems to be suggesting that the truth exists both in each version of a story and somewhere in the unspoken narrative or in the spaces between stories.

17   A hallmark of *The Hundred Secret Senses* is the novel's precarious position somewhere between the real and the surreal, between the prosaic and the magical. When Kwan as Nunumu first hears Miss Banner's life story told in fractured stumbling Chinese, she forms the impression that Miss Banner has come from a peculiarly skewed and topsy-turvy universe. Miss Banner's little brothers chase a chicken into a deep hole and fall all the way to the other side of the world; her father picks scented money that grows like flowers and makes people happy; her mother puffs out her neck like a rooster, calls for her sons, and climbs down the hole that has swallowed them. After her mother's disappearance, Miss Banner's father takes her first to a palace governed by little Jesuses, and later to an island ruled by mad dogs. At length, the father vanishes and Miss Banner lives with a succession of uncles, including one who cuts off pieces of China and sails off on a floating island. The reality—which Kwan learns after Miss Banner becomes more fluent in Chinese—is that Miss Banner's brothers died of chicken pox and her mother of a goiter disease; her father was an opium trader who put her in a school for Jesus-worshipping children in India; father and daughter left India for Malacca; and the uncles were actually a series of lovers. Tan's clever juxtaposition of fact and whimsy complements the surrealism that pervades the entire novel and validates for the reader the simultaneous existence of twentieth century and nineteenth century, Chinese and American, Kwan and Nunumu, and the *yin* people in Tan's fictional universe.

18   Tan also employs multiple versions of a story to create uncertainty and to describe a world in which no definite answers are possible. Jack Yee,

the shadowy father that Kwan and Olivia barely remember, is an enigma to both daughters, but for different reasons. In Olivia's version of Jack's story—passed on to her by the American-born adults in the family—Jack was a good-looking university student in Guilin who was forced to marry a young market vendor when she became pregnant with his child. Five years later, when his wife died of a lung disease, the grief-stricken Jack left his young daughter with an aunt and went to Hong Kong to begin a new life. Before he could send for his beloved daughter, the Communist takeover in China destroyed all hope for a reunion between father and child, and the despondent Jack emigrated to America. Kwan's arrival replaces the sad story with an even more disturbing one. According to Kwan, her mother did not die of a lung disease; she died of "heartsickness" when her husband abandoned her with a four-year-old daughter and another child on the way. Kwan tells Olivia that all the water in her mother's belly "poured out as tears from her eyes. . . . That poor starving baby in her belly ate a hole in my mother's heart, and they both died" (14). In this way, years later, Olivia learns what Kwan has always known. Their father had no legal or hereditary claim to the name Jack Yee. The name belonged to the owner of a stolen overcoat that the young university student who became their father purloined from a drunken man who had been trying to sell it for whatever cash he could get. In the coat's pockets were immigration permits, academic records, notification of admission to an American university, a ticket for passage on a ship, and cash—documents that would facilitate a new life in a wealthy country full of opportunity, far away from poverty, factory work, a pregnant wife, and a child. Donning the coat and the spectacles he found in one pocket, and appropriating the documents, the student became Jack Yee. But Amy Tan does not privilege Kwan's version. Kwan, in fact, prefaces her tale by saying that she heard it from Li Bin-bin, her mother's sister who raised her—and who, under the circumstances, would be unlikely to feel kindly toward the bogus Jack Yee. Thus the question remains: Who is the man behind the identity of Jack Yee? Kwan says that she has never known his true name, and she clearly knows almost nothing of his origins. And by extension, then, who are Olivia and Kwan? Who are their true ancestors? And who are Miss Banner and Nunumu? And, ultimately, how are all of these individuals connected?

19   Finally, Tan employs the many-layered triple narrative to interrogate the accounts of actual historical events, perhaps even to suggest that such accounts are unstable because they are the productions of gendered, class-defined, or racially constructed language. The Taiping Rebellion of the mid-nineteenth century is well known to Sinologists as well as to historians and geographers, but the standard texts tend toward factual, Westernized accounts of military battles, descriptions of territory gained or lost, and tallies of victories and defeats. Kwan's version of the Rebellion privileges the perspective of a half-blind orphan who notices far more than battles between Manchu and Hakka. For one-eyed

Nunumu, the Rebellion means the loss of her entire family, and life in a half-deserted village populated only by the elderly and the very young, the physically and mentally disabled, and the cowardly; the Heavenly King and his armies succeed only in bringing her hunger and cold, and a life of servitude in a house full of missionaries. Nunumu's experiences factor the personal element into a historical equation, revealing the frequently overlooked truth that military and political battles are always won or lost at the expense of thousands of individuals whose lives are forever disrupted by the ambitions of a powerful minority and their followers.

Works Cited

Goldman, Marlene. "Naming the Unspeakable: The Mapping of Female Identity in Maxine Hong Kingston's *The Woman Warrior.*" *International Women's Writing: New Landscapes of Identity.* Eds. Anne E. Brown and Marjanne E. Goozé. Westport, CT: Greenwood Press, 1995. 223–32.

Hsaio, Ruth. "Facing the Incurable: Patriarchy in *Eat a Bowl of Tea.*" In *Reading the Literature of Asian America.* Eds. Shirley Geok-lin Lim and Amy Ling. Philadelphia: Temple University Press, 1992. 151–62.

Kim, Elaine. *Asian American Literature: An Introduction to the Writings and their Social Context.* Philadelphia: Temple University Press, 1982.

Lim, Shirley G., and Amy Ling. *Reading the Literatures of Asian America.* Philadelphia: Temple University Press, 1992.

Ling, Amy. *Between Worlds: Women Writers of Chinese Ancestry.* New York: Pergamon, 1990.

CHINESE AMERICAN WOMEN, LANGUAGE, AND MOVING SUBJECTIVITY

VICTORIA CHEN

To imagine a language means to imagine a form of life.

WITTGENSTEIN, *PHILOSOPHICAL INVESTIGATIONS*

Philosophical Investigations

1   It was not until the 1970s that Asian American literature became recognized as a separate canon and a "new tradition" of writing. While this "new" form of expression created a new political consciousness and identity, the images and stories that abound in pioneer literature such as Maxine Hong Kingston's *The Woman Warrior* and *China Men* are paradoxically located in "recovered" ethnic history. More recently, Amy Tan's *The Joy Luck Club* also takes the reader through a journey back to a specific set of ethnic memories as the mothers in the stories interweave

their experiences struggling for survival and dignity in China and for coherence and hope in America. Part of the reason for the celebration of Asian American women's literature is that it provides an alternative way to think about issues such as language, subjectivity, cultural voice, and ethnic/gender identity.

2   For Chinese American women such as Kingston, Tan, and the female characters in *The Joy Luck Club*, speaking in a double voice and living in a bicultural world characterize their dual cultural enmeshment. While striving to maintain a relationship with their Chinese immigrant parents, the Chinese American daughters also live in a society where one is expected to speak in a "standard" form of English and to "succeed" in the middle class Euro-American way. For Kingston and Tan, writing about their immigrant mothers' neglected pasts and their own tumultuous presents becomes a powerful way to recreate their own identities as Chinese Americans and to confront the dilemma of living biculturally in a society that insists on a homogeneous identity. If a language indeed is intrinsically connected with a form of life, and speaking and writing in a given language necessitates one to participate in that cultural world, how then do these Chinese American women authors position themselves in linguistic/cultural borderlands through the use of language? What are some forms of language and life that make their storytelling possible and intelligible? How do different languages function in their own lives and in their storytelling? How do they use languages to interweave and mediate their multiple identities? This essay attempts to address some of these issues. I will draw upon essays written by and about Kingston and Tan as well as narratives from *The Joy Luck Club* and *The Woman Warrior* in my discussion.

3   Amy Tan (1991) in her essay "Mother Tongue" discusses that as someone who has always loved language, she celebrates using "all the Englishes I grew up with" in her living and her writing. The English that she hears from her mother, despite its "imperfection," has become their "language of intimacy, a different sort of English that relates to family talk, the language I grew up with." There is a discrepancy, both linguistically and culturally, between the "standard" English that she learns from school and uses in her professional world and the "simple" and "broken" English that is used in her interaction with her mother. However, as Tan points out, speaking her mother's version of English gives her bicultural insight and strength, and she sees the beauty and wisdom in her mother's language: "Her language, as I hear it, is vivid, direct, full of observation and imagery"; "I wanted to capture what language ability tests can never reveal: her intent, her passion, her imagery, the rhythms of her speech and the nature of her thoughts." Kingston also grew up in two languages, her family's Chinese dialect and the public American English in which she was educated. *The Woman Warrior* reveals the disjunction that Kingston experienced in moving between these two languages. While her mother marked her growing up with stories of nameless Chinese women,

multiple cultural ghosts, Kingston wrote, "To make my waking life American-normal . . . I push the deformed into my dreams, which are in Chinese, the language of impossible stories." The entire book is devoted to Kingston's ongoing struggle to enter the Chinese cultural world composed of impossible stories and to figure out what it meant to be a Chinese American woman in this society.

4   Tan's *The Joy Luck Club* is a segmented novel, set in San Francisco in the 1980s, powerfully blending the voices of four Chinese immigrant mothers and their American-born daughters. The book opens with a story of a swan and a woman sailing across an ocean toward America saying, "In America I will have a daughter just like me. But over there . . . nobody will look down on her, because I will make her speak only perfect American English. And over there she will always be too full to swallow any sorrow! She will know my meaning. . . ." The tale symbolizes not only the geographic separation from the woman's motherland but also the alienation later felt by both the mother and daughter in America. The woman's desire for her daughter to speak perfect American English foregrounds the problems and difficulties of communicating and translating between the different languages that they speak. The American dream eventually eludes the immigrant woman beyond her best intentions. Mastering this imaginary perfect English for the American-born daughter turns out not to be a simple ticket to American success. This linguistic competency, ironically, signifies her departure from her mother (and her motherland), deepening the chasm between generations and cultures. Moreover, learning to speak perfect American English may also entail the complex journey of "successful" acculturation which often masks the racism and sexism that belie the American dream.

5   Although Tan's essay celebrates the two Englishes with which she grew up, and that dual languages and cultures can indeed enrich and enlighten one's life, coherence and double voice do not always come without personal struggle and emotional trauma. As we enter the hyphenated world of the "Chinese-American" women in *The Joy Luck Club*, much of the mothers' and daughters' conversations seem to be focused on debating, negotiating, and wandering between the two disparate cultural logics. Lindo shared her daughter's concern that she cannot say whether her Chinese or American face is better: "I think about our two faces. I think about my intentions. Which one is American? Which one is Chinese? Which one is better? If you show one, you must always sacrifice the other." Tan (1990), in her essay "The Language of Discretion," pointed out a special kind of double bind attached to knowing two languages and vehemently rebelled against seeing cultural descriptions as dichotomous categories: "It's dangerous business, this sorting out of language and behavior. Which one is English? Which is Chinese? . . . Reject them all!" "Having listened to both Chinese and English, I also tend to be suspicious of any comparisons between Chinese and English languages." Tan argued: "Typically, one language—that of the person doing the

comparing—is often used as the standard, the benchmark for a logical form of explanation."

6   Speaking a language is inherently political. In the case of Chinese American women, while straddling and juggling along the fault lines of gender and culture, the truth is that the two Englishes that Tan cherished are not valued equally in this society. Despite the creative use of imaginative metaphors in her English, as Tan humorously presented, her mother would never score high in a standard English test that insists on one correct way of linguistic construction. It is no secret that in much of our social discourse and communication practice, the myth persists that what counts as the "normal" standards and criteria for comparing and discussing cultural difference is still the mainstream Eurocentric mode of thinking and doing. In her writing about Asian American women's experience of racism, Shah (1994) said, "For me, the experience of 'otherness,' the formative discrimination in my life, has resulted from culturally different people thinking they were culturally central; thinking that *my* house smelled funny, that *my* mother talked weird, that *my* habits were strange. They were normal; I wasn't." Similarly, in a discussion of the difficult dialogues between black and white women, Houston (1994) points out that when a white woman says "We're all alike," she usually means "I can see how you, a black woman, are like me, a white woman." She does not mean "I can see how I am like you." In other words, whether explicitly or implicitly, "just people" often means "just white people."

7   Language and identity are always positioned within a hierarchical power structure in which the Chinese American immigrants' form of life has never been granted a status equal to that of their European counterparts in the history of this country. It is one thing to embrace the philosophical wisdom of "having the best of both worlds" but another to confront the real ongoing struggle between languages and identities that most Chinese Americans experience. Bicultural identity cannot be reduced to two neutral, pristine, and equal linguistic domains that one simply picks and chooses to participate in without personal, relational, social, and political consequences. We need to understand the tension and conflict between generations of Chinese American women within the ideological cultural context of racial and sexual inequality and their ongoing contestation of their positions in it.

8   Through Tan's storytelling in *The Joy Luck Club*, the meaning of "perfect English" is transformed from the mother's naive American dream to the daughter's awakening bicultural disillusionment, as the daughter June laments: "These kinds of explanations made me feel my mother and I spoke two different languages, which we did. I talked to her in English, she answered back in Chinese," and later, "My mother and I never really understood one another. We translated each other's meanings and I seemed to hear less than what was said, while my mother heard more." The lack of shared languages and cultural logics remains a central theme throughout all the narratives in Tan's book. This absence transcends the

simple linguistic dichotomies or cultural misunderstandings; both mothers and daughters are negotiating their relational and social positions and contesting their identities as Chinese American women in the languages that can enhance or undermine their power, legitimacy, and voice.

9   In a similar vein, in *The Woman Warrior* Kingston describes "abnormal" discourse as constructed and experienced by both parents and children in her family. The children in Kingston's family often spoke in English language which their parents "didn't seem to hear"; "the Chinese can't hear American at all; the language is too soft and Western music unhearable." Exasperated and bemused by their Chinese aunt's behavior, the children told each other that "Chinese people are very weird." Angry at the fact that the Chinese were unable, unwilling, or did not see the need to explain things to the children, Kingston writes, "I thought talking and not talking made the differences between sanity and insanity. Insane people were the ones who couldn't explain themselves." While the Chinese American children were frustrated by the impenetrable wisdom spoken or unspoken in the Chinese language, the parents teased the children about the way they spoke in the "ghost's" language and of the craziness and absurdity of doing things in American ways. Insane and absurd in what language(s) and from what cultural perspective(s)? Who has the authority to tell Kingston that Chinese girls are worthless growing up in a society that is supposed to be more egalitarian and liberating for women? What constitutes "normal" and "abnormal" discourse for Chinese American women? What price do they have to pay for being a full participant in either or both cultural worlds?

10   One intriguing feature in learning to speak and hear incommensurate languages is the process of adjudicating conflicting voices. In Chinese American families, communication can often be characterized by a lack of a shared universe of discourse or a set of mutually intelligible vocabularies. For Kingston, even attempting to engage in a meaningful dialogue with her parents about her confusions and their conflicts became a problem, as she told us, "I don't know any Chinese I can ask without getting myself scolded or teased." Silent and silenced, Kingston was angry at the sexist trivialization of her intellectual interests and academic accomplishment. She writes, "I've stopped checking 'bilingual' on job applications. I could not understand any of the dialects the interviewer at China Airlines tried on me, and he didn't understand me either." Family language almost became a "burden" as Kingston strived to make sense of what it meant to occupy two linguistic and cultural spaces as a Chinese American woman in a patriarchal system. Could her surrender allude to the disappointment and frustration that Chinese Americans as a group feel within the larger society?

11   In Tan's novel, when one of the daughters, June, did not comply with her mother's wishes, her mother shouted at her in Chinese: "Only two kinds of daughters. Those who are obedient and those who follow their own mind! Only one kind of daughter can live in this house. Obedient

daughter!" The mother's injunction is an enactment of her personal power within the family structure, and in this language and cultural logic, June is powerless even if she could speak "perfect" American English, which would give her positional power in a different situation.

12   Toward the end of the book when Kingston finally confronted her mother with her long list of feelings of guilt being a Chinese American daughter, the linguistic gap and cultural intranslatability resonated throughout their shouting match. Angry, frustrated, hurt, sad, and disappointed, Kingston realized that the confrontation was futile: "And suddenly I got very confused and lonely because I was at the moment telling her my list, and in the telling, it grew. No higher listener. No listener but myself." Once again, their voices did not intermesh, and neither could enter the cultural logic that was specifically structured within the primary language that they spoke. There was no possibility for Kingston to articulate her silence, nor was there space for displaying her mother's good intentions. The celebration of the multiple languages and polyphonic voices seemed elusive. Two generations of women were ultimately torn apart and yet inextricably bonded by the unspeakable cultural tongue. Each in their own way sounded strange, incoherent, crazy, abnormal, and stubborn to the other.

13   The end of the story of the swan in *The Joy Luck Club* says, "Now the woman was old. And she had a daughter who grew up speaking only English and swallowing more Coca-Cola than sorrow. For a long time now the woman had wanted to give her daughter the single swan feather and tell her, 'This feather may look worthless, but it comes from afar and carries with it all my good intentions.' And she waited, year after year, for the day she could tell her daughter this in perfect American English." As one of the mothers Lindo lamented, "I wanted my children to have the best combination, American circumstances and Chinese character. How could I know these two things do not mix?"

14   If indeed Chinese Americans are steeped in two languages and two forms of life, one public and dominant, another private and submerged, what is the symbolic significance of using these languages as constructed from various social positions? For the immigrant parents, educating their American-born children to speak the family language is a way to continue the cultural tradition and to instill ethnic pride. Speaking a private language is also an attempt to mark one's difference from the mainstream culture and to resist racism, hegemony, and the overwhelming power of homogenization in this society. In Tan's and Kingston's storytelling, speaking Chinese also becomes simply functional for the older immigrants who do not want to participate or/and are not perceived as full participants in the public language. As a result, they remain outsiders within the system; their use of private language marks the central feature of their identity.

15   Although for many American-born Chinese, using family language can affirm their cultural ties to their ancestors, Kingston also grew up hear-

ing all the derogatory comments about girls in Chinese, the language of foreign and impossible stories to her ear. While speaking her family dialect gives her a sense of connection and intimacy, the private language also symbolizes the oppression, confusion, frustration, madness, and silence that were associated with her coming of age. Using English to speak and write signifies Kingston's rebellion against the patriarchal tradition; it forced her to take a non-Chinese and non-female position in her family and community. For Chinese American women, speaking English affirms their public identity and gives them a legitimate cultural voice to claim for a space in this society. English gives them a means to assert their independence and a tool to fight against sexism and racism that they encounter. Trinh Minh-ha, in an interview, insisted that identity remains as a political/personal strategy of resistance and survival; "the reflexive question asked . . . is no longer: who am I? but when, where, how am I (so and so)?"

16   It is important to remember that a discussion of uses of language needs to be understood in a political context. Chinese Americans strive for polyphonic coherence within a society that celebrates conformity and homogeneity despite its rhetoric of diversity and pluralism. To mainstream ears, Chinese languages may sound a cacophony of unfamiliar tones and words; this unintelligibility can be associated with foreignness, exotic cultural others, lack of education, or powerlessness. This perceived absence of a shared language and culture (and therefore of disparate social and national interests) can lead to hostility or discrimination toward Chinese Americans.

17   Through the use of language we create and maintain our social relationships. We accomplish this goal only if an intersubjective discourse exists so that our words and actions are intelligible to others within the community. In Chinese American bicultural experience, this shared language often cannot be taken for granted. In *The Woman Warrior*, Kingston confronted her mother about telling her that she was ugly all the time, to which her mother replied, "That's what we're supposed to say. That's what Chinese say. We like to say the opposite." Here in the mother's language, "truth" is characterized by the logic of the opposite; this "indirect" approach works only if one knows how to hear the statement within the context of a certain kind of relationship. Saying the opposite is what the mother felt obligated to perform; in fact, it was the only language that she could use in order to demonstrate her affection and care for her daughter. Unfortunately, lacking the cultural insight to reverse the logic of her mother's statement, Kingston felt shamed, outraged, and was in turn accused by her mother of not being able to "tell a joke from real life"; her mother shouts at her, "You're not so smart. Can't even tell real from false." Real from false in what language? Where does the humor of this apparent joke for the mother—and humiliation for the daughter—lie in perfect American English?

18   In *The Joy Luck Club*, the young women's innocence, ignorance, and apathy toward their mother's language seemed to frighten the mothers. June tried to understand her three aunties at the mah jong table:

> And then it occurs to me. They are frightened. In me, they see their own daughters, just as ignorant, just as unmindful of all the truths and hopes they have brought to America. They see daughters who grow impatient when their mothers talk in Chinese, who think they are stupid when they explain things in fractured English. They see that joy and luck do not mean the same to their daughters, that to these closed American-born minds "joy luck" is not a word, it does not exist. They see daughters who will bear grandchildren born without any connecting hope passed from generation to generation.

19   Failure to translate between languages can cost emotional turmoil; it can also silence someone who depends on the English translation to negotiate or accomplish his/her goals. In one of the stories in *The Joy Luck Club*, the daughter Lena was unable to translate her mother's words to her Caucasian stepfather who did not speak Chinese. Since Lena understood the Chinese words spoken by her mother but not the implications, she made up something in her translation and as a result rewrote her mother's story in that episode. Tan intentionally constructed this scene to illustrate the nature of the mother-daughter relationship. Lena was ignorant of both the story that her mother was hinting at and of the Chinese language that her mother was speaking. Kingston's and Tan's writings are characterized by untold stories written in untranslatable language between the two generations of women. McAlister (1992) argued that by failing to translate between languages and stories, Chinese American daughters can participate in the silencing of their mothers. This position seems incongruous in view of Tan's overall agenda in her storytelling. By having all the women narrate their own stories, Tan treats language not just as a tool to reflect upon the past or to celebrate the present, but as a political means to allow Chinese American women to articulate their silenced lives, their otherwise voiceless positions in this society.

20   Tan writes *The Joy Luck Club* in a language that demands the reader recognize the distinctness of each character, each story and voice, and each mother-daughter relationship. The women in her creation are not just nameless, faceless, or interchangeable Chinese Americans. The interrelated narratives make sense only if readers can discern the specificities of each woman's story as located within the novel. Therefore, "Tan confronts an Orientalist discourse that depends on the sameness of Chinese difference." By granting subjectivity to each woman, Tan compels each to tell her own story in her own words, thus (re)creating the meanings of her life. The mother-daughter tensions as constructed in their own discourse are fraught with complexities of racial, gender, and class issues, not just the simple binary opposition of Americanness and Chineseness, mothers and daughters.

21   The ability to tell one's own story, to speak one's mind, is the best antidote to powerlessness. Tan's writing instills agency and visibility in Chi-

nese American women. The silence is broken, and their new voices are constructed in collective storytelling, a language of community, without denying or erasing the different positions such collaboration encounters. In a similar vein, Kingston gave the no name woman in her mother's storytelling a voice and a life, a permanent place in American culture; she immortalized this silent woman through her writing: "My aunt haunts me— her ghost drawn to me because now, after fifty years of neglect, I alone devote pages of paper to her." Both Tan and Kingston allow their female characters to reclaim and recreate their identity. "Storytelling heals past experiences of loss and separation; it is also a medium for rewriting stories of oppression and victimization into parables of self-affirmation and individual empowerment." It is possible to celebrate the present without forgetting the past. In an interview when Kingston was contrasting her own American voice in *Tripmaster Monkey* and her translation of Chinese voices in her previous two books, she said, "When I wrote *The Woman Warrior* and *China Men*, as I look back on it, I was trying to find an American language that would translate the speech of the people who are living their lives with the Chinese language. They carry on their adventures and their emotional life and everything in Chinese. I had to find a way to translate all that into a graceful American language, which is my language." Perhaps the boundary between Kingston's two languages/voices is not so clear; of *Tripmaster Monkey*, [a Chinese poet] she said that "I was writing in the tradition of the past." "And I spent this lifetime working on roots. So what they were saying was that I was their continuity."

22   Both Kingston's and Tan's writings point to the multiplicity and instability of cultural identity for Chinese American women, oscillating and crisscrossing between different Englishes and Chinese dialects that they speak. Although cultural borderlands can be a useful metaphor for "home" for these individuals, we must realize that this home does not rest in a fixed location, nor is it constructed in any one unified language or perfect American English. Neither of the authors is searching for a definitive Chinese American voice. Through interweaving their own bicultural tongues and multiple imaginative voices, Kingston and Tan focus on women's experiences in their writings and position their uses of languages as central to our understanding of Chinese American women's bicultural world.

23   Ultimately we see the transformation of double voice in both *The Woman Warrior* and *The Joy Luck Club*. As Trinh put it nicely, "the fact one is always marginalized in one's own language and areas of strength is something that one has to learn to live with." Therefore, fragmentation in one's identity becomes "a way of living with differences without turning them into opposites, nor trying to assimilate them out of insecurity." Chinese American women need to cultivate not simply multiple subjectivities but also the ability to move between different languages and positions. As Trinh suggested, this fluidity is a form of challenge and reconstruction of power relations, and women need to learn to use language as a poetic arena of struggle of possibility for transformation. "Ethnic identity is twin skin to linguistic identity—I am my language." Unless

Chinese American women acknowledge and celebrate all the Englishes that they grew up with, they cannot accept the legitimacy of their bicultural identity. When asked if she still felt the same contradictions that the protagonist did in *The Woman Warrior*, Kingston said "No, no. I feel much more integrated . . . It takes decades of struggle. When you are a person who comes from a multicultural background it just means that you have more information coming in from the universe. And it's your task to figure out how it all integrates, figure out its order and its beauty. It's a harder, longer struggle."

THE SALON INTERVIEW

AMY TAN: THE SPIRIT WITHIN

"My sister Kwan believes she has yin eyes. She sees those who have died and now dwell in the World of Yin, ghosts who leave the mists just to visit her kitchen on Balboa Street in San Francisco. 'Libby-ah,' she'll say to me. 'Guess who I see yesterday, you guess.' And I don't have to guess that she's talking about someone dead."

1 So begins Amy Tan's third novel, *The Hundred Secret Senses*. Although it has flown up the best-seller lists in the month since its release, the book is a risky departure for the 43-year-old writer, with its emphasis on spirits, magical time-shifts and other unearthly phenomena.

2 Tan spoke enthusiastically about her book, but admitted that she feared it would be ridiculed as "Chinese superstition." She sat for an interview on the balcony of her San Francisco home, where she surreptitiously lit up a cigarette.

3 "I don't smoke in public, it's not a good image, it's not a good role model," she apologized. "Not that I actively set out to be one."

4 With her tiny Yorkshire terrier, Babbazo, snugly ensconced in her lap, Tan, a brilliant smile often belying the frankness of her words, talked about the burdens of fame, the world of Yin, and her struggles with her own emotional demons.

5 Q. Have you felt the need to be a role model ever since the success of your first book, *The Joy Luck Club*, in 1989?

6 A. I don't feel the need to be a role model, it's just something that's been thrust upon me. Teachers and a lot of Asian American organizations, for example, say to me, "We need you to come and speak to us because you're a role model."

7 Q. Are you comfortable with that?

8 A. No. Placing on writers the responsibility to represent a culture is an onerous burden. Someone who writes fiction is not necessarily writing a depiction of any generalized group, they're writing a very specific story. There's also a danger in balkanizing literature, as if it should be read as sociology, or politics, or that it should answer ques-

tions like, "What does *The Hundred Secret Senses* have to teach us about Chinese culture?" As opposed to treating it as literature—as a story, language, memory.

9 Q. Are you finding more or less of that pressure to be categorized?

10 A. It's lessening in the United States. Other Asian American writers just shudder when they are compared to me; it really denigrates the uniqueness of their own work. I find it happening less here partly because people are more aware now of the flaws of political correctness—that literature has to do something to educate people. I don't see myself, for example, writing about cultural dichotomies, but about human connections. All of us go through angst and identity crises. And even when you write in a specific context, you still tap into that subtext of emotions that we all feel about love and hope, and mothers and obligations and responsibilities.

11 Q. Speaking of mothers, do you get a hard time from relatives or close friends who think they see themselves in your books? Any accusations of personal secrets being told or confidences betrayed?

12 A. I did, at one point. One relative felt that the story of my grandmother should not have been revealed. My grandmother was the woman (in *The Kitchen God's Wife*) who had been raped, forced to be a concubine, and finally killed herself. My mother, though, got equally angry at the relative and said, "For so many years, I carried this shame on my back, and my mother suffered, because she couldn't say anything to anybody." And she said, "It's not too late; tell the world, tell the world what happened to her." And I take her mandate to be the one that is in my heart, the one that I should follow.

13 Q. In *The Hundred Secret Senses*, you draw much more on the world of the spirit than in your previous books. Was that a theme that you had always wanted to tackle as a writer, or did more personal experiences compel you to address it?

14 A. It's been a part of my life for at least the past 20 years. I've had a lot of death in my life, of people who have been close to me. So I've long thought about how life is influenced by death, how it influences what you believe in and what you look for. Yes, I think I was pushed in a way to write this book by certain spirits—the yin people—in my life. They've always been there, I wouldn't say to help, but to kick me in the ass to write.

15 Q. Yin people?

16 A. Yin people is the term Kwan uses, because "ghosts" is politically incorrect. People have such terrible assumptions about ghosts—you know, phantoms that haunt you, that make you scared, that turn the house upside down. Yin people are not in our living presence but are around, and kind of guide you to insights. Like in Las Vegas when the bells go off, telling you you've hit the jackpot. Yin people ring the bells, saying, "Pay attention." And you say, "Oh, I see now." Yet I'm a fairly skeptical person. I'm educated, I'm reasonably sane, and I know that this subject is fodder for ridicule.

17 Q. Does that worry you?

18 A. To write the book, I had to put that aside. As with any book. I go through the anxiety, "What will people think of me for writing something like this?" But ultimately, I have to write what I have to write about, including the question of life continuing beyond our ordinary senses.

19 Q. You have a very optimistic way of looking at life and death. But these concerns have also been a cause for deep distress in your life, including bouts with serious depression.

20 A. Some of it is probably biochemical, but I think it's also in my family tree. I mean, my grandmother killed herself; she certainly had depression in her life. And anyone, like my mother, who witnessed her own mother killing herself, is going to be prone to the same disease. My own father died of a brain tumor when I was 14. My brother died of the same disease. I didn't do anything about it for a long time, because, like many people, I worried about altering my psyche with drugs. As a writer, I was especially concerned with that. A lot of writers believe that the trauma and the angst that you feel is an essential part of the craft.

21 Q. And depression is still not respectable—especially taking medication for it.

22 A. People look at me as this very, I don't know, Confucius-like wise person—which I'm not. They don't see all the shit that I've been through (laughs). And going back to the question of being a role model, well, my life hasn't been perfect. I needed help.

23 Q. What do you take?

24 A. Zoloft. I don't think it's made me a Pollyanna. I can still get angry and upset, but I don't fall into the abyss. I'm grateful that I have some traction now. It doesn't change essentially who you are, but it fixes things just the way insulin does for people with diabetes.

25 Q. In *The Hundred Secret Senses*, the central character, Kwan, is packed off to a California mental hospital for seeing "ghosts." She is somewhat weird, often embarrassing, and doesn't exactly look like Joan Chen. Where did Kwan come from?

26 A. Kwan comes strictly from my imagination, from that world of yin that I write about. I don't know anybody in my life like Kwan, although I feel Kwan-like characters all round me. I would find myself laughing and wondering where these ideas came from. You can call it imagination, I suppose. But I was grateful for wherever they came from.

27 Q. Olivia, Kwan's American half-sister is not so happy-go-lucky. Pained, needy, she accidentally pulls heads off pet turtles and has a hard time with other people.

28 A. I took my own skepticism and embedded it into Olivia. Some of her—or the questions that trouble her—are drawn from friends who have the usual existential questions about life and relationships and work and success, and "Why are we here?" and "Why are we with this person?" I've already had interviewers wondering if Olivia's relationship with her husband, Simon, is like my marriage, and I think, "Wait a minute, that's not my husband, that's not my relationship." Certainly all of us have gone through fights with partners in our life, but that's

not drawn from my relationships per se. But I know that I'm going to be subject to that assumption.

29 Q. You write that Olivia's mother suffers "from a kind heart compounded by seasonal rashes of volunteerism." She thinks of her step-daughter Kwan "as a foreign exchange student she would host for a year." In other words, she's a somewhat self-centered ditz—like some of your other less-than-appealing Caucasian characters, in *The Joy Luck Club*, for example. Is there a problem between you and white characters?

30 A. (Laughs). No. Some of these characters have to be foils. I needed a mother who was kind of undependable, so that Kwan could become that fount of love that Olivia is looking for. There was no intention—unless there is something subconscious—in trying to depict a Caucasian mother as not so great. I'd have to go through psychotherapy to explore that one. No, some of my best friends are Caucasian.

Fowler 1

Gael Fowler

Professor Henderson

English 1102

May 1, 2008

Agony from the Heart

1   The short story "Heart," written by the Chinese-American author Amy Tan, illustrates the theme of grief and loss resulting from the deaths of close family members. Three tragic deaths portrayed in this story are those of a child, a spouse, and a parent. The narrator, Lu Ling, reveals her nursemaid's experiences with these types of losses before she realizes her own vulnerability. Lu Ling and Precious Auntie, her nursemaid, have a terrible argument toward the end of the story, and Lu Ling speaks harshly to her servant. When Lu Ling realizes that she has been unkind to her friend and wants to apologize for her cruel behavior, she discovers Precious Auntie dead in a ravine and mourns the loss of the woman she has known as her nursemaid. Later, she learns that Precious Auntie was actually her biological mother. Both mother and daughter become intensely aware of their vulnerability as they experience tragic losses and have to deal with powerful grief.

2   The most painful event that a parent can ever experience is
the death of his child. In this story, Precious Auntie's father
is an extremely gifted bonesetter who fails to save his four sons
from a deadly disease. The loss of his children is devastating to
him, and as a result "he spent his entire fortune and went into a
lifetime of debt to pay for their funerals" (Tan 659). The death
of Precious Auntie's brothers causes her father to be plagued
with grief for the remainder of his life. The bonesetter survives
the death of his sons by living through the happiness of his
daughter. According to Precious Auntie, "*he spoiled me, let me do
whatever a son might do*" (Tan 659). She also comments, "*My father
was used to seeing pain of the worst kinds. But with me he was
helpless. He couldn't bear to see me cry*" (Tan 659). Losing four
sons is extremely difficult for the bonesetter, but this tragedy
results in the birth of a stronger relationship with his daughter
as he struggles to endure the pain.

3   The loss of an intended spouse is also a catastrophic and
traumatic experience. On the day of Precious Auntie's marriage
to Baby Uncle, a horse kicks Baby Uncle in the head. This fatal
blow changes Precious Auntie's life drastically. She continually
hears the horrendous sound of the accident "in the breaking of
twigs, the crackling of fire, [and] whenever a melon was split
in two" (Tan 665). Precious Auntie is hysterical for days and
weeks after her lover's death. She even tries to commit suicide
in order "to cause pain greater than what she already felt" (Tan
665-66). Fortunately, Precious Auntie has a daughter who gives
her a purpose for living during the remainder of her years.

4   Losing a mother or a father is devastating for a child. When
a parent dies, a child feels as if a vital part of her existence
is missing. Precious Auntie never really knows her mother because
she loses her mother at a young age. Therefore, her relationship

with her father becomes that much closer. Seeing her father "lying [dead] in a ditch" (Tan 665) is the worst nightmare that Precious Auntie can imagine. For days, she "apologized to the [corpse] of her father" (Tan 665) because she feels responsible for her father's death. Even though Precious Auntie cannot prevent the accident that kills her father, she lives the rest of her life with agonizing feelings of guilt.

5   Death has always been a dominant theme in literature. Amy Tan's excellence at portraying basic literary themes is seen throughout her writing. According to Elaine Kim, Asian authors like Tan write masterfully about the topics of "'love, desire for personal freedom and acceptance, and struggles against oppression and injustice'" (qtd. in Huntley 668). Several of Tan's stories depict the lives of common people who experience severe tragedies, such as the loss of loved ones. Some people, like the bonesetter, lose a child. Many people like Precious Auntie will watch in horror as their lovers or parents slip away from them. A few unfortunate people like Lu Ling will even have to learn devastating secrets about their family relationships. Amy Tan addresses these classic themes of literature by delving into her own personal and cultural history. Amy Tan's style of writing is perfectly described in the following statement by E. D. Huntley:

> Tan's novels reify and reinterpret traditional
> genres by casting them in a variety of modes—
> realistic, comic, tragic, tragicomic,
> allegorical, fantastic, naturalistic, and
> heroic—that metamorphose seamlessly into each
> other in Tan's signature narrative style. (667)

Fowler 4

Perhaps Amy Tan's greatest strength as an author is the ability to make readers identify with her characters by writing from her heart.

[New Page]

Fowler 5

Works Cited

Henderson, Gloria Mason, Anna Dunlap Higgins, Bill Day, and Sandra Stevenson Waller, eds. *Literature and Ourselves: A Thematic Introduction for Readers and Writers*. 6th ed. New York: ABLongman, 2009.

Huntley, E. D. *Amy Tan: A Critical Companion*. Westport, Connecticut: Greenwood P, 1998. Henderson, Higgins, Day, and Waller 667–75.

Tan, Amy. "Heart." *The Bonesetter's Daughter*. New York: G. P. Putnam's Sons, 2001. Henderson, Higgins, Day, and Waller 651–67.

Crafting Arguments

1. Each of the stories in this unit is now part of a novel. Write an essay arguing that each is nevertheless a unified, well-structured story.
2. Using one or more of the critical essays in the casebook, write an essay explaining Simon's role in "Young Girl's Wish."
3. "Young Girl's Wish" and "Heart" portray vulnerability on many levels. Use one or both of the stories and at least one of the critical essays to discuss the theme of vulnerability in these two works.
4. Write an essay analyzing Tan's use of point of view in the two stories.
5. Examine the use of Chinese superstitions in the two stories. Then, after forming your own opinions, craft an essay supporting your conclusions about their use to develop the plots or portray the characters.

Vulnerability: Crafting Arguments

1. One theme in several of the works in this unit is that death is the ultimate equalizer. In an essay, analyze the use of this theme in one or more of the works.

2. Use one or more of the works in this unit to write an essay analyzing racial, cultural, or gender vulnerability.

3. Select at least two works that deal with the reaction of the living to the death of a loved one and analyze the ways in which the authors portray the survivors' emotions.

4. Human beings often react in violent or bizarre ways when they realize their own vulnerability. Using one or more of the selections in this unit to illustrate and support your claims, describe the author's use of these reactions to create the theme.

5. Write an essay using three poems or three essays from this unit to illustrate three different types of vulnerability.

6. Four of the works in this unit—Faulkner's "A Rose for Emily," Robinson's "Richard Cory," Dunbar's "We Wear the Mask," and McCrae's "In Flanders Field"—are written in first-person plural. After carefully re-reading each work, analyze each author's reasons for choosing this particular point of view.

7. Using Sloan's and Weinberg's definitions of terrorism and terrorists, write an essay in which you give your definition.

Vulnerability: Writing about Film

See Appendix B: Writing about Film for help with these essays.

1. Several of John Grisham's and Stephen King's novels have been adapted to film. Select an adaptation of a work by one of these authors and prepare a paper that analyzes the ways in which the film portrays the central character's vulnerability.

2. War movies are a staple of the Hollywood genre films. Many of these are actually adaptations from literary pieces, including *Gone with the Wind, All Quiet on the Western Front, The Sands of Iwo Jima, From Here to Eternity, The Naked and the Dead, Paths of Glory, War and Peace, Little Big Man, Apocalypse Now, Dr. Zhivago, Last of the Mohicans, Farewell to Arms, For Whom the Bell Tolls*, and *Full Metal Jacket*. View a war film and craft a paper that analyzes the film techniques used to express the vulnerability that war introduces into the lives of the characters.

3. There are several film versions of *Othello*. Watch two versions and write a paper that compares two or three of the directors' choices. For you, which version is the most effective? Why?

4. Several film adaptations are based on literary works that explore the vulnerability caused by fear. Considering film adaptations as diverse as *Deliverance, The Exorcist, Dracula, The Innocents, Sleepy Hollow*, and *The Natural*, select a film adaptation and craft a paper analyzing the ways in which a particular scene captures a character's terror.

Freedom and Responsibility

A scene from *The Shawshank Redemption*. Photofest.

We are accustomed to celebrating our freedom as Americans without much thought. Seldom do we stop to realize what that freedom means or requires of us. The most seminal of American documents, the Declaration of Independence, espouses a doctrine that even today in this country seems astoundingly revolutionary—the idea that governments "derive their just powers from the consent of the governed" and that when they fail to serve their purpose in protecting citizens' rights, those citizens have the right, even the responsibility, to overthrow such governments. When Martin Luther King Jr. led peaceful protests against the segregation and brutal treatment of African-Americans, he was simply acting on ideas contained in Jefferson's great founding document.

Often we fail to realize the extent to which those great American values, freedom and equality, both of which originate in the Declaration of Independence, may be mutually exclusive. As Kurt Vonnegut's "Harrison Bergeron" demonstrates, an exact and universal equality may not only reduce our freedom but also produce a world that is culturally sterile. Asserting our freedom, as the fate of Harrison Bergeron illustrates, may be very costly. In John Updike's "A & P," Sammy's refusal to conform and his assertion of independence cost him his job. Nowhere is the terrible cost of freedom more graphically exemplified than in Ursula Le Guin's "The Ones Who Walk Away from Omelas," where the freedom and comfortable lives of a whole society depend on the brutal suffering of a single poor wretch. One person's freedom may mean another's subjugation.

What, then, are the limits to freedom? To what degree should we be subject to our government, and to what degree should the government be subject to us? Sometimes the desire for freedom may compete with personal responsibilities to family and community. In "On the Rainy River," Tim O'Brien faces an agonizing choice. If he goes to Canada because of his opposition to the Vietnam War, he fears being perceived by his parents, friends, and neighbors as a coward, not a principled objector. On the other hand, to fight in a war he considers wrong will violate his conscience. Hence, O'Brien's story raises extremely important issues. When must we submerge our individuality in deference to the community? Where does our individual freedom end, and where do the perceived needs of the community begin? When should communal decisions, expressed as government policy, supersede individual conscience?

Writing about Freedom and Responsibility

In writing about the selections in Freedom and Responsibility, you will have a wide variety of choices. As you study the works, you will probably notice that several use satire or irony. You might start by reviewing the definitions of these two terms included in the glossary. Then you might use Jonathan Swift's "A Modest Proposal," which offers a perfect example of a caustic satire written about a real-life situation, to write an essay illustrating the literary devices that Swift uses to make his points or a researched paper about the situation in Ireland that is the subject of Swift's satire. If you prefer to write about short stories, and especially if you enjoy fantasy, you might choose Vonnegut's "Harrison Bergeron," which combines satire with humor; you might examine the real-life tendencies that he satirizes and explore the ways in which the author uses humor in his satire.

After reviewing the Questions for Engagement, Response, and Analysis in the Introduction, you might write an essay comparing or classifying the choices and lack of choices recognized by the speakers in Karl Shapiro's "The Conscientious Objector" and Anne Sexton's "Ringing the Bells." Or you might discuss problems faced by immigrants portrayed in Pat Mora's "Immigrants" and Dwight Okita's "In Response to Executive Order 9066." As in any of the thematic units, you might write an essay examining the distinctive tone or the sound and metaphorical devices used by the poets to create the overall effects they desire. Or you might compare Shapiro's "The Conscientious Objector" to one of Tim O'Brien's stories in terms of freedom and duties.

All sections in this unit suggest arguments that might appeal to your sense of freedom and the responsibility that goes with freedom. For example, in "Letter From Birmingham City Jail," King feels he has a responsibility to confront the clergy and other leaders about his concerns. But what are the boundaries of responsibilities? Do the townspeople have the right to make one person responsible for the happiness of all in LeGuin's "Those Who Walk Away From Omelas"? Although Sammy in "A&P" chooses to quit his job because of the three young ladies, does he really have an obligation to stay because of his parents' reputation in that New England town? Will he indeed feel "how hard the world was going to be to [him] hereafter"?

If your professor asks you to use the Casebook on Tim O'Brien to write a documented paper, you should, of course, begin by reading the stories. You might list ideas for topics as you read and then add to the list when you have completed your reading and have a more complete view of the possibilities. After writing down some of your own ideas for future reference, you should then read the critical essays. Using this technique will help you remember which ideas were yours and which the essays influenced. When Nick Hembree was asked to write a documented essay using some of the stories and critical essays in the casebook, he began by trying to detail the interesting and provocative techniques used by O'Brien. He also wanted to emphasize the meanings of the stories. Nick decided to use three of the stories to write an essay about the nature of truth and its general elusiveness and complexity. He gave the first draft of the essay to his professor, who made a few suggestions. Then he polished the final draft and checked his documentation before submitting it. After you have read the O'Brien stories, you will probably enjoy reading Nick's essay to see if your perceptions are similar to his.

ESSAYS

Jonathan Swift (1667–1745)

Though Jonathan Swift's parents were English, he was born in Dublin and became one of the most ardent defenders of Ireland. As dean of St. Patrick's Cathedral in Dublin from 1726 to 1739, Swift was a major force in the religious and political affairs of Ireland. A man of great intellect, Swift is recognized as a true master of style and as one of the world's foremost satirists. His most famous work, Gulliver's Travels, *satirizes many of the social, political, and religious practices of his time. "A Modest Proposal" reveals the extreme hardships the peasants of Ireland suffered at the hands of greedy English landlords.*

A MODEST PROPOSAL   (1729)

FOR PREVENTING THE CHILDREN OF POOR PEOPLE IN IRELAND FROM BEING A BURDEN TO THEIR PARENTS OR COUNTRY, AND FOR MAKING THEM BENEFICIAL TO THE PUBLIC

1   It is a melancholy object to those who walk through this great town, or travel in the country, when they see the streets, the roads and cabin-doors crowded with beggars of the female sex, followed by three, four, or six children, all in rags, and importuning every passenger for an alms. These mothers, instead of being able to work for their honest livelihood, are forced to employ all their time in strolling, to beg sustenance for their helpless infants, who, as they grow up, either turn thieves for want of work, or leave their dear native country to fight for the Pretender in Spain, or sell themselves to the Barbadoes.

2   I think it is agreed by all parties that this prodigious number of children, in the arms, or on the backs, or at the heels of their mothers, and frequently of their fathers, is in the present deplorable state of the kingdom a very great additional grievance; and therefore whoever could find out a fair, cheap, and easy method of making these children sound and useful members of the commonwealth would deserve so well of the public as to have his statue set up for a preserver of the nation.

3   But my intention is very far from being confined to provide only for the children of professed beggars; it is of a much greater extent, and shall take in the whole number of infants at a certain age who are born of parents in effect as little able to support them as those who demand our charity in the streets.

4   As to my own part, having turned my thoughts for many years upon this important subject, and maturely weighed the several schemes of other projectors, I have always found them grossly mistaken in their

computation. It is true a child just dropped from its dam may be supported by her milk for a solar year with little other nourishment, at most not above the value of two shillings, which the mother may certainly get, or the value in scraps, by her lawful occupation of begging, and it is exactly at one year old that I propose to provide for them, in such a manner as, instead of being a charge upon their parents, or the parish, or wanting food and raiment for the rest of their lives, they shall, on the contrary, contribute to the feeding and partly to the clothing of many thousands.

5   There is likewise another great advantage in my scheme, that it will prevent those voluntary abortions, and that horrid practice of women murdering their bastard children, alas, too frequent among us, sacrificing the poor innocent babes, I doubt, more to avoid the expense than the shame, which would move tears and pity in the most savage and inhuman breast.

6   The number of souls in Ireland being usually reckoned one million and a half, of these I calculate there may be about two hundred thousand couples whose wives are breeders, from which number I subtract thirty thousand couples who are able to maintain their own children, although I apprehend there cannot be so many under the present distresses of the kingdom, but this being granted, there will remain an hundred and seventy thousand breeders. I again subtract fifty thousand for those women who miscarry, or whose children die by accident or disease within the year. There only remain an hundred and twenty thousand children of poor parents annually born: the question therefore is, how this number shall be reared, and provided for, which, as I have already said, under the present situation of affairs is utterly impossible by all the methods hitherto proposed, for we can neither employ them in handicraft or agriculture; we neither build houses (I mean in the country), nor cultivate land: they can very seldom pick up a livelihood by stealing until they arrive at six years old, except where they are of towardly parts, although I confess they learn the rudiments much earlier, during which time they can however be properly looked upon only as probationers, as I have been informed by a principal gentleman in the County of Cavan, who protested to me that he never knew above one or two instances under the age of six, even in a part of the kingdom so renowned for the quickest proficiency in that art.

7   I am assured by our merchants that a boy or a girl before twelve years old, is no saleable commodity, and even when they come to this age, they will not yield above three pounds, or three pounds and half-a-crown at most on the Exchange, which cannot turn to account either to the parents or the kingdom, the charge of nutriment and rags having been at least four times that value.

8   I shall now therefore humbly propose my own thoughts, which I hope will not be liable to the least objection.

9   I have been assured by a very knowing American of my acquaintance in London, that a young healthy child well nursed is at a year old a most delicious, nourishing and wholesome food, whether stewed, roasted, baked, or boiled, and I make no doubt that it will equally serve in a fricassee, or a ragout.

10   I do therefore humbly offer it to public consideration, that of the hundred and twenty thousand children already computed, twenty thousand may be reserved for breed, whereof only one fourth part to be males, which is more than we allow to sheep, black-cattle, or swine, and my reason is that these children are seldom the fruits of marriage, a circumstance not much regarded by our savages, therefore one male will be sufficient to serve four females. That the remaining hundred thousand may at a year old be offered in sale to the persons of quality, and fortune, through the kingdom, always advising the mother to let them suck plentifully in the last month, so as to render them plump, and fat for a good table. A child will make two dishes at an entertainment for friends, and when the family dines alone, the fore or hind quarter will make a reasonable dish, and seasoned with a little pepper or salt will be very good boiled on the fourth day, especially in winter.

11   I have reckoned upon a medium, that a child just born will weigh twelve pounds, and in a solar year if tolerably nursed increaseth to twenty-eight pounds.

12   I grant this food will be somewhat dear, and therefore very proper for landlords, who, as they have already devoured most of the parents, seem to have the best title to the children.

13   Infant's flesh will be in season throughout the year, but more plentiful in March, and a little before and after, for we are told by a grave author, an eminent French physician, that fish being a prolific diet, there are more children born in Roman Catholic countries about nine months after Lent than at any other season; therefore reckoning a year after Lent, the markets will be more glutted than usual, because the number of Popish infants is at least three to one in this kingdom, and therefore it will have one other collateral advantage by lessening the number of Papists among us.

14   I have already computed the charge of nursing a beggar's child (in which list I reckon all cottagers, labourers, and four-fifths of the farmers) to be about two shillings *per annum*, rags included, and I believe no gentleman would repine to give ten shillings for the carcass of a good fat child, which, as I have said, will make four dishes of excellent nutritive meat, when he hath only some particular friend or his own family to dine with him. Thus the Squire will learn to be a good landlord and grow popular among his tenants, the mother will have eight shillings net profit, and be fit for work until she produces another child.

15   Those who are more thrifty (as I must confess the times require) may flay the carcass; the skin of which artificially dressed, will make admirable gloves for ladies, and summer boots for fine gentlemen.

16   As to our city of Dublin, shambles may be appointed for this purpose, in the most convenient parts of it, and butchers we may be assured will not be wanting, although I rather recommend buying the children alive, and dressing them hot from the knife, as we do roasting pigs.

17   A very worthy person, a true lover of his country, and whose virtues I highly esteem, was lately pleased, in discoursing on this matter to offer a refinement upon my scheme. He said that many gentlemen of this kingdom, having of late destroyed their deer, he conceived that the want of venison might be well supplied by the bodies of young lads and maidens, not exceeding fourteen years of age, nor under twelve, so great a number of both sexes in every county being now ready to starve, for want of work and service: and these to be disposed of by their parents if alive, or otherwise by their nearest relations. But with due deference to so excellent a friend, and so deserving a patriot, I cannot be altogether in his sentiments. For as to the males, my American acquaintance assured me from frequent experience that their flesh was generally tough and lean, like that of our schoolboys, by continual exercise, and their taste disagreeable, and to fatten them would not answer the charge. Then as to the females, it would, I think with humble submission, be a loss to the public, because they soon would become breeders themselves: and besides, it is not improbable that some scrupulous people might be apt to censure such a practice (although indeed very unjustly) as a little bordering upon cruelty, which I confess, hath always been with me the strongest objection against any project, howsoever well intended.

18   But in order to justify my friend, he confessed that this expedient was put into his head by the famous Psalmanazar, a native of the island Formosa, who came from thence to London, above twenty years ago, and in conversation told my friend that in his country when any young person happened to be put to death, the executioner sold the carcass to persons of quality, as a prime dainty, and that, in his time, the body of a plump girl of fifteen, who was crucified for an attempt to poison the emperor, was sold to his Imperial Majesty's Prime Minister of State, and other great Mandarins of the Court, in joints from the gibbet, at four hundred crowns. Neither indeed can I deny that if the same use were made of several plump young girls in this town who, without one single groat to their fortunes, cannot stir abroad without a chair, and appear at the playhouse and assemblies in foreign fineries, which they never will pay for, the kingdom would not be the worse.

19   Some persons of a desponding spirit are in great concern about that vast number of poor people, who are aged, diseased, or maimed, and I have been desired to employ my thoughts what course may be taken to ease the nation of so grievous an encumbrance. But I am not in the least pain upon that matter, because it is very well known that they are every day dying, and rotting, by cold, and famine, and filth, and vermin, as fast as can be reasonably expected. And as to the younger labourers they are now in almost as hopeful a condition. They cannot get work, and

consequently pine away from want of nourishment, to a degree that if at any time they are accidentally hired to common labour, they have not strength to perform it; and thus the country and themselves are in a fair way of being soon delivered from the evils to come.

20   I have too long digressed, and therefore shall return to my subject. I think the advantages by the proposal which I have made are obvious and many, as well as of the highest importance.

21   For first, as I have already observed, it would greatly lessen the number of Papists, with whom we are yearly over-run, being the principal breeders of the nation, as well as our most dangerous enemies, and who stay at home on purpose with a design to deliver the kingdom to the Pretender, hoping to take their advantage by the absence of so many good Protestants, who have chosen rather to leave their country than stay at home and pay tithes against their conscience to an idolatrous Episcopal curate.

22   Secondly, the poorer tenants will have something valuable of their own, which by law may be made liable to distress, and help to pay their landlord's rent, their corn and cattle being already seized, and money a thing unknown.

23   Thirdly, whereas the maintenance of an hundred thousand children, from two years old, and upwards, cannot be computed at less than ten shillings a piece *per annum*, the nation's stock will be thereby increased fifty thousand pounds *per annum* besides the profit of a new dish, introduced to the tables of all gentlemen of fortune in the kingdom, who have any refinement in taste, and the money will circulate among ourselves, the goods being entirely of our own growth and manufacture.

24   Fourthly, the constant breeders, besides the gain of eight shillings sterling *per annum*, by the sale of their children, will be rid of the charge of maintaining them after the first year.

25   Fifthly, this food would likewise bring great custom to taverns, where the vintners will certainly be so prudent as to procure the best receipts for dressing it to perfection, and consequently have their houses frequented by all the fine gentlemen, who justly value themselves upon their knowledge in good eating; and a skilful cook, who understands how to oblige his guests, will contrive to make it as expensive as they please.

26   Sixthly, this would be a great inducement to marriage, which all wise nations have either encouraged by rewards, or enforced by laws and penalties. It would increase the care and tenderness of mothers towards their children, when they were sure of a settlement for life, to the poor babes, provided in some sort by the public to their annual profit instead of expense. We should soon see an honest emulation among the married women, which of them could bring the fattest child to the market. Men would become as fond of their wives, during the time of their pregnancy, as they are now of their mares in foal, their cows in calf, or sows when they are ready to farrow, nor offer to beat or kick them (as it is too frequent a practice) for fear of a miscarriage.

27   Many other advantages might be enumerated. For instance, the addition of some thousand carcasses in our exportation of barrelled beef; the propagation of swine's flesh, and improvement in the art of making good bacon, so much wanted among us by the great destruction of pigs, too frequent at our tables, which are no way comparable in taste or magnificence to a well-grown, fat, yearling child, which roasted whole will make a considerable figure at a Lord Mayor's feast, or any other public entertainment.

28   Supposing that one thousand families in this city would be constant customers for infants' flesh, besides others who might have it at merry meetings, particularly weddings and christenings; I compute that Dublin would take off annually about twenty thousand carcasses, and the rest of the kingdom (where probably they will be sold somewhat cheaper) the remaining eighty thousand.

29   I can think of no one objection that will possibly be raised against this proposal, unless it should be urged that the number of people will be thereby much lessened in the kingdom. This I freely own, and it was indeed one principal design in offering it to the world. I desire the reader will observe, that I calculate my remedy *for this one individual Kingdom of* Ireland, *and for no other that ever was, is, or, I think, ever can be upon earth.* Therefore let no man talk to me of other expedients: *Of taxing our absentees at five shillings a pound: Of using neither clothes, nor household furniture, except what is of our own growth and manufacture: Of utterly rejecting the materials and instruments that promote foreign luxury: Of curing the expensiveness of pride, vanity, idleness, and gaming in our women: Of introducing a vein of parsimony, prudence, and temperance: Of learning to love our country, wherein we differ even from* Laplanders, *and the inhabitants of* Topinamboo: *Of quitting our animosities and factions, nor act any longer like the* Jews, *who were murdering one another at the very moment their city was taken: Of being a little cautious not to sell our country and consciences for nothing: Of teaching landlords to have at least one degree of mercy towards their tenants.* Lastly, *of putting a spirit of honesty, industry, and skill into our shopkeepers, who, if a resolution could now be taken to buy only our native goods, would immediately unite to cheat and exact upon us in the price, the measure and the goodness, nor could ever yet be brought to make one fair proposal of just dealing, though often and earnestly invited to it.*

30   Therefore I repeat, let no man talk to me of these and the like expedients, till he hath at least a glimpse of hope that there will ever be some hearty and sincere attempt to put them in practice.

31   But as to myself, having been wearied out for many years with offering vain, idle, visionary thoughts, and at length utterly despairing of success, I fortunately fell upon this proposal, which as it is wholly new, so it hath something solid and real, of no expense and little trouble, full in our own power, and whereby we can incur no danger in disobliging England.

For this kind of commodity will not bear exportation, the flesh being of too tender a consistence to admit a long continuance in salt, *although perhaps I could name a country which would be glad to eat up our whole nation without it.*

32   After all I am not so violently bent upon my own opinion as to reject any offer, proposed by wise men, which shall be found equally innocent, cheap, easy and effectual. But before some thing of that kind shall be advanced in contradiction to my scheme, and offering a better, I desire the author, or authors, will be pleased maturely to consider two points. First, as things now stand, how they will be able to find food and raiment for a hundred thousand useless mouths and backs? And secondly, there being a round million of creatures in human figure, throughout this kingdom, whose whole subsistence put into a common stock would leave them in debt two millions of pounds sterling; adding those who are beggars by profession, to the bulk of farmers, cottagers, and labourers with their wives and children, who are beggars in effect; I desire those politicians who dislike my overture, and may perhaps be so bold to attempt an answer, that they will first ask the parents of these mortals whether they would not at this day think it a great happiness to have been sold for food at a year old, in the manner I prescribe, and thereby have avoided such a perpetual scene of misfortunes as they have since gone through, by the oppression of landlords, the impossibility of paying rent without money or trade, the want of common sustenance, with neither house nor clothes to cover them from the inclemencies of weather, and the most inevitable prospect of entailing the like, or greater miseries upon their breed for ever.

33   I profess in the sincerity of my heart that I have not the least personal interest in endeavouring to promote this necessary work, having no other motive than the *public good of my country, by advancing our trade, providing for infants, relieving the poor, and giving some pleasure to the rich.* I have no children by which I can propose to get a single penny; the youngest being nine years old, and my wife past child-bearing.

Questions for Engagement, Response, and Analysis

1. Look up satire in the glossary. After reading the definitions of Horatian and Juvenalian satire, identify the tone of this essay.

2. At what point in the essay does Swift's narrator present his proposal?

3. Why would older children not be just as good as younger children for Swift's plan?

4. Outline the "advantages" of the "Modest Proposal," according to the narrator.

5. List the other suggestions for solving Ireland's problem included in paragraph 29. Swift, in other essays, had suggested all of these solutions. Why does the narrator reject them?

Crafting Arguments

1. Using the information in Swift's essay to support each of your claims, analyze Swift's essay as an indictment of both the Irish and the English.
2. Write an essay analyzing the devices that Swift uses to make his satire effective.

Thomas Jefferson (1743–1826)

Thomas Jefferson, the third president of the United States and author of the Declaration of Independence, was truly a Renaissance man—a statesman, a scientist, an architect, and an author. The son of a successful planter and a member of the famous Randolph family of Virginia, Jefferson spent most of his life in Virginia. As an architect, he designed both his home, Monticello, and the buildings of the University of Virginia. Jefferson is considered by many historians to be the foremost symbol of the American desire for individual freedom.

THE DECLARATION OF INDEPENDENCE   (1776)

1   When in the course of human events, it becomes necessary for one people to dissolve the political bands which have connected them with another, and to assume among the powers of the earth, the separate and equal station to which the Laws of Nature and of Nature's God entitle them, a decent respect to the opinions of mankind requires that they should declare the causes which impel them to the separation.

2   We hold these truths to be self-evident, that all men are created equal, that they are endowed by their Creator with certain inalienable rights, that among these are life, liberty, and the pursuit of happiness. That to secure these rights, governments are instituted among men, deriving their just powers from the consent of the governed. That whenever any form of government becomes destructive of these ends, it is the right of the people to alter or to abolish it, and to institute new government, laying its foundation on such principles and organizing its powers in such form, as to them shall seem most likely to effect their safety and happiness. Prudence, indeed, will dictate that governments long established should not be changed for light and transient causes; and accordingly all experience hath shown, that mankind are more disposed to suffer, while evils are sufferable, than to right themselves by abolishing the forms to which they are accustomed. But when a long train of abuses and usurpations, pursuing invariably the same object, evinces a design to reduce them under absolute despotism, it is their right, it is their duty, to throw off such government, and to provide new guards for their future security. Such has been the patient sufferance of these Colonies; and such is now

the necessity which constrains them to alter their former systems of government. The history of the present King of Great Britain is a history of repeated injuries and usurpations, all having in direct object the establishment of an absolute tyranny over these States. To prove this, let facts be submitted to a candid world.

3   He has refused his assent to laws, the most wholesome and necessary for the public good.

4   He has forbidden his Governors to pass laws of immediate and pressing importance, unless suspended in their operation till his assent should be obtained; and when so suspended, he has utterly neglected to attend to them.

5   He has refused to pass other laws for the accommodation of large districts of people, unless those people would relinquish the right of representation in the legislature, a right inestimable to them and formidable to tyrants only.

6   He has called together legislative bodies at places unusual, uncomfortable, and distant from the depository of their public records, for the sole purpose of fatiguing them into compliance with his measures.

7   He has dissolved representative houses repeatedly, for opposing with manly firmness his invasions on the rights of the people.

8   He has refused for a long time, after such dissolutions, to cause others to be elected; whereby the legislative powers, incapable of annihilation, have returned to the people at large for their exercise; the State remaining in the meantime exposed to all the dangers of invasion from without and convulsions within.

9   He has endeavoured to prevent the population of these states; for that purpose obstructing the laws for naturalization of foreigners; refusing to pass others to encourage their migration hither, and raising the conditions of new appropriations of lands.

10   He has obstructed the administration of justice, by refusing his assent to laws for establishing judiciary powers.

11   He has made judges dependent on his will alone, for the tenure of their office, and the amount and payment of their salaries.

12   He has erected a multitude of new offices, and sent hither swarms of officers to harass our people, and eat out their substance.

13   He has kept among us, in times of peace, standing armies without the consent of our legislatures.

14   He has affected to render the military independent of and superior to the civil power.

15   He has combined with others to subject us to a jurisdiction foreign of our constitution, and unacknowledged by our laws; giving his assent to their acts of pretended legislation:

16   For quartering large bodies of armed troops among us:

17   For protecting them, by a mock trial, from punishment for any murders which they should commit on the inhabitants of these States:

18   For cutting off our trade with all parts of the world:

19   For imposing taxes on us without our consent:

20   For depriving us in many cases of the benefits of trial by jury:

21   For transporting us beyond seas to be tried for pretended offenses:

22   For abolishing the free system of English laws in a neighbouring Province, establishing therein an arbitrary government, and enlarging its boundaries so as to render it at once an example and fit instrument for introducing the same absolute rule into these Colonies:

23   For taking away our Charters, abolishing our most valuable laws, and altering fundamentally the forms of our governments:

24   For suspending our own legislatures, and declaring themselves invested with power to legislate for us in all cases whatsoever.

25   He has abdicated government here, by declaring us out of his protection and waging war against us.

26   He has plundered our seas, ravaged our coasts, burnt our towns, and destroyed the lives of our people.

27   He is at this time transporting large armies of foreign mercenaries to complete the works of death, desolation, and tyranny, already begun with circumstances of cruelty and perfidy scarcely paralleled in the most barbarous ages, and totally unworthy the head of a civilized nation.

28   He has constrained our fellow citizens taken captive on the high seas to bear arms against their country, to become the executioners of their friends and brethren, or to fall themselves by their hands.

29   He has excited domestic insurrections amongst us, and has endeavored to bring on the inhabitants of our frontiers, the merciless Indian savages, whose known rule of warfare, is an undistinguished destruction of all ages, sexes, and conditions.

30   In every stage of these oppressions we have petitioned for redress in the most humble terms: our repeated petitions have been answered only by repeated injury. A prince whose character is thus marked by every act which may define a tyrant is unfit to be the ruler of a free people.

31   Nor have we been wanting in attention to our British brethren. We have warned them from time to time of attempts by their legislature to extend an unwarrantable jurisdiction over us. We have reminded them of the circumstances of our emigration and settlement here. We have appealed to their native justice and magnanimity, and we have conjured them by the ties of our common kindred to disavow these usurpations, which would inevitably interrupt our connections and correspondence. They too have been deaf to the voice of justice and of consanguinity. We must, therefore, acquiesce in the necessity, which denounces our separation, and hold them, as we hold the rest of mankind, enemies in war, in peace friends.

32   We, therefore, the Representatives of the United States of America, in General Congress assembled, appealing to the Supreme Judge of the world for the rectitude of our intentions, do, in the name, and by authority of the good people of these Colonies, solemnly publish and declare, That these United Colonies are, and of right ought to be, Free

and Independent States; that they are absolved from all allegiance to the British Crown, and that all political connection between them and the state of Great Britain, is and ought to be totally dissolved; and that as Free and Independent States, they have full power to levy war, conclude peace, contract alliances, establish commerce, and to do all other acts and things which Independent States may of right do. And for the support of this declaration, with a firm reliance on the protection of Divine Providence, we mutually pledge to each other our lives, our fortunes, and our sacred honor.

Questions for Engagement, Response, and Analysis

1. Because the outcome of the rebellion will be determined by war in any case, why do Jefferson and his fellow patriots feel compelled to explain their reasons for rebellion?

2. What are the premises of Jefferson's argument?

3. What, according to Jefferson, is the purpose of government?

4. What are the abuses of power with which the Declaration charges King George III of England?

5. Jefferson says government derives its "just powers from the consent of the governed." In your Reader's Journal, freewrite about the degree to which governments and government agencies in the United States today—local, state, and federal—have lived up to Jefferson's claim or have failed in their purpose and ignored the source of their power.

Crafting Arguments

1. In an essay, analyze the techniques Jefferson uses to craft this famous argument.

Abraham Lincoln (1809–1865)

Abraham Lincoln, the sixteenth president of the United States, led his country through the difficult times of the Civil War. With the Emancipation Proclamation on January 1, 1863, Lincoln declared that all slaves were free. Even before he became president, Lincoln was noted for his powerful speeches; probably his most famous is the Gettysburg Address, delivered on November 19, 1863, at the site of the Battle of Gettysburg in honor of those who had died there for their country. This speech combines the best of Lincoln's rhetorical abilities in a powerful tribute and challenge. On April 14, 1865, while attending a performance of Our American Cousin *at Ford's Theatre in Washington, D.C., Lincoln was assassinated.*

THE GETTYSBURG ADDRESS   (1863)

1   Four score and seven years ago our fathers brought forth on this continent a new nation, conceived in liberty and dedicated to the proposition that all men are created equal. Now we are engaged in a great civil war, testing whether that nation or any nation so conceived and so dedicated can long endure. We are met on a great battlefield of that war. We have come to dedicate a portion of that field as a final resting-place for those who here gave their lives that the nation might live. It is altogether fitting and proper that we should do this. But in a larger sense, we cannot dedicate, we cannot consecrate, we cannot hallow this ground. The brave men, living and dead, who struggled here have consecrated it far above our poor power to add or detract. The world will little note nor long remember what we say here, but it can never forget what they did here. It is for us the living rather to be dedicated here to the unfinished work which they who fought here have thus far so nobly advanced. It is rather for us to be here dedicated to the great task remaining before us—that from these honored dead we take increased devotion to that cause for which they gave the last full measure of devotion—that we here highly resolve that these dead shall not have died in vain, that this nation under God shall have a new birth of freedom, and that government of the people, by the people, for the people shall not perish from the earth.

Questions for Engagement, Response, and Analysis

1. Explain Lincoln's claim that "we cannot consecrate, we cannot hallow this ground."

2. Notice the many examples of parallel structure in this famous speech. How does this parallelism affect the meaning of Lincoln's speech?

Crafting Arguments

1. Write an essay comparing Lincoln's challenge here with that in McCrae's "In Flanders Fields" or with Jefferson's claims in the Declaration of Independence.

2. Using the information in Lincoln's address to support each of your claims, write an essay explaining how Lincoln's description of the American government as "of the people, by the people, for the people" can be not just an ideal but a reality.

Martin Luther King Jr. (1929–1968)

Martin Luther King Jr., an ordained minister at the age of eighteen, was born in Atlanta, Georgia. He received degrees from Morehouse College, Crozer Theological Seminary, and

Boston University. A leader of the civil rights movement, King organized the Montgomery, Alabama, bus boycott after Rosa Parks refused to give up her seat on a bus to a white person. He was also the founder and president of the Southern Christian Leadership Conference (SCLC), which espoused his philosophy of nonviolence. This letter from jail was written in response to the local clergy who had questioned King's approach and methodology.

LETTER FROM BIRMINGHAM CITY JAIL   (1963)

1   My dear Fellow Clergymen,

2   While confined here in Birmingham city jail, I came across your recent statement calling our present activities "unwise and untimely." Seldom, if ever, do I pause to answer criticism of my work and ideas. If I sought to answer all of the criticisms that cross my desk, my secretaries would be engaged in little else in the course of the day, and I would have no time for constructive work. But since I feel that you are men of genuine good will and your criticisms are sincerely set forth, I would like to answer your statement in what I hope will be patient and reasonable terms.

3   I think I should give the reason for my being in Birmingham, since you have been influenced by the argument of "outsiders coming in." I have the honor of serving as president of the Southern Christian Leadership Conference, an organization operating in every southern state, with headquarters in Atlanta, Georgia. We have some eighty-five affiliate organizations all across the South—one being the Alabama Christian Movement for Human Rights. Whenever necessary and possible we share staff, educational and financial resources with our affiliates. Several months ago our local affiliate here in Birmingham invited us to be on call to engage in a nonviolent direct-action program if such were deemed necessary. We readily consented and when the hour came we lived up to our promises. So I am here, along with several members of my staff, because we were invited here. I am here because I have basic organizational ties here.

4   Beyond this, I am in Birmingham because injustice is here. Just as the eighth century prophets left their little villages and carried their "thus saith the Lord" far beyond the boundaries of their hometowns; and just as the Apostle Paul left his little village of Tarsus and carried the gospel of Jesus Christ to practically every hamlet and city of the Graeco-Roman world, I too am compelled to carry the gospel of freedom beyond my particular hometown. Like Paul, I must constantly respond to the Macedonian call for aid.

5   Moreover, I am cognizant of the interrelatedness of all communities and states. I cannot sit idly by in Atlanta and not be concerned about what happens in Birmingham. Injustice anywhere is a threat to justice every-where. We are caught in an inescapable network of mutuality, tied in a single garment of destiny. Whatever affects one directly affects all

indirectly. Never again can we afford to live with the narrow, provincial "outside agitator" idea. Anyone who lives in the United States can never be considered an outsider anywhere in this country.

6   You deplore the demonstrations that are presently taking place in Birmingham. But I am sorry that your statement did not express a similar concern for the conditions that brought the demonstrations into being. I am sure that each of you would want to go beyond the superficial social analyst who looks merely at effects, and does not grapple with underlying causes. I would not hesitate to say that it is unfortunate that so-called demonstrations are taking place in Birmingham at this time, but I would say in more emphatic terms that it is even more unfortunate that the white power structure of this city left the Negro community with no other alternative.

7   In any nonviolent campaign there are four basic steps: (1) collection of the facts to determine whether injustices are alive, (2) negotiation, (3) self-purification, and (4) direct action. We have gone through all of these steps in Birmingham. There can be no gainsaying of the fact that racial injustice engulfs this community.

8   Birmingham is probably the most thoroughly segregated city in the United States. Its ugly record of police brutality is known in every section of this country. Its injust treatment of Negroes in the courts is a notorious reality. There have been more unsolved bombings of Negro homes and churches in Birmingham than any city in this nation. These are the hard, brutal and unbelievable facts. On the basis of these conditions Negro leaders sought to negotiate with the city fathers. But the political leaders consistently refused to engage in good faith negotiation.

9   Then came the opportunity last September to talk with some of the leaders of the economic community. In these negotiating sessions certain promises were made by the merchants—such as the promise to remove the humiliating racial signs from the stores. On the basis of these promises Rev. Shuttlesworth and the leaders of the Alabama Christian Movement for Human Rights agreed to call a moratorium on any type of demonstrations. As the weeks and months unfolded we realized that we were the victims of a broken promise. The signs remained. Like so many experiences of the past we were confronted with blasted hopes, and the dark shadow of a deep disappointment settled upon us. So we had no alternative except that of preparing for direct action, whereby we would present our very bodies as a means of laying our case before the conscience of the local and national community. We were not unmindful of the difficulties involved. So we decided to go through a process of self-purification. We started having workshops on nonviolence and repeatedly asked ourselves the questions, "Are you able to accept blows without retaliating?" "Are you able to endure the ordeals of jail?" We decided to set our direct-action program around the Easter season, realizing that with the exception of Christmas, this was the largest shopping period of the year. Knowing that a strong economic withdrawal program

would be the by-product of direct action, we felt that this was the best time to bring pressure on the merchants for the needed changes. Then it occurred to us that the March election was ahead and so we speedily decided to postpone action until after election day. When we discovered that Mr. Connor was in the run-off, we decided again to postpone action so that the demonstrations could not be used to cloud the issues. At this time we agreed to begin our nonviolent witness the day after the run-off.

10   This reveals that we did not move irresponsibly into direct action. We too wanted to see Mr. Connor defeated; so we went through postponement after postponement to aid in this community need. After this we felt that direct action could be delayed no longer.

11   You may well ask, "Why direct action? Why sit-ins, marches, etc.? Isn't negotiation a better path?" You are exactly right in your call for negotiation. Indeed, this is the purpose of direct action. Nonviolent direct action seeks to create such a crisis and establish such creative tension that a community that has constantly refused to negotiate is forced to confront the issue. It seeks so to dramatize the issue that it can no longer be ignored. I just referred to the creation of tension as a part of the work of the nonviolent resister. This may sound rather shocking. But I must confess that I am not afraid of the word tension. I have earnestly worked and preached against violent tension, but there is a type of constructive nonviolent tension that is necessary for growth. Just as Socrates felt that it was necessary to create a tension in the mind so that individuals could rise from the bondage of myths and half-truths to the unfettered realm of creative analysis and objective appraisal, we must see the need of having nonviolent gadflies to create the kind of tension in society that will help men to rise from the dark depths of prejudice and racism to the majestic heights of understanding and brotherhood. So the purpose of the direct action is to create a situation so crisis-packed that it will inevitably open the door to negotiation. We, therefore, concur with you in your call for negotiation. Too long has our beloved Southland been bogged down in the tragic attempt to live in monologue rather than dialogue.

12   One of the basic points in your statement is that our acts are untimely. Some have asked, "Why didn't you give the new administration time to act?" The only answer that I can give to this inquiry is that the new administration must be prodded about as much as the outgoing one before it acts. We will be sadly mistaken if we feel that the election of Mr. Boutwell will bring the millennium to Birmingham. While Mr. Boutwell is much more articulate and gentle than Mr. Connor, they are both segregationists, dedicated to the task of maintaining the status quo. The hope I see in Mr. Boutwell is that he will be reasonable enough to see the futility of massive resistance to desegregation. But he will not see this without pressure from the devotees of civil rights. My friends, I must say to you that we have not made a single gain in civil rights without determined legal and nonviolent pressure. History is the long and tragic story

of the fact that privileged groups seldom give up their privileges voluntarily. Individuals may see the moral light and voluntarily give up their unjust posture; but as Reinhold Niebuhr has reminded us, groups are more immoral than individuals.

13   We know through painful experience that freedom is never voluntarily given by the oppressor; it must be demanded by the oppressed. Frankly, I have never yet engaged in a direct action movement that was "well-timed," according to the timetable of those who have not suffered unduly from the disease of segregation. For years now I have heard the words "Wait!" It rings in the ear of every Negro with a piercing familiarity. This "Wait" has almost always meant "Never." It has been a tranquilizing thalidomide, relieving the emotional stress for a moment, only to give birth to an ill-formed infant of frustration. We must come to see with the distinguished jurist of yesterday that "justice too long delayed is justice denied." We have waited for more than 340 years for our constitutional and God-given rights. The nations of Asia and Africa are moving with jetlike speed toward the goal of political independence, and we still creep at horse and buggy pace toward the gaining of a cup of coffee at a lunch counter. I guess it is easy for those who have never felt the stinging darts of segregation to say, "Wait." But when you have seen vicious mobs lynch your mothers and fathers at will and drown your sisters and brothers at whim; when you have seen hate-filled policemen curse, kick, brutalize and even kill your black brothers and sisters with impunity; when you see the vast majority of your twenty million Negro brothers smothering in an airtight cage of poverty in the midst of an affluent society; when you suddenly find your tongue twisted and your speech stammering as you seek to explain to your six-year-old daughter why she can't go to the public amusement park that has just been advertised on television, and see tears welling up in her little eyes when she is told that Funtown is closed to colored children, and see the depressing clouds of inferiority begin to form in her little mental sky, and see her begin to distort her little personality by unconsciously developing a bitterness toward white people; when you have to concoct an answer for a five-year-old son asking in agonizing pathos: "Daddy, why do white people treat colored people so mean?"; when you take a cross-country drive and find it necessary to sleep night after night in the uncomfortable corners of your automobile because no motel will accept you; when you are humiliated day in and day out by nagging signs reading "white" and "colored"; when your first name becomes "nigger" and your middle name becomes "boy" (however old you are) and your last name becomes "John," and when your wife and mother are never given the respected title "Mrs."; when you are harried by day and haunted by night by the fact that you are a Negro, living constantly at tiptoe stance never quite knowing what to expect next, and plagued with inner fears and outer resentments; when you are forever fighting a degenerating sense of "nobodiness"; then you will understand why we find it difficult to wait. There comes a time when

the cup of endurance runs over, and men are no longer willing to be plunged into an abyss of injustice where they experience the blackness of corroding despair. I hope, sirs, you can understand our legitimate and unavoidable impatience.

14   You express a great deal of anxiety over our willingness to break laws. This is certainly a legitimate concern. Since we so diligently urge people to obey the Supreme Court's decision of 1954 outlawing segregation in the public schools, it is rather strange and paradoxical to find us consciously breaking laws. One may well ask, "How can you advocate breaking some laws and obeying others?" The answer is found in the fact that there are two types of laws: there are *just* and there are *unjust* laws. I would agree with Saint Augustine that "An unjust law is no law at all."

15   Now what is the difference between the two? How does one determine when a law is just or unjust? A just law is a man-made code that squares with the moral law or the law of God. An unjust law is a code that is out of harmony with the moral law. To put it in the terms of Saint Thomas Aquinas, an unjust law is a human law that is not rooted in eternal and natural law. Any law that uplifts human personality is just. Any law that degrades human personality is unjust. All segregation statutes are unjust because segregation distorts the soul and damages the personality. It gives the segregator a false sense of superiority, and the segregated a false sense of inferiority. To use the words of Martin Buber, the great Jewish philosopher, segregation substitutes an "I-it" relationship for the "I-thou" relationship, and ends up relegating persons to the status of things. So segregation is not only politically, economically and sociologically unsound, but it is morally wrong and sinful. Paul Tillich has said that sin is separation. Isn't segregation an existential expression of man's tragic separation, an expression of his awful estrangement, his terrible sinfulness? So I can urge men to disobey segregation ordinances because they are morally wrong.

16   Let us turn to a more concrete example of just and unjust laws. An unjust law is a code that a majority inflicts on a minority that is not binding on itself. This is difference made legal. On the other hand a just law is a code that a majority compels a minority to follow that it is willing to follow itself. This is sameness made legal.

17   Let me give another explanation. An unjust law is a code inflicted upon a minority which that minority had no part in enacting or creating because they did not have the unhampered right to vote. Who can say that the legislature of Alabama which set up the segregation laws was democratically elected? Throughout the state of Alabama all types of conniving methods are used to prevent Negroes from becoming registered voters and there are some counties without a single Negro registered to vote despite the fact that the Negro constitutes a majority of the population. Can any law set up in such a state be considered democratically structured?

18   These are just a few examples of unjust and just laws. There are some instances when a law is just on its face and unjust in its application. For instance, I was arrested Friday on a charge of parading without a permit. Now there is nothing wrong with an ordinance which requires a permit for a parade, but when the ordinance is used to preserve segregation and to deny citizens the First Amendment privilege of peaceful assembly and peaceful protest, then it becomes unjust.

19   I hope you can see the distinction I am trying to point out. In no sense do I advocate evading or defying the law as the rabid segregationist would do. This would lead to anarchy. One who breaks an unjust law must do it *openly*, *lovingly* (not hatefully as the white mothers did in New Orleans when they were seen on television screaming, "nigger, nigger, nigger"), and with a willingness to accept the penalty. I submit that an individual who breaks a law that conscience tells him is unjust, and willingly accepts the penalty by staying in jail to arouse the conscience of the community over its injustice, is in reality expressing the very highest respect for law.

20   Of course, there is nothing new about this kind of civil disobedience. It was seen sublimely in the refusal of Shadrach, Meshach and Abednego to obey the laws of Nebuchadnezzar because a higher moral law was involved. It was practiced superbly by the early Christians who were willing to face hungry lions and the excruciating pain of chopping blocks, before submitting to certain unjust laws of the Roman Empire. To a degree academic freedom is a reality today because Socrates practiced civil disobedience.

21   We can never forget that everything Hitler did in Germany was "legal" and everything the Hungarian freedom fighters did in Hungary was "illegal." It was "illegal" to aid and comfort a Jew in Hitler's Germany. But I am sure that if I had lived in Germany during that time I would have aided and comforted my Jewish brothers even though it was illegal. If I lived in a Communist country today where certain principles dear to the Christian faith are suppressed, I believe I would openly advocate disobeying these anti-religious laws. I must make two honest confessions to you, my Christian and Jewish brothers. First, I must confess that over the last few years I have been gravely disappointed with the white moderate. I have almost reached the regrettable conclusion that the Negro's great stumbling block in the stride toward freedom is not the White Citizen's Counciler or the Ku Klux Klanner, but the white moderate who is more devoted to "order" than to justice; who prefers a negative peace which is the absence of tension to a positive peace which is the presence of justice; who constantly says, "I agree with you in the goal you seek, but I can't agree with your methods of direct action"; who paternalistically feels that he can set the timetable for another man's freedom; who lives by the myth of time and who constantly advised the Negro to wait until a "more convenient season." Shallow understanding from people of good will is more frustrating than absolute misunderstanding from

people of ill will. Lukewarm acceptance is much more bewildering than outright rejection.

22   I had hoped that the white moderate would understand that law and order exist for the purpose of establishing justice, and that when they fail to do this they become dangerously structured dams that block the flow of social progress. I had hoped that the white moderate would understand that the present tension of the South is merely a necessary phase of the transition from an obnoxious negative peace, where the Negro passively accepted his unjust plight, to a substance-filled positive peace, where all men will respect the dignity and worth of human personality. Actually, we who engage in nonviolent direct action are not the creators of tension. We merely bring to the surface the hidden tension that is already alive. We bring it out in the open where it can be seen and dealt with. Like a boil that can never be cured as long as it is covered up but must be opened with all its pus-flowing ugliness to the natural medicines of air and light, injustice must likewise be exposed, with all of the tension its exposing creates, to the light of human conscience and the air of national opinion before it can be cured.

23   In your statement you asserted that our actions, even though peaceful, must be condemned because they precipitate violence. But can this assertion be logically made? Isn't this like condemning the robbed man because his possession of money precipitated the evil act of robbery? Isn't this like condemning Socrates because his unswerving commitment to truth and his philosophical delvings precipitated the misguided popular mind to make him drink the hemlock? Isn't this like condemning Jesus because His unique God-consciousness and never-ceasing devotion to his will precipitated the evil act of crucifixion? We must come to see, as federal courts have consistently affirmed, that it is immoral to urge an individual to withdraw his efforts to gain his basic constitutional rights because the quest precipitates violence. Society must protect the robbed and punish the robber.

24   I had also hoped that the white moderate would reject the myth of time. I received a letter this morning from a white brother in Texas which said: "All Christians know that the colored people will receive equal rights eventually, but it is possible that you are in too great of a religious hurry. It has taken Christianity almost two thousand years to accomplish what it has. The teachings of Christ take time to come to earth." All that is said here grows out of a tragic misconception of time. It is the strangely irrational notion that there is something in the very flow of time that will inevitably cure all ills. Actually time is neutral. It can be used either destructively or constructively. I am coming to feel that the people of ill will have used time much more effectively than the people of good will. We will have to repent in this generation not merely for the vitriolic words and actions of the bad people, but for the appalling silence of the good people. We must come to see that human progress never rolls in on wheels of inevitability. It comes through the tireless efforts and persistent

work of men willing to be co-workers with God, and without this hard work time itself becomes an ally of the forces of social stagnation. We must use time creatively, and forever realize that the time is always ripe to do right. Now is the time to make real the promise of democracy, and transform our pending national elegy into a creative psalm of brotherhood. Now is the time to lift our national policy from the quicksand of racial injustice to the solid rock of human dignity.

25   You spoke of our activity in Birmingham as extreme. At first I was rather disappointed that fellow clergymen would see my nonviolent efforts as those of the extremist. I started thinking about the fact that I stand in the middle of two opposing forces in the Negro community. One is a force of complacency made up of Negroes who, as a result of long years of oppression, have been so completely drained of self-respect and a sense of "somebodiness" that they have adjusted to segregation, and, of a few Negroes in the middle class who, because of a degree of academic and economic security, and because at points they profit by segregation, have unconsciously become insensitive to the problems of the masses. The other force is one of bitterness and hatred, and comes perilously close to advocating violence. It is expressed in the various black nationalist groups that are springing up over the nation, the largest and best known being Elijah Muhammad's Muslim movement. This movement is nourished by the contemporary frustration over the continued existence of racial discrimination. It is made up of people who have lost faith in America, who have absolutely repudiated Christianity, and who have concluded that the white man is an incurable "devil." I have tried to stand between these two forces, saying that we need not follow the "do-nothingism" of the complacent or the hatred and despair of the black nationalist. There is the more excellent way of love and nonviolent protest. I'm grateful to God that, through the Negro church, the dimension of nonviolence entered our struggle. If this philosophy had not emerged, I am convinced that by now many streets of the South would be flowing with floods of blood. And I am further convinced that if our white brothers dismiss us as "rabble-rousers" and "outside agitators," those of us who are working through the channels of nonviolent direct action, and refuse to support our nonviolent efforts, millions of Negroes, out of frustration and despair, will seek solace and security in black nationalist ideologies, a development that will lead inevitably to a frightening racial nightmare.

26   Oppressed people cannot remain oppressed forever. The urge for freedom will eventually come. This is what happened to the American Negro. Something within has reminded him of his birthright of freedom; something without has reminded him that he can gain it. Consciously and unconsciously, he has been swept in by what the Germans call the *Zeitgeist*, and with his black brothers of Africa, and his brown and yellow brothers of Asia, South America and the Caribbean, he is moving with a sense of cosmic urgency toward the promised land of racial

justice. Recognizing this vital urge that has engulfed the Negro community, one should readily understand public demonstrations. The Negro has many pent-up resentments and latent frustrations. He has to get them out. So let him march sometime; let him have his prayer pilgrimages to the city hall; understand why he must have sit-ins and freedom rides. If his repressed emotions do not come out in these nonviolent ways, they will come out in ominous expressions of violence. This is not a threat; it is a fact of history. So I have not said to my people "get rid of your discontent." But I have tried to say that this normal and healthy discontent can be channelized through the creative outlet of nonviolent direct action. Now this approach is being dismissed as extremist. I must admit that I was initially disappointed in being so categorized.

27   But as I continued to think about the matter I gradually gained a bit of satisfaction from being considered an extremist. Was not Jesus an extremist in love—"Love your enemies, bless them that curse you, pray for them that despitefully use you." Was not Amos an extremist for justice—"Let justice roll down like waters and righteousness like a mighty stream." Was not Paul an extremist for the gospel of Jesus Christ—"I bear in my body the marks of the Lord Jesus." Was not Martin Luther an extremist—"Here I stand; I can do none other so help me God." Was not John Bunyan an extremist—"I will stay in jail to the end of my days before I make a butchery of my conscience." Was not Abraham Lincoln an extremist—"This nation cannot survive half slave and half free." Was not Thomas Jefferson an extremist—"We hold these truths to be self-evident, that all men are created equal." So the question is not whether we will be extremists but what kind of extremist will we be. Will we be extremists for hate or will we be extremists for love? Will we be extremists for the preservation of injustice—or will we be extremists for the cause of justice? In that dramatic scene on Calvary's hill, three men were crucified. We must not forget that all three were crucified for the same crime—the crime of extremism. Two were extremists for immorality, and thusly fell below their environment. The other, Jesus Christ, was an extremist for love, truth and goodness, and thereby rose above his environment. So, after all, maybe the South, the nation and the world are in dire need of creative extremists.

28   I had hoped that the white moderate would see this. Maybe I was too optimistic. Maybe I expected too much. I guess I should have realized that few members of a race that has oppressed another race can understand or appreciate the deep groans and passionate yearnings of those that have been oppressed and still fewer have the vision to see that injustice must be rooted out by strong, persistent and determined action. I am thankful, however, that some of our white brothers have grasped the meaning of this social revolution and committed themselves to it. They are still all too small in quantity, but they are big in quality. Some like Ralph McGill, Lillian Smith, Harry Golden and James Dabbs have written about our struggle in eloquent, prophetic and understanding

terms. Others have marched with us down nameless streets of the South. They have languished in filthy roach-infested jails, suffering the abuse and brutality of angry policemen who see them as "dirty nigger-lovers." They, unlike so many of their moderate brothers and sisters, have recognized the urgency of the moment and sensed the need for powerful "action" antidotes to combat the disease of segregation.

29   Let me rush on to mention my other disappointment. I have been so greatly disappointed with the white church and its leadership. Of course, there are some notable exceptions. I am not unmindful of the fact that each of you has taken some significant stands on this issue. I commend you, Rev. Stallings, for your Christian stance on this past Sunday, in welcoming Negroes to your worship service on a non-segregated basis. I commend the Catholic leaders of this state for integrating Springhill College several years ago.

30   But despite these notable exceptions I must honestly reiterate that I have been disappointed with the church. I do not say that as one of the negative critics who can always find something wrong with the church. I say it as a minister of the gospel, who loves the church; who was nurtured in its bosom; who has been sustained by its spiritual blessing and who will remain true to it as long as the cord of life shall lengthen.

31   I had the strange feeling when I was suddenly catapulted into the leadership of the bus protest in Montgomery several years ago that we would have the support of the white church. I felt that the white ministers, priests and rabbis of the South would be some of our strongest allies. Instead, some have been outright opponents, refusing to understand the freedom movement and misrepresenting its leaders; all too many others have been more cautious than courageous and have remained silent behind the anesthetizing security of the stained-glass windows.

32   In spite of my shattered dreams of the past, I came to Birmingham with the hope that the white religious leadership of this community would see the justice of our cause, and with deep moral concern, serve as the channel through which our just grievances would get to the power structure. I had hoped that each of you would understand. But again I have been disappointed. I have heard numerous religious leaders of the South call upon their worshippers to comply with a desegregation decision because it is the *law*, but I have longed to hear white ministers say, "Follow this decree because integration is morally *right* and the Negro is your brother." In the midst of blatant injustices inflicted upon the Negro, I have watched white churches stand on the sideline and merely mouth pious irrelevancies and sanctimonious trivialities. In the midst of a mighty struggle to rid our nation of racial and economic injustice, I have heard so many ministers say, "Those are social issues with which the gospel has no concern," and I have watched so many churches commit themselves to a completely otherworldly religion which made a strange distinction between body and soul, the sacred and the secular.

33   So here we are moving toward the exit of the twentieth century with a religious community largely adjusted to the status quo, standing as a taillight behind other community agencies rather than a headlight leading men to higher levels of justice.

34   I have traveled the length and breadth of Alabama, Mississippi and all the other southern states. On sweltering summer days and crisp autumn mornings I have looked at her beautiful churches with their lofty spires pointing heavenward. I have beheld the impressive outlay of her massive religious education buildings. Over and over again I have found myself asking: "What kind of people worship here? Who is their God? Where were their voices when the lips of Governor Barnett dripped with words of interposition and nullification? Where were they when Governor Wallace gave the clarion call for defiance and hatred? Where were their voices of support when tired, bruised and weary Negro men and women decided to rise from the dark dungeons of complacency to the bright hills of creative protest?"

35   Yes, these questions are still in my mind. In deep disappointment, I have wept over the laxity of the church. But be assured that my tears have been tears of love. There can be no deep disappointment where there is not deep love. Yes, I love the church; I love her sacred walls. How could I do otherwise? I am in the rather unique position of being the son, the grandson and the great-grandson of preachers. Yes, I see the church as the body of Christ. But, oh! How we have blemished and scarred that body through social neglect and fear of being nonconformists.

36   There was a time when the church was very powerful. It was during that period when the early Christians rejoiced when they were deemed worthy to suffer for what they believed. In those days the church was not merely a thermometer that recorded the ideas and principles of popular opinion; it was a thermostat that transformed the mores of society. Wherever the early Christians entered a town the power structure got disturbed and immediately sought to convict them for being "disturbers of the peace" and "outside agitators." But they went on with the conviction that they were "a colony of heaven," and had to obey God rather than man. They were small in number but big in commitment. They were too God-intoxicated to be "astronomically intimidated." They brought an end to such ancient evils as infanticide and gladiatorial contests.

37   Things are different now. The contemporary church is often a weak, ineffectual voice with an uncertain sound. It is so often the archsupporter of the status quo. Far from being disturbed by the presence of the church, the power structure of the average community is consoled by the church's silent and often vocal sanction of things as they are.

38   But the judgment of God is upon the church as never before. If the church of today does not recapture the sacrificial spirit of the early church, it will lose its authentic ring, forfeit the loyalty of millions, and be dismissed as an irrelevant social club with no meaning for the twentieth century. I am meeting young people every day whose disappointment with the church has risen to outright disgust.

39   Maybe again, I have been too optimistic. Is organized religion too inextricably bound to the status quo to save our nation and the world? Maybe I must turn my faith to the inner spiritual church, the church within the church, as the true *ecclesia* and the hope of the world. But again I am thankful to God that some noble souls from the ranks of organized religion have broken loose from the paralyzing chains of conformity and joined us as active partners in the struggle for freedom. They have left their secure congregations and walked the streets of Albany, Georgia, with us. They have gone through the highways of the South on tortuous rides for freedom. Yes, they have gone to jail with us. Some have been kicked out of their churches, and lost support of their bishops and fellow ministers. But they have gone with the faith that right defeated is stronger than evil triumphant. These men have been the leaven in the lump of the race. Their witness has been the spiritual salt that has preserved the true meaning of the gospel in these troubled times. They have carved a tunnel of hope through the dark mountain of disappointment.

40   I hope the church as a whole will meet the challenge of this decisive hour. But even if the church does not come to the aid of justice, I have no despair about the future. I have no fear about the outcome of our struggle in Birmingham, even if our motives are presently misunderstood. We will reach the goal of freedom in Birmingham and all over the nation, because the goal of America is freedom. Abused and scorned though we may be, our destiny is tied up with the destiny of America. Before the Pilgrims landed at Plymouth, we were here. Before the pen of Jefferson etched across the pages of history the majestic words of the Declaration of Independence, we were here. For more than two centuries our foreparents labored in this country without wages; they made cotton king; and they built the homes of their masters in the midst of brutal injustice and shameful humiliation—and yet out of a bottomless vitality they continued to thrive and develop. If the inexpressible cruelties of slavery could not stop us, the opposition we now face will surely fail. We will win our freedom because the sacred heritage of our nation and the eternal will of God are embodied in our echoing demands.

41   I must close now. But before closing I am impelled to mention one other point in your statement that troubled me profoundly. You warmly commended the Birmingham police force for keeping "order" and "preventing violence." I don't believe you would have so warmly commended the police force if you had seen its angry violent dogs literally biting six unarmed, nonviolent Negroes. I don't believe you would so quickly commend the policemen if you would observe their ugly and inhuman treatment of Negroes here in the city jail; if you would watch them push and curse old Negro women and young Negro girls; if you would see them slap and kick old Negro men and young boys; if you will observe them, as they did on two occasions, refuse to give us food because we wanted to sing our grace together. I'm sorry that I can't join you in your praise for the police department.

42   It is true that they have been rather disciplined in their public handling of the demonstrators. In this sense they have been rather publicly "non-violent." But for what purpose? To preserve the evil system of segregation. Over the last few years I have consistently preached that nonviolence demands that the means we use must be as pure as the ends we seek. So I have tried to make it clear that it is wrong to use immoral means to attain moral ends. But now I must affirm that it is just as wrong, or even more so, to use moral means to preserve immoral ends. Maybe Mr. Connor and his policemen have been rather publicly nonviolent, as Chief Pritchett was in Albany, Georgia, but they have used the moral means of nonviolence to maintain the immoral end of flagrant racial injustice. T. S. Eliot has said that there is no greater treason than to do the right deed for the wrong reason.

43   I wish you had commended the Negro sit-inners and demonstrators of Birmingham for their sublime courage, their willingness to suffer and their amazing discipline in the midst of the most inhuman provocation. One day the South will recognize its real heroes. They will be the James Merediths, courageously and with a majestic sense of purpose facing jeering and hostile mobs and the agonizing loneliness that characterizes the life of the pioneer. They will be old, oppressed, battered Negro women, symbolized in the seventy-two-year-old woman of Montgomery, Alabama, who rose up with a sense of dignity and with her people decided not to ride the segregated buses, and responded to one who inquired about her tiredness with ungrammatical profundity: "My feet is tired, but my soul is rested." They will be the young high school and college students, young ministers of the gospel and a host of their elders courageously and nonviolently sitting-in at lunch counters and willingly going to jail for conscience's sake. One day the South will know that when these disinherited children of God sat down at lunch counters they were in reality standing up for the best in the American dream and the most sacred values in our Judeo-Christian heritage, and thusly, carrying our whole nation back to those great wells of democracy which were dug deep by the Founding Fathers in the formulation of the Constitution and the Declaration of Independence.

44   Never before have I written a letter this long (or should I say a book?). I'm afraid that it is much too long to take your precious time. I can assure you that it would have been much shorter if I had been writing from a comfortable desk, but what else is there to do when you are alone for days in the dull monotony of a narrow jail cell other than write long letters, think strange thoughts, and pray long prayers?

45   If I have said anything in this letter that is an overstatement of the truth and is indicative of an unreasonable impatience, I beg you to forgive me. If I have said anything in this letter that is an understatement of the truth and is indicative of my having a patience that makes me patient with anything less than brotherhood, I beg God to forgive me.

46   I hope this letter finds you strong in the faith. I also hope that circumstances will soon make it possible for me to meet each of you, not

as an integrationist or a civil rights leader, but as a fellow clergyman and a Christian brother. Let us all hope that the dark clouds of racial prejudice will soon pass away and the deep fog of misunderstanding will be lifted from our fear-drenched communities and in some not too distant tomorrow the radiant stars of love and brotherhood will shine over our great nation with all of their scintillating beauty.

47   Yours for the cause of Peace and Brotherhood,

48   Martin Luther King Jr.

Questions for Engagement, Response, and Analysis

1. What are the conditions King and others in Birmingham are protesting? How does King respond to the charge that he is an "outside agitator"?

2. What are the four basic steps in a nonviolent action campaign? How were they carried out in Birmingham?

3. How does King use the word *untimely*? Explain his claim that the charge that the demonstrations are untimely is invalid.

4. Under what circumstances does King consider breaking the law justified? What precedents does he cite for doing so? Discuss the dichotomy between *just* and *unjust* law and the difference between "*difference* made legal" and "*sameness* made legal."

5. Explain King's claim that "Injustice anywhere is a threat to justice everywhere."

6. Explain King's statement that "tension in the mind" can "help men to rise from the dark depths of prejudice and racism to the majestic heights of understanding and brotherhood."

Crafting Arguments

1. Select one of the following quotations from King's letter and support or challenge it:

   • History is the long and tragic story of the fact that privileged groups seldom give up their privileges voluntarily.

   • Shallow understanding from people of good will is more frustrating than absolute misunderstanding from people of ill will. Lukewarm acceptance is much more bewildering than outright rejection.

2. Both the Bible and the Declaration of Independence influenced King. In an essay, show how King's letter reflects the ideas and styles of one of these documents.

3. Analyze the style of this letter, showing how the rhythmic cadences of a sermon, the rhetorical questions, and the metaphors help to make the letter persuasive.

FICTION

Luke

Although few facts about the life of Luke are positively known, scholars believe that Luke, "the beloved physician," wrote the New Testament books Luke and Acts. They believe that Luke was from Antioch in Syria and that he was a close companion of Paul. Although the exact date is unknown, the book of Luke was probably written between 63 and 68 C.E. Scholars also comment on Luke's skill in writing correct Greek. The following is from the King James version of the Bible.

THE PARABLE OF THE PRODIGAL SON
LUKE 15:11–32

11   And he said, A certain man had two sons:

12   And the younger of them said to *his* father, Father, give me the portion of goods that falleth to *me*. And he divided unto them *his* living.

13   And not many days after the younger son gathered all together, and took his journey into a far country, and there wasted his substance with riotous living.

14   And when he had spent all, there arose a mighty famine in that land; and he began to be in want.

15   And he went and joined himself to a citizen of that country; and he sent him into his fields to feed swine.

16   And he would fain have filled his belly with the husks that the swine did eat: and no man gave unto him.

17   And when he came to himself, he said, How many hired servants of my father's have bread enough and to spare, and I perish with hunger!

18   I will arise and go to my father, and will say unto him, Father, I have sinned against heaven, and before thee.

19   And am no more worthy to be called thy son: make me as one of thy hired servants.

20   And he arose, and came to his father. But when he was yet a great way off, his father saw him, and had compassion, and ran, and fell on his neck, and kissed him.

21   And the son said unto him, Father, I have sinned against heaven, and in thy sight, and am no more worthy to be called thy son.

22   But the father said to his servants, Bring forth the best robe, and put *it* on him; and put a ring on his hand, and shoes on *his* feet:

23   And bring hither the fatted calf, and kill *it*; and let us eat, and be merry:

24   For this my son was dead, and is alive again; he was lost, and is found. And they began to be merry.

25   Now his elder son was in the field: and as he came and drew nigh to the house, he heard musick and dancing.

26 And he called one of the servants, and asked what these things meant.

27 And he said unto him, Thy brother is come; and thy father hath killed the fatted calf, because he hath received him safe and sound.

28 And he was angry, and would not go in: therefore came his father out, and intreated him.

29 And he answering said to *his* father, Lo, these many years do I serve thee, neither transgressed I at any time thy commandment: and yet thou never gavest me a kid, that I might make merry with my friends:

30 But as soon as this thy son was come, which hath devoured thy living with harlots, thou hast killed for him the fatted calf.

31 And he said unto him, Son, thou art ever with me, and all that I have is thine.

32 It was meet that we should make merry, and be glad: for this thy brother was dead, and is alive again; and was lost, and is found.

Questions for Engagement, Response, and Analysis

1. What is a parable? How does this form differ from the form of the modern short story?

2. Why would the son choose to give up the security of home and family for "riotous living" in a "far country"? Is his behavior responsible?

3. The father, upon his son's return, prepares a rich feast and gives the returning son the "best robe" and a ring. Is the father being fair to the son who stayed at home? Explain the reasons for your answer.

4. What does the father mean when he tells the older son, "Son, thou art ever with me, and all that I have is thine"? In what ways does this comment speak to the older son's freedom?

Crafting Arguments

1. In an essay, explain your interpretation of this parable.

2. Write an essay using this parable to compare responsible behavior with unconditional love.

Kurt Vonnegut Jr. (1922–2007)

Kurt Vonnegut Jr., a self-acknowledged pessimist and humanist, was one of America's foremost science fiction writers. In his short stories and novels, he satirized the dilemmas people have created: unimaginably destructive wars, out-of-control technology, pollution, and racism. A great admirer of Mark Twain, Vonnegut named his son Mark. His most famous novels are Cat's Cradle *(1963), which ends with the freezing of the world, and* Slaughterhouse-Five *(1969), inspired by his experiences as a prisoner of war in Germany during the Dresden bombings. Vonnegut's last novel was* Timequake *(1999); and* A Man Without a Country *(2005), a collection of biographical essays, was his last published work. Vonnegut also wrote essays, plays, and film and television adaptations of his works. A popular speaker on college campuses, Vonnegut always challenged students to become critical thinkers.*

HARRISON BERGERON   (1961)

1   The year was 2081, and everybody was finally equal. They weren't only equal before God and the law. They were equal every which way. Nobody was smarter than anybody else. Nobody was better looking than anybody else. Nobody was stronger or quicker than anybody else. All this equality was due to the 211th, 212th, and 213th Amendments to the Constitution, and to the unceasing vigilance of agents of the United States Handicapper General.

2   Some things about living still weren't quite right, though. April, for instance, still drove people crazy by not being springtime. And it was in that clammy month that the H-G men took George and Hazel Bergeron's fourteen-year-old son, Harrison, away.

3   It was tragic, all right, but George and Hazel couldn't think about it very hard. Hazel had a perfectly average intelligence, which meant she couldn't think about anything except in short bursts. And George, while his intelligence was way above normal, had a little mental handicap radio in his ear. He was required by law to wear it at all times. It was tuned to a government transmitter. Every twenty seconds or so, the transmitter would send out some sharp noise to keep people like George from taking unfair advantage of their brains.

4   George and Hazel were watching television. There were tears on Hazel's cheeks, but she'd forgotten for the moment what they were about.

5   On the television screen were ballerinas.

6   A buzzer sounded in George's head. His thoughts fled in panic, like bandits from a burglar alarm.

7   "That was a really pretty dance, that dance they just did," said Hazel.

8   "Huh?" said George.

9   "That dance—it was nice," said Hazel.

10   "Yup," said George. He tried to think a little about the ballerinas. They weren't really very good—no better than anybody else would have been, anyway. They were burdened with sashweights and bags of birdshot, and their faces were masked, so that no one, seeing a free and graceful gesture or a pretty face, would feel like something the cat drug in. George was toying with the vague notion that maybe dancers shouldn't be handicapped. But he didn't get very far with it before another noise in his ear radio scattered his thoughts.

11   George winced. So did two out of the eight ballerinas.

12   Hazel saw him wince. Having no mental handicap herself, she had to ask George what the latest sound had been.

13   "Sounded like somebody hitting a milk bottle with a ball peen hammer," said George.

14   "I'd think it would be real interesting, hearing all the different sounds," said Hazel, a little envious. "All the things they think up."

15   "Um," said George.

16   "Only, if I was Handicapper General, you know what I would do?" said Hazel. Hazel, as a matter of fact, bore a strong resemblance to the Handicapper General, a woman named Diana Moon Glampers. "If I was Diana Moon Glampers," said Hazel, "I'd have chimes on Sunday—just chimes. Kind of in honor of religion."

17   "I could think, if it was just chimes," said George.

18   "Well—maybe make 'em real loud," said Hazel. "I think I'd make a good Handicapper General."

19   "Good as anybody else," said George.

20   "Who knows better'n I do what normal is?" said Hazel.

21   "Right," said George. He began to think glimmeringly about his abnormal son who was now in jail, about Harrison, but a twenty-one-gun salute in his head stopped that.

22   "Boy!" said Hazel, "that was a doozy, wasn't it?"

23   It was such a doozy that George was white and trembling, and tears stood on the rims of his red eyes. Two of the eight ballerinas had collapsed to the studio floor, were holding their temples.

24   "All of a sudden you look so tired," said Hazel. "Why don't you stretch out on the sofa, so's you can rest your handicap bag on the pillows, honeybunch." She was referring to the forty-seven pounds of birdshot in a canvas bag, which was padlocked around George's neck. "Go on and rest the bag for a little while," she said. "I don't care if you're not equal to me for a while."

25   George weighed the bag with his hands. "I don't mind it," he said. "I don't notice it any more. It's just a part of me."

26   "You been so tired lately—kind of wore out," said Hazel. "If there was just some way we could make a little hole in the bottom of the bag, and just take out a few of them lead balls. Just a few."

27   "Two years in prison and two thousand dollars fine for every ball I took out," said George. "I don't call that a bargain."

28   "If you could just take a few out when you came home from work," said Hazel. "I mean—you don't compete with anybody around here. You just set around."

29   "If I tried to get away with it," said George, "then other people'd get away with it—and pretty soon we'd be right back to the dark ages again, with everybody competing against everybody else. You wouldn't like that, would you?"

30   "I'd hate it," said Hazel.

31   "There you are," said George. "The minute people start cheating on laws, what do you think happens to society?"

32   If Hazel hadn't been able to come up with an answer to this question, George couldn't have supplied one. A siren was going off in his head.

33   "Reckon it'd fall all apart," said Hazel.

34   "What would?" said George blankly.

35   "Society," said Hazel uncertainly. "Wasn't that what you just said?"

36   "Who knows?" said George.

37   The television program was suddenly interrupted for a news bulletin. It wasn't clear at first as to what the bulletin was about, since the announcer, like all announcers, had a serious speech impediment. For about half a minute, and in a state of high excitement, the announcer tried to say, "Ladies and gentlemen—"

38   He finally gave up, handed the bulletin to a ballerina to read.

39   "That's all right—" Hazel said of the announcer, "he tried. That's the big thing. He tried to do the best he could with what God gave him. He should get a nice raise for trying so hard."

40   "Ladies and gentlemen—" said the ballerina, reading the bulletin. She must have been extraordinarily beautiful, because the mask she wore was hideous. And it was easy to see that she was the strongest and most graceful of all the dancers, for her handicap bags were as big as those worn by two-hundred-pound men.

41   And she had to apologize at once for her voice, which was a very unfair voice for a woman to use. Her voice was a warm, luminous, time-less melody. "Excuse me—" she said, and she began again, making her voice absolutely uncompetitive.

42   "Harrison Bergeron, age fourteen," she said in a grackle squawk, "has just escaped from jail, where he was held on suspicion of plotting to over-throw the government. He is a genius and an athlete, is underhandi-capped, and should be regarded as extremely dangerous."

43   A police photograph of Harrison Bergeron was flashed on the screen—upside down, then sideways, upside down again, then right side up. The picture showed the full length of Harrison against a background calibrated in feet and inches. He was exactly seven feet tall.

44   The rest of Harrison's appearance was Halloween and hardware. Nobody had ever borne heavier handicaps. He had outgrown hindrances faster than the H-G men could think them up. Instead of a little ear radio for a mental handicap, he wore a tremendous pair of earphones, and spectacles with thick wavy lenses. The spectacles were intended to make him not only half blind, but to give him whanging headaches besides.

45   Scrap metal was hung all over him. Ordinarily, there was a certain symmetry, a military neatness to the handicaps issued to strong people, but Harrison looked like a walking junkyard. In the race of life, Harrison carried three hundred pounds.

46   And to offset his good looks, the H-G men required that he wear at all times a red rubber ball for a nose, keep his eyebrows shaved off, and cover his even white teeth with black caps at snaggle-tooth random.

47   "If you see this boy," said the ballerina, "do not—I repeat, do not—try to reason with him."

48   There was the shriek of a door being torn from its hinges.

49   Screams and barking cries of consternation came from the television set. The photograph of Harrison Bergeron on the screen jumped again and again, as though dancing to the tune of an earthquake.

50   George Bergeron correctly identified the earthquake, and well he might have—for many was the time his own home had danced to the same crashing tune. "My God—" said George, "that must be Harrison."

51   The realization was blasted from his mind instantly by the sound of an automobile collision in his head.

52   When George could open his eyes again, the photograph of Harrison was gone. A living, breathing Harrison filled the screen.

53   Clanking, clownish, and huge, Harrison stood in the center of the studio. The knob of the uprooted studio door was still in his hand. Ballerinas, technicians, musicians, and announcers cowered on their knees before him, expecting to die.

54   "I am the Emperor!" cried Harrison. "Do you hear? I am the Emperor! Everybody must do what I say at once!" He stamped his foot and the studio shook.

55   "Even as I stand here—" he bellowed, "crippled, hobbled, sickened— I am a greater ruler than any man who ever lived! Now watch me become what I *can* become!"

56   Harrison tore the straps of his handicap harness like wet tissue paper, tore straps guaranteed to support five thousand pounds.

57   Harrison's scrap-iron handicaps crashed to the floor.

58   Harrison thrust his thumbs under the bar of the padlock that secured his head harness. The bar snapped like celery. Harrison smashed his headphones and spectacles against the wall.

59   He flung away his rubber-ball nose, revealed a man that would have awed Thor, the god of thunder.

60   "I shall now select my Empress!" he said, looking down on the cowering people. "Let the first woman who dares rise to her feet claim her mate and her throne!"

61   A moment passed, and then a ballerina arose, swaying like a willow.

62   Harrison plucked the mental handicap from her ear, snapped off her physical handicaps with marvellous delicacy. Last of all, he removed her mask.

63   She was blindingly beautiful.

64   "Now—" said Harrison, taking her hand, "shall we show the people the meaning of the word dance? Music!" he commanded.

65   The musicians scrambled back into their chairs, and Harrison stripped them of their handicaps, too. "Play your best," he told them, "and I'll make you barons and dukes and earls."

66   The music began. It was normal at first—cheap, silly, false. But Harrison snatched two musicians from their chairs, waved them like batons as he sang the music as he wanted it played. He slammed them back into their chairs.

67   The music began again and was much improved.

68   Harrison and his Empress merely listened to the music for a while—listened gravely, as though synchronizing their heartbeats with it.

69   They shifted their weights to their toes.

70   Harrison placed his big hands on the girl's tiny waist, letting her sense the weightlessness that would soon be hers.

71   And then, in an explosion of joy and grace, into the air they sprang!

72   Not only were the laws of the land abandoned, but the law of gravity and the laws of motion as well.

73   They reeled, whirled, swiveled, flounced, capered, gamboled, and spun.

74   They leaped like deer on the moon.

75   The studio ceiling was thirty feet high, but each leap brought the dancers nearer to it.

76   It became their obvious intention to kiss the ceiling.

77   They kissed it.

78   And then, neutralizing gravity with love and pure will, they remained suspended in air inches below the ceiling, and they kissed each other for a long, long time.

79   It was then that Diana Moon Glampers, the Handicapper General, came into the studio with a double-barreled ten-gauge shotgun. She fired twice, and the Emperor and the Empress were dead before they hit the floor.

80   Diana Moon Glampers loaded the gun again. She aimed it at the musicians and told them they had ten seconds to get their handicaps back on.

81   It was then that the Bergerons' television tube burned out.

82   Hazel turned to comment about the blackout to George. But George had gone out into the kitchen for a can of beer.

83   George came back in with the beer, paused while a handicap signal shook him up. And then he sat down again. "You been crying?" he said to Hazel.

84   "Yup," she said.

85   "What about?" he said.

86   "I forget," she said. "Something real sad on television."

87   "What was it?" he said.

88   "It's all kind of mixed up in my mind," said Hazel.

89   "Forget sad things," said George.

90   "I always do," said Hazel.

91   "That's my girl," said George. He winced. There was the sound of a rivetting gun in his head.

92   "Gee—I could tell that one was a doozy," said Hazel.

93   "You can say that again," said George.

94   "Gee—" said Hazel, "I could tell that one was a doozy."

Questions for Engagement, Response, and Analysis

1. What is the setting of the story? Why is it significant that the same thing happens every normal day?

2. What effect would 213 amendments have on the U.S. Constitution?

3. What are the effects of enforced equality in this story? What is lost in this society because of enforced equality? What is Vonnegut saying about equality as a viable ideal?

4. What is the theme of the story?

5. What is the effect of seeing the story through George's and Hazel's eyes? How would the story be different if told from Harrison's point of view?

Crafting Arguments

1. Vonnegut uses a variety of symbols to emphasize his theme. Write an essay in which you first state what you believe to be the theme, then list the symbols, give your interpretation of each, and explain how they unify and stress Vonnegut's theme.

2. The society of "Harrison Bergeron" extends to its logical conclusion Jefferson's premise that "all men are created equal." In what ways does the society described in this story violate other principles enunciated in the Declaration of Independence?

Ursula K. Le Guin (b. 1929)

Ursula K. Le Guin is one of America's most prolific writers and one of the hardest to classify. She has written poetry, short stories, novels, and children's books. At times, the genres seem to overlap, for her fiction is beautifully lyric, often symbolic, and philosophically titillating. Though she is usually classified as a writer of science fiction or fantasy, Le Guin's works are sometimes based on recorded mythology; however, often the myths are Le Guin originals. Her most famous and most admired novels are those included in the Earthsea Series—A Wizard of Earthsea (1968), The Tombs of Atuan (1971), The Farthest Shore (1972), Tehanu (1990), and The Other Wind (2001)—and the Hainish Series, which includes two of her most famous novels—The Left Hand of Darkness (1969) and The Dispossessed (1974). Her most recent publications are The Wave in the Mind: Talks and Essays on the Writer, the Reader, and the Imagination (2004), Incredible Good Fortune: New Poems (2006), and the three volumes of Annals of the Western Shore (2004, 2006, 2007).

THE ONES WHO WALK AWAY FROM OMELAS   (1973)

1   With a clamor of bells that set the swallows soaring, the Festival of Summer came to the city Omelas, bright-towered by the sea. The rigging of the boats in harbor sparkled with flags. In the streets between houses

with red roofs and painted walls, between old moss-grown gardens and under avenues of trees, past great parks and public buildings, processions moved. Some were decorous: old people in long stiff robes of mauve and grey, grave master workmen, quiet, merry women carrying their babies and chatting as they walked. In other streets the music beat faster, a shimmering of gong and tambourine, and the people went dancing, the procession was a dance. Children dodged in and out, their high calls rising like the swallows' crossing flights over the music and the singing. All the processions wound towards the northside of the city, where on the great water-meadow called the Green Fields boys and girls, naked in the bright air, with mud-stained feet and ankles and long, lithe arms, exercised their restive horses before the race. The horses wore no gear at all but a halter without bit. Their manes were braided with streamers of silver, gold, and green. They flared their nostrils and pranced and boasted to one another; they were vastly excited, the horse being the only animal who has adopted our ceremonies as his own. Far off to the north and west the mountains stood up half encircling Omelas on her bay. The air of morning was so clear that the snow still crowning the Eighteen Peaks burned with white-gold fire across the miles of sunlit air, under the dark blue of the sky. There was just enough wind to make the banners that marked the race-course snap and flutter now and then. In the silence of the broad green meadows one could hear the music winding through the city streets, farther and nearer and ever approaching, a cheerful faint sweetness of the air that from time to time trembled and gathered together and broke into the great joyous clanging of the bells.

2   Joyous! How is one to tell about joy? How describe the citizens of Omelas?

3   They were not simple folk, you see, though they were happy. But we do not say the words of cheer much any more. All smiles have become archaic. Given a description such as this one tends to make certain assumptions. Given a description such as this one tends to look next for the King, mounted on a splendid stallion and surrounded by his noble knights, or perhaps in a golden litter borne by great-muscled slaves. But there was no king. They did not use swords, or keep slaves. They were not barbarians. I do not know the rules and laws of their society, but I suspect that they were singularly few. As they did without monarchy and slavery, so they also got on without the stock exchange, the advertisement, the secret police, and the bomb. Yet I repeat that these were not simple folk, not dulcet shepherds, noble savages, bland utopians. They were not less complex than us. The trouble is that we have a bad habit, encouraged by pedants and sophisticates, of considering happiness as something rather stupid. Only pain is intellectual, only evil interesting. This is the treason of the artist: a refusal to admit the banality of evil and the terrible boredom of pain. If you can't lick 'em, join 'em. If it hurts, repeat it. But to praise despair is to condemn delight, to embrace violence is to lose hold of everything else. We have almost lost hold; we can no

longer describe a happy man, nor make any celebration of joy. How can I tell you about the people of Omelas? They were not naïve and happy children—though their children were, in fact, happy. They were mature, intelligent, passionate adults whose lives were not wretched. O miracle! but I wish I could describe it better. I wish I could convince you. Omelas sounds in my words like a city in a fairy tale, long ago and far away, once upon a time. Perhaps it would be best if you imagined it as your own fancy bids, assuming it will rise to the occasion, for certainly I cannot suit you all. For instance, how about technology? I think that there would be no cars or helicopters in and above the streets; this follows from the fact that the people of Omelas are happy people. Happiness is based on a just discrimination of what is necessary, what is neither necessary nor destructive, and what is destructive. In the middle category, however—that of the unnecessary but undestructive, that of comfort, luxury, exuberance, etc.—they could perfectly well have central heating, subway trains, washing machines, and all kinds of marvelous devices not yet invented here, floating light-sources, fuelless power, a cure for the common cold. Or they could have none of that: it doesn't matter. As you like it. I incline to think that people from towns up and down the coast have been coming in to Omelas during the last days before the Festival on very fast little trains and double-decked trams, and that the train station of Omelas is actually the handsomest building in town, though plainer than the magnificent Farmer's Market. But even granted trains, I fear that Omelas so far strikes some of you as goody-goody. Smiles, bells, parades, horses, bleh. If so, please add an orgy. If an orgy would help, don't hesitate. Let us not, however, have temples from which issue beautiful nude priests and priestesses already half in ecstasy and ready to copulate with any man or woman, lover or stranger, who desires union with the deep godhead of the blood, although that was my first idea. But really it would be better not to have any temples in Omelas—at least, not manned temples. Religion yes, clergy no. Surely the beautiful nudes can just wander about, offering themselves like divine soufflés to the hunger of the needy and the rapture of the flesh. Let them join the processions. Let tambourines be struck above the copulations, and the glory of desire be proclaimed upon the gongs, and (a not unimportant point) let the offspring of these delightful rituals be beloved and looked after by all. One thing I know there is none of in Omelas is guilt. But what else should there be? I thought at first there were no drugs, but that is puritanical. For those who like it, the faint insistent sweetness of *drooz* may perfume the ways of the city, *drooz* which first brings a great lightness and brilliance to the mind and limbs, and then after some hours a dreamy languor, and wonderful visions at least of the very arcana and inmost secrets of the Universe, as well as exciting the pleasure of sex beyond all belief; and it is not habit-forming. For more modest tastes I think there ought to be beer. What else, what else belongs in the joyous city? The sense of victory, surely, the celebration of courage. But as we did without clergy, let us do without soldiers. The joy built upon successful slaughter is not the right kind of joy; it will not do; it is fearful and it is trivial. A boundless and generous contentment, a magnanimous triumph felt not against some outer enemy but in communion with the finest and fairest in the souls of all men everywhere and the splendor of the world's summer: this is what swells the hearts of the people of Omelas, and the victory they celebrate is that of life. I really don't think many of them need to take *drooz*.

4   Most of the processions have reached the Green Fields by now. A marvelous smell of cooking goes forth from the red and blue tents of the provisioners. The faces of small children are amiably sticky; in the benign grey beard of a man a couple of crumbs of rich pastry are entangled. The youths and girls have mounted their horses and are beginning to group around the starting line of the course. An old woman, small, fat, and laughing, is passing out flowers from a basket, and tall young men wear her flowers in their shining hair. A child of nine or ten sits at the edge of the crowd, alone, playing on a wooden flute. People pause to listen, and they smile, but they do not speak to him, for he never ceases playing and never sees them, his dark eyes wholly rapt in the sweet, thin magic of the tune.

5   He finishes, and slowly lowers his hands holding the wooden flute.

6   As if that little private silence were the signal, all at once a trumpet sounds from the pavilion near the starting line: imperious, melancholy, piercing. The horses rear on their slender legs, and some of them neigh in answer. Sober-faced, the young riders stroke the horses' necks and soothe them, whispering, "Quiet, quiet, there my beauty, my hope. . . ." They begin to form in rank along the starting line. The crowds along the race-course are like a field of grass and flowers in the wind. The Festival of Summer has begun.

7   Do you believe? Do you accept the festival, the city, the joy? No? Then let me describe one more thing.

8   In a basement under one of the beautiful public buildings of Omelas, or perhaps in the cellar of one of its spacious private homes, there is a room. It has one locked door, and no window. A little light seeps in dustily between cracks in the boards, secondhand from a cobwebbed window somewhere across the cellar. In one corner of the little room a couple of mops, with stiff, clotted, foul-smelling heads, stand near a rusty bucket. The floor is dirt, a little damp to the touch, as cellar dirt usually is. The room is about three paces long and two wide: a mere broom closet or disused tool room. In the room a child is sitting. It could be a boy or a girl. It looks about six, but actually is nearly ten. It is feeble-minded. Perhaps it was born defective, or perhaps it has become imbecile through fear, malnutrition, and neglect. It picks its nose and occasionally fumbles vaguely with its toes or genitals, as it sits hunched in the corner farthest from the bucket and the two mops. It is afraid of the mops. It finds them horrible. It shuts its eyes, but it knows the mops are still standing there;

and the door is locked; and nobody will come. The door is always locked; and nobody ever comes, except that sometimes—the child has no understanding of time or interval—sometimes the door rattles terribly and opens, and a person, or several people, are there. One of them may come in and kick the child to make it stand up. The others never come close, but peer in at it with frightened, disgusted eyes. The food bowl and the water jug are hastily filled, the door is locked, the eyes disappear. The people at the door never say anything, but the child, who has not always lived in the tool room, and can remember sunlight and its mother's voice, sometimes speaks. "I will be good," it says. "Please let me out. I will be good!" They never answer. The child used to scream for help at night, and cry a good deal, but now it only makes a kind of whining, "eh-haa, eh-haa," and it speaks less and less often. It is so thin there are no calves to its legs; its belly protrudes; it lives on a half-bowl of corn meal and grease a day. It is naked. Its buttocks and thighs are a mass of festered sores, as it sits in its own excrement continually.

9   They all know it is there, all the people of Omelas. Some of them have come to see it, others are content merely to know it is there. They all know that it has to be there. Some of them understand why, and some do not, but they all understand that their happiness, the beauty of their city, the tenderness of their friendships, the health of their children, the wisdom of their scholars, the skill of their makers, even the abundance of their harvest and the kindly weathers of their skies, depend wholly on this child's abominable misery.

10   This is usually explained to children when they are between eight and twelve, whenever they seem capable of understanding; and most of those who come to see the child are young people, though often enough an adult comes, or comes back, to see the child. No matter how well the matter has been explained to them, these young spectators are always shocked and sickened at the sight. They feel disgust, which they had thought themselves superior to. They feel anger, outrage, impotence, despite all the explanations. They would like to do something for the child. But there is nothing they can do. If the child were brought up into the sunlight out of that vile place, if it were cleaned and fed and comforted, that would be a good thing, indeed; but if it were done, in that day and hour all the prosperity and beauty and delight of Omelas would wither and be destroyed. Those are the terms. To exchange all the goodness and grace of every life in Omelas for that single, small improvement: to throw away the happiness of thousands for the chance of the happiness of one: that would be to let guilt within the walls indeed.

11   The terms are strict and absolute; there may not even be a kind word spoken to the child.

12   Often the young people go home in tears, or in a tearless rage, when they have seen the child and faced this terrible paradox. They may brood over it for weeks or years. But as time goes on they begin to realize that even if the child could be released, it would not get much good of its

freedom: a little vague pleasure of warmth and food, no doubt, but little more. It is too degraded and imbecile to know any real joy. It has been afraid too long ever to be free of fear. Its habits are too uncouth for it to respond to humane treatment. Indeed, after so long it would probably be wretched without walls about it to protect it, and darkness for its eyes, and its own excrement to sit in. Their tears at the bitter injustice dry when they begin to perceive the terrible justice of reality, and to accept it. Yet it is their tears and anger, the trying of their generosity and the acceptance of their helplessness, which are perhaps the true source of the splendor of their lives. Theirs is no vapid, irresponsible happiness. They know that they, like the child, are not free. They know compassion. It is the existence of the child, and their knowledge of its existence, that makes possible the nobility of their architecture, the poignancy of their music, the profundity of their science. It is because of the child that they are so gentle with children. They know that if the wretched one were not there snivelling in the dark, the other one, the flute-player, could make no joyful music as the young riders line up in their beauty for the race in the sunlight of the first morning of summer.

13   Now do you believe in them? Are they not more credible? But there is one more thing to tell, and this is quite incredible.

14   At times one of the adolescent girls or boys who go to see the child does not go home to weep or rage, does not, in fact, go home at all. Sometimes also a man or woman much older falls silent for a day or two, and then leaves home. These people go out into the street, and walk down the street alone. They keep walking, and walk straight out of the city of Omelas, through the beautiful gates. They keep walking across the farmlands of Omelas. Each one goes alone, youth or girl, man or woman. Night falls; the traveler must pass down village streets, between the houses with yellow-lit windows, and on out into the darkness of the fields. Each alone, they go west or north, towards the mountains. They go on. They leave Omelas, they walk ahead into the darkness, and they do not come back. The place they go towards is a place even less imaginable to most of us than the city of happiness. I cannot describe it at all. It is possible that it does not exist. But they seem to know where they are going, the ones who walk away from Omelas.

Questions for Engagement, Response, and Analysis

1. What is the setting? What descriptive details might lead you to infer that Omelas is a utopia? How does the narrator involve you in making her description of Omelas believable? What is the significance of telling you what the people are *not?*

2. Why does the happiness of Omelas depend on the misery of a feeble-minded child locked in a closet? Why is the child referred to as "it"?

3 Omelas has religion but no clergy. What is the logic behind this proposal? Similarly, Omelas has no soldiers. Why?

4. Why are the young and some others offended, and why do some eventually walk away from Omelas? Why does the story emphasize the people who stay and the title emphasize those who walk away?

5. Le Guin's narrator accuses writers and artists of having a bias against happiness and joy, of seeing happiness as simple-minded. Which writers whom you have read in this anthology seem to have such a bias?

Crafting Arguments

1. Write an essay discussing the theme of the story. What questions does the story raise without answering them? How do your answers to those questions affect your theories about the theme?

John Updike (b. 1932)

Born in Reading, Pennsylvania, John Updike attended Harvard and edited the Harvard Lampoon. *As a Knox Fellow, he traveled and studied in England; as a Fulbright Lincoln Lecturer, he traveled to Ghana, Nigeria, Tanzania, Kenya, and Ethiopia. A prolific writer of short stories and poetry, Updike is best known for his novels.* The Poorhouse Fair *(1959) won the Rosenthal Foundation Award, and* The Witches of Eastwick *(1984) was later made into a movie. The Rabbit series, which won Updike critical acclaim, includes* Rabbit, Run *(1960);* Rabbit Redux *(1971);* Rabbit Is Rich *(1981), which won the Pulitzer Prize in 1982;* Rabbit at Rest *(1990); and* Rabbit Remembered *(2001), a novella. Among his recent works are the novels* Seek My Face *(2002) and* Terrorist *(2006) and* Due Consideration: Essays and Criticism *(2007). He is one of the very few artists to have been awarded both the National Medal of Arts (1989) and the National Medal for the Humanities (2003) at the White House. In 1998, Updike was awarded the National Book Foundation Medal for Distinguished Contribution to American Letters.*

A & P   (1959)

1   In walks these three girls in nothing but bathing suits. I'm in the third checkout slot, with my back to the door, so I don't see them until they're over by the bread. The one that caught my eye first was the one in the plaid green two-piece. She was a chunky kid, with a good tan and a sweet broad soft-looking can with those two crescents of white just under it, where the sun never seems to hit, at the top of the backs of her legs. I stood there with my hand on a box of HiHo crackers trying to remember if I rang it up or not. I ring it up again and the customer starts giving me hell. She's one of these cash-register-watchers, a witch about fifty with

rouge on her cheekbones and no eyebrows, and I know it made her day to trip me up. She'd been watching cash registers for fifty years and probably never seen a mistake before.

2   By the time I got her feathers smoothed and her goodies into a bag— she gives me a little snort in passing, if she'd been born at the right time they would have burned her over in Salem—by the time I get her on her way the girls had circled around the bread and were coming back, without a pushcart, back my way along the counters, in the aisle between the checkouts and the Special bins. They didn't even have shoes on. There was this chunky one, with the two-piece—it was bright green and the seams on the bra were still sharp and her belly was still pretty pale so I guessed she just got it (the suit)—there was this one, with one of those chubby berry-faces, the lips all bunched together under her nose, this one, and a tall one, with black hair that hadn't quite frizzed right, and one of these sunburns right across under the eyes, and a chin that was too long—you know, the kind of girl other girls think is very "striking" and "attractive" but never quite makes it, as they very well know, which is why they like her so much—and then the third one, that wasn't quite so tall. She was the queen. She kind of led them, the other two peeking around and making their shoulders round. She didn't look around, not this queen, she just walked straight on slowly, on these long white prima-donna legs. She came down a little hard on her heels, as if she didn't walk in her bare feet that much, putting down her heels and then letting the weight move along to her toes as if she was testing the floor with every step, putting a little deliberate extra action into it. You never know for sure how girls' minds work (do you really think it's a mind in there or just a little buzz like a bee in a glass jar?) but you got the idea she had talked the other two into coming in here with her, and now she was showing them how to do it, walk slow and hold yourself straight.

3   She had on a kind of dirty-pink—beige maybe, I don't know—bathing suit with a little nubble all over it and, what got me, the straps were down. They were off her shoulders looped loose around the cool tops of her arms, and I guess as a result the suit had slipped a little on her, so all around the top of the cloth there was this shining rim. If it hadn't been there you wouldn't have known there could have been anything whiter than those shoulders. With the straps pushed off, there was nothing between the top of the suit and the top of her head except just *her*, this clean bare plane of the top of her chest down from the shoulder bones like a dented sheet of metal tilted in the light. I mean, it was more than pretty.

4   She had sort of oaky hair that the sun and salt had bleached, done up in a bun that was unravelling, and a kind of prim face. Walking into the A & P with your straps down, I suppose it's the only kind of face you *can* have. She held her head so high her neck, coming up out of those white shoulders, looked kind of stretched, but I didn't mind. The longer her neck was, the more of her there was.

5   She must have felt in the corner of her eye me and over my shoulder Stokesie in the second slot watching, but she didn't tip. Not this queen.

She kept her eyes moving across the racks, and stopped, and turned so slow it made my stomach rub the inside of my apron, and buzzed to the other two, who kind of huddled against her for relief, and then they all three of them went up the cat-and-dog-food-breakfast-cereal-macaroni-rice-raisins-seasonings-spreads-spaghetti-soft-drinks-crackers-and-cookies aisle. From the third slot I look straight up this aisle to the meat counter, and I watched them all the way. The fat one with the tan sort of fumbled with the cookies, but on second thought she put the package back. The sheep pushing their carts down the aisle—the girls were walking against the usual traffic (not that we have one-way signs or anything)—were pretty hilarious. You could see them, when Queenie's white shoulders dawned on them, kind of jerk, or hop, or hiccup, but their eyes snapped back to their own baskets and on they pushed. I bet you could set off dynamite in an A & P and the people would by and large keep reaching and checking oatmeal off their lists and muttering "Let me see, there was a third thing, began with A, asparagus, no, ah, yes, applesauce!" or whatever it is they do mutter. But there was no doubt, this jiggled them. A few houseslaves in pin curlers even looked around after pushing their carts past to make sure what they had seen was correct.

6   You know, it's one thing to have a girl in a bathing suit down on the beach, where what with the glare nobody can look at each other much anyway, and another thing in the cool of the A & P, under the fluorescent lights, against all those stacked packages, with her feet paddling along naked over our checkerboard green-and-cream rubber-tile floor.

7   "Oh Daddy," Stokesie said beside me. "I feel so faint."

8   "Darling," I said. "Hold me tight." Stokesie's married, with two babies chalked up on his fuselage already, but as far as I can tell that's the only difference. He's twenty-two, and I was nineteen this April.

9   "Is it done?" he asks, the responsible married man finding his voice. I forgot to say he thinks he's going to be manager some sunny day, maybe in 1990 when it's called the Great Alexandrov and Petrooshki Tea Company or something.

10   What he meant was, our town is five miles from a beach, with a big summer colony out on the Point, but we're right in the middle of town, and the women generally put on a shirt or shorts or something before they get out of the car into the street. And anyway these are usually women with six children and varicose veins mapping their legs and nobody, including them, could care less. As I say, we're right in the middle of town, and if you stand at our front doors you can see two banks and the Congregational church and the newspaper store and three real-estate offices and about twenty-seven old freeloaders tearing up Central Street because the sewer broke again. It's not as if we're on the Cape; we're north of Boston and there's people in this town haven't seen the ocean for twenty years.

11   The girls had reached the meat counter and were asking McMahon something. He pointed, they pointed, and they shuffled out of sight behind a pyramid of Diet Delight peaches. All that was left for us to see was old

McMahon patting his mouth and looking after them sizing up their joints. Poor kids, I began to feel sorry for them, they couldn't help it.

12   Now here comes the sad part of the story, at least my family says it's sad, but I don't think it's so sad myself. The store's pretty empty, it being Thursday afternoon, so there was nothing much to do except lean on the register and wait for the girls to show up again. The whole store was like a pinball machine and I didn't know which tunnel they'd come out of. After a while they come around out of the far aisle, around the light bulbs, records at discount of the Caribbean Six or Tony Martin Sings or some such gunk you wonder they waste the wax on, sixpacks of candy bars, and plastic toys done up in cellophane that fall apart when a kid looks at them anyway. Around they come, Queenie still leading the way, and holding a little gray jar in her hand. Slots Three through Seven are unmanned and I could see her wondering between Stokes and me, but Stokesie with his usual luck draws an old party in baggy gray pants who stumbles up with four giant cans of pineapple juice (what do these bums *do* with all that pineapple juice? I've often asked myself) so the girls come to me. Queenie puts down the jar and I take it into my fingers icy cold. Kingfish Fancy Herring Snacks in Pure Sour Cream: 49¢. Now her hands are empty, not a ring or a bracelet, bare as God made them, and I wonder where the money's coming from. Still with that prim look she lifts a folded dollar bill out of the hollow at the center of her nubbled pink top. The jar went heavy in my hand. Really, I thought that was so cute.

13   Then everybody's luck begins to run out. Lengel comes in from haggling with a truck full of cabbages on the lot and is about to scuttle into that door marked MANAGER behind which he hides all day when the girls touch his eye. Lengel's pretty dreary, teaches Sunday school and the rest, but he doesn't miss that much. He comes over and says, "Girls, this isn't the beach."

14   Queenie blushes, though maybe it's just a brush of sunburn I was noticing for the first time, now that she was so close. "My mother asked me to pick up a jar of herring snacks." Her voice kind of startled me, the way voices do when you see the people first, coming out so flat and dumb yet kind of tony, too, the way it ticked over "pick up" and "snacks." All of a sudden I slid right down her voice into her living room. Her father and the other men were standing around in ice-cream coats and bow ties and the women were in sandals picking up herring snacks on toothpicks off a big glass plate and they were all holding drinks the color of water with olives and sprigs of mint in them. When my parents have somebody over they get lemonade and if it's a real racy affair Schlitz in tall glasses with "They'll Do It Every Time" cartoons stencilled on.

15   "That's all right," Lengel said. "But this isn't the beach." His repeating this struck me as funny, as if it had just occurred to him, and he had been thinking all these years the A & P was a great big dune and he was the head lifeguard. He didn't like my smiling—as I say he doesn't miss much—but he concentrates on giving the girls that sad Sunday-school-superintendent stare.

16   Queenie's blush is no sunburn now, and the plump one in plaid, that I liked better from the back—a really sweet can—pipes up. "We weren't doing any shopping. We just came in for the one thing."

17   "That makes no difference," Lengel tells her, and I could see from the way his eyes went that he hadn't noticed she was wearing a two-piece before. "We want you decently dressed when you come in here."

18   "We *are* decent," Queenie says suddenly, her lower lip pushing, getting sore now that she remembers her place, a place from which the crowd that runs the A & P must look pretty crummy. Fancy Herring Snacks flashed in her very blue eyes.

19   "Girls, I don't want to argue with you. After this come in here with your shoulders covered. It's our policy." He turns his back. That's policy for you. Policy is what the kingpins want. What the others want is juvenile delinquency.

20   All this while, the customers had been showing up with their carts but, you know, sheep, seeing a scene, they had all bunched up on Stokesie, who shook open a paper bag as gently as peeling a peach, not wanting to miss a word. I could feel in the silence everybody getting nervous, most of all Lengel, who asks me, "Sammy, have you rung up their purchase?"

21   I thought and said "No" but it wasn't about that I was thinking. I go through the punches, 4, 9, GROC, TOT—it's more complicated than you think, and after you do it often enough, it begins to make a little song, that you hear words to, in my case "Hello (*bing*) there, you (*gung*) happy *pee*-pul (*splat*)!"—the *splat* being the drawer flying out. I uncrease the bill, tenderly as you may imagine, it just having come from between the two smoothest scoops of vanilla I had ever known were there, and pass a half and a penny into her narrow pink palm, and nestle the herrings in a bag and twist its neck and hand it over, all the time thinking.

22   The girls, and who'd blame them, are in a hurry to get out, so I say "I quit" to Lengel quick enough for them to hear, hoping they'll stop and watch me, their unsuspected hero. They keep right on going, into the electric eye; the door flies open and they flicker across the lot to their car, Queenie and Plaid and Big Tall Goony-Goony (not that as raw material she was so bad), leaving me with Lengel and a kink in his eyebrow.

23   "Did you say something, Sammy?"

24   "I said I quit."

25   "I thought you did."

26   "You didn't have to embarrass them."

27   "It was they who were embarrassing us."

28   I started to say something that came out "Fiddle-de- doo." It's a saying of my grandmother's, and I know she would have been pleased.

29   "I don't think you know what you're saying," Lengel said.

30   "I know you don't," I said. "But I do." I pull the bow at the back of my apron and start shrugging it off my shoulders. A couple customers that had been heading for my slot begin to knock against each other, like scared pigs in a chute.

31   Lengel sighs and begins to look very patient and old and gray. He's been a friend of my parents for years. "Sammy, you don't want to do this to your Mom and Dad," he tells me. It's true, I don't. But it seems to me that once you begin a gesture it's fatal not to go through with it. I fold the apron, "Sammy" stitched in red on the pocket, and put it on the counter, and drop the bow tie on top of it. The bow tie is theirs, if you've ever wondered. "You'll feel this for the rest of your life," Lengel says, and I know that's true, too, but remembering how he made that pretty girl blush makes me so scrunchy inside I punch the No Sale tab and the machine whirs "pee-pul" and the drawer splats out. One advantage to this scene taking place in summer, I can follow this up with a clean exit, there's no fumbling around getting your coat and galoshes, I just saunter into the electric eye in my white shirt that my mother ironed the night before, and the door heaves itself open, and outside the sunshine is skating around on the asphalt.

32   I look around for my girls, but they're gone, of course. There wasn't anybody but some young married screaming with her children about some candy they didn't get by the door of a powder-blue Falcon station wagon. Looking back in the big windows, over the bags of peat moss and aluminum lawn furniture stacked on the pavement, I could see Lengel in my place in the slot, checking the sheep through. His face was dark gray and his back stiff, as if he'd just had an injection of iron, and my stomach kind of fell as I felt how hard the world was going to be to me hereafter.

Questions for Engagement, Response, and Analysis

1. What is the point of view in this story? How does Sammy's age shape the effect this experience has on him? How would the story have differed if the narrator had been Lengel?

2. Describe Sammy's feelings about his job. Why does Sammy call the customers sheep?

3. Other than the obvious physical attraction, what is appealing to Sammy about the three girls "in nothing but bathing suits"? What does Sammy see as the significance of their wearing bathing suits in the A & P?

Crafting Arguments

1. In an essay, analyze Sammy's reasons for quitting his job at the A & P.

2. Write an essay analyzing the changes that take place in Sammy and arguing that his experience is or is not an epiphany.

Madison Smartt Bell (b. 1957)

A prolific writer, Madison Smartt Bell has published twelve novels and two collections of short stories, one of which, Barking Man and Other Stories *(1990), includes "Customs of the Country." His fiction creates a dark world of often violent characters who frequently live or die in the face of apparent hopelessness. Among Bell's novels are* Waiting for the World *(1985);* The Year of Silence *(1987);* Soldier's Joy *(1989), which received a Lillian Smith Award, and* Save Me, Joe Louis *(1993).* All Souls' Rising *(1995), the first novel in Bell's Haitian Revolutionary trilogy, received a National Book Award nomination. Bell is a professor of English at Goucher College in Baltimore, Maryland.*

CUSTOMS OF THE COUNTRY (1988)

1   I don't remember much about that place anymore. It was nothing but somewhere I came to put in some pretty bad time, though that was not what I had planned on when I went there. I had it in mind to improve things, but I didn't think you could fairly claim that's what I did. So that's one reason I might just as soon forget about it. And I didn't stay there all that long, not more than about nine months or so, about the same time, come to think, that the child I was there to try to get back had lived inside my body.

2   It was a cluster-housing thing a little ways north out of town from Roanoke, on a two-lane road that crossed the railroad cut and went about a mile farther up through the woods. The buildings looked something like a motel, a little raw still, though they weren't new. My apartment was no more than a place that would barely look all right and yet cost me little enough so I had something left over to give the lawyer. There was fresh paint on the walls and the trim in the kitchen and bathroom was in fair shape. And it was real quiet mostly, except that the man next door used to beat up his wife a couple of times a week. The place was soundproof enough I couldn't usually hear talk but I could hear yelling plain as day and when he got going good he would slam her bang into our common wall. If she hit in just the right spot it would send my pots and pans flying off the pegboard where I'd hung them above the stove.

3   Not that it mattered to me that the pots fell down, except for the noise and the time it took to pick them up again. Living alone like I was, I didn't have the heart to do much cooking and if I did fix myself something I mostly used an old iron skillet that hung there on the same wall. All the others I only had out for show. The whole apartment was done about the same way, made into something I kept spotless and didn't much care to use. I wore my hands out scrubbing everything clean and then saw to it that it stayed that way. I sewed slipcovers for that threadbare batch of Goodwill furniture I'd put in the place, and I hung curtains and found some sunshiny posters to tack on the walls, and I never cared a damn

about any of it. It was an act, and I wasn't putting it on for me or for Davey, but for all the other people I expected to come to see it and judge it. And however good I could get it looking, it never felt quite right.

4   I felt even less at home there than I did at my job, which was waitressing three snake-bends of the counter at the Truckstops of America out at the I-81 interchange. The supervisor was a man named Tim that used to know my husband Patrick from before we had the trouble. He was nice about letting me take my phone calls there and giving me time off to see the lawyer, and in most other ways he was a decent man to work for, except that now and then he would have a tantrum over something or other and try to scream the walls down. Still, it never went beyond yelling, and he always acted sorry once he got through. The other waitress on my shift was an older lady named Prissy, and I liked her all right in spite of the name.

5   We were both on a swing shift that rolled over every ten days, which was the main thing I didn't like about that job. The six-to-two I hated the worst because it would have me getting back to my apartment building around three in the morning, not the time it looked its best. It was the kind of place where at that time of night I could expect to find the deputies out there looking for somebody, or else some other kind of trouble. I never got to know the neighbors any too well, but a lot of them were pretty sorry—small-time criminals, dope dealers and thieves, none of them much good at whatever it was they did. There was one check forger that I knew of, and a man who would break into the other apartments looking for whiskey. One thing and another, along that line.

6   The man next door, the one that beat up his wife, didn't do crimes or work either that I ever heard. He just seemed to lay around the place, maybe drawing some kind of welfare. There wasn't a whole lot of him, he was just a stringy little man, hair and mustache a dishwater-brown, cheap green tatoos running up his arms. Maybe he was stronger than he looked, but I did wonder how come his wife would take it from him, since she was about a head taller and must have outweighed him an easy ten pounds. I might have thought she was whipping on him—stranger things have been known to go on—but she was the one that seemed like she might break out crying if you looked at her crooked. She was a big fine-looking girl with a lovely shape, and long brown hair real smooth and straight and shiny. I guess she was too hammered down most of the time to pay much attention to how she dressed, but still she had pretty brown eyes, big and long-lashed and soft, sort of like a cow's eyes, except I never saw a cow that looked that miserable.

7   At first I thought maybe I might make a friend of her, she was about the only one around there I felt like I might want to. Our paths crossed pretty frequent, either around the apartment building or in the Kwik Sack back toward town, where I'd find her running the register some days. But she was shy of me, shy of anybody I suppose. She would flinch if you did so much as say hello. So after a while I quit trying. She'd get hers about

twice a week, maybe other times I wasn't around to hear it happen. It's a wonder all the things you can learn to ignore, and after a month or so I was that accustomed I barely noticed when they would start in. I would just wait till I thought they were good and through, and then get up and hang those pans back on the wall where they were supposed to go. And all the while I would just be thinking about some other thing, like what might be going on with my Davey.

8   The place where he had been fostered out was not all that far away, just about ten or twelve miles up the road, out there in the farm country. The people were named Baker. I never got to first names with them, just called them Mr. and Mrs. They were older than me, both just into their forties, and they didn't have any children of their own. The place was only a small farm but Mr. Baker grew tobacco on the most of it and I'm told he made it a paying thing. Mrs. Baker kept a milk cow or two and she grew a garden and canned in the old-time way. Thrifty people. They were real sweet to Davey and he seemed to like being with them pretty well. He had been staying there almost the whole two years, which was lucky too, since most children usually got moved around a whole lot more than that.

9   And that was the trouble, like the lawyer explained to me, it was just too good. Davey was doing too well out there. He'd made out better in the first grade than anybody would have thought. So nobody really felt like he needed to be moved. The worst of it was the Bakers had got to like him well enough they were saying they wanted to adopt him if they could. Well, it would have been hard enough for me without that coming into it.

10   Even though he was so close, I didn't go out to see Davey near as much as I would have liked to. The lawyer kept telling me it wasn't a good idea to look like I was pressing too hard. Better take it easy till all the evaluations came in and we had our court date and all. Still, I would call and go on out there maybe a little more than once a month, most usually on the weekends, since that seemed to suit the Bakers better. They never acted like it was any trouble, and they were always pleasant to me, or polite might be a better word yet. The way it sometimes seemed they didn't trust me did bother me a little. I would have liked to take him out to the movies a time or two, but I could see plain enough the Bakers wouldn't have been easy about me having him off their place.

11   But I can't remember us having a bad time, any of those times I went. He was always happy to see me, though he'd be quiet when we were in the house, with Mrs. Baker hovering. So I would get us outside quick as ever I could and, once we were out, we would just play like both of us were children. There was an open pasture, a creek with a patch of woods, a hay barn where we would play hide-and-go-seek. I don't know what all else we did, silly things mostly. That was how I could get near him the easiest, he didn't get a whole lot of playing in, way out there. The Bakers weren't what you would call playful and there weren't any other children

living near. So that was the thing I could give him that was all mine to give. When the weather was good we would stay outside together most all the day and he would just wear me out. But over the winter those visits seemed to get shorter and shorter, like the days.

12   Davey called me Momma still, but I suppose he had come to think your mother was something more like a big sister or just some kind of a friend. Mrs. Baker was the one doing for him all the time. I don't know just what he remembered from before, or if he remembered any of the bad part. He would always mind me but he never acted scared around me, and if anybody says he did they lie. But I never really did get to know what he had going on in the back of his mind about the past. At first I worried the Bakers might have been talking against me, but after I had seen a little more of them I knew they wouldn't have done anything like that, wouldn't have thought it right. So I expect whatever Davey knew about the other time he remembered on his own. He never mentioned Patrick hardly and I think he really had forgotten about him. Thinking back I guess he never saw that much of Patrick even when we were all living together. But Davey had Patrick's mark all over him, the same eyes and the same red hair.

13   Patrick had thick wavy hair the shade of an Irish setter's, and a big rolling mustache the same color. Maybe that was his best feature, but he was a good-looking man altogether, still is I suppose, though the prison haircut don't suit him. If he ever had much of a thought in his head I suspect he had knocked it clean out with dope, yet he was always fun to be around. I wasn't but seventeen when I married him and I didn't have any better sense myself. Right to the end I never thought anything much was the matter, all his vices looked so small to me. He was good-tempered almost all the time, and good with Davey when he did notice him. Never once did he raise his hand to either one of us. In little ways he was unreliable, late, not showing up at all, gone out of the house for days sometimes. Hindsight shows me he ran with other women, but I managed not to know anything about that at the time. He had not quite finished high school and the best job he could hold was being an orderly down at the hospital, but he made a good deal of extra money stealing pills out of there and selling them on the street.

14   That was something else I didn't allow myself to think on much back then. Patrick never told me a lot about it anyhow, always acted real mysterious about whatever he was up to in that line. He would disappear on one of his trips and come back with a whole mess of money, and I would spend up my share and be glad I had it too. I never thought much about where it was coming from, the money or the pills either one. He used to keep all manner of pills around the house, Valium and ludes and a lot of different kinds of speed, and we both took what we felt like whenever we felt in the mood. But what Patrick made the most on was Dilaudid. I used to take it without ever knowing what it really was, but once everything fell in on us I found out it was a bad thing, bad as heroin they

said, and not much different, and it was what they gave Patrick most of his time for.

15   I truly was surprised to find out that it was the strongest dope we had, because I never really even felt like it made you all that high. You would just take one and kick back on a long slow stroke and whatever trouble you might have, it would not be able to find you. It came on like nothing but it was the hardest habit to lose, and I was a long time shaking it. I might be thinking about it yet if I would let myself, and there were times, all through the winter I spent in that apartment, I'd catch myself remembering the feeling.

16   You couldn't call it a real bad winter, there wasn't much snow or anything, but I was cold just about all the time, except when I was at work. All I had in the apartment was some electric baseboard heaters, and they cost too much for me to leave them running very long at a stretch. I'd keep it just warm enough so I couldn't see my breath, and spent my time in a hot bathtub or under a big pile of blankets on the bed. Or else I would just be cold.

17   There was some kind of strange quietness about that place all during the cold weather. If the phone rang it would make me jump. Didn't seem like there was any TV or radio ever playing next door. The only sound coming out of there was Susan getting beat up once in a while. That was her name, a sweet name, I think. I found it out from hearing him say it, which he used to do almost every time before he started on her. "Susan," he'd call out, loud enough I could hear him through the wall. He'd do it a time or two, he might have been calling her to him, and I suppose she went. After that would come a bad silence that reminded you of a snake being somewhere around. Then a few minutes' worth of hitting sounds and then the big slam as she hit the wall, and the clatter of my pots falling on the floor. He'd throw her at the wall maybe once or twice, usually when he was about to get rough. By the time the pots had quit spinning on the floor it would be real quiet over there again, and the next time I saw Susan she'd be walking in that ginger way people have when they're hiding a hurt, and if I said hello to her she'd give a little jump and look away.

18   After a while I quit paying it much mind, it didn't feel any different to me than hearing the news on the radio. All their carrying on was not any more to me than a bump in the rut I had worked myself into, going back and forth from the job, cleaning that apartment till it hurt, calling up the lawyer about once a week to find out what was happening, which never was much. He was forever trying to get our case before some particular doctor or social worker or judge who'd be more apt to help us than another, so he said. I would call him up from the TOA, all eager to hear what news he had, and every time it was another delay. In the beginning I used to talk it all over with Tim or Prissy after I hung up, but after a while I got out of the mood to discuss it. I kept ahead making those calls but every one of them just wore out my hope a little more, like a drip of

water wearing down a stone. And little by little I got in the habit of thinking that nothing really was going to change.

19   Somehow or other that winter passed by, with me going from one phone call to the next, going out to wait on that TOA counter, coming home to shiver and hold hands with myself and lie awake all through the night, or the day, depending what shift I was on. It was springtime, well into warm weather, before anything really happened at all. That was when the lawyer called *me*, for a change, and told me he had some people lined up to see me at last.

20   Well, I was all ready for them to come visit, come see how I'd fixed up my house and all the rest of my business to get set for having Davey back with me again. But as it turned out, nobody seemed to feel like they were called on to make that trip. "I don't think that will be necessary" was what one of them said, I don't recall which. They both talked about the same, in voices that sounded like filling out forms.

21   So all I had to do was drive downtown a couple of times and see them in their offices. That child psychologist was the first and I doubt he kept me more than half an hour. I couldn't tell the point of most of the questions he asked. My second trip I saw the social worker, who turned out to be a black lady once I got down there, though I never could have told it over the phone. Her voice sounded like it was coming out of the TV. She looked me in the eye while she was asking her questions, but I couldn't tell a thing about what she thought. It wasn't till I was back in the apartment that I understood that she must have already had her mind made up.

22   That came to me in a sort of a flash, while I was standing in the kitchen washing out a cup. Soon as I walked back in the door I saw my coffee mug left over from breakfast, and I kicked myself for letting it sit out. I was giving it a hard scrub with a scouring pad when I realized it didn't matter anymore. I might just as well have dropped it on the floor and got what kick I could out of watching it smash, because it wasn't going to make any difference to anybody now. But all the same I rinsed it and set it in the drainer, careful as if it was an eggshell. Then I stepped backward out of the kitchen and took a long look around that cold shabby place and thought it might be for the best that nobody was coming. How could I have expected it to fool anybody else when it wasn't even good enough to fool me? A lonesomeness came over me, I felt like I was floating all alone in the middle of cold air, and then I began to remember some things I would just as soon have not.

23   No, I never did like to think about this part, but I have had to think about it time and again, with never a break for a long, long time, because I needed to get to understand it at least well enough to believe it never would ever happen anymore. And I had come to believe that, in the end. If I hadn't, I never would have come back at all. I had found a way to trust myself again, though it took me a full two years to do it, and though of course it still didn't mean that anybody else would trust me.

24   What had happened was that Patrick went off on one of his mystery trips and stayed gone a deal longer than usual. Two nights away, I was used to that, but on the third I did start to wonder. He normally would have called at least, if he was going to be gone that long of a stretch. But I didn't hear a peep until about halfway through the fourth day. And it wasn't Patrick himself that called, but one of those public-assistance lawyers from downtown.

25   Seemed like the night before Patrick had got himself stopped on the interstate loop down there. The troopers said he was driving like a blind man, and he was so messed up on whiskey and ludes I suppose he must have been pretty near blind at that. Well, maybe he would have just lost his license or something like that, only that the backseat of the car was loaded up with all he had lately stole out of the hospital.

26   So it was bad. It was so bad my mind just could not contain it, and every hour it seemed to be getting worse. I spent the next couple of days running back and forth between the jail and that lawyer, and I had to haul Davey along with me wherever I went. He was too little for school and I couldn't find anybody to take him right then, though all that running around made him awful cranky. Patrick was just grim, he would barely speak. He already knew pretty well for sure that he'd be going to prison. The lawyer had told him there wasn't no use in getting a bondsman, he might just as well stay on in there and start pulling his time. I don't know how much he really saved himself that way, though, since what they ended up giving him was twenty-five years.

27   That was when all my troubles found me, quick. Two days after Patrick got arrested, I came down real sick with something. I thought at first it was a bad cold or the flu. My nose kept running and I felt so wore out I couldn't hardly get up off the bed and yet at the same time I felt real restless, like all my nerves had been scraped bare. Well, I didn't really connect it up to the fact that I'd popped the last pill in the house a couple of days before. What was really the matter was me coming off that Dilaudid, but I didn't have any notion of that at the time.

28   I was laying there in bed not able to get up and about ready to jump right out of my skin at the same time when Davey got the drawer underneath the stove open. Of course he was getting restless himself with all that had been going on, and me not able to pay him much mind. All our pots and pans were down in that drawer then, and he began to take them out one at a time and throw them on the floor. It made a hell of a racket, and the shape I was in, I felt like he must be doing it on purpose to devil me. I called out to him and asked him to quit. Nice at first: "You stop that, now, Davey. Momma don't feel good." But he kept right ahead. All he wanted was to have my attention, I know, but my mind wasn't working right just then. I knew I should get up and just go lead him away from there, but I couldn't seem to get myself to move. I had a picture of myself doing the right thing, but I just wasn't doing it. I was still lying there calling to him to quit and he was still banging those pots around

and before long I was screaming at him outright, and starting to cry at the same time. But he never stopped a minute. I guess I had scared him some already and he was just locked into doing it, or maybe he wanted to drown me out. Every time he flung a pot it felt like I was getting shot at. And the next thing I knew I got myself in the kitchen someway and I was snatching him up off the floor.

29 To this day I don't remember doing it, though I have tried and tried. I thought if I could call it back then maybe I could root it out of myself and be shed of it for good and all. But all I ever knew was one minute I was grabbing a hold of him and the next he was laying on the far side of the room with his right leg folded up funny where it was broke, not even crying, just looking surprised. And I knew that it had to be me that threw him over there because as sure as hell is real there was nobody else around that could have done it.

30 I drove him to the hospital myself. I laid him straight on the front seat beside me and drove with one hand all the way so I could hold on to him with the other. He was real quiet and real brave the whole time, never cried the least bit, just kept a tight hold on my hand with his. Well, after a while, we got there and they ran him off somewhere to get his leg set and pretty soon the doctor came back out and asked me how it had happened.

31 It was the same hospital where Patrick had worked and I even knew that doctor a little bit. Not that being connected to Patrick would have done me a whole lot of good around there at that time. Still, I have often thought since then that things might have come out better for me and Davey both if I just could have lied to that man, but I was not up to telling a lie that anybody would be apt to believe. All I could do was start to scream and jabber like a crazy person, and it ended up I stayed in that hospital quite a few days myself. They took me for a junkie and I guess I really was one too, though I hadn't known it till that very day. And I never saw Davey again for a whole two years, not till the first time they let me go out to the Bakers'.

32 Sometimes you don't get but one mistake, if the one you pick is bad enough. Do as much as step in the road one time without looking, and your life could be over with then and there. But during those two years I taught myself to believe that this mistake of mine could be wiped out, that if I struggled hard enough with myself and the world I could make it like it never had been.

33 Three weeks went by after I went to see that social worker, and I didn't have any idea what was happening, or if anything was. Didn't call anybody, I expect I was afraid to. Then one day the phone rang for me out there at the TOA. It was the lawyer and I could tell right off from the sound of his voice I wasn't going to care for his news. Well, he told me all the evaluations had come in now, sure enough and they weren't running in our favor. They weren't against *me*, he made sure to say that, it was more like they were *for* the Bakers. And his judgment was it wouldn't pay

me anything if we went on to court. It looked like the Bakers would get Davey for good anyhow, and they were likely to be easier about visitation if there wasn't any big tussle. But if I drug them into court, then we would have to start going back over the whole case history—

34   That was the word he used, *case history*, and it was around about there that I hung up. I went walking stiff-legged back across to the counter and just let myself sort of drop on a stool. Prissy had been covering my station while I was on the phone and she came right over to me then.

35   "What is it?" she said. I guess she could tell it was something by the look on my face.

36   "I lost him," I said.

37   "Oh, hon, you know I'm so sorry," she said. She reached out for my hand but I snatched it back. I know she meant it well but I just was not in the mood to be touched.

38   "There's no forgiveness," I said. I felt bitter about it. It had been a hard road for me to come as near forgiving myself as I ever could. And Davey forgave me, I really knew that, I could tell it in the way he acted when we were together. And if us two could do it, I didn't feel like it ought to be anybody else's business but ours. Tim walked up then and Prissy whispered something to him, and then he took a step nearer to me.

39   "I'm sorry," he told me.

40   "Not like I am," I said. "You don't know the meaning of the word."

41   "Go ahead and take off the rest of your shift if you feel like it," he said. "I'll wait on these tables myself, need be."

42   "I don't know it would make any difference," I said.

43   "Better take it easy on yourself," he said. "No use in taking it so hard. You're just going to have to get used to it."

44   "Is that a fact?" I said. And I lit myself a cigarette and turned my face away. We had been pretty busy, it was lunchtime, and the people were getting restless seeing all of us standing around there not doing a whole lot about bringing them their food. Somebody called out something to Tim, I didn't hear just what it was, but it set off one of his temper fits.

45   "Go on and get out of here if that's how you feel," he said. He was getting red in the face and waving his arms around to include everybody there in what he was saying. "Go on and clear out of here, every last one of you, and we don't care if you never come back. There's not one of you couldn't stand to miss a meal anyhow. Take a look at yourselves, you're all fat as hogs . . ."

46   It seemed like he might be going to keep it up a good while, and he had already said I could leave, so I hung up my apron and got my purse and I left. It was the first time he ever blew up at the customers that way, it had always been me or Prissy or one of the cooks. I never did find out what came of it all because I never went back to that place again.

47   I drove home in such a poison mood I barely knew I was driving a car or that there were any others on the road. I was ripe to get killed or kill

somebody, and I wouldn't have cared much either way. I kept thinking about what Tim had said about having to get used to it. It came to me that I was used to it already, I really hadn't been all that surprised. That's what I'd been doing all those months, just gradually getting used to losing my child forever.

48   When I got back to the apartment I just fell in a chair and sat there staring across at the kitchen wall. It was in my mind to pack my traps and leave that place, but I hadn't yet figured out where I could go. I sat there a good while, I guess. The door was ajar from me not paying attention, but it wasn't cold enough out to make any difference. If I turned my head that way I could see a slice of the parking lot. I saw Susan drive up and park and come limping toward the building with an armload of groceries. Because of the angle I couldn't see her go into their apartment but I heard the door open and shut and after that it was quiet as a tomb. I kept on sitting there thinking about how used to everything I had got. There must have been generous numbers of other people too, I thought, who had got themselves accustomed to all kinds of things. Some were used to taking the pain and the rest were used to serving it up. About half of the world was screaming in misery, and it wasn't anything but a habit.

49   When I started to hear the hitting sounds come toward me through the wall, a smile came on my face like it was cut there with a knife. I'd been expecting it, you see, and the mood I was in I felt satisfied to see what I had expected was going to happen. So I listened a little more carefully than I'd been inclined to do before. It was *hit hit hit* going along together with a groan and a hiss of the wind being knocked out of her. I had to strain pretty hard to hear that breathing part, and I could hear him grunt too, when he got in a good one. There was about three minutes of that with some little breaks, and then a longer pause. When she hit the wall it was the hardest she had yet, I think. It brought down every last one of my pots at one time, including the big iron skillet that was the only one I ever used.

50   It was the first time they'd managed to knock that skillet down, and I was so impressed that I went over and stood looking down at it like I needed to make sure it was a real thing. I stared at the skillet so long it went out of focus and started looking more like a big black hole in the floor. That's when it dawned on me that this was one thing I didn't really have to keep on being used to.

51   It took three or four knocks before he came to the door, but that didn't worry me at all. I had faith, I knew he was going to come. I meant to stay right there till he did. When he came, he opened the door wide and stood there with his arms folded and his face all stiff with his secrets. It was fairly dark behind him, they had all the curtains drawn. I had that skillet held out in front of me in both my hands, like maybe I had come over to borrow a little hot grease or something. It was so heavy it kept wanting to dip down toward the floor like a water witch's rod. When I saw he wasn't expecting anything, I twisted the skillet back over my

shoulder like baseball players do their bat, and I hit him bang across the face as hard as I knew how. He went down and out at the same time and fetched up on his back clear in the middle of the room.

52   Then I went in after him with the skillet cocked and ready in case he made to get up. But he didn't look like there was a whole lot of fight left in him right then. He was awake, at least partly awake, but his nose was just spouting blood and it seemed like I'd knocked out a few of his teeth. I wish I could tell you I was sorry or glad, but I didn't feel much of anything really, just that high lonesome whistle in the blood I used to get when I took all that Dilaudid. Susan was sitting on the floor against the wall, leaning down on her knees and sniveling. Her eyes were red but she didn't have any bruises where they showed. He never did hit her on the face, that was the kind he was. There was a big crack coming down the wall behind her and I remember thinking it probably wouldn't be too much longer before it worked through to my side.

53   "I'm going to pack and drive over to Norfolk," I told her. I hadn't thought of it before but once it came out my mouth I knew it was what I would do. "You can ride along with me if you want to. With your looks you could make enough money serving drinks to the sailors to buy that Kwik Sack and blow it up."

54   She didn't say anything, just raised her head up and stared at me kind of bug-eyed. And after a minute I turned around and went out. It didn't take me any time at all to get ready. All I had was a suitcase and a couple of boxes of other stuff. The sheets and blankets I just pulled off the bed and stuffed in the trunk all in one big wad. I didn't care a damn about that furniture, I would have lit it on fire on a dare.

55   When I was done I stuck my head back into the other apartment. The door was still open like I had left it. What was she doing but kneeling down over that son of a bitch and trying to clean off his face with a washrag. I noticed he was making a funny sound when he breathed, and his nose was still bleeding pretty quick, so I thought maybe I had broke it. Well, I can't say that worried me much.

56   "Come on now if you're coming, girl," I said. She looked up at me, not telling me one word, just giving me a stare out of those big cow eyes of hers like I was the one had been beating on her that whole winter through. And I saw then that they were both of them stuck in their groove and that she would not be the one to step out of it. So I pulled back out of the doorway and went on down the steps to my car.

57   I was speeding on the road to Norfolk, doing seventy, seventy-five. I'd have liked to gone faster if the car had been up to it. I can't say I felt sorry for busting that guy, though I didn't enjoy the thought of it either. I just didn't know what difference it had made, and chances were it had made none at all. Kind of a funny thing, when you thought about it that way. It was the second time in my life I'd hurt somebody bad, and the other time I hadn't meant to do it at all. This time I'd known what I was doing for sure, but I still didn't know what I'd done.

Questions for Engagement, Response, and Analysis

1. What is the point of view in this story? How would this story be different if it were told from another point of view? Could it be as effective?

2. Describe the narrator's personality. What is her opinion of herself? What events led to the narrator's treatment of Davey?

3. What kind of future can the narrator anticipate?

Crafting Arguments

1. Is the narrator, a child abuser and drug addict, simply an evil person, or does she have some redeeming qualities?

2. After carefully examining the behavior and comments of the narrator, write an essay about her responsibility for her choices and about the actions that limit her future choices.

POETRY

William Wordsworth (1770–1850)

William Wordsworth was a leading poet of the Romantic movement in England. His collaboration with Samuel Taylor Coleridge on the book of poems Lyrical Ballads *in 1798 is often cited as the beginning of the Romantic movement in England. Wordsworth rebelled against the order and restraint of the Enlightenment, supported the French Revolution, and sought in nature and in the lives of ordinary people an answer to the complexity and materialism of industrial England. In his poetry, he tried to use the plain language of ordinary people. As the supreme English nature poet, Wordsworth changed forever the view of nature in his culture and in ours.*

THE WORLD IS TOO MUCH WITH US   (1807)

The world is too much with us; late and soon,
Getting and spending, we lay waste our powers;
Little we see in Nature that is ours;
We have given our hearts away, a sordid boon!
5   This Sea that bares her bosom to the moon;
The winds that will be howling at all hours,
And are up-gathered now like sleeping flowers;
For this, for everything, we are out of tune;

It moves us not. Great God! I'd rather be
10 A Pagan suckled in a creed outworn;
So might I, standing on this pleasant lea,
Have glimpses that would make me less forlorn;
Have sight of Proteus rising from the sea;
Or hear old Triton blow his wreathed horn.

Questions for Engagement, Response, and Analysis

1. The traditional Italian sonnet form asks a question in the octave and answers it in the sestet. Analyze whether or not Wordsworth follows this traditional form.

2. Examine Wordsworth's allusions to pagan beliefs, interpret them, and give your theories about his reasons for using them.

3. Compare the theme and subject of this poem to those of Hopkins' "God's Grandeur" in the Quest unit.

Crafting Arguments

1. Write an essay explicating this poem. Be sure to examine all aspects of form—such as rhyme, rhythm, and sound devices—as well as metaphorical devices and allusions.

Walt Whitman (1819–1892)

Born on Long Island to Quaker parents, Walt Whitman is one of the most influential poets in American literature. Often referred to as the great egalitarian bard because of his democratic ideals, Whitman began his career writing for newspapers. During the Civil War, Whitman served as a nurse. He was a great admirer of Abraham Lincoln, and two of his most famous poems are about Lincoln's death. He first published his revolutionary book of poetry, Leaves of Grass, *in 1855, and he continued to revise and republish* Leaves of Grass *for the rest of his life. The first poem in the book, later titled "Song of Myself," celebrates many of the Transcendental ideas for which Whitman was praised by Ralph Waldo Emerson. However, many nineteenth-century critics were shocked by both the content and the free verse form of the poetry.* Drum Taps, *first published in 1865 and later incorporated into* Leaves of Grass, *includes many of Whitman's poems about the Civil War.*

FOR YOU O DEMOCRACY (1856)

Come, I will make the continent indissoluble,
I will make the most splendid race the sun ever shone upon,
I will make divine magnetic lands,

With the love of comrades,
5   With the life-long love of comrades.

I will plant companionship thick as trees along all the rivers
    of America, and along the shores of the great lakes, and
    all over the prairies,
I will make inseparable cities with their arms about each
10   other's necks,
    By the love of comrades,
    By the manly love of comrades.

For you these from me, O Democracy, to serve you ma
femme!
15   For you, for you I am trilling these songs.

Questions for Engagement, Response, and Analysis

1. In your opinion, who is the speaker in this poem?
2. What does the speaker wish for this democracy?
3. What is the theme?
4. Taking into consideration that many readers of Whitman's poetry have pointed out that he was influenced by the Bible and by Shakespeare, examine the style of this brief poem.

Crafting Arguments

1. Using your answers to questions two and three above, write an essay in which you argue that Whitman's style reflects his subject matter and creates an appropriate tone.

Rudyard Kipling (1865–1936)

Born in Bombay, India, Kipling was educated in England; in 1882, he returned to India to work as an editor of a newspaper. In 1889, he went back to England to continue his writing career. Some of his early poems were collected in Departmental Ditties *(1886) and* Barrack-Room Ballads *(1892); his short stories from this period were* Soldiers Three *(1888) and* Plain Tales from the Hills *(1888). His novel,* The Light That Failed *(1890), also met with success. Kipling's stories of India made him a popular writer because of his romantic notions of the Englishman and the Indian people. These views are reflected in some of his poems such as "Mandalay," "The White Man's Burden," and "Gunga Din" and in* Recessional *(1897). After marrying an American, Kipling moved to Vermont, where he lived for four years and wrote the children's stories* The Jungle Book *(1894),* Second Jungle Book *(1895),* Captains Courageous *(1897),* Kim *(1901), and* Just So Stories *(1902). In 1900, he returned to England and continued to write. His later works include* Puck of Pook's Hill *(1906) and his famous poem "If"* *(1910). Kipling was England's first Nobel Prize winner in literature (1907).*

IF   (1910)

If you can keep your head when all about you
Are losing theirs and blaming it on you,
If you can trust yourself when all men doubt you
But make allowance for their doubting too,
5   If you can wait and not be tired by waiting,
Or being lied about, don't deal in lies,
Or being hated, don't give way to hating,
And yet don't look too good, nor talk too wise:

If you can dream—and not make dreams your
10   master,
If you can think—and not make thoughts your aim;
If you can meet with Triumph and Disaster
And treat those two impostors just the same;
If you can bear to hear the truth you've spoken
15   Twisted by knaves to make a trap for fools,
Or watch the things you gave your life to, broken,
And stoop and build 'em up with worn-out tools:

If you can make one heap of all your winnings
And risk it all on one turn of pitch-and-toss,
20   And lose, and start again at your beginnings
And never breathe a word about your loss;
If you can force your heart and nerve and sinew
To serve your turn long after they are gone,
And so hold on when there is nothing in you
25   Except the Will which says to them: "Hold on!"

If you can talk with crowds and keep your virtue,
Or walk with kings—nor lose the common touch,
If neither foes nor loving friends can hurt you;
If all men count with you, but none too much,
30   If you can fill the unforgiving minute
With sixty seconds' worth of distance run,
Yours is the Earth and everything that's in it,
And—which is more—you'll be a Man, my son!

Questions for Engagement, Response, and Analysis

1. How many sentences make up this poem? Examine the sentence structure and explain the effect of this structure on the poem.

2. What is the form of the poem? How does Kipling's use of **anaphora** serve to unify the poem and emphasize his points?

3. Look at each one of the "If" clauses and try to select one noun that names the characteristic you would have if you could accomplish the task described.

Crafting Arguments

1. Use the nouns you listed for the question above to write an essay about what qualities, according to Kipling, would make "a Man."
2. In an essay, compare the qualities of a man suggested here with those of a woman described by Maya Angelou in "Phenomenal Woman."

W. H. Auden (1907–1973)

W. H. Auden, a major twentieth-century poet who was born in England, became a citizen of the United States in 1946. A precocious writer, he published Poems *in 1930 and* Orators *in 1932. Also in the 1930s, Auden experimented with different forms of drama, including verse plays and plays that used music. A winner of many literary prizes, he was praised for his expertise in lyrical poetry and for his technical proficiency. Auden, who influenced many of the poets of his age, is noted as a poet, critic, essayist, and playwright.*

THE UNKNOWN CITIZEN   (1940)
(To JS/07/M/378 THIS MARBLE MONUMENT
IS ERECTED BY THE STATE)

He was found by the Bureau of Statistics to be
One against whom there was no official complaint,
And all the reports on his conduct agree
That, in the modern sense of an old-fashioned word, he was a saint,
5   For in everything he did he served the Greater Community.
Except for the War till the day he retired
He worked in a factory and never got fired
But satisfied his employers, Fudge Motors Inc.
Yet he wasn't a scab or odd in his views,
10   For his Union reports that he paid his dues,
(Our report on his Union shows it was sound)
And our Social Psychology workers found
That he was popular with his mates and liked a drink.
The Press are convinced that he bought a paper every day
15   And that his reactions to advertisements were normal in every way.
Policies taken out in his name prove that he was fully insured,
And his Health-card shows he was once in hospital but left it cured.
Both Producers Research and High-Grade Living declare
He was fully sensible to the advantages of the Installment Plan

20   And had everything necessary to the Modern Man,
      A phonograph, a radio, a car and a frigidaire.
      Our researchers into Public Opinion are content
      That he held the proper opinions for the time of year;
      When there was peace, he was for peace; when there was war, he went.
25   He was married and added five children to the population,
      Which our Eugenist says was the right number for a parent of his
          generation.
      And our teachers report that he never interfered with their education.
      Was he free? Was he happy? The question is absurd:
      Had anything been wrong, we should certainly have heard.

Questions for Engagement, Response, and Analysis

1. What is the point of view in this poem? What is the occasion?

2. What is the tone of the poem? Does it change?

3. What, according to the poem, is "the modern sense" of the word "saint"? In what ways is this man saintly?

4. Why does the speaker describe the questions "Was he free? Was he happy?" as absurd? How would you answer these questions about the unknown citizen?

5. What is missing in this eulogy?

6. If the Unknown Citizen were a character in "Harrison Bergeron," what handicaps might he wear?

Crafting Arguments

1. In an essay, select three of the "normal" facets of the Unknown Citizen's life applauded by the speaker and argue that they truly are admirable.

2. Write an essay specifying what Auden is satirizing in this poem.

Karl Shapiro (1913–2000)

American poet and literary critic Karl Shapiro was born in Baltimore, Maryland. He is known for his independence and iconoclasm. He disliked and opposed the great modern poets Ezra Pound, William Butler Yeats, and T. S. Eliot, regarding Eliot's Christianity as a sellout to an outmoded worldview. Shapiro taught at many universities, including Johns Hopkins, the University of Nebraska, the University of Illinois at Chicago, and the University of California, Davis. His collections of poems include V-Letter and Other Poems *(1945), a collection of poems about World War II that*

won a Pulitzer Prize; Poems of a Jew *(1958); and* The Bourgeois Poet *(1964).*

THE CONSCIENTIOUS OBJECTOR   (1978)

The gates clanged and they walked you into jail
More tense than felons but relieved to find
The hostile world shut out, flags that dripped
From every mother's windowpane, obscene
5   The bloodlust sweating from the public heart,
The dog authority slavering at your throat.
A sense of quiet, of pulling down the blind
Possessed you. Punishment you felt was clean.

The decks, the catwalks, and the narrow light
10   Composed a ship. This was a mutinous crew
Troubling the captains for plain decencies,
A *Mayflower* brim with pilgrims headed out
To establish new theocracies to west,
A Noah's ark coasting the topmost seas
15   Ten miles above the sodomites and fish.
These inmates loved the only living doves.

Like all men hunted from the world you made
A good community, voyaging the storm
To no safe Plymouth or green Ararat;
20   Trouble or calm, the men with Bibles prayed,
The gaunt politicals construed our hate.
The opposite of all armies, you were best
Opposing uniformity and yourselves;
Prison and personality were your fate.
25   You suffered not so physically but knew
Maltreatment, hunger, ennui of the mind.
Well might the soldier kissing the hot beach
Erupting in his face damn all your kind.
Yet you who saved neither yourselves nor us
30   Are equally with those who shed the blood
The heroes of our cause. Your conscience is
What we come back to in the armistice.

Questions for Engagement, Response, and Analysis

1. Who is speaking in the poem? To whom is the poem addressed? Define
   a conscientious objector.

2. Examine the loaded language in the first six lines. To whom is it
   applied? Why?

3. Identify the allusions and explain what they suggest in the context of
   the poem.

Crafting Arguments

1. Write an essay explicating this poem, examining the way in which all aspects of form—such as rhythm and sound devices—as well as metaphorical devices and diction work together to create the tone and emphasize the theme.

2. O'Brien in "On the Rainy River" describes his decision to allow himself to be drafted. In an essay, compare O'Brien's decision with the conscientious objector's decision.

Anne Sexton (1928–1974)

Anne Sexton believed that as a child she had been unwanted and rejected. Before she was twenty years old, she married Alfred Muller Sexton III. In 1954, shortly after the birth of her first daughter, Sexton suffered her first mental breakdown. The birth of her second daughter in 1955 was followed by a second breakdown. The psychiatrist who treated her at this time convinced her that she was intelligent and talented, and he encouraged her to write poetry. Sexton found a form of salvation in writing poems about her tendency toward suicide, her mental breakdowns, and the problems she faced as a woman. In 1974, after a lifetime of feeling that death was calling her, Sexton committed suicide. The following poem was included in her first collection, To Bedlam and Part Way Back *(1960).*

RINGING THE BELLS   (1960)

And this is the way they ring
the bells in Bedlam
and this is the bell-lady
who comes each Tuesday morning
5   to give us a music lesson
and because the attendants make you go
and because we mind by instinct,
like bees caught in the wrong hive,
we are the circle of the crazy ladies
10   who sit in the lounge of the mental house
and smile at the smiling woman
who passes us each a bell,
who points at my hand
that holds my bell, E flat,
15   and this is the gray dress next to me
who grumbles as if it were special
to be old, to be old,
and this is the small hunched squirrel girl
on the other side of me

20   who picks at the hairs over her lip.
       who picks at the hairs over her lip all day,
       and this is how the bells really sound,
       as untroubled and clean
       as a workable kitchen,
25   and this is always my bell responding
       to my hand that responds to the lady
       who points at me, E flat;
       and although we are no better for it,
       they tell you to go. And you do.

Questions for Engagement, Response, and Analysis

1. Who is the speaker in the poem? What is the situation?

2. What is the music lesson supposed to do for the "crazy ladies"? How does the speaker feel about the music lesson?

3. What does the animal imagery suggest about the women in the poem?

Crafting Arguments

1. Examine the structure, diction, and imagery of the poem. Then, supporting each of your claims with quotations, write an essay illustrating how all three combine to create the tone and theme of the poem.

Pat Mora (b. 1942)

Pat Mora, a Southwestern poet from El Paso, Texas, was educated at Texas Western College and University of Texas, El Paso. Of Mexican American parentage, she has written several books of poems, including Chants *(1984),* Borders *(1986), and* Communion *(1991). In* House of Houses *(1997), Mora reveals her family in first-person narratives; and a children's book,* The Rainbow Tulip *(1999), tells the story of her mother's childhood.* My Own True Name *(2000) collects her poems for young adults. In many of her works, Mora celebrates her bicultural heritage and encourages Chicana women to accept their identity.*

IMMIGRANTS   (1986)

       wrap their babies in the American flag,
       feed them mashed hot dogs and apple pie,
       name them Bill and Daisy,
       buy them blonde dolls that blink blue
5   eyes or a football and tiny cleats
       before the baby can even walk,
       speak to them in thick English,
           hallo, babee, hallo,

10   whisper in Spanish or Polish
   when the babies sleep, whisper
   in a dark parent bed, that dark
   parent fear, "Will they like
   our boy, our girl, our fine american
   boy, our fine american girl?"

Questions for Engagement, Response, and Analysis

1. Who is the speaker in the poem? What is the subject of the one sentence in the poem?

2. What American qualities do the immigrants seek for their children? Why?

3. What is the source of the immigrants' anxiety?

Crafting Arguments

1. Identify the theme of this poem and write an essay showing how the details of the poem support your choice.

Dwight Okita (b. 1958)

Poet and playwright Dwight Okita, a lifelong resident of Chicago, is of Japanese American descent. His mother spent four years during World War II in a relocation center, one of ten in which the United States government interned more than 100,000 Japanese Americans in response to the Japanese attack on Pearl Harbor. Ironically, during the same time, Okita's father was serving in the 442nd Battalion, composed of Japanese American citizens. Okita's Crossing with the Light *was published in paperback in 1992.*

IN RESPONSE TO EXECUTIVE ORDER 9066: ALL AMERICANS OF JAPANESE DESCENT MUST REPORT TO RELOCATION CENTERS   (1983)

Dear Sirs:
Of course I'll come. I've packed my galoshes
and three packets of tomato seeds. Janet calls them
"love apples." My father says where we're going

5   they won't grow.
I am a fourteen-year-old girl with bad spelling
and a messy room. If it helps any, I will tell you
I have always felt funny using chopsticks
and my favorite food is hot dogs.

10   My best friend is a white girl named Denise—
we look at boys together. She sat in front of me

all through grade school because of our names:
O'Connor, Ozawa. I know the back of Denise's head very well.
I tell her she's going bald. She tells me I copy on tests.
15   We're best friends.

I saw Denise today in Geography class.
She was sitting on the other side of the room.
"You're trying to start a war," she said, "giving secrets away
to the Enemy, Why can't you keep your big mouth shut?"
20   I didn't know what to say.
I gave her a packet of tomato seeds
and asked her to plant them for me, told her
when the first tomato ripened
she'd miss me.

Questions for Engagement, Response, and Analysis

1. Who is the speaker in this epistolary poem? What seems to be the speaker's attitude toward the executive order to report to a relocation center?
2. Contrast the relationship between the speaker and Denise in stanza 2 with their relationship in stanza 3.
3. How does the attitude of the speaker in this poem compare to that of the speaker in "Immigrants"?
4. Explain the symbolism of the tomato seeds.
5. What is the tone of the poem? What elements contribute to creation of this tone?

Crafting Arguments

1. In an essay, analyze the techniques that Okita uses to craft this epistolary poem.

D R A M A

Susan Glaspell (1882–1948)

Susan Glaspell wrote many plays for the Provincetown Players in Cape Cod, Massachusetts. She won a Pulitzer Prize for Alison's House *(1931), a play based loosely on the family and lifestyle of Emily Dickinson.* Trifles *(1916), written in ten days for the Provincetown Players, was inspired by a murder trial that Glaspell encountered while she was a reporter for a Des Moines newspaper. One year later she wrote the short story version, "A Jury of Her Peers."*

TRIFLES (1916)

Characters

GEORGE HENDERSON: county attorney
HENRY: sheriff
LEWIS HALE: a neighboring farmer
MRS. PETERS
MRS. HALE

SCENE

The kitchen in the now abandoned farmhouse of John Wright, a gloomy kitchen, and left without having been put in order— unwashed pans under the sink, a loaf of bread outside the breadbox, a dish towel on the table—other signs of incompleted work. At the rear the outer door opens and the Sheriff comes in followed by the County Attorney and Hale. The Sheriff and Hale are men in middle life, the County Attorney is a young man; all are much bundled up and go at once to the stove. They are followed by two women—the Sheriff's wife first; she is a slight wiry woman, a thin nervous face. Mrs. Hale is larger and would ordinarily be called more comfortable looking, but she is disturbed now and looks fearfully about as she enters. The women have come in slowly, and stand close together near the door.

COUNTY ATTORNEY (*Rubbing his hands*): This feels good. Come up to the fire, ladies.

MRS. PETERS (*After taking a step forward*): I'm not—cold.

SHERIFF (*Unbuttoning his overcoat and stepping away from the stove as if to mark the beginning of official business*): Now, Mr. Hale, before we move things about, you explain to Mr. Henderson just what you saw when you came here yesterday morning.

COUNTY ATTORNEY: By the way, has anything been moved? Are things just as you left them yesterday?

SHERIFF (*Looking about*): It's just the same. When it dropped below zero last night I thought I'd better send Frank out this morning to make a fire for us—no use getting pneumonia with a big case on, but I told him not to touch anything except the stove—and you know Frank.

COUNTY ATTORNEY: Somebody should have been left here yesterday.

SHERIFF: Oh—yesterday. When I had to send Frank to Morris Center for that man who went crazy—I want you to know I had my hands full yesterday, I knew you could get back from Omaha by today and as long as I went over everything here myself—

COUNTY ATTORNEY: Well, Mr. Hale, tell just what happened when you came here yesterday morning.

20 HALE: Harry and I had started to town with a load of potatoes. We came along the road from my place and as I got here I said, "I'm going to see if I can't get John Wright to go in with me on a party telephone." I spoke to Wright about it once before and he put me off, saying folks talked too much anyway, and all he asked was peace and quiet—I guess you know about how much he talked himself; but I thought maybe if I went to the house and talked about it before his wife, though I said to Harry that I didn't know as what his wife wanted made much difference to John—

COUNTY ATTORNEY: Let's talk about that later, Mr. Hale. I do want to talk
30   about that, but tell now just what happened when you got to the house.

HALE: I didn't hear or see anything; I knocked at the door, and still it was all quiet inside. I knew they must be up, it was past eight o'clock. So I knocked again, and I thought I heard somebody say, "Come in." I wasn't sure, I'm not sure yet, but I opened the door—this door (*Indicating the door by which the two women are still standing*) and there in that rocker—(*Pointing to it*) sat Mrs. Wright.

COUNTY ATTORNEY: What—was she doing?

HALE: She was rockin' back and forth. She had her apron in her hand and was kind of—pleating it.

40 COUNTY ATTORNEY: And how did she—look?

HALE: Well, she looked queer.

COUNTY ATTORNEY: How do you mean—queer?

HALE: Well, as if she didn't know what she was going to do next. And kind of done up.

COUNTY ATTORNEY: How did she seem to feel about your coming?

HALE: Why, I don't think she minded—one way or other. She didn't pay much attention. I said, "How do, Mrs. Wright, it's cold, ain't it?" and she said, "Is it?"—and went on kind of pleating at her apron. Well, I was surprised; she didn't ask me to come up to the stove, or to set
50   down, but just sat there, not even looking at me, so I said, "I want to see John." And then she—laughed. I guess you would call it a laugh. I thought of Harry and the team outside, so I said a little sharp: "Can't I see John?" "No," she says, kind o' dull like. "Ain't he home?" says I. "Yes," says she, "He's home." "Then why can't I see him?" I asked her, out of patience. "'Cause he's dead," says she. "Dead?"

says I. She just nodded her head, not getting a bit excited, but rockin' back and forth. "Why—where is he?" says I, not knowing what to say. She just pointed upstairs—like that (*Himself pointing to the room above*) I got up, with the idea of going up there. I walked from there to here—then I says, "Why, what did he die of?" "He died of a rope round his neck," says she, and just went on pleatin' at her apron. Well, I went out and called Harry. I thought I might—need help. We went upstairs and there he was lyin'—

COUNTY ATTORNEY: I think I'd rather have you go into that upstairs, where you can point it all out. Just go on now with the rest of the story.

HALE: Well, my first thought was to get that rope off. It looked . . . (*Stops, his face twitches*) . . . but Harry, he went up to him, and he said, "No, he's dead all right, and we'd better not touch anything." So we went back down stairs. She was still sitting that same way. "Has anybody been notified?" I asked. "No," says she, unconcerned. "Who did this, Mrs. Wright?" said Harry. He said it businesslike—and she stopped pleatin' of her apron. "I don't know," she says. "You don't *know*?" says Harry. "No," says she. "Weren't you sleepin' in the bed with him?" says Harry. "Yes," says she, "but I was on the inside." "Somebody slipped a rope around his neck and strangled him and you didn't wake up?" says Harry. "I didn't wake up," she said after him. We must 'a looked as if we didn't see how that could be, for after a minute she said, "I sleep sound." Harry was going to ask her more questions but I said maybe we ought to let her tell her story first to the coroner, or the sheriff, so Harry went fast as he could to Rivers' place, where there's a telephone.

COUNTY ATTORNEY: And what did Mrs. Wright do when she knew that you had gone for the coroner?

HALE: She moved from that chair to this one over here (*Pointing to a small chair in the corner*) and just sat there with her hands held together and looking down. I got a feeling that I ought to make some conversation, so I said I had come in to see if John wanted to put in a telephone, and at that she started to laugh, and then she stopped and looked at me—scared. (*The County Attorney, who has had his notebook out, makes a note.*) I dunno, maybe it wasn't scared. I wouldn't like to say it was. Soon Harry got back, and then Dr. Lloyd came, and you, Mr. Peters, and so I guess that's all I know that you don't.

COUNTY ATTORNEY (*Looking around*): I guess we'll go upstairs first—and then out to the barn and around there. (*To the Sheriff*) You're convinced that there was nothing important here—nothing that would point to any motive.

SHERIFF: Nothing here but kitchen things.

(*The County Attorney, after again looking around the kitchen, opens the door of a cupboard closet. He gets up on a chair and looks on a shelf. Pulls his hand away, sticky.*)

COUNTY ATTORNEY: Here's a nice mess.

(The women draw nearer.)

MRS. PETERS *(To the other woman):* Oh, her fruit; it did freeze. *(To the County Attorney)* She worried about that when it turned so cold. She said the fire'd go out and her jars would break.

SHERIFF: Well, can you beat the women! Held for murder and worryin' about her preserves.

COUNTY ATTORNEY: I guess before we're through she may have something more serious than preserves to worry about.

HALE: Well, women are used to worrying over trifles.

(The two women move a little closer together.)

COUNTY ATTORNEY *(With the gallantry of a young politician):* And yet, for all their worries, what would we do without the ladies? *(The women do not unbend. He goes to the sink, takes a dipperful of water from the pail and pouring it into a basin, washes his hands. Starts to wipe them on the roller towel, turns it for a cleaner place.)* Dirty towels! *(Kicks his foot against the pans under the sink.)* Not much of a housekeeper, would you say, ladies?

MRS. HALE *(Stiffly):* There's a great deal of work to be done on a farm.

COUNTY ATTORNEY: To be sure. And yet *(With a little bow to her)* I know there are some Dickson county farmhouses which do not have such roller towels.

(He gives it a pull to expose its full length again.)

MRS. HALE: Those towels get dirty awful quick. Men's hands aren't always as clean as they might be.

COUNTY ATTORNEY: Ah, loyal to your sex, I see. But you and Mrs. Wright were neighbors. I suppose you were friends, too.

MRS. HALE *(Shaking her head):* I've not seen much of her of late years. I've not been in this house—it's more than a year.

COUNTY ATTORNEY: And why was that? You didn't like her?

MRS. HALE: I liked her all well enough. Farmers' wives have their hands full, Mr. Henderson. And then—

COUNTY ATTORNEY: Yes—?

MRS. HALE *(Looking about):* It never seemed a very cheerful place.

COUNTY ATTORNEY: No—it's not cheerful. I shouldn't say she had the homemaking instinct.

MRS. HALE: Well, I don't know as Wright had, either.

COUNTY ATTORNEY: You mean that they didn't get on very well?

MRS. HALE: No, I don't mean anything. But I don't think a place'd be any cheerfuller for John Wright's being in it.

COUNTY ATTORNEY: I'd like to talk more of that a little later. I want to get the lay of things upstairs now.

(He goes to the left, where three steps lead to a stair door.)

SHERIFF: I suppose anything Mrs. Peters does'll be all right. She was to take in some clothes for her, you know, and a few little things. We left in such a hurry yesterday.

COUNTY ATTORNEY: Yes, but I would like to see what you take, Mrs. Peters, and keep an eye out for anything that might be of use to us.

MRS. PETERS: Yes, Mr. Henderson.

(The women listen to the men's steps on the stairs, then look about the kitchen.)

MRS. HALE: I'd hate to have men coming into my kitchen, snooping around and criticizing.

(She arranges the pans under sink which the County Attorney had shoved out of place.)

MRS. PETERS: Of course it's no more than their duty.

MRS. HALE: Duty's all right, but I guess that deputy sheriff that came out to make the fire might have got a little of this on. *(Gives the roller towel a pull.)* Wish I'd thought of that sooner. Seems mean to talk about her for not having things slicked up when she had to come away in such a hurry.

MRS. PETERS *(Who has gone to a small table in the left rear corner of the room, and lifted one end of a towel that covers a pan.)*: She had bread set.

(Stands still.)

MRS. HALE *(Eyes fixed on a loaf of bread beside the breadbox, which is on a low shelf at the other side of the room. Moves slowly toward it):* She was going to put this in there. *(Picks up loaf, then abruptly drops it. In a manner of returning to familiar things)* It's a shame about her fruit. I wonder if it's all gone. *(Gets up on the chair and looks.)* I think there's some here that's all right, Mrs. Peters. Yes— here; *(Holding it toward the window)* this is cherries, too. *(Looking again)* I declare I believe that's the only one. *(Gets down, bottle in her hand. Goes to the sink and wipes it off on the outside.)* She'll feel awful bad after all her hard work in the hot weather. I remember the afternoon I put up my cherries last summer.

(She puts the bottle on the big kitchen table, center of the room. With a sigh, is about to sit down in the rocking-chair. Before she is seated realizes what chair it is; with a slow look at it, steps back. The chair which she has touched rocks back and forth.)

MRS. PETERS: Well, I must get those things from the front room closet. *(She goes to the door at the right, but after looking into the other room, steps back.)* You coming with me, Mrs. Hale? You could help me carry them.

(They go in the other room; reappear, Mrs. Peters carrying a dress and skirt, Mrs. Hale following with a pair of shoes.)

MRS. PETERS: My, it's cold in there.

(She puts the clothes on the big table, and hurries to the stove.)

MRS. HALE *(Examining her skirt)*: Wright was close. I think maybe that's why she kept so much to herself. She didn't even belong to the Ladies Aid. I suppose she felt she couldn't do her part, and then you don't enjoy things when you feel shabby. She used to wear pretty

170   clothes and be lively, when she was Minnie Foster, one of the town girls singing in the choir. But that—oh, that was thirty years ago. This all you was to take in?

MRS. PETERS: She said she wanted an apron. Funny thing to want, for there isn't much to get you dirty in jail, goodness knows. But I suppose just to make her feel more natural. She said they was in the top drawer in this cupboard. Yes, here. And then her little shawl that always hung behind the door. *(Opens stair door and looks)* Yes, here it is.

(Quickly shuts door leading upstairs.)

MRS. HALE *(Abruptly moving toward her.)*: Mrs. Peters?

MRS. PETERS: Yes, Mrs. Hale?

MRS. HALE: Do you think she did it?

180   MRS. PETERS: *(In a frightened voice.)*: Oh, I don't know.

MRS. HALE: Well, I don't think she did. Asking for an apron and her little shawl. Worrying about her fruit.

MRS. PETERS *(Starts to speak, glances up, where footsteps are heard in the room above. In a low voice)*: Mr. Peters says it looks bad for her. Mr. Henderson is awful sarcastic in a speech and he'll make fun of her sayin' she didn't wake up.

MRS. HALE: Well, I guess John Wright didn't wake when they was slipping that rope under his neck.

MRS. PETERS: No, it's strange. It must have been done awful crafty and still. They say it was such a—funny way to kill a man, rigging it all

190   up like that.

MRS. HALE: That's just what Mr. Hale said. There was a gun in the house. He says that's what he can't understand.

MRS. PETERS: Mr. Henderson said coming out that what was needed for the case was a motive; something to show anger, or—sudden feeling.

MRS. HALE *(Who is standing by the table)*: Well, I don't see any signs of anger around here. *(She puts her hand on the dish towel which lies on the table, stands looking down at table, one half of which is clean, the other half messy.)* It's wiped to here. *(Makes a move as if to finish work, then turns and looks at loaf of bread outside the breadbox. Drops towel. In that voice of coming back to familiar*

200   *things)* Wonder how they are finding things upstairs. I hope she had it a little more redup there. You know, it seems kind of *sneaking.*

Locking her up in town and then coming out here and trying to get her own house to turn against her!

MRS. PETERS: But Mrs. Hale, the law is the law.

MRS. HALE: I s'pose 'tis. *(Unbuttoning her coat)* Better loosen up your things, Mrs. Peters. You won't feel them when you go out.

(Mrs. Peters takes off her fur tippet, goes to hang it on hook at back of room, stands looking at the under part of the small corner table.)

MRS. PETERS: She was piecing a quilt.

(She brings the large sewing basket and they look at the bright pieces.)

MRS. HALE: It's log cabin pattern. Pretty, isn't it? I wonder if she was goin' to quilt it or just knot it?

(Footsteps have been heard coming down the stairs. The Sheriff enters followed by Hale and the County Attorney.)

SHERIFF: They wonder if she was going to quilt it or just knot it!

(The men laugh; the women look abashed.)

210   COUNTY ATTORNEY *(Rubbing his hands over the stove)*: Frank's fire didn't do much up there, did it? Well, let's go out to the barn and get that cleared up.

(The men go outside.)

MRS. HALE *(Resentfully)*: I don't know as there's anything so strange, our takin' up our time with little things while we're waiting for them to get the evidence. *(She sits down at the big table smoothing out a block with decision.)* I don't see as it's anything to laugh about.

MRS. PETERS *(Apologetically)*: Of course they've got awful important things on their minds.

(Pulls up a chair and joins Mrs. Hale at the table.)

MRS. HALE *(Examining another block)*: Mrs. Peters, look at this one.
220   Here, this is the one she was working on, and look at the sewing! All the rest of it has been so nice and even. And look at this! It's all over the place! Why, it looks as if she didn't know what she was about!

(After she has said this they look at each, then start to glance back at the door. After an instant Mrs. Hale has pulled at a knot and ripped the sewing.)

MRS. PETERS: Oh, what are you doing, Mrs. Hale?

MRS. HALE *(Mildly)*: Just pulling out a stitch or two that's not sewed very good. *(Threading a needle)* Bad sewing always made me fidgety.

MRS. PETERS *(Nervously)*: I don't think we ought to touch things.

230 MRS. HALE: I'll just finish up this end. (*Suddenly stopping and leaning forward*) Mrs. Peters?

MRS. PETERS: Yes, Mrs. Hale?

MRS. HALE: What do you suppose she was so nervous about?

MRS. PETERS: Oh—I don't know. I don't know as she was nervous. I sometimes sew awful queer when I'm just tired. (*Mrs. Hale starts to say something, looks at Mrs. Peters, then goes on sewing.*) Well, I must get these things wrapped up. They may be through sooner than we think. (*Putting apron and other things together*) I wonder where I can find a piece of paper, and string.

MRS. HALE: In that cupboard, maybe.

MRS. PETERS: (*Looking in cupboard*): Why, here's a birdcage. (Holds it up) Did she have a bird, Mrs. Hale?

240 MRS. HALE: Why, I don't know whether she did or not—I've not been here for so long. There was a man around last year selling canaries cheap, but I don't know as she took one; maybe she did. She used to sing real pretty herself.

MRS. PETERS (*Glancing around*): Seems funny to think of a bird here. But she must have had one, or why would she have a cage? I wonder what happened to it.

MRS. HALE: I s'pose maybe the cat got it.

MRS. PETERS: No, she didn't have a cat. She's got that feeling some people have about cats—being afraid of them. My cat got in her room

250 and she was real upset and asked me to take it out.

MRS. HALE: My sister Bessie was like that. Queer, ain't it?

MRS. PETERS (*Examining the cage*): Why, look at this door. It's broke. One hinge is pulled apart.

MRS. HALE (*Looking too*): Looks as if someone must have been rough with it.

MRS. PETERS: Why, yes.

(*She brings the cage forward and puts it on the table.*)

MRS. HALE: I wish if they're going to find any evidence they'd be about it. I don't like this place.

MRS. PETERS: But I'm awful glad you came with me, Mrs. Hale. It would

260 be lonesome for me sitting here alone.

MRS. HALE: It would, wouldn't it? (*Dropping her sewing*) But I tell you what I do wish, Mrs. Peters. I wish I had come over sometimes when *she* was here. I—(*Looking round the room*)—wish I had.

MRS. PETERS: But of course you were awful busy, Mrs. Hale—your house and your children.

MRS. HALE: I could've come. I stayed away because it weren't cheerful— and that's why I ought to have come. I—I've never liked this place. Maybe because it's down in a hollow and you don't see the road. I

270 dunno what it is but it's a lonesome place and always was. I wish I had come over to see Minnie Foster sometimes. I can see now—

(Shakes her head).

MRS. PETERS: Well, you mustn't reproach yourself, Mrs. Hale. Somehow we just don't see how it is with other folks until—something comes up.

MRS. HALE: Not having children makes less work—but it makes a quiet house, and Wright out to work all day, and no company when he did come in. Did you know John Wright, Mrs. Peters?

MRS. PETERS: Not to know him; I've seen him in town. They say he was a good man.

MRS. HALE: Yes—good; he didn't drink, and kept his word as well as most, I guess, and paid his debts. But he was a hard man, Mrs.
280   Peters. Just to pass the time of day with him—*(Shivers)* Like a raw wind that gets to the bone. *(Pauses, her eye falling on the cage)* I should think she would'a wanted a bird. But what do you suppose went with it?

MRS. PETERS: I don't know, unless it got sick and died.

(She reaches over and swings the broken door, swings it again. Both women watch it.)

MRS. HALE: You weren't raised round here, were you? *(Mrs. Peters shakes her head).* You didn't know—her?

MRS. PETERS: Not till they brought her yesterday.

MRS. HALE: She—come to think of it, she was kind of a like a bird herself—real sweet and pretty, but kind of timid and—fluttery. How—she—
290   did—change. *(Silence, then as if struck by a happy thought and relieved to get back to everyday things).* Tell you what, Mrs. Peters, why don't you take the quilt in with you? It might take up her mind.

MRS. PETERS: Why, I think that's a real nice idea, Mrs. Hale. There couldn't possibly be an objection to it, could there? Now, just what would I take? I wonder if her patches are in here—and her things.

(They look in the sewing basket.)

MRS. HALE: Here's some red. I expect this has got sewing things in it. *(Brings out a fancy box)* What a pretty box. Looks like something somebody would give you. Maybe her scissors are in here. *(Opens box. Suddenly puts her hand to her nose)* Why—*(Mrs. Peters bends nearer, then turns her face away).* There's something wrapped up
300   in this piece of silk.

MRS. PETERS: Why, this isn't her scissors.

MRS. HALE *(Lifting the silk):* Oh, Mrs. Peters—it's—

(Mrs. Peters bends closer).

MRS. PETERS: It's the bird.

MRS. HALE *(Jumping up):* But, Mrs. Peters—look at it! Its neck! Look at its neck! It's all—other side *to.*

MRS. PETERS: Somebody—wrung—its—neck.

(Their eyes meet. A look of growing comprehension, of horror. Steps are heard outside. Mrs. Hale slips the box under quilt pieces, and sinks into her chair. Enter Sheriff and County Attorney. Mrs. Peters rises.)

COUNTY ATTORNEY: *(As one turning from serious things to little pleasantries)*: Well, ladies, have you decided whether she was going to quilt it or knot it?

310 MRS. PETERS: We think she was going to—knot it.

COUNTY ATTORNEY: Well, that's interesting, I'm sure. *(Seeing the birdcage)* Has the bird flown?

MRS. HALE *(Putting more quilt pieces over the box)*: We think the—cat got it.

COUNTY ATTORNEY *(Preoccupied)*: Is there a cat?

(Mrs. Hale glances in a quick covert way at Mrs. Peters.)

MRS. PETERS: Well, not now. They're superstitious, you know. They leave.

COUNTY ATTORNEY: *(To Sheriff Peters, continuing an interrupted conversation)*: No sign at all of anyone having come from the outside. Their own rope. Now let's go up again and go over it piece by piece. *(They start upstairs)*. It would have to have been someone who knew just the—

(Mrs. Peters sits down. The two women sit there not looking at one another, but as if peering into something and at the same time holding back. When they talk now it is in the manner of feeling their way over strange ground, as if afraid of what they are saying, but as if they can not help saying it.)

320 MRS. HALE: She liked the bird. She was going to bury it in that pretty box.

MRS. PETERS *(In a whisper)*: When I was a girl—my kitten—there was a boy took a hatchet, and before my eyes—and before I could get there—*(Covers her face an instant)* If they hadn't held me back I would have—*(Catches herself, looks upstairs where steps are heard, falters weakly)*—hurt him.

MRS. HALE *(With a slow look around her)*: I wonder how it would seem never to have had any children around. *(Pause)* No, Wright wouldn't like the bird—a thing that sang. She used to sing. He killed that, too.

MRS. PETERS *(Moving uneasily)*: We don't know who killed the bird.

330 MRS. HALE: I knew John Wright.

MRS. PETERS: It was an awful thing was done in this house that night, Mrs. Hale. Killing a man while he slept, slipping a rope around his neck that choked the life out of him.

MRS. HALE: His neck. Choked the life out of him.

(Her hand goes out and rests on the birdcage.)

MRS. PETERS *(With rising voice)*: We don't know who killed him. We don't know.

MRS. HALE (*Her own feeling not interrupted*): If there'd been years and years of nothing, then a bird to sing to you, it would be awful—still, after the bird was still.

340 MRS. PETERS (*Something within her speaking*): I know what stillness is. When we homesteaded in Dakota, and my first baby died—after he was two years old, and me with no other then—

MRS. HALE (*Moving*): How soon do you suppose they'll be through, looking for the evidence?

MRS. PETERS: I know what stillness is. (*Pulling herself back*) The law has got to punish crime, Mrs. Hale.

MRS. HALE (*Not as if answering that*): I wish you'd seen Minnie Foster when she wore a white dress with blue ribbons and stood up there in the choir and sang. (*A look around the room*) Oh, I *wish* I'd come

350 over here once in a while! That was a crime! That was a crime! Who's going to punish that?

MRS. PETERS (*Looking upstairs*): We mustn't—take on.

MRS. HALE: I might have known she needed help! I know how things can be—for women. I tell you, it's queer, Mrs. Peters. We live close together and we live far apart. We all go through the same things— it's all just a different kind of the same thing. (*Brushes her eyes; noticing the bottle of fruit, reaches out for it*) If I was you I wouldn't tell her her fruit was gone. Tell her it *ain't*. Tell her it's all right. Take this in to prove it to her. She—she may never know whether it was broke or not.

MRS. PETERS (*Takes the bottle, looks about for something to wrap it in; takes petticoat from the clothes brought from the other room, very*

360 *nervously begins winding this around the bottle. In a false voice*): My, it's a good thing the men couldn't hear us. Wouldn't they just laugh! Getting all stirred up over a little thing like a—dead canary. As if that could have anything to do with—with—wouldn't they *laugh*!

(*The men are heard coming down stairs*).

MRS. HALE (*Under her breath*): Maybe they would—maybe they wouldn't.

COUNTY ATTORNEY: No, Peters, it's all perfectly clear except a reason for doing it. Something to show—something to make a story about—a thing that would connect up with this strange way of doing it—

(*The women's eyes meet for an instant. Enter Hale from outer door*).

HALE: Well, I've got the team around. Pretty cold out there.

370 COUNTY ATTORNEY: I'm going to stay here a while myself. (*To the Sheriff*) You can send Frank out for me, can't you? I want to go over everything. I'm not satisfied that we can't do better.

SHERIFF: Do you want to see what Mrs. Peters is going to take in?

(*The County Attorney goes to the table, picks up the apron, laughs.*)

COUNTY ATTORNEY: Oh, I guess they're not very dangerous things the ladies have picked out. *(Moves a few things about, disturbing the quilt pieces which cover the box. Steps back)* No, Mrs. Peters doesn't need supervising. For that matter, a sheriff's wife is married to the law. Ever think of it that way, Mrs. Peters?

MRS. PETERS: Not—just that way.

380 SHERIFF *(Chuckling)*: Married to the law. (Moves toward the other room) I just want you to come in here a minute, George. We ought to take a look at these windows.

COUNTY ATTORNEY *(Scoffingly)*: Oh, windows!

SHERIFF: We'll be right out, Mr. Hale.

> *(Hale goes outside. The Sheriff follows the County Attorney into the other room. Then Mrs. Hale rises, hands tight together, looking intensely at Mrs. Peters, whose eyes make a slow turn, finally meeting Mrs. Hale's. A moment Mrs. Hale holds her, then her own eyes point the way to where the box is concealed. Suddenly Mrs. Peters throws back quilt pieces and tries to put the box in the bag she is wearing. It is too big. She opens box, starts to take bird out, cannot touch it, goes to pieces, stands there helpless. Sound of a knob turning in the other room. Mrs. Hale snatches the box and puts it in the pocket of her big coat. Enter County Attorney and Sheriff.)*

COUNTY ATTORNEY: *(Facetiously)*: Well, Henry, at least we found out that she was not going to quilt it. She was going to—what is it you call it, ladies?

MRS. HALE: *(Her hand against her pocket)*: We call it—knot it, Mr. Henderson.

Curtain.

Questions for Engagement, Response, and Analysis

1. What is the setting of the play? How is it central to the situation portrayed?

2. How do the approaches of the men investigating the death differ from the women's approach? What do these differences reveal about them?

3. What is the attitude of the men in the story toward the women?

4. Putting together all the signs in the play, what conclusions can you draw about who killed Mr. Wright and about the killer's motive?

5. Explain the examples of both verbal and situational irony in the play.

6. Glaspell changed the title of the play, *Trifles*, when she wrote the short story, "A Jury of Her Peers." Which title do you consider more appropriate? Why?

Crafting Arguments

1. In an essay, contrast the men's manner and approach to the investigation with that of the women. Why are the women able to solve the murder when the men are not?

2. In an essay, argue that Mrs. Peters and Mrs. Hale do or do not make the right decision when they decide to withhold evidence from the men. Do their reasons justify their becoming, in effect, Minnie's judge and jury?

3. Write an essay explaining how the objects in the kitchen are symbolic of Minnie's life after her marriage.

Casebook
on Tim O'Brien

Perhaps more vividly and convincingly than any other writer, Tim O'Brien, in his stories and novels on Vietnam, graphically illustrates William Tecumseh Sherman's statement, "War is hell." This casebook, containing three of O'Brien's stories as well as critical analyses of O'Brien's work, enables you to explore in class discussion and in writing the soul-searching, sometimes gut-wrenching dilemma of young people unwillingly drafted to fight in the Vietnam War, a war many did not believe in and very few understood.

Tim O'Brien (b. 1946)

Upon graduation from Macalester College in Minnesota in 1968, O'Brien was drafted into the infantry and, though he strongly opposed the war, went to Vietnam as a foot soldier. During part of his time in Vietnam, O'Brien and his platoon were stationed at My Lai, where, the previous year, panicking American soldiers had killed in cold blood every living thing in the village. Vietnam has been the primary focus of O'Brien's fiction. His books include If I Die in a Combat Zone, Box Me Up and Ship Me Home *(1973);* Northern Lights *(1975);* Going After Cacciato *(1978), which won the National Book Award;* The Things They Carried *(1990), a collection of interconnected stories, including the three printed here; and* In the Lake of the Woods *(1990), which, in an effort to portray the tragic truth of the My Lai massacre, mixes fact and fiction.* More recent works are Tomcat in Love *(1998), a comic novel, and* July, July *(2002). O'Brien teaches Creative Writing at Southwest Texas State University.*

ON THE RAINY RIVER (1990)

1   This is one story I've never told before. Not to anyone. Not to my parents, not to my brother or sister, not even to my wife. To go into it, I've always thought, would only cause embarrassment for all of us, a sudden need to be elsewhere, which is the natural response to a confession. Even now, I'll admit, the story makes me squirm. For more than twenty years I've had to live with it, feeling the shame, trying to push it away, and so by this act of remembrance, by putting the facts down on paper, I'm hoping to relieve at least some of the pressure on my dreams. Still, it's a hard story to tell. All of us, I suppose, like to believe that in a moral emergency we will behave like the heroes of our youth, bravely and forthrightly, without thought of personal loss or discredit. Certainly that was my conviction back in the summer of 1968. Tim O'Brien: a secret hero. The Lone Ranger. If the stakes ever became high enough—if the evil were evil enough, if the good were good enough—I would simply tap a secret reservoir of courage that had been accumulating inside me over the years. Courage, I seemed to think, comes to us in finite quantities, like an inheritance, and by being frugal and stashing it away and letting it earn interest, we steadily increase our moral capital in preparation for that day when the account must be drawn down. It was a comforting theory. It dispensed with all those bothersome little acts of daily courage; it offered hope and grace to the repetitive coward; it justified the past while amortizing the future.

2   In June of 1968, a month after graduating from Macalester College, I was drafted to fight a war I hated. I was twenty-one years old. Young, yes, and politically naive, but even so the American war in Vietnam seemed to me wrong. Certain blood was being shed for uncertain reasons. I saw no unity of purpose, no consensus on matters of philosophy or history or law. The very facts were shrouded in uncertainty: Was it a civil war? A war of national liberation or simple aggression? Who started it, and when, and why? What really happened to the USS *Maddox* on that dark night in the Gulf of Tonkin? Was Ho Chi Minh a Communist stooge, or a nationalist savior, or both, or neither? What about the Geneva Accords? What about SEATO and the Cold War? What about dominoes? America was divided on these and a thousand other issues, and the debate had spilled out across the floor of the United States Senate and into the streets, and smart men in pinstripes could not agree on even the most fundamental matters of public policy. The only certainty that summer was moral confusion. It was my view then, and still is, that you don't

make war without knowing why. Knowledge, of course, is always imperfect, but it seemed to me that when a nation goes to war it must have reasonable confidence in the justice and imperative of its cause. You can't fix your mistakes. Once people are dead, you can't make them undead.

3   In any case those were my convictions, and back in college I had taken a modest stand against the war. Nothing radical, no hothead stuff, just ringing a few doorbells for Gene McCarthy, composing a few tedious, uninspired editorials for the campus newspaper. Oddly, though, it was almost entirely an intellectual activity. I brought some energy to it, of course, but it was the energy that accompanies almost any abstract endeavor; I felt no personal danger; I felt no sense of an impending crisis in my life. Stupidly, with a kind of smug removal that I can't begin to fathom, I assumed that the problems of killing and dying did not fall within my special province.

4   The draft notice arrived on June 17, 1968. It was a humid afternoon, I remember, cloudy and very quiet, and I'd just come in from a round of golf. My mother and father were having lunch out in the kitchen. I remember opening up the letter, scanning the first few lines, feeling the blood go thick behind my eyes. I remember a sound in my head. It wasn't thinking, just a silent howl. A million things all at once—I was too *good* for this war. Too smart, too compassionate, too everything. It couldn't happen. I was above it. I had the world dicked—Phi Beta Kappa and summa cum laude and president of the student body and a full-ride scholarship for grad studies at Harvard. A mistake, maybe—a foul-up in the paperwork. I was no soldier. I hated Boy Scouts. I hated camping out. I hated dirt and tents and mosquitoes. The sight of blood made me queasy, and I couldn't tolerate authority, and I didn't know a rifle from a slingshot. I was a *liberal*, for Christ sake: If they needed fresh bodies, why not draft some back-to-the-stone-age hawk? Or some dumb jingo in his hard hat and Bomb Hanoi button, or one of LBJ's pretty daughters, or Westmoreland's whole handsome family—nephews and nieces and baby grandson. There should be a law, I thought. If you support a war, if you think it's worth the price, that's fine, but you have to put your own precious fluids on the line. You have to head for the front and hook up with an infantry unit and help spill the blood. And you have to bring along your wife, or your kids, or your lover. A law, I thought.

5   I remember the rage in my stomach. Later it burned down to a smoldering self-pity, then to numbness. At dinner that night my father asked what my plans were.

6   "Nothing," I said. "Wait."

7   I spent the summer of 1968 working in an Armour meatpacking plant in my hometown of Worthington, Minnesota. The plant specialized in pork products, and for eight hours a day I stood on a quarter-mile assembly line—more properly, a disassembly line—removing blood clots from the necks of dead pigs. My job title, I believe, was Declotter. After slaughter,

the hogs were decapitated, split down the length of the belly, pried open, eviscerated, and strung up by the hind hocks on a high conveyer belt. Then gravity took over. By the time a carcass reached my spot on the line, the fluids had mostly drained out, everything except for thick clots of blood in the neck and upper chest cavity. To remove the stuff, I used a kind of water gun. The machine was heavy, maybe eighty pounds, and was suspended from the ceiling by a heavy rubber cord. There was some bounce to it, and elastic up-and-down give, and the trick was to maneuver the gun with your whole body, not lifting with the arms, just letting the rubber cord do the work for you. At one end was a trigger; at the muzzle end was a small nozzle and a steel roller brush. As a carcass passed by, you'd lean forward and swing the gun up against the clots and squeeze the trigger, all in one motion, and the brush would whirl and water would come shooting out and you'd hear a quick splattering sound as the clots dissolved into a fine red mist. It was not pleasant work. Goggles were a necessity, and a rubber apron, but even so it was like standing for eight hours a day under a lukewarm blood-shower. At night I'd go home smelling of pig. It wouldn't go away. Even after a hot bath, scrubbing hard, the stink was always there—like old bacon, or sausage, a dense greasy pig-stink that soaked deep into my skin and hair. Among other things, I remember, it was tough getting dates that summer. I felt isolated; I spent a lot of time alone. And there was also that draft notice tucked away in my wallet.

8   In the evenings I'd sometimes borrow my father's car and drive aimlessly around town, feeling sorry for myself, thinking about the war and the pig factory and how my life seemed to be collapsing toward slaughter. I felt paralyzed. All around me the options seemed to be narrowing, as if I were hurtling down a huge black funnel, the whole world squeezing in tight. There was no happy way out. The government had ended most graduate school deferments; the waiting lists for the National Guard and Reserves were impossibly long; my health was solid; I didn't qualify for CO status—no religious grounds, no history as a pacifist. Moreover, I could not claim to be opposed to war as a matter of general principle. There were occasions, I believed, when a nation was justified in using military force to achieve its ends, to stop a Hitler or some comparable evil, and I told myself that in such circumstances I would've willingly marched off to the battle. The problem, though, was that a draft board did not let you choose your war.

9   Beyond all this, or at the very center, was the raw fact of terror. I did not want to die. Not ever. But certainly not then, not there, not in a wrong war. Driving up Main Street, past the courthouse and the Ben Franklin store, I sometimes felt the fear spreading inside me like weeds. I imagined myself dead. I imagined myself doing things I could not do—charging an enemy position, taking aim at another human being.

10   At some point in mid-July I began thinking seriously about Canada. The border lay a few hundred miles north, an eight-hour drive. Both my conscience and my instincts were telling me to make a break for it, just

take off and run like hell and never stop. In the beginning the idea seemed purely abstract, the word Canada printing itself out in my head; but after a time I could see particular shapes and images, the sorry details of my own future—a hotel room in Winnipeg, a battered old suitcase, my father's eyes as I tried to explain myself over the telephone. I could almost hear his voice, and my mother's. Run, I'd think. Then I'd think, Impossible. Then a second later I'd think, *Run*.

11   It was a kind of schizophrenia. A moral split. I couldn't make up my mind. I feared the war, yes, but I also feared exile. I was afraid of walking away from my own life, my friends and my family, my whole history, everything that mattered to me. I feared losing the respect of my parents. I feared the law. I feared ridicule and censure. My hometown was a conservative little spot on the prairie, a place where tradition counted, and it was easy to imagine people sitting around a table down at the old Gobbler Café on Main Street, coffee cups poised, the conversation slowly zeroing in on the young O'Brien kid, how the damned sissy had taken off for Canada. At night, when I couldn't sleep, I'd sometimes carry on fierce arguments with those people. I'd be screaming at them, telling them how much I detested their blind, thoughtless, automatic acquiescence to it all, their simple-minded patriotism, their prideful ignorance, their love-it-or-leave-it platitudes, how they were sending me off to fight a war they didn't understand and didn't want to understand. I held them responsible. By God, yes, I *did*. All of them—I held them personally and individually responsible—the polyestered Kiwanis boys, the merchants and farmers, the pious churchgoers, the chatty housewives, the PTA and the Lions club and the Veterans of Foreign Wars and the fine upstanding gentry out at the country club. They didn't know Bao Dai from the man in the moon. They didn't know history. They didn't know the first thing about Diem's tyranny, or the nature of Vietnamese nationalism, or the long colonialism of the French—this was all too damned complicated, it required some reading—but no matter, it was a war to stop the Communists, plain and simple, which was how they liked things, and you were a treasonous pussy if you had second thoughts about killing or dying for plain and simple reasons.

12   I was bitter, sure. But it was so much more than that. The emotions went from outrage to terror to bewilderment to guilt to sorrow and then back again to outrage. I felt a sickness inside me. Real disease.

13   Most of this I've told before, or at least hinted at, but what I have never told is the full truth. How I cracked. How at work one morning, standing on the pig line, I felt something break open in my chest. I don't know what it was. I'll never know. But it was real, I know that much, it was a physical rupture—a cracking-leaking-popping feeling. I remember dropping my water gun. Quickly, almost without thought, I took off my apron and walked out of the plant and drove home. It was midmorning, I remember, and the house was empty. Down in my chest there was still that leaking sensation, something very warm and precious spilling out, and I

was covered with blood and hog-stink, and for a long while I just concentrated on holding myself together. I remember taking a hot shower. I remember packing a suitcase and carrying it out to the kitchen, standing very still for a few minutes, looking carefully at the familiar objects all around me. The old chrome toaster, the telephone, the pink and white Formica on the kitchen counters. The room was full of bright sunshine. Everything sparkled. My house, I thought. My life. I'm not sure how long I stood there, but later I scribbled out a short note to my parents.

14   What it said, exactly, I don't recall now. Something vague. Taking off, will call, love Tim.

15   I drove north.

16   It's a blur now, as it was then, and all I remember is a sense of high velocity and the feel of the steering wheel in my hands. I was riding on adrenaline. A giddy feeling, in a way, except there was the dreamy edge of impossibility to it—like running a dead-end maze—no way out—it couldn't come to a happy conclusion and yet I was doing it anyway because it was all I could think of to do. It was pure flight, fast and mindless. I had no plan. Just hit the border at high speed and crash through and keep on running. Near dusk I passed through Bemidji, then turned northeast toward International Falls. I spent the night in the car behind a closed-down gas station a half mile from the border. In the morning, after gassing up, I headed straight west along the Rainy River, which separates Minnesota from Canada, and which for me separated one life from another. The land was mostly wilderness. Here and there I passed a motel or bait shop, but otherwise the country unfolded in great sweeps of pine and birch and sumac. Though it was still August, the air already had the smell of October, football season, piles of yellow-red leaves, everything crisp and clean. I remember a huge blue sky. Off to my right was the Rainy River, wide as a lake in places, and beyond the Rainy River was Canada.

17   For a while I just drove, not aiming at anything, then in the late morning I began looking for a place to lie low for a day or two. I was exhausted, and scared sick, and around noon I pulled into an old fishing resort called the Tip Top Lodge. Actually it was not a lodge at all, just eight or nine tiny yellow cabins clustered on a peninsula that jutted northward into the Rainy River. The place was in sorry shape. There was a dangerous wooden dock, an old minnow tank, a flimsy tar paper boathouse along the shore. The main building, which stood in a cluster of pines on high ground, seemed to lean heavily to one side, like a cripple, the roof sagging toward Canada. Briefly, I thought about turning around, just giving up, but then I got out of the car and walked up to the front porch.

18   The man who opened the door that day is the hero of my life. How do I say this without sounding sappy? Blurt it out—the man saved me. He offered exactly what I needed, without questions, without any words at all. He took me in. He was there at the critical time—a silent, watchful presence. Six days later, when it ended, I was unable to find a proper way

to thank him, and I never have, and so, if nothing else, this story represents a small gesture of gratitude twenty years overdue.

19   Even after two decades I can close my eyes and return to that porch at the Tip Top Lodge. I can see the old guy staring at me. Elroy Berdahl: eighty-one years old, skinny and shrunken and mostly bald. He wore a flannel shirt and brown work pants. In one hand, I remember, he carried a green apple, a small paring knife in the other. His eyes had the bluish gray color of a razor blade, the same polished shine, and as he peered up at me I felt a strange sharpness, almost painful, a cutting sensation, as if his gaze were somehow slicing me open. In part, no doubt, it was my own sense of guilt, but even so I'm absolutely certain that the old man took one look and went right to the heart of things—a kid in trouble. When I asked for a room, Elroy made a little clicking sound with his tongue. He nodded, led me out to one of the cabins, and dropped a key in my hand. I remember smiling at him. I also remember wishing I hadn't. The old man shook his head as if to tell me it wasn't worth the bother.

20   "Dinner at five-thirty," he said. "You eat fish?"

21   "Anything," I said.

22   Elroy grunted and said, "I'll bet."

23   We spent six days together at the Tip Top Lodge. Just the two of us. Tourist season was over, and there were no boats on the river, and the wilderness seemed to withdraw into a great permanent stillness. Over those six days Elroy Berdahl and I took most of our meals together. In the mornings we sometimes went out on long hikes into the woods, and at night we played Scrabble or listened to records or sat reading in front of his big stone fireplace. At times I felt the awkwardness of an intruder, but Elroy accepted me into his quiet routine without fuss or ceremony. He took my presence for granted, the same way he might've sheltered a stray cat—no wasted sighs or pity—and there was never any talk about it. Just the opposite. What I remember more than anything is the man's willful, almost ferocious silence. In all that time together, all those hours, he never asked the obvious questions: Why was I there? Why alone? Why so preoccupied? If Elroy was curious about any of this, he was careful never to put it into words.

24   My hunch, though, is that he already knew. At least the basics. After all, it was 1968, and guys were burning draft cards, and Canada was just a boat ride away. Elroy Berdahl was no hick. His bedroom, I remember, was cluttered with books and newspapers. He killed me at the Scrabble board, barely concentrating, and on those occasions when speech was necessary he had a way of compressing large thoughts into small, cryptic packets of language. One evening, just at sunset, he pointed up at an owl circling over the violet-lighted forest to the west.

25   "Hey, O'Brien," he said. "There's Jesus."

26   The man was sharp—he didn't miss much. Those razor eyes. Now and then he'd catch me staring out at the river, at the far shore, and I could almost hear the tumblers clicking in his head. Maybe I'm wrong, but I doubt it.

27   One thing for certain, he knew I was in desperate trouble. And he knew I couldn't talk about it. The wrong word—or even the right word—and I would've disappeared. I was wired and jittery. My skin felt too tight. After supper one evening I vomited and went back to my cabin and lay down for a few moments and then vomited again; another time, in the middle of the afternoon, I began sweating and couldn't shut it off. I went through whole days feeling dizzy with sorrow. I couldn't sleep; I couldn't lie still. At night I'd toss around in bed, half awake, half dreaming, imagining how I'd sneak down to the beach and quietly push one of the old man's boats out into the river and start paddling my way toward Canada. There were times when I thought I'd gone off the psychic edge. I couldn't tell up from down, I was just falling, and late in the night I'd lie there watching weird pictures spin through my head. Getting chased by the Border Patrol—helicopters and searchlights and barking dogs—I'd be crashing through the woods, I'd be down on my hands and knees—people shouting out my name—the law closing in on all sides—my hometown draft board and the FBI and the Royal Canadian Mounted Police. It all seemed crazy and impossible. Twenty-one years old, an ordinary kid with all the ordinary dreams and ambitions, and all I wanted was to live the life I was born to—a mainstream life—I loved baseball and hamburgers and cherry Cokes—and now I was off on the margins of exile, leaving my country forever, and it seemed so impossible and terrible and sad.

28   I'm not sure how I made it through those six days. Most of it I can't remember. On two or three afternoons, to pass some time, I helped Elroy get the place ready for winter, sweeping down the cabins and hauling in the boats, little chores that kept my body moving. The days were cool and bright. The nights were very dark. One morning the old man showed me how to split and stack firewood, and for several hours we just worked in silence out behind his house. At one point, I remember, Elroy put down his maul and looked at me for a long time, his lips drawn as if framing a difficult question, but then he shook his head and went back to work. The man's self-control was amazing. He never pried. He never put me in a position that required lies or denials. To an extent, I suppose, his reticence was typical of that part of Minnesota, where privacy still held value, and even if I'd been walking around with some horrible deformity—four arms and three heads—I'm sure the old man would've talked about everything except those extra arms and heads. Simple politeness was part of it. But even more than that, I think, the man understood that words were insufficient. The problem had gone beyond discussion. During that long summer I'd been over and over the various arguments, all the pros and cons, and it was no longer a question that could be decided by an act of pure reason. Intellect had come up against emotion. My conscience told me to run, but some irrational and powerful force was resisting, like a weight pushing me toward the war. What it came down to, stupidly, was a sense of shame. Hot, stupid shame. I did not

want people to think badly of me. Not my parents, not my brother and sister, not even the folks down at the Gobbler Café. I was ashamed to be there at the Tip Top Lodge. I was ashamed of my conscience, ashamed to be doing the right thing.

29   Some of this Elroy must've understood. Not the details, of course, but the plain fact of crisis.

30   Although the old man never confronted me about it, there was one occasion when he came close to forcing the whole thing out into the open. It was early evening, and we'd just finished supper, and over coffee and dessert I asked him about my bill, how much I owed so far. For a long while the old man squinted down at the tablecloth.

31   "Well, the basic rate," he said, "is fifty bucks a night. Not counting meals. This makes four nights, right?"

32   I nodded. I had three hundred and twelve dollars in my wallet.

33   Elroy kept his eyes on the tablecloth. "Now that's an onseason price. To be fair, I suppose we should knock it down a peg or two." He leaned back in his chair. "What's a reasonable number, you figure?"

34   "I don't know," I said. "Forty?"

35   "Forty's good. Forty a night. Then we tack on food—say another hundred? Two hundred sixty total?"

36   "I guess."

37   He raised his eyebrows. "Too much?"

38   "No, that's fair. It's fine. Tomorrow, though . . . I think I'd better take off tomorrow."

39   Elroy shrugged and began clearing the table. For a time he fussed with the dishes, whistling to himself as if the subject had been settled. After a second he slapped his hands together.

40   "You know what we forgot?" he said. "We forgot wages. Those odd jobs you done. What we have to do, we have to figure out what your time's worth. Your last job—how much did you pull in an hour?"

41   "Not enough," I said.

42   "A bad one?"

43   "Yes. Pretty bad."

44   Slowly then, without intending any long sermon, I told him about my days at the pig plant. It began as a straight recitation of the facts, but before I could stop myself I was talking about the blood clots and the water gun and how the smell had soaked into my skin and how I couldn't wash it away. I went on for a long time. I told him about wild hogs squealing in my dreams, the sounds of butchery, slaughter-house sounds, and how I'd sometimes wake up with that greasy pig-stink in my throat.

45   When I was finished, Elroy nodded at me.

46   "Well, to be honest," he said, "when you first showed up here, I wondered about all that. The aroma, I mean. Smelled like you was awful damned fond of pork chops." The old man almost smiled. He made a snuffling sound, then sat down with a pencil and a piece of paper. "So what'd this crud job pay? Ten bucks an hour? Fifteen?"

47   "Less."

48   Elroy shook his head. "Let's make it fifteen. You put in twenty-five hours here, easy. That's three hundred seventy-five bucks total wages. We subtract the two hundred sixty for food and lodging, I still owe you a hundred and fifteen."

49   He took four fifties out of his shirt pocket and laid them on the table.

50   "Call it even," he said.

51   "No."

52   "Pick it up. Get yourself a haircut."

53   The money lay on the table for the rest of the evening. It was still there when I went back to my cabin. In the morning, though, I found an envelope tacked to my door. Inside were the four fifties and a two-word note that said EMERGENCY FUND.

54   The man knew.

55   Looking back after twenty years, I sometimes wonder if the events of that summer didn't happen in some other dimension, a place where your life exists before you've lived it, and where it goes afterward. None of it ever seemed real. During my time at the Tip Top Lodge I had the feeling that I'd slipped out of my own skin, hovering a few feet away while some poor yo-yo with my name and face tried to make his way toward a future he didn't understand and didn't want. Even now I can see myself as I was then. It's like watching an old home movie: I'm young and tan and fit. I've got hair—lots of it. I don't smoke or drink. I'm wearing faded blue jeans and a white polo shirt. I can see myself sitting on Elroy Berdahl's dock near dusk one evening, the sky a bright shimmering pink, and I'm finishing up a letter to my parents that tells what I'm about to do and why I'm doing it and how sorry I am that I'd never found the courage to talk to them about it. I ask them not to be angry. I try to explain some of my feelings, but there aren't enough words, and so I just say that it's a thing that has to be done. At the end of the letter I talk about the vacations we used to take up in this north country, at a place called Whitefish Lake, and how the scenery here reminds me of those good times. I tell them I'm fine. I tell them I'll write again from Winnipeg or Montreal or wherever I end up.

56   On my last full day, the sixth day, the old man took me out fishing on the Rainy River. The afternoon was sunny and cold. A stiff breeze came in from the north, and I remember how the little fourteen-foot boat made sharp rocking motions as we pushed off from the dock. The current was fast. All around us, I remember, there was a vastness to the world, an unpeopled rawness, just the trees and the sky and the water reaching out toward nowhere. The air had the brittle scent of October.

57   For ten or fifteen minutes Elroy held a course upstream, the river choppy and silver-gray, then he turned straight north and put the engine on full throttle. I felt the bow lift beneath me. I remember the wind in my ears, the sound of the old outboard Evinrude. For a time I didn't pay attention to anything, just feeling the cold spray against my face, but then

it occurred to me that at some point we must've passed into Canadian waters, across that dotted line between two different worlds, and I remember a sudden tightness in my chest as I looked up and watched the far shore come at me. This wasn't a daydream. It was tangible and real. As we came in toward land, Elroy cut the engine, letting the boat fishtail lightly about twenty yards off shore. The old man didn't look at me or speak. Bending down, he opened up his tackle box and busied himself with a bobber and a piece of wire leader, humming to himself, his eyes down.

58   It struck me then that he must've planned it. I'll never be certain, of course, but I think he meant to bring me up against the realities, to guide me across the river and to take me to the edge and to stand a kind of vigil as I chose a life for myself.

59   I remember staring at the old man, then at my hands, then at Canada. The shoreline was dense with brush and timber. I could see tiny red berries on the bushes. I could see a squirrel up in one of the birch trees, a big crow looking at me from a boulder along the river. That close— twenty yards—and I could see the delicate latticework of the leaves, the texture of the soil, the browned needles beneath the pines, the configurations of geology and human history. Twenty yards. I could've done it. I could've jumped and started swimming for my life. Inside me, in my chest. I felt a terrible squeezing pressure. Even now, as I write this, I can still feel that tightness. And I want you to feel it—the wind coming off the river, the waves, the silence, the wooded frontier. You're at the bow of a boat on the Rainy River. You're twenty-one years old, you're scared, and there's a hard squeezing pressure in your chest.

60   What would you do?

61   Would you jump? Would you feel pity for yourself? Would you think about your family and your childhood and your dreams and all you're leaving behind? Would it hurt? Would it feel like dying? Would you cry, as I did?

62   I tried to swallow it back. I tried to smile, except I was crying.

63   Now, perhaps, you can understand why I've never told this story before. It's not just the embarrassment of tears. That's part of it, no doubt, but what embarrasses me much more, and always will, is the paralysis that took my heart. A moral freeze: I couldn't decide, I couldn't act, I couldn't comport myself with even a pretense of modest human dignity.

64   All I could do was cry. Quietly, not bawling, just the chest-chokes.

65   At the rear of the boat Elroy Berdahl pretended not to notice. He held a fishing rod in his hands, his head bowed to hide his eyes. He kept humming a soft, monotonous little tune. Everywhere, it seemed, in the trees and water and sky, a great worldwide sadness came pressing down on me, a crushing sorrow, sorrow like I had never known it before. And what was so sad, I realized, was that Canada had become a pitiful fantasy. Silly and hopeless. It was no longer a possibility. Right then, with

the shore so close, I understood that I would not do what I should do. I would not swim away from my hometown and my country and my life. I would not be brave. That old image of myself as a hero, as a man of conscience and courage, all that was just a threadbare pipe dream. Bobbing there on the Rainy River, looking back at the Minnesota shore, I felt a sudden swell of helplessness come over me, a drowning sensation, as if I had toppled overboard and was being swept away by the silver waves. Chunks of my own history flashed by. I saw a seven-year-old boy in a white cowboy hat and a Lone Ranger mask and a pair of holstered six-shooters; I saw a twelve-year-old Little League shortstop pivoting to turn a double play; I saw a sixteen-year- old kid decked out for his first prom, looking spiffy in a white tux and a black bow tie, his hair cut short and flat, his shoes freshly polished. My whole life seemed to spill out into the river, swirling away from me, everything I had ever been or ever wanted to be. I couldn't get my breath; I couldn't stay afloat; I couldn't tell which way to swim. A hallucination, I suppose, but it was as real as anything I would ever feel. I saw my parents calling to me from the far shoreline. I saw my brother and sister, all the townsfolk, the mayor and the entire Chamber of Commerce and all my old teachers and girlfriends and high school buddies. Like some weird sporting event: everybody screaming from the side-lines, rooting me on—a loud stadium roar. Hotdogs and popcorn—stadium smells, stadium heat. A squad of cheerleaders did cartwheels along the banks of the Rainy River; they had megaphones and pompoms and smooth brown thighs. The crowd swayed left and right. A marching band played fight songs. All my aunts and uncles were there, and Abraham Lincoln, and Saint George, and a nine-year-old girl named Linda who had died of a brain tumor back in fifth grade, and several members of the United States Senate, and a blind poet scribbling notes, and LBJ, and Huck Finn, and Abbie Hoffman, and all the dead soldiers back from the grave, and the many thousands who were later to die—villagers with terrible burns, little kids without arms or legs—yes, and the Joint Chiefs of Staff were there, and a couple of popes, and a first lieutenant named Jimmy Cross, and the last surviving veteran of the American Civil War, and Jane Fonda dressed up as Barbarella, and an old man sprawled beside a pigpen, and my grandfather, and Gary Cooper, and a kind-faced woman carrying an umbrella and a copy of Plato's *Republic*, and a million ferocious citizens waving flags of all shapes and colors—people in hard hats, people in headbands— they were all whooping and chanting and urging me toward one shore or the other. I saw faces from my distant past and distant future. My wife was there. My unborn daughter waved at me, and my two sons hopped up and down, and a drill sergeant named Blyton sneered and shot up a finger and shook his head. There was a choir in bright purple robes. There was a cabbie from the Bronx. There was a slim young man I would one day kill with a hand grenade along a red clay trail outside the village of My Khe.

66   The little aluminum boat rocked softly beneath me. There was the wind and the sky.

67   I tried to will myself overboard.

68   I gripped the edge of the boat and leaned forward and thought, *Now*.

69   I did try. It just wasn't possible.

70   All those eyes on me—the town, the whole universe—and I couldn't risk the embarrassment. It was as if there were an audience to my life, that swirl of faces along the river, and in my head I could hear people screaming at me. Traitor! they yelled. Turncoat! Pussy! I felt myself blush. I couldn't tolerate it. I couldn't endure the mockery, or the disgrace, or the patriotic ridicule. Even in my imagination, the shore just twenty yards away, I couldn't make myself be brave. It had nothing to do with morality. Embarrassment, that's all it was.

71   And right then I submitted.

72   I would go to the war—I would kill and maybe die—because I was embarrassed not to.

73   That was the sad thing. And so I sat in the bow of the boat and cried.

74   It was loud now. Loud, hard crying.

75   Elroy Berdahl remained quiet. He kept fishing. He worked his line with the tips of his fingers, patiently, squinting out at his red and white bobber on the Rainy River. His eyes were flat and impassive. He didn't speak. He was simply there, like the river and the late-summer sun. And yet by his presence, his mute watchfulness, he made it real. He was the true audience. He was a witness, like God, or like the gods, who look on in absolute silence as we live our lives, as we make our choices or fail to make them.

76   "Ain't biting," he said.

77   Then after a time the old man pulled in his line and turned the boat back toward Minnesota.

78   I don't remember saying goodbye. That last night we had dinner together, and I went to bed early, and in the morning Elroy fixed breakfast for me. When I told him I'd be leaving, the old man nodded as if he already knew. He looked down at the table and smiled.

79   At some point later in the morning it's possible that we shook hands—I just don't remember—but I do know that by the time I'd finished packing the old man had disappeared. Around noon, when I took my suitcase out to the car, I noticed that his old black pickup truck was no longer parked in front of the house. I went inside and waited for a while, but I felt a bone certainty that he wouldn't be back. In a way, I thought, it was appropriate. I washed up the breakfast dishes, left his two hundred dollars on the kitchen counter, got into the car, and drove south toward home.

80   The day was cloudy. I passed through towns with familiar names, through the pine forests and down to the prairie, and then to Vietnam, where I was a soldier, and then home again. I survived, but it's not a happy ending. I was a coward. I went to the war.

Questions for Engagement, Response, and Analysis

1. Who is the narrator? What is his youthful theory about courage?

2. Describe the narrator's summer job, examine the imagery of the pig stench, and relate it to the stench of war.

3. What are the narrator's reasons for leaving the job and driving north? What is his dilemma?

4. In what way is the Tip Top Lodge misnamed? In what way is the name appropriate?

5. Referring to the summer of 1968 when he received his draft notice, the narrator says, "The only certainty that summer was moral confusion." What are some of the uncertainties that contributed to his opposition to the war?

6. What is a conscientious objector? Why does the narrator not apply for conscientious objector status?

7. How does the fishing trip on Rainy River precipitate the narrator's decision? What does Elroy Berdahl do that causes the narrator to regard Berdahl as "the hero of [his] life"?

How to Tell a True War Story   (1990)

1   This is true.

2   I had a buddy in Vietnam. His name was Bob Kiley, but everybody called him Rat.

3   A friend of his gets killed, so about a week later Rat sits down and writes a letter to the guy's sister. Rat tells her what a great brother she had, how together the guy was, a number one pal and comrade. A real soldier's soldier, Rat says. Then he tells a few stories to make the point, how her brother would always volunteer for stuff nobody else would volunteer for in a million years, dangerous stuff, like doing recon or going out on these really badass night patrols. Stainless steel balls, Rat tells her. The guy was a little crazy, for sure, but crazy in a good way, a real daredevil, because he liked the challenge of it, he liked testing himself, just man against gook. A great, great guy, Rat says.

4   Anyway, it's a terrific letter, very personal and touching. Rat almost bawls writing it. He gets all teary telling about the good times they had together, how her brother made the war seem almost fun, always raising hell and lighting up villes and bringing smoke to bear every which way. A great sense of humor, too. Like the time at this river when he went fishing with a whole damn crate of hand grenades. Probably the funniest thing in world history, Rat says, all that gore, about twenty zillion dead gook fish. Her brother, he had the right attitude. He knew how to have a good time. On Halloween, this real hot spooky night, the dude paints up his body all different colors and puts on this weird mask and hikes over to a ville and goes trick-or-treating almost stark naked, just boots and

balls and an M–16. A tremendous human being, Rat says. Pretty nutso sometimes, but you could trust him with your life.

5   And then the letter gets very sad and serious. Rat pours his heart out. He says he loved the guy. He says the guy was his best friend in the world. They were like soul mates, he says, like twins or something, they had a whole lot in common. He tells the guy's sister he'll look her up when the war's over.

6   So what happens?

7   Rat mails the letter. He waits two months. The dumb cooze never writes back.

8   A true war story is never moral. It does not instruct, nor encourage virtue, nor suggest models of proper human behavior, nor restrain men from doing the things men have always done. If a story seems moral, do not believe it. If at the end of a war story you feel uplifted, or if you feel that some small bit of rectitude has been salvaged from the larger waste, then you have been made the victim of a very old and terrible lie. There is no rectitude whatsoever. There is no virtue. As a first rule of thumb, therefore, you can tell a true war story by its absolute and uncompromising allegiance to obscenity and evil. Listen to Rat Kiley. Cooze, he says. He does not say bitch. He certainly does not say woman, or girl. He says cooze. Then he spits and stares. He's nineteen years old—it's too much for him—so he looks at you with those big sad gentle killer eyes and says cooze, because his friend is dead, and because it's so incredibly sad and true: she never wrote back.

9   You can tell a true war story if it embarrasses you. If you don't care for obscenity, you don't care for the truth; if you don't care for the truth, watch how you vote. Send guys to war, they come home talking dirty.

10   Listen to Rat: "Jesus Christ, man, I write this beautiful fuckin' letter, I slave over it, and what happens? The dumb cooze never writes back."

11   The dead guy's name was Curt Lemon. What happened was, we crossed a muddy river and marched west into the mountains, and on the third day we took a break along a trail junction in deep jungle. Right away, Lemon and Rat Kiley started goofing. They didn't understand about the spookiness. They were kids; they just didn't know. A nature hike, they thought, not even a war, so they went off into the shade of some giant trees—quadruple canopy, no sunlight at all—and they were giggling and calling each other yellow mother and playing a silly game they'd invented. The game involved smoke grenades, which were harmless unless you did stupid things, and what they did was pull out the pin and stand a few feet apart and play catch under the shade of those huge trees. Whoever chickened out was a yellow mother. And if nobody chickened out, the grenade would make a light popping sound and they'd be covered with smoke and they'd laugh and dance around and then do it again.

12   It's all exactly true.

13   It happened, to *me*, nearly twenty years ago, and I still remember that trail junction and those giant trees and a soft dripping sound somewhere

beyond the trees. I remember the smell of moss. Up in the canopy there were tiny white blossoms, but no sunlight at all, and I remember the shadows spreading out under the trees where Curt Lemon and Rat Kiley were playing catch with smoke grenades. Mitchell Sanders sat flipping his yo-yo. Norman Bowker and Kiowa and Dave Jensen were dozing, or half dozing, and all around us were those ragged green mountains.

14   Except for the laughter things were quiet.

15   At one point, I remember, Mitchell Sanders turned and looked at me, not quite nodding, as if to warn me about something, as if he already *knew*, then after a while he rolled up his yo-yo and moved away.

16   It's hard to tell you what happened next.

17   They were just goofing. There was a noise, I suppose, which must've been the detonator, so I glanced behind me and watched Lemon step from the shade into bright sunlight. His face was suddenly brown and shining. A handsome kid, really. Sharp gray eyes, lean and narrow-waisted, and when he died it was almost beautiful, the way the sunlight came around him and lifted him up and sucked him high into a tree full of moss and vines and white blossoms.

18   In any war story, but especially a true one, it's difficult to separate what happened from what seemed to happen. What seems to happen becomes its own happening and has to be told that way. The angles of vision are skewed. When a booby trap explodes, you close your eyes and duck and float outside yourself. When a guy dies, like Curt Lemon, you look away and then look back for a moment and then look away again. The pictures get jumbled; you tend to miss a lot. And then afterward, when you go to tell about it, there is always that surreal seemingness, which makes the story seem untrue, but which in fact represents the hard and exact truth as it *seemed*.

19   In many cases a true war story cannot be believed. If you believe it, be skeptical. It's a question of credibility. Often the crazy stuff is true and the normal stuff isn't, because the normal stuff is necessary to make you believe the truly incredible craziness.

20   In other cases you can't even tell a true war story. Sometimes it's just beyond telling.

21   I heard this one, for example, from Mitchell Sanders. It was near dusk and we were sitting at my foxhole along a wide muddy river north of Quang Ngai. I remember how peaceful the twilight was. A deep pinkish red spilled out on the river, which moved without sound, and in the morning we would cross the river and march west into the mountains. The occasion was right for a good story.

22   "God's truth," Mitchell Sanders said. "A six-man patrol goes up into the mountains on a basic listening-post operation. The idea's to spend a week up there, just lie low and listen for enemy movement. They've got a radio along, so if they hear anything suspicious—anything—they're supposed to call in artillery or gunships, whatever it takes. Otherwise they keep strict field discipline. Absolute silence. They just listen."

23　　Sanders glanced at me to make sure I had the scenario. He was playing with his yo-yo, dancing it with short, tight little strokes of the wrist.

24　　His face was blank in the dusk.

25　　"We're talking regulation, by-the-book LP. These six guys, they don't say boo for a solid week. They don't got tongues. *All* ears."

26　　"Right," I said.

27　　"Understand me?"

28　　"Invisible."

29　　Sanders nodded.

30　　"Affirm," he said. "Invisible. So what happens is, these guys get themselves deep in the bush, all camouflaged up, and they lie down and wait and that's all they do, nothing else, they lie there for seven straight days and just listen. And man, I'll tell you—it's spooky. This is mountains. You don't *know* spooky till you been there. Jungle, sort of, except it's way up in the clouds and there's always this fog—like rain, except it's not raining—everything's all wet and swirly and tangled up and you can't see jack, you can't find your own pecker to piss with. Like you don't even have a body. Serious spooky. You just go with the vapors—the fog sort of takes you in . . . And the sounds, man. The sounds carry forever. You hear stuff nobody should *ever* hear."

31　　Sanders was quiet for a second, just working the yo-yo, then he smiled at me.

32　　"So after a couple days the guys start hearing this real soft, kind of wacked-out music. Weird echoes and stuff. Like a radio or something, but it's not a radio, it's this strange gook music that comes right out of the rocks. Faraway, sort of, but right up close, too. They try to ignore it. But it's a listening post, right? So they listen. And every night they keep hearing that crazyass gook concert. All kinds of chimes and xylophones. I mean, this is wilderness—no way, it can't be real—but there it *is*, like the mountains are tuned in to Radio fucking Hanoi. Naturally they get nervous. One guy sticks Juicy Fruit in his ears. Another guy almost flips. Thing is, though, they can't report music. They can't get on the horn and call back to base and say, 'Hey, listen, we need some firepower, we got to blow away this weirdo gook rock band.' They can't do that. It wouldn't go down. So they lie there in the fog and keep their mouths shut. And what makes it extra bad, see, is the poor dudes can't horse around like normal. Can't joke it away. Can't even talk to each other except maybe in whispers, all hush-hush, and that just revs up the willies. All they do is listen."

33　　Again there was some silence as Mitchell Sanders looked out on the river. The dark was coming on hard now, and off to the west I could see the mountains rising in silhouette, all the mysteries and unknowns.

34　　"This next part," Sanders said quietly, "you won't believe."

35　　"Probably not," I said.

36　　"You won't. And you know why?" He gave me a long, tired smile. "Because it happened. Because every word is absolutely dead-on true."

37   Sanders made a sound in his throat, like a sigh, as if to say he didn't care if I believed him or not. But he did care. He wanted me to feel the truth, to believe by the raw force of feeling. He seemed sad, in a way.

38   "These six guys," he said, "they're pretty fried out by now, and one night they start hearing voices. Like at a cocktail party. That's what it sounds like, this big swank gook cocktail party somewhere out there in the fog. Music and chitchat and stuff. It's crazy, I know, but they hear the champagne corks. They hear the actual martini glasses. Real hoity-toity, all very civilized, except this isn't civilization. This is Nam.

39   "Anyway, the guys try to be cool. They just lie there and groove, but after a while they start hearing—you won't believe this—they hear chamber music. They hear violins and cellos. They hear this terrific mama-san soprano. Then after a while they hear gook opera and a glee club and the Haiphong Boys Choir and a barbershop quartet and all kinds of weird chanting and Buddha-Buddha stuff. And the whole time, in the background, there's still that cocktail party going on. All these different voices. Not human voices, though. Because it's the mountains. Follow me? The rock—it's *talking*. And the fog, too, and the grass and the goddamn mongooses. Everything talks. The trees talk politics, the monkeys talk religion. The whole country. Vietnam. The place talks. It talks. Understand? Nam—it truly *talks*.

40   "The guys can't cope. They lose it. They get on the radio and report enemy movement—a whole army, they say—and they order up the firepower. They get arty and gunships. They call in air strikes. And I'll tell you, they fuckin' crash that cocktail party. All night long, they just smoke those mountains. They make jungle juice. They blow away trees and glee clubs and whatever else there is to blow away. Scorch time. They walk napalm up and down the ridges. They bring in the Cobras and F-4s, they use Willie Peter and HE and incendiaries. It's all fire. They make those mountains burn.

41   "Around dawn things finally get quiet. Like you never even *heard* quiet before. One of those real thick, real misty days—just clouds and fog, they're off in this special zone—and the mountains are absolutely dead-flat silent. Like *Brigadoon*—pure vapor, you know? Everything's all sucked up inside the fog. Not a single sound, except they still *hear* it.

42   "So they pack up and start humping. They head down the mountain, back to base camp, and when they get there they don't say diddly. They don't talk. Not a word, like they're deaf and dumb. Later on this fat bird colonel comes up and asks what the hell happened out there. What'd they hear? Why all the ordnance? The man's ragged out, he gets down tight on their case. I mean, they spent six trillion dollars on firepower, and this fatass colonel wants answers, he wants to know what the fuckin' story is.

43   "But the guys don't say zip. They just look at him for a while, sort of funny like, sort of amazed, and the whole war is right there in that stare. It says everything you can't ever say. It says, man, you got *wax* in your

ears. It says, poor bastard, you'll never know—wrong frequency—you don't *even* want to hear this. Then they salute the fucker and walk away, because certain stories you don't ever tell."

44   You can tell a true war story by the way it never seems to end. Not then, not ever. Not when Mitchell Sanders stood up and moved off into the dark.

45   It all happened.

46   Even now, at this instant, I remember that yo-yo. In a way, I suppose, you had to be there, you had to hear it, but I could tell how desperately Sanders wanted me to believe him, his frustration at not quite getting the details right, not quite pinning down the final and definitive truth.

47   And I remember sitting at my foxhole that night, watching the shadows of Quang Ngai, thinking about the coming day and how we would cross the river and march west into the mountains, all the ways I might die, all the things I did not understand.

48   Late in the night Mitchell Sanders touched my shoulder. "Just came to me," he whispered. "The moral, I mean. Nobody listens. Nobody hears nothin'. Like that fatass colonel. The politicians, all the civilian types. Your girlfriend. My girlfriend. Everybody's sweet little virgin girlfriend. What they need is to go out on LP. The vapors, man. Trees and rocks— you got to *listen* to your enemy."

49   And then again, in the morning, Sanders came up to me. The platoon was preparing to move out, checking weapons, going through all the little rituals that preceded a day's march. Already the lead squad had crossed the river and was filing off toward the west.

50   "I got a confession to make," Sanders said. "Last night, man, I had to make up a few things."

51   "I know that."

52   "The glee club. There wasn't any glee club."

53   "Right."

54   "No opera."

55   "Forget it, I understand."

56   "Yeah, but listen, it's still true. Those six guys, they heard wicked sound out there. They heard sound you just plain won't believe."

57   Sanders pulled on his rucksack, closed his eyes for a moment, then almost smiled at me. I knew what was coming.

58   "All right," I said, "what's the moral?"

59   "Forget it."

60   "No, go ahead."

61   For a long while he was quiet, looking away, and the silence kept stretching out until it was almost embarrassing. Then he shrugged and gave me a stare that lasted all day.

62   "Hear that quiet, man?" he said. "That quiet—just listen. There's your moral."

63   In a true war story, if there's a moral at all, it's like the thread that makes the cloth. You can't tease it out. You can't extract the meaning without unraveling the deeper meaning. And in the end, really, there's nothing much to say about a true war story, except maybe "Oh."

64   True war stories do not generalize. They do not indulge in abstraction or analysis.

65   For example: War is hell. As a moral declaration the old truism seems perfectly true, and yet because it abstracts, because it generalizes, I can't believe it with my stomach. Nothing turns inside.

66   It comes down to gut instinct. A true war story, if truly told, makes the stomach believe.

67   This one does it for me. I've told it before—many times, many versions—but here's what actually happened.

68   We crossed that river and marched west into the mountains. On the third day, Curt Lemon stepped on a booby-trapped 105 round. He was playing catch with Rat Kiley, laughing, and then he was dead. The trees were thick; it took nearly an hour to cut an LZ for the dustoff.

69   Later, higher in the mountains, we came across a baby VC water buffalo. What it was doing there I don't know—no farms or paddies—but we chased it down and got a rope around it and led it along to a deserted village where we set up for the night. After supper Rat Kiley went over and stroked its nose.

70   He opened up a can of C rations, pork and beans, but the baby buffalo wasn't interested.

71   Rat shrugged.

72   He stepped back and shot it through the right front knee. The animal did not make a sound. It went down hard, then got up again, and Rat took careful aim and shot off an ear. He shot it in the hindquarters and in the little hump at its back. He shot it twice in the flanks. It wasn't to kill; it was to hurt. He put the rifle muzzle up against the mouth and shot the mouth away. Nobody said much. The whole platoon stood there watching, feeling all kinds of things, but there wasn't a great deal of pity for the baby water buffalo. Curt Lemon was dead. Rat Kiley had lost his best friend in the world. Later in the week he would write a long personal letter to the guy's sister, who would not write back, but for now it was a question of pain. He shot off the tail. He shot away chunks of meat below the ribs. All around us there was the smell of smoke and filth and deep greenery, and the evening was humid and very hot. Rat went to automatic. He shot randomly, almost casually, quick little spurts in the belly and butt. Then he reloaded, squatted down, and shot it in the left front knee. Again the animal fell hard and tried to get up, but this time it couldn't quite make it. It wobbled and went down sideways. Rat shot it in the nose. He bent forward and whispered something, as if talking to a pet, then he shot it in the throat. All the while the baby buffalo was silent, or almost silent, just a light bubbling sound where the nose had been. It lay very still. Nothing moved except the eyes, which were enormous, the pupils shiny black and dumb.

73   Rat Kiley was crying. He tried to say something, but then cradled his rifle and went off by himself.

74   The rest of us stood in a ragged circle around the baby buffalo. For a time no one spoke. We had witnessed something essential, something brand-new and profound, a piece of the world so startling there was not yet a name for it.

75   Somebody kicked the baby buffalo.

76   It was still alive, though just barely, just in the eyes.

77   "Amazing," Dave Jensen said. "My whole life, I never seen anything like it."

78   "Never?"

79   "Not hardly. Not once."

80   Kiowa and Mitchell Sanders picked up the baby buffalo. They hauled it across the open square, hoisted it up, and dumped it in the village well.

81   Afterward, we sat waiting for Rat to get himself together.

82   "Amazing," Dave Jensen kept saying. "A new wrinkle. I never seen it before."

83   Mitchell Sanders took out his yo-yo. "Well, that's Nam," he said. "Garden of Evil. Over here, man, every sin's real fresh and original."

84   How do you generalize?

85   War is hell, but that's not the half of it, because war is also mystery and terror and adventure and courage and discovery and holiness and pity and despair and longing and love. War is nasty; war is fun. War is thrilling; war is drudgery. War makes you a man; war makes you dead.

86   The truths are contradictory. It can be argued, for instance, that war is grotesque. But in truth war is also beauty. For all its horror, you can't help but gape at the awful majesty of combat. You stare out at tracer rounds unwinding through the dark like brilliant red ribbons. You crouch in ambush as a cool, impassive moon rises over the nighttime paddies. You admire the fluid symmetries of troops on the move, the harmonies of sound and shape and proportion, the great sheets of metal-fire streaming down from a gunship, the illumination rounds, the white phosphorus, the purply orange glow of napalm, the rocket's red glare. It's not pretty, exactly. It's astonishing. It fills the eye. It commands you. You hate it, yes, but your eyes do not. Like a killer forest fire, like cancer under a micro-scope, any battle or bombing raid or artillery barrage has the aesthetic purity of absolute moral indifference—a powerful, implacable beauty—and a true war story will tell the truth about this, though the truth is ugly.

87   To generalize about war is like generalizing about peace. Almost everything is true. Almost nothing is true. At its core, perhaps, war is just another name for death, and yet any soldier will tell you, if he tells the truth, that proximity to death brings with it a corresponding proximity to life. After a firefight, there is always the immense pleasure of aliveness. The trees are alive. The grass, the soil—everything. All around you things are purely living, and you among them, and the aliveness makes you tremble. You feel an intense, out-of-the-skin awareness of your living

self—your truest self, the human being you want to be and then become by the force of wanting it. In the midst of evil you want to be a good man. You want decency. You want justice and courtesy and human concord, things you never knew you wanted. There is a kind of largeness to it, a kind of godliness. Though it's odd, you're never more alive than when you're almost dead. You recognize what's valuable. Freshly, as if for the first time, you love what's best in yourself and in the world, all that might be lost. At the hour of dusk you sit at your foxhole and look out on a wide river turning pinkish red, and at the mountains beyond, and although in the morning you must cross the river and go into the mountains and do terrible things and maybe die, even so, you find yourself studying the fine colors on the river, you feel wonder and awe at the setting of the sun, and you are filled with a hard, aching love for how the world could be and always should be, but now is not.

88   Mitchell Sanders was right. For the common soldier, at least, war has the feel—the spiritual texture—of a great ghostly fog, thick and permanent. There is no clarity. Everything swirls. The old rules are no longer binding, the old truths no longer true. Right spills over into wrong. Order blends into chaos, love into hate, ugliness into beauty, law into anarchy, civility into savagery. The vapors suck you in. You can't tell where you are, or why you're there, and the only certainty is overwhelming ambiguity.

89   In war you lose your sense of the definite, hence your sense of truth itself, and therefore it's safe to say that in a true war story nothing is ever absolutely true.

90   Often in a true war story there is not even a point, or else the point doesn't hit you until twenty years later, in your sleep, and you wake up and shake your wife and start telling the story to her, except when you get to the end you've forgotten the point again. And then for a long time you lie there watching the story happen in your head. You listen to your wife's breathing. The war's over. You close your eyes. You smile and think, Christ, what's the *point?*

91   This one wakes me up.

92   In the mountains that day, I watched Lemon turn sideways. He laughed and said something to Rat Kiley. Then he took a peculiar half step, moving from shade into bright sunlight, and the booby-trapped 105 round blew him into a tree. The parts were just hanging there, so Dave Jensen and I were ordered to shinny up and peel him off. I remember the white bone of an arm. I remember pieces of skin and something wet and yellow that must've been the intestines. The gore was horrible, and stays with me. But what wakes me up twenty years later is Dave Jensen singing "Lemon Tree" as we threw down the parts.

93   You can tell a true war story by the questions you ask. Somebody tells a story, let's say, and afterward you ask, "Is it true?" and if the answer matters, you've got your answer.

94   For example, we've all heard this one. Four guys go down a trail. A grenade sails out. One guy jumps on it and takes the blast and saves his three buddies.

95   Is it true?

96   The answer matters.

97   You'd feel cheated if it never happened. Without the grounding reality, it's just a trite bit of puffery, pure Hollywood, untrue in the way all such stories are untrue. Yet even if it did happen—and maybe it did, anything's possible—even then you know it can't be true, because a true war story does not depend upon that kind of truth. Absolute occurrence is irrelevant. A thing may happen and be a total lie; another thing may not happen and be truer than the truth. For example: Four guys go down a trail. A grenade sails out. One guy jumps on it and takes the blast, but it's a killer grenade and everybody dies anyway. Before they die, though, one of the dead guys says, "The fuck you do *that* for?" and the jumper says, "Story of my life, man," and the other guy starts to smile but he's dead.

98   That's a true story that never happened.

99   Twenty years later, I can still see the sunlight on Lemon's face. I can see him turning, looking back at Rat Kiley, then he laughed and took that curious half step from shade into sunlight, his face suddenly brown and shining, and when his foot touched down, in that instant, he must've thought it was the sunlight that was killing him. It was not the sunlight. It was a rigged 105 round. But if I could ever get the story right, how the sun seemed to gather around him and pick him up and lift him high into a tree, if I could somehow re-create the fatal whiteness of that light, the quick glare, the obvious cause and effect, then you would believe the last thing Curt Lemon believed, which for him must've been the final truth.

100   Now and then, when I tell this story, someone will come up to me afterward and say she liked it. It's always a woman. Usually it's an older woman of kindly temperament and humane politics. She'll explain that as a rule she hates war stories; she can't understand why people want to wallow in all the blood and gore. But this one she liked. The poor baby buffalo, it made her sad. Sometimes, even, there are little tears. What I should do, she'll say, is put it all behind me. Find new stories to tell.

101   I won't say it but I'll think it.

102   I'll picture Rat Kiley's face, his grief, and I'll think, *You dumb cooze.*

103   Because she wasn't listening.

104   It *wasn't* a war story. It was a *love* story.

105   But you can't say that. All you can do is tell it one more time, patiently, adding and subtracting, making up a few things to get at the real truth. No Mitchell Sanders, you tell her. No Lemon, no Rat Kiley. No trail junction. No baby buffalo. No vines or moss or white blossoms. Beginning to end, you tell her, it's all made up. Every goddamn detail—the mountains and the river and especially that poor dumb baby buffalo. None of it happened. *None* of it. And even if it did happen, it didn't

happen in the mountains, it happened in this little village on the Batan-
gan Peninsula, and it was raining like crazy, and one night a guy named
Stink Harris woke up screaming with a leech on his tongue. You can tell
a true war story if you just keep on telling it.

106   And in the end, of course, a true war story is never about war. It's about
sunlight. It's about the special way that dawn spreads out on a river when
you know you must cross the river and march into the mountains and do
things you are afraid to do. It's about love and memory. It's about sorrow.
It's about sisters who never write back and people who never listen.

Questions for Engagement, Response, and Analysis

1. Why would a story that instructs on moral virtues, teaches the right way
   to do things, and causes a listener or reader to "feel uplifted" not be "a
   true war story"? What does O'Brien mean when he says the "stomach
   [must] believe" for a war story to be true? How do the stories the narrator tells exemplify what he says about the nature of a "true war story"?

2. Describe Mitchell Sanders' story about a platoon on a listening post.
   Why does the narrator regard Sanders' story as true? What does
   Sanders mean when he says the meaning of his story is in the "quiet"?

3. Explain the narrator's description of war as having "a powerful,
   implacable beauty" that is simultaneously an "ugly" "truth."

4. What does the narrator mean when he says, "in the end . . . a true war
   story is never about war"?

5. Explain whether you think O'Brien is telling the truth about war.

THE MAN I KILLED   (1990)

1   His jaw was in his throat, his upper lip and teeth were gone, his one
eye was shut, his other eye was a star-shaped hole, his eyebrows were
thin and arched like a woman's, his nose was undamaged, there was a
slight tear at the lobe of one ear, his clean black hair was swept upward
into a cowlick at the rear of the skull, his forehead was lightly freckled,
his fingernails were clean, the skin at his left cheek was peeled back in
three ragged strips, his right cheek was smooth and hairless, there was
a butterfly on his chin, his neck was open to the spinal cord and the blood
there was thick and shiny and it was this wound that had killed him. He
lay face-up in the center of the trail, a slim, dead, almost dainty young
man. He had bony legs, a narrow waist, long shapely fingers. His chest
was sunken and poorly muscled—a scholar, maybe. His wrists were the
wrists of a child. He wore a black shirt, black pajama pants, a gray ammunition belt, a gold ring on the third finger of his right hand. His rubber
sandals had been blown off. One lay beside him, the other a few meters
up the trail. He had been born, maybe, in 1946 in the village of My Khe
near the central coastline of Quang Ngai Province, where his parents
farmed, and where his family had lived for several centuries, and where,
during the time of the French, his father and two uncles and many

neighbors had joined in the struggle for independence. He was not a Communist. He was a citizen and a soldier. In the village of My Khe, as in all of Quang Ngai, patriotic resistance had the force of tradition, which was partly the force of legend, and from his earliest boyhood the man I killed would have listened to stories about the heroic Trung sisters and Tran Hung Dao's famous rout of the Mongols and Le Loi's final victory against the Chinese at Tot Dong. He would have been taught that to defend the land was a man's highest duty and highest privilege. He had accepted this. It was never open to question. Secretly, though, it also frightened him. He was not a fighter. His health was poor, his body small and frail. He liked books. He wanted someday to be a teacher of mathematics. At night, lying on his mat, he could not picture himself doing the brave things his father had done, or his uncles, or the heroes of the stories. He hoped in his heart that he would never be tested. He hoped the Americans would go away. Soon, he hoped. He kept hoping and hoping, always, even when he was asleep.

2   "Oh, man, you fuckin' trashed the fucker," Azar said. "You scrambled his sorry self, look at that, you *did*, you laid him out like Shredded fuckin' Wheat."

3   "Go away," Kiowa said.

4   "I'm just saying the truth. Like oatmeal."

5   "Go," Kiowa said.

6   "Okay, then. I take it back," Azar said. He started to move away, then stopped and said, "Rice Krispies, you know? On the dead test, this particular individual gets A-plus."

7   Smiling at this, he shrugged and walked up the trail toward the village behind the trees.

8   Kiowa kneeled down.

9   "Just forget that crud," he said. He opened up his canteen and held it out for a while and then sighed and pulled it away. "No sweat, man. What else could you do?"

10   Later, Kiowa said, "I'm serious. Nothing *anybody* could do. Come on, stop staring."

11   The trail junction was shaded by a row of trees and tall brush. The slim young man lay with his legs in the shade. His jaw was in his throat. His one eye was shut and the other was a star-shaped hole.

12   Kiowa glanced at the body.

13   "All right, let me ask a question," he said. "You want to trade places with him? Turn it all upside down—you *want* that? I mean, be honest."

14   The star-shaped hole was red and yellow. The yellow part seemed to be getting wider, spreading out at the center of the star. The upper lip and gum and teeth were gone. The man's head was cocked at a wrong angle, as if loose at the neck, and the neck was wet with blood.

15   "Think it over," Kiowa said.

16   Then later he said, "Tim, it's a *war*. The guy wasn't Heidi—he had a weapon, right? It's a tough thing, for sure, but you got to cut out that staring."

17   Then he said, "Maybe you better lie down a minute."

18   Then after a long empty time he said, "Take it slow. Just go wherever the spirit takes you."

19   The butterfly was making its way along the young man's forehead, which was spotted with small dark freckles. The nose was undamaged. The skin on the right cheek was smooth and fine-grained and hairless. Frail-looking, delicately boned, the young man would not have wanted to be a soldier and in his heart would have feared performing badly in battle. Even as a boy growing up in the village of My Khe, he had often worried about this. He imagined covering his head and lying in a deep hole and closing his eyes and not moving until the war was over. He had no stomach for violence. He loved mathematics. His eyebrows were thin and arched like a woman's, and at school the boys sometimes teased him about how pretty he was, the arched eyebrows and long shapely fingers, and on the playground they mimicked a woman's walk and made fun of his smooth skin and his love for mathematics. The young man could not make himself fight them. He often wanted to, but he was afraid, and this increased his shame. If he could not fight little boys, he thought, how could he ever become a soldier and fight the Americans with their airplanes and helicopters and bombs? It did not seem possible. In the presence of his father and uncles, he pretended to look forward to doing his patriotic duty, which was also a privilege, but at night he prayed with his mother that the war might end soon. Beyond anything else, he was afraid of disgracing himself, and therefore his family and village. But all he could do, he thought, was wait and pray and try not to grow up too fast.

20   "Listen to me," Kiowa said. "You feel terrible, I know that."

21   Then he said, "Okay, maybe I *don't* know."

22   Along the trail there were small blue flowers shaped like bells. The young man's head was wrenched sideways, not quite facing the flowers, and even in the shade a single blade of sunlight sparkled against the buckle of his ammunition belt. The left cheek was peeled back in three ragged strips. The wounds at his neck had not yet clotted, which made him seem animate even in death, the blood still spreading out across his shirt.

23   Kiowa shook his head.

24   There was some silence before he said, "Stop *staring.*"

25   The young man's fingernails were clean. There was a slight tear at the lobe of one ear, a sprinkling of blood on the forearm. He wore a gold ring on the third finger of his right hand. His chest was sunken and poorly muscled—a scholar, maybe. His life was now a constellation of possibilities. So, yes, maybe a scholar. And for years, despite his family's poverty, the man I killed would have been determined to continue his education in mathematics. The means for this were arranged, perhaps, through the village liberation cadres, and in 1964 the young man began attending classes at the university in Saigon, where he avoided politics and paid attention to the problems of calculus. He devoted himself to his

studies. He spent his nights alone, wrote romantic poems in his journal, took pleasure in the grace and beauty of differential equations. The war, he knew, would finally take him, but for the time being he would not let himself think about it. He had stopped praying; instead, now, he waited. And as he waited, in his final year at the university, he fell in love with a classmate, a girl of seventeen, who one day told him that his wrists were like the wrists of a child, so small and delicate, and who admired his narrow waist and the cowlick that rose up like a bird's tail at the back of his head. She liked his quiet manner; she laughed at his freckles and bony legs. One evening, perhaps, they exchanged gold rings.

26   Now one eye was a star.

27   "You okay?" Kiowa said.

28   The body lay almost entirely in shade. There were gnats at the mouth, little flecks of pollen drifting above the nose. The butterfly was gone. The bleeding had stopped except for the neck wounds.

29   Kiowa picked up the rubber sandals, clapping off the dirt, then bent down to search the body. He found a pouch of rice, a comb, a fingernail clipper, a few soiled piasters, a snapshot of a young woman standing in front of a parked motorcycle. Kiowa placed these items in his rucksack along with the gray ammunition belt and rubber sandals.

30   Then he squatted down.

31   "I'll tell you the straight truth," he said. "The guy was dead the second he stepped on the trail. Understand me? We all had him zeroed. A good kill—weapon, ammunition, everything." Tiny beads of sweat glistened at Kiowa's forehead. His eyes moved from the sky to the dead man's body to the knuckles of his own hands. "So listen, you best pull your shit together. Can't just sit here all day."

32   Later he said, "Understand?"

33   Then he said, "Five minutes, Tim. Five more minutes and we're moving out."

34   The one eye did a funny twinkling trick, red to yellow. His head was wrenched sideways, as if loose at the neck, and the dead young man seemed to be staring at some distant object beyond the bell-shaped flowers along the trail. The blood at the neck had gone to a deep purplish black. Clean fingernails, clean hair—he had been a soldier for only a single day. After his years at the university, the man I killed returned with his new wife to the village of My Khe, where he enlisted as a common rifleman with the 48th Vietcong Battalion. He knew he would die quickly. He knew he would see a flash of light. He knew he would fall dead and wake up in the stories of his village and people.

35   Kiowa covered the body with a poncho.

36   "Hey, you're looking better," he said. "No doubt about it. All you needed was time—some mental R&R."

37   Then he said, "Man, I'm sorry."

38   Then later he said, "Why not talk about it?"

39   Then he said, "Come on, man, talk."

40   He was a slim, dead, almost dainty young man of about twenty. He lay with one leg bent beneath him, his jaw in his throat, his face neither expressive nor inexpressive. One eye was shut. The other was a star-shaped hole.

41   "Talk," Kiowa said.

Questions for Engagement, Response, and Analysis

1. What is the effect of the opening of the story? Why does O'Brien mix ordinary and brutal details?

2. Why does the narrator discuss in detail the past life of the dead Vietnamese, a past that is obviously fictional, as the narrator could have no way of knowing it? What effect does O'Brien create by using these details?

3. Kiowa insists that the narrator had no choice but to kill the Vietnamese soldier. Explain whether you agree or disagree.

4. How does the narrator feel about the death of the Vietnamese soldier? If he had no choice, why does he dwell so extensively on the killing?

THE UNDYING UNCERTAINTY OF THE NARRATOR IN TIM O'BRIEN'S *THE THINGS THEY CARRIED*

STEVEN KAPLAN, UNIVERSITY OF SOUTHERN COLORADO

1   Before the United States became militarily involved in defending the sovereignty of South Vietnam, it had to, as one historian recently put it, "invent" (Baritz 142–43) the country and the political issues at stake there. The Vietnam War was in many ways a wild and terrible work of fiction written by some dangerous and frightening storytellers. First the United States decided what constituted good and evil, right and wrong, civilized and uncivilized, freedom and oppression for Vietnam, according to American standards; then it traveled the long physical distance to Vietnam and attempted to make its own notions about these things clear to the Vietnamese people—ultimately by brute, technological force. For the U.S. military and government, the Vietnam that they had in effect invented became fact. For the soldiers that the government then sent there, however, the facts that their government had created about who was the enemy, what were the issues, and how the war was to be won were quickly overshadowed by a world of uncertainty. Ultimately, trying to stay alive long enough to return home in one piece was the only thing that made any sense to them. As David Halberstam puts it in his novel, *One Very Hot Day*, the only fact of which an American soldier in Vietnam could be certain was that "yes was no longer yes, no was no longer no, maybe was more certainly maybe" (127). Almost all of the literature on the war, both fictional and nonfictional, makes clear that the only certain thing during the Vietnam War was that nothing was certain. Philip Beidler has pointed out in an impressive study of the literature of that

war that "most of the time in Vietnam, there were some things that seemed just too terrible and strange to be true and others that were just too terrible and true to be strange" (4).

2   The main question that Beidler's study raises is how, in light of the overwhelming ambiguity that characterized the Vietnam experience, could any sense or meaning be derived from what happened and, above all, how could this meaning, if it were found, be conveyed to those who had not experienced the war? The answer Beidler's book offers, as Beidler himself recently said at a conference on writing about the war, is that "words are all we have. In the hands of true artists . . . they may yet preserve us against the darkness" (Lomperis 87). Similarly, for the novelist Tim O'Brien, the language of fiction is the most accurate means for conveying, as Beidler so incisively puts it, "what happened [in Vietnam] . . . what might have happened, what could have happened, what should have happened, and maybe also what can be kept from happening or what can be made to happen" (87). If the experience of Vietnam and its accompanying sense of chaos and confusion can be shown at all, then for Tim O'Brien it will not be in the fictions created by politicians but in the stories told by writers of fiction.

3   One of Tim O'Brien's most important statements about the inherent problems of understanding and writing about the Vietnam experience appears in a chapter of his novel, Going After Cacciato, appropriately titled "The Things They Didn't Know." The novel's protagonist, Paul Berlin, briefly interrupts his fantasy about chasing the deserter Cacciato, who is en route from Vietnam to Paris, to come to terms with the fact that although he is physically in Vietnam and fighting a war, his understanding of where he is and what he is doing there is light-years away. At the center of the chapter is a long catalogue of the things that Berlin and his comrades did not know about Vietnam, and the chapter closes with the statement that what "they" knew above all else were the "uncertainties never articulated in war stories" (319). In that chapter Tim O'Brien shows that recognizing and exploring the uncertainties about the war is perhaps the closest one can come to finding anything certain at all. Paul Berlin, in his fantasy about escaping the war and chasing Cacciato to Paris, is in fact attempting to confront and, as far as possible, understand the uncertainties of the Vietnam War through the prism of his imagination. Once inside his make-believe world, Berlin has the opportunity to explore all of the things that he did not know about the war: The elusive enemy suddenly becomes his partner in a long debate about the meaning of the war; he explores the mysterious tunnels of the Vietcong; one of the victims of the war becomes Berlin's tour guide as he and his fellow soldiers go after Cacciato; and, most important of all, Berlin is given a chance to test and ultimately reject his own thoughts of desertion by imagining how he would react to the desertion of another soldier.

4   In his most recent work of fiction, *The Things They Carried*,[1] Tim O'Brien takes the act of trying to reveal and understand the uncertainties

about the war one step further, by looking at it through the imagination. He completely destroys the fine line dividing fact from fiction and tries to show, even more so than in *Cacciato*, that fiction (or the imagined world) can often be truer, especially in the case of Vietnam, than fact. In the first chapter, an almost documentary account of the items referred to in the book's title, O'Brien introduces the reader to some of the things, both imaginary and concrete, emotional and physical, that the average foot soldier had to carry through the jungles of Vietnam. All of the "things" are depicted in a style that is almost scientific in its precision. We are told how much each subject weighs, either psychologically or physically, and, in the case of artillery, we are even told how many ounces each round weighed:

> As PFCs or Spec 4s, most of them were common grunts and carried the standard M-16 gas operated assault rifle. The weapon weighed 7.5 pounds, 8.2 pounds with its full 20-round magazine. Depending on numerous factors, such as topography and psychology, the rifleman carried anywhere from 12 to 20 magazines, usually in cloth bandoliers, adding on another 8.4 pounds at minimum, 14 pounds at maximum. (Carried 7)

5   Even the most insignificant details seem worth mentioning. One main character is not just from Oklahoma City but from "Oklahoma City, Oklahoma" (5), as if mentioning the state somehow makes the location more factual, more certain. More striking than this obsession with even the minutest detail, however, is the academic tone that at times makes the narrative sound like a government report. We find such transitional phrases as "for instance" (5) and "in addition" (7), and whole paragraphs are dominated by sentences that begin with "because" (5). These strengthen our impression that the narrator is striving, above all else, to convince us of the reality, of the concrete certainty, of the things they carried.

6   In the midst of this factuality and certainty, however, are signals that all the information in this opening chapter will not amount to much: that the certainties are merely there to conceal uncertainties and that the words following the frequent "becauses" do not provide an explanation of anything. We are told in the opening page that the most important thing that First Lieutenant Jimmy Cross carried were some letters from a girl he loved. The narrator, one of Cross's friends in the war and now a forty-three-year-old writer named Tim O'Brien, tells us that the girl did not love Cross, but that he constantly indulged in "hoping" and "pretending" (3) in an effort to turn her love into fact. We are also told "she was a virgin," but this is immediately qualified by the statement that "he was almost sure" of this (3). On the next page, Cross becomes increasingly uncertain as he sits at "night and wonder(s) if Martha was a virgin" (4). Shortly after

---

[1]The reviewers of this book are split on whether to call it a novel or a collection of short stories. In a recent interview. I asked Tim O'Brien what he felt was the most adequate designation. He said that The *Things They Carried* is neither a collection of stories nor a novel; he preferred to call it a work of fiction.

this, Cross wonders who had taken the pictures he now holds in his hands "because he knew she had boyfriends" (5), but we are never told how he "knew" this. At the end of the chapter, after one of Cross's men has died because Cross was too busy thinking of Martha, Cross sits at the bottom of his foxhole crying, not so much for the member of his platoon who has been killed "but mostly it was for Martha, and for himself, because she belonged to another world, and because she was . . . a poet and a virgin and uninvolved" (17).

7   This pattern of stating facts and then quickly calling them into question that is typical of Jimmy Cross's thoughts in these opening pages characterizes how the narrator portrays events throughout this book; the facts about an event are given; they then are quickly qualified or called into question; from this uncertainty emerges a new set of facts about the same subject that are again called into question—on and on, without end. O'Brien catalogues the weapons that the soldiers carried, down to their weight, thus making them seem important and their protective power real. However, several of these passages are introduced by the statement that some of these same weapons were also carried by the character Ted Lavender; each of the four sections of the first chapter that tells us what he carried is introduced by a qualifying phrase that reveals something about which Lavender himself was not at all certain when he was carrying his weapons: "Until he was shot . . ." (4, 7, 10).

8   Conveying the average soldier's sense of uncertainty about what actually happened in Vietnam by presenting the what-ifs and maybes as if they were facts, and then calling these facts back into question again, can be seen as a variation of the haunting phrase used so often by American soldiers to convey their own uncertainty about what happened in Vietnam: "there it is." They used it to make the unspeakable and indescribable and the uncertain real and present for a fleeting moment. Similarly, O'Brien presents facts and stories that are only temporarily certain and real; the strange "balance" in Vietnam between "crazy and almost crazy" (20) always creeps back in and forces the mind that is remembering and retelling a story to remember and retell it one more time in a different form, adding different nuances, and then to tell it again one more time.

9   Storytelling in this book is something in which "the whole world is rearranged" (39) in an effort to get at the "full truth" (49) about events that themselves deny the possibility of arriving at something called the "full," meaning certain and fixed, "truth." By giving the reader facts and then calling those facts into question, by telling stories and then saying that those stories happened (147), and then that they did not happen (203), and then that they might have happened (204), O'Brien puts more emphasis in *The Things They Carried* on the question that he first posed in *Going After Cacciato*: how can a work of fiction become paradoxically more real than the events upon which it is based, and how can the confusing experiences of the average soldier in Vietnam be conveyed in such a way that they will acquire at least a momentary sense of certainty?

In *The Things They Carried*, this question is raised even before the novel begins. The book opens with a reminder: "This is a work of fiction. Except for a few details regarding the author's own life, all the incidents, names, and characters are imaginary." Two pages later we are told that "this book is lovingly dedicated to the men of Alpha Company, and in particular to Jimmy Cross, Norman Bowker, Rat Kiley, Mitchell Sanders, Henry Dobbins, and Kiowa." We discover only a few pages after this dedication that those six men are the novel's main characters.

10   These prefatory comments force us simultaneously to consider the unreal (the fictions that follow) as real because the book is dedicated to the characters who appear in it, and the "incidents, names, and characters" are unreal or "imaginary." O'Brien informs us at one point that in telling these war stories he intends to get at the "full truth" (49) about them; yet from the outset he has shown us that the full truth as he sees it is in itself something ambiguous. Are these stories and the characters in them real or imaginary, or does the "truth" hover somewhere between the two? A closer look at the book's narrative structure reveals that O'Brien is incapable of answering the questions that he initially raises, because the very act of writing fiction about the war, of telling war stories, as he practices it in *The Things They Carried*, is determined by the nature of the Vietnam War and ultimately by life in general where "the only certainty is overwhelming ambiguity" (88).

11   The emphasis on ambiguity behind O'Brien's narrative technique in *The Things They Carried* is thus similar to the pattern used by Joseph Conrad's narrator, Marlow, in *Heart of Darkness*, so incisively characterized by J. Hillis Miller as a lifting of veils to reveal a truth that is quickly obscured again by the dropping of a new veil (158). Over and over again, O'Brien tells us that we are reading "the full and exact truth" (181), and yet, as we make our way through this book and gradually find the same stories being retold with new facts and from a new perspective, we come to realize that there is no such thing as the full and exact truth. Instead, the only thing that can be determined at the end of the story is its own indeterminacy.

12   O'Brien calls telling stories in this manner "Good Form" in the title of one of the chapters of *The Things They Carried*: This is good form because "telling stories" like this "can make things present" (204). The stories in this book are not truer than the actual things that happened in Vietnam because they contain some higher, metaphysical truth: "True war stories do not generalize. They do not indulge in abstractions or analysis" (84). Rather, these stories are true because the characters and events within them are being given a new life each time they are told and retold. This approach to storytelling echoes Wolfgang Iser's theory of representation in his essay "Representation: A Performative Act":

13   Whatever shape or form these various (philosophical or fictional) conceptualizations (of life) may have, their common denominator is the attempt to explain origins. In this respect they close off those very potentialities that literature holds open. Of course literature also springs from

the same anthropological need, since it stages what is inaccessible, thus compensating for the impossibility of knowing what it is to be. But literature is not an explanation of origins; it is a staging of the constant deferment of explanation, which makes the origin explode into its multifariousness.

14   It is at this point that aesthetic semblance makes its full impact. Representation arises out of and thus entails the removal of difference, whose irremovability transforms representation into a performative act of staging something. This staging is almost infinitely variable, for in contrast to explanations, no single staging could ever remove difference and so explain origin. On the contrary, its very multiplicity facilitates an unending mirroring of what man is, because no mirrored manifestation can ever coincide with our actual being. (245)

15   When we conceptualize life, we attempt to step outside ourselves and look at who we are. We constantly make new attempts to conceptualize our lives and uncover our true identities because looking at who we might be is as close as we can come to discovering who we actually are. Similarly, representing events in fiction is an attempt to understand them by detaching them from the "real world" and placing them in a world that is being staged. In *The Things They Carried*, Tim O'Brien desperately struggles to make his readers believe that what they are reading is true because he wants them to step outside their everyday reality and participate in the events that he is portraying; he wants us to believe in his stories to the point where we are virtually in the stories so that we might gain a more thorough understanding of, or feeling for, what is being portrayed in them. Representation as O'Brien practices it in this book is not a mimetic act but a "game," as Iser also calls it in a more recent essay, "The Play of the Text," a process of acting things out:

> Now since the latter [the text] is fictional, it automatically invokes a convention-governed contract between author and reader indicating that the textual world is to be viewed not as reality but as if it were reality. And so whatever is repeated in the text is not meant to denote the world, but merely a world enacted. This may well repeat an identifiable reality, but it contains one all-important difference: what happens within it is relieved of the consequences inherent in the real world referred to. Hence in disclosing itself, fictionality signalizes that everything is only to be taken as if it were what it seems to be, to be taken—in other words—as play. (251)

16   In *The Things They Carried*, representation includes staging what might have happened in Vietnam while simultaneously questioning the accuracy and credibility of the narrative act itself. The reader is thus made fully aware of being made a participant in a game, in a "performative act," and thereby also is asked to become immediately involved in the incredibly frustrating act of trying to make sense of events that resist understanding. The reader is permitted to experience at first hand the uncertainty that characterized being in Vietnam. We are being forced to "believe" (79) that the only "certainty" was the "overwhelming ambiguity."

17   This process is nowhere clearer than in a chapter appropriately called "How to Tell A True War Story." O'Brien opens this chapter by telling us "This Is True." Then he takes us through a series of variations of the story about how Curt Lemon stepped on a mine and was blown up into a tree. The only thing true or certain about the story, however, is that it is being constructed and then deconstructed and then reconstructed right in front of us. The reader is given six different versions of the death of Curt Lemon, and each version is so discomforting that it is difficult to come up with a more accurate statement to describe his senseless death than "there it is," or as O'Brien puts it—"in the end, really there's nothing much to say about a true war story, except maybe 'oh'" (84).

18   Before we learn in this chapter how Curt Lemon was killed, we are told the "true" story that Rat Kiley apparently told to the character-narrator O'Brien about how Kiley wrote to Lemon's sister and "says he loved the guy. He says the guy was his best friend in the world" (76). Two months after writing the letter, Kiley has not heard from Lemon's sister, and so he writes her off as a "dumb cooze" (76). This is what happened according to Kiley, and O'Brien assures us that the story is "incredibly sad and true" (77). However, when Rat Kiley tells a story in another chapter we are warned that he

> swore up and down to its truth, although in the end, I'll admit, that doesn't amount to much of a warranty. Among the men in Alpha Company, Rat had a reputation for exaggeration and overstatement, a compulsion to rev up the facts, and for most of us it was normal procedure to discount sixty or seventy percent of anything he had to say. (101)

19   Rat Kiley is an unreliable narrator, and his facts are always distorted, but this does not affect storytelling truth as far as O'Brien is concerned. The passage above on Rat Kiley's credibility as a storyteller concludes: "It wasn't a question of deceit. Just the opposite: he wanted to heat up the truth, to make it burn so hot that you would feel exactly what he felt" (101). This summarizes O'Brien's often confusing narrative strategy in *The Things They Carried*; the facts about what actually happened, or whether anything happened at all, are not important. They cannot be important because they themselves are too uncertain, too lost in a world in which certainty had vanished somewhere between the "crazy and almost crazy." The important thing is that any story about the war, any "true war story," must "burn so hot" when it is told that it becomes alive for the listener-reader in the act of its telling.

20   In Rat Kiley's story about how he wrote to Curt Lemon's sister, the details we are initially given are exaggerated to the point where, in keeping with O'Brien's fire metaphor, they begin to heat up. Curt Lemon, we are told, "would always volunteer for stuff nobody else would volunteer for in a million years" (75). And once Lemon went fishing with a crate of hand grenades, "the funniest thing in world history . . . about twenty zillion dead gook fish" (76). But the story does not get so hot that it burns, it does not become so "incredibly sad and true," as O'Brien puts

it, until we find out at the story's close that, in Rat's own words, "I write this beautiful fuckin' letter, I slave over it, and what happens? The dumb cooze never writes back" (77). It is these words and not the facts that come before them that make the story true for O'Brien.

21   At the beginning of this chapter, O'Brien asks us several times to "Listen to Rat," to listen how he says things more than to what he says. And of all of the words that stand out in his story, it is the word "cooze," (which is repeated four times in two pages), that makes his story come alive for O'Brien. "You can tell a true war story by its absolute and uncompromising allegiance to obscenity and evil" (76). This is just one way that O'Brien gives for determining what constitutes a true war story. The unending list of possibilities includes reacting to a story with the ambiguous words "Oh" and "There it is." Rat Kiley's use of "cooze" is another in the sequence of attempts to utter some truth about the Vietnam experience and, by extension, about war in general. There is no moral to be derived from this word, such as war is obscene or corrupt: "A true war story is never moral. It does not instruct" (76). There is simply the real and true fact that the closest thing to certainty and truth in a war story is a vague utterance, a punch at the darkness, an attempt to rip momentarily through the veil that repeatedly re-covers the reality and truth of what actually happened.

22   It is thus probably no coincidence that in the middle of this chapter on writing a true war story, O'Brien tells us that "Even now, at this instant," Mitchell Sanders's "yo-yo" is the main thing he can remember from the short time encompassing Lemon's death (83). This object, associated with games and play, becomes a metaphor for the playful act of narration that O'Brien practices in this book, a gamestory that he plays by necessity. The only way to tell a true war story, according to O'Brien, is to keep telling it "one more time, patiently, adding and subtracting, making up a few things to get at the real truth" (91), which ultimately is impossible because the real truth, the full truth, as the events themselves, are lost forever in "a great ghostly fog, thick and permanent" (88). You only "tell a true war story" "if you just keep on telling it" (91) because "absolute occurrence is irrelevant" (89). The truth, then, is clearly not something that can be distinguished or separated from the story itself, and the reality or non-reality of the story's events is not something that can be determined from a perspective outside of the story. As the critic Geoffrey Hartman says about poetry: "To keep a poem in mind is to keep it there, not to resolve it into available meanings" (274). Similarly, for O'Brien it is not the fact that a story happened that makes it true and worth remembering, any more than the story itself can be said to contain a final truth. The important thing is that a story becomes so much a part of the present that "there is nothing to remember (while we are reading it) except the story" (40). This is why O'Brien's narrator is condemned, perhaps in a positive sense, to telling and then retelling numerous variations of the same story over and over and over

again. This is also why he introduces each new version of a story with such comments as: "This one does it for me. I have told it before many times, many versions—but here is what actually happened" (85). What actually happened, the story's truth, can only become apparent for the fleeting moment in which it is being told; that truth will vanish back into the fog just as quickly as the events that occurred in Vietnam were sucked into a realm of uncertainty the moment they occurred.

23   O'Brien demonstrates nothing new about trying to tell war stories— that the "truths" they contain "are contradictory" (87), elusive, and thus indeterminate. Two hundred years ago, Goethe, as he tried to depict the senseless bloodshed during the allied invasion of revolutionary France, also reflected in his autobiographical essay "Campaign in France" on the same inevitable contradictions that arise when one speaks of what happened or might have happened in battle. Homer's *Iliad* is, of course, the ultimate statement on the contradictions inherent in war. However, what is new in O'Brien's approach in *The Things They Carried* is that he makes the axiom that in war "almost everything is true. Almost nothing is true" (87) the basis for the act of telling a war story.

24   The narrative strategy that O'Brien uses in this book to portray the uncertainty of what happened in Vietnam is not restricted to depicting war, and O'Brien does not limit it to the war alone. He concludes his book with a chapter titled "The Lives of the Dead" in which he moves from his experiences in Vietnam back to when he was nine years old. On the surface, the book's last chapter is about O'Brien's first date, his first love, a girl named Linda who died of a brain tumor a few months after he had taken her to see the movie *The Man Who Never Was*. What this chapter is really about, however, as its title suggests, is how the dead (which also includes people who may never have actually existed) can be given life in a work of fiction. In a story, O'Brien tells us, "memory and imagination and language combine to make spirits in the head. There is the illusion of aliveness" (260). Like the man who never was in the film of that title, the people that never were except in memories and the imagination can become real or alive, if only for a moment, through the act of storytelling.

25   According to O'Brien, when you tell a story, really tell it, "you objectify your own experience. You separate it from yourself" (178). By doing this you are able to externalize "a swirl of memories that might otherwise have ended in paralysis or worse" (179). However, the storyteller does not just escape from the events and people in a story by placing them on paper; as we have seen, the act of telling a given story is an on-going and never-ending process. By constantly involving and then re-involving the reader in the task of determining what "actually" happened in a given situation, in a story, and by forcing the reader to experience the impossibility of ever knowing with any certainty what actually happened, O'Brien liberates himself from the lonesome responsibility of remembering and trying to understand events. He also creates a community of

26   individuals immersed in the act of experiencing the uncertainty or indeterminacy of all events, regardless of whether they occurred in Vietnam, in a small town in Minnesota (253–73), or somewhere in the reader's own life.

O'Brien thus saves himself, as he puts it in the last sentence of his book, from the fate of his character Norman Bowker who, in a chapter called "Speaking of Courage," kills himself because he cannot find some lasting meaning in the horrible things he experienced in Vietnam. O'Brien saves himself by demonstrating in this book that the most important thing is to be able to recognize and accept that events have no fixed or final meaning and that the only meaning that events can have is one that emerges momentarily and then shifts and changes each time that the events come alive as they are remembered or portrayed.

27   The character Norman Bowker hangs himself in the locker room of the local YMCA after playing basketball with some friends (181), partially because he has a story locked up inside of himself that he feels he cannot tell because no one would want to hear it. It is the story of how he failed to save his friend Kiowa[2] from drowning in a field of human excrement: "A good war story, he thought, but it was not a war for war stories, not for talk of valor, and nobody in town wanted to know about the stink. They wanted good intentions and good deeds" (169). Bowker's dilemma is remarkably similar to that of Krebs in Hemingway's story "Soldier's Home": "At first Krebs [. . .] did not want to talk about the war at all. Later he felt the need to talk but no one wanted to hear about it. His town had heard too many atrocity stories to be thrilled by actualities" (Hemingway 145).

28   O'Brien, after his war, took on the task "of grabbing people by the shirt and explaining exactly what had happened to me" (179). He explains in *The Things They Carried* that it is impossible to know "exactly what had happened." He wants us to know all of the things he/they/we did not know about Vietnam and will probably never know. He wants us to feel the sense of uncertainty that his character/narrator Tim O'Brien experiences twenty years after the war when he returns to the place where his friend Kiowa sank into a "field of shit" and tries to find "something meaningful and right" (212) to say but ultimately can only say, "well . . . there it is" (212). Each time we, the readers of *The Things They Carried*, return to Vietnam through O'Brien's labyrinth of stories, we become more and more aware that this statement is the closest we probably ever will come to knowing the "real truth," the undying uncertainty of the Vietnam War.

[2]In the "Notes" to this chapter, O'Brien typically turns the whole story upside down "in the interest of truth" and tells us that Norman Bowker was not responsible for Kiowa's horrible death: "That part of the story is my own" (182). This phrase could be taken to mean that this part of the story is his own creation or that he was the one responsible for Kiowa's death.

Works Cited

Baritz, Loren. *Backfire: A History of How American Culture Led Us into Vietnam and Made Us Fight the Way We Did.* New York: Morrow, 1985.

Beidler, Philip. *American Literature and the Experience of Vietnam.* Athens: University of Georgia Press, 1982.

Halberstam, David. *One Very Hot Day.* New York: Houghton, 1967.

Hartman, Geoffrey. *Criticism in the Wilderness: The Study of Literature Today.* New Haven: Yale UP, 1980.

Hemingway, Ernest. *Short Stories.* New York: Scribner, 1953.

Iser, Wolfgang. *Prospecting: From Reader Response to Literary Anthropology.* Baltimore, MD: Johns Hopkins University Press, 1989.

Lomperis, Timothy, *"Reading the Wind": The Literature of the Vietnam War: An Interpretative Critique.* Durham, NC: Duke University Press, 1989.

Miller, J. Hillis. "Heart of Darkness Revisited." In *Heart of Darkness: A Case Study in Contemporary Criticism,* edited by Ross C. Murfin. New York: St. Martin's, 1989.

O'Brien, Tim. *Going After Cacciato.* New York: Dell, 1978.

———. *The Things They Carried.* Boston: Houghton, 1990.

"HOW TO TELL A TRUE WAR STORY": METAFICTION IN *THE THINGS THEY CARRIED*

CATHERINE CALLOWAY

1   Tim O'Brien's most recent book, *The Things They Carried*, begins with a litany of items that the soldiers "hump" in the Vietnam War—assorted weapons, dog tags, flak jackets, car plugs, cigarettes, insect repellent, letters, can openers, C-rations, jungle boots, maps, medical supplies, and explosives as well as memories, reputations, and personal histories. In addition, the reader soon learns, the soldiers also carry stories: stories that connect "the past to the future" (40), stories that can "make the dead talk" (261), stories that "never seem . . . to end" (83), stories that are "beyond telling" (79), and stories "that swirl back and forth across the border between trivia and bedlam, the mad and the mundane" (101). Although perhaps few of the stories in *The Things They Carried* are as brief as the well-known Vietnam War tale related by Michael Herr in *Dispatches*—"Patrol went up the mountain. One man came back. He died before he could tell us what happened," (6)—many are in their own way as enigmatic. The tales included in O'Brien's twenty-two chapters range from several lines to many pages and demonstrate well the impossibility of knowing the reality of the war in absolute terms. Sometimes stories are abandoned, only to be continued pages or chapters later. At other times, the narrator begins to tell a story, only to have another character finish the tale. Still other stories are told as if true accounts, only for their validity to be immediately questioned or denied. O'Brien draws the

reader into the text, calling the reader's attention to the process of invention and challenging him to determine which, if any, of the stories are true. As a result, the stories become epistemological tools, multidimensional windows through which the war, the world, and the ways of telling a war story can be viewed from many different angles and visions.

2   The epistemological ambivalence of the stories in *The Things They Carried* is reinforced by the book's ambiguity of style and structure. What exactly is *The Things They Carried* in terms of technique? Many reviewers refer to the work as a series of short stories, but it is much more than that. *The Things They Carried* is a combat novel, yet it is not a combat novel. It is also a blend of traditional and untraditional forms—a collection, Gene Lyons says, of "short stories, essays, anecdotes, narrative fragments, jokes, fables, biographical and autobiographical sketches, and philosophical asides" (52). It has been called both "a unified narrative with chapters that stand perfectly on their own" (Coffey 60) and a series of "22 discontinuous sections" (Bawer A 13).

3   Also ambiguous is the issue of how much of the book is autobiography. The relationship between fiction and reality arises early in the text when the reader learns the first of many parallels that emerge as the book progresses: that the protagonist and narrator, like the real author of *The Things They Carried*, is named Tim O'Brien. Both the real and the fictional Tim O'Brien are in their forties and are natives of Minnesota, writers who graduated Phi Beta Kappa from Macalester College, served as grunts in Vietnam after having been drafted at age twenty-one, attended graduate school at Harvard University, and wrote books entitled *If I Die in a Combat Zone* and *Going After Cacciato*. Other events of the protagonist's life are apparently invention. Unlike the real Tim O'Brien, the protagonist has a nine-year-old daughter named Kathleen and makes a return journey to Vietnam years after the war is over.[1] However, even the other supposedly fictional characters of the book sound real because of an epigraph preceding the stories that states, "This book is lovingly dedicated to the men of Alpha Company, and in particular to Jimmy Cross, Norman Bowker, Rat Kiley, Mitchell Sanders, Henry Dobbins, and Kiowa," leading the reader to wonder if the men of Alpha Company are real or imaginary.

4   Clearly O'Brien resists a simplistic classification of his latest work. In both the preface to the book and in an interview with Elizabeth Mehren, he terms *The Things They Carried* "fiction . . . a novel" (Mehren El), but in an interview with Martin Naparsteck, he refers to the work as a "sort of half novel, half group of stories. It's part nonfiction, too," he insists (7).

[1]Biographical information on the real Tim O'Brien is taken from published facts of his life. See, for instance, Michael Coffey, "Tim O'Brien," *Publishers Weekly*, 237, 16 Feb. 1990, 60–61, and Everett C. Wilkie Jr., "Tim O'Brien." *Dictionary of Literary Biography Yearbook: 1980*, eds. Karen L. Rood, Jean W. Ross, and Richard Ziegfeld (Detroit: Gale, 1981), 286–90.

And, as Naparsteck points out, the work "resists easy categorization: it is part novel, part collection of stories, part essays, part journalism; it is, more significantly, all at the same time" (1).

5   As O'Brien's extensive focus on storytelling indicates, *The Things They Carried* is also a work of contemporary metafiction, what Robert Scholes first termed fabulation or "ethically controlled fantasy" (3). According to Patricia Waugh,

> Metafiction is a term given to fictional writing which self-consciously and systematically draws attention to its status as an artefact in order to pose questions about the relationship between fiction and reality. In providing a critique of their own methods of construction, such writings not only examine the fundamental structures of narrative fiction, they also explore the possible fictionality of the world outside the literary fictional text. (2)

6   Like O'Brien's earlier novel, the critically acclaimed *Going After Cacciato*,[2] *The Things They Carried* considers the process of writing; it is, in fact, as much about the process of writing as it is the text of a literary work. By examining imagination and memory, two main components that O'Brien feels are important to a writer of fiction (Schroeder 143), and by providing so many layers of technique in one work, O'Brien delves into the origins of fictional creation. In focusing so extensively on what a war story is or is not, O'Brien writes a war story as he examines the process of writing one. To echo what Philip Beidler has stated about *Going After Cacciato*, "the form" of *The Things They Carried* thus becomes "its content" (172); the medium becomes the message.

7   "I'm forty-three years old, and a writer now," O'Brien's protagonist states periodically throughout the book, directly referring to his role as author and to the status of his work as artifice. "Much of it [the war] is hard to remember," he comments. "I sit at this typewriter and stare through my words and watch Kiowa sinking into the deep muck of a shit field, or Curt Lemon hanging in pieces from a tree, and as I write about these things, the remembering is turned into a kind of rehappening" (36). The "rehappening" takes the form of a number of types of stories: some happy, some sad, some peaceful, some bloody, some wacky. We learn of Ted Lavender, who is "zapped while zipping" (17) after urinating, of the paranoid friendship of Dave Jensen and Lee Strunk, of the revenge plot against Bobby Jorgenson, an unskilled medic who almost accidentally kills the narrator, of the moral confusion of the protagonist who fishes on the Rainy River and dreams of desertion to Canada, and Mary Ann Bell, Mark Fossie's blue-eyed, blonde, seventeen-year-old girlfriend, who is chillingly attracted to life in a combat zone.

8   Some stories only indirectly reflect the process of writing; other selections include obvious metafictional devices. In certain sections of the book, entire chapters are devoted to discussing form and technique.

---

[2]O'Brien, *Going After Cacciato* (New York: Delta/Seymour Lawrence, 1978). *Going After Cacciato* received the National Book Award in 1979.

A good example is "Notes," which elaborates on "Speaking of Courage," the story that precedes it. The serious reader of the real Tim O'Brien's fiction recognizes "Speaking of Courage" as having first been published in the Summer 1976 issue of *Massachusetts Review*.[3] This earlier version of the story plays off chapter 14 of *Going After Cacciato*, "Upon Almost Winning the Silver Star," in which the protagonist, Paul Berlin, is thinking about how he might have won the Silver Star for bravery in Vietnam had he had the courage to rescue Frenchie Tucker, a character shot while searching a tunnel. However, in *The Things They Carried*'s version of "Speaking of Courage," the protagonist is not Paul Berlin, but Norman Bowker, who wishes he had had the courage to save Kiowa, a soldier who dies in a field of excrement during a mortar attack.[4] Such shifts in character and events tempt the reader into textual participation, leading him to question the ambiguous nature of reality. Who really did not win the Silver Star for bravery? Paul Berlin, Norman Bowker, or Tim O'Brien? Who actually needed saving? Frenchie Tucker or Kiowa? Which version of the story, if either, is accurate? The inclusion of a metafictional chapter presenting the background behind the tale provides no definite answers or resolutions. We learn that Norman Bowker, who eventually commits suicide, asks the narrator to compose the story and that the author has revised the tale for inclusion in *The Things They Carried* because a postwar story is more appropriate for the later book than for *Going After Cacciato*. However, O'Brien's admission that much of the story is still invention compels the reader to wonder about the truth. The narrator assures us that the truth is that "Norman did not experience a failure of nerve that night . . . or lose the Silver Star for valor" (182). Can even this version be believed? Was there really a Norman Bowker, or is he, too, only fictional?

9   Even more significant, the reader is led to question the reality of many, if not all, of the stories in the book. The narrator insists that the story of Curt Lemon's death, for instance, is "all exactly true" (77), then states

[3]*Massachusetts Review* 17 (Spring 1976): 243–53. The earlier version of the story has also been published in *Prize Stories 1978: The O'Henry Awards*. Ed. and intro. William Abrahams (Garden City: Doubleday, 1978), 159–68. A later version of "Speaking of Courage" appeared in *Granta* 29 (Winter 1989): 135–154, along with "Notes."

[4]O'Brien frequently makes changes between versions of his stories that are published in literary magazines and chapters of his books. The version of "Spin" that was published in the Spring 1990 issue of *The Quarterly* (3–13), for example, combines several of the individual stories from *The Things They Carried* into one longer tale. In addition, O'Brien makes changes between the hardback and paperback versions of his books. In both the "Field Trip" chapter of the hardback edition of *The Things They Carried* and the short story version of "Field Trip" (*McCalls* 17, Aug. 1990: 78–79), the narrator returns Kiowa's hatchet to the site of Kiowa's death, but in the paperback edition of *The Things They Carried* (New York Penguin, 1990), the narrator carries a pair of Kiowa's moccasins. For references to changes in O'Brien's earlier works, see my "Pluralities of Vision: *Going After Cacciato* and Tim O'Brien's Short Fiction," *America Rediscovered: Critical Essays on Literature and Film of the Vietnam War*, eds. Owen W. Gilman Jr. and Lorrie Smith (New York: Garland, 1990), 213–24.

eight pages later that he has told Curt's story previously—"many times, many versions" (85)—before narrating yet another version. As a result, any and all accounts of the incident are questionable. Similarly, the reader is led to doubt the validity of many of the tales told by other characters in the book. The narrator remarks that Rat Kiley's stories, such as the one about Mary Ann Bell in "Sweetheart of the Song Tra Bong," are particularly ambiguous:

> For Rat Kiley . . . facts were formed by sensation, not the other way around, and when you listened to one of his stories, you'd find yourself performing rapid calculations in your head, subtracting superlatives, figuring the square root of an absolute and then multiplying by maybe. (101)

10   Still other characters admit the fictionality of their stories. Mitchell Sanders, in the ironically titled "How to Tell a True War Story," confesses to the protagonist that although his tale is the truth, parts of it are pure invention. "Last night, man," Sanders states, "I had to make up a few things . . . The glee club. There wasn't any glee club . . . No opera," either (83–84). "But," he adds, "it's still true" (84).

11   O'Brien shares the criteria with which the writer or teller and the reader or listener must be concerned by giving an extended definition of what a war story is or is not. The chapter "How to Tell a True War Story" focuses most extensively on the features that might be found in a "true" war tale. "A true war story is never moral," the narrator states. "It does not instruct, nor encourage virtue, nor suggest models of proper human behavior, nor restrain men from doing the things men have always done" (76).

12   Furthermore, a true war story has an "absolute and uncompromising allegiance to obscenity and evil" (76), is embarrassing, may not be believable, seems to go on forever, does "not generalize" or "indulge in abstraction or analysis" (84), does not necessarily make "a point" (88), and sometimes cannot even be told. True war stories, the reader soon realizes, are like the nature of the Vietnam War itself; "the only certainty is overwhelming ambiguity" (88). "The final and definitive truth" (83) cannot be derived, and any "truths are contradictory" (87).

> By defining a war story so broadly, O'Brien writes more stories, interspersing the definitions with examples from the war to illustrate them. What is particularly significant about the examples is that they are given in segments, a technique that actively engages the readers in the process of textual creation. Characters who are mentioned as having died early in the work are brought back to life through flashbacks in other parts of the text so that we can see who these characters are, what they are like, and how they die. For instance, in the story "Spin," the narrator first refers to the death of Curt Lemon, a soldier blown apart by a booby trap, but the reader does not learn the details of the tragedy until four stories later, in "How to Tell a True War Story." Even then, the reader must piece together the details of Curt's death throughout that particular tale. The first reference to Lemon appears on the third page of the story, when O'Brien matter-of-factly states,

"The dead guy's name was Curt Lemon" (77). Lemon's death is briefly mentioned a few paragraphs later, but additional details surrounding the incident are not given at once but are revealed gradually throughout the story, in between digressive stories narrated by two other soldiers, Rat Kiley and Mitchell Sanders. Each fragment about Curt's accident illustrates the situation more graphically. Near the beginning of the tale, O'Brien describes the death somewhat poetically. Curt is "a handsome kid, really. Sharp grey eyes, lean and narrow-waisted, and when he died it was almost beautiful, the way the sunlight came around him and lifted him up and sucked him high into a tree full of moss and vines and white blossoms" (78). Lemon is not mentioned again for seven pages, at which time O'Brien illustrates the effect of Lemon's death upon the other soldiers by detailing how Rat Kiley, avenging Curt's death, mutilates and kills a baby water buffalo. When later in the story Lemon's accident is narrated for the third time, the reader is finally told what was briefly alluded to in the earlier tale "Spin": how the soldiers had to peel Curt Lemon's body parts from a tree.

13   The story of Curt Lemon does not end with "How to Tell a True War Story" but is narrated further in two other stories, "The Dentist" and "The Lives of the Dead." In "The Lives of the Dead," for example, Curt is resurrected through a story of his trick-or-treating in Vietnamese hootches on Halloween for whatever goodies he can get: "candles and joss sticks and a pair of black pajamas and statuettes of the smiling Buddha" (268). To hear Rat Kiley tell it, the narrator comments, "you'd never know that Curt Lemon was dead. He was still out there in the dark, naked and painted up, trick-or-treating, sliding from hootch to hootch in that crazy white ghost mask" (268). To further complicate matters, in "The Lives of the Dead," O'Brien alludes to a soldier other than Curt, Stink Harris, from a previous literary work, *Going After Cacciato*, written over a decade before *The Things They Carried*. Thus, the epistemological uncertainty in the stories is mirrored by the fact that O'Brien presents events that take place in a fragmented form rather than in a straightforward, linear fashion. The reader has to piece together information, such as the circumstances surrounding the characters' deaths, in the same manner that the characters must piece together the reality of the war, or, for that matter, Curt Lemon's body.

14   The issue of truth is particularly a main crux of the events surrounding "The Man I Killed," a story that O'Brien places near the center of the book. Gradually interspersed throughout the stories that make up *The Things They Carried* are references to a Vietnamese soldier, "A slim, dead, dainty young man of about twenty" (40) with "a star-shaped hole" (141) in his face, who is first mentioned in the story "Spin" and whose death still haunts the narrator long after the end of the war. Nine chapters after "Spin," in "The Man I Killed," the protagonist graphically describes the dead Vietnamese youth as well as creates a personal history for him; he envisions the young man to have been a reluctant soldier who hated violence and "loved mathematics" (142), a university-educated man who "had been a soldier for only a single day" (144) and who, like

the narrator, perhaps went to war only to avoid "disgracing himself, and therefore his family and village" (142).[5] "Ambush," the story immediately following "The Man I Killed," provides yet another kaleidoscopic fictional frame of the incident, describing in detail the events that lead up to the narrator's killing of the young soldier and ending with a version of the event that suggests that the young man does not die at all. The reader is forced to connect the threads of the story in between several chapters that span over a hundred pages; not until a later chapter, "Good Form," where the protagonist narrates three more stories of the event, does the reader fully question the truth of the incident. In the first version in "Good Form," the narrator reverses the details of the earlier stories and denies that he was the thrower of the grenade that killed the man. "Twenty years ago I watched a man die on a trail near the village of My Khe," he states. "I did not kill him. But I was present, you see, and my presence was guilt enough" (203). However, he immediately admits that "Even that story is made up" (203) and tells instead what he terms "the happening-truth":

> I was once a soldier. There were many bodies, real bodies with real faces, but I was young then and I was afraid to look. And now, twenty years later, I'm left with faceless responsibility and faceless grief. (203)

15   In still a third version, "the happening-truth" is replaced with "the story-truth." According to the protagonist, the Vietnamese soldier

> was a slim, dead, almost dainty young man of about twenty. He lay in the center of a red clay trail near the village of My Khe. His jaw was in his throat. His one eye was shut, the other eye was a star-shaped hole. I killed him. (204)

16   But the reader wonders, did the narrator kill the young man? When the narrator's nine-year-old daughter demands, "Daddy, tell the truth . . . did you ever kill anybody?" the narrator reveals that he "can say, honestly, 'Of course not,'" or he "can say, honestly, 'Yes'" (204).

17   According to Inger Christensen, one of the most important elements of metafiction is "the novelist's message" (10). At least one reviewer has reduced O'Brien's message in *The Things They Carried* to the moral "'Death sucks'" (Melmoth H6); the book, however, reveals an even greater thematic concern. "Stories can save us," asserts the protagonist in "The Lives of the Dead," the concluding story of the text (255), where fiction is used as a means of resurrecting the deceased. In this multiple narrative, O'Brien juxtaposes tales of death in Vietnam with an account of the death of Linda, a nine-year-old girl who had a brain tumor. As the protagonist tells Linda's story, he also comments on the nature and power of fiction. Stories, he writes, are "a kind of dreaming, [where] the dead

---

[5]O'Brien develops the figure of the young Vietnamese youth who opposes the war more fully in *Going After Cacciato*, where Li Van Hgoc, a Vietnamese major, has been imprisoned in a tunnel complex for ten years for fleeing from the war and refusing to fight. The major, in a sense, mirrors Paul Berlin and the Third Squad. Theoretically, the soldiers have one main factor in common with Li Van Hgoc; they are all deserters from the war.

sometimes smile and sit up and return to the world" (255). The narrator of "The Lives of the Dead" thus seeks to keep his own friends alive through the art of storytelling. "As a writer now," he asserts,

> I want to save Linda's life. Not her body—her life . . . in a story I can steal her soul. I can revive, at least briefly, that which is absolute and unchanging . . . in a story, miracles can happen. Linda can smile and sit up. She can reach out, touch my wrist, and say, "Timmy, stop crying." (265)

18   Past, present, and future merge into one story as through fiction O'Brien zips "across the surface of . . . [his] own history, moving fast, riding the melt beneath the blades, doing loops and spins . . . as Tim trying to save Timmy's life with a story" (273). His story mirrors his own creative image of history, "a blade tracing loops on ice" (265), as his metafictive narrative circles on three levels: the war of a little boy's soul as he tries to understand the death of a friend, the Vietnam War of a twenty-three-year-old infantry sergeant, and the war of "guilt and sorrow" (265) faced by "a middle-aged writer" (265) who must deal with the past.

19   In focusing so extensively on the power of fiction and on what a war story is or is not in *The Things They Carried*, O'Brien writes a multidimensional war story even as he examines the process of writing one. His tales become stories within stories or multilayered texts within texts within texts. The book's genius is a seeming inevitability of form that perfectly embodies its theme—the miracle of vision—the eternally protean and volatile capacity of the imagination, which may invent that which it has the will and vision to conceive.[6] "In the end," the narrator states,

> a true war story is never about war. It's about sunlight. It's about the special way that dawn spreads out on a river when you know you must cross the river and march into the mountains and do things you are afraid to do. It's about love and memory. It's about sorrow. It's about sisters who never write back and people who never listen. (91)

20   How, then, can a true war story be told? Perhaps the best way, O'Brien says, is to "just keep on telling it" (91).

Works Cited

Bawer, Bruce. "Confession or Fiction? Stories from Vietnam." *Wall Street Journal* 215, 23 Mar. 1990: A13.

Beidler, Philip D. *American Literature and the Experience of Vietnam*. Athens: University of Georgia Press, 1982.

---

[6]This theme is also a main theme of *Going After Cacciato*, which examines issues such as how war affects the imagination and how the imagination affects war, how reality cannot be escaped even in the imagination, how the imagination is used to invent rather than to discover, how the imagination must be used as a responsible tool, and how the imagination can be a force for remaking reality.

Christensen, Inger. *The Meaning of Metafiction*. Bergen: Universitets-forlaget, 1981.

Herr, Michael. *Dispatches*. New York: Vintage, 1977.

Lyons, Gene. "No More Bugles, No More Drums." *Entertainment Weekly* 23 Feb. 1990: 50–52.

Mehren, Elizabeth. "Short War Stories." *Los Angeles Times* 11 Mar. 1990: E1, E12.

Melmoth, John. "Muck and Bullets." *The Sunday Times* (London) 20 May 1990: H6.

Naparsteck, Martin. "An Interview with Tim O'Brien." *Contemporary Literature* 32 (Spring 1991): 1–11.

O'Brien, Tim. *The Things They Carried*. New York: Houghton, 1990.

Scholes, Robert. *Fabulation and Metafiction*. Urbana: University of Illinois Press, 1983.

Schroeder, Eric James. "Two Interviews: Talks with Tim O'Brien and Robert Stone." *Modern Fiction Studies 30* (Spring 1984): 135–64.

Waugh, Patricia. *Metafiction: The Theory and Practice of Self-Conscious Fiction*. New York: Methuen, 1984.

GETTING IT RIGHT: THE SHORT FICTION OF TIM O'BRIEN

DANIEL ROBINSON

But it's true even if it didn't happen—

—KEN KESEY

1   In his introduction to *Men at War*, Ernest Hemingway states that a "writer's job is tell the truth. His standard of fidelity to the truth should be so high that his inventions . . . should produce a truer account than anything factual can be" (xi). Tim O'Brien, for whose writing the Vietnam War is the informing principle, returns to this notion of truth in his short fiction.[1] His stories revolve around multiple centers of interest—at once stories in the truest sense, with a core of action and character, and also metafictional stories on the precise nature of writing war stories.

2   For O'Brien, like Hemingway in his introduction, the notion of absolute fidelity to facts almost becomes a non sequitur when considering truth. Facts might provide a chronology of events (and even then, we may disagree on the validity of the facts), but alone they cannot reveal the hidden truths found in a true war story. As Hemingway writes, facts "can be observed badly; but when a good writer is creating something, he has time and scope to make of it an absolute truth" (xi–xii). That is

---

[1]In this essay, I consider only those stories of Tim O'Brien's that were previously published as separate short stories and are substantially different from any counterparts in later novels. Thus, I exclude stories that appeared in *Going After Cacciato* in much the same form as when they were published earlier as well as those stories in *The Things They Carried* that were not separately published.

also true for O'Brien: He sometimes writes stories that contradict the facts of other stories; yet the essential, underlying truth of each story is intact and illuminating. Those truths lie as much in the fragmented, impressionistic stories he tells as in the narrative technique he chooses for the telling.

3   O'Brien does not deliver Vietnam in neatly packaged truisms. The same words that rang obscene for Frederic Henry in Hemingway's *A Farewell to Arms*, "abstract words such as glory, honor, courage, or hallow," become empty in O'Brien's fiction. Those words imply a rational order to war that does not exist, and the absence of those words mirrors the horror of a world at its most irrational. As O'Brien writes in "How to Tell a True War Story," "[O]ften in a true war story there is not even a point" (88). What O'Brien prefers are the images that make "the stomach believe" (89), images of men at war who are too afraid not to kill.

4   The true reasons that bring O'Brien's characters to Vietnam are far from the abstract words that Frederic Henry dismisses and equally far from the Hollywood notion of heroism so prevalent in war movies prior to American involvement in Vietnam. The average age of the company of foot soldiers O'Brien writes about is nineteen or twenty, and most were probably drafted, as is the case of the fictional Tim O'Brien through whom author O'Brien often tells his stories. Thus, we see boys becoming men before they have had the opportunity to understand what manhood involves. And among the many things each soldier carried—the weapons, charms, diseases, and emotions—they "carried the soldier's greatest fear, which was the fear of blushing. Men killed, and died, because they were embarrassed not to" ("Things" 20–21). Even the enemy soldiers, the Viet Cong, exhibit that moral dichotomy and fight out of fear as much as nationalism:

> In the presence of his father and uncles, he pretended to look forward to doing his patriotic duty, which was also a privilege, but at night he prayed with his mother that the war might end soon. Beyond anything else, he was afraid of disgracing himself, and therefore his family and village. ("Man" 142)

5   However, quite different from most of O'Brien's characters driven by fear is Azar, the nineteen-year-old draftee who straps a puppy to a Claymore antipersonnel mine and blows the dog to pieces. Azar, still a teenager, loves Vietnam because it makes him "feel like a kid again." "The Vietnam experience," he says, "I mean, wow, I love this shit" ("Ghost" 237). O'Brien's characters choose war for entirely negative reasons, not for unselfish love of country or of basic freedoms but from fear of embarrassment and cowardice or the love of war as if it were a child's game. Even the decision to go to Vietnam is determined not through an examination of positive motives but, again, for negative reasons: "I would go to the war . . . because I was embarrassed not to. . . . I was a coward. I went to war" ("River" 63).

6   That inability in O'Brien's characters to establish a positive purpose in their reasons for going to war mirrors the historical ambiguities surrounding American involvement in Vietnam. Like the chaotic and morally ambiguous war they fight, O'Brien's characters are unsure of their purpose or even their actions. Azar explains blowing up the puppy as simple childish exuberance: "What's everybody so upset about? I mean, Christ, I'm just a boy" ("Spin" 40). After one of his men dies, "Lieutenant Jimmy Cross led his men into the village of Than Ke. They burned everything. They shot chickens and dogs, they trashed the village well, they called in artillery and watched the wreckage, then they marched for several hours through the hot afternoon" to a place where they set up camp for the night ("Things" 16). Those men act not from forethought but from some measure of selective emotion: Azar, the sadist, experiences delight from torturing the puppy and, in "The Ghost Soldiers," torture—prankstering a medic on guard duty who had nearly allowed another soldier to die through inaction; and the troop, following Lavender's sniper-death, razes the nearest village not for some strategic reason but out of an apparent need for revenge. The chauvinistic clichés that so often accompany patriotic fervor are missing. These characters have no center around which they can construct a reason for their involvement, and the only absolute is that resupply helicopters will arrive soon with more things for them to carry: For "all the ambiguities of Vietnam, all the mysteries and unknowns, there was at least the single abiding certainty that they would never be at a loss for things to carry" ("Things" 16).

7   As Lorrie Smith writes in "Disarming the War Story," "The 'story' of World War II . . . has meaning for our culture as a heroic quest, and it forms a coherent narrative in which the soldier's sacrifices are redemptive" (90). All of that coherence of purpose is lost in O'Brien's stories of Vietnam, as his characters stumble through a landscape of disjointed experiences and realities. And though we may, as Smith asserts, "feel acutely the disjunction between ideals and realities" (90) when we attempt to consider Vietnam in terms of heroic quests, coherent actions, and redemptive sacrifices, O'Brien's characters seldom articulate any distinctions. For them, the realities are too overpowering to place against any abstract notions based upon cultural and societal ideals. Only Lt. Jimmy Cross, in "The Things They Carried," and Tim,[2] in "On the Rainy River," consider that disjunction, and then only in personal terms, excluding any real notion of established codes.

---

[2]Any use of "Tim" in this essay refers to the fictional character, and the use of "O'Brien" refers to Tim O'Brien the author. In an interview with Steven Kaplan, O'Brien discusses the similarities and differences between him and his fictional character: "Everything I have written has come partly out of my own concerns . . . but the story lines themselves, the events . . . the characters . . . the places . . . are almost all invented. . . . Ninety percent or more of the material . . . is invented, and I invented ninety percent of a new Tim O'Brien, maybe even more than that" (95).

8   One often expects writers of war stories to present antithetical abstractions in a concrete form to establish some moral or ethical base. O'Brien, however, fuses abstracts such as reality and surreality and right and wrong in an effort to emphasize the lack of firm moral ground supporting his characters in a war lacking in definable purposes. To stop his own pain at seeing his best friend blown up, Rat Kiley systematically dismembers a baby water buffalo by shooting pieces from its body—its mouth, tail, ears, nose—until all that remains alive and moving are its eyes. The reaction by Rat's stunned comrades is restrained amazement: "A new wrinkle. I never seen it before. . . . Well, that's Nam" (86). A group of Green Berets keep a pile of enemy bones stacked in a corner of their barracks underneath a sign that reads, "ASSEMBLE YOUR OWN GOOK!! FREE SAMPLE KIT!" ("Sweetheart" 119). That distillation of moral or ethical standards, an "aesthetic purity of moral indifference" ("True" 87), illustrates a general loss of humanity in any war, but possibly more so in a war that lacks any underlying absolutes, any real reasons for having gone to war. Thus the moral confusion Tim feels (in "On the Rainy River") after finding out he has been drafted becomes a moral indifference once exposed to the brutalities and absurdities of war.

9   Those apparent indifferences extend even to how the soldiers deal with the death of their comrades. When a man dies, he is not killed, but "greased. . . . offed, lit up, zapped." ("Things" 19). Somehow, by verbally denying the reality of death through hyperbolic misnomers, they reject the death itself. At one point in "The Lives of the Dead," Tim's unit enters a village it has calmly watched being bombed and burned by air strikes for thirty minutes. When the unit enters, the only person in the village is a dead old man who is missing an arm and whose face is covered by swarming flies and gnats. Each man, as he walks past the dead Vietnamese, offers a greeting and shakes the remaining hand: "How-dee-doo. . . . Gimme five. . . . A real honor. . . . Pleased as punch" (256). After Tim refuses to introduce himself or even offer a toast to the old man's health, he is ridiculed for not showing respect for his elders: "Maybe it's too real for you?" he is asked. "That's right," he replies. "Way too real" (256). It is only his fourth day, and Tim soon realizes that he must develop the cynical sense of humor he will eventually need to cope with the realities of death. Paul Berlin, on his first day in Vietnam, in "Where Have You Gone, Charming Billy?" watches one of his comrades die of a heart attack brought on by the fear of dying. In his attempt to deal with witnessing his first death, he tries to transform the event into something that had not happened. Eventually, however, as the realities of the experience eat at him, he places the death in comic terms by imagining the official death notification:

SORRY TO INFORM YOU THAT YOUR SON BILLY BOY WAS YESTERDAY SCARED TO DEATH IN ACTION IN THE REPUBLIC OF VIETNAM, VALIANTLY SUCCUMBING TO A HEART ATTACK SUFFERED WHILE UNDER ENORMOUS STRESS. . . . (130)

10   Berlin finally concludes that the death will make "a good joke" and "a funny war story" for his father (132). Not superficial male posturing, but overwhelming fear forces O'Brien's characters purposefully to detach themselves from death. They use any method possible, from keeping the dead alive through absurd ceremonial greetings to parodying government form letters to, as Albert Wilhelm writes, "keep the horrors of war at bay" (221).

11   Ironically, one of the deaths that breaks through the fabricated veneer of insulation is the death of an enemy in "The Man I Killed." In explicit detail bordering on the religious, Tim vividly recalls the man he killed—maybe the first man or maybe just the first he had an opportunity to study afterwards. Azar dismisses the death in the common distancing dialogue discussed above, "Oh, man, you fuckin' trashed the fucker. . . . You laid him out like Shredded fuckin' Wheat. . . . Rice Krispies, you know? On the dead test, this particular individual gets A-plus" (140); And Kiowa tries moving Tim beyond his dumbstruck staring at the bloody corpse to talk about his emotions. Only here and in "Speaking of Courage," where Norman Bowker, back home in Iowa on the Fourth of July, recounts the death of Kiowa in a swampy field, is the examination of death not covered under false layers of fear. O'Brien the writer must now dredge up those deaths that Tim the young soldier tried so hard to bury, which may explain why O'Brien returns to Vietnam in his fiction with such force and passion: he is reliving the horrors he suppressed decades earlier.

12   As in "The Man I Killed" and "Speaking of Courage," O'Brien often uses a spiraling narrative technique to draw out the realism of death, even if this characters continue to refute that death. O'Brien revolves those stories around a specific death, as Joseph Heller revolves the first part of *Catch-22* around Snowden's death, covering the same ground yet illuminating the moment's particular horror with each movement back to the death. The effect is at once numbing and oddly positive. We sense the overwhelming totality of death on the one hand, but we also imagine the narrator attempting to place a new order to his story, one that will somehow exclude the death. In "The Man I Killed," the effect is an increasing horror at seeing the dead man; whereas in "Speaking of Courage," Norman realizes that he failed to save his friend's life. "The Things They Carried" revolves around the sniper death of Lavender, and in so doing shows Lt. Jimmy Cross's movement from the innocence of his insular world in which, to keep the war at a distance, he pretends that a girl back home in the United States is in love with him. However, with Lavender's death, he must face the reality that his lack of focus in leading his men may in part have caused that death. As many initiations do, Cross's initiation into the realities surrounding him results also in his need to destroy something of his past, which he does when he burns Martha's letters and photographs.

13   Kiowa's death becomes the center point for Norman Bowker in "Speaking of Courage" and is also the death around which the action

revolves in "In the Field." Ironically, here two other soldiers feel the responsibility for Kiowa's death, which adds an interesting layer of multiplicity of perception to O'Brien's stories. O'Brien further explores that notion of multiplicity of perception through Jimmy Cross's drafting a letter to Kiowa's parents. His first draft places blame on some ubiquitous "They" who sent him and his men to bivouac in a tactically indefensible position; in his second draft, he accepts the blame; and finally, he revises the letter to express "an officer's condolences. No apologies necessary" (197–98). All three drafts are accurate and true, underscoring the inability to write about war in absolute terms.

14   O'Brien's cyclical pattern that places death as the center point around which many of his stories revolve reinforces a permanence to war that a more linear narrative structure would necessarily exclude. O'Brien's characters cannot leave the deaths behind them and trudge on through a strictly chronological story. "The bad stuff," O'Brien writes in "Spin," "never stops happening: it lives in its own dimension, replaying itself over and over" (36). And even when the war is over, it is not over; even though "the war occurred half a lifetime ago, . . . the remembering makes it now" (40). So the cyclical pattern established in many of these stories continues to revolve long after the story stops, and the things they carried during the war become eclipsed by the things they carry following the war.

15   The deaths, of course, form the most visually unforgettable parts of O'Brien's stories. They are, first of all, not Hollywood war deaths: They are not scripted to show grace under pressure or to elevate the human reaction to the horrors of war. O'Brien's characters do not die filled with the notions of courage, honor, and camaraderie: they just die. Ted Lavender dies while zipping up his pants after urinating on a bus; Kiowa dies from drowning in the muddy human filth of a village's sewage field; Billy Boy Watkins dies of a heart attack brought on by the fear of dying after stepping on a land mine; Lemon dies from stepping on a land mine while playing an innocent game of catch and is literally blown into a nearby tree; and Jorgenson, who dies after eluding enemy patrols and taking a midnight swim, swallows bad water. None of the deaths are the deaths of heroes; and like the ritualized shooting of the water buffalo following Lemon's death, they serve to show a major theme connecting O'Brien's work—how isolated events of cruelty define war. Azar killing the puppy, Bowker shooting the water buffalo, a little girl dancing to an unheard rhythm outside her burned-out hut following a napalm raid, the first enemy killed, and the singular deaths of friends accrue as acts of cruelty to, as O'Brien says, "touch [the] reader's heart more than a grandiose description of the fire bombing of a village, or the napalming of a village, where you don't see corpses, you don't know the corpses, you don't witness the death in any detail. It is somehow made abstract, bloodless" (Kaplan 102). By focusing on the character—the individual coming in close contact with what death looks like—and allowing the surrounding

scenes and events to take secondary importance, O'Brien increases the absurdity and horror. His plots are determined not by incident and event, but by the changing moral attitudes and development of his characters.

16   Likewise, "declarations about war, such as war is hell" (Kaplan 101) or war is immoral seem, in O'Brien's fiction, just as hollow as the declarations of war that place men in battle. These declarations, while possibly true, are little more than abstract generalities that fail to turn something deep within the reader. "A true war story," as O'Brien wrote, "if truly told, makes the stomach believe" (84). A true war story, then, may not have a point, and it certainly does not exist in the narrative vacuum of beginning-middle-end, but it functions at a level of truth beyond that found in the story's words. Often, you doubt whether an O'Brien story can be true. Can a man actually transport his girlfriend to an isolated medical post in the Central Highlands and then lose her to the war as she slowly matriculates into the jungle? Some things, Pederson says in "Keeping Watch by Night," "you just see and you got to believe in what you see" (66). A true war story has no moral, no instruction, no virtue, no suggestion of proper behavior; there is only a revelation of the possible evil in the nature of man: "You can tell a true war story," O'Brien tells us, "by its absolute and uncompromising allegiance to obscenity and evil" ("True" 76). True war stories, as O'Brien writes in his nonfiction narrative *If I Die in a Combat Zone*, offer "simple, unprofound scraps of truth" that lack any lessons to teach about war. The writer, then, according to O'Brien, must "simply tell stories" (32). However, within that apparent lack of pretense to message lies the phenomenological truths of O'Brien's fiction, which strike much deeper than, as Lorrie Smith writes, an exploitation of "war's larger political implications" (94). By suppressing the abstract in favor of the concrete, O'Brien allows his stories to exist as commentary through the "complex tangles and nuances of actual experience" (Calloway 222).

17   Beyond that, moreover, as O'Brien tells Steven Kaplan, "good stories somehow have to do with an awakening into a new world, something new and true, where someone is jolted out of . . . complacency and forced to confront a new set of circumstances or a new self" (99). The archetypal pattern that O'Brien here alludes to of initiation into the complexities of the real world forms an underlying basis of much of O'Brien's fiction. Paul Berlin's witnessing Billy Boy's death signals his loss of innocence, his transition into manhood, and an unwelcome realization of the world's potential for cruelty. And Tim, who may realize that his only options are kill or be killed, cannot be comforted by that knowledge as his world of relative innocence is shattered by the realities of this new world he inhabits. Correspondingly, that separation between men and boys is also shown by the physical appearance of the soldiers as they trudge along under the weight of all they carry: "The most recent arrivals had pasty skin burnt at the shoulder blades and clavicle and neck; their boots were not yet red with clay, and they walked more carefully than

the rest, and they looked more vulnerable" ("Spin" 36). As their appearance evolves and their movements change, so, too, their character changes in the "effort to establish a new order" to their life (Kaplan 99)—one in which the vulnerability of youth is replaced by the cynicism and hardness of manhood.

18   That also may be why O'Brien still returns to Vietnam in his fiction—because he is still trying to make sense of the new order established in his life over twenty years ago. In his stories, in the futile attempt to regain what he had before the war, he can still dream alive the people who died; unfortunately, though, that also necessitates his reliving their deaths. That need may be what still hits O'Brien: "twenty years later, in your sleep, and you wake up and shake your wife and start telling the story to her, except when you get to the end you've forgotten the point again. And then for a long time you lie there watching the story happen in your head. You listen to your wife's breathing. The war's over. You close your eyes. You smile and think, Christ, what's the point?" ("True" 88–89). The point, however, is all in the telling, as is the healing. In his stories, O'Brien answers his characters' desire to make sense out of their experiences: Kiowa imploring Tim to just talk after killing an enemy soldier instead of dumbly staring at the corpse, or Rat Kiley—not wanting to have to listen to the silence of the night—asking Kiowa to tell once again how Lavender fell like a sack of cement, or the platoon waiting once more for Rat to tell his story about the sweetheart of Song Tra Bong. O'Brien's characters, like O'Brien himself, carry their stories with them, sometimes damning the unimaginable weight of relived experience and sometimes extolling the outlet allowed through storytelling, which becomes at times a life-support system and a salvation from the moral complexities of the war.

19   Those moral complexities required of O'Brien "an innovative form rather than the conventional chronological narrative" (Slabey 206). In presenting stories from a war that lacked a traditional progression or a logical structure, O'Brien demands more from his writing than strict realism can provide. He blurs the distinctions in his stories to present truths coalesced in memory and imagination to, "get things right"—not in the absolute terms of packaged truisms and simplistic judgments but through the inner landscape of experiential truth telling.

Works Cited

Beidler, Philip D. *Re-Writing America: Vietnam Authors in Their Generation*. Athens: University of Georgia Press, 1991.

Calloway, Catherine. "Pluralities of Vision: *Going After Cacciato* and Tim O'Brien's Short Fiction." In *America Rediscovered*, edited by Gilman and Smith, 213–22.

Gilman, Owen W., and Lorrie Smith, eds. *America Rediscovered: Critical Essays on Literature and Film of the Vietnam War*. New York: Garland, 1990.

Kaplan, Steven. "An Interview with *Tim O'Brien*." *Missouri Review* *14.3* (1991): 95–108.

O'Brien, Tim. "The Ghost Soldiers." O'Brien, *Things* 215–44.

———. "How to Tell a True War Story." O'Brien, *Things*, 73–92.

———. "In the Field." O'Brien, *Things*, 183–200.

———. "Keeping Watch by Night." *Redbook* 148 (Dec. 1976): 65–67.

———. "The Lives of the Dead." O'Brien, *Things*, 253–73.

———. "The Man I Killed." O'Brien, *Things*, 137–44.

———. "On the Rainy River." O'Brien, *Things*, 41–64.

———. "Speaking of Courage." O'Brien, *Things*, 155–74.

———. "Spin." O'Brien, *Things*, 33–40.

———. "Style." O'Brien, *Things*, 151–54.

———. "Sweetheart of Song Tra Bong." O'Brien, *Things*, 99–126.

———. "The Things They Carried." O'Brien, *Things*, 1–26.

———. *The Things They Carried*. New York: Penguin, 1991.

———. "Where Have You Gone, Charming Billy?" *Redbook* 145 (May 1975): 81, 127–32.

Slabey, Robert M. "*Going After Cacciato*: Tim O'Brien's 'Separate Peace.'" In *America Rediscovered*, edited by Gilman and Smith, 205–11.

Smith, Lorrie. "Disarming the War Story." In *America Rediscovered*, edited by Gilman and Smith, 87–99.

Wilhelm, Albert. "Ballad Allusions in Tim O'Brien's 'Where Have You Gone, Charming Billy?'" *Studies in Short Fiction* 28.2 (Spring 1991): 218–22.

Nick Hembree

Professor Henderson

English 1102

3 May 2006

Dreams of Truth, Reality, and War

1   Tim O'Brien seamlessly blends fact and fiction in his
stories set in the Vietnam conflict, weaving a horridly
beautiful tapestry of war and of life. He creates truths that
transcend what is and what is not, and in his own words, "[w]hat
stories can do, I guess, is make things present" ("Good Form"
180). Many critics of his work agree that his masterful
storytelling ability confers some special sense of what it was
like to be there, deep in the foggy mountains and torrid jungles
of Vietnam. Catherine Calloway says, "Clearly O'Brien resists a
simplistic classification of his latest work [*The Things They
Carried*]" (814), and Daniel Robinson comments, "[Tim O'Brien]
sometimes writes stories that contradict the facts of other
stories; yet the essential underlying truth of each story is
intact and illuminating" (822).

2   As O'Brien himself often repeats throughout his works,
there are no morals to his stories—only truths. A moral is a
simple truism that can be applied to a limited situation; a
truth, on the other hand, allows those who understand it
properly to be more aware of the nature of humanity. With that
idea in mind, O'Brien probes deeply into his own inner psyche in
"On the Rainy River," delving deeply into powerful emotional
currents that sweep past all of the thoughts and ideals that he
has tried to construct around them. He begins the story with an
explanation of why he has never told this particular tale to
anyone before:

> To go into it, I always thought, would only
> cause embarrassment for all of us, a sudden
> need to be elsewhere, which is the natural
> response to a confession. . . . For nearly
> twenty years I've had to live with it, feeling
> the shame, trying to push it away, and so by
> this act of remembrance, by putting the facts
> down on paper, I hope to relieve at least some
> of the pressure of my dreams. (777)

3   This passage gives the reader some small idea of how
profoundly O'Brien's acts in the story have affected even his
present day life. The price of cowardice to one's self is one
not easily repaid, as O'Brien discovers from the events of his
past. Morally and intellectually against the fighting in
Vietnam, Tim O'Brien has found himself suddenly with a draft
notice and having finally to come to grips with who he is and
what he is personally going to do about the war, yet indecision
is the only solution he can come up with, and "[b]eyond all
this, or at the very center, was the raw fact of terror" (779),
the terror of facing death for a reason that cannot be
understood or believed in. Eventually, O'Brien heads north in a
vain attempt to escape his reality, only to find the Canadian
border, and the ultimate need to make a decision to run from the
war or to take a part in it. At the very end of the story, the
choice is made: "[e]ven in my imagination, the shore [of Canada]
just twenty yards away, I couldn't make myself be brave. It had
nothing to do with morality. Embarrassment, that's all it was"
(788). It is nice to believe in ideals of what is right and what
is wrong, but in the end, sometimes we simply do what our
overwhelming internal forces drive us to, for better or for

worse. Tim O'Brien would likely argue for the worst, yet the
past has already been, and we can only take care of the present.

4   Of all his stories, "On the Rainy River" rings with the
clearest sound of fact, yet this is not always the case with
O'Brien's writings. In fact, one of his greatest attributes as a
writer is his excellent use of metafiction, drawing the reader's
attention to a fundamental truth that might otherwise be missed.
All throughout the story "How to Tell a True War Story," in *The
Things They Carried*, O'Brien repeats the account of how Curt
Lemon came to die: "he must've thought it was the sunlight
killing him. It was not the sunlight. It was a rigged 105 round"
(798). Every time he repeats the story, it comes a small step
closer to a truth, becoming more full with the telling, yet also
becoming less believable. Rat Kiley, a friend of Curt, writes to
his sister after he dies, expressing his love and anguish for
Curt, yet the "dumb cooze" never writes back, despite Rat's
pouring his heart out into the letter. The reader later learns
that Curt is the same man who trick-or-treated completely nude
(save only his boots and gun) in a small Vietnamese village, and
he is also the same man who traipses about the jungle, as if on a
school field trip instead of a military mission. Later on, after
Curt's death, Rat mercilessly tortures a water buffalo, shooting
it in various places and watching it collapse, as all of his
fellow soldiers sit back and watch, sickened at the display, yet
simply letting it pass. Finally, O'Brien tells of how whenever he
tells this particular story, someone will always come up and say
to him how touching it was and that he should also move on with
his life, but "[a]ll you can do is tell it one more time,
patiently, adding and subtracting, making up a few things to get
at the real truth. . . . No Lemon, no Rat Kiley. No trail
junction. No baby buffalo" (798). Simply telling the facts can be

a poor way of getting people to understand what the speaker is
trying to tell them; rather, it is when he changes the way that
he tells a story, the exact details of it, that he can more
easily allow people to understand truth, and not simple truisms
or facts.

5   Yet another technique that O'Brien uses in his writings is
that of complete focus upon one thing all throughout a story,
such as in "The Man I Killed," as well as a complete rejection
of the facts to his readers, making them completely uncertain
that the story has any factual base yet at the same time,
reinforcing the abstract idea behind the story. In "The Man I
Killed," O'Brien begins with telling the physical details of a
dead body lying on a trail, a man stripped of his very life,
moving on to personal details of the Vietnamese youth that he
could not possibly know, such as where he was born, where he
went to school, who his fiancée was. Throughout the story, a
mental image of what the youth was like slowly collects in the
reader's mind: "He was not a fighter. His health was poor, his
body small and frail. He liked books. He wanted someday to be a
teacher of mathematics" (800). There is nothing especially evil
about the youth, as he was not unlike O'Brien himself, afraid of
war, but more afraid to fight tradition and ridicule;
nevertheless, he has been killed, and O'Brien sits and ponders
the death of the youth, wondering who the young Vietnamese boy
was, what his future might have been. However, in another short
story in *The Things They Carried*, O'Brien refutes the fact that
the incident ever occurred, yet at the same time making it clear
that the story truth is more real than the happening-truth:

            Here is the happening-truth. I was once a
            soldier. There were many bodies, real bodies
            with real faces, but I was young then and I

was afraid to look. And now, twenty years

later, I'm left with faceless responsibility

and faceless grief.

    Here is the story-truth. He was a slim,

dead, almost dainty young man of about twenty.

He lay in the center of a red clay trail near

the village of My Khe. His jaw was in his

throat. His one eye was shut, the other eye was

a star-shaped hole. I killed him. ("Good Form"

180)

O'Brien manages again to twist reality and fiction into

something more real than either, and transcending both, reaching

for some celestial absolute that tantalizes the mind.

6   Tim O'Brien's use of fiction and storytelling is a work of

genius, extracting and manipulating its reader's thoughts and

feelings in an incredibly powerful way. His stories do not have

morals; as he says in "How to Tell a True War Story": "A true war

story is never moral. It does not instruct, nor encourage virtue,

nor suggest models of proper human behavior, nor restrain men

from doing the things that men have always done" (790). A good

story merely tells truth, and O'Brien has done the job elegantly

in his savagely beautiful *The Things They Carried*, a book that

should be read by anyone who wants to understand better the

workings of the human mind under the stresses of war and

conflict, be they physical, mental, or emotional.

Works Cited

Calloway, Catherine. "'How To Tell a True War Story': Metafiction in *The Things They Carried*." *Critique* 36.4 (Summer 1995): 249ff. Henderson, Higgins, Day, and Waller 813-21.

Henderson, Gloria Mason, Anna Dunlap Higgins, Bill Day, and Sandra Stevenson Waller, eds. *Literature and Ourselves: A Thematic Introduction for Readers and Writers*. 6th ed. New York: ABLongman, 2009.

O'Brien, Tim. "Good Form." *The Things They Carried*. New York: Broadway Books, 1990. 179-80.

——. "How to Tell a True War Story." *The Things They Carried*. New York: Broadway Books, 1990. Henderson, Higgins, Day, and Waller 789-99.

——. "The Man I Killed." *The Things They Carried*. New York: Broadway Books, 1990. Henderson, Higgins, Day, and Waller 799-803.

——. "On the Rainy River." *The Things They Carried*. New York: Broadway Books, 1990. Henderson, Higgins, Day and Waller. 777-88.

Robinson, "Getting It Right: The Short Fiction of Tim O'Brien." *Critique* 40.3 (Spring 1999): 257ff. Henderson, Higgins, Day, and Waller 821-29.

Crafting Arguments

1. After reading the three stories by O'Brien, write an essay giving your opinion of what the themes are and how O'Brien illuminates them.
2. The men in O'Brien's stories have both extraordinary restrictions on their freedom and simultaneously the freedom to commit acts they would never consider at home. Using O'Brien's stories and the secondary sources, analyze how war changes men's sense of freedom and responsibility.

3. Using at least one of the stories and the secondary essays, analyze O'Brien's use of first-person narrators.

4. The narrator asserts that "the truths [about war] are contradictory" and says of war, "The old rules are no longer binding, the old truths no longer hold true. Right spills over into wrong." Use one or both of these statements to write an evaluation of the behavior of the men in O'Brien's stories.

5. O'Brien says that he thought, "There should be a law. . . . If you support a war, if you think it's worth the price, . . . you have to put your own precious fluids on the line. You have to head for the front and hook up with an infantry unit and help spill the blood." Using his story, write an essay explaining why you agree or disagree with this statement.

6. In an essay, analyze the moral dilemma O'Brien describes in "On the Rainy River."

7. Write a character sketch of Elroy Berdahl, explaining his wisdom and understanding.

Freedom and Responsibility: Crafting Arguments

1. Using one selection from this unit, discuss how the author shows the delicate balance between freedom and responsibility.

2. Choose one short story from this section and show how that work reveals the responsibilities a person has to others in society.

3. Use at least one work from this section to write an essay arguing that sometimes a person is morally obligated to disobey government regulations or laws.

4. Several of the narrators or characters in the poems in this unit are imprisoned, either literally or figuratively. Use one or more of the poems to write an essay arguing one of the following:
   Sometimes prison is preferable to another choice.
   Many individuals create their own prisons.
   Often people fail to realize that they lack freedom.

Freedom & Responsibility: Writing about Film

See Appendix B: Writing about Film for help with these essays.

1. View a war movie that is an adaptation. You may want to consider *Gone with the Wind, All Quiet on the Western Front, The Sands of Iwo Jima, From Here to Eternity, The Naked and the Dead, Paths of Glory, War and Peace, Little Big Man, Apocalypse Now, Dr. Zhivago, Last of the Mohicans, A Farewell to Arms, For Whom the Bell Tolls,* or *Full Metal Jacket.* Prepare a paper that analyzes the

ways in which the film speaks to the issues of freedom and responsibility.

2. Frank Darabont's *The Shawshank Redemption* (1994) is an adaptation of a novella by Stephen King. How does this film portray the protagonist's fight for freedom? What scenes are especially compelling; what film techniques allow the director to create such heightened moments?

3. The films *To Kill a Mockingbird* and *The Crucible* are based on literary works that examine themes stemming from the human tendency to look for scapegoats. View one of these films and compare its presentation of theme with the literary source's.

4. Stanley Kubrick's *A Clockwork Orange* (1972) is a popular film adaptation of Antony Burgess' novel that offers an intriguing comment on freedom and responsibility. The Ludovico technique scene is an especially provocative part of the movie. View this adaptation and offer your analysis of its comment on freedom and responsibility.

Creativity

A scene from *Enchanted*. Buena Vista Pictures/Everett Collection.

What is creativity? Although no one definition could fully describe something so mysterious and wonderful, perhaps the following comments will add to your understanding. Creativity refers to an ability to bring into existence something where there had been nothing. In theological terms, the word *creativity* speaks to an aspect of God's nature that He also shared with humans. Figures on cave walls fleeing from prehistoric beasts and artifacts unearthed from ancient soil testify to the long history of human creativity: humans have always been creative beings. Some of the world's most famous thinkers and inventors, such as da Vinci, Beethoven, Newton, Einstein, and Franklin, also possessed great creativity. They imagined that which had never been before. Parents and educators go to great lengths to stimulate a child's creativity and to encourage imagination precisely because doing so prepares a child to deal creatively with life.

This unit celebrates creativity, as does the entire anthology—literature is, after all, born out of human creativity. You will find in these works a great wealth of commentary about this mysterious and wonderful human faculty. Some texts in this unit speak especially to the eternal aspect of creativity. For example, Genesis I opens the unit with the words "In the beginning God created" and then chronicles the epic creation of all things, nature, animals, and humans, who were then "blessed" with their own creative longing and the ability to create. In John Keats' "Ode to a Grecian Urn," the speaker praises the eternal quality of the urn's beauty: "Beauty is truth, truth beauty, that is all / Ye know on earth, and all ye need to know."

Some works in this unit address the power of the creative force. The poet Emily Dickinson claims that her extraordinary outpouring of creativity is as "full as Opera." For her, the imagination is the one part of herself that neither her family nor her culture can imprison; regardless of her physical situation, she cannot truly be "Shut up" because her creative mind continues to "go round." Ursula K. LeGuin's "The Child and the Shadow" applauds the creative genius of one of the world's most famous chroniclers of fairy tales, Hans Christian Anderson, and the ways in which his creativity has taught generations of children. In

her essay, LeGuin argues that the archetypes found in fantasy literature—certainly one of the most imaginative genres—are the perfect
medium for translating the concepts of good and evil to children. In
"Beauty Laid Bare: Aesthetics in the Ordinary," bell hooks examines
the politics of the beauty inherent in the creative force, applauding
those whose imaginations can find restorative powers in the things of
everyday life. Even in poverty, hooks argues, the urge to create beauty
out of the everyday exists.

Still other works focus on readers' imaginative response to literature.
For the poet Emily Dickinson, reading can "take us Lands away." Likewise, Billy Collins' "Marginalia" comments on the creative leap we make
in reading. When responding to literature by jotting down notes in a
text's margins, readers imaginatively take part in the literature. A few of
the works in this unit take a humorous approach. In his "Girl Copy,"
David Mamet describes the limits of his creative force: like a hot house
flower, creativity can demand its proper atmosphere and soil. In Woody
Allen's "The Kugelmass Episode," the main character, by letting his creativity run wild, becomes the subject of an imaginative pursuit. Mark
Twain's ass offers a vivid commentary on reader response.

Writing about Creativity

As you begin to interpret literature and to craft papers that articulate
what you think about a text, you will take part in the creative force: ideas
and sentences you do not have one day will appear the next. If you are
asked to craft a paper based on works in this unit, you will have many
choices. If you choose to prepare a paper that focuses on thematic concerns, for example, you could examine works such as those by Keats and
Collins. What do these works have to say about the creative participation
that occurs between art and audience/reader? You could select to write
about Wendy Wasserstein's play "Tender Offer" and examine the ways
that the dance the girl creates forms a space for healing between father
and daughter. You might want to examine the metaphor that Emily Dickinson uses in her poem "There is no Frigate like a Book." How, according to this poem, does poetry "take us Lands away"? You could examine
what happens when someone like Kugelmass in Allen's short story or the
ass in Mark Twain's fable indulges too much in the power of our creative
minds. You might want to look closely at the ways Margaret Atwood's
"Happy Endings" and Sylvia Plath's "Metaphors" encourage—perhaps
demand—a reader's creative participation.

If you prefer to craft a Comparison/Contrast or a Classification paper,
there are many possible approaches. You could examine two works, for

example those by Keats and Alberto Rios, that focus on an object. In what ways do these works make similar comments about our creative productions? What is unique about each author's approach? You could also look at the works of two or three authors who seem to be commenting on the nature of creativity. For instance, what do Emily Dickinson, Seamus Heaney, and Lawrence Ferlinghetti have to say about the powers and the risks of a life dedicated to allowing the imagination its room to roam? You could select characters who seem to you to offer differing perspectives on the creative impulse and prepare a Comparison/Contrast essay. A few good choices for such an assignment are Dee and Maggie or Gracie Mae and Traynor from Alice Walker's "Everyday Use" and "Nineteen Fifty Five," respectively.

When Graphics Design major Taylor Magusiak was asked to contribute a sample student paper to the Casebook on Alice Walker, she first read the primary materials in the Casebook and then met with her professor to discuss possible approaches. From the beginning, Taylor was attracted to the art objects in "Everyday Use" and "1955," specifically the quilts and the lyrics. Next she performed a freewrite on those topics, which generated lots of ideas, especially about the creative force behind those products. Then Taylor began drafting, but she immediately experienced writer's block. As happens to many students, Taylor found herself tempted to "prove" that one character's approach to art was "right" and another's was "wrong." A quick meeting with her professor cleared up this issue: the goal of a strong argument is not to "prove" that someone— or some other interpretation—is wrong. Great literature often stirs up far more questions than it answers. After this second meeting with her professor, Taylor began drafting in earnest. Once she had a draft she liked, she read the secondary sources and selected quotations that supported or illustrated her points. A final conference with her professor helped Taylor polish her paper, add documentation, and insert some transition phrases before putting together her final draft. Her paper is included at the end of the Alice Walker Casebook in this unit.

E S S A Y S

Genesis I

Genesis, the first book of the Old Testament, is appropriately a book of beginnings. Though scholars have advanced several theories about its authorship, with some attributing it to Moses, they have reached no consensus. Originally written in Hebrew, it has been translated into almost every language. The version included here is from the King James translation.

1   In the beginning God created the heaven and the earth.

2   And the earth was without form, and void; and darkness was upon the face of the deep. And the Spirit of God moved upon the face of the waters.

3   And God said, Let there be light: and there was light.

4   And God saw the light, that it was good: and God divided the light from the darkness.

5   And God called the light Day, and the darkness he called Night. And the evening and the morning were the first day.

6   And God said, Let there be a firmament in the midst of the waters, and let it divide the waters from the waters.

7   And God made the firmament, and divided the waters which were under the firmament from the waters which were above the firmament: and it was so.

8   And God called the firmament Heaven. And the evening and the morning were the second day.

9   And God said, Let the waters under the heaven be gathered together unto one place, and let the dry land appear: and it was so.

10   And God called the dry land Earth; and the gathering together of the waters called he Seas: and God saw that it was good.

11   And God said, Let the earth bring forth grass, the herb yielding seed, and the fruit tree yielding fruit after his kind, whose seed is in itself, upon the earth: and it was so.

12   And the earth brought forth grass, and herb yielding seed after his kind, and the tree yielding fruit, whose seed was in itself, after his kind: and God saw that it was good.

13   And the evening and the morning were the third day.

14   And God said, Let there be lights in the firmament of the heaven to divide the day from the night; and let them be for signs, and for seasons, and for days, and years:

15   And let them be for lights in the firmament of the heaven to give light upon the earth: and it was so.

16   And God made two great lights; the greater light to rule the day, and the lesser light to rule the night: he made the stars also.

17   And God set them in the firmament of the heaven to give light upon the earth,

18   And to rule over the day and over the night, and to divide the light from the darkness: and God saw that it was good.

19   And the evening and the morning were the fourth day.

20   And God said, Let the waters bring forth abundantly the moving creature that hath life, and fowl that may fly above the earth in the open firmament of heaven.

21   And God created great whales, and every living creature that moveth, which the waters brought forth abundantly, after their kind, and every winged fowl after his kind: and God saw that it was good.

22   And God blessed them, saying, Be fruitful, and multiply, and fill the waters in the seas, and let fowl multiply in the earth.

23   And the evening and the morning were the fifth day.

24   And God said, Let the earth bring forth the living creature after his kind, cattle, and creeping thing, and beast of the earth after his kind: and it was so.

25   And God made the beast of the earth after his kind, and cattle after their kind, and every thing that creepeth upon the earth after his kind: and God saw that it was good.

26   And God said, Let us make man in our image, after our likeness: and let them have dominion over the fish of the sea, and over the fowl of the air, and over the cattle, and over all the earth, and over every creeping thing that creepeth upon the earth.

27   So God created man in his own image, in the image of God created he him; male and female created he them.

28   And God blessed them, and God said unto them, Be fruitful, and multiply, and replenish the earth, and subdue it: and have dominion over the fish of the sea, and over the fowl of the air, and over every living thing that moveth upon the earth.

29   And God said, Behold, I have given you every herb bearing seed, which is upon the face of all the earth, and every tree, in the which is the fruit of a tree yielding seed; to you it shall be for meat.

30   And to every beast of the earth, and to every fowl of the air, and to every thing that creepeth upon the earth, wherein there is life, I have given every green herb for meat: and it was so.

31   And God saw every thing that he had made, and, behold, it was very good. And the evening and the morning were the sixth day.

Questions for Engagement, Response, and Analysis

1. According to Genesis, what was the first great act of creation?

2. Make a chart of all God's creations described in this chapter, separating them by the days in which they were created.

3. Identify and explain the pattern of what happens at the end of each day.

4. What are the charges that God gives Adam and Eve?

Crafting Arguments

1. Recognizing that the King James version is a translation, write an essay examining the stylistic patterns that add meaning and beauty to Genesis I, either quoting or giving verse numbers for your illustrations.

Ursula K. Le Guin (b. 1929)

The biography of Ursula Le Guin appears before "The Ones Who Walk Away from Omelas" in the Freedom and Responsibility Unit.

THE CHILD AND THE SHADOW   (1975)

1   Once upon a time, says Hans Christian Andersen, there was a kind, shy, learned young man from the North, who came south to visit the hot countries, where the sun shines fiercely and all shadows are very black.

2   Now across the street from the young man's window is a house, where he once glimpses a beautiful girl tending beautiful flowers on the balcony. The young man longs to go speak to her, but he's too shy. One night, while his candle is burning behind him, casting his shadow onto the balcony across the way, he "jokingly" tells his shadow to go ahead, go on into that house. And it does. It enters the house across the street and leaves him.

3   The young man's a bit surprised, naturally, but he doesn't do anything about it. He presently grows a new shadow and goes back home. And he grows older, and more learned; but he's not a success. He talks about beauty and goodness, but nobody listens to him.

4   Then one day when he's a middle-aged man, his shadow comes back to him—very thin and rather swarthy, but elegantly dressed. "Did you go into the house across the street?" the man asks him, first thing; and the shadow says, "Oh, yes, certainly." He claims that he saw everything, but he's just boasting. The man knows what to ask. "Were the rooms like the starry sky when one stands on the mountaintops?" he asks, and all the shadow can say is, "Oh, yes, everything was there." He doesn't know how to answer. He never got in any farther than the anteroom, being, after all, only a shadow. "I should have been annihilated by that flood of light had I penetrated into the room where the maiden lived," he says.

5   He is, however, good at blackmail and such arts; he is a strong unscrupulous fellow, and he dominates the man completely. They go traveling, the shadow as master and the man as servant. They meet a princess who suffers "because she sees too clearly." She sees that the shadow casts no shadow and distrusts him, until he explains that the man is really his shadow, which he allows to walk about by itself. A peculiar arrangement, but logical; the princess accepts it. When she and the shadow

engage to marry, the man rebels at last. He tries to tell the princess the truth, but the shadow gets there first, with explanations: "The poor fellow is crazy, he thinks he's a man and I'm his shadow!"—"How dreadful," says the princess. A mercy killing is definitely in order. And while the shadow and the princess get married, the man is executed.

6   Now that is an extraordinarily cruel story. A story about insanity, ending in humiliation and death.

7   Is it a story for children? Yes, it is. It's a story for anybody who's listening.

8   If you listen, what do you hear?

9   The house across the street is the House of Beauty, and the maiden is the Muse of Poetry; the shadow tells us that straight out. And that the princess who sees too clearly is pure, cold reason, is plain enough. But who are the man and the shadow? That's not so plain. They aren't allegorical figures. They are symbolic or archetypal figures, like those in a dream. Their significance is multiple, inexhaustible. I can only hint at the little I'm able to see of it.

10   The man is all that is civilized—learned, kindly, idealistic, decent. The shadow is all that gets suppressed in the process of becoming a decent, civilized adult. The shadow is the man's thwarted selfishness, his unadmitted desires, the swearwords he never spoke, the murders he didn't commit. The shadow is the dark side of his soul, the unadmitted, the inadmissible.

11   And what Andersen is saying is that this monster is an integral part of the man and cannot be denied—not if the man wants to enter the House of Poetry.

12   The man's mistake is in not following his shadow. It goes ahead of him, as he sits there at his window, and he cuts it off from himself, telling it, "jokingly," to go on without him. And it does. It goes on into the House of Poetry, the source of all creativity—leaving him outside, on the surface of reality.

13   So, good and learned as he is, he can't do any good, can't act, because he has cut himself off at the roots. And the shadow is equally helpless; it can't get past the shadowy anteroom to the light. Neither of them, without the other, can approach the truth.

14   When the shadow returns to the man in middle life, he has a second chance. But he misses it, too. He confronts his dark self at last, but instead of asserting equality or mastery, he lets it master him. He gives in. He does, in fact, become the shadow's shadow, and his fate then is inevitable. The Princess Reason is cruel in having him executed, and yet she is just.

15   Part of Andersen's cruelty is the cruelty of reason—of psychological realism, radical honesty, the willingness to see and accept the consequences of an act or a failure to act. There is a sadistic depressive streak in Andersen also, which is his own shadow; it's there, it's part of him, but not all of him, nor is he ruled by it. His strength, his subtlety, his creative genius, come precisely from his acceptance of and cooperation with the

dark side of his own soul. That's why Andersen the fabulist is one of the great realists of literature.

16   Now I stand here, like the princess herself, and tell you what the story of the shadow means to me at age forty-five. But what did it mean to me when I first read it, at age ten or eleven? What does it mean to children? Do they "understand" it? Is it "good" for them—this bitter, complex study of a moral failure?

17   I don't know. I hated it when I was a kid. I hated all the Andersen stories with unhappy endings. That didn't stop me from reading them, and rereading them. Or from remembering them . . . so that after a gap of over thirty years, when I was pondering this talk, a little voice suddenly said inside my left ear, "You'd better dig out that Andersen story, you know, about the shadow."

18   At age ten I certainly wouldn't have gone on about reason and repression and all that. I had no critical equipment, no detachment, and even less power of sustained thought than I have now. I had somewhat less conscious mind than I have now. But I had as much, or more, of an unconscious mind, and was perhaps in better touch with it than I am now. And it was to that, to the unknown depths in me, that the story spoke; and it was the depths which responded to it and, nonverbally, irrationally, understood it, and learned from it.

19   The great fantasies, myths, and tales are indeed like dreams: they speak *from* the unconscious *to* the unconscious, in the *language* of the unconscious—symbol and archetype. Though they use words, they work the way music does: they short-circuit verbal reasoning, and go straight to the thoughts that lie too deep to utter. They cannot be translated fully into the language of reason, but only a Logical Positivist, who also finds Beethoven's Ninth Symphony meaningless, would claim that they are therefore meaningless. They are profoundly meaningful, and usable—practical—in terms of ethics; of insight; of growth.

20   Reduced to the language of daylight, Andersen's story says that a man who will not confront and accept his shadow is a lost soul. It also says something specifically about itself, about art. It says that if you want to enter the House of Poetry, you have to enter it in the flesh, the solid, imperfect, unwieldy body, which has corns and colds and greeds and passions, the body that casts a shadow. It says that if the artist tries to ignore evil, he will never enter into the House of Light.

21   That's what one great artist said to me about shadows. Now if I may move our candle and throw the shadows in a different direction, I'd like to interrogate a great psychologist on the same subject. Art has spoken, let's hear what science has to say. Since art is the subject, let it be the psychologist whose ideas on art are the most meaningful to most artists, Carl Gustav Jung.

22   Jung's terminology is notoriously difficult, as he kept changing meanings the way a growing tree changes leaves. I will try to define a few of the key terms in an amateurish way without totally misrepresenting

them. Very roughly, then, Jung saw the ego, what we usually call the self, as only a part of the Self, the part of it which we are consciously aware of. The ego "revolves around the Self as the earth around the Sun," he says. The Self is transcendent, much larger than the ego; it is not a private possession, but collective—that is, we share it with all other human beings, and perhaps with all beings. It may indeed be our link with what is called God. Now this sounds mystical, and it is, but it's also exact and practical. All Jung is saying is that we are fundamentally alike; we all have the same general tendencies and configurations in our psyche, just as we all have the same general kind of lungs and bones in our body. Human beings all look roughly alike; they also think and feel alike. And they are all part of the universe.

23   The ego, the little private individual consciousness, knows this, and it knows that if it's not to be trapped in the hopeless silence of autism it must identify with something outside itself, beyond itself, larger than itself. If it's weak, or if it's offered nothing better, what it does is identify with the "collective consciousness." That is Jung's term for a kind of lowest common denominator of all the little egos added together, the mass mind, which consists of such things as cults, creeds, fads, fashions, status-seeking, conventions, received beliefs, advertising, popcult, all the isms, all the ideologies, all the hollow forms of communication and "togetherness" that lack real communion or real sharing. The ego, accepting these empty forms, becomes a member of the "lonely crowd." To avoid this, to attain real community, it must turn inward, away from the crowd, to the source: it must identify with *its own* deeper regions, the great unexplored regions of the Self. These regions of the psyche Jung calls the "collective unconscious," and it is in them, where we all meet, that he sees the source of true community; of felt religion; of art, grace, spontaneity, and love.

24   How do you get there? How do you find your own private entrance to the collective unconscious? Well, the first step is often the most important, and Jung says that the first step is to turn around and follow your own shadow.

25   Jung saw the psyche as populated with a group of fascinating figures, much livelier than Freud's grim trio of Id, Ego, Superego; they're all worth meeting. The one we're concerned with is the shadow.

26   The shadow is on the other side of our psyche, the dark brother of the conscious mind. It is Cain, Caliban, Frankenstein's monster, Mr. Hyde. It is Vergil who guided Dante through hell, Gilgamesh's friend Enkidu, Frodo's enemy Gollum. It is the Doppelgänger. It is Mowgli's Grey Brother; the werewolf; the wolf, the bear, the tiger of a thousand folktales; it is the serpent, Lucifer. The shadow stands on the threshold between the conscious and the unconscious mind, and we meet it in our dreams, as sister, brother, friend, beast, monster, enemy, guide. It is all we don't want to, can't, admit into our conscious self, all the qualities and tendencies within us which have been repressed, denied, or not used. In

describing Jung's psychology, Jolande Jacobi wrote that "the development of the shadow runs parallel to that of the ego; qualities which the ego does not need or cannot make use of are set aside or repressed, and thus they play little or no part in the conscious life of the individual. Accordingly, a child has no real shadow, but his shadow becomes more pronounced as his ego grows in stability and range."[1] Jung himself said, "Everyone carries a shadow, and the less it is embodied in the individual's conscious life, the blacker and denser it is."[2] The less you look at it, in other words, the stronger it grows, until it can become a menace, an intolerable load, a threat within the soul.

27   Unadmitted to consciousness, the shadow is projected outward, onto others. There's nothing wrong with me—it's *them*. I'm not a monster, other people are monsters. All foreigners are evil. All communists are evil. All capitalists are evil. It was the cat that made me kick him, Mommy.

28   If the individual wants to live in the real world, he must withdraw his projections; he must admit that the hateful, the evil, exists within himself. This isn't easy. It is very hard not to be able to blame anybody else. But it may be worth it. Jung says, "If he only learns to deal with his own shadow he has done something real for the world. He has succeeded in shouldering at least an infinitesimal part of the gigantic, unsolved social problems of our day."[3]

29   Moreover, he has grown toward true community, and self-knowledge and creativity. For the shadow stands on the threshold. We can let it bar the way to the creative depths of the unconscious, or we can let it lead us to them. For the shadow is not simply evil. It is inferior, primitive, awkward, animallike, childlike; powerful, vital, spontaneous. It's not weak and decent, like the learned young man from the North; it's dark and hairy and unseemly; but, without it, the person is nothing. What is a body that casts no shadow? Nothing, a formlessness, two-dimensional, a comic-strip character. The person who denies his own profound relationship with evil denies his own reality. He cannot do, or make; he can only undo, unmake.

30   Jung was especially interested in the second half of life, when this conscious confrontation with a shadow that's been growing for thirty or forty years can become imperative—as it did for the poor fellow in the Andersen story. As Jung says, the child's ego and shadow are both still ill defined; a child is likely to find his ego in a ladybug, and his shadow lurking horribly under his bed. But I think that when in pre-adolescence and adolescence the conscious sense of self emerges, often quite overwhelmingly, the shadow darkens right with it. The normal adolescent ceases to project so blithely as the little child did; he realizes that you

[1]Jolande Jacobi, *The Psychology of C. G. Jung* (New Haven: Yale University Press, 1962), 107.

[2]Carl Gustav Jung, *Psychology and Religion: West and East*, Bollingen Series XX, *The Collected Works of C. G. Jung*, vol. 11 (New York: Pantheon Books, 1958), 76.

[3]Jung, *Psychology and Religion*, 83.

can't blame everything on the bad guys with the black Stetsons. He begins
to take responsibility for his acts and feelings. And with it he often shoulders a terrible load of guilt. He sees his shadow as much blacker, more
wholly evil, than it is. The only way for a youngster to get past the paralyzing self-blame and self-disgust of this stage is really to look at that
shadow, to face it, warts and fangs and pimples and claws and all—to
accept it as himself—as *part* of himself. The ugliest part, but not the
weakest. For the shadow is the guide. The guide inward and out again;
downward and up again; there, as Bilbo the Hobbit said, and back again.
The guide of the journey to self-knowledge, to adulthood, to the light.

31   "Lucifer" means the one who carries the light.

32   It seems to me that Jung described, as the individual's imperative need
and duty, that journey which Andersen's learned young man failed to
make.

33   It also seems to me that most of the great works of fantasy are about
that journey; and that fantasy is the medium best suited to a description
of that journey, its perils and rewards. The events of a voyage into the
unconscious are not describable in the language of rational daily life: only
the symbolic language of the deeper psyche will fit them without trivial-
izing them.

34   Moreover, the journey seems to be not only a psychic one, but a moral
one. Most great fantasies contain a very strong, striking moral dialectic,
often expressed as a struggle between the Darkness and the Light. But
that makes it sound simple, and the ethics of the unconscious—of the
dream, the fantasy, the fairy tale—are not simple at all. They are, indeed,
very strange.

35   Take the ethics of the fairy tale, where the shadow figure is often
played by an animal—horse, wolf, bear, snake, raven, fish. In her article
"The Problem of Evil in Fairytales," Mary Louise von Franz—a Jungian—
points out the real strangeness of morality in folktales. There *is no right
way* to act when you're the hero or heroine of a fairy tale. There is no
system of conduct, there are no standards of what a nice prince does and
what a good little girl doesn't do. I mean, do good little girls usually push
old ladies into baking ovens, and get rewarded for it? Not in what we call
"real life," they don't. But in dreams and fairy tales they do. And to judge
Gretel by the standards of conscious, daylight virtue is a complete and
ridiculous mistake.

36   In the fairy tale, though there is no "right" and "wrong," there is a different standard, which is perhaps best called "appropriateness." Under
no conditions can we say that it is morally right and ethically virtuous to
push an old lady into a baking oven. But, under the conditions of fairy
tale, in the language of the archetypes, we can say with perfect conviction that it may be *appropriate* to do so. Because, in those terms, the
witch is not an old lady, nor is Gretel a little girl. Both are psychic factors,
elements of the complex soul. Gretel is the archaic child-soul, innocent,
defenseless; the witch is the archaic crone, the possessor and destroyer,

the mother who feeds you cookies and who must be destroyed before she eats you like a cookie, so that you can grow up and be a mother too. And so on and so on. All explanations are partial. The archetype is unexhaustible. And children understand it as fully and surely as adults do—often more fully, because they haven't got minds stuffed full of the one-sided, shadowless half-truths and conventional moralities of the collective consciousness.

37   Evil, then, appears in the fairy tale not as something diametrically opposed to good, but as inextricably involved with it, as in the yang-yin symbol. Neither is greater than the other, nor can human reason and virtue separate one from the other and choose between them. The hero or heroine is the one who sees what is appropriate to be done, because he or she sees the *whole*, which is greater than either evil or good. Their heroism is, in fact, their certainty. They do not act by rules; they simply know the way to go.

38   In this labyrinth where it seems one must trust to blind instinct, there is, von Franz points out, one—only one—consistent rule or "ethic": "Anyone who earns the gratitude of animals, or whom they help for any reason, invariably wins out. This is the only unfailing rule that I have been able to find."

39   Our instinct, in other words, is not blind. The animal does not reason, but it sees. And it acts with certainty; it acts "rightly," appropriately. That is why all animals are beautiful. It is the animal who knows the way, the way home. It is the animal within us, the primitive, the dark brother, the shadow soul, who is the guide.

40   There is often a queer twist to this in folktales, a kind of final secret. The helpful animal, often a horse or a wolf, says to the hero, "When you have done such-and-so with my help, then you must kill me, cut off my head." And the hero must trust his animal guide so wholly that he is willing to do so. Apparently the meaning of this is that when you have followed the animal instincts far enough, then they must be sacrificed, so that the true self, the whole person, may step forth from the body of the animal, reborn. That is von Franz's explanation, and it sounds fair enough; I am glad to have any explanation of that strange episode in so many tales, which has always shocked me. But I doubt that that's all there is to it—or that any Jungian would pretend it was. Neither rational thought nor rational ethics can "explain" these deep strange levels of the imagining mind. Even in merely reading a fairy tale, we must let go our daylight convictions and trust ourselves to be guided by dark figures, in silence; and when we come back, it may be very hard to describe where we have been.

41   In many fantasy tales of the nineteenth and twentieth centuries the tension between good and evil, light and dark, is drawn absolutely clearly, as a battle, the good guys on one side and the bad guys on the other, cops and robbers, Christians and heathens, heroes and villains. In such fantasies I believe the author has tried to force reason to lead him where

reason cannot go, and has abandoned the faithful and frightening guide he should have followed, the shadow. These are false fantasies, rationalized fantasies. They are not the real thing. Let me, by way of exhibiting the real thing, which is always much more interesting than the fake one, discuss *The Lord of the Rings* for a minute.

42   Critics have been hard on Tolkien for his "simplisticness," his division of the inhabitants of Middle Earth into the good people and the evil people. And indeed he does this, and his good people tend to be entirely good, though with endearing frailties, while his Orcs and other villains are altogether nasty. But all this is a judgment by daylight ethics, by conventional standards of virtue and vice. When you look at the story as a psychic journey, you see something quite different, and very strange. You see then a group of bright figures, each one with its black shadow. Against the Elves, the Orcs. Against Aragorn, the Black Rider. Against Gandalf, Saruman. And above all, against Frodo, Gollum. Against him— and with him.

43   It is truly complex, because both the figures are already doubled. Sam is, in part, Frodo's shadow, his inferior part. Gollum is two people, too, in a more direct, schizophrenic sense; he's always talking to himself, Slinker talking to Stinker, Sam calls it. Sam understands Gollum very well, though he won't admit it and won't accept Gollum as Frodo does, letting Gollum be their guide, trusting him. Frodo and Gollum are not only both hobbits; they are the same person—and Frodo knows it. Frodo and Sam are the bright side, Smeagol-Gollum the shadow side. In the end Sam and Smeagol, the lesser figures, drop away, and all that is left is Frodo and Gollum, at the end of the long quest. And it is Frodo the good who fails, who at the last moment claims the Ring of Power for himself; and it is Gollum the evil who achieves the quest, destroying the Ring, and himself with it. The Ring, the archetype of the Integrative Function, the creative-destructive, returns to the volcano, the eternal source of creation and destruction, the primal fire. When you look at it that way, can you call it a simple story? I suppose so. *Oedipus Rex* is a fairly simple story, too. But it is not simplistic. It is the kind of story that can be told only by one who has turned and faced his shadow and looked into the dark.

44   That it is told in the language of fantasy is not an accident, or because Tolkien was an escapist, or because he was writing for children. It is a fantasy because fantasy is the natural, the appropriate, language for the recounting of the spiritual journey and the struggle of good and evil in the soul.

45   That has been said before—by Tolkien himself, for one—but it needs repeating. It needs lots of repeating, because there is still, in this country, a deep puritanical distrust of fantasy, which comes out often among people truly and seriously concerned about the ethical education of children. Fantasy, to them, is escapism. They see no difference between the Batmen and Supermen of the commercial dope-factories and the timeless

archetypes of the collective unconscious. They confuse fantasy, which in the psychological sense is a universal and essential faculty of the human mind, with infantilism and pathological regression. They seem to think that shadows are something that we can simply do away with, if we can only turn on enough electric lights. And so they see the irrationality and cruelty and strange amoralities of fairy tale, and they say: "But this is very bad for children, we must teach children right from wrong, with realistic books, books that are true to life!"

46   I agree that children need to be—and usually want very much to be—taught right from wrong. But I believe that realistic fiction for children is one of the very hardest media in which to do it. It's hard not to get entangled in the superficialities of the collective consciousness, or simplistic moralism, in projections of various kinds, so that you end up with the baddies and the goodies all over again. Or you get that business about "there's a little bit of bad in the best of us and a little bit of good in the worst of us," a dangerous banalization of the fact, which is that there is incredible potential for good and for evil in every one of us. Or writers are encouraged to merely capitalize on sensationalism, upsetting the child reader without themselves being really involved in the violence of the story, which is shameful. Or you get the "problem books." The problem of drugs, of divorce, of race prejudice, of unmarried pregnancy, and so on—as if evil were a problem, something that can be solved, that has an answer, like a problem in fifth grade arithmetic. If you want the answer, you just look in the back of the book.

47   *That* is escapism, that posing evil as a "problem," instead of what it is: all the pain and suffering and waste and loss and injustice we will meet all our lives long, and must face and cope with over and over and over, and admit, and live with, in order to live human lives at all.

48   But what, then, is the naturalistic writer for children to do? Can he present the child with evil as an *insoluble* problem—something neither the child nor any adult can do anything about at all? To give the child a picture of the gas chambers of Dachau, or the famines of India, or the cruelties of a psychotic parent, and say, "Well, baby, this is how it is, what are you going to make of it?"—that is surely unethical. If you suggest that there is a "solution" to these monstrous facts, you are lying to the child. If you insist that there isn't, you are overwhelming him with a load he's not strong enough yet to carry.

49   The young creature does need protection and shelter. But it also needs the truth. And it seems to me that the way you can speak absolutely honestly and factually to a child about both good and evil is to talk about himself. Himself, his inner self, his deep, the deepest Self. That is something he can cope with; indeed, his job in growing up is to become himself. He can't do this if he feels the task is hopeless, nor can he if he's led to think there isn't any task. A child's growth will be stunted

and perverted if he is forced to despair or if he is encouraged in false hope, if he is terrified or if he is coddled. What he needs to grow up is reality, the wholeness which exceeds all our virtue and all our vice. He needs knowledge; he needs self-knowledge. He needs to see himself and the shadow he casts. That is something he can face, his own shadow; and he can learn to control it and to be guided by it. So that, when he grows up into his strength and responsibility as an adult in society, he will be less inclined, perhaps, either to give up in despair or to deny what he sees, when he must face the evil that is done in the world, and the injustices and grief and suffering that we all must bear, and the final shadow at the end of all.

50   Fantasy is the language of the inner self. I will claim no more for fantasy than to say that I personally find it the appropriate language in which to tell stories to children—and others. But I say that with some confidence, having behind me the authority of a very great poet, who put it much more boldly. "The great instrument of moral good," Shelley said, "is the imagination."

Questions for Engagement, Response, and Analysis

1. Look up **symbol** and **archetype** in the glossary. Using the definitions, discuss Le Guin's interpretation of Andersen's story.

2. According to Le Guin, what is the difference between Jung's "'collective consciousness'" and his "'collective unconscious'"?

3. Le Guin says, "[T]he shadow is not simply evil. It is inferior, primitive, animal-like, childlike; powerful, vital, spontaneous." Why, according to Le Guin, is it nevertheless essential?

4. What is the journey that Le Guin describes in paragraphs 30 through 34?

5. Explain why you agree or disagree with Le Guin's definition of evil in paragraphs 46 and 47.

6. Le Guin believes that fantasy is "the appropriate language in which to tell stories to children—and others." What are her reasons? Explain why you agree or disagree.

Crafting Arguments

1. Explain Le Guin's claim that fantasies in which the lines between good and evil are clearly drawn are "false fantasies."

2. In this essay, Le Guin describes fantasy as "the natural, the appropriate, language for the recounting of the spiritual journey and the struggle of good and evil in the soul." Using one or more works from this anthology, support or dispute this statement.

David Mamet (b. 1947)

Multitalented writer and director David Mamet has been recognized for his work as playwright, screenwriter, essayist, director, and novelist. His plays Glengarry Glen Ross *and* Speed-the-Plow *were nominated for Tony awards in 1984 and 1988, respectively, and Mamet won a Pulitzer Prize for the former. In film, Mamet received an Academy Award nomination for* The Verdict *in 1982. His other outstanding screenplays include* The Postman Always Rings Twice *(1981),* The Untouchables *(1987),* Glengarry Glen Ross *(1992),* Wag the Dog *(1998) and* Redbelt *(2008). Mamet's novel* The Old Religion *(1997) portrays the 1915 lynching of Leo Frank in Marietta, Georgia. Recently Mamet has been recognized as creator, producer, and writer of the acclaimed television series* The Unit. *In these and his many other works, Mamet is noted for his distinctive style, often described as sparse, almost minimalist prose.*

GIRL COPY
(1996)

1   I sat for a year in a cork-lined office and looked at photos of naked women.

2   I did it for a living.

3   I got the job at a party given by a friend of a friend.

4   A man came up to me, he said he knew my plays, and asked me to come work for him as a contributing editor of his men's magazine.

5   I told him I had no idea what such a job might be supposed to entail. He said my duties would be these: to come to the office and offer innovative solutions to various problems, and to suggest projects of my own.

6   This explanation left me no better informed than I had been prior to my question. "Look," I said, "I don't want to mislead or disappoint you. I am not a good 'company' man, I've never worked on a magazine before, and, though I'm flattered by your offer . . ."

7   I went on in this vein for a while, warmed by my own candor, until he stopped and assured me that there was nothing in the job beyond my capabilities, that I could make my own hours, and that he would pay me $20,000 a year.

8   The magazine took up a floor in the Playboy Building.

9   It was decorated in an informal but serious style; and that, of course, was the manner in which we were supposed to function while in it.

10   We contributing editors, men and women in our twenties, were being paid to pitch in and be witty and creative promptly, and in service of the Issue and its deadlines.

11   I wrote my share of letters to the editor. Each letter, either through agreement or through disagreement with the policies of the Rag, was to function as entertainment; and I and the others strove to make it so. We cranked them out, and made up names and hometowns for our faithful

correspondents, checking the telephone books of those hometowns to insure that each burg housed at least three people of the name we had appropriated. This tactic, the legal department informed us, lessened the chance of a lawsuit by someone who felt offended seeing his name borrowed by a girlie mag.

12   I wrote captions for cartoons. Who would have thought it? I'd always assumed that a cartoonist dreamt up the idea whole; but, however it came about, there were these drawings of folks in what would prove to be a comic situation after the caption had been applied, and there I was straining to find a caption.

13   I wrote "service features"; that is, surveys of a particular gadget or service—toiletries or resorts, for example. The items surveyed were, in the main, sold by our mag's advertisers; and these gratuities I found both easy and enjoyable to write. Perhaps because I felt I was dispensing patronage, I don't know.

14   I wrote puns and gags, and one-liners, and photo captions; my favorite of the last: We had a shot of a house trailer that had been turned into a helicopter; I titled it "Upwardly mobile homes." I talked on the phone to Henny Youngman. I had coffee and croissants with Eddie Constantine; I created the fictitious craze that was supposedly sweeping the swinging North Side of Chicago: strip darts; I invented the American joke. Yes. This sounds like the pompous posturing of a garrulous old Fool—is he so bereft of kudos that he would stoop to garner that owing to the creator of "How many Americans does it take to change a lightbulb? One." Well, yes. I would so stoop, and there it is in print in 1976. Where did I get the energy for these bons mots? For this, finally, this "humor"? The energy came as a counterirritant to the despair caused by my attempts to write Girl Copy.

15   Fran Lebowitz wrote that as a child, she detested homework; and then she grew up and became a writer; which, she found, is a life of constant homework.

16   All over the country adolescent boys and frustrated married men were looking at the sexy photos of the sexy naked women, and these men were having fantasies about them.

17   Here I was, getting twenty grand a year to look at the same photos and create those fantasies, and it felt to me like work.

18   I would be given "the blues," blue-and-gray first runs of what would later be glorious color spreads of the said naked women, and I would tack them on the cork-lined walls, and I would strive to have fantasies about them. For it was all a fiction, all that stuff; their names were made up, their biographies, their likes and peeves. It was whole cloth, like the letters to the editor. Someone made it up, and that year, that was my job.

19   I think my personal best was "Katya with her pants down"; and there was also "Anna is a palindrome," but I'm not sure if that was mine.

20   I did write: "Tolstoy said that a nap after dinner is silver, a nap before dinner gold. Gretchen prefers a nap to dinner altogether."

21   Workmanlike, as you see.

22   Others did better. The office consensus favorite concerned French women, and informed us that French women have eyes like chocolate horses, that they wear white socks and harbor a fear of being frightened by an orangutan that has gained entrance to their flat by means of the chimney. I butcher the above-referenced work, with apologies to its author, whose name I have forgotten. The original can be found in an issue of *Oui*, nineteen seventy-four or -five.

23   No, I never did better than the acceptable "Katya."

24   I toyed with "London britches" and "London derriere," neither of which ever progressed beyond the title. I spent too much time staring at the blues—much too much to achieve that effortlessness that, unfortunately, usually denotes lack of effort.

25   They were my homework. Photos of naked women feigning sexual interest in something or other—their people, the camera, or, in what was considered quite daring in those forgotten times, themselves.

26   For there were two plateaus, it seems to me, in those bygone days, two Rubiconim, which we approached with utmost caution.

27   My editor, the bloke who gave me the job, was, by the way, good as his word. He was generous and helpful, and made a point of both aiding and appreciating my efforts. Our editor, I say, would come to this meeting or that, and display a copy of some rival and less prestigious men's mag, and say: "They've Gone Pink."

28   To "Go Pink," was, of course, to reveal, in a photo, the Labia; the existence of which was, one would think, a secret to no one, but to which photographic reference was felt, in that time, to be Non-U.

29   We at the mag considered ourselves gentlemen—and -women. We held to the crypto-British, which is to say wry, self-deprecating, view of our work.

30   We tried to be funny and smart, and put out a book diverting and honestly, if mildly, erotic. What then of this Going Pink?

31   But the decision was not ours. It came from on high, and devolved upon the photographic rather than the verbal portion of the floor, and Pink we went—the ensuing consequence of which can be seen all around us in the savage immorality of the American Culture and the general falling-away-from-God.

32   The second Rubicon was Missing Fingers.

33   And what was the intent and what the effect of That Magazine, Brute that I am?

34   I am reminded of a passage in a Kurt Vonnegut book. A young man is admiring the centerfold of some girlie mag. He shows it to an older man and says, "Look at that woman!" "Son, that's not a woman," the older man says, "that's a photograph."

35   And they were lovely, those photographs. And their subjects were lovely, too.

36   The models came to the office infrequently; and had I jotted down my fantasies about the models rather than staring at the blues, I would have got home earlier all that year.

37   I always hoped that the gentle collegiality of the office hid a raucous sexual nightlife, and that in time, I would be invited to share it. I looked, through the year, for signs that I was being accepted and, in fact, for signs that such a secret life went on—that the editorial staff, Chicagoan P. G. Wodehouses, when the Lindbergh Beacon went on, turned to diversions worthy of Arthur Schnitzler.

38   I more than fantasized about it; I *knew* that it happened somewhere north of Division Street and after midnight. And I knew that I was never going to be invited.

39   For I was an interloper; I was a Ringer, brought in by the kindness of the Editor, and how could I hope to be given the Office to come to a soiree if I couldn't even get my Girl Copy right?

40   The invite never came. My closest approach came out of my "strip darts" gag.

41   I wrote the copy, and the photo folks set up a shoot.

42   We went, at nine AM, to some studio around State Street, and various people took their clothes off and pretended to play darts, and we drank the warm prop champagne and went home at lunch feeling foolish.

43   "Yes," you might say, "that's how you should have felt during that whole year."

44   And looking back, I think that I did, and my Schnitzler fantasies were signals of my anomie.

45   I wasn't as funny as the people who were funny, nor as sexy as those who were gifted in that way; what I chose to recognize as Fantasy was boring, and my true fantasies never made it past the superego and onto the page.

46   I made friends with one of the senior editors, and we bummed cigarettes and talked about Poetry.

47   I rented a room on Lake Shore Drive and saw the sun pop out of the lake most mornings during the Bicentennial summer. The editor still expressed approval of me, and I got offered a gig teaching drama at Yale.

48   I went to the man who gave me the job, and he congratulated me and said that he'd still like me, at the same salary, that I would only have to work three days a week, which left four for Yale, and that the mag would pay the airfare.

49   Once again I told him that he had the wrong guy, that I wasn't worth it, and he once again said that he didn't share my feelings.

50   I was very much surprised by his interest and endorsement after a year of my work. But it never occurred to me to accept his offer.

51   So I left Chicago, that most wonderful of towns, and went to Yale to discover that teaching writing was yet one more thing that I could not do.

52   Now, going on twenty years later, I browse sometimes through old magazines in a bookstore, looking for copies of jokes and gags and my Girl Copy, and I remember those long afternoons sitting in my office, looking at the blurred photographs of naked women.

Questions for Engagement, Response, and Analysis

1. Describe Mamet's job and his expectations of it.
2. What is the tone of the essay? How is the tone influenced by Mamet's memories of the job and of his expectations and misconceptions?
3. What is the state of Mamet's creativity while he is working at the magazine? What would you suppose is the reason for this state?
4. What is the theme of this essay?

Crafting Arguments

1. Starting with your answer to number two above, write an essay examining the ways Mamet creates the tone of the essay, giving specific examples to support each of your claims.

bell hooks (b. 1952)

Gloria Jean Watkins was born and raised in Hopkinsville, Kentucky. She was educated at Stanford (B.A.), the University of Wisconsin–Madison (M.A.), and the University of California, Santa Cruz (Ph.D.), where she wrote her dissertation on Toni Morrison. She adopted the name bell hooks in honor of her mother and her grandmother. As an educator, bell hooks has taught at the University of California, Santa Cruz; San Francisco State University; Yale University; Oberlin College; and the City College of New York. In 1981, she published Ain't I a Woman?: Black Women and Feminism, *a book that has been influential in feminist thought. She has written books for children and for juvenile readers as well as many books on feminism, aesthetics, and the importance of education. Some of the more recent books are* Art on My Mind *(1995), from which the essay included here is taken;* Cultural Criticism and Transformation *(1997);* Remembered Rapture: The Writer at Work *(1999); and* Is Feminism Dead? *(2004).*

BEAUTY LAID BARE: AESTHETICS
IN THE ORDINARY   (1995)

1   Growing up in conservative working-class and poor Southern black communities, I had no notion that black folks were inherently more radical or "cool" than any other marginalized or oppressed group. While the folks I lived amongst were often militant in their condemnation of racism, they were pretty much in agreement with many of the other values that trickled down from the worlds of the conservative ruling classes, from the white or black bourgeois world. When it came to materialism, across class it was clear that success in diverse black communities was measured by having nice things. Whether or not something was perceived as "nice" depended on one's social environment.

2   One of the intense pressures I experienced as an adolescent was caused by my longing to cultivate my own style and taste, clashing with the pressure to conform to set bourgeois standards. Sarah Oldham, my mother's mother, was the "style radical." Her aesthetic sensibility was grounded in a more traditional appreciation for the natural world, for color and harmony. As a quiltmaker she was constantly creating new worlds, discovering new patterns, different shapes. To her it was the uniqueness of the individual body, look, and soul that mattered. From her I learned the appropriateness of being myself.

3   The example of personal freedom and creative courage set by my grandmother was constantly challenged by the bourgeois aspirations of my mother, whereby she insisted on conformity, on imitating acceptable appearances and styles. To my mother, "nice things" were not the earth, the sky, the eggs in the henhouse, a fishing worm uncovered in dark, moist dirt, the sight of a tomato growing on a vine; "nice things" were the objects seen in advertisements, on the screen, and in catalogues.

4   My grandmother and her daughter, my mother, did agree on the basic principle that beautiful objects enhanced life, even if their aesthetic standards differed. Although we came from a poor and working-class background, from a history of squatting, sharecropping, and working in white folks' houses, among the traditional Southern black folks I grew up around there was a shared belief in the idea that beautiful things, objects that could be considered luxurious, that were expensive and difficult to own, were necessary for the spirit. The more downtrodden and unfortunate the circumstances, the more "beauty" was needed to uplift, to offer a vision of hope, to transform. When it came to the issue of desiring and longing for the beautiful object, whether it was a house, a car, furniture, clothing, shoes, etc., everyone agreed, across class, that folks needed to be in touch with beauty. When I was a child, this did not seem to be a radical idea. It was such a common way of thinking about life it seemed "natural." There was never a need to make someone feel guilty when he or she did without the basic necessities of life in order to acquire an object deemed beautiful, healing to the spirit. At times those objects were luxury items, not intrinsically aesthetically beautiful, but desired because the culture of consumerism had deemed them lovely symbols of power and possibility. Even though folks sometimes laughed at the individual who bought a shiny car bigger than the wood frame shack he or she lived in, underneath the mockery was the understanding that this symbol of luxury was a balm to a depressed and wounded spirit. This stance was in every way oppositional.

5   The black elders in our community, like Sarah my grandmother and Gus my grandfather, believed it was better to seek beauty in a world that was not subject to monetary exchange. For Sarah, beauty was there in the growing of flowers in her elaborate garden, or in the making of her quilts. Alice Walker, in her insightful essay "In Search of Our Mothers' Gardens," acknowledges the way poor black women

expressed their concern with beauty in the growing and arranging of flower gardens. Offering the example of her own mother, Walker declares: "Her face, as she prepared the Art that is her gift, is a legacy of respect she leaves to me, for all that illuminates and cherishes life. She has handed down respect of the possibilities—and the will to grasp them." This legacy had been handed down through generations in traditional Southern black folk culture. These were notions of beauty and wealth grounded in a worldview that was in opposition to excessive materialism.

6   Southern black males who had an oppositional aesthetic were often economically deprived but rich in spirit. When the forces of white supremacy and capitalism denied them access to meaningful work, they cultivated ways to care for the soul that sustained them. For my grandfather, Daddy Gus, the will to create was life-sustaining. To him beauty was present in found objects, discarded objects that he rescued and restored because, as he put it, "spirits lived there." His room—a luxurious, welcoming place for us as children—was full of "treasures." Entering that sanctuary of precious "beautiful" objects, we were embraced by an atmosphere of peace and serenity. In *Shambala: The Sacred Path of the Warrior*, Buddhist monk Chogyam Trungpa teaches that we create this atmosphere by expressing gentleness and precision in our environment: "You may live in a dirt hut with no floor and only one window, but if you regard that space as sacred, if you care for it with your heart and mind, then it will be a palace." This caretaking promotes "awareness and attention to detail." There can be a sacred place in everyone's life where beauty can be laid bare, where our spirits can be moved and lifted up by the creation and presence of a beautiful object.

7   When I first began to travel to different continents, I was fascinated by how, in most parts of the world, especially in places that the United States designates as "Third World," no matter how poor the surroundings, individuals create beautiful objects. In the deserts of North Africa, beautiful woven rugs were present in every abode, no matter how humble. In countries where folks are ravished by genocidal war and famine, suffering, anguished bodies shroud themselves in beautiful cloth. Indians in Mexico and the United States, living in various states of impoverishment, make clay pots that reveal artistic skill and vision.

8   In contrast, in the United States, contemporary African-Americans have been increasingly socialized by the mass media to leave behind attachments to the oppositional worldviews of our elders, especially to those having to do with beauty, and to assimilate into the mainstream. Hedonistic consumerism is offered as a replacement for healing and life-sustaining beauty. Unlike the global nonwhite poor, who manage to retain an awareness of the need for beauty despite imperialist devastation, the vast majority of the black poor in the United States do not

harbor uplifting cultural objects in their homes. This group has been overwhelmingly encouraged to abandon, destroy, or sell artifacts from the past. And this destruction has brought in its wake the loss of an aesthetic sensibility that is redemptive. For example, today's concrete state-designed and -operated homogenous housing for the poor takes away the opportunity for creativity that was characteristic of the rural shack, its porch and gardens.

9   Black liberation movement has not addressed the issue of aesthetics in everyday life. Militant black power movements in the 1960s and 1970s did not encourage a reclamation of attitudes about beauty common in traditional black folk culture. While obsessive materialism has been consistently critiqued in antiracist movements, as well as by radicals on the left, the issue of aesthetics has not received much attention, nor has the relationship between the desire for beauty and the longing for material goods.

10   At the outset of the contemporary feminist movement there was significant interrogation of consumerism, of women's addiction to materialism, and of the issue of money, both its distribution along gendered lines and its use. Early feminist anthologies such as *Women in Sexist Society*, edited by Vivian Gornick and Barbara Moran, included discussions of consumerism and beauty in relation to appearances. An anonymous "red-stocking sister" made the useful point that feminist discussions of female obsession with consumerism would be useful if they began from a standpoint that depicted Americans as mere dupes of patriarchal advertising culture, "oppressed" by an infatuation with goods. She suggested: "The consumerism theory is the outgrowth of an aristocratic, European-oriented antimaterialism based on upperclass *ressentiment* against the rise of the vulgar bourgeois. Radical intellectuals have been attracted to this essentially reactionary position . . . because it appeals to both their dislike of capitalism and their feeling of superiority to the working class . . .Oddly, no one claims that the ruling class is oppressed by commodity choices; it seems that rich people consume out of free choice." As was the case in black liberation struggles, there was no discussion of aesthetics, of the place of beauty in everyday life, within feminist debates about materialism, money, etc. Progressive feminist thinkers are more likely to critique the dangers of excessive materialism without discussing in a concrete way how we can balance a desire for beauty or luxury within an anticapitalist, antisexist agenda.

11   As revolutionary and radical feminism becomes less visible, and as more reformist thinking, such as Naomi Wolf's *Fire with Fire*, prevails as the feminist order of the day, there is hardly any discussion among feminists about the politics of materialism or money. Contemporary feminists, myself included, can receive more financial rewards for feminist work than has ever been possible, yet we remain relatively silent about these issues. Wolf is not silent. She advocates a brand of "power

feminism" that sees nothing problematic about both pursuing and achieving wealth and opposing patriarchal domination. Certainly there is a distinction to be made between the processes by which material privilege can be acquired and wealth accumulated.

12   Most radical or revolutionary feminists continue to believe that living simply, the equitable distribution of resources, and communalism are necessary to the progressive struggle to end sexism while ending class exploitation. All too often in the past, living simply was made synonymous with a vulgar antimaterialism or anti-aestheticism that privileged living without attention to beauty, to decoration, either of one's person or one's space. Although nowadays the tendency seems to be toward the other extreme, toward indulging to excess, some radical feminists, myself included, grapple with the place of beauty in revolutionary struggle, with our materialism and with our longing for luxury. Just as my Southern black ancestors recognized that in the midst of exploitation and oppression suffering could be endured if transforming encounters with beauty took place, many revolutionary feminists recognize that we need these same values within the progressive feminist movement. Since it is so easy for those of us with material privilege to hoard resources, to have an attachment to wealth or privileged class power, we need to be vigilant in creating an ethical approach to consumerism that sustains and affirms radical agendas for social change.

13   Rather than surrendering our passion for the beautiful, for luxury, we need to envision ways those passions can be fulfilled that do not reinforce the structures of domination we seek to change. Hopefully, feminist thinkers will begin to engage in more discussion and theorizing about the place of beauty in revolutionary struggle. Many of us who have a degree of material privilege find that sharing resources, sharing objects we find beautiful that enhance our lives, is one way to resist falling into a privatized, hedonistic consumerism that is self-serving. Those of us who engage in barter, conscious gift giving, tithing, sharing of living space and money, celebrate the luxurious if that which we deem luxurious is not acquired by harming others.

14   Females in white-supremacist patriarchal society are most often socialized to consume in an unmindful manner. We are encouraged to value goods, especially luxury goods, over our well-being and safety. Many women remain in domestic situations where we are being hurt and even abused by sexist men because of an attachment to material wealth and privilege. While there are many poor women who remain in abusive households because they plainly lack the economic means to leave, there are also some women who remain in such settings because they fear leaving behind material abundance. This kind of thinking is life-threatening and must be challenged.

15   Beauty can be and is present in our lives irrespective of our class status. Learning to see and appreciate the presence of beauty is an act

of resistance in a culture of domination that recognizes the production of a pervasive feeling of lack, both material and spiritual, as a useful colonizing strategy. Individuals who feel constant lack will consume more, will submit more readily. As feminist thinkers construct feminist theory and practice to guide us into a revolutionary, revitalized feminist future, we need to place aesthetics on our agenda. We need to theorize the meaning of beauty in our lives so that we can educate for critical consciousness, talking through the issues: how we acquire and spend money, how we feel about beauty, what the place of beauty is in our lives when we lack material privilege and even basic resources for living, the meaning and significance of luxury, and the politics of envy. Interrogating these issues will enable feminist thinkers to share certain strategies of resistance that will illuminate the ways we can create a balanced, harmonious life where we know the joy of collective, progressive struggle, where the presence of beauty uplifts and renews the spirit.

Questions for Engagement, Response, and Analysis

1. What were the two differing points of view about "nice things" and beauty exemplified by hooks' mother and grandmother?
2. Define the following terms in the context of hooks' essay:
    Creative courage
    Aesthetic sensibility
    Culture of consumerism
    Hedonistic consumerism
3. In what ways is hooks like Dee in Alice Walker's "Everyday Use"? In what ways is she like Maggie?
4. What is the main point of this essay?
5. Freewrite in your Reader's Journal about the joys of surrounding yourself with beauty or about the transforming power of beauty.

Crafting Arguments

1. Analyze hooks' claims that "beautiful objects [enhance] life" and that they are "necessary for the spirit."
2. Using hooks' essay, Alice Walker's essay "In Search of Our Mothers' Gardens," and Walker's story "Everyday Use," explain how quilts serve the double purpose of adding beauty to one's life and preserving one's cultural history.
3. According to Hooks, "the black poor in the United States" no longer "harbor uplifting cultural objects in their homes" and this situation has "brought in its wake the loss of an aesthetic sensibility that is redemptive." Write an essay in which you explain her claims and support or challenge them.

FICTION

Mark Twain (1835–1910)

*Mark Twain is the pseudonym adopted by Samuel Lang-
horne Clemens. Twain grew up on the banks of the Mississippi River in Hannibal, Missouri, a locale that forms the
backdrop for two of his finest novels,* The Adventures of Tom
Sawyer *(1876) and* The Adventures of Huckleberry Finn
*(1885). By the time he published his first story at the age of
thirty, Twain had already worked as a printer's apprentice,
a riverboat pilot on the Mississippi River, and a reporter on
the wild frontier in the 1860s in Nevada and California. In
addition to* Tom Sawyer *and* Huckleberry Finn, *his books
include* Innocents Abroad *(1869), a hilarious account of
Americans in Europe;* Roughing It *(1872), comic nonfiction
about his work as a reporter in the American West; and such
cynical but thought-provoking later fiction as "The Man
That Corrupted Hadleyburg" (1900) and* The Mysterious
Stranger, *published posthumously in 1916.*

A FABLE   (1909)

1   Once upon a time an artist who had painted a small and very beautiful picture placed it so that he could see it in the mirror. He said, "This
doubles the distance and softens it, and it is twice as lovely as it was
before."

2   The animals out in the woods heard of this through the housecat, who
was greatly admired by them because he was so learned, and so refined
and civilized, and so polite and high-bred, and could tell them so much
which they didn't know before, and were not certain about afterward.
They were much excited about this new piece of gossip, and they asked
questions, so as to get at a full understanding of it. They asked what a picture was, and the cat explained.

3   "It is a flat thing," he said; "wonderfully flat, marvelously flat, enchant-
ingly flat and elegant. And, oh, so beautiful!"

4   That excited them almost to a frenzy, and they said they would give
the world to see it. Then the bear asked:

5   "What is it that makes it so beautiful?"

6   "It is the looks of it," said the cat.

7   This filled them with admiration and uncertainty, and they were more
excited than ever. Then the cow asked:

8   "What is a mirror?"

9   "It is a hole in the wall," said the cat. "You look in it, and there you see
the picture, and it is so dainty and charming and ethereal and inspiring
in its unimaginable beauty that your head turns round and round, and you
almost swoon with ecstasy."

10   The ass had not said anything as yet; he now began to throw doubts. He said there had never been anything as beautiful as this before, and probably wasn't now. He said that when it took a whole basketful of sesquipedalian adjectives to whoop up a thing of beauty, it was time for suspicion.

11   It was easy to see that these doubts were having an effect upon the animals, so the cat went off offended. The subject was dropped for a couple of days, but in the meantime curiosity was taking a fresh start, and there was a revival of interest perceptible. Then the animals assailed the ass for spoiling what could possibly have been a pleasure to them, on a mere suspicion that the picture was not beautiful, without any evidence that such was the case. The ass was not troubled; he was calm, and said there was one way to find out who was in the right, himself or the cat: he would go and look in that hole, and come back and tell what he found there. The animals felt relieved and grateful, and asked him to go at once—which he did.

12   But he did not know where he ought to stand; and so, through error, he stood between the picture and the mirror. The result was that the picture had no chance, and didn't show up. He returned home and said:

13   "The cat lied. There was nothing in that hole but an ass. There wasn't a sign of a flat thing visible. It was a handsome ass, and friendly, but just an ass, and nothing more."

14   The elephant asked:

15   "Did you see it good and clear? Were you close to it?"

16   "I saw it good and clear, O Hathi, King of Beasts. I was so close that I touched noses with it."

17   "This is very strange," said the elephant; "the cat was always truthful before—as far as we could make out. Let another witness try. Go, Baloo, look in the hole, and come and report."

18   So the bear went. When he came back, he said:

19   "Both the cat and the ass have lied; there was nothing in the hole but a bear."

20   Great was the surprise and puzzlement of the animals. Each was now anxious to make the test himself and get at the straight truth. The elephant sent them one at a time.

21   First, the cow. She found nothing in the hole but a cow.

22   The tiger found nothing in it but a tiger.

23   The lion found nothing in it but a lion.

24   The leopard found nothing in it but a leopard.

25   The camel found a camel, and nothing more.

26   Then Hathi was wroth, and said he would have the truth, if he had to go and fetch it himself. When he returned, he abused his whole subjectry for liars, and was in an unappeasable fury with the moral and mental blindness of the cat. He said that anybody but a near-sighted fool could see that there was nothing in the hole but an elephant.

Moral, By the Cat

27   You can find in a text whatever you bring, if you will stand between it
and the mirror of your imagination. You may not see your ears, but they
will be there.

Questions for Engagement, Response, and Analysis

1. Why does the artist position the picture across from the mirror?
2. Contrast the perceptions of the other animals with those of the cat;
   then agree or disagree with their evaluations of the cat and of the
   picture.
3. What does Twain mean by "You may not see your ears, but they will
   be there"?
4. What is the theme of this essay?

Crafting Arguments

1. Twain says that "You can find in a text whatever you bring, if you
   will stand between it and the mirror of your imagination." In an
   essay, explain how you found meaning in a work in this text or in a
   work of literature you have previously read because of your own
   experience.

James Grover Thurber (1894–1961)

*Humorist and cartoonist James Thurber was born in
Columbus, Ohio, and attended Ohio State University.
Thurber was unable to serve in active combat during World
War II because of a childhood accident in which his brother
shot him in the eye with an arrow during a game of
William Tell, so he worked as a code clerk for the Depart-
ment of State. He began his writing career at the* Columbus
Dispatch *in a column he called "Credos and Curios." After
moving to New York, he worked first at the* New York
Evening Post *and later at* The New Yorker. *There, his friend
E. B. White discovered Thurber's unique cartoons and
encouraged him to publish them along with his humorous
stories. Among his most famous stories are "The Secret Life
of Walter Mitty," "The Unicorn in the Garden," "The Dog
Who Bit People," "The Night the Bed Fell," "The Catbird
Seat," and "The Greatest Man in the World." Several of
Thurber's works were made into film:* The Male Animal *was
first a Broadway comedy and then a film, starring Henry
Fonda and Olivia de Havilland.* The Secret Life of Walter
Mitty, *a loose adaptation of Thurber's story, starred Danny
Kaye. Thurber's career at* The New Yorker *lasted until the
mid-twentieth century.*

THE SECRET LIFE OF WALTER MITTY   (1939)

1   We're going through!" The Commander's voice was like thin ice breaking. He wore his full-dress uniform, with the heavily braided white cap pulled down rakishly over one cold gray eye. "We can't make it, sir. It's spoiling for a hurricane, if you ask me." "I'm not asking you, Lieutenant Berg," said the Commander. "Throw on the power lights! Rev her up to 8,500! We're going through!" The pounding of the cylinders increased: ta-pocketa-pocketa-pocketa-*pocketa-pocketa*. The Commander stared at the ice forming on the pilot window. He walked over and twisted a row of complicated dials. "Switch on No. 8 auxiliary!" he shouted. "Switch on No. 8 auxiliary!" repeated Lieutenant Berg. "Full strength in No. 8 turret!" shouted the Commander. "Full strength in No. 8 turret!" The crew, bending to their various tasks in the huge, hurtling eight-engined Navy hydroplane, looked at each other and grinned. "The Old Man'll get us through," they said to one another. "The Old Man ain't afraid of Hell!" . . .

2   "Not so fast! You're driving too fast!" said Mrs. Mitty. "What are you driving so fast for?"

3   "Hmm?" said Walter Mitty. He looked at his wife, in the seat beside him, with shocked astonishment. She seemed grossly unfamiliar, like a strange woman who had yelled at him in a crowd. "You were up to fifty-five," she said. "You know I don't like to go more than forty. You were up to fifty-five." Walter Mitty drove on toward Waterbury in silence, the roaring of the SN202 through the worst storm in twenty years of Navy flying fading in the remote, intimate airways of his mind. "You're tensed up again," said Mrs. Mitty. "It's one of your days. I wish you'd let Dr. Renshaw look you over."

4   Walter Mitty stopped the car in front of the building where his wife went to have her hair done. "Remember to get those overshoes while I'm having my hair done," she said. "I don't need overshoes," said Mitty. She put her mirror back into her bag. "We've been all through that," she said, getting out of the car. "You're not a young man any longer." He raced the engine a little. "Why don't you wear your gloves? Have you lost your gloves?" Walter Mitty reached in a pocket and brought out the gloves. He put them on, but after she had turned and gone into the building and he had driven on to a red light, he took them off again. "Pick it up, brother!" snapped a cop as the light changed, and Mitty hastily pulled on his gloves and lurched ahead. He drove around the streets aimlessly for a time, and then he drove past the hospital on his way to the parking lot.

5   . . ."It's the millionaire banker, Wellington McMillan," said the pretty nurse. "Yes?" said Walter Mitty, removing his gloves slowly. "Who has the case?" "Dr. Renshaw and Dr. Benbow, but there are two specialists here, Dr. Remington from New York and Mr. Pritchard-Mitford from London. He flew over." A door opened down a long, cool corridor and Dr. Renshaw came out. He looked distraught and haggard. "Hello, Mitty," he said. "We're having the devil's own time with McMillan, the millionaire banker

and close personal friend of Roosevelt. Obstreosis of the ductal tract. Tertiary. Wish you'd take a look at him." "Glad to," said Mitty.

6   In the operating room there were whispered introductions: "Dr. Remington, Dr. Mitty. Mr. Pritchard-Mitford, Dr. Mitty." "I've read your book on streptothricosis." said Pritchard-Mitford, shaking hands. "A brilliant performance, sir." "Thank you," said Walter Mitty. "Didn't know you were in the States, Mitty," grumbled Remington. "Coals to Newcastle, bringing Mitford and me up here for a tertiary." "You are very kind," said Mitty. A huge, complicated machine, connected to the operating table, with many tubes and wires, began at this moment to go pocketa-pocketa-pocketa. "The new anesthetizer is giving way!" shouted an intern. "There is no one in the East who knows how to fix it!" "Quiet, man!" said Mitty, in a low, cool voice. He sprang to the machine, which was now going pocketa-pocketa-queep-pocketa-queep. He began fingering delicately a row of glistening dials. "Give me a fountain pen!" he snapped. Someone handed him a fountain pen. He pulled a faulty piston out of the machine and inserted the pen in its place. "That will hold for ten minutes," he said. "Get on with the operation." A nurse hurried over and whispered to Renshaw, and Mitty saw the man turn pale. "Coreopsis has set in," said Renshaw nervously. "If you would take over, Mitty?" Mitty looked at him and at the craven figure of Benbow, who drank, and at the grave, uncertain faces of the two great specialists. "If you wish," he said. They slipped a white gown on him; he adjusted a mask and drew on thin gloves; nurses handed him shining . . .

7   "Back it up, Mac! Look out for that Buick!" Walter Mitty jammed on the brakes. "Wrong lane, Mac," said the parking-lot attendant, looking at Mitty closely. "Gee. Yeh," muttered Mitty. He began cautiously to back out of the lane marked "Exit Only." "Leave her sit there," said the attendant. "I'll put her away." Mitty got out of the car. "Hey, better leave the key." "Oh," said Mitty, handing the man the ignition key. The attendant vaulted into the car, backed it up with insolent skill, and put it where it belonged.

8   They're so damn cocky, thought Walter Mitty, walking along Main Street; they think they know everything. Once he had tried to take his chains off, outside New Milford, and he had got them wound around the axles. A man had had to come out in a wrecking car and unwind them, a young, grinning garageman. Since then Mrs. Mitty always made him drive to a garage to have the chains taken off. The next time, he thought, I'll wear my right arm in a sling; they won't grin at me then. I'll have my right arm in a sling and they'll see I couldn't possibly take the chains off myself. He kicked at the slush on the sidewalk. "Overshoes," he said to himself, and he began looking for a shoe store.

9   When he came out into the street again, with the overshoes in a box under his arm, Walter Mitty began to wonder what the other thing was his wife had told him to get. She had told him, twice, before they set out from their house for Waterbury. In a way he hated these weekly trips to

town—he was always getting something wrong. Kleenex, he thought, Squibb's, razor blades? No. Toothpaste, toothbrush, bicarbonate, carborundum, initiative and referendum? He gave it up. But she would remember it. "Where's the what's-its-name?" she would ask. "Don't tell me you forgot the what's-its-name." A newsboy went by shouting something about the Waterbury trial.

10   . . ."Perhaps this will refresh your memory." The District Attorney suddenly thrust a heavy automatic at the quiet figure on the witness stand. "Have you ever seen this before?" Walter Mitty took the gun and examined it expertly. "This is my Webley-Vickers 50.80," he said calmly. An excited buzz ran around the courtroom. The Judge rapped for order. "You are a crack shot with any sort of firearms, I believe?" said the District Attorney, insinuatingly. "Objection!" shouted Mitty's attorney. "We have shown that the defendant could not have fired the shot. We have shown that he wore his right arm in a sling on the night of the fourteenth of July." Walter Mitty raised his hand briefly and the bickering attorneys were stilled. "With any known make of gun," he said evenly, "I could have killed Gregory Fitzhurst at three hundred feet *with my left hand*." Pandemonium broke loose in the courtroom. A woman's scream rose above the bedlam and suddenly a lovely, dark-haired girl was in Walter Mitty's arms. The District Attorney struck at her savagely. Without rising from his chair, Mitty let the man have it on the point of the chin. "You miserable cur!" . . .

11   "Puppy biscuit," said Walter Mitty. He stopped walking and the buildings of Waterbury rose up out of the misty courtroom and surrounded him again. A woman who was passing laughed. "He said 'Puppy biscuit,'" she said to her companion. "That man said 'Puppy biscuit' to himself." Walter Mitty hurried on. He went into an A. & P., not the first one he came to but a smaller one farther up the street. "I want some biscuit for small, young dogs," he said to the clerk. "Any special brand, sir?" The greatest pistol shot in the world thought a moment. "It says 'Puppies Bark for It' on the box," said Walter Mitty.

12   His wife would be through at the hairdresser's in fifteen minutes, Mitty saw in looking at his watch, unless they had trouble drying it; sometimes they had trouble drying it. She didn't like to get to the hotel first; she would want him to be there waiting for her as usual. He found a big leather chair in the lobby, facing a window, and he put the overshoes and the puppy biscuit on the floor beside it. He picked up an old copy of *Liberty* and sank down into the chair. "Can Germany Conquer the World Through the Air?" Walter Mitty looked at the pictures of bombing planes and of ruined streets.

13   . . ."The cannonading has got the wind up in young Raleigh, sir," said the sergeant. Captain Mitty looked up at him through touseled hair. "Get him to bed," he said wearily. "With the others. I'll fly alone." "But you can't, sir," said the sergeant anxiously. "It takes two men to handle that bomber and the Archies are pounding hell out of the air.

Von Richtman's circus is between here and Saulier." "Somebody's got to get that ammunition dump," said Mitty. "I'm going over. Spot of brandy?" He poured a drink for the sergeant and one for himself. War thundered and whined around the dugout and battered at the door. There was a rending of wood and splinters flew through the room. "A bit of a near thing," said Captain Mitty carelessly. "The box barrage is closing in," said the sergeant. "We only live once, Sergeant," said Mitty, with his faint, fleeting smile. "Or do we?" He poured another brandy and tossed it off. "I never see a man could hold his brandy like you, sir," said the sergeant. "Begging your pardon, sir." Captain Mitty stood up and strapped on his huge Webley-Vickers automatic. "It's forty kilometers through hell, sir," said the sergeant. Mitty finished one last brandy. "After all," he said softly, "what isn't?" The pounding of the cannon increased; there was the rat-tat-tatting of machine guns, and from somewhere came the menacing pocketa-pocketa-pocketa of the new flame-throwers. Walter Mitty walked to the door of the dugout humming "Auprès de Ma Blonde." He turned and waved to the sergeant. "Cheerio!" he said. . . .

14 Something struck his shoulder. "I've been looking all over this hotel for you," said Mrs. Mitty. "Why do you have to hide in this old chair? How did you expect me to find you?" "Things close in," said Walter Mitty vaguely. "What?" Mrs. Mitty said. "Did you get the what's-its-name? The puppy biscuit? What's in that box?" "Overshoes," said Mitty. "Couldn't you have put them on in the store?" "I was thinking," said Walter Mitty. "Does it ever occur to you that I am sometimes thinking?" She looked at him. "I'm going to take your temperature when I get you home," she said.

15 They went out through the revolving doors that made a faintly derisive whistling sound when you pushed them. It was two blocks to the parking lot. At the drugstore on the corner she said, "Wait here for me. I forgot something. I won't be a minute." She was more than a minute. Walter Mitty lighted a cigarette. It began to rain, rain with sleet in it. He stood up against the wall of the drugstore, smoking. . . . He put his shoulders back and his heels together. "To hell with the handkerchief," said Walter Mitty scornfully. He took one last drag on his cigarette and snapped it away. Then, with that faint, fleeting smile playing about his lips, he faced the firing squad; erect and motionless, proud and disdainful, Walter Mitty the Undefeated, inscrutable to the last.

Questions for Engagement, Response, and Analysis

1. What is the point of view of this story?
2. What is the tone? How does Thurber create it?
3. Examine each of Walter Mitty's fantasies. What characteristics do they have in common? What characteristics do the protagonists all share?

Crafting Arguments

1. In an essay, argue that in this battle of the sexes, Walter Mitty wins, that like Thurber, Mitty is a creator.

2. Write an essay comparing Walter Mitty with the heroes of his fantasies and identifying the tone created by the contrast.

Ray Bradbury (b. 1920)

One of America's most prolific writers of science fiction and fantasy, Ray Bradbury was born in Waukegan, Illinois, but has spent most of his life in Los Angeles, California. His novels and short stories have won numerous awards, including the Nebula, O. Henry Memorial, Prometheus, Benjamin Franklin, and Aviation-Space Writers and World Fantasy Lifetime Achievement Awards. His works have often been adapted for television and film. The most notable adaptations include The Martian Chronicles, *a 1980 miniseries;* Fahrenheit 451 *(1966), adapted from the 1953 novel;* The Illustrated Man *(1969);* It Came from Outer Space *(1953) and* It Came from Outer Space II *(1996);* Quest *(1983); and* Something Wicked This Way Comes *(1983), from the 1962 novel. His recent works include novels—*Let's All Kill Constance *(2003) and* Forever Summer *(2006)—and short story collections—*The Cat's Pajamas *(2004) and* Now and Forever *(2006).*

THERE WILL COME SOFT RAINS   (1950)

1   In the living room the voice-clock sang, *Tick-tock, seven o'clock, time to get up, time to get up, seven o'clock!* as if it were afraid that nobody would. The morning house lay empty. The clock ticked on, repeating and repeating its sounds into the emptiness. *Seven-nine, breakfast time, seven-nine!*

2   In the kitchen the breakfast stove gave a hissing sigh and ejected from its warm interior eight pieces of perfectly browned toast, eight eggs sunnyside up, sixteen slices of bacon, two coffees, and two cool glasses of milk.

3   "Today is August 4, 2026," said a second voice from the kitchen ceiling, "in the city of Allendale, California." It repeated the date three times for memory's sake. "Today is Mr. Featherstone's birthday. Today is the anniversary of Tilita's marriage. Insurance is payable, as are the water, gas, and light bills."

4   Somewhere in the walls, relays clicked, memory tapes glided under electric eyes.

5   *Eight-one, tick-tock, eight-one o'clock, off to school, off to work, run, run, eight-one!* But no doors slammed, no carpets took the soft tread of rubber heels. It was raining outside. The weather box on the front door

sang quietly: "Rain, rain, go away; rubbers, raincoats for today . . ." And the rain tapped on the empty house, echoing.

6   Outside, the garage chimed and lifted its door to reveal the waiting car. After a long wait the door swung down again.

7   At eight-thirty the eggs were shriveled and the toast was like stone. An aluminum wedge scraped them into the sink, where hot water whirled them down a metal throat which digested and flushed them away to the distant sea. The dirty dishes were dropped into a hot washer and emerged twinkling dry.

8   *Nine-fifteen,* sang the clock, *time to clean.*

9   Out of warrens in the wall, tiny robot mice darted. The rooms were acrawl with the small cleaning animals, all rubber and metal. They thudded against chairs, whirling their mustached runners, kneading the rug nap, sucking gently at hidden dust. Then, like mysterious invaders, they popped into their burrows. Their pink electric eyes faded. The house was clean.

10   *Ten o'clock.* The sun came out from behind the rain. The house stood alone in a city of rubble and ashes. This was the one house left standing. At night the ruined city gave off a radioactive glow which could be seen for miles.

11   *Ten-fifteen.* The garden sprinklers whirled up in golden founts, filling the soft morning air with scatterings of brightness. The water pelted windowpanes, running down the charred west side where the house had been burned evenly free of its white paint. The entire west face of the house was black, save for five places. Here the silhouette in paint of a man mowing a lawn. Here, as in a photograph, a woman bent to pick flowers. Still farther over, their images burned on wood in one titanic instant, a small boy, hands flung into the air; higher up, the image of a thrown ball, and opposite him a girl, hands raised to catch a ball which never came down.

12   The five spots of paint—the man, the woman, the children, the ball—remained. The rest was a thin charcoaled layer.

13   The gentle sprinkler rain filled the garden with falling light.

14   Until this day, how well the house had kept its peace. How carefully it had inquired, "Who goes there? What's the password?" and, getting no answer from lonely foxes and whining cats, it had shut up its windows and drawn shades in an old-maidenly preoccupation with self-protection which bordered on a mechanical paranoia.

15   It quivered at each sound, the house did. If a sparrow brushed a window, the shade snapped up. The bird, startled, flew off! No, not even a bird must touch the house!

16   The house was an altar with ten thousand attendants, big, small, servicing, attending, in choirs. But the gods had gone away, and the ritual of the religion continued senselessly, uselessly.

17   *Twelve noon.*

18   A dog whined, shivering, on the front porch.

19   The front door recognized the dog voice and opened. The dog, once huge and fleshy, but now gone to bone and covered with sores, moved in and through the house, tracking mud. Behind it whirred angry mice, angry at having to pick up mud, angry at inconvenience.

20   For not a leaf fragment blew under the door but what the wall panels flipped open and the copper scrap rats flashed swiftly out. The offending dust, hair, or paper, seized in miniature steel jaws, was raced back to the burrows. There, down tubes which fed into the cellar, it was dropped into the sighing vent of an incinerator which sat like evil Baal in a dark corner.

21·   The dog ran upstairs, hysterically yelping to each door, at last realizing, as the house realized, that only silence was here.

22   It sniffed the air and scratched the kitchen door. Behind the door, the stove was making pancakes which filled the house with a rich baked odor and the scent of maple syrup.

23   The dog frothed at the mouth, lying at the door, sniffing, its eyes turned to fire. It ran wildly in circles, biting at its tail, spun in a frenzy, and died. It lay in the parlor for an hour.

24   *Two o'clock*, sang a voice.

25   Delicately sensing decay at last, the regiments of mice hummed out as softly as blown gray leaves in an electrical wind.

26   *Two-fifteen.*

27   The dog was gone.

28   In the cellar, the incinerator glowed suddenly and a whirl of sparks leaped up the chimney.

29   *Two thirty-five.*

30   Bridge tables sprouted from patio walls. Playing cards fluttered onto pads in a shower of pips. Martinis manifested on an oaken bench with egg-salad sandwiches. Music played.

31   But the tables were silent and the cards untouched.

32   At four o'clock the tables folded like great butterflies back through the paneled walls.

33   *Four-thirty.*

34   The nursery walls glowed.

35   Animals took shape: yellow giraffes, blue lions, pink antelopes, lilac panthers cavorting in crystal substance. The walls were glass. They looked out upon color and fantasy. Hidden films clocked through well-oiled sprockets, and the walls lived. The nursery floor was woven to resemble a crisp, cereal meadow. Over this ran aluminum roaches and iron crickets, and in the hot still air butterflies of delicate red tissue wavered among the sharp aromas of animal spoors! There was the sound like a great matted yellow hive of bees within a dark bellows, the lazy bumble of a purring lion. And there was the patter of okapi feet and the murmur of a fresh jungle rain, like other hoofs, falling upon the summer-starched grass. Now the walls dissolved into distances of parched weed,

mile on mile, and warm endless sky. The animals drew away into thorn brakes and water holes.

36   It was the children's hour.

37   *Five o'clock.* The bath filled with clear hot water.

38   *Six, seven, eight o'clock.* The dinner dishes manipulated like magic tricks, and in the study a *click.* In the metal stand opposite the hearth where a fire now blazed up warmly, a cigar popped out, half an inch of soft gray ash on it, smoking, waiting.

39   *Nine o'clock.* The beds warmed their hidden circuits, for nights were cool here.

40   *Nine-five.* A voice spoke from the study ceiling:

41   "Mrs. McClellan, which poem would you like this evening?"

42   The house was silent.

43   The voice said at last, "Since you express no preference, I shall select a poem at random." Quiet music rose to back the voice. "Sara Teasdale. As I recall, your favorite. . . .

There will come soft rains and the smell of the ground,
And swallows circling with their shimmering sound;

And frogs in the pools singing at night,
And wild plum trees in tremulous white;

Robins will wear their feathery fire,
Whistling their whims on a low fence-wire;

And not one will know of the war, not one
Will care at last when it is done.

Not one would mind, neither bird nor tree,
If mankind perished utterly;

And Spring herself, when she woke at dawn
Would scarcely know that we were gone."

44   The fire burned on the stone hearth and the cigar fell away into a mound of quiet ash on its tray. The empty chairs faced each other between the silent walls, and the music played.

45   At ten o'clock the house began to die.

46   The wind blew. A falling tree bough crashed through the kitchen window. Cleaning solvent, bottled, shattered over the stove. The room was ablaze in an instant!

47   "Fire!" screamed a voice. The house lights flashed, water pumps shot water from the ceilings. But the solvent spread on the linoleum, licking, eating, under the kitchen door, while the voices took it up in chorus: "Fire, fire, fire!"

48   The house tried to save itself. Doors sprang tightly shut, but the windows were broken by the heat and the wind blew and sucked upon the fire.

49   The house gave ground as the fire in ten billion angry sparks moved with flaming ease from room to room and then up the stairs. While scurrying water rats squeaked from the walls, pistoled their water, and ran for more. And the wall sprays let down showers of mechanical rain.

50   But too late. Somewhere, sighing, a pump shrugged to a stop. The quenching rain ceased. The reserve water supply which had filled baths and washed dishes for many quiet days was gone.

51   The fire crackled up the stairs. It fed upon Picassos and Matisses in the upper halls, like delicacies, baking off the oily flesh, tenderly crisping the canvases into black shavings.

52   Now the fire lay in beds, stood in windows, changed the colors of drapes!

53   And then, reinforcements.

54   From attic trapdoors, blind robot faces peered down with faucet mouths gushing green chemical.

55   The fire backed off, as even an elephant must at the sight of a dead snake. Now there were twenty snakes whipping over the floor, killing the fire with a clear cold venom of green froth.

56   But the fire was clever. It had sent flame outside the house, up through the attic to the pumps there. An explosion! The attic brain which directed the pumps was shattered into bronze shrapnel on the beams.

57   The fire rushed back into every closet and felt of the clothes hung there.

58   The house shuddered, oak bone on bone, its bared skeleton cringing from the heat, its wire, its nerves revealed as if a surgeon had torn the skin off to let the red veins and capillaries quiver in the scalded air. Help, help! Fire! Run, run! Heat snapped mirrors like the first brittle winter ice. And the voices wailed, Fire, fire, run, run, like a tragic nursery rhyme, a dozen voices, high, low, like children dying in a forest, alone, alone. And the voices fading as the wires popped their sheathings like hot chestnuts. One, two, three, four, five voices died.

59   In the nursery the jungle burned. Blue lions roared, purple giraffes bounded off. The panthers ran in circles, changing color, and ten million animals, running before the fire, vanished off toward a distant steaming river. . . .

60   Ten more voices died. In the last instant under the fire avalanche, other choruses, oblivious, could be heard announcing the time, playing music, cutting the lawn by remote-control mower, or setting an umbrella frantically out and in, the slamming and opening front door, a thousand things happening, like a clock shop when each clock strikes the hour insanely before or after the other, a scene of maniac confusion, yet unity; singing, screaming, a few last cleaning mice darting bravely out to carry the horrid ashes away! And one voice, with sublime disregard for the situation, read poetry aloud in the fiery study, until all the film spools burned, until all the wires withered and the circuits cracked.

61   The fire burst the house and let it slam flat down, puffing out skirts of spark and smoke.

62   In the kitchen, an instant before the rain of fire and timber, the stove could be seen making breakfasts at a psychopathic rate, ten dozen eggs, six loaves of toast, twenty dozen bacon strips, which, eaten by fire, started the stove working again, hysterically hissing!

63   The crash. The attic smashing into kitchen and parlor. The parlor into cellar, cellar into sub-cellar. Deep freeze, armchair, film tapes, circuits, beds, and all like skeletons thrown in a cluttered mound deep under.

64   Smoke and silence. A great quantity of smoke.

65   Dawn showed faintly in the east. Among the ruins, one wall stood alone. Within the wall, a last voice said, over and over again and again, even as the sun rose to shine upon the heaped rubble and steam:

66   "Today is August 5, 2026, today is August 5, 2026, today is . . ."

Questions for Engagement, Response, and Analysis

1. What is the setting of this story?
2. List the clues to the end of the story that Bradbury gives even before paragraph 10.
3. Reread paragraph 16. Then, explain the analogy in this paragraph.
4. What is the effect of the personification of the fire?
5. What is the theme of this story?

Crafting Arguments

1. Using the details Bradbury gives to describe the house, write an essay describing the family that lived there.
2. After carefully re-reading the story and Teasdale's poem, write an essay explaining why, in your opinion, Bradbury chose this poem's opening words as the title and included the poem in the story.

Woody Allen (b. 1935)

Born Allen Stewart Konigsberg, Woody Allen exhibited an early interest in writing and at the age of seventeen joined NBC as a staff writer. There he wrote for The Garry Moore Show *and* Sid Caesar's Your Show of Shows. *His first screenplay,* What's New, Pussycat? *(1964), decided his future as a director. Since then he has written, directed, and starred in many of his own films as an Academy Award–winning filmmaker; he is one of the few directors with total control over production. Many of Allen's films and stories are parodies, science fiction, and spoofs of nineteenth-century Russian novels; they often use wordplay, allusions, and juxtapositions of unusual elements. Among his most influential films are* Bananas *(1971),* Annie Hall *(1977),* Hannah and Her Sisters *(1986),* Crimes and Misdemeanors *(1989), and* Match Point *(2005). Allen is still a prolific writer*

and producer. "The Kugelmass Episode," first published in
The New Yorker, won an O. Henry Award as one of the best
stories of 1978.

THE KUGELMASS EPISODE   (1977)

1   Kugelmass, a professor of humanities at City College, was unhappily married for the second time. Daphne Kugelmass was an oaf. He also had two dull sons by his first wife, Flo, and was up to his neck in alimony and child support.

2   "Did I know it would turn out so badly?" Kugelmass whined to his analyst one day. "Daphne had promise. Who suspected she'd let herself go and swell up like a beach ball? Plus she had a few bucks, which is not in itself a healthy reason to marry a person, but it doesn't hurt, with the kind of operating nut I have. You see my point?"

3   Kugelmass was bald and as hairy as a bear, but he had soul.

4   "I need to meet a new woman," he went on. "I need to have an affair. I may not look the part, but I'm a man who needs romance. I need softness, I need flirtation. I'm not getting younger, so before it's too late I want to make love in Venice, trade quips at '21,' and exchange coy glances over red wine and candlelight. You see what I'm saying?"

5   Dr. Mandel shifted in his chair and said, "An affair will solve nothing. You're so unrealistic. Your problems run much deeper."

6   "And also this affair must be discreet," Kugelmass continued. "I can't afford a second divorce. Daphne would really sock it to me."

7   "Mr. Kugelmass—"

8   "But it can't be anyone at City College, because Daphne also works there. Not that anyone on the faculty at C.C.N.Y. is any great shakes, but some of those co- eds . . ."

9   "Mr. Kugelmass—"

10   "Help me. I had a dream last night. I was skipping through a meadow holding a picnic basket and the basket was marked 'Options.' And then I saw there was a hole in the basket."

11   "Mr. Kugelmass, the worst thing you could do is act out. You must simply express your feelings here, and together we'll analyze them. You have been in treatment long enough to know there is no overnight cure. After all, I'm an analyst, not a magician."

12   "Then perhaps what I need is a magician," Kugelmass said, rising from his chair. And with that he terminated his therapy.

13   A couple of weeks later, while Kugelmass and Daphne were moping around in their apartment one night like two pieces of old furniture, the phone rang.

14   "I'll get it," Kugelmass said. "Hello."

15   "Kugelmass?" a voice said. "Kugelmass, this is Persky."

16   "Who?"

17   "Persky. Or should I say The Great Persky?"

18   "Pardon me?"

19   "I hear you're looking all over town for a magician to bring a little exotica into your life? Yes or no?"

20   "Sh-h-h," Kugelmass whispered. "Don't hang up. Where are you calling from, Persky?"

21   Early the following afternoon, Kugelmass climbed three flights of stairs in a broken-down apartment house in the Bushwick section of Brooklyn. Peering through the darkness of the hall, he found the door he was looking for and pressed the bell. I'm going to regret this, he thought to himself.

22   Seconds later, he was greeted by a short, thin, waxy-looking man.

23   "*You're* Persky the Great?" Kugelmass said.

24   "The Great Persky. You want a tea?"

25   "No, I want romance. I want music. I want love and beauty."

26   "But not tea, eh? Amazing. O.K., sit down."

27   Persky went to the back room, and Kugelmass heard the sounds of boxes and furniture being moved around. Persky reappeared, pushing before him a large object on squeaky roller-skate wheels. He removed some old silk handkerchiefs that were lying on its top and blew away a bit of dust. It was a cheap-looking Chinese cabinet, badly lacquered.

28   "Persky," Kugelmass said, "what's your scam?"

29   "Pay attention," Persky said. "This is some beautiful effect. I developed it for a Knights of Pythias date last year, but the booking fell through. Get into the cabinet."

30   "Why, so you can stick it full of swords or something?"

31   "You see any swords?"

32   Kugelmass made a face and, grunting, climbed into the cabinet. He couldn't help noticing a couple of ugly rhinestones glued onto the raw plywood just in front of his face. "If this is a joke," he said.

33   "Some joke. Now, here's the point. If I throw any novel into this cabinet with you, shut the doors, and tap it three times, you will find yourself projected into that book."

34   Kugelmass made a grimace of disbelief.

35   "It's the emess," Persky said "My hand to God. Not just a novel, either. A short story, a play, a poem. You can meet any of the women created by the world's best writers. Whoever you dreamed of. You could carry on all you like with a real winner. Then when you've had enough you give a yell, and I'll see you're back here in a split second."

36   "Persky, are you some kind of outpatient?"

37   "I'm telling you it's on the level," Persky said.

38   Kugelmass remained skeptical. "What are you telling me—that this cheesy homemade box can take me on a ride like you're describing?"

39   "For a double sawbuck."

40   Kugelmass reached for his wallet. "I'll believe this when I see it," he said.

41   Persky tucked the bills in his pants pocket and turned toward his bookcase. "So who do you want to meet? Sister Carrie?[1] Hester Prynne?[2] Ophelia?[3] Maybe someone by Saul Bellow?[4] Hey, what about Temple Drake?[5] Although for a man your age she'd be a workout."

42   "French. I want to have an affair with a French lover."

43   "Nana?"[6]

44   "I don't want to have to pay for it."

45   "What about Natasha in *War and Peace*?"

46   "I said French. I know! What about Emma Bovary?[7] That sounds to me perfect."

47   "You got it Kugelmass. Give me a holler when you've had enough." Persky tossed in a paperback copy of Flaubert's novel.

48   "You sure this is safe?" Kugelmass asked as Persky began shutting the cabinet doors.

49   "Safe. Is anything safe in this crazy world?" Persky rapped three times on the cabinet and then flung open the doors.

50   Kugelmass was gone. At the same moment, he appeared in the bedroom of Charles and Emma Bovary's house at Yonville. Before him was a beautiful woman, standing alone with her back turned to him as she folded some linen. I can't believe this, thought Kugelmass, staring at the doctor's ravishing wife. This is uncanny. I'm here. It's her.

51   Emma turned in surprise. "Goodness, you startled me," she said. "Who are you?" She spoke in the same fine English translation as the paperback.

52   It's simply devastating, he thought. Then, realizing that it was he whom she had addressed, he said, "Excuse me. I'm Sidney Kugelmass. I'm from City College. A professor of humanities. C.C.N.Y.? Uptown. I—oh, boy!"

53   Emma Bovary smiled flirtatiously and said, "Would you like a drink? A glass of wine, perhaps?"

54   She is beautiful, Kugelmass thought. What a contrast with the troglodyte who shared his bed! He felt a sudden impulse to take this vision into his arms and tell her she was the kind of woman he had dreamed of all his life.

55   "Yes, some wine," he said hoarsely. "White. No, red. No, white. Make it white."

56   "Charles is out for the day," Emma said, her voice full of playful implication.

57   After the wine, they went for a stroll in the lovely French countryside. "I've always dreamed that some mysterious stranger would appear and

---

[1]Sister Carrie, a character in Theodore Dreiser's novel of the same name, becomes a prostitute.

[2]Hester Prynne, a character in Hawthorne's *The Scarlet Letter*, wears an "A" for adultery.

[3]Ophelia in Shakespeare's *Hamlet* is the young woman whom Hamlet loves.

[4]Saul Bellow is a contemporary American novelist.

[5]In William Faulkner's novel *Sanctuary*, Popeye rapes Temple Drake with a corncob.

[6]Nana is the sensuous heroine of Zola's *Nana*.

[7]Emma Bovary is the faithless wife in Flaubert's *Madame Bovary*.

rescue me from the monotony of this crass rural existence," Emma said, clasping his hand. They passed a small church. "I love what you have on," she murmured. "I've never seen anything like it around here. It's so . . . so modern."

58   "It's called a leisure suit," he said romantically. "It was marked down." Suddenly he kissed her. For the next hour they reclined under a tree and whispered together and told each other deeply meaningful things with their eyes. Then Kugelmass sat up. He had just remembered he had to meet Daphne at Bloomingdale's. "I must go," he told her. "But don't worry, I'll be back."

59   "I hope so," Emma said.

60   He embraced her passionately, and the two walked back to the house. He held Emma's face cupped in his palms, kissed her again, and yelled, "O.K., Persky! I got to be at Bloomingdale's by three-thirty."

61   There was an audible pop, and Kugelmass was back in Brooklyn.

62   "So? Did I lie?" Persky asked triumphantly.

63   "Look, Persky, I'm right now late to meet the ball and chain at Lexington Avenue, but when can I go again? Tomorrow?"

64   "My pleasure. Just bring a twenty. And don't mention this to anybody."

65   "Yeah. I'm going to call Rupert Murdoch."[8]

66   Kugelmass hailed a cab and sped off to the city. His heart danced on point. I am in love, he thought, I am the possessor of a wonderful secret. What he didn't realize was that at this very moment students in various classrooms across the country were saying to their teachers, "Who is this character on page 100? A bald Jew is kissing Madame Bovary?" A teacher in Sioux Falls, South Dakota, sighed and thought, Jesus, these kids, with their pot and acid. What goes through their minds!

67   Daphne Kugelmass was in the bathroom-accessories department at Bloomingdale's when Kugelmass arrived breathlessly. "Where've you been?" she snapped. "It's four-thirty."

68   "I got held up in traffic," Kugelmass said.

69   Kugelmass visited Persky the next day, and in a few minutes was again passing magically to Yonville. Emma couldn't hide her excitement at seeing him. The two spent hours together, laughing and talking about their different backgrounds. Before Kugelmass left, they made love. "My God, I'm doing it with Madame Bovary!" Kugelmass whispered to himself. "Me, who failed freshman English."

70   As the months passed, Kugelmass saw Persky many times and developed a close and passionate relationship with Emma Bovary. "Make sure and always get me into the book before page 120," Kugelmass said to the magician one day. "I always have to meet her before she hooks up with this Rodolphe character."

71   "Why?" Persky asked. "You can't beat his time?"

---

[8]Rupert Murdoch is a wealthy Australian publisher and owner of several sensational tabloids.

72   "Beat his time. He's landed gentry. Those guys have nothing better to do than flirt and ride horses. To me, he's one of those faces you see in the pages of *Women's Wear Daily*. With the Helmut Berger hairdo. But to her he's hot stuff."

73   "And her husband suspects nothing?"

74   "He's out of his depth. He's a lacklustre little paramedic who's thrown in his lot with a jitterbug. He's ready to go to sleep by ten, and she's putting on her dancing shoes. Oh, well . . . See you later."

75   And once again Kugelmass entered the cabinet and passed instantly to the Bovary estate at Yonville. "How you doing, cupcake?" he said to Emma.

76   "Oh, Kugelmass," Emma sighed. "What I have to put up with. Last night at dinner, Mr. Personality dropped off to sleep in the middle of the dessert course. I'm pouring my heart out about Maxim's and the ballet, and out of the blue I hear snoring."

77   "It's O.K., darling. I'm here now," Kugelmass said, embracing her. I've earned this, he thought, smelling Emma's French perfume and burying his nose in her hair. I've suffered enough. I've paid enough analysts. I've searched till I'm weary. She's young and nubile, and I'm here a few pages after Leon and just before Rodolphe. By showing up during the correct chapters, I've got the situation knocked.

78   Emma, to be sure, was just as happy as Kugelmass. She had been starved for excitement, and his tales of Broadway night life, of fast cars and Hollywood and TV stars, enthralled the young French beauty.

79   "Tell me again about O. J. Simpson," she implored that evening, as she and Kugelmass strolled past Abbé Bournisien's church.

80   "What can I say? The man is great. He sets all kinds of rushing records. Such moves. They can't touch him."

81   "And the Academy Awards?" Emma said wistfully. "I'd give anything to win one."

82   "First you've got to be nominated."

83   "I know. You explained it. But I'm convinced I can act. Of course, I'd want to take a class or two. With Strasberg maybe. Then if I had the right agent—"

84   "We'll see, we'll see. I'll speak to Persky."

85   That night, safely returned to Persky's flat, Kugelmass brought up the idea of having Emma visit him in the big city.

86   "Let me think about it," Persky said. "Maybe I could work it. Stranger things have happened." Of course, neither of them could think of one.

87   "Where the hell do you go all the time?" Daphne Kugelmass barked at her husband as he returned home late that evening. "You got a chippie stashed somewhere?"

88   "Yeah, sure, I'm just the type," Kugelmass said wearily. "I was with Leonard Popkin. We were discussing Socialist agriculture in Poland. You know Popkin. He's a freak on the subject."

89   "Well, you've been very odd lately," Daphne said. "Distant. Just don't forget about my father's birthday. On Saturday?"

90   "Oh, sure, sure," Kugelmass said, heading for the bathroom.

91   "My whole family will be there. We can see the twins. And Cousin Hamish. You should be more polite to Cousin Hamish—he likes you."

92   "Right, the twins," Kugelmass said, closing the bathroom door and shutting out the sound of his wife's voice. He leaned against it and took a deep breath. In a few hours, he told himself, he would be back in Yonville again, back with his beloved. And this time, if all went well, he would bring Emma back with him.

93   At three-fifteen the following afternoon, Persky worked his wizardry again. Kugelmass appeared before Emma, smiling and eager. The two spent a few hours at Yonville with Binet and then remounted the Bovary carriage. Following Persky's instructions, they held each other tightly, closed their eyes, and counted to ten. When they opened them, the carriage was just drawing up at the side door of the Plaza Hotel, where Kugelmass had optimistically reserved a suite earlier in the day.

94   "I love it! It's everything I dreamed it would be," Emma said as she swirled joyously around the bedroom, surveying the city from their window. "There's F.A.O. Schwarz. And there's Central Park, and the Sherry is which one? Oh, there—I see. It's too divine."

95   On the bed there were boxes from Halston and Saint Laurent. Emma unwrapped a package and held up a pair of black velvet pants against her perfect body.

96   "The slacks suit is by Ralph Lauren," Kugelmass said. "You'll look like a million bucks in it. Come on, sugar, give us a kiss."

97   "I've never been so happy!" Emma squealed as she stood before the mirror. "Let's go out on the town. I want to see *Chorus Line* and the Guggenheim and this Jack Nicholson character you always talk about. Are any of his flicks showing?"

98   "I cannot get my mind around this," a Stanford professor said. "First a strange character named Kugelmass, and now she's gone from the book. Well, I guess the mark of a classic is that you can reread it a thousand times and always find something new."

99   The lovers passed a blissful weekend. Kugelmass had told Daphne he would be away at a symposium in Boston and would return Monday. Savoring each moment, he and Emma went to the movies, had dinner in Chinatown, passed two hours at a discothèque, and went to bed with a TV movie. They slept till noon on Sunday, visited SoHo, and ogled celebrities at Elaine's. They had caviar and champagne in their suite on Sunday night and talked until dawn. That morning, in the cab taking them to Persky's apartment, Kugelmass thought, It was hectic, but worth it. I can't bring her here too often, but now and then it will be a charming contrast with Yonville.

100   At Persky's, Emma climbed into the cabinet, arranged her new boxes of clothes neatly around her, and kissed Kugelmass fondly. "My place next time," she said with a wink. Persky rapped three times on the cabinet. Nothing happened.

101   "Hmmm," Persky said, scratching his head. He rapped again, but still no magic. "Something must be wrong," he mumbled.

102   "Persky, you're joking!" Kugelmass cried. "How can it not work?"

103   "Relax, relax. Are you still in the box, Emma?"

104   "Yes."

105   Persky rapped again—harder this time.

106   "I'm still here, Persky."

107   "I know, darling. Sit tight."

108   "Persky, we *have* to get her back," Kugelmass whispered. "I'm a married man, and I have a class in three hours. I'm not prepared for anything more than a cautious affair at this point."

109   "I can't understand it," Persky muttered. "It's such a reliable little trick."

110   But he could do nothing. "It's going to take a little while," he said to Kugelmass. "I'm going to have to strip it down. I'll call you later."

111   Kugelmass bundled Emma into a cab and took her back to the Plaza. He barely made it to his class on time. He was on the phone all day, to Persky and to his mistress. The magician told him it might be several days before he got to the bottom of the trouble.

112   "How was the symposium?" Daphne asked him that night.

113   "Fine, fine," he said, lighting the filter end of a cigarette.

114   "What's wrong? You're as tense as a cat."

115   "Me? Ha, that's a laugh. I'm as calm as a summer night. I'm just going to take a walk." He eased out the door, hailed a cab, and flew to the Plaza.

116   "This is no good," Emma said. "Charles will miss me."

117   "Bear with me, sugar," Kugelmass said. He was pale and sweaty. He kissed her again, raced to the elevators, yelled at Persky over a pay phone in the Plaza lobby, and just made it home before midnight.

118   "According to Popkin, barley prices in Kraków have not been this stable since 1971," he said to Daphne, and smiled wanly as he climbed into bed.

119   The whole week went by like that.

120   On Friday night, Kugelmass told Daphne there was another symposium he had to catch, this one in Syracuse. He hurried back to the Plaza, but the second weekend there was nothing like the first. "Get me back into the novel or marry me," Emma told Kugelmass. "Meanwhile, I want to get a job or go to class, because watching TV all day is the pits."

121   "Fine. We can use the money," Kugelmass said. "You consume twice your weight in room service."

122   "I met an Off Broadway producer in Central Park yesterday, and he said I might be right for a project he's doing," Emma said.

123   "Who is this clown?" Kugelmass asked.

124   "He's not a clown. He's sensitive and kind and cute. His name's Jeff Something-or-Other, and he's up for a Tony."

125   Later that afternoon, Kugelmass showed up at Persky's drunk.

126   "Relax," Persky told him. "You'll get a coronary."

127   "Relax. The man says relax. I've got a fictional character stashed in a hotel room, and I think my wife is having me tailed by a private shamus."

128   "O.K., O.K. We know there's a problem." Persky crawled under the cabinet and started banging on something with a large wrench.

129   "I'm like a wild animal." Kugelmass went on. "I'm sneaking around town, and Emma and I have had it up to here with each other. Not to mention a hotel tab that reads like the defense budget."

130   "So what should I do? This is the world of magic," Persky said. "It's all nuance."

131   "Nuance, my foot. I'm pouring Dom Pérignon and black eggs into this little mouse, plus her wardrobe, plus she's enrolled at the Neighborhood Playhouse and suddenly needs professional photos. Also, Persky, Professor Fivish Kopkind, who teaches Comp Lit and who has always been jealous of me, has identified me as the sporadically appearing character in the Flaubert book. He's threatened to go to Daphne. I see ruin and alimony; jail. For adultery with Madame Bovary, my wife will reduce me to beggary."

132   "What do you want me to say? I'm working on it night and day. As far as your personal anxiety goes, that I can't help you with. I'm a magician, not an analyst."

133   By Sunday afternoon, Emma had locked herself in the bathroom and refused to respond to Kugelmass's entreaties. Kugelmass stared out the window at the Wollman Rink and contemplated suicide. Too bad this is a low floor, he thought, or I'd do it right now. Maybe if I ran away to Europe and started life over. . . . Maybe I could sell the *International Herald Tribune*, like those young girls used to.

134   The phone rang. Kugelmass lifted it to his ear mechanically.

135   "Bring her over," Persky said. "I think I got the bugs out of it."

136   Kugelmass's heart leaped. "You're serious?" he said. "You got it licked?"

137   "It was something in the transmission. Go figure."

138   "Persky, you're a genius. We'll be there in a minute. Less than a minute."

139   Again the lovers hurried to the magician's apartment, and again Emma Bovary climbed into the cabinet with her boxes. This time there was no kiss. Persky shut the doors, took a deep breath, and tapped the box three times. There was the reassuring popping noise, and when Persky peered inside, the box was empty. Madame Bovary was back in her novel. Kugelmass heaved a great sigh of relief and pumped the magician's hand.

140   "It's over," he said. "I learned my lesson. I'll never cheat again, I swear it." He pumped Persky's hand again and made a mental note to send him a necktie.

141   Three weeks later, at the end of a beautiful spring afternoon, Persky answered his doorbell. It was Kugelmass, with a sheepish expression on his face.

142   "O.K., Kugelmass," the magician said. "Where to this time?"

143   "It's just this once," Kugelmass said. "The weather is so lovely, and I'm not getting any younger. Listen, you've read *Portnoy's Complaint?*[9] Remember The Monkey?"[10]

---

[9]*Portnoy's Complaint* is a novel by Philip Roth that, when it was first published, was a favorite of undergraduates because of its sexual explicitness.

[10]The Monkey is a sexually athletic young woman in *Portnoy's Complaint*.

144   "The price is now twenty-five dollars, because the cost of living is up, but I'll start you off with one freebie, due to all the trouble I caused you."

145   "You're good people," Kugelmass said, combing his few remaining hairs as he climbed into the cabinet again. "This'll work all right?"

146   "I hope. But I haven't tried it much since all that unpleasantness."

147   "Sex and romance," Kugelmass said from inside the box. "What we go through for a pretty face."

148   Persky tossed in a copy of *Portnoy's Complaint* and rapped three times on the box. This time, instead of a popping noise there was a dull explosion, followed by a series of crackling noises and a shower of sparks. Persky leaped back, was seized by a heart attack, and dropped dead. The cabinet burst into flames, and eventually the entire house burned down.

149   Kugelmass, unaware of this catastrophe, had his own problems. He had not been thrust into *Portnoy's Complaint*, or into any other novel, for that matter. He had been projected into an old textbook, *Remedial Spanish*, and was running for his life over a barren, rocky terrain as the word *tener* ("to have")—a large and hairy irregular verb—raced after him on its spindly legs.

Questions for Engagement, Response, and Analysis

1. What is the effect of Persky's mentioning as choices for Kugelmass such characters as Hester Prynne, Ophelia, Temple Drake, or Nana?
2. Describe Kuglemass' character. What are his motivations?
3. Analyze the ending of the story and explain its irony.
4. What is the tone of the story? What techniques does Allen use to create it?
5. What is the theme of the story?

Crafting Arguments

1. What relationship between life and art does this story suggest? In an essay, analyze this relationship and the way it compares to the moral in Mark Twain's "A Fable."
2. Examine Allen's style of writing, especially the way he uses description, allusions, and irony to create tone. Use specific examples from the story to support your claims.

Margaret Atwood (b. 1939)

Canadian writer Margaret Atwood is recognized as an outstanding poet, novelist, and short story writer. Since 1964, she has published numerous highly acclaimed books of poetry. Her novels, often described as feminist, include The Handmaid's Tale *(1985), a futuristic novel filmed in 1990;* The Robber Bride *(1993);* The Blind Assassin, *winner of the 2000 Booker Prize;* Oryx and Crake *(2003); and* The Penelopiad *(2005). As a story writer who is often compared to Chekhov, Atwood creates complex, believable characters. She is also a literary critic; her* Survival: A Thematic Guide to Canadian Literature *(1972) was an astonishing, if controversial, success. Atwood's major themes include loneliness, love, and the individual's quest for identity. Her mastery of and love of language are clearly exhibited in her stories and novels.*

Happy Endings
(1983)

1   John and Mary meet.

2   What happens next?

3   If you want a happy ending, try A.

4   A. John and Mary fall in love and get married. They both have worthwhile and remunerative jobs which they find stimulating and challenging. They buy a charming house. Real estate values go up. Eventually, when they can afford live-in help, they have two children, to whom they are devoted. The children turn out well. John and Mary have a stimulating and challenging sex life and worthwhile friends. They go on fun vacations together. They retire. They both have hobbies which they find stimulating and challenging. Eventually they die. This is the end of the story.

5   B. Mary falls in love with John but John doesn't fall in love with Mary. He merely uses her body for selfish pleasure and ego gratification of a tepid kind. He comes to her apartment twice a week and she cooks him dinner, you'll notice that he doesn't even consider her worth the price of a dinner out, and after he's eaten the dinner he fucks her and after that he falls asleep, while she does the dishes so he won't think she's untidy, having all those dirty dishes lying around, and puts on fresh lipstick so she'll look good when he wakes up, but when he wakes up he doesn't even notice, he puts on his socks and his shorts and his pants and his shirt and his tie and his shoes, the reverse order from the one in which he took them off. He doesn't take off Mary's clothes, she takes them off herself, she acts as if she's dying for it every time, not because she likes sex exactly, she doesn't, but she wants John to think she does because if they do it often enough surely he'll get used to her, he'll come to depend on her and they will get married, but John goes out the door with hardly so much as a goodnight and three days later he turns up at six o'clock and they do the whole thing over again.

6   Mary gets run down. Crying is bad for your face, everyone knows that and so does Mary but she can't stop. People at work notice. Her friends tell her John is a rat, a pig, a dog, he isn't good enough for her, but she can't believe it. Inside John, she thinks, is another John, who is much nicer. This other John will emerge like a butterfly from a cocoon, a Jack from a box, a pit from a prune, if the first John is only squeezed enough.

7   One evening John complains about the food. He has never complained about the food before. Mary is hurt.

8   Her friends tell her they've seen him in a restaurant with another woman, whose name is Madge. It's not even Madge that finally gets to Mary; it's the restaurant. John has never taken Mary to a restaurant. Mary collects all the sleeping pills and aspirins she can find, and takes them and half a bottle of sherry. You can see what kind of a woman she is by the fact that it's not even whiskey. She leaves a note for John. She hopes he'll discover her and get her to the hospital in time and repent and then they can get married, but this fails to happen and she dies.

9   John marries Madge and everything continues as in A.

10   C. John, who is an older man, falls in love with Mary, and Mary, who is only twenty-two, feels sorry for him because he's worried about his hair falling out. She sleeps with him even though she's not in love with him. She met him at work. She's in love with someone called James, who is twenty-two also and not yet ready to settle down.

11   John on the contrary settled down long ago: this is what is bothering him. John has a steady respectable job and is getting ahead in his field, but Mary isn't impressed by him, she's impressed by James, who has a motorcycle and a fabulous record collection. But James is often away on his motorcycle, being free. Freedom isn't the same for girls, so in the meantime Mary spends Thursday evenings with John. Thursdays are the only days John can get away.

12   John is married to a woman called Madge and they have two children, a charming house which they bought just before the real estate values went up, and hobbies which they find stimulating and challenging, when they have the time. John tells Mary how important she is to him, but of course he can't leave his wife because a commitment is a commitment. He goes on about this more than is necessary and Mary finds it boring, but older men can keep it up longer so on the whole she has a fairly good time.

13   One day James breezes in on his motorcycle with some top-grade California hybrid and James and Mary get higher than you'd believe possible and they climb into bed. Everything becomes very underwater, but along comes John, who has a key to Mary's apartment. He finds them stoned and entwined. He's hardly in any position to be jealous, considering Madge, but nevertheless he's overcome with despair. Finally he's middle-aged, in two years he'll be bald as an egg, and he can't stand it. He purchases a handgun, saying he needs it for target practice—this is the thin part of the plot, but it can be dealt with later—and shoots the two of them and himself.

14   Madge, after a suitable period of mourning, marries an understanding man called Fred and everything continues as in A, but under different names.

15   D. Fred and Madge have no problems. They get along exceptionally well and are good at working out any little difficulties that may arise. But their charming house is by the seashore and one day a giant tidal wave

approaches. Real estate values go down. The rest of the story is about what caused the tidal wave and how they escape from it. They do, though thousands drown. Some of the story is about how the thousands drown, but Fred and Madge are virtuous and lucky. Finally on high ground they clasp each other, wet and dripping and grateful, and continue as in A.

16   E. Yes, but Fred has a bad heart. The rest of the story is about how kind and understanding they both are until Fred dies. Then Madge devotes herself to charity work until the end of A. If you like, it can be "Madge," "cancer," "guilty and confused," and "bird watching."

17   F. If you think this is all too bourgeois, make John a revolutionary and Mary a counterespionage agent and see how far that gets you. Remember, this is Canada. You'll still end up with A, though in between you may get a lustful brawling saga of passionate involvement, a chronicle of our times, sort of.

18   You'll have to face it, the endings are the same however you slice it. Don't be deluded by any other endings, they're all fake, either deliberately fake, with malicious intent to deceive, or just motivated by excessive optimism if not by downright sentimentality.
     The only authentic ending is the one provided here:

19   *John and Mary die. John and Mary die. John and Mary die.*

20   So much for endings. Beginnings are always more fun. True connoisseurs, however, are known to favor the stretch in between, since it's the hardest to do anything with.

21   That's about all that can be said for plots, which anyway are just one thing after another, a what and a what and a what.

22   Now try How and Why.

Questions for Engagement, Response, and Analysis

1. In your opinion, why does Atwood offer alternate endings to the story?
2. What is the tone of the story?
3. Why, after focusing on the *what* in the story, does Atwood, in the last line, say, "Now try How and Why"?
4. In your Reader's Journal, freewrite your own ending to the story.

Crafting Arguments

1. Carefully examine each of the choices of endings, looking for things such as repeated phrases, elements that are common to all versions, and unrealistic expectations. Then, write an essay comparing the endings and explaining how they create the theme of the story.

POETRY

John Keats (1795–1821)

John Keats was, along with William Wordsworth, Samuel Taylor Coleridge, Lord Byron, and Percy Bysshe Shelley, one of the leading poets of the Romantic period in England. Nearly all of his greatest poems were written in one year, 1818–1819, and published in Lamia, Isabella, and Other Poems *(1820). Keats' poetry celebrates beauty in rich, lush images; his magnificent collected letters, a work of art in their own right, gained increasing attention in the twentieth century. Keats was stricken with tuberculosis and died at the age of twenty-five.*

ODE ON A GRECIAN URN   (1819)

I

Thou still unravish'd bride of quietness,
   Thou foster-child of silence and slow time,
Sylvan historian, who canst thus express
   A flowery tale more sweetly than our rhyme:
5   What leaf-fring'd legend haunts about thy shape
     Of deities or mortals, or of both,
       In Tempe or the dales of Arcady?
   What men or gods are these? What maidens loth?
     What mad pursuit? What struggle to escape?
10   What pipes and timbrels? What wild ecstasy?

II

Heard melodies are sweet, but those unheard
   Are sweeter; therefore, ye soft pipes, play on;
Not to the sensual ear, but, more endear'd,
   Pipe to the spirit ditties of no tone:
15   Fair youth, beneath the trees, thou canst not leave
     Thy song, nor ever can those trees be bare;
       Bold Lover, never, never canst thou kiss,
   Though winning near the goal—yet, do not grieve;
     She cannot fade, though thou hast not thy bliss,
20   For ever wilt thou love, and she be fair!

III

Ah, happy, happy boughs! that cannot shed
   Your leaves, nor ever bid the Spring adieu;

And, happy melodist, unwearied,
    For ever piping songs for ever new;
25   More happy love! more happy, happy love!
      For ever warm and still to be enjoy'd,
        For ever panting, and for ever young;
All breathing human passion far above,
    That leaves a heart high-sorrowful and cloy'd,
30   A burning forehead, and a parching tongue.

IV

Who are these coming to the sacrifice?
    To what green altar, O mysterious priest,
Lead'st thou that heifer lowing at the skies,
    And all her silken flanks with garlands drest?
35 What little town by river or sea shore,
    Or mountain-built with peaceful citadel,
      Is emptied of this folk, this pious morn?
And, little town, thy streets for evermore
Will silent be; and not a soul to tell
40   Why thou art desolate, can e'er return.

V

O Attic shape! Fair attitude! with brede
    Of marble men and maidens overwrought,
With forest branches and the trodden weed;
    Thou, silent form, dost tease us out of thought
45 As doth eternity: Cold Pastoral!
    When old age shall this generation waste,
      Thou shalt remain, in midst of other woe
Than ours, a friend to man, to whom thou say'st,
    'Beauty is truth, truth beauty,'—that is all
50   Ye know on earth, and all ye need to know.

Questions for Engagement, Response, and Analysis

1. Whom or what is the speaker in the poem addressing?
2. What is the theme of this poem?

Crafting Arguments

1. In an essay, list each of the people the speaker addresses and analyze
   (1) the conclusions that the speaker draws about each situation and
   (2) their relation to the theme.

Emily Dickinson (1830–1886)

Although very sociable as a girl and young woman, Emily Dickinson slowly became reclusive. In fact, she and her younger sister, Lavinia, lived their whole lives in their father's house, with their brother, Austin, living a mere stone's throw away. Despite her later tendency to "dwell" only in her house and the grounds surrounding it, Dickinson maintained close friendships with her sister-in-law, Susan Gilbert Dickinson, and with others who corresponded with her but whom she seldom or never saw. The reasons for the poet's seclusion are nowhere stated clearly, though literary critics and lovers of her poetry are fascinated by the possibilities: was she agoraphobic; was she suffering from a broken heart; or was she choosing to avoid a patriarchal world that little valued women's writing? Few people in Amherst, Massachusetts, where Emily Dickinson spent most of her life, would have dreamed that within the confines of her yard a revolution in American poetry was taking place. Her poetry was far ahead of her time in form and content. The great bulk of her work—close to two thousand poems— was discovered only after her death, most in little packets sewn together with thread, some on scraps of paper. Her brief poems, rich in metaphor and punctuated primarily by dashes, present a wealth of startling images and an intensity of thought that make her one of America's most loved and studied poets.

326[1]

I cannot dance upon my Toes—
No Man instructed me—
But oftentimes, among my mind,
A Glee possesseth me,

5   That had I Ballet knowledge—
Would put itself abroad
In Pirouette to blanch a Troupe—
Or lay a Prima, mad,

And though I had no Gown of Gauze—
10   No Ringlet, to my Hair,
Nor hopped to Audiences—like Birds,
One Claw upon the Air,

---

[1]In his *The Poems of Emily Dickinson*, Variorum Edition, R. W. Franklin numbers these four poems 381, 445, 466, and 1286.

Nor tossed my shape in Eider Balls,
Nor rolled on wheels of snow
15   Till I was out of sight, in sound,
The House encore me so—

Nor any know I know the Art
I mention—easy—Here—
Nor any Placard boast me—
20   It's full as Opera—

Questions for Engagement, Response, and Analysis

1. Does there seem to be any identifiable situation in this poem?
2. How would you describe the poet's level of diction and the word choices?
3. What is the controlling image in this poem? What other figurative language is there?
4. What is the theme of this poem?

613

They shut me up in Prose—
As when a little Girl
They put me in the Closet—
Because they liked me "still"—

5   Still! Could themself have peeped—
And seen my Brain—go round—
They might as wise have lodged a Bird
For Treason—in the Pound—

Himself has but to will
10   And easy as a Star
Abolish his Captivity—
And laugh—No more have I—

Questions for Engagement, Response, and Analysis

1. Who are the "They" of the first line? Is it the same "They" as in line 3?
2. What is the controlling image in this poem? Explain its meaning in the poem.
3. According to the poem, how can we escape "Captivity"?

657

I dwell in Possibility—
A fairer House than Prose—
More numerous of Windows—
Superior—for Doors—

5 Of Chambers as the Cedars—
Impregnable of Eye—
And for an Everlasting Roof
The Gambrels of the Sky—

Of Visitors—the fairest—
10 For Occupation—This—
The spreading wide my narrow Hands
To gather Paradise—

Questions for Engagement, Response, and Analysis

1. How does the metrical pattern and rhyme in this poem compare with the other Dickinson poems?

2. What is the controlling image? What does Dickinson seem to be saying with that image?

3. Interpret the lines "For Occupation—This— / The spreading wide my narrow Hands / To gather Paradise"?

1263

There is no Frigate like a Book
To take us Lands away
Nor any Coursers like a Page
Of prancing Poetry—
5 This Traverse may the poorest take
Without oppress of Toll—
How frugal is the Chariot
That bears the Human soul.

Questions for Engagement, Response, and Analysis

1. Read this poem out loud. How would you define its sound?

2. Define the words "Frigate," "Coursers," and "Frugal."

3. What is the controlling image of the poem, and what message does it convey?

Crafting Arguments

1. In an essay, explicate one of Emily Dickinson's poems. How do all the poetic elements come together to express the poem's theme?

2. Craft a paper in which you analyze an image in one of Dickinson's poems. How does that image function within the context of the poem, and why do you think the poet chose that particular one?

3. Analyze the images in two of the poems and write a Comparison/Contrast paper.

4. Using the poems in this unit, write a paper that offers your interpretation of the power of poetry as Dickinson defines it.

Archibald MacLeish (1892–1982)

Archibald MacLeish was an American scholar, teacher, poet, essayist, critic, and playwright. He served for five years (1939–1944) as Librarian of Congress. Primarily known for his short poems, MacLeish also received a Pulitzer Prize for J.B., a verse dramatization of the biblical story of Job. Though MacLeish was not one of the first Imagists, his "Ars Poetica" is often mentioned as one of the best examples of Imagist writing.

Ars Poetica   (1926)

A poem should be palpable and mute
As a globed fruit,

Dumb
As old medallions to the thumb,
5   Silent as the sleeve-worn stone
Of casement ledges where the moss has grown—

A poem should be wordless
As the flight of birds.

A poem should be motionless in time
10   As the Moon climbs,

Leaving, as the Moon releases
Twig by twig the night-entangled trees,

Leaving, as the Moon behind the winter leaves,
Memory by memory the mind—
15   A poem should be motionless in time
As the Moon climbs.

A poem should be equal to:
Not true.

For all the history of grief
20   An empty doorway and a maple leaf.

For love
The leaning grasses and two lights above the sea—

A poem should not mean
But be.

Questions for Engagement, Response, and Analysis

1. Explain each of the three statements that MacLeish makes about poetry.
2. What pictures do the similes and metaphors provide? In what ways do these devices communicate, even more clearly than expository writing can, a definition of poetry?

Crafting Arguments

1. Beginning with your answer to number two above, interpret each of the metaphorical devices and explain how each adds to the description of what a poem should be. If possible, select examples from other poems as well to illustrate your claims.

Countee Cullen (1903-1948)

A New Yorker by birth, Cullen was a Phi Beta Kappa graduate of New York University. He wrote his first collection of poems, Color *(1925), while he was in college. Cullen also wrote a novel,* One Way to Heaven *(1932), and a version of Euripides's play* Medea. *A member of the Harlem Renaissance, Cullen later turned to teaching to earn a living.*

Yet Do I Marvel   (1925)

I doubt not God is good, well-meaning, kind,
And did he stoop to quibble could tell why
The little buried mole continues blind,
Why flesh that mirrors him must some day die,
5   Make plain the reason tortured Tantalus
Is baited with the fickle fruit, declare
If merely brute caprice dooms Sisyphus
To struggle up a never-ending stair.

Inscrutable His ways are and immune
10 To catechism by a mind too strewn
With petty cares to slightly understand
What awful brain compels His awful hand;
Yet do I marvel at this curious thing:
To make a poet black, and bid him sing!

Questions for Engagement, Response, and Analysis

1. What acts of God puzzle the narrator?

2. To Cullen, what is the most "inscrutable" and "curious" of all of God's creations? Explain why.

3. Research the myths of Tantalus and Sisyphus and explain the last four lines of the octave.

4. What limitations does Cullen suggest the human brain has?

5. Explain the double meaning of the word *awful* in line 12.

6. Taking into consideration the time in which the poet lived, explain the last two lines.

Crafting Arguments

1. How does Cullen use the traditional form of the sonnet and sound devices such as alliteration, assonance, and consonance to create tone?

W. H. Auden (1907–1973)

A brief biography of W. H. Auden precedes "The Unknown Citizen" in the Freedom and Responsibility Unit.

MUSÉE DES BEAUX ARTS   (1940)

About suffering they were never wrong,
The Old Masters: how well they understood
Its human position; how it takes place
While someone else is eating or opening a window or just walking
5   dully along;
How, when the aged are reverently, passionately waiting
For the miraculous birth, there always must be
Children who did not specially want it to happen, skating
On a pond at the edge of the wood:
10   They never forgot
That even the dreadful martyrdom must run its course
Anyhow in a corner, some untidy spot
Where the dogs go on with their doggy life and the torturer's horse
Scratches its innocent behind on a tree.
15   In Brueghel's *Icarus*, for instance: how everything turns away
Quite leisurely from the disaster; the ploughman may
Have heard the splash, the forsaken cry,
But for him it was not an important failure; the sun shone
As it had to on the white legs disappearing into the green
20   Water; and the expensive delicate ship that must have seen
Something amazing, a boy falling out of the sky,
Had somewhere to get to and sailed calmly on.

Questions for Engagement, Response, and Analysis

1. What is the theme of the poem?
2. After carefully examining a reproduction of Brueghel's *The Fall of Icarus*, explain how it conveys the same point as Auden's poem.

Crafting Arguments

1. Auden says, "About suffering they [the Old Masters] were never wrong." Select one work of literature in this anthology and discuss what it says about human suffering.
2. MacLeish, in "Ars Poetica," says, "A poem should not mean / But be." In an essay compare MacLeish's definition with Auden's theme in "Musée des Beaux Arts."

Lawrence Ferlinghetti (b. 1919)

Lawrence Ferlinghetti is an American poet, novelist, play- wright, and painter who was an important member of the Beat movement, a movement that climaxed in 1956 in San Francisco and New York City, and whose members, dis- gusted by the crass commercialism of society, dropped out, invented their own vocabulary, and experimented with illegal drugs. Ferlinghetti received his B.A. in journalism at the University of North Carolina. During World War II, he served in the navy, participating in the invasion at Nor- mandy and visiting Nagasaki shortly after it was devas- tated by the atomic bomb. Because of this experience, he became a pacifist. In 1953, he opened the City Lights Book- store, the first paperback bookstore in the United States, a shop that became a center for jazz performances and poetry readings. The San Francisco bookstore also pub- lished Ferlinghetti's first book, Pictures of the Gone World *(1955), and many of the works of the Beat poets. Fer- linghetti's most famous book of poetry is* A Coney Island of the Mind *(1958).*

CONSTANTLY RISKING ABSURDITY (1958)

Constantly risking absurdity
        and death
whenever he performs
    above the heads
        of his audience
the poet like an acrobat
    climbs on rime
        to a high wire of his own making
and balancing on eyebeams

10   above a sea of faces

paces his way

to the other side of day

performing entrechats

and sleight-of-foot tricks

15   and other high theatrics

and all without mistaking

any thing

for what it may not be

For he's the super realist

20   who must perforce perceive

taut truth

before the taking of each stance or step

in his supposed advance

toward that still higher perch

25   where Beauty stands and waits

with gravity

to start her death-defying leap

And he

a little charleychaplin man

who may or may not catch

30   her fair eternal form

spreadeagled in the empty air

of existence

Questions for Engagement, Response, and Analysis

1. What effect does the reading aloud of "must perforce perceive / taut truth" have on the speed of the poem? How is this speed relevant to that of a tightrope walker? A poet?
2. In what ways is a poet a "super realist"?
3. What is the effect of the arrangement of the lines?
4. What is the tone of the poem?

Crafting Arguments

1. Ferlinghetti uses one controlling metaphor in one long sentence. In an essay, analyze the ways that Ferlinghetti blends the metaphor and the form to make an accurate description of a poet.

Sylvia Plath

A brief biography of Sylvia Plath precedes "Daddy" in the Family Unit.

METAPHORS   (1960)

I'm a riddle in nine syllables,
An elephant, a ponderous house,
A melon strolling on two tendrils.
O red fruit, ivory, fine timbers!
5   This loaf's big with its yeasty rising.
Money's new-minted in this fat purse.
I'm a means, a stage, a cow in calf.
I've eaten a bag of green apples,
Boarded the train there's no getting off.

Questions for Engagement, Response, and Analysis

1. What is the tone of the poem? How can you tell?
2. What does the image included in each line suggest? What do the images have in common?
3. What is the answer to the poem's riddle? In what way does the form of the poem help reveal the answer?

Crafting Arguments

1. Write an essay analyzing the images in the poems and explaining how Plath uses form and metaphors to create the theme and tone of the poem.

Seamus Heaney (b. 1939)

Seamus Heaney was born in County Derry in Northern Ireland, where his father was a farmer and cattle dealer; this locale has been influential in his writing. He has described his move away from the farm as a removal from "the earth of farm labour to the heaven of education." At St. Columb's College and Queen's University, Belfast, he learned Latin, Irish, and Anglo-Saxon, languages that have influenced his poetry. In addition to poetry, Heaney writes incisive literary criticism, influenced by his awareness of the importance of the poet as part of the world of creativity. His works of criticism include The Government of the Tongue *(1988) and* The Redress of Poetry *(1995). Heaney's 1999 verse translation of* Beowulf *has received remarkable academic acclaim. Heaney has taught at several universities, including the University of California at Berkeley, Carysfort College, and Harvard University. In 1995, Heaney was awarded the Nobel Prize in Literature.*

DIGGING   (1966)

Between my finger and my thumb
The squat pen rests; snug as a gun.
Under my window, a clean rasping sound
When the spade sinks into gravelly ground:
5   My father, digging. I look down

Till his straining rump among the flowerbeds
Bends low, comes up twenty years away
Stooping in rhythm through potato drills
Where he was digging.
10   The coarse boot nestled on the lug, the shaft
Against the inside knee was levered firmly.
He rooted out tall tops, buried the bright edge deep
To scatter new potatoes that we picked
Loving their cool hardness in our hands.
15   By God, the old man could handle a spade.
Just like his old man.
My grandfather cut more turf in a day
Than any other man on Toner's bog.
Once I carried him milk in a bottle
20   Corked sloppily with paper. He straightened up
To drink it, then fell to right away
Nicking and slicing neatly, heaving sods
Over his shoulder, going down and down
For the good turf. Digging.
25   The cold smell of potato mould, the squelch and slap
Of soggy peat, the curt cuts of an edge
Through living roots awaken in my head.
But I've no spade to follow men like them.
Between my finger and my thumb
30   The squat pen rests.
I'll dig with it.

Questions for Engagement, Response, and Analysis

1. The speaker uses most of the poem to describe his father's and his grandfather's profession. What parallels does he then draw with his own profession?

2. What is the speaker's attitude toward his father and grandfather? What is the tone of the poem? How does Heaney convey this tone?

3. What is the theme of the poem?

Crafting Arguments

1. Read Whitelock's "Future Connected By" in the Family Unit and write an essay comparing the attitudes of the speakers toward their fathers and the decisions made by the sons.

2. Write an essay in which you compare Heaney's implications about
   what it takes to be a poet with Ferlinghetti's description of the poet.

Billy Collins (b. 1941)

*A brief biography of Billy Collins appears in the Vulnera-
bility Unit.*

MARGINALIA

Sometimes the notes are ferocious,
skirmishes against the author
raging along the borders of every page
in tiny black script.
5   If I could just get my hands on you,
Kierkegaard, or Conor Cruise O'Brien,
they seem to say,
I would bolt the door and beat some logic into your head.

Other comments are more offhand, dismissive—
10   "Nonsense." "Please!" "HA!!"—
that kind of thing.
I remember once looking up from my reading,
my thumb as a bookmark,
trying to imagine what the person must look like
15   who wrote "Don't be a ninny"
alongside a paragraph in *The Life of Emily Dickinson*.

Students are more modest
needing to leave only their splayed footprints
along the shore of the page.
20   One scrawls "Metaphor" next to a stanza of Eliot's.
Another notes the presence of "Irony"
fifty times outside the paragraphs of *A Modest Proposal*.

Or they are fans who cheer from the empty bleachers,
hands cupped around their mouths.
25   "Absolutely," they shout
to Duns Scotus and James Baldwin.
"Yes." "Bull's-eye." "My man!"
Check marks, asterisks, and exclamation points
rain down along the sidelines.

30   And if you have managed to graduate from college
without ever having written "Man vs. Nature"
in a margin, perhaps now
is the time to take one step forward.

We have all seized the white perimeter as our own
35   and reached for a pen if only to show

we did not just laze in an armchair turning pages;
we pressed a thought into the wayside,
planted an impression along the verge.

Even Irish monks in their cold scriptoria
40   jotted along the borders of the Gospels
brief asides about the pains of copying,
a bird singing near their window,
or the sunlight that illuminated their page—
anonymous men catching a ride into the future
45   on a vessel more lasting than themselves.

And you have not read Joshua Reynolds,
they say, until you have read him
enwreathed with Blake's furious scribbling.

Yet the one I think of most often,
50   the one that dangles from me like a locket,
was written in the copy of *Catcher in the Rye*
I borrowed from the local library
one slow, hot summer.
I was just beginning high school then,
55   reading books on a davenport in my parents' living room,
and I cannot tell you
how vastly my loneliness was deepened,
how poignant and amplified the world before me seemed,
when I found on one page

60   a few greasy looking smears
and next to them, written in soft pencil—
by a beautiful girl, I could tell,
whom I would never meet—
"Pardon the egg salad stains, but I'm in love."

Questions for Engagement, Response, and Analysis

1. Annotate this poem by looking up any allusions that you do not already recognize and explaining them in the context of the poem.

2. List and explain all the metaphors Collins uses for margins.

3. What is the tone of the poem? How does Collins create it?

Crafting Arguments

1. In an essay, discuss the devices—such as allusions, metaphors, and stanza—that Collins uses to craft his poem and emphasize the theme and the tone.

Alberto Ríos (b. 1952)

Ríos, a highly respected modern Hispanic American writer,
was born in Nogales, Arizona, to an English mother and a
Mexican American father. He has received the Walt Whit-
man Award of the Academy of American Poets (1981), the
Western States Book Award (1984), six Pushcart Prizes, and
the Mountain Plains Library Author of the Year Award
(1991). Ríos' poetry includes Whispering to Fool the Wind
(1981) and The Smallest Muscle in the Human Body *(2002).*
His fiction includes The Iguana Killer *(1984) and* Pig Cookies and Other Stories *(1995).*

THE VIETNAM WALL   (1985)

I

Have seen it
And I like it: The magic,
The way like cutting onions
5 It brings water out of nowhere.
Invisible from one side, a scar
Into the skin of the ground
From the other, a black winding
Appendix line.
10   A dig.
      An archaeologist can explain.
The walk is slow at first
Easy, a little black marble wall
Of a dollhouse,
15 A smoothness, a shine
The boys in the street want to give.
One name. And then more
Names, long lines, lines of names until
They are the shape of the U.N. building
20 Taller than I am: I have walked
Into a grave.
And everything I expect has been taken away, like that, quick:
      The names are not alphabetized.
      They are in the order of dying,
25   An alphabet of—somewhere—screaming.
I start to walk out. I almost leave
But stop to look up names of friends,
My own name. There is somebody
Severiano Ríos.
30 Little kids do not make the same noise
Here, junior high school boys don't run

Or hold each other in headlocks.
No rules, something just persists
Like pinching on St. Patrick's Day
35   Every year for no green.
   No one knows why.
Flowers are forced
Into the cracks
Between sections.
40   Men have cried
At this wall.
I have
Seen them.

Questions for Engagement, Response, and Analysis

1. Who is the speaker in this poem?
2. What is the tone? Give specific examples of how it is created early in the poem and intensified as the poem builds to its conclusion.

Crafting Arguments

1. List each of the metaphors for the wall and in an essay, give your interpretation of each and explain how they combine to create the theme of the poem.

D R A M A

Wendy Wasserstein (1950–2006)

Wendy Wasserstein was born in Brooklyn, New York, and educated at Mount Holyoke College (B.A.), City College of New York (M.A.), and Yale School of Drama (M.F.A.). Wassertein fell in love with the theater early in her life. In 1977, a production of her play Uncommon Women, *first performed at the Phoenix Theater, was filmed and broadcast on PBS's* Great Performances. *This play, starring Glenn Close (Meryl Streep in the television version) and Swoosie Kurtz, revealed a major theme of Wasserstein's drama: the struggle of women to find their identities in a world that expects them to be ideal mothers and wives but also offeres them the challenges and opportunities of careers. Her most successful play,* The Heidi Chronicles, *which opened on Broadway in 1989, won a Tony and a Pulitzer Prize. Theater critics repeatedly praised Wasserstein for her humor and her obvious affection for and sympathy with her characters. Wasserstein also wrote two collections of essays:* Batchelor Girls *(1990) and* Shiksa Goddess *(2001). An essay included in* Shiksa Goddess *movingly describes her pregnancy at age forty-eight and her premature baby girl's health struggles. When Wasserstein died in 2006, the lights on Broadway were dimmed.*

TENDER OFFER (1983)

Lisa is alone in a dance studio. She is nine, dressed in traditional leotards and tights. She begins singing to herself, "Nothing Could Be Finer Than to Be in Carolina." She maps out a dance routine, including parts for the chorus. She builds to a finale. A man, Paul, around 35, walks in. He has a sweet, though distant, demeanor. As he walks in, Lisa notices him and stops.

PAUL. You don't have to stop, sweetheart.

LISA. That's okay.

PAUL. Looked very good.

LISA. Thanks.

PAUL. Don't I get a kiss hello?

LISA. Sure.

PAUL. *(Embraces her.)* Hi, Tiger.

LISA. Hi, Dad.

PAUL. I'm sorry I'm late.

10 LISA. That's okay.

PAUL. How'd it go?

LISA. Good.

PAUL. Just good?

LISA. Pretty good.

PAUL. "Pretty good." You mean you got a lot of applause or "pretty good" you could have done better.

LISA. Well, Courtney Palumbo's mother thought I was pretty good. But you know the part in the middle when everybody's supposed to freeze and the big girl comes out. Well, I think I moved a little bit.

20 PAUL. I thought what you were doing looked very good.

LISA. Daddy, that's not what I was doing. That was tap-dancing. I made that up.

PAUL. Oh. Well it looked good. Kind of sexy.

LISA. Yuch!

PAUL. What do you mean "yuch"?

LISA. Just yuch!

PAUL. You don't want to be sexy?

LISA. I don't care.

PAUL. Let's go, Tiger. I promised your mother I'd get you home in time

30 for dinner.

LISA. I can't find my leg warmers.

PAUL. You can't find your what?

LISA. Leg warmers. I can't go home till I find my leg warmers.

PAUL. I don't see you looking for them.

LISA. I was waiting for you.

PAUL. Oh.

LISA. Daddy.

PAUL. What?

LISA. Nothing.

40   PAUL. Where do you think you left them?

LISA. Somewhere around here. I can't remember.

PAUL. Well, try to remember, Lisa. We don't have all night.

LISA. I told you. I think somewhere around here.

PAUL. I don't see them. Let's go home now. You'll call the dancing school
    tomorrow.

LISA. Daddy, I can't go home till I find them. Miss Judy says it's not pro-
    fessional to leave things.

PAUL. Who's Miss Judy?

LISA. She's my ballet teacher. She once danced the lead in *Swan Lake*,
50   and she was a June Taylor dancer.

PAUL. Well, then, I'm sure she'll understand about the leg warmers.

LISA. Daddy, Miss Judy wanted to know why you were late today.

PAUL. Hmmmmmmmmm?

LISA. Why were you late?

PAUL. I was in a meeting. Business. I'm sorry.

LISA. Why did you tell Mommy you'd come instead of her if you knew
    you had business?

PAUL. Honey, something just came up. I thought I'd be able to be here. I
    was looking forward to it.

60   LISA. I wish you wouldn't make appointments to see me.

PAUL. Hmmmmmmmm.

LISA. You shouldn't make appointments to see me unless you know
    you're going to come.

PAUL. Of course I'm going to come.

LISA. No, you're not. Talia Robbins told me she's much happier living
    without her father in the house. Her father used to come home late
    and go to sleep early.

PAUL. Lisa, stop it. Let's go.

LISA. I can't find my leg warmers.

70   PAUL. Forget your leg warmers.

LISA. Daddy.

PAUL. What is it?

LISA. I saw this show on television, I think it was WPIX Channel 11.
    Well, the father was crying about his daughter.

PAUL. Why was he crying? Was she sick?

LISA. No. She was at school. And he was at business. And he just missed
    her, so he started to cry.

PAUL. What was the name of this show?

LISA. I don't know. I came in in the middle.

80 PAUL. Well, Lisa, I certainly would cry if you were sick or far away, but I know that you're well and you're home. So no reason to get maudlin.

LISA. What's maudlin?

PAUL. Sentimental, soppy. Frequently used by children who make things up to get attention.

LISA. I am sick! I am sick! I have Hodgkin's disease and a bad itch on my leg.

PAUL. What do you mean you have Hodgkin's disease? Don't say things like that.

LISA. Swoosie Kurtz, she had Hodgkin's disease on a TV movie last year,
90 but she got better and now she's on *Love Sidney*.

PAUL. Who is Swoosie Kurtz?

LISA. She's an actress named after an airplane. I saw her on *Live at Five*.

PAUL. You watch too much television; you should do your homework. Now, put your coat on.

LISA. Daddy, I really do have a bad itch on my leg. Would you scratch it?

PAUL. Lisa, you're procrastinating.

LISA. Why do you use words I don't understand? I hate it. You're like Daria Feldman's mother. She always talks in Yiddish to her husband
100 so Daria won't understand.

PAUL. Procrastinating is not Yiddish.

LISA. Well, I don't know what it is.

PAUL. Procrastinating means you don't want to go about your business.

LISA. I don't go to business. I go to school.

PAUL. What I mean is you want to hang around here until you and I are late for dinner and your mother's angry and it's too late for you to do your homework.

LISA. I do not.

PAUL. Well, it sure looks that way. Now put your coat on and let's go.

110 LISA. Daddy.

PAUL. Honey, I'm tired. Really, later.

LISA. Why don't you want to talk to me?

PAUL. I do want to talk to you. I promise when we get home we'll have a nice talk.

LISA. No, we won't. You'll read the paper and fall asleep in front of the news.

PAUL. Honey, we'll talk on the weekend, I promise. Aren't I taking you to the theater this weekend? Let me look. (*He takes out appointment book.*) Yes. Sunday. *Joseph and the Amazing Technicolor*
120 *Raincoat* with Lisa. Okay, Tiger?

LISA. Sure. It's Dreamcoat.

PAUL. What?

LISA. Nothing, I think I see my leg warmers. (*She goes to pick them up, and an odd-looking trophy.*)

PAUL. What's that?

LISA. It's stupid. I was second best at the dance recital, so they gave me this thing. It's stupid.

PAUL. Lisa.

LISA. What?

PAUL. What did you want to talk about?

130 LISA. Nothing.

PAUL. Was it about my missing your recital? I'm really sorry, Tiger. I would have liked to have been here.

LISA. That's okay.

PAUL. Honest?

LISA. Daddy, you're prostrastinating.

PAUL. I'm procrastinating. Sit down. Let's talk. So. How's school?

LISA. Fine.

PAUL. You like it?

LISA. Yup.

140 PAUL. You looking forward to camp this summer?

LISA. Yup.

PAUL. Is Daria Feldman going back?

LISA. Nope.

PAUL. Why not?

LISA. I don't know. We can go home now. Honest, my foot doesn't itch anymore.

PAUL. Lisa, you know what you do in business when it seems like there's nothing left to say? That's when you really start talking. Put a bid on the table.

150 LISA. What's a bid?

PAUL. You tell me what you want and I'll tell you what I've got to offer. Like Monopoly. You want Boardwalk, but I'm only willing to give you the Railroads. Now, because you are my daughter I'd throw in Water Works and Electricity. Understand, Tiger?

LISA. No. I don't like board games. You know, Daddy, we could get Space Invaders for our home for 35 dollars. In fact, we could get an Osborne System for two thousand. Daria Feldman's parents . . .

PAUL. Daria Feldman's parents refuse to talk to Daria, so they bought a computer to keep Daria busy so they won't have to speak in Yid-

160 dish. Daria will probably grow up to be a homicidal maniac lesbian prostitute.

LISA. I know what that word prostitute means.

PAUL. Good. *(Pause.)* You still haven't told me about school. Do you still like your teacher?

LISA. She's okay.

PAUL. Lisa, if we're talking try to answer me.

LISA. I am answering you. Can we go home now, please?

PAUL. Damn it, Lisa, if you want to talk to me . . . Talk to me!

LISA. I can't wait till I'm old enough so I can make my own money and
170   never have to see you again. Maybe I'll become a prostitute.

PAUL. Young lady, that's enough.

LISA. I hate you, Daddy! I hate you! *(She throws her trophy into the trash bin.)*

PAUL. What'd you do that for?

LISA. It's stupid.

PAUL. Maybe I wanted it.

LISA. What for?

PAUL. Maybe I wanted to put it where I keep your dinosaur and the picture you made of Mrs. Kimbel with the chicken pox.

LISA. You got mad at me when I made that picture. You told me I had to
180   respect Mrs. Kimbel because she was my teacher.

PAUL. That's true. But she wasn't my teacher. I liked her better with the chicken pox. *(Pause.)* Lisa, I'm sorry. I was very wrong to miss your recital, and you don't have to become a prostitute. That's not the type of profession Miss Judy has in mind for you.

LISA. *(Mumbles.)* No.

PAUL. No. *(Pause.)* So Talia Robbins is really happy her father moved out?

LISA. Talia Robbins picks open the eight-grade lockers during gym period. But she did that before her father moved out.

190   PAUL. You can't always judge someone by what they do or what they don't do. Sometimes you come home from dancing school and run upstairs and shut the door, and when I finally get to talk to you, everything is "okay" or "fine." Yup or nope?

LISA. Yup.

PAUL. Sometimes, a lot of times, I come home and fall asleep in front of the television. So you and I spend a lot of time being a little scared of each other. Maybe?

LISA. Maybe.

PAUL. Tell you what. I'll make you a tender offer.

200   LISA. What?

PAUL. I'll make you a tender offer. That's when one company publishes in the newspaper that they want to buy another company. And the company that publishes is called the Black Knight because they want to gobble up the poor little company. So the poor little company needs to be rescued. And then a White Knight comes along and makes a bigger and better offer so the shareholders won't have to tender shares to the Big Black Knight. You with me?

LISA. Sort of.

PAUL. I'll make you a tender offer like the White Knight. But I don't
210   want to own you. I just want to make a much better offer. Okay?

LISA. *(Sort of understanding.)* Okay. *(Pause. They sit for a moment.)* Sort of, Daddy, what do you think about? I mean, like when you're quiet what do you think about?

PAUL. Oh, business usually. If I think I made a mistake or if I think I'm
doing okay. Sometimes I think about what I'll be doing five years
from now and if it's what I hoped it would be five years ago. Sometimes I think about what your life will be like, if Mount Saint Helen's
will erupt again. What you'll become if you'll study penmanship or
word processing. If you speak kindly of me to your psychiatrist
220   when you are in graduate school. And how the hell I'll pay for your
graduate school. And sometimes I try and think what it was I
thought about when I was your age.

LISA. Do you ever look out your window at the clouds and try to see
which kinds of shapes they are? Like one time, honest, I saw the
head of Walter Cronkite in a flower vase. Really! Like look don't
those kinda look like if you turn it upside down, two big elbows or
two elephant trunks dancing?

PAUL. Actually still looks like Walter Cronkite in a flower vase to me.
But look up a little. See the one that's still moving? That sorta looks
230   like a whale on a thimble.

LISA. Where?

PAUL. Look up. To your right.

LISA. I don't see it. Where?

PAUL. The other way.

LISA. Oh, yeah! There's the head and there's the stomach. Yeah! *(Lisa
picks up her trophy.)* Hey, Daddy.

PAUL. Hey, Lisa.

LISA. You can have this thing if you want it. But you have to put it like
this, because if you put it like that it is gross.

240   PAUL. You know what I'd like? So I can tell people who come into my
office why I have this gross stupid thing on my shelf, I'd like it if you
could show me your dance recital.

LISA. Now?

PAUL. We've got time. Mother said she won't be home till late.

LISA. Well, Daddy, during a lot of it I freeze and the big girl in front
dances.

PAUL. Well, how 'bout the number you were doing when I walked in?

LISA. Well, see, I have parts for a lot of people in that one, too.

PAUL. I'll dance the other parts.

250   LISA. You can't dance.

PAUL. Young lady, I played Yvette Mimimeux in a Hasty Pudding Show.

LISA. Who's Yvette Mimimeux?

PAUL. Watch more television. You'll find out. *(Paul stands up.)* So I'm
ready. *(He begins singing.)* "Nothing could be finer than to be in
Carolina."

LISA. Now I go. "In the morning." And now you go. Dum-da.

PAUL. *(Obviously not a tap dancer.)* Da-da-dum.

LISA. *(Whines.)* Daddy!

PAUL. *(Mimics her.)* Lisa! "Nothing could be finer . . . "

260   LISA. That looks dumb.

PAUL. Oh, yeah? You think they do this better in *The Amazing Minkcoat*? No way! Now you go — da da da dum.

LISA. Da da da dum.

PAUL. "If I had Aladdin's lamp for only a day, I'd make a wish . . . "

LISA. Daddy, that's maudlin!

PAUL. I know it's maudlin. And here's what I'd say:

LISA AND PAUL. I'd say that "nothing could be finer than to be in Carolina
270   in the moooooooooooornin'."

Questions for Engagement, Response, and Analysis

1. Explain the significance of the setting of the play.

2. If you do not already know it, look up the ballet term *pas de deux*. In what ways is the exchange between Lisa and Paul a verbal equivalent of a *pas de deux*?

3. Analyze the personalities of Lisa and Paul.

4. What is the theme of the play?

Crafting Arguments

1. In an essay, describe the relationship between Lisa and Paul, analyze their replies to one another, and interpret the final dance.

Casebook
on Alice Walker

Because Alice Walker has, from the beginning of her career, been fascinated with creativity in its many different forms, a careful examination of her works can lead readers to examine their own views about both the creator and the object created. In the stories and essays included in this casebook, Walker presents creators who use fabrics, seeds, words, and music in their attempts to express themselves and to share their cultures with others. In addition, she illustrates different interpretations of what it means to appreciate the results of creativity. The scholarly essays about her works should also help you to craft interesting and revealing papers about Walker's works.

Alice Walker (b. 1944)

Alice Walker, writer of novels, short stories, poems, and essays, is perhaps best known for her popular novel The Color Purple (1982), *which was made into a 1985 movie directed by Steven Spielberg. Walker was born in Eatonton, Georgia, and received a scholarship to the prestigious Spellman College, partially as a result of having a handicap: her brother had accidentally blinded one of Walker's eyes in a gun accident. Many of her early works, including* The Color

*Purple and "Everyday Use," draw on her rural Southern
upbringing and celebrate the complex, rich art of rural
Southern African American women. Unlike most of her previous work,* Possessing the Secret of Joy *(1992) is set in
Africa. Her 1998 novel,* By the Light of My Father's Smile,
*uses multiple narrators to examine father-daughter rela-
tionships. In 2000, Walker published* The Way Forward Is
with a Broken Heart, *from which the second essay here is
taken; and in 2005 she published the novel* Now Is the Time
to Open Your Heart. *In 2003, she published two books of
poetry,* Absolute Trust in the Goodness of the Earth *and* A
Poem Traveled Down My Arm: Poems and Drawings. *Her
recent works frequently blend autobiography with fiction.*

EVERYDAY USE (1973)

FOR YOUR GRANDMAMA

1   I will wait for her in the yard that Maggie and I made so clean and wavy
yesterday afternoon. A yard like this is more comfortable than most people know. It is not just a yard. It is like an extended living room. When
the hard clay is swept clean as a floor and the fine sand around the edges
lined with tiny, irregular grooves, anyone can come and sit and look up
into the elm tree and wait for the breezes that never come inside
the house.

2   Maggie will be nervous until after her sister goes: she will stand hopelessly in corners, homely and ashamed of the burn scars down her arms
and legs, eying her sister with a mixture of envy and awe. She thinks her
sister has held life always in the palm of one hand, that "no" is a word the
world never learned to say to her.

3   You've no doubt seen those TV shows where the child who has "made
it" is confronted, as a surprise, by her own mother and father, tottering
in weakly from backstage. (A pleasant surprise, of course: What would
they do if parent and child came on the show only to curse out and insult
each other?) On TV mother and child embrace and smile into each other's
faces. Sometimes the mother and father weep, the child wraps them in
her arms and leans across the table to tell how she would not have made
it without their help. I have seen these programs.

4   Sometimes I dream a dream in which Dee and I are suddenly brought
together on a TV program of this sort. Out of a dark and soft-seated lim-
ousine I am ushered into a bright room filled with many people. There I
meet a smiling, gray, sporty man like Johnny Carson who shakes my hand
and tells me what a fine girl I have. Then we are on the stage and Dee is
embracing me with tears in her eyes. She pins on my dress a large orchid,
even though she has told me once that she thinks orchids are tacky flowers.

5   In real life I am a large, big-boned woman with rough, man-working
hands. In the winter I wear flannel nightgowns to bed and overalls during the day. I can kill and clean a hog as mercilessly as a man. My fat

keeps me hot in zero weather. I can work outside all day, breaking ice to get water for washing; I can eat pork liver cooked over the open fire minutes after it comes steaming from the hog. One winter I knocked a bull calf straight in the brain between the eyes with a sledge hammer and had the meat hung up to chill before nightfall. But of course all this does not show on television. I am the way my daughter would want me to be: a hundred pounds lighter, my skin like an uncooked barley pancake. My hair glistens in the hot bright lights. Johnny Carson has much to do to keep up with my quick and witty tongue.

6   But that is a mistake. I know even before I wake up. Who ever knew a Johnson with a quick tongue? Who can even imagine me looking a strange white man in the eye? It seems to me I have talked to them always with one foot raised in flight, with my head turned in whichever way is farthest from them. Dee, though. She would always look anyone in the eye. Hesitation was no part of her nature.

7   "How do I look, Mama?" Maggie says, showing just enough of her thin body enveloped in pink skirt and red blouse for me to know she's there, almost hidden by the door.

8   "Come out into the yard," I say.

9   Have you ever seen a lame animal, perhaps a dog run over by some careless person rich enough to own a car, sidle up to someone who is ignorant enough to be kind to him? That is the way my Maggie walks. She has been like this, chin on chest, eyes on ground, feet in shuffle, ever since the fire that burned the other house to the ground.

10   Dee is lighter than Maggie, with nicer hair and a fuller figure. She's a woman now, though sometimes I forget. How long ago was it that the other house burned? Ten, twelve years? Sometimes I can still hear the flame and feel Maggie's arms sticking to me, her hair smoking and her dress falling off her in little black papery flakes. Her eyes seemed stretched open, blazed open by the flames reflected in them. And Dee. I see her standing off under the sweet gum tree she used to dig gum out of; a look of concentration on her face as she watched the last dingy gray board of the house fall in toward the red-hot brick chimney. Why don't you do a dance around the ashes? I'd wanted to ask her. She had hated the house that much.

11   I used to think she hated Maggie, too. But that was before we raised the money, the church and me, to send her to Augusta to school. She used to read to us without pity; forcing words, lies, other folks' habits, whole lives upon us two, sitting trapped and ignorant underneath her voice. She washed us in a river of make-believe, burned us with a lot of knowledge we didn't necessarily need to know. Pressed us to her with the serious way she read, to shove us away at just the moment, like dimwits, we seemed about to understand.

12   Dee wanted nice things. A yellow organdy dress to wear to her graduation from high school; black pumps to match a green suit she'd made from an old suit somebody gave me. She was determined to stare down

any disaster in her efforts. Her eyelids would not flicker for minutes at a time. Often I fought off the temptation to shake her. At sixteen she had a style of her own: and knew what style was.

13   I never had an education myself. After second grade the school was closed down. Don't ask me why: in 1927 colored asked fewer questions than they do now. Sometimes Maggie reads to me. She stumbles along good-naturedly but can't see well. She knows she is not bright. Like good looks and money, quickness passed her by. She will marry John Thomas (who has mossy teeth in an earnest face) and then I'll be free to sit here and I guess just sing church songs to myself. Although I never was a good singer. Never could carry a tune. I was always better at a man's job. I used to love to milk till I was hooked in the side in '49. Cows are soothing and slow and don't bother you, unless you try to milk them the wrong way.

14   I have deliberately turned my back on the house. It is three rooms, just like the one that burned, except the roof is tin; they don't make shingle roofs any more. There are no real windows, just some holes cut in the sides, like the portholes in a ship, but not round and not square, with rawhide holding the shutters up on the outside. This house is in a pasture too, like the other one. No doubt when Dee sees it she will want to tear it down. She wrote me once that no matter where we "choose" to live, she will manage to come see us. But she will never bring her friends. Maggie and I thought about this and Maggie asked me, "Mama, when did Dee ever have any friends?"

15   She had a few. Furtive boys in pink shirts hanging about on washday after school. Nervous girls who never laughed. Impressed with her they worshiped the well-turned phrase, the cute shape, the scalding humor that erupted like bubbles in lye. She read to them.

16   When she was courting Jimmy T she didn't have much time to pay to us, but turned all her faultfinding power on him. He flew to marry a cheap city girl from a family of ignorant flashy people. She hardly had time to recompose herself.

17   When she comes I will meet—but there they are!

18   Maggie attempts to make a dash for the house, in her shuffling way, but I stay her with my hand. "Come back here," I say. And she stops and tries to dig a well in the sand with her toe.

19   It is hard to see them clearly through the strong sun. But even the first glimpse of leg out of the car tells me it is Dee. Her feet were always neat-looking, as if God himself had shaped them with a certain style. From the other side of the car comes a short, stocky man. Hair is all over his head a foot long and hanging from his chin like a kinky mule tail. I hear Maggie suck in her breath. "Uhnnnh," is what it sounds like. Like when you see the wriggling end of a snake just in front of your foot on the road. "Uhnnnh."

20   Dee next. A dress down to the ground, in this hot weather. A dress so loud it hurts my eyes. There are yellows and oranges enough to throw back the light of the sun. I feel my whole face warming from the heat

waves it throws out. Earrings gold, too, and hanging down to her shoulders. Bracelets dangling and making noises when she moves her arm up to shake the folds of the dress out of her armpits. The dress is loose and flows, and as she walks closer, I like it. I hear Maggie go "Uhnnnh" again. It is her sister's hair. It stands straight up like the wool on a sheep. It is black as night and around the edges are two long pigtails that rope about like small lizards disappearing behind her ears.

21   "Wa-su-zo-Tean-o!" she says, coming on in that gliding way the dress makes her move. The short stocky fellow with the hair to his navel is all grinning and he follows up with "Asalamalakim, my mother and sister!" He moves to hug Maggie but she falls back, right up against the back of my chair. I feel her trembling there and when I look up I see the perspiration falling off her chin.

22   "Don't get up," says Dee. Since I am stout it takes something of a push. You can see me trying to move a second or two before I make it. She turns, showing white heels through her sandals, and goes back to the car. Out she peeks next with a Polaroid. She stoops down quickly and lines up picture after picture of me sitting there in front of the house with Maggie cowering behind me. She never takes a shot without making sure the house is included. When a cow comes nibbling around the edge of the yard she snaps it and me and Maggie and the house. Then she puts the Polaroid in the back seat of the car, and comes up and kisses me on the forehead.

23   Meanwhile Asalamalakim is going through motions with Maggie's hand. Maggie's hand is as limp as a fish, and probably as cold, despite the sweat, and she keeps trying to pull it back. It looks like Asalamalakim wants to shake hands but wants to do it fancy. Or maybe he don't know how people shake hands. Anyhow, he soon gives up on Maggie.

24   "Well," I say. "Dee."

25   "No, Mama," she says. "Not 'Dee,' Wangero Leewanika Kemanjo!"

26   "What happened to 'Dee'?" I wanted to know.

27   "She's dead," Wangero said. "I couldn't bear it any longer, being named after the people who oppress me."

28   "You know as well as me you was named after your aunt Dicie," I said. Dicie is my sister. She named Dee. We called her "Big Dee" after Dee was born.

29   "But who was she named after?" asked Wangero.

30   "I guess after Grandma Dee," I said.

31   "And who was she named after?" asked Wangero.

32   "Her mother," I said, and saw Wangero was getting tired. "That's about as far back as I can trace it," I said. Though, in fact, I probably could have carried it back beyond the Civil War through the branches.

33   "Well," said Asalamalakim, "there you are."

34   "Uhnnnh," I heard Maggie say.

35   "There I was not," I said, "before 'Dicie' cropped up in our family, so why should I try to trace it that far back?"

36   He just stood there grinning, looking down on me like somebody inspecting a Model A car. Every once in a while he and Wangero sent eye signals over my head.

37   "How do you pronounce this name?" I asked.

38   "You don't have to call me by it if you don't want to," said Wangero.

39   "Why shouldn't I?" I asked. "If that's what you want us to call you, we'll call you."

40   "I know it might sound awkward at first," said Wangero.

41   "I'll get used to it," I said. "Ream it out again."

42   Well, soon we got the name out of the way. Asalamalakim had a name twice as long and three times as hard. After I tripped over it two or three times he told me to just call him Hakim-a-barber. I wanted to ask him was he a barber, but I didn't really think he was, so I didn't ask.

43   "You must belong to those beef-cattle peoples down the road," I said. They said "Asalamalakim" when they met you, too, but they didn't shake hands. Always too busy: feeding the cattle, fixing the fences, putting up salt-lick shelters, throwing down hay. When the white folks poisoned some of the herd the men stayed up all night with rifles in their hands. I walked a mile and a half just to see the sight.

44   Hakim-a-barber said, "I accept some of their doctrines, but farming and raising cattle is not my style." (They didn't tell me, and I didn't ask, whether Wangero (Dee) had really gone and married him.)

45   We sat down to eat and right away he said he didn't eat collards and pork was unclean. Wangero, though, went on through the chitlins and corn bread, the greens and everything else. She talked a blue streak over the sweet potatoes. Everything delighted her. Even the fact that we still used the benches her daddy made for the table when we couldn't afford to buy chairs.

46   "Oh, Mama!" she cried. Then turned to Hakim-a-barber. "I never knew how lovely these benches are. You can feel the rump prints," she said, running her hands underneath her and along the bench. Then she gave a sigh and her hand closed over Grandma Dee's butter dish. "That's it!" she said. "I knew there was something I wanted to ask you if I could have." She jumped up from the table and went over in the corner where the churn stood, the milk in it clabber by now. She looked at the churn and looked at it.

47   "This churn top is what I need," she said. "Didn't Uncle Buddy whittle it out of a tree you all used to have?"

48   "Yes," I said.

49   "Uh huh," she said happily. "And I want the dasher, too."

50   "Uncle Buddy whittle that, too?" asked the barber.

51   Dee (Wangero) looked up at me.

52   "Aunt Dee's first husband whittled the dash," said Maggie so low you almost couldn't hear her. "His name was Henry, but they called him Stash."

53   "Maggie's brain is like an elephant's," Wangero said, laughing. "I can use the churn top as a centerpiece for the alcove table," she said, sliding

a plate over the churn, "and I'll think of something artistic to do with the dasher."

54   When she finished wrapping the dasher the handle stuck out. I took it for a moment in my hands. You didn't even have to look close to see where hands pushing the dasher up and down to make butter had left a kind of sink in the wood. In fact, there were a lot of small sinks; you could see where thumbs and fingers had sunk into the wood. It was a beautiful light yellow wood, from a tree that grew in the yard where Big Dee and Stash had lived.

55   After dinner Dee (Wangero) went to the trunk at the foot of my bed and started rifling through it. Maggie hung back in the kitchen over the dishpan. Out came Wangero with two quilts. They had been pieced by Grandma Dee and then Big Dee and me had hung them on the quilt frames on the front porch and quilted them. One was in the Lone Star pattern. The other was Walk Around the Mountain. In both of them were scraps of dresses Grandma Dee had worn fifty and more years ago. Bits and pieces of Grandpa Jarrell's Paisley shirts. And one teeny faded blue piece, about the size of a penny matchbox, that was from Great Grandpa Ezra's uniform that he wore in the Civil War.

56   "Mama," Wangero said sweet as a bird. "Can I have these old quilts?"

57   I heard something fall in the kitchen, and a minute later the kitchen door slammed.

58   "Why don't you take one or two of the others?" I asked. "These old things was just done by me and Big Dee from some tops your grandma pieced before she died."

59   "No," said Wangero. "I don't want those. They are stitched around the borders by machine."

60   "That'll make them last better," I said.

61   "That's not the point," said Wangero. "These are all pieces of dresses Grandma used to wear. She did all this stitching by hand. Imagine!" She held the quilts securely in her arms, stroking them.

62   "Some of the pieces, like those lavender ones, come from old clothes her mother handed down to her," I said, moving up to touch the quilts. Dee (Wangero) moved back just enough so that I couldn't reach the quilts. They already belonged to her.

63   "Imagine!" she breathed again, clutching them closely to her bosom.

64   "The truth is," I said, "I promised to give them quilts to Maggie, for when she marries John Thomas."

65   She gasped like a bee had stung her.

66   "Maggie can't appreciate these quilts!" she said. "She'd probably be backward enough to put them to everyday use."

67   "I reckon she would," I said. "God knows I been saving 'em for long enough with nobody using 'em. I hope she will!" I didn't want to bring up how I had offered Dee (Wangero) a quilt when she went away to college. Then she had told me they were old-fashioned, out of style.

68   "But they're *priceless*!" she was saying now, furiously; for she has a temper. "Maggie would put them on the bed and in five years they'd be in rags. Less than that!"

69   "She can always make some more," I said. "Maggie knows how to quilt."

70   Dee (Wangero) looked at me with hatred. "You just will not understand. The point is these quilts, *these* quilts!"

71   "Well," I said, stumped. "What would *you* do with them?"

72   "Hang them," she said. As if that was the only thing you *could* do with quilts.

73   Maggie by now was standing in the door. I could almost hear the sound her feet made as they scraped over each other.

74   "She can have them, Mama," she said, like somebody used to never winning anything, or having anything reserved for her. "I can 'member Grandma Dee without the quilts."

75   I looked at her hard. She had filled her bottom lip with checkerberry snuff and it gave her face a kind of dopey, hangdog look. It was Grandma Dee and Big Dee who taught her how to quilt herself. She stood there with her scarred hands hidden in the folds of her skirt. She looked at her sister with something like fear but she wasn't mad at her. This was Maggie's portion. This was the way she knew God to work.

76   When I looked at her like that something hit me in the top of my head and ran down to the soles of my feet. Just like when I'm in church and the spirit of God touches me and I get happy and shout. I did something I never had done before: hugged Maggie to me, then dragged her on into the room, snatched the quilts out of Miss Wangero's hands and dumped them into Maggie's lap. Maggie just sat there on my bed with her mouth open.

77   "Take one or two of the others," I said to Dee.

78   But she turned without a word and went out to Hakim-a-barber.

79   "You just don't understand," she said, as Maggie and I came out to the car.

80   "What don't I understand?" I wanted to know.

81   "Your heritage," she said. And then she turned to Maggie, kissed her, and said, "You ought to try to make something of yourself, too, Maggie. It's really a new day for us. But from the way you and Mama still live you'd never know it."

82   She put on some sunglasses that hid everything above the tip of her nose and her chin.

83   Maggie smiled; maybe at the sunglasses. But a real smile, not scared. After we watched the car dust settle I asked Maggie to bring me a dip of snuff. And then the two of us sat there just enjoying, until it was time to go in the house and go to bed.

Questions for Engagement, Response, and Analysis

1. What is the setting of the story? What does it suggest about this family?

2. What do the mother's recurring dream and her response to it reveal about her relationship to Dee?

3. Examine Dee's interaction with her mother and her sister. What does her behavior suggest about her attitudes toward them? Toward her heritage?

4. How does the narrator's style change after the arrival of Dee? Why might Walker have chosen to change the style here?

5. What is Maggie's attitude toward her heritage? How does it differ from Dee's?

6. What is the theme of this story? What does the title suggest?

NINETEEN FIFTY-FIVE   (1981)

1955

1   The car is a brandnew red Thunderbird convertible, and it's passed the house more than once. It slows down real slow now, and stops at the curb. An older gentleman dressed like a Baptist deacon gets out on the side near the house, and a young fellow who looks about sixteen gets out on the driver's side. They are white, and I wonder what in the world they are doing in this neighborhood.

2   Well, I say to J. T., put your shirt on, anyway, and let me clean these glasses offa the table.

3   We had been watching the ballgame on TV. I wasn't actually watching, I was sort of daydreaming, with my foots up in J. T.'s lap.

4   I seen 'em coming on up the walk, brisk, like they coming to sell something, and then they rung the bell, and J. T. declined to put on a shirt but instead disappeared into the bedroom where the other television is. I turned down the one in the living room; I figured I'd be rid of these two double quick and J. T. could come back out again.

5   Are you Gracie Mae Still? asked the old guy, when I opened the door and put my hand on the lock inside the screen.

6   And I don't need to buy a thing, said I.

7   What makes you think we're sellin'? he asks, in that hearty Southern way that makes my eyeballs ache.

8   Well, one way or another and they're inside the house and the first thing the young fellow does is raise the TV a couple of decibels. He's about five feet nine, sort of womanish looking, with real dark white skin and a red pouting mouth. His hair is black and curly and he looks like a Loosianna creole.

9   About one of your songs, says the deacon. He is maybe sixty, with white hair and beard, white silk shirt, black linen suit, black tie, and black shoes. His cold gray eyes look like they're sweating.

10   One of my songs?

11   Traynor here just *loves* your songs. Don't you, Traynor? He nudges Traynor with his elbow. Traynor blinks, says something I can't catch in a pitch I don't register.

12   The boy learned to sing and dance livin' round you people out in the country. Practically cut his teeth on you.

13   Traynor looks up at me and bites his thumbnail.

14   I laugh.

15   Well, one way or another they leave with my agreement that they can record one of my songs. The deacon writes me a check for five hundred dollars, the boy grunts his awareness of the transaction, and I am laughing all over myself by the time I rejoin J. T.

16   Just as I am snuggling down beside him though I hear the front door bell going off again.

17   Forgit his hat? asks J. T.

18   I hope not, I say.

19   The deacon stands there leaning on the door frame and once again I'm thinking of those sweaty-looking eyeballs of his. I wonder if sweat makes your eyeballs pink because his are sure pink. Pink and gray and it strikes me that nobody I'd care to know is behind them.

20   I forgot one little thing, he says pleasantly. I forgot to tell you Traynor and I would like to buy up all of those records you made of the song. I tell you we sure do love it.

21   Well, love it or not, I'm not so stupid as to let them do that without making 'em pay. So I says, Well, that's gonna cost you. Because, really, that song never did sell all that good, so I was glad they was going to buy it up. But on the other hand, them two listening to my song by themselves, and nobody else getting to hear me sing it, give me a pause.

22   Well, one way or another the deacon showed me where I would come out ahead on any deal he had proposed so far. Didn't I give you five hundred dollars? he asked. What white man—and don't even mention colored—would give you more? We buy up all your records of that particular song: first, you git royalties. Let me ask you, how much you sell that song for in the first place? Fifty dollars? A hundred, I say. And no royalties from it yet, right? Right. Well, when we buy up all of them records you gonna git royalties. And that's gonna make all them race record shops sit up and take notice of Gracie Mae Still. And they gonna push all them other records of yourn they got. And you no doubt will become one of the big name colored recording artists. And then we can offer you another five hundred dollars for letting us do all this for you. And by God you'll be sittin' pretty! You can go out and buy you the kind of outfit a star should have. Plenty sequins and yards of red satin.

23   I had done unlocked the screen when I saw I could get some more money out of him. Now I held it wide open while he squeezed through the opening between me and the door. He whipped out another piece of paper and I signed it.

24　　He sort of trotted out to the car and slid in beside Traynor, whose head was back against the seat. They swung around in a u-turn in front of the house and then they was gone.

25　　J. T. was putting his shirt on when I got back to the bedroom. Yankees beat the Orioles 10–6, he said. I believe I'll drive out to Paschal's pond and go fishing. Wanta go?

26　　While I was putting on my pants J. T. was holding the two checks.

27　　I'm real proud of a woman that can make cash money without leavin' home, he said. And I said *Umph*. Because we met on the road with me singing in first one little low-life jook after another, making ten dollars a night for myself if I was lucky, and sometimes bringin' home nothing but my life. And J. T. just loved them times. The way I was fast and flashy and always on the go from one town to another. He loved the way my singin' made the dirt farmers cry like babies and the womens shout Honey, hush! But that's mens. They loves any style to which you can get 'em accustomed.

1956

28　　My little grandbaby called me one night on the phone: Little Mama, Little Mama, there's a white man on the television singing one of your songs! Turn on channel 5.

29　　Lord, if it wasn't Traynor. Still looking half asleep from the neck up, but kind of awake in a nasty way from the waist down. He wasn't doing too bad with my song either, but it wasn't just the song that people in the audience was screeching and screaming over, it was that nasty little jerk he was doing from the waist down.

30　　Well, Lord have mercy, I said, listening to him. If I'da closed my eyes, it could have been me. He had followed every turning of my voice, side streets, avenues, red lights, train crossings and all. It give me a chill.

31　　Everywhere I went I heard Traynor singing my song, and all the little white girls just eating it up. I never had so many ponytails switched across my line of vision in my life. They was so *proud*. He was a *genius*.

32　　Well, all that year I was trying to lose weight anyway and that and high blood pressure and sugar kept me pretty well occupied. Traynor had made a smash from a song of mine, I still had seven hundred dollars of the original one thousand dollars in the bank, and I felt if I could just bring my weight down, life would be sweet.

1957

33　　I lost ten pounds in 1956. That's what I give myself for Christmas. And J. T. and me and the children and their friends and grandkids of all description had just finished dinner—over which I had put on nine and a half of my lost ten—when who should appear at the front door but Traynor. Little Mama, Little Mama! It's that white man who sings ＿＿＿＿＿＿＿＿＿. The children didn't call it my song anymore. Nobody did. It was funny how that happened. Traynor and the deacon had bought up all my records, true, but on his record he had put "written by Gracie Mae Still." But that was just another name on the label, like "produced by Apex Records."

34   On the TV he was inclined to dress like the deacon told him. But now he looked presentable.

35   Merry Christmas, said he.

36   And same to you, Son.

37   I don't know why I called him Son. Well, one way or another they're all our sons. The only requirement is that they be younger than us. But then again, Traynor seemed to be aging by the minute.

38   You looks tired, I said. Come on in and have a glass of Christmas cheer.

39   J. T. ain't never in his life been able to act decent to a white man he wasn't working for, but he poured Traynor a glass of bourbon and water, then he took all the children and grandkids and friends and whatnot out to the den. After while I heard Traynor's voice singing the song, coming from the stereo console. It was just the kind of Christmas present my kids would consider cute.

40   I looked at Traynor, complicit. But he looked like it was the last thing in the world he wanted to hear. His head was pitched forward over his lap, his hands holding his glass and his elbows on his knees.

41   I done sung that song seem like a million times this year, he said. I sung it on the Grand Ole Opry, I sung it on the Ed Sullivan show. I sung it on Mike Douglas, I sung it at the Cotton Bowl, the Orange Bowl. I sung it at Festivals. I sung it at Fairs. I sung it overseas in Rome, Italy, and once in a submarine *underseas*. I've sung it and sung it, and I'm making forty thousand dollars a day offa it, and you know what, I don't have the faintest notion what that song means.

42   Whatchumean, what do it mean? It mean what it says. All I could think was: These suckers is making forty thousand a *day* offa my song and now they gonna come back and try to swindle me out of the original thousand.

43   It's just a song, I said. Cagey. When you fool around with a lot of no count mens you sing a bunch of 'em. I shrugged.

44   Oh, he said. Well. He started brightening up. I just come by to tell you I think you are a great singer.

45   He didn't blush, saying that. Just said it straight out.

46   And I brought you a little Christmas present too. Now you take this little box and you hold it until I drive off. Then you take it outside under that first streetlight back up the street aways in front of that greenhouse. Then you open the box and see . . . Well, just *see*.

47   What had come over this boy, I wondered, holding the box. I looked out the window in time to see another white man come up and get in the car with him and then two more cars full of white mens start out behind him. They was all in long black cars that looked like a funeral procession.

48   Little Mama, Little Mama, what it is? One of my grandkids come running up and started pulling at the box. It was wrapped in gay Christmas paper—the thick, rich kind that's hard to picture folks making just to throw away.

49   J. T. and the rest of the crowd followed me out of the house, up the street to the streetlight and in front of the greenhouse. Nothing was there but somebody's gold-grilled white Cadillac. Brandnew and most distracting. We got to looking at it so till I almost forgot the little box in my hand. While the others were busy making 'miration I carefully took off the paper and ribbon and folded them up and put them in my pants pocket. What should I see but a pair of genuine solid gold caddy keys.

50   Dangling the keys in front of everybody's nose, I unlocked the caddy, motioned for J. T. to git in on the other side, and us didn't come back home for two days.

1960

51   Well, the boy was sure nuff famous by now. He was still a mite shy of twenty but already they was calling him the Emperor of Rock and Roll.

52   Then what should happen but the draft.

53   Well, says J. T. There goes all the Emperor of Rock and Roll business.

54   But even in the army the womens was on him like white on rice. We watched it on the News.

55   *Dear Gracie Mae* [he wrote from Germany],

56   *How you? Fine I hope as this leaves me doing real well. Before I come in the army I was gaining a lot of weight and gitting jittery from making all them dumb movies. But now I exercise and eat right and get plenty of rest. I'm more awake than I been in ten years.*

57   *I wonder if you are writing any more songs?*

58   *Sincerely,*
59   *Traynor*

60   I wrote him back:

61   *Dear Son,*

62   *We is all fine in the Lord's good grace and hope this finds you the same. J. T. and me be out all times of the day and night in that car you give me—which you know you didn't have to do. Oh, and I do appreciate the mink and the new self-cleaning oven. But if you send anymore stuff to eat from Germany I'm going to have to open up a store in the neighborhood just to get rid of it. Really, we have more than enough of everything. The Lord is good to us and we don't know Want.*

63   *Glad to here you is well and gitting your right rest. There ain't nothing like exercising to help that along. J. T. and me work some part of every day that we don't go fishing in the garden.*

64   *Well, so long Soldier.*

65   *Sincerely,*
66   *Gracie Mae*

67 He wrote:

68 *Dear Gracie Mae,*

69   *I hope you and J. T. like that automatic power tiller I had one of the stores back home send you. I went through a mountain of catalogs looking for it—I wanted something that even a woman could use.*

70   *I've been thinking about writing some songs of my own but every time I finish one it don't seem to be about nothing I've actually lived myself. My agent keeps sending me other people's songs but they just sound mooney. I can hardly git through 'em without gagging.*

71   *Everybody still loves that song of yours. They ask me all the time what do I think it means, really. I mean, they want to know just what I want to know. Where out of your life did it come from?*

72   *Sincerely,*
73   *Traynor*

1968

74   I didn't see the boy for seven years. No. Eight. Because just about everybody was dead when I saw him again. Malcolm X, King, the president and his brother, and even J. T. J. T. died of a head cold. It just settled in his head like a block of ice, he said, and nothing we did moved it until one day he just leaned out the bed and died.

75   His good friend Horace helped me put him away, and then about a year later Horace and me started going together. We was sitting out on the front porch swing one summer night, dusk-dark, and I saw this great procession of lights winding to a stop.

76   Holy Toledo! said Horace. (He's got a real sexy voice like Ray Charles.) Look *at* it. He meant the long line of flashy cars and the white men in white summer suits jumping out on the drivers' sides and standing at attention. With wings they could pass for angels, with hoods they could be the Klan.

77   Traynor comes waddling up the walk.

78   And suddenly I know what it is he could pass for. An Arab like the ones you see in storybooks. Plump and soft and with never a care about weight. Because with so much money, who cares? Traynor is almost dressed like someone from a storybook too. He has on, I swear, about ten necklaces. Two sets of bracelets on his arms, at least one ring on every finger, and some kind of shining buckles on his shoes, so that when he walks you get a quite a few twinkling lights.

79   Gracie Mae, he says, coming up to give me a hug. J. T.

80   I explain that J. T. passed. That this is Horace.

81   Horace, he says, puzzled but polite, sort of rocking back on his heels, Horace.

82   That's it for Horace. He goes in the house and don't come back.

83   Looks like you and me is gained a few, I say.

84   He laughs. The first time I ever heard him laugh. It don't sound much like a laugh and I can't swear that it's better than no laugh a'tall.

85   He's gitting fat for sure, but he's still slim compared to me. I'll never see three hundred pounds again and I've just about said (excuse me) fuck it. I got to thinking about it one day an' I thought: aside from the fact that they say it's unhealthy, my fat ain't never been no trouble. Mens always have loved me. My kids ain't never complained. Plus they's fat. And fat like I is I looks distinguished. You see me coming and know somebody's *there*.

86   Gracie Mae, he says, I've come with a personal invitation to you to my house tomorrow for dinner. He laughed. What did it sound like? I couldn't place it. See them men out there? he asked me. I'm sick and tired of eating with them. They don't never have nothing to talk about. That's why I eat so much. But if you come to dinner tomorrow we can talk about the old days. You can tell me about that farm I bought you.

87   I sold it, I said.

88   You did?

89   Yeah, I said, I did. Just cause I said I liked to exercise by working in a garden didn't mean I wanted five hundred acres! Anyhow, I'm a city girl now. Raised in the country it's true. Dirt poor—the whole bit—but that's all behind me now.

90   Oh well, he said, I didn't mean to offend you.

91   We sat a few minutes listening to the crickets.

92   Then he said: You wrote that song while you was still on the farm, didn't you, or was it right after you left?

93   You had somebody spying on me? I asked.

94   You and Bessie Smith got into a fight over it once, he said.

95   You *is* been spying on me!

96   But I don't know what the fight was about, he said. Just like I don't know what happened to your second husband. Your first one died in the Texas electric chair. Did you know that? Your third one beat you up, stole your touring costumes and your car and retired with a chorine to Tuskegee. He laughed. He's still there.

97   I had been mad, but suddenly I calmed down. Traynor was talking very dreamily. It was dark but seems like I could tell his eyes weren't right. It was like some*thing* was sitting there talking to me but not necessarily with a person behind it.

98   You gave up on marrying and seem happier for it. He laughed again. I married but it never went like it was supposed to. I never could squeeze any of my own life either into it or out of it. It was like singing somebody else's record. I copied the way it was sposed to be *exactly* but I never had a clue what marriage meant.

99   I bought her a diamond ring big as your fist. I bought her clothes. I built her a mansion. But right away she didn't want the boys to stay there. Said they smoked up the bottom floor. Hell, there were *five* floors.

100   No need to grieve, I said. No need to. Plenty more where she come from.

101   He perked up. That's part of what that song means, ain't it? No need to grieve. Whatever it is, there's plenty more down the line.

102   I never really believed that way back when I wrote that song, I said. It was all bluffing then. The trick is to live long enough to put your young bluffs to use. Now if I was to sing that song today I'd tear it up. 'Cause I done lived long enough to know it's *true*. Them words could hold me up.

103   I ain't lived that long, he said.

104   Look like you on your way, I said. I don't know why, but the boy seemed to need some encouraging. And I don't know, seem like one way or another you talk to rich white folks and you end up reassuring *them*. But what the hell, by now I feel something for the boy. I wouldn't be in his bed all alone in the middle of the night for nothing. Couldn't be nothing worse than being famous the world over for something you don't even understand. That's what I tried to tell Bessie. She wanted that same song. Overheard me practicing it one day, said, with her hands on her hips: Gracie Mae, I'ma sing your song tonight. I *likes* it.

105   Your lips be too swole to sing, I said. She was mean and she was strong, but I trounced her.

106   Ain't you famous enough with your own stuff? I said. Leave mine alone. Later on, she thanked me. By then she was Miss Bessie Smith to the World, and I was still Miss Gracie Mae Nobody from Notasulga.

107   The next day all these limousines arrived to pick me up. Five cars and twelve bodyguards. Horace picked that morning to start painting the kitchen.

108   Don't paint the kitchen, fool, I said. The only reason that dumb boy of ours is going to show me his mansion is because he intends to present us with a new house.

109   What you gonna do with it? he asked me, standing there in his shirt-sleeves stirring the paint.

110   Sell it. Give it to the children. Live in it on weekends. It don't matter what I do. He sure don't care.

111   Horace just stood there shaking his head. Mama you sure looks *good*, he says. Wake me up when you git back.

112   *Fool*, I say, and pat my wig in front of the mirror.

113   The boy's house is something else. First you come to this mountain, and then you commence to drive and drive up this road that's lined with magnolias. Do magnolias grow on mountains? I was wondering. And you come to lakes and you come to ponds and you come to deer and you come up on some sheep. And I figure these two is sposed to represent England and Wales. Or something out of Europe. And you just keep on coming to stuff. And it's all pretty. Only the man driving my car don't look at nothing but the road. Fool. And then *finally*, after all this time, you begin to go up the driveway. And there's more magnolias–only they're not in such good shape. It's sort of cool up this high and I don't think they're gonna make it. And then I see this building that looks like if it had a name it would be The Tara Hotel. Columns and steps and outdoor chandeliers

and rocking chairs. Rocking chairs? Well, and there's the boy on the steps dressed in a dark green satin jacket like you see folks wearing on TV late at night, and he looks sort of like a fat Dracula with all that house rising behind him, and standing beside him there's this little white vision of loveliness that he introduces as his wife.

114   He's nervous when he introduces us and he says to her: This is Gracie Mae Still, I want you to know me. I mean . . . and she gives him a look that would fry meat.

115   Won't you come in, Gracie Mae, she says, and that's the last I see of her.

116   He fishes around for something to say or do and decides to escort me to the kitchen. We go through the entry and the parlor and the breakfast room and the dining room and the servants' passage and finally get there. The first thing I notice is that, altogether, there are five stoves. He looks about to introduce me to one.

117   Wait a minute, I say. Kitchens don't do nothing for me. Let's go sit on the front porch.

118   Well, we hike back and we sit in the rocking chairs rocking until dinner.

119   Gracie Mae, he says down the table, taking a piece of fried chicken from the woman standing over him, I got a little surprise for you.

120   It's a house, ain't it? I ask, spearing a chitlin.

121   You're getting *spoiled*, he says. And the way he says *spoiled* sounds funny. He slurs it. It sounds like his tongue is too thick for his mouth. Just that quick he's finished the chicken and is now eating chitlins *and* a pork chop. *Me* spoiled, I'm thinking.

122   I already got a house. Horace is right this minute painting the kitchen. I bought that house. My kids feel comfortable in that house.

123   But this one I bought you is just like mine. Only a little smaller.

124   I still don't need no house. And anyway who would clean it?

125   He looks surprised.

126   Really, I think, some peoples advance *so* slowly.

127   I hadn't thought of that. But what the hell, I'll get you somebody to live in.

128   I don't want other folks living 'round me. Makes me nervous.

129   You *don't*? It *do*?

130   What I want to wake up and see folks I don't even know for?

131   He just sits there downtable staring at me. Some of that feeling is in the song, ain't it? Not the words, the *feeling*. What I want to wake up and see folks I don't even know for? But I see twenty folks a day I don't even know, including my wife.

132   This food wouldn't be bad to wake up to though, I said. The boy had found the genius of corn bread.

133   He looked at me real hard. He laughed. Short. They want what you got but they don't want you. They want what I got only it ain't mine. That's what makes 'em so hungry for me when I sing. They getting the flavor of

something but they ain't getting the thing itself. They like a pack of hound dogs trying to gobble up a scent.

134   You talking 'bout your fans?

135   Right. Right. He says.

136   Don't worry 'bout your fans, I say. They don't know their asses from a hole in the ground. I doubt there's a honest one in the bunch.

137   That's the point. Dammit, that's the point! He hits the table with his fist. It's so solid it don't even quiver. You need a honest audience! You can't have folks that's just gonna lie right back to you.

138   Yeah, I say, it was small compared to yours, but I had one. It would have been worth my life to try to sing 'em somebody else's stuff that I didn't know nothing about.

139   He must have pressed a buzzer under the table. One of his flunkies zombies up.

140   Git Johnny Carson, he says.

141   On the phone? asks the zombie.

142   On the phone, says Traynor, what you think I mean, git him offa the front porch? Move your ass.

143   So two weeks later we's on the Johnny Carson show.

144   Traynor is all corseted down nice and looks a little bit fat but mostly good. And all the women that grew up on him and my song squeal and squeal. Traynor says: The lady who wrote my first hit record is here with us tonight, and she's agreed to sing it for all of us, just like she sung it forty-five years ago. Ladies and Gentlemen, the great Gracie Mae Still!

145   Well, I had tried to lose a couple of pounds my own self, but failing that I had me a very big dress made. So I sort of rolls over next to Traynor, who is dwarfted by me, so that when he puts his arm around back of me to try to hug me it looks funny to the audience and they laugh.

146   I can see this pisses him off. But I smile out there at 'em. Imagine squealing for twenty years and not knowing why you're squealing? No more sense of endings and beginnings than hogs.

147   It don't matter, Son, I say. Don't fret none over me.

148   I commence to sing. And I sound—wonderful. Being able to sing good ain't all about having a good singing voice a'tall. A good singing voice helps. But when you come up in the Hard Shell Baptist church like I did you understand early that the fellow that sings is the singer. Them that waits for programs and arrangements and letters from home is just good voices occupying body space.

149   So there I am singing my own song, my own way. And I give it all I got and enjoy every minute of it. When I finish Traynor is standing up clapping and clapping and beaming at first me and then the audience like I'm his mama for true. The audience claps politely for about two seconds.

150   Traynor looks disgusted.

151   He comes over and tries to hug me again. The audience laughs.

152   Johnny Carson looks at us like we both weird.

153   Traynor is mad as hell. He's supposed to sing something called a love ballad. But instead he takes the mike, turns to me and says: Now see if my imitation still holds up. He goes into the same song, *our song*, I think, looking out at his flaky audience. And he sings it just the way he always did. My voice, my tone, my inflection, everything. But he forgets a couple of lines. Even before he's finished the matronly squeals begin.

154   He sits down next to me looking whipped.

155   It don't matter, Son, I say, patting his hand. You don't even know those people. Try to make the people you know happy.

156   Is that in the song? he asks.

157   Maybe. I say.

1977

158   For a few years I hear from him, then nothing. But trying to lose weight takes all the attention I got to spare. I finally faced up to the fact that my fat is the hurt I don't admit, not even to myself, and that I been trying to bury it from the day I was born. But also when you git real old, to tell the truth, it ain't as pleasant. It gits lumpy and slack. Yuck. So one day I said to Horace, I'ma git this shit offa me.

159   And he fell in with the program like he always try to do and Lord such a procession of salads and cottage cheese and fruit juice!

160   One night I dreamed Traynor had split up with his fifteenth wife. He said: *You meet 'em for no reason. You date 'em for no reason. You marry 'em for no reason. I do it all but I swear it's just like somebody else doing it. I feel like I can't remember Life.*

161   The boy's in trouble, I said to Horace.

162   You've always said that, he said.

163   I have?

164   Yeah. You always said he looked asleep. You can't sleep through life if you wants to live it.

165   You not such a fool after all, I said, pushing myself up with my cane and hobbling over to where he was. Let me sit down on your lap, I said, while this salad I ate takes effect.

166   In the morning we heard Traynor was dead. Some said fat, some said heart, some said alcohol, some said drugs. One of the children called from Detroit. Them dumb fans of his is on a crying rampage, she said. You just ought to turn on the t.v.

167   But I didn't want to see 'em. They was crying and crying and didn't even know what they was crying for. One day this is going to be a pitiful country, I thought.

Questions for Engagement, Response, and Analysis

1. Describe the narrator of the story.
2. What do Traynor's experiences reveal about him?
3. What is the effect of having the story take place over a period of several years—from 1955 to 1977? What is the significance of this time period?
4. What is the theme of the story?

IN SEARCH OF OUR MOTHERS' GARDENS   (1970)

I described her own nature and temperament. Told how they needed a larger life for their expression. . . . I pointed out that in lieu of proper channels, her emotions had overflowed into paths that dissipated them. I talked, beautifully I thought, about an art that would be born, an art that would open the way for women the likes of her. I asked her to hope, and build up an inner life against the coming of that day. . . . I sang, with a strange quiver in my voice, a promise song.

—JEAN TOOMER, "AVEY,"

CANE

1   The poet speaking to a prostitute who falls asleep while he's talking—

2   When the poet Jean Toomer walked through the South in the early twenties, he discovered a curious thing: black women whose spirituality was so intense, so deep, so *unconscious*, that they were themselves unaware of the richness they held. They stumbled blindly through their lives; creatures so abused and mutilated in body, so dimmed and confused by pain, that they considered themselves unworthy even of hope. In the selfless abstractions their bodies became to the men who used them, they became more than "sexual objects," more even than mere women: they became "Saints." Instead of being perceived as whole persons, their bodies became shrines: what was thought to be their minds became temples suitable for worship. These crazy Saints stared out at the world, wildly, like lunatics—or quietly, like suicides; and the "God" that was in their gaze was as mute as a great stone.

3   Who were these Saints? These crazy, loony, pitiful women?

4   Some of them, without a doubt, were our mothers and grandmothers.

5   In the still heat of the post-Reconstruction South, this is how they seemed to Jean Toomer: exquisite butterflies trapped in an evil honey, toiling away their lives in an era, a century, that did not acknowledge them, except as "the *mule* of the world." They dreamed dreams that no one knew—not even themselves, in any coherent fashion—and saw visions no one could understand. They wandered or sat about the

countryside crooning lullabies to ghosts, and drawing the mother of Christ in charcoal on courthouse walls.

6   They forced their minds to desert their bodies and their striving spirits sought to rise, like frail whirlwinds from the hard red clay. And when those frail whirlwinds fell, in scattered particles, upon the ground, no one mourned. Instead, men lit candles to celebrate the emptiness that remained, as people do who enter a beautiful but vacant space to resurrect a God.

7   Our mothers and grandmothers, some of them: moving to music not yet written. And they waited.

8   They waited for a day when the unknown thing that was in them would be made known; but guessed, somehow in their darkness, that on the day of their revelation they would be long dead. Therefore to Toomer they walked, and even ran, in slow motion. For they were going nowhere immediate, and the future was not yet within their grasp. And men took our mothers and grandmothers, "but got no pleasure from it." So complex was their passion and their calm.

9   To Toomer, they lay vacant and fallow as autumn fields, with harvest time never in sight: and he saw them enter loveless marriages, without joy; and become prostitutes, without resistance; and become mothers of children, without fulfillment.

10   For these grandmothers and mothers of ours were not Saints, but Artists; driven to a numb and bleeding madness by the springs of creativity in them for which there was no release. They were Creators, who lived lives of spiritual waste, because they were so rich in spirituality—which is the basis of Art—that the strain of enduring their unused and unwanted talent drove them insane. Throwing away this spirituality was their pathetic attempt to lighten the soul to a weight their work-worn, sexually abused bodies could bear.

11   What did it mean for a black woman to be an artist in our grandmothers' time? In our great-grandmothers' day? It is a question with an answer cruel enough to stop the blood.

12   Did you have a genius of a great-great-grandmother who died under some ignorant and depraved white overseer's lash? Or was she required to bake biscuits for a lazy backwater tramp, when she cried out in her soul to paint watercolors of sunsets, or the rain falling on the green and peaceful pasturelands? Or was her body broken and forced to bear children (who were more often than not sold away from her)—eight, ten, fifteen, twenty children—when her one joy was the thought of modeling heroic figures of rebellion, in stone or clay?

13   How was the creativity of the black woman kept alive, year after year and century after century, when for most of the years black people have been in America, it was a punishable crime for a black person to read or write? And the freedom to paint, to sculpt, to expand the mind with action did not exist. Consider, if you can bear to imagine it, what might have been the result if singing, too, had been forbidden by law. Listen to

the voices of Bessie Smith, Billie Holiday, Nina Simone, Roberta Flack, and Aretha Franklin, among others, and imagine those voices muzzled for life. Then you may begin to comprehend the lives of our "crazy," "Sainted" mothers and grandmothers. The agony of the lives of women who might have been Poets, Novelists, Essayists, and Short-Story Writers (over a period of centuries) who died with their great gifts stifled within them.

14   And, if this were the end of the story, we would have cause to cry out in my paraphrase of Okot p'Bitek's great poem:

> O, my clanswomen
> Let us all cry together!
> Come,
> Let us mourn the death of our mother,
> The death of a Queen
> The ash that was produced
> By a great fire!
> O, this homestead is utterly dead
> Close the gates
> With *lacari* thorns,
> For our mother
> The creator of the Stool is lost!
> And all the young women
> Have perished in the wilderness!

15   But this is not the end of the story, for all the young women—our mothers and grandmothers, *ourselves*—have not perished in the wilderness. And if we ask ourselves why, and search for and find the answer, we will know beyond all efforts to erase it from our minds, just exactly who, and of what, we black American women are.

16   One example, perhaps the most pathetic, most misunderstood one, can provide a backdrop for our mothers' work: Phillis Wheatley, a slave in the 1700s.

17   Virginia Woolf, in her book *A Room of One's Own*, wrote that in order for a woman to write fiction she must have two things, certainly: a room of her own (with key and lock) and enough money to support herself.

18   What then are we to make of Phillis Wheatley, a slave, who owned not even herself? This sickly, frail black girl who required a servant of her own at times—her health was so precarious—and who, had she been white, would have been easily considered the intellectual superior of all the women and most of the men in the society of her day.

19   Virginia Woolf wrote further, speaking of course not of our Phillis, that "any woman born with a great gift in the sixteenth century [insert "eighteenth century," insert "black woman," insert "born or made a slave"] would certainly have gone crazed, shot herself, or ended her days in some lonely cottage outside the village, half witch, half wizard [insert "Saint,"], feared and mocked at. For it needs little skill and psychology

to be sure that a highly gifted girl who had tried to use her gift for poetry would have been so thwarted and hindered by contrary instincts [add "chains, guns, the lash, the ownership of one's body by someone else, submission to an alien religion"], that she must have lost her health and sanity to a certainty."

20   The key words, as they relate to Phillis, are "contrary instincts." For when we read the poetry of Phillis Wheatley—as when we read the novels of Nella Larsen or the oddly false-sounding autobiography of that freest of all black women writers, Zora Hurston—evidence of "contrary instincts" is everywhere. Her loyalties were completely divided, as was, without question, her mind.

21   But how could this be otherwise? Captured at seven, a slave of wealthy, doting whites who instilled in her the "savagery" of the Africa they "rescued" her from . . . one wonders if she was even able to remember her homeland as she had known it, or as it really was.

22   Yet, because she did try to use her gift for poetry in a world that made her a slave, she was "so thwarted and hindered by . . . contrary instincts, that she . . . lost her health. . . ." In the last years of her brief life, burdened not only with the need to express her gift but also with a penniless, friendless "freedom" and several small children for whom she was forced to do strenuous work to feed, she lost her health, certainly. Suffering from malnutrition and neglect and who knows what mental agonies, Phillis Wheatley died.

23   So torn by "contrary instincts" was black, kidnapped, enslaved Phillis that her description of "the Goddess"—as she poetically called the Liberty she did not have—is ironically, cruelly humorous. And, in fact, has held Phillis up to ridicule for more than a century. It is usually read prior to hanging Phillis's memory as that of a fool. She wrote:

> The Goddess comes, she moves divinely fair,
> Olive and laurel binds her *golden* hair.
> Wherever shines this native of the skies,
> Unnumber'd charms and recent graces rise. [My italics]

24   It is obvious that Phillis, the slave, combed the "Goddess's" hair every morning; prior, perhaps, to bringing in the milk, or fixing her mistress's lunch. She took her imagery from the one thing she saw elevated above all others.

25   With the benefit of hindsight we ask, "How could she?"

26   But at last, Phillis, we understand. No more snickering when your stiff, struggling, ambivalent lines are forced on us. We know now that you were not an idiot or a traitor; only a sickly little black girl, snatched from your home and country and made a slave; a woman who still struggled to sing the song that was your gift, although in a land of barbarians who praised you for your bewildered tongue. It is not so much what you sang, as that you kept alive, in so many of our ancestors, *the notion of song.*

27   Black women are called, in the folklore that so aptly identifies one's status in society, "the *mule* of the world," because we have been handed the burdens that everyone else—*everyone* else—refused to carry. We have also been called "Matriarchs," "Superwomen," and "Mean and Evil Bitches." Not to mention "Castraters" and "Sapphire's Mama." When we have pleaded for understanding, our character has been distorted; when we have asked for simple caring, we have been handed empty inspirational appellations, then stuck in the farthest corner. When we have asked for love, we have been given children. In short, even our plainer gifts, our labors of fidelity and love, have been knocked down our throats. To be an artist and a black woman, even today, lowers our status in many respects, rather than raises it: and yet, artists we will be.

28   Therefore we must fearlessly pull out of ourselves and look at and identify with our lives the living creativity some of our great-grandmothers were not allowed to know. I stress *some* of them because it is well known that the majority of our great-grandmothers knew, even without "knowing" it, the reality of their spirituality, even if they didn't recognize it beyond what happened in the singing at church—and they never had any intention of giving it up.

29   How they did it—those millions of black women who were not Phillis Wheatley, or Lucy Terry or Frances Harper or Zora Hurston or Nella Larsen or Bessie Smith; or Elizabeth Catlett, or Katherine Dunham, either—brings me to the title of this essay, "In Search of Our Mothers' Gardens," which is a personal account that is yet shared, in its theme and its meaning, by all of us. I found, while thinking about the far-reaching world of the creative black woman, that often the truest answer to a question that really matters can be found very close.

30   In the late 1920s my mother ran away from home to marry my father. Marriage, if not running away, was expected of seventeen-year-old girls. By the time she was twenty, she had two children and was pregnant with a third. Five children later, I was born. And this is how I came to know my mother: she seemed a large, soft, loving-eyed woman who was rarely impatient in our home. Her quick, violent temper was on view only a few times a year, when she battled with the white landlord who had the misfortune to suggest to her that her children did not need to go to school.

31   She made all the clothes we wore, even my brothers' overalls. She made all the towels and sheets we used. She spent the summers canning vegetables and fruits. She spent the winter evenings making quilts enough to cover all our beds.

32   During the "working" day, she labored beside—not behind—my father in the fields. Her day began before sunup, and did not end until late at night. There was never a moment for her to sit down, undisturbed, to unravel her own private thoughts; never a time free from interruption—by work or the noisy inquiries of her many children. And yet, it is to my

mother—and all our mothers who were not famous—that I went in search of the secret of what has fed that muzzled and often mutilated, but vibrant, creative spirit that the black woman has inherited, and that pops out in wild and unlikely places to this day.

33   But when, you will ask, did my overworked mother have time to know or care about feeding the creative spirit?

34   The answer is so simple that many of us have spent years discovering it. We have constantly looked high, when we should have looked high—and low.

35   For example: in the Smithsonian Institution in Washington, D.C., there hangs a quilt unlike any other in the world. In fanciful, inspired, and yet simple and identifiable figures, it portrays the story of the Crucifixion. It is considered rare, beyond price. Though it follows no known pattern of quilt-making, and though it is made of bits and pieces of worthless rags, it is obviously the work of a person of powerful imagination and deep spiritual feeling. Below this quilt I saw a note that says it was made by "an anonymous Black woman in Alabama, a hundred years ago."

36   If we could locate this "anonymous" black woman from Alabama, she would turn out to be one of our grandmothers—an artist who left her mark in the only materials she could afford, and in the only medium her position in society allowed her to use.

37   As Virginia Woolf wrote further, in *A Room of One's Own*:

> Yet genius of a sort must have existed among women as it must have existed among the working class. [Change this to "slaves" and "the wives and daughters of sharecroppers."] Now and again an Emily Brontë or a Robert Burns [change this to "a Zora Hurston or a Richard Wright"] blazes out and proves its presence. But certainly it never got itself on to paper. When, however, one reads of a witch being ducked, of a woman possessed by devils [or "Sainthood"], of a wise woman selling herbs [our root workers], or even a very remarkable man who had a mother, then I think we are on the track of a lost novelist, a suppressed poet, of some mute and inglorious Jane Austen. . . . Indeed, I would venture to guess that Anon, who wrote so may poems without signing them, was often a woman. . . .

38   And so our mothers and grandmothers have, more often than not anonymously, handed on the creative spark, the seed of the flower they themselves never hoped to see; or like a sealed letter they could not plainly read.

39   And so it is, certainly, with my own mother. Unlike "Ma" Rainey's songs, which retained their creator's name even while blasting forth from Bessie Smith's mouth, no song or poem will bear my mother's name. Yet so many of the stories that I write, that we all write, are my mother's stories. Only recently did I fully realize this: that through years of listening to my mother's stories of her life, I have absorbed not only the stories themselves, but something of the manner in which she spoke, something of the urgency that involves the knowledge that her stories—like her life—must be recorded. It is probably for this reason that so much of what I have written is about characters whose counterparts in real life are so much older than I am.

40   But the telling of these stories, which came from my mother's lips as naturally as breathing, was not the only way my mother showed herself as an artist. For stories, too, were subject to being distracted, to dying without conclusion. Dinners must be started, and cotton must be gathered before the big rains. The artist that was and is my mother showed itself to me only after many years. This is what I finally noticed:

41   Like Mem, a character in *The Third Life of Grange Copeland*, my mother adorned with flowers whatever shabby house we were forced to live in. And not just your typical straggly country stand of zinnias, either. She planted ambitious gardens—and still does—with over fifty different varieties of plants that bloom profusely from early March until late November. Before she left home for the fields, she watered her flowers, chopped up the grass, and laid out new beds. When she returned from the fields she might divide clumps of bulbs, dig a cold pit, uproot and replant roses, or prune branches from her taller bushes or trees—until night came and it was too dark to see.

42   Whatever she planted grew as if by magic, and her fame as a grower of flowers spread over three counties. Because of her creativity with her flowers, even my memories of poverty are seen through a screen of blooms—sunflowers, petunias, roses, dahlias, forsythia, spirea, delphiniums, verbena . . . and on and on.

43   And I remember people coming to my mother's yard to be given cuttings from her flowers; I hear again the praise showered on her because whatever rocky soil she landed on, she turned into a garden. A garden so brilliant with colors, so original in its design, so magnificent with life and creativity, that to this day people drive by our house in Georgia—perfect strangers and imperfect strangers—and ask to stand or walk among my mother's art.

44   I notice that it is only when my mother is working in her flowers that she is radiant, almost to the point of being invisible except as Creator: hand and eye. She is involved in work her soul must have. Ordering the universe in the image of her personal conception of Beauty.

45   Her face, as she prepares the Art that is her gift, is a legacy of respect she leaves to me, for all that illuminates and cherishes life. She had handed down respect for the possibilities—and the will to grasp them.

46   For her, so hindered and intruded upon in so many ways, being an artist has still been a daily part of her life. This ability to hold on, even in very simple ways, is work Black women have done for a very long time.

47   This poem is not enough, but it is something, for woman who literally covered the holes in our walls with sunflowers:

They were women then
My mama's generation
Husky of voice—Stout of Step
With fists as well as
Hands
How they battered down
Doors
And ironed

Starched white
Shirts
How they led
Armies
Headragged Generals
Across mined
Fields
Booby-trapped
Ditches
To discover books
Desks
A place for us
How they knew what we
Must know
Without knowing a page
Of it
Themselves.

48   Guided by my heritage of a love of beauty and a respect for strength—
in search of my mother's garden, I found my own.

49   And perhaps in Africa over 200 years ago, there was just such a mother;
perhaps she painted vivid and daring decorations in oranges and yellows
and greens on the walls of her hut; perhaps she sang in a voice like Roberta
Flack's—sweetly over the compounds of her village; perhaps she wove the
most stunning mats or told the most ingenious stories of all the village storytellers. Perhaps she was herself a poet—though only her daughter's name
is signed to the poems that we know.

50   Perhaps Phillis Wheatley's mother was also an artist.

51   Perhaps in more than Phillis Wheatley's biological life is her mother's
signature made clear.

Questions for Engagement, Response, and Analysis

1. Explain Walker's claim that "spirituality . . . is the basis of art."

2. What did Southern black women have to endure during the years
   Walker describes? Why were they sometimes referred to as "the mule
   of the world"?

3. List the creative outlets these women found when creativity requiring
   language skills was thwarted.

4. What is the theme of this essay?

THE WAY FORWARD IS WITH A BROKEN HEART   (2000)

TO THE HUSBAND OF MY YOUTH

1   It is the sixteenth of July 1999. John Kennedy Jr.'s body has been found
in waters off the coast of Martha's Vineyard. They say he "hit a square"
while flying his small aircraft; a situation in which it is impossible to tell

up from down or earth from sky and that he lost his way. I've never heard this description before, and I don't immediately believe this is what happened to him; I am more inclined to think "sabotage" or "preemptive assassination," but I like it immensely. Instantly I think of all the "squares" I have hit. I think of you, from whom there is no word. No response to my call expressing concern for you after your mother's recent death.

2   Thinking of your mother, who never had the faintest notion what to make of me, non-Jewish, non-repentant, I know it is time to lay the past to rest. I say that, but am stunned to feel the absence, not of your mother, whom I rarely saw, but of a young man I never knew. Someone I never thought that much about. Saw only fleetingly on television or in the news, though his image was, apparently, everywhere, selling television, selling news. It's not that I wasn't aware of him; I just never pried into his life. The look I remembered came from thirty-five years ago when he was wearing snowsuits. The little face behind the smart military salute as his father's coffin rolled by. I look at his picture now and see someone who looks, above all, *decent*. A young man with good eyes and an open, honest face. Someone who barely noticed his own press.

3   I wonder how you are feeling about this? Did you gaze, as I did, at the faces of the three who died, trying to see if they had, before death, succeeded in finding the secret of life? To live it boldly, fully, without stinginess to the self? To find love and hold on to it until it walks away? To know that today is all we have, and maybe only a fraction of today? And that living life to the hilt is the best praise of it?

4   We have seen so many deaths! Our battered, trying to do our best with the mess we were left, generation. By now, not unlike the Kennedys, I imagine we are almost at the point of viewing the relentless approach of the Grim Reaper among those we love, coming ever closer to ourselves, as farce. We've wept so much. Up begins to rise in us something of the absurd.

5   I certainly feel this. I also feel, as someone I know has said, that these are the losses that mature us. They are also the losses that make us old. Did any of us expect to outlive the boy we called, as we assumed his family did, "John-John"? Many of us never expected to outlive his father or his uncle or his cousins. It feels "old" that we have. Remember how Bobby Kennedy came to Mississippi to find out for himself that black children were starving? And that he cried? And that he too, dying, was young?

6   We are no longer young, Stranger who was the husband of my youth. It is as elders that we are left behind by the young who are everywhere dying ahead of us, whether from starvation, war, assassination, or hitting "squares," of all forms. My heart aches for them.

7   We are not even the only ones not speaking to each other. Across America elders are not speaking to each other, though most of us will find we have a lot to say, after we've cried in each other's arms. We are a frightened, a brokenhearted nation; some of us wanting desperately to run back to the illusory "safety" of skin color, money or the nineteen fifties. We've never seen weather like the weather there is today. We've never seen

violence like the violence we see today. We've never seen greed or evil like the greed and evil we see today. We've never seen tomatoes either, like the ones being created today. There is much from which to recoil.

8   And yet, Stranger who perhaps I am never to know, the past doesn't exist. It cannot be sanctuary. Skin color has always been a tricky solace, more so now that the ozone has changed. After Nature is destroyed, money will remain inedible. We have reached a place of deepest emptiness and sorrow. We look at the destruction around us and perceive our collective poverty. We see that everything that is truly needed by the world is too large for individuals to give. We find we have only ourselves. Our experience. Our dreams. Our simple art. Our memories of better ways. Our knowledge that the world cannot be healed in the abstract. That healing begins where the wound was made.

9   Now it seems to me we might begin to understand something of the meaning of earnest speaking and fearless listening; something of the purpose of the most ancient form of beginning to remake the world: remembering what the world we once made together was like.

10   I send you my sorrow. And my art.

11   In the sure knowledge that our people, the American race, lovers who falter and sometimes fail, are good.

Questions for Engagement, Response, and Analysis

1. To whom does Alice Walker address this epilogue to *The Way Forward Is with a Broken Heart?* Why does she call him a stranger? Why did she choose this particular day to write the epilogue?

2. What does it mean to "hit a square" in aviation terms? In what way does Walker perceive hitting a square as a metaphor for certain times in life?

3. What is the tone of this essay? How is it created?

4. What is the theme?

5. In your Reader's Journal, freewrite about one or more times in your life that you "hit a square."

ALICE WALKER

DONNA HAISTY WINCHELL

1   In Walker's earlier collection, *In Love and Trouble*, one of the few women who exhibit spiritual health is the narrator of "Everyday Use," perhaps the most often anthologized of all Walker's short stories. The story seems oddly out of place in a volume about the suffering caused by misplaced loyalty to black men, because Mrs. Johnson manages quite well without a man and seems more at peace with herself than the vast majority of early Walker women. Yet Mrs. Johnson exists in the story as a foil for her daughter Dee, who, like other women in *In Love and Trouble*, suffers from misplaced loyalties or, perhaps more accurately in her

case, misplaced priorities, although Dee remains blind to the falsity and shallowness of the life she lives as a modern young black woman.

2 Dee makes the mistake of believing that one's heritage is something that one puts on display if and when such a display is fashionable. The very name that she prefers, Wangero Leewanika Kemanjo, is one "put on" to replace the one passed down to her through generations of Johnson women. Dee has taken on a fashionable African name, fashionable African clothing and hairstyles, a fashionable Muslim boyfriend, and a fashionable desire to show off the primitive lifestyle of those whose name she rejects. When Dee comes home to visit her mother and her sister Maggie, she takes photographs of them, being careful to capture in the background her mother's three-room house with no real windows but rather with jagged holes cut in the sides and covered with shutters secured only with rawhide. Dee and her boyfriend exchange knowing glances that reveal that they perceive Dee's mother as a quaint yet entertaining artifact.

3 Dee wants to take home with her some bits and pieces of her heritage. She wants the churn top to make into a centerpiece for her alcove table and the dasher for "something artistic." She never stops to consider that these pieces of "art" are also useful. They are valuable to Dee because they are old and vaguely connected with members of her family now dead and gone. When Maggie quietly speaks up to explain the family history behind the churn, it is clear that, for her, heritage is more than art. Maggie, badly burned in the fire that claimed the Johnsons' previous house, has never gone out into the world as Dee has, but she lives her heritage every day. Even a churn handle, priceless because it bears the handprints of generations of Johnsons, can still be used to make butter. Such simple arts are the stuff of Maggie's daily life.

4 If Walker's portrayal of Dee draws her story into line with the others in *In Love and Trouble* because of her easy vulnerability to the fad of the moment, which gives a false and shallow picture of who she is, both as a black woman and as a member of the Johnson family, her mother is more at home with the women of *You Can't Keep a Good Woman Down*. In both size and spirit she is linked most directly with Gracie Mae Still, the main character of "Nineteen Fifty-Five," which opens the later volume.

5 Mrs. Johnson is Walker's introduction to the type of androgynous figure that in *The Color Purple* strikes a successful balance between male and female. In spite of her dream of appearing svelte and smooth talking on a late night talk show, Mrs. Johnson accepts the reality of her existence, and her pride in her strength comes through in her description of herself:

> In real life I am a large, big-boned woman with rough, man-working hands. In the winter I wear flannel nightgowns to bed and overalls during the day. I can kill and clean a hog as mercilessly as a man. My fat keeps me hot in zero weather. I can work outside all day, breaking ice to get water for washing; I can eat pork liver cooked over the open fire minutes after it comes steaming from the hog. One winter I knocked a bull calf straight in the brain between the eyes with a sledge hammer and had the meat hung up to chill before nightfall. But of course all this does not show on television. (*Trouble*, 48)

6   Although Dee finds her mother and sister woefully backward and ignorant, the knowledge of the outside world Dee tries to force on them is
knowledge they probably do not need. Mrs. Johnson can take an objective look at who and what she is and find not disillusionment but an easy
satisfaction. Simple pleasures—a dip of snuff, a cooling breeze across a
clean swept yard, church songs, the soothing movements of milk cows—
are enough. In her dreams she may be someone else, but she realizes that
phantom self for the fantasy that it is.

7   Gracie Mae Still shares with Mrs. Johnson a sense of health and wholeness; with Gracie Mae, it is the health and wholeness that come with
being an artist whose works are outpourings of honest emotion. In a 1981
interview with Kay Bonetti, Walker discussed her envy of musicians, who
"can put so much of themselves into what they sing. There's nothing
between what they feel and what they say, if it's really good, and I like
that . . . because it means a type of freedom for them."

8   Gracie Mae has written songs that have been the envy of such greats
as Bessie Smith, but her music is successful only when Traynor, a young
man described in terms that make him sound suspiciously like Elvis Presley, records one of her songs. Walker leaves it up to her readers to draw
any parallels between Elvis and Traynor, preferring to view Traynor as a
more general symbol of white exploitation of black music. Traynor is a
pitiable character, however, because he cannot understand the songs that
he sings. He is trying to sing something that he lacks the experience to
sing or to interpret. He says of Gracie Mae's song:

> I done sung that song seem like a million times this year. . . . I sung it on
> the Grand Ole Opry, I sung it on the Ed Sullivan show. I sung it on Mike
> Douglas, I sung it at the Cotton Bowl, the Orange Bowl. I sung it at Festi-
> vals. I sung it at Fairs. I sung it overseas in Rome, Italy, and once in a sub-
> marine *underseas*. I've sung it and sung it, and I'm making forty thousand
> dollars a day offa it, and you know what, I don't have the faintest notion
> what that song means. (*GW*, 8)

9   In "Everyday Use" art, when it is more than simply a fad, is inextricably bound up with life. Traynor is a commerical success as an artist, the
latest fad on the rock-and-roll scene, yet he is a spiritual failure because
for him the link between art and life is never forged. Traynor has no more
understanding of life than he has of the songs he is famous for. He tells
Gracie Mae, "I married but it never went like it was supposed to. I never
could squeeze any of my own life either into it or out of it. It was like
singing somebody else's record. I copied the way it was sposed to be
exactly but I never had a clue what marriage meant" (*GW*, 13). His lack
of understanding reaches its broadest implications when Gracie Mae
dreams that Traynor has just split up with his fifteenth wife and he says,
"*You meet 'em for no reason. You date 'em for no reason. I do it all but
I swear it's just like somebody else doing it. I feel like I can't remember
Life*" (*GW*, 19): Of his own music, he writes to Gracie Mae, "*I've been
thinking about writing some songs of my own but every time I finish one*

*it don't seem to be about nothing I've actually lived myself. . . . Every-
body still loves that song of yours. They ask me all the time what do I
think it means, really. I mean, they want to know just what I want to
know. Where out of your life did it come from?" (GW*, 11).

10   Gracie Mae achieved her understanding of both art and life by way of
suffering. Her audience may have been small compared to Traynor's, but
as she explains to him, "It would have been worth my life to try to sing
'em somebody else's stuff that I didn't know nothing about" and
"Couldn't be nothing worse than being famous the world over for something you don't even understand" (*GW*, 17, 14). The aging Gracie Mae
knows even more about life than did the young one. She knows that
much of what she wrote early was a bluff, but she explains, "The trick
is to live long enough to put your young bluffs to use. Now if I was to
sing that song today I'd tear it up. 'Cause I done lived long enough to
know it's true. Them words could hold me up." Traynor responds, "I ain't
lived that long" (*GW*, 14).

11   Walker contends that white America has not lived long enough either.
In her interview with Bonetti, Walker says, "Whites are going to have to
go through a whole lot to be able to sing, but that's what singing is, I
think—having to go through a lot, understand a lot, and suffer a lot." Art,
on the other hand, helps some fortunate individuals through the suffering: "One of the functions of art really is to help you grow, to help you
become whole, and to help you become a better person, and if it doesn't
do that, I think you should plant peanuts or something" (Bonetti).
Traynor might have been happier planting peanuts. Through her music,
though, Gracie Mae has found a type of freedom that all of Traynor's fame
and money cannot buy. Part of her freedom is the freedom to be her content if overweight self. She occasionally diets, but at one point she concludes, "I'll never seen three hundred pounds again. . . . I got to thinking
about it one day an' I thought: aside from the fact that they say it's
unhealthy, my fat ain't never been no trouble. Mens always have loved
me. My kids ain't never complained. Plus they's fat. And fat like I is I looks
distinguished. You see me coming and know somebody's *there*" (*GW*, 12).
Gracie Mae may be unhealthy physically because of her fat, but she is
spiritually as healthy and whole as they come.

PATCHES: QUILTS AND COMMUNITY IN ALICE WALKER'S "EVERYDAY USE"

HOUSTON A. BAKER JR., AND CHARLOTTE PIERCE-BAKER

*During the Depression and really hard time, people often
paid their debts with quilts, and sometimes their tithe to
the church too.*

—THE QUILTERS

1   A patch is a fragment. It is a vestige of wholeness that stands as a sign of loss and a challenge to creative design. As remainder or remnant, the patch may symbolize rupture and impoverishment; it may be defined by the faded glory of the already gone. But as a fragment, it is also rife with explosive potential of the yet-to-be-discovered. Like woman, it is a liminal element between wholes.

2   Weaving, shaping, sculpting, or quilting in order to create a kaleidoscopic and momentary array is tantamount to providing an improvisational response to chaos. Such activity represents a nonce response to ceaseless scattering; it constitutes survival strategy and motion in the face of dispersal. A patchwork quilt, laboriously and affectionately crafted from bits of worn overalls, shredded uniforms, tattered petticoats, and outgrown dresses stands as a signal instance of a patterned wholeness in the African diaspora.

3   Traditional African cultures were scattered by the European slave trade throughout the commercial time and space of the New World. The transmutation of quilting, a European, feminine tradition, into a black women's folk art, represents an innovative fusion of African cloth manufacture, piecing, and appliqué with awesome New World experiences—and expediencies. The product that resulted was, in many ways, a double patch. The hands that pieced the master's rigidly patterned quilts by day were often the hands that crafted a more functional design in slave cabins by night. The quilts of Afro-America offer a *sui generis* context (a weaving together) of experiences and a storied, vernacular representation of lives conducted in the margins, ever beyond an easy and acceptable wholeness. In many ways, the quilts of Afro-America resemble the work of all those dismembered gods who transmute fragments and remainders into the light and breath of a new creation. And the sorority of quiltmakers, fragment weavers, holy patchers, possesses a sacred wisdom that it hands down from generation to generation of those who refuse the center for the ludic and unconfined spaces of the margins.

4   Those positioned outside the sorority and enamored of wholeness often fail to comprehend the dignity inherent in the quiltmakers' employment of remnants and conversion of fragments into items of everyday use. Just as the mysteries of, say, the blues remain hidden from those in happy circumstances, so the semantic intricacies of quiltmaking remain incomprehensible to the individualistic sensibility invested in myths of a postindustrial society. All of the dark, southern energy that manifests itself in the conversion of a sagging cabin—a shack really—into a "happy home" by stringing a broom wire between two nails in the wall and making the joint jump, or that shows itself in the "crazy quilt" patched from crumbs and remainders, seems but a vestige of outmoded and best-forgotten customs.

5   To relinquish such energy, however, is to lose an enduring resourcefulness that has ensured a distinctive aesthetic tradition and a unique code of everyday, improvisational use in America. The tradition-bearers of the type of Afro-American energy we have in mind have always

included ample numbers of southern, black women who have transmuted fragments of New World displacement into a quilted eloquence
scarcely appreciated by traditional spokespersons for wholeness . . . .

6   Southern black women have not only produced quilts of stunning
beauty, they have also crafted books of monumental significance, works
that have made them appropriately famous. In fact, it has been precisely
the appropriation of energy drawn from sagging cabins and stitched
remainders that has constituted the world of the quiltmakers' sorority.
The energy has flowed through such women as Harriet Brent Jacobs,
Zora Neale Hurston, and Margaret Walker, enabling them to continue an
ancestral line elegantly shared by Alice Walker.

7   In a brilliant essay entitled "Alice Walker: The Black Woman Artist as
Wayward," Professor Barbara Christian writes: "Walker is drawn to the
integral and economical process of quilt making as a model for her own
craft. For through it, one can create out of seemingly disparate everyday
materials patterns of clarity, imagination, and beauty." Professor Christian goes on to discuss Walker's frequently cited "In Search of Our Mothers' Gardens" and her short story "Everyday Use." She convincingly
argues that Walker employs quilts as signs of functional beauty and spiritual heritage that provide exemplars of challenging convention and radical individuality, or "artistic waywardness."

8   The patchwork quilt as a trope for understanding black women's creativity in the United States, however, presents an array of interpretive
possibilities that is not exhausted by Professor Christian's adept criticism
of Walker. For example, if one takes a different tack and suggests that
the quilt as metaphor presents not a stubborn contrariness, a wayward
individuality, but a communal bonding that confounds traditional definitions of art and of the artist, then one plays on possibilities in the quilting trope rather different from those explored by Christian. What we
want to suggest in our own adaptation of the trope is that it opens a fascinating interpretive window on vernacular dimensions of lived, creative
experience in the United States. Quilts, in their patched and many-
colored glory offer not a counter to tradition, but, in fact, an instance of
the only legitimate tradition of "the people" that exists. They are repre-
sentations of the stories of the vernacular natives who make up the
ninety-nine percent of the American population unendowed with money
and control. The class distinction suggested by "vernacular" should not
overshadow the gender specificity of quilts as products of a universal
woman's creativity—what Pattie Chase in *The Contemporary Quilt* calls
"an ancient affinity between women and cloth." They are the testimony
of "mute and inglorious" generations of women gone before. The quilt as
interpretive sign opens up a world of *difference*, a nonscripted territory
whose creativity with fragments is less a matter of "artistic" choice than
of economic and functional necessity. "So much in the habit of sewing
something," says Walker's protagonist in the remarkable novel *The Color
Purple*, "[that] I stitch up a bunch of scraps, try to see what I can make."

9   The Johnson women, who populate the generations represented in Walker's short story "Everyday Use," are inhabitants of southern cabins who have always worked with "scraps" and seen what they could make of them. The result of their labor has been a succession of mothers and daughters surviving the ignominies of Jim Crow life and passing on ancestral blessings to descendants. The guardians of the Johnson homestead when the story commences are the mother—"a large, big-boned woman with rough, man-working hands"—and her daughter Maggie, who has remained with her "chin on chest, eyes on ground, feet in shuffle, ever since the fire that burned the other house to the ground" ten or twelve years ago. The mood at the story's beginning is one of ritualistic "waiting": "I will wait for her in the yard that Maggie and I made so clean and wavy yesterday afternoon." The subject awaited is the other daughter, Dee. Not only has the yard (as ritual ground) been prepared for the arrival of a goddess, but the sensibilities and costumes of Maggie and her mother have been appropriately attuned for the occasion. The mother daydreams of television shows where parents and children are suddenly—and pleasantly—reunited, banal shows where chatty hosts oversee tearful reunions. In her fantasy, she weighs a hundred pounds less, is several shades brighter in complexion, and possesses a devastatingly quick tongue. She returns abruptly to real life meditation, reflecting on her own heroic, agrarian accomplishments in slaughtering hogs and cattle and preparing their meat for winter nourishment. She is a robust provider who has gone to the people of her church and raised money to send her light-complexioned, lithe-figured, and ever-dissatisfied daughter Dee to college. Today, as she waits in the purified yard, she notes the stark differences between Maggie and Dee and recalls how the "last dingy gray board of the house [fell] in toward the red-hot brick chimney" when her former domicile burned. Maggie was scarred horribly by the fire, but Dee, who had hated the house with an intense fury, stood "off under the sweet gum tree . . . a look of concentration on her face." A scarred and dull Maggie, who has been kept at home and confined to everyday offices, has but one reaction to the fiery and vivacious arrival of her sister: "I hear Maggie suck in her breath. 'Uhnnnh,' is what it sounds like. Like when you see the wriggling end of a snake just in front of your foot on the road. 'Uhnnnh.' "

10   Indeed, the question raised by Dee's energetic arrival is whether there are words adequate to her flair, her brightness, her intense colorfulness of style which veritably blocks the sun. She wears "a dress so loud it hurts my eyes. There are yellows and oranges enough to throw back the light of the sun. I feel my whole face warming from the heat waves it throws out." Dee is both serpent and fire introduced with bursting esprit into the calm pasture that contains the Johnsons' tin-roofed, three-room, windowless shack and grazing cows. She has joined the radical, black nationalists of the 1960s and 1970s, changing her name from Dee to Wangero and cultivating a suddenly fashionable, or stylish, interest in what she

passionately describes as her "heritage." If there is one quality that Dee (Wangero) possesses in abundance, it is "style": "At sixteen she had a style of her own: and knew what style was."

11   But in her stylishness, Dee is not an example of the indigenous rapping and styling out of Afro-America. Rather, she is manipulated by the style-makers, the fashion designers whose semiotics the French writer Roland Barthes has so aptly characterized. "Style" for Dee is the latest vogue—the most recent fantasy perpetuated by American media. When she left for college, her mother had tried to give her a quilt whose making began with her grandmother Dee, but the bright daughter felt such patched coverings were "old-fashioned and out of style." She has returned at the commencement of "Everyday Use," however, as one who now purports to know the value of the work of black women as holy patchers.

12   The dramatic conflict of the story surrounds the definition of holiness. The ritual purification of earth and expectant atmosphere akin to that of Beckett's famous drama ("I will wait for her in the yard that Maggie and I made so clean and wavy yesterday afternoon.") prepare us for the narrator's epiphanic experience at the story's conclusion.

13   Near the end of "Everyday Use," the mother (who is the tale's narrator) realizes that Dee (a.k.a, Wangero) is a *fantasy* child, a perpetrator and victim of: "words, lies, other folks's habits." The energetic daughter is as frivolously careless of other peoples' lives as the fiery conflagration that she had watched ten years previously. Assured by the makers of American fashion that "black" is currently "beautiful," she has conformed her own "style" to that notion. Hers is a trendy "blackness" cultivated as "art" and costume. She wears "a dress down to the ground . . . bracelets dangling and making noises when she moves her arm up to shake the folds of the dress out of her armpits." And she says of quilts she has removed from a trunk at the foot of her mother's bed: "Maggie can't appreciate these quilts! She'd probably be backward enough to put them to everyday use." "Art" is, thus, juxtaposed with "everyday use" in Walker's short story, and the fire goddess Dee, who has achieved literacy only to burn "us with a lot of knowledge we didn't necessarily need to know," is revealed as a perpetuator of institutional theories of aesthetics. (Such theories hold that "art" is, in fact, defined by social institutions such as museums, book reviews, and art dealers.) Of the two quilts that she has extracted from the trunk, she exclaims: "But they're 'priceless.'" And so the quilts are by "fashionable" standards of artistic value, standards that motivate the answer that Dee provides to her mother's question: "'Well,' I said, stumped. 'What would *you* do with them?'" Dee's answer: "Hang them." The stylish daughter's entire life has been one of "framed" experience; she has always sought a fashionably "aesthetic" distance from southern expediencies. (And how unlike quilt frames that signal social activity and a coming to completeness are her *frames*.) Her concentrated detachment from the fire, which so nearly symbolizes her

role vis-à-vis the Afro-American community (her black friends "worshipped . . . the scalding humor that erupted like bubbles in lye") is characteristic of her attitude. Her goals include the appropriation of exactly what *she* needs to remain fashionable in the eyes of a world of pretended wholeness, a world of banal television shows, framed and institutionalized art, and polaroid cameras—devices that instantly process and record experience as "framed" photograph. Ultimately, the framed polaroid photograph represents the limits of Dee's vision.

14   Strikingly, the quilts whose *tops* have been stitched by her grandmother from fragments of outgrown family garments and quilted after the grandmother's death by Aunt Dee and her sister (the mother who narrates the story) are perceived in Dee's polaroid sensibility as merely "priceless" works of an institutionally, or stylishly, defined "art world." In a reversal of perception tantamount to the acquisition of sacred knowledge by initiates in a rite of passage, the mother/narrator realizes that she has always worshipped at the altars of a "false" goddess. As her alter ego, Dee has always expressed that longing for the "other" that characterizes inhabitants of oppressed, "minority" cultures. Situated in an indisputably black and big-boned skin, the mother has secretly admired the "good hair," full figure, and well-turned (i.e., "whitely trim") ankle of Dee (Wangero). Sacrifices and sanctity have seemed in order. But in her epiphanic moment of recognition, she perceives the fire-scarred Maggie—the stay-at-home victim of southern scarifications—in a revised light. When Dee grows belligerent about possessing the quilts, Maggie emerges from the kitchen and says with a contemptuous gesture of dismissal: "She can have them, Mama. . . . I can 'member Grandma Dee without quilts." The mother's response to what she wrongly interprets as Maggie's hang-dog resignation before Dee is a radical awakening to godhead:

> When I looked at her . . . something hit me in the top of my head and ran down to the soles of my feet. Just like when I'm in church and the spirit of God touches me and I get happy and shout. I did something I never had done before: hugged Maggie to me, then dragged her into the room, snatched the quilts out of Miss Wangero's hands and dumped them into Maggie's lap.

15   Maggie is the arisen goddess of Walker's story; she is the sacred figure who bears the scarifications of experience and knows how to convert patches into robustly patterned and beautifully quilted wholes. As an earth-rooted and quotidian goddess, she stands in dramatic contrast to the stylishly fiery and other-oriented Wangero. The mother says in response to Dee's earlier cited accusation that Maggie would reduce quilts to rags by putting them to everyday use: "'She can always make some more,' I said. 'Maggie knows how to quilt.'" And, indeed, Maggie, the emergent goddess of New World improvisation and long ancestral memory, does know how to quilt. Her mind and imagination are capable of preserving the wisdom of grandmothers and aunts without material prompts:

"I can 'member . . . without the quilts," she says. The secret to employing beautiful quilts as items of everyday use is the secret of crafty dues.

16   In order to comprehend the transient nature of all wholes, one must first become accustomed to living and working with fragments. Maggie has learned the craft of fragment weaving from her women ancestors: "It was Grandma Dee and Big Dee who taught her how to quilt herself." The conjunction of "quilt" and "self" in Walker's syntax may be simply a serendipitous accident of style. Nonetheless, the conjunction works magnificently to capture the force of black woman's quilting in "Everyday Use." Finally, it is the "self," or a version of humanness that one calls the Afro-American self, that must, in fact, be crafted from fragments on the basis of wisdom gained from preceding generations.

17   What is at stake in the world of Walker's short story, then, is not the prerogatives of Afro-American women as "wayward artists." Individualism and a flouting of convention in order to achieve "artistic" success constitute acts of treachery in "Everyday Use." For Dee, if she is anything, *is* a fashionable denizen of America's art/fantasy world. She is removed from the "everyday uses" of a black community that she scorns, misunderstands, burns. Certainly, she is "unconventionally" black. As such, however, she is an object of holy contempt from the archetypal weaver of black wholeness from tattered fragments. Maggie's "Uhnnnh" and her mother's designation "Miss Wangero" are gestures of utter contempt. Dee's sellout to fashion and fantasy in a television-manipulated world of "artistic" frames is a representation of the *complicity of the clerks.* Not "art," then, but use or function is the signal in Walker's fiction of sacred creation.

18   Quilts designed for everyday use, pieced wholes defying symmetry and pattern, are signs of the scarred generations of women who have always been alien to a world of literate words and stylish fantasies. The crafted fabric of Walker's story is the very weave of blues and jazz traditions in the Afro-American community, daringly improvisational modes that confront breaks in the continuity of melody (or theme) by riffing. The asymmetrical quilts of southern black women are like the off-centered stomping of the jazz solo or the innovative musical showmanship of the blues interlude. They speak a world in which the deceptively shuffling Maggie is capable of a quick change into goddess, an unlikely holy figure whose dues are paid in full. Dee's anger at her mother is occasioned principally by the mother's insistence that paid dues make Maggie a more likely bearer of sacredness, tradition, and true value than the "brighter" sister. "You just don't understand," she says to her mother. Her assessment is surely correct where institutional theories and systems of "art" are concerned. The mother's cognition contains no categories for framed art. The mother works according to an entirely different scale of use and value, finally assigning proper weight to the virtues of Maggie and to the ancestral importance of the pieced quilts that she has kept out of use for so many years. Smarting, perhaps, from Dee's designation of the quilts as "old-fashioned," the mother has buried the covers away in a trunk. At the

end of Walker's story, however, she has become aware of her own mistaken value judgments, and she pays homage that is due to Maggie. The unlikely daughter is a *griot* of the vernacular who remembers actors and events in a distinctively black "historical" drama.

19   Before Dee departs, she "put on some sunglasses that hid everything above the tip of her nose and her chin." Maggie smiles at the crude symbolism implicit in this act, for she has always known that her sister saw "through a glass darkly." But it is the mother's conferral of an ancestral blessing (signaled by her deposit of the quilts in Maggie's lap) that constitutes the occasion for the daughter's first "real smile." Maggie knows that it is only communal recognition by elders of the tribe that confers ancestral privileges on succeeding generations. The mother's holy recognition of the scarred daughter's sacred status as quilter is the best gift of a hard-pressed womankind to the fragmented goddess of the present.

20   At the conclusion of "Everyday Use," which is surely a fitting precursor to *The Color Purple*, with its sewing protagonist and its scenes of sisterly quilting, Maggie and her mother relax in the ritual yard after the dust of Dee's departing car has settled. They dip snuff in the manner of African confreres sharing cola nuts. The moment is past when a putatively "new" generation has confronted scenes of black, everyday life. A change has taken place, but it is a change best described by Amiri Baraka's designation for Afro-American music's various styles and discontinuities. The change in Walker's story is the "changing same." What has been reaffirmed at the story's conclusion is the value of the quiltmaker's motion and strategy in the precincts of a continuously undemocratic South.

21   But the larger appeal of "Everyday Use" is its privileging of a distinctively woman's craft as *the* signal mode of confronting chaos through a skillful blending of patches. In *The Color Purple*, Celie's skill as a fabric worker completely transmutes the order of Afro-American existence. Not only do her talents with a needle enable her to wear the pants in the family, they also allow her to become the maker of pants par excellence. Hence, she becomes a kind of unifying goddess of patch and stitch, an instructress of mankind who bestows the gift of consolidating fragments. Her abusive husband Albert says: "When I was growing up . . . I use to try to sew along with mama cause that's what she was always doing. But everybody laughed at me. But you know, I liked it." "Well," says Celie, "nobody gon laugh at you now . . . . Here, help me stitch in these pockets."

22   A formerly "patched" separateness of woman is transformed through fabric craft into a new unity. Quilting, sewing, stitching are bonding activities that begin with the godlike authority and daring of women, but that are given (as a gift toward community) to men. The old disparities are transmuted into a vision best captured by the scene that Shug suggests to Celie: "But, Celie, try to imagine a city full of these shining, blueblack people wearing brilliant blue robes with designs like fancy quilt patterns." The heavenly city of quilted design is a form of unity wrested by the sheer force of the woman quiltmaker's will from chaos. As a community, it stands as both a sign of the potential effects of black women's creativity in America,

and as an emblem of the effectiveness of women's skillful confrontation of patches. Walker's achievement as a southern, black, woman novelist is her own successful application of the holy patching that was a staple of her grandmother's and great-grandmother's hours of everyday ritual. "Everyday Use" is, not surprisingly, dedicated to "your grandmama": to those who began the line of converting patches into works of southern genius.

HERITAGE AND DERACINATION IN WALKER'S "EVERYDAY USE"

DAVID COWART

1   "Everyday Use," a story included in Alice Walker's 1973 collection *In Love and Trouble*, addresses itself to the dilemma of African Americans who, in striving to escape prejudice and poverty, risk a terrible deracination, a sundering from all that has sustained and defined them. The story concerns a young woman who, in the course of a visit to the rural home she thinks she has outgrown, attempts unsuccessfully to divert some fine old quilts, earmarked for the dowry of a sister, into her own hands. This character has changed her given name, "Dee Johnson," to the superficially more impressive "Wangero Leewanika Kemanjo"—and thereby created difficulties for the narrator (her mother), who recognizes the inappropriateness of the old name but cannot quite commit herself to the new. She tries to have it both ways, referring to her daughter now by one name, now by the other, now by parenthetically hybridized combinations of both. The critic, sharing Mrs. Johnson's confusion, may learn from her example to avoid awkwardness by calling the character more or less exclusively by one name. I have opted here for "Wangero"—without, I hope, missing the real significance of the confusion. Indeed, in this confusion one begins to see how the fashionable politics espoused by the central character of Walker's story becomes the foil to an authorial vision of the African American community, past and present, and its struggle for liberation.

2   Walker contrives to make the situation of Wangero, the visitor, analogous to the cultural position of the minority writer who, disinclined to express the fate of the oppressed in the language and literary structures of the oppressor, seeks a more authentic idiom and theme. Such a writer, Walker says, must not become a literary Wangero. Only by remaining in touch with a proximate history and an immediate cultural reality can one lay a claim to the quilts—or hope to produce the authentic art they represent. Self-chastened, Walker presents her own art—the piecing of linguistic and literary intertexts—as quilt-making with words, an art as imbued with the African American past as the literal quilt-making of the grandmother for whom Wangero was originally named.

3   The quilts that Wangero covets link her generation to prior generations, and thus they represent the larger African American past. The quilts contain scraps of dresses worn by the grandmother and even the great grandmother, as well as a piece of the uniform worn by the great grandfather

who served in the Union Army in the War Between the States. The visitor rightly recognizes the quilts as part of a fragile heritage, but she fails to see the extent to which she herself has traduced that heritage. Chief among the little gestures that collectively add up to a profound betrayal is the changing of her name. Mrs. Johnson thinks she could trace the name Dee in their family "back beyond the Civil War" (54), but Wangero persists in seeing the name as little more than the galling reminder that African Americans have been denied authentic names. "I couldn't bear it any longer, being named after the people who oppress me" (53). She now styles and dresses herself according to the dictates of a faddish Africanism and thereby demonstrates a cultural Catch-22: an American who attempts to become an African succeeds only in becoming a phony. In her name, her clothes, her hair, her sunglasses, her patronizing speech, and her black Muslim companion, Wangero proclaims a deplorable degree of alienation from her rural origins and family. The story's irony is not subtle: the visitor who reproaches others for an ignorance of their own heritage (a word that probably does not figure in the lexicon of either her mother or her sister) is herself almost completely disconnected from a nurturing tradition.

4   Wangero has realized the dream of the oppressed: she has escaped the ghetto. Why, then, is she accorded so little maternal or authorial respect? The reason lies in her progressive repudiation of the very heritage she claims to revere. I say progressive because Walker makes clear that Wangero's flirtation with Africa is only the latest in a series of attempts to achieve racial and cultural autonomy, attempts that prove misguided insofar as they promote an erosion of all that is most real—and valuable—in African American experience. Wangero's mental traveling, moreover, replicates that of an entire generation. Her choices follow the trends in African American cultural definition from the simple integrationist imperative that followed *Brown v. Board of Education* (1954) to the collective outrage of the "long hot summer" of 1967 and the rise of an Islamic alternative to the Christianity that black America had hitherto embraced . . . In 1964, Walker herself traveled to Africa, and one imagines her character Wangero among the enthusiastic readers of the enormously popular *Roots* (1976), in which Alex Haley memorably describes the researches that eventually led him to the African village from which his ancestor, Kunta Kinte, had been abducted by slavers.

5   In other words, the Africa-smitten Wangero one meets in the opening pages of the story is a precipitate of the cultural struggles of a generation—struggles adumbrated in the stages of this character's education. She had left home to attend school in Augusta, where apparently she immersed herself in the liberating culture she would first urge on her bewildered mother and sister, then denounce as oppressive. Now, with her black Muslim boyfriend or husband in tow (her mother hears his name as "Hakim-a-barber"), she has progressed to an idea of nationality radically at odds with all that has hitherto defined the racial identity of African Americans.

6   Though Walker depicts "Hakim-a-barber" as something of a fool, a person who has embraced a culture as alien as anything imposed on black people by white America, her quarrel is not with Islam, for she hints

(through the perceptions of Wangero's mother) that a nearby Muslim commune is an admirable, even heroic, institution. But the neighboring Muslims have immersed themselves in agrarian practicality. They are unlikely to view relics of the rural life as collectors' items. Their sense of purpose, their identity, seems to contain no element of pose. Wangero and her companion, on the other hand, are all pose.

7   Wangero despises her sister, her mother, and the church that helped to educate her. Her quest is ultimately selfish, and Walker focuses the reader's growing dislike for the heroine in her indifference to Maggie, the pathetic sister she seems prepared to ignore in a kind of moral triage. Maggie represents the multitude of black women who must suffer while the occasional lucky "sister" escapes the ghetto. Scarred, graceless, "not bright" (50), and uneducated, Maggie is a living reproach to a survivor like her sister. Maggie is the aggregate underclass that has been left behind as a handful of Wangeros achieve their independence—an underclass scarred in the collective disasters Walker symbolizes neatly in the burning of the original Johnson home. Wangero had welcomed that conflagration. Her mother remembers the "look of concentration on her face as she watched the last dingy gray board of the house fall in toward the red-hot brick chimney. Why don't you do a dance around the ashes? I'd wanted to ask her. She had hated the house that much" (49–50). Wangero did not set the fire, but she delighted in its obliteration of the house that represented everything she sought to escape. When, predictably, the house reappears as before, she may have understood that fire alone cannot abolish a ghetto. This burned house, however, represents more than a failed attempt to eradicate poverty. It subsumes a whole African American history of violence, from slavery (one thinks of Maggie's scars multiplied among the escaped or emancipated slaves in Morrison's *Beloved*) through the ghetto-torching riots of 1964, 1965, 1967, and 1968 ("Burn, Baby, Burn!") to the pervasive inner-city violence of subsequent decades. The fire, that is, is the African American past, a conflagration from which assorted survivors stumble forward, covered like Maggie with scars of the body or like Wangero with scars of the soul.

8   Assimilation, torching the ghetto, Islam, the Africanist vision—Walker treats these alternatives with respect, even as she satirizes her character's uncritical embracing of one after another of them. The author knows that each represents an attempt to restore a sense of identity terribly impaired by the wrongs visited on black people in the new world. Wangero, however, fails properly to appreciate the black community's transformation of these wrongs into moral capital. She does not see the integrity of African American cultural institutions that evolved as the creative and powerful response to the general oppression. In simpler terms, she is ashamed of a mother and a sister who, notwithstanding their humble circumstances, exemplify character bred in adversity.

9   "It all comes back to houses," Walker remarks in her essay on Flannery O'Connor (*In Search* 58). Freud associates houses with women, and this story of three women is also the story of three houses, one that burned, one that shelters two of the fire's survivors, and one, never directly

described, that is to be the repository of various articles of this family's past, its heritage. This last house, owned by and symbolic of Wangero, embodies also the cultural problem Walker seeks to address in her story. How, she asks, can one escape the margins without a catastrophic deracination? Is the freedom Wangero achieves somehow at odds with proper valuation of the immediate cultural matrix out of which she comes? Can she, like Dickens's Pip, embrace a grand heritage only by betraying the simpler heritage necessary to emotional and psychological wholeness?

10   Wangero claims to value heritage, and Walker is surely sympathetic to someone who seems to recognize, however clumsily, the need to preserve the often fragile artifacts of the African American past. But Walker exposes Wangero's preservationism as hopelessly selfish and misguided. Though the author elsewhere laments the paucity of photographs in the African American historical record (*Living by the Word* 63), she evinces little patience with Wangero's desire to photograph mother and cow in front of the house. Wangero's desire is to have a record of how far she has come. No doubt she will view as "quaint" these images of a rural past. She wants the photographs—and presently the churn lid, the dasher, and the quilts— for purposes of display, reminders that she no longer has to live in such a house, care for such a cow, have daily intercourse with such a mother and sister. She "makes the mistake," says Donna Haisty Winchell, "of believing that one's heritage is something that one puts on display if and when such a display is fashionable" (81). Wangero seems to think the African American past can be rescued only by being commodified. She wants to make the lid of the butter churn into a centerpiece for her table. She wants to hang quilts on the wall. She wants, in short, to do what white people do with the cunning and quaint implements and products of the past. Wangero fails to see the mote in her own eye when she reproaches her mother and her sister for a failure to value their heritage—she, who wants only to preserve that heritage as the negative index to her own sophistication.

11   One wonders if Wangero's house, unlike the houses of her childhood, will have a lawn. Doubtless she has never paused to think about the humble yard of her mother's house as anything more than another shabby badge of poverty. But like the more obviously significant quilts, this yard—a description of which opens the story—is another symbol of the cultural something produced out of nothing by people lacking everything:

> A yard like this is more comfortable than most people know. It is not just a yard. It is like an extended living room. When the hard clay is swept clean as a floor and the fine sand around the edges lined with tiny, irregular grooves, anyone can come and sit and look up into the elm tree and wait for the breezes that never come inside the house. (47)

12   A paragon of meaningful simplicity, this yard. The grooved borders even put one in mind of the artfully raked sand in a Japanese *hira-niwa* garden (indeed, the breezes sound like a plural visitation of *kamikaze*, the "divine wind"). In Japan, such a garden affords emotional balm and spiritual serenity to those who tend or contemplate it, and Walker implies

similar restorative properties in the uncluttered plainness of the narrator's yard. Mrs. Johnson mentions neither grass, nor shrubs, nor (surprisingly for Walker) flowers. In its stark vacuity the yard evokes the minimalist lives of poor people; yet the author describes that emptiness in terms suggestive of spiritual wealth.

13   If conversely Wangero is described in language evocative of spiritual poverty or confusion, the reader does not completely despise her, for even as it satirizes her pretensions, "Everyday Use" hints at an affinity between its author and its central character. "Walker's *writing*," says Marianne Hirsch, "constitutes a form of distance" (207) from the real-life mother and home on which she bases the story. The story can be read, in fact, as a cautionary tale the author tells herself: a parable, so to speak, about the perils of writing one's impoverished past from the vantage of one's privileged present. The deracination of Wangero, that is, can represent the fate of anyone who, like the author, goes from sharecropper's daughter to literary sophisticate. I refer here to an autobiographical dimension that proves interestingly unstable, for Walker's self-depiction as Wangero actually displaces an intended self-depiction as Maggie. That Walker would represent herself in the backward, disfigured Maggie strains credulity only if one forgets that the author was herself a disfigured child, an eye having been shot out with a B.B. gun. In a 1973 interview, moreover, Walker makes clear the autobiographical genesis of a poem ("For My Sister Molly Who in the Fifties" in *Revolutionary Petunias*) in which an ignorant and unglamorous girl discovers that her "brilliant" older sister, home for a visit, is ashamed of their uncouth family (*In Search* 269–70). "Everyday Use" is the prose version of that poem. . . .

14   Walker refuses, then, to write "protest literature," in which the shallow is passed off as the profoundest truth. She credits Tolstoy with showing her the practical wisdom of partaking in the socio-political process in order to delve into the essential nature of individual disposition. In "Everyday Use" Walker explores with great subtlety the demands—often conflicting—of ideology and art. She contemplates the culturally distorting pressures brought to bear on another kind of language, another vehicle whereby African American experience is embodied and transmitted. This other language—the quilts—exhibits a special integrity resembling that of the language in which the author writes her story. As this story engages the theme of heritage, it resolves the dilemma inherent in ideologically self-conscious art (how simultaneously to be politically engaged and free of a limiting topicality) by inviting a connection between writing and quilt-making, a connection between types of textuality that prove complementary.

15   "In contemporary writing," Elaine Showalter observes, "the quilt stands for a vanished past experience to which we have a troubled and ambivalent cultural relationship" (228). Certainly the quilts over which Wangero and her mother quarrel represent a heritage vastly more personal and immediate than the intellectual and deracinated daughter can see; indeed, they represent a heritage she has already discarded, for she no longer

shares a name with those whose lives, in scraps of cast-off clothing, the quilts transmute. Moreover, Wangero herself has not learned to quilt—the art will die if women like Maggie do not keep it up. Yet as Barbara Christian observes, a "heritage must continually be renewed rather than fixed in the past" (87). Thus for Maggie and her mother the idea of heritage is perpetually subordinate to the fact of a living tradition, a tradition in which one generation remains in touch with its predecessors by means of homely skills—quilt-making and butter-churning, among others—that get passed on. The quilts remain appropriate for "everyday use" so long as the art of their manufacture remains alive. They can be quite utilitarian, and indeed, they are supposed to be a practical dowry for Maggie.

16   Of course the quilts, like this story, are beautiful and merit preservation. Walker seems to intimate, however, even in her own literary art, a belief in the idea of a living, intertextual tradition, a passing on of values as well as skills that ought only occasionally to issue in canonization or any of the other processes whereby something intended for "everyday use" ends up framed, on a wall, on a shelf, in a library or museum. Indeed, as Faith Pullin notes with regard to the quilts, "the mother is the true African here, since the concept of art for art's sake is foreign to Africa—all objects are for use. Dee has taken over a very Western attitude towards art and its material value" (185). Walker, by the same token, seems to conceive of her own art as part of a dynamic process in which utility (domestic, political) meets and bonds with an aesthetic ideal. Her story/quilt is intended as much for immediate consumption—that is, reading—by the brothers and sisters of these sisters as for sacralization on some library shelf or college syllabus.

17   Thus Walker, though she mocks Wangero's idea of heritage, nevertheless aspires to project herself as sensitive artist of the African American experience, and she does so by inviting recognition of a further parallel between the contested quilts and her own fictive art. Quilts are the "texts" (the word means *weave*) of American rural life. Moreover, they are palpably "intertextual," inasmuch as they contain literal scraps of past lives. Engaged in her own version of quilt-making, Walker weaves in stories like this one a simple yet richly heteroglossic text on patterns set by a literary tradition extending into communities black and white, American and international. The interested reader may detect in Walker's work the intertextual presence of a number of writers she names as influences in the 1973 interview mentioned previously: Tolstoy, Turgenev, Gorky, Gogol, Camara Laye, García Márquez, Flannery O'Connor, Elechi Ahmadi, Bessie Head, Jean Toomer, and especially Zora Neale Hurston (*In Search* 257–260). Like any other writer, any other user of language. Walker "pieces" her literary quilts out of all that she has previously read or heard. Perhaps it is with Maggie after all that the author exhibits the most comprehensive affinity.

18   African American writing, according to Henry Louis Gates, enjoys its own distinctive brand of intertextuality, and I should like to conclude this discussion by glancing at a couple of the ways in which "Everyday Use" exemplifies the theory developed by Gates in *The Signifying Monkey*. Borrowing a term from the vernacular, Gates argues that texts by African Amer-

ican writers "Signify" on prior texts: they play with their predecessors in a perpetual and parodic evolution of meanings congenial to a people whose latitude for direct expression has been historically hedged about by innumerable sanctions. Gates explains Signifyin(g) with reference to Bakhtin's idea of a "double-voiced" discourse, in which one hears simultaneously the present text and the text being augmented or ironically revised. Not that Signifyin(g) need always be at the expense of its intertext: in one of the analytic set pieces of his book, as it happens, Gates reads Walker's *The Color Purple* as what he calls "unmotivated" (that is, non-disparaging) Signifying on texts by Rebecca Cox Jackson and Zora Neale Hurston.

19   In "Everyday Use" one encounters Signifyin(g) in both its street sense and its literary sense. "To rename is to revise," says Gates, "and to revise is to Signify" (xxiii). Thus Wangero thinks she is Signifyin(g) on white culture when she revises her name, but inadvertently she plays false with her own familial culture, as her mother's remarks about the history of the name Dee allow the reader to see. Indeed, if the mother were not so thoroughly innocent, one would suspect her of Signifying on her daughter's misguided aspirations. The master manipulator of the intertexts is of course Walker herself as she Signifies on Africanist pretension, calling into question the terms with which a number of her contemporaries are repudiating the language and culture of what Wangero calls "the oppressor." . . .

20   . . . Surely, then, one can legitimately consider the possibility that Walker plays the Signifying Monkey to a white literary Lion more or less literally in her own Georgia back yard. To come to cases: what is the relationship between Walker's story and the respected and influential body of short fiction about the rural South written by Flannery O'Connor?

21   As noted previously, Walker considers O'Connor an influence, and Margaret D. Bauer, who has remarked some of the parallels in the work of these two artists, tends to see their relationship as healthily non-agonistic (149–150). But anyone who dips into the essay on O'Connor that appears in *In Search of Our Mothers' Gardens* will be struck by the ambivalence of the younger author's feelings about the elder. While admitting that she has long admired her writing, she at the same time gauges feelings of fury and bitterness when she visits O'Connor's house outside Milledgeville, Georgia. Thus one should not be surprised to discover something other than simple homage in "Everyday Use," the little comedy of superficial sophistication and rural manners in which Walker replicates and plays with the many such fictions of O'Connor.

22   O'Connor contrasts intellectual pretension with certain transcendent realities: Original Sin, Grace, prospects for redemption. Walker, meanwhile, assesses ideas of cultural identity within a community only a few minutes drive from the home in which O'Connor spent her last years. O'Connor relentlessly exposes liberal pieties—notably regarding race—as humanistic idols that obscure the spiritual realities central to her vision. Writing at the height of Civil Rights agitation, she delights in characters like Asbury in "The Enduring Chill" or Julian in "Everything that Rises Must Converge"— characters who have embraced the new ideas about race only to be exposed for their concurrent spiritual folly. I have been arguing all along that Walker,

too, satirizes the heady rhetoric of late 60s black consciousness, deconstructing its pieties (especially the rediscovery of Africa) and asserting neglected values. At the same time, however, she revises—Signifies on—the O'Connor diagesis, which allows so little real value to black aspiration. Thus Walker parodies the iconoclastic tricks that O'Connor uses over and over again. As Wangero meets in Maggie the self she wants to deny, Walker Signifies on O'Connor's fondness for characters that psychologically double each other. Walker Signifies, too, on the O'Connor moment of divine insight, for Mrs. Johnson's decision to reaffirm the gift of the quilts to Maggie comes as heaven-sent enlightenment. Mrs. Johnson, however, enjoys a positive moment of revelation—unlike Mrs. May in "Greenleaf," Mrs. Turpin in "Revelation," or the Grandmother in "A Good Man Is Hard to Find." When, finally, Walker represents Wangero's intellectual posturing as shallow beside the simple integrity of her mother and sister, she plays with the standard O'Connor plot of the alienated and superficially intellectual young person (Hulga, in "Good Country People," is the definitive example) who fails conspicuously to justify the contempt in which she or he holds a crass, materialistic, and painfully unimaginative female parent. Walker tropes even the O'Connor meanness. Where O'Connor allows at best that the petty complacency and other failings of the mothers in "The Comforts of Home" and "The Enduring Chill" are venial flaws beside the arrogance, the intellectual posturing, and the spiritual blindness of their children, Walker declines to qualify her sympathy and admiration for Maggie and Mrs. Johnson.

23   One of the ironies here is that both Walker and O'Connor are themselves intellectuals struggling to make their way in a world of competitive ideas and talents—not to mention competing ideologies. Each critiques herself through mocking self-projection, and each stakes out an ideological position at odds with prevailing, thought. O'Connor addresses herself to the spiritual folly of a godless age, Walker to a kind of social shortsightedness. The measure of Walker's success may be that one comes to care as much about the question she poses—"Who shall inherit the quilts?"—as about the nominally grander question posed by O'Connor: "Who shall inherit the Kingdom of Heaven?"

24   In "Everyday Use," then, Walker addresses herself to the problems of African Americans who risk deracination in their quest for personal authenticity. At the same time she makes the drama of Wangero and Maggie emblematic of the politically charged choices available in minor/minority writing. With wit and indirection, she probes the problem of post-colonial writers who, as they struggle with a cultural imperative to repudiate the language and the institutions of the colonizer, simultaneously labor under the necessity—born in part of a desire to address an audience that includes the colonizer and his inheritors—of expressing themselves in that language and deferring to those institutions. In her problematic repudiation of oppressor culture, Wangero represents, among other things, the marginalized individual who fails to see this dilemma as false. She seems willing to lose her soul to be free of the baleful influences that she thinks have shaped it.

25   Walker hints that the false dilemma behind Wangero's blindness
afflicts the narrowly political writer as well. The alternative to the
dilemma is the same in both instances: a living tradition that preserves a
true heritage even as it appropriates what it needs from the dominant culture it may be engaged in subverting. African Americans, Walker says,
can take pride in the living tradition of folk art, seen here in the example
of the quilts, and they can learn from a literary art like her own, a literary art committed at once to political responsibility and to the means—
through simple appropriation of linguistic tools—of its own permanence.

Works Cited

Baker, Houston, and Charlotte Pierce-Baker. "Patches: Quills and Community in Alice Walker's 'Everyday Use.'" *Alice Walker: Critical Perspectives Past and Present*. Ed. Henry Louis Gates and K. A. Appiah,
   New York: Amistad. 1993. 309–316.

Bauer, Margaret D. "Alice Walker: Another Southern Writer Criticizing
   Codes Not Put to 'Everyday Use.'" *Studies in Short Fiction* 29 (1992):
   143–151.

Christian, Barbara. *Black Feminist Criticism: Perspectives on Black
   Women Writers*. New York: Pergamon, 1985.

Deleuze, Gilles, and Felix Guattari. *Kafka: Toward a Minor Literature*.
   Minneapolis: University of Minnesota Press, 1986.

Gates, Henry Louis. *The Signifying Monkey: A Theory of Afro-American
   Literary Criticism*. New York: Oxford University Press, 1988.

Hirsch, Marianne. "Clytemnestra's Anger: Writing (Out) the Mother's
   Anger." *Alice Walker*. Ed. Harold Bloom. New York: Chelsea House,
   1989. 195–213.

Petry, Alice Hall. "Alice Walker: The Achievement of the Short Fiction."
   Modern Language Studies 19 (Winter 1989): 12–27.

Pifer, Ellen. "Toni Morrison's *Beloved*: Twain's Mississippi Recollected
   and Rewritten." Ed. Francois Piquet. Paris: Didier, 1993, 511–514.

Pullin, Faith. "Landscapes of Reality: The Fiction of Contemporary
   Afro-American Women. *Black Fiction: New Studies in the Afro-
   American Novel since 1945*. Ed. A. Robert Lee. New York: Barnes
   and Noble, 1980. 173–203.

Showalter, Elaine. "Piecing and Writing." *The Poetics of Gender*. Ed.
   Nancy K. Miller. New York: Columbia University Press. 1986.
   222–247.

Walker, Alice. *In Love and Trouble: Stories of Black Women*. New York:
   Harcourt Brace Jovanovich, 1973.

———. *In Search of Our Mothers' Gardens*. San Diego: Harcourt Brace
   Jovanovich, 1983.

———. *Living by the Word: Selected Writings 1973–1987*. San Diego:
   Harcourt Brace Jovanovich, 1988.

———. *Revolutionary Petunias and Other Poems*. New York: Harcourt
   Brace Jovanovich, 1973.

Winchell, Donna Haisty. *Alice Walker*. Boston: Twayne, 1990.

Taylor Magusiak

Professor Higgins

English 1101

15 November 2007

Creative Scraps

1   When people take artwork from others, whether they desire
to keep it or just to enjoy it, how can they really understand
the original meaning of it? The artist can try to explain the
feelings and emotions that went into the work, but can others
really feel the same way about it? Some might say that while the
original feelings of the work are something only the artist can
experience, others who share the artist's work may relate the
art to their own personal lives. In Alice Walker's stories
"Everyday Use" and "Nineteen Fifty-five," the quilts, the
physical forms of art, are almost taken and are given two very
different meanings, and the lyrics, the verbal form of art, are
used as if owned but never given a new meaning,

2   The quilts in "Everyday Use" show a family's history.
Grandma Dee, Aunt Dee, and Mrs. Johnson stitched the quilts by
hand. Though they have different patterns, the Lone Star pattern
and the Walk Around the Mountain pattern, "in both of them were
scraps of dresses Grandma Dee had worn fifty or more years ago.
Bits and pieces of Grandpa Jarrell's Paisley shirts. And one
teeny faded blue piece about the size of a penny matchbox, that
was from Great Grandpa Ezra's uniform from the Civil War" (918).
The quilts are pieces of art that connect the heritage of the
family. They are a group project that has taken years to create.
Dee tells Mama, "'Maggie would put them on the bed and in five
years they'd be rags'" (919), but because Maggie knows how to
quilt, she can take the rags and scraps of clothing to combine
and make new quilts, thus adding another generation to the

heritage represented by the quilts. Each scrap tells a story; and once they come together as one, they are a beautiful remembrance of the past.

3   Though the quilts illustrate a family history, they also represent a family conflict about how to accept that heritage. Dee and Maggie have different expectations about how the quilts should be treated. Dee plans to hang them, and her statement that the quilts are "priceless," suggests that she wants them for social acceptance. They are part of black history and a big fad at the time. Perhaps Dee thinks if she has the quilts, she will be priceless. As Baker Jr. and Pierce-Baker point out, "the quilts . . . are perceived in Dee's polaroid sensibility as merely 'priceless' works of an institutionally, or stylishly, defined 'art world'" (948). Maggie's saying that she "'can 'member Grandma Dee without the quilts'" (919) suggests that she does not want them only for show but would put them to "everyday use." Mama even says, "'God knows I been saving 'em for long enough with nobody using 'em'" (918). Both Mama and Maggie believe that the quilts are made to be used. In contrast, Dee tells Mama and Maggie that they don't understand their heritage: "'You ought to try and make something of yourself, too, Maggie. It's really a new day for us. But from the way you and Mama still live you'd never know it'" (919). Dee values her heritage primarily as a way to climb the social ladder. Maggie "knows how to convert patches into robustly patterned and beautifully quilted wholes" (Baker Jr. and Pierce-Baker 948).

4   Like the scraps in the quilt, the words in the song come from a mixture of emotions resulting from different experiences. The lyrics in "Nineteen Fifty-five" come from the life experiences of Gracie Mae Still. Though the reader never finds out the name or the lyrics of the song, the small details Traynor gives, such as "You wrote that song while you was still on the farm" (926) suggest

that it is based on Gracie Mae's personal life lessons. The lyrics
in Gracie Mae's songs express her suffering and happiness. They
show parts of her life that affected her in ways she does not want
to forget. Traynor truthfully writes Gracie Mae during the war,
*"I've been thinking about writing some songs of my own but every
time I finish one it don't seem to be about anything I've actually
lived myself"* (925). Traynor's being moved more by Gracie Mae's
life experiences and his inability to write meaningful songs
suggest that, at least in his opinion, he is not living. When he
asks her if part of the song is about "No need to grieve," Gracie
Mae claims, "I never really believed that way back when I wrote
that song. . . . It was all bluffing then. The trick is to live
long enough to put your young bluffs to work" (927). Gracie Mae's
songs are so meaningful because she has lived and is living the
experiences she sings about. The songs reflect her life, and as she
as a person grows, her understanding of her own songs grows. She
doesn't go out and try to buy her feelings; she writes them first
and then lives to see if they are true.

5   Though Traynor as a singer and performer is also an artist,
he tries to find his life story in Gracie Mae's song. When Gracie
Mae says that she has "lived long enough to know [the bluffs are]
true" (927), Traynor responds, "I ain't lived that long" (927).
He says that he bought the song and sang it a million times, but
he still does not "have the faintest notion what that song means"
(923). Trying to help him understand, Gracie Mae tells him, "It
would have been worth my life to try to sing 'em somebody else's
stuff that I didn't know nothing about" (929). Traynor still
thinks that if he can find meaning in the song, he will find
meaning in his life. The problem is he sleeps through life hoping
for inspiration. Even Horace states, "You can't sleep through

life if you wants to live it" (930). The song never brings what
Traynor is looking for. After she sings the song on the Johnny
Carson show, Gracie Mae comments that Traynor "goes into the same
song, *our* song" (930). She understands that Traynor is trying to
sing about experiences before he has them, but she also feels she
is growing as a person by trying to help Traynor live his life.
Gracie Mae feels a bond with Traynor, perhaps because of his
persistence with trying to understand her songs. She also
sympathizes with him, saying, "Couldn't be nothing worse than
being famous the world over for something you don't understand"
(927). As Donna Haisty Winchell points out, "Through her music,
. . . Gracie Mae has found a type of freedom that all of
Traynor's fame and money cannot buy" (943).

6   Who really decides what artwork means when it takes on a new
meaning with every person? Both the artist and those who
appreciate the art are creating the meaning. To Maggie the quilts
are a reminder of the family she loves and something to use every
day, but to Dee they are a fashionable reminder of her racial
history. For Traynor the lyrics are a reminder of his desire to
find life, but to Gracie Mae the lyrics are real life. No matter
what form or meaning, art is a way to remember times of the past,
as the quilts reflect black history and the lyrics are true-life
experiences and a way to live fully in the present.

Works Cited

Baker, Houston A., Jr., and Charlotte Pierce-Baker. "Patches: Quilts and Community in Alice Walker's 'Everyday Use.'" *The Southern Review* 21 (July 1985). 706-20. Henderson, Higgins, Day, and Waller 943-51.

Henderson, Gloria Mason, Anna Dunlap Higgins, Bill Day, and Sandra Stevenson Waller, eds. *Literature and Ourselves: A Thematic Introduction for Readers and Writers.* 6th Ed. New York: ABLongman, 2009.

Walker, Alice. "Everyday Use." *In Love and Trouble: Stories of Black Women.* New York: Harcourt Brace Jovanovich, 1973. Henderson, Higgins, Day, and Waller 913-19.

———. "Nineteen Fifty-Five." *You Can't Keep a Good Woman Down.* New York: Harcourt Brace Jovanovich, 1981. Henderson, Higgins, Day, and Waller 920-30.

Winchell, Donna Haisty. *Alice Walker.* New York: Twayne Publishers, 1992. Henderson and Higgins 940-43.

Crafting Arguments

1. In an essay on "Everyday Use," contrast the distinctively different lifestyles of Dee and her companion with those of their hosts, Mama and Maggie, and explain how these lifestyles affect their attitudes toward art and heritage.

2. Using the contrasting conceptions of "heritage" exemplified by Dee and by Maggie, explain in a persuasive essay whether a heritage is best preserved by protecting it or by living it.

3. Contrast Gracie Mae Still's singing, attitudes toward life, and experiences with those of Traynor in "1955."

4. Write an essay comparing Walker's two narrators: the mother in "Everyday Use" and Gracie Mae Still in "1955."

5. Examine the things for which Walker mourns in the epilogue to *The Way Forward Is with a Broken Heart.* Then write an essay describing the "deepest emptiness and sorrow" and the ways that, according to Walker, the wounds might be healed.

6. Write an essay comparing Walker's concept of creativity and art with that of bell hooks in "Beauty Laid Bare: Aesthetics in the Ordinary."

Creativity: Crafting Arguments

1. In an essay apply any of bell hooks' claims about beauty and aesthetics to one or more of the works in this unit.
2. Because it balances both inner experience and outer experience, both the human imagination and the world it discovers, art raises profound questions about the nature of truth, the essence of reality. Select one or more of the works in this unit and write an essay that illustrates how art can raise questions about truth or reality.
3. In the Freedom and Responsibility Unit, Tim O'Brien's narrator in "How to Tell a True War Story" insists that the truth of art does not depend on factual accuracy. Use at least two of the works in this unit to support the claim that art, through imagination, sometimes reveals truth that transcends fact.
4. Select two or more works in this unit to illustrate that imagination and creativity can lead to discovery—of self, of others, or of truth.
5. Select any work in this unit that especially appeals to you and write an essay arguing that you as reader are part of the creative process.
6. Using any three works in this unit, explain the relationship of creator (writer, artist, reader, etc.) to creation.
7. Le Guin describes symbol and archetype in "The Child and the Shadow." Apply these terms to "The Ones Who Walk Away from Omelas" in the Freedom and Responsibility Unit or to another work in this anthology.

Creativity: Writing about Film

See Appendix B: Writing about Film for help with these essays.
1. View Wolfgang Petersen's fantasy adaptation *The Neverending Story* (1984). Then read Ursula K. Le Guin's "The Child and the Shadow." Using Le Guin's essay as background, craft a paper arguing that the characters created for this film do or do not convey truths that children would otherwise find incomprehensible.
2. Curtis Hanson's adaptation *Wonder Boys* (2000) examines the nature of creativity, creative genius, and wasted creative talent. View the film, focusing especially on scenes that seem symbolic, for example, the greenhouse scene. How do dialogue and film techniques convey theme?
3. Fantasy and science fiction films are certainly creative. View a favorite fantasy or science fiction adaptation, analyzing the director's incorporation of computer-generated special effects to enhance thematic issues. You may want to consider such popular films as *Blade Runner; Total Recall; The Chronicles of Narnia: The Lion, the Witch and the Wardrobe* or *Prince Caspian; Minority Report; Jumanji;* or *I, Robot.*
4. Sequels are a Hollywood staple. You might enjoy analyzing a director's interpretation of character development and the progression of story line in such trilogies and sequels as *The Lord of the Rings* or the *Harry Potter* films.

Quest

A scene from *Lord of the Rings: The Fellowship of the Ring*. New Line Cinema/Photofest.

Awareness that humanity cannot "live by bread alone" (Matthew 4:4) predates Christ by thousands of years. The theme of the quest, which ultimately reveals humanity in a search for meaning, for a truth beyond the purely physical, is older than written literature. It finds expression in ancient religions and myths, in the Babylonian epic of *Gilgamesh*, and in the great oral epics of Homer, particularly *The Odyssey*. A recurring theme in art, mythology, and religion is the human need and resulting search for a defining direction, order, and meaning. In a sense, the quest, the search for an ultimate truth, might be seen as one defining characteristic of humanity.

The quest for truth begins not in certainty but in doubt, in questioning. In Sophocles's great tragedy, Oedipus insists on asking questions despite dire warnings, proceeding from question to question to a shocking revelation about his own identity. Plato's quest for truth—his philosophy—begins, proceeds, and ends with question after question. The wisdom of the "Beatitudes" arises out of Jesus' questioning of received wisdom, his refusal to accept the status quo. Blake raises without answering the question whether the God who made the lamb could make the tiger.

Anguished questioning torments even writers and characters of profound faith. Faith often seems not to end the quest but to begin it anew. Hopkins' "God's Grandeur," though written in praise of God and though ending in a strongly affirmative sestet, nevertheless reveals in its second quatrain grave doubts about our capacity to know God. Flannery O'Connor, a devout Catholic, sees modern men and women as so immersed in the world as to be wholly unaware of their own inadequacy. For O'Connor, only the inexplicable and often violent grace of God can give a person some sense of order and meaning. O'Connor's quest cannot even begin without grace.

The quest for truth may sometimes be quite costly. Socrates' insistence on questioning received wisdom led to his being condemned to death. Oedipus' fateful quest for truth leads to his wife's hanging herself and his blinding himself. Because he regards his quest as too costly, Prufrock, the narrator of T. S. Eliot's "The Love Song of J. Alfred Prufrock," is unable even to ask his most superficial question. We see in him the predicament of many people today, unable to believe in God or any ultimate truth, thoroughly disoriented, searching in spite of themselves for truth and direction in a world that apparently offers neither.

Despite the difficulty of the quest, the search for a truth that transcends the merely physical world continues. Plato's philosopher finds his way out of the cave. Writers as different as Matthew, William Butler Yeats, and Gerard Manley Hopkins offer us a vision of what we might attain, of a transcendent existence beyond the ravages of pain and age.

As the persistent questioning of Socrates, the endless searching of Alfred, Lord Tennyson's Ulysses, and the eloquent frozen action of John Keats' Grecian urn make clear, often the joy, meaning, and order we seek are in the quest itself. Even one of the most devout of medieval mystics, the monk Brother Lawrence, saw his vocation not as resting in God but as constantly practicing God's presence. Like Tennyson's Ulysses, we feel compelled to search: "to strive, to seek, to find, and not to yield."

Writing about Quest

The theme of the quest—whether for knowledge of self, knowledge of the nature of humanity, or knowledge of God—is perhaps the richest source of writing topics. Many works tell of more than one quest, and each genre in this unit offers you a wide variety of subjects. You might select the work that appeals to you most and let that work determine your subject and the type of essay you will write, or you might decide that you would prefer to write about one quest and then select one or more works that illustrate that quest. For example, if you wanted to write about the search for knowledge of self, you might select James Joyce's "Araby," an initiation story. If you prefer to write about poetry, you might write an essay classifying the types of sterility and loneliness portrayed in "The Love Song of J. Alfred Prufrock."

If you choose to write about the quest for the nature of humanity, you will find that it is often inextricably intertwined with the other two types of quests mentioned above. For example, you might write an essay about Tennyson's poem showing how Ulysses, in setting goals for himself, challenges his men to share in his quest. Another essay about the nature of humanity might explain how Hazel in Toni Cade Bambara's "Raymond's Run," while enjoying the talent that gives her personal satisfaction, learns a new admiration for and understanding of her brother. You might write an essay claiming that elements of Oedipus' character that helped to make him great also drive him to a relentless pursuit of the murderer of Laius, the former king of Thebes.

The quest for a satisfactory relationship with God permeates great literature, and this unit offers a wide variety of works on this subject. You might, for example, write about the ironic point of view in Arthur C. Clarke's "The Star," which tells of a moral crisis faced by a Jesuit priest. The stories in the Flannery O'Connor Casebook offer startling accounts of women who are shocked into a recognition of their own nature and their relationship to God. The questions at the end of the casebook suggest a variety of types of essays and subjects. You might, for example, write a character sketch of the Misfit, the grandmother, or Mrs. May; analyze the Misfit as a violent agent of change; or interpret the symbolism in either of the stories.

When Quimby Melton, an English major, was asked to write an essay using the O'Connor casebook, he was already familiar with Flannery O'Connor's fiction, having previously read several of her stories; however, he selected a story he had not read before: "Greenleaf." After reading the story carefully, he thought about the symbolism, themes, and characterization. Then he read the critical essays and constructed his thesis statement based on his interpretation of the story and on his decision about what would make a workable topic. The thesis that he chose allowed him to use his previous knowledge about O'Connor's religious beliefs and about the American South as he discussed the symbols in the story and the ways in which they clarify and vivify the theme. Once he had selected his subject, Quimby wrote the whole essay in one night. His professor suggested a few minor changes, but the essay required little revision. Quimby's essay is included at the end of the O'Connor casebook.

ESSAYS

Plato (c. 429–347 B.C.)

*The philosopher and teacher Plato was a high-born Athen-
ian who studied under Socrates and taught Aristotle. Plato
founded a school in the grove sacred to the hero Academus
and called it the Academy. The Republic, Plato's plan for a
utopia, includes one of the most famous of all allegories, the allegory of the cave, which delineates his philosophical view of
reality. Plato customarily wrote in dialogues, often using
Socrates as a character. Because of its emphasis on the transcendent, Plato's philosophy influenced many later religions, including Christianity and Islam.*

ALLEGORY OF THE CAVE[1]   (FOURTH CENTURY B.C.E.)

1   And now, I said, let me show in a figure how far our nature is enlightened or unenlightened:—Behold! human beings living in an underground
den, which has a mouth open towards the light and reaching all along the
den; here they have been from their childhood, and have their legs and
necks chained so that they cannot move, and can only see before them,
being prevented by the chains from turning round their heads. Above and
behind them a fire is blazing at a distance, and between the fire and the
prisoners there is a raised way; and you will see, if you look, a low wall
built along the way, like the screen which marionette players have in
front of them, over which they show the puppets.

2   I see.

3   And do you see, I said, men passing along the wall carrying all sorts of
vessels, and statues and figures of animals made of wood and stone and
various materials, which appear over the wall? Some of them are talking,
others silent.

4   You have shown me a strange image, and they are strange prisoners.

5   Like ourselves, I replied; and they see only their own shadows, or the
shadows of one another, which the fire throws on the opposite wall of
the cave?

6   True, he said; how could they see anything but the shadows if they
were never allowed to move their heads?

7   And of the objects which are being carried in like manner they would
only see the shadows?

8   Yes, he said.

9   And if they were able to converse with one another, would they not
suppose that they were naming what was actually before them?

---

[1]From Plato's *The Republic*, translated by Benjamin Jowett.

10   Very true.

11   And suppose further that the prison had an echo which came from the other side, would they not be sure to fancy when one of the passers-by spoke that the voice which they heard came from the passing shadow?

12   No question, he replied.

13   To them, I said, the truth would be literally nothing but the shadows of the images.

14   That is certain.

15   And now look again, and see what will naturally follow if the prisoners are released and disabused of their error. At first, when any of them is liberated and compelled suddenly to stand up and turn his neck round and walk and look towards the light, he will suffer sharp pains; the glare will distress him, and he will be unable to see the realities of which in his former state he had seen the shadows; and then conceive some one saying to him, that what he saw before was an illusion, but that now, when he is approaching nearer to being and his eye is turned towards more real existence, he has a clearer vision,—what will be his reply? And you may further imagine that his instructor is pointing to the objects as they pass and requiring him to name them,—will he not be perplexed? Will he not fancy that the shadows which he formerly saw are truer than the objects which are now shown to him?

16   Far truer.

17   And if he is compelled to look straight at the light, will he not have a pain in his eyes which will make him turn away to take refuge in the objects of vision which he can see, and which he will conceive to be in reality clearer than the things which are now being shown to him?

18   True, he said.

19   And suppose once more, that he is reluctantly dragged up a steep and rugged ascent, and held fast until he is forced into the presence of the sun himself, is he not likely to be pained and irritated? When he approaches the light his eyes will be dazzled, and he will not be able to see anything at all of what are now called realities.

20   Not all in a moment, he said.

21   He will require to grow accustomed to the sight of the upper world. And first he will see the shadows best, next the reflections of men and other objects in the water, and then the objects themselves; then he will gaze upon the light of the moon and the stars and the spangled heaven; and he will see the sky and the stars by night better than the sun or the light of the sun by day?

22   Certainly.

23   Last of all he will be able to see the sun, and not mere reflections of him in the water, but he will see him in his own proper place, and not in another; and he will contemplate him as he is.

24   Certainly.

25   He will then proceed to argue that this is he who gives the season and the years, and is the guardian of all that is in the visible world, and in a

certain way the cause of all things which he and his fellows have been accustomed to behold?

26   Clearly, he said, he would first see the sun and then reason about him.

27   And when he remembered his old habitation, and the wisdom of the den and his fellow-prisoners, do you not suppose that he would felicitate himself on the change, and pity them?

28   Certainly, he would.

29   And if they were in the habit of conferring honours among themselves on those who were quickest to observe the passing shadows and to remark which of them went before, and which followed after, and which were together; and who were therefore best able to draw conclusions as to the future, do you think that he would care for such honours and glories, or envy the possessors of them? Would he not say with Homer,

> "Better to be the poor servant of a poor master,"

and to endure anything, rather than think as they do and live after their manner?

30   Yes, he said, I think that he would rather suffer anything than entertain these false notions and live in this miserable manner.

31   Imagine once more, I said, such an one coming suddenly out of the sun to be replaced in his old situation; would he not be certain to have his eyes full of darkness?

32   To be sure, he said.

33   And if there were a contest, and he had to compete in measuring the shadows with the prisoners who had never moved out of the den, while his sight was still weak, and before his eyes had become steady (and the time which would be needed to acquire this new habit of sight might be very considerable), would he not be ridiculous? Men would say of him that up he went and down he came without his eyes; and that it was better not even to think of ascending; and if any one tried to loose another and lead him up to the light, let them only catch the offender, and they would put him to death.

34   No question, he said.

35   This entire allegory, I said, you may now append, dear Glaucon, to the previous argument; the prison-house is the world of sight, the light of the fire is the sun, and you will not misapprehend me if you interpret the journey upwards to be the ascent of the soul into the intellectual world according to my poor belief, which, at your desire, I have expressed—whether rightly or wrongly God knows. But, whether true or false, my opinion is that in the world of knowledge the idea of good appears last of all, and is seen only with an effort; and, when seen, is also inferred to be the universal author of all things beautiful and right, parent of light and of the lord of light in this visible world, and the immediate source of reason and truth in the intellectual; and that this is the power upon which he who would act rationally either in public or private life must have his eye fixed.

36   I agree, he said, as far as I am able to understand you.

37   Moreover, I said, you must not wonder that those who attain to this beatific vision are unwilling to descend to human affairs; for their souls are ever hastening into the upper world where they desire to dwell; which desire of theirs is very natural, if our allegory may be trusted.

38   Yes, very natural.

39   And is there anything surprising in one who passes from divine contemplations to the evil state of man, misbehaving himself in a ridiculous manner; if, while his eyes are blinking and before he has become accustomed to the surrounding darkness, he is compelled to fight in courts of law, or in other places, about the images or the shadows of images of justice, and is endeavouring to meet the conceptions of those who have never yet seen absolute justice?

40   Anything but surprising, he replied.

41   Any one who has common sense will remember that the bewilderments of the eyes are of two kinds, and arise from two causes, either from coming out of the light or from going into the light, which is true of the mind's eye, quite as much as of the bodily eye; and he who remembers this when he sees any one whose vision is perplexed and weak, will not be too ready to laugh; he will first ask whether that soul of man has come out of the brighter life, and is unable to see because unaccustomed to the dark, or having turned from darkness to the day is dazzled by excess of light. And he will count the one happy in his condition and state of being, and he will pity the other; or, if he have a mind to laugh at the soul which comes from below into the light, there will be more reason in this than in the laugh which greets him who returns from above out of the light into the den.

42   That, he said, is a very just distinction.

43   But then, if I am right, certain professors of education must be wrong when they say that they can put a knowledge into the soul which was not there before, like sight into blind eyes.

44   They undoubtedly say this, he replied.

45   Whereas, our argument shows that the power and capacity of learning exists in the soul already; and that just as the eye was unable to turn from darkness to light without the whole body, so too the instrument of knowledge can only by the movement of the whole soul be turned from the world of becoming into that of being, and learn by degrees to endure the sight of being, and of the brightest and best of being, or in other words, of the good.

46   Very true.

47   And must there not be some art which will effect conversion in the easiest and quickest manner; not implanting the faculty of sight, for that exists already, but has been turned in the wrong direction, and is looking away from the truth?

48   Yes, he said, such an art may be presumed.

49   And whereas the other so-called virtues of the soul seem to be akin to bodily qualities, for even when they are not originally innate they can be

implanted later by habit and exercise, the virtue of wisdom more than anything else contains a divine element which always remains, and by this conversion is rendered useful and profitable; or, on the other hand, hurtful and useless. Did you never observe the narrow intelligence flashing from the keen eye of a clever rogue—how eager he is, how clearly his paltry soul sees the way to his end; he is the reverse of blind, but his keen eyesight is forced into the service of evil, and he is mischievous in proportion to his cleverness?

50   Very true, he said.

51   But what if there had been a circumcision of such natures in the days of their youth; and they had been severed from those sensual pleasures, such as eating and drinking, which, like leaden weights, were attached to them at their birth, and which drag them down and turn the vision of their souls upon the things that were below—if, I say, they had been released from these impediments and turned in the opposite direction, the very same faculty in them would have seen the truth as keenly as they see what their eyes are turned to now.

52   Very likely.

53   Yes, I said; and there is another thing which is likely, or rather a necessary inference from what has preceded, that neither the uneducated and uninformed of the truth, nor yet those who never make an end of their education, will be able ministers of State; not the former, because they have no single aim of duty which is the rule of all their actions, private as well as public; nor the latter, because they will not act at all except upon compulsion, fancying that they are already dwelling apart in the Islands of the Blest.

54   Very true, he replied.

55   Then, I said, the business of us who are the founders of the State will be to compel the best minds to attain that knowledge which we have already shown to be the greatest of all—they must continue to ascend until they arrive at the good; but when they have ascended and seen enough we must not allow them to do as they do now.

56   What do you mean?

57   I mean that they remain in the upper world: but this must not be allowed; they must be made to descend again among the prisoners in the den, and partake of their labours and honours, whether they are worth having or not.

58   But is not this unjust? he said; ought we to give them a worse life, when they might have a better?

59   You have again forgotten, my friend, I said, the intention of the legislator, who did not aim at making any one class in the State happy above the rest; the happiness was to be in the whole State, and he held the citizens together by persuasion and necessity, making them benefactors of the State, and therefore benefactors of one another; to this end he created them, not to please themselves, but to be his instruments in binding up the State.

60   True, he said, I had forgotten.

61   Observe, Glaucon, that there will be no injustice in compelling our philosophers to have a care and providence of others; we shall explain to them that in other States, men of their class are not obliged to share in the toils of politics: and this is reasonable, for they grow up at their own sweet will, and the government would rather not have them. Being self-taught, they cannot be expected to show any gratitude for a culture which they have never received. But we have brought you into the world to be rulers of the hive, kings of yourselves and of the other citizens, and have educated you far better and more perfectly than they have been educated, and you are better able to share in the double duty. Wherefore each of you, when his turn comes, must go down to the general underground abode, and get the habit of seeing in the dark. When you have acquired the habit, you will see ten thousand times better than the inhabitants of the den, and you will know what the several images are, and what they represent, because you have seen the beautiful and just and good in their truth. And thus our State which is also yours will be a reality, and not a dream only, and will be administered in a spirit unlike that of other States, in which men fight with one another about shadows only and are distracted in the struggle for power, which in their eyes is a great good. Whereas the truth is that the State in which the rulers are most reluctant to govern is always the best and most quietly governed, and the State in which they are most eager, the worst.

62   Quite true, he replied.

63   And will our pupils, when they hear this, refuse to take their turn at the toils of State, when they are allowed to spend the greater part of their time with one another in the heavenly light?

64   Impossible, he answered; for they are just men, and the commands which we impose upon them are just; there can be no doubt that every one will take office as a stern necessity, and not after the fashion of our present rulers of State.

65   Yes, my friend, I said; and there lies the point. You must contrive for your future rulers another and a better life than that of a ruler, and then you may have a well ordered State; for only in the State which offers this, will they rule who are truly rich, not in silver and gold, but in virtue and wisdom, which are the true blessings of life. Whereas if they go to the administration of public affairs, poor and hungering after their own private advantage, thinking that hence they are to snatch the chief good, order there can never be; for they will be fighting about office, and the civil and domestic broils which thus arise will be the ruin of the rulers themselves and of the whole State.

66   Most true, he replied.

67   And the only life which looks down upon the life of political ambition is that of true philosophy. Do you know of any other?

68   Indeed, I do not, he said.

69   And those who govern ought not to be lovers of the task? For, if they are, there will be rival lovers, and they will fight.

70   No question.

71   Who then are those whom we shall compel to be guardians? Surely they will be the men who are wisest about affairs of State, and by whom the State is best administered, and who at the same time have other honours and another and a better life than that of politics?

72   They are the men, and I will choose them, he replied.

73   And now shall we consider in what way such guardians will be produced, and how they are to be brought from darkness to light,—as some are said to have ascended from the world below to the gods?

74   By all means, he replied.

Questions for Engagement, Response, and Analysis

1. Why does Socrates, the first-person narrator of this dialogue, ask questions rather than make statements?

2. An allegory is a story in which concrete elements signify specific things or ideas other than themselves. Explain the significance of the following elements in Plato's allegory: the cave, the sun, the men in the cave, the one man who escapes, his first reaction to the sun's light, and his subsequent actions and their results.

3. Why, according to Socrates, do those who attain knowledge of "the idea of the good" have difficulty concentrating on ordinary human affairs?

4. According to Socrates, how valid is the justice of most societies?

5. What difficulty in finding ideal rulers does Socrates see?

Crafting Arguments

1. Supporting your claims with this dialogue plus your knowledge of contemporary governments, argue for or against the following statement: "The State in which the rulers are most reluctant to govern is always the best and most quietly governed, and the State in which they are most eager, the worst."

Matthew

Little is known about Matthew, the author of the first gospel in the New Testament. In fact, he is not mentioned elsewhere in the New Testament. Traditionally called "Matthew the tax collector," he has been identified with Levi, a Jew of Galilee, who was a tax-gatherer. The fifth chapter of Matthew, which is the first chapter of the Sermon on the Mount, is probably the clearest exposition of Jesus' moral teachings in the four gospels.

BEATITUDES

1 And seeing the multitudes, he went up into a mountain: and when he was set, his disciples came unto him:

2 And he opened his mouth, and taught them, saying,

3 Blessed are the poor in spirit: for theirs is the kingdom of heaven.

4 Blessed are they that mourn: for they shall be comforted.

5 Blessed are the meek: for they shall inherit the earth.

6 Blessed are they which do hunger and thirst after righteousness: for they shall be filled.

7 Blessed are the merciful: for they shall obtain mercy.

8 Blessed are the pure in heart: for they shall see God.

9 Blessed are the peacemakers: for they shall be called the children of God.

10 Blessed are they which are persecuted for righteousness' sake: for theirs is the kingdom of heaven.

11 Blessed are ye, when men shall revile you, and persecute you, and shall say all manner of evil against you falsely, for my sake.

12 Rejoice, and be exceeding glad: for great is your reward in heaven: for so persecuted they the prophets which were before you.

Questions for Engagement, Response, and Analysis

1. Examine the structure of the Beatitudes. What relationship among the Beatitudes does the structure make clear without the author's having to point it out?

2. Several of the Beatitudes are **paradoxes**. If you are not already familiar with paradoxes, check the definition in the Glossary; then explain each of these paradoxes.

3. What is the tone of this passage?

Crafting Arguments

1. In an essay, discuss what the Beatitudes reveal about the beliefs and attitudes of Christianity.

William Golding (1911–1993)

British novelist and essayist William Golding is best known for his first novel, Lord of the Flies *(1954). His works, usually allegorical, are enriched with image clusters and symbols and often have unique points of view. The Inheritors (1955), for example, takes place around a symbolic waterfall and is seen primarily through the eyes of Neanderthals. Golding received the Nobel Prize for Literature in 1983 and was knighted by Queen Elizabeth in 1988.*

THINKING AS A HOBBY (1961)

1   While I was still a boy, I came to the conclusion that there were three grades of thinking; and since I was later to claim thinking as my hobby, I came to an even stranger conclusion—namely, that I myself could not think at all.

2   I must have been an unsatisfactory child for grownups to deal with. I remember how incomprehensible they appeared to me at first, but not, of course, how I appeared to them. It was the headmaster of my grammar school who first brought the subject of thinking before me—though neither in the way, nor with the result he intended. He had some statuettes in his study. They stood on a high cupboard behind his desk. One was a lady wearing nothing but a bath towel. She seemed frozen in an eternal panic lest the bath towel slip down any farther; and since she had no arms, she was in an unfortunate position to pull the towel up again. Next to her, crouched the statuette of a leopard, ready to spring down at the top drawer of a filing cabinet labeled A–AH. My innocence interpreted this as the victim's last, despairing cry. Beyond the leopard was a naked, muscular gentleman, who sat, looking down, with his chin on his fist and his elbow on his knee. He seemed utterly miserable.

3   Some time later, I learned about these statuettes. The headmaster had placed them where they would face delinquent children, because they symbolized to him the whole of life. The naked lady was the Venus of Milo. She was Love. She was not worried about the towel. She was just busy being beautiful. The leopard was Nature, and he was being natural. The naked, muscular gentleman was not miserable. He was Rodin's Thinker, an image of pure thought. It is easy to buy small plaster models of what you think life is like.

4   I had better explain that I was a frequent visitor to the headmaster's study, because of the latest thing I had done or left undone. As we now say, I was not integrated. I was, if anything, disintegrated; and I was puzzled. Grownups never made sense. Whenever I found myself in a penal position before the headmaster's desk, with the statuettes glimmering whitely above him, I would sink my head, clasp my hands behind my back and writhe one shoe over the other.

5   The headmaster would look opaquely at me through flashing spectacles.

6   "What are we going to do with you?"

7   Well, what *were* they going to do with me? I would writhe my shoe some more and stare down at the worn rug.

8   "Look up, boy! Can't you look up?"

9   Then I would look up at the cupboard, where the naked lady was frozen in her panic and the muscular gentleman contemplated the hindquarters of the leopard in endless gloom. I had nothing to say to the headmaster. His spectacles caught the light so that you could see nothing human behind them. There was no possibility of communication.

10   "Don't you ever think at all?"

11   No, I didn't think, wasn't thinking, couldn't think—I was simply waiting in anguish for the interview to stop.

12   "Then you'd better learn—hadn't you?"

13   On one occasion the headmaster leaped to his feet, reached up and plunked Rodin's masterpiece on the desk before me.

14   "That's what a man looks like when he's really thinking."

15   I surveyed the gentleman without interest or comprehension.

16   "Go back to your class."

17   Clearly there was something missing in me. Nature had endowed the rest of the human race with a sixth sense and left me out. This must be so, I mused, on my way back to the class, since whether I had broken a window, or failed to remember Boyle's Law, or been late for school, my teachers produced me one, adult answer: "Why can't you think?"

18   As I saw the case, I had broken the window because I had tried to hit Jack Arney with a cricket ball and missed him; I could not remember Boyle's Law because I had never bothered to learn it; and I was late for school because I preferred looking over the bridge into the river. In fact, I was wicked. Were my teachers, perhaps, so good that they could not understand the depths of my depravity? Were they clear, untormented people who could direct their every action by this mysterious business of thinking? The whole thing was incomprehensible. In my earlier years, I found even the statuette of the Thinker confusing. I did not believe any of my teachers were naked, ever. Like someone born deaf, but bitterly determined to find out about sound, I watched my teachers to find out about thought.

19   There was Mr. Houghton. He was always telling me to think. With a modest satisfaction, he would tell me that he had thought a bit himself. Then why did he spend so much time drinking? Or was there more sense in drinking than there appeared to be? But if not, and if drinking were in fact ruinous to health—and Mr. Houghton was ruined, there was no doubt about that—why was he always talking about the clean life and the virtues of fresh air? He would spread his arms wide with the action of a man who habitually spent his time striding along mountain ridges.

20   "Open air does me good, boys—I know it!"

21   Sometimes, exalted by his own oratory, he would leap from his desk and hustle us outside into a hideous wind.

22   "Now, boys! Deep breaths! Feel it right down inside you—huge draughts of God's good air!"

23   He would stand before us, rejoicing in his perfect health, an open-air man. He would put his hands on his waist and take a tremendous breath. You could hear the wind, trapped in the cavern of his chest and struggling with all the unnatural impediments. His body would reel with shock and his ruined face go white at the unaccustomed visitation. He would stagger back to his desk and collapse there, useless for the rest of the morning.

24   Mr. Houghton was given to high-minded monologues about the good life, sexless and full of duty. Yet in the middle of one of these monologues,

if a girl passed the window, tapping along on her neat little feet, he would interrupt his discourse, his neck would turn of itself and he would watch her out of sight. In this instance, he seemed to me ruled not by thought but by an invisible and irresistible spring in his nape.

25   His neck was an object of great interest to me. Normally it bulged a bit over his collar. But Mr. Houghton had fought in the First World War alongside both Americans and French, and had come—by who knows what illogic?—to a settled detestation of both countries. If either country happened to be prominent in current affairs, no argument could make Mr. Houghton think well of it. He would bang the desk, his neck would bulge still further and go red. "You can say what you like," he would cry, "but I've thought about this—and I know what I think!"

26   Mr. Houghton thought with his neck.

27   There was Miss Parsons. She assured us that her dearest wish was our welfare, but I knew even then, with the mysterious clairvoyance of childhood, that what she wanted most was the husband she never got. There was Mr. Hands—and so on.

28   I have dealt at length with my teachers because this was my introduction to the nature of what is commonly called thought. Through them I discovered that thought is often full of unconscious prejudice, ignorance and hypocrisy. It will lecture on disinterested purity while its neck is being remorselessly twisted toward a skirt. Technically, it is about as proficient as most businessmen's golf, as honest as most politicians' intentions, or—to come near my own preoccupation—as coherent as most books that get written. It is what I came to call grade-three thinking, though more properly, it is feeling, rather than thought.

29   True, often there is a kind of innocence in prejudices, but in those days I viewed grade-three thinking with an intolerant contempt and an incautious mockery. I delighted to confront a pious lady who hated the Germans with the proposition that we should love our enemies. She taught me a great truth in dealing with grade-three thinkers; because of her, I no longer dismiss lightly a mental process which for nine-tenths of the population is the nearest they will ever get to thought. They have immense solidarity. We had better respect them, for we are outnumbered and surrounded. A crowd of grade-three thinkers, all shouting the same thing, all warming their hands at the fire of their own prejudices, will not thank you for pointing out the contradictions in their beliefs. Man is a gregarious animal, and enjoys agreement as cows will graze all the same way on the side of a hill.

30   Grade-two thinking is the detection of contradictions. I reached grade two when I trapped the poor, pious lady. Grade-two thinkers do not stampede easily, though often they fall into the other fault and lag behind. Grade-two thinking is a withdrawal, with eyes and ears open. It became my hobby and brought satisfaction and loneliness in either hand. For grade-two thinking destroys without having the power to create. It set me watching the crowds cheering His Majesty the King and asking myself

what all the fuss was about, without giving me anything positive to put in the place of that heady patriotism. But there were compensations. To hear people justify their habit of hunting foxes and tearing them to pieces by claiming that the foxes liked it. To hear our Prime Minister talk about the great benefit we conferred on India by jailing people like Pandit Nehru and Gandhi. To hear American politicians talk about peace in one sentence and refuse to join the League of Nations in the next. Yes, there were moments of delight.

31   But I was growing toward adolescence and had to admit that Mr. Houghton was not the only one with an irresistible spring in his neck. I, too, felt the compulsive hand of nature and began to find that pointing out contradiction could be costly as well as fun. There was Ruth, for example, a serious and attractive girl. I was an atheist at the time. Grade-two thinking is a menace to religion and knocks down sects like skittles. I put myself in a position to be converted by her with an hypocrisy worthy of grade three. She was a Methodist—or at least, her parents were, and Ruth had to follow suit. But, alas, instead of relying on the Holy Spirit to convert me, Ruth was foolish enough to open her pretty mouth in argument. She claimed that the Bible (King James Version) was literally inspired. I countered by saying that the Catholics believed in the literal inspiration of Saint Jerome's *Vulgate*,[1] and the two books were different. Argument flagged.

32   At last she remarked that there were an awful lot of Methodists, and they couldn't be wrong, could they—not all those millions? That was too easy, said I restively (for the nearer you were to Ruth, the nicer she was to be near to) since there were more Roman Catholics than Methodists anyway; and they couldn't be wrong, could they—not all those hundreds of millions? An awful flicker of doubt appeared in her eyes. I slid my arm around her waist and murmured breathlessly that if we were counting heads, the Buddhists were the boys for my money. But Ruth had *really* wanted to do me good, because I was so nice. She fled. The combination of my arm and those countless Buddhists was too much for her.

33   That night her father visited my father and left, red-cheeked and indignant. I was given the third degree to find out what had happened. It was lucky we were both of us only fourteen. I lost Ruth and gained an undeserved reputation as a potential libertine.

34   So grade-two thinking could be dangerous. It was in this knowledge, at the age of fifteen, that I remember making a comment from the heights of grade two, on the limitations of grade three. One evening I found myself alone in the school hall, preparing it for a party. The door of the headmaster's study was open. I went in. The headmaster had ceased to thump Rodin's Thinker down on the desk as an example to the young. Perhaps he had not found any more candidates, but the statuettes were still there, glimmering

[1]The Latin Bible as revised in the fourth century A.D. by Jerome and used thereafter as the authoritative text for Roman Catholic ritual.

and gathering dust on top of the cupboard. I stood on a chair and rearranged them. I stood Venus in her bath towel on the filing cabinet, so that now the top drawer caught its breath in a gasp of sexy excitement. "A-ah!" The portentous Thinker I placed on the edge of the cupboard so that he looked down at the bath towel and waited for it to slip.

35   Grade-two thinking, though it filled life with fun and excitement, did not make for content. To find out the deficiencies of our elders bolsters the young ego but does not make for personal security. I found that grade two was not only the power to point out contradictions. It took the swimmer some distance from the shore and left him there, out of his depth. I decided that Pontius Pilate was a typical grade-two thinker. "What is truth?" he said, a very common grade-two thought, but one that is used always as the end of an argument instead of the beginning. There is still a higher grade of thought which says, "What is truth?" and sets out to find it.

36   But these grade-one thinkers were few and far between. They did not visit my grammar school in the flesh though they were there in books. I aspired to them, partly because I was ambitious and partly because I now saw my hobby as an unsatisfactory thing if it went no further. If you set out to climb a mountain, however high you climb, you have failed if you cannot reach the top.

37   I *did* meet an undeniably grade-one thinker in my first year at Oxford. I was looking over a small bridge in Magdalen Deer Park, and a tiny mustached and hatted figure came and stood by my side. He was a German who had just fled from the Nazis to Oxford as a temporary refuge. His name was Einstein.

38   But Professor Einstein knew no English at that time and I knew only two words of German. I beamed at him, trying wordlessly to convey by my bearing all the affection and respect that the English felt for him. It is possible—and I have to make the admission—that I felt here were two grade-one thinkers standing side by side; yet I doubt if my face conveyed more than a formless awe. I would have given my Greek and Latin and French and a good slice of my English for enough German to communicate. But we were divided; he was as inscrutable as my headmaster. For perhaps five minutes we stood together on the bridge, undeniable grade-one thinker and breathless aspirant. With true greatness, Professor Einstein realized that my contact was better than none. He pointed to a trout wavering in midstream.

39   He spoke: "*Fisch.*"

40   My brain reeled. Here I was, mingling with the great, and yet helpless as the veriest grade-three thinker. Desperately I sought for some sign by which I might convey that I, too, revered pure reason. I nodded vehemently. In a brilliant flash I used up half of my German vocabulary.

41   "*Fisch. Ja Ja.*"

42   For perhaps another five minutes we stood side by side. Then Professor Einstein, his whole figure still conveying good will and amiability, drifted away out of sight.

43   I, too, would be a grade-one thinker. I was irreverent at the best of times. Political and religious systems, social customs, loyalties and traditions, they all came tumbling down like so many rotten apples off a tree. This was a fine hobby and a sensible substitute for cricket, since you could play it all the year round. I came up in the end with what must always remain the justification for grade-one thinking, its sign, seal and charter. I devised a coherent system for living. It was a moral system, which was wholly logical. Of course, as I readily admitted, conversion of the world to my way of thinking might be difficult, since my system did away with a number of trifles, such as big business, centralized government, armies, marriage. . . .

44   It was Ruth all over again. I had some very good friends who stood by me, and still do. But my acquaintances vanished, taking the girls with them. Young women seemed oddly contented with the world as it was. They valued the meaningless ceremony with a ring. Young men, while willing to concede the chaining sordidness of marriage, were hesitant about abandoning the organizations which they hoped would give them a career. A young man on the first rung of the Royal Navy, while perfectly agreeable to doing away with big business and marriage, got as red-necked as Mr. Houghton when I proposed a world without any battleships in it.

45   Had the game gone too far? Was it a game any longer? In those prewar days, I stood to lose a great deal, for the sake of a hobby.

46   Now you are expecting me to describe how I saw the folly of my ways and came back to the warm nest, where prejudices are so often called loyalties, where pointless actions are hallowed into custom by repetition, where we are content to say we think when all we do is feel.

47   But you would be wrong. I dropped my hobby and turned professional.

48   If I were to go back to the headmaster's study and find the dusty statuettes still there, I would arrange them differently. I would dust Venus and put her aside, for I have come to love her and know her for the fair thing she is. But I would put the Thinker, sunk in his desperate thought, where there were shadows before him—and at his back, I would put the leopard, crouched and ready to spring.

Questions for Engagement, Response, and Analysis

1. Golding uses the three statuettes both symbolically and structurally. Explain what they mean to him as a young boy, as an adolescent, and as an adult.

2. Define the three grades of thinkers according to Golding.

3. Why, according to Golding, are grade-three thinkers dangerous? What is unsatisfactory about grade-two thinking?

4. How does Golding's assessment of most human intelligence compare to that of Socrates in the allegory of the cave?

5. In your Reader's Journal, freewrite about what your classifications of thinkers would be, which classification you would belong in, and why.

Crafting Arguments

1. Write an essay analyzing Golding's use of structure, symbolism, and metaphorical devices to organize his essay and to clarify his ideas.

FICTION

James Joyce (1882–1941)

One of the most famous, influential, and controversial writers of the twentieth century, James Joyce was born in Dublin in 1882. Joyce excelled at the Irish Catholic schools where he was educated, and his experiences at these schools were a major influence on his later work, especially on his first novel, Portrait of the Artist As a Young Man *(1916). Joyce spent most of his life in Trieste, Rome, and Paris. Both his novels and his short stories are justly ranked as works that, though unique, were major influences on later writers. His collection of stories in* Dubliners, *ending with "The Dead," appeared in 1914. The American magazine* Little Review *began publication of Joyce's novel* Ulysses *in 1920, but the courts stopped publication when the publishers were convicted of obscenity; it was finally published in 1922.* Finnegan's Wake, *his last novel, was published in 1939, three years before his death.*

ARABY

(1914)

1   North Richmond Street, being blind, was a quiet street except at the hour when the Christian Brothers' School set the boys free. An uninhabited house of two stories stood at the blind end, detached from its neighbors in a square ground. The other houses of the street, conscious of decent lives within them, gazed at one another with brown imperturbable faces.

2   The former tenant of our house, a priest, had died in the back drawing room. Air, musty from having been long enclosed, hung in all the rooms, and the waste room behind the kitchen was littered with old useless papers. Among these I found a few paper-covered books, the pages of which were curled and damp: *The Abbot*, by Walter Scott, *The Devout Communicant*, and *The Memoirs of Vidocq*. I liked the last best because its leaves were yellow. The wild garden behind the house contained a central apple tree and a few straggling brushes under one of which I found the late tenant's rusty bicycle pump. He had been a very charitable priest;

in his will he had left all his money to institutions and the furniture of his house to his sister.

3   When the short days of winter came dusk fell before we had well eaten our dinners. When we met in the street the houses had grown somber. The space of sky above us was the color of ever-changing violet and towards it the lamps of the street lifted their feeble lanterns. The cold air stung us and we played till our bodies glowed. Our shouts echoed in the silent street. The career of our play brought us through the dark muddy lanes behind the houses where we ran the gauntlet of the rough tribes from the cottages, to the back doors of the dark odorous stables where a coachman smoothed and combed the horse or shook music from the buckled harness. When we returned to the street, light from the kitchen windows had filled the areas. If my uncle was seen turning the corner we hid in the shadow until we had seen him safely housed. Or if Mangan's sister came out on the doorstep to call her brother in to his tea we watched her from our shadow peer up and down the street. We waited to see whether she would remain or go in and, if she remained, we left our shadow and walked up to Mangan's steps resignedly. She was wait-ing for us, her figure defined by the light from the half-opened door. Her brother always teased her before he obeyed and I stood by the railings looking at her. Her dress swung as she moved her body and the soft rope of her hair tossed from side to side.

4   Every morning I lay on the floor in the front parlor watching her door. The blind was pulled down to within an inch of the sash so that I could not be seen. When she came out on the doorstep my heart leaped. I ran to the hall, seized my books and followed her. I kept her brown figure always in my eye and, when we came near the point at which our ways diverged, I quickened my pace and passed her. This happened morning after morning. I had never spoken to her, except for a few casual words, and yet her name was like a summons to all my foolish blood.

5   Her image accompanied me even in places the most hostile to romance. On Saturday evenings when my aunt went marketing I had to go to carry some of the parcels. We walked through the flaring streets, jostled by drunken men and bargaining women, amid the curses of labor-ers, the shrill litanies of shop boys who stood on guard by the barrels of pigs' cheeks, the nasal chanting of street singers, who sang a *come-all-you* about O'Donovan Rossa, or a ballad about the troubles in our native land. These noises converged in a single sensation of life for me: I imag-ined that I bore my chalice safely through a throng of foes. Her name sprang to my lips at moments in strange prayers and praises which I myself did not understand. My eyes were often full of tears (I could not tell why) and at times a flood from my heart seemed to pour itself out into my bosom. I thought little of the future. I did not know whether I would ever speak to her or not or, if I spoke to her, how I could tell her of my confused adoration. But my body was like a harp and her words and gestures were like fingers running upon the wires.

6   One evening I went into the back drawing room in which the priest had died. It was a dark rainy evening and there was no sound in the house. Through one of the broken panes I heard the rain impinge upon the earth, the fine incessant needles of water playing in the sodden beds. Some distant lamp or lighted window gleamed below me. I was thankful that I could see so little. All my senses seemed to desire to veil themselves and, feeling that I was about to slip from them, I pressed the palms of my hands together until they trembled, murmuring: *"O love! O love!"* many times.

7   At last she spoke to me. When she addressed the first words to me I was so confused that I did not know what to answer. She asked me was I going to *Araby*. I forgot whether I answered yes or no. It would be a splendid bazaar, she said; she would love to go.

8   "And why can't you?" I asked.

9   While she spoke she turned a silver bracelet round and round her wrist. She could not go, she said, because there would be a retreat that week in her convent. Her brother and two other boys were fighting for their caps and I was alone at the railings. She held one of the spikes, bowing her head towards me. The light from the lamp opposite our door caught the white curve of her neck, lit up her hair that rested there and, falling, lit up the hand upon the railing. It fell over one side of her dress and caught the white border of a petticoat, just visible as she stood at ease.

10   "It's well for you," she said.

11   "If I go," I said, "I will bring you something."

12   What innumerable follies laid waste my waking and sleeping thoughts after that evening! I wished to annihilate the tedious intervening days. I chafed against the work of school. At night in my bedroom and by day in the classroom her image came between me and the page I strove to read. The syllables of the word *Araby* were called to me through the silence in which my soul luxuriated and cast an Eastern enchantment over me. I asked for leave to go to the bazaar on Saturday night. My aunt was surprised and hoped it was not some Freemason affair. I answered few questions in class. I watched my master's face pass from amiability to sternness; he hoped I was not beginning to idle. I could not call my wandering thoughts together. I had hardly any patience with the serious work of life which, now that it stood between me and my desire, seemed to me child's play, ugly monotonous child's play.

13   On Saturday morning I reminded my uncle that I wished to go to the bazaar in the evening. He was fussing at the hall stand, looking for the hat brush, and answered me curtly:

14   "Yes, boy, I know."

15   As he was in the hall I could not go into the front parlor and lie at the window. I left the house in bad humor and walked slowly towards the school. The air was pitilessly raw and already my heart misgave me.

16   When I came home to dinner my uncle had not yet been home. Still it was early. I sat staring at the clock for some time and, when its ticking

began to irritate me, I left the room. I mounted the staircase and gained the upper part of the house. The high cold empty gloomy rooms liberated me and I went from room to room singing. From the front window I saw my companions playing below in the street. Their cries reached me weakened and indistinct and, leaning my forehead against the cool glass, I looked over at the dark house where she lived. I may have stood there for an hour, seeing nothing but the brown-clad figure cast by my imagination, touched discreetly by the lamplight at the curved neck, at the hand upon the railings and at the border below the dress.

17   When I came downstairs again I found Mrs. Mercer sitting at the fire. She was an old garrulous woman, a pawnbroker's widow, who collected used stamps for some pious purpose. I had to endure the gossip of the tea table. The meal was prolonged beyond an hour and still my uncle did not come. Mrs. Mercer stood up to go; she was sorry she couldn't wait any longer, but it was after eight o'clock and she did not like to be out late, as the night air was bad for her. When she had gone I began to walk up and down the room, clenching my fists. My aunt said:

18   "I'm afraid you may put off your bazaar for this night of Our Lord."

19   At nine o'clock I heard my uncle's latchkey in the hall door. I heard him talking to himself and heard the hall stand rocking when it had received the weight of his overcoat. I could interpret these signs. When he was midway through his dinner I asked him to give me the money to go to the bazaar. He had forgotten.

20   "The people are in bed and after their first sleep now," he said.

21   I did not smile. My aunt said to him energetically:

22   "Can't you give him the money and let him go? You've kept him late enough as it is."

23   My uncle said he was very sorry he had forgotten. He said he believed in the old saying: "All work and no play makes Jack a dull boy." He asked me where I was going and, when I had told him a second time he asked me did I know *The Arab's Farewell to His Steed*. When I left the kitchen he was about to recite the opening lines of the piece to my aunt.

24   I held a florin tightly in my hand as I strode down Buckingham Street towards the station. The sight of the streets thronged with buyers and glaring with gas recalled to me the purpose of my journey. I took my seat in a third-class carriage of a deserted train. After an intolerable delay the train moved out of the station slowly. It crept onward among ruinous houses and over the twinkling river. At Westland Row Station a crowd of people pressed to the carriage doors; but the porters moved them back, saying that it was a special train for the bazaar. I remained alone in the bare carriage. In a few minutes the train drew up beside an improvised wooden platform. I passed out on to the road and saw by the lighted dial of a clock that it was ten minutes to ten. In front of me was a large building which displayed the magical name.

25   I could not find any sixpenny entrance and, fearing that the bazaar would be closed, I passed in quickly through a turnstile, handing a shilling

to a weary-looking man. I found myself in a big hall girdled at half its height by a gallery. Nearly all the stalls were closed and the greater part of the hall was in darkness. I recognized a silence like that which pervades a church after a service. I walked into the center of the bazaar timidly. A few people were gathered about the stalls which were still open. Before a curtain, over which the words *Café Chantant* were written in colored lamps, two men were counting money on a salver. I listened to the fall of the coins.

26   Remembering with difficulty why I had come I went over to one of the stalls and examined porcelain vases and flowered tea sets. At the door of the stall a young lady was talking and laughing with two young gentlemen. I remarked their English accents and listened vaguely to their conversation.

27   "O, I never said such a thing!"

28   "O, but you did!"

29   "O, but I didn't!"

30   "Didn't she say that?"

31   "Yes, I heard her."

32   "O, there's a . . . fib!"

33   Observing me, the young lady came over and asked me did I wish to buy anything. The tone of her voice was not encouraging; she seemed to have spoken to me out of a sense of duty. I looked humbly at the great jars that stood like eastern guards at either side of the dark entrance to the stall and murmured:

34   "No, thank you."

35   The young lady changed the position of one of the vases and went back to the two young men. They began to talk of the same subject. Once or twice the young lady glanced at me over her shoulder.

36   I lingered before her stall, though I knew my stay was useless, to make my interest in her wares seem the more real. Then I turned away slowly and walked down the middle of the bazaar. I allowed the two pennies to fall against the sixpence in my pocket. I heard a voice call from one end of the gallery that the light was out. The upper part of the hall was now completely dark.

37   Gazing up into the darkness I saw myself as a creature driven and derided by vanity; and my eyes burned with anguish and anger.

Questions for Engagement, Response, and Analysis

1. What is the point of view and how is it crucial to this story?

2. How does the description of the neighborhood set the tone and prepare for the conclusion?

3. What do the many references to the church and religion suggest about the boy's attitude and his sense of mission?

4. What does Araby symbolize for the narrator?

5. What is the theme of the story?

Crafting Arguments

1. In an essay, analyze the ways in which the narrator changes as the story progresses and the causes of the changes.

2. Write an essay describing the narrator's quest in "Araby." Does he experience an epiphany? If so, what is it?

Arthur C. Clarke (1917–2008)

Arthur C. Clarke, a British physicist and mathematician, writes fiction and nonfiction. His works, selling in the millions, have been translated into dozens of languages. A 1945 paper published in Wireless World *helped to set the stage for modern telecommunications. Clarke is, however, probably best known for the screenplay for Stanley Kubrick's* 2001: A Space Odyssey, *based on Clarke's short story "Sentinel of Eternity." "The Star," published in 1955, won a Hugo award for excellence in science fiction.*

THE STAR (1955)

1   It is three thousand light years to the Vatican. Once, I believed that space could have no power over faith, just as I believed that the heavens declared the glory of God's handiwork. Now I have seen that handiwork, and my faith is sorely troubled. I stare at the crucifix that hangs on the cabin wall above the Mark VI Computer, and for the first time in my life I wonder if it is no more than an empty symbol.

2   I have told no one yet, but the truth cannot be concealed. The facts are there for all to read, recorded on the countless miles of magnetic tape and the thousands of photographs we are carrying back to Earth. Other scientists can interpret them as easily as I can, and I am not one who would condone that tampering with the truth which often gave my order a bad name in the olden days.

3   The crew are already sufficiently depressed: I wonder how they will take this ultimate irony. Few of them have any religious faith, yet they will not relish using this final weapon in their campaign against me—that private, good-natured, but fundamentally serious, war which lasted all the way from Earth. It amused them to have a Jesuit as chief astrophysicist: Dr. Chandler, for instance, could never get over it (why are medical men such notorious atheists?). Sometimes he would meet me on the observation deck, where the lights are always low so that the stars shine with undiminished glory. He would come up to me in the gloom and stand staring out of the great oval port, while the heavens crawled slowly around us as the ship turned end over end with the residual spin we had never bothered to correct.

4   "Well, Father," he would say at last, "it goes on forever and forever, and perhaps *Something* made it. But how you can believe that Something

has a special interest in us and our miserable little world—that just beats me." Then the argument would start, while the stars and nebulae would swing around us in silent, endless arcs beyond the flawlessly clear plastic of the observation port.

5   It was, I think, the apparent incongruity of my position that caused most amusement to the crew. In vain I would point to my three papers in the *Astrophysical Journal,* my five in the *Monthly Notices of the Royal Astronomical Society.* I would remind them that my order has long been famous for its scientific works. We may be few now, but ever since the eighteenth century we have made contributions to astronomy and geophysics out of all proportion to our numbers. Will my report on the Phoenix Nebula end our thousand years of history? It will end, I fear, much more than that.

6   I do not know who gave the nebula its name, which seems to me a very bad one. If it contains a prophecy, it is one that cannot be verified for several billion years. Even the word nebula is misleading: this is a far smaller object than those stupendous clouds of mist—the stuff of unborn stars— that are scattered throughout the length of the Milky Way. On the cosmic scale, indeed, the Phoenix Nebula is a tiny thing—a tenuous shell of gas surrounding a single star.

7   Or what is left of a star . . .

8   The Rubens engraving of Loyola seems to mock me as it hangs there above the spectrophotometer tracings. What would *you,* Father, have made of this knowledge that has come into my keeping, so far from the little world that was all the universe you knew? Would your faith have risen to the challenge, as mine has failed to do?

9   You gaze into the distance, Father, but I have traveled a distance beyond any that you could have imagined when you founded our order a thousand years ago. No other survey ship has been so far from Earth: we are at the very frontiers of the explored universe. We set out to reach the Phoenix Nebula, we succeeded, and we are homeward bound with our burden of knowledge. I wish I could lift that burden from my shoulders, but I call to you in vain across the centuries and the light-years that lie between us.

10   On the book you are holding the words are plain to read. AD MAJOREM DEI GLORIAM, the message runs, but it is a message I can no longer believe. Would you still believe it, if you could see what we have found?

11   We knew, of course, what the Phoenix Nebula was. Every year, in our galaxy alone, more than a hundred stars explode, blazing for a few hours or days with thousands of times their normal brilliance before they sink back into death and obscurity. Such are the ordinary novae— the commonplace disasters of the universe. I have recorded the spectrograms and light curves of dozens since I started working at the Lunar Observatory.

12   But three or four times in every thousand years occurs something beside which even a nova pales into total insignificance.

13   When a star becomes a *supernova,* it may for a little while outshine all the massed suns of the galaxy. The Chinese astronomers watched this happen in A.D. 1054, not knowing what it was they saw. Five centuries later, in 1572, a supernova blazed in Cassiopeia so brilliantly that it was visible in the daylight sky. There have been three more in the thousand years that have passed since then.

14   Our mission was to visit the remnants of such a catastrophe, to reconstruct the events that led up to it, and, if possible, to learn its cause. We came slowly in through the concentric shells of gas that had been blasted out six thousand years before, yet were expanding still. They were immensely hot, radiating even now with a fierce violet light, but were far too tenuous to do us any damage. When the star had exploded, its outer layers had been driven upward with such speed that they had escaped completely from its gravitational field. Now they formed a hollow shell large enough to engulf a thousand solar systems, and at its center burned the tiny, fantastic object which the star had now become—a White Dwarf, smaller than the Earth, yet weighing a million times as much.

15   The glowing gas shells were all around us, banishing the normal night of interstellar space. We were flying into the center of a cosmic bomb that had detonated millennia ago and whose incandescent fragments were still hurling apart. The immense scale of the explosion, and the fact that the debris already covered a volume of space many billions of miles across, robbed the scene of any visible movement. It would take decades before the unaided eye could detect any motion in these tortured wisps and eddies of gas, yet the sense of turbulent expansion was overwhelming.

16   We had checked our primary drive hours before, and were drifting slowly toward the fierce little star ahead. Once it had been a sun like our own, but it had squandered in a few hours the energy that should have kept it shining for a million years. Now it was a shrunken miser, hoarding its resources as if trying to make amends for its prodigal youth.

17   No one seriously expected to find planets. If there had been any before the explosion, they would have been boiled into puffs of vapor, and their substance lost in the greater wreckage of the star itself. But we made the automatic search, as we always do when approaching an unknown sun, and presently we found a single small world circling the star at an immense distance. It must have been the Pluto of this vanished solar system, orbiting on the frontiers of the night. Too far from the central sun ever to have known life, its remoteness had saved it from the fate of all its lost companions.

18   The passing fires had seared its rocks and burned away the mantle of frozen gas that must have covered it in the days before the disaster. We landed, and we found the Vault.

19   Its builders had made sure that we should. The monolithic marker that stood above the entrance was now a fused stump, but even the first long-range photographs told us that here was the work of intelligence. A little later we detected the continent-wide pattern of radio-activity that had

been buried in the rock. Even if the pylon above the Vault had been destroyed, this would have remained, an immovable and all but eternal beacon calling to the stars. Our ship fell toward this gigantic bull's-eye like an arrow into its target.

20   The pylon must have been a mile high when it was built, but now it looked like a candle that had melted down into a puddle of wax. It took us a week to drill through the fused rock, since we did not have the proper tools for a task like this. We were astronomers, not archaeologists, but we could improvise. Our original purpose was forgotten: this lonely monument, reared with such labor at the greatest possible distance from the doomed sun, could have only one meaning. A civilization that knew it was about to die had made its last bid for immortality.

21   It will take us generations to examine all the treasures that were placed in the Vault. They had plenty of time to prepare, for their sun must have given its first warnings many years before the final detonation. Everything that they wished to preserve, all the fruit of their genius, they brought here to this distant world in the days before the end, hoping that some other race would find it and that they would not be utterly forgotten. Would we have done as well, or would we have been too lost in our own misery to give thought to a future we could never see or share?

22   If only they had had a little more time! They could travel freely enough between the planets of their own sun, but they had not yet learned to cross the interstellar gulfs, and the nearest solar system was a hundred light-years away. Yet even had they possessed the secret of the Transfinite Drive, no more than a few millions could have been saved. Perhaps it was better thus.

23   Even if they had not been so disturbingly human as their sculpture shows, we could not have helped admiring them and grieving for their fate. They left thousands of visual records and the machines for projecting them, together with elaborate pictorial instructions from which it will not be difficult to learn their written language. We have examined many of these records, and brought to life for the first time in six thousand years the warmth and beauty of a civilization that in many ways must have been superior to our own. Perhaps they only showed us the best, and one can hardly blame them. But their words were very lovely, and their cities were built with a grace that matches anything of man's. We have watched them at work and play, and listened to their musical speech sounding across the centuries. One scene is still before my eyes—a group of children on a beach of strange blue sand, playing in the waves as children play on Earth. Curious whiplike trees line the shore, and some very large animal is wading in the shadows yet attracting no attention at all.

24   And sinking into the sea, still warm and friendly and life-giving, is the sun that will soon turn traitor and obliterate all this innocent happiness.

25   Perhaps if we had not been so far from home and so vulnerable to loneliness, we should not have been so deeply moved. Many of us had seen the ruins of ancient civilizations on other worlds, but they had never

affected us so profoundly. This tragedy was unique. It is one thing for a race to fail and die, as nations and cultures have done on Earth. But to be destroyed so completely in the full flower of its achievement, leaving no survivors—how could that be reconciled with the mercy of God?

26   My colleagues have asked me that, and I have given what answers I can. Perhaps you could have done better, Father Loyola, but I have found nothing in the *Exercitia Spiritualia* that helps me here. They were not an evil people: I do not know what gods they worshiped, if indeed they worshiped any. But I have looked back at them across the centuries, and have watched while the loveliness they used their last strength to preserve was brought forth again into the light of their shrunken sun. They could have taught us much: why were they destroyed?

27   I know the answers that my colleagues will give when they get back to Earth. They will say that the universe has no purpose and no plan, that since a hundred suns explode every year in our galaxy, at this very moment some race is dying in the depths of space. Whether that race has done good or evil during its lifetime will make no difference in the end: there is no divine justice, for there is no God.

28   Yet, of course, what we have seen proves nothing of the sort. Anyone who argues thus is being swayed by emotion, not logic. God has no need to justify His actions to man. He who built the universe can destroy it when He chooses. It is arrogance—it is perilously near blasphemy—for us to say what He may or may not do.

29   This I could have accepted, hard though it is to look upon whole worlds and peoples thrown into the furnace. But there comes a point when even the deepest faith must falter, and now, as I look at the calculations lying before me, I know I have reached that point at last.

30   We could not tell, before we reached the nebula, how long ago the explosion took place. Now, from the astronomical evidence and the record in the rocks of that one surviving planet, I have been able to date it very exactly. I know in what year the light of this colossal conflagration reached our Earth. I know how brilliantly the supernova whose corpse now dwindles behind our speeding ship once shone in terrestrial skies. I know how it must have blazed low in the east before sunrise, like a beacon in that oriental dawn.

31   There can be no reasonable doubt: the ancient mystery is solved at last. Yet, oh God, there were so many stars you could have used. What was the need to give these people to the fire, that the symbol of their passing might shine above Bethlehem?

Questions for Engagement, Response, and Analysis

1. What is the point of view in "The Star"? What is the tone? How is it created and controlled by the point of view?
2. What characteristics and talents are expected of a Jesuit priest? At what point in the story is the reader made aware that this priest is

facing a spiritual crisis? At what point does Clarke reveal the source of the crisis?

3. What is the theme of "The Star"?

Crafting Arguments

1. Analyze in an essay how Clarke's use of a Jesuit priest as narrator is vital to the irony in the story.

Toni Cade Bambara (1939–1995)

Toni Cade adopted the name Bambara from a name she found in a sketchbook in her great-grandmother's trunk. This renaming of herself, with an emphasis on personal history, demonstrates her fascination with the myths, music, and history of African Americans. After receiving a bachelor of arts degree in theater art and English from Queens College and studying at Commedia del'Arte in Milan, Italy, Bambara taught at several colleges throughout the Northeast. She settled in Atlanta and taught at Spelman College. Many of her works skillfully portray adolescents coming to grips with their environment and show the politics and cultural activities of the urban community.

RAYMOND'S RUN   (1960)

1   I don't have much work to do around the house like some girls. My mother does that. And I don't have to earn my pocket money by hustling; George runs errands for the big boys and sells Christmas cards. And anything else that's got to get done, my father does. All I have to do in life is mind my brother Raymond, which is enough.

2   Sometimes I slip and say my little brother Raymond. But as any fool can see he's much bigger and he's older too. But a lot of people call him my little brother cause he needs looking after cause he's not quite right. And a lot of smart mouths got lots to say about that too, especially when George was minding him. But now, if anybody has anything to say to Raymond, anything to say about his big head, they have to come by me. And I don't play the dozens or believe in standing around with somebody in my face doing a lot of talking. I much rather just knock you down and take my chances even if I am a little girl with skinny arms and a squeaky voice, which is how I got the name Squeaky. And if things get too rough, I run. And as anybody can tell you, I'm the fastest thing on two feet.

3   There is no track meet that I don't win the first-place medal. I used to win the twenty-yard dash when I was a little kid in kindergarten. Nowadays, it's the fifty-yard dash. And tomorrow I'm subject to run the quarter-meter relay all by myself and come in first, second, and third. The big kids call me Mercury cause I'm the swiftest thing in the neighborhood.

Everybody knows that—except two people who know better, my father and me. He can beat me to Amsterdam Avenue with me having a two-fire-hydrant head start and him running with his hands in his pockets and whistling. But that's private information. Cause can you imagine some thirty-five-year-old man stuffing himself into PAL shorts to race little kids? So as far as everyone's concerned, I'm the fastest and that goes for Gretchen, too, who has put out the tale that she is going to win the first-place medal this year. Ridiculous. In the second place, she's got short legs. In the third place, she's got freckles. In the first place, no one can beat me and that's all there is to it.

4   I'm standing on the corner admiring the weather and about to take a stroll down Broadway so I can practice my breathing exercises, and I've got Raymond walking on the inside close to the buildings, cause he's sub-ject to fits of fantasy and starts thinking he's a circus performer and that the curb is a tightrope strung high in the air. And sometimes after a rain he likes to step down off his tightrope right into the gutter and slosh around getting his shoes and cuffs wet. Then I get hit when I get home. Or sometimes if you don't watch him he'll dash across traffic to the island in the middle of Broadway and give the pigeons a fit. Then I have to go behind him apologizing to all the old people sitting around trying to get some sun and getting all upset with the pigeons fluttering around them, scattering their newspapers and upsetting the wax paper lunches in their laps. So I keep Raymond on the inside of me, and he plays like he's dri-ving a stage-coach which is O.K. by me so long as he doesn't run me over or interrupt my breathing exercises, which I have to do on account of I'm serious about my running, and I don't care who knows it.

5   Now some people like to act like things come easy to them, won't let on that they practice. Not me. I'll high-prance down 34th Street like a rodeo pony to keep my knees strong even if it does get my mother uptight so that she walks ahead like she's not with me, don't know me, is all by herself on a shopping trip, and I am somebody else's crazy child. Now you take Cynthia Procter for instance. She's just the opposite. If there's a test tomorrow, she'll say something like, "Oh, I guess I'll play handball this afternoon and watch television tonight," just to let you know she ain't thinking about the test. Or like last week when she won the spelling bee for the millionth time, "A good thing you got 'receive,' Squeaky, cause I would have got it wrong. I completely forgot about the spelling bee." And she'll clutch the lace on her blouse like it was a narrow escape. Oh, brother. But of course when I pass her house on my early morning trots around the block, she is practicing the scales on the piano over and over and over and over. Then in music class she always lets herself get bumped around so she falls accidently on purpose onto the piano stool and is so surprised to find herself sitting there that she decides just for fun to try out the ole keys. And what do you know—Chopin's waltzes just spring out of her fingertips and she's the most surprised thing in the world. A regular prodigy. I could kill people like that. I stay up all night

studying the words for the spelling bee. And you can see me any time of day practicing running. I never walk if I can trot, and shame on Raymond if he can't keep up. But of course he does, cause if he hangs back someone's liable to walk up to him and get smart, or take his allowance from him, or ask him where he got that great big pumpkin head. People are so stupid sometimes.

6   So I'm strolling down Broadway breathing out and breathing in on counts of seven, which is my lucky number, and here comes Gretchen and her sidekicks: Mary Louise, who used to be a friend of mine when she first moved to Harlem from Baltimore and got beat up by everybody till I took up for her on account of her mother and my mother used to sing in the same choir when they were young girls, but people ain't grateful, so now she hangs out with the new girl Gretchen and talks about me like a dog; and Rosie, who is as fat as I am skinny and has a big mouth where Raymond is concerned and is too stupid to know that there is not a big deal of difference between herself and Raymond and that she can't afford to throw stones. So they are steady coming up Broadway and I see right away that it's going to be one of those Dodge City scenes cause the street ain't that big and they're close to the buildings just as we are. First I think I'll step into the candy store and look over the new comics and let them pass. But that's chicken and I've got a reputation to consider. So then I think I'll just walk straight on through them or even over them if necessary. But as they get to me, they slow down. I'm ready to fight, cause like I said I don't feature a whole lot of chitchat, I much prefer to just knock you down right from the jump and save everybody a lotta precious time.

7   "You signing up for the May Day races?" smiles Mary Louise, only it's not a smile at all. A dumb question like that doesn't deserve an answer. Besides, there's just me and Gretchen standing there really, so no use wasting my breath talking to shadows.

8   "I don't think you're going to win this time," says Rosie, trying to signify with her hands on her hips all salty, completely forgetting that I have whupped her behind many times for less salt than that.

9   "I always win cause I'm the best," I say straight at Gretchen who is, as far as I'm concerned, the only one talking in this ventriloquist-dummy routine. Gretchen smiles, but it's not a smile, and I'm thinking that girls never really smile at each other because they don't know how and don't want to know how and there's probably no one to teach us how, cause grownup girls don't know either. Then they all look at Raymond who has just brought his mule team to a standstill. And they're about to see what trouble they can get into through him.

10   "What grade you in now, Raymond?"

11   "You got anything to say to my brother, you say it to me, Mary Louise Williams of Raggedy Town, Baltimore."

12   "What are you, his mother?" sasses Rosie.

13   "That's right, Fatso. And the next word out of anybody and I'll be *their* mother too." So they just stand there and Gretchen shifts from one leg to

the other and so do they. Then Gretchen puts her hands on her hips and is about to say something with her freckle-face self but doesn't. Then she walks around me looking me up and down but keeps walking up Broadway, and her sidekicks follow her. So me and Raymond smile at each other and he says "Giddyap" to his team and I continue with my breathing exercises, strolling down Broadway toward the ice man on 145th with not a care in the world cause I am Miss Quicksilver herself.

14   I take my time getting to the park on May Day because the track meet is the last thing on the program. The biggest thing on the program is the Maypole dancing, which I can do without, thank you, even if my mother thinks it's a shame I don't take part and act like a girl for a change. You'd think my mother'd be grateful not to have to make me a white organdy dress with a big satin sash and buy me new white baby-doll shoes that can't be taken out of the box till the big day. You'd think she'd be glad her daughter ain't out there prancing around a Maypole getting the new clothes all dirty and sweaty and trying to act like a fairy or a flower or whatever you're supposed to be when you should be trying to be yourself, whatever that is, which is, as far as I am concerned, a poor black girl who really can't afford to buy shoes and a new dress you only wear once a lifetime cause it won't fit next year.

15   I was once a strawberry in a Hansel and Gretel pageant when I was in nursery school and didn't have no better sense than to dance on tiptoe with my arms in a circle over my head doing umbrella steps and being a perfect fool just so my mother and father could come dressed up and clap. You'd think they'd know better than to encourage that kind of nonsense. I am not a strawberry. I do not dance on my toes. I run. That is what I am all about. So I always come late to the May Day program, just in time to get my number pinned on and lay in the grass till they announce the fifty-yard dash.

16   I put Raymond in the little swings, which is a tight squeeze this year and will be impossible next year. Then I look around for Mr. Pearson, who pins the numbers on. I'm really looking for Gretchen if you want to know the truth, but she's not around. The park is jam-packed. Parents in hats and corsages and breast-pocket handkerchiefs peeking up. Kids in white dresses and light blue suits. The parkees unfolding chairs and chasing the rowdy kids from Lenox as if they had no right to be there. The big guys with their caps on backwards, leaning against the fence swirling the basketballs on the tips of their fingers, waiting for all these crazy people to clear out the park so they can play. Most of the kids in my class are carrying bass drums and glockenspiels and flutes. You'd think they'd put in a few bongos or something for real like that.

17   Then here comes Mr. Pearson with his clipboard and his cards and pencils and whistles and safety pins and fifty million other things he's always dropping all over the place with his clumsy self. He sticks out in a crowd because he's on stilts. We used to call him Jack and the Beanstalk to get him mad. But I'm the only one that can outrun him and get away, and I'm too grown for that silliness now.

18   "Well, Squeaky," he says, checking my name off the list and handing me number seven and two pins. And I'm thinking he's got no right to call me Squeaky, if I can't call him Beanstalk.

19   "Hazel Elizabeth Deborah Parker," I correct him and tell him to write it down on his board.

20   "Well, Hazel Elizabeth Deborah Parker, going to give someone else a break this year?" I squint at him real hard to see if he is seriously thinking I should lose the race on purpose just to give someone else a break. "Only six girls running this time," he continues, shaking his head sadly like it's my fault all of New York didn't turn out in sneakers. "That new girl should give you a run for your money." He looks around the park for Gretchen like a periscope in a submarine movie. "Wouldn't it be a nice gesture if you were . . . to ahhh . . ."

21   I give him such a look he couldn't finish putting that idea into words. Grownups got a lot of nerve sometimes. I pin number seven to myself and stomp away, I'm so burnt. And I go straight for the track and stretch out on the grass while the band winds up with "Oh, the Monkey Wrapped His Tail Around the Flagpole," which my teacher calls by some other name. The man on the loudspeaker is calling everyone over to the track and I'm on my back looking at the sky, trying to pretend I'm in the country, but I can't because even grass in the city feels hard as sidewalk, and there's just no pretending you are anywhere but in a "concrete jungle" as my grandfather says.

22   The twenty-yard dash takes all of two minutes cause most of the little kids don't know no better than to run off the track or run the wrong way or run smack into the fence and fall down and cry. One little kid, though, has got the good sense to run straight for the white ribbon up ahead so he wins. Then the second-graders line up for the thirty-yard dash and I don't even bother to turn my head to watch cause Raphael Perez always wins. He wins before he even begins by psyching the runners, telling them they're going to trip on their shoelaces and fall on their faces or lose their shorts or something, which he doesn't really have to do since he is very fast, almost as fast as I am. After that is the forty-yard dash which I used to run when I was in first grade. Raymond is hollering from the swings cause he knows I'm about to do my thing cause the man on the loudspeaker has just announced the fifty-yard dash, although he might just as well be giving a recipe for angel food cake cause you can hardly make out what he's saying for the static. I get up and slip off my sweat pants and then I see Gretchen standing at the starting line, kicking her legs out like a pro. Then as I get into place I see that ole Raymond is on the line on the other side of the fence, bending down with his fingers on the ground just like he knew what he was doing. I was going to yell at him but then I didn't. It burns up your energy to holler.

23   Every time, just before I take off in a race, I always feel like I'm in a dream, the kind of dream you have when you're sick with fever and feel all hot and weightless. I dream I'm flying over a sandy beach in the early

morning sun, kissing the leaves of the trees as I fly by. And there's always the smell of apples, just like in the country when I was little and used to think I was a choo-choo train, running through the fields of corn and chugging up the hill to the orchard. And all the time I'm dreaming this, I get lighter and lighter until I'm flying over the beach again, getting blown through the sky like a feather that weighs nothing at all. But once I spread my fingers in the dirt and crouch over the Get on Your Mark, the dream goes and I am solid again and am telling myself, Squeaky you must win, you must win, you are the fastest thing in the world, you can even beat your father up Amsterdam if you really try. And then I feel my weight coming back just behind my knees then down to my feet then into the earth and the pistol shot explodes in my blood and I am off and weight-less again, flying past the other runners, my arms pumping up and down and the whole world is quiet except for the crunch as I zoom over the gravel of the track. I glance to my left and there is no one. To the right, a blurred Gretchen, who's got her chin jutting out as if it would win the race all by itself. And on the other side of the fence is Raymond with his arms down to his side and the palms tucked up behind him, running in his very own style, and it's the first time I ever saw that and I almost stop to watch my brother Raymond on his first run. But the white ribbon is bouncing toward me and I tear past it, racing into the distance till my feet with a mind of their own start digging up footfuls of dirt and brake me short. Then all the kids standing on the side pile on me, banging me on the back and slapping my head with their May Day programs, for I have won again and everybody on 151st Street can walk tall for another year.

24   "In first place . . ." the man on the loudspeaker is clear as a bell now, but then he pauses and the loudspeaker starts to whine. Then static. And I lean down to catch my breath and here comes Gretchen walking back, for she's overshot the finish line too, huffing and puffing with her hands on her hips taking it slow, breathing in steady time like a real pro and I sort of like her a little for the first time. "In first place . . ." and then three or four voices get all mixed up on the loudspeaker and I dig my sneaker into the grass and stare at Gretchen who's staring back, we both won-dering just who did win. I can hear old Beanstalk arguing with the man on the loudspeaker and then a few others running their mouths about what the stopwatches say. Then I hear Raymond yanking at the fence to call me and I wave to shush him, but he keeps rattling the fence like a gorilla in a cage like in them gorilla movies, but then like a dancer or something he starts climbing hand over hand and remembering how he looked running with his arms down to his side and with the wind pulling his mouth back and his teeth showing and all, it occurred to me that Ray-mond would make a very fine runner. Doesn't he always keep up with me on my trots? And he surely knows how to breathe in counts of seven cause he's always doing it at the dinner table, which drives my brother George up the wall. And I'm smiling to beat the band cause if I've lost this race, or if me and Gretchen tied, or even if I've won, I can always retire

as a runner and begin a whole new career as a coach with Raymond as my champion. After all, with a little more study I can beat Cynthia and her phony self at the spelling bee. And if I bugged my mother, I could get piano lessons and become a star. And I have a big rep as the baddest thing around. And I've got a roomful of ribbons and medals and awards. But what has Raymond got to call his own?

25   So I stand there with my new plans, laughing out loud by this time as Raymond jumps down from the fence and runs over with his teeth showing and his arms down to the side, which no one before him has quite mastered as a running style. And by the time he comes over I'm jumping up and down so glad to see him—my brother Raymond, a great runner in the family tradition. But of course everyone thinks I'm jumping up and down because the men on the loudspeaker have finally gotten themselves together and compared notes and are announcing "In first place—Miss Hazel Elizabeth Deborah Parker." (Dig that.) "In second place—Miss Gretchen P. Lewis." And I look at Gretchen wondering what the "P" stands for. And I smile. Cause she's good, no doubt about it. Maybe she'd like to help me coach Raymond; she obviously is serious about running, as any fool can see. And she nods to congratulate me and then she smiles. And I smile. We stand there with this big smile of respect between us. It's about as real a smile as girls can do for each other, considering we don't practice real smiling every day, you know, cause maybe we too busy being flowers or fairies or strawberries instead of something honest and worthy of respect . . . you know . . . like being people.

Questions for Engagement, Response, and Analysis

1. Describe the first-person narrator in this story.
2. What is the relationship between Hazel and her brother Raymond? Between Hazel and her father? Between Hazel and her mother?
3. What do Hazel's opinions of others—Cynthia Procter and Mr. Pearson, for example—reveal about her?
4. What is the theme of this story?

Crafting Arguments

1. Write an essay describing in detail Hazel's epiphany and supporting your claims about the changes this epiphany has made in her.

Isabel Allende (b. 1942)

Born in Lima, Peru, Isabel Allende moved with her family to Chile in 1945. Her uncle, Salvador Allende, was president of Chile until 1973, when he was assassinated. A few years later, Allende, her husband, and their children moved to Venezuela. Allende combines in her fiction realistic and

*brutal political observation, a feminist vision, and the
imaginative detail of magical realism. She is among the
most highly regarded of contemporary Latin American novelists. Among her books are* The House of the Spirits *(1982);*
Of Love and Shadows *(1984);* Eva Luna *(1989), a novel;* The
Stories of Eva Luna *(1990), from which the story below is
taken; and* My Invented Country *(2003). Her most recent
novels are* Zorro *(2005) and* Inez of My Soul *(2006). Several
of her novels, including* The House of the Spirits *and* Of Love
and Shadows, *have been adapted for film. Though she writes
in Spanish, translations of her works have been very popular in the United States.*

AND OF CLAY ARE WE CREATED (1989)

1   They discovered the girl's head protruding from the mudpit, eyes wide
open, calling soundlessly. She had a First Communion name, Azucena.
Lily. In that vast cemetery where the odor of death was already attracting vultures from far away, and where the weeping of orphans and wails
of the injured filled the air, the little girl obstinately clinging to life
became the symbol of the tragedy. The television cameras transmitted so
often the unbearable image of the head budding like a black squash from
the clay that there was no one who did not recognize her and know her
name. And every time we saw her on the screen, right behind her was
Rolf Carlé, who had gone there on assignment, never suspecting that he
would find a fragment of his past, lost thirty years before.

2   First a subterranean sob rocked the cotton fields, curling them like
waves of foam. Geologists had set up their seismographs weeks before
and knew that the mountain had awakened again. For some time they
had predicted that the heat of the eruption could detach the eternal ice
from the slopes of the volcano, but no one heeded their warnings; they
sounded like tales of frightened old women. The towns in the valley went
about their daily life, deaf to the moaning of the earth, until that fateful
Wednesday night in November when a prolonged roar announced the end
of the world, and walls of snow broke loose, rolling in an avalanche of
clay, stones, and water that descended on the villages and buried them
beneath unfathomable meters of telluric vomit. As soon as the survivors
emerged from the paralysis of that first awful terror, they could see that
houses, plazas, churches, white cotton plantations, dark coffee forests,
cattle pastures—all had disappeared. Much later, after soldiers and volunteers had arrived to rescue the living and try to assess the magnitude
of the cataclysm, it was calculated that beneath the mud lay more than
twenty thousand human beings and an indefinite number of animals
putrefying in a viscous soup. Forests and rivers had also been swept
away, and there was nothing to be seen but an immense desert of mire.

3   When the station called before dawn, Rolf Carlé and I were together.
I crawled out of bed, dazed with sleep, and went to prepare coffee while

he hurriedly dressed. He stuffed his gear in the green canvas backpack he always carried, and we said goodbye, as we had so many times before. I had no presentiments. I sat in the kitchen, sipping my coffee and planning the long hours without him, sure that he would be back the next day.

4   He was one of the first to reach the scene, because while other reporters were fighting their way to the edges of that morass in jeeps, bicycles, or on foot, each getting there however he could, Rolf Carlé had the advantage of the television helicopter, which flew him over the avalanche. We watched on our screens the footage captured by his assistant's camera, in which he was up to his knees in muck, a microphone in his hand, in the midst of a bedlam of lost children, wounded survivors, corpses, and devastation. The story came to us in his calm voice. For years he had been a familiar figure in newscasts, reporting live at the scene of battles and catastrophes with awesome tenacity. Nothing could stop him, and I was always amazed at his equanimity in the face of danger and suffering; it seemed as if nothing could shake his fortitude or deter his curiosity. Fear seemed never to touch him, although he had confessed to me that he was not a courageous man, far from it. I believe that the lens of the camera had a strange effect on him; it was as if it transported him to a different time from which he could watch events without actually participating in them. When I knew him better, I came to realize that this fictive distance seemed to protect him from his own emotions.

5   Rolf Carlé was in on the story of Azucena from the beginning. He filmed the volunteers who discovered her, and the first persons who tried to reach her; his camera zoomed in on the girl, her dark face, her large desolate eyes, the plastered-down tangle of her hair. The mud was like quicksand around her, and anyone attempting to reach her was in danger of sinking. They threw a rope to her that she made no effort to grasp until they shouted to her to catch it; then she pulled a hand from the mire and tried to move, but immediately sank a little deeper. Rolf threw down his knapsack and the rest of his equipment and waded into the quagmire, commenting for his assistant's microphone that it was cold and that one could begin to smell the stench of corpses.

6   "What's your name?" he asked the girl, and she told him her flower name. "Don't move, Azucena," Rolf Carlé directed, and kept talking to her, without a thought for what he was saying, just to distract her, while slowly he worked his way forward in mud up to his waist. The air around him seemed as murky as the mud.

7   It was impossible to reach her from the approach he was attempting, so he retreated and circled around where there seemed to be firmer footing. When finally he was close enough, he took the rope and tied it beneath her arms, so they could pull her out. He smiled at her with that smile that crinkles his eyes and makes him look like a little boy; he told her that everything was fine, that he was here with her now, that soon they would have her out. He signaled the others to pull, but as soon as the cord tensed, the girl screamed. They tried again, and her shoulders

and arms appeared, but they could move her no farther; she was trapped. Someone suggested that her legs might be caught in the collapsed walls of her house, but she said it was not just rubble, that she was also held by the bodies of her brothers and sisters clinging to her legs.

8   "Don't worry, we'll get you out of here," Rolf promised. Despite the quality of the transmission, I could hear his voice break, and I loved him more than ever. Azucena looked at him, but said nothing.

9   During those first hours Rolf Carlé exhausted all the resources of his ingenuity to rescue her. He struggled with poles and ropes, but every tug was an intolerable torture for the imprisoned girl. It occurred to him to use one of the poles as a lever but got no result and had to abandon the idea. He talked a couple of soldiers into working with him for a while, but they had to leave because so many other victims were calling for help. The girl could not move, she barely could breathe, but she did not seem desperate, as if an ancestral resignation allowed her to accept her fate. The reporter, on the other hand, was determined to snatch her from death. Someone brought him a tire, which he placed beneath her arms like a life buoy, and then laid a plank near the hole to hold his weight and allow him to stay closer to her. As it was impossible to remove the rubble blindly, he tried once or twice to dive toward her feet, but emerged frustrated, covered with mud, and spitting gravel. He concluded that he would have to have a pump to drain the water, and radioed a request for one, but received in return a message that there was no available transport and it could not be sent until the next morning.

10   "We can't wait that long!" Rolf Carlé shouted, but in the pandemonium no one stopped to commiserate. Many more hours would go by before he accepted that time had stagnated and reality had been irreparably distorted.

11   A military doctor came to examine the girl, and observed that her heart was functioning well and that if she did not get too cold she could survive the night.

12   "Hang on, Azucena, we'll have the pump tomorrow," Rolf Carlé tried to console her.

13   "Don't leave me alone," she begged.

14   "No, of course I won't leave you."

15   Someone brought him coffee, and he helped the girl drink it, sip by sip. The warm liquid revived her and she began telling him about her small life, about her family and her school, about how things were in that little bit of world before the volcano had erupted. She was thirteen, and she had never been outside her village. Rolf Carlé, buoyed by a premature optimism, was convinced that everything would end well: the pump would arrive, they would drain the water, move the rubble, and Azucena would be transported by helicopter to a hospital where she would recover rapidly and where he could visit her and bring her gifts. He thought, She's already too old for dolls, and I don't know what would please her; maybe a dress. I don't know much about women, he

concluded, amused, reflecting that although he had known many women in his lifetime, none had taught him these details. To pass the hours he began to tell Azucena about his travels and adventures as a newshound, and when he exhausted his memory, he called upon imagination, inventing things he thought might entertain her. From time to time she dozed, but he kept talking in the darkness, to assure her that he was still there and to overcome the menace of uncertainty.

16   That was a long night.

🍃

17   Many miles away, I watched Rolf Carlé and the girl on a television screen. I could not bear the wait at home, so I went to National Television, where I often spent entire nights with Rolf editing programs. There, I was near his world, and I could at least get a feeling of what he lived through during those three decisive days. I called all the important people in the city, senators, commanders of the armed forces, the North American ambassador, and the president of National Petroleum, begging them for a pump to remove the silt, but obtained only vague promises. I began to ask for urgent help on radio and television, to see if there wasn't *someone* who could help us. Between calls I would run to the newsroom to monitor the satellite transmissions that periodically brought new details of the catastrophe. While reporters selected scenes with most impact for the news report, I searched for footage that featured Azucena's mudpit. The screen reduced the disaster to a single plane and accentuated the tremendous distance that separated me from Rolf Carlé; nonetheless, I was there with him. The child's every suffering hurt me as it did him; I felt his frustration, his impotence. Faced with the impossibility of communicating with him, the fantastic idea came to me that if I tried, I could reach him by force of mind and in that way give him encouragement. I concentrated until I was dizzy—a frenzied and futile activity. At times I would be overcome with compassion and burst out crying; at other times, I was so drained I felt as if I were staring through a telescope at the light of a star dead for a million years.

18   I watched that hell on the first morning broadcast, cadavers of people and animals awash in the current of new rivers formed overnight from the melted snow. Above the mud rose the tops of trees and the bell towers of a church where several people had taken refuge and were patiently awaiting rescue teams. Hundreds of soldiers and volunteers from the Civil Defense were clawing through rubble searching for survivors, while long rows of ragged specters awaited their turn for a cup of hot broth. Radio networks announced that their phones were jammed with calls from families offering shelter to orphaned children. Drinking water was in scarce supply, along with gasoline and food. Doctors, resigned to amputating arms and legs without anesthesia, pled that at least they be sent serum and painkillers and antibiotics; most of the roads, however, were impassable, and worse were the bureaucratic obstacles that stood

in the way. To top it all, the clay contaminated by decomposing bodies threatened the living with an outbreak of epidemics.

19   Azucena was shivering inside the tire that held her above the surface. Immobility and tension had greatly weakened her, but she was conscious and could still be heard when a microphone was held out to her. Her tone was humble, as if apologizing for all the fuss. Rolf Carlé had a growth of beard, and dark circles beneath his eyes; he looked near exhaustion. Even from that enormous distance I could sense the quality of his weariness, so different from the fatigue of other adventures. He had completely forgotten the camera; he could not look at the girl through a lens any longer. The pictures we were receiving were not his assistant's but those of other reporters who had appropriated Azucena, bestowing on her the pathetic responsibility of embodying the horror of what had happened in that place. With the first light Rolf tried again to dislodge the obstacles that held the girl in her tomb, but he had only his hands to work with; he did not dare use a tool for fear of injuring her. He fed Azucena a cup of the cornmeal mush and bananas the Army was distributing, but she immediately vomited it up. A doctor stated that she had a fever, but added that there was little he could do: antibiotics were being reserved for cases of gangrene. A priest also passed by and blessed her, hanging a medal of the Virgin around her neck. By evening a gentle, persistent drizzle began to fall.

20   "The sky is weeping," Azucena murmured, and she, too, began to cry.

21   "Don't be afraid," Rolf begged. "You have to keep your strength up and be calm. Everything will be fine. I'm with you, and I'll get you out somehow."

22   Reporters returned to photograph Azucena and ask her the same questions, which she no longer tried to answer. In the meanwhile, more television and movie teams arrived with spools of cable, tapes, film, videos, precision lenses, recorders, sound consoles, lights, reflecting screens, auxiliary motors, cartons of supplies, electricians, sound technicians, and cameramen: Azucena's face was beamed to millions of screens around the world. And all the while Rolf Carlé kept pleading for a pump. The improved technical facilities bore results, and National Television began receiving sharper pictures and clearer sound; the distance seemed suddenly compressed, and I had the horrible sensation that Azucena and Rolf were by my side, separated from me by impenetrable glass. I was able to follow events hour by hour; I knew everything my love did to wrest the girl from her prison and help her endure her suffering; I overheard fragments of what they said to one another and could guess the rest; I was present when she taught Rolf to pray, and when he distracted her with the stories I had told him in a thousand and one nights beneath the white mosquito netting of our bed.

23   When darkness came on the second day, Rolf tried to sing Azucena to sleep with old Austrian folk songs he had learned from his mother, but she was far beyond sleep. They spent most of the night talking, each in a stupor of exhaustion and hunger, and shaking with cold. That night, imperceptibly, the unyielding floodgates that had contained Rolf Carlé's

past for so many years began to open, and the torrent of all that had lain hidden in the deepest and most secret layers of memory poured out, leveling before it the obstacles that had blocked his consciousness for so long. He could not tell it all to Azucena; she perhaps did not know there was a world beyond the sea or time previous to her own; she was not capable of imagining Europe in the years of the war. So he could not tell her of defeat, nor of the afternoon the Russians had led them to the concentration camp to bury prisoners dead from starvation. Why should he describe to her how the naked bodies piled like a mountain of firewood resembled fragile china? How could he tell this dying child about ovens and gallows? Nor did he mention the night that he had seen his mother naked, shod in stiletto-heeled red boots, sobbing with humiliation. There was much he did not tell, but in those hours he relived for the first time all the things his mind had tried to erase. Azucena had surrendered her fear to him and so, without wishing it, had obliged Rolf to confront his own. There, beside that hellhole of mud, it was impossible for Rolf to flee from himself any longer, and the visceral terror he had lived as a boy suddenly invaded him. He reverted to the years when he was the age of Azucena, and younger, and, like her, found himself trapped in a pit without escape, buried in life, his head barely above ground; he saw before his eyes the boots and legs of his father, who had removed his belt and was whipping it in the air with the never-forgotten hiss of a viper coiled to strike. Sorrow flooded through him, intact and precise, as if it had lain always in his mind, waiting. He was once again in the armoire where his father locked him to punish him for imagined misbehavior, there where for eternal hours he had crouched with his eyes closed, not to see the darkness, with his hands over his ears, to shut out the beating of his heart, trembling, huddled like a cornered animal. Wandering in the mist of his memories he found his sister Katharina, a sweet, retarded child who spent her life hiding, with the hope that her father would forget the disgrace of her having been born. With Katharina, Rolf crawled beneath the dining room table, and with her hid there under the long white tablecloth, two children forever embraced, alert to footsteps and voices. Katharina's scent melded with his own sweat, with aromas of cooking, garlic, soup, freshly baked bread, and the unexpected odor of putrescent clay. His sister's hand in his, her frightened breathing, her silk hair against his cheek, the candid gaze of her eyes. Katharina . . . Katharina materialized before him, floating on the air like a flag, clothed in the white tablecloth, now a winding sheet, and at last he could weep for her death and for the guilt of having abandoned her. He understood then that all his exploits as a reporter, the feats that had won him such recognition and fame, were merely an attempt to keep his most ancient fears at bay, a stratagem for taking refuge behind a lens to test whether reality was more tolerable from that perspective. He took excessive risks as an exercise of courage, training by day to conquer the monsters that tormented him by night. But he had come face to face with the moment of truth; he could not continue to escape his past. He *was* Azucena; he was buried in the clayey mud; his terror was not the distant emotion of an almost forgotten childhood, it was a claw sunk in his throat. In the flush of his tears he saw his mother, dressed in black and clutching her imitation-crocodile pocketbook to her bosom, just as he had last seen her on the dock when she had come to put him on the boat to South America. She had not come to dry his tears, but to tell him to pick up a shovel: the war was over and now they must bury the dead.

24   "Don't cry. I don't hurt anymore. I'm fine," Azucena said when dawn came.

25   "I'm not crying for you," Rolf Carlé smiled. "I'm crying for myself. I hurt all over."

26   The third day in the valley of the cataclysm began with a pale light filtering through storm clouds. The President of the Republic visited the area in his tailored safari jacket to confirm that this was the worst catastrophe of the century; the country was in mourning; sister nations had offered aid; he had ordered a state of siege; the Armed Forces would be merciless, anyone caught stealing or committing other offenses would be shot on sight. He added that it was impossible to remove all the corpses or count the thousands who had disappeared; the entire valley would be declared holy ground, and bishops would come to celebrate a solemn mass for the souls of the victims. He went to the Army field tents to offer relief in the form of vague promises to crowds of the rescued, then to the improvised hospital to offer a word of encouragement to doctors and nurses worn down from so many hours of tribulations. Then he asked to be taken to see Azucena, the little girl the whole world had seen. He waved to her with a limp statesman's hand, and microphones recorded his emotional voice and paternal tone as he told her that her courage had served as an example to the nation. Rolf Carlé interrupted to ask for a pump, and the President assured him that he personally would attend to the matter. I caught a glimpse of Rolf for a few seconds kneeling beside the mudpit. On the evening news broadcast, he was still in the same position; and I, glued to the screen like a fortune-teller to her crystal ball, could tell that something fundamental had changed in him. I knew somehow that during the night his defenses had crumbled and he had given in to grief; finally he was vulnerable. The girl had touched a part of him that he himself had no access to, a part he had never shared with me. Rolf had wanted to console her, but it was Azucena who had given him consolation.

27   I recognized the precise moment at which Rolf gave up the fight and surrendered to the torture of watching the girl die. I was with them, three days and two nights, spying on them from the other side of life. I was there when she told him that in all her thirteen years no boy had ever loved her and that it was a pity to leave this world without knowing love.

Rolf assured her that he loved her more than he could ever love anyone, more than he loved his mother, more than his sister, more than all the women who had slept in his arms, more than he loved me, his life companion, who would have given anything to be trapped in that well in her place, who would have exchanged her life for Azucena's, and I watched as he leaned down to kiss her poor forehead, consumed by a sweet, sad emotion he could not name. I felt how in that instant both were saved from despair, how they were freed from the clay, how they rose above the vultures and helicopters, how together they flew above the vast swamp of corruption and laments. How, finally, they were able to accept death. Rolf Carlé prayed in silence that she would die quickly, because such pain cannot be borne.

28   By then I had obtained a pump and was in touch with a general who had agreed to ship it the next morning on a military cargo plane. But on the night of that third day, beneath the unblinking focus of quartz lamps and the lens of a hundred cameras, Azucena gave up, her eyes locked with those of the friend who had sustained her to the end. Rolf Carlé removed the life buoy, closed her eyelids, held her to his chest for a few moments and then let her go. She sank slowly, a flower in the mud.

29   You are back with me, but you are not the same man. I often accompany you to the station and we watch the videos of Azucena again; you study them intently, looking for something you could have done to save her, something you did not think of in time. Or maybe you study them to see yourself as if in a mirror, naked. Your cameras lie forgotten in a closet; you do not write or sing; you sit long hours before the window, staring at the mountains. Beside you, I wait for you to complete the voyage into yourself, for the old wounds to heal. I know that when you return from your nightmares, we shall again walk hand in hand, as before.

Questions for Engagement, Response, and Analysis

1. Who is the narrator of the story? How does her particular perspective on the events—both her relationship to Rolf and her location—affect the story? What does her statement "I felt as if I were staring through a telescope at the light of a star dead for a million years" suggest about her perspective?

2. Why do the media, in the midst of such widespread tragedy, focus so much attention on one little girl? Why can they get all of their elaborate equipment to the site when no one seems to be able to bring the needed pump? How and why does she become "the symbol of the tragedy"?

3. Explain the narrator's comment that Rolf Carlé "accepted that time had stagnated and reality had been irreparably distorted."

4. In what ways is this a story of an accidental quest?

5. Explain the significance of the title of the story.

Crafting Arguments

1. The narrator says that Rolf "was Azucena; he was buried in the clayey mud" and that he had "[taken] refuge behind a lens to test whether reality was more tolerable from that perspective." Write an essay in which you examine the theme of perspective in this story, using specific examples of the narrator's perspective and of Rolf's.

2. In an essay, analyze Allende's use of vivid images and metaphors to help readers visualize and empathize with the characters.

3. After rereading the last four paragraphs of this story, discuss Rolf's quest, examining his epiphany, explaining what it involves, and supporting your theories about its results, whether complete or incomplete.

4. Craft an essay in which you state what you believe to be the theme of the story and support your claim.

Louise Erdrich (b. 1954)

Award-winning writer Louise Erdrich is a native of Minnesota. Her mother was French and Ojibwe Indian. As Erdrich was growing up, her parents worked at the Bureau of Indian Affairs School in Wahpeton, North Dakota. Her grandfather was the Tribal Chairman of the Turtle Mountain Reservation in North Dakota, and Erdrich is a member of the Turtle Mountain Band of Chippewa. She was married to author Michael Dorris, with whom she had three children in addition to his three adopted children. Her fiction is influenced by the stories she heard as a child and by the perceptions she has gained as a mother. Her works include nonfiction, such as The Blue Jay's Dance: A Birth Year *(1995), and fiction, such as* Love Medicine *(1984),* The Bingo Palace *(1994), and* Tales of Burning Love *(1996). Erdrich published her first children's book,* Grandmother's Pigeon, *in 1996. She won the Wordcraft circle writer of the year award in 2000 for her children's book* The Birchbark House *(1999).*

NAKED WOMAN PLAYING CHOPIN   (1998)

A FARGO ROMANCE

1   The street that runs along the Red River follows the curves of a stream that is muddy and shallow, full of brush, silt, and oxbows that throw the whole town off the strict clean grid laid out by railroad plat. The river floods most springs and drags local back yards into its flow, even though its banks are strengthened with riprap and piled high with concrete torn from reconstructed streets and basements. It is a hopelessly complicated river, one that freezes deceptively, breaks rough, drowns one or two every year in its icy flow. It is a dead river in some places, one that

harbors only carp and bullheads. Wild in others, it lures moose down from Canada into the city limits. At one time, when the land along its banks was newly broken, paddleboats and barges of grain moved grandly from its source to Winnipeg, for the river flows inscrutably north. And, over on the Minnesota side, across from what is now church land and the town park, a farm spread generously up and down the river and back into wide hot fields.

2   The bonanza farm belonged to Easterners who had sold a foundry in Vermont and with their money bought the flat vastness that lay along the river. They raised astounding crops when the land was young—rutabagas that weighed sixty pounds, wheat unbearably lush, corn on cobs like truncheons. Then there were six grasshopper years during which even the handles on the hoes and rakes were eaten and a cavalry soldier, too, was partially devoured while he lay drunk in the insects' path. The enterprise suffered losses on a grand scale. The farm was split among four brothers, eventually, who then sold off half each so that, by the time Berndt Vogel escaped the trench war of Europe where he'd been chopped mightily but inconclusively in six places by a British cavalry sabre and then kicked by a horse so that his jaw never shut right again, there was just one beautiful and peaceful swatch of land about to go for grabs. In the time it took him to gather—by forswearing women, drinking low beers only, and working twenty-hour days—the money to retrieve the farm from the local bank, its price had dropped further and further, as the earth rose up in a great ship of destruction. Sails of dust carried half of Berndt's lush dirt over the horizon, but enough remained for him to plant and reap six fields.

3   So Berndt survived. On his land there stood an old hangar-like barn, with only one small part still in use—housing a cow, chickens, one depressed pig. Berndt kept the rest in decent repair, not only because as a good German he must waste nothing that came his way, but also because he saw in those grand, dust-filled shafts of light something that he could worship. It had once housed teams of great blue Percherons and Belgian draft horses. Only one horse was left, old and made of brutal velvet, but the others still moved in the powerful synchronicity of his dreams. He fussed over the remaining mammoth and imagined his farm one day entire, vast and teeming, crews of men under his command, a cookhouse, a bunkhouse, equipment, a woman and children sturdily determined to their toil, and a garden in which seeds bearing the scented pinks and sharp red geraniums of his childhood were planted and thrived.

4   How surprised he was to find, one afternoon, as though sown by the wind and summoned by his dreams, a woman standing barefoot, starved and frowsy in the doorway of his barn. She was a pale flower, nearly bald and dressed in a rough shift. He blinked stupidly at the vision. Light poured around her like smoke and swirled at her gesture of need. She spoke.

5   *"Ich habe Hunger."*

6   By the way she said it, he knew she was a Swabian and therefore—he tried to thrust the thought from his mind—liable to have certain unruly habits in bed. He passed his hand across his eyes. Through the gown of nearly transparent muslin he could see that her breasts were, excitingly, bound tightly to her chest with strips of cloth. He blinked hard. Looking directly into her eyes, he experienced the vertigo of confronting a female who did not blush or look away but held him with an honest human calm. He thought at first that she must be a loose woman, fleeing a brothel—had Fargo got so big? Or escaping an evil marriage, perhaps. He didn't know she was from God.

7   In the center of the town on the other side of the river there stood a convent made of yellow bricks. Hauled halfway across Minnesota from Little Falls by pious drivers, they still held the peculiar sulfurous moth gold of the clay outside that town. The word "Fleisch" was etched in shallow letters on each one: Fleisch Company Brickworks. Donated to the nuns at cost. The word, of course, was covered by mortar each time a brick was laid. However, because she had organized a few discarded bricks behind the convent into the base for a small birdbath, one of the younger nuns knew, as she gazed at the mute order of the convent's wall, that she lived within the secret repetition of that one word.

8   She had once been Agnes DeWitt and now was Sister Cecellia, shorn, houseled, clothed in black wool and bound in starched linen of heatless white. She not only taught but lived music, existed for those hours when she could be concentrated in her being—which was half music, half divine light, flesh only to the degree that she could not admit otherwise. At the piano keyboard, absorbed into the notes that rose beneath her hands, she existed in her essence, a manifestation of compelling sound. Her hands were long and thick-veined, very white, startling against her habit. She rubbed them with lard and beeswax nightly to keep them supple. During the day, when she graded papers or used the blackboard her hands twitched and drummed, patterned and repatterned difficult fingerings. She was no trouble to live with and her obedience was absolute. Only, and with increasing concentration, she played Brahms, Beethoven, Debussy, Schubert, and Chopin.

9   It wasn't that she neglected her other duties; rather, it was the playing itself—distilled of longing—that disturbed her sisters. In her music Sister Cecellia explored profound emotions. She spoke of her faith and doubt, of her passion as the bride of Christ, of her loneliness, shame, ultimate redemption. The Brahms she played was thoughtful, the Schubert confounding. Debussy was all contrived nature and yet as gorgeous as a meadowlark. Beethoven contained all messages, but her crescendos lacked conviction. When it came to Chopin, however, she did not use the flowery ornamentation or the endless trills and insipid floribunda of so many of her day. Her playing was of the utmost sincerity. And Chopin, played simply, devastates the heart. Sometimes a pause between the piercing sorrows of minor notes made a sister scrubbing the floor weep

into the bucket where she dipped her rag so that the convent's boards, washed in tears, seemed to creak in a human tongue. The air of the house thickened with sighs.

10   Sister Cecellia, however, was emptied. Thinned. It was as though her soul were neatly removed by a drinking straw and siphoned into the green pool of quiet that lay beneath the rippling cascade of notes. One day, exquisite agony built and released, built higher, released more forcefully until slow heat spread between her fingers, up her arms, stung at the points of her bound breasts, and then shot straight down.

11   Her hands flew off the keyboard—she crouched as though she had been shot, saw yellow spots, and experienced a peaceful wave of oneness in which she entered pure communion. She was locked into the music, held there safely, entirely understood. Such was her innocence that she didn't know she was experiencing a sexual climax, but believed, rather, that what she felt was the natural outcome of this particular nocturne played to the utmost of her skills—and so it came to be. Chopin's spirit became her lover. His flats caressed her. His whole notes sank through her body like clear pebbles. His atmospheric trills were the flicker of a tongue. His pauses before the downward sweep of notes nearly drove her insane.

12   The Mother Superior knew something had to be done when she herself woke, her face bathed with sweat and tears, to the insinuating soft largo of the Prelude in E Minor. In those notes she remembered the death of her mother and sank into an endless afternoon of her loss. The Mother Superior then grew, in her heart, a weed of rage against the God who had taken a mother from a seven-year-old child whose world she was, entirely, without question—heart, arms, guidance, soul—until by evening she felt fury steaming from the hot marrow of her bones and stopped herself.

13   "Oh, God, forgive me," the Superior prayed. She considered humunculation, but then rushed down to the piano room instead, and with all of the strength in her wide old arms gathered and hid from Cecellia every piece of music but the Bach.

14   After that, for some weeks, there was relief. Sister Cecellia turned to the Two-Part Inventions. Her fingers moved on the keys with the precision of an insect building its nest. She played each as though she were constructing an airtight box. Stealthily, once Cecellia had moved on to Bach's other works, the Mother Superior removed from the music cabinet and destroyed the Goldberg Variations—clearly capable of lifting subterranean complexities into the mind. Life in the convent returned to normal. The cook, to everyone's gratitude, stopped preparing the rancid, goose-fat-laced beet soup of her youth and stuck to overcooked string beans, cabbage, potatoes. The floors stopped groaning and absorbed fresh wax. The doors ceased to fly open for no reason and closed discreetly. The water stopped rushing through the pipes as the sisters no longer took continual advantage of the new plumbing to drown out the sounds of their emotions.

15   And then one day Sister Cecellia woke with a tightness in her chest. Pain shot through her and the red lump in her rib cage beat like a wild thing caught in a snare of bones. Her throat shut. She wept. Her hands, drawn to the keyboard, floated into a long appoggiatura. Then, crash, she was inside a thrusting mazurka. The music came back to her. There was the scent of faint gardenias—his hothouse boutonnière. The silk of his heavy brown hair. His sensuous drawing-room sweat. His voice—she heard it—avid and light. It was as if the composer himself had entered the room. Who knows? Surely there was no more desperate, earthly, exacting heart than Cecellia's. Surely something, however paltry, lies beyond the grave.

16   At any rate, she played Chopin. Played him in utter naturalness until the Mother Superior was forced to shut the cover to the keyboard and gently pull the stool away. Cecellia lifted the lid and played upon her knees. The poor scandalized dame dragged her from the keys. Cecellia crawled back. The Mother, at her wit's end, sank down and urged the young woman to pray. She herself spoke first in fear and then in certainty, saying that it was the very Devil who had managed to find a way to Cecellia's soul through the flashing doors of sixteenth notes. Her fears were confirmed when, not moments later, the gentle sister raised her arms and fists and struck the keys as though the instrument were stone and from the rock her thirst would be quenched. But only discord emerged.

17   "My child, my dear child," the Mother comforted, "come away and rest yourself."

18   The younger nun, breathing deeply, refused. Her severe gray eyes were rimmed in a smoky red. Her lips bled purple. She was in torment. "There is no rest," she declared. She unpinned her veil and studiously dismantled her habit, folding each piece with reverence and setting it upon the piano bench. The Mother remonstrated with Cecellia in the most tender and compassionate tones. However, just as in the depth of her playing the virgin had become the woman, so now the woman in the habit became a woman to the bone. She stripped down to her shift, but no further.

19   "He wouldn't want me to go out unprotected," she told her Mother Superior.

20   "God?" the older woman asked, bewildered.

21   "Chopin," Cecellia answered.

22   Kissing her dear Mother's trembling fingers, Cecellia knelt. She made a true genuflection, murmured an act of contrition, and then walked away from the convent made of bricks with the secret word pressed between yellow mortar, and from the music, her music, which the Mother Superior would from then on keep under lock and key.

23   So it was Sister Cecellia, or Agnes DeWitt of rural Wisconsin, who appeared before Berndt Vogel in the cavern of the barn and said in her mother's dialect, for she knew a German when she met one, that she was hungry. She wanted to ask whether he had a piano, but it was clear to her that he wouldn't and at any rate she was exhausted.

24   *"Jetzt muss ich schlafen,"* she said after eating half a plate of scalded oatmeal with new milk.

25   So he took her to his bed, the only bed there was, in the corner of the otherwise empty room. He went out to the barn he loved, covered himself with hay, and lay awake all night listening to the rustling of mice and sensing the soundless predatory glide of the barn owls and the stiff erratic flutter of bats. By morning, he had determined to marry her if she would have him, just so that he could unpin and then unwind the long strip of cloth that bound her torso. She refused his offer, but she did speak to him of who she was and where from, and in that first summary she gave of her life she concluded that she must never marry again, for not only had she wed herself soul to soul to Christ, but she had already been unfaithful—with her phantom lover, the Polish composer. She had already lived out too grievous a destiny to become a bride again. By explaining this to Berndt, however, she had merely moved her first pawn in a long game of words and gestures that the two would play over the course of many months. What she didn't know was that she had opened to a dogged and ruthless opponent.

26   Berndt Vogel's passion engaged him, mind and heart. He prepared himself. Having dragged Army caissons through hip-deep mud after the horses died in torment, having seen his best friend suddenly uncreated into a mass of shrieking pulp, having lived intimately with pouring tumults of eager lice and rats plump with a horrifying food, he was rudimentarily prepared for the suffering he would experience in love. She, however, had also learned her share of discipline. Moreover—for the heart of her gender is stretched, pounded, molded, and tempered for its hot task from birth—she was a woman.

27   The two struck a temporary bargain, and set up housekeeping. She still slept in the indoor bed. He stayed in the barn. A month passed. Three. Six. Each morning she lit the stove and cooked, then heated water in a big tank for laundry and swept the cool linoleum floors. Monday she sewed. She baked all day Tuesday. On Wednesdays she churned and scrubbed. She sold the butter and the eggs Thursdays. Killed a chicken every Friday. Saturdays she walked into town and practiced the piano in the school basement. Sunday she played the organ for Mass and then at the close of the day started the next week's work. Berndt paid her. At first she spent her salary on clothing. When with her earnings she had acquired shoes, stockings, a full set of cotton underclothing and then a woollen one, too, and material for two housedresses—one patterned with twisted leaves and tiny blue berries, and the other of an ivy lattice print—and a sweater and, at last, a winter coat, after she had earned a blanket, quilted overalls, a pair of boots, she decided on a piano.

28   This is where Berndt thought he could maneuver her into marriage, but she proved too cunning for him. It was early in the evening and the yard was pleasant with the sound of grasshoppers. The two sat on the porch drinking glasses of sugared lemon water. Every so often, in the ancient

six-foot grasses that survived at the margin of the yard, a firefly signalled or a dove cried out its five hollow notes.

29   They drank slowly, she in her sprigged-berry dress that skimmed her waist. He noted with disappointment that she wore normal underclothing now, had stopped binding her breasts. Perhaps, he thought, he could persuade her to resume her old ways, at least occasionally, just for him. It was a wan hope. She looked so comfortable, so free. She'd taken on a little weight and lost her anemic pallor. Her arms were brown, muscular. In the sun, her straight fine hair glinted with green-gold sparks of light and her eyes were deceptively clear.

30   "I can teach music," she told him. She had decided that her suggestion must sound merely practical, a money-making ploy. She did not express any pleasure or zeal, though at the very thought each separate tiny muscle in her hands ached. "It would be a way of bringing in some money."

31   He was left to absorb this. He might have believed her casual proposition, except that her restless fingers gave her away, and he noted their insistent motions. She was playing the Adagio of the "Pathétique" on the tablecloth, a childhood piece that nervously possessed her from time to time.

32   "You would need a piano," he told her. She nodded and held his gaze in that aloof and unbearably sexual way that had first skewered him.

33   "It's the sort of thing a husband gives his wife," he dared.

34   Her fingers stopped moving. She cast down her eyes in contempt.

35   "I can use the school instrument. I've spoken to the school principal already."

36   Berndt looked at the Moon-shaped bone of her ankle, at her foot in the brown, thick-heeled shoe she'd bought. He ached to hold her foot in his lap, untie her oxford shoe with his teeth, cover her calf with kisses, and breathe against the delicate folds of berry cloth.

37   He offered marriage once again. His heart. His troth. His farm. She spurned the lot. She would simply walk into town. He let her know that he would like to buy the piano, it wasn't that, but there was not a store for many miles where it could be purchased. She knew better and with exasperated heat described the way that she would, if he would help financially, go about locating and then acquiring the best piano for the best price. She vowed that she would purchase the instrument not in Fargo but in Minneapolis. From there, she could have it hauled for less than the freight markup. She would make her arrangements in one day and return by night in order not to spend one extra dime either on food she couldn't carry or on a hotel room. When he resisted to the last, she told him that she was leaving. She would find a small room in town and there she would acquire students, give lessons.

38   She betrayed her desperation. Some clench of her fingers gave her away, and it was as much Berndt's unconfused love of her and wish that she might be happy as any worry she might leave him that finally caused him to agree. In the six months that he'd known Agnes DeWitt she had become someone to reckon with, and even he, who understood

desperation and self-denial, was finding her proximity most difficult. He worked himself into exhaustion, and his farm prospered. Sleeping in the barn was difficult, but he had set into one wall a bunk room for himself and his hired man and installed a stove that burned red hot on cold nights; only, sometimes, as he looked sleepily into the glowering flanks of iron, he could not keep his own fingers from moving along the rough mattress in faint imitation of the way he would, if he ever could, touch her hips. He, too, was practicing.

39   The piano moved across the August desert of drought-sucked wheat like a shield, a dark upended black thing, an ebony locust. Agnes made friends with a hauler out of Morris and he gave her a slow-wagon price. Both were to accompany into Fargo the last grand piano made by Cara-macchione. It had been shipped to Minneapolis, unsold until Agnes entered with her bean sock of money. She accompanied the instrument back to the farm during the dog days. Hot weather was beloved by this particular piano. It tuned itself on muggy days. And so, as it moved across the flat expanse, Miss Agnes DeWitt mounted the back of the wagon and played to the clouds.

40   They had to remove one side of the house to get the piano into the front room, and it took six strong men a full day to do the job. By the time the instrument was settled into place by the window, Berndt was per-suaded of its necessary presence, and proud. He sent the men away, although the side of the house was still open to the swirling light of stars. Dark breezes moved the curtains; he asked her to play for him. She did, the music gripped her, and she did not, could not, stop.

41   Late that night she turned from the last chord of the simple Nocturne in C Minor into the silence of Berndt's listening presence. Three slow claps from his large hands died in the waiting quiet. His eyes rested upon her and she returned his gaze with a long and mysterious stare of gentle regard. The side of the house admitted a great swatch of Moonlight. Spi-ders built their webs of phosphorescence across black space. Berndt ticked through what he knew—she would not marry him because she had been married and unfaithful, in her mind at least. He was desperate not to throw her off, repel her, damage the mood set by the boom of nighthawks flying in, swooping out, by the rustle of black oak and wil-low, by the scent of the blasted petals of summer's last wild roses. His courage was at its lowest ebb. Fraught with sheer need and emotion he stood before Agnes, finally, and asked in a low voice, *"Schlaf mit mir. Bitte, Schlaf mit mir."*

42   Agnes looked into his face, openly at last, showing him the great weight of feeling she carried. As she had for her Mother Superior, she removed her clothing carefully and folded it, only she did not stop undressing at her shift but continued until she had slipped off her large tissuey bloomers and seated herself naked at the piano. Her body was a pale blush of silver, and her hands, when they began to move, rose and fell with the simplicity of water.

43   It became clear to Berndt Vogel, as the music slowly wrapped around him, that he was engaged in something that he would have had to pay a whore in Fargo—if there really were any whores in Fargo—a great sum to perform. A snake of hair wound down her spine. Her pale buttocks seemed to float off the invisible bench. Her legs moved like a swimmer's, and he thought he heard her moan. He watched her fingers spin like white shadows across the keys, and found that his body was responding as though he lay fully twined with her underneath a quilt of music and stars. His breath came short, shorter, rasping and ragged. Beyond control, he gasped painfully and gave himself into some furtive cleft of halftones and anger that opened beneath the ice of high keys.

44   Shocked, weak and wet, Berndt rose and slipped through the open side wall. He trod aimless crop lines until he could allow himself to collapse in the low fervor of night wheat. It was true, wasn't it, that the heart was a lying cheat? And as the songs Chopin invented were as much him as his body, so it followed that Berndt had just watched the woman he loved make love to a dead man. Now, as he listened to the music, he thought of returning. Imagined the meal of her white shoulders. Shut his eyes and entered the confounding depth between her legs.

45   Then followed their best years. Together, they constructed a good life in which the erotic merged into the daily so that every task and even small kindness was charged with a sexual humor. Some mornings the two staggered from the bedroom disoriented, still half drunk on the unlikely eagerness of the other's body. These frenzied periods occurred every so often, like spells in the weather. They would be drawn, sink, disappear into their greed, until the cow groaned for milking or the hired man swore and banged on the outside gate. If nothing else intervened, they'd stop from sheer exhaustion. Then they would look at one another oddly, questingly, as if the other person were a complete stranger, and gradually resume their normal interaction, which was off-hand and distracted, but upheld by the assurance of people who thought alike.

46   Agnes gave music lessons, and although the two weren't married, even the Catholics and the children came to her. This was because it was wellknown that Miss DeWitt's first commitment had been to Christ. It was understandable that she would have no other marriage. Although she did not take the Holy Eucharist on her tongue, she was there at church each Sunday morning, faithful and devout, to play the organ. There, she, of course, played Bach, with a purity of intent purged of any subterranean feeling, strictly, and for God.

47   So when the river began to rise one spring, Berndt had already gone where life was deepest many times, and he did not particularly fear the rain. But what began as a sheer mist became an even sprinkle and then developed into a slow, pounding shower that lasted three days, then four, then on the fifth day, when it should have tapered off, increased.

48   The river boiled along swiftly, a gray soup still contained, just barely, within its high banks. On day six the rain stopped, or seemed to. The

storm had moved upstream. All day while the sun shone pleasantly the river heaved itself up, tore into its flow new trees and boulders, created tip-ups, washouts, areas of singing turbulence, and crawled, like an infant, toward the farm. Berndt rushed around uneasily, pitching hay into the high loft, throwing chickens up after the hay, wishing he could throw the horse up as well, and the house, and—because Agnes wrung her hands—the piano. But the piano was earth-anchored and well-tuned by the rainy air, so, instead of worrying, Agnes practiced.

49   Once the river started to move, it gained confidence. It had no problem with fences or gates, wispy windbreaks, ditches. It simply levelled or attained the level of whatever stood in its path. Water jumped up the lawn and collected behind the sacks of sand that Berndt had desperately filled and laid. The river tugged itself up the porch and into the house from one side. From the other side it undermined an already weak foundation that had temporarily shored up the same wall once removed to make way for the piano. The river tore against the house and then, like a child tipping out a piece of candy from a box, it surged underneath and rocked the floor, and the piano crashed through the weakened wall.

50   It landed in the swift current of the yard, Agnes with it. Berndt saw only the white treble clef of her dress as she spun away, clutching the curved lid. It bobbed along the flower beds first, and then, as muscular new eddies caught it, touched down on the shifting lanes of Berndt's wheat fields, and farther, until the revolving instrument and the woman on it reached the original river and plunged in. They were carried not more than a hundred feet before the piano lost momentum and sank. As it went down, Agnes thought at first of crawling into its box, nestling for safety among the cold, dead strings. But, as she struggled with the hinged cover, she lost her grip and was swept north. She should have drowned, but there was a snag of rope, a tree, two men in a fishing skiff risking themselves to save a valuable birding dog. They pulled Agnes out and dumped her in the bottom of the boat, impatient to get the dog. She gagged, coughed, and passed out in a roil of feet and fishing tackle.

51   When she came to, she was back in the convent, which was on high ground and open to care for victims of the flood. Berndt was not among the rescued. When the river went down and the heat rose, he was found snagged in a tip-up of roots, tethered to his great blue steaming horse. As Agnes recovered her strength, did she dream of him? Think of him entering her and her receiving him? Long for the curve of his hand on her breast? Yes and no. She thought again of music. Chopin. Berndt. Chopin.

52   He had written a will, in which he declared her his common-law wife and left to her the farm and all upon it. There, she raised Rosecomb Bantams, Dominikers, Reds. She bought another piano and played with an isolated intensity that absorbed her spirit.

53   A year or so after Berndt's death, her students noticed that she would stop in the middle of a lesson and smile out the window as though welcoming a long-expected visitor. One day the neighbor children went to pick up the usual order of eggs and were most struck to see the white-and-black-flecked Dominikers flapping up in alarm around Miss DeWitt as she stood magnificent upon the green grass.

54   Tall, slender, legs slightly bowed, breasts jutting a bit to either side, and the flare of hair flicking up the center of her—naked. She looked at the children with remote kindness. Asked, "How many dozen?" Walked off to gather the eggs.

55   That episode made the gossip-table rounds. People put it off to Berndt's death and a relapse of nerves. She lost only a Lutheran student or two. She continued playing the organ for Mass, and at home, in the black, black nights, Chopin. And if she was asked, by an innocent pupil too young to understand the meaning of discretion, why she sometimes didn't wear clothes, Miss DeWitt would answer that she removed her clothing when she played the music of a particular bare-souled composer. She would nod meditatively and say in her firmest manner that when one enters into such music, one should be naked. And then she would touch the keys.

Questions for Engagement, Response, and Analysis

1. Explain the foreshadowing in the opening paragraph.

2. What is the setting of the story?

3. Describe the relationship between Agnes and the other nuns. What is the Mother Superior's motivation?

4. What is the relationship between Agnes and Berndt? Who or what stands in the way of her marrying him?

5. What is the tone of the story? List some of the details that help to create this tone.

6. What is Agnes' quest?

Crafting Arguments

1. Erdrich's says of Agnes' relationship to music: "She not only taught but lived music, existed for those hours when she could be concentrated in her being—which was half music, half divine light, flesh only to the degree that she could not admit otherwise." Write an essay using this and other specific examples from the story to analyze what music means to Agnes.

2. In an essay, state what you believe to be the theme of this story and support your claim.

POETRY

John Donne (1572–1631)

John Donne, an Anglican priest highly regarded for his sermons, wrote conversational, sometimes tortuous, but carefully controlled poetry. His works include cynical court poetry such as the Satires, *strikingly sensual love poems in* Songs and Sonnets, *and powerful, often anguished religious poems such as the* Holy Sonnets. *Foremost among those poets later called metaphysical by Samuel Johnson, Donne often joins quite disparate concepts in elaborate images or conceits. The speaker's comparison of himself and his beloved to a compass in "A Valediction: Forbidding Mourning" is among the most famous of Donne's conceits.*

HOLY SONNET 14   (c. 1610)

Batter my heart, three person'd God; for, you
As yet but knocke, breathe, shine, and seeke to mend;
That I may rise, and stand, o'erthrow mee, and bend
Your force, to breake, blowe, burn and make me new.
5 I, like an usurpt towne, to another due,
Labour to admit You, but Oh, to no end;
Reason Your viceroy in mee, mee should defend
But is captiv'd, and proves weake or untrue,
Yet dearely I love You, and would be lov'd faine,
10 But am betroth'd unto Your enemie,
Divorce mee, untie, or breake that knot againe,
Take mee to You, imprison mee, for I
Except You enthrall mee, never shall be free,
Nor ever chaste, except You ravish mee.

Questions for Engagement, Response, and Analysis

1. What is the speaker asking God to do? Why?
2. What is the effect of the strong action verbs and the alliterative *b*s in the first four lines of the sonnet?
3. Explain the extended simile developed in the second quatrain.
4. Explain the paradoxes in the last two lines.

Crafting Arguments

1. In an analysis, show how imagery, sound, diction, and syntax develop the tone of Donne's "Holy Sonnet 14."

John Milton (1608–1674)

*John Milton, educated at Cambridge and a master of Greek,
Latin, Italian, and Hebrew, isolated himself after graduation from college to read the great books. After writing several controversial pamphlets, including* Areopagitica
*(1644), an argument for freedom of the press, he served as
foreign secretary under Oliver Cromwell, Puritan Lord Protector of England from 1653 to 1658. Milton's* Paradise Lost
*(1667), based on the Genesis account of humanity's fall, is
regarded as the greatest epic poem written in English. Both*
Paradise Lost *and* Paradise Regained *(1671) were written
during Milton's last years in spite of his having lost his
sight in 1652. Milton wrote the following sonnet shortly
after becoming blind.*

SONNET 16   (1655)

When I consider how my light is spent,
  Ere half my days, in this dark world and wide,
  And that one talent which is death to hide,
  Lodged with me useless, though my soul more bent
5 To serve therewith my Maker, and present
  My true account, lest he returning chide,
  Doth God exact day-labour, light denied,
  I fondly ask; but Patience to prevent
That murmur, soon replies, "God doth not need
10 Either man's work or his own gifts, who best
  Bear his mild yoke, they serve him best. His state
Is kingly. Thousands at his bidding speed
  And post o'er land and ocean without rest:
  They also serve who only stand and wait."

Questions for Engagement, Response, and Analysis

1. To what does Milton refer when he speaks of "that one talent which is
   death to hide / Lodged with me useless"? What effect has this loss had
   on his attitude? How is it reflected in the tone of the poem?

2. Explain the last line of the poem.

3. What is the theme of Milton's sonnet?

Crafting Arguments

1. In an essay, analyze the ways in which Donne and Milton use the
   Italian sonnet form, metaphor, sound devices, and powerful diction to
   make a statement about their relationship with God.

William Blake (1757–1827)

William Blake was an English mystical poet and engraver. He sought to release Christianity from the constraints of early industrial materialism, Enlightenment rationalism, and puritanical sexual repression. He developed his own philosophical and mythological system expressed in such long, complex, and extremely difficult prophetic works as The Book of Thel *(1789) and* Jerusalem *(1804–1820). Much more accessible are the lyrics in* Songs of Innocence *(1789) and its companion volume,* Songs of Experience *(1794), poems that express Blake's sympathy with the oppressed and his rage at the human institutions that perpetuate oppression.*

THE LAMB   (1789)

Little Lamb, who made thee?
Dost thou know who made thee?
Gave thee life & bid thee feed,
By the stream & o'er the mead;
5   Gave thee clothing of delight,
Softest clothing wooly bright;
Gave thee such a tender voice,
Making all the vales rejoice!
Little Lamb I'll tell thee,
10   Little Lamb I'll tell thee!
He is callèd by thy name,
For he calls himself a Lamb:
He is meek & he is mild,
He became a little child:
15   I a child & thou a lamb,
We are callèd by his name.
Little Lamb God bless thee.
Little Lamb God bless thee.

Questions for Engagement, Response, and Analysis

1. Who is the speaker in this poem?
2. What is the tone? How do sound, imagery, and diction develop the tone?
3. Who or what does the Lamb symbolize?

THE TYGER   (1794)

Tyger! Tyger! burning bright
In the forests of the night,

What immortal hand or eye
Could frame thy fearful symmetry?

5   In what distant deeps or skies
Burnt the fire of thine eyes?
On what wings dare he aspire?
What the hand, dare seize the fire?

And what shoulder, & what art,
10 Could twist the sinews of thy heart?
And when thy heart began to beat,
What dread hand? & what dread feet?

What the hammer? what the chain?
In what furnace was thy brain?
15 What the anvil? what dread grasp
Dare its deadly terrors clasp?

When the stars threw down their spears,
And water'd heaven with their tears,
Did he smile his work to see?
20 Did he who made the Lamb make thee?

Tyger! Tyger! burning bright
In the forests of the night,
What immortal hand or eye
Dare frame thy fearful symmetry?

Questions for Engagement, Response, and Analysis

1. What is the tone? How do stanza form, rhythm, sound, imagery, and diction develop the tone?

2. What event is Blake alluding to in the lines "When the stars threw down their spears / And water'd heaven with their tears"?

3. How would you explain the reasons for the difference in stanza 1 and stanza 6?

4. Who or what does the tiger symbolize?

Crafting Arguments

1. Write an essay comparing the form, tone, imagery, and diction of "The Lamb" and "The Tyger" and giving your interpretation of the reasons for the differences.

2. In an essay, analyze "The Lamb" and "The Tyger" as representing two contrasting but complementary visions of God and of the created world.

Alfred, Lord Tennyson (1809–1892)

*Tennyson succeeded Wordsworth as English Poet Laureate.
Tennyson's early poems were not acclaimed; however, after
the death of a friend caused him to write an extended elegy,*
In Memoriam *(1853), and Queen Victoria named him a
Lord, Tennyson became one of the most popular poets of his
day. Among his works are* Maud, and Other Poems *(1855)*
and Idylls of the King *(1859), an extended poem about King
Arthur.*

ULYSSES   (1833)

It little profits that an idle king,
By this still hearth, among these barren crags,
Match'd with an aged wife, I mete and dole
Unequal laws unto a savage race,
5   That hoard, and sleep, and feed, and know not me.
I cannot rest from travel: I will drink
Life to the lees: all times I have enjoy'd
Greatly, have suffer'd greatly, both with those
That loved me, and alone; on shore, and when
10   Thro' scudding drifts the rainy Hyades
Vext the dim sea: I am become a name;
For always roaming with a hungry heart
Much have I seen and known; cities of men
And manners, climates, councils, governments,
15   Myself not least, but honour'd of them all;
And drunk delight of battle with my peers,
Far on the ringing plains of windy Troy.
I am a part of all that I have met;
Yet all experience is an arch wherethro'
20   Gleams that untravell'd world, whose margin fades
For ever and for ever when I move.
How dull it is to pause, to make an end,
To rust unburnish'd, not to shine in use!
As tho' to breathe were life. Life piled on life
25   Were all too little, and of one to me
Little remains: but every hour is saved
From that eternal silence, something more,
A bringer of new things; and vile it were
For some three suns to store and hoard myself,
30   And this gray spirit yearning in desire
To follow knowledge like a sinking star,
Beyond the utmost bound of human thought.
    This is my son, mine own Telemachus,
To whom I leave the sceptre and the isle—

35 Well-loved of me, discerning to fulfil
This labour, by slow prudence to make mild
A rugged people, and thro' soft degrees
Subdue them to the useful and the good.
Most blameless is he, centred in the sphere
40 Of common duties, decent not to fail
In offices of tenderness, and pay
Meet adoration to my household gods
When I am gone. He works his work, I mine.
  There lies the port; the vessel puffs her sail:
45 There gloom the dark broad seas. My mariners,
Souls that have toil'd, and wrought, and thought with me—
That ever with a frolic welcome took
The thunder and the sunshine, and opposed
Free hearts, free foreheads—you and I are old;
50 Old age hath yet his honour and his toil;
Death closes all: but something ere the end,
Some work of noble note, may yet be done,
Not unbecoming men that strove with Gods.
The lights begin to twinkle from the rocks:
55 The long day wanes: the slow moon climbs: the deep
Moans round with many voices. Come, my friends,
'Tis not too late to seek a newer world.
Push off, and sitting well in order smite
The sounding furrows; for my purpose holds
60 To sail beyond the sunset, and the baths
Of all the western stars, until I die.
It may be that the gulfs will wash us down:
It may be we shall touch the Happy Isles,
And see the great Achilles, whom we knew.
65 Tho' much is taken, much abides; and tho'
We are not now that strength which in old days
Moved earth and heaven, that which we are, we are;
One equal temper of heroic hearts,
Made weak by time and fate, but strong in will
70 To strive, to seek, to find, and not to yield.

Questions for Engagement, Response, and Analysis

1. Who is the speaker in this dramatic monologue? Who is the audience?
2. What is Ulysses trying to persuade his audience to do? What persuasive techniques does he use?
3. What is the tone of the poem? How is it created?
4. In what ways is Telemachus Ulysses' ideal heir?
5. Explain Ulysses' claim, "I am a part of all that I have met."

Crafting Arguments

1. After examining what Ulysses says about himself and what he challenges his men to do, write an essay giving your interpretation of Ulysses' philosophy of life.

2. "Do Not Go Gentle into That Good Night" by Dylan Thomas has a similar message. In an essay, compare the themes of these two poems.

Gerard Manley Hopkins (1844–1889)

Born into a High Anglican family in England, Gerard Manley Hopkins in 1866 converted to Catholicism. Two years later, he entered the Jesuit order and in 1877 was ordained a Jesuit priest. His sometimes anguished poems, which were not published until 1918, reveal a man of strong faith sometimes racked by doubts about the adequacy of his devotion and service. Hopkins developed an experimental metrical system he called sprung rhythm, basing his lines on the number of accents rather than the number of syllables.

GOD'S GRANDEUR (1877)

The world is charged with the grandeur of God.
    It will flame out, like shining from shook foil;
    It gathers to a greatness, like the ooze of oil
Crushed. Why do men then now not reck his rod?
5   Generations have trod, have trod, have trod;
    And all is seared with trade; bleared, smeared with toil;
    And wears man's smudge and shares man's smell: the soil
Is bare now, nor can foot feel, being shod.
And for all this, nature is never spent;
10   There lives the dearest freshness deep down things;
And though the last lights off the black West went
    Oh, morning, at the brown brink eastward, springs—
Because the Holy Ghost over the bent
World broods with warm breast and with ah! bright wings.

Questions for Engagement, Response, and Analysis

1. What is the tone of the octave in this Italian sonnet? What is the tone of the sestet?

2. What kinds of images does Hopkins use in the octave?

3. What is Hopkins' answer to the question in line 4? Compare his answer to Wordsworth's lament in "The World Is Too Much with Us."

4. What images does Hopkins use to characterize the grandeur of God? Explain the final image.

Crafting Arguments

1. In an essay, compare the tone, diction, and images in the octave with those in the sestet and explain how together they create the theme of the poem.

T. S. Eliot (1888–1965)

Eliot, born an American and the grandson of a Unitarian minister, changed his nationality and his religion, becoming a British citizen and a devout Anglican. Eliot's early poems, like "The Love Song of J. Alfred Prufrock" and "The Hollow Men," expressed the disenchantment and disillusionment of many people in the early twentieth century. The Waste Land (1922) is considered by many critics to be the ultimate expression of the modern condition. Eliot's conversion to the Anglican faith, however, changed his outlook completely; and his later works such as "Ash Wednesday" and Four Quartets (1934–1944) depict human beings' search for a sustaining faith. An ardent admirer of Dante, Eliot learned medieval Italian in order to read The Divine Comedy in its original form. The quotation with which Eliot begins "The Love Song of J. Alfred Prufrock" is a statement of Guido da Montefeltro, a sinner in Dante's Inferno, who says that he would not tell Dante his story if he thought that there was any chance that Dante would return to earth to repeat it.

THE LOVE SONG OF J. ALFRED PRUFROCK   (1917)

S' io credessi che mia risposta fosse
A persona che mai tornasse al mondo,
Questa fiamma staria senza piú scosse.
Ma perciocchè giammai di questo fondo
Non tornò vivo alcum, s' i' odo il vero,
Senza tema d'infamia ti rispondo.

Let us go then, you and I,
When the evening is spread out against the sky
Like a patient etherized upon a table;
Let us go, through certain half-deserted streets,
5   The muttering retreats
Of restless nights in one-night cheap hotels
And sawdust restaurants with oyster-shells:
Streets that follow like a tedious argument
Of insidious intent
10 To lead you to an overwhelming question . . .

Oh, do not ask, "What is it?"
Let us go and make our visit.

In the room the women come and go
Talking of Michelangelo.

15   The yellow fog that rubs its back upon the window panes,
The yellow smoke that rubs its muzzle on the window panes,
Licked its tongue into the corners of the evening,
Lingered upon the pools that stand in drains,
Let fall upon its back the soot that falls from chimneys,
20   Slipped by the terrace, made a sudden leap,
And seeing that it was a soft October night,
Curled once about the house, and fell asleep.

And indeed there will be time
For the yellow smoke that slides along the street,
25   Rubbing its back upon the window panes;
There will be time, there will be time
To prepare a face to meet the faces that you meet;
There will be time to murder and create,
And time for all the works and days of hands
30   That lift and drop a question on your plate:
Time for you and time for me,
And time yet for a hundred indecisions,
And for a hundred visions and revisions,
Before the taking of a toast and tea.

35   In the room the women come and go
Talking of Michelangelo.

And indeed there will be time
To wonder, "Do I dare?" and, "Do I dare?"—
Time to turn back and descend the stair,
40   With a bald spot in the middle of my hair—
(They will say: "How his hair is growing thin!")
My morning coat, my collar mounting firmly to the chin,
My necktie rich and modest, but asserted by a simple pin—
(They will say: "But how his arms and legs are thin!")
45   Do I dare
Disturb the universe?
In a minute there is time
For decisions and revisions which a minute will reverse.

For I have known them all already, known them all:
50   Have known the evenings, mornings, afternoons,
I have measured out my life with coffee spoons;
I know the voices dying with a dying fall
Beneath the music from a farther room.
So how should I presume?

55   And I have known the eyes already, known them all—
The eyes that fix you in a formulated phrase.

And when I am formulated, sprawling on a pin,
When I am pinned and wriggling on the wall,
Then how should I begin
To spit out all the butt-ends of my days and ways?
    And how should I presume?

    And I have known the arms already, known them all—
Arms that are braceleted and white and bare
(But in the lamplight, downed with light brown hair!)
    Is it perfume from a dress
    That makes me so digress?
Arms that lie along a table, or wrap about a shawl.
    And should I then presume?
    And how should I begin?

    Shall I say, I have gone at dusk through narrow streets,
And watched the smoke that rises from the pipes
Of lonely men in shirtsleeves, leaning out of windows? . . .
I should have been a pair of ragged claws
Scuttling across the floors of silent seas.
    And the afternoon, the evening, sleeps so peacefully!
Smoothed by long fingers,
Asleep . . . tired . . . or it malingers,
Stretched on the floor, here beside you and me.
Should I, after tea and cakes and ices,
Have the strength to force the moment to its crisis?
But though I have wept and fasted, wept and prayed,
Though I have seen my head (grown slightly bald) brought
        in upon a platter,
I am no prophet—and here's no great matter;
I have seen the moment of my greatness flicker,
And I have seen the eternal Footman hold my coat, and snicker,
        And in short, I was afraid.

    And would it have been worth it, after all,
After the cups, the marmalade, the tea,
Among the porcelain, among some talk of you and me,
    Would it have been worth while
To have bitten off the matter with a smile,
To have squeezed the universe into a ball
To roll it toward some overwhelming question,
To say: "I am Lazarus, come from the dead,
Come back to tell you all, I shall tell you all"—
If one, settling a pillow by her head,
    Should say: "That is not what I meant at all;
        That is not it, at all."

    And would it have been worth it, after all,

60
65
70
75
80
85
90
95

100　　Would it have been worth while,
　　　After the sunsets and the dooryards and the sprinkled streets,
　　　After the novels, after the teacups, after the skirts that trail
　　　　　along the floor—
　　　And this, and so much more?—
　　　It is impossible to say just what I mean!
105　　But as if a magic lantern threw the nerves in patterns on a screen:
　　　Would it have been worth while
　　　If one, settling a pillow or throwing off a shawl,
　　　And turning toward the window, should say: "That is not it at all,
　　　　　That is not what I meant, at all."

110　　　　No! I am not Prince Hamlet, nor was meant to be;
　　　Am an attendant lord, one that will do
　　　To swell a progress, start a scene or two,
　　　Advise the prince: withal, an easy tool,
　　　Deferential, glad to be of use,
115　　Politic, cautious, and meticulous;
　　　Full of high sentence, but a bit obtuse;
　　　At times, indeed, almost ridiculous—
　　　Almost, at times, the Fool.

　　　I grow old . . . I grow old . . .
120　　I shall wear the bottoms of my trousers rolled.

　　　　Shall I part my hair behind? Do I dare to eat a peach?
　　　I shall wear white flannel trousers, and walk upon the beach.
　　　I have heard the mermaids singing, each to each.
　　　I do not think that they will sing to me.

125　　I have seen them riding seaward on the waves,
　　　Combing the white hair of the waves blown back
　　　When the wind blows the water white and black.
　　　We have lingered in the chambers of the sea
　　　By seagirls wreathed with seaweed red and brown,
130　　Till human voices wake us, and we drown.

Questions for Engagement, Response, and Analysis

1. What does Eliot suggest about Prufrock by beginning the poem with a quotation from Dante's *Inferno?*

2. Explain the effect of the description in the opening ten lines. What does this description tell you about Prufrock's world?

3. What is Prufrock afraid to ask? Why is he afraid to ask it?

4. What is the tone of the poem? In what way is it especially appropriate for this subject?

Crafting Arguments

1. Identify all of the allusions in the poem. Then write an essay explaining how Eliot uses the allusions, metaphors, and images to create the theme of the poem.

2. Examine Prufrock's statements about himself. Then write an essay explaining how the contrast between his knowledge of heroic figures in literature and his self-knowledge affects Prufrock's self-concept and confidence.

3. Write an essay comparing Prufrock's attitudes toward life with those of Ulysses in Tennyson's poem.

Langston Hughes (1902–1967)

Born in Joplin, Missouri, James Langston Hughes was a novelist, poet, and playwright who often wrote in dialect to reflect what he considered to be the language of the ordinary "Negro." He graduated from Lincoln University in 1929 after attending Columbia University and after working with some of the most famous black writers of the Harlem Renaissance. Hughes founded theaters, produced plays, and traveled to such locales as Haiti, the Soviet Union, and Spain, where he covered the Spanish Civil War. His many works include the Semple tales, the novels Not Without Laughter *(1930) and* Ask Your Mama *(1961), and the gospel musical* Tambourines to Glory *(1959). Hughes' poetry reflects several recurring themes: the racial tension that the black man experiences, the glorification of the common man or woman, and the importance of music, especially jazz and the blues.*

HARLEM   (1951)

What happens to a dream deferred?

    Does it dry up
    like a raisin in the sun?
    Or fester like a sore—
5   And then run?
    Does it stink like rotten meat?
    Or crust and sugar over—
    like a syrupy sweet?

    Maybe it just sags
10   like a heavy load.

    Or does it explode?

Questions for Engagement, Response, and Analysis

1. What is the tone of this poem? How does Hughes create it?
2. What is the theme?
3. Why does Hughes never identify the kind of dream he has in mind?

Crafting Arguments

1. In an essay, analyze and explain each of the similes Hughes uses to describe the possible effects of "a dream deferred."

John Ciardi (1916–1986)

John Ciardi was a man of many talents. He was born into an Italian family living in Boston and raised by his mother and sisters, who lived frugally in order to save enough money to send Ciardi to college. During World War II, he joined the Army Air Corps and flew more than twenty missions over Japan. Ciardi taught at several colleges, including Harvard and Rutgers, and he was director of the Bread Loaf Writer's Conference for seventeen years. He published his first book of poetry, Homeward to America, *in 1940 and wrote of his experiences in the war in his second book of poetry,* Other Skies *(1947). In addition to many other poetry colletions, he published several books of poetry for children. Though Ciardi's primary talent was as a poet, he also published two very influential works. The first,* How Does a Poem Mean? *(1959), was used extensively in college literature classes. The second—his translation of the three books of Dante's* Divine Comedy *(1954, 1961, 1970)—is celebrated as probably the best verse rendition of Dante in contemporary English.*

IN PLACE OF A CURSE   (1989)

At the next vacancy for God, if I am elected,
I shall forgive last the delicately wounded
who, having been slugged no harder than anyone else,
never got up again, neither to fight back,
5   nor to finger their jaws in painful admiration.

They who are wholly broken, and they in whom
mercy is understanding, I shall embrace at once
and lead to pillows in heaven. But they who are
the meek by trade, baiting the best of their betters
10   with the extortions of a mock-helplessness

I shall take last to love, and never wholly.
Let them all into Heaven—I abolish Hell—

but let it be read over them as they enter:
"Beware the calculations of the meek, who gambled nothing,
15   gave nothing, and could never receive enough."

Questions for Engagement, Response, and Analysis

1. How would you characterize the speaker in this poem? In what ways would the speaker be a different kind of god from the Judeo-Christian God?

2. To which of the Beatitudes is this poem a response? How does Ciardi alter this Beatitude?

3. Who, according to the speaker, will inherit heaven? According to Matthew, who will inherit "the kingdom of heaven"? Who will "inherit the earth"?

4. What is the tone of the poem? How does Ciardi's use of diction and alliteration help to create the tone?

5. What is the significance of the title?

Crafting Arguments

1. In an essay, explain Ciardi's differentiation between the two types of the meek and show how this differentiation emphasizes Ciardi's theme.

N. Scott Momaday (b. 1934)

N. Scott Momaday, a Kiowa, studied at the University of New Mexico and received his doctorate from Stanford University in 1963. His first novel, House Made of Dawn *(1968), won a Pulitzer Prize and brought him accolades for bringing prestige to Native American writers. The Way to* Rainy Mountain *(1969) describes the oral histories and migration stories of his ancestors as imagined by his grandmother. His second novel,* The Ancient Child *(1989), is a story about a spiritual journey. Other recent works include* In the Presence of the Sun *(1991) and* Circle of Wonder: A Native American Christmas Story *(1994). In 2006, he produced* The Indolent Boys, *a play written for radio. Currently, Momaday teaches at the University of Arizona.*

CARRIERS OF THE DREAM WHEEL   (1992)

This is the Wheel of Dreams
Which is carried on their voices,
By means of which their voices turn
And center upon being.

5   It encircles the First World,
   This powerful wheel.
   They shape their songs upon the wheel
   And spin the names of the earth and sky,
   The aboriginal names.
10 They are old men, or men
   Who are old in their voices,
   And they carry the wheel among the camps,
   Saying: Come, come,
   Let us tell the old stories,
15 Let us sing the sacred songs.

Questions for Engagement, Response, and Analysis

1. Explain what Momaday means when he says that the "Wheel of Dreams" is "carried on their voices." Who are "they"?

2. In Kiowa cosmology, the wheel suggests the continuing cycle of oral tales and songs. Why are these dreams, tales, and songs important to the Kiowa?

3. Interpret the imagery of the wheel.

Crafting Arguments

1. In an essay, explain how Momaday uses the elements of poetry in order to emphasize the importance of tradition to the Kiowa.

D RA M A

Sophocles (496?–406 B.C.)

Sophocles, the second of the three great Greek tragedians, wrote at least 120 plays, and his tragedies won first place at the festival of Dionysus twenty-four times. Sophocles' long life spanned the time in history when the culture of Athens was at its peak. Born to a wealthy Athenian family, Sophocles was honored as a producer of tragedies and as a citizen. He was selected for the highest elective office as one of the ten generals of Athens and was awarded priesthoods for his religious piety. Three of the seven extant plays of Sophocles, Oedipus the King, Oedipus at Colonus, *and* Antigone, *tell the story of the royal family of Thebes. Aristotle gave* Oedipus Rex *the highest praise of any extant*

*Greek tragedy, and it is often described as the best example
of dramatic irony in literature.*

ANCIENT GREEK DRAMA

*Ancient Greek drama was performed in huge outdoor amphithe-
aters that seated as many as 20,000 spectators on great semicir-
cular stone benches that climbed the slope of a hill. At the bottom
center was the skene building, which served both as a dressing
room for the actors and as the scenery, most often as the front of
a palace or temple. In front of the skene was a circular acting
space, the orchestra.*

*Because of the massive size of such amphitheaters, where many
spectators would have been hundreds of feet from the stage,
ancient Greek drama emphasizes large, clearly visible, and stylized effects. Actors declaimed their lines through the amplifying
mouthpieces of masks and apparently later, in tragedies, wore elevated shoes to enhance their stature. Probably, because of the size
of the theaters and the masks, ancient Greek drama relied on bold
and dramatic movements rather than on subtle gestures, facial
expressions, and asides.*

*Deriving from the worship of the god Dionysus, Athenian
drama was a community celebration. Audiences apparently were
quite volatile and deeply involved in the drama. Because almost
the only subjects accepted for performance were the Greek myths,
the audience already knew the stories behind each play; therefore,
Greek drama provided the perfect vehicle for dramatic irony, a
form of irony made possible by the audience's knowledge of events
and relationships of which the characters were often ignorant. In
dramatic irony, the character's words have a double meaning
unknown to the character but known to the audience or to other
characters. Apparently, too, the audience had extraordinary attention spans; on each of the last three days of the Dionysian festival,
they would sit through five plays—three tragedies, one satyr play,
and one comedy.*

OEDIPUS REX   (FIFTH CENTURY B.C.)

ENGLISH VERSION BY DUDLEY FITTS AND ROBERT FITZGERALD

Persons Represented

OEDIPUS
A PRIEST
CREON
TEIRESIAS
IOCASTE [JOCASTA]

MESSENGER
SHEPHERD OF LAÏOS
SECOND MESSENGER
CHORUS OF THEBAN ELDERS

THE SCENE—*Before the palace of* OEDIPUS, *King of Thebes. A central door and two lateral doors open onto a platform which runs the length of the façade. On the platform, right and left, are altars; and three steps lead down into the "*ORCHESTRA,*" or chorus-ground. At the beginning of the action these steps are crowded by suppliants who have brought branches and chaplets of olive leaves and who lie in various attitudes of despair.* OEDIPUS *enters.*

PROLOGUE

OEDIPUS: My children, generations of the living
In the line of Kadmos, nursed at his ancient hearth:
Why have you strewn yourselves before these altars
In supplication, with your boughs and garlands?
The breath of incense rises from the city
With a sound of prayer and lamentation.
Children,
I would not have you speak through messengers,
And therefore I have come myself to hear you—
10   I, Oedipus, who bear the famous name.

(To a Priest.)

You, there, since you are eldest in the company,
Speak for them all, tell me what preys upon you,
Whether you come in dread, or crave some blessing:
Tell me, and never doubt that I will help you
In every way I can; I should be heartless
Were I not moved to find you suppliant here.
PRIEST: Great Oedipus, O powerful King of Thebes!
You see how all the ages of our people
20   Cling to your altar steps: here are boys
Who can barely stand alone, and here are priests
By weight of age, as I am a priest of God,
And young men chosen from those yet unmarried;
As for the others, all that multitude,
They wait with olive chaplets in the squares,
At the two shrines of Pallas, and where Apollo
Speaks in the glowing embers.
Your own eyes
Must tell you: Thebes is tossed on a murdering sea
30   And can not lift her head from the death surge.
A rust consumes the buds and fruits of the earth;
The herds are sick; children die unborn,

And labor is vain. The god of plague and pyre
Raids like detestable lightning through the city,
And all the house of Kadmos is laid waste,
All emptied, and all darkened; Death alone
Battens upon the misery of Thebes.
You are not one of the immortal gods, we know;
Yet we have come to you to make our prayer
40   As to the man surest in mortal ways
And wisest in the ways of God. You saved us
From the Sphinx, that flinty singer, and the tribute
We paid to her so long; yet you were never
Better informed than we, nor could we teach you:
It was some god breathed in you to set us free.
Therefore, O mighty King, we turn to you:
Find us our safety, find us a remedy,
Whether by counsel of the gods or men.
A king of wisdom tested in the past
50   Can act in a time of troubles, and act well.
Noblest of men, restore
Life to your city! Think how all men call you
Liberator for your triumph long ago;
Ah, when your years of kingship are remembered,
Let them not say *We rose, but later fell*—
Keep the State from going down in the storm!
Once, years ago, with happy augury,
You brought us fortune; be the same again!
No man questions your power to rule the land:
60   But rule over men, not over a dead city!
Ships are only hulls, citadels are nothing,
When no life moves in the empty passageways.
   OEDIPUS: Poor children! You may be sure I know
All that you longed for in your coming here.
I know that you are deathly sick; and yet,
Sick as you are, not one is as sick as I.
Each of you suffers in himself alone
His anguish, not another's; but my spirit
Groans for the city, for myself, for you.
70   I was not sleeping, you are not waking me.
No, I have been in tears for a long while
And in my restless thought walked many ways.
In all my search, I found one helpful course,
And that I have taken: I have sent Creon,
Son of Menoikeus, brother of the Queen,
To Delphi, Apollo's place of revelation,
To learn there, if he can,
What act or pledge of mine may save the city.

I have counted the days, and now, this very day,
80　　I am troubled, for he has overstayed his time.
What is he doing? He has been gone too long.
Yet whenever he comes back, I should do ill
To scant whatever duty God reveals.

PRIEST: It is a timely promise. At this instant
They tell me Creon is here.

OEDIPUS: O Lord Apollo!
May his news be fair as his face is radiant!

PRIEST: It could not be otherwise: he is crowned with bay,
The chaplet is thick with berries.

90　　OEDIPUS: We shall soon know;
He is near enough to hear us now.

(Enter Creon.)

O Prince: Brother: son of Menoikeus:
What answer do you bring us from the god?

CREON: A strong one. I can tell you, great afflictions
Will turn out well, if they are taken well.

OEDIPUS: What was the oracle? These vague words
Leave me still hanging between hope and fear.

100　　CREON: Is it your pleasure to hear me with all these
Gathered around us? I am prepared to speak,
But should we not go in?

OEDIPUS: Let them all hear it.
It is for them I suffer, more than for myself.

CREON: Then I will tell you what I heard at Delphi.
In plain words
The god commands us to expel from the land of Thebes
An old defilement we are sheltering.
It is a deathly thing, beyond cure;
We must not let it feed upon us longer.

OEDIPUS: What defilement? How shall we rid ourselves of it?

110　　CREON: By exile or death, blood for blood. It was
Murder that brought the plague-wind on the city.

OEDIPUS: Murder of whom? Surely the god has named him?

CREON: My lord: long ago Laïos was our king,
Before you came to govern us.

OEDIPUS: I know;
I learned of him from others; I never saw him.

CREON: He was murdered; and Apollo commands us now
To take revenge upon whoever killed him.

OEDIPUS: Upon whom? Where are they? Where shall we find a clue
120　　To solve that crime, after so many years?

CREON: Here in this land, he said.
If we make enquiry,

We may touch things that otherwise escape us.

OEDIPUS: Tell me: Was Laïos murdered in his house,
Or in the fields, or in some foreign country?

CREON: He said he planned to make a pilgrimage.
He did not come home again.

OEDIPUS: And was there no one,
No witness, no companion, to tell what happened?

130 CREON: They were all killed but one, and he got away
So frightened that he could remember one thing only.

OEDIPUS: What was that one thing? One may be the key
To everything, if we resolve to use it.

CREON: He said that a band of highwaymen attacked them,
Outnumbered them, and overwhelmed the King.

OEDIPUS: Strange, that a highwayman should be so daring—
Unless some faction here bribed him to do it.

CREON: We thought of that. But after Laïos' death
New troubles arose and we had no avenger.

140 OEDIPUS: What troubles could prevent your hunting down the killers?

CREON: The riddling Sphinx's song
Made us deaf to all mysteries but her own.

OEDIPUS: Then once more I must bring what is dark to light.
It is most fitting that Apollo shows,
As you do, this compunction for the dead.
You shall see how I stand by you, as I should,
To avenge the city and the city's god,
And not as though it were for some distant friend,
But for my own sake, to be rid of evil.

150 Whoever killed King Laïos might—who knows?—
Decide at any moment to kill me as well.
By avenging the murdered king I protect myself.
Come, then, my children: leave the altar steps,
Lift up your olive boughs!
One of you go
And summon the people of Kadmos to gather here.
I will do all that I can; you may tell them that.

(Exit a page.)

So, with the help of God,
We shall be saved—or else indeed we are lost.

160 PRIEST: Let us rise, children. It was for this we came,
And now the King has promised it himself.
Phoibos has sent us an oracle; may he descend
Himself to save us and drive out the plague.

*(Exeunt Oedipus and Creon into the palace by the central door. The
priest and the suppliants disperse R and L. After a short pause the
chorus enters the orchestra.)*

PARODOS

CHORUS: What is God singing in his profound

(STROPHE 1)

Delphi of gold and shadow?
What oracle for Thebes, the sunwhipped city?
Fear unjoints me, the roots of my heart tremble.
Now I remember, O Healer, your power, and wonder:
Will you send doom like a sudden cloud. or weave it
170   Like nightfall of the past?
Speak, speak to us, issue of holy sound:
Dearest to our expectancy: be tender!
Let me pray to Athené, the immortal daughter of Zeus,

(ANTISTROPHE 1)

And to Artemis her sister
Who keeps her famous throne in the market ring,
And to Apollo, bowman at the far butts of heaven—
O gods, descend! Like three streams leap against
The fires of our grief, the fires of darkness;
Be swift to bring us rest!
180   As in the old time from the brilliant house
Of air you stepped to save us, come again!

(STROPHE 2)

Now our afflictions have no end,
Now all our stricken host lies down
And no man fights off death with his mind;
The noble plowland bears no grain,
And groaning mothers can not bear—
See, how our lives like birds take wing,
Like sparks that fly when a fire soars,
To the shore of the god of evening.

(ANTISTROPHE 2)
190   The plague burns on, it is pitiless,
Though pallid children laden with death
Lie unwept in the stony ways,
And old gray women by every path
Flock to the strand about the altars
There to strike their breasts and cry
Worship of Phoibos in wailing prayers:
Be kind, God's golden child!

(STROPHE 3)

There are no swords in this attack by fire,
No shields, but we are ringed with cries.

200   Send the besieger plunging from our homes
        Into the vast sea-room of the Atlantic
        Or into the waves that foam eastward of Thrace—
        For the day ravages what the night spares—
        Destroy our enemy, lord of the thunder!
        Let him be riven by lightning from heaven!

        (ANTISTROPHE 3)

        Phoibos Apollo, stretch the sun's bowstring,
        That golden cord, until it sing for us,
        Flashing arrows in heaven!
        Artemis, Huntress,
210   Race with flaring lights upon our mountains!
        O scarlet god, O golden-banded brow,
        O Theban Bacchos in a storm of Maenads,

        (Enter Oedipus, C.)

        Whirl upon Death, that all the Undying hate!
        Come with blinding torches, come in joy!

        SCENE I

        OEDIPUS: Is this your prayer? It may be answered. Come,
        Listen to me, act as the crisis demands,
        And you shall have relief from all these evils.
220   Until now I was a stranger to this tale,
        As I had been a stranger to the crime.
        Could I track down the murderer without a clue?
        But now, friends,
        As one who became a citizen after the murder,
        I make this proclamation to all Thebans:
        If any man knows by whose hand Laïos, son of Labdakos,
        Met his death, I direct that man to tell me everything,
        No matter what he fears for having so long withheld it.
        Let it stand as promised that no further trouble
        Will come to him, but he may leave the land in safety.
        Moreover: If anyone knows the murderer to be foreign,
        Let him not keep silent: he shall have his reward from me.
        However, if he does conceal it; if any man
230   Fearing for his friend or for himself disobeys this edict,
        Hear what I propose to do:
        I solemnly forbid the people of this country,
        Where power and throne are mine, ever to receive that man
        Or speak to him, no matter who he is, or let him
        Join in sacrifice, lustration, or in prayer.
        I decree that he be driven from every house,
        Being, as he is, corruption itself to us: the Delphic

240 Voice of Zeus has pronounced this revelation.
 Thus I associate myself with the oracle
 And take the side of the murdered king.
 As for the criminal, I pray to God—
 Whether it be a lurking thief, or one of a number—
 I pray that that man's life be consumed in evil and wretchedness.
 And as for me, this curse applies no less
 If it should turn out that the culprit is my guest here,
 Sharing my hearth.
 You have heard the penalty.
250 I lay it on you now to attend to this
 For my sake, for Apollo's, for the sick
 Sterile city that heaven has abandoned.
 Suppose the oracle had given you no command:
 Should this defilement go uncleansed for ever?
 You should have found the murderer: your king,
 A noble king, had been destroyed!
 Now I,
 Having the power that he held before me,
 Having his bed, begetting children there
260 Upon his wife, as he would have, had he lived—
 Their son would have been my children's brother,
 If Laïos had had luck in fatherhood!
 (But surely ill luck rushed upon his reign)—
 I say I take the son's part, just as though
 I were his son, to press the fight for him
 And see it won! I'll find the hand that brought
 Death to Labdakos' and Polydoros' child,
 Heir of Kadmos' and Agenor's line.
 And as for those who fail me,
270 Many the gods deny them the fruit of the earth,
 Fruit of the womb, and may they rot utterly!
 Let them be wretched as we are wretched, and worse!
 For you, for loyal Thebans, and for all
 Who find my actions right, I pray the favor
 Of justice, and of all the immortal gods.
 CHORAGOS: Since I am under oath, my lord, I swear
 I did not do the murder, I can not name
 The murderer. Might not the oracle
 That has ordained the search tell where to find him?
280 OEDIPUS: An honest question. But no man in the world
 Can make the gods do more than the gods will.
 CHORAGOS: There is one last expedient—
 OEDIPUS: Tell me what it is.
 Though it seem slight, you must not hold it back.
 CHORAGOS: A lord clairvoyant to the lord Apollo,

As we all know, is the skilled Teiresias.
One might learn much about this from him, Oedipus.
OEDIPUS: I am not wasting time:
Creon spoke of this, and I have sent for him—
290   Twice, in fact; it is strange that he is not here.
CHORAGOS: The other matter—that old report—seems useless.
OEDIPUS: Tell me. I am interested in all reports.
CHORAGOS: The King was said to have been killed by highwaymen.
OEDIPUS: I know. But we have no witnesses to that.
CHORAGOS: If the killer can feel a particle of dread,
Your curse will bring him out of hiding!
OEDIPUS: No.
The man who dared that act will fear no curse.

(Enter the blind seer Teiresias, led by a page.)

CHORAGOS: But there is one man who may detect the criminal.
300   This is Teiresias, this is the holy prophet
In whom, alone of all men, truth was born.
OEDIPUS: Teiresias: seer: student of mysteries,
Of all that's taught and all that no man tells,
Secrets of Heaven and secrets of the earth:
Blind though you are, you know the city lies
Sick with plague; and from this plague, my lord,
We find that you alone can guard or save us.
Possibly you did not hear the messengers?
Apollo, when we sent to him,
310   Sent us back word that this great pestilence
Would lift, but only if we established clearly
The identity of those who murdered Laïos.
They must be killed or exiled.
Can you use
Birdflight or any art of divination
To purify yourself, and Thebes, and me
From this contagion? We are in your hands.
There is no fairer duty
Than that of helping others in distress.
320   TEIRESIAS: How dreadful knowledge of the truth can be
When there's no help in truth! I knew this well,
But made myself forget. I should not have come.
OEDIPUS: What is troubling you? Why are your eyes so cold?
TEIRESIAS: Let me go home. Bear your own fate, and I'll
Bear mine. It is better so: trust what I say.
OEDIPUS: What you say is ungracious and unhelpful
To your native country. Do not refuse to speak.
TEIRESIAS: When it comes to speech, your own is neither temperate
Nor opportune. I wish to be more prudent.

330   OEDIPUS: In God's name, we all beg you—
 TEIRESIAS: You are all ignorant.
  No; I will never tell you what I know.
  Now it is my misery; then, it would be yours.
 OEDIPUS: What! You do know something, and will not tell us?
  You would betray us all and wreck the State?
 TEIRESIAS: I do not intend to torture myself, or you.
  Why persist in asking? You will not persuade me.
 OEDIPUS: What a wicked old man you are! You'd try a stone's
  Patience! Out with it! Have you no feeling at all?
340   TEIRESIAS: You call me unfeeling. If you could only see
  The nature of your own feelings . . .
 OEDIPUS: Why,
  Who would not feel as I do? Who could endure
  Your arrogance toward the city?
 TEIRESIAS: What does it matter!
  Whether I speak or not, it is bound to come.
 OEDIPUS: Then, if "it" is bound to come, you are bound to tell me.
 TEIRESIAS: No, I will not go on. Rage as you please.
 OEDIPUS: Rage? Why not!
350   And I'll tell you what I think:
  You planned it, you had it done, you all but
  Killed him with your own hands: if you had eyes,
  I'd say the crime was yours, and yours alone.
 TEIRESIAS: So? I charge you, then,
  Abide by the proclamation you have made:
  From this day forth
  Never speak again to these men or to me;
  You yourself are the pollution of this country.
 OEDIPUS: You dare say that! Can you possibly think you have
360   Some way of going free, after such insolence?
 TEIRESIAS: I have gone free. It is the truth sustains me.
 OEDIPUS: Who taught you shamelessness? It was not your craft.
 TEIRESIAS: You did. You made me speak. I did not want to.
 OEDIPUS: Speak what? Let me hear it again more clearly.
 TEIRESIAS: Was it not clear before? Are you tempting me?
 OEDIPUS: I did not understand it. Say it again.
 TEIRESIAS: I say that you are the murderer whom you seek.
 OEDIPUS: Now twice you have spat out infamy. You'll pay for it!
 TEIRESIAS: Would you care for more? Do you wish to be really angry?
370   OEDIPUS: Say what you will. Whatever you say is worthless.
 TEIRESIAS: I say you live in hideous shame with those
  Most dear to you. You can not see the evil.
 OEDIPUS: It seems you can go on mouthing like this for ever.
 TEIRESIAS: I can, if there is power in truth.

OEDIPUS: There is:
    But not for you, not for you,
    You sightless, witless, senseless, mad old man!

TEIRESIAS: You are the madman. There is no one here
    Who will not curse you soon, as you curse me.

380 OEDIPUS: You child of endless night! You can not hurt me
    Or any other man who sees the sun.

TEIRESIAS: True: it is not from me your fate will come.
    That lies within Apollo's competence.
    As it is his concern.

OEDIPUS: Tell me.
    Are you speaking for Creon, or for yourself?

TEIRESIAS: Creon is no threat. You weave your own doom.

OEDIPUS: Wealth, power, craft of statesmanship!
    Kingly position, everywhere admired!

390   What savage envy is stored up against these,
    If Creon, whom I trusted, Creon my friend,
    For this great office which the city once
    Put in my hands unsought—if for this power
    Creon desires in secret to destroy me!

    He has bought this decrepit fortune-teller, this
    Collector of dirty pennies, this prophet fraud—
    Why, he is no more clairvoyant than I am!

    Tell us.
    Has your mystic mummery ever approached the truth?

400   When that hellcat the Sphinx was performing here,
    What help were you to these people?
    Her magic was not for the first man who came along:
    It demanded a real exorcist. Your birds—
    What good were they? or the gods, for the matter of that?
    But I came by,
    Oedipus, the simple man, who knows nothing—
    I thought it out for myself, no birds helped me!
    And this is the man you think you can destroy,
    That you may be close to Creon when he's king!

410   Well, you and your friend Creon, it seems to me,
    Will suffer most. If you were not an old man,
    You would have paid already for your plot.

CHORAGOS: We can not see that his words or yours
    Have been spoken except in anger, Oedipus,
    And of anger we have no need. How can God's will
    Be accomplished best? That is what most concerns us.

TEIRESIAS: You are a king. But where argument's concerned
    I am your man, as much a king as you.
    I am not your servant, but Apollo's.

420   I have no need of Creon to speak for me.

Listen to me. You mock my blindness, do you?
But I say that you, with both your eyes, are blind:
You can not see the wretchedness of your life,
Nor in whose house you live, no, nor with whom.
Who are your father and mother? Can you tell me?
You do not even know the blind wrongs
That you have done them, on earth and in the world below.
But the double lash of your parents' curse will whip you
Out of this land some day, with only night

430   Upon your precious eyes.
Your cries then—where will they not be heard?
What fastness of Kithairon will not echo them?
And that bridal-descant of yours—you'll know it then,
The song they sang when you came here to Thebes
And found your misguided berthing.
All this, and more, that you can not guess at now,
Will bring you to yourself among your children.
Be angry, then. Curse Creon. Curse my words.
I tell you, no man that walks upon the earth

440   Shall be rooted out more horribly than you.

OEDIPUS: Am I to bear this from him?—Damnation
    Take you! Out of this place! Out of my sight!

TEIRESIAS: I would not have come at all if you had not asked me.

OEDIPUS: Could I have told that you'd talk nonsense, that
    You'd come here to make a fool of yourself, and of me?

TEIRESIAS: A fool? Your parents thought me sane enough.

OEDIPUS: My parents again!—Wait: who were my parents?

TEIRESIAS: This day will give you a father, and break your heart.

OEDIPUS: Your infantile riddles! Your damned abracadabra!

450 TEIRESIAS: You were a great man once at solving riddles.

OEDIPUS: Mock me with that if you like; you will find it true.

TEIRESIAS: It was true enough. It brought about your ruin.

OEDIPUS: But if it saved this town?

TEIRESIAS: (to the Page) Boy, give me your hand.

OEDIPUS: Yes, boy; lead him away.
    —While you are here
    We can do nothing. Go; leave us in peace.

TEIRESIAS: I will go when I have said what I have to say.
    How can you hurt me? And I tell you again:

460 The man you have been looking for all this time,
The damned man, the murderer of Laïos,
That man is in Thebes. To your mind he is foreign-born,
But it will soon be shown that he is a Theban,
A revelation that will fail to please.
A blind man,
Who has his eyes now; a penniless man, who is rich now;

And he will go tapping the strange earth with his staff
To the children with whom he lives now he will be
Brother and father—the very same; to her
470   Who bore him, son and husband—the very same
Who came to his father's bed, wet with his father's blood.
Enough. Go think that over.
If later you find error in what I have said,
You may say that I have no skill in prophecy.

(Exit Teiresias, led by his page. Oedipus goes into the palace.)

ODE I

CHORUS: The Delphic stone of prophecies

(STROPHE 1)

Remembers ancient regicide
And a still bloody hand.
That killer's hour of flight has come.
He must be stronger than riderless
340   Coursers of untiring wind,
For the son of Zeus armed with his father's thunder
Leaps in lightning after him;
And the Furies follow him, the sad Furies.
Holy Parnassos' peak of snow

(ANTISTROPHE 1)

Flashes and blinds that secret man,
That all shall hunt him down:
Though he may roam the forest shade
Like a bull wild from pasture
To rage through glooms of stone.
490   Doom comes down on him; flight will not avail him;
For the world's heart calls him desolate,
And the immortal Furies follow, for ever follow.
But now a wilder thing is heard

(STROPHE 2)

From the old man skilled at hearing Fate in the wingbeat of a bird.
Bewildered as a blown bird, my soul hovers and can not find
Foothold in this debate, or any reason or rest of mind.
But no man ever brought—none can bring
Proof of strife between Thebes' royal house,
Labdakos' line, and the son of Polybos;
500   And never until now has any man brought word
Of Laïos' dark death staining Oedipus the King.
Divine Zeus and Apollo hold

(ANTISTROPHE 2)

Perfect intelligence alone of all tales ever told;
And well though this diviner works, he works in his own night;
No man can judge that rough unknown or trust in second sight,
For wisdom changes hands among the wise.
Shall I believe my great lord criminal
At a raging word that a blind old man let fall?
I saw him, when the carrion woman faced him of old,

510   Prove his heroic mind! These evil words are lies.

SCENE II

CREON: Men of Thebes:
I am told that heavy accusations
Have been brought against me by King Oedipus.
I am not the kind of man to bear this tamely.
If in these present difficulties
He holds me accountable for any harm to him
Through anything I have said or done—why, then,
I do not value life in this dishonor.
It is not as though this rumor touched upon

520   Some private indiscretion. The matter is grave.
The fact is that I am being called disloyal
To the State, to my fellow citizens, to my friends.
CHORAGOS: He may have spoken in anger, not from his mind.
CREON: But did you not hear him say I was the one
Who seduced the old prophet into lying?
CHORAGOS: The thing was said; I do not know how seriously.
CREON: But you were watching him! Were his eyes steady?
Did he look like a man in his right mind?
CHORAGOS: I do not know.

530   I can not judge the behavior of great men.
But here is the King himself.

(enter Oedipus.)

OEDIPUS: So you dared come back.
Why? How brazen of you to come to my house,
You murderer!
Do you think I do not know
That you plotted to kill me, plotted to steal my throne?
Tell me, in God's name: am I coward, a fool,
That you should dream you could accomplish this?

540   A fool who could not see your slippery game?
A coward, not to fight back when I saw it?
You are the fool, Creon, are you not? hoping
Without support or friends to get a throne?
Thrones may be won or bought: you could do neither.

CREON: Now listen to me. You have talked; let me talk, too.
    You can not judge unless you know the facts.
OEDIPUS: You speak well: there is one fact; but I find it hard
    To learn from the deadliest enemy I have.
CREON: That above all I must dispute with you.
550   OEDIPUS: That above all I will not hear you deny.
CREON: If you think there is anything good in being stubborn
    Against all reason, then I say you are wrong.
OEDIPUS: If you think a man can sin against his own kind
    And not be punished for it, I say you are mad.
CREON: I agree. But tell me: what have I done to you?
OEDIPUS: You advised me to send for that wizard, did you not?
CREON: I did. I should do it again.
OEDIPUS: Very well. Now tell me:
    How long has it been since Laïos—
560   CREON: What of Laïos?
OEDIPUS: Since he vanished in that onset by the road?
CREON: It was long ago, a long time.
OEDIPUS: And this prophet,
    Was he practicing here then?
CREON: He was; and with honor, as now.
OEDIPUS: Did he speak of me at that time?
CREON: He never did;
    At least, not when I was present.
OEDIPUS: But . . . the enquiry?
570   I suppose you held one?
CREON: We did, but we learned nothing.
OEDIPUS: Why did the prophet not speak against me then?
CREON: I do not know; and I am the kind of man
    Who holds his tongue when he has no facts to go on.
OEDIPUS: There's one fact that you know, and you could tell it.
CREON: What fact is that? If I know it, you shall have it.
OEDIPUS: If he were not involved with you, he could not say
    That it was I who murdered Laïos.
CREON: If he says that, you are the one that knows it!—
580   But now it is my turn to question you.
OEDIPUS: Put your questions. I am no murderer.
CREON: First, then: You married my sister?
OEDIPUS: I married your sister.
CREON: And you rule the kingdom equally with her?
OEDIPUS: Everything that she wants she has from me.
CREON: And I am the third, equal to both of you?
OEDIPUS: That is why I call you a bad friend.
CREON: No. Reason it out, as I have done.
    Think of this first: Would any sane man prefer
590   Power, with all a king's anxieties,

To that same power and the grace of sleep?
Certainly not I.
I have never longed for the king's power—only his rights.
Would any wise man differ from me in this?
As matters stand, I have my way in everything
With your consent, and no responsibilities.
If I were king. I should be a slave to policy.
How could I desire a scepter more
Than what is now mine—untroubled influence?

600   No, I have not gone mad; I need no honors,
Except those with the perquisites I have now.
I am welcome everywhere; every man salutes me,
And those who want your favor seek my ear,
Since I know how to manage what they ask.
Should I exchange this case for that anxiety?
Besides, no sober mind is treasonable.
I hate anarchy
And never would deal with any man who likes it.
Test what I have said. Go to the priestess

610   At Delphi, ask if I quoted her correctly.
And as for this other thing: if I am found
Guilty of treason with Teiresias,
Then sentence me to death! You have my word
It is a sentence I should cast my vote for—
But not without evidence!
You do wrong
When you take good men for bad, bad men for good.
A true friend thrown aside—why, life itself
Is not more precious!

620   In time you will know this well:
For time, and time alone, will show the just man,
Though scoundrels are discovered in a day.

CHORAGOS: This is well said, and a prudent man would ponder it.
    Judgments too quickly formed are dangerous.

OEDIPUS: But is he not quick in his duplicity?
    And shall I not be quick to parry him?
    Would you have me stand still, hold my peace, and let
    This man win everything, through my inaction?

CREON: And you want—what is it, then? To banish me?

630   OEDIPUS: No, not exile. It is your death I want,
    So that all the world may see what treason means.

CREON: You will persist, then? You will not believe me?

OEDIPUS: How can I believe you?

CREON: Then you are a fool.

OEDIPUS: To save myself?

CREON: In justice, think of me.

OEDIPUS: You are evil incarnate.

CREON: But suppose that you are wrong?

OEDIPUS: Still I must rule.

640 CREON: But not if you rule badly.

OEDIPUS: O city, city!

CREON: It is my city, too!

CHORAGOS: Now, my lords, be still. I see the Queen,
　　Iocaste, coming from her palace chambers;
　　And it is time she came, for the sake of you both.
　　This dreadful quarrel can be resolved through her.

(enter Iocaste.)

IOCASTE: Poor foolish men, what wicked din is this?
　　With Thebes sick to death, is it not shameful
　　That you should rake some private quarrel up?

(to Oedipus:)

650　Come into the house.
　　—And you, Creon, go now:
　　Let us have no more of this tumult over nothing.

CREON: Nothing? No, sister: what your husband plans for me
　　Is one of two great evils: exile or death.

OEDIPUS: He is right.
　　Why, woman I have caught him squarely
　　Plotting against my life.

CREON: No! Let me die
　　Accurst if ever I have wished you harm!

660　IOCASTE: Ah, believe it, Oedipus!
　　In the name of the gods, respect this oath of his
　　For my sake, for the sake of these people here!

(STROPHE 1)

CHORAGOS: Open your mind to her, my lord. Be ruled by her, I beg you!

OEDIPUS: What would you have me do?

CHORAGOS: Respect Creon's word. He has never spoken like a fool,
　　And now he has sworn an oath.

OEDIPUS: You know what you ask?

CHORAGOS: I do.

670　OEDIPUS: Speak on, then.

CHORAGOS: A friend so sworn should not be baited so,
　　In blind malice, and without final proof.

OEDIPUS: You are aware, I hope, that what you say
　　Means death for me, or exile at the least.

CHORAGOS: No, I swear by Helios, first in Heaven!

(STROPHE 2)

　　May I die friendless and accurst,
　　The worst of deaths, if ever I meant that!

It is the withering fields
That hurt my sick heart:
Must we bear all these ills,
680   And now your bad blood as well?
OEDIPUS: Then let him go. And let me die, if I must,
Or be driven by him in shame from the land of Thebes.
It is your unhappiness, and not his talk,
That touches me.
As for him—
Wherever he goes, hatred will follow him.
CREON: Ugly in yielding, as you were ugly in rage!
Natures like yours chiefly torment themselves.
OEDIPUS: Can you not go? Can you not leave me?
690   CREON: I can.
You do not know me; but the city knows me,
And in its eyes, I am just, if not in yours.

(Exit Creon.)

(ANTISTROPHE 1)

CHORAGOS: Lady Iocaste, did you not ask the King to go to his chambers?
IOCASTE: First tell me what has happened.
CHORAGOS: There was suspicion without evidence, yet it rankled
As even false charges will.
IOCASTE: On both sides?
CHORAGOS: On both.
700   IOCASTE: But what was said?
CHORAGOS: Oh let it rest, let it be done with!
Have we not suffered enough?
OEDIPUS: You see to what your decency has brought you:
You have made difficulties where my heart saw none.
CHORAGOS: Oedipus, it is not once only I have told you—

(ANTISTROPHE 2)

You must know I should count myself unwise
To the point of madness, should I now forsake you—
You, under whose hand,
In the storm of another time,
710   Our dear land sailed out free.
But now stand fast at the helm!
IOCASTE: In God's name, Oedipus, inform your wife as well:
Why are you so set in this hard anger?
OEDIPUS: I will tell you, for none of these men deserves
My confidence as you do. It is Creon's work,
His treachery, his plotting against me.
IOCASTE: Go on, if you can make this clear to me.

OEDIPUS: He charges me with the murder of Laïos.

IOCASTE: Has he some knowledge? Or does he speak from hearsay?

720 OEDIPUS: He would not commit himself to such a charge,
But he has brought in that damnable soothsayer
To tell his story.

IOCASTE: Set your mind at rest.
If it is a question of soothsayers, I tell you
That you will find no man whose craft gives knowledge
Of the unknowable.

Here is my proof:
An oracle was reported to Laïos once
(I will not say from Phoibos himself, but from
730 His appointed ministers, at any rate)
That his doom would be death at the hands of his own son—
His son, born of his flesh and of mine!
Now, you remember the story: Laïos was killed
By marauding strangers where three highways meet.
But his child had not been three days in this world
Before the King had pierced the baby's ankles
And left him to die on a lonely mountainside.
Thus, Apollo never caused that child
To kill his father, and it was not Laïos' fate
740 To die at the hands of his son, as he had feared.
This is what prophets and prophecies are worth!
Have no dread of them.
It is God himself
Who can show us what he wills, in his own way.

OEDIPUS: How strange a shadowy memory crossed my mind,
Just now while you were speaking; it chilled my heart.

IOCASTE: What do you mean? What memory do you speak of?

OEDIPUS: If I understand you, Laïos was killed
At a place where three roads meet.

750 IOCASTE: So it was said;
We have no later story.

OEDIPUS: Where did it happen?

IOCASTE: Phokis, it is called: at a place where the Theban Way
Divides into the roads toward Delphi and Daulia.

OEDIPUS: When?

IOCASTE: We had the news not long before you came
And proved the right to your succession here.

OEDIPUS: Ah, what net has God been weaving for me?

760 IOCASTE: Oedipus! Why does this trouble you?

OEDIPUS: Do not ask me yet.
First, tell me how Laïos looked, and tell me
How old he was.

IOCASTE: He was tall, his hair just touched

With white; his form was not unlike your own.

OEDIPUS: I think that I myself may be accurst
By my own ignorant edict.

IOCASTE: You speak strangely.
It makes me tremble to look at you, my King.

OEDIPUS: I am not sure that the blind man can not see.

770   But I should know better if you were to tell me—

IOCASTE: Anything—though I dread to hear you ask it.

OEDIPUS: Was the King lightly escorted, or did he ride
With a large company, as a ruler should?

IOCASTE: There were five men with him in all: one was a herald,
And a single chariot, which he was driving.

OEDIPUS: Alas, that makes it plain enough!
But who—
Who told you how it happened?

IOCASTE: A household servant,

780   The only one to escape.

OEDIPUS: And is he still
A servant of ours?

IOCASTE: No; for when he came back at last
And found you enthroned in the place of the dead king,
He came to me, touched my hand with his, and begged
That I would send him away to the frontier district
Where only the shepherds go—
As far away from the city as I could send him.
I granted his prayer; for although the man was a slave,

790   He had earned more than this favor at my hands.

OEDIPUS: Can he be called back quickly?

IOCASTE: Easily.
But why?

OEDIPUS: I have taken too much upon myself
Without enquiry; therefore I wish to consult him.

IOCASTE: Then he shall come.
But am I not one also
To whom you might confide these fears of yours?

OEDIPUS: That is your right; it will not be denied you,

800   Now least of all; for I have reached a pitch
Of wild foreboding. Is there anyone
To whom I should sooner speak?
Polybos of Corinth is my father.
My mother is a Dorian: Meropê.
I grew up chief among the men of Corinth
Until a strange thing happened—
Not worth my passion, it may be, but strange.
At a feast, a drunken man maundering in his cups
Cries out that I am not my father's son!

810 I contained myself that night, though I felt anger
And a sinking heart. The next day I visited
My father and mother, and questioned them. They stormed,
Calling it all the slanderous rant of a fool;
And this relieved me. Yet the suspicion
Remained always aching in my mind;
I knew there was talk; I could not rest;
And finally, saying nothing to my parents,
I went to the shrine at Delphi.
The god dismissed my question without reply;
820 He spoke of other things.
Some were clear,
Full of wretchedness, dreadful, unbearable:
As, that I should lie with my own mother, breed
Children from whom all men would turn their eyes;
And that I should be my father's murderer.
I heard all this, and fled. And from that day
Corinth to me was only in the stars
Descending in that quarter of the sky,
As I wandered farther and farther on my way
830 To a land where I should never see the evil
Sung by the oracle. And I came to this country
Where, so you say, King Laïos was killed.
I will tell you all that happened there, my lady.
There were three highways
Coming together at a place I passed;
And there a herald came towards me, and a chariot
Drawn by horses, with a man such as you describe
Seated in it. The groom leading the horses
Forced me off the road at his lord's command;
840 But as this charioteer lurched over towards me
I struck him in my rage. The old man saw me
And brought his double goad down upon my head
As I came abreast.
He was paid back, and more!
Swinging my club in this right hand I knocked him
Out of his car, and he rolled on the ground.
I killed him.
I killed them all.
Now if that stranger and Laïos were—kin,
850 Where is a man more miserable than I?
More hated by the gods? Citizen and alien alike
Must never shelter me or speak to me—
I must be shunned by all.
And I myself
Pronounced this malediction upon myself!

Think of it: I have touched you with these hands,
These hands that killed your husband. What defilement!
Am I all evil, then? It must be so,
Since I must flee from Thebes, yet never again
860　See my own countrymen, my own country,
For fear of joining my mother in marriage
And killing Polybos, my father.
Ah,
If I was created so, born to this fate,
Who could deny the savagery of God?
O holy majesty of heavenly powers!
May I never see that day! Never!
Rather let me vanish from the race of men
Than know the abomination destined me!

870　CHORAGOS: We too, my lord, have felt dismay at this.
But there is hope: you have yet to hear the shepherd.
OEDIPUS: Indeed, I fear no other hope is left me.
IOCASTE: What do you hope from him when he comes?
OEDIPUS: This much:
If his account of the murder tallies with yours,
Then I am cleared.
IOCASTE: What was it that I said
Of such importance?
OEDIPUS: Why, "marauders," you said,
880　Killed the King, according to this man's story.
If he maintains that still, if there were several,
Clearly the guilt is not mine: I was alone.
But if he says one man, singlehanded, did it,
Then the evidence all points to me.
IOCASTE: You may be sure that he said there were several;
And can he call back that story now? He can not.
The whole city heard it as plainly as I.
But suppose he alters some detail of it:
He can not ever show that Laïos' death
890　Fulfilled the oracle: for Apollo said
My child was doomed to kill him; and my child—Poor
baby!—it was my child that died first.
No. From now on, where oracles are concerned,
I would not waste a second thought on any.
OEDIPUS: You may be right.
But come: let someone go
For the shepherd at once. This matter must be settled.
IOCASTE: I will send for him.
I would not wish to cross you in anything,
900　And surely not in this.—Let us go in.

(Exeunt into the palace.)

ODE II

CHORUS: Let me be reverent in the ways of right,

(STROPHE 1)

Lowly the paths I journey on;
Let all my words and actions keep
The laws of the pure universe
From highest Heaven handed down.
For Heaven is their bright nurse,
Those generations of the realms of light;
Ah, never of mortal kind were they begot,
Nor are they slaves of memory, lost in sleep;
910   Their Father is greater than Time, and ages not.
The tyrant is a child of Pride

(ANTISTROPHE 1)

Who drinks from his great sickening cup
Recklessness and vanity,
Until from his high crest headlong
He plummets to the dust of hope.
That strong man is not strong.
But let no fair ambition be denied;
May God protect the wrestler for the State
In government, in comely policy,
920   Who will fear God, and on His ordinance wait.
Haughtiness and the high hand of disdain

(STROPHE 2)

Tempt and outrage God's holy law;
And any mortal who dares hold
No immortal Power in awe
Will be caught up in a net of pain:
The price for which his levity is sold.
Let each man take due earnings, then,
And keep his hands from holy things,
And from blasphemy stand apart—
930   Else the crackling blast of heaven
Blows on his head, and on his desperate heart;
Though fools will honor impious men,
In their cities no tragic poet sings.
Shall we lose faith in Delphi's obscurities,

(ANTISTROPHE 2)

We who have heard the world's core
Discredited, and the sacred wood
Of Zeus at Elis praised no more?

The deeds and the strange prophecies
Must make a pattern yet to be understood.
940 Zeus, if indeed you are lord of all,
Throned in light over night and day,
Mirror this in your endless mind:
Our masters call the oracle
Words on the wind, and the Delphic vision blind!
Their hearts no longer know Apollo,
And reverence for the gods has died away.

SCENE III

(Enter Iocaste.)

IOCASTE: Princes of Thebes, it has occurred to me
To visit the altars of the gods, bearing
These branches as a suppliant, and this incense.
950 Our King is not himself: his noble soul
Is overwrought with fantasies of dread,
Else he would consider
The new prophecies in the light of the old.
He will listen to any voice that speaks disaster,
And my advice goes for nothing.

(She approaches the altar, R.)

To you, then, Apollo,
Lycean lord, since you are nearest, I turn in prayer.
Receive these offerings, and grant us deliverance
From defilement. Our hearts are heavy with fear
960 When we see our leader distracted, as helpless sailors
Are terrified by the confusion of their helmsman.

(Enter Messenger.)

MESSENGER: Friends, no doubt you can direct me:
Where shall I find the house of Oedipus,
Or, better still, where is the King himself?
CHORAGOS: It is this very place, stranger, he is inside.
This is his wife and mother of his children.
MESSENGER: I wish her happiness in a happy house,
Blest in all the fulfillment of her marriage.
IOCASTE: I wish as much for you: your courtesy
970 Deserves a like good fortune. But now, tell me:
Why have you come? What have you to say to us?
MESSENGER: Good news, my lady, for your house and your husband.
IOCASTE: What news? Who sent you here?
MESSENGER: I am from Corinth.
The news I bring ought to mean joy for you,
Though it may be you will find some grief in it.

IOCASTE: What is it? How can it touch us in both ways?
MESSENGER: The word is that the people of the Isthmus
    Intend to call Oedipus to be their king.
980 IOCASTE: But old King Polybos—is he not reigning still?
MESSENGER: No. Death holds him in his sepulchre.
IOCASTE: What are you saying? Polybos is dead?
MESSENGER: If I am not telling the truth, may I die myself.
IOCASTE: (*to a maidservant:*) Go in, go quickly; tell this to your master.
    O riddlers of God's will, where are you now!
    This was the man whom Oedipus, long ago,
    Feared so, fled so, in dread of destroying him—
    But it was another fate by which he died.

    (Enter Oedipus, C.)

990 OEDIPUS: Dearest Iocaste, why have you sent for me?
IOCASTE: Listen to what this man says, and then tell me
    What has become of the solemn prophecies.
OEDIPUS: Who is this man? What is his news for me?
IOCASTE: He has come from Corinth to announce your father's death!
OEDIPUS: Is it true, stranger? Tell me in your own words.
MESSENGER: I can not say it more clearly: the King is dead.
OEDIPUS: Was it by treason? Or by an attack of illness?
MESSENGER: A little thing brings old men to their rest.
OEDIPUS: It was sickness, then?
1000 MESSENGER: Yes, and his many years.
OEDIPUS: Ah!
    Why should a man respect the Pythian hearth, or
    Give heed to the birds that jangle above his head?
    They prophesied that I should kill Polybos,
    Kill my own father, but he is dead and buried,
    And I am here—I never touched him, never,
    Unless he died of grief for my departure,
    And thus, in a sense, through me. No. Polybos
    Has packed the oracles off with him underground.
1010 They are empty words.
IOCASTE: Had I not told you so?
OEDIPUS: You had; it was my faint heart that betrayed me.
IOCASTE: From now on never think of those things again.
OEDIPUS: And yet—must I not fear my mother's bed?
IOCASTE: Why should anyone in this world be afraid,
    Since Fate rules us and nothing can be foreseen?
    A man should live only for the present day.
    Have no more fear of sleeping with your mother:
    How many men, in dreams, have lain with their mothers!
1020 No reasonable man is troubled by such things.
OEDIPUS: That is true; only—

If only my mother were not still alive!
But she is alive. I can not help my dread.

IOCASTE: Yet this news of your father's death is wonderful.

OEDIPUS: Wonderful. But I fear the living woman.

MESSENGER: Tell me, who is this woman that you fear?

OEDIPUS: It is Meropê, man; the wife of King Polybos.

MESSENGER: Meropê? Why should you be afraid of her?

OEDIPUS: An oracle of the gods, a dreadful saying.

1030   MESSENGER: Can you tell me about it or are you sworn to silence?

OEDIPUS: I can tell you, and I will.

Apollo said through his prophet that I was the man
Who should marry his own mother, shed his father's blood
With his own hands. And so, for all these years
I have kept clear of Corinth, and no harm has come—
Though it would have been sweet to see my parents again.

MESSENGER: And is this the fear that drove you out of Corinth?

OEDIPUS: Would you have me kill my father?

MESSENGER: As for that

1040   You must be reassured by the news I gave you.

OEDIPUS: If you could reassure me, I would reward you.

MESSENGER: I had that in mind, I will confess: I thought
I could count on you when you returned to Corinth.

OEDIPUS: No: I will never go near my parents again.

MESSENGER: Ah, son, you still do not know what you are doing—

OEDIPUS: What do you mean? In the name of God tell me!

MESSENGER: —If these are your reasons for not going home.

OEDIPUS: I tell you, I fear the oracle may come true.

MESSENGER: And guilt may come upon you through your parents?

1050   OEDIPUS: That is the dread that is always in my heart.

MESSENGER: Can you not see that all your fears are groundless?

OEDIPUS: How can you say that? They are my parents, surely?

MESSENGER: Polybos was not your father.

OEDIPUS: Not my father?

MESSENGER: No more your father than the man speaking to you.

OEDIPUS: But you are nothing to me!

MESSENGER: Neither was he.

OEDIPUS: Then why did he call me son?

MESSENGER: I will tell you:

1060   Long ago he had you from my hands, as a gift.

OEDIPUS: Then how could he love me so, if I was not his?

MESSENGER: He had no children, and his heart turned to you.

OEDIPUS: What of you? Did you buy me? Did you find me by chance?

MESSENGER: I came upon you in the crooked pass of Kithairon.

OEDIPUS: And what were you doing there?

MESSENGER: Tending my flocks.

OEDIPUS: A wandering shepherd?

MESSENGER: But your savior, son, that day.

OEDIPUS: From what did you save me?

1070   MESSENGER: Your ankles should tell you that.

OEDIPUS: Ah, stranger, why do you speak of that childhood pain?

MESSENGER: I cut the bonds that tied your ankles together.

OEDIPUS: I have had the mark as long as I can remember.

MESSENGER: That was why you were given the name you bear.

OEDIPUS: God! Was it my father or my mother who did it?
    Tell me!

MESSENGER: I do not know. The man who gave you to me
    Can tell you better than I.

OEDIPUS: It was not you that found me, but another?

1080   MESSENGER: It was another shepherd gave you to me.

OEDIPUS: Who was he? Can you tell me who he was?

MESSENGER: I think he was said to be one of Laïos' people.

OEDIPUS: You mean the Laïos who was king here years ago?

MESSENGER: Yes; King Laïos; and the man was one of his herdsmen.

OEDIPUS: Is he still alive? Can I see him?

MESSENGER: These men here
    Know best about such things.

OEDIPUS: Does anyone here
    Know this shepherd that he is talking about?

1090   Have you seen him in the fields, or in the town?
    If you have, tell me. It is time things were made plain.

CHORAGOS: I think the man he means is that same shepherd
    You have already asked to see. Iocaste perhaps
    Could tell you something.

OEDIPUS: Do you know anything
    About him, Lady? Is he the man we have summoned?
    Is that the man this shepherd means?

IOCASTE: Why think of him?
    Forget this herdsman. Forget it all.

1100   This talk is a waste of time.

OEDIPUS: How can you say that,

IOCASTE: For God's love, let us have no more questioning!
    Is your life nothing to you?
    My own is pain enough for me to bear.

OEDIPUS: You need not worry. Suppose my mother a slave,
    And born of slaves: no baseness can touch you.

IOCASTE: Listen to me, I beg you: do not do this thing!

OEDIPUS: I will not listen; the truth must be made known.

IOCASTE: Everything that I say is for your own good!

1110   OEDIPUS: My own good
    Snaps my patience, then; I want none of it.

IOCASTE: You are fatally wrong! May you never learn who you are!

OEDIPUS: Go, one of you, and bring the shepherd here.

Let us leave this woman to brag of her royal name.

IOCASTE: Ah, miserable!

That is the only word I have for you now.

That is the only word I can ever have.

(Exit into the palace.)

CHORAGOS: Why has she left us, Oedipus? Why has she gone

In such a passion of sorrow? I fear this silence:

¹¹²⁰ Something dreadful may come of it.

OEDIPUS: Let it come!

However base my birth, I must know about it.

The Queen, like a woman, is perhaps ashamed

To think of my low origin. But I

Am a child of Luck; I can not be dishonored.

Luck is my mother; the passing months, my brothers,

Have seen me rich and poor.

If this is so,

How could I wish that I were someone else?

¹¹³⁰ How could I not be glad to know my birth?

ODE III

(STROPHE)

CHORUS: If ever the coming time were known

To my heart's pondering,

Kithairon, now by Heaven I see the torches

At the festival of the next full moon,

And see the dance, and hear the choir sing

A grace to your gentle shade:

Mountain where Oedipus was found,

O mountain guard of a noble race!

May the god who heals us lend his aid,

¹¹⁴⁰ And let that glory come to pass

For our king's cradling-ground.

(ANTISTROPHE)

Of the nymphs that flower beyond the years,

Who bore you, royal child,

To Pan of the hills or the timberline Apollo,

Cold in delight where the upland clears,

Or Hermês for whom Kyllenê's heights are piled?

Or flushed as evening cloud,

Great Dionysos, roamer of mountains,

He—was it he who found you there,

¹¹⁵⁰ And caught you up in his own proud

Arms from the sweet god-ravisher

Who laughed by the Muses' fountains?

SCENE IV

OEDIPUS: Sirs: though I do not know the man,
    I think I see him coming, this shepherd we want:
    He is old, like our friend here, and the men
    Bringing him seem to be servants of my house.
    But you can tell, if you have ever seen him.

(Enter Shepherd escorted by servants.)

CHORAGOS: I know him, he was Laïos' man. You can trust him.
OEDIPUS: Tell me first, you from Corinth: is this the shepherd
1160   We were discussing?
MESSENGER: This is the very man.
Oedipus: (to *Shepherd*) Come here. No, look at me. You must answer
    Everything I ask. —You belonged to Laïos?
SHEPHERD: Yes: born his slave, brought up in his house.
OEDIPUS: Tell me: what kind of work did you do for him?
SHEPHERD: I was a shepherd of his, most of my life.
OEDIPUS: Where mainly did you go for pasturage?
SHEPHERD: Sometimes Kithairon, sometimes the hills near-by.
OEDIPUS: Do you remember ever seeing this man out there?
1170 SHEPHERD: What would he be doing there? This man?
OEDIPUS: This man standing here. Have you ever seen him before?
SHEPHERD: No. At least, not to my recollection.
MESSENGER: And that is not strange, my lord. But I'll refresh
    His memory: he must remember when we two
    Spent three whole seasons together, March to September,
    On Kithairon or thereabouts. He had two flocks;
    I had one. Each autumn I'd drive mine home
    And he would go back with his to Laïos' sheepfold.—
    Is this not true, just as I have described it?
1180 SHEPHERD: True, yes; but it was all so long ago.
MESSENGER: Well, then: do you remember, back in those days,
    That you gave me a baby boy to bring up as my own?
SHEPHERD: What if I did? What are you trying to say?
MESSENGER: King Oedipus was once that little child.
SHEPHERD: Damn you, hold your tongue!
OEDIPUS: No more of that!
    It is your tongue needs watching, not this man's.
SHEPHERD: My King, my Master, what is it I have done wrong?
OEDIPUS: You have not answered his question about the boy.
1190 SHEPHERD: He does not know . . . He is only making trouble . . .
OEDIPUS: Come, speak plainly, or it will go hard with you.
SHEPHERD: In God's name, do not torture an old man!
OEDIPUS: Come here, one of you; bind his arms behind him.
SHEPHERD: Unhappy king! What more do you wish to learn?
OEDIPUS: Did you give this man the child he speaks of?

SHEPHERD: I did.

    And I would to God I had died that very day.

OEDIPUS: You will die now unless you speak the truth.

SHEPHERD: Yet if I speak the truth, I am worse than dead.

1200 OEDIPUS: Very well; since you insist upon delaying—

SHEPHERD: No! I have told you already that I gave him the boy.

OEDIPUS: Where did you get him? From your house? From somewhere
    else?

SHEPHERD: Not from mine, no. A man gave him to me.

OEDIPUS: Is that man here? Do you know whose slave he was?

SHEPHERD: For God's love, my King, do not ask me any more!

OEDIPUS: You are a dead man if I have to ask you again.

SHEPHERD: Then . . . Then the child was from the palace of Laïos.

OEDIPUS: A slave child? or a child of his own line?

1210 SHEPHERD: Ah, I am on the brink of dreadful speech!

OEDIPUS: And I of dreadful hearing. Yet I must hear.

SHEPHERD: If you must be told, then . . .

    They said it was Laïos' child;

    But it is your wife who can tell you about that.

OEDIPUS: My wife!—Did she give it to you?

SHEPHERD: My lord, she did.

OEDIPUS: Do you know why?

SHEPHERD: I was told to get rid of it.

OEDIPUS: An unspeakable mother!

1220 SHEPHERD: There had been prophecies . . .

OEDIPUS: Tell me.

SHEPHERD: It was said that the boy would kill his own father.

OEDIPUS: Then why did you give him over to this old man?

SHEPHERD: I pitied the baby, my King,

    And I thought that this man would take him far away

    To his own country.

    He saved him—but for what a fate!

    For if you are what this man says you are,

    No man living is more wretched than Oedipus.

1230 OEDIPUS: Ah God!

    It was true!

    All the prophecies!

    —Now,

    O Light, may I look on you for the last time!

    I, Oedipus,

    Oedipus, damned in his birth, in his marriage damned,

    Damned in the blood he shed with his own hand!

(He rushes into the palace.)

ODE IV

CHORUS: Alas for the seed of men.

(STROPHE 1)

What measure shall I give these generations
1240   That breathe on the void and are void
And exist and do not exist?
Who bears more weight of joy
Than mass of sunlight shifting in images,
Or who shall make his thought stay on
That down time drifts away?
Your splendor is all fallen.
O naked brow of wrath and tears,
O change of Oedipus!
I who saw your days call no man blest—
1250   Your great days like ghósts góne.
That mind was a strong bow.

(ANTISTROPHE 1)

Deep, how deep you drew it then, hard archer,
At a dim fearful range,
And brought dear glory down!
You overcame the stranger—
The virgin with her hooking lion claws—
And though death sang, stood like a tower
To make pale Thebes take heart.
Fortress against our sorrow!
1260   True king, giver of laws,
Majestic Oedipus!
No prince in Thebes had ever such renown,
No prince won such grace of power.
And now of all men ever known

(STROPHE 2)

Most pitiful is this man's story:
His fortunes are most changed, his state
Fallen to a low slave's
Ground under bitter fate.
O Oedipus, most royal one!
1270   The great door that expelled you to the light
Gave at night—ah, gave night to your glory:
As to the father, to the fathering son.
All understood too late.
How could that queen whom Laïos won,
The garden that he harrowed at his height,
Be silent when that act was done?
But all eyes fail before time's eye,

(ANTISTROPHE 2)

All actions come to justice there.

Though never willed, though far down the deep past,
1260 Your bed, your dread sirings,
Are brought to book at last.
Child by Laïos doomed to die,
Then doomed to lose that fortunate little death,
Would God you never took breath in this air
That with my wailing lips I take to cry:
For I weep the world's outcast.
I was blind, and now I can tell why:
Asleep, for you had given ease of breath
To Thebes, while the false years went by.

EXODOS

(Enter, from the palace, second messenger.)

1290 SECOND MESSENGER: Elders of Thebes, most honored in this land,
What horrors are yours to see and hear, what weight
Of sorrow to be endured, if, true to your birth,
You venerate the line of Labdakos!
I think neither Istros nor Phasis, those great rivers,
Could purify this place of the corruption
It shelters now, or soon must bring to light—
Evil not done unconsciously, but willed.
The greatest griefs are those we cause ourselves.
CHORAGOS: Surely, friend, we have grief enough already;
1300 What new sorrow do you mean?
SECOND MESSENGER: The Queen is dead.
CHORAGOS: Iocaste? Dead? But at whose hand?
SECOND MESSENGER: Her own.
The full horror of what happened you can not know,
For you did not see it; but I, who did, will tell you
As clearly as I can how she met her death.
When she had left us,
In passionate silence, passing through the court,
She ran to her apartment in the house,
1310 Her hair clutched by the fingers of both hands.
She closed the doors behind her; then, by that bed
Where long ago the fatal son was conceived—
That son who should bring about his father's death—
We hear her call upon Laïos, dead so many years,
And heard her wail for the double fruit of her marriage,
A husband by her husband, children by her child.
Exactly how she died I do not know:
For Oedipus burst in moaning and would not let us
Keep vigil to the end: it was by him
1320 As he stormed about the room that our eyes were caught.
From one to another of us he went, begging a sword,

Cursing the wife who was not his wife, the mother
Whose womb had carried his own children and himself.
I do not know: it was none of us aided him,
But surely one of the gods was in control!
For with a dreadful cry
He hurled his weight, as though wrenched out of himself,
At the twin doors: the bolts gave, and he rushed in.
And there we saw her hanging, her body swaying
1330   From the cruel cord she had noosed about her neck.
A great sob broke from him, heartbreaking to hear,
As he loosed the rope and lowered her to the ground.
I would blot out from my mind what happened next!
For the King ripped from her gown the golden brooches
That were her ornament, and raised them, and plunged them down
Straight into his own eyeballs, crying, "No more,
No more shall you look on the misery about me,
The horrors of my own doing! Too long you have known
The faces of those whom I should never have seen,
1340   Too long been blind to those for whom I was searching!
From this hour, go in darkness!;" And as he spoke,
He struck at his eyes—not once, but many times;
And the blood spattered his beard,
Bursting from his ruined sockets like red hail.
So from the unhappiness of two this evil has sprung,
A curse on the man and woman alike. The old
Happiness of the house of Labdakos
Was happiness enough: where is it today?
It is all wailing and ruin, disgrace, death—all
1350   The misery of mankind that has a name—
And it is wholly and for ever theirs.
CHORAGOS: Is he in agony still? Is there no rest for him?
SECOND MESSENGER: He is calling for someone to lead him to the gates
So that all the children of Kadmos may look upon
His father's murderer, his mother's—no,
I can not say it!
And then he will leave Thebes,
Self-exiled, in order that the curse
Which he himself pronounced may depart from the house.
1360   He is weak, and there is none to lead him,
So terrible is his suffering.
But you will see:
Look, the doors are opening; in a moment
You will see a thing that would crush a heart of stone.

(The central door is opened; OEDIPUS, blinded, is led in.)

CHORAGOS: Dreadful indeed for men to see.

Never have my own eyes
Looked on a sight so full of fear.
Oedipus!
What madness came upon you, what daemon
1370   Leaped on your life with heavier
Punishment than a mortal man can bear?
No: I can not even
Look at you, poor ruined one.
And I would speak, question, ponder,
If I were able. No.
You make me shudder.

OEDIPUS: God. God.
Is there a sorrow greater?
Where shall I find harbor in this world?
1380   My voice is hurled far on a dark wind.
What has God done to me?

CHORAGOS: Too terrible to think of, or to see.

OEDIPUS: O cloud of night,

(STROPHE 1)

Never to be turned away: night coming on,
I can not tell how: night like a shroud!
My fair winds brought me here.
O God. Again
The pain of the spikes where I had sight,
1390   The flooding pain
Of memory, never to be gouged out.

CHORAGOS: This is not strange.
You suffer it all twice over, remorse in pain,
Pain in remorse.

(ANTISTROPHE 1)

OEDIPUS: Ah dear friend
Are you faithful even yet, you alone?
Are you still standing near me, will you stay here,
Patient, to care for the blind?
The blind man!
1400   Yet even blind I know who it is attends me,
By the voice's tone—
Though my new darkness hide the comforter.

CHORAGOS: Oh fearful act!
What god was it drove you to rake black
Night across your eyes?

(STROPHE 2)

OEDIPUS: Apollo. Apollo. Dear
Children, the god was Apollo.

He brought my sick, sick fate upon me.
But the blinding hand was my own!
1410   How could I bear to see
When all my sight was horror everywhere?
CHORAGOS: Everywhere; that is true.
OEDIPUS: And now what is left?
Images? Love? A greeting even,
Sweet to the senses? Is there anything?
Ah, no, friends: lead me away.
Lead me away from Thebes.
Lead the great wreck
And hell of Oedipus, whom the gods hate.
1420   CHORAGOS: Your fate is clear, you are not blind to that.
Would God you had never found it out!

(ANTISTROPHE 2)

OEDIPUS: Death take the man who unbound
My feet on that hillside
And delivered me from death to life! What life?
If only I had died,
This weight of monstrous doom
Could not have dragged me and my darlings down.
CHORAGOS: I would have wished the same.
OEDIPUS: Oh never to have come here
1430   With my father's blood upon me! Never
To have been the man they call his mother's husband!
Oh accurst! Oh child of evil,
To have entered that wretched bed—
The selfsame one!
More primal than sin itself, this fell to me.
CHORAGOS: I do not know how I can answer you.
You were better dead than alive and blind.
OEDIPUS: Do not counsel me any more. This punishment
That I have laid upon myself is just.
1440   If I had eyes,
I do not know how I could bear the sight
Of my father, when I came to the house of Death,
Or my mother: for I have sinned against them both
So vilely that I could not make my peace
By strangling my own life.
Or do you think my children,
Born as they were born, would be sweet to my eyes?
Ah never, never! Nor this town with its high walls,
Nor the holy images of the gods.
1450   For I,
Thrice miserable!—Oedipus, noblest of all the line
Of Kadmos, have condemned myself to enjoy

These things no more, by my own malediction
Expelling that man whom the gods declared
To be a defilement in the house of Laïos.
After exposing the rankness of my own guilt,
How could I look men frankly in the eyes?
No, I swear it,
If I could have stifled my hearing at its source,
1460   I would have done it and made all this body
A tight cell of misery, blank to light and sound:
So I should have been safe in a dark agony
Beyond all recollection.
Ah Kithairon!
Why did you shelter me? When I was cast upon you,
Why did I not die? Then I should never
Have shown the world my execrable birth.
Ah Polybos! Corinth, city that I believed
The ancient seat of my ancestors: how fair
1470   I seemed, your child! And all the while this evil
Was cancerous within me!
For I am sick
In my daily life, sick in my origin.
O three roads, dark ravine, woodland and way
Where three roads met: you, drinking my father's blood,
My own blood, spilled by my own hand: can you remember
The unspeakable things I did there, and the things
I went on from there to do?
O marriage, marriage!
1480   The act that engendered me, and again the act
Performed by the son in the same bed—
Ah, the net
Of incest, mingling fathers, brothers, sons,
With brides, wives, mothers: the last evil
That can be known by men: no tongue can say
How evil!
No. For the love of God, conceal me
Somewhere far from Thebes; or kill me; or hurl me
Into the sea, away from men's eyes for ever.
1490   Come, lead me. You need not fear to touch me.
Of all men, I alone can bear this guilt.

(Enter Creon.)

CHORAGOS: We are not the ones to decide; but Creon here
    May fitly judge of what you ask. He only
    Is left to protect the city in your place.
OEDIPUS: Alas, how can I speak to him? What right have I
    To beg his courtesy whom I have deeply wronged?

CREON: I have not come to mock you, Oedipus,
    Or to reproach you, either.
    (*To attendants:*)—You, standing there:
1500   If you have lost all respect for man's dignity,
    At least respect the flame of Lord Helios:
    Do not allow this pollution to show itself
    Openly here, an affront to the earth
    And Heaven's rain and the light of day. No, take him
    Into the house as quickly as you can.
    For it is proper
    That only the close kindred see his grief.
OEDIPUS: I pray you in God's name, since your courtesy
    Ignores my dark expectation, visiting
1510   With mercy this man of all men most execrable:
    Give me what I ask—for your good, not for mine.
CREON: And what is it that you would have me do?
OEDIPUS: Drive me out of this country as quickly as may be
    To a place where no human voice can ever greet me.
CREON: I should have done that before now—only,
    God's will had not been wholly revealed to me.
OEDIPUS: But his command is plain: the parricide
    Must be destroyed. I am that evil man.
CREON: That is the sense of it, yes; but as things are,
1520   We had best discover clearly what is to be done.
OEDIPUS: You would learn more about a man like me?
CREON: You are ready now to listen to the god.
OEDIPUS: I will listen. But it is to you
    That I must turn for help. I beg you, hear me.
    The woman in there—
    Give her whatever funeral you think proper:
    She is your sister.
    —But let me go, Creon!
    Let me purge my father's Thebes of the pollution
1530   Of my living here, and go out to the wild hills,
    To Kithairon, that has won such fame with me,
    The tomb my mother and father appointed for me,
    And let me die there, as they willed I should.
    And yet I know
    Death will not ever come to me through sickness
    Or in any natural way: I have been preserved
    For some unthinkable fate. But let that be.
    As for my sons, you need not care for them.
    They are men, they will find some way to live.
1540   But my poor daughters, who have shared my table,
    Who never before have been parted from their father—
    Take care of them. Creon; do this for me.

And will you let me touch them with my hands
A last time, and let us weep together?
Be kind, my lord,
Great prince, be kind! Could I but touch them,
They would be mine again, as when I had my eyes.

(Enter Antigone and Ismene, attended.)

Ah, God!
Is it my dearest children I hear weeping?
1550   Has Creon pitied me and sent my daughters?
CREON: Yes, Oedipus: I knew that they were dear to you
In the old days, and know you must love them still.
OEDIPUS: May God bless you for this—and be a friendlier
Guardian to you than he has been to me!
Children, where are you?
Come quickly to my hands: they are your brother's—
Hands that have brought your father's once clear eyes
To this way of seeing—
Ah dearest ones,
1560   I had neither sight nor knowledge then, your father
By the woman who was the source of his own life!
And I weep for you—having no strength to see you—,
I weep for you when I think of the bitterness
That men will visit upon you all your lives.
What homes, what festivals can you attend
Without being forced to depart again in tears?
And when you come to marriageable age,
Where is the man, my daughters, who would dare
Risk the bane that lies on all my children?
1570   Is there any evil wanting? Your father killed
His father; sowed the womb of her who bore him;
Engendered you at the fount of his own existence!
That is what they will say of you.
Then, whom
Can you ever marry? There are no bridegrooms for you,
And your lives must wither away in sterile dreaming.
O Creon, son of Menoikeus!
You are the only father my daughters have,
Since we, their parents, are both of us gone for ever.
1580   They are your own blood: you will not let them
Fall into beggary and loneliness;
You will keep them from the miseries that are mine!
Take pity on them; see, they are only children,
Friendless except for you. Promise me this,
Great Prince, and give me your hand in token of it.

(Creon clasps his right hand.)

Children: I could say much, if you could understand me,
But as it is, I have only this prayer for you:
Live where you can, be as happy as you can—
1590   Happier, please God, than God has made your father!
CREON: Enough. You have wept enough. Now go within.
OEDIPUS: I must; but it is hard.
CREON: Time eases all things.
OEDIPUS: But you must promise—
CREON: Say what you desire.
OEDIPUS: Send me from Thebes!
CREON: God grant that I may!
OEDIPUS: But since God hates me . . .
CREON: No, he will grant your wish
1600   OEDIPUS: You promise?
CREON: I can not speak beyond my knowledge.
OEDIPUS: Then lead me in.
CREON: Come now, and leave your children.
OEDIPUS: No! Do not take them from me!
CREON: Think no longer
    That you are in command here, but rather think
    How, when you were, you served your own destruction.

*(Exeunt into the house all but the chorus; the choragos chants
directly to the audience:)*

CHORAGOS: Men of Thebes: look upon Oedipus.
    This is the king who solved the famous riddle
1610   And towered up, most powerful of men.
    No mortal eyes but looked on him with envy,
    Yet in the end ruin swept over him.
    Let every man in mankind's frailty
    Consider his last day; and let none
    Presume on his good fortune until he find
    Life, at his death, a memory without pain.

Questions for Engagement, Response, and Analysis

1. How would you describe the relationship between Oedipus and the
   people of Thebes as the play begins? What kind of ruler has Oedipus
   been? What is his perception of himself as king?

2. What is the condition of Thebes as the play begins? Look up the myth
   of the fisher king and explain how it applies to this condition.

3. Explain Oedipus' behavior toward Teiresias and Creon.

4. Explain why Oedipus insists on hearing what he must know will be
   horrifying news.

Crafting Arguments

1. Discuss in detail the changing attitudes of the chorus in the play. Why is the accusation against Oedipus so terrifying to them? What dilemma does the accusation pose for them?

2. Contrast Iocaste's skepticism with Oedipus' insistence on knowing the truth.

3. Discuss the degree to which Oedipus is triumphant at the end of the play. Does Oedipus maintain his position as savior and father to his people? What kind of father does he appear to be to his daughters? Discuss whether he retains nobility and dignity in his fall.

4. In an essay, analyze Sophocles' use of image clusters of light and dark and/or of sight and blindness.

5. Both Creon and Teiresias act as dramatic foils to Oedipus: they emphasize characteristics of Oedipus through marked contrast. In an essay show how one of these characters is an effective dramatic foil.

Casebook
on Flannery O'Connor

The final casebook in this text combines several quests seen in other works in this unit: the quest for God, the quest for knowledge of oneself, and the quest for ways in which to understand one's relationships with others. Though Flannery O'Connor writes from the point of view of a woman who grew up in the South and who was a devout Catholic, the questions her very unusual characters seek to answer are universal. O'Connor's comments in her essay "The Fiction Writer and His Country" will help you to gain insight into her own views about writing, and the essays by literary scholars will help you write your own essays about the stories.

Flannery O'Connor (1925–1964)

Flannery O'Connor was a devout Catholic who, in the short time that she lived, wrote two novels and many short stories that vividly portray the incompleteness of human beings without God. Except for her graduate study at the University of Iowa, O'Connor spent most of her life in Milledgeville, Georgia, where she observed the people and the land that would become the basis for most of her works. Because her characters are far from ordinary and because their fates are often disastrous, O'Connor is frequently described as a Southern Gothic writer. Her characters range from

*unbelievers, like Mrs. May in "Greenleaf" and the grand-
mother in "A Good Man Is Hard to Find" who, in spite of
their superficiality and self-centeredness, believe themselves
to be good Christians, to committed if unorthodox Christians, like Mrs. Greenleaf. O'Connor's stories tell of events
that cause arrogant and imperceptive people to see more
clearly into reality and to begin their quest for truth.*

A GOOD MAN IS HARD TO FIND   (1953)

1   The grandmother didn't want to go to Florida. She wanted to visit
some of her connections in east Tennessee and she was seizing at every
chance to change Bailey's mind. Bailey was the son she lived with, her
only boy. He was sitting on the edge of his chair at the table, bent over
the orange sports section of the *Journal.* "Now look here, Bailey," she
said, "see here, read this," and she stood with one hand on her thin hip
and the other rattling the newspaper at his bald head. "Here this fellow
that calls himself The Misfit is aloose from the Federal Pen and headed
toward Florida and you read here what it says he did to these people. Just
you read it. I wouldn't take my children in any direction with a criminal
like that aloose in it. I couldn't answer to my conscience if I did."

2   Bailey didn't look up from his reading so she wheeled around then and
faced the children's mother, a young woman in slacks, whose face was
as broad and innocent as a cabbage and was tied around with a green
headkerchief that had two points on the top like rabbit's ears. She was
sitting on the sofa, feeding the baby his apricots out of a jar. "The children have been to Florida before," the old lady said. "You all ought to take
them somewhere else for a change so they would see different parts of
the world and be broad. They never have been to east Tennessee."

3   The children's mother didn't seem to hear her but the eight-year-old
boy, John Wesley, a stocky child with glasses, said, "If you don't want to
go to Florida, why dontcha stay at home?" He and the little girl, June Star,
were reading the funny papers on the floor.

4   "She wouldn't stay at home to be queen for a day," June Star said without raising her yellow head.

5   "Yes and what would you do if this fellow, The Misfit, caught you?" the
grandmother said.

6   "I'd smack his face," John Wesley said.

7   "She wouldn't stay at home for a million bucks," June Star said "Afraid
she'd miss something. She has to go everywhere we go."

8   "All right, Miss," the grandmother said. "Just remember that the next
time you want me to curl your hair."

9   June Star said her hair was naturally curly.

10   The next morning the grandmother was the first one in the car, ready to
go. She had her big black valise that looked like the head of a hippopotamus in one corner, and underneath it she was hiding a basket with Pity
Sing, the cat, in it. She didn't intend for the cat to be left alone in the house

for three days because he would miss her too much and she was afraid he might brush against one of the gas burners and accidentally asphyxiate himself. Her son, Bailey, didn't like to arrive at a motel with a cat.

11   She sat in the middle of the back seat with John Wesley and June Star on either side of her. Bailey and the children's mother and the baby sat in front and they left Atlanta at eight forty-five with the mileage on the car at 55890. The grandmother wrote this down because she thought it would be interesting to say how many miles they had been when they got back. It took them twenty minutes to reach the outskirts of the city.

12   The old lady settled herself comfortably, removing her white cotton gloves and putting them up with her purse on the shelf in front of the back window. The children's mother still had on slacks and still had her hair tied up in a green kerchief, but the grandmother had on a navy blue straw sailor hat with a bunch of white violets on the brim and a navy blue dress with a small white dot in the print. Her collars and cuffs were white organdy trimmed with lace and at her neckline she had pinned a purple spray of cloth violets containing a sachet. In case of an accident, anyone seeing her dead on the highway would know at once that she was a lady.

13   She said she thought it was going to be a good day for driving, neither too hot nor too cold, and she cautioned Bailey that the speed limit was fifty-five miles an hour and that the patrolmen hid themselves behind billboards and small clumps of trees and sped out after you before you had a chance to slow down. She pointed out interesting details of the scenery: Stone Mountain; the blue granite that in some places came up to both sides of the highway; the brilliant red clay banks slightly streaked with purple; and the various crops that made rows of green lacework on the ground. The trees were full of silver-white sunlight and the meanest of them sparkled. The children were reading comic magazines and their mother had gone back to sleep.

14   "Let's go through Georgia fast so we won't have to look at it much," John Wesley said.

15   "If I were a little boy," said the grandmother, "I wouldn't talk about my native state that way. Tennessee has the mountains and Georgia has the hills."

16   "Tennessee is just a hillbilly dumping ground," John Wesley said, "and Georgia is a lousy state too."

17   "You said it," June Star said.

18   "In my time," said the grandmother, folding her thin veined fingers, "children were more respectful of their native states and their parents and everything else. People did right then. Oh look at the cute little pickaninny!" she said and pointed to a Negro child standing in the door of a shack. "Wouldn't that make a picture, now?" she asked and they all turned and looked at the little Negro out of the back window. He waved.

19   "He didn't have any britches on," June Star said.

20   "He probably didn't have any," the grandmother explained. "Little niggers in the country don't have things like we do. If I could paint, I'd paint that picture," she said.

21   The children exchanged comic books.

22   The grandmother offered to hold the baby and the children's mother passed him over the front seat to her. She set him on her knee and bounced him and told him about the things they were passing. She rolled her eyes and screwed up her mouth and stuck her leathery thin face into his smooth bland one. Occasionally he gave her a faraway smile. They passed a large cotton field with five or six graves fenced in the middle of it, like a small island. "Look at the graveyard!" the grandmother said, pointing it out. "That was the old family burying ground. That belonged to the plantation."

23   "Where's the plantation?" John Wesley asked.

24   "Gone With the Wind," said the grandmother. "Ha. Ha."

25   When the children finished all the comic books they had brought, they opened the lunch and ate it. The grandmother ate a peanut butter sandwich and an olive and would not let the children throw the box and the paper napkins out the window. When there was nothing else to do they played a game by choosing a cloud and making the other two guess what shape it suggested. John Wesley took one the shape of a cow and June Star guessed a cow and John Wesley said, no, an automobile, and June Star said he didn't play fair, and they began to slap each other over the grandmother.

26   The grandmother said she would tell them a story if they would keep quiet. When she told a story, she rolled her eyes and waved her head and was very dramatic. She said once when she was a maiden lady she had been courted by a Mr. Edgar Atkins Teagarden from Jasper, Georgia. She said he was a very good-looking man and a gentleman and that he brought her a watermelon every Saturday afternoon with his initials cut in it, E. A. T. Well, one Saturday, she said, Mr. Teagarden brought the watermelon and there was nobody at home and he left it on the front porch and returned in his buggy to Jasper, but she never got the watermelon, she said, because a nigger boy ate it when he saw the initials, E. A. T.! This story tickled John Wesley's funny bone and he giggled and giggled but June Star didn't think it was any good. She said she wouldn't marry a man that just brought her a watermelon on Saturday. The grandmother said she would have done well to marry Mr. Teagarden because he was a gentlemen and had bought Coca-Cola stock when it first came out and that he had died only a few years ago, a very wealthy man.

27   They stopped at The Tower for barbecued sandwiches. The Tower was a part stucco and part wood filling station and dance hall set in a clearing outside of Timothy. A fat man named Red Sammy Butts ran it and there were signs stuck here and there on the building and for miles up and down the highway saying, TRY RED SAMMY'S FAMOUS BARBECUE. NONE LIKE FAMOUS RED SAMMY'S! RED SAM! THE FAT BOY WITH THE HAPPY LAUGH. A VETERAN! RED SAMMY'S YOUR MAN!

28   Red Sammy was lying on the bare ground outside The Tower with his head under a truck while a gray monkey about a foot high, chained to a small chinaberry tree, chattered nearby. The monkey sprang back into

the tree and got on the highest limb as soon as he saw the children jump out of the car and run toward him.

29   Inside, The Tower was a long dark room with a counter at one end and tables at the other and dancing space in the middle. They all sat down at a board table next to the nickelodeon and Red Sam's wife, a tall burnt-brown woman with hair and eyes lighter than her skin, came and took their order. The children's mother put a dime in the machine and played "The Tennessee Waltz," and the grandmother said that tune always made her want to dance. She asked Bailey if he would like to dance but he only glared at her. He didn't have a naturally sunny disposition like she did and trips made him nervous. The grandmother's brown eyes were very bright. She swayed her head from side to side and pretended she was dancing in her chair. June Star said play something she could tap to so the children's mother put in another dime and played a fast number and June Star stepped out onto the dance floor and did her tap routine.

30   "Ain't she cute?" Red Sam's wife said, leaning over the counter. "Would you like to come be my little girl?"

31   "No I certainly wouldn't," June Star said. "I wouldn't live in a broken-down place like this for a million bucks!" and she ran back to the table.

32   "Ain't she cute?" the woman repeated, stretching her mouth politely.

33   "Aren't you ashamed?" hissed the grandmother.

34   Red Sam came in and told his wife to quit lounging on the counter and hurry up with these people's order. His khaki trousers reached just to his hip bones and his stomach hung over them like a sack of meal swaying under his shirt. He came over and sat down at a table nearby and let out a combination sigh and yodel. "You can't win," he said. "You can't win," and he wiped his sweating red face off with a gray handkerchief. "These days you don't know who to trust," he said. "Ain't that the truth?"

35   "People are certainly not nice like they used to be," said the grandmother.

36   "Two fellers come in here last week," Red Sammy said, "driving a Chrysler. It was a old beat-up car but it was a good one and these boys looked all right to me. Said they worked at the mill and you know I let them fellers charge the gas they bought? Now why did I do that?"

37   "Because you're a good man!" the grandmother said at once.

38   "Yes'm, I suppose so," Red Sam said as if he were struck with this answer.

39   His wife brought the orders, carrying the five plates all at once without a tray, two in each hand and one balanced on her arm. "It isn't a soul in this green world of God's that you can trust," she said. "And I don't count nobody out of that, not nobody," she repeated, looking at Red Sammy.

40   "Did you read about that criminal, The Misfit, that's escaped?" asked the grandmother.

41   "I wouldn't be a bit surprised if he didn't attack this place right here," said the woman. "If he hears about it being here, I wouldn't be none

surprised to see him. If he hears it's two cent in the cash register, I wouldn't be a tall surprised if he . . ."

42   "That'll do," Red Sam said. "Go bring these people their Co'-Colas," and the woman went off to get the rest of the order.

43   "A good man is hard to find," Red Sammy said. "Everything is getting terrible. I remember the day you could go off and leave your screen door unlatched. Not no more."

44   He and the grandmother discussed better times. The old lady said that in her opinion Europe was entirely to blame for the way things were now. She said the way Europe acted you would think we were made of money and Red Sam said it was no use talking about it, she was exactly right. The children ran outside into the white sunlight and looked at the monkey in the lacy chinaberry tree. He was busy catching fleas on himself and biting each one carefully between his teeth as if it were a delicacy.

45   They drove off again into the hot afternoon. The grandmother took cat naps and woke up every five minutes with her own snoring. Outside of Toombsboro she woke up and recalled an old plantation that she had visited in this neighborhood once when she was a young lady. She said the house had six white columns across the front and that there was an avenue of oaks leading up to it and two little wooden trellis arbors on either side in front where you sat down with your suitor after a stroll in the garden. She recalled exactly which road to turn off to get to it. She knew that Bailey would not be willing to lose any time looking at an old house, but the more she talked about it, the more she wanted to see it once again and find out if the little twin arbors were still standing. "There was a secret panel in this house," she said craftily, not telling the truth but wishing that she were, "and the story went that all the family silver was hidden in it when Sherman came through but it was never found . . ."

46   "Hey!" John Wesley said. "Let's go see it! We'll find it! We'll poke all the woodwork and find it! Who lives there? Where do you turn off at? Hey, Pop, can't we turn off there?"

47   "We never have seen a house with a secret panel!" June Star shrieked. "Let's go to the house with the secret panel! Hey Pop, can't we go see the house with the secret panel!"

48   "It's not far from here, I know," the grandmother said. "It wouldn't take over twenty minutes."

49   Bailey was looking straight ahead. His jaw was as rigid as a horseshoe. "No," he said.

50   The children began to yell and scream that they wanted to see the house with the secret panel. John Wesley kicked the back of the front seat and June Star hung over her mother's shoulder and whined desperately into her ear that they never had any fun even on their vacation, that they could never do what THEY wanted to do. The baby began to scream and John Wesley kicked the back of the seat so hard that his father could feel the blows in his kidney.

51   "All right!" he shouted and drew the car to a stop at the side of the road. "Will you all shut up? Will you all just shut up for one second? If you don't shut up, we won't go anywhere."

52   "It would be very educational for them," the grandmother murmured.

53   "All right," Bailey said, "but get this: this is the only time we're going to stop for anything like this. This is the one and only time."

54   "The dirt road that you have to turn down is about a mile back," the grandmother directed. "I marked it when we passed."

55   "A dirt road," Bailey groaned.

56   After they had turned around and were headed toward the dirt road, the grandmother recalled other points about the house, the beautiful glass over the front doorway and the candle-lamp in the hall. John Wesley said that the secret panel was probably in the fireplace.

57   "You can't go inside this house," Bailey said. "You don't know who lives there."

58   "While you all talk to the people in front, I'll run around behind and get in a window," John Wesley suggested.

59   "We'll all stay in the car," his mother said.

60   They turned onto the dirt road and the car raced roughly along in a swirl of pink dust. The grandmother recalled the times when there were no paved roads and thirty miles was a day's journey. The dirt road was hilly and there were sudden washes in it and sharp curves on dangerous embankments. All at once they would be on a hill, looking down over the blue tops of trees for miles around, then the next minute, they would be in a red depression with the dust-coated trees looking down on them.

61   "This place had better turn up in a minute," Bailey said, "or I'm going to turn around."

62   The road looked as if no one had traveled on it for months.

63   "It's not much farther," the grandmother said and just as she said it, a horrible thought came to her. The thought was so embarrassing that she turned red in the face and her eyes dilated and her feet jumped up, upsetting her valise in the corner. The instant the valise moved, the newspaper top she had over the basket under it rose with a snarl and Pity Sing, the cat, sprang onto Bailey's shoulder.

64   The children were thrown to the floor and their mother, catching the baby, was thrown out the door onto the ground; the old lady was thrown into the front seat. The car turned over once and landed right-side-up in a gulch off the side of the road. Bailey remained in the driver's seat with the cat—gray-striped with a broad white face and an orange nose—clinging to his neck like a caterpillar.

65   As soon as the children saw they could move their arms and legs, they scrambled out of the car, shouting, "We've had an ACCIDENT!" The grandmother was curled up under the dashboard, hoping she was injured so that Bailey's wrath would not come down on her all at once. The horrible thought she had had before the accident was that the house she had remembered so vividly was not in Georgia but in Tennessee.

66   Bailey removed the cat from his neck with both hands and flung it out the window against the side of a pine tree. Then he got out of the car and started looking for the children's mother. She was sitting against the side of the red gutted ditch, holding the screaming baby, but she only had a cut down her face and a broken shoulder. "We've had an ACCIDENT!" the children screamed in a frenzy of delight.

67   "But nobody's killed," June Star said with disappointment as the grandmother limped out of the car, her hat still pinned to her head but the broken front brim standing up at a jaunty angle and the violet spray hanging off the side. They all sat down in the ditch, except the children, to recover from the shock. They were all shaking.

68   "Maybe a car will come along," said the children's mother hoarsely.

69   "I believe I have injured an organ," said the grandmother, pressing her side, but no one answered her. Bailey's teeth were clattering. He had on a yellow sport shirt with bright blue parrots designed in it and his face was as yellow as the shirt. The grandmother decided that she would not mention that the house was in Tennessee.

70   The road was about ten feet above and they could see only the tops of the trees on the other side of it. Behind the ditch they were sitting in there were more woods, tall and dark and deep. In a few minutes they saw a car some distance away on top of a hill, coming slowly as if the occupants were watching them. The grandmother stood up and waved both her arms dramatically to attract their attention. The car continued to come on slowly, disappeared around a bend and appeared again, moving even slower, on top of the hill they had gone over. It was a big black battered hearse-like automobile. There were three men in it.

71   It came to a stop just over them and for some minutes, the driver looked down with a steady expressionless gaze to where they were sitting, and didn't speak. Then he turned his head and muttered something to the other two and they got out. One was a fat boy in black trousers and a red sweat shirt with a silver stallion embossed on the front of it. He moved around on the right side of them and stood staring, his mouth partly open in a kind of loose grin. The other had on khaki pants and a blue striped coat and a gray hat pulled down very low, hiding most of his face. He came around slowly on the left side. Neither spoke.

72   The driver got out of the car and stood by the side of it, looking down at them. He was an older man than the other two. His hair was just beginning to gray and he wore silver-rimmed spectacles that gave him a scholarly look. He had a long creased face and didn't have on any shirt or undershirt. He had on blue jeans that were too tight for him and was holding a black hat and a gun. The two boys also had guns.

73   "We've had an ACCIDENT!" the children screamed.

74   The grandmother had the peculiar feeling that the bespectacled man was someone she knew. His face was as familiar to her as if she had known him all her life but she could not recall who he was. He moved away from the car and began to come down the embankment, placing his

feet carefully so that he wouldn't slip. He had on tan and white shoes and no socks, and his ankles were red and thin. "Good afternoon," he said. "I see you all had you a little spill."

75   "We turned over twice!" said the grandmother.

76   "Oncet," he corrected. "We seen it happen. Try their car and see will it run, Hiram," he said quietly to the boy with the gray hat.

77   "What you got that gun for?" John Wesley asked. "Whatcha gonna do with that gun?"

78   "Lady," the man said to the children's mother, "would you mind calling them children to sit down by you? Children make me nervous. I want all you all to sit down right together there where you're at."

79   "What are you telling US what to do for?" June Star asked.

80   Behind them the line of woods gaped like a dark open mouth. "Come here," said their mother.

81   "Look here now," Bailey began suddenly, "we're in a predicament! We're in . . ."

82   The grandmother shrieked. She scrambled to her feet and stood staring. "You're The Misfit!" she said. "I recognized you at once!"

83   "Yes'm," the man said, smiling slightly as if he were pleased in spite of himself to be known, "but it would have been better for all of you, lady, if you hadn't of reckernized me."

84   Bailey turned his head sharply and said something to his mother that shocked even the children. The old lady began to cry and The Misfit reddened.

85   "Lady," he said, "don't you get upset. Sometimes a man says things he don't mean. I don't reckon he meant to talk to you thataway."

86   "You wouldn't shoot a lady, would you?" the grandmother said and removed a clean handkerchief from her cuff and began to slap at her eyes with it.

87   The Misfit pointed the toe of his shoe into the ground and made a little hole and then covered it up again. "I would hate to have to," he said.

88   "Listen," the grandmother almost screamed, "I know you're a good man. You don't look a bit like you have common blood. I know you must come from nice people!"

89   "Yes ma'am," he said, "finest people in the world." When he smiled he showed a row of strong white teeth. "God never made a finer woman than my mother and my daddy's heart was pure gold," he said. The boy with the red sweat shirt had come around behind them and was standing with his gun at his hip. The Misfit squatted down on the ground. "Watch them children, Bobby Lee," he said. "You know they make me nervous." He looked at the six of them huddled together in front of him and he seemed to be embarrassed as if he couldn't think of anything to say. "Ain't a cloud in the sky," he remarked, looking up at it. "Don't see no sun but don't see no cloud neither."

90   "Yes, it's a beautiful day," said the grandmother. "Listen," she said, "you shouldn't call yourself The Misfit because I know you're a good man at heart. I can just look at you and tell."

91   "Hush!" Bailey yelled. "Hush! Everybody shut up and let me handle this!" He was squatting in the position of a runner about to sprint forward but he didn't move.

92   "I pre-chate that, lady," the Misfit said and drew a little circle in the ground with the butt of his gun.

93   "It'll take a half a hour to fix this here car," Hiram called, looking over the raised hood of it.

94   "Well, first you and Bobby Lee get him and that little boy to step over yonder with you," The Misfit said, pointing to Bailey and John Wesley. "The boys want to ast you something," he said to Bailey. "Would you mind stepping back in them woods there with them?"

95   "Listen," Bailey began, "we're in a terrible predicament! Nobody realizes what this is," and his voice cracked. His eyes were as blue and intense as the parrots in his shirt and he remained perfectly still.

96   The grandmother reached up to adjust her hat brim as if she were going to the woods with him but it came off in her hand. She stood staring at it and after a second she let it fall on the ground. Hiram pulled Bailey up by the arm as if he were assisting an old man. John Wesley caught hold of his father's hand and Bobby Lee followed. They went off toward the woods and just as they reached the dark edge, Bailey turned and supporting himself against a gray naked pine trunk, he shouted, "I'll be back in a minute, Mamma, wait on me!"

97   "Come back this instant!" his mother shrilled but they all disappeared into the woods.

98   "Bailey Boy!" the grandmother called in a tragic voice but she found she was looking at The Misfit squatting on the ground in front of her. "I just know you're a good man," she said desperately. "You're not a bit common!"

99   "Nome, I ain't a good man," The Misfit said after a second as if he had considered her statement carefully, "but I ain't the worst in the world neither. My daddy said I was a different breed of dog from my brothers and sisters. 'You know,' Daddy said, 'it's some that can live their whole life out without asking about it and it's others has to know why it is, and this boy is one of the latters. He's going to be into everything!'" He put on his black hat and looked up suddenly and then away deep into the woods as if he were embarrassed again. "I'm sorry I don't have on a shirt before you ladies," he said, hunching his shoulders slightly. "We buried our clothes that we had on when we escaped and we're just making do until we can get better. We borrowed these from some folks we met," he explained.

100   "That's perfectly all right," the grandmother said. "Maybe Bailey has an extra shirt in his suitcase."

101   "I'll look and see terrectly," The Misfit said.

102   "Where are they taking him?" the children's mother screamed.

103   "Daddy was a card himself," The Misfit said. "You couldn't put anything over on him. He never got in trouble with the Authorities though. Just had the knack of handling them."

104   "You could be honest too if you'd only try," said the grandmother. "Think how wonderful it would be to settle down and live a comfortable life and not have to think about somebody chasing you all the time."

105   The Misfit kept scratching in the ground with the butt of his gun as if he were thinking about it. "Yes'm, somebody is always after you," he murmured.

106   The grandmother noticed how thin his shoulder blades were just behind his hat because she was standing up looking down on him. "Do you ever pray?" she asked.

107   He shook his head. All she saw was the black hat wiggle between his shoulder blades. "Nome," he said.

108   There was a pistol shot from the woods, followed closely by another. Then silence. The old lady's head jerked around. She could hear the wind move through the tree tops like a long satisfied insuck of breath. "Bailey Boy!" she called.

109   "I was a gospel singer for a while," The Misfit said. "I been most everything. Been in the arm service, both land and sea, at home and abroad, been twict married, been an undertaker, been with the railroads, plowed Mother Earth, been in a tornado, seen a man burnt alive oncet," and he looked up at the children's mother and the little girl who were sitting close together, their faces white and their eyes glassy; "I even seen a woman flogged," he said.

110   "Pray, pray," the grandmother began, "pray, pray . . ."

111   "I never was a bad boy that I remember of," The Misfit said in an almost dreamy voice, "But somewheres along the line I done something wrong and got sent to the penitentiary. I was buried alive," and he looked up and held her attention to him by a steady stare.

112   "That's when you should have started to pray," she said. "What did you do to get sent up to the penitentiary that first time?"

113   "Turn to the right, it was a wall," The Misfit said, looking up again at the cloudless sky. "Turn to the left, it was a wall. Look up it was a ceiling, look down it was a floor. I forget what I done, lady. I set there and set there, trying to remember what it was I done and I ain't recalled it to this day. Oncet in a while, I would think it was coming to me, but it never come."

114   "Maybe they put you in by mistake," the old lady said vaguely.

115   "Nome," he said. "It wasn't no mistake. They had the papers on me."

116   "You must have stolen something," she said.

117   The Misfit sneered slightly. "Nobody had nothing I wanted," he said. "It was a head-doctor at the penitentiary said what I had done was kill my daddy but I known that for a lie. My daddy died in nineteen ought nineteen of the epidemic flu and I never had a thing to do with it. He was buried in the Mount Hopewell Baptist churchyard and you can go there and see for yourself."

118   "If you would pray," the old lady said, "Jesus would help you."

119   "That's right," The Misfit said.

120   "Well then, why don't you pray?" she asked trembling with delight suddenly.

121   "I don't want no hep," he said. "I'm doing all right by myself."

122   Bobby Lee and Hiram came ambling back from the woods. Bobby Lee was dragging a yellow shirt with bright blue parrots in it.

123   "Thow me that shirt, Bobby Lee," The Misfit said. The shirt came flying at him and landed on his shoulder and he put it on. The grandmother couldn't name what the shirt reminded her of. "No, lady," The Misfit said while he was buttoning it up, "I found out the crime don't matter. You can do one thing or you can do another, kill a man or take a tire off his car, because sooner or later you're going to forget what it was you done and just be punished for it."

124   The children's mother had begun to make heaving noises as if she couldn't get her breath. "Lady," he asked, "would you and that little girl like to step off yonder with Bobby Lee and Hiram and join your husband?"

125   "Yes, thank you," the mother said faintly. Her left arm dangled helplessly and she was holding the baby, who had gone to sleep, in the other. "Hep that lady up, Hiram," The Misfit said as she struggled to climb out of the ditch, "and Bobby Lee, you hold onto that little girl's hand."

126   "I don't want to hold hands with him," June Star said. "He reminds me of a pig."

127   The fat boy blushed and laughed and caught her by the arm and pulled her off into the woods after Hiram and her mother.

128   Alone with The Misfit, the grandmother found that she had lost her voice. There was not a cloud in the sky nor any sun. There was nothing around her but woods. She wanted to tell him that he must pray. She opened and closed her mouth several times before anything came out. Finally she found herself saying, "Jesus, Jesus," meaning, Jesus will help you, but the way she was saying it, it sounded as if she might be cursing.

129   "Yes'm," The Misfit said as if he agreed. "Jesus thown everything off balance. It was the same case with Him as with me except He hadn't committed any crime and they could prove I had committed one because they had the papers on me. Of course," he said, "they never shown me my papers. That's why I sign myself now. I said long ago, you get you a signature and sign everything you do and keep a copy of it. Then you'll know what you done and you can hold up the crime to the punishment and see do they match and in the end you'll have something to prove you ain't been treated right. I call myself The Misfit," he said, "because I can't make what all I done wrong fit what all I gone through in punishment."

130   There was a piercing scream from the woods, followed closely by a pistol report. "Does it seem right to you, lady, that one is punished a heap and another ain't punished at all?"

131   "Jesus!" the old lady cried. "You've got good blood! I know you wouldn't shoot a lady! I know you come from nice people! Pray! Jesus, you ought not to shoot a lady. I'll give you all the money I've got!"

132   "Lady," The Misfit said, looking beyond her far into the woods, "there never was a body that give the undertaker a tip."

133   There were two more pistol reports and the grandmother raised her head like a parched old turkey hen crying for water and called "Bailey Boy, Bailey Boy!" as if her heart would break.

134   "Jesus was the only One that ever raised the dead," The Misfit continued, "and He shouldn't have done it. He thown everything off balance. If He did what He said, then it's nothing for you to do but thow away everything and follow Him, and if He didn't, then it's nothing for you to do but enjoy the few minutes you got left the best way you can—by killing somebody or burning down his house or doing some other meanness to him. No pleasure but meanness," he said and his voice had become almost a snarl.

135   "Maybe He didn't raise the dead," the old lady mumbled, not knowing what she was saying and feeling so dizzy that she sank down in the ditch with her legs twisted under her.

136   "I wasn't there so I can't say He didn't," The Misfit said. "I wisht I had of been there," he said, hitting the ground with his fist. "It ain't right I wasn't there because if I had of been there I would of known. Listen lady," he said in a high voice, "if I had of been there I would of known and I wouldn't be like I am now." His voice seemed about to crack and the grandmother's head cleared for an instant. She saw the man's face twisted close to her own as if he were going to cry and she murmured, "Why you're one of my babies. You're one of my own children!" she reached out and touched him on the shoulder. The Misfit sprang back as if a snake had bitten him and shot her three times through the chest. Then he put his gun down on the ground and took off his glasses and began to clean them.

137   Hiram and Bobby Lee returned from the woods and stood over the ditch, looking down at the grandmother who half sat and half lay in a puddle of blood with her legs crossed under her like a child's and her face smiling up at the cloudless sky.

138   Without his glasses, The Misfit's eyes were red- rimmed and pale and defenseless-looking. "Take her off and thow her where you thown the others," he said picking up the cat that was rubbing itself against his leg.

139   "She was a talker, wasn't she?" Bobby Lee said, sliding down the ditch with a yodel.

140   "She would of been a good woman," The Misfit said, "if it had been somebody there to shoot her every minute of her life."

141   "Some fun!" Bobby Lee said.

142   "Shut up, Bobby Lee," The Misfit said. "It's no real pleasure in life."

Questions for Engagement, Response, and Analysis

1. How is the end of the story foreshadowed in the events that precede it?

2. What is the purpose of the incident at Red Sammy's? What do this incident and the story about Mr. Teagarden reveal about the grandmother?

3. Explain the significance of the title. Why does the grandmother tell Red Sammy and the Misfit that they are good men? On what does the grandmother base her moral judgments of people?

4. Discuss whether the grandmother is to blame for what happens to the family.

5. Explain the symbolism of the hearse, the woods, and the sky without a sun.

6. Why does the Misfit call himself by that name? What characteristics make the Misfit a misfit? In what way does the Misfit's assessment of Christianity here accord with Jesus' gospel?

7. What evidence is there that the Misfit is the only character in "A Good Man Is Hard to Find" who has truly thought about the meaning of life?

8. Explain why the grandmother says to the Misfit, "Why you're one of my babies. You're one of my own children"? Why does he kill her when she touches him?

9. Explain the Misfit's statement that the grandmother "'would of been a good woman . . . if it had been somebody there to shoot her every minute of her life.'"

GREENLEAF   (1956)

1   Mrs. May's bedroom window was low and faced on the east and the bull, silvered in the moonlight, stood under it, his head raised as if he listened—like some patient god come down to woo her—for a stir inside the room. The window was dark and the sound of her breathing too light to be carried outside. Clouds crossing the moon blackened him and in the dark he began to tear at the hedge. Presently they passed and he appeared again in the same spot, chewing steadily, with a hedge-wreath that he had ripped loose for himself caught in the tips of his horns. When the moon drifted into retirement again, there was nothing to mark his place but the sound of steady chewing. Then abruptly a pink glow filled the window. Bars of light slid across him as the venetian blind was slit. He took a step backward and lowered his head as if to show the wreath across his horns.

2   For almost a minute there was no sound from inside, then as he raised his crowned head again, a woman's voice, guttural as if addressed to a dog, said, "Get away from here, Sir!" and in a second muttered, "Some nigger's scrub bull."

3   The animal pawed the ground and Mrs. May, standing bent forward behind the blind, closed it quickly lest the light make him charge into the shrubbery. For a second she waited, still bent forward, her nightgown hanging loosely from her narrow shoulders. Green rubber curlers sprouted neatly over her forehead and her face beneath them was

smooth as concrete with an egg-white paste that drew the wrinkles out while she slept.

4   She had been conscious in her sleep of a steady rhythmic chewing as if something were eating one wall of the house. She had been aware that whatever it was had been eating as long as she had had the place and had eaten everything from the beginning of her fence line up to the house and now was eating the house and calmly with the same steady rhythm would continue through the house, eating her and the boys, and then on, eating everything but the Greenleafs, on and on, eating everything until nothing was left but the Greenleafs on a little island all their own in the middle of what had been her place. When the munching reached her elbow, she jumped up and found herself, fully awake, standing in the middle of her room. She identified the sound at once: a cow was tearing at the shrubbery under her window. Mr. Greenleaf had left the lane gate open and she didn't doubt that the entire herd was on her lawn. She turned on the dim pink table lamp and then went to the window and slit the blind. The bull, gaunt and long-legged, was standing about four feet from her, chewing calmly like an uncouth country suitor.

5   For fifteen years, she thought as she squinted at him fiercely, she had been having shiftless people's hogs root up her oats, their mules wallow on her lawn, their scrub bulls breed her cows. If this one was not put up now, he would be over the fence, ruining her herd before morning—and Mr. Greenleaf was soundly sleeping a half mile down the road in the tenant house. There was no way to get him unless she dressed and got in her car and rode down there and woke him up. He would come but his expression, his whole figure, his every pause, would say: "Hit looks to me like one or both of them boys would not make their maw ride out in the middle of the night thisaway. If hit was my boys, they would have got thet bull up theirself."

6   The bull lowered his head and shook it and the wreath slipped down to the base of his horns where it looked like a menacing prickly crown. She had closed the blind then; in a few seconds she heard him move off heavily.

7   Mr. Greenleaf would say, "If hit was my boys they would never have allowed their maw to go after hired help in the middle of the night. They would have did it theirself."

8   Weighing it, she decided not to bother Mr. Greenleaf. She returned to bed thinking that if the Greenleaf boys had risen in the world it was because she had given their father employment when no one else would have him. She had had Mr. Greenleaf fifteen years but no one else would have had him five minutes. Just the way he approached an object was enough to tell anybody with eyes what kind of a worker he was. He walked with a high-shouldered creep and he never appeared to come directly forward. He walked on the perimeter of some invisible circle and if you wanted to look him in the face, you had to move and get in front of him. She had not fired him because she had always doubted she could do better. He was too shiftless to go out and look for another job; he didn't have the initiative to steal, and after she had told him three or four times

to do a thing, he did it; but he never told her about a sick cow until it was too late to call the veterinarian and if her barn had caught on fire, he would have called his wife to see the flames before he began to put them out. And of the wife, she didn't even like to think. Beside the wife, Mr. Greenleaf was an aristocrat.

9   "If it had been my boys," he would have said, "they would have cut off their right arm before they would have allowed their maw to . . ."

10   "If your boys had any pride, Mr. Greenleaf," she would like to say to him some day, "there are many things that they would not *allow* their mother to do."

11   The next morning as soon as Mr. Greenleaf came to the back door, she told him there was a stray bull on the place and that she wanted him penned up at once.

12   "Done already been here three days," he said, addressing his right foot which he held forward, turned slightly as if he were trying to look at the sole. He was standing at the bottom of the three back steps while she leaned out the kitchen door, a small woman with pale near-sighted eyes and grey hair that rose on top like the crest of some disturbed bird.

13   "Three days!" she said in the restrained screech that had become habitual with her.

14   Mr. Greenleaf, looking into the distance over the near pasture, removed a package of cigarets from his shirt pocket and let one fall into his hand. He put the package back and stood for a while looking at the cigaret. "I put him in the bull pen but he torn out of there," he said presently. "I didn't see him none after that." He bent over the cigaret and lit it and then turned his head briefly in her direction. The upper part of his face sloped gradually into the lower which was long and narrow, shaped like a rough chalice. He had deep-set fox-colored eyes shadowed under a grey felt hat that he wore slanted forward following the line of his nose. His build was insignificant.

15   "Mr. Greenleaf," she said, "get that bull up this morning before you do anything else. You know he'll ruin the breeding schedule. Get him up and keep him up and the next time there's a stray bull on this place, tell me at once. Do you understand?"

16   "Where you want him put at?" Mr. Greenleaf asked.

17   "I don't care where you put him," she said. "You are supposed to have some sense. Put him where he can't get out. Whose bull is he?"

18   For a moment Mr. Greenleaf seemed to hesitate between silence and speech. He studied the air to the left of him. "He must be somebody's bull," he said after a while.

19   "Yes, he must!" she said and shut the door with a precise little slam.

20   She went into the dining room where the two boys were eating breakfast and sat down on the edge of her chair at the head of the table. She never ate breakfast but she sat with them to see that they had what they wanted. "Honestly!" she said, and began to tell about the bull, aping Mr. Greenleaf saying, "It must be *somebody's* bull."

21   Wesley continued to read the newspaper folded beside his plate but Scofield interrupted his eating from time to time to look at her and laugh. The two boys never had the same reaction to anything. They were as different, she said, as night and day. The only thing they did have in common was that neither of them cared what happened on the place. Scofield was a business type and Wesley was an intellectual.

22   Wesley, the younger child, had had rheumatic fever when he was seven and Mrs. May thought that this was what had caused him to be an intellectual. Scofield, who had never had a day's sickness in his life, was an insurance salesman. She would not have minded his selling insurance if he had sold a nicer kind but he sold the kind that only Negroes buy. He was what Negroes call a "policy man." He said there was more money in nigger-insurance than any other kind, and before company, he was very loud about it. He would shout, "Mamma don't like to hear me say it but I'm the best nigger-insurance salesman in this county!"

23   Scofield was thirty-six and he had a broad pleasant smiling face but he was not married. "Yes," Mrs. May would say, "and if you sold decent insurance, some *nice* girl would be willing to marry you. What nice girl wants to marry a nigger-insurance man? You'll wake up some day and it'll be too late."

24   And at this Scofield would yodel and say, "Why Mamma, I'm not going to marry until you're dead and gone and then I'm going to marry me some nice fat farm girl that can take over this place!" And once he had added, "—some nice lady like Mrs. Greenleaf." When he had said this, Mrs. May had risen from her chair, her back stiff as a rake handle, and had gone to her room. There she had sat down on the edge of her bed for some time with her small face drawn. Finally she had whispered, "I work and slave, I struggle and sweat to keep this place for them and soon as I'm dead, they'll marry trash and bring it in here and ruin everything. They'll marry trash and ruin everything I've done," and she had made up her mind at that moment to change her will. The next day she had gone to her lawyer and had had the property entailed so that if they married, they could not leave it to their wives.

25   The idea that one of them might marry a woman even remotely like Mrs. Greenleaf was enough to make her ill. She had put up with Mr. Greenleaf for fifteen years, but the only way she had endured his wife had been by keeping entirely out of her sight. Mrs. Greenleaf was large and loose. The yard around her house looked like a dump and her five girls were always filthy; even the youngest one dipped snuff. Instead of making a garden or washing their clothes, her preoccupation was what she called "prayer healing."

26   Every day she cut all the morbid stories out of the newspaper—the accounts of women who had been raped and criminals who had escaped and children who had been burned and of train wrecks and plane crashes and the divorces of movie stars. She took these to the woods and dug a hole and buried them and then she fell on the ground over them and mumbled and groaned for an hour or so, moving her huge arms back and

forth under her and out again and finally just lying down flat and, Mrs. May suspected, going to sleep in the dirt.

27   She had not found out about this until the Greenleafs had been with her a few months. One morning she had been out to inspect a field that she had wanted planted in rye but that had come up in clover because Mr. Greenleaf had used the wrong seeds in the grain drill. She was returning through a wooded path that separated two pastures, muttering to herself and hitting the ground methodically with a long stick she carried in case she saw a snake. "Mr. Greenleaf," she was saying in a low voice, "I cannot afford to pay for your mistakes. I am a poor woman and this place is all I have. I have two boys to educate. I cannot . . . ."

28   Out of nowhere a guttural agonized voice groaned, "Jesus! Jesus!" In a second it came again with a terrible urgency. "Jesus! Jesus!"

29   Mrs. May stopped still, one hand lifted to her throat. The sound was so piercing that she felt as if some violent unleashed force had broken out of the ground and was charging toward her. Her second thought was more reasonable: somebody had been hurt on the place and would sue her for everything she had. She had no insurance. She rushed forward and turning a bend in the path, she saw Mrs. Greenleaf sprawled on her hands and knees off the side of the road, her head down.

30   "Mrs. Greenleaf!" she shrilled, "what's happened?"

31   Mrs. Greenleaf raised her head. Her face was a patchwork of dirt and tears and her small eyes, the color of two field peas, were red-rimmed and swollen, but her expression was as composed as a bulldog's. She swayed back and forth on her hands and knees and groaned. "Jesus, Jesus."

32   Mrs. May winced. She thought the word, Jesus, should be kept inside the church building like other words inside the bedroom. She was a good Christian woman with a large respect for religion, though she did not, of course, believe any of it was true. "What is the matter with you?" she asked sharply.

33   "You broken my healing," Mrs. Greenleaf said, waving her aside. "I can't talk to you until I finish."

34   Mrs. May stood, bent forward, her mouth open and her stick raised off the ground as if she were not sure what she wanted to strike with it.

35   "Oh Jesus, stab me in the heart!" Mrs. Greenleaf shrieked. "Jesus, stab me in the heart!" and she fell back flat in the dirt, a huge human mound, her legs and arms spread out as if she were trying to wrap them around the earth.

36   Mrs. May felt as furious and helpless as if she had been insulted by a child. "Jesus," she said, drawing herself back, "would be *ashamed* of you. He would tell you to get up from there this instant and go wash your children's clothes!" and she had turned and walked off as fast as she could.

37   Whenever she thought of how the Greenleaf boys had advanced in the world, she had only to think of Mrs. Greenleaf sprawled obscenely on the

ground, and say to herself, "Well, no matter how far they *go*, they *came* from that."

38   She would like to have been able to put in her will that when she died, Wesley and Scofield were not to continue to employ Mr. Greenleaf. She was capable of handling Mr. Greenleaf; they were not. Mr. Greenleaf had pointed out to her once that her boys didn't know hay from silage. She had pointed out to him that they had other talents, that Scofield was a successful business man and Wesley a successful intellectual. Mr. Greenleaf did not comment, but he never lost an opportunity of letting her see, by his expression or some simple gesture, that he held the two of them in infinite contempt. As scrub-human as the Greenleafs were, he never hesitated to let her know that in any like circumstance in which his own boys might have been involved, they—O. T. and E. T. Greenleaf—would have acted to better advantage.

39   The Greenleaf boys were two or three years younger than the May boys. They were twins and you never knew when you spoke to one of them whether you were speaking to O. T. or E. T., and they never had the politeness to enlighten you. They were long-legged and raw-boned and red-skinned, with bright grasping fox-colored eyes like their father's. Mr. Greenleaf's pride in them began with the fact that they were twins. He acted, Mrs. May said, as if this were something smart they had thought of themselves. They were energetic and hard-working and she would admit to anyone that they had come a long way—and that the Second World War was responsible for it.

40   They had both joined the service and, disguised in their uniforms, they could not be told from other people's children. You could tell, of course, when they opened their mouths but they did that seldom. The smartest thing they had done was to get sent overseas and there to marry French wives. They hadn't married French trash either. They had married nice girls who naturally couldn't tell that they murdered the king's English or that the Greenleafs were who they were.

41   Wesley's heart condition had not permitted him to serve his country but Scofield had been in the army for two years. He had not cared for it and at the end of his military service, he was only a Private First Class. The Greenleaf boys were both some kind of sergeants, and Mr. Greenleaf, in those days, had never lost an opportunity of referring to them by their rank. They had both managed to get wounded and now they both had pensions. Further, as soon as they were released from the army, they took advantage of all the benefits and went to the school of agriculture at the university—the taxpayers meanwhile supporting their French wives. The two of them were living now about two miles down the highway on a piece of land that the government had helped them to buy and in a brick duplex bungalow that the government had helped to build and pay for. If the war had made anyone, Mrs. May said, it had made the Greenleaf boys. They each had three little children apiece, who spoke Greenleaf English and French, and who, on account of their mothers'

background, would be sent to the convent school and brought up with manners. "And in twenty years," Mrs. May asked Scofield and Wesley, "do you know what those people will be?

42   "*Society*," she said blackly.

43   She had spent fifteen years coping with Mr. Greenleaf and, by now, handling him had become second nature with her. His disposition on any particular day was as much a factor in what she could and couldn't do as the weather was, and she had learned to read his face the way real country people read the sunrise and sunset.

44   She was a country woman only by persuasion. The late Mr. May, a business man, had bought the place when land was down, and when he died it was all he had to leave her. The boys had not been happy to move to the country to a broken-down farm, but there was nothing else for her to do. She had the timber on the place cut and with the proceeds had set herself up in the dairy business after Mr. Greenleaf had answered her ad. "i seen yor add and i will come have 2 boys," was all his letter said, but he arrived the next day in a pieced-together truck, his wife and five daughters sitting on the floor in back, himself and the two boys in the cab.

45   Over the years they had been on her place, Mr. and Mrs. Greenleaf had aged hardly at all. They had no worries, no responsibilities. They lived like the lilies of the field, off the fat that she struggled to put into the land. When she was dead and gone from overwork and worry, the Greenleafs, healthy and thriving, would be just ready to begin draining Scofield and Wesley.

46   Wesley said the reason Mrs. Greenleaf had not aged was because she released all her emotions in prayer healing. "You ought to start praying, Sweetheart," he had said in the voice that, poor boy, he could not help making deliberately nasty.

47   Scofield only exasperated her beyond endurance but Wesley caused her real anxiety. He was thin and nervous and bald and being an intellectual was a terrible strain on his disposition. She doubted if he would marry until she died but she was certain that then the wrong woman would get him. Nice girls didn't like Scofield but Wesley didn't like nice girls. He didn't like anything. He drove twenty miles every day to the university where he taught and twenty miles back every night, but he said he hated the twenty-mile drive and he hated the second-rate university and he hated the morons who attended it. He hated the country and he hated the life he lived; he hated living with his mother and his idiot brother and he hated hearing about the damn dairy and the damn help and the damn broken machinery. But in spite of all he said, he never made any move to leave. He talked about Paris and Rome but he never went even to Atlanta.

48   "You'd go to those places and you'd get sick," Mrs. May would say. "Who in Paris is going to see that you get a salt-free diet? And do you think if you married one of those odd numbers you take out that *she* would cook a salt-free diet for you? No indeed, she would not!" When she took this line, Wesley would turn himself roughly around in his chair and

ignore her. Once when she had kept it up too long, he had snarled, "Well, why don't you do something practical, Woman? Why don't you pray for me like Mrs. Greenleaf would?"

49   "I don't like to hear you boys make jokes about religion," she had said. "If you would go to church, you would meet some nice girls."

50   But it was impossible to tell them anything. When she looked at the two of them now, sitting on either side of the table, neither one caring the least if a stray bull ruined her herd—which was their herd, their future— when she looked at the two of them, one hunched over a paper and the other teetering back in his chair, grinning at her like an idiot, she wanted to jump up and beat her fist on the table and shout, "You'll find out one of these days, you'll find out what *Reality* is when it's too late!"

51   "Mamma," Scofield said, "don't you get excited now but I'll tell you whose bull that is." He was looking at her wickedly. He let his chair drop forward and he got up. Then with his shoulders bent and his hands held up to cover his head, he tiptoed to the door. He backed into the hall and pulled the door almost to so that it hid all of him but his face. "You want to know, Sugarpie?" he asked.

52   Mrs. May sat looking at him coldly.

53   "That's O. T. and E. T.'s bull," he said. "I collected from their nigger yesterday and he told me they were missing it," and he showed her an exaggerated expanse of teeth and disappeared silently.

54   Wesley looked up and laughed.

55   Mrs. May turned her head forward again, her expression unaltered. "I am the only *adult* on this place," she said. She leaned across the table and pulled the paper from the side of his plate. "Do you see how it's going to be when I die and you boys have to handle him?" she began. "Do you see why he didn't know whose bull that was? Because it was theirs. Do you see what I have to put up with? Do you see that if I hadn't kept my foot on his neck all these years, you boys might be milking cows every morning at four o'clock?"

56   Wesley pulled the paper back toward his plate and staring at her full in the face, he murmured, "I wouldn't milk a cow to save your soul from hell."

57   "I know you wouldn't," she said in a brittle voice. She sat back and began rapidly turning her knife over at the side of her plate. "O. T. and E. T. are fine boys," she said. "They ought to have been my sons." The thought of this was so horrible that her vision of Wesley was blurred at once by a wall of tears. All she saw was his dark shape, rising quickly from the table. "And you two," she cried, "you two should have belonged to that woman!"

58   He was heading for the door.

59   "When I die," she said in a thin voice, "I don't know what's going to become of you."

60   "You're always yapping about when-you-die," he growled as he rushed out, "but you look pretty healthy to me."

61   For some time she sat where she was, looking straight ahead through the window across the room into a scene of indistinct greys and greens. She stretched her face and her neck muscles and drew in a long breath but the scene in front of her flowed together anyway into a watery grey mass. "They needn't think I'm going to die any time soon," she muttered, and some more defiant voice in her added: I'll die when I get good and ready.

62   She wiped her eyes with the table napkin and got up and went to the window and gazed at the scene in front of her. The cows were grazing on two pale green pastures across the road and behind them, fencing them in, was a black wall of trees with a sharp sawtooth edge that held off the indifferent sky. The pastures were enough to calm her. When she looked out any window in her house, she saw the reflection of her own character. Her city friends said she was the most remarkable woman they knew, to go, practically penniless and with no experience, out to a rundown farm and make a success of it. "Everything is against you," she would say, "the weather is against you and the dirt is against you and the help is against you. They're all in league against you. There's nothing for it but an iron hand!"

63   "Look at Mamma's iron hand!" Scofield would yell and grab her arm and hold it up so that her delicate blue-veined little hand would dangle from her wrist like the head of a broken lily. The company always laughed.

64   The sun, moving over the black and white grazing cows, was just a little brighter than the rest of the sky. Looking down, she saw a darker shape that might have been its shadow cast at an angle, moving among them. She uttered a sharp cry and turned and marched out of the house.

65   Mr. Greenleaf was in the trench silo, filling a wheelbarrow. She stood on the edge and looked down at him. "I told you to get up that bull. Now he's in with the milk herd."

66   "You can't do two thangs at oncet," Mr. Greenleaf remarked.

67   "I told you to do that first."

68   He wheeled the barrow out of the open end of the trench toward the barn and she followed close behind him. "And you needn't think, Mr. Greenleaf," she said, "that I don't know exactly whose bull that is or why you haven't been in any hurry to notify me he was here. I might as well feed O. T. and E. T.'s bull as long as I'm going to have him here ruining my herd."

69   Mr. Greenleaf paused with the wheelbarrow and looked behind him. "Is that them boys' bull?" he asked in an incredulous tone.

70   She did not say a word. She merely looked away with her mouth taut.

71   "They told me their bull was out but I never known that was him," he said.

72   "I want that bull put up now," she said, "and I'm going to drive over to O. T. and E. T.'s and tell them they'll have to come get him today. I ought to charge for the time he's been here—then it wouldn't happen again."

73   "They didn't pay but seventy-five dollars for him," Mr. Greenleaf offered.

74   "I wouldn't have had him as a gift," she said.

75   "They was just going to beef him," Mr. Greenleaf went on, "but he got loose and run his head into their pickup truck. He don't like cars and trucks. They had a time getting his horn out the fender and when they finally got him loose, he took off and they was too tired to run after him—but I never known that was him there."

76   "It wouldn't have paid you to know, Mr. Greenleaf," she said. "But you know now. Get a horse and get him."

77   In a half hour, from her front window she saw the bull, squirrel-colored, with jutting hips and long light horns, ambling down the dirt road that ran in front of the house. Mr. Greenleaf was behind him on the horse. "That's a Greenleaf bull if I ever saw one," she muttered. She went out on the porch and called, "Put him where he can't get out."

78   "He likes to bust loose," Mr. Greenleaf said, looking with approval at the bull's rump. "This gentleman is a sport."

79   "If those boys don't come for him, he's going to be a dead sport," she said. "I'm just warning you."

80   He heard her but he didn't answer.

81   "That's the awfullest looking bull I ever saw," she called but he was too far down the road to hear.

82   It was mid-morning when she turned into O. T. and E. T.'s driveway. The house, a new red-brick, low-to-the-ground building that looked like a warehouse with windows, was on top of a treeless hill. The sun was beating down directly on the white roof of it. It was the kind of house that everybody built now and nothing marked it as belonging to the Greenleafs except three dogs, part hound and part spitz, that rushed out from behind it as soon as she stopped her car. She reminded herself that you could always tell the class of people by the class of dog, and honked her horn. While she sat waiting for someone to come, she continued to study the house. All the windows were down and she wondered if the government could have air-conditioned the thing. No one came and she honked again. Presently a door opened and several children appeared in it and stood looking at her, making no move to come forward. She recognized this as a true Greenleaf trait—they could hang in a door, looking at you for hours.

83   "Can't one of you children come here?" she called.

84   After a minute they all began to move forward, slowly. They had on overalls and were barefooted but they were not as dirty as she might have expected. There were two or three that looked distinctly like Greenleafs; the others not so much so. The smallest child was a girl with untidy black hair. They stopped about six feet from the automobile and stood looking at her.

85   "You're mighty pretty," Mrs. May said, addressing herself to the smallest girl.

86   There was no answer. They appeared to share one dispassionate expression between them.

87   "Where's your Mamma?" she asked.

88   There was no answer to this for some time. Then one of them said something in French. Mrs. May did not speak French.

89   "Where's your daddy?" she asked.

90   After a while, one of the boys said, "He ain't hyar neither."

91   "Ahhhh," Mrs. May said as if something had been proven. "Where's the colored man?"

92   She waited and decided no one was going to answer. "The cat has six little tongues," she said. "How would you like to come home with me and let me teach you how to talk?" She laughed and her laugh died on the silent air. She felt as if she were on trial for her life, facing a jury of Greenleafs. "I'll go down and see if I can find the colored man," she said.

93   "You can go if you want to," one of the boys said.

94   "Well, thank you," she murmured and drove off.

95   The barn was down the lane from the house. She had not seen it before but Mr. Greenleaf had described it in detail for it had been built according to the latest specifications. It was a milking parlor arrangement where the cows are milked from below. The milk ran in pipes from the machines to the milk house and was never carried in no bucket, Mr. Greenleaf said, by no human hand. "When you gonter get you one?" he had asked.

96   "Mr. Greenleaf," she had said, "I have to do for myself. I am not assisted hand and foot by the government. It would cost me $20,000 to install a milking parlor. I barely make ends meet as it is."

97   "My boys done it," Mr. Greenleaf had murmured, and then—"but all boys ain't alike."

98   "No indeed!" she had said. "I thank God for that!"

99   "I thank Gawd for ever-thang," Mr. Greenleaf had drawled.

100   You might as well, she had thought in the fierce silence that followed; you've never done anything for yourself.

101   She stopped by the side of the barn and honked but no one appeared. For several minutes she sat in the car, observing the various machines parked around, wondering how many of them were paid for. They had a forage harvester and a rotary hay baler. She had those too. She decided that since no one was here, she would get out and have a look at the milking parlor and see if they kept it clean.

102   She opened the milking room door and stuck her head in and for the first second she felt as if she were going to lose her breath. The spotless white concrete room was filled with sunlight that came from a row of windows head-high along both walls. The metal stanchions gleamed ferociously and she had to squint to be able to look at all. She drew her head out of the room quickly and closed the door and leaned against it, frowning. The light outside was not so bright but she was conscious that the sun was directly on top of her head, like a silver bullet ready to drop into her brain.

103   A Negro carrying a yellow calf-feed bucket appeared from around the corner of the machine shed and came toward her. He was a light yellow boy dressed in the cast-off army clothes of the Greenleaf twins. He stopped at a respectable distance and set the bucket on the ground.

104   "Where's Mr. O. T. and Mr. E. T.?" she asked.

105   "Mist O. T. he in town, Mist E. T. he off yonder in the field," the Negro said, pointing first to the left and then to the right as if he were naming the position of two planets.

106   "Can you remember a message?" she asked, looking as if she thought this doubtful.

107   "I'll remember it if I don't forget it," he said with a touch of sullenness.

108   "Well, I'll write it down then," she said. She got in her car and took a stub of pencil from her pocket book and began to write on the back of an empty envelope. The Negro came and stood at the window. "I'm Mrs. May," she said as she wrote. "Their bull is on my place and I want him off *today*. You can tell them I'm furious about it."

109   "That bull lef here Sareday," the Negro said, "and none of us ain't seen him since. We ain't knowed where he was."

110   "Well, you know now," she said, "and you can tell Mr. O. T. and Mr. E. T. that if they don't come get him today, I'm going to have their daddy shoot him the first thing in the morning. I can't have that bull ruining my herd." She handed him the note.

111   "If I knows Mist O. T. and Mist E. T.," he said, taking it, "they goin to say you go ahead on and shoot him. He done busted up one of our trucks already and we be glad to see the last of him."

112   She pulled her head back and gave him a look from slightly bleared eyes. "Do they expect me to take my time and my worker to shoot their bull?" she asked. "They don't want him so they just let him loose and expect somebody else to kill him? He's eating my oats and ruining my herd and I'm expected to shoot him too?"

113   "I speck you is," he said softly. "He done busted up . . . ."

114   She gave him a very sharp look and said, "Well, I'm not surprised. That's just the way some people are," and after a second she asked, "Which is boss, Mr. O. T. or Mr. E. T.?" She had always suspected that they fought between themselves secretly.

115   "They never quarls," the boy said. "They like one man in two skins."

116   "Hmp. I expect you just never heard them quarrel."

117   "Nor nobody else heard them neither," he said, looking away as if this insolence were addressed to some one else.

118   "Well," she said, "I haven't put up with their father for fifteen years not to know a few things about Greenleafs."

119   The Negro looked at her suddenly with a gleam of recognition. "Is you my policy man's mother?" he asked.

120   "I don't know who your policy man is," she said sharply. "You give them that note and tell them if they don't come for that bull today, they'll be making their father shoot it tomorrow," and she drove off.

121   She stayed at home all afternoon waiting for the Greenleaf twins to come for the bull. They did not come. I might as well be working for them, she thought furiously. They are simply going to use me to the limit. At the supper table, she went over it again for the boys' benefit because

she wanted them to see exactly what O. T. and E. T. would do. "They don't want that bull," she said, "—pass the butter—so they simply turn him loose and let somebody else worry about getting rid of him for them. How do you like that? I'm the victim. I've always been the victim."

122   "Pass the butter to the victim," Wesley said. He was in a worse humor than usual because he had had a flat tire on the way home from the university.

123   Scofield handed her the butter and said, "Why Mamma, ain't you ashamed to shoot an old bull that ain't done nothing but give you a little scrub strain in your herd? I declare," he said, "with the Mamma I got it's a wonder I turned out to be such a nice boy!"

124   "You ain't her boy, Son," Wesley said.

125   She eased back in her chair, her fingertips on the edge of the table.

126   "All I know is," Scofield said, "I done mighty well to be as nice as I am seeing what I come from."

127   When they teased her they spoke Greenleaf English but Wesley made his own particular tone come through it like a knife edge. "Well lemme tell you one thang, Brother," he said, leaning over the table, "that if you had half a mind you would already know."

128   "What's that, Brother?" Scofield asked, his broad face grinning into the thin constricted one across from him.

129   "That is," Wesley said, "that neither you nor me is her boy . . . ," but he stopped abruptly as she gave a kind of hoarse wheeze like an old horse lashed unexpectedly. She reared up and ran from the room.

130   "Oh, for God's sake," Wesley growled. "What did you start her off for?"

131   "I never started her off," Scofield said. "You started her off."

132   "Hah."

133   "She's not as young as she used to be and she can't take it."

134   "She can only give it out," Wesley said. "I'm the one that takes it."

135   His brother's pleasant face had changed so that an ugly family resemblance showed between them. "Nobody feels sorry for a lousy bastard like you," he said and grabbed across the table for the other's shirtfront.

136   From her room she heard a crash of dishes and she rushed back through the kitchen into the dining room. The hall door was open and Scofield was going out of it. Wesley was lying like a large bug on his back with the edge of the over-turned table cutting him across the middle and broken dishes scattered on top of him. She pulled the table off him and caught his arm to help him rise but he scrambled up and pushed her off with a furious charge of energy and flung himself out of the door after his brother.

137   She would have collapsed but a knock on the back door stiffened her and she swung around. Across the kitchen and back porch, she could see Mr. Greenleaf peering eagerly through the screenwire. All her resources returned in full strength as if she had only needed to be challenged by the devil himself to regain them. "I heard a thump," he called, "and I thought the plastering might have fell on you."

138   If he had been wanted someone would have had to go on a horse to find him. She crossed the kitchen and the porch and stood inside the

screen and said, "No, nothing happened but the table turned over. One of the legs was weak," and without pausing, "the boys didn't come for the bull so tomorrow you'll have to shoot him."

139   The sky was crossed with thin red and purple bars and behind them the sun was moving down slowly as if it were descending a ladder. Mr. Greenleaf squatted down on the step, his back to her, the top of his hat on a level with her feet. "Tomorrow I'll drive him home for you," he said.

140   "Oh no, Mr. Greenleaf," she said in a mocking voice, "you drive him home tomorrow and next week he'll be back here. I know better than that." Then in a mournful tone, she said, "I'm surprised at O. T. and E. T. to treat me this way. I thought they'd have more gratitude. Those boys spent some mighty happy days on this place, didn't they, Mr. Greenleaf?"

141   Mr. Greenleaf didn't say anything.

142   "I think they did," she said. "I think they did. But they've forgotten all the nice little things I did for them now. If I recall, they wore my boys' old clothes and played with my boys' old toys and hunted with my boys' old guns. They swam in my pond and shot my birds and fished in my stream and I never forgot their birthday and Christmas seemed to roll around very often if I remember it right. And do they think of any of those things now?" she asked. "NOOOOO," she said.

143   For a few seconds she looked at the disappearing sun and Mr. Greenleaf examined the palms of his hands. Presently as if it had just occurred to her, she asked, "Do you know the real reason they didn't come for that bull?"

144   "Naw I don't," Mr. Greenleaf said in a surly voice.

145   "They didn't come because I'm a woman," she said. "You can get away with anything when you're dealing with a woman. If there were a man running this place . . ."

146   Quick as a snake striking Mr. Greenleaf said, "You got two boys. They know you got two men on the place."

147   The sun had disappeared behind the tree line. She looked down at the dark crafty face, upturned now, and at the wary eyes, bright under the shadow of the hatbrim. She waited long enough for him to see that she was hurt and then she said, "Some people learn gratitude too late, Mr. Greenleaf, and some never learn it at all," and she turned and left him sitting on the steps.

148   Half the night in her sleep she heard a sound as if some large stone were grinding a hole on the outside wall of her brain. She was walking on the inside, over a succession of beautiful rolling hills, planting her stick in front of each step. She became aware after a time that the noise was the sun trying to burn through the tree line and she stopped to watch, safe in the knowledge that it couldn't, that it had to sink the way it always did outside of her property. When she first stopped it was a swollen red ball, but as she stood watching it began to narrow and pale until it looked like a bullet. Then suddenly it burst through the tree line and raced down the hill toward her. She woke up with her hand over her mouth and the

same noise, diminished but distinct, in her ear. It was the bull munching under her window. Mr. Greenleaf had let him out.

149   She got up and made her way to the window in the dark and looked out through the slit blind, but the bull had moved away from the hedge and at first she didn't see him. Then she saw a heavy form some distance away, paused as if observing her. This is the last night I am going to put up with this, she said, and watched until the iron shadow moved away in the darkness.

150   The next morning she waited until exactly eleven o'clock. Then she got in her car and drove to the barn. Mr. Greenleaf was cleaning milk cans. He had seven of them standing up outside the milk room to get the sun. She had been telling him to do this for two weeks. "All right, Mr. Greenleaf," she said, "go get your gun. We're going to shoot that bull."

151   "I thought you wanted theseyer cans . . ."

152   "Go get your gun, Mr. Greenleaf," she said. Her voice and face were expressionless.

153   "That gentleman torn out of there last night," he murmured in a tone of regret and bent again to the can he had his arm in.

154   "Go get your gun, Mr. Greenleaf," she said in the same triumphant toneless voice. "The bull is in the pasture with the dry cows. I saw him from my upstairs window. I'm going to drive you up to the field and you can run him into the empty pasture and shoot him there."

155   He detached himself from the can slowly. "Ain't nobody ever ast me to shoot my boys' own bull!" he said in a high rasping voice. He removed a rag from his back pocket and began to wipe his hands violently, then his nose.

156   She turned as if she had not heard this and said, "I'll wait for you in the car. Go get your gun."

157   She sat in the car and watched him stalk off toward the harness room where he kept a gun. After he had entered the room, there was a crash as if he had kicked something out of his way. Presently he emerged again with the gun, circled behind the car, opened the door violently and threw himself onto the seat beside her. He held the gun between his knees and looked straight ahead. He'd like to shoot me instead of the bull, she thought, and turned her face away so that he could not see her smile.

158   The morning was dry and clear. She drove through the woods for a quarter of a mile and then out into the open where there were fields on either side of the narrow road. The exhilaration of carrying her point had sharpened her senses. Birds were screaming everywhere, the grass was almost too bright to look at, the sky was an even piercing blue. "Spring is here!" she said gaily. Mr. Greenleaf lifted one muscle somewhere near his mouth as if he found this the most asinine remark ever made. When she stopped at the second pasture gate, he flung himself out of the car door and slammed it behind him. Then he opened the gate and she drove through. He closed it and flung himself back in, silently, and she drove around the rim of the pasture until she spotted the bull, almost in the center of it, grazing peacefully among the cows.

159   "The gentleman is waiting on you," she said and gave Mr. Greenleaf's furious profile a sly look. "Run him into that next pasture and when you get him in, I'll drive in behind you and shut the gate myself."

160   He flung himself out again, this time deliberately leaving the car door open so that she had to lean across the seat and close it. She sat smiling as she watched him make his way across the pasture toward the opposite gate. He seemed to throw himself forward at each step and then pull back as if he were calling on some power to witness that he was being forced. "Well," she said aloud as if he were still in the car, "it's your own boys who are making you do this, Mr. Greenleaf." O. T. and E. T. were probably splitting their sides laughing at him now. She could hear their identical nasal voices saying, "Made Daddy shoot our bull for us. Daddy don't know no better than to think that's a fine bull he's shooting. Gonna kill Daddy to shoot that bull!"

161   "If those boys cared a thing about you, Mr. Greenleaf," she said, "they would have come for that bull. I'm surprised at them."

162   He was circling around to open the gate first. The bull, dark among the spotted cows, had not moved. He kept his head down, eating constantly. Mr. Greenleaf opened the gate and then began circling back to approach him from the rear. When he was about ten feet behind him, he flapped his arms at his sides. The bull lifted his head indolently and then lowered it again and continued to eat. Mr. Greenleaf stooped again and picked up something and threw it at him with a vicious swing. She decided it was a sharp rock for the bull leapt and then began to gallop until he disappeared over the rim of the hill. Mr. Greenleaf followed at his leisure.

163   "You needn't think you're going to lose him!" she cried and started the car straight across the pasture. She had to drive slowly over the terraces and when she reached the gate, Mr. Greenleaf and the bull were nowhere in sight. This pasture was smaller than the last, a green arena, encircled almost entirely by woods. She got out and closed the gate and stood looking for some sign of Mr. Greenleaf but he had disappeared completely. She knew at once that his plan was to lose the bull in the woods. Eventually, she would see him emerge somewhere from the circle of trees and come limping toward her and when he finally reached her, he would say, "If you can find that gentleman in them woods, you're better than me."

164   She was going to say, "Mr. Greenleaf, if I have to walk into those woods with you and stay all afternoon, we are going to find that bull and shoot him. You are going to shoot him if I have to pull the trigger for you." When he saw she meant business he would return and shoot the bull quickly himself.

165   She got back into the car and drove to the center of the pasture where he would not have so far to walk to reach her when he came out of the woods. At this moment she could picture him sitting on a stump, marking lines in the ground with a stick. She decided she would wait exactly ten minutes by her watch. Then she would begin to honk. She got out of the car and walked around a little and then sat down on the front bumper to wait and rest. She was very tired and she lay her head back against the

hood and closed her eyes. She did not understand why she should be so tired when it was only mid-morning. Through her closed eyes, she could feel the sun, red-hot overhead. She opened her eyes slightly but the white light forced her to close them again.

166   For some time she lay back against the hood, wondering drowsily why she was so tired. With her eyes closed, she didn't think of time as divided into days and nights but into past and future. She decided she was tired because she had been working continuously for fifteen years. She decided she had every right to be tired, and to rest for a few minutes before she began working again. Before any kind of judgement seat, she would be able to say: I've worked, I have not wallowed. At this very instant while she was recalling a life-time of work, Mr. Greenleaf was loitering in the woods and Mrs. Greenleaf was probably flat on the ground, asleep over her holeful of clippings. The woman had got worse over the years and Mrs. May believed that now she was actually demented. "I'm afraid your wife has let religion warp her," she said once tactfully to Mr. Greenleaf. "Everything in moderation, you know."

167   "She cured a man once that half his gut was eat out with worms," Mr. Greenleaf said, and she had turned away, half-sickened. Poor souls, she thought now, so simple. For a few seconds she dozed.

168   When she sat up and looked at her watch, more than ten minutes had passed. She had not heard any shot. A new thought occurred to her: suppose Mr. Greenleaf had aroused the bull chunking stones at him and the animal had turned on him and run him up against a tree and gored him? The irony of it deepened: O. T. and E. T. would then get a shyster lawyer and sue her. It would be the fitting end to her fifteen years with the Greenleafs. She thought of it almost with pleasure as if she had hit on the perfect ending for a story she was telling her friends. Then she dropped it, for Mr. Greenleaf had a gun with him and she had no insurance.

169   She decided to honk. She got up and reached inside the car window and gave three sustained honks and two or three shorter ones to let him know she was getting impatient. Then she went back and sat down on the bumper again.

170   In a few minutes something emerged from the tree line, a black heavy shadow that tossed its head several times and then bounded forward. After a second she saw it was the bull. He was crossing the pasture toward her at a slow gallop, a gay almost rocking gait as if he were overjoyed to find her again. She looked beyond him to see if Mr. Greenleaf was coming out of the woods too but he was not. "Here he is, Mr. Greenleaf!" she called and looked on the other side of the pasture to see if he could be coming out there but he was not in sight. She looked back and saw that the bull, his head lowered, was racing toward her. She remained perfectly still, not in fright, but in a freezing unbelief. She stared at the violent black streak bounding toward her as if she had no sense of distance, as if she could not decide at once what his intention was, and the bull had buried his head in her lap, like a wild tormented lover, before

her expression changed. One of his horns sank until it pierced her heart and the other curved around her side and held her in an unbreakable grip. She continued to stare straight ahead but the entire scene in front of her had changed—the tree line was a dark wound in a world that was nothing but sky—and she had the look of a person whose sight has been suddenly restored but who finds the light unbearable.

171   Mr. Greenleaf was running toward her from the side with his gun raised and she saw him coming though she was not looking in his direction. She saw him approaching on the outside of some invisible circle, the tree line gaping behind him and nothing under his feet. He shot the bull four times through the eye. She did not hear the shots but she felt the quake in the huge body as it sank, pulling her forward on its head, so that she seemed, when Mr. Greenleaf reached her, to be bent over whispering some last discovery into the animal's ear.

Questions for Engagement, Response, and Analysis

1. What is the point of view in this story?

2. Examine Mrs. May's comments about and attitudes toward the Greenleafs. What do these reveal about her?

3. What are the standards Mrs. May uses to classify people? Compare her standards with those of the grandmother in "A Good Man Is Hard to Find."

4. Describe the relationship between Mrs. May and her sons. Then compare Mrs. May's sons with E. T. and O. T. Greenleaf.

5. Explain the significance of the scene in which Mrs. Greenleaf prays to Jesus as she lies on the ground. How does it foreshadow the end of the story?

6. Analyze O'Connor's comment when the bull gores Mrs. May that "she had the look of a person whose sight has been suddenly restored but who finds the light unbearable."

THE FICTION WRITER AND HIS COUNTRY   (1957)

1   . . . I am no disbeliever in spiritual purpose and no vague believer. I see from the standpoint of Christian orthodoxy. This means that for me the meaning of life is centered in our Redemption by Christ and what I see in the world I see in its relation to that. I don't think that this is a position that can be taken halfway or one that is particularly easy in these times to make transparent in fiction.

2   Some may blame preoccupation with the grotesque on the fact that here we have a Southern writer and that this is just the type of imagination that Southern life fosters. I have written several stories which did not seem to me to have any grotesque characters in them at all, but which have immediately been labeled grotesque by non-Southern

readers. I find it hard to believe that what is observable behavior in one section can be entirely without parallel in another. At least, of late, Southern writers have had the opportunity of pointing out that none of us invented Elvis Presley and that that youth is himself probably less an occasion for concern than his popularity, which is not restricted to the Southern part of the country. The problem may well become one of finding something that is *not* grotesque and of deciding what standards we would use in looking.

3   My own feeling is that writers who see by the light of their Christian faith will have, in these times, the sharpest eyes for the grotesque, for the perverse, and for the unacceptable. In some cases, these writers may be unconsciously infected with the Manichean spirit of the times and suffer the much-discussed disjunction between sensibility and belief, but I think that more often the reason for this attention to the perverse is the difference between their beliefs and the beliefs of their audience. Redemption is meaningless unless there is cause for it in the actual life we live, and for the last few centuries there has been operating in our culture the secular belief that there is no such cause.

4   The novelist with Christian concerns will find in modern life distortions which are repugnant to him, and his problem will be to make these appear as distortions to an audience which is used to seeing them as natural; and he may well be forced to take ever more violent means to get his vision across to this hostile audience. When you can assume that your audience holds the same beliefs you do, you can relax a little and use more normal means of talking to it; when you have to assume that it does not, then you have to make your vision apparent by shock—to the hard of hearing you shout, and for the almost-blind you draw large and startling figures.

5   Unless we are willing to accept our artists as they are, the answer to the question, "Who speaks for America today?" will have to be: the advertising agencies. They are entirely capable of showing us our unparalleled prosperity and our almost classless society, and no one has ever accused them of not being affirmative. Where the artist is still trusted, he will not be looked to for assurance. Those who believe that art proceeds from a healthy, and not from a diseased, faculty of the mind will take what he shows them as a revelation, not of what we ought to be but of what we are at a given time and under given circumstances; that is, as a limited revelation but revelation nevertheless.

6   When we talk about the writer's country we are liable to forget that no matter what particular country it is, it is inside as well as outside him. Art requires a delicate adjustment of the outer and inner worlds in such a way that, without changing their nature, they can be seen through each other. To know oneself is to know one's region. It is also to know the world, and it is also, paradoxically, a form of exile from that world. The writer's value is lost, both to himself and to his country, as soon as he ceases to see that country as a part of himself, and to

know oneself is, above all, to know what one lacks. It is to measure one-self against Truth, and not the other way around. The first product of self-knowledge is humility, and this is not a virtue conspicuous in any national character.

7   St. Cyril of Jerusalem, in instructing catechumens, wrote: "The dragon sits by the side of the road, watching those who pass. Beware lest he devour you. We go to the Father of Souls, but it is necessary to pass by the dragon." No matter what form the dragon may take, it is of this mysterious passage past him, or into his jaws, that stories of any depth will always be concerned to tell, and this being the case, it requires considerable courage at any time, in any country, not to turn away from the storyteller.

Questions for Engagement, Response, and Analysis

1. List and explain O'Connor's statements about the grotesque.

2. According to O'Connor, what is the duty of the Christian novelist?

3. Explain O'Connor's metaphor of the dragon and the passage.

THE SEARCH FOR REDEMPTION: FLANNERY O'CONNOR'S FICTION

FREDERICK J. HOFFMAN

1   The first impression one has of Flannery O'Connor's work is of its extraordinary lucidity; given, that is, what she expects to communicate, she does communicate it with most remarkable clarity and ease. Of course, one needs to know just what it is; she is concerned with the problem of how a writer, "by indirections, finds directions out." She has a reputation for obscurity, for not giving the expected turn to the reader, for not rewarding him for his having taken the trouble to read her.

2   The best statement she has given of her purpose and method is a talk she gave at the College of Saint Teresa (Winona, Minnesota) in the fall of 1960. Responding to a critic's suggestion that she is probably not a "Catholic novelist" because she doesn't write on "Catholic subjects," she said:

> The Catholic novelist in the South is forced to follow the spirit into strange places and to recognize it in many forms not totally congenial to him. But the fact that the South is the Bible Belt increases rather than decreases his sympathy for what he sees. His interest will in all likelihood go immediately to those aspects of Southern life where the religious feeling is most intense and where its outward forms are farthest from the Catholic.[1]

---

[1] Flannery O'Connor, "The Role of the Catholic Novelist," *Greyfriar* [Siena Studies in Literature] 7 (1964): 8.

3   Her major subjects are the struggle for redemption, the search for Jesus, and the meaning of "prophecy": all of these in an intensely evangelical Protestant South, where the need for Christ is expressed without shyness and where "prophecy" is intimately related to the ways in which men are daily challenged to define themselves.[2] The literary problem raised by this peculiarity of "place" (though it may be located elsewhere as well, as a "need for ceremony," or a desperate desire to "ritualize" life) is neatly described by Miss O'Connor: she must, she says, define in unnaturally emphatic terms what would not otherwise be accepted, or what might be misunderstood. The sentiment (or some emotional reaction) will get in the way. "There is something in us," she said, in the same talk, "as storytellers and as listeners to stories, that demands the redemptive act, that demands that what falls at least be offered the chance to be restored."[3] But the rituals of any church are not comprehended by a large enough majority of readers; therefore,

> When I write a novel in which the central action is a baptism, I know that for the larger percentage of my readers, baptism is a meaningless rite: therefore I have to imbue this action with an awe and terror which will suggest its awful mystery.[4]

4   Miss O'Connor writes about intensely religious acts and dilemmas in a time when people are much divided on the question of what actually determines a "religious act." Definitions are not easy, and, frequently, what is being done with the utmost seriousness seems terribly naive, or simple-minded, to the reader. She must, therefore, force the statement of it into a pattern of "grotesque" action, which reminds one somewhat of Franz Kafka,[5] at least in its violation of normal expectations.

[2]See Sister M. Bernetta Quinn, "View from a Rock: The Fiction of Flannery O'Connor and J. F. Powers," *Critique* 2 (Fall 1958): 19–27: "The center of all Catholic fiction is the Redemption. However mean or miserable or degraded human life may seem to the natural gaze, it must never be forgotten that God considered it valuable enough to send His only Son that He might reclaim it" (21). See *A Handbook of Christian Theology* (New York: Meridian Books, 1958), 296: "Thus the God who ransoms, redeems, and delivers Israel out of her bondage is the God who, in Christ, pays the price which restores sinful mankind to freedom and new life. In this act of redemption two interrelated theological emphases are dominant: God's *love* by which He takes the initiative, and man's sin which occasions the situation from which God redeems him."

[3]"The Role of the Catholic Novelist," pp. 10–11.

[4]Ibid., p. 11.

[5]See Melvin J. Friedman, in *Recent American Fiction*, ed. Joseph J. Waldmeir (Boston: Houghton Mifflin, 1963), 241. Friedman also cites Nathanael West, as does John Hawkes, "Flannery O'Connor's Devil," *Sewanee Review* 70 (Summer 1962): 396. Hawkes mentions an interesting conjunction of influences on himself: "it was Melville's granddaughter [Eleanor Melville Metcalf], a lady I was privileged to know in Cambridge, Massachusetts, who first urged me to read the fiction of Flannery O'Connor, and—further—[. . .] this experience occurred just at the time I had discovered the short novels of Nathanael West."

5   We have the phenomenon of a Catholic writer describing a Protestant, an evangelical, world, to a group of readers who need to be forced or shocked and/or amused into accepting the validity of religious states. The spirit of evil abounds, and the premonition of disaster is almost invariably confirmed. Partly, this is because the scene is itself grotesquely exaggerated (though eminently plausible at the same time); partly it is because Christian sensibilities have been, not so much blunted as rendered bland and over-simple. The contrast of the fumbling grandmother and The Misfit, in Miss O'Connor's most famous story, "A Good Man Is Hard to Find," is a case in point. The grandmother is fully aware of the expected terror, but she cannot react "violently" to it. She must therefore use commonplaces to meet a most uncommon situation:

> "If you would pray," the old lady said, "Jesus would help you."
> "That's right," The Misfit said.
> "Well then, why don't you pray?" she asked trembling with delight suddenly.
> "I don't want no hep," he said. "I'm doing all right by myself."

6   Another truth about Miss O'Connor's fiction is its preoccupation with the Christ figure, a use of Him that is scarcely equalled by her contemporaries. The Misfit offers an apparently strange but actually a not uncommon observation:

> "Jesus was the only One that ever raised the dead, . . . and He shouldn't have done it. He thown everything off balance. If He did what He said, then it's nothing for you to do but thow away everything and follow Him, and if He didn't, then it's nothing for you to do but enjoy the few minutes you got left the best you can—by killing somebody or burning down his house or doing some other meanness to him. No pleasure but meanness," he said and his voice became almost a snarl.

7   One of Paul Tillich's most effective statements has to do with the relationship of man to Jesus Christ, in volume two of his most impressive *Systematic Theology.* "Jesus Christ," he says, "combines the individual name with the title, 'the Christ,'" and "Jesus as the Christ is both a historical fact and a subject of believing reception."[6] Perhaps more important, and in line with his attempt to review theology in existentialist terms, Tillich says, "Son of God becomes the title of the one in whom the essential unity of God and man has appeared under the conditions of existence. The essentially universal becomes existentially unique."[7]

---

[6]*Systematic Theology* (Chicago: University of Chicago Press, 1951), vol. 2, 98. It is interesting that many of Miss O'Connor's characters want to "see a sign": that is, they want Christ's divinity manifested directly. The Misfit is such a one; Hazel Motes of *Wise Blood* struggles against a Christian mission on the grounds that Christ as God has never revealed Himself; Mr. Head and his grandson have a remarkable experience of illumination when they see the plaster statue of a Negro (in "The Artificial Nigger"); and the young Tarwater of *The Violent Bear It Away* has a "voice" (variously called "stranger," "friend," and "mentor") who tries to deny Jesus because there has been no "sign" of Him.

[7]Ibid., p. 110.

8   As all of us know, the crucifixion was historically a defeat for the messianic cause, whose followers wanted Jesus literally to triumph over the Romans and to restore the Jews to power. But it was also, and most importantly, the source of grace; or, as Tillich puts it, "'Christ' became an individual with supernatural powers who, through a voluntary sacrifice, made it possible for God to save those who believe in him."[8] It is this latter figure whom Miss O'Connor's heroes spend so much energy and time denying; many of them also are on the way to accepting Him.

9   In almost all of Miss O'Connor's fiction, the central crisis involves a confrontation with Jesus, "the Christ." In the manner of Southern Protestantism, these encounters are quite colloquial and intimate. The "Jesus" on the lips of her characters is someone who hovers very near; with Him, her personalities frequently carry on a personal dialogue. The belief, or the disbelief, in Him is almost immediate. He is "Jesus" made almost entirely human and often limited in theological function. Man often "takes over" from Him, or threatens to do so. The so-called "grotesques" of Flannery O'Connor's fiction are most frequently individual souls, imbued with religious sentiments of various kinds, functioning in the role of the surrogate Christ or challenging Him to prove Himself. Not only for literary strategy, but also because such manifestations *are* surreal, Miss O'Connor makes these acts weird demonstrations of human conduct: "irrational" in the sense of their taking issue with a rational view of events. . . .

10   The figure of Jesus haunts almost all of her characters. They are, half the time, violently opposed to Him (or, in His image, opposed to some elder who has tried to force His necessity upon them), because they cannot see beyond themselves to a transcendent existence. Hazel Motes and Tarwater are both haunted by the rank and stinking corporeality of their elders, whom they have seen dead and—in dream or in reality—been obliged to bury.

11   These experiences serve to make them resist the compunctions of grace and turn away from the prospects of redemption. But the alternative is singularly uninviting. Hazel Motes has no success preaching the new church "without Christ," and Tarwater finds his uncle either pathetic or farcical. They react violently at the turn of their journeys: Motes blinds himself in a mixture of the desire for penitence and the will to prove his courage; Tarwater has recourse both to water and fire, from mixed motives of defiance and fear.

12   This clarity of vision comes in part from Miss O'Connor's having herself had a satisfactory explanation of these religious drives, and therefore being in a position to portray the violent acts of those who possess the drives but are unable to define goals or direct energies toward them. The grotesqueries of her fiction are in effect a consequence of her seeing what she calls "the Manichean spirit of the times," in which the religious metaphors retain their power but cannot be precisely delineated by

[8]Ibid., p. 111.

persons driven by the necessities they see in them. Violence, in this setting, assumes a religious meaning; it is, in effect, the sparks caused by the clash of religious desire and disbelief.

> The novelist with Christian concerns will find in modern life distortions which are repugnant to him, and his problem will be to make these appear as distortions to an audience which is used to seeing them as natural; and he may well be forced to take ever more violent means to get his vision across to his hostile audience.[9]

13   The matter becomes extremely delicate, in the light of her other observations: for example, that "Art requires a delicate adjustment of the outer and inner worlds in such a way that, without changing their nature, they can be seen through each other.[10] This remark suggests that the religious metaphors are, above all, psychological realities; that these are dramatized in the desperate struggles her characters have, at one time against but finally in the mood of accepting the Christian demands and rewards. When Miss O'Connor makes the following summary of her vision, therefore, she is simply defining the ultimate goals of her characters, whether they have been represented or not in the act of achieving them.

> I see from the standpoint of Christian orthodoxy. This means that for me the meaning of life is centered in our Redemption by Christ and that what I see in the world I see in its relation to that. I don't think that this is a position that can be taken halfway or one that is particularly easy in these times to make transparent in fiction.[11]

VIOLENCE AND THE GROTESQUE

GILBERT H. MULLER

1   Miss O'Connor's technical strategy in the application of violence is to show precisely how the destructive impulse brings the horror of man's grotesque state home to him. Because this kind of violence is religiously motivated, it differs considerably from those gratuitous forms of violence in fiction which are used to exploit current tastes. The violence in Miss O'Connor's fiction is real, yet it has a metaphysical dimension arising from man's loss of theological identity. If in terms of effect this violence partakes of exaggeration, sensationalism, and shock, it nevertheless raises problems which treat the moral and religious order of the universe. The author was quick to distinguish violence in the pure grotesque from its presence in other adulterated forms. She objected to the attempts of some critics to place her within the School of Southern Degeneracy, and she

[9]"The Fiction Writer and His Country," in *The Living Novel, A Symposium,* ed. Granville Hicks (New York: Macmillan, 1957), 162–63.

[10]Ibid., p. 163.

[11]Ibid., p. 162.

asserted that every time she was associated with this gothic beast she "felt like Br'er Rabbit stuck on the tarbaby."[1] She was emphatic in denying that she utilized violence as a gothic contrivance, remarking that gothicism was a degeneracy which was rarely recognized as such. Fictional assessment of violence in ethical and theological terms is one quality which sets the grotesque apart from a gothic aesthetic, since the violence implicit in gothic fiction has little moral foundation: it exists to satisfy itself and does not serve as a meaningful vision. Conversely, when violence appears in the grotesque, as in the hecatomb which frames "A Good Man Is Hard to Find," it is used to suggest the lack of any framework of order in the universe; it reinforces the grotesque by working *against* the ideals of social and moral order to create an alienated perspective. . . .

2   Acts of violence in Miss O'Connor's fiction illuminate a world of continual spiritual warfare. The Misfit in "A Good Man Is Hard to Find" kills people not because he enjoys murder, but because like Meursault in *L'Etranger* he is powerless to control his impulses when faced with the indifference of the universe. His act of violence is not totally irrational because its manifestation points toward the spiritual disorder of the world. The Misfit therefore is not presented merely as a pathological murderer, but as a crazed latter-day anchorite, wielding a gun instead of a gnarled club. Still he is without grace, and he complicates the grotesque situation of the Bailey family as well as of himself by ignoring the cardinal commandment—"Thou shalt not kill." Slaughter is a part of the natural process, and modern war demonstrates that it is a part of the human process as well. Yet from a Catholic perspective the injunction placed upon man not to kill is a radical one—and one which must be obeyed. In human and theological terms to kill is to lapse into evil.

3   Ultimately violence in Flannery O'Connor's fiction forces the reader to confront the problem of evil and to seek alternatives to it. Because Miss O'Connor uses violence to shock her characters (and readers), it becomes the most singular expression of sin within her grotesque landscape. Time and again in her stories violence intrudes suddenly upon the familiar and seemingly secure world and turns the landscape into a secular hell. Thus the slow pastoral seduction planned by Hulga in "Good Country People" is disrupted by Manley Pointer's outrages against her body and spirit. Similarly Julian's world in "Everything That Rises Must Converge" suddenly becomes chaotic when violence ruins what previously had been an innocuous, albeit distasteful, bus trip. Obviously violence of this type occupies a crucial position in making the world seem strange, terrifying, and deprived of grace. As Frederick J. Hoffman remarks in what is perhaps the finest book on violence in contemporary literature, "Surprise is an indispensable element of the fact of violence in modern life. A carefully plotted pattern

[1]"Some Aspects of the Grotesque in Southern Fiction," in *Mystery and Manners*, ed. Sally Fitzgerald and Robert Fitzgerald (New York: Farrar, Strauss & Giroux, 1969), 38.

of expected events has always been needed to sustain a customary existence. A sudden break in the routine challenges the fullest energy of man's power of adjustment. Suddenness is a quality of violence. It is a sign of force breaking through the design established to contain it."[2] . . .

4   The violent figure frequently becomes an extension of the world that he inhabits. His spiritual desolation is reflected in the very landscape through which he moves, for in this landscape images of violence and disorder prevail. Flannery O'Connor pays strict attention to scene, to landscape in disarray, because by being a reflection of the interior self of the character, it assumes a complicity, despite its supposedly inanimate nature, in the bizarre disjunctiveness of the universe. The potentially violent and hostile landscape is a mark of Miss O'Connor's fiction and serves as a vivid image of a worldly Inferno. And of course with the author, a violent landscape is almost by extension a grotesque landscape. In other words the reductive power of violence unleashes essentially grotesque currents of feeling. In "A Good Man Is Hard to Find," for instance, the deranged mind of the Misfit, and the secular impulses of a family preordained to destruction, find an objective correlative in images of a distorted and inimical wasteland. The twisted setting in the story mirrors spiritual and moral decay, and the peaceful rhythms usually associated with a family trip are continually undercut by the images of destruction which are juxtaposed against it. Cotton fields with small islands of graves, the dirt road with "sudden washes in it and sharp curves on dangerous embankments," the line of woods which gapes "like a dark open mouth" create a landscape which is menacing and alien. Even the diner the family stops at for lunch is a precarious structure, lacking any solidarity or harmony, and is presided over by a sadistic monkey that bites fleas between its teeth with delight. Here, and in other stories such as "A Circle in the Fire" (1954) and "A View of the Woods" (1957), the environment impinges upon characters and is potentially violent: physical description consistently works in opposition to people's desire for harmony and order, and it also affords a premonition of disaster.

5   Flannery O'Connor's technique of description is terse and severe, tending always toward the impressionistic, in which landscape is distilled into primary images that render a picture of a violent physical world. Miss O'Connor, a watercolorist of considerable talent, concentrates upon line and color to evoke locale swiftly; considering the premium she placed upon the stark outlines of her fiction, any profusion of description would work against her overall narrative intentions, and thus she relied upon the synthetic method of drawing objects in the physical world together to achieve a concentrated effect. Whether describing the countryside or the metropolis, the author is carefully selective and austere, building up

[2]*The Mortal No: Death and the Modern Imagination* (Princeton, N.J.: Princeton University Press, 1964), 292.

a pattern of imagery and frequently counterpointing these images in order to create a charged atmosphere and to make a thematic statement.

6   The landscapes depicted in Flannery O'Connor's fiction seem to intensify man's propensity for physical, psychological, and spiritual violence. In a world deprived of meaning, in a world which is ruthless and cruel, the only consolation which her characters have is an ability to exploit others through violence. Arson, rape, mutilation, suicide, and murder are some of the extremes of violent behavior that appear in O'Connor's fiction, and what is curious about these manifestations is that characters such as Rufus, Shiftlet, and the Bible salesman actually take pleasure in wanton acts of destruction. This pleasure in violence, a phenomenon which preoccupies many behavioral scientists and such philosophers as Karl Jaspers, deprives men of being, although the malefactors believe mistakenly that it serves to define their lives. As such, violence becomes a manifestation of the demonic, understood in the medieval sense of the word, as a force which obliterates identity and damns human beings. Even the Misfit, with his debased logic, comprehends a world without meaning, and in such a world, where it is impossible to attach one's loyalties to any overriding ethical or theological position, the only pleasure and consolation for the lack of meaning must come from amoral acts of violence. Unlike the Hemingway protagonist, who attempts to channel violence into such acceptable institutions as war, hunting, and the bullfight, the characters in O'Connor's fiction rarely seek social justification for their destructive acts. If any justification is required, it exists in the universe itself, in a fallen and grotesque world where a perverse Creator forces man to attest to his damnation every moment of his life.

7   At the root of violence in Miss O'Connor's fiction lies this concept of the depraved and potentially lethal world, in which the destiny of man is seemingly imposed upon him by a vaguely apprehended source. W. M. Frohock in *The Novel of Violence in America* cogently explains the dilemma facing the violent protagonist: "The hero finds himself in a predicament such that the only possible exit is through infliction of harm on some other human. In the infliction of harm he also finds the way to his own destruction. But still he accepts the way of violence because life, as he sees it, is like that: violence is man's fate." Life—in the existential sense of the word—is like that, even at the most mundane level. . . .

8   The entire strategy of violence in Flannery O'Connor's stories of the grotesque is to reveal how complicity in destruction carries men away from God, away from that center of mystery she was constantly trying to define and which Catholics term grace. This is why violent death is the one act of paramount importance in O'Connor's fiction: it serves to define evil in society. The feud violence that exists in "Greenleaf," for example, is clearly delineated not only in terms of class hatreds but also in terms of good and evil. The pervasive aura of violence in this story reveals the corruption of the will and the need of grace. This kind of violence is a form of spiritual punishment, and in "Revelation," "The Lame Shall Enter First," and many other of her tales it is admonitory. Mrs. May obviously

disdains the low origins and primitive ways of the Greenleafs as well as their newly acquired success. With their fox-colored eyes and dark crafty faces, they seem to be cast in the mold of Faulkner's tenacious Snopes clan. Yet the Greenleafs, as their name implies, are in basic harmony with nature. More importantly Mrs. Greenleaf embraces a variety of worship which is reminiscent of early mystery religions based on vegetation and on earth. Her mortification and ecstasy, which are appalling to Mrs. May, are ways of experiencing the spiritual through nature; moreover, Mrs. Greenleaf thinks in terms of a primitive salvation for mankind. Mrs. May's failure to understand the rituals that Mrs. Greenleaf enacts before her eyes signifies the modern failure to integrate religious mystery with culture. It also explains why Mrs. May's destiny of necessity must be violent, because hers is the fate of the individual who is estranged from the basic forces of the community and from grace.

9   Another indication of evil in "Greenleaf" is the alienation that exists among the members of the May family. Estrangement within the family is of course one of the most common forms of sublimated violence and overt feuding in Flannery O'Connor's fiction. In "Greenleaf" Mrs. May's two sons loathe their mother and hate each other as well. Wesley, the younger of the brothers, bears spiritual kinship to Hulga, Asbury, and other effete intellectuals who are encountered frequently in Miss O'Connor's stories. He is sickly, sardonic, ill-natured, and rude—a vacuous academician consumed by a brutal sense of determinism. Scofield is much coarser than his brother; patterned after Jason Compson, he displays a marked degeneracy in his manners. Both brothers are perversely preoccupied with their mother's death, and this act suggests how individuals can consciously choose to perform or to wish acts of evil. . . .

10   The ultimate battle is against evil—and against the devil incarnated in concrete forms—in the figure of a Bible salesman, an old man with a peppermint cane, or a friendly figure in a panama hat. In this situation violence becomes a mark of faith. As the noted historian Jacques Ellul has written, "The whole meaning of the violence of love is contained in Paul's word that evil is to be overcome with good (Romans 12:17–21). This is a generalization of the Sermon on the Mount. And it is important for us to understand that this sermon shows what the violence of love is. Paul says, 'Do not let yourself be overcome by evil.' This then is the fight—and not only spiritual, for Paul and the whole Bible are very realistic and see that evil is constantly incarnated."[3]

---

[3]*Violence: Reflections from a Christian Perspective* (New York: Seabury, 1969), 172–73. I am indebted to Mr. Ellul for his concept of love as a spiritual force and also for his cogent explanation of the incarnation of spiritual forms. The latter, of course, is standard Catholic doctrine. Miss O'Connor, for instance, in referring to Christ rather than the devil, states, "Christ didn't redeem us by a direct intellectual act, but became incarnate in human form, and he speaks to us now through the mediation of a visible Church. All this may seem a long way from the subject of fiction, but it is not, for the main concern of the fiction writer is with mystery as it is incarnated in human life" (*Mystery and Manners*, 176).

11   The violence of love is synonymous with faith, and only this sort of violence is effectual in face of the grotesque. Characters like Thomas in "The Comforts of Home" and Hulga in "Good Country People" fail to recognize the true battle. But others accept it reluctantly, undergo violence and suffering, and rage successfully against the absurd. All O'Connor's protagonists are denied basic needs. A few perceive the grotesque nature of the world; they demand recognition of their own worthiness in this world, sense the futility and frustration arising from this need, and consequently embrace what seemingly is the most lucid course of action—violence. In short, whether we are speaking of the Misfit or of Francis Marion Tarwater, this kind of antagonist revolts against an unsatisfactory state of affairs. He indulges in violence because he wants to see if faith can survive. Flannery O'Connor considers all her characters—and the society they compose—as ruled by this harsh geometry of religion. Against the potential framework of religious order she sets violence and disorder, and then she tries to resolve the ambiguity by forcing her characters into those varieties of extreme situation which test the limits of the grotesque.

12   The extreme situation reveals the paradoxical nature of violence in O'Connor's fiction. Young Bevel's drowning in "The River," for instance, permits him a unique salvation, as does the drowning of Bishop in *The Violent Bear It Away*. Guizac's crucifixion in "The Displaced Person" is also his sacrifice for a depraved culture. The Misfit's murders reveal the horror of a world without Christ. The flagellation of O. E. Parker, the physical assaults of Manley Pointer, the depravities of Rufus Johnson are all examples of violence operating from the shifting and highly ambiguous perspective, for we see in these stories that the infliction of pain and suffering leads to purification and self- knowledge, either for the victimizer or the victim, or for that curious figure, like the Misfit and Shiftlet, Tarwater and Hazel Motes, who is both victim and victimizer, who initiates violence only to discover that it rebounds upon him. . . .

13   Revelation of the true kingdom—or, as Miss O'Connor called it, the true country—is a primary concern in her fiction, and it is for this reason that she utilized motifs of violence to get at the incongruous nature of reality and to reveal the vitality of the grotesque as technique and vision. In a paragraph that has become a classic statement on the value of the grotesque, one can see how the concept of violence fits into Flannery O'Connor's vision:

> The novelist with Christian concerns will find in modern life distortions which are repugnant to him, and his problem will be to make these appear as distortions to an audience which is used to seeing them as natural; and he may well be forced to take ever more violent means to get his vision across to this hostile audience. When you assume that your audience holds the same beliefs you do, you can relax a little and use more normal ways of talking to it; when you have to assume that it does not, then you have to make your vision apparent by shock—to the hard

of hearing you shout, and for the almost-blind you draw large and star-tling figures.[4]

14   The world of the grotesque, whether we are talking about O'Connor and Faulkner, Thomas Pynchon and James Purdy, or Vladimir Nabokov and Jorge Borges, is a world of distortions—in character and landscape and also in spirit. Demonic and violent acts therefore are a means whereby we can fix the precise limits of meaning in this alien and mysterious world. At the same time violence becomes a source of hope whereby man can transcend his grotesque condition. As Miss O'Connor has written in reference to "A Good Man Is Hard to Find":

> We hear many complaints about the prevalence of violence in modern fic-tion, and it is always assumed that this violence is a bad thing and meant to be an end in itself. With the serious writer, violence is never an end in itself. It is the extreme situation that best reveals what we are essentially, and I believe these are times when writers are most interested in what we are essentially, than in the tenor of our daily lives. Violence is a force which can be used for good or evil, and among the things taken by it is the kingdom of heaven. But regardless of what can be taken by it, the man in the violent situation reveals those qualities least dispensable in his personality, those qualities which are all he will have to take into eternity with him; and since the characters in this story are all on the verge of eter-nity, it is appropriate to think of what they take with them.[5]

15   In the broadest sense, to reflect on the grotesque is to reflect upon violence: essentially the modern condition reveals that violence creates a perilous balance between the horrifying and the ludicrous. Flannery O'Connor knew that the grotesque, by descending into the claustral world of violence, of the incongruous and irrational, contains within itself the germ whereby a transcendent order can be discovered: in an ambigu-ous world you look for absolutes, and when you face the unknown you invariably recognize spiritual mystery. Violence speaks to us about our experience of such a world by revealing the human need for something beyond a purely secular vision.

UNDERSTANDING FLANNERY O'CONNOR: GREENLEAF

MARGARET EARLEY WHITT

1   "Greenleaf" is the earliest story of the collection [*Everything That Rises Must Converge*] and her first top-award recipient for the O. Henry. It was published first in the summer 1956 issue of the *Kenyon Review*, appearing a year after the publication of *A Good Man Is Hard to Find*. The story was also included in *The Best American Short Stories of 1957*. "Greenleaf" joins three earlier stories in featuring a lone woman who

---

[4]*Mystery and Manners*, pp. 33–34.
[5]Ibid., pp. 113–14.

seeks to protect her farm property and to control the people who live on it. Mrs. May has hired some "good country people" to assist in working the land, whose irritating ways irk the stubborn landowner. "Greenleaf" is O'Connor's last story that features a hard-working farm-owning woman who has problems of control with both the hired help and her children. As a transition story, it is the first of four stories that O'Connor writes about a single mother struggling with an adult still-at-home son.

2   All of the single threads of the story line—Mrs. May's struggling dynamics with her sons, their constant comparisons to the more successful Greenleaf boys, the striking contrast of Mrs. May's and Mrs. Greenleaf's responses to religion—converge in the momentary dilemma of this story: the scrub bull that has come to court Mrs. May and to invade her property and her herd of cows. This bull has connections with the myth in which Zeus disguises himself as a white bull and carries off Europa to Crete,[1] as well as biblical connections to the holy hunt of the unicorn, where the courting animal becomes a symbolic Christ figure that pierces Mrs. May through the heart with a deeper understanding of Christian reality.[2] Before the bull and Mrs. May have a final and fatal meeting, O'Connor makes clear the limited perspective with which Mrs. May views the world.

3   Mrs. May, "a small woman with pale near-sighted eyes and grey hair that [rises] on top like the crest of some disturbed bird" (503), has sole responsibility for the success of her farm. Her two adult sons—thirty-six-year-old Scofield, the "nigger-insurance salesman" (504), and Wesley, the younger intellectual—have one thing in common: "neither of them care[s] what happen[s] on the place" (504). Both sons verbally abuse their mother at every opportunity. Scofield suggests that she can easily be replaced by some "nice fat farm girl" wife that he will choose upon her death (505). Wesley, who causes her "real anxiety" (509), "wouldn't milk a cow to save [her] soul from hell" (510). As a final blow in this daily barrage, he also strips his mother of parenthood; to Scofield, he taunts: "Neither you nor me is her boy" (517). Mrs. May, on the other hand, remains foremost a Southern mother. She feels a duty to her sons and takes whatever treatment they offer. Although she does not eat breakfast with them, she sits "with them to see that they [have] what they wanted" (504). She makes sure that Wesley maintains his salt-free diet. Mrs. May's downfall, however, is that she constantly reminds her sons how great her own sacrifice has been, and she stands at the ready with plenty of good advice about how they could improve their lives. For example, if Scofield

---

[1]See John C. Shields, "Flannery O'Connor's 'Greenleaf' and the Myth of Europa and the Bull," *Studies in Short Fiction* 18 (1981): 421–31. Shields presents a detailed study of how the myth's portrayal of the union of sky and earth informs a reading of this story.

[2]See Kristen Meek, "Flannery O'Connor's 'Greenleaf' and the Holy Hunt for the Unicorn," *Flannery O'Connor Bulletin* 19 (1990): 30–37. Meek's essay makes a biblical connection with the events of the story.

would sell "decent insurance, some *nice* girl would be willing to marry [him]. What nice girl wants to marry a nigger-insurance man?" (505). Mrs. May does not hear her racist comments. Her simplistic worldview extends to every aspect of her life and beyond: "I'll die when I get good and ready"(511).

4   Mrs. May's relationship with her sons is complicated by the success of her hired people's twin sons, a few years younger than her own. Mr. Greenleaf, her employee for fifteen years, is always quick to point out what his sons would do by comparison. Because of the rigid class structure that so permeated the South of O'Connor's day, the upper-class land-owning Mrs. May has to endure the comeuppance from a lower class that refuses to adhere to old rules: "As scrub-human as the Greenleafs were, [Mr. Greenleaf] never hesitated to let her know that in any like circumstance in which his own boys might have been involved—O. T. and E. T. Greenleaf—would have acted to better advantage" (507). Mrs. May is prepared to credit anything outside and beyond the boys with their elevated place in the world: the war that sent them to Europe, where they could "disguise" themselves in uniform (507), court and marry French women who do not realize they are "murder[ing] the king's English" (508), and "manage" to get wounded and receive a pension (508). She takes credit as well for her contribution to their rise and wants to hold it over them when she discovers that the scrub bull on her property belongs to O. T. and E. T. She reminds Mr. Greenleaf, with a repetition of the first person possessive pronoun, that his boys "wore my boys' old clothes and played with my boys' old toys and hunted with my boys' old guns"; further, for Mrs. May, those twins had access to "my pond . . . , my birds . . . , my stream" (518). Mrs. May is without subtlety or nuance; her only deficiency is that she is a woman: "You can get away with anything when you're dealing with a woman. If there were a man running this place" (519). She tolerates her own sons' fighting: "Nobody feels sorry for a lousy bastard like you" (517), shouts one to the other before the dishes crash, the table is overturned, and the boys are grabbing each other's shirtfronts. Because her own boys fight, Mrs. May is sure the Greenleafs do, but according to their hired help, "they never quarls. [. . .] They like one man in two skins" (516). Mrs. May and her sons are denied the superiority she feels is the privilege of her class.

5   Mrs. May carries her superficial thinking into matters of religion as well. She has reduced religion to attending church, a "proper" place for her boys to "meet some nice girls" (510). Mrs. Greenleaf, by contrast, takes religion to the "preoccupation" of "prayer healing" (505). By clipping appropriate stories from the paper—rape, burned children, escaped criminals, train wrecks, plane crashes, and movie star divorces—burying them in the ground, and praying over them, she is in direct communication with the healing power of her Jesus: "Oh Jesus, stab me in the heart!" (506). Mrs. May is shocked at her first encounter with Mrs. Greenleaf's ritual, for her Jesus is a practical man. She knows that Jesus would be "*ashamed*"

of Mrs. Greenleaf and tell her to "get up from there this instant and go wash [her] children's clothes!" (507). Mrs. Greenleaf, with her backwoods fundamentalist perspective, values the mystery of Jesus as deity, accepting his power to right the wrongs of the day. Mrs. May understands the language of the Christian religion where it fits in society, and how she might work it to her advantage, but "she [does] not, of course, believe any of it [is] true" (506).

6   Into the melee of these relationships comes the bull, an "uncouth country suitor" (502). The May boys have the advantage over their mother as Scofield knows it is the Greenleaf boys' bull. The Greenleaf boys have no intention of reclaiming the bull and are willing to let Mrs. May assume the responsibility of having their father kill it. As O'Connor closes in on the activity of the killing scene, she advances the bull to symbol. From the opening scene with his Christlike hedge wreath "caught in the tips of his horns" (501), his presumptuous invasion of her property, until the end when he picks up the pace of his wooing, no longer the "patient god" (501), the bull, as an image of Christ, crosses at a "slow gallop" and then, suddenly, is "racing toward her" (523). Until this point in the story, Mrs. May has set her own schedule and controlled her world, but now the bull changes everything. Mrs. May moves from "freezing unbelief" (523), not just her response to the bull's charge but her response to religion's role in her life, to "the look of a person whose sight has been suddenly restored but who finds the light unbearable" (523). O'Connor uses repetition of language and image to draw the parallel between Mrs. May's response to the earlier scene of Mrs. Greenleaf in her prayer healing and the charging bull. With Mrs. Greenleaf, Mrs. May stops still: "The sound was so piercing that she felt as if some violent unleashed force had broken out of the ground and was charging toward her" (506). Facing the bull, Mrs. May remains perfectly still: "She stared at the violent black streak bounding toward her as if she had no sense of distance" until his horn "sank until it pierced her heart" (523). Mrs. Greenleaf's figurative chant for Jesus to stab her in the heart takes on a literal action as the bull stabs Mrs. May through her heart. O'Connor has set up the scene of the "last discovery" of Mrs. May, as she whispers "into the animal's ear" (524), to be the beginning of understanding her own limitations. O'Connor suggests that Mrs. May reaches the Teilhardian Omega Point of God in the "unbearable" light.

Works Cited

Meek, Kristen. "Flannery O'Connor's 'Greenleaf' and the Holy Hunt of the Unicorn." *Flannery O'Connor Bulletin* 19 (1990): 30–37.

Shields, John C. "Flannery O'Connor's 'Greenleaf' and the Myth of Europa and the Bull." *Studies in Short Fiction* 18 (1981): 421–31.

Quimby Melton IV

Professor Henderson

English 1102

3 May 2007

Greenleaf's Destructive Bull and Paean to the Common Man

1   Beyond a field of common travail lies a structure of human
social interaction which divides worker and owner. Though both
work the field, though both love and bleed in the common field,
one owns and one does not. Taken with the linguistic, financial,
familial-historic, and general physical appearances that divide
human society, this owner versus worker relationship seems quite
unjust. The relationship between the owner/worker and his quasi-
serf employee is nowhere better seen than in the rural, post-
reconstruction American South. This "rigid class structure that
so [permeates] the South of O'Connor's day" (Whitt 1119) serves
as a perfect canvas for the story "Greenleaf," which exists as a
song of praise for the worker and the injustice he and his
family face from the higher social strata: a stratification upon
which O'Connor seemingly frowns throughout the story as she
lauds the common man. O'Connor is not content, however, simply
to frown upon this injustice; rather, through the use of the
bull as both symbolic and manifest character of Greenleaf, she
destroys those who would denounce the common man.

2   O'Connor uses the Greenleafs as her embodiment of the
common man, i.e., the common laborer. She fixes the social
standing of her characters early in the story as Mrs. May is
awakened by a bull, crowned by a wreath of greenery, chewing on
a bush directly outside her bedroom window. She immediately
curses her worker, Mr. Greenleaf, for "[leaving] the lane gate
open" (O'Connor 1089) as if all problems on her farm are

Mr. Greenleaf's fault. However, directly before this curse, O'Connor has defended the Greenleafs by establishing their safety in the strange dream Mrs. May is having. In this apocalyptic dream, the bull is eating Mrs. May's entire surroundings. Her whole world, as it is in this dream, is in danger of being consumed by this bull. "[E]verything from the beginning of [Mrs. May's] fence line up to the house" has been eaten by the bull; and now, "with the same steady rhythm" (1089), the bull is threatening the house, Mrs. May, and her two sons. The bull, a continued symbol of destruction throughout the story, threatens to destroy Mrs. May's world much like the Apocalyptic Dragoons of the Christian faith: a faith "she [does] not, of course, believe . . . [is] true" (1092). The Greenleafs, symbols of the simple faithful as well as of the common worker, will be safe from the apocalyptic bull's destruction "on a little island all their own in the middle of what [was Mrs. May's] place" (1089). By placing the bull as a symbol of apocalyptic destruction, O'Connor establishes the saved and the damned: the "salt-of-the-earth" (Matthew 5:13) Greenleafs will be saved while the hypocritical and judgmental Mays will be consumed.

3   O'Connor also praises the simple faith of the common laborer. The Greenleafs will be saved from the apocalypse because their earthly religion is a living, active one built on the pillars of prayer, practice, and faith. Mrs. Greenleaf buries the evil she sees in the daily paper not to overlook the negativity but to give to God of the problems of the world. Like Donne's cry, "Batter my heart, three person'd God," Mrs Greenleaf cries to God to "stab [her] in the heart" (1092) as she prays over the buried newspaper clippings. Mr. Greenleaf

also shows his religious faith when he softly mentions to Mrs.

May, "I thank Gawd for ever-thang" (1098). The Greenleafs are

not ashamed of their faith and do not believe, as Mrs. May does,

that Jesus, "should be kept inside the church building" (1092).

Mrs. May respects religion but is "shocked at . . . Mrs.

Greenleaf's ritual . . . and understands . . . where [the

Christian religion] fits in society and how she might work it to

her advantage" (Whitt 1120); but she does not understand the

spiritual fervor of the Greenleafs. Even O. T. and E. T.

Greenleaf's children will be "sent to a convent school and

brought up with manners" (1094) by the religious faithful.

Ironically, through hard work, sacrifice, and the final honing

of religious education, the common worker Greenleafs will have

achieved in two generations the status of "society," which Mrs.

May has lost in one.

4   O'Connor praises the unity of the Greenleafs and uses the

symbols of unity versus disunity to further separate the class

of worker and owner/worker. The Greenleafs are unified as a

family unit. They have peace not strife; Mrs. May notices that

"over the years [the Greenleafs] had been on her place, [they]

had aged hardly at all." The Greenleafs have "no worries, no

responsibilities" and live "like the lilies of the field"

(1094). The Greenleaf boys, O. T. and E. T., are "fine boys"

(1095), according to Mrs. May; according to O. T. and E. T.'s

hired hand, they never quarrel as if they are "one man in two

skins" (1099). Unity pervades the Greenleafs in religion,

brotherhood, and peace. The May boys, however, are "as different

. . . as night and day" (1091) and there is constant strife in

the May family. The boys fight with their mother and are

dissatisfied with life; as a culmination of the strife, Scofield

and Wesley physically assault one another at the dinner table.
Through the great corpus of evidence O'Connor supplies, it is
obvious that the unity and simple wants and needs as well as
faith of the Greenleafs afford their happiness. O'Connor praises
them for this by showing the alternative to their happiness
through the form of the Mays and their disunity and resulting
strife.

5   Between the families, there is also strife, not unity.
Mrs. May does not like the Greenleafs, and Mr. Greenleaf is
quite sardonic in his unspoken way towards his boss. The bull
as destroyer furthers the separation of the families. Because
of the bull, Mrs. May judges and dislikes the Greenleafs even
more, and Mr. Greenleaf further despises his boss. The bull
sweeps in and destroys the already fragile relationship that
exists between owner/worker and worker, thus pushing
reconciliation further from their grasp. The bull also creates
the final destruction as he destroys the person and life of
Mrs. May. Mrs. May, by the end of the story, has created for
herself a grand inferiority to the Greenleafs. She feels she is
neither appreciated for her work nor any longer in control of
her farm. By commanding the destruction of the bull, Mrs. May
feels that she will reassert her authority and destroy the bull
before he both symbolically and literally destroys her.
Ultimately, the bull is reasserted as destroyer and true
authority, for he takes the life of Mrs. May and teaches her
the truth of life and religion. The bull is enrobed in a
Christ-like persona as he stabs Mrs. May's heart in a final
revelation of Mrs. Greenleaf's prayer. She who supposed she
would "die when [she got] good and ready" (1096) is taught a
lesson on the fragility of life by a pesky, charging bull with

an aversion to automobiles. The light she sees is radiant
because of the religious and mortal lessons Mrs. May has
learned about truth and the mutability of life.

6   In the final moments of life, Mrs. May realizes the truth
and inherent goodness of the Greenleaf way of life. She forgets
her petty worries and injuries and, for an instant, is human. In
the moment of death, she is neither rich nor poor, neither
simple nor educated. Mrs. May transcends the temporal aspects of
life and is shown the truth of life: all are human and equally
susceptible to death and resurrection. Ultimately both bull and
Mrs. May are destroyed by the common man in the form of Mr.
Greenleaf in a final cry of victory and praise for the worker
over the oppressive elite. Victory, at the end of "Greenleaf,"
belongs to the Greenleafs: O'Connor's final affirmation of the
superiority of the common man.

Melton 6

Works Cited

Henderson, Gloria Mason, Anna Dunlap Higgins, Bill Day, and

Sandra Stevenson Waller, eds. *Literature and Ourselves:*

A Thematic Introduction for Readers and Writers. 6th ed.

New York: ABLongman, 2009.

O'Connor, Flannery. "Greenleaf." In *The Complete Stories.* New

York: The Noonday Press, 1998. 311-34. Henderson, Higgins,

Day, and Waller. 1088-1105.

Whitt, Margaret Earley. *Understanding Flannery O'Connor.*

Columbia: University of South Carolina Press, 1995. 121-26.

Henderson, Higgins, Day, and Waller. 1117-20.

Crafting Arguments

1. In an essay, argue that in "A Good Man Is Hard to Find," the grand-mother's behavior is responsible for her family's fate.

2. Write an essay suggesting some of the things that the bull, appearing at the beginning and the ending of "Greenleaf," might symbolize.

3. In a character analysis, illustrate how Mrs. May's jealousy, rage, self-pity, and obsession with control define her character.

4. Write an essay comparing the grandmother and Mrs. May.

5. O'Connor is especially skillful at using irony to portray the problems faced by people who lack a sincere belief in God. Using the critical essays in this Casebook and O'Connor's essay, discuss her use of irony in "A Good Man Is Hard to Find" and/or "Greenleaf."

6. Each of the protagonists in the O'Connor stories reaches a point where she realizes her personal inadequacy and helplessness. O'Connor might say that each experiences divine grace. After reading O'Connor's stories and the critical essays in this Casebook, write an essay analyzing the nature of divine grace as manifested in O'Connor's fiction.

7. O'Connor has a good eye for the humorously grotesque, seemingly irrelevant details that realistically characterize people. Carefully examine her use of such detail in the stories, and explain how her grotesque descriptions of people express her religious vision.

8. Examine O'Connor's use of vivid descriptive details and their often ironic implications in one or both of the stories. Then write an essay analyzing this aspect of her style.

9. The Misfit and the bull are violent agents of change in O'Connor's protagonists' lives. With the help of the critical sources in the

Casebook, discuss what each appears to represent in O'Connor's Christian vision.

Quest: Crafting Arguments

1. Several characters in this section think they have all the answers they need about the meaning and purpose of their lives. In an essay, show how these characters are made to see that they, like others, are pilgrims or seekers, that their lives must be a continual quest for meaning.

2. Taking into consideration that the goals of the quest can be defined in a number of ways, choose two selections from this unit and show how they define two different aspects of the quest.

3. Using at least two of the works in this unit, discuss one quest that seems to be universal.

4. The individual's search for his or her own identity is a major theme in literature. Using two stories and/or the play from this section, write an essay discussing this theme.

5. Notice that four of the five short stories in the Quest unit are written in first person. Use at least two of these stories to explain why first person point of view is especially effective in writing about quests.

Quest: Writing about Film

See Appendix B: Writing About Film for help with these essays.

1. The quest, whether it be for a holy purpose or for self-knowledge, has always been a part of literature. View one of the versions of Sophocles' *Oedipus Rex* and craft an analysis that examines the ways in which the filmmaker translates this classic quest into movie format.

2. You might prefer to view a movie with a contemporary twist on the quest theme. Consider film adaptations as varied as *Brokeback Mountain, Silence of the Lambs, Forrest Gump, Sleepy Hollow, Under the Tuscan Sun,* and *Evan Almighty.* Prepare a paper that offers your definition of the quest in one such adaptation.

3. Action-adventure movies with a quest theme are very popular. In these movies, often a single character overcomes unbelievable odds to accomplish a task or quest; in other films, this quest is a group effort. Write a Comparison/Contrast paper in which you examine the characters and events in the adaptation and the characters and events in the literary source. You might want to consider such adaptations as *Beowulf, Last of the Mohicans,* the *Harry Potter* films, and *The Lord of the Rings* trilogy.

4. Film adaptations appropriate for children also often showcase a quest theme. View an adaptation such as *The Wizard of Oz, Hook, Pocahontas: The Legend, The Polar Express,* or *Enchanted* and analyze the message the movie presents.

Appendix A

CRITICAL APPROACHES TO LITERATURE

Literary theorists have developed a variety of approaches to literature that are more narrowly defined than the three general approaches described in our introduction—author-oriented, reader-oriented, and text-oriented approaches. These critical approaches to literature often overlap and frequently have more than one name. Some of the most important are formalism (or New Criticism), biographical criticism, historical criticism, sociological criticism, psychological criticism, archetypal (or mythic) criticism, gender criticism, deconstructionist criticism, and cultural studies criticism.

Formalism

Formalism, or *New Criticism*, describes the work of literature as the sum of its parts. Formalism developed in part as a reaction to what its proponents saw as an excessive emphasis on autobiographical, historical, and sociological criticism. Formalists reject analysis of a work of literature that is based on whether or not the author achieved his or her goals, labeling this form of analysis the "intentional fallacy" because it is based on what is unknowable and irrelevant. Similarly, they reject reader-response criticism as irrelevant and overly subjective, labeling it the "affective fallacy." Instead, formalism focuses on a close reading, or *explication*, of the literary work itself.

Formalism also emphasizes an examination of the words and patterns within the work, especially as they are used as images and symbols. Formalists often examine the ways in which irony and paradox are used to develop theme. For example, a formalist approach might consider the ways in which the words, images, symbols, paradoxes, and irony effectively create the tone in Edwin Arlington Robinson's "Richard Cory" or might examine Flannery O'Connor's use of dialogue between the Misfit and the grandmother in "A Good Man Is Hard to Find" to reveal the shallowness of the grandmother's definition of goodness and the emptiness of both characters' lives without divine grace. Furthermore, formalism recognizes the differences in genres and may examine whether a work fulfills the expectations for its genre.

Biographical Criticism

Other critics examine influences outside the literature in order to analyze and interpret the works. *Biographical criticism* focuses on how the author's life has influenced the work. Biographical critics believe that a reader who is familiar with details about the author's family, education, career, or religion may know which clues to look for in interpreting a work or may have added insight into the meaning of that work. For example, knowing that Ursula K. Le Guin's father was an anthropologist may aid the reader in understanding the moral implications of the worlds she creates in her novels and in "The Ones Who Walk Away from Omelas." Similarly, knowing about the differences between Alice Walker's background and her mother's life may help the reader to understand how members of the same family can have such differing lifestyles and views of heritage in "Everyday Use."

Historical Criticism

Historical criticism reminds readers that authors are influenced by the cultural milieus in which they live and that their works reflect these milieus. Historical critics contend that the reader who knows details about the specific time, place, and events depicted in a work can read it with greater understanding. For example, a historical critic might examine the history of the Negro leagues in order to illuminate the way Troy has been treated and to explain Troy's behavior in August Wilson's *Fences*. Historical critics also examine the ways in which interpretations may have changed over the life of the work.

Sociological Criticism

Sociological criticism begins by examining the cultures and beliefs of the time during which a work of literature was created. Believing that art imitates life, sociological critics point out that both the artist and the work of art are directly influenced by the artist's values, belief systems, roles, mores, and demographics. Sociological critics may consider the way in which the work reflects its society. For example, these critics might compare the drug culture as it existed within the musical community in Harlem during the 1930s and 1940s with James Baldwin's description in "Sonny's Blues" or might compare the concept of a "fit mother" in the second half of the twentieth century in the United States with Madison Smartt Bell's portrayal of the mother in "Customs of the Country"—a story that suggests a sociological approach even in its title. Because sociological critics believe that an author's knowledge of and concern for his or her audience invariably affect that author's work, they also assess information about that audience.

One sociological approach, *Marxist criticism*, takes an exclusively political point of view in interpreting literature. Marxist critics believe that every work of literature, whether intentionally or unintentionally, promotes or espouses a political ideology. Thus, a Marxist critic might examine the lack of productive action on the part of the politicians in Isabel Allende's "And of Clay Are We Created." For the Marxist critic, the ideal work of art will make readers aware of the class struggle so as to encourage them to side with the proletariat.

Psychological Criticism

Psychological criticism is based mainly on the theories of Freud and his followers. Freud himself began the psychological examination into the nature of creativity, describing it as an escape into fantasy that can provide insights for both the author and the reader. Freud's theory that a work of literature is an expression of the author's unconscious desires is the basis for much psychological criticism; a good example is the critical discussion of Charlotte Perkins Gilman's portrayal of a mental breakdown in "The Yellow Wallpaper."

Another psychological approach suggested by Freud's work focuses on using psychoanalytic techniques to interpret fictional characters. For example, a critic interpreting Shakespeare's tragedy *Othello* might use Freud's concept of the id, ego, and superego to explain Iago's vengeful and destructive actions. A psychological critic might study the reasons for Connie's choices in Joyce Carol Oates' "Where Are You Going, Where Have You Been?"

Archetypal Criticism

Another approach, which grew partially out of psychological theory, is *archetypal*, or *mythic, criticism*. In his theory of the "collective unconscious," Swiss psychologist Carl Jung asserted that all humans unconsciously share in the total experience of the human race. Jung also suggested that this collective unconscious reveals itself in the form of "archetypes," universal symbols or images that occur repeatedly in creative human history. These recurring archetypes often take the form of opposites, such as light and dark or heaven and hell. An example of the light/dark dichotomy is found in the imagery of James Baldwin's "Sonny's Blues." A few archetypal figures include the hero; the villain; the woman as earth mother, platonic ideal, or temptress; and the scapegoat, of which Ursula K. Le Guin's "The Ones Who Walk Away from Omelas" presents an excellent example.

Jung's theory of archetypes reinforces Sir James George Frazer's earlier work, published in *The Golden Bough*, the first anthropological study of myth and ritual. Through his studies, Frazer found that cultures with no common history and no physical contact have similar mythic explanations for their experiences and for the natural phenomena that puzzle them. For example, almost all cultures believe in a destruction myth, the most frequent describing the destruction of humanity by flood. The death–rebirth myth, which follows the cycle of the seasons and the life cycle, is the most universal of archetypes. Other archetypal motifs include the quest, the initiation, and the journey. The final thematic section of *Literature and Ourselves* includes examples of the quest. The Jesuit priest in Arthur C. Clarke's "The Star" seeks to reconcile his religious faith with his newly acquired scientific knowledge. The initiation rite is illustrated by Squeaky's growing awareness of herself and of the joy of sharing her knowledge and ability with others in Toni Cade Bambara's "Raymond's Run." Because the archetypal or mythic approach examines recurring universal figures and motifs, it offers an effective way to compare literature over the centuries.

Gender Criticism

Gender criticism explores the effects of gender roles, attitudes, and dynamics on writers, works, and audiences. Feminist critics in particular believe that literature previously has been written primarily by men for men, and they see one of the roles of their criticism as including women writers and the "woman's point of view." These critics have also focused attention on previously neglected works by women authors, including Zora Neale

Hurston and Charlotte Perkins Gilman. Virginia Woolf pointed out difficulties faced by women writers who had not been allowed to reach their creative potential; her essay "Professions for Women" tells of the Victorian woman's struggles with the "Angel in the House." Feminist critics also attempt to expose hidden sexual biases in literary works and to help readers identify and question stereotypes of women. Feminist criticism of Emily Dickinson has revealed previously overlooked meanings in many of the poems. Almost all of the works in the Men and Women thematic unit could be subjects of gender criticism. For example, Kate Chopin's story describes a situation faced by a woman who lives in a world dominated by men, and the poems of Maya Angelou and Janice Mirikitani illustrate some of the new freedoms of women.

Gender criticism has not, however, been exclusively feminist criticism. In response to feminist criticism, other critics have begun to examine the impact of male authorship, the masculine point of view, and male stereotypes on literature. David Osborne in "Beyond the Cult of Fatherhood" examines the expanding roles of modern men. Gender criticism can shed new light on older works or influence new authors.

Deconstructionist Criticism

Like the formalists, the *deconstructionists* begin with a close reading of the text; however, the deconstructionists believe that textual explication is not enough. These critics believe that accurate readings of a work entail a distrust of both the language and the author. Such a reading may result in a discovery that the work has no organic unity and indeed no distinct boundaries. The deconstructionist critic views the work and the author with great skepticism and unravels the text in order to uncover hidden truths that even the author may not be aware of. For example, a deconstructionist critic might contend that the attitudes of other characters toward Othello reveal a racism beyond that directly stated in Shakespeare's play and perhaps beyond anything that Shakespeare himself had imagined. Deconstructionists attempt to expose the inability of the text to achieve closure or to reveal "objective" truth. In other words, deconstructionists claim that the work cannot validate itself.

Cultural Studies Criticism

Cultural studies criticism applies the methods of literary criticism to previously overlooked or undervalued areas of our common everyday culture. Cultural studies "reads," or critically analyzes, more than just literary texts; cultural studies critics examine both textual and nontextual subjects from beyond the scope of the literary canon. Semiotics (the science of signs) allows cultural critics to "read" common objects as texts in order to investigate the underlying meanings and assumptions that guide our day-to-day existence. For example, wearing blue jeans to the mall is now considered acceptable, whereas wearing blue jeans to church might be seen as disrespectful. Blue jeans still convey some of the rebel reputation they possessed during the 1950s, when blue-jean-wearing teenagers were often viewed as juvenile delinquents. The negative connotations have faded sufficiently so that blue jeans are common casual wear, yet enough of the old interpretation remains that few would find them acceptable in more formal situations. The people frowning at the teenagers wearing blue jeans in church are, in a way, performing a semiotic analysis of their clothing and reading them as disrespectful. Cultural studies critics are interested in how the underlying meanings of common objects and practices are created and conveyed. From fast food to fashion trends, from punk rock to hip-hop, from television commercials to romance novels, cultural studies calls into question the dividing lines between "high" and "low" art and literature while investigating the assumptions that shape our attitudes and behaviors.

When applied to literary texts, cultural studies analysis seeks to clarify the contexts in which any literary work is composed and understood. A critic analyzing Joyce Carol Oates' "Where Are You Going, Where Have You Been?" from a cultural studies perspective might investigate aspects of 1960s youth culture in the story such as rock 'n' roll, fashion, and teen slang in order to gain a deeper perspective of the character of Connie. A critic might utilize lyrics from rock songs of the time to illustrate the nature of the "glow of slow pulsed joy" that Connie feels when she listens to the music. Many popular songs of the period resonate with sexual double entendres, and Connie herself is beginning to explore a newfound sexuality as part of her defiance of parental authority. Further, a cultural studies critic might interpret Arnold Friend, with his promise of sexual violence coupled with an awkward use of teen slang and mock-worship of rock 'n' roll, as a representation of Connie's own insecurities and fears regarding her disavowal of her family's values and behaviors. In sum, a cultural studies critic is willing to go outside the boundaries of the text in order to explore the contexts in which a literary work is conveyed or portrayed.

Appendix B

WRITING ABOUT FILM

Americans go to the movies more than any other people in the world, spending over one billion dollars per year for admission tickets. Almost five hundred movies are released per year to the over 35,000 movie theaters in the country. The average American sees six films per year. You are probably very experienced in viewing movies. The Introduction of *Literature and Ourselves* speaks of the critical thinking that happens as you read a text. Your mind works the same way when you view a film: you engage with it, respond to it, analyze it, and then argue about it. Think about the last time you went to a movie with a friend or family member. As the closing credits were rolling, your mind was probably racing. This scene scared you; this stunt held you spellbound. If the film was an adaptation of a piece of literature that you had already read, you probably spent most of the movie writing a Comparison/Contrast paper in your head. Your internal dialogue perhaps ran like this: "that's not what the character would look like; that line is right from the book; that's not where it should be filmed; that scene is just like the description in the story."

Films affect us. Because they are a visual medium, they are immediately engaging. The volume and surround-sound of the darkened theater, combined with the computer-generated special effects, make them even more engaging. The images you see and the sounds you hear, whether they are sexy, heart-warming, inspiring, or frightening, haunt your memory for days. You want a kiss like that, a home like that. You are afraid to be alone at night. You hum the songs. A movie works its way into both your conscious and your subconscious mind. Thinking about what you are viewing and being affected by will make you a wiser, more careful consumer; it will also heighten your appreciation of the art of filmmaking. As an added bonus, the confidence you acquire in analysis will reassure you that you can interpret a text, be it film or literature.

The Elements of Film

The Introduction defines **analysis** as breaking something down into component parts in order to study the whole more deeply. The Introduction's review of the elements of Essay, Fiction, Poetry, and Drama improves your critical reading skills because you understand the individual techniques at a writer's disposal. The study of film begins with the same analytical step. The

1133

elements of film are numerous, far too many to review thoroughly here; fortunately, you do not have to be a Film Studies scholar to enjoy watching a film closely. The goal of this appendix is to offer a brief overview of the conventions of film so that you may view an adaptation more carefully and then argue more effectively about your opinions.

Auteur, Adaptation, and Actor

Literature has its essayists, fiction writers, poets, and dramatists. They are known for their particular gifts with the written word: their style; their tone; and their handling of theme, plot, setting, and character development. Cinema has its auteur, or filmmaker, the creative force behind the film. In American cinema, specific attention is almost always given to the director as auteur, although the director is frequently not the author of the screenplay. Steven Spielberg, Spike Lee, Ang Lee, Quentin Tarantino, Penny Marshall, George Lucas, and Sophia Coppola are names you may recognize. If you like "classic" films, you may also know the names Orson Welles and Alfred Hitchcock. Film Studies speaks of the signature "vision" of certain directors. Perhaps you know immediately that you are watching a Tarantino or Hitchcock movie because you recognize the special way those directors use the camera, manipulate light, or create atmosphere. If so, you are already familiar with the signature vision of the auteur.

A film can be an original screenplay, or it can be based on or adapted from a literary source. Adaptation means a composition recast into a new form. If you enjoy "Bloopers" and other behind-the-scenes movie footage, you already appreciate the artistic way that film offers its version of reality. You can think of an adaptation as an auteur's version of an author's version of reality. The medium of the written word is quite different from the medium of film. Ultimately, what the filmmaker creates is an interpretation of the piece of literature, the recasting of art from one medium into another. By taking a trip to your library or to the nearest movie rental store, you will find a great many "film versions" of literary works. These versions attempt to reproduce almost exactly the literary source. Especially popular with literature teachers, these films are versions of the works of authors usually considered "classic," such as Sophocles, William Shakespeare, Nathaniel Hawthorne, Ambrose Bierce, Kate Chopin, and William Faulkner. If you prefer to study adaptations that are based more loosely on the source or that are updated or changed in some way to appeal to contemporary audiences, your choices are vast. You may be acquainted with a good many of these adaptations, for example Robert Zemeckis' *Beowulf* (2007), based on the Anglo-Saxon poem *Beowulf*; Tim Burton's *Sleepy Hollow* (1999), based on Washington Irving's "The Legend of Sleepy Hollow"; Rob Minkoff's *Stuart Little* (1999), based on E. B. White's novel of the same name; Amy Heckerling's *Clueless* (1995), based on Jane Austen's *Emma*; and Barry Levinson's *The Natural* (1984), based on Bernard Malamud's novel of the same title.

Despite the decisive role that an auteur plays in creating an adaptation, you may recognize other names more easily than those of directors. In America, moviegoers pay a lot for "star" quality portrayal of character: Julia Roberts, Reese Witherspoon, and Will Smith reportedly can earn twenty to thirty million dollars per film. When moviegoers have already read the literary source, casting and characterization can become hot areas of debate because readers have expectations of what a character will look and act like. Perhaps you enjoy films that follow character description carefully. Some viewers applaud Oprah Winfrey's portrayal of Celie in Steven Spielberg's adaptation of Alice Walker's *The Color Purple* (1985) because they feel Winfrey's no-makeup appearance accurately reflects Walker's description of the character. Other viewers applaud the selection of Daniel Day-Lewis to play Hawkeye in Michael Mann's adaptation of James Fennimore Cooper's *Last of the Mohicans* (1992) precisely because Lewis does not fit any description of the character given in any of the five novels in which he appears.

Because casting decisions are so hotly debated, Film Studies textbooks often recommend that viewers keep in mind that literature and film are different mediums. Such texts suggest that moviegoers learn to appreciate film as a separate medium and to view the adaptation as a new piece of art, not as a poor copy of an original. When you note differences between the source's description of characters and an actor's physical appearance, mannerisms, and/or speech patterns, you may choose to focus on the ways in which those differences allow you to enjoy the character in a new way. Whether you prefer the new version or the old version, try to keep in mind what the director is attempting to portray. Ask yourself what the cinematic version of the character has to offer.

Cinematography

Broadly defined, cinematography refers to the art of filmmaking. While an understanding of all the intricacies of cinematography is certainly not necessary in order to write a strong argument about an adaptation, you will benefit from knowing a few important terms, such as those in italics in this section. In literature, point of view determines what readers know and what they do not know. In film, the camera achieves this feat: the auteur films the movie on meticulously designed sets, using certain lenses and film types and manipulating the camera in particular ways. The result is that the filmmaker is able to control what you see and even how you see it. Much more than in literary works, cinematic point of view manipulates you.

Consider framing and mise-en-scène. What you see when you watch a movie is simply the *frame*, the rectangular image projected on to the screen in a theatre. *Framing* refers to the auteur's craft of producing that frame, or image. Behind and beyond the frame is the set, either studio or on-location. *Mise-en-scène* is a French term that means "putting on stage," and it refers to everything that creates the image within the frame: sets, costumes, props, lighting, acting, and techniques of framing the image by aiming the camera. An auteur carefully considers every prop, every camera angle, every lighting effect so that you will see and be affected by only what the auteur has designed.

Next, consider the image created by an auteur's decisions concerning film and lens selection—decisions you yourself make if you like photography. Whereas slow film creates a clear, crisp image, fast film produces the grainy quality of some horror or dream sequences. Color film has its effect; black-and-white, another. A *zoom lens* is special lens whose focal length can be quickly changed. By using a zoom lens, a director can rapidly alter the size of an image or create the illusion of camera movement: the director can zoom in toward the object, creating the effect that the viewer is moving toward the object; the director can also zoom out, creating the effect that the viewer is moving away from the object. A *wide-angle lens* is a lens of short focal length. Selecting this type of lens allows the director to fit more into the frame. A *telephoto lens* is a lens of long focal length. With this lens, the director can create a large image of even the smallest detail.

An auteur's techniques in manipulating the camera also affect us. *High angle* camera work takes place when the camera is positioned high and aims downward. The resulting effect is usually that the subject filmed seems small, helpless, or powerless. A *low angle* shot, with the camera positioned low and aimed up, often gives the subject an air of magnitude, power, or evil intention. Also known as an establishing shot, a *long shot*, filmed with the camera far from the subject, allows you to view the entire character and much of the surroundings. Usually, the effect of this kind of camera work is that you feel oriented. A *medium shot* is created by moving the camera closer to the subject, with only immediate surroundings visible. This shot provides a view of the character from the waist or knees up. A *close-up* occurs when the camera closes in on the character. Several camera techniques create the sensation that you are actually in the scene. In a *traveling shot* the camera follows action, either by a track much like a train track or by any number of innovative means. The effect is that you seem to be moving also. A *crane shot* creates the illusion that you are hovering above the film's action; a *helicopter shot* gives you a bird's eye view, even allowing you to fly alongside characters with super powers and view the landscape below you. A *shot-reverse-shot* shows first the speaker and then the listener. A *point of view shot* forces you to see what the character sees, even if what the character sees is something you would prefer not to see, such as a headless body. Certain shots can mimic the movements of your head: a *pan shot* occurs when the camera is fixed but pans side to side, as if you are shaking your head "no"; a *tilt shot* occurs when the camera is fixed but tilts up and down, as though you are nodding "yes."

Sound and Special Effects

The Introduction covers many of the sounds and special effects, so to speak, at the writer's disposal: figurative language, imagery, rhythm, and rhyme. Some of these elements are immediately noticeable; others are not. Such elements often create the tone in a piece of literature and add to the overall theme. A film's atmosphere is created by mis-en-scène and camera techniques, but sound and special effects also play an important part. Sounds in a movie can be either *direct* or *post-dubbed* (recorded in a studio and added at the editing stage). Some sounds are immediately noticeable, and some are not. For example, most film audiences are very aware of *soundtracks*, the music used in movies during dialogue-free sequences. *Vocal elements* are sounds produced by the combined efforts of actors speaking lines and directors giving advice in order to achieve certain effects. These elements are quite noticeable: your favorite actor's voice can sound sleepily confused, threatening, sexy, or terrified. The *voice-over* technique allows a filmmaker the opportunity to use vocal commentary for any number of ends, and it is a very obvious sound effect. On the other hand, some *background music* is so unobtrusive that you may not even notice it. Some *sound effects* seem so natural—a slamming door, footsteps—that you may not even think about them. Such sound effects are important elements in creating the film's reality. Think about descriptive passages in literature. Adaptation presents such descriptions in a medium that is both visual and aural. You see and hear words brought to life. As you begin to listen carefully to films, you will be amazed at what you hear. The auteur has created an entire world of sound.

You may think of *special effects* as being the province of only the big-budget action and sci-fi movies: bad guys appear to melt into a pile of metal, characters morph into aliens, and the *Titanic* sails again. Yet, adaptations can showcase powerful special effects. Consider Zemeckis' *Beowulf*, Andrew Adamson's *The Chronicles of Narnia: The Lion, the Witch and the Wardrobe* (2005) and *Prince Caspian* (2008), Burton's *Sleepy Hollow*, Joe Johnston's *Jumanji* (1995), and the *Harry Potter* and *Lord of the Rings* films, all of which have captivating special effects.

Editing

Have you ever watched an entertainment show that focused on the reactions of actors as they emerged from the gala premiere of their own movie? Even the actors in an adaptation do not know exactly what the finished film will look like or what overall message it will ultimately convey until all the pieces are glued together in the process of editing. Technically speaking, *editing* is the means by which footage is assembled. *Footage* is the term for the shots taken during the filming, or production, stage. A *shot* is a photographic view or exposure that has not been edited in any way. During the editing stage, individual shots are arranged into sequences and scenes. A *sequence* creates the illusion of one continuous conversation or one continuous action. A *scene* is built by editing together shots that create the illusion that you are watching an action taking place continuously at one location. You will want to take note of editing that calls attention to itself. Flashbacks and crosscutting are editing techniques that you have probably noticed. A *flashback* is just what it sounds like: one minute you are in the movie's narrative present and the next you have flashed back in time. *Crosscutting* alternates between two different scenes. Editing techniques such as these are supposed to affect you. Once you begin to notice editing practices, you may never be the malleable viewer you were before. You will, however, probably be more appreciative of the many of decisions that took place on the other side of the camera so that the movie is as powerful as it is.

You are now ready to read the literary source and view the film so that you can write your paper. The following questions follow the pattern of those in the literary elements section of the Introduction. Their purpose is to assist you in preparing a strong argument about your film.

The Viewer's Box

Questions for Engagement, Response, and Analysis: Film

Auteur, Adaptation, and Actor

1. If you are familiar with other works directed by the auteur of the film you are studying, consider how this literary adaptation compares with those other works. What does this particular director bring to the film?
2. What does casting say about the filmmaker's decisions? Do characters look, sound, and act like the descriptions of their literary counterparts?

3. What do the actors bring to the adaptation? Consider their age, gender, race, previous roles, and any other aspects that you feel affect their present characterization.

4. Study the characters as they are developed in the film. For now, do not concern yourself with the literary counterpart; simply examine the characterization that you see before you. How would you describe the characters? Do they experience growth or change? How do they speak to the film's overall theme?

5. If the literary source is from another time and place, ask yourself whether you can see the influence of contemporary culture. Are contemporary values, gender ideas, or political concerns visible in the adaptation? For example, if the piece of literature was written by an author who used terms acceptable at that time that are now offensive, how did the filmmaker handle this situation?

Cinematography

1. What is the genre of this film? What do viewers expect from this genre? In what ways does the filmmaker meet and/or fail to meet genre expectations?

2. Is the literary source the same genre? What is the effect of the filmmaker's decision to adhere to or to break from the source's genre? What is the effect on the story's theme?

3. How does the filmmaker achieve the point of view? Consider film and lens choices, shot distances, and camera work. What is the effect of point of view in the film?

4. Did the filmmaker attempt to capture the literary work's point of view? What is the effect of that decision?

5. What are the settings in the film? Did the filmmaker attempt to create settings that in some way reflect the atmosphere of the literary source? Does the filmmaker take advantage of both studio and on-location filming? What is the effect of setting on plot, characterization, atmosphere, and/or theme?

6. Consider the mise-en-scène. What details add to the film's plot, character development, theme, and/or atmosphere? How?

Sound and Special Effects

1. Listen to the film. If need be, leave the room and listen from an adjoining room. In what ways does the filmmaker take advantage of auditory effects in order to achieve thematic or characterization development?

2. In what ways does the soundtrack add to the effects of cinematography? What does it add to plot, theme, atmosphere, and characterization?

3. To what degree does the filmmaker take advantage of sound elements in order to capture some aspect of the literary source? If the adaptation is markedly different from the literature that inspired it, what elements did the filmmaker use to ensure this separation?

Editing

1. Theme is the major idea, moral precept, or abstract principle underlying a literary piece. What themes does the film suggest? What cinematic elements convey the theme(s)?

2. How is the narrative told through editing? Is there a movement from exposition to rising action and crises to resolution? Are there flashbacks?

3. In what ways does editing affect character development, plot, atmosphere, and/or theme?

4. Whether the adaptation attempts to capture a great deal of the literary source or generally ignores it, does the film attempt to convey a similar theme?

Writing about Film

The Introduction focuses on crafting arguments about literature. Perhaps you have written a paper using the four steps suggested: Establishing Purpose and Audience; Generating a Working Thesis; Gathering Evidence; and Drafting, Revising, and Editing. If you have not yet read that part of the Introduction, you may want to do so now. The same basic processes—reconfigured a bit to accommodate a different medium—assist you in writing about a film adaptation. In preparing your paper, you may want to follow these three basic steps: Preparing to Watch the Film; Viewing a Film Critically and Generating a Thesis; and Drafting, Revising, and Editing the Paper.

Step One: Preparing to Watch the Film

You may never have thought about preparing to see a movie. You see the trailer or hear friends talk about a film, and you go. When you need to write a paper about a film, a bit of preparation will enhance your understanding of the movie and improve your argument as well, although the exact preparation will depend on timing and personal preference. If you have at least a few days before you need to view the film, you can begin studying the movie by researching prerelease and preview materials, interviews with directors and actors, and any critical commentaries. Find out the adaptation's genre. Often you can find a film's credits on the Internet; sometimes you can also find a version of the screenplay. Make as extensive a list of characters and scenes as you can so that you will already be familiar with names and know a bit about plot.

Exactly how you are planning to view the adaptation depends on the film's release status: DVD, dollar theater, or big screen. If you are allowed to select your own film, consider choosing one that has been released on DVD. Writing is a bit tricky when it focuses on a medium which by its very nature unwinds quickly past your eyes and involves you at such a deep emotional level. Unless you have a home theater, a film on DVD will not be as emotionally impacting, but it makes your work a bit easier. You can view the DVD as many times as needed, pausing any time you need to in order to catch a quote or write down a description of complex camera work. You can even allow yourself the pleasure of watching the film once before you ever begin any research so that you can enjoy the experience of surprise plot twists or altered endings. If the movie has been released to a dollar theater, you can at least afford to see it several times and still experience the big screen effect. Do not be discouraged if you are required to write about a movie that is coming out in theaters. Pay attention to the film's advertisements, interviews, and other prerelease promotional information so that you will know as much as possible about the film before arriving at the theater.

Step Two: Viewing a Film Critically and Generating a Thesis

Viewing a film critically can be challenging, especially in a movie theatre. When you read critically, you annotate and, perhaps, write in your journal. Taking analytical notes during a film is the equivalent of trying to write down your feelings while experiencing an amusement park ride in the dark. Relax. Having done your previewing homework, you already know the basics. Combine these basics with a few handy items, and your job at the theater is fairly simple. You will need a notepad, a couple of pens, and a tiny pen light. Sitting on the very back row will help ensure that you do not get involved in an altercation with an irate moviegoer. Whether you take notes at the theater or at home, a shorthand notation system will increase your chances of capturing what you need as the film races past you. You will find many examples in Film Studies textbooks, most of which simply either abbreviate terms or use a few letters from a cinematic term. You may choose to think up your own shorthand system. Think of this process as you would instant messages: instead of BFF and LOL, you can say CUS (close-up shot) and LAS (low angle shot).

What exactly do you need to note? No viewer can record every visual and auditory detail of every frame. Do not worry; you do not need every detail. Think about the steps in writing an argument about literature. Your goal is to mine the film for evidence to support your ideas, just as you mined the literature for the same purpose. You may want to turn back to Part Two of the Introduction to refresh your memory. Your first job, as always, is to follow the particulars of your assignment, meeting all requirements that your teacher provides for purpose or mode. Some popular assignments include movie reviews; historical, cultural, or gender studies; explications of particular scenes; character analyses; Comparison/ Contrasts of literary source and adaptation; and thematic arguments. The sample student paper at the end of this appendix is an argument that analyzes the symbolic meaning of water in an adaptation of a work from this anthology.

In general, the process of gathering evidence from a film for a paper that offers an argument is as follows. Because you first need a debatable topic, either perform your prewriting research or watch the film once without taking notes. Either activity combined with your familiarity with the literary source will probably prompt an idea. You may then want to do some prewriting work on that idea to move closer to your tentative thesis. Cluster or list ideas and as many details as you can recall. This prewriting work will help you know exactly what scenes you need to focus on carefully, what nuances of camera work you need to examine closely, what details of sound or special effects you want to note. Then watch the movie again, taking notes this time.

The primary source of your film paper is the movie itself. If your assignment requires secondary sources, those will include books, articles, reviews, or electronic sources that discuss your film. Your teacher and your school's librarian can help you locate good basic reference works such as *The Oxford Companion to Film, The Oxford Guide to Film Studies, The World Encyclopedia of Film, The Film Index,* and *Magill's Survey of Cinema.* Useful journals include *Film Quarterly, The Journal of Popular Film and Television, Film Criticism,* and *Cinema Journal.* Reliable Internet sources include the Internet Movie Database, All Movie Guide, Cinema Sites, and American Film Institute.

Step Three: Drafting, Revising, and Editing the Paper

Your main goal always is to follow your teacher's assignment. If your assignment allows a good deal of freedom in structuring your paper, you may want to make use of the following information. A common method for a film paper includes beginning with an introductory paragraph. You may want to open this paragraph with one of the stylistic devices covered in the Introduction and/or offer a very brief summary of the adaptation to acquaint your readers with the topic. You may also want to deal here with any opposing views. Often, the thesis is placed at the end of this introductory paragraph. Body paragraphs usually open with warrants–topic sentences that support the thesis, introduce the point of the individual paragraph, and link paragraphs together. Within the body paragraphs, you will need to develop each paragraph's claim with your own ideas and explanations, with evidence from the film, and (if the assignment calls for it) with research. End the paper by concluding your overall point, perhaps closing with flair by using one of the stylistic devices mentioned in the Introduction. Proof thoroughly, taking advantage of both the spelling and grammar checks on your computer and the tutoring center at your institution.

The bulleted list below offers a few guidelines concerning essays about film. You may also want to review the sample student paper at the end of this Appendix, as it includes examples of smoothly integrated quotations, internal documentation, and proper works cited format.

- Movie titles are underlined or italicized.
- The first time you mention a film's title, provide also the director's name and the year of release in parentheses right after the title.
- Movies are the collaborative work of many creative minds; refer to whomever you need to in order to make particular points. You can often find the full credit listing on the Internet—an important tool given the speed at which the credits roll once the "big names" are past.
- Give the filmmaker's entire name the first time you refer to him or her; afterward, use only the last name.
- Throughout your paper, use the literary present tense.
- Quote dialogue just as you would quote a character speaking in a piece of literature, being sure to anchor all quotes.
- When you first mention a character's name, also provide the actor's name in parentheses, being careful to differentiate between actor and character.

Films are powerful cultural "texts." They document the time and place of their creation, condemning or condoning everything from fashion to gender expectation to racial stereotype and recording a culture's likes and dislikes. Movies also affect us, establishing what is hot and what is not and transforming "unknowns" into overnight stars. Blockbusters, with their big budgets, big effects, big sounds, and big-name celebrities open to record audiences. *Harry Potter and the Prisoner of Azkaban* (2004) is reported to have earned more than ninety million dollars in its first weekend, *Harry Potter and the Goblet of Fire* (2005), more than one hundred million. You are watching the movies. You are paying the prices. Viewing carefully, with an appreciation for the elements of film, just makes sense.

Sample Student Essay

Business major Stephanie Minter was asked to read the selection from Frances Mayes' *Under the Tuscan Sun* located in the Family Unit of this anthology and then watch the adaptation. She was offered the opportunity to review both the novel in its entirety and relevant secondary sources. Then, Stephanie was asked to select a persuasive topic from this list of possible modes: an explication of a scene, a character analysis, a Comparison/Contrast of literary source and adaptation, or a study of a symbol of her choice. In all but the Comparison/Contrast approach, she was asked to focus on the cinematic version of Mayes' work. Stephanie chose to focus on the symbol of water, especially as it speaks to the development of the film's protagonist. Below is the essay that she prepared for this assignment.

Minter 1

Stephanie Minter

Professor Henderson

English 1102

1 May 2008

Under the Tuscan Sun

Audrey Wells' film *Under the Tuscan Sun* (2003) portrays the life of Frances Mayes (Diane Lane), a 35-year-old divorcee, through water, a necessity of life. Frances matures throughout the film from a scared, childlike woman into a full-grown, vibrant woman. Although the film is extremely different from Frances Mayes's biographical novel, several aspects were also brought into the comedic and romantic film such as the beautiful scenery, the magnificent Signor Martini, and even the exquisite culinary masterpieces. A connotative aspect of water is often biblical in the sense that water is used for baptismal purposes to

cleanse and give new life. Three specific instances
where water is present symbolize Frances's rebirth from
a childlike woman gradually into a more mature woman
through her own various trials and tribulations, a sort
of self-discovery. Water is used to symbolize the steps
necessary to moving on throughout the film. These
steps, however, take time.

Frances experiences a lot of grief after she
divorces her cheating husband, Tom. She, like her ex-
husband, expresses her childish ways in various forms.
Tom shows his immaturity through reliving his teenage
fantasies by committing adultery with a significantly
younger female. Frances expresses her lack of mature
development through a simple act involving water. In
the final scene in her San Franciscan home, a long
shot depicts Frances's maturity level as she picks up
a small blue vase from the table, empties the contents
(flowers), and pours the water all over the hardwood
floors in the foyer as she conspicuously looks around
and across the ceilings. Frances's act of intentionally dumping the water shows her immature actions
despite her actual age. This behavior shows that, as
in life, people must grow from specific events to
fully recover and resume a "normal" lifestyle again.
Upon the entrance into the Bramasole estate in Cortona, Italy, Frances walks into an antique faucet that
protrudes from the wall. This specific faucet symbolically portrays Frances' life in that when she first
appears in Bramasole, she is slightly harmed and taken
aback by the faucet (much as her husband's infidelity

took her by surprise). The framing of the faucet
centers it before Lane's character (Frances) even
enters the villa. As Frances appears from stage left,
she brushes against the spigot with her left shoulder.
Her attention is drawn to this faucet, this outlet of
a long-repressed force; it is as though the faucet is
a burden in dire need of being released and lifted.
Water and lack thereof represent one of the many steps
Frances must take in the stages of her recovery.

Through her upcoming challenges in the film, Frances
encounters many varied ups and downs in Italy. In a
humorous scene while in Rome, she introduces herself to
a handsome Italian named Marcello (Raoul Bora), who then
takes her to his family's hometown in Positano. This
lovely town is one of the country's most beautiful
peninsular cities. Frances is surrounded by breathtaking
oceanic views, only one of the many "painting-like
landscape[s]" the film captures, throughout her brief,
but most eventful, weekend getaway (Toscano, par. 2). The
panoramic framing of the natural landscape expands the
viewer's perception of the remarkable beauty of the
peninsula. The water is so abundant and changing, yet
ever powerful. Frances and Marcello's lust-filled weekend
proves to be just the medicine necessary to mend a broken
heart; unfortunately, the treatment proves also to be
temporary as she will soon after be filled with hurt
again. Throughout this time, the faucet in her Tuscan home
begins gradually to drip, symbolically showing Frances's
personal improvement in moving on with her life and her
gradual emergence as a new and stronger woman. The

dripping faucet is a sound element to the featured film.
Whether the sound is "direct" or "postdubbed" (recorded
then or added later), Frances first notices the nuisance
of a noise while she is in her library. This is a dramatic change from the fact that, when she first moved
into the rundown villa, the faucet showed no sign of
working just as Frances showed no sign of being able to
move on from her divorce. After this vast and exciting
incident (in the eyes of a remodeling homeowner), there
is a final step to be taken in order for Frances to be
like the woman she once was and to be fully recovered.

The final scenes of Under the Tuscan Sun are filled
with love, joy, and happiness; yet, Frances still feels
lonely and, in essence, unhappy in the romance department
of her life. In one of the scenes of the reception after
the wedding celebration of Chiara (Giulia Steigerwalt)
and Pawel (Pawel Szajda) a new character is introduced:
Ed (David Sutcliffe). Ed enters the mid-life fairy tale
while Frances, lying in her lawn chair, is absorbing all
the realities and celebrations she is experiencing and
has experienced. As he picks a ladybug off Frances's arm,
he introduces himself as a fellow writer who, long
before, received a poor review from Frances that motivated him to try again. Ed fatefully finds himself at the
little Tuscan villa and takes on the role, eventually, of
Frances's well-needed and desired male companion and soul
mate. The scenes lapse into celebration in the Tuscan
household at Christmastime where, surrounding the table,
there are all of the people who were necessary in the
full development of Frances' final character: Chiara,

Pawel, Patti (Sandra Oh), Alexandra, and most importantly, Ed. The scenes finally fade into the most symbolic finale—the faucet pouring water all over the tiled
floors. The shot begins with the framing focusing on the
splattering water on the floors, slowly pans over to
Frances's bare feet and the joyous sounds of Frances
giggling as the cold water floods over and around her
feet. The final shot centers the faucet as its main focal
point in a sort of medium shot. The concept that this
antique, almost 300-year-old faucet is now flooding the
tiled entryway captures the excitement and the changes in
Frances's life. Just as the faucet needed time to exert
the raging force it had held back for years, Frances's
timely progression into a woman who is now capable of
being, once again, romantically involved with another man
is measured through the changes of this faucet.

Despite the mediocre reviews received, *Under the
Tuscan Sun* thematically and visually evokes a great number
of viewers' arousals and connections with the cultural
compilations and with the artistic composition. Director
Audrey Wells symbolically uses water, a sign of cleansing
and new birth, to illustrate Frances's growth from the
shattered, naive woman she was before into a new and
improved woman. A "[s]impler but no less memorable
image . . . , a water faucet on the wall," acts as a
growth chart, emotionally and spiritually, for Frances's
rebirth (Putman, par. 4). Through time and various stages,
she becomes vibrant, alive, and outgoing once again just
as the faucet in her Bramasole villa becomes again a
source of life-giving water. Frances finds sadness, hurt,

and happiness through her interactions with water in her
San Franciscan home, in her sexual encounters at the
beaches of Positano, and in her glorious celebration of
the once unpromising antique faucet which, through the
times, the hopes, and the adventures surrounding it,
becomes functional. *Under the Tuscan Sun* is a classic
tale of Cinderella with a twist in which the damsel in
distress rescues herself, thus, recreating a self-
discovery through water.

Works Cited

Putman, Dustin. Rev. of *Under the Tuscan Sun* (2003). 14

    May 2004 <http://www.URL>.

Toscano, Tony. Rev. of *Under the Tuscan Sun* (2003). 14

    May 2004

    <http://www.rottentomatoes.com/click/movie-

    1125789/reviews.php?critic=columns&sortby=default&page

    =2&rid=1201299>.

Under the Tuscan Sun. Dir. Audrey Wells. Perf. Diane Lang,

    Sandra Oh, Lindsay Duncan, Vincent Riotta. 2003.

    Videocassette. Touchstone Pictures, 2004.

Under the Tuscan Sun. Internet Movie Database. May 2004.

    14 May 2004 <http://us.imdb.com/title/tt0328589>.

Appendix C

DOCUMENTING A RESEARCH PAPER: MLA FORMAT

When your teacher assigns a documented paper, first ask your teacher what documentation system you should use in your paper. Several excellent formats are available, some designed primarily for particular disciplines. Two of the most often used for papers in the humanities are *The MLA [Modern Language Association] Handbook for Writers of Research Papers* and *The Chicago Manual of Style*. In this text, the *MLA Handbook* will be the basis for documentation in the student essays. The MLA format is briefly summarized in this section. You might want to consult the *MLA Handbook* for more extensive information and more examples.

Documentation of Quotations, Paraphrases, and Summaries

Unless the information is common knowledge, you *must* document any information borrowed from other sources, whether quoted, paraphrased, or summarized. Any material quoted must be put in quotation marks, must be exactly like the original source unless ellipses or brackets (explained later in this appendix) are used, and must be clearly and correctly documented. Use quotations judiciously, and avoid back-to-back quotations. Most teachers prefer that no more than one-fifth of your paper be in quotation marks. To prevent your paper from becoming a string of quotations, you should develop the technique of blending paraphrase with short quotations. **Paraphrasing** is retelling the original material *in your own words*; if your paraphrase includes any of the original wording, those words must be put in quotation marks. In paraphrasing, be careful not to alter the author's tone or meaning. A paraphrase differs from a summary primarily in length: a paraphrase is about the same length as the original source, but a summary is a concise overview. Because paraphrases and summaries are based on ideas that are not your own, you must document them, making sure that the reader can tell where they begin and end, even though you are not quoting the author directly. Failure to do so is **plagiarism**, the academic equivalent of stealing. It is extremely important to remember that if you fail to document any ideas or words that you have borrowed from other sources—whether they are quoted, paraphrased, or summarized—you are guilty of plagiarism; and at the very least, your paper will receive a failing grade.

Parenthetical Citations

MLA format uses parenthetical in-text citations containing information that will lead your readers to the correct alphabetical entry on the Works Cited page and give them the specific page, paragraph, or screen for your reference.

You should always introduce your quotations, making sure that they connect with your sentences grammatically. One method of introducing quotations is simply to mention the speaker or writer:

> Prufrock repeats, "In the room the women come
>
> and go / Talking of Michelangelo" (Eliot 35–36).

You may also use a whole sentence followed by a colon to introduce a quotation:

> Walker's narrator realizes that her younger
>
> daughter is uncomfortable about Dee's visit: "Maggie
>
> will be nervous until after her sister goes: she will
>
> stand hopelessly in corners, homely and ashamed of the
>
> burn scars down her arms and legs, eying her sister
>
> with a mixture of envy and awe" (913).

If the material quoted is already in quotation marks, put a single quotation inside the double quotation marks:

> The woman "whose hands are gnarled by arthritis,"
>
> says, "'These same intellectuals tried to breed our
>
> mules! . . . we'd try to keep our faces serious but
>
> encouraging'" (Tan, "Young Girl's Wish" 650).

As these examples show, the *MLA Handbook* requires parenthetical citation immediately following a quotation, paraphrase, or summary. The citations correspond to titles listed on the Works Cited page at the end of the paper. After a paraphrase, the documentation precedes any appropriate punctuation. After quotations, the parenthetical documentation follows quotation marks and precedes terminal punctuation. If the final punctuation is a question mark or an exclamation point, some teachers prefer that you include the parenthetical documentation earlier in the sentence in order to avoid double terminal punctuation:

> The grandmother (O'Connor 1083) asks, "'You
>
> wouldn't shoot a lady, would you?'"

Your parenthetical citation must give the reader (1) enough information to locate the complete bibliographical information on the Works Cited page and (2) the exact page or line where the cited material appears in the source. If you are documenting Internet sources, your professor may direct you to use paragraph or screen numbers. Of course, if you are documenting a film or television show, you cannot include a page number, line, or paragraph. If the Works Cited page lists only one source by an author and the author's name has not already been mentioned in the sentence, your citation will consist of the author's last name and the page number. If the author's name has been given in the sentence, you need give only the page number. Notice that no comma appears before the page number. In paraphrases, an effective technique is to introduce the borrowed material with the author's name and to add the page number at the end of the borrowed material. This method lets the reader know exactly where the paraphrase begins. The following examples illustrate correct documentation where a paraphrase or quotation is introduced with the author's name:

> In Gilman's "The Yellow Wallpaper," the narrator
>
> implies that, although her husband loves her, he wants
>
> to tell her exactly what to do (277).
>
> Didion says, "Marriage is the classic betrayal"
>
> (44).

If the Works Cited page includes two or more works by the same author, your parenthetical citation must include a title. Long titles may be shortened. In the following examples, the full title is "A Good Man Is Hard to Find."

> O'Connor describes the Misfit: "He was an older
>
> man than the other two. His hair was just beginning to
>
> gray and he wore silver-rimmed spectacles that gave
>
> him a scholarly look" ("A Good Man" 1082).
>
> The grandmother says, "'If you would pray, . . .
>
> Jesus would help you'" (O'Connor, "A Good Man" 1085).

If you want to use information that is already quoted, you should first try to find the original source. If you cannot find the original, however, you may use the material by giving credit to both sources, as in the following example:

> James Russell Lowell decided to omit Thoreau's
>
> last sentence in The Maine Woods, which says, "It [the
>
> pine tree] is as immortal as I am, and perchance will
>
> go to as high a heaven, there to tower above me still"
>
> (qtd. in Matthews 251).

The complete bibliographical material on the Works Cited page would be listed under Matthews, not under Thoreau.

If your source has two or three authors, all last names are listed in the parenthetical citation; if there are more than three authors, the first author is listed followed by "et al.," meaning " and others."

> According to the article, "The group has a
> suspicious history" (McGee et al. 29).

If the source has no author, use its title. Thus, the citation should be as follows: ("Wife Is Not Convicted of Murder" B20).

If the work referred to has more than one volume, the volume number must be included: (Graves 1: 256).

If several works provide the same information that is being paraphrased, the documentation should give credit to all: (Graves 1: 256; Campbell 112; Hamilton 29). If more than three authors give the same information and it is not considered general knowledge, content notes are effective (see below).

Quoting Poetry

When you are quoting poetry, if you cite one or two lines, include the quotation in the text, using a slash to show where the line ended:

> In "A Prayer for My Daughter," Yeats wishes, "And
> may her bridegroom bring her to a house / Where all's
> accustomed" (74-75).

If you quote more than two lines of poetry, indent the quotation and set up the lines as the poet does:

> Yeats prays that his daughter will have beauty
> but know how to value it:
> May she be granted beauty and yet not
> Beauty to make a stranger's eye distraught,
> Or hers before a looking glass. (17-19)

Notice that citations to poetry list line rather than page numbers.

Quoting Religious Texts and Plays

When you quote from the Bible or similar religious texts and include parenthetical documentation, you should include the name of the book, the chapter, and the verse, for example (Job 42.12-17). Similarly, when you quote from Shakespearean plays and other long plays, you list act, scene, and lines: (Oth. 5.2.1-19). Note that *Othello* is underlined and abbreviated.

The longer names of books of the Bible are also abbreviated, but they are not underlined: (Matt. 5.3–16).

Quoting Electronic Sources

Electronic sources are documented in a variety of ways. If the electronic source has page numbers, you can include the page number. If it has paragraph or screen numbers, use them instead of page numbers: (Wilcox, "Buffy," par. 8). If the source has none of these, you may identify it by author or title alone, depending on how the source is alphabetized on the Works Cited page. Note that some professors may require that you print the electronic sources and number the paragraphs yourself.

Quoting Television and Film

If you are documenting a television show or film, you should include whatever information you used to alphabetize the Works Cited entry. For a television show, that is usually the title of the episode (in quotation marks) or of the program (underlined). Similarly, for a film, it is usually the title. However, if you are focusing throughout on a particular actor or on the director, you may have alphabetized by that name. Your parenthetical documentation may look like one of these: (*Apocalypse Now*), (Streep), or (Speilberg).

Long Quotations

If your quotation is long, more than four lines, you must indent it on the left. The indentation indicates that the information is quoted. Therefore, quotation marks are not needed unless the material quoted was already in quotation marks, as in the second example below. Note that in an indented quotation final punctuation precedes the parenthetical citation.

```
Capote's narrator says,

     This is our last Christmas together.

     Life separates us. Those who Know Best decide

     that I belong in a military school. . . . I have

     a new home too. But it doesn't count. Home is

     where my friend is, and there I never go.

     (105)

In "Thinking as a Hobby," Golding says,

     Then I would look up at the cupboard, where

     the naked lady was frozen in her panic and the

     muscular gentleman contemplated the hindquarters
```

```
of the leopard in endless gloom. I had noth-

ing to say to the headmaster....

    "Don't you ever think at all?"

    No, I didn't think, wasn't thinking, couldn't

think—I was simply waiting in anguish for the

interview to stop. (1022)
```

Note that quotation marks are necessary here because part of the passage is quoted in the source.

Remember that you must reproduce quotations *exactly* unless you indicate that changes have been made. Changes may be indicated by using ellipses or brackets.

If you omit something from a quotation, let the reader know by using ellipses (three spaced dots). If you omit a whole sentence, use four dots (three ellipses and a period). If you omit a line or more of poetry, include an entire line of spaced dots. Most teachers prefer that if you quote only a few words and make them a grammatical part of your sentence, you omit the ellipses. If the source that you are quoting already has ellipses, you should put your ellipses inside brackets.

```
    Greiner describes Frost's "An Old Man's Winter

Night" as "nothing if not a poem of despair, and . . . a

companion piece . . . to T. S. Eliot's equally fine

'Gerontion'" (231).

    Frost, in his poem "Out, Out—," personifies the

saw, saying,

    . . . At the word, the saw,

    As if to prove saws knew what supper meant,

    Leaped out at the boy's hand, . . .

    . . . . . . . . . . . . . . . . . . . . . . . . . . .

    Neither refused the meeting. (13-17)

    Gerber believes that Frost's "Home Burial" is

"modern in theme" (229).
```

Brackets are used to add information inside a quotation for clarification or grammatical correctness or to indicate that the original material contains an error:

When Kugelmass visits Persky the Great, Persky
"[removes] some old silk handkerchiefs that were
lying on [the cabinet's] top" (Allen 341).

The Latin word *sic* is used to indicate an error in quoted material.

The reporter accused the senator of "having
forgotten his principals [sic]" (Johnson A1).

Works Cited Page

On the Works Cited page, list alphabetically *all* sources for your paper.

Books

Basic citations for books include the following information if it is available
or applicable: author, title, editor, edition, place, publisher, publication date,
and volume. Examples of some book citations follow:

Book with One Author

Keillor, Garrison. *Happy to Be Here: Stories and Comic Pieces.*

New York: Atheneum, 1982.

Two or More Works by the Same Author

O'Connor, Flannery. *The Violent Bear It Away.* New York:
Farrar, Straus & Cudahy, 1960.

___. *Wise Blood.* 2nd ed. New York: Farrar, Straus &
Cudahy, 1962.

Work with Two Authors or Editors

Andrew, Malcolm, and Ronald Waldron, eds. *The Poems of
the Pearl Manuscript: Pearl, Cleanness, Patience, Sir
Gawain and the Green Knight.* Berkeley: U of California
P, 1979.

Work with More Than Three Authors or Editors

Abrams, M. H., et al., eds. *The Norton Anthology of English
Literature.* New York, W. W. Norton, 1968.

Work with Both Author and Editor

Webster, John. *The White Devil*. Ed. John Russell Brown.

　　Oxford: Manchester UP, 1968.

Work with a Translator

Mann, Thomas. *The Magic Mountain*. Trans. H. T. Lowe-Porter.

　　New York: Knopf, 1953.

An Introduction or Preface

Woollcott, Alexander. Introduction. *The Complete Works of*

　　Lewis Carroll. New York: Modern Library, n.d.

Notice the use of n.d. when the book does not include a publication date. Similarly, n.p. means no place or no publisher is given in the book.

Article or Story Printed as a Part of a Book

Money, Mary Alice. "The Undemonization of Supporting Char-

　　acters in *Buffy*." *Fighting the Forces: What's at Stake*

　　in Buffy the Vampire Slayer. Ed. Rhonda V. Wilcox and

　　David Lavery. Lanham, MD: Rowman and Littlefield,

　　2002. 98–107.

Poem, Story, or Article Reprinted in a Book

Kenny, Maurice. "Wild Strawberry." *Dancing Back Strong the*

　　Nation. Fredonia, NY: White Pine Press, 1981. Rpt. in

　　Harper's Anthology of 20th Century Native American

　　Poetry. Ed. Duane Niatum. New York: Harper and Row,

　　1988. 37–38.

Notice that when a work is published or reprinted as a part of a book, as illustrated in the two entries above, specific pages are given. Some professors prefer that you not include the information about the original publication, in which case the Works Cited entry would look like this:

Kenny, Maurice. "Wild Strawberry." *Harper's Anthology*

　　of 20th Century Native American Poetry. Ed. Duane

　　Niatum. New York: Harper and Row, 1988. 37–38.

Play in a Collection

Shakespeare, William. *Othello, the Moor of Venice*. *The*

   Complete Works of Shakespeare. Ed. David Bevington.

   4th ed. New York: Addison Wesley Longman, 1992.

Work of Several Volumes

Bullough, Geoffrey, ed. *Narrative and Dramatic Sources of*

   Shakespeare. 8 vols. London: Routledge and Kegan Paul,

   1966–1975.

One Volume of a Multiple Volume Set

Bullough, Geoffrey, ed. *The Comedies: 1597–1603*. London:

   Routledge and Kegan Paul, 1968. Vol. 3 of *Narrative*

   and Dramatic Sources of Shakespeare. 8 vols.

   1966–1975.

Periodicals

Basic citations for periodicals include the following information: author, article title, periodical name, series number or name, volume number (for a scholarly journal), publication date, and page numbers.

Article in a Scholarly Journal

Licala, Elizabeth. "Charles Clough's Dreampix." *Art in*

   America 80 (July 1992): 94–97.

Article from a Monthly Magazine

Barrett, Michael J. "The Case for More School Days."

   Atlantic Monthly Nov. 1990: 78, 80–81.

Article in a Weekly Magazine

Gates, David. "War and Remembrance." *Newsweek* 24 Sept.

   2007: 55–59.

Article from a Journal Found on Microfilm

Marston, Jane. "Epistemology and the Solipsistic Conscious-

   ness in Flannery O'Connor's 'Greenleaf.'" Microfilm.

   Studies in Short Fiction 21 (Fall 1984): 375–82.

Newspaper Article

Dart, Bob. "Long Road Home: Nothing Comes Easy in New

Orleans." *Atlanta Journal-Constitution* 19 Feb. 2006: A1.

CD-ROM

If you are documenting material that you found in full text form on a CD-ROM, use an entry like the following, taken from the Government Reporter section of SIRS, on your Works Cited page.

Grant, Agnes, and LaVina Gillespie. "Using Literature by

American Indians and Alaska Natives in Secondary

Schools." *ERIC Digest* Sept. 1992: n.p. *SIRS Government*

Reporter. CD-ROM. Social Issues Resources Series. May

1996.

Film, Videocassette, or DVD

A Works Cited entry for a film usually begins with the underlined title, then adds the director, distributor, and year of release. It may also include the names of the writer, performers, or producer. However, if you are referring to the contribution a particular person has made to the film—such as the director, the composer, or an actor or actress—you should put that person's name first. An entry for a videotape or DVD includes the same information but may add the release date and the medium.

Film

Bram Stoker's Dracula. Dir. Francis Ford Coppola. Columbia,

1992.

Videotape

Barnburning. Dir. Peter Werner. Prod. Calvin Scaggs. Ameri-

can Short Story Series. Videocassette. Monterey Home

Video. 1980.

DVD

Memoirs of a Geisha. Dir. Rob Marshall. 2005. DVD. Colum-

bia, 2006.

Electronic Sources

A wealth of material is also available on the Internet, from indexes to full text articles, accessible through the World Wide Web. In addition to the materials available through search engines, you may be able to access materials from other libraries such as the Library of Congress or the British Library, from any branch of the federal government, or from current news sources, such as CNN. To document sources that have previously been published but that you found through a Web source, first follow the directions for documenting the book or article. Then add the following information, when it is available or pertinent:

1. Name of the author or editor, if available
2. Title of work: in quotation marks if an article, a poem, or a short story; underlined if a book
3. Publication information if previously published, arranged as it would be if it were not on the Internet
4. Name of the database or professional site
5. Version number, if given
6. Date of the posting of the electronic publication
7. Name of the sponsor of the Web page (university or institution, for example)
8. Date on which the material was found during research
9. Electronic address of the source in angle brackets

Scholarly Database

Martinez, Z. Nelly. "Isabel Allende's Fictional World: Roads to Freedom." *Latin American Literary Review* 30.60 (July–Dec. 2002): 51ff. *Research Library.* GALILEO. ProQuest. Hightower Lib., Gordon College. 24 Jul. 2004 <http://proquest.umi.com Path: Isabel Allende>.

Short Work within a Scholarly Project

Heaney, Seamus. "Bogland." *Seamus Heaney.* Ed. Paul Jones. April 1997. University of North Carolina. 29 June 1998 <http://sunsite.unc.edu/ipa/heaney/bogland.html>.

Personal or Professional Site

Atwood, Margaret. "Spotty-Handed Villainesses." O. W. Toad, Ltd., 1994. 12 April 1998 <http://www.io.org-toadaly/vlness.htm>.

Oliver, Betty. Artworks. 29 October 2007 <http://www.spsu.edu/htc/bseabolt/artworks/artworks%20default.htm>.

Book

Austen, Jane. *Pride and Prejudice*. cit 1813. Ed. R. W.

Chapman. 23 Aug. 1998 <http://ftp://wiretap.area.com/

Library/Classic/pride.ja>.

Article in a Scholarly Journal

Churchill, Mary Faggan. "Alice Walker and Zora Neale

Hurston: The Common Bond." *MELUS* 22.3 (Fall 1997).

29 June 1998 <callisto.gsu.edu:4000/

QUERY:fel+1:Chkscreen+11:bad+html/>.

Bilger, Audrey. "Goblin Laughter: Violent Comedy and the

Condition of Women in Fanney Burney and Jane Austen."

Women's Studies 24.4 (1995): n.pag. 14 Feb. 1998

<http://www.cognito.com/0003/articles/00016736/16736229.htm>.

Online Posting

Blackmon, Samantha. "Human Element." Online posting. 4 May

2003. Computers & Writing Online. 3 Feb. 2005 <http://

www.cw-online.org/lists/cw-online/ archives. May

2003>.

Synchronous Communication

Thorne. Online discussion of *Literature and Ourselves*

Greeting." 2 Feb 2005. Nouspace. 3 Feb. 2005

<http:// nouspace.net:7000/5956>.

Home Page for a Course

Koch, Jr., Robert T. English 1102. Spring 2005. 1 Feb.

2005 <http://www.gdn.edu/faculty/rkoch/teach.htm-

pdf/e1102sHsp05.pdf>.

Unsigned Article in a Newspaper or on a Newswire

"Pathfinder Mission Reshaped Knowledge About Mars."

CNNinteractive 29 June 1998. 4 May 2005 <http://cnn.

com.TECH/space/9806/29/pathfinder.whatwelearned/>.

Article in a Magazine

VanBiema, David. "In Search of Moses." *Time* 14 Dec. 1998.

    16 Dec. 1998 <http://cgi.pathfinder.com/time/maga-

    zine/1998/dom/981214/cover1.htm>.

E-mail (Electronic mail)

Sample, Maxine. "Re: African Writers." E-mail to Sandra

    Waller. 1 July 2004.

Other Sources

There are many other sources of information, including computer software, television and radio programs, recordings, performances, works of art, letters, interviews, and films. Consult the *MLA Handbook* for complete details. Representative samples are shown here:

Personal Interview

Montgomery, Michael. Personal interview. 25 June 2007.

Works from One Book

If you are using several works from one book—for example, if you are writing a documented essay using one of the Casebooks in this textbook— you have a choice of three forms for the Works Cited page. You may give the complete information about the textbook in each entry, or you may include one complete entry for the textbook and list only the editor or editors and page numbers at the end of each additional entry. The first form would look like this:

Works Cited

Melton, Quimby, IV. "Greenleaf's Destructive Bull and Paean

    to the Common Man." *Literature and Ourselves: A Thematic*

    Introduction for Readers and Writers. 6th ed. Ed. Gloria

    Mason Henderson, Anna Dunlap Higgins, Bill Day, and San-

    dra Stevenson Waller. New York: ABLongman, 2009.

    1121-26.

Muller, Gilbert H. "Violence and the Grotesque." *Nightmares*

    and Visions: Flannery O'Conner and the Catholic

    Grotesque. Athens: U of Georgia P., 1972. Rpt. in

    Literature and Ourselves: A Thematic Introduction for

    Readers and Writers. 6th ed. Ed. Gloria Mason Henderson,

Anna Dunlap Higgins, Bill Day, and Sandra Stevenson
Waller. New York: ABLongman, 2009. 1111-17.

O'Connor, Flannery. "Greenleaf." *The Complete Stories*. New
York: Noonday Press, 1998. 311-34. Rpt. in *Literature
and Ourselves: A Thematic Introduction for Readers and
Writers*. 6th ed. Ed. Gloria Mason Henderson, Anna Dun-
lap Higgins, Bill Day, and Sandra Stevenson Waller.
New York: ABLongman, 2009. 1088-1105.

The same Works Cited page using the second form would look like this:

Works Cited

Henderson, Gloria Mason, Anna Dunlap Higgins, Bill Day, and
Sandra Waller, eds. *Literature and Ourselves: A
Thematic Introduction for Readers and Writers*. 6th ed.
New York: ABLongman, 2009.

Melton, Quimby, IV. "Greenleaf's Destructive Bull and Paean
to the Common Man." Henderson, Higgins, Day, and
Waller 1121-26.

Muller, Gilbert H. "Violence and the Grotesque." *Nightmares
and Visions: Flannery O'Conner and the Catholic
Grotesque*. Athens: U of Georgia P., 1972. Henderson,
Higgins, Day, and Waller 1111-17.

O'Connor, Flannery. "Greenleaf." *The Complete Stories*. New
York: Noonday Press, 1998. 311-34. Henderson, Higgins, Day, and Waller 1088-1105.

If your professor does not require the original publication information,
your Works Cited page would look like this:

Works Cited

Henderson, Gloria Mason, Anna Dunlap Higgins, Bill Day, and
Sandra Stevenson Waller, eds. *Literature and
Ourselves: A Thematic Introduction for Readers and
Writers*. 6th ed. New York: ABLongman, 2009.

Melton, Quimby, IV. "Greenleaf's Destructive Bull and Paean

    to the Common Man." Henderson, Higgins, Day, and

    Waller 1121-26.

Muller, Gilbert H. "Violence and the Grotesque." Henderson,

    Higgins, Day, and Waller 1111-17.

O'Connor, Flannery. "Greenleaf." Henderson, Higgins, Day,

    and Waller 1088-1105.

If you use either of the first two forms, any reference to materials written by the editors of the text would look like this: (Henderson, Higgins, Day, and Waller xxx–xxx).

Note that when a work has more than three authors, you may list all of them or you may list the first author followed by a comma and et al. as in the following example.

Henderson, Gloria Mason, et al, eds. *Literature and*

    Ourselves: A Thematic Introduction for Readers and

    Writers. 6th ed. New York: ABLongman, 2009.

If you use this form, your parenthetical citation would look like this: (Henderson et al. 234).

You should select the parenthetical documentation to match the form used in your Works Cited page.

Content Notes

You may use content notes to add information that you would like the reader to know but that would interfere with the flow or organization of your paper. Content notes do not, as a rule, give documentation, but if you are citing so many sources that listing them in the text would be awkward, you could list them in content notes instead. Also, if the content note itself includes a quotation, give the citation and list the source in the Works Cited page. Include the notes on a separate page before the Works Cited page. Indicate notes in the text with consecutive numbers one-half space above the line, like this:[1] On the Content Notes page, indent the first line of each note and precede it with a raised number corresponding to the number in the text.

Some examples of content notes follow:

Acknowledgments

[1]The author would like to thank Maxine Sample for lending her essential materials on Alice Walker.

Comparison

[2]Cf. Carlos Baker's comment on Hemingway's return (121–22).

Note: Baker must be listed on the Works Cited page. (The abbreviation "cf." means "compare.")

[3]Similar opinions are expressed by Marcus (123–27), Johnston (14–19), and Wilcox (211–21).

Exceptions to Prevailing Point of View

[4]Wilson disagrees with this interpretation (198–203).

Glossary

Allegory A work in which concrete elements such as characters, objects, or incidents represent abstract qualities. This form of writing is often used to teach religious principles or ethical behavior or to espouse political agendas. Allegories were very popular in the Middle Ages. The play *Everyman* and Dante's *Divine Comedy* are examples. A more modern allegory is George Orwell's *Animal Farm*.

Alliteration Repetition at close intervals of consonant sounds in phrases or lines of poetry: for example, "*b*end / Your force to *b*reake, *b*low, *b*urn, and *m*ake *m*e new."

Allusion An indirect reference to literature, a historical event, a famous person or character, or a work of art.

Anagnorisis In tragedy, the point at which a character reaches recognition, discovery, or self-awareness; the change from ignorance to knowledge.

Analogy Comparison of things otherwise thought to be dissimilar; point-by-point comparison.

Analysis Examination of a subject by separating it or breaking it down into parts.

Anaphora Rhetorical device that repeats a word, phrase, or clause at the beginning of consecutive sentences. For an example, see Elizabeth Barrett Browning's Sonnet 43, lines 7–9.

Antagonist An opposing force or character; that element which opposes or clashes with the main character or protagonist.

Apostrophe An address to a real or fictional person or thing.

Archetype A prototype (situation, character, image, or action) or model on which all others are patterned; a pattern that appears repeatedly in literature, such as a legend, quest, or situation.

Aside A dramatic device in which a character delivers a short speech or remark to the audience. This remark usually reveals the speaker's emotions or thoughts; the assumption is that no one except the audience can hear the remark.

Assonance Repetition at close intervals of similar vowel sounds in phrases or in lines of poetry; for example, "I love thee to the d*e*pth, and br*ea*dth and height / My soul can r*ea*ch, when f*ee*ling. . . ."

Blank verse Unrhymed poetry in iambic pentameter (ten syllables with the stress on every second syllable).

Blocking Grouping and arranging action and characters on stage.

Caesura A natural, strong pause within a line of poetry.

Character A person in a work; the personality traits or qualities of that person.

Characterization Development and presentation of the personality of a character, usually through actions, speech, reputation, appearance, and the author's attitude toward this person.

Claim A thesis statement; a debatable proposal; a judgment about what must, should, or needs to be done; a controversial statement in an argument; a statement that has a counterclaim.

Classification Organization according to a methodical division into groups or clusters; the system of grouping or arranging.

Climax The moment of greatest excitement, interest, or tension before the resolution of a play or narrative; a turning point.

Comedy A literary work, usually a play, that ends happily and that often includes humor and laughter.

Complication A plot stage in which a conflict appears; a part of the rising action of the narrative.

Concession An acknowledgment that the opposition in an argument has a good or strong point.

Conflict The opposition between protagonist and antagonist in a play or narrative; the opposition between the protagonist and another force, either within him- or herself or without, e.g., between the person and the environment, the person and society, or the person and the cosmic.

Connotation Suggestive, implied, or emotional meaning of a word or phrase.

Consonance Repetition of consonant sounds in a line of verse either at the beginning of or within the words.

Counterclaim An argumentative statement made by those who oppose your thesis or claim; some argumentative essays include at least one counterclaim showing respect for the opposition.

Couplet A pair of consecutive rhymed lines in verse. A closed couplet has two self-contained, rhymed lines that express a complete thought. An open couplet contains two rhymed lines that do not form a complete thought. A heroic couplet consists of a closed couplet in iambic pentameter.

Crisis A turning point or crucial moment in literature when the protagonist has to make a decision or resolve friction; crisis and climax may arrive at the same time or at entirely different times.

Denotation The dictionary, literal, or exact meaning of a word.

Denouement A French term meaning resolution or settlement of loose ends; the untangling of the plot.

Dialect Speech or speech patterns of a particular region, occupational or social group, or culture. Dialect is usually perceived as deviating from "standard" speech.

Dialogue Conversation between at least two characters.

Diction An author's choice and arrangement of words and phrases.

Dramatic foil In drama, a character who sets off or intensifies the qualities of another character through a marked contrast.

Dramatic irony Marked difference in knowledge between the audience and a character in the play. The audience understands the meaning of certain words or events that the character does not understand. The most famous example of dramatic irony appears in Sophocles's *Oedipus the King*.

Dramatic monologue Poem spoken by one person but addressed to one or more listeners, revealing the speaker's character.

Dynamic Term used to refer to a character who undergoes a change in personality or behavior by the end of the literary work.

Elegy Lyric poem meditating on or celebrating a death.

Enjambment The running on of one line of poetry to the next line without end punctuation.

Epic A long narrative poem written in a dignified style on a majestic theme, relating the exploits of a national hero.

Epigram A short, witty poem or saying that makes a satirical point.

Epiphany In literature, a sudden manifestation or revelation of meaning; an instinctive perception of reality.

Epistolary Written in the form of a letter; poetry or fiction composed as one or more letters.

Ethos Appeal to ethics.

Evidence In literary argumentation, the passages from the primary source and/or the secondary source(s) that support the warrants, and help to prove the overall claim.

Exposition The beginning or opening of a play or a story; the introduction of characters, conflicts, and other information important to the reader.

Fable A short narrative that usually teaches a moral; a short story that has an uplifting message. Fables often use animals to make a point.

Fiction An imaginative narrative such as a short story or novel.

Figurative language Language not taken literally; image conveyed through nonliteral language, such as with a metaphor or simile.

Film *See* definitions and explanations in Appendix B.

First-person point of view Narration using *I* or *we*. *See* unreliable narrator.

Flashback A break in the chronological presentation of a story to return to the past or to an earlier episode.

Flat character A character who is not fully developed; the character is often one-dimensional.

Foil A character who, through sharply defined opposing traits, emphasizes the characteristics of another; a foil is usually a minor character.

Foot In poetry, a unit of stressed and unstressed syllables or heavy and light stresses. The metrical patterns include the following: *Anapest*: two unstressed syllables followed by one stressed syllable. *Dactyl*: a stressed syllable followed by two unstressed syllables. *Iamb*: an unstressed syllable followed by a stressed syllable. *Trochee*: a stressed syllable followed by an unstressed syllable. *Spondee*: two stressed syllables.

Foreshadowing Hints or clues that help to predict a later event.

Genre Literary type or kind of literature; the four most general kinds are fiction, drama, poetry, and nonfiction. Genres can be further subdivided, such as nonfiction into the essay or the autobiography, and fiction into the novel or the short story.

Hamartia The Greek term for the hero's flaw in character or for an error in judgment leading to the hero's downfall.

Hubris Excessive pride.

Hyperbole Figurative language that uses exaggeration for effect: for example, "It's raining cats and dogs."

Image A mental or visual impression that employs an appeal to one of the five senses.

Imagists Poets and other artists belonging to a movement that rebelled against Romanticism in the early 1900s. These artists focused on free verse (unrhymed verse without a metrical pattern) and imagery.

Initiation story A narrative in which a character undergoes some ordeal that leads to maturity.

Irony Contradiction; discrepancy or contrast between what is implied and what is real. Verbal irony is the use of words to impart double or opposite meanings. Situational irony relates to an event that turns out contrary to what is expected. *See also* dramatic irony.

Logos Appeal to logic.

Lyric A short poem expressing the emotions of the writer or singer. In the past, a lyric was usually accompanied by the lyre, a musical instrument.

Metaphor Figure of speech that uses an implied comparison between two distinctly different things; one term is defined in relationship to another term: for example, life is a cabaret.

Metaphysical poets A group of seventeenth-century English poets (especially John Donne and Robert Herrick) whose works are characterized by incredible and subtle imagery.

Meter The rhythm or beat of verse; a measured pattern of stressed and unstressed syllables. *See also* foot.

Metonymy Figurative language that uses a closely associated attribute to represent the thing itself. For example, the White House often symbolizes the president of the United States.

Monologue A long speech by a person or character to the audience, to a character not present, or to him- or herself.

Motivation The reason a character behaves, talks, or becomes what he or she is; the driving force or forces behind a character's actions.

Mystery A narrative whose plot involves the solution of a puzzle or crime and usually creates suspense.

Narration A story, fictional or nonfictional; the process of telling a story.

Narrator The teller of a story or novel.

Nonfiction novel A novel that deals with real rather than fictional characters or situations.

Novel A long work of fiction with a complex plot.

Objective point of view The simple reporting of observable events, similar to unbiased newspaper reporting.

Octave An eight-line stanza or the first eight lines of a sonnet.

Ode A long lyrical poem addressing or exalting a person or object using a distinguished style and elaborate format.

Omniscient point of view Literally all-knowing point of view whereby the author can recall the thoughts and actions of all characters and can be in several places at one time.

Onomatopoeia The use of words that sound like the actions they name; for example, *splash* or *buzz*.

Oxymoron A figure of speech that joins two words with contradictory meaning; for example, a heavy lightness or a thunderous silence.

Parable A short story that illustrates a moral or religious lesson.

Paradox A seemingly contradictory or unbelievable statement that, upon reflection, reveals a truth.

Parody A satirical or humorous imitation of another work; a literary work that imitates the style of another work; ridiculing something through imitation.

Pathos Appeal to emotion.

Peripeteia A sudden reversal of the protagonist's fortune.

Personification Figurative language giving an inanimate object, animal, or abstraction human characteristics; for example, the jungle swallowed him.

Plot The sequence of events in a narrative. Elements of plot include exposition, conflict/complication, climax, and resolution/denouement.

Poem An arrangement of written or spoken words in lines with or without rhyme or meter and typically using figurative language.

Point of view The perspective from which a story is narrated.

Primary source The text (essay, short story or novel, poem or play) that the writer is concentrating on, writing about, or discussing.

Props, properties Furniture or other movable articles in a play.

Protagonist The main or central character in fiction or drama.

Pun Rhetorical device humorously using a word or words with different meanings but with similar sounds; sometimes referred to as a play on words.

Quatrain A four-line stanza of poetry.

Quintet A five-line stanza of poetry.

Resolution *See* denouement.

Rhetorical question A question that does not require an answer; a question that is asked for effect or to make a point.

Rhyme In poetry, the repetition of sounds at the ends of lines or within lines.

Rhythm Pattern of stressed and unstressed sounds in poetry.

Round character A character who is fully developed; a multidimensional character.

Satire A literary work that ridicules some aspect of society or some human folly or vice. Horatian satire is light, humorous satire in which the author often makes fun of himself as well as his society. Juvenalian satire is harsh, bitter, biting satire.

Satirist A person who writes satires.

Secondary source Anything that is written about a text that is under study or concentration.

Sestet A six-line stanza or the last six lines of a Petrarchan sonnet, which usually rhyme *cde, cde.*

Set The scenery and properties on the stage.

Setting The time, place, and physical and cultural environment of a story, play, or poem.

Simile Figure of speech that compares two distinctly different things using the words *as* or *like.*

Situation The details of who is talking to whom and why.

Soliloquy A stylistic technique in which a character voices thoughts aloud to the audience.

Sonnet A fourteen-line poem in iambic pentameter.

Speaker The person who speaks in a poem.

Sprung rhythm A highly irregular metrical pattern developed by English poet Gerard Manley Hopkins. A metrical foot may consist either of a single stressed syllable or of a stressed syllable followed by one or more unstressed syllables; for example, "Oh, morning at the brown brink eastward springs—"

Stage directions Instructions given by the playwright to the stage manager, director, actors, and all others involved in the production of a play.

Static A term used to refer to a stereotypical, simplified character who fails to grow or change in personality or behavior by the end of the work.

Stereotype A fixed or traditional conception of a person, group, or idea held by a number of people without allowing for individuality.

Style The manner in which the author expresses himself or herself. Style includes diction, tone, syntax, and figurative language.

Symbol An object, person, or action that suggests something else, usually a feeling or abstract quality.

Symbolism The use of symbols in a literary work.

Synaesthesia Concurrent responses to senses; blending of two or more senses, as in "green-black smear of smell" or "a sweet cold silver noise."

Synecdoche A figure of speech in which the whole stands for a part (e.g., Italy defeated France, for soccer teams) or a part stands for the whole (e.g., wheels for a car).

Syntax Sentence structure and word order; planned arrangement of words to show relationships.

Terza rima A stanza form utilizing three-line units (tercets) with interlocking rhymes; *aba, bcb, cdc, ded,* and so forth.

Theater of the absurd Drama movement of the mid-twentieth century that used absurd, inconsistent, often meaningless situations and conversations expressing existentialism or isolation.

Theme Major idea, moral precept, or abstract principle underlying a work; the main idea expressed in a work of literature.

Thesis The claim or central idea of an essay, usually expressed in one sentence in the introduction and then developed in the body paragraphs.

Third-person-limited point of view Narration of a story in the third person strictly limited to the thoughts and perceptions of a single character.

Tone The attitude of author, speaker, and/or narrator toward the subject or situation of a literary work; for example, ironic, nonchalant, humorous, melancholy, objective, or sarcastic.

Tragedy A play (or other work) showing the protagonist in an internal or external struggle that eventually leads to his downfall or ruin; a work in which the protagonist goes from happiness to misery.

Tragic hero or heroine Protagonist in a tragedy who, according to Aristotle, must be basically good but flawed, must be aristocratic, must be believable, and must behave consistently. Modern tragic heroes and heroines do not always fit Aristotle's definition; in particular, they are often working-class people.

Unreliable narrator The teller of a story whose narration is biased or limited.

Warrant The reasons for the writer's position, stated so that the warrant may be supported with evidence from the literature; topic sentence.

Credits

FAMILY

Essays

"On Going Home," from *Slouching Towards Bethlehem* by Joan Didion. Copyright © 1966, 1968, renewed 1996 by Joan Didion. Reprinted by permission of Farrar, Straus and Giroux, LLC.

"Dr. Spock Never Promised Us a Rose Garden," "My Wife's Clean Hands," and "Tales from the Funny Farm", from *Fatherhood* by Bill Cosby. From FATHERHOOD by Bill Cosby, copyright © 1986 by William H. Cosby, Jr. Used by permission of Doubleday, a division of Random House, Inc.

"*Bramare:* (Archaic) To Yearn For," from *Under the Tuscan Sun,* © 1996 by Frances Mayes. Used with permission of Chronicle Books LLC, San Francisco. Visit ChronicleBooks.com.

Fiction

"A Domestic Dilemma," from *The Ballad of the Sad Café and Collected Short Stories* by Carson McCullers. Copyright © 1936, 1941, 1942, 1950, 1951, © 1955 by Carson McCullers, renewed 1979 by Floria V. Lasky. Reprinted by permission of Houghton Mifflin Company. All rights reserved.

"Sonny's Blues," © 1957 by James Baldwin was originally published in *Partisan Review.* Copyright renewed. Collected in *Going to Meet the Man,* published by Vintage Books. Reprinted by arrangement with the James Baldwin Estate.

"A Christmas Memory," from *A Christmas Memory* by Truman Capote, copyright © 1956 by Truman Capote. Used by permission of Random House, Inc.

"Where Are You Going, Where Have You Been?" by Joyce Carol Oates. Copyright © 1970 Ontario Review. Reprinted by permission of John Hawkins & Associates, Inc.

"Because My Father Always Said He Was the Only Indian Who Saw Jimi Hendrix Play *The Star Spangled Banner,*" from *The Lone Ranger and Tonto Fistfight in Heaven* by Sherman Alexie. Copyright © 1993 by Sherman Alexie. Used by permission of Grove/Atlantic, Inc.

Poetry

"A Prayer for My Daughter," reprinted with the permission of Scribner, an imprint of Simon & Schuster Adult Publishing Group, from *The Collected Works of W.B. Yeats, Volume 1: The Poems, Revised,* edited by Richard Finneran. Copyright © 1924 by The Macmillan Company; copyright renewed © 1952 by Bertha Georgie Yeats.

"My Papa's Waltz," copyright 1942 by Hearst Magazine, Inc., from *The Collected Poems of Theodore Roethke* by Theodore Roethke. Used by permission of Doubleday, a division of Random House, Inc.

"The Mother" by Gwendolyn Brooks. Reprinted by consent of Brooks Permissions.

Drama

Casebook on August Wilson

MEN AND WOMEN

Essays

Fiction

Poetry

"Why Do People Become Terrorist" from *Global Terrorism: A Beginner's Guide* by Leonard Wineberg pp. 82-85. Oneworld Publications, 2005. Reprinted by permission of the publisher.

Fiction

"The Lottery Ticket" from *The Wife and Other Stories* by Anton Chekov, translated by Constance Garnett (1862-1946) in 1918.

"A Rose for Emily," copyright 1930 and renewed 1958 by William Faulkner, from *Collected Stories of William Faulkner* by William Faulkner. Used by permission of Random House, Inc.

"Dead Men's Path," from *Girls At War and Other Stories* by Chinua Achebe, copyright © 1972, 1973 by Chinua Achebe. Used by permission of Harold Ober Associates Incorporated and Doubleday, a division of Random House, Inc.

"The Management of Grief," from *The Middleman and Other Stories* by Bharati Mukherjee. Copyright © Bharati Mukherjee, 1988. Reprinted by permission of Penguin Group (Canada) and Grove/Atlantic, Inc.

"Newsworld" from *Newsworld* by Todd James Pierce, © 2006. Reprinted by permission of the University of Pittsburgh Press.

Poetry

"If We Must Die," from *Selected Poems of Claude McKay* (Harcourt Brace, 1981), by Claude McKay. Reprinted by permission of Archives of Claude McKay, Carl Cowl, Administrator.

"Dulce et Decorum Est," by Wilfred Owen, from *The Collected Poems of Wilfred Owen,* copyright © 1963 by Chatto & Windus, Ltd. Reprinted by permission of New Directions Publishing Corp.

"Buffalo Bill's Defunct," "anyone lived in a pretty how town," copyright 1923, 1951, © 1991 by the Trustees for the e. e. cummings Trust. Copyright © 1976 by George James Firmage, "anyone lived in a pretty how town". Copyright 1940, © 1968, 1991 by the Trustees for the e. e. cummings Trust, from *Complete Poems: 1904–1962* by e. e. cummings, edited by George J. Firmage. Used by permission of Liveright Publishing Corporation.

"The Death of the Ball Turret Gunner," from *The Complete Poems* by Randall Jarrell. Copyright © 1969, renewed 1997 by Mary von S. Jarrell. Reprinted by permission of Farrar, Straus and Giroux, LLC.

"Do Not Go Gentle Into That Good Night," from *Dylan Thomas: Poems of Dylan Thomas* by Dylan Thomas. Copyright 1945 by The Trustees for the Estate of Dylan Thomas. Reprinted by permission of David Higham Associates LTD and New Directions Publishing Corp.

"Forgetfulness," from *Questions About Angels*, by Billy Collins, © 1991. Reprinted by permission of the University of Pittsburgh Press.

"On the Subway," from *The Gold Cell* by Sharon Olds, copyright © 1987 by Sharon Olds. Used by permission of Alfred A. Knopf, a division of Random House, Inc.

"Last Service" from *Raising the Dead* by Ron Rash. Originally published in Southwest Review. Reprinted by permission of the author.

"Try to Praise the Mutilated World," from *Without End* by Adam Zagajewski, translated by Clare Cavanagh. Copyright © 2002 by Adam Zagajewski. Translation copyright © 2002 by Farrar, Straus and Giroux, LLC.

Drama

Othello, the Moor of Venice from *The Complete Works of Shakespeare*, Fourth Edition, edited by David Bevington. Copyright © 1992 by Addison Wesley Longman. Reprinted by permission of Pearson Education, Inc.

Casebook on Amy Tan

"Young Girl's Wish," copyright © 1995 by Amy Tan. First appeared in *The New Yorker*. Reprinted with permission of the author and the Sandra Dikjstra Literary Agency.

"Heart," from *The Bonesetter's Daughter* by Amy Tan, copyright © 2001 by Amy Tan. Used by permission of G.P. Putnam's Sons, a division of Penguin Group (USA) Inc.

"Amy Tan: A Critical Companion," pages 19–31 and 113–121 from *Amy Tan: A Critical Companion* by E.D. Huntley. Copyright © 1998 by Greenwood Publishing Group. Reprinted by permission of Greenwood Publishing Group.

"Chinese American Women, Language, and Moving Subjectivity," by Victoria Chen from *Modern Critical Views, Amy Tan*, edited by Harold Bloom.

The Salon Interview: Amy Tan, The Spirit Within. This article first appeared in Salon.com, at http://www.salon.com. An online version remains in the Salon archives. Reprinted with permission.

FREEDOM AND RESPONSIBILITY

Essays

"Letter from Birmingham City Jail," reprinted by arrangement with the Estate of Martin Luther King Jr., c/o Writers House as agent for the proprietor New York, NY. Copyright 1963 Martin Luther King Jr., copyright renewed 1991 Coretta Scott King.

Fiction

"The Parable of the Prodigal Son" Luke 15: 11-32.

"Harrison Bergeron," from *Welcome To The Monkey House* by Kurt Vonnegut, Jr, copyright © 1961 by Kurt Vonnegut Jr. Used by permission of Dell Publishing, a division of Random House, Inc.

"The Ones Who Walk Away from Omelas," from *The Wind's Twelve Quarters* by Ursula K. LeGuin. Copyright © 1973 by Ursula K. LeGuin; first appeared in *New Dimensions 3*. Reprinted by permission of the author and the author's agent, Virginia Kidd.

"A&P," from *Pigeon Feathers And Other Stories* by John Updike, copyright © 1962 and renewed 1990 by John Updike. Used by permission of Alfred A. Knopf, a division of Random House, Inc.

"Customs of the Country" from *Barking Man and Other Stories* by Madison Bell, © 1988 by Madison Bell Ticknor and Fields, 1990, first published in Harper's Magazine. Used by permission of the Author.

Poetry

"The Unknown Citizen", copyright 1940 & renewed 1968 by W.H. Auden, "Musee des Beaux Arts", copyright 1940 & renewed 1968 by W.H. Auden, from *Collected Poems* by W.H. Auden. Used by permission of Random House, Inc.

"The Conscientious Objector," © 1978 Estate of Karl Shapiro c/o Wieser & Elwell, Inc., New York.

Drama

Casebook on Tim O'Brien

CREATIVITY

Essays

"Metaphors" from *Crossing the Water* by Sylvia Plath. Copyright © 1960 by Ted Hughes. Reprinted by permission of HarperCollins Publishers Inc. and Faber and Faber Ltd.

"Digging," from *Opened Ground: Selected Poems 1966–1996* by Seamus Heaney. Reprinted by permission of Farrar, Straus and Giroux, LLC, and Faber and Faber Ltd.

"Marginalia" from *Picnic Lightning* by Billy Collins, © 1998. Reprinted by permission of the University of Pittsburgh Press.

"Poem," from *The Apple that Astonished Paris* by Billy Collins. Copyright 1988 by Billy Collins. Reprinted by permission of The University of Arkansas Press.

"The Vietnam Wall," by Alberto Ríos from *Currents from the Dancing River: Contemporary Latino Fiction, Nonfiction, and Poetry.* Published originally in *The Lime Orchard Woman.* Copyright © 1988 by Alberto Ríos. Reprinted by permission of the author.

Drama

"Tender Offer," © 1991 by Wendy Wasserstein. First published in Antaeus, Issue #66, *Plays In One Act.* Used by permission of The Gersh Agency. No part of this material may be reproduced in whole or part, without the express written permission of the author's agent.

Casebook on Alice Walker

"Everyday Use" from *In Love & Trouble: Stories of Black Women*, copyright © 1973 by Alice Walker, reprinted by permission of Harcourt, Inc.

"Nineteen Fifty-Five" from *You Can't Keept a Good Woman Down*, Copyright © 1981 by Alice Walker, reprinted by permission of Harcourt, Inc.

"In Search of Our Mothers' Gardens" from *In Search of Our Mothers' Gardens: A Womanist Prose*, copyright © 1970 and renewed 1998 by Alice Walker, reprinted by permission of Harcourt, Inc.

"Woman" from *Revolutionary Petunias & Other Poems*, copyright © 1970 and renewed 1998 by Alice Walker, reprinted by permission of Harcourt, Inc.

"Epilogue: To the Husband of My Youth" from *The Way Forward Is With a Broken Heart* by Alice Walker, copyright © 2000 by Alice Walker. Used by permission of Random House, Inc.

"Alice Walker" from *United States Authors Series*, 1st edition by Donna Hairsty Winchell, 1992. Reprinted with permission of Gale, a division of Thomson Learning.

"Patches: Quilts and Community in Alice Walker's 'Everyday Use' " by Houston A. Baker, Jr., and Charlotte Pierce-Baker. Originally published in *The Southern Review*, Vol. 21, No. 3, July 1985. Reprinted by permission of the authors.

"Heritage and Deracination in Walker's 'Everyday Use'" by David Cowart, published in *Studies in Short Fiction*, No. 33, 1996. Copyright © 1996 by Studies in Short Fiction. Reprinted by permission.

"Creative Scraps" by Taylor Magusiak.

QUEST

Essays

"Allegory of the Cave" from *The Republic* by Plato, translated by Benjamin Jowett.

"Beatitudes" Matthew V, 1-12.

Index

Key Terms Index

Italic numbers refer to the Glossary, pages 1165-1170.